CRIMINAL PROCEDURES: THE POLICE

ASPEN CASEBOOK SERIES

CRIMINAL PROCEDURES: THE POLICE

Cases, Statutes, and Executive Materials

Fourth Edition

MARC L. MILLER
Vice Dean for Faculty and Ralph W. Bilby Professor of Law
The University of Arizona James E. Rogers College of Law

RONALD F. WRIGHT
Professor of Law
Wake Forest University School of Law

Wolters Kluwer
Law & Business

Published by Wolters Kluwer Law & Business in New York.

Wolters Kluwer Law & Business serves customers worldwide with CCH, Aspen Publishers, and Kluwer Law International products. (www.wolterskluwerlb.com)

To contact Customer Service, e-mail customer.service@wolterskluwer.com, call 1-800-234-1660, fax 1-800-901-9075, or mail correspondence to:

Wolters Kluwer Law & Business
Attn: Order Department
PO Box 990
Frederick, MD 21705

Printed in the United States of America.

1 2 3 4 5 6 7 8 9 0

ISBN 978-0-7355-0721-0

Library of Congress Cataloging-in-Publication Data

Miller, Marc (Marc Louis)
Criminal procedures—the police : cases, statutes, and executive materials / Marc L. Miller, Ronald F. Wright. — 4th ed.
p. cm.
Includes index.
ISBN 978-0-7355-0721-0
1. Criminal procedure—United States—Cases. 2. Police questioning—United States. 3. Casebooks. I. Wright, Ronald F., 1959- II. Title.

KF9619.M53 2011
345.73'05—dc23

2011025714

SUSTAINABLE FORESTRY INITIATIVE
Certified Chain of Custody
Promoting Sustainable Forestry
www.sfiprogram.org
SFI-00756

About Wolters Kluwer Law & Business

Wolters Kluwer Law & Business is a leading global provider of intelligent information and digital solutions for legal and business professionals in key specialty areas, and respected educational resources for professors and law students. Wolters Kluwer Law & Business connects legal and business professionals as well as those in the education market with timely, specialized authoritative content and information-enabled solutions to support success through productivity, accuracy and mobility.

Serving customers worldwide, Wolters Kluwer Law & Business products include those under the Aspen Publishers, CCH, Kluwer Law International, Loislaw, Best Case, ftwilliam.com and MediRegs family of products.

CCH products have been a trusted resource since 1913, and are highly regarded resources for legal, securities, antitrust and trade regulation, government contracting, banking, pension, payroll, employment and labor, and healthcare reimbursement and compliance professionals.

Aspen Publishers products provide essential information to attorneys, business professionals and law students. Written by preeminent authorities, the product line offers analytical and practical information in a range of specialty practice areas from securities law and intellectual property to mergers and acquisitions and pension/benefits. Aspen's trusted legal education resources provide professors and students with high-quality, up-to-date and effective resources for successful instruction and study in all areas of the law.

Kluwer Law International products provide the global business community with reliable international legal information in English. Legal practitioners, corporate counsel and business executives around the world rely on Kluwer Law journals, looseleafs, books, and electronic products for comprehensive information in many areas of international legal practice.

Loislaw is a comprehensive online legal research product providing legal content to law firm practitioners of various specializations. Loislaw provides attorneys with the ability to quickly and efficiently find the necessary legal information they need, when and where they need it, by facilitating access to primary law as well as state-specific law, records, forms and treatises.

Best Case Solutions is the leading bankruptcy software product to the bankruptcy industry. It provides software and workflow tools to flawlessly streamline petition preparation and the electronic filing process, while timely incorporating ever-changing court requirements.

ftwilliam.com offers employee benefits professionals the highest quality plan documents (retirement, welfare and non-qualified) and government forms (5500/PBGC, 1099 and IRS) software at highly competitive prices.

MediRegs products provide integrated health care compliance content and software solutions for professionals in healthcare, higher education and life sciences, including professionals in accounting, law and consulting.

Wolters Kluwer Law & Business, a division of Wolters Kluwer, is headquartered in New York. Wolters Kluwer is a market-leading global information services company focused on professionals.

Summary of Contents

Contents

Preface

The American criminal justice system is huge, complex, and varied. Federal, state, and local governments together spend over $200 billion each year on policing, prosecution, trial, and punishment. Well over 2.3 million persons are incarcerated in federal and state prisons, and state and local jails, in the United States at any one time. Another 5 million are on probation or parole.

There are almost 18,000 separate police agencies in the United States, with around 800,000 sworn officers. There are even more "private police" and security agents. In an average year, these officers and agents make more than 14 million arrests.

Criminal cases are prosecuted by more than 2,400 prosecutors' offices, employing about 35,000 attorneys and more than 50,000 additional staff. They obtain about 1 million felony convictions every year, and even more misdemeanor convictions. Thousands of attorneys work as public defenders or as defense counsel in private practice. Thousands of judges hear cases in trial and appellate courts. Lawyers often find their first jobs in the criminal justice system. Some stay for life.

Criminal procedure is the body of law governing this collection of systems. The law of criminal procedure directs — or at least attempts to direct — the actions of police officers, prosecutors, defense attorneys, judges, and other government officials. Criminal procedure limits the way the government may interact with citizens, suspects, defendants, convicted offenders, and victims.

The federal government, every state government, and many local governments operate criminal justice systems. They all spend time, effort, and money each year running and reshaping their respective systems. Although the federal system is one of the largest systems standing alone, the state and local systems collectively are much larger. Virtually all misdemeanors are processed in state courts, along with almost 95 percent of all felony convictions. Criminal justice in the United States is overwhelmingly a state and local function.

There is no one criminal procedure: Each system follows its own set of rules, controlled to different degrees by outside authorities. Procedural rules come from many sources, including constitutions, legislatures, courts, and executive branch agencies. Because the issues of criminal procedure are common and accessible — unlike, say, antitrust law — a wealth of less formal constraints, including community views and the media, also shape procedure. We have titled this casebook "Criminal Procedures" to reflect these multiple layers and sources of law.

The Approach in This Casebook

A criminal procedure casebook must impose some order on the morass of cases, rules, and practices that characterize criminal justice systems. One accepted way to make this material accessible for newcomers is to focus on the role of one important institution, the United States Supreme Court, and on one important source of law, the United States Constitution.

Since the days of the Warren Court, starting in 1953, the Supreme Court has influenced criminal justice systems in profound ways. It made the Bill of Rights in the federal Constitution a shaping force for every criminal justice system. The Warren Court made the story of criminal procedure, told from the point of view of the Supreme Court, compelling. The main topics of controversy were police practices: stops, searches, and interrogations. Other decisions of the Court created a basic framework for providing defendants with counsel and for conducting criminal trials. For years, the focus on the Supreme Court's constitutional rulings guided students through the questions that most concerned judges and lawyers.

But the story of this one institution offers less explanatory power as time passes. Traditional issues on the Court's constitutional criminal procedure docket now occupy less of the attention of judges, attorneys, defendants, victims, and others concerned with criminal justice. Most criminal defendants do not go to trial. Many have no complaints about illegal searches or coerced confessions. These defendants and their lawyers care about improper use of force, local police responses to domestic violence, the allocation of police patrols, the plea agreements defendants can reach with the prosecutor, and their sentences.

The central questions have shifted in light of changes in the workload, politics, funding, and structure of criminal justice institutions. New crime-fighting strategies — such as community policing and curfews — advances in technology, and changes in the political and social order raise new questions and place old questions in a new light.

The U.S. Supreme Court leaves important dimensions of most procedural issues unresolved and thus leaves other institutions free to innovate; they have done so. The issues of current importance in criminal procedure are being shaped in multiple institutions, including state courts, legislatures, and executive branch agencies.

This book adopts a panoramic view of criminal procedure, emphasizing the interaction among, and variety within, criminal justice systems. In our opinion, students in an upper-level course such as criminal procedure can and should move beyond the skills of case synthesis and beyond the ability to appreciate the role of only one institution. Our materials emphasize the following themes and objectives:

- *Procedural variety.* In each area we present competing rules from the federal and state systems. We also occasionally examine procedures from earlier times or from non-U.S. systems. Reviewing different possible procedural rules encourages critical analysis and helps identify the assumptions held and judgments made in the design of each criminal system.
- *Materials from multiple institutions.* In addition to leading U.S. Supreme Court cases, we make extensive use of state high court cases, statutes, rules of procedure, and police and prosecutorial policies, and we encourage readers to consider the interactions among multiple institutions. Examining the efforts of different institutions to achieve similar goals highlights the reality of procedural innovation and reform.
- *Real-world perspective.* We focus on procedures and issues of current importance to defendants, lawyers, courts, legislators, and the public. We devote the most attention to the issues arising in the largest number of cases.
- *Street-level federalism.* Federal law, typically in the form of constitutional decisions by the U.S. Supreme Court, still plays an important role in guiding the investigation and prosecution of high-volume street crimes. The interactions of police with citizens and suspects form the workaday setting for issues of criminal justice. The impact of abstract constitutional doctrine on these daily interactions raises important theoretical questions about federal-state relations and interactions among jurisdictions and governmental institutions.
- *Political context.* Materials trace the political environment surrounding different institutions and issues. We explore the impact of public concerns such as terrorism, drug trafficking, domestic abuse, and treatment of crime victims on procedural rules. Funding decisions with regard to criminal justice systems also offer a window into the political setting.
- *Impact of procedures.* We consider the effects that different procedures have on law enforcers, lawyers, courts, communities, defendants, and victims. We emphasize primary materials but include social science studies as well, especially when they have been the basis for procedural reform. This perspective keeps in mind the managerial needs of criminal justice: Any legal rule must apply to multitudes of defendants in overcrowded systems.

By studying the various ways in which state and local systems have answered crucial procedural questions, students become aware of a broader range of policy alternatives. They form a more complete picture of the complex and interactive workings of the criminal justice system. Our goal in emphasizing the variety within criminal procedure is to produce lawyers who know both the current law and the way to shape better law down the road.

Conceptual Anchors

Our emphasis on variety does not mean that we will survey the practices of all 50 states on each issue; this casebook is not a treatise. Rather, the materials highlight the majority and minority views on each topic, as well as the federal view. The major positions on a topic are usually summarized in the first note following the principal materials. Truly distinctive answers to problems are mentioned occasionally as a point of comparison with the leading approach, but the uniqueness of the position is always highlighted.

The book addresses a wide range of U.S. Supreme Court precedents, including the recognized core of essential cases and many of the most recent important decisions. State supreme court decisions summarizing and critiquing a U.S. Supreme Court decision, or a line of cases, represent effective teaching tools since the state cases tend to highlight the competing doctrinal positions. State supreme court opinions by and large show less interest in the positions of individual justices than do U.S. Supreme Court decisions and devote less attention to questions about consistency with past decisions. State supreme court opinions often provide provocative settings that show how principles operate in practice. They tend to present succinctly the textual and institutional arguments favoring a procedural requirement, the values furthered by the rules, and their likely effects on police, suspects, and communities.

Studying a variety of possible answers to important procedural questions has an unexpected effect: through criticism and contrast it provides students with a firmer grasp of the federal approach, including current federal constitutional criminal procedure, than does presentation of federal law alone. Students become better equipped to understand what is truly important about the current norms. Short "problems" throughout the book also enable readers to apply and integrate basic concepts.

The state cases appearing in this book take every conceivable position with respect to Supreme Court precedent, ranging from total agreement to complete rejection, and encompassing subtle variations in interpretation and emphasis. For a large number of state cases that focus on state constitutional or statutory questions, the position of the U.S. Supreme Court is simply irrelevant. The case selection does not favor decisions merely because they reject the U.S. Supreme Court view — the "new federalism" approach. These materials are not a battle cry for state court independence; they simply reflect the vibrancy of state supreme courts and state law.

The Fourth Edition

The fourth edition of this book is a response to changes in the field, incorporating emerging themes and major issues. Such themes and issues — the turning points in the law — result as often from dramatic events outside the courtroom as from blockbuster judicial decisions. Such dramatic and unexpected "drivers" of change in criminal procedure over the years since the first edition of this book appeared include increasing attention to issues of race, especially the so-called DWB (driving while black) stops on American highways and the "innocence" projects that have revealed strings of wrongful convictions. The fourth edition continues to explore the legal echoes within domestic criminal procedure of the attacks on September 11, 2001, and the ongoing war on terrorism.

We have made changes in every chapter. Some of those changes reflect actual shifts in doctrine, while others are the result of suggestions by teachers and students about cases and materials that worked well in the classroom, and others that might be improved.

Our attention to developments in the states provides a large pool of new cases, statutes, and rules to draw from, keeping the discussion anchored to current reality in criminal justice. For example, many of the cases in this book were decided after 2000. Recent federal developments also find their place in these pages. Significant

U.S. Supreme Court cases added to this edition include Arizona v. Gant, Berghuis v. Thompkins, Herring v. United States, and Maryland v. Shatzer.

The overall goal of these changes has been to produce a book that remains fresh and engaging.

Criminal Procedure Courses

This book examines police activities, including stops, investigations, searches, arrests, interrogations, and identifications. This coverage is the heart of the basic criminal procedure course, often labeled "Criminal Procedure I" or the "police practices" course. It is typically taught in three or four classroom hours.

Most law schools now offer a second procedure course — often called the bail-to-jail course — that focuses on the regulation of prosecutors, defense counsel, and courts before and during trial. A companion volume, Criminal Procedures: Prosecution and Adjudication, uses the same basic approach as this text to support the Criminal Procedure II course.

The materials throughout this volume address interrelated themes; criminal procedure is a relatively coherent field. It is not necessary, however, to study the materials in a set order. The teacher can approach topics from a variety of perspectives and using a number of different doctrinal starting points. Students should not be surprised if their professor presents the chapters in an order different from the one we have used or adds chapters, cases, or other materials to the course.

Procedure, Politics, and Reform

This book reminds readers regularly about the political environment shaping the work of every institutional actor in criminal justice. The materials consider the changing political priorities that make enforcement especially urgent for certain criminal laws — those punishing drug trafficking, environmental crimes, and sexual assault, to name a few. Such high-priority enforcement efforts influence criminal procedure more generally. Terrorism is the newest and most tragic law enforcement priority, and we consider the potential impact of new approaches and doctrines aimed at terrorists on domestic criminal procedure and the implications for more typical crimes.

The theme of jurisdictional and institutional variation draws critical attention to the role of states, whose systems handle 94 percent of the felonies prosecuted in the United States. But while the federal and state systems are the most appropriate levels at which to consider constitutional and statutory constraints, the local level is the true locus of criminal justice power. It is also the place where criminal justice systems in the United States engage most citizens. There are roughly 3,000 counties in the United States, including 254 in Texas and 168 in Georgia.

The local foundations of discretionary power in U.S. criminal justice systems are reflected in the funding for those systems. Just over half of all criminal justice funding comes from the local level, just over 30 percent from the state level, and just under 20 percent from the federal level. But funding is not spread evenly across system components. Police services are primarily funded at the local level, prisons are funded at the state level, and the costs of prosecution and adjudication are funded primarily at both the local and state levels. There has been much legal and public debate over the 30-year expansion in the federal prosecution of what traditionally would have been local drug offenses; today, immigration and drug crimes dominate the federal criminal docket, although the federal courts do continue to handle traditional areas of federal interest such as bank robbery and large-scale fraud.

Students who appreciate the handful of basic political struggles that time and again shape procedural debates will be better able to direct changes in the system and to influence decisions in close cases. The struggles center on questions such as these: What are the purposes of the criminal justice system? In particular, what is the relevance of criminal law and procedure to the social goals of crime control and prevention? How does the theory and practice of federalism inform criminal justice theory and practice? Can we trust the police? How vital is the adversary system and the role of defense counsel to the success of that system? Are we comfortable with the broad discretion exercised on a daily basis by police and prosecutors? How important is it to treat suspects similarly? Should we explicitly consider the costs of procedures?

The priorities inherent in this textbook suggest a return to the study of criminal procedure as a genuine procedure course, not a course in constitutional adjudication. The constitutional component remains an indispensable part of the course but is not the sum total of criminal procedure.

The return to a fuller conception of criminal procedure offers enormous opportunities to those who study the system and to those who will soon participate in its operation and evolution. When many institutions are able to shape a legal system, there are many opportunities for change. We hope each student will leave this course with a sense of the drama and the special challenges of each case and of the entire process. We hope each student will finish school ready to create procedures more sound than those that exist today.

Marc Miller
Ron Wright

Tucson, Arizona
Winston-Salem, North Carolina
May 2011

Acknowledgments

Creating a new edition of this book powerfully reminded us of how communities make work more fun and make final products better. Our debts extend to our friends and colleagues, our institutions, our students, our teachers, and our families.

Some of the teachers who use this book contact us on occasion to suggest improvements for future editions. They include Laura Appleman, Doug Berman, Stephanos Bibas, Frank Bowman, Irus Braverman, Darryl Brown, Jenny Carroll, Steve Chanenson, Jack Chin, Jennifer Collins, Steve Easton, Nancy Gertner, Aya Gruber, Thaddeus Hoffmeister, Jim Jacobs, Sam Kamin, Elizabeth Ludwin King, Tamara Lave, Kay Levine, Dan Markel, Tracey Meares, Alan Michaels, Tommy Miller, Kenneth Nunn, Jenny Roberts, Kami Simmons, Jonathan Simon, Shandrea Solomon, Kate Stith, Paul Stokstad, Andrew Taslitz, Sandra Guerra Thompson, Robert Wagner, Jonathan Witmer-Rich, David Yellen, and Tung Yin. It is a great joy for us as editors to learn from them what is happening in classrooms all over the world.

Scholars who provided wise counsel on earlier editions, which is still very evident in the revised volume, include Albert Alschuler, Akhil Amar, Barbara Babcock, Adolph Dean, Nora Demleitner, George Fisher, Dan Freed, Mark Hall, Mark Harris, Lenese Herbert, Andrew Kull, Gerard Lynch, William Mayton, David Orentlicher, Leonard Orland, Alan Palmiter, Anne Poulin, Aaron Rappaport, Sadiq Reza, Natsu Saito, Stephen Schulhofer, Charles Shanor, Rick Singer, Michael Smith, Charles Weisselberg, Bert Westbrook, and Deborah Young. We have also learned from two extensive published reviews of this book. See Robert Weisberg, A New Legal Realism for Criminal Procedure, 49 Buff. L. Rev. 909 (2001), and Stephanos Bibas, The Real-World Shift in Criminal Procedure, 93 J. Crim. L. & Criminology 789 (2003).

We have both been graced with great teachers, all of whom became friends. We can trace in these pages the influence of Norval Morris, Frank Zimring, Edward Levi, Richard Epstein, Philip Kurland, David Currie, James Boyd White, Owen Fiss, Robert Burt, Peter Schuck, Steven Duke, and Judges Frank Johnson and John Godbold.

Over the years we have worked on this project with many fine students whose energy renewed our own. They include Liz Asplund, Amber Byers, Ryan Carter, Pablo Clarke, Perry Coumas, Don Donelson, Ben Durie, Joseph Ezzo, Alexandra Ford, Heather Gaw, Jennifer Gibbons, Kaitlyn Girard, Elizabeth Goodwin, Whitney Hendrix, Antoine Marshall, Emily Parish, Russ Rotondi, Ramie Shalabi, and Rebecca Stahl. Exceptional research help on earlier editions came from Roger Abramson, Nathan Adams, Wes Camden, Sean Monaghan, Tyronia Morrison, Alice Shanlever, and Daniel Terner.

We have made heavy demands on our libraries and technology experts, and owe thanks to Marcia Baker, Terry Gordon, Sarah Gotschall, Will Haines, Deborah Keene, Lori Levy, William Morse, Stuart Myerberg, Holliday Osborne, John Perkins, and Erika Wayne. Steve Turner, the former director of the Wilsonville, Oregon, public library, helped us achieve greater clarity throughout the book. Kristie Gallardo, Barbara Lopez, Beverly Marshall, Radine Robinson, and Marissa White provided timely administrative support for this edition and earlier ones: It is a miracle they did not ask to work with faculty other than us.

We also have debts to many of the hard-working and visionary lawyers and judges in the criminal justice system. A few who provided special assistance are Harry Connick and Tim McElroy of the District Attorney's office in New Orleans; Numa Bertel of the Orleans Indigent Defender Program; Judge Camille Buras of the District Court in New Orleans; Lawson Lamar and William Vose of the State Attorney's office in Orange County, Florida; Russell Hauge of the Kitsap County Prosecutor's Office in Washington; Peter Gilchrist of the District Attorney's Office in Mecklenburg County, North Carolina; Patricia Jessamy of the State's Attorney's office in Baltimore, Maryland; and Chief Judge James Carr of the U.S. District Court for the Northern District of Ohio. We appreciate the willingness of police departments and prosecutorial and defender's offices to give us copies of their policies and manuals. We have also gained insight from our conversations with skilled reporters and criminal justice reformers, including Kevin Corcoran.

Family debts for so consuming a project are hard to recognize in print, and even harder to repay in life. Joanna Wright, ever the curious one, shows an interest in everything from exclusionary rules to font sizes. Andrew Wright keeps reminding us that justice for real people must be the bottom line for any legal procedure. Owen Miller (age 8) is full of questions about everything, starting with the basics: "What is a bad guy?" and "Why do police officers carry guns?" Evelyn Miller (4) wants to know why this book has so many words and so few pictures. Wyatt Miller (2) is still focused on questions of even a more fundamental nature. Conversations with our brothers Travis Wright, who is a police officer, and Craig Miller, who for years worked on justice reform projects and now teaches inner-city high school students history and government, helped us remember that criminal procedure rules guide the behavior of people in very different settings. Other family members (especially Alex Miller, Renata Miller, Katy Miller, Denis Wright, Kyung Ah Wright, and the Ohlingers and Mannings) read parts of the manuscript and forgave us for the piles of papers and disks at every family gathering.

Our parents have been our teachers, our friends, and our models. Ron's father, Ronald F. Wright, Sr., died when Ron was a law student, but his energy and optimism pervade this book. Marc's father, Howard, for many years a law professor, provided steady advice from beginning to end. Our mothers, Marian and Shirley, showed a confidence that helped us keep our destination in mind when work seemed nothing but roads.

This book sits between covers only because of the daily encouragement and advice of Amy Wright and Christina Cutshaw. Putting up with writing projects is not part of the wedding vows; perhaps it should be.

CRIMINAL PROCEDURES: THE POLICE

I

The Border of Criminal Procedure: Daily Interactions Between Citizens and Police

Criminal procedure shapes the behavior of police, prosecutors, defense attorneys, and courts as they investigate crimes, prosecute, defend, and adjudge defendants, and sentence criminals. Many institutions create procedural rules to regulate the criminal justice process.

Looking at police work, for example, there are rules about when police can stop, search, and arrest suspects. But not all police activities are subject to rules. For example, no state has a body of law telling police officers how they should talk with people on their rounds. Why not? Legal systems are supposed to prevent extraordinary and undesirable police actions. Thus, when a legal system allows some kinds of police activities to fall outside the bounds of formal legal rules, it is an indication of what society considers to be ordinary and desirable policing.

A society's vision of ordinary and desirable police behavior determines the "border" of criminal procedure — that is, the point where the law, in the form of rules from whatever source, starts to guide and limit police activity. This chapter explores that border. It suggests that assumptions about the *ordinary* behavior of the police shape the procedures we will study in later chapters, procedures that govern the *exceptional* confrontations between citizens and officers.

Modern criminal procedure assumes that the police initiate contact with citizens while "engaged in the often competitive enterprise of ferreting out crime." Johnson v. United States, 333 U.S. 10 (1948). But the police do many things in addition to ferreting out crime. The cases in Section A involve police-initiated actions that pursue some purpose other than enforcing the criminal law — actions often referred to as the "community caretaker" function of police. Should police and citizens have different powers and responsibilities when the police act outside their law enforcement mode? In the cases in Section B, citizens initiate the relationship by commenting on police behavior, usually in colorful (though rarely original) terms. In Section C, we consider the power of police to control the movement of kids, gang members, and other people. The chapter concludes with an examination of different philosophies of policing (in particular the currently dominant "community policing" model), asking whether a change in overall philosophy should produce changes in the relevant procedural rules governing the police.

A. POLICE AS COMMUNITY CARETAKERS

Any description of police work (and, therefore, any set of procedural rules to control the police) must reckon with the wide variety of functions that the police perform. Most of the time, police officers interact with citizens without giving a thought to making an arrest or gathering evidence of a crime. It is estimated that police officers devote roughly 70 percent of their time to matters other than criminal enforcement. The following materials — drawn from statutes, police department manuals, and cases — offer concrete images of police trying to accomplish something other than enforcing the criminal law. The police might view their task as defusing domestic disputes, or moving people out of dangerous or unhealthy situations, or offering guidance to young people, or something else. How should procedural rules that apply to the police account for these different functions? Should there be different rules for the police when they pursue "community caretaker" objectives rather than "law enforcement" objectives?

■ OREGON REVISED STATUTES §133.033

(1) [Any] peace officer of this state . . . is authorized to perform community caretaking functions.

(2) As used in this section, "community caretaking functions" means any lawful acts that are inherent in the duty of the peace officer to serve and protect the public. "Community caretaking functions" includes, but is not limited to:

(a) The right to enter or remain upon the premises of another if it reasonably appears to be necessary to:

(A) Prevent serious harm to any person or property;

(B) Render aid to injured or ill persons; or

(C) Locate missing persons.

(b) The right to stop or redirect traffic or aid motorists or other persons when such action reasonably appears to be necessary to:

(A) Prevent serious harm to any person or property;

(B) Render aid to injured or ill persons; or

(C) Locate missing persons. . . .

INDIANAPOLIS POLICE DEPARTMENT JOB DESCRIPTION: PATROL OFFICER

% TIME	*CRITICAL TASKS*
15%	1. Patrols assigned area in vehicle and on foot; maintains high patrol visibility to assist in crime prevention; actively performs routine beat patrol, concentrating on high incident areas, to detect possible criminal activities or needs for service; regularly checks businesses and residential areas; monitors radio broadcasts by Communications and other officers to ensure awareness of activities in area and to provide assistance, if needed; identifies, reports, and responds to suspicious activities or needs for service.
14%	2. Performs variety of police-community relations functions; meets and talks with citizens, providing information and advising of safety measures; visits local businesses to determine needs for service; assists motorists, providing directions; talks with juveniles in district to establish rapport; makes presentations to neighborhood organizations and block clubs. . . .
12%	3. Performs duties relating to service and assistance (lost child, injured persons, walk-aways, prowlers, abandoned vehicles, dog bites, civil law disputes, vehicle inspections, etc.). . . .
10%	4. Receives emergency and non-emergency radio runs and information from Communications; . . . responds to run, using siren and/or red lights in emergencies. . . .
10%	5. Prepares reports (incident reports, capias information sheets, probable cause affidavits, accident reports, arrest slips, [uniform traffic tickets], property slips, inter-departments, etc.) relating to activities in accordance with General Orders/Department Directives; observes and records events. . . .
8%	6. Performs duties relating to criminal investigation and apprehension; responds to scenes of possible criminal activity through radio runs, notification, or observation; assesses scene to determine situation needs (assistance from other officers, ambulance, detective, K-9, etc.); provides assistance to victim(s); searches and secures crime scene; interviews victims and witnesses to determine and verify nature of offense and identify suspect(s); notifies Communications of descriptions for broadcast; assists in pursuit (foot and vehicular) and/or apprehension of suspects; interrogates suspects, advising of Constitutional rights; makes arrests using only that force necessary; conducts search of arrested suspects; ensures suspects are transported to appropriate detention area and evidence is secured; advises victims of procedures to follow in prosecution.

% TIME	*CRITICAL TASKS*
6%	7. Performs duties relating to disturbances and domestic violence; . . . evaluates situation to determine needs (assistance from other officers, ambulance, etc.); administers first aid, if needed; assists in resolution of conflicts; subdues violent subject using only that physical force necessary; makes arrests as needed to preserve peace . . . ; advises victim of possible courses of action.
5%	8. Performs duties relating to traffic enforcement; observes traffic violations; stops vehicles; checks registration and licenses for status; advises driver of violation committed and need to maintain safe driving practices; conducts or requests breathalyzer tests, if indicated; issues citations and makes arrests to enforce law, advising violator of rights. . . .
5%	9. Performs duties relating to accident investigation and assistance; . . . assists in extraction of victims and provision of first aid; secures scene to prevent further incidents; conducts investigation, gathering evidence, taking statements, and preparing diagrams; conducts or requests breathalyzer tests, if indicated; issues citations and makes arrests to enforce law, advising violator of rights. . . .
5%	10. Testifies in court; prepares for testimony, reviewing reports and notes; meets with victims, witnesses, detectives, defense attorneys, and representatives from Prosecutor's Office to review case; . . . presents testimony in accordance with Department policy. . . .

■ STATE v. MICHAEL DUBE

655 A.2d 338 (Me. 1995)

WATHEN, C.J.

Michael Dube appeals from his conviction of endangering the welfare of a child, entered in the District Court following Dube's conditional guilty plea. The defendant challenges the District Court's denial of his motion to suppress [evidence that he claims was] obtained as a result of an illegal search. We vacate the Judgment of conviction.

On July 4, 1993, two officers of the Sanford Police Department responded to a call from the custodian of the apartment building in which defendant lived with his family. Defendant was not at home and the custodian needed to enter the apartment to stop sewage or water from leaking into the apartments below. The custodian had his own key but asked the police officers to accompany him to verify that he was only dealing with the emergency. When they entered the kitchen, the officers were struck with an "incredible smell of urine and feces." There was a puddle of urine on the kitchen floor, and an open diaper containing human feces that appeared to have been walked through by a baby. The feces had been tracked throughout the apartment. The officers watched the custodian [work on toilets on the first and second floors]. From where they stood on the landing, the officers could see into the three bedrooms. In the baby's bedroom and the children's bedroom, they saw clothes strewn on the floor covered with animal and human feces. There were at least 75-100 individual feces "right beside the baby's crib," and a similar number around the bunk beds and more in the hallway.

Officer Beaulieu called the Sanford Police Department to request that the Department of Human Services (DHS) send a caseworker to the apartment. He also radioed for another police unit to bring a camera. The officers asked the custodian to "stand by," and when he finished with the repairs the custodian waited on the sidewalk. About five minutes later, two officers arrived with a camera and Officer Beaulieu took pictures of parts of the apartment, and then went outside to wait with the custodian. When two DHS workers arrived, they were shown around the apartment by Officer Beaulieu. Thereafter, defendant and his family returned home, and he was charged with endangering the welfare of a child. . . .

Defendant argues that the initial entry into the apartment by the police officers was unlawful and a violation of the fourth amendment proscription against unreasonable searches. [We have noted] that a police officer has a legitimate role as a public servant to assist those in distress and to maintain and foster public safety. Local police officers frequently engage in community caretaking functions, totally divorced from the detection, investigation, or acquisition of evidence relating to the violation of a criminal statute.

In this case, the custodian had a statutory right to enter the apartment in response to an emergency, and the court found that it was reasonable for the police to accompany him. During the time that the officers were on the premises performing a lawful police function, their observations, made with their natural senses, without acting to enhance their view, [were proper].

Defendant next argues that even if the officers' initial entry was lawful, their continued presence at some point became unlawful. We agree. Although the officers were lawfully on the premises during the time the custodian was dealing with the plumbing emergency, their continued presence after the repairs were completed was unlawful. [The law required them at that point to leave the apartment and obtain a warrant before proceeding with any further searches. Although the photographs only recorded what was in plain sight,] the photographs were taken after the custodian had finished his repairs. [Once] the repairs were complete, the justification for the presence of the police in the apartment ceased. . . . We are required to vacate the judgment. . . .

STATE v. MICHAEL LOVEGREN

51 P.3d 471 (Mont. 2002)

NELSON, J.

. . . ¶3 On the night of October 31, 1998, Officer Gary Hofer of the Richland County Sheriff's Department was on routine patrol. At approximately 3:05 A.M., he came upon a vehicle parked on the side of Highway 16 South in Richland County between Crane and Sidney. The vehicle's motor was running, but its headlights were off. Officer Hofer stopped to investigate.

¶4 When Officer Hofer approached the vehicle and looked in the window, he saw Lovegren sitting in the driver's seat. Lovegren appeared to be asleep. Officer Hofer knocked on the window and, when Lovegren did not respond, Officer Hofer opened the door. Lovegren suddenly woke up and stated: "I was drinking." Officer Hofer smelled a strong odor of alcohol and he noticed that Lovegren's eyes were bloodshot, so he had Lovegren perform various field sobriety tests. Lovegren failed both the one-legged stand and the heel-to-toe test. Hence, Officer Hofer transported Lovegren to the station, where a breath test was performed. The test results showed that Lovegren's blood alcohol content was 0.115. Officer Hofer read Lovegren his *Miranda* rights and wrote out a citation charging him with driving under the influence of alcohol in violation of §61-8-401, MCA. . . .

¶6 On May 12, 1999, Lovegren filed a motion in the District Court asking the court to suppress all of the evidence obtained in the investigative stop on the grounds that Officer Hofer lacked a particularized suspicion of any wrongdoing on Lovegren's part, thus the stop was not justified. On May 26, 1999, the District Court denied Lovegren's motion, stating that a particularized suspicion was not required in this situation, as Officer Hofer had a duty to investigate for Lovegren's own safety.

¶7 . . . Lovegren was subsequently convicted of the charge and the District Court [fined Lovegren $420 and sentenced him to 60 days in jail with all but one day suspended. The court also suspended Lovegren's driver's license for six months. Lovegren appeals.]

¶10 . . . Lovegren contends that this investigative stop was not justified because Officer Hofer did not have a particularized suspicion that Lovegren had committed, was committing, or was about to commit an offense.

¶11 Lovegren also contends that the District Court overstepped its authority by inferring more from the police reports than what they actually said. Lovegren notes that in the police report, Officer Hofer clearly stated that the driver of the vehicle "appeared to be asleep" and that there were no references in the report to any signs of struggle or trauma to indicate the need of further assistance. Thus, Lovegren argues that the District Court erred in concluding that although the report indicates that the driver appeared to be asleep, the officer could not know whether the driver was asleep, ill, unconscious or even dead.

¶12 The State argues, on the other hand, that the District Court correctly determined that Officer Hofer did not need a particularized suspicion of criminal activity in this situation. The State maintains that the court correctly applied the "community caretaker doctrine" — even though the court did not identify it as such — in determining that Officer Hofer was justified in stopping to check on Lovegren's welfare and that Officer Hofer would have been derelict in his duties had he not done so. . . .

¶16 [Many courts recognize that some of the least intrusive police-citizen encounters do not] involve any form of detention at all and, therefore, [do] not involve a seizure. This category is generally referred to as the "community caretaker" or "public safety" function. . . .

¶18 Because this Court has not squarely addressed the community caretaker doctrine, we take this opportunity to survey the law from other jurisdictions in this area and to set forth our own test for application of this doctrine.

¶19 Of the many jurisdictions that have addressed this doctrine, a majority have adopted it in some form. However, the boundaries of this doctrine that control the judgment exercised by the officers in these situations are not consistent across all of the jurisdictions. Indeed, our review of the cases leads us to conclude that some jurisdictions have expanded the doctrine beyond what would likely be acceptable given the enhanced protection of the right of individual privacy and against unreasonable searches and seizures guaranteed under Article II, Sections 10 and 11 of the Montana Constitution. . . .

¶20 [T]he majority of the jurisdictions that have adopted the community caretaker doctrine have determined that a peace officer has a duty to investigate situations in which a citizen may be in peril or need some type of assistance from an officer. [The opinion cited cases from Minnesota, Alaska, New Jersey, Vermont, and Washington State.]

¶21 [T]he caretaking duties that come under this doctrine are varied and range from assisting a driver slumped over in his car to stopping a man walking alongside a road. [The opinion cited cases from Alaska, Arkansas, Illinois, North Dakota, Virginia, Wyoming, Alabama, and Wisconsin.]

¶22 In addition, many jurisdictions have recognized that the scope of any intrusion following the stop must be limited to those actions necessary to carry out the purposes of the stop, unless particularized suspicion or probable cause subsequently arises. See State v. Dube, 655 A.2d 338 (Me. 1995) (initial entry into apartment by police as they accompanied building custodian so he could make emergency repairs was lawful, but squalid conditions of apartment did not create exigent circumstances justifying officers' continued presence in apartment after repairs were completed). . . .

¶24 [W]hen an officer claims that he or she acted under the community caretaker doctrine, many jurisdictions use a two-step approach to analyze the officer's actions. First, if an officer states that he stopped to assist a person who appeared to be in need of assistance, an objective view of the specific and articulable facts must be examined to determine whether they support the officer's statements. And, second, a determination must be made regarding at what moment the officer "seized" the person and thereby implicated Fourth Amendment protections. . . .

¶25 With this survey of the foregoing case law in mind, we adopt the following test in relation to the community caretaker doctrine. First, as long as there are objective, specific and articulable facts from which an experienced officer would suspect that a citizen is in need of help or is in peril, then that officer has the right to stop and investigate. Second, if the citizen is in need of aid, then the officer may take appropriate action to render assistance or mitigate the peril. Third, once, however, the officer is assured that the citizen is not in peril or is no longer in need of assistance or that the peril has been mitigated, then any actions beyond that constitute a seizure implicating not only the protections provided by the Fourth Amendment, but more importantly, those greater guarantees afforded under Article II, Sections 10 and 11 of the Montana Constitution as interpreted in this Court's decisions.

¶26 Applying this test in the present case, the facts support the conclusion that Officer Hofer had objective, specific and articulable facts suggesting that Lovegren might be in need of assistance. While Lovegren might simply have been asleep, he might just as likely have been ill and unconscious and in need of help. Under these circumstances, Officer Hofer had the right to check on Lovegren's welfare and to open the door of Lovegren's vehicle when Lovegren failed to respond to a knock on the window of his vehicle. As the State points out, it would have been a dereliction of Officer Hofer's duties if, after knocking on the window and obtaining no response, Officer Hofer walked away and continued on his patrol. Thus, under the community caretaker doctrine, when Officer Hofer opened the door to check on Lovegren, Officer Hofer had not yet "seized" Lovegren.

¶27 However, when Officer Hofer opened the door, not only did Lovegren awake, but he voluntarily stated that he had been drinking. At that time, Officer Hofer also noticed other signs of intoxication giving him a particularized suspicion to make a further investigatory stop — i.e., the field sobriety tests — which eventually developed into probable cause for an arrest. This escalation of events leading to Lovegren's arrest is proper. . . .

¶28 Accordingly, we hold that the District Court did not err when it denied Lovegren's motion to suppress.

Problem 1-1. The Right to Be Left Alone?

Officer Gary Taylor of the Olla Police Department responded to a report of an injured person walking along Highway 125. Upon arriving at the scene, Officer Taylor observed two men: Reverend Allen Scott McDowell, who was responsible for placing the call, and Robert Stowe. Stowe, who was intoxicated, had fought with his wife earlier and punched through a window, resulting in a deep cut on his right arm, which was dripping blood. Officer Taylor wrapped a towel around Stowe's arm in an attempt to stop the blood flow. Stowe responded in a belligerent manner, cursing loudly. Officer Taylor tried to take him to get medical attention for his arm. Stowe refused and became increasingly hostile and threatening. Traffic began to back up, because Stowe and the officer were standing in the middle of the highway. Realizing that he was unable to reason with Stowe, Officer Taylor told him that he was under arrest for disturbing the peace. At this point, Stowe hit Officer Taylor in the head, knocking him backward across the road and into a roadside ditch. Eventually, with the assistance of Reverend McDowell and a bystander, the officer handcuffed Stowe and placed him in the patrol car.

Stowe was charged with disturbing the peace, under a statute that prohibits people from acting "in a manner which would foreseeably disturb or alarm the public." Stowe claims that he was minding his own business, disturbing no one. He made it apparent to all of his "rescuers" that he wanted no help and resented their interference in his personal misery. He argues that the police officer's attempt to force medical attention on him was an unconstitutional seizure of his person in violation of the Fourth Amendment of the U.S. Constitution. The Fourth Amendment guarantees a citizen's right to be free from "unreasonable" searches or seizures. How would you rule? Cf. State v. Stowe, 635 So. 2d 168 (La. 1994).

Notes

1. *Community caretakers: majority view.* The majority of the states have applied some form of the community caretaker doctrine to police. As we saw in *Dube* and *Lovegren*, this concept often arises when courts relax the usual restrictions on searches and seizures that apply during a criminal investigation. The community caretaker function has been used to justify entry into homes and stops of automobiles, with police officers pursuing various "caretaker" missions. See Laney v. State, 117 S.W.3d 854 (Tex. Crim. App. 2003) (officer entered trailer after midnight to determine where two young boys lived); State v. Deneui, 775 N.W.2d 221 (S.D. 2009) (during investigation of theft of natural gas, officers noticed ammonia fumes emanating from home and entered based on concern that potential occupants may have succumbed to fumes). Does an energetic community caretaker function provide a convenient after-the-fact rationale for searches that would not otherwise be legal?

Does the community caretaker function interfere with a citizen's right to be let alone, perhaps by sleeping in a car? Is it built on a faulty premise, "We're from the government, and we're here to help you"? One way to think about these questions is to identify the precise crime that should form the basis for charges against Stowe in Problem 1-1. Is it fair to say that Stowe's only crime was "bleeding in public" after he made it "apparent to all of his 'rescuers' that he did not require their assistance, and resented their intrusion into his personal misery"? See State v. Stowe, 635 So. 2d 168 (La. 1994) (Ortique, J., dissenting).

The U.S. Supreme Court has also recognized the community caretaking function. In Brigham City v. Stuart, 547 U.S. 398 (2006), the Court held that the Fourth Amendment does not bar law enforcement officers from entering a residence without a warrant if they have "an objectively reasonable basis to believe that an occupant is seriously injured or imminently threatened" with a serious injury. See also Colorado v. Bertine, 479 U.S. 367 (1987) (noting community caretaker value of inventory searches, which are not subject to the warrant requirement because they are "totally divorced from the detection, investigation, or acquisition of evidence relating to the violation of a criminal statute") (quoting Cady v. Dombrowski, 413 U.S. 433 (1973)).

2. *Distinguishing community caretaker functions from criminal enforcement.* As suggested by the Oregon statute, the Indianapolis job description, and the *Dube* and *Lovegren* cases, the community caretaker function of the police can cover a wide variety of activities. As explained in *Dube,* a community caretaker function can change to a crime control function. What factors might identify such a shift in function? See Williams v. State, 962 A.2d 210 (Del. 2008) (officer who stopped person who appeared to need assistance did not convert the stop into an illegal detention by asking for person's name and date of birth; officer must have record of who receives assistance to respond to later claims of officer wrongdoing or to further later criminal investigations). If a police department receives a 911 call reporting unusual noises behind the neighbor's house, should that be treated as a "crime control" or a community caretaker episode? What if a patrol officer responds to a burglar alarm? What if 95 percent of burglar alarm calls are false calls? Review the job description of a patrol officer in Indianapolis, and attempt to sort the various duties into the community caretaker or the crime control category. Courts usually declare that the officer's subjective intent when performing an action does not determine whether the courts will treat it as community caretaking or a criminal investigation. See State v. Kramer, 759 N.W.2d 598 (Wis. 2009).

There is debate among courts about whether the community caretaker doctrine should apply to the entry of homes, or whether it should remain limited to police encounters with individuals inside vehicles. For a survey of this debate about the proper boundaries of the community caretaker doctrine and a description of the related concept known as the "emergency aid" doctrine, see the web extension for this chapter at *http://www.crimpro.com/extension/ch01*.

Should statutes or ordinances, rather than judicial decisions, define the boundaries of community caretaker authority? Would the Oregon statute provide a different outcome in *Dube*?

3. *Adjusted procedural controls for different police roles.* The *Dube* court suggests that it is appropriate to have higher procedural requirements for police officers who are investigating a crime, and to apply more lax requirements to officers acting in a community caretaker function. What features of community caretaker functions

might justify this different treatment? Are caretaker functions less intrusive for citizens? Do those activities produce less severe consequences than a criminal investigation? Do police encounter a greater variety of situations during community caretaking, making it less amenable to general rules than the conduct of a criminal investigation? Could a legal system subject all police activity — whether or not directed toward criminal law enforcement — to the same procedural requirements? See Debra Livingston, Police, Community Caretaking and the Fourth Amendment, 1998 U. Chi. Legal F. 261; Michael R. Dimino, Sr., Police Paternalism: Community Caretaking, Assistance Searches, and Fourth Amendment Reasonableness, 66 Wash. & Lee L. Rev. 1485 (2009).

B. POLICE ENFORCEMENT OF CIVILITY

Police and citizens have very many exchanges that do not enter the casebooks and that are not governed by statutes or other rules. Because of the informal and personal nature of many of these exchanges, they will often be resolved in the streets, or in police precincts and prosecutors' offices, without ever becoming a source of formal (or traceable) conflict. But the lack of formality in day-to-day exchanges between police and citizens does not mean the exchanges are unimportant. These low-level interactions — at the border of criminal procedure — may be the place where trust and distrust, abuse and respect, are firmly established in the public mind.

■ STATE v. SHARON MATSON

818 A.2d 213 (Me. 2003)

Procedural history

CALKINS, J.

Sharon Matson appeals from a judgment of conviction of obstructing government administration. . . . On appeal, Matson argues that there was insufficient evidence that her rude and disruptive conduct toward a police officer who was in the process of arresting her companion constituted "intimidation" within the meaning of section 751. We agree and vacate the judgment.

At approximately 2 A.M. on December 7, 2001, Rockland Police Officer Finnegan stopped a car for having a license plate light out, illegal attachment of plates, and suspicion of operating under the influence (OUI). Finnegan testified that he smelled alcohol on the breath of the driver, Gifford Campbell, and Finnegan asked Gifford to step out and walk to the front of Finnegan's cruiser for field sobriety tests. Campbell's passenger, Sharon Matson, came out of the car yelling, "No, no fucking way. You're not doing to him what you did to me," a reference to the fact that Finnegan had arrested her for OUI a few months before. Finnegan told Matson to sit in the car, to calm down, and not to interfere, but she refused and kept shouting. Finnegan performed a horizontal gaze nystagmus test on Campbell but did no additional field sobriety tests because Matson continued yelling at him and no back-up officers were available. As Finnegan told Campbell he was under arrest for operating after suspension, Matson "charged forward," saying, "No, no fucking way. You're not arresting him." Matson stepped to within a couple of feet of Finnegan; as he began walking Campbell to the cruiser, she stepped in his way and refused to move, shouting all the while. Finnegan warned her she could be arrested for obstructing government administration and told her to step back, get out of the way, and stop interfering. She responded by saying, "Arrest me." He moved her out of the way with his left hand while holding Campbell with his right and walked past her to the cruiser. She followed, shouting. Finnegan stopped to search Campbell, and then moved him toward the rear door of the cruiser. Matson stepped in front of them, stood with her back against the door, spread her arms, and said, "No, no way, you're not taking him to jail." Finnegan told her to get out of the way, and she refused and again told him to arrest her. He moved her aside again, this time with his right hand, put Campbell in the cruiser, and arrested her. Matson said, "Good, I wanted you to arrest me." On cross-examination, Finnegan stated that he was not in fear of Matson at any time and that she never struck him, threatened him, or called him names.

The court took judicial notice of the file in Matson's OUI case, which indicated that she had been released on bail, with conditions, in May 2001, and that the conditions remained in effect until the court found her not guilty in January 2002. Campbell and Matson testified to a story different from Finnegan's, in which Finnegan used excessive force against Matson. In its closing, the State noted that it did not allege disorderly conduct and that Matson had a right to say what she said, but it argued that Matson had interfered with Finnegan's arrest of Campbell by intimidation and force. The court found that Finnegan's testimony was credible, that Matson's testimony was inconsistent, and that it was unlikely that the events transpired as she had described them. The court found that Matson's conduct involved intimidation but not force and found her guilty of obstructing government administration. . . . The court sentenced Matson to pay fines. . . .

Title 17-A M.R.S.A. §751(1) provides: "A person is guilty of obstructing government administration if the person uses force, violence or intimidation or engages in any criminal act with the intent to interfere with a public servant performing or purporting to perform an official function." Because the court based its determination of guilt on a finding that Matson had used intimidation, not force, and because there is no doubt that, in arresting Campbell, Finnegan was a public servant performing an official function and that Matson intended to interfere with that arrest, the issue on appeal is whether the evidence supports a finding that her conduct involved intimidation within the meaning of the statute.

We have interpreted the intimidation provision in section 751 once, in State v. Janisczak, 579 A.2d 736 (Me. 1990). The defendant in that case interfered with an arrest by yelling profanities at officers, who were struggling with a large, violent suspect. We adopted a definition of intimidation as "unlawful coercion, extortion, duress, or putting in fear." We then applied that definition to hold that

> no reasonable trier of fact could find on the evidence presented that Janisczak's actions constituted unlawful coercion, extortion, or duress. Further, although all five of the officers who were present at the scene testified at trial, none stated that he was put in fear by the defendant. Nor did any officer present testimony from which a jury reasonably could infer that one or more of the officers was afraid of Janisczak or his actions.

The State attempts to distinguish *Janisczak* on the basis that the defendant's conduct there consisted solely of speech, whereas Matson physically interfered with the arrest here. This argument is unconvincing. In holding in *Janisczak* that the evidence was insufficient to prove intimidation, we focused not on the lack of physical interference, but on the fact that the officers were not actually intimidated by the defendant's conduct. That analysis is controlling here. Finnegan admitted that he was not put in fear by Matson's conduct, and there is no basis for concluding that her actions constituted coercion, much less duress or extortion. The State presented no evidence that Finnegan was intimidated.

The State seems to suggest that Matson must have been guilty of obstructing government administration because she physically interfered with an arrest. However, physical interference without the use of force, violence, or the commission of a crime and which does not actually intimidate the police officer has not been made a crime. The Legislature could have drafted section 751 to prohibit any physical interference with a public servant performing an official function, but it chose not to do so. Cf. Model Penal Code §242.1 ("A person commits a misdemeanor if he purposely obstructs, impairs or perverts the administration of law or other governmental function by force, violence, physical interference or obstacle."). . . . Instead, 17-A M.R.S.A. §751-A only prohibits refusal to submit to arrest by the arrestee himself, and then only if it involves physical force or substantial risk of bodily injury. The Legislature chose to draft section 751 narrowly, and we have construed it narrowly.

The evidence was insufficient to support Matson's conviction for obstructing government administration. . . .

SAUFLEY, C.J., dissenting.

I respectfully dissent. In reviewing a sufficiency of the evidence challenge to a criminal conviction, we must view the evidence and any inferences that can be drawn from the evidence most favorably to the result reached by the trial court. . . . The Court's opinion does not directly address the defense evidence. However, that evidence, interpreted most favorably to the trial court's result, suggests a considerably more violent and forceful confrontation between the defendant and the police officer than is suggested by the State's evidence which is the focus of the Court's discussion. . . .

As the officer was moving the arrested driver towards the cruiser, Matson blocked his way and his entrance to the cruiser door. She refused the officer's request to move out of the way at which point, according to the defense evidence, the officer had to forcibly push or pull Matson to the side, causing her to fall down. According to the defense evidence, Matson then got back up and came at the officer again, either as he was placing the arrestee in the cruiser or after he had placed the arrestee in the cruiser. Again, the officer had to push Matson back. . . . Further shouting then occurred with Matson swearing at the officer and inviting him to arrest her. Matson was arrested at about the same time as a back-up officer arrived on the scene.

The sum of this evidence indicates that Matson obstructed the officer's efforts to conduct field sobriety tests and take the driver into custody. The evidence indicates, essentially without dispute, that the officer was sufficiently intimidated by Matson's actions that he ceased doing field sobriety tests before he otherwise would have done so and he called for back-up assistance. Further, as the officer was attempting to put the arrestee into his vehicle, Matson physically obstructed the officer's efforts, leading to a physical confrontation between Matson and the officer requiring him to use force — Matson's evidence indicates considerable force — to move her out of the way and place the arrestee in the police cruiser. . . .

The Court's opinion indicates that there was insufficient evidence to support a finding that Matson used "force, violence or intimidation." Certainly, the officer's ceasing field sobriety tests and calling for back-up as a result of Matson's shouting, swearing, insults and confrontational behavior can reasonably be construed to support a finding of at least some degree of intimidation. Further, Matson's physical blocking of the officer's efforts to place the arrestee in his cruiser required the officer to deviate from what otherwise would have been his normal practice and to forcibly move Matson aside so he could complete his arrest. The evidence indicates that Matson then came at the officer a second time and again had to be restrained as she was objecting to the arrest.

The Court cites State v. Janisczak, 579 A.2d 736 (Me. 1990), to suggest that this evidence is insufficient to support a finding of fear, violence or intimidation. However, *Janisczak* must be distinguished from this case. The Court's opinion in *Janisczak* indicates that the confrontation there involved five officers and the one defendant and that no officer stated that he was "put in fear by the defendant." Here, a lone officer was faced with two people, one who he was arresting and another who was completely out of control, combative and physically attempting to prevent the officer from performing his function. The officer certainly had sufficient concerns about the safety of the situation to deviate from his normal practice, suspend field sobriety tests, call for back-up and forcibly move Matson aside to terminate her physical obstruction of his arrest. These circumstances demonstrate sufficient force and intimidating behavior by Matson to support the conviction beyond a reasonable doubt. Accordingly, I would affirm the judgment of conviction on the charge of obstructing government administration. . . .

Notes

1. *Police enforcement of civility: majority view.* Appellate cases involving arrests for incivility toward police officers are rare. One reason might be that citizens are rarely uncivil toward police, though this seems unlikely. Sometimes police arrest citizens for direct interference with their duties and charge them with obstruction or interfering with an arrest or assault, but in the absence of physical contact police more often respond with the indirect charge of disorderly conduct. Prosecutors refuse to charge some of these arrests, and trial courts dismiss others.

Most state appellate decisions reverse disorderly conduct convictions based solely on profane insults directed toward police officers. See Jones v. State, 798 So. 2d 1241 (Miss. 2001). But a few sustain such convictions. In City of St. Paul v. Morris, 104 N.W.2d 902 (Minn. 1960), two officers entered a restaurant at 1:30 A.M. and arrested three people (including the half brother of the defendant, Robert Morris) for consuming liquor in a restaurant not licensed for such consumption. As the officers left the restaurant, Morris walked behind them asking the officers why they were arresting his brother. The defendant then said to the officers two or three times, "You white motherfuckers, what are you picking on us for, why don't you pick on the white people?" The officers then arrested Morris. Other patrons of the restaurant were close enough to hear what Morris said, but he used a normal tone of voice and there was no noise, fighting, violence, or threats among the other patrons. The ordinance in question made it a misdemeanor for a person to make "any noise, riot, disturbance or improper diversion." The appellate court upheld Morris' conviction because the ordinance "embraces acts which corrupt the public morals or outrage the sense of public decency." The officers had no special duty to tolerate such verbal abuse: "there is no sound reason why officers must be subjected to indignities such as present here, indignities that go far beyond what any other citizen might reasonably be expected to endure." Although the dissenting opinion stressed the racial tension evident in the conflict, the majority believed that the case raised no racial issue: "under the particular facts involved, we have no doubt that the expression would be equally provocative and offensive to any citizen, regardless of race." For a more recent example of a court sustaining a conviction based on abusive language directed at a police officer, see Spry v. State, 396 Md. 682 (Md. 2007) (affirming arrest for disturbance of the peace one day after Spry initially refused an officer's request to leave the scene of a fight and said to the police officer, "Fuck you, bitch").

What differences might explain the different outcomes in *Matson* and *Morris*? Could you imagine a court today not seeing a racial issue involved based on facts like those in *Morris*? What has changed?

2. *Nonjudicial procedural rules for enforcing civility.* Were the officers in these cases really concerned with "disorderly conduct," or were they concerned with something else? If you were responsible for training police, would you recommend that officers enforce civility, both among citizens and toward officers? Would you draft a policy that offers guidance on this question?

3. *The capacity of the police to tolerate abuse.* How does the Maine court in *Matson* view the need for police officers to tolerate abusive outbursts by citizens? Does the court hold police officers to higher standards of tolerance than might be expected of ordinary citizens? Should the tolerance expected of an officer depend on rank and experience?

4. *The capacity of the police to impose punishment.* How upset do you think Officer Finnegan was after the appellate court reversed Matson's conviction for resisting arrest? Appellate courts often dismiss charges of disorderly conduct or resisting arrest after a citizen directs profanity toward an officer. Why might such decisions not deter officers from making such arrests? Perhaps the answer comes from the observation made by some police officers that "If you can't give 'em a rap, you can still give 'em a ride."

C. CONTROL OF GANGS AND KIDS

Not everyone will respond civilly to police requests, and the police often desire more formal control than the combination of words, fear, and respect allow. Laws such as gang and loitering ordinances and curfews provide a more formal and enforceable basis for control of citizens by police. These laws exist not only at the border of criminal procedure, but at the borders of government powers and individual rights more generally. These cases raise the most basic questions of our government: What powers *must* government have? What powers *may* government have? What powers must government *not* have?

In 1992, the city of Chicago passed an ordinance, §8-4-015 of the Municipal Code, giving police authority to disrupt loitering by gang members.

(a) Whenever a police officer observes a person whom he reasonably believes to be a criminal street gang member loitering in any public place with one or more other persons, he shall order all such persons to disperse and remove themselves from the area. Any person who does not promptly obey such an order is in violation of this section. . . .

(c) As used in this section:

(1) "Loiter" means to remain in any one place with no apparent purpose.

(2) "Criminal street gang" means any ongoing organization, association in fact or group of three or more persons, whether formal or informal, having as one of its substantial activities the commission of one or more [enumerated] criminal acts . . . , and whose members individually or collectively engage in or have engaged in a pattern of criminal gang activity. . . .

(e) Any person who violates this section is subject to a fine of not less than $100 and not more than $500 for each offense, or imprisonment for not more than six months, or both. In addition to or instead of the above penalties, any person who violates this section maybe required to perform up to 120 hours of community service. . . .

In 1997 the Illinois Supreme Court held that the ordinance violated the U.S. Constitution. City of Chicago v. Jesus Morales, 687 N.E.2d 53 (Ill. 1997). The city petitioned the U.S. Supreme Court for certiorari. The Supreme Court's decision follows.

■ CITY OF CHICAGO v. JESUS MORALES

527 U.S. 41 (1999)

STEVENS, J.*

In 1992, the Chicago City Council enacted the Gang Congregation Ordinance, which prohibits "criminal street gang members" from "loitering" with one another or with other persons in any public place. The question presented is whether the Supreme Court of Illinois correctly held that the ordinance violates the Due Process Clause of the Fourteenth Amendment to the Federal Constitution.

Issue

I.

Before the ordinance was adopted, the city council's Committee on Police and Fire conducted hearings to explore the problems created by the city's street gangs, and more particularly, the consequences of public loitering by gang members. Witnesses included residents of the neighborhoods where gang members are most active, as well as some of the aldermen who represent those areas. . . . The council found that a continuing increase in criminal street gang activity was largely responsible for the city's rising murder rate, as well as an escalation of violent and drug-related crimes. It noted that in many neighborhoods throughout the city, "the burgeoning presence of street gang members in public places has intimidated many law abiding citizens." Furthermore, the council stated that gang members "establish

* [Justices O'Connor, Breyer, and Kennedy joined Parts I, II, and V of the opinion. Justices Souter and Ginsburg joined the opinion in its entirety. — EDS.]

control over identifiable areas . . . by loitering in those areas and intimidating others from entering those areas; and [m]embers of criminal street gangs avoid arrest by committing no offense punishable under existing laws when they know the police are present. . . ."

Two months after the ordinance was adopted, the Chicago Police Department promulgated General Order 92-4 to provide guidelines to govern its enforcement. That order purported to establish limitations on the enforcement discretion of police officers "to ensure that the anti-gang loitering ordinance is not enforced in an arbitrary or discriminatory way." The limitations confine the authority to arrest gang members who violate the ordinance to sworn "members of the Gang Crime Section" and certain other designated officers, and establish detailed criteria for defining street gangs and membership in such gangs. In addition, the order directs district commanders to "designate areas in which the presence of gang members has a demonstrable effect on the activities of law abiding persons in the surrounding community," and provides that the ordinance "will be enforced only within the designated areas." The city, however, does not release the locations of these "designated areas" to the public.

II.

During the three years of its enforcement, the police issued over 89,000 dispersal orders and arrested over 42,000 people for violating the ordinance.[7] . . .

III.

The basic factual predicate for the city's ordinance is not in dispute. As the city argues in its brief, "the very presence of a large collection of obviously brazen, insistent, and lawless gang members and hangers-on on the public ways intimidates residents, who become afraid even to leave their homes and go about their business. That, in turn, imperils community residents' sense of safety and security, detracts from property values, and can ultimately destabilize entire neighborhoods." The findings in the ordinance explain that it was motivated by these concerns. We have no doubt that a law that directly prohibited such intimidating conduct would be constitutional,[17] but this ordinance broadly covers a significant amount of additional activity. Uncertainty about the scope of that additional coverage provides the basis for respondents' claim that the ordinance is too vague. . . .

Vagueness may invalidate a criminal law for either of two independent reasons. First, it may fail to provide the kind of notice that will enable ordinary people to understand what conduct it prohibits; second, it may authorize and even encourage arbitrary and discriminatory enforcement.

7. City of Chicago, R. Daley & T. Hillard, Gang and Narcotic Related Violent Crime: 1993-1997, p.7 (June 1998). The city believes that the ordinance resulted in a significant decline in gang-related homicides. It notes that in 1995, the last year the ordinance was enforced, the gang-related homicide rate fell by 26%. In 1996, after the ordinance had been held invalid, the gang-related homicide rate rose 11%. However, gang-related homicides fell by 19% in 1997, over a year after the suspension of the ordinance. . . .

17. In fact the city already has several laws that serve this purpose. See, e.g., Ill. Comp. Stat. ch. 720 §§5/12-6 (1998) (Intimidation); 570/405.2 (Street gang criminal drug conspiracy); 147/1 et seq. (Illinois Street Gang Terrorism Omnibus Prevention Act); 5/25-1 (Mob action). . . .

IV.

[The] term "loiter" may have a common and accepted meaning, but the definition of that term in this ordinance — "to remain in any one place with no apparent purpose" — does not. It is difficult to imagine how any citizen of the city of Chicago standing in a public place with a group of people would know if he or she had an "apparent purpose." If she were talking to another person, would she have an apparent purpose? If she were frequently checking her watch and looking expectantly down the street, would she have an apparent purpose? . . .

The city's principal response to this concern about adequate notice is that loiterers are not subject to sanction until after they have failed to comply with an officer's order to disperse. "[Whatever] problem is created by a law that criminalizes conduct people normally believe to be innocent is solved when persons receive actual notice from a police order of what they are expected to do." We find this response unpersuasive for at least two reasons.

First, the purpose of the fair notice requirement is to enable the ordinary citizen to conform his or her conduct to the law. No one may be required at peril of life, liberty or property to speculate as to the meaning of penal statutes. Although it is true that a loiterer is not subject to criminal sanctions unless he or she disobeys a dispersal order, the loitering is the conduct that the ordinance is designed to prohibit. If the loitering is in fact harmless and innocent, the dispersal order itself is an unjustified impairment of liberty. . . . Because an officer may issue an order only after prohibited conduct has already occurred, it cannot provide the kind of advance notice that will protect the putative loiterer from being ordered to disperse. Such an order cannot retroactively give adequate warning of the boundary between the permissible and the impermissible applications of the law.

Second, the terms of the dispersal order compound the inadequacy of the notice afforded by the ordinance. It provides that the officer "shall order all such persons to disperse and remove themselves from the area." This vague phrasing raises a host of questions. After such an order issues, how long must the loiterers remain apart? How far must they move? If each loiterer walks around the block and they meet again at the same location, are they subject to arrest or merely to being ordered to disperse again? . . .

The Constitution does not permit a legislature to set a net large enough to catch all possible offenders, and leave it to the courts to step inside and say who could be rightfully detained, and who should be set at large. This ordinance is therefore vague not in the sense that it requires a person to conform his conduct to an imprecise but comprehensible normative standard, but rather in the sense that no standard of conduct is specified at all.

V.

The broad sweep of the ordinance also violates the requirement that a legislature establish minimal guidelines to govern law enforcement. . . .

It is true, as the city argues, that the requirement that the officer reasonably believe that a group of loiterers contains a gang member does place a limit on the authority to order dispersal. That limitation would no doubt be sufficient if the ordinance only applied to loitering that had an apparently harmful purpose or effect, or possibly if it only applied to loitering by persons reasonably believed to be criminal gang members. But this ordinance, for reasons that are not explained in the findings of the city council, requires no harmful purpose and applies to non-gang members as well as suspected gang members. . . .

VI.

. . . We recognize the serious and difficult problems testified to by the citizens of Chicago that led to the enactment of this ordinance. We are mindful that the preservation of liberty depends in part on the maintenance of social order. However, in this instance the city has enacted an ordinance that affords too much discretion to the police and too little notice to citizens who wish to use the public streets. . . .

O'CONNOR, J., concurring in part.

[The ordinance] fails to provide police with any standard by which they can judge whether an individual has an "apparent purpose." Indeed, because any person standing on the street has a general "purpose" — even if it is simply to stand — the ordinance permits police officers to choose which purposes are permissible. Under this construction the police do not have to decide that an individual is "threaten[ing] the public peace" to issue a dispersal order. [The] ordinance applies to hundreds of thousands of persons who are not gang members, standing on any sidewalk or in any park, coffee shop, bar, or other location open to the public. . . .

Nevertheless, there remain open to Chicago reasonable alternatives to combat the very real threat posed by gang intimidation and violence. For example, the Court properly and expressly distinguishes the ordinance from laws that require loiterers to have a "harmful purpose," from laws that target only gang members, and from laws that incorporate limits on the area and manner in which the laws may be enforced. In addition, the ordinance here is unlike a law that "directly prohibit[s]" the "presence of a large collection of obviously brazen, insistent, and lawless gang members and hangers-on on the public ways" that intimidates residents. Indeed, as the plurality notes, the city of Chicago has several laws that do exactly this. . . .

BREYER, J., concurring in part.

[The ordinance does not] limit in any way the range of conduct that police may prohibit. . . . Since one always has some apparent purpose, the so-called limitation invites, in fact requires, the policeman to interpret the words "no apparent purpose" as meaning "no apparent purpose except for. . . ." And it is in the ordinance's delegation to the policeman of open-ended discretion to fill in that blank that the problem lies. To grant to a policeman virtually standardless discretion to close off major portions of the city to an innocent person is, in my view, to create a major, not a "minor," limitation upon the free state of nature. . . .

The ordinance is unconstitutional, not because a policeman applied this discretion wisely or poorly in a particular case, but rather because the policeman enjoys too much discretion in every case. [The] city of Chicago may no more apply this law to the defendants, no matter how they behaved, than could it apply an (imaginary) statute that said, "It is a crime to do wrong," even to the worst of murderers. . . .

SCALIA, J., dissenting

The citizens of Chicago were once free to drive about the city at whatever speed they wished. At some point Chicagoans (or perhaps Illinoisans) decided this would not do, and imposed prophylactic speed limits designed to assure safe operation by the average (or perhaps even subaverage) driver with the average (or perhaps even subaverage) vehicle. This infringed upon the "freedom" of all citizens, but was not unconstitutional.

Similarly, the citizens of Chicago were once free to stand around and gawk at the scene of an accident. At some point Chicagoans discovered that this obstructed traffic and caused more accidents. They did not make the practice unlawful, but they did authorize police officers to order the crowd to disperse, and imposed penalties for refusal to obey such an order. Again, this prophylactic measure infringed upon the "freedom" of all citizens, but was not unconstitutional.

Until the ordinance that is before us today was adopted, the citizens of Chicago were free to stand about in public places with no apparent purpose — to engage, that is, in conduct that appeared to be loitering. In recent years, however, the city has been afflicted with criminal street gangs. . . . Once again, Chicagoans decided that to eliminate the problem it was worth restricting some of the freedom that they once enjoyed. The means they took was similar to the second, and more mild, example given above rather than the first: Loitering was not made unlawful, but when a group of people occupied a public place without an apparent purpose and in the company of a known gang member, police officers were authorized to order them to disperse, and the failure to obey such an order was made unlawful. The minor limitation upon the free state of nature that this prophylactic arrangement imposed upon all Chicagoans seemed to them (and it seems to me) a small price to pay for liberation of their streets. The majority today invalidates this perfectly reasonable measure . . . by elevating loitering to a constitutionally guaranteed right, and by discerning vagueness where . . . none exists.

[The ordinance is not vague.] The criteria for issuance of a dispersal order under the Chicago Ordinance could hardly be clearer. . . .

The Court [argues] that the "apparent purpose" test is too elastic because it presumably allows police officers to treat de minimis "violations" as not warranting enforcement. But such discretion . . . is no different with regard to the enforcement of this clear ordinance than it is with regard to the enforcement of all laws in our criminal-justice system. Police officers (and prosecutors) have broad discretion over what laws to enforce and when. . . .

The fact is that the present ordinance is entirely clear in its application, cannot be violated except with full knowledge and intent, and vests no more discretion in the police than innumerable other measures authorizing police orders to preserve the public peace and safety. [The] majority's real quarrel with the Chicago Ordinance is simply that it permits (or indeed requires) too much harmless conduct by innocent citizens to be proscribed. . . .

But in our democratic system, how much harmless conduct to proscribe is not a judgment to be made by the courts. So long as constitutionally guaranteed rights are not affected, and so long as the proscription has a rational basis, all sorts of perfectly harmless activity by millions of perfectly innocent people can be forbidden — riding a motorcycle without a safety helmet, for example, starting a campfire in a national forest, or selling a safe and effective drug not yet approved by the FDA. All of these acts are entirely innocent and harmless in themselves, but because of the risk of harm that they entail, the freedom to engage in them has been abridged. The citizens of Chicago have decided that depriving themselves of the freedom to "hang out" with a gang member is necessary to eliminate pervasive gang crime and intimidation — and that the elimination of the one is worth the deprivation of the other. This Court has no business second-guessing either the degree of necessity or the fairness of the trade. . . .

THOMAS, J., dissenting.

. . . Gangs fill the daily lives of many of our poorest and most vulnerable citizens with a terror that the Court does not give sufficient consideration, often relegating them to the status of prisoners in their own homes. The city of Chicago has suffered the devastation wrought by this national tragedy. Last year, in an effort to curb plummeting attendance, the Chicago Public Schools hired dozens of adults to escort children to school. The youngsters had become too terrified of gang violence to leave their homes alone. The children's fears were not unfounded. In 1996, the Chicago Police Department estimated that there were 132 criminal street gangs in the city. Between 1987 and 1994, these gangs were involved in 63,141 criminal incidents, including 21,689 nonlethal violent crimes and 894 homicides. Many of these criminal incidents and homicides result from gang "turf battles," which take place on the public streets and place innocent residents in grave danger. . . .

As part of its ongoing effort to curb the deleterious effects of criminal street gangs, the citizens of Chicago sensibly decided to return to basics. The ordinance does nothing more than confirm the well-established principle that the police have the duty and the power to maintain the public peace, and, when necessary, to disperse groups of individuals who threaten it.

[It] is important to note that the ordinance does not criminalize loitering per se. Rather, it penalizes loiterers' failure to obey a police officer's order to move along. A majority of the Court believes that this scheme vests too much discretion in police officers. Nothing could be further from the truth. Far from according officers too much discretion, the ordinance merely enables police officers to fulfill one of their traditional functions. Police officers are not, and have never been, simply enforcers of the criminal law. They wear other hats — importantly, they have long been vested with the responsibility for preserving the public peace.

In order to perform their peace-keeping responsibilities satisfactorily, the police inevitably must exercise discretion. Indeed, by empowering them to act as peace officers, the law assumes that the police will exercise that discretion responsibly and with sound judgment. That is not to say that the law should not provide objective guidelines for the police, but simply that it cannot rigidly constrain their every action. By directing a police officer not to issue a dispersal order unless he "observes a person whom he reasonably believes to be a criminal street gang member loitering in any public place," Chicago's ordinance strikes an appropriate balance between those two extremes. Just as we trust officers to rely on their experience and expertise in order to make spur-of-the-moment determinations about amorphous legal standards such as "probable cause" and "reasonable suspicion," so we must trust them to determine whether a group of loiterers contains individuals (in this case members of criminal street gangs) whom the city has determined threaten the public peace. . . . Today, the Court focuses extensively on the "rights" of gang members and their companions. It can safely do so — the people who will have to live with the consequences of today's opinion do not live in our neighborhoods. Rather, the people who will suffer from our lofty pronouncements are people . . . who have seen their neighborhoods literally destroyed by gangs and violence and drugs. They are good, decent people who must struggle to overcome their desperate situation, against all odds, in order to raise their families, earn a living, and remain good citizens. As one resident described, "There is only about maybe one or two percent of the people in the city causing these problems maybe, but it's keeping 98 percent of us in our houses and off the streets and afraid to shop." By focusing exclusively on the imagined "rights" of the two percent, the Court today has denied our most vulnerable citizens the very thing that Justice Stevens elevates above all else — the "freedom of movement." And that is a shame. I respectfully dissent.

TRACEY L. MEARES, NORMS, LEGITIMACY AND LAW ENFORCEMENT

79 Or. L. Rev. 391 (2000)

Why do some communities exhibit high crime rates while others do not? As an answer, I have looked to social disorganization theory. This is a theory developed by Clifford Shaw and Henry McKay to explain why juvenile delinquency remained high in certain areas of central cities over time despite population turnover. In Shaw and McKay's classic work, they maintained that low economic status, ethnic heterogeneity and residential mobility led to the disruption of community social organization, which, in turn, accounted for variation in crime and delinquency rates in a given area. See Clifford R. Shaw & Henry D. McKay, Juvenile Delinquency and Urban Areas (rev. ed. 1969). To support this theory, the researchers demonstrated that high rates of juvenile delinquency were specific to certain areas in the cities they studied and that these rates persisted over time despite population turnover. This finding motivated the researchers to reject individual-level explanations of delinquency and focus instead on the features of the communities in which the juveniles lived in order to explain the high crime rates.

Contemporary researchers have applied Shaw and McKay's insights to the longstanding problematic observation that African-Americans are under criminal justice system control out of proportion to their representation in the general population. . . . [They] have documented that major differences often exist between the ecological contexts in which poor African-Americans typically reside on the one hand, and those in which poor whites typically reside on the other. Poor white families tend to reside in communities that feature more family-stable contexts than poor black families. . . . Indeed, Professors Robert Sampson and William Julius Wilson have noted, "[R]acial difference in poverty and family disruption are so strong that the 'worst' urban contexts in which whites reside are considerably better than the average context of black communities." Robert J. Sampson & William Julius Wilson, Toward a Theory of Race, Crime, and Urban Inequality, in Crime and Inequality 37, 42 (John Hagan & Ruth D. Peterson eds., 1995).

In terms of social organization theory, these different contexts translate into different levels of capacity of neighborhoods to resist and reduce crime. This is in large part because ecological contexts affect the extent to which neighborhood residents exert social control — informal mechanisms rather than formal regulation imposed by police and courts — to achieve public order. . . .

Norm enforcement is easier when individuals in a community have social linkages and trust one another. Individuals who reside in communities in which there are few social linkages and where distrust is rampant will have difficulty exerting social control over one another. Empirical work bears this out. While ecological factors such as poverty, joblessness and family disruption are associated with crime, criminologists have shown that such factors are mediated by community-type social capital factors such as prevalence of friendship networks, participation in formal and informal organizations like churches and PTAs and the like. Such social structural factors provide the linkages along which norms of law abidingness can travel. They are "norm highways."

It is critical to understand, however, that the norms on social highways can travel in any direction. There is no necessary reason why community norms must be directed toward the project of crime control. In fact, one can easily imagine tight social networks supporting criminogenic conduct on a community-wide basis. . . .

Because social capital factors appear to matter more to explaining high crime rates in communities than individual-level factors, it makes sense to engineer crime policy that takes account of this reality. The social capital thesis calls into question policies that attempt to control crime simply by manipulating an individual's calculus regarding whether "crime pays" in the particular instance. In fact, deterrence-based strategies directed toward individual law breakers may even exacerbate the very activity the strategy purports to curb. For example, if lawmakers choose to address illegal drug selling by increasing the number of those convicted for drug selling and by increasing prison sentences for those convicted of such activity (which is basically the current American approach to drug crimes), then one expected consequence is that more individuals will be imprisoned for longer periods of time. Although the standard economic conception of crime suggests that this strategy should make a dent in the level of illegal drug activity, social organization theory's emphasis on social capital and norms suggests that this strategy will backfire. The highest numbers of those caught under this approach will tend to be street-level dealers, who are not evenly distributed throughout a city, but who are geographically concentrated in disadvantaged, minority neighborhoods. . . . Removal of these individuals in large numbers from their communities will be associated with higher levels of joblessness, low economic status, and family disruption, which in turn will disrupt the social structural and cultural determinants of community-based social control. . . .

The best norm-based strategies will maximize social organization benefits without visiting as high a cost on disadvantaged communities as high rates of imprisonment do. Drug enforcement strategies, such as reverse drug stings, redistribute enforcement costs to communities that have the capacity to absorb the consequences of possible imprisonment. These, and strategies that attempt to disrupt illegal drug markets without relying at all on imprisonment, such as using loitering ordinances to make it difficult for drug buyers to find street sellers, can address illegal drug markets without concentrating the costs of imprisonment on the communities least prepared to absorb those costs. . . .

Norms and Compliance

Do people obey the law because they fear the consequences if they do not? Or, do they obey the law for other reasons? Focusing on the former question, economists have looked primarily to deterrence theory to explain compliance. The foundations of this theory are well-known. People rationally maximize their utility, and they, therefore, shape their behavior in response to incentives and penalties associated with the criminal code. . . . This view suggests that compliance is instrumental. This view also fuels the current trend toward "get tough on crime" approaches, which feature policies such as truth-in-sentencing, long sentences for drug offending, and so-called "three-strikes-and-you're-out" sentences.

Social psychologists have offered another view of compliance with the law. By pointing to normative bases for compliance rather than instrumental ones, these researchers have connected voluntary compliance with the law to the fact that individuals believe the law is "just" or because they believe that the authority enforcing the law has the right to do so. See Tom R. Tyler, Why People Obey the Law 3-4 (1990). . . . In contrast to the individual who complies with the law because she is responding to externally imposed punishments, the individual who complies for normative reasons does so because she feels an internal obligation. [There] is empirical work demonstrating that legitimacy matters more to compliance than instrumental factors, such as sanctions imposed by authorities on individuals who fail to follow the law or private rules.

[This is good news] because relying only on carrots and sticks to produce compliance can be a costly strategy. [Instrumental] means of producing compliance are not self-sustaining. Authorities must be willing to maintain mechanisms of instrumental compliance. For example, if deterrence is to be produced by maintaining a certain probability of detection of rule-breakers, then authorities must be willing to devote resources to maintenance (or increase) of the desired level of police to ensure that the requisite probability of detection is met. Therefore, instrumental means of producing compliance always depend on resource limits.

Legitimacy . . . can be acquired simply by changing procedures and practices of current officials in ways that require almost no additional resources. For example, some research indicates that police who regularly treat arrestees with courtesy are more likely than those who do not to be viewed as legitimate. While police officers may not like to be told to be more polite to arrestees, this research suggests that law enforcement gains could be achieved more cheaply than through more instrumental means simply by telling officers to "be nice." . . .

A legitimacy-based program of law enforcement will focus more on persuasion than it will focus on punishment. And, in order to persuade, authorities will have to pay attention to the creation of the necessary social capital that engenders trust relationships between governors and the governed. . . .

COMMUNITY PARTICIPATION IN POLICING

Generation of participation by stakeholders in criminal justice processes is a feature of . . . law enforcement that should enhance legitimacy of government. [A key aspect of creating participation is] the leveling of authority between government officials and the governed. [The process described here] requires government officials to cede some of their exclusive power to enforce laws.

In an attempt to address the complaints of residents concerned about gang violence and open-air drug selling, the City of Chicago has recently adopted an ordinance that empowers police officers to approach groups of people involved in gang loitering or narcotics-related loitering, inform those individuals that they are engaged in prohibited loitering, order the individuals to disperse from within sight and hearing of the place which the order was issued, and inform the individuals ordered to disperse that they will be subject to arrest if they fail to obey the order or return to the area during the next three hours. This ordinance is a revised version of another anti-gang loitering ordinance adopted by Chicago. The original ordinance was struck down by the Supreme Court as unconstitutionally vague. While the original ordinance defined loitering as staying in one place "with no apparent purpose," the revised ordinance defines gang loitering as "remaining in any one place under circumstances that would warrant a reasonable person to believe that the purpose or effect of that behavior is to enable a criminal street gang to establish control over identifiable areas, to intimidate others from entering those areas, or to conceal illegal activities." Similarly, narcotics-related loitering means "remaining in any one place under circumstances that would warrant a reasonable person to believe that the purpose or effect of that behavior is to facilitate the distribution of substances in violation of the Cannabis Control Act or the Illinois Controlled Substances Act." The definitions of both types of loitering incorporate specific language from both Justice Stevens' opinion for the plurality and Justice O'Connor's concurrence, which was joined by Justice Breyer.

[The] revised ordinance contains language that has both social organization benefits and legitimacy benefits. Consider social organization first. The sociology explained above suggests that law enforcement strategies that depend on imprisonment of a large number of geographically concentrated individuals should be avoided if possible. Of course, some criminal offenses demand imprisonment, such as murder or robbery. But other offenses likely are better dealt with through norm-focused strategies. Open-air drug selling is an example. The anti-gang, anti-narcotics loitering ordinance adopted by Chicago empowers police officers to disrupt drug markets without arresting large numbers of low-level dealers who retail in open areas and who are concentrated in minority, poor areas of the City. These dealers depend on confederates to stand in strategic areas to advertise the drugs they are selling to the many buyers who come from outside the particular community in which the drugs are sold — often the suburbs. Without the "advertisers" these outsiders cannot find the dealers. So, enforcement of the anti-narcotics provision of the ordinance can disrupt the market without arrest and potential subsequent conviction and imprisonment of the dealer. This is a social organization benefit. . . .

The City Council recognized that drug selling and gang clashes are intimately bound up in place. Therefore, the ordinance provides that the Superintendent of Police shall designate areas of the city for enforcement by written directive. In order to make this designation, the ordinance also provides that the Superintendent "shall consult as he or she deems appropriate with persons who are knowledgeable. . . . Such persons may include . . . elected and appointed officials of the area [and] community-based organizations . . . who are familiar with the area." . . .

The consultation provision provides a key opening for increased perceptions of legitimacy of Chicago police among the communities in which this ordinance will be enforced. By its very structure the ordinance reduces the hierarchy inherent to municipal policing. This ordinance creates a partnership in the law enforcement process, and through that process creates greater accountability of the police to the members of affected communities. . . . [This] process provides both invitations to participation as well as meaningful signals to community members that their opinions count.

COOPERATION BETWEEN THE CHURCH AND THE POLICE

. . . There has been an ongoing effort in Chicago to create more ties between the pastors of African-American churches on Chicago's impoverished West side and the police. To create these bonds the commander of Chicago's highest-crime Police District tried an extremely innovative strategy. Three years ago, he facilitated a community-wide prayer vigil. In groups of ten, the participants stood on designated corners — the same corners where lookouts often hawked their wares by calling out, "Rocks and Blows!" — and prayed. Following the prayer vigil, the whole group and over 7,000 more community residents went to a large park for a "praise celebration," where there was music provided by a 400-member gospel choir, food, and inspirational speeches.

Importantly, it is not the vigil itself that creates the legitimacy benefits; rather, it is the organization process — the monthly meetings in the police roll call room and regular contact between ministers and police officials — that generated the social capital that drives assessments of trust. Of course, there would have been no meetings but for the prayer vigil, so the vigil is a necessary component. [But] the process of putting on the vigil was an opportunity for both the police and the ministers to begin to see themselves as part of the same group — a necessary component to trust generation. . . .

Our current approach to crime control is basically inconsistent with the project of improving community capacity for social control — especially the capacity of those communities that possess the highest crime rates. The United States imprisons more people than any other country in the world, and the bulk of those imprisoned are African-American males, who likely come from urban areas. Social organization theory tells us that this approach is dangerously counterproductive.

Notes

1. *Order maintenance.* Is order maintenance (or as Justice Thomas labels it, "peace-keeping") a crime control function or a community caretaker function? Should police have the general authority to ask citizens to "move on"? If you were a member of the Chicago City Council, could you draft a constitutional gang ordinance that would serve similar purposes to the ordinance struck down in *Morales*? State and federal cases on gang and order maintenance provisions are uncommon. Why?

As Professor Meares points out, the city of Chicago amended its anti-loitering ordinance to address the Court's concerns as expressed in *Morales.* The ordinance itself now requires the police superintendent to designate "hot zones" of gang or narcotics activity, where the police may enforce the ordinance. The superintendent must consult community groups (along with various law enforcement officials) when designating the hot zones. See Chicago Police Department General Order No. 00-02. Would the amended ordinance survive a constitutional challenge? (No challenges have succeeded so far.) Does it reinforce community crime control efforts?

2. *Community control of police.* The opinions of the Justices in *Morales* reveal different visions of "ordinary" policing and the ordinary methods of controlling police. For the plurality and concurring justices, pre-announced rules of law are necessary to hold police discretion to an acceptable minimum; legislators and judges control

the police through formal sources of law. For the dissenting justices, police discretion is perfectly ordinary, even desirable. Control of the police comes from political pressure on elected officials at the local level rather than from pre-announced rules. Are these visions realistic about the power of legal rules or political pressure to influence police operations? Professors Dan Kahan and Tracey Meares argue that doctrines granting broad discretion to police officers (including loitering laws) are more defensible today than in the 1960s because of the rising political power of African Americans in the nation's inner cities. Techniques formerly used to harass and exclude African Americans from public life could now become the tools of minority communities to free themselves from rampant criminality. Kahan & Meares, The Coming Crisis of Criminal Procedure, 86 Geo. L.J. 1153 (1998); see also Debra Livingston, Police Discretion and the Quality of Life in Public Places: Courts, Communities, and the New Policing, 97 Colum. L. Rev. 551 (1997). Is their vision of democratic accountability realistic?

3. *Social norms and the sources of crime.* As the excerpt above implies, Meares assigns only a secondary role to the police in the prevention of crime. The police (and the criminal procedure rules that structure their behavior) can contribute best to the control of crime if they ultimately strengthen the *community's* own ability to control crime. Thus, the "disorganization" of a community is the most salient source of crime, and the best rules for the police are built around an awareness of that source.

What are some other accounts of the sources of crime, and how might those accounts change your views on the proper role of the police? Several criminological theories over the years have emphasized the genetic and biological components of crime. (Sometimes this leads to searches for identifiable traits among a criminal "type," an enterprise that too often has degenerated into racial stereotyping or other unsound generalizations.) If you believe that some individuals have a biological or psychological predisposition to commit crimes, how might that affect the rules you would expect the police to follow? If the causes of female crime are different from the causes of male crime, does that have implications for policing?

Other criminological theories emphasize various aspects of the criminal's social environment. For instance, according to "strain theory," unemployment, poverty and other sources of stress induce many people to commit crimes. "Social learning" theory suggests that many criminals learn to commit their crimes because the people around them reinforce criminal actions and attitudes. The influence of these theories and many other explanations for crime have waxed and waned among criminologists over the years. See Robert Agnew, Crime Causation: Sociological Theories, in Encyclopedia of Crime and Justice (Joshua Dressler ed., 2002). For each of these accounts of the sources of crime, how might the police best contribute to the control of crime? For a survey of the leading criminological accounts of crime, see the web extension for this chapter at *http://www.crimpro.com/extension/ch01*.

4. *Community crime control antecedents.* There are historic antecedents for today's forms of community crime control. Professor Jonathan Simon describes the thousand-year-old tradition of "frankpledge" in England, where each frankpledge group (originally 100 households) was held collectively responsible for crime control. From the tenth through the fifteenth centuries, free adult males had a legal obligation to "report offenses committed by other members of the group and to be financially obligated for any failure to produce the offender at presentment." During the "view of the frankpledge," the male population gathered before representatives

of the crown and local elites. The officials collected taxes and fines, registered newcomers, and took reports on crime. In this way, the frankpledge system "integrated crime control into the everyday lives of the common people and local government." Simon, Poor Discipline: Parole and the Social Control of the Underclass 18-20 (1993). The frankpledge system created strong incentive for private social control of criminal behavior. Does it resemble crime control in small towns in the United States today? Is the frankpledge compatible with a mobile society? How does the relationship between citizen and police officer in a community policing model resemble the frankpledge?

Problem 1-2. Juvenile Curfews

At 10:35 P.M., 15-year-old David Simmons and a friend were skateboarding in a Panora, Iowa, shopping center. A police officer issued citations to them for violating a Panora juvenile curfew ordinance, which provided as follows:

1. It is unlawful for any minor [under 18] to be or remain upon any of the alleys, streets or public places or places of business and amusement in the city between the hours of 10 P.M. and 5 A.M. of the following day.
2. The curfew shall not apply to any minor who is accompanied by a guardian, parent or other person charged with the care and custody of such minor, or other responsible person over 18 years of age, nor shall the restriction apply to any minor who is traveling between his home or place of residence and the place where any approved place of employment, church, municipal or school function is being held.
3. It is unlawful for any parent, guardian or other person charged with the care and custody of any minor to allow or permit such minor to be in or upon any of the streets, alleys, places of business or amusement, or other public places within the curfew hours except as provided in subsection 2.
4. It is unlawful for any person, firm or corporation operating a place of business or amusement to allow or permit any minor to be in or upon any place of business or amusement operated by them within the curfew hours except as provided in subsection 2.
5. Any peace officer of this city while on duty is hereby empowered to arrest any minor who violates the curfew. Upon arrest, the minor shall be returned to the custody of the parent, guardian or other person charged with the care and custody of the minor.

Simmons was found guilty of violating the curfew ordinance. The penalty imposed was a $1 fine plus surcharge and costs. Simmons appealed the conviction, with strong support from his parents. The Simmons family also asked the city council to repeal or amend the curfew ordinance.

As an appellate court judge, how would you rule on his appeal? Is the ordinance constitutional? As a member of the city council, would you vote to repeal or amend the ordinance? Compare City of Panora v. Simmons, 445 N.W.2d 363 (Iowa 1989).

Notes

1. *Juvenile curfews: majority position.* Many state and local governments have passed laws empowering the police to enforce a "curfew" on persons less than 18 years old. The practice is now commonplace: A 2005 survey by the National League of Cities showed that over half of the cities surveyed had enacted juvenile curfew laws, and two-thirds of the cities with curfew laws passed them within the last 20 years. Children and parents who challenge the validity of these laws argue that the curfews are unconstitutionally vague and interfere with fundamental rights such as the "right to travel" or the right of parents to make basic parenting decisions without governmental interference. The state court response has been mixed, with the largest group of states upholding the statutes or ordinances, noting that they do not simply ban juveniles from being "present" in public after dark. Instead, they allow juveniles to be outdoors for certain legitimate reasons or in the company of a parent. See Ramos v. Town of Vernon, 761 A.2d 705 (Conn. 2000). A few state courts have struck down the juvenile curfew laws. See City of Sumner v. Walsh, 61 P.3d 1111 (Wash. 2003); State v. J.P., 907 So. 2d 1011 (Fla. 2004). To gain a better sense of this debate among state courts and lower federal courts, along with some historical background on the use of juvenile curfews, see the web extension for this chapter at *http://www.crimpro.com/extension/ch01*.

2. *Adult curfews.* There is a long and largely disreputable history of adult curfews in the United States. Before the Civil War, curfew laws in the South designated times when slaves could be on the streets. During the late 1800s, curfew ordinances flourished in places where there were large numbers of immigrants, because of fears that immigrants would not properly supervise their children. In 1941, emergency curfews were imposed on American citizens of Japanese ancestry. A variety of adult curfew, loitering, and vagrancy laws were invalidated in the late 1960s through the early 1980s as violations of the basic right of adult citizens to go where they want, whenever they want. See Papachristou v. City of Jacksonville, 405 U.S. 156 (1972) (striking down a vagrancy ordinance); Kolender v. Lawson, 461 U.S. 352 (1983) (rejecting a California statute requiring citizens who loiter to account for their presence and show "reasonable and reliable" identification when required by a police officer; Lawson was detained about 15 times during two-year period for walking in isolated areas at late hours). The Supreme Court reaffirmed this line of cases by striking down the gang loitering ordinance in Chicago v. Morales, 527 U.S. 41 (1999). In a society searching urgently for ways to control crime, should courts reconsider the validity of adult curfew laws? Is the right to prowl at 3 A.M. essential to a free country?

3. *Police as parents.* As a parent, how would you feel about a local curfew law? Would your decision depend on the sanctions attached to the law? Would it depend on your view of the police purpose when enforcing a curfew? Are police exercising a crime control function or a community caretaker function (or something else entirely) when they enforce a curfew?

D. TRADITIONAL AND COMMUNITY POLICING

The idea of what police do, and how they do it, is far from a static concept. From the introduction of police into municipalities in the mid-nineteenth century until the 1940s, local political leaders controlled police departments through job patronage and through investigating complaints from citizens. Police officers in this period responded to a wide variety of social needs including, but not limited to, crime control. The "reform era" followed, lasting from the 1940s until the 1980s. During this period, according to scholars George Kelling and Mark Moore,

> [reformers] rejected politics as the basis of police legitimacy. . . . Civil service eliminated patronage and ward influences in hiring and firing police officers.
>
> [Police] in the reform era moved to narrow their functioning to crime control and criminal apprehension. Police agencies became *law enforcement* agencies. Their goal was to control crime. Their principal means was the use of criminal law to apprehend and deter offenders. Activities that drew the police into solving other kinds of community problems . . . were identified as "social work," and became the object of derision. . . .
>
> During the era of reform policing, the new model demanded an impartial law enforcer who related to citizens in professionally neutral and distant terms. No better characterization of this model can be found than television's Sergeant Friday, whose response, "Just the facts, ma'am," typified the idea: impersonal and oriented toward crime solving rather than responsive to the emotional crisis of a victim.

Kelling and Moore, From Political to Reform to Community: The Evolving Strategy of Police, in Community Policing: Rhetoric or Reality (Jack Greene and Stephen Mastrofski eds., 1988).

In the past 30 years a new conception of the police function has emerged: "community policing." In its broadest outlines, community policing shifts control over police resources from central police management to the community level. Community policing broadens the goals of policing to include community order beyond crime control, and recognizes that fear of crime is a serious matter in its own right. In these sweeping terms, it is difficult to find many police officers, or many departments, that have not embraced this change.

As these changes in police function become pervasive, the trend toward community policing may shift individual and public perceptions of what the police do. In turn, this change may require us to rethink much of modern criminal procedure, which is firmly anchored to the reform-era conception of policing.

The following materials describe in more detail the shifts in policing models over the last generation. The first piece, written during the heyday of reform-era professionalized policing, sets out a classic dichotomy between the "crime control" and "due process" models of criminal justice — two ways of evaluating the work of law enforcement officers and other criminal justice actors. The second piece, written by a national coalition of police chiefs and other police administrators, lays out the distinctive features of the newer community policing model.

As you read the description below of this changing philosophy of policing, keep in mind its possible effect on procedural rules. If you were a city council member, would you pass an ordinance to give the police greater powers to "problem solve"?

For instance, recall the curfew and "civility" cases from the previous sections. It is possible that departments adopting the community policing philosophy should get greater leeway in enforcing civility or juvenile curfews. With the shift to community policing, are procedural controls on the police *less* important or feasible, or are they *more* important than ever — to prevent the officers from making arbitrary and discriminatory use of their more frequent interactions with the public?

■ HERBERT L. PACKER, TWO MODELS OF THE CRIMINAL PROCESS

113 U. Pa. L. Rev. 1 (1964)

. . . The kind of criminal process we have depends importantly on certain value choices that are reflected, explicitly or implicitly, in its habitual functioning. The kind of model we need is one that permits us to recognize explicitly the value choices that underlie the details of the criminal process. In a word, what we need is a *normative* model, or rather two models, to let us perceive the normative antinomy that runs deep in the life of the criminal law. These models may not be labeled Good and Bad, and I hope they will not be taken in that sense. Rather, they represent an attempt to abstract two separate value systems that compete for attention in the operation of the criminal process. . . . I call these two models the Due Process Model and the Crime Control Model. . . .

CRIME CONTROL VALUES

The value system that underlies the Crime Control Model is based on the proposition that the repression of criminal conduct is by far the most important function to be performed by the criminal process. The failure of law enforcement to bring criminal conduct under tight control is viewed as leading to the breakdown of public order and thence to the disappearance of an important condition of human freedom. . . . The claim ultimately is that the criminal process is a positive guarantor of social freedom. In order to achieve this high purpose, the Crime Control Model requires that primary attention be paid to the efficiency with which the criminal process operates to screen suspects, determine guilt, and secure appropriate dispositions of persons convicted of crime. . . .

The model, in order to operate successfully, must produce a high rate of apprehension and conviction and must do so in a context where the magnitudes being dealt with are very large, and the resources for dealing with them are very limited. There must then be a premium on speed and finality. Speed, in turn, depends on informality and on uniformity; finality depends on minimizing the occasions for challenge. The process must not be cluttered with ceremonious rituals that do not advance the progress of a case. Facts can be established more quickly through interrogation in a police station than through the formal process of examination and cross-examination in a court; it follows that extrajudicial processes should be preferred to judicial processes, informal to formal operations. Informality is not enough; there must also be uniformity. Routine stereotyped procedures are essential if large numbers are being handled. The model that will operate successfully on these presuppositions must be an administrative, almost a managerial, model. The image that comes to mind is an assembly line or a conveyor belt down which moves an endless stream of cases, never stopping, carrying the cases to workers who stand at fixed stations and who perform on each case as it comes by the same small but essential operation that brings it one step closer to being a finished product, or, to exchange the metaphor for the reality, a closed file.

The criminal process, on this model, is seen as a screening process in which each successive stage — prearrest investigation, arrest, post-arrest investigation, preparation for trial, trial or entry of plea, conviction, and disposition — involves a series of routinized operations whose success is gauged primarily by their tendency to pass the case along to a successful conclusion.

What is a successful conclusion? One that throws off at an early stage those cases in which it appears unlikely that the person apprehended is an offender and then secures, as expeditiously as possible, the conviction of the rest with a minimum of occasions for challenge, let alone postaudit. By the application of administrative expertness, primarily that of the police and prosecutors, an early determination of probable innocence or guilt emerges. The probably innocent are screened out. The probably guilty are passed quickly through the remaining stages of the process. The key to the operation of the model as to those who are not screened out is what I shall call a presumption of guilt. . . .

The presumption of guilt allows the Crime Control Model to deal efficiently with large numbers. The supposition is that the screening processes operated by police and prosecutors are reliable indicators of probable guilt. Once a man has been investigated without being found to be probably innocent, or, to put it differently, once a determination has been made that there is enough evidence of guilt so that he should be held for further action rather than released from the process, then all subsequent activity directed toward him is based on the view that he is probably guilty. . . .

It would be a mistake to think of the presumption of guilt as the opposite of the presumption of innocence. [The] two concepts embody different rather than opposite ideas. . . . The presumption of innocence is really a direction to the authorities to ignore the presumption of guilt in their treatment of the suspect. It tells them, in effect, to close their eyes to what will frequently seem to be factual probabilities. . . .

For this model . . . the preliminary screening processes operated by the police and the prosecuting officials contain adequate guarantees of reliable factfinding. Indeed, the position is a stronger one. It is that subsequent processes, particularly of a formal adjudicatory nature, are unlikely to produce as reliable factfinding as the expert administrative process that precedes them. . . . It becomes important, then, to place as few restrictions as possible on the character of the administrative factfinding processes and to limit restrictions to those that enhance reliability, excluding those designed for other purposes. . . .

The complementary proposition is that the subsequent stages are relatively unimportant and should be truncated as much as possible. [There] have to be devices for dealing with the suspect after the preliminary screening process has resulted in a determination of probable guilt. The focal device . . . is the plea of guilty; through its use adjudicative factfinding is reduced to a minimum. It might be said of the Crime Control Model that, reduced to its barest essentials and when operating at its most successful pitch, it consists of two elements: (a) an administrative factfinding process leading to exoneration of the suspect, or to (b) the entry of a plea of guilty.

Due Process Values

If the Crime Control Model resembles an assembly line, the Due Process Model looks very much like an obstacle course. Each of its successive stages is designed to present formidable impediments to carrying the accused any further along in the process. . . .

The Due Process Model [takes] a view of informal, nonadjudicative factfinding that stresses the possibility of error: people are notoriously poor observers of disturbing events — the more emotion-arousing the context, the greater the possibility that recollection will be incorrect; confessions and admissions by persons in police custody may be induced by physical or psychological coercion, so that the police end up hearing what the suspect thinks they want to hear rather than the truth; witnesses may be animated by a bias or interest that no one would trouble to discover except one specially charged with protecting the interests of the accused — which the police are not. Considerations of this kind all lead to the rejection of informal factfinding processes as definitive of factual guilt and to the insistence on formal, adjudicative, adversary factfinding processes in which the factual case against the accused is publicly heard by an impartial tribunal and is evaluated only after the accused has had a full opportunity to discredit the case against him. Even then the distrust of factfinding processes that animates the Due Process Model is not dissipated. The possibilities of human error being what they are, further scrutiny is necessary, or at least must be available, lest in the heat of battle facts have been overlooked or suppressed. . . . The demand for finality is thus very low in the Due Process Model.

[Under the Due Process Model, if] efficiency suggests shortcuts around reliability, those demands must be rejected. The aim of the process is at least as much to protect the factually innocent as it is to convict the factually guilty. It somewhat resembles quality control in industrial technology: tolerable deviation from standard varies with the importance of conformity to standard in the destined use of the product. The Due Process Model resembles a factory that has to devote a substantial part of its input to quality control. This necessarily reduces quantitative output.

[The Due Process Model has evolved] from an original matrix of concern with the maximization of reliability into something quite different and more far-reaching. This complex of values can be symbolized although not adequately described by the concept of the primacy of the individual and the complementary concept of limitation on official power.

The combination of stigma and loss of liberty that is embodied in the end result of the criminal process is viewed as being the heaviest deprivation that government can inflict on the individual. Furthermore, the processes that culminate in these highly afflictive sanctions are in themselves coercive, restricting, and demeaning. Power is always subject to abuse, sometimes subtle, other times, as in the criminal process, open and ugly. Precisely because of its potency in subjecting the individual to the coercive power of the state, the criminal process must, on this model, be subjected to controls and safeguards that prevent it from operating with maximal efficiency. According to this ideology, maximal efficiency means maximal tyranny. . . .

The most modest-seeming but potentially far-reaching mechanism by which the Due Process Model implements these antiauthoritarian values is the doctrine of legal guilt. According to this doctrine, an individual is not to be held guilty of crime merely on a showing that in all probability, based upon reliable evidence, he did factually what he is said to have done. Instead, he is to be held guilty if and only if these factual determinations are made in procedurally regular fashion and by authorities acting within competences duly allocated to them. . . .

Another strand in the complex of attitudes that underlies the Due Process Model is the idea — itself a shorthand statement for a complex of attitudes — of equality. . . . Stated most starkly, the ideal of equality holds that "there can be no equal justice where the kind of trial a man gets depends on the amount of money he has." . . . The demands made by a norm of this kind are likely by its very nature to be quite sweeping. . . .

There is a final strand of thought in the Due Process Model whose presence is often ignored but which needs to be candidly faced if thought on the subject is not to be obscured. That is a mood of skepticism about the morality and the utility of the criminal sanction. [We] are told that the criminal law's notion of just condemnation and punishment is a cruel hypocrisy visited by a smug society on the psychologically and economically crippled; that its premise of a morally autonomous will with at least some measure of choice whether to comply with the values expressed in a penal code is unscientific and outmoded. [Doubts] about the ends for which power is being exercised create pressure to limit the discretion with which that power is exercised. . . .

What assumptions do we make about the sources of authority to shape the real-world operations of the criminal process? . . . Because the Crime Control Model is basically an affirmative model, emphasizing at every turn the existence and exercise of official power, its validating authority is ultimately legislative (although proximately administrative). Because the Due Process Model is basically a negative model, asserting limits on the nature of official power and on the modes of its exercise, its validating authority is judicial and requires an appeal to supra-legislative law, to the law of the Constitution. . . . That is at once the strength and the weakness of the Due Process Model: its strength because in our system the appeal to the Constitution provides the last and the overriding word; its weakness because saying no in specific cases is an exercise in futility unless there is a general willingness on the part of the officials who operate the process to apply negative prescriptions across the board. . . .

■ COMMUNITY POLICING CONSORTIUM, UNDERSTANDING COMMUNITY POLICING: A FRAMEWORK FOR ACTION

Bureau of Justice Assistance (1994)

. . . Experience and research reveal that community institutions are the first line of defense against disorder and crime. Thus, it is essential that the police work closely with all facets of the community to identify concerns and to find the most effective solutions. This is the essence of community policing.

THE ROLE OF THE POLICE: A HISTORICAL PERSPECTIVE

. . . Researchers have suggested that the reform era in government, which began in the early 1900's, coupled with a nationwide move toward professionalization, resulted in the separation of the police from the community. Police managers assigned officers to rotating shifts and moved them frequently from one geographical location to another to eliminate corruption. Management also instituted a policy of centralized control, designed to ensure compliance with standard operating procedures and to encourage a professional aura of impartiality.

This social distancing was also reinforced by technological developments. The expanding role of automobiles replaced the era of the friendly foot patrol officer. By the 1970's, rapid telephone contact with police through 911 systems allowed them to respond quickly to crimes. Answering the overwhelming number of calls for service, however, left police little time to prevent crimes from occurring. As increasingly sophisticated communications technology made it possible for calls to be transmitted almost instantaneously, officers had to respond to demands for assistance regardless of the urgency of the situation. Answering calls severely limited a broad police interaction with the community. The advent of the computer also contributed to the decrease in police contact with the community. Statistics, rather than the type of service provided or the service recipients, became the focus for officers and managers. As computers generated data on crime patterns and trends, counted the incidence of crimes, increased the efficiency of dispatch, and calculated the rapidity and outcome of police response, rapid response became an end in itself.

Random patrolling also served to further break the link between communities and police. Police were instructed to change routes constantly, in an effort to thwart criminals. However, community members also lost the ability to predict when they might be able to interact with their local police. . . .

The police and the public had become so separated from one another that in some communities an attitude of "us versus them" prevailed between the police and community members. One observer of the urban scene characterized the deteriorating police-community relationship this way: "For the urban poor the police are those who arrest you." . . .

COMMUNITY PARTNERSHIP: CORE COMPONENT ONE

Establishing and maintaining mutual trust is the central goal of the first core component of community policing — community partnership. Police recognize the need for cooperation with the community. In the fight against serious crime, police have encouraged community members to come forth with relevant information. In addition, police have spoken to neighborhood groups, participated in business and civic events, worked with social agencies, and taken part in educational and recreational programs for school children. . . . So how then do the cooperative efforts of community policing differ from the actions that have taken place previously? The fundamental distinction is that, in community policing, the police become an integral part of the community culture, and the community assists in defining future priorities and in allocating resources. The difference is substantial and encompasses basic goals and commitments.

Community partnership . . . recognizes the value of activities that contribute to the orderliness and well-being of a neighborhood. These activities could include:

helping accident or crime victims, providing emergency medical services, helping resolve domestic and neighborhood conflicts (e.g., family violence, landlord-tenant disputes, or racial harassment), working with residents and local businesses to improve neighborhood conditions, controlling automobile and pedestrian traffic, providing emergency social services and referrals to those at risk (e.g., adolescent runaways, the homeless, the intoxicated, and the mentally ill), protecting the exercise of constitutional rights (e.g., guaranteeing a person's right to speak, protecting lawful assemblies from disruption), and providing a model of citizenship (helpfulness, respect for others, honesty, and fairness). . . .

To build this trust for an effective community partnership police must treat people with respect and sensitivity. The use of unnecessary force and arrogance, aloofness, or rudeness at any level of the agency will dampen the willingness of community members to ally themselves with the police.

The effective mobilization of community support requires different approaches in different communities. Establishing trust and obtaining cooperation are often easier in middle-class and affluent communities than in poorer communities, where mistrust of police may have a long history. Building bonds in some neighborhoods may involve supporting basic social institutions (e.g., families, churches, schools) that have been weakened by pervasive crime or disorder. . . .

For the patrol officer, police-community partnership entails talking to local business owners to help identify their problems and concerns, visiting residents in their homes to offer advice on security, and helping to organize and support neighborhood watch groups and regular community meetings. For example, the patrol officer will canvass the neighborhood for information about a string of burglaries and then revisit those residents to inform them when the burglar is caught. . . .

Problem Solving: Core Component Two

. . . The theory behind problem-oriented policing is simple. Underlying conditions create problems. These conditions might include the characteristics of the people involved (offenders, potential victims, and others), the social setting in which these people interact, the physical environments, and the way the public deals with these conditions.

A problem created by these conditions may generate one or more incidents. These incidents, while stemming from a common source, may appear to be different. For example, social and physical conditions in a deteriorated apartment complex may generate burglaries, acts of vandalism, intimidation of pedestrians by rowdy teenagers, and other incidents. These incidents, some of which come to police attention, are symptoms of the problems. The incidents will continue so long as the problem that creates them persists. . . .

Determining the underlying causes of crime depends, to a great extent, on an in-depth knowledge of community. Therefore, community participation in identifying and setting priorities will contribute to effective problem-solving efforts by the community and the police. . . .

Neighborhood groups and the police will not always agree on which specific problems deserve attention first. Police may regard robberies as the biggest problem in a particular community, while residents may find derelicts who sleep in doorways, break bottles on sidewalks, and pick through garbage cans to be the number one problem. Under community policing, the problem with derelicts should also receive early attention from the police. . . .

In community policing, the problem-solving process is dependent on input from both the police and the community. Problem solving can involve:

- Eliminating the problem entirely. This type of solution is usually limited to disorder problems. Examples include eliminating traffic congestion by erecting traffic control signs, and destroying or rehabilitating abandoned buildings that can provide an atmosphere conducive to crime.
- Reducing the number of the occurrences of the problem. Drug-dealing and the accompanying problems of robbery and gang violence will be decreased if the police and community work together to set up drug counseling and rehabilitation centers. Longer-range solutions might include intensifying drug education in schools, churches, and hospitals.
- Reducing the degree of injury per incident. For example, police can teach store clerks how to act during a robbery in order to avoid injury or death and can advise women in the community on ways to minimize the chances of being killed or seriously injured if attacked. . . .

The best solutions are those that satisfy community members, improve safety, diminish anxiety, lead to increased order, strengthen the ties between the community and the police, and minimize coercive actions. The following example describes such a solution: A patrol officer faced with chronic nighttime robberies of convenience stores discovered that a major contributing factor was that cash registers could not be seen from the street, either because of their location within the store or because of posters plastered on front windows. The officer did not identify the "root cause" or ultimate cause of crime, but instead identified an underlying condition that, once addressed, held promise of reducing the number of future convenience store robberies. . . .

To maximize the time that the patrol officer can spend interacting with community members, community policing encourages the use of the 911 system only for true emergencies. Non-emergency calls should be handled through other means, including delays in responding and report handling by the police station or sheriff's office over the telephone or by mail. . . .

Implications for Management and the Organizational Structure

. . . Community policing emphasizes the value of the patrol function and the patrol officer as an individual. Patrol officers have traditionally been accorded low status despite the scope and sensitivity of the tasks they perform. Community policing requires the shifting of initiative, decisionmaking, and responsibility downward within the police organization. . . . Assignment stability of these neighborhood officers is also essential if they are to develop close working relationships within their communities because they are expected to engage in activities other than simply reacting to calls for service. . . .

Systems for evaluating personnel performance should reflect the goals of community policing. Emphasizing quality over quantity represents a major difference between traditional policing and community-oriented policing. Patrol officers could be evaluated on how well they know their beats — a prerequisite for identification of problems — and how effectively they and their supervisors have adopted problem-solving techniques. Other relevant performance measures include the extent to which personnel have formed partnerships with the community and the nature of their contributions to this team effort. Since officers are working as part of a team, they should not be evaluated as if they were operating alone. The occasional mistake made by an officer seeking to solve community issues in a proactive manner would be an inappropriate measure of performance. . . .

The backbone of community policing is the patrol officer, and the status, pay, and working conditions of this position should encourage people to spend an entire career in patrol. In effect, what is needed is a system that rewards advancement through skill levels in the same job as much or more than it rewards advancement through the ranks. . . .

The problem-solving orientation of community policing requires a greater emphasis on analytic skills and expert systems management to obtain the most valuable information support. . . . Strategic analysis will require that information be collected by a number of unconventional methods, e.g., conducting neighborhood victimization surveys, canvassing rehabilitation centers and hospitals, interacting with school officials, and assessing the impact of environmental changes on criminal activity. . . .

Wide dissemination and information sharing are essential components of community policing. Pertinent and appropriate information should be made available to members of the community whenever possible. For example, statistics showing an increase in burglaries or rapes in a specific section of town should be shared with the community to further the problem-solving process. . . .

Effective community collaboration and interaction will require patrol officers to be more accessible to community members. "Storefront" police offices or "mini-stations" within neighborhoods can be established quite inexpensively, particularly with assistance from the community. The duties of staffing storefront facilities can be shared among officers, civilian employees, and community residents. [Police departments may supplement automobile patrols with foot, bicycle, scooter, and horseback patrols.]

Assessing Internal Changes

. . . In the past, police efforts usually have been evaluated on a traditional and narrow set of criteria (e.g., crime statistics, the number of 911 calls, the length of police response, the number of arrests and citations, etc.). These assessments were often taken only at times of serious crime increases. Many of the traditional methods of assessment remain valid, but can measure only the effectiveness of crime-fighting tactics and cannot gauge the effect of crime-prevention efforts. . . .

An important goal of community policing is to provide higher-quality service to neighborhoods; therefore, customer satisfaction becomes an important measure of effectiveness. The perception of progress among community members and ongoing feedback from all elements of the community are essential parts of the assessment process. Randomly and routinely conducted surveys will inform the agency of the public view of police performance, the level of fear and concern, and will make the agency aware of the extent to which community members feel as if they are participants in the community policing effort. . . .

Increased levels of community participation in crime reduction and prevention efforts is another indication of program success. Community members will not act if they are afraid or suspicious. Community members should become more willing to work with the police in a variety of ways, ranging from converting abandoned buildings to community assets to involving police actively in neighborhood watch groups. They might also be more comfortable providing information on criminal activity in the area. In fact, calls to report crime may increase considerably during the early phases of community policing implementation, as community confidence in police capability rises and community trust increases. However, the number of 911 calls will likely decrease over time, which will provide a quantitative measure of the strategy's effect. . . .

Notes

1. *Are your police community police?* Do you recognize the community policing approach in the activities and attitudes of your local police? Are there any dangers in the community policing approach?

Periodic surveys of local police departments show that the rhetoric and practices of community policing have become the norm in the United States. As of 2000, about 95 percent of the larger police departments (and about two-thirds of all local police departments) employed at least some "community police" officers. More than three-fourths of larger police departments trained all new officer recruits in community policing methods. On an operational level, police departments in 2000 reported growing use of foot and bicycle patrol, assignment of officers to fixed geographic beats, outreach to neighborhood associations and other community organizations, surveys of citizens about their satisfaction with police services, and use of computers for crime mapping. Bureau of Justice Statistics, Law Enforcement Management and Administrative Statistics, 2000: Data for Individual State and Local Agencies with 100 or More Officers (April 2004, NCJ 203350). How might each of these activities carry out the community policing philosophy?

2. *Community policing and measures of success.* There are theoretical reasons (such as those discussed by Tracey Meares earlier in this chapter) to believe that community policing actually reduces crime. Experience with this concept also offers some encouragement. Once the community policing model became firmly established in the 1990s, the United States also saw a remarkable drop in crime rates. Perhaps more effective policing can take credit for at least part of this good news.

On the other hand, the success or failure of community policing is terribly difficult to measure — especially when police administrators use the label "community policing" to describe virtually any change in management or department structure. Do the advocates of community policing make claims about its social effects that are measurable and verifiable? How would you measure the success of your local "community" police department?

3. *Potential impact on criminal procedure.* Community policing tends to give more authority to the officer on the beat and to give supervisors less control over daily activities and choices of patrol officers. Does this development make it difficult to enforce procedural requirements? Is the decentralizing of authority inconsistent with the very idea of uniform rules of procedure influencing all police officers? As you read cases on searches and seizures in Chapters 2-7, ask yourself how many of the police officers in these cases were acting in a community policing mode. Would

your view of the cases, or the proper rules, change if the police adopted a different philosophy?

4. *Herbert Packer's models of criminal procedure and the community policing philosophy.* Professor Herbert Packer created a way of thinking about criminal procedure that has remained highly influential to this day. His "Crime Control" and "Due Process" models offer a way to identify some of the values and assumptions associated with different approaches to procedural controversies. You might find it useful to refer to these models as organizing principles from time to time as you think about difficult procedural questions later in this course. How do Packer's two models differ in their description of police work? Do the two models share any assumptions about policing? Would a shift to community policing be more appealing to a Crime Control advocate or to a Due Process advocate? Or does community policing promote forms of policing that Packer's account does not address at all? Consider an alternative method of thinking about the criminal process, proposed by John Griffiths:

> . . . Packer's [model] rests not upon two but upon a single, albeit unarticulated, basic conception of the nature of the criminal process — that it is a battleground of fundamentally hostile forces, where the only relevant variable is the "balance of advantage." [Packer] assumes disharmony, fundamentally irreconcilable interests, a state of war. We can start from an assumption of reconcilable — even mutually supportive — interests, a state of love. [There is] a "real-world" institution which occasionally inflicts punishments on offenders for their offenses but which is nonetheless built upon a fundamental assumption of harmony of interest and love. [I therefore offer] a "Family Model" of the criminal process. [People operating within the Family Model would accept] the idea that criminals are just people who are deemed to have offended — that we are all . . . both actual and potential criminals. . . .
>
> What other implications would follow from a Family Model? For one thing, that ideology would necessarily be accompanied by a basic faith in public officials; everyone would assume, as a general matter, that if a public official has a particular role or duty, he can be expected to carry it out in good faith and using his best judgment. . . . Basic faith in public officials would revolutionize American criminal procedure. We are all used to the proposition that legal procedures — indeed, the organization of government in general — must be designed with the bad man, or the man who will unwittingly misuse his powers, primarily in mind. . . . Our assumption that the state and the individual are in battle compels us to believe that any "discretion" — any active responsibility going beyond the umpiring role of a judge — will necessarily be exercised either on behalf of the individual's interest or on behalf of the state's. We see only Packer's two poles as the possible outcomes of discretion.

Griffiths, Ideology in Criminal Procedure, or a Third "Model" of the Criminal Process, 79 Yale L.J. 359 (1970). Is the "family" model more consistent with the realities of police-community relations in a world dominated by the community policing model?

Does Packer's model suggest anything about different ways in which victims of alleged crimes might become involved in criminal investigations or adjudications? For two efforts to supplement the Packer models, see Kent Roach, Four Models of the Criminal Process, 89 J. Crim. L. & Criminology 671 (1999) (proposing "punitive" and "non-punitive" models of victim involvement); Douglas Beloof, The Third Model of Criminal Process: The Victim Participation Model, 1999 Utah L. Rev. 289.

II

Brief Searches and Stops

Police officers sometimes restrict the movement of individuals ("seize" them) or intrude into their privacy to obtain information ("search" them). But in most of these encounters, the stop or search does not last very long or intrude very deeply. Courts and legislatures have established rules to control these encounters between government agents and the public. Yet the restrictions on this police behavior are not as demanding as the rules that apply when government agents attempt to carry out a full-blown search or seizure. This chapter deals with efforts to regulate these lesser searches and seizures.

One of the most important legal constraints on these brief searches and seizures comes from the Fourth Amendment to the U.S. Constitution, which provides as follows:

> The right of the people to be secure in their persons, houses, papers, and effects, against unreasonable searches and seizures, shall not be violated, and no Warrants shall issue, but upon probable cause, supported by Oath or affirmation, and particularly describing the place to be searched, and the persons or things to be seized.

The Fourth Amendment and its analogs in state constitutions have spawned a huge and complex case law. They have also shaped many state and federal statutes, as well as prosecutorial office guidelines and police department directives and training manuals. To understand the complex law of search and seizure, it is helpful (and probably necessary) to approach the material with some general conceptual framework. Two different frameworks for organizing the extensive modern law of search and seizure suggest themselves in the cases and other legal materials.

The traditional framework for searches and seizures begins with the oft-repeated remark that the Fourth Amendment incorporates a strong preference for search warrants (that is, a judicial determination that a proposed search is justified), that warrantless searches are generally considered unreasonable, and that exceptions to the "warrant requirement" are "jealously and carefully drawn." State and federal courts invoke this theme. This preference for warrants grows out of the apparent emphasis on limited warrants in the constitutional text. Some statutes also implicitly make warrants the standard and unwarranted searches the exceptions. For example, Mont. Code Ann. §46-5-101 provides that

> [a] search of a person, object, or place may be made and evidence, contraband, and persons may be seized . . . when a search is made: (1) by the authority of a search warrant; or (2) in accordance with judicially recognized exceptions to the warrant requirement.

Before the late 1960s, the recognized exceptions to the warrant requirement were indeed fairly few. Most prominent were two umbrella categories, exigent circumstances and consent. Warrants were generally required unless the police could show exigent circumstances or consent to search or seize. Within the category of exigent circumstances, courts developed exceptions to the warrant requirement such as risk of flight, destruction of evidence, or an officer's personal observation of a crime.

In the traditional framework, the justification necessary to proceed with a valid search or seizure, whether carried out with or without a warrant, was probable cause. Once a court was convinced that the government's activity amounted to a "search" or "seizure," the court insisted that the government show probable cause to justify its action. A sensible approach for the study of search and seizure in such a legal system is to start with the foundational elements — the process for warrants and the standard of probable cause — and then to identify and study the exceptions.

Organizing a field according to its foundational rules and exceptions works well if the rules are ordinarily followed and the exceptions are modest. But in the modern law of search and seizure the exceptions have swallowed the traditional rules. In doing so, they have changed the entire framework and the best way to study searches and seizures.

Modern search and seizure law is astoundingly complex and contradictory. A survey of current "exceptions" to the warrant requirement — some of which appear in this chapter, and others in Chapters 3 and 4 — suggests how unwieldy the traditional framework has become. A partial list would include exigent circumstances (such as flight or destruction of evidence), plain view, open fields, community caretaker functions, brief frisks for weapons, inventory searches, protective sweeps, automobile searches, border searches, school searches, prison searches, searches incident to arrest, fire investigations, and administrative searches. See Craig Bradley, Two Models of the Fourth Amendment, 83 Mich. L. Rev. 1468 (1985).

What has caused such complexity in this area of the law? Three changes, marked by three U.S. Supreme Court cases decided in 1967 and 1968, rearranged the doctrinal foundations of search and seizure law. Because these cases appear at different points in this volume, a preview here is useful.

The first key case was Katz v. United States, 389 U.S. 347 (1967). In *Katz,* the U.S. Supreme Court changed the method of deciding whether a person had an interest that the Fourth Amendment would protect. In other words, it redefined the basic *conceptual framework* for deciding whether the government had engaged in a "search" that is subject to constitutional limitations. In doing so, the Court moved away from concepts of protected physical spaces (property) and toward concepts of individual privacy.

Katz was convicted of transmitting gambling information by telephone across state lines; crucial evidence in the case came from a wiretap of a public phone booth. The intermediate appeals court found no Fourth Amendment violation and upheld Katz's conviction because the listening device had been placed on the outside of the telephone booth, and thus there was "no physical entrance into the area occupied" by Katz. This was a straightforward application of the "trespass" theory of unreasonable searches, with historical origins in the tort suits that the targets of unreasonable searches filed against the officers who had improperly invaded their property interests. But the Supreme Court reversed Katz's conviction, finding that the Fourth Amendment protected Katz from the government recording his conversation in a telephone booth. The Court described the key doctrinal shift as follows:

> [The] parties have attached great significance to the characterization of the telephone booth from which the petitioner placed his calls. The petitioner has strenuously argued that the booth was a "constitutionally protected area." The Government has maintained with equal vigor that it was not. But this effort to decide whether or not a given "area," viewed in the abstract, is "constitutionally protected" deflects attention from the problem presented by this case. For the Fourth Amendment protects people, not places. What a person knowingly exposes to the public, even in his own home or office, is not a subject of Fourth Amendment protection. But what he seeks to preserve as private, even in an area accessible to the public, may be constitutionally protected.

What are the implications of deciding that the Fourth Amendment "protects people, not places"? The shift to a privacy analysis has drawn a larger number and variety of governmental actions into Fourth Amendment territory. It is far easier to make a claim about "expectations of privacy" in a host of situations than it would be to make a claim based on property interests. As the courts have applied the Fourth Amendment to new settings, they have generated new law and departed more frequently from the concepts of probable cause and warrants.

The second key case to transform search and seizure doctrine is Terry v. Ohio, 392 U.S. 1 (1968), which we will study in section D of this chapter. *Terry* moved beyond the relative simplicity of having a single *standard* — probable cause — to assess the validity of searches and seizures. *Terry* recognized a major category of limited stops and searches that law enforcement officers could conduct on the basis of reasonable suspicion — a standard less than probable cause. By recognizing that standards other than probable cause would be appropriate for justifying various kinds of searches and seizures, the Court invited more deviations from the traditional doctrinal core of the Fourth Amendment.

The third key case is Camara v. Municipal Court, 387 U.S. 523 (1967), which created a new *method* for determining what justification the government would need for a search and what process it would follow to establish that justification. In *Camara,* the Supreme Court approved the granting of warrants for municipal building code enforcement inspections. These inspections took place on the basis of general administrative needs for inspecting an area, without requiring any individualized suspicion that a property owner was violating the law. The Court in *Camara* declared that the Fourth Amendment applied to both civil and criminal law enforcement efforts. With such a diversity of governmental purposes and activities at issue, the complexity of search and seizure doctrine was bound to increase. Furthermore, the opinion in *Camara* announced that it would "balance" competing interests to determine the level of justification and the type of warrant process the government would need to follow before conducting a search: "[There] can be no ready test for determining reasonableness other than by balancing the need to search against the invasion which the search entails."

These cases have fractured search and seizure doctrine and increased the overall complexity of the law. Whether these changes are good or bad, they have made search and seizure law more difficult to learn and apply.

Perhaps some new principle or calculus offers a more satisfying synthesis of these changes in the law than the traditional framework of warrants and probable cause can offer. As you study the materials in the next few chapters, try to construct a coherent explanation for the cases and laws that govern searches and seizures.

In particular, consider the explanatory value of a calculus that weighs three recurring factors in determining the "reasonableness" of a search or seizure: (1) the privacy interest of the person subject to a search; (2) the government's interest in conducting the search; and (3) the degree of intrusion from the search. The balancing of these three factors may solve such crucial puzzles as the level of justification necessary to support the search (such as probable cause, reasonable suspicion, or no individualized suspicion) and the time when the government must give its justification (before the search to obtain a warrant, or after the fact when the target challenges the search).

You will have the opportunity to test this conceptual framework, along with the more traditional framework that emphasizes probable cause and warrants, and to analyze a wide array of government efforts to collect information. The following materials begin with the briefest and most common government searches and seizures.

A. BRIEF INVESTIGATIVE STOPS OF SUSPECTS

Countless times each day, a police officer or some other government agent stops to talk with a member of the general public. Some citizens take part in these conversations willingly; others are more reluctant but feel obliged to stay and continue the conversation. A few do not cooperate at all. What authority does the officer have to insist that a citizen stop for a few moments during an investigation?

■ DELAWARE CODE TIT. 11, §1902

(a) A peace officer may stop any person abroad, or in a public place, who the officer has reasonable ground to suspect is committing, has committed or is about to commit a crime, and may demand the person's name, address, business abroad and destination.

(b) Any person so questioned who fails to give identification or explain the person's actions to the satisfaction of the officer may be detained and further questioned and investigated.

ALASKA STATUTES §28.35.182(b)

A person commits the offense of failure to stop at the direction of a peace officer . . . if the person, while driving or operating a vehicle or motor vehicle . . . knowingly fails to stop as soon as practical and in a reasonably safe manner under the circumstance when requested or signaled to do so by a peace officer.

Notes

1. *Three types of encounters: conversations, stops, and arrests.* These statutes set out a typical set of requirements for police officers who stop a person in a vehicle or on foot in public. While more than 30 states codify these requirements in statutes or rules of criminal procedure, others announce the requirements in judicial opinions. Most are not recent innovations; for instance, the Delaware statute above was adopted in 1951 and is based on the Uniform Arrest Act of 1940. The Supreme Court ratified the constitutionality of this framework in Terry v. Ohio, 392 U.S. 1 (1968), a case we discuss later in this chapter. If you were a police officer, would you prefer explicit statutory authority to stop suspects, or would you rather see the power established and developed in case law? See George Dix, Nonarrest Investigatory Detentions in Search and Seizure Law, 1985 Duke L.J. 849.

These statutes assume the existence of three different levels of controls on the officer. On the first level, where the police officer does not "stop" a person at all but merely engages in a conversation, the officer does not need to justify the decision to focus attention on one person. On the second level, where the officer "stops" a person for a brief time but not long enough to qualify as an arrest, the officer must have "reasonable suspicion" before making the stop. Reasonable suspicion has also been described as "individualized" or "articulable" suspicion. On the third level, where the officer detains a person for a longer time or in a more coercive way, there is an "arrest." Constitutions, statutes, and rules of procedure all require that the officer show "probable cause" that the arrestee has committed a crime.

Thus, for the brief encounters we are now exploring, there are two questions to resolve: Was the interaction between the police officer and the individual a consensual encounter, a limited "stop," or a full arrest? If the incident was a stop, did the government agent have the "reasonable suspicion" needed to justify the stop?

2. *The prevalence of stops and consensual encounters.* Consensual conversations and stops (particularly traffic stops) are the two most common forms of interaction between the police and the public. According to a 2005 national survey, about 19 percent of all persons age 16 or older had at least one contact with a police officer during the year. Just over 40 percent of those contacts occurred during a motor vehicle stop; another 24 percent of the contacts happened when people reported a crime to the police. Only about 3 percent of the contacts occurred because the officer suspected the person of a crime. Bureau of Justice Statistics, Contacts Between Police and the Public, 2005 (April 2007, NCJ 215243).

3. *Ambiguous statutory language.* Will defense counsel and prosecutors in Delaware agree on what constitutes a "reasonable ground" for a stop under the statute? Will they agree on how long the "further" questioning can last under the statute? How should the trial court resolve their disagreements? What sources will be relevant? Is the court's task here the same as when parties dispute the meaning

of some phrase that has developed through the common law? As you read further in this chapter, take special note of the methods courts use to resolve conflicts about the meaning of ambiguous statutory language.

1. *Consensual Encounters and "Stops"*

Conversations change direction. Sometimes a conversation between a police officer and a member of the public will begin as a "consensual encounter" but will transform into a "stop" without the officer's announcement of this fact in so many words. What marks the difference between consensual encounters and coercive stops?

■ UNITED STATES v. SYLVIA MENDENHALL

446 U.S. 544 (1980)

STEWART, J.*

. . . I.

[Sylvia Mendenhall] arrived at the Detroit Metropolitan Airport on a commercial airline flight from Los Angeles early in the morning on February 10, 1976. As she disembarked from the airplane, she was observed by two agents of the Drug Enforcement Administration (DEA), who were present at the airport for the purpose of detecting unlawful traffic in narcotics. After observing the respondent's conduct, which appeared to the agents to be characteristic of persons unlawfully carrying narcotics,[1] the agents approached her as she was walking through the concourse, identified themselves as federal agents, and asked to see her identification and airline ticket. The respondent produced her driver's license, which was in the name of Sylvia Mendenhall, and, in answer to a question of one of the agents, stated that she resided at the address appearing on the license. The airline ticket was issued in the name of "Annette Ford." When asked why the ticket bore a name different from her own, the respondent stated that she "just felt like using that name." In response to a further question, the respondent indicated that she had been in California only two days. Agent Anderson then specifically identified himself as a federal narcotics agent and, according to his testimony, the respondent "became quite shaken, extremely nervous. She had a hard time speaking."

* [Chief Justice Burger and Justices Blackmun and Powell concurred in part and joined in parts I, IIB, IIC, and III of the opinion; Justice Rehnquist joined the opinion, including part IA. — EDS.]

1. The agent testified that the respondent's behavior fit the so-called "drug courier profile" — an informally compiled abstract of characteristics thought typical of persons carrying illicit drugs. In this case the agents thought it relevant that (1) the respondent was arriving on a flight from Los Angeles, a city believed by the agents to be the place of origin for much of the heroin brought to Detroit; (2) the respondent was the last person to leave the plane, "appeared to be very nervous," and "completely scanned the whole area where [the agents] were standing"; (3) after leaving the plane the respondent proceeded past the baggage area without claiming any luggage; and (4) the respondent changed airlines for her flight out of Detroit.

After returning the airline ticket and driver's license to her, Agent Anderson asked the respondent if she would accompany him to the airport DEA office for further questions. She did so, although the record does not indicate a verbal response to the request. The office, which was located up one flight of stairs about 50 feet from where the respondent had first been approached, consisted of a reception area adjoined by three other rooms. At the office the agent asked the respondent if she would allow a search of her person and handbag and told her that she had the right to decline the search if she desired. She responded: "Go ahead." She then handed Agent Anderson her purse, which contained a receipt for an airline ticket that had been issued to "F. Bush" three days earlier for a flight from Pittsburgh through Chicago to Los Angeles. The agent asked whether this was the ticket that she had used for her flight to California, and the respondent stated that it was.

A female police officer then arrived to conduct the search of the respondent's person. . . . The policewoman explained that the search would require that the respondent remove her clothing. . . . As the respondent removed her clothing, she took from her undergarments two small packages, one of which appeared to contain heroin, and handed both to the policewoman. The agents then arrested the respondent for possessing heroin. It was on the basis of this evidence that the District Court denied the respondent's motion to suppress. . . .

II.

The Fourth Amendment provides that "the right of the people to be secure in their persons, houses, papers, and effects, against unreasonable searches and seizures, shall not be violated. . . ."

A.

The Fourth Amendment's requirement that searches and seizures be founded upon an objective justification, governs all seizures of the person, including seizures that involve only a brief detention short of traditional arrest. Terry v. Ohio, 392 U.S. 1 (1968). Accordingly, if the respondent was "seized" when the DEA agents approached her on the concourse and asked questions of her, the agents' conduct in doing so was constitutional only if they reasonably suspected the respondent of wrongdoing. But "obviously, not all personal intercourse between policemen and citizens involves 'seizures' of persons. Only when the officer, by means of physical force or show of authority, has in some way restrained the liberty of a citizen may we conclude that a 'seizure' has occurred." *Terry*, 392 U.S., at 19, n.16.

The distinction between an intrusion amounting to a "seizure" of the person and an encounter that intrudes upon no constitutionally protected interest is illustrated by the facts of Terry v. Ohio, which the Court recounted as follows: "Officer McFadden approached the three men, identified himself as a police officer and asked for their names. . . . When the men 'mumbled something' in response to his inquiries, Officer McFadden grabbed petitioner Terry, spun him around so that they were facing the other two, with Terry between McFadden and the others, and patted down the outside of his clothing." Obviously the officer "seized" Terry and subjected him to a "search" when he took hold of him, spun him around, and patted down the outer surfaces of his clothing. What was not determined in that case, however, was that a seizure had taken place before the officer physically restrained Terry for purposes of searching his person for weapons. The Court "assume[d] that up to that point no intrusion upon constitutionally protected rights had occurred." The Court's assumption appears entirely correct in view of the fact [that police officers enjoy the liberty possessed by every citizen] to address questions to other persons. . . .

We adhere to the view that a person is "seized" only when, by means of physical force or a show of authority, his freedom of movement is restrained. Only when such restraint is imposed is there any foundation whatever for invoking constitutional safeguards. The purpose of the Fourth Amendment is not to eliminate all contact between the police and the citizenry, but to prevent arbitrary and oppressive interference by enforcement officials with the privacy and personal security of individuals. As long as the person to whom questions are put remains free to disregard the questions and walk away, there has been no intrusion upon that person's liberty or privacy as would under the Constitution require some particularized and objective justification.

Moreover, characterizing every street encounter between a citizen and the police as a "seizure," while not enhancing any interest secured by the Fourth Amendment, would impose wholly unrealistic restrictions upon a wide variety of legitimate law enforcement practices. The Court has on other occasions referred to the acknowledged need for police questioning as a tool in the effective enforcement of the criminal laws. Without such investigation, those who were innocent might be falsely accused, those who were guilty might wholly escape prosecution, and many crimes would go unsolved. In short, the security of all would be diminished.

We conclude that a person has been "seized" within the meaning of the Fourth Amendment only if, in view of all of the circumstances surrounding the incident, a reasonable person would have believed that he was not free to leave.[6] Examples of circumstances that might indicate a seizure, even where the person did not attempt to leave, would be the threatening presence of several officers, the display of a weapon by an officer, some physical touching of the person of the citizen, or the use of language or tone of voice indicating that compliance with the officer's request might be compelled. In the absence of some such evidence, otherwise inoffensive contact between a member of the public and the police cannot, as a matter of law, amount to a seizure of that person.

On the facts of this case, no "seizure" of the respondent occurred. The events took place in the public concourse. The agents wore no uniforms and displayed no weapons. They did not summon the respondent to their presence, but instead approached her and identified themselves as federal agents. They requested, but did not demand to see the respondent's identification and ticket. Such conduct without more, did not amount to an intrusion upon any constitutionally protected interest. The respondent was not seized simply by reason of the fact that the agents approached her, asked her if she would show them her ticket and identification, and posed to her a few questions. Nor was it enough to establish a seizure that the person asking the questions was a law enforcement official. In short, nothing in the record suggests that the respondent had any objective reason to believe that she was not free to end the conversation in the concourse and proceed on her way, and for that reason we conclude that the agents' initial approach to her was not a seizure.

6. We agree with the District Court that the subjective intention of the DEA agent in this case to detain the respondent, had she attempted to leave, is irrelevant except insofar as that may have been conveyed to the respondent.

Our conclusion that no seizure occurred is not affected by the fact that the respondent was not expressly told by the agents that she was free to decline to cooperate with their inquiry, for the voluntariness of her responses does not depend upon her having been so informed. We also reject the argument that the only inference to be drawn from the fact that the respondent acted in a manner so contrary to her self-interest is that she was compelled to answer the agents' questions. It may happen that a person makes statements to law enforcement officials that he later regrets, but the issue in such cases is not whether the statement was self-protective, but rather whether it was made voluntarily. [The court also held that Mendenhall had "voluntarily" proceeded to the DEA office, and consented to the search of her person.]

WESLEY WILSON v. STATE

874 P.2d 215 (Wyo. 1994)

TAYLOR, J.

[Limping] severely, Wesley Wilson . . . walked rapidly eastbound on 12th Street in Casper, Wyoming on the morning of June 21, 1991. At 12:31 A.M., Officer Kamron Ritter . . . of the Casper Police Department watched Wilson's "lunging" steps and pulled his patrol car over to the sidewalk. Officer Ritter, believing that a fight may have taken place, asked if Wilson was okay and what happened to his leg. Wilson responded that he had twisted his ankle at a party. Smelling alcohol on Wilson's breath, Officer Ritter requested identification, which Wilson provided. Officer Ritter radioed for a routine warrants check with the National Crime Information Center (NCIC) and local files. This initial encounter with Wilson lasted about a minute and a half.

The conversation with Wilson was interrupted when Officer Ritter detected smoke coming from 12th Street, west of where he was standing. At the same time, two motorcyclists stopped and reported to Officer Ritter that a fire was burning in a building [one block] up the street. Before leaving to check on the fire, Officer Ritter told Wilson to "stay in the area."

Officer Ritter reported the fire to the police dispatcher. . . . After about eight minutes at the scene of the fire, Officer Ritter returned to check on Wilson. He had limped about 40 feet farther east and was attempting to cross 12th Street. As additional fire trucks approached, Officer Ritter helped Wilson cross the street. Officer Ritter then told Wilson to go to a nearby corner and "wait" while the officer returned to the fire scene.

As Officer Ritter provided traffic control, the police dispatcher radioed, at 12:41 A.M., that Wilson had two outstanding arrest warrants. Officer Ritter and Officer Terry Van Oordt then walked down the block to where Wilson was sitting on a lawn at the corner watching the fire. When the officers approached Wilson, they informed him of the outstanding warrants and asked him to stand. Wilson told the officers it was difficult to stand with his injured ankle. The officers noticed an oily patch on the right shoulder of the shirt Wilson was wearing. Both officers touched the stained area and found an oily substance. Wilson volunteered, "What are you doing? I don't smell like smoke." The officers proceeded to arrest Wilson on the outstanding warrants. The following morning, in custody, Wilson made a voluntary statement implicating himself in starting the fire.

At a suppression hearing, Officer Ritter testified about his concerns for Wilson's safety during their initial encounter and that he had no suspicions of Wilson's involvement in the fire or of arresting him for public intoxication. Officer Ritter stated he followed routine Casper Police Department procedure to get the names of subjects police come in "contact" with "at that time of night" and "always" run a warrants check. Officer Ritter said he wanted Wilson to wait until the results of the warrants check were received. During their second encounter, when Officer Ritter helped Wilson cross the street, the officer testified he still had no suspicion of Wilson's potential involvement in the fire but wanted Wilson to wait for the completion of the warrants check. . . .

Wilson, who did not testify at the hearing, argued that the stop was illegal and the evidence gathered from the stop [including his statements about smoke and his confession] should be suppressed.* [The district court denied the suppression motion, and the jury convicted Wilson of felony property destruction.]

Wilson's statement of the issues presumes his appeal is one based on provisions of both the United States Constitution and the Wyoming Constitution. The language of Wyo. Const, art. 1, §4 differs somewhat from its federal counterpart in providing:

> The right of the people to be secure in their persons, houses, papers and effects against unreasonable searches and seizures shall not be violated, and no warrant shall issue but upon probable cause, supported by affidavit, particularly describing the place to be searched or the person or thing to be seized.

[However,] we are unable to consider the impact of those differences in this situation because Wilson . . . failed to offer any argument supporting an independent state constitutional claim. . . . The Fourth Amendment to the United States Constitution grants

> the right of the people to be secure in their persons, houses, papers, and effects, against unreasonable searches and seizures, shall not be violated, and no Warrants shall issue, but upon probable cause, supported by Oath or affirmation, and particularly describing the place to be searched, and the persons or things to be seized.

[The] decision of the United States Supreme Court in Terry v. Ohio, 392 U.S. 1 (1968) marked the initial recognition by the United States Supreme Court of some lesser standard than probable cause for intrusion upon constitutionally guaranteed rights. In *Terry*, a police officer, observing specific conduct which his training and experience taught him was indicative of criminal behavior, conducted a limited seizure to investigate his reasonable suspicions. In the course of such a seizure, the United States Supreme Court approved a limited search for weapons for the protection of the police officer. . . .

From this genesis, a general recognition of the rich diversity of police-citizen encounters has emerged. [Three] categories or tiers of interaction between police and citizens may be characterized. The most intrusive encounter, an arrest, requires

* [The ordinary remedy for the violation of the defendant's constitutional rights is the exclusion of the evidence obtained as a result of the improper seizure during the prosecution's case at trial. Exclusion is not the only possible remedy. See discussion in Chapter 6. — EDS.]

justification by probable cause to believe that a person has committed or is committing a crime. The investigatory stop represents a seizure which invokes Fourth Amendment safeguards, but, by its less intrusive character, requires only the presence of specific and articulable facts and rational inferences which give rise to a reasonable suspicion that a person has committed or may be committing a crime. The least intrusive police-citizen contact, a consensual encounter, involves no restraint of liberty and elicits the citizen's voluntary cooperation with non-coercive questioning.

The proper test for determining when a police-citizen encounter implicates Fourth Amendment rights as a seizure was initially outlined in United States v. Mendenhall, 446 U.S. 544 (1980). [The Court] found no seizure had occurred where federal drug agents approached a woman walking through an airport and requested her identification. [The *Mendenhall* standard] creates an objective test, which makes the subjective intent of the police officer irrelevant unless it is conveyed to the person being detained, and like all search and seizure cases, the inquiry is very fact oriented. The reasonable person standard also means the subjective perceptions of the suspect are irrelevant to the court's inquiry.

[An] analytical difficulty imposed by [this] standard lies in the determination of whether a reasonable person "would have believed that he was not free to leave" when being questioned by a police officer. We find useful instruction in the Model Code of Pre-Arraignment Procedure, §110.1 commentary at 259-60 (A.L.I. 1975):

> The motives that lead one to cooperate with the police are various. To put an extreme case, the police may in purely precatory language request a person to give information. Even if he is guilty, such a person might accede to the request because he has been trained to submit to the wishes of persons in authority, or because he fears that a refusal will focus suspicion, or because he believes that concealment is no longer possible and a cooperative posture tactically or psychologically preferable. Regardless of the particular motive, the cooperation is clearly a response to the authority of the police.
>
> By specifically authorizing law enforcement officers . . . to seek cooperation, the Code rejects the notion that a damaging response to an inquiry from a policeman can never be "voluntary." . . . The extra pressures to cooperate with what is known to be an official request require no further justification than that the request was made in the performance of law enforcement functions. That there exist such pressures seems to us, far from being regrettable, to be a necessary condition of the police's capacity to operate reasonably effectively within their limited grant of powers.

The critical distinction between the position advanced by Wilson and that argued by the State is which type of encounter occurred in this case. Wilson basically contends that he was seized without reasonable suspicion during the period when his identification was being checked for possible warrants. The State asserts that Wilson was never seized in a manner that would implicate Fourth Amendment rights, until he was validly arrested on the outstanding warrants. . . .

The initial encounter between Officer Ritter and Wilson was prompted by the officer's concerns for the safety of a citizen. The officer conducted himself in a reasonable manner by simply pulling his patrol car to the curb to talk with Wilson. No flashing lights or siren sounds were used to signal Wilson to stop. The community caretaker function . . . permits police to act in a manner that enhances public safety. The police officer's observation of specific and articulable facts, Wilson's lunging walk with a severe limp, reasonably justified a brief inquiry into his condition and the possible cause, such as whether Wilson was a victim of criminal conduct. This portion of the initial encounter between Officer Ritter and Wilson occurred in a consensual atmosphere which implicates no Fourth Amendment interest.

When Officer Ritter requested Wilson's name and identification and Wilson complied, the encounter remained consensual. A request for identification is not, by itself, a seizure. Indeed, a reasonable person in physical distress should feel less intimidated by a police officer's offer to help and a request for identification than someone stopped at random. . . .

After obtaining Wilson's identification, Officer Ritter radioed for the NCIC and local warrants check. Despite the request for the computerized warrants check, the encounter remained consensual. Officer Ritter had not imposed any restriction on Wilson's freedom to leave as the warrants check was instituted. . . .

The initial encounter ended when Officer Ritter detected smoke and the two motorcyclists stopped to report a fire. At that point, Officer Ritter told Wilson to "stay in the area." [No seizure occurred at this point] because, when left unattended, [Wilson] limped away from the immediate area where the questioning had occurred. . . .

When Officer Ritter left the fire scene and returned to check on Wilson for the second time, [he] assisted Wilson across the street by grabbing him at the elbow and supporting his weight. [The] physical touching in this instance did not effect a seizure. A reasonable person would not believe that an officer's assistance in crossing a street would represent a restriction on the person's freedom to leave. The aid Officer Ritter provided ensured Wilson's safety by removing him from the path of emergency vehicles.

After Officer Ritter and Wilson crossed the street, the officer instructed Wilson to go to a specific street corner and wait. We hold a seizure occurred at the point when Wilson complied with the instruction to wait given by Officer Ritter in their second encounter. As Officer Ritter directed traffic, he could see Wilson sitting in front of a retail store at the specific corner the officer had directed. The persistence of Officer Ritter in returning to check on Wilson only supplements the determination that a seizure occurred. The show of authority by Officer Ritter restrained Wilson's liberty. A reasonable person would have believed he or she was not free to leave. With his seizure, Wilson's Fourth Amendment right to be free of unreasonable intrusions was implicated.

The narrow issue remaining is whether a brief detention for the purpose of completing a computerized warrants check is an unreasonable seizure. [It] is Casper Police Department policy to conduct NCIC and local warrants checks of everyone police "contact" late at night. The meaning of a "contact" was never defined. However, a seizure to conduct a computerized identification check without reasonable suspicion is not permitted. We acknowledge that where police have been unable to locate a person suspected of involvement in a past crime, the ability to briefly stop that person, ask questions, or check identification in the absence of probable cause promotes the strong government interest in solving crimes and bringing offenders to justice. However, we do not find in the circumstances of Officer Ritter's encounter with Wilson justification for a seizure . . . for the purpose of investigating past crime. . . . Officer Ritter questioned Wilson and requested his identification solely on the basis of the officer's concern for a citizen's safety. The officer lacked any reasonable suspicion of past criminal conduct. . . . When no observed violation of law is present, the intrusion required to run an NCIC or warrants check requires reasonable suspicion of criminal conduct. . . .

Officer Ritter admitted in his testimony that at no time during the first or second encounters did he possess any articulable facts sufficient to create a reasonable suspicion of past or present criminal conduct. Acting in a community caretaker function, Officer Ritter stopped Wilson to inquire about his condition and ensure his safety. A seizure for the purpose of completing an NCIC and local warrants check was impermissible as a matter of law. . . .

In a society burdened by crime, the protection of individual liberties requires difficult choices. All of us want to be able to freely walk the streets of our cities and towns. While we cannot and should not tolerate crime and lawlessness, we equally cannot tolerate the abrogation of basic liberties. Permitting a seizure, without reasonable suspicion of criminal behavior, to complete a computerized identification check of a police "contact" represents an unreasonable intrusion on basic liberties. . . .

The decision of the district court to deny suppression is reversed and this case is remanded for retrial without the tainted evidence.

THOMAS, J., dissenting.

I must dissent from the majority opinion in this case. . . . The contact between the officer and Wilson never went beyond the elicitation of Wilson's voluntary cooperation so as to become a seizure. [Wilson never asked to leave.] The officer testified he would not have pursued Wilson if he had chosen to leave because he had no reason to detain him if Wilson did not consent. . . . Laying aside the question whether there was any constraint upon Wilson's freedom to leave, an elapsed period of ten minutes, during which the officer's attention was devoted to the fire and traffic direction, is not unreasonable. The record reveals, of the ten minutes, Wilson was in the presence of the officer less than three minutes. . . .

The American bench needs to understand that its invocation of the premise of protecting Constitutional rights in reversing criminal convictions has contributed to the development of a society in which violence stalks our streets and fear permeates our neighborhoods. Every decision that tightens the cuffs with which we shackle our law enforcement officers contributes to such evolution. We must remember this rule applies to serial killers and multiple rapists as well as to inept firebugs who are simply a nuisance to property, until someone dies in the fire. . . .

In my judgment, the real question to be addressed in this case is: What was going on that was wrong? The obvious answer is it was wrong for Wilson to set fire to another citizen's garage-workshop. . . . The conclusion Wilson's conviction should not be upheld because of an academic fascination with the supposed wrongful conduct of the police officer does not serve the interests of the citizens of Wyoming and their property rights, which are not constitutionally subordinated to the rights of their persons. . . . I most vigorously dissent.

Notes

1. *Definition of a "stop": majority position.* Most American jurisdictions define a "stop" along the lines set out in United States v. Mendenhall, 446 U.S. 544 (1980). An encounter between a police officer and a citizen becomes a "stop" when a

reasonable person in that situation would not "feel free to leave" or to refuse to cooperate. Jurisdictions have generally adopted this definition in judicial decisions construing the state constitution rather than settling the question through statutes or rules of procedure. Is this the same "reasonable person" you met in Torts?

2. *Does reality matter?* Empirical inquiries could help us answer the question of whether a reasonable person would "feel free to leave" in a given situation. How would you gather such information for a court to use? See David K. Kessler, Free to Leave? An Empirical Look at the Fourth Amendment's Seizure Standard, 99 J. Crim. L. & Criminology 51 (2009) (survey of Boston residents regarding encounters with police). Did the Wyoming court in *Wilson* show any curiosity about the best method for finding a psychologically realistic answer to the question?

3. *The relevant pool.* The concept of the "reasonable person" is familiar in tort law and substantive criminal law. Courts applying the reasonable person concept are sometimes willing to consider particular features of the victim (age or gender, for instance) in their definition of a reasonable person. In effect, courts will sometimes narrow the relevant "pool" of persons from which the reasonable person is drawn.

Should the reasonable person standard for purposes of defining a "stop" consider the experiences and perceptions of different racial groups in their dealings with the police? Different genders? There is ample sociological and survey evidence that black males perceive the police to be more discriminatory and abusive than do white males. If a court is convinced that black males are more likely than other groups to submit passively to police encounters, should it account for this in the totality of the circumstances that go into the definition of a "stop"? See Devon W. Carbado, (E)Racing the Fourth Amendment, 100 Mich. L. Rev. 946, 974-1003 (2002).

4. *Routine check for warrants.* The court ultimately found that Ritter did not seize Wilson when he first requested a warrant check. Do you agree? Did Ritter "seize" Wilson without reasonable suspicion when he followed police department policy and requested an NCIC and warrant check on the person he "contacted" at night? The court concludes that Ritter later detained Wilson for the purpose of "completing" the warrant check. Did Ritter ever tell Wilson that he intended to complete the warrant check before releasing him? Does the status of a warrant check as a "stop" depend on how often police officers allow the individual to walk away before the check is complete? Or is it more important to know how this particular citizen (or a "reasonable" citizen) *believes* the officer would react? See Golphin v. State, 945 So. 2d 1174 (Fla. 2006) (officer's retention of person's identification card while running computer check for outstanding warrants did not necessarily convert consensual encounter into seizure); Montague v. Commonwealth, 684 S.E.2d 583 (Va. 2009) (no "stop" when officers approached suspect in common area of apartment complex, asked for his identity and whether he lived in apartments, and ran a warrants check without informing suspect of that fact).

5. *Limiting stops to investigations of serious crimes.* Should stops be available to police officers investigating misdemeanors? Most states have granted this power to the police, although there are exceptions. See N.Y. Crim. Proc. Law §140.50 (grants power to stop only when officer suspects commission of felony or the most serious misdemeanors); State v. Duvernoy, 195 S.E.2d 631 (W. Va. 1973) (limiting power to stop to investigate nonviolent offenses). Does your position on this issue depend on how effective a policy of investigative stops can be in preventing specific crimes? See Gordon Whitaker, Charles Phillips, Peter Haas & Robert Worden, Aggressive

Policing and the Deterrence of Crime, 7 Law & Pol'y 395 (1985) (investigative stops have strong negative effects on rate of robberies, auto theft, vandalism; smaller effects on rates of burglaries and thefts of property from autos). Does it depend on the racial makeup of the police force?

6. *Duration of stop and subject matter of questions.* When an officer stops a car based on reasonable suspicion that a traffic violation has occurred, it creates an opportunity to investigate other crimes. But the opportunity is limited. It is clear that the stop can only last as long as it would ordinarily take to complete a routine traffic citation. See State v. Joyce, 986 A.2d 642 (N.H. 2009) (motorist seized when officer called for narcotics-sniffing dog after police had been on scene for 10 to 15 minutes). State and federal courts have wrestled with the question of whether there are any limits on the subjects that an officer can discuss during the limited time available during a traffic stop. A rich case law has developed to trace the boundaries of the police power to stop a person, including the power to stop witnesses rather than suspects. For insights into these debates, see the web extension for this chapter at *http://www.crimpro.com/extension/ch02*.

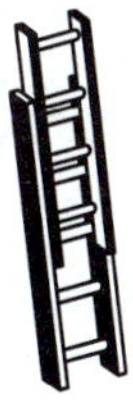

Problem 2-1. Tickets, Please

At 3:30 A.M. on January 23, Mark Battaglia, an investigator from the Sheriff's Department, boarded a bus just as it arrived in Albany from New York City. Battaglia wore civilian clothing with his police badge displayed on his coat. Two uniformed officers accompanied him. Battaglia announced to the 15 passengers on board that he was conducting a drug interdiction. He said that he would ask everyone to produce bus tickets and identification. Battaglia then walked to the rear of the bus and saw Rawle McIntosh and a female companion sitting in the last row of seats. Battaglia noticed that McIntosh pushed a black jacket between himself and his companion. He asked McIntosh for his identification and bus ticket. Battaglia inspected the driver's license and ticket he provided, and asked him about his travel plans. Battaglia then returned the identification and the ticket to McIntosh, and asked the two passengers to stand. As they stood, the jacket remained on the seat. Noticing a bulge in the pocket of the jacket, Battaglia reached into the pocket and found cocaine.

Did Battaglia "stop" McIntosh? If so, exactly when did the stop happen? Would there be a stop if Battaglia questioned McIntosh about his identity and his travel plans without requesting or holding the ticket and identification document? See People v. McIntosh, 755 N.E.2d 329 (N.Y. 2001).

Now suppose that McIntosh refuses to provide the proof of his identity when Officer Battaglia requests it, and he is prosecuted under a statute punishing any person for refusing to provide proof of identity when a police officer makes such a request. The state legislature passed this statute in the aftermath of the terrorist attacks in New York City on September 11, 2001. Is the statute constitutional?

Notes

1. *Asking for name and identification.* Does a stop occur whenever a police officer asks for a person to produce proof of identity? Does it matter how the officer asks

for the identification card or how quickly she returns the card? How could anyone feel free to leave when an officer is holding his driver's license? More than 20 state legislatures have passed statutes empowering police officers to ask for identification. In other states, the judiciary has permitted the police to make this request without specific statutory authority. If a statute authorizes a request for identification only upon reasonable suspicion (as statutes typically do), does that suggest that any police request for a citizen's identification is a stop? Apart from asking for name and identification, are there certain questions a police officer might ask that should automatically convert a conversation into a stop?

Could a statute explicitly oblige citizens to comply with the request for identification and allow officers to restrain citizens who refuse to do so? Is that what the Delaware statute allows? There is little litigation so far over the question of whether such a statute is constitutional. The questions become more immediate in light of the September 11 terrorist attacks. The law in other countries, such as Germany and France, explicitly empowers police officers to insist that people identify themselves. What would you want to know about the operation of such laws to determine whether they offer useful guidance for legislatures in the United States?

2. *Seizures in close quarters.* In Florida v. Bostick, 501 U.S. 429 (1991), the Court considered an encounter between police officers and a suspected drug courier who consented to a search of his luggage during questioning on a bus. Terrance Bostick was reclining on the back seat of the Greyhound bus bound from Miami to Atlanta when two officers wearing badges and sheriff's department jackets boarded the bus during a rest stop. The officers proceeded to the rear of the bus, stood in the aisle in front of Bostick, and questioned him about his destination. They asked to see his ticket and identification. After returning the documents, the officers stated that they were narcotics agents in search of illegal drugs. Then they asked for Bostick's consent to search his bag, telling him that he did not have to consent. He did consent, and they discovered cocaine in the bag. The Supreme Court decided that the agents did not "stop" Bostick when they questioned him on the bus. Although Bostick was not literally "free to leave" during the questioning because the officers were blocking the aisle of the bus, the Court concluded that a reasonable person in Bostick's position could have felt "free to decline the officers' requests or otherwise terminate the encounter." Compare United States v. Drayton, 536 U.S. 194 (2002) (no "stop" when two officers question passengers on bus while standing behind passenger's seat, one officer remains at front of bus watching passengers). Do the police "stop" the driver of a parked car when they position their patrol cars to block the vehicle from moving? Cases analyzing these and other potential stop scenarios appear on the web extension for this chapter at *http://www.crimpro.com/extension/ch02*.

3. *The reasonable person standard and the guilty suspect.* When trying to determine whether police seized a person during a conversation, courts have often stated that the exchange amounts to a seizure only if a "reasonable person" would conclude that he is not free to go. In Florida v. Bostick, the defendant argued that any person carrying contraband in a piece of luggage would not freely consent to a search of the luggage in his presence. Hence, he argued, his agreement to allow the search of his bag demonstrated that he did not feel free to leave. The court replied that the reasonable person standard "presupposes an innocent person." Does this standard lead to the conclusion that *any* refusal to engage in a conversation with a police officer amounts to reasonable suspicion for a stop?

2. *Grounds for Stops: Articulable, Individualized Reasonable Suspicion*

To justify a "stop," the government agent must be able to articulate a reasonable suspicion that the person has committed or will commit a crime. Exactly how can an officer establish reasonable suspicion? This concept is among the most commonly invoked in criminal procedure. Judges and lawyers applying the concept speak with apparent assurance about its meaning. Yet it is surprisingly difficult to find a precise definition of reasonable suspicion. And even a precise standard will leave enormous difficulties when applied to varied circumstances.

Judicial decisions, statutes, and rules of procedure use somewhat different verbal formulations to describe the justification needed for a low-level stop. Some formulations, especially those of the U.S. Supreme Court, emphasize the difference between reasonable suspicion and probable cause (the level of proof necessary to justify an arrest or a full-blown search):

> The Fourth Amendment requires some minimal level of objective justification for making the stop [that] is considerably less than proof of wrongdoing by a preponderance of the evidence. We have held that probable cause means a fair probability that contraband or evidence of a crime will be found, and the level of suspicion required for [reasonable suspicion] is obviously less demanding than that for probable cause. The concept of reasonable suspicion, like probable cause, is not readily, or even usefully, reduced to a neat set of legal rules. . . . In evaluating the validity of a stop such as this, we must consider the totality of the circumstances — the whole picture. [United States v. Sokolow, 490 U.S. 1 (1989).]

Some formulations emphasize that reasonable suspicion must be more than a guess and that it must be based on objective and articulable facts about an individual:

> [In] justifying the particular intrusion the police officer must be able to point to specific and articulable facts which, taken together with rational inferences from those facts, reasonably warrant that intrusion. . . . And in determining whether the officer acted reasonably in such circumstances, due weight must be given, not to his inchoate and unparticularized suspicion or "hunch," but to the specific reasonable inferences which he is entitled to draw from the facts in light of his experience. [Terry v. Ohio, 392 U.S. 1 (1968).]

Still other formulations insist that the reasonable suspicion standard is fact-sensitive, and the facts necessary to meet the standard will change from one context to another.

> The following are among the factors to be considered in determining if the officer has grounds to "reasonably suspect": (1) The demeanor of the suspect; (2) The gait and manner of the suspect; (3) Any knowledge the officer may have of the suspect's background or character; (4) Whether the suspect is carrying anything, and what he is carrying; (5) The manner in which the suspect is dressed, including bulges in clothing, when considered in light of all of the other factors; (6) The time of the day or night the suspect is observed; (7) Any overheard conversation of the suspect; (8) The particular streets and areas involved; (9) Any information received from third persons, whether they are known or unknown; (10) Whether the suspect is consorting with others whose

conduct is "reasonably suspect"; (11) The suspect's proximity to known criminal conduct; (12) Incidence of crime in the immediate neighborhood; (13) The suspect's apparent effort to conceal an article; (14) Apparent effort of the suspect to avoid identification or confrontation by a law enforcement officer. [Ark. Stat. §16-81-203.]

As used in [the following sections], unless the context requires otherwise: . . . "Reasonably suspects" means that a peace officer holds a belief that is reasonable under the totality of the circumstances existing at the time and place the peace officer acts. [Oregon Rev. Stat. §131.605.]

■ STATE v. THEODORE NELSON

638 A.2d 720 (Me. 1994)

GLASSMAN, J.

Theodore Nelson appeals from the judgment entered . . . on a jury verdict finding him guilty of operating a motor vehicle while under the influence of intoxicating liquor. . . . We agree with Nelson that because the stop of his motor vehicle was unlawful, the District Court erred in not granting Nelson's motion to suppress the evidence secured as a result of the stop and we vacate the judgment. . . .

At the hearing before the District Court on Nelson's motion to suppress, the sole witness presented was Officer Michael Holmes, who testified as follows: On December 24, 1991, at approximately 1:30 A.M., while on patrol . . . , he observed an unoccupied automobile he knew belonged to Bruce Moore, a former neighbor of his, in a well-lit parking lot at a housing complex for the elderly located on North Main Street. Because the police department within the prior two weeks had received several complaints of theft during the nighttime, Officer Holmes took up an observation post in a small parking lot adjacent to the driveway to the complex and approximately 50 to 100 yards from the Moore automobile. He observed a white pickup truck occupied by a driver, later identified as Nelson, and one passenger enter the driveway to the complex. The pickup was backed into a parking space beside the Moore vehicle, the motor was shut off, and the headlights extinguished leaving the parking lights illuminated. With the use of binoculars, Officer Holmes recognized the passenger as Moore. He observed each of the occupants of the pickup starting to drink from a 16-ounce Budweiser can. There was no evidence that Officer Holmes observed anything unusual about the appearance of either occupant. After approximately forty-five to fifty minutes, Moore left the pickup truck and entered his own vehicle. The headlights of the pickup truck were turned on and it was again driven past Officer Holmes onto North Main Street. As the pickup passed his observation site, Officer Holmes immediately "pulled out behind it, and turned on [his] blue lights, [and] made an enforcement stop." Nelson promptly brought the pickup to a stop. At no time did Officer Holmes observe anything unusual about the operation of the pickup. There was no evidence of mechanical defects to the pickup or of excessive speed. He stopped the pickup because he "observed the operator . . . drinking a can of beer [and suspected that] the person may be under the influence of intoxicating liquor." The District Court held "Officer Holmes had reasonable articulable suspicion to stop the Defendant's vehicle," and denied Nelson's motion to suppress evidence secured as a result of the claimed illegal stop. . . .

Every person is protected from unreasonable intrusions by police officers and other governmental agents by the Fourth Amendment to the United States Constitution and article I, section 5 of the Maine Constitution. An investigatory stop is justified if at the time of the stop the officer has an articulable suspicion that criminal conduct has taken place, is occurring, or imminently will occur, and the officer's assessment of the existence of specific and articulable facts sufficient to warrant the stop is objectively reasonable in the totality of the circumstances. . . . It is well established that the suspicion for the stop must be based on information available to the officer at the time of the stop and cannot be bolstered by evidence secured by the stop. . . .

In the instant case, we find a clear deficiency in the evidence supporting the reasonableness of the suspicion. The record reveals that the officer observed nothing to support his suspicion that Nelson was operating under the influence of alcohol other than Nelson's consumption of a single can of beer over the course of nearly one hour. An adult's consumption of liquor in a motor vehicle is neither a crime nor a civil violation. The reasonable suspicion standard requires more than mere speculation. There was no evidence that the officer observed indicia of physical impairment or anything unusual in Nelson's appearance. Officer Holmes testified that the pickup truck was not being operated in an erratic manner. The officer offered no reason for his stop of the motor vehicle other than his suspicion that Nelson was under the influence of alcohol.

Based on the whole picture presented by this case, it cannot be said that it was objectively reasonable to believe that criminal activity was afoot. Accordingly, the court should have granted Nelson's motion to suppress the evidence secured as a result of the illegal stop. Judgment vacated.

COLLINS, J., dissenting.

. . . The stop in this instance was not based on mere speculation that Nelson was driving while under the influence. Rather, the officer had observed Nelson drinking a 16-ounce beer, at 1:30 in the morning on Christmas Eve, while parked in the parking lot of a housing complex for the elderly from which several complaints of theft had been registered. These observed facts, in combination with the recognition of the common practice in American society of having a second beer, gave the officer an articulable suspicion that Nelson was operating his truck while under the influence of alcohol. The officer's suspicion was objectively reasonable given the totality of the circumstances. As such, I believe the stop was justified and I would affirm the trial court.

■ STATE v. DAVID DEAN

645 A.2d 634 (Me. 1994)

RUDMAN, J.

[David Dean entered a conditional plea of guilty to charges of operating a vehicle under the influence of alcohol. He now appeals on the ground that the stop was not justified by reasonable suspicion.] The underlying facts are undisputed. At approximately 11:00 P.M. on Tuesday, April 13, 1993, Officer Dennis Sampson of the South Paris Police Department spotted Dean's car while Sampson was patrolling a new residential development on Cobble Hill Road. The road is a dead end, and the development was uninhabited during weekdays. Sampson was patrolling the area at the request of the development's property owners after a number of complaints of vandalism. No complaint had been made that night, and Dean's driving was unremarkable. Sampson stopped him solely because of his presence at that particular time and place. Sampson "wanted to see what they was up to, see if they were landowners or property owners, get some names in case we did have problems up in that area." The District Court, in a well-reasoned opinion, ruled that Sampson had the necessary "reasonable suspicion" to justify the stop. . . .

Dean's contention is that Officer Sampson did not entertain any suspicion that Dean was engaged in criminal activity. Dean raises the specter of random stops in any high-crime area, justified solely by the fact that the person detained happens to be in that area. The District Court, however, understood Dean's contentions and explicitly made the required findings:

> Now, I'll point out that the facts in this case suggest that this particular defendant was driving along a dead-end road at nighttime. The — the structures in the area were uninhabited, and it had been an area which had been the scene of a variety of criminal behavior which, in fact, brought . . . if not residents then the property owners to the police. They asked for increased surveillance. Ordinarily, the officer could not have stopped this particular vehicle. But under the circumstances, given the fact that this occurred well after dark, that the place was virtually uninhabited, that it was a dead-end street and [an area] in which a substantial amount of crime had been perpetrated in the recent past — I find that the officer acted properly because he reasonably suspected, based on prior reports of criminal activity in the area, that this particular Defendant could be engaged in such behavior. . . .

The only real issue is whether the two articulable facts relied on by the court can yield a reasonable suspicion. Those two facts are: (1) Dean's presence in an area of recent crime reports; and (2) the apparent absence of any reason to be in an uninhabited area at night. It is well-settled that a person's mere presence in a high crime area does not justify an investigatory stop. However, the combination of the recent criminal activity with other articulable facts — in this case, the time of day and the fact that the area was uninhabited — creates a reasonable suspicion. Many cases uphold a finding of a reasonable suspicion on similar facts.

In a recent decision, also involving police surveillance of an area due to several complaints, we held that the District Court erred by failing to grant the defendant's motion to suppress. State v. Nelson (Me. 1994). . . . In the *Nelson* case, however, the defendant was sitting in a truck in the parking lot of an occupied housing complex. Dean, in contrast, was driving through an uninhabited development site on a dead end street at 11:00 at night. His situation is distinguishable from that of the defendant in *Nelson*.

Dean's situation is more analogous to that of the defendant in State v. Fitzgerald, 620 A.2d 874 (Me. 1993). After dark, a police officer spotted Fitzgerald's car entering a private turn-around, known to be the site of frequent illegal trash dumping, and posted with "no trespassing" signs by the owner. When the officer's vehicle drove into the turn-around, the defendant was standing next to his car. The defendant then got into his car and drove away. The officer stopped the defendant's vehicle, saw that the defendant displayed evidence of being under the influence of alcohol, and arrested him for operating under the influence. Although the officer never witnessed any illegality or impropriety (Fitzgerald never violated the no trespassing signs), we affirmed the finding that the officer had a reasonable and articulable suspicion, "based on the previous littering and trespassing," the fact that Fitzgerald was outside his car in the dark when the officer approached, and the fact that Fitzgerald tried to leave when he saw the cruiser. Similarly, Officer Sampson's suspicion of Dean was engendered by prior complaints combined with other facts — the time of night and the absence of any apparent reason to be in an uninhabited housing development.

But for Dean's intoxication, this would have been a brief investigatory stop. An investigatory stop of a motor vehicle is normally a minimal intrusion by the state into a person's affairs. Balancing the facts on which Officer Sampson relied to make the stop against Dean's right to be free from any arbitrary intrusions by the State, we find the District Court's findings that the officer's suspicion was reasonable and the stop was justified are not clearly erroneous.

GLASSMAN, J., dissenting.

I respectfully dissent. We have recently reemphasized that the reasonable articulable suspicion standard requires "more than mere speculation" on the part of the police officer to sustain an investigatory stop. State v. Nelson (Me. 1994). Dean's behavior in driving out of a dead-end street at 11:00 P.M. on a Tuesday was in no sense illegal or even inherently suspicious, and the officer's desire to "see what [Dean] was up to" stems, at best, from a hunch.[1] A mere hunch will not justify a stop, and the officer's reasons for stopping the vehicle must not be a mere pretext or ruse. . . .

As the court notes, it is well settled that a person's mere presence in a high-crime area does not justify an investigatory stop. What the court regards as "other articulable facts" justifying the stop, in reality, are mere speculations entertained by the officer because of Dean's presence on a public way in an area where there had been complaints of vandalism or other damage to property. Each of the cases cited by the court to support its position involves additional facts beyond the defendant's mere presence in a crime area, e.g., police observed unusual behavior by the defendant, intrusion onto private property, the unusual operation of a vehicle, or the vehicle's unusual location. The constitutional right to be free from an illegal stop should not be abridged solely on the basis of the day of the week or time of day a car is being operated on a public way. . . .

Notes

1. *Components of reasonable suspicion: majority position.* Courts typically do not specify the general categories of facts that could support a finding of reasonable suspicion. In virtually all cases, however, the conduct of the suspect said to be the basis

1. The court seeks to distinguish *Nelson* by noting that Nelson was sitting in a pickup truck parked in the parking lot of an occupied housing complex whereas Dean was observed driving a motor vehicle on a public way leading out of a largely uninhabited residential development site. This is inapposite because the surroundings in which the police observed Nelson were not at issue in that case, which turned on whether merely drinking a can of beer in a parked car provided a reasonably articulable suspicion that a crime had taken place. This case turns on the site of the stop.

for reasonable suspicion does not violate the criminal law. The observer must infer from the observed facts that there is some correlation between the legal conduct observed and the suspected criminal acts. The officer may observe something resembling criminal conduct (such as the legal acts necessary to prepare for a crime); she might also observe the suspect taking an action that could be designed to hide a crime or to avoid contact with the police (such as avoiding eye contact with the officer or running away from the scene). See Sibron v. New York, 392 U.S. 40 (1968); but cf. State v. Hall, 115 P.3d 908 (Ore. 2005) (fact that suspect repeatedly turned to look at officer's patrol vehicle and then averted his gaze did not amount to reasonable suspicion). The surroundings of the suspect are another common component of reasonable suspicion: For instance, presence near a crime scene soon after the time of a crime would be significant, especially if the suspect has no other apparent reason to be in that location. See State v. Miller, 207 P.3d 541 (Alaska 2009) (officer observed man and woman in vehicle exiting parking lot of tavern soon after receiving 911 call about couple arguing loudly in parking lot). How strong should the correlation be between this innocent conduct and the suspected criminal conduct to establish reasonable suspicion? Why do courts and other legal institutions scrupulously avoid answering this question in terms of numeric probabilities?

A study of stops in New York City gives us one indication of the level of certainty police officers believe in practice to be enough for reasonable suspicion. During a two-year period, a specialized Street Crimes Unit made 45,000 stops, with about 20 percent of those stops resulting in an arrest or criminal charges. See Jeffrey Goldberg, "The Color of Suspicion," N.Y. Times Magazine, June 20, 1999, at 85. Do these figures indicate that police officers have 20 percent confidence that a crime has been or is about to be committed when they make a stop? If so, is that enough certainty?

2. *Do standards matter?* Are *Nelson* and *Dean* consistent; that is, do they reflect a single standard of reasonable suspicion? If you were representing Nelson and Dean, where would you rather argue the case: under the statutory definition of reasonable suspicion in Oregon or Arkansas, or the judicial definition in Maine? Do different formulations of the reasonable suspicion standard make any difference in the outcomes?

3. *Objective basis.* The basis for reasonable suspicion turns on the facts available to the officer; it does not matter whether the officer holds an actual suspicion. In fact, the officer might wrongly believe that reasonable suspicion exists for one crime, when in fact reasonable suspicion exists for another crime. Does an objective "reasonable suspicion" standard promote more careful evaluation of facts by police officers?

4. *Seriousness of crime.* Would the reasonable suspicion determination in *Dean* have turned out differently if the suspected crime had been murder instead of vandalism of property? Was the police officer in *Nelson* concerned about a different crime from the one he ultimately charged? Should the seriousness of the crime committed or soon to be committed affect the determination of reasonable suspicion? See Commonwealth v. Hawkins, 692 A.2d 1068 (Pa. 1997) (rejects concept of fluctuating reasonable suspicion standard based on seriousness of crime suspected; no "gun exception" to reasonable suspicion requirement).

5. *Codified definitions of reasonable suspicion.* This section began with examples of statutes defining reasonable suspicion. Similar definitions appear in some states' rules of criminal procedure. The statutory examples draw on language familiar in

judicial opinions defining the same concept; that is, they codify the common law. Would the presence of such a statute or rule affect a court's willingness to elaborate on the meaning of reasonable suspicion or to adjust it over time?

6. *Role of appellate courts in defining reasonable suspicion.* Under the "totality of the circumstances" test, the factfinder at the trial level takes a central role in deciding whether reasonable suspicion exists. What contributions might an appellate court make? Could an appeals court bring more predictability to the process by describing the sorts of factors that should receive more or less weight? For instance, should an appellate court declare that conduct "as consistent with innocent activity as with criminal activity" should receive little or no weight? See Irwin v. Superior Court of Los Angeles County, 462 P.2d 12, 14 (Cal. 1969) (adopting innocent conduct limit); State v. O'Meara, 9 P.3d 325 (Ariz. 2000) ("totality of circumstances" test for reasonable suspicion allows court to consider conduct susceptible of an innocent explanation; here, unusual meeting in parking lot with drivers switching among four vehicles established reasonable suspicion for stop).

In Ornelas v. United States, 517 U.S. 690 (1996), the U.S. Supreme Court held that appellate courts would determine for themselves, under a de novo standard, the presence or absence of reasonable suspicion. This standard, the Court said, would allow appellate courts to unify precedent and clarify the legal principles at stake, providing law enforcement officers with the tools to reach correct determinations beforehand. At the same time, the Court declared that a reviewing court must give "due weight" to factual inferences drawn by resident judges. In United States v. Arvizu, 534 U.S. 266 (2002), the Court applied this standard of review to affirm a trial judge's finding of reasonable suspicion. A Border Patrol agent stopped Arvizu while driving on an unpaved road in a remote area of southeastern Arizona, and discovered over 100 pounds of marijuana in the minivan. The officer became suspicious when the driver of the minivan slowed dramatically after the patrol car appeared, and the children in the back seat waved to the officer in an "abnormal" and "mechanical" fashion, off and on for about five minutes. While each of these facts was "susceptible to innocent explanations" when viewed in isolation, the trial judge nevertheless could consider them as part of the "totality of the circumstances" to establish reasonable suspicion. An appellate court should not "casually" reject factors such as these "in light of the District Court's superior access to the evidence and the well-recognized inability of reviewing courts to reconstruct what happened in the courtroom." Is this a de novo standard of review at work?

7. *Anonymous tips as the basis for reasonable suspicion.* Ordinarily, the police obtain reasonable suspicion based on their own observations and investigations. But on occasion, the police receive information from an anonymous informant that might contribute later to a finding of "reasonable suspicion." The U.S. Supreme Court has stated that anonymous tips can contribute to a reasonable suspicion finding only if the police can find independent corroboration of "significant details" of the informant's information. Alabama v. White, 496 U.S. 325 (1990). Those significant details must amount to more than innocent conduct that any person could observe. The anonymous tip, standing alone without corroboration, cannot justify a brief seizure of the suspect. See Florida v. J.L., 529 U.S. 266 (2000) (anonymous tip says that young black male standing at a particular bus stop and wearing a plaid shirt was carrying a gun; not enough for reasonable suspicion). You can get a flavor of the state court decisions regarding anonymous tips and reasonable suspicion on the web extension for this chapter at *http://www.crimpro.com/extension/ch02*.

■ ILLINOIS v. WILLIAM aka "SAM" WARDLOW

525 U.S. 119 (2000)

REHNQUIST, C.J.[*]

Respondent Wardlow fled upon seeing police officers patrolling an area known for heavy narcotics trafficking. Two of the officers caught up with him, stopped him and conducted a protective pat-down search for weapons. Discovering a .38-caliber handgun, the officers arrested Wardlow. We hold that the officers' stop did not violate the Fourth Amendment to the United States Constitution.

On September 9, 1995, Officers Nolan and Harvey were working as uniformed officers in the special operations section of the Chicago Police Department. The officers were driving the last car of a four car caravan converging on an area known for heavy narcotics trafficking in order to investigate drug transactions. The officers were traveling together because they expected to find a crowd of people in the area, including lookouts and customers.

As the caravan passed 4035 West Van Buren, Officer Nolan observed respondent Wardlow standing next to the building holding an opaque bag. Respondent looked in the direction of the officers and fled. Nolan and Harvey turned their car southbound, watched him as he ran through the gangway and an alley, and eventually cornered him on the street. Nolan then exited his car and stopped respondent. He immediately conducted a protective pat-down search for weapons because in his experience it was common for there to be weapons in the near vicinity of narcotics transactions. During the frisk, Officer Nolan squeezed the bag respondent was carrying and felt a heavy, hard object similar to the shape of a gun. The officer then opened the bag and discovered a .38-caliber handgun with five live rounds of ammunition. The officers arrested Wardlow. The Illinois trial court denied respondent's motion to suppress, finding the gun was recovered during a lawful stop and frisk. Following a stipulated bench trial, Wardlow was convicted of unlawful use of a weapon by a felon. The [Illinois Supreme Court] reversed Wardlow's conviction, concluding that the gun should have been suppressed because Officer Nolan did not have reasonable suspicion. . . .

This case, involving a brief encounter between a citizen and a police officer on a public street, is governed by the analysis we first applied in Terry v. Ohio, 392 U.S. 1 (1968). In *Terry,* we held that an officer may, consistent with the Fourth Amendment, conduct a brief, investigatory stop when the officer has a reasonable, articulable suspicion that criminal activity is afoot. While "reasonable suspicion" is a less demanding standard than probable cause and requires a showing considerably less than preponderance of the evidence, the Fourth Amendment requires at least a minimal level of objective justification for making the stop. The officer must be able to articulate more than an inchoate and unparticularized suspicion or hunch of criminal activity.

Nolan and Harvey were among eight officers in a four car caravan that was converging on an area known for heavy narcotics trafficking, and the officers anticipated encountering a large number of people in the area, including drug customers and individuals serving as lookouts. It was in this context that Officer Nolan decided to investigate Wardlow after observing him flee. An individual's presence in an area

* [Justices O'Connor, Scalia, Kennedy, and Thomas joined in the opinion. — EDS.]

of expected criminal activity, standing alone, is not enough to support a reasonable, particularized suspicion that the person is committing a crime. Brown v. Texas, 443 U.S. 47 (1979). But officers are not required to ignore the relevant characteristics of a location in determining whether the circumstances are sufficiently suspicious to warrant further investigation. Accordingly, we have previously noted the fact that the stop occurred in a "high crime area" among the relevant contextual considerations in a *Terry* analysis.

In this case, moreover, it was not merely respondent's presence in an area of heavy narcotics trafficking that aroused the officers' suspicion but his unprovoked flight upon noticing the police. Our cases have also recognized that nervous, evasive behavior is a pertinent factor in determining reasonable suspicion. Headlong flight — wherever it occurs — is the consummate act of evasion: it is not necessarily indicative of wrongdoing, but it is certainly suggestive of such. In reviewing the propriety of an officer's conduct, courts do not have available empirical studies dealing with inferences drawn from suspicious behavior, and we cannot reasonably demand scientific certainty from judges or law enforcement officers where none exists. Thus, the determination of reasonable suspicion must be based on commonsense judgments and inferences about human behavior. We conclude Officer Nolan was justified in suspecting that Wardlow was involved in criminal activity, and, therefore, in investigating further.

Such a holding is entirely consistent with our decision in Florida v. Royer, 460 U.S. 491 (1983), where we held that when an officer, without reasonable suspicion or probable cause, approaches an individual, the individual has a right to ignore the police and go about his business. And any refusal to cooperate, without more, does not furnish the minimal level of objective justification needed for a detention or seizure. But unprovoked flight is simply not a mere refusal to cooperate. Flight, by its very nature, is not "going about one's business"; in fact, it is just the opposite. Allowing officers confronted with such flight to stop the fugitive and investigate further is quite consistent with the individual's right to go about his business or to stay put and remain silent in the face of police questioning. . . .

STEVENS, J., concurring in part and dissenting in part.*

The State of Illinois asks this Court to announce a "bright-line rule" authorizing the temporary detention of anyone who flees at the mere sight of a police officer. Respondent counters by asking us to adopt the opposite per se rule — that the fact that a person flees upon seeing the police can never, by itself, be sufficient to justify a temporary investigative stop of the kind authorized by *Terry.* The Court today wisely endorses neither per se rule. . . .

Although I agree with the Court's rejection of the per se rules proffered by the parties, unlike the Court, I am persuaded that in this case the brief testimony of the officer who seized respondent does not justify the conclusion that he had reasonable suspicion to make the stop.

. . . The question in this case concerns "the degree of suspicion that attaches to" a person's flight — or, more precisely, what "commonsense conclusions" can be drawn respecting the motives behind that flight. A pedestrian may break into a run for a variety of reasons — to catch up with a friend a block or two away, to seek

* [Justices Souter, Ginsburg, and Breyer joined in this opinion. — EDS.]

shelter from an impending storm, to arrive at a bus stop before the bus leaves, to get home in time for dinner, to resume jogging after a pause for rest, to avoid contact with a bore or a bully, or simply to answer the call of nature — any of which might coincide with the arrival of an officer in the vicinity. A pedestrian might also run because he or she has just sighted one or more police officers. [There] are unquestionably circumstances in which a person's flight is suspicious, and undeniably instances in which a person runs for entirely innocent reasons.[3]

Given the diversity and frequency of possible motivations for flight, it would be profoundly unwise to endorse either per se rule. The inference we can reasonably draw about the motivation for a person's flight, rather, will depend on a number of different circumstances. Factors such as the time of day, the number of people in the area, the character of the neighborhood, whether the officer was in uniform, the way the runner was dressed, the direction and speed of the flight, and whether the person's behavior was otherwise unusual might be relevant in specific cases. . . .

[A] reasonable person may conclude that an officer's sudden appearance indicates nearby criminal activity. And where there is criminal activity there is also a substantial element of danger — either from the criminal or from a confrontation between the criminal and the police. These considerations can lead to an innocent and understandable desire to quit the vicinity with all speed. Among some citizens, particularly minorities and those residing in high crime areas, there is also the possibility that the fleeing person is entirely innocent, but, with or without justification, believes that contact with the police can itself be dangerous, apart from any criminal activity associated with the officer's sudden presence.[7]

[In this case, the] entire justification for the stop is articulated in the brief testimony of Officer Nolan, [who stated,] "He looked in our direction and began fleeing." No other factors sufficiently support a finding of reasonable suspicion. Though respondent was carrying a white, opaque bag under his arm, there is nothing at all suspicious about that. Certainly the time of day — shortly after noon — does not support Illinois' argument. Nor were the officers responding to any call or report of suspicious activity in the area. . . .

The State, along with the majority of the Court, relies as well on the assumption that this flight occurred in a high crime area. Even if that assumption is accurate, it is insufficient because even in a high crime neighborhood unprovoked flight does not invariably lead to reasonable suspicion. On the contrary, because many factors providing innocent motivations for unprovoked flight are concentrated in high crime areas, the character of the neighborhood arguably makes an inference of guilt less appropriate, rather than more so. . . .

3. Compare, e.g., Proverbs 28:1 ("The wicked flee when no man pursueth: but the righteous are as bold as a lion") with Proverbs 22:3 ("A shrewd man sees trouble coming and lies low; the simple walk into it and pay the penalty"). I have rejected reliance on the former proverb in the past, because its "ivory-towered analysis of the real world" fails to account for the experiences of many citizens of this country, particularly those who are minorities. See California v. Hodari D., 499 U.S. 621, 630, n.4 (1991) (Stevens, J., dissenting). That this pithy expression fails to capture the total reality of our world, however, does not mean it is inaccurate in all instances.

7. See Johnson, Americans' Views on Crime and Law Enforcement: Survey Findings, National Institute of Justice Journal 13 (Sept.1997) (reporting study by the Joint Center for Political and Economic Studies in April 1996, which found that 43% of African-Americans consider "police brutality and harassment of African-Americans a serious problem" in their own community); Casimir, Minority Men: We Are Frisk Targets, N.Y. Daily News, Mar. 26,1999, p. 34 (informal survey of 100 young black and Hispanic men living in New York City; 81 reported having been stopped and frisked by police at least once; none of the 81 stops resulted in arrests).

Notes

1. *"Bad neighborhoods" and reasonable suspicion: majority position.* An officer trying to establish reasonable suspicion will at times rely on the amount of crime occurring recently in the neighborhood. The government typically does not support the assertion with any statistical analysis of reported crimes, but bases the claim on the impressions of the officer about neighborhoods. See State v. Moore, 853 A.2d 903 (N.J. 2004) (nature of crime in area may contribute to reasonable suspicion to stop men engaged in suspicious street-side transaction). If you were a judge evaluating the claim of reasonable suspicion, would the reputation of the neighborhood for crime play any part in your decision? If you were a police officer, how might you strengthen such claims? See Margaret Raymond, Down on the Corner, Out in the Street: Considering the Character of the Neighborhood in Evaluating Reasonable Suspicion, 60 Ohio St. L.J. 99 (1999); cf. Brown v. Texas, 443 U.S. 47 (1979) ("The fact that appellant was in a neighborhood frequented by drug users, standing alone, is not a basis for concluding that appellant himself was engaged in criminal conduct").

2. *Neighborhood as proxy for race?* The neighborhoods described in court as "high crime" areas are often the homes for poor and minority residents. Do the demographics of some neighborhoods make crimes committed or reported there easier to notice or remember? Do more crimes occur in poorer neighborhoods because of subtle signals that disorder is tolerated there — the so-called "broken windows" theory of policing? If this is true, then it would make sense to direct more stop-and-frisk activity in places where police find the greatest physical and social disorder. A study of New York City policing by Jeffrey Pagan and Garth Davies, however, found that neighborhood characteristics such as racial composition and poverty levels are better predictors of stop-and-frisk activity than the presence of physical disorder in the neighborhood. They conclude that policing in New York City "is not about disorderly places . . . but about policing poor people in poor places." Fagan & Davies, Street Stops and Broken Windows: *Terry,* Race and Disorder in New York City, 28 Fordham Urban L.J. 457 (2000). If you were a police chief and a reporter called a similar study about your department to your attention, how would you respond?

3. *Avoiding or fleeing the police as basis for reasonable suspicion.* The officers in *Wardlow* noted that the suspect tried to flee the scene and considered the flight to be one factor contributing to reasonable suspicion. Would a suspect's flight from the police be enough, standing alone, to establish reasonable suspicion of criminal activity? A strong majority of state courts have decided that flight contributes to reasonable suspicion, but few cases arise in which flight alone is the basis for a claim of reasonable suspicion. Compare Bost v. State, 958 A.2d 356 (Md. 2008) (reasonable suspicion present when police approached group drinking on side of city street, man immediately walked away, "clutching" something at waistband, picked up pace as he crossed street, looked back at officers), with State v. Hicks, 488 N.W.2d 359 (Neb. 1992) (flight upon approach of police vehicle not sufficient to justify investigative stop).

4. *Seizure by pursuit.* In California v. Hodari D., 499 U.S. 621 (1991), the Court assumed that a suspect's flight, standing alone, did not create reasonable suspicion. Nevertheless, the Court ruled that the officer needed no individualized suspicion

to pursue Hodari because the pursuit did not amount to a "seizure" under the federal constitution. Two officers wearing police department jackets rounded a corner in their patrol car and saw four or five young men gathered around a small car parked at the curb. When the group saw the officers' car approaching, they began to run away. The officers were suspicious and gave chase. One officer left the patrol car and took a route that placed him in front of one of the fleeing suspects. The suspect, looking behind as he ran, did not turn and see the officer until the two were quite close. At that point, he tossed away what appeared to be a small rock and ran in the opposite direction. A moment later, the officer tackled the suspect, handcuffed him, and radioed for assistance. The rock the suspect had discarded was crack cocaine. The Court held that there was no "stop" until the officer tackled Hodari; the pursuit by the officer was not enough.

Courts in about 30 states, reviewing similar cases under their state constitutions, have reached the same conclusion. See State v. Smith, 39 S.W.3d 739 (Ark. 2001). However, most of the remaining states insist that pursuit might sometimes qualify as a seizure. Seizures occur when the "totality of the circumstances" reasonably indicate that the person is not free to leave. See State v. Garcia, 217 P.3d 1032 (N.M. 2009). How might a court reach the conclusion that a person can feel "free to leave," despite the fact that a police officer is chasing her and shouting "stop"? Is it because the suspect is in fact trying to leave? Would it matter if the suspect paused momentarily before or during flight? See State v. Rogers, 924 P.2d 1027 (Ariz. 1996).

5. *Discretion to stop and the definition of crimes.* There is a powerful relationship between reasonable suspicion and the substantive criminal law. If a legislature creates a crime such as "drug loitering," it empowers the police to stop people based on innocent behavior (such as standing on a corner or making signals) that is often a precursor to more harmful criminal activity, such as drug trafficking. See Mich. Comp. L. §750.167(1)(j) (disorderly conduct where a person knowingly loiters in or about a place where an illegal occupation or business is being conducted); Andrew D. Leipold, Targeted Loitering Laws, 3 U. Pa. J. Const. L. 474 (2001). If you were counsel to a police department, would you ask the city council to pass such an ordinance, or would you rather formulate a profile within the department itself?

3. *Pretextual Stops*

An officer needs reasonable suspicion that a crime has been or will be committed before stopping a person for an investigation. But when the officer has multiple reasons to stop a person, including reasonable suspicion of one crime and a hunch that the person has committed another crime, must the suspicion and the purpose match? In other words, does the police officer invalidate a stop when the crime that she reasonably suspects is only a "pretext" to justify a stop that she intends to use while investigating some other crime? State courts were split on this subject until the U.S. Supreme Court addressed it in Whren v. United States, 517 U.S. 806 (1996). The case created a new shorthand term in criminal procedure: "*Whren* stops" refer to traffic stops based on reasonable suspicion of a traffic violation, but intended to further the investigation of some other crime. Now virtually all state courts addressing this question respond much like the New York court in the following case.

PEOPLE v. FRANK ROBINSON

767 N.E.2d 638 (N.Y. 2001)

SMITH, J.

The issue [in these consolidated cases] is whether a police officer who has probable cause to believe a driver has committed a traffic infraction violates article I, §12 of the New York State Constitution when the officer, whose primary motivation is to conduct another investigation, stops the vehicle. We conclude that there is no violation, and we adopt Whren v. United States, 517 U.S. 806 (1996), as a matter of state law.

People v. Robinson. On November 22, 1993, New York City police officers in the Street Crime Unit, Mobile Taxi Homicide Task Force were on night patrol in a marked police car in the Bronx. Their main assignment was to follow taxicabs to make sure that no robberies occurred. After observing a car speed through a red light, the police activated their high intensity lights and pulled over what they suspected was a livery cab. After stopping the cab, one officer observed a passenger, the defendant, look back several times. The officers testified that they had no intention of giving the driver a summons but wanted to talk to him about safety tips. The officers approached the vehicle with their flashlights turned on and their guns holstered. One of the officers shined his flashlight into the back of the vehicle, where defendant was seated, and noticed that defendant was wearing a bullet proof vest. After the officer ordered defendant out of the taxicab, he observed a gun on the floor where defendant had been seated. Defendant was arrested and charged with criminal possession of a weapon and unlawfully wearing a bullet proof vest. Defendant moved to suppress the vest and gun, arguing that the officers used a traffic infraction as a pretext to search the occupant of the taxicab. The Court denied the motion, and defendant was convicted of both charges. . . .

People v. Reynolds. On March 6, 1999, shortly after midnight, a police officer, on routine motor patrol in the City of Rochester, saw a man he knew to be a prostitute enter defendant's truck. The officer followed the truck and ran a computer check on the license plate. Upon learning that the vehicle's registration had expired two months earlier, the officer stopped the vehicle. The resulting investigation did not lead to any charges involving prostitution. Nevertheless, because the driver's eyes were bloodshot, his speech slurred and there was a strong odor of alcohol, police performed various field sobriety tests, with defendant failing most. . . . Defendant was charged with driving while intoxicated, an unclassified misdemeanor, and operating an unregistered motor vehicle, a traffic infraction. Defendant's motion to suppress was granted by the Rochester City Court, which dismissed all charges.

People v. Glenn. On November 7, 1997, plainclothes police officers were on street crime patrol in an unmarked car in Manhattan. They observed a livery cab make a right hand turn without signaling. An officer noticed one of three passengers in the back seat lean forward. The police stopped the vehicle to investigate whether or not a robbery was in progress. A police officer subsequently found cocaine on the rear seat and, after he arrested defendant, found additional drugs on his person. Defendant was charged with criminal possession of a controlled substance in the third degree and criminally using drug paraphernalia in the second degree. He contended that the drugs should be suppressed, asserting that the traffic infraction was a pretext to investigate a robbery. After his motion to suppress was denied, he pleaded guilty to one count of criminal possession of a controlled substance. . . .

Discussion. The Supreme Court, in Whren v. United States, 517 U.S. 806 (1996), unanimously held that where a police officer has probable cause to detain a person temporarily for a traffic violation, that seizure does not violate the Fourth Amendment to the United States Constitution even though the underlying reason for the stop might have been to investigate some other matter. In *Whren,* officers patrolling a known drug area of the District of Columbia became suspicious when several young persons seated in a truck with temporary license plates remained at a stop sign for an unusual period of time, and the driver was looking down into the lap of the passenger seated on his right. After the car made a right turn without signaling, the police stopped it, assertedly to warn the driver of traffic violations, and saw two plastic bags of what appeared to be crack cocaine in Whren's hands.

After arresting the occupants, the police found several quantities of drugs in the car. The petitioners were charged with violating federal drug laws. The petitioners moved to suppress the drugs, arguing that the stop was not based upon probable cause or even reasonable suspicion that they were engaged in illegal drug activity and that the police officer's assertion that he approached the car in order to give a warning was pretextual. The District Court denied suppression. . . .

The Supreme Court held that the Fourth Amendment had not been violated because "as a general matter, the decision to stop an automobile is reasonable where the police have probable cause to believe that a traffic violation has occurred." The stop of the truck was based upon probable cause that the petitioners had violated provisions of the District of Columbia traffic code. The Court rejected any effort to tie the legality of the officers' conduct to their primary motivation or purpose in making the stop, deeming irrelevant whether a reasonable traffic police officer would have made the stop. According to the Court, "Subjective intentions play no role in ordinary, probable-cause Fourth Amendment analysis." Thus, the "Fourth Amendment's concern with 'reasonableness' allows certain actions to be taken in certain circumstances, whatever the subjective intent." More than forty states and the District of Columbia have adopted the objective standard approved by *Whren* or cited it with approval.

In each of the cases before us, defendant argues that the stop was pretextual and in violation of New York State Constitution, article I, §12. . . . We hold that where a police officer has probable cause to believe that the driver of an automobile has committed a traffic violation, a stop does not violate article I, §12 of the New York State Constitution. In making that determination of probable cause, neither the primary motivation of the officer nor a determination of what a reasonable traffic officer would have done under the circumstances is relevant. . . .

The real concern of those opposing pretextual stops is that police officers will use their authority to stop persons on a selective and arbitrary basis. *Whren* recognized that the answer to such action is the Equal Protection Clause of the Constitution. We are not unmindful of studies . . . which show that certain racial and ethnic groups are disproportionately stopped by police officers, and that those stops do not end in the discovery of a higher proportion of contraband than in the cars of other groups. The fact that such disparities exist is cause for both vigilance and concern about the protections given by the New York State Constitution. Discriminatory law enforcement has no place in our law. . . .

The alternatives to upholding a stop based solely upon reasonable cause to believe a traffic infraction has been committed put unacceptable restraints on law enforcement. This is so whether those restrictions are based upon the primary motivation of an officer or upon what a reasonable traffic police officer would have done under the circumstances. Rather than restrain the police in these instances, the police should be permitted to do what they are sworn to do — uphold the law. . . .

To be sure, the story does not end when the police stop a vehicle for a traffic infraction. Our holding in this case addresses only the initial police action upon which the vehicular stop was predicated. The scope, duration and intensity of the seizure, as well as any search made by the police subsequent to that stop, remain subject to the strictures of article I, §12, and judicial review. . . .

The dissenters concede that . . . an individualized determination of probable cause will generally provide an objective evidentiary floor circumscribing police conduct and thereby prevent the arbitrary exercise of search and seizure power. However, [the] dissenters assert that because motor vehicle travel is so much a part of our lives and is minutely regulated, total compliance with the law is impossible. We see no basis for this differentiation. While New Yorkers may ubiquitously disobey parts of the Vehicle and Traffic Law, that does not render its commands unenforceable. As noted by the unanimous United States Supreme Court, "we are aware of no principle that would allow us to decide at what point a code of law becomes so expansive and so commonly violated that infraction itself can no longer be the ordinary measure of the lawfulness of enforcement." *Whren,* 517 U.S. at 818.

Because the Vehicle and Traffic Law provides an objective grid upon which to measure probable cause, a stop based on that standard is not arbitrary in the context of constitutional search and seizure jurisprudence. Contrary to the dissent's view, probable cause stops are not based on the discretion of police officers. They are based on violations of law. An officer may choose to stop someone for a "minor" violation after considering a number of factors, including traffic and weather conditions, but the officer's authority to stop a vehicle is circumscribed by the requirement of a violation of a duly enacted law. In other words, it is the violation of a statute that both triggers the officer's authority to make the stop and limits the officer's discretion. . . .

The dissent also raises the spectre of "repeatedly documented" racial profiling in the search and seizure context. There is no claim in any of the three cases before us that the police officers engaged in racial profiling. But, if racial profiling is the analytical pivot of our colleagues' dissent, their remedy misses the mark. The dissenters' "reasonable police officer" standard does little to combat or reduce the likelihood of racially motivated traffic stops, since, in their view, an officer's primary motivation is irrelevant.

We conclude, for a number of reasons, that the "reasonable police officer" test should not be followed. The dissenters maintain that under the "reasonable police officer" test, prosecution of a traffic violation would be appropriate even if the stop were pretextual and the other evidence suppressed. . . . We do not see how, in the context before us, a court may separate the fruits of a stop (often a gun or drugs) from the supposed illegality of the stop itself. It would seem that if the stop is arbitrary and, therefore, unlawful, it must be so for all purposes. In the name of protecting the rights of New Yorkers, the dissenters' result would be all too ironic: A police officer could "arbitrarily" stop someone for speeding and the stop would be valid, but a gun seen in plain view in the car during the stop would be suppressed as unlawfully seized.

The invention of the automobile has changed the fabric of American life. While the vast majority of New Yorkers own or drive vehicles, the frequency of their time on the road cannot recast the functional parameters of the Fourth Amendment or article 1, §12. We agree with *Whren* that the reasonable officer standard would result in inappropriate selective enforcement of traffic laws. How is a court to know which laws to enforce? . . . We are simply not free to pick and choose which laws deserve our adherence. If a statute improperly impairs our constitutional liberties, whatever the source, there is a remedy.

We are not confounded by the proposition that police officers must exercise their discretion on a daily basis. Nor are we surprised at the assertion that many New Yorkers often violate some provision of the Vehicle and Traffic Law. But we cannot equate the combination of police officer discretion and numerous traffic violations as arbitrary police conduct. . . . In the cases before us, [we have] a standard that constrains police conduct — probable cause under the Vehicle and Traffic Law and its related regulations that govern the safe use of our highways. . . .

LEVINE, J., dissenting.

[In] the context of pretextual traffic stops — traffic infraction stops that would not have been made but for the aim of the police to accomplish an otherwise unlawful investigative seizure or search — the existence of probable cause that the infraction was committed is manifestly insufficient to protect against arbitrary police conduct. That is so for two reasons. First, motor vehicle travel is one of the most ubiquitous activities in which Americans engage outside the home. Second, it is, by an overwhelming margin, the most pervasively regulated activity engaged in by Americans. . . .

The confluence of the foregoing factors — the dependency of the vast majority of Americans upon private automobile transportation and the virtual impossibility of sustained total compliance with the traffic laws — gives the police wide discretion to engage in investigative seizures, only superficially checked by the probable cause requirement for the traffic infraction that is the ostensible predicate for the stop. . . . Sadly, the pretext stop decisions in lower State and Federal courts confirm that the traffic infraction probable cause standard has left the police with the ability to stop vehicles at will for illegitimate investigative purposes. Typically, the stops are conducted as part of a drug interdiction program by a law enforcement agency. The vehicle and occupants appear to fit within a "drug courier" profile and the driver or occupants may have engaged in some other innocuous behavior which arouses a surmise of criminal conduct. The officer then follows the vehicle until some traffic code violation is observed. At that point, or even later, the vehicle is pulled over and the officer proceeds with the investigation. All occupants may be directed to exit the vehicle; the driver also may be interrogated and asked to consent to a search of the vehicle. . . .

Moreover, as has been repeatedly documented, . . . drug courier interdiction through traffic infraction stops has a dramatically disproportionate impact on young African-American males. Yet both the majority and the *Whren* Court dismiss the relevance of such disparate treatment in the constitutional search and seizure context. They instead suggest that the remedy lies in invoking the Federal Constitution's Equal Protection Clause. The same studies that recognize the existence of a disparate racial impact, however, also demonstrate the inadequacy of the Equal Protection Clause as a remedy for those abuses. A racial profiling claim under the Equal Protection Clause is difficult, if not impossible, to prove. The Equal Protection Clause prohibits race-based selective enforcement of the law only when such enforcement "had a discriminatory effect and . . . was motivated by a discriminatory purpose." United States v Armstrong, 517 U.S. 456 (1996). . . . Moreover, the problems of proof in establishing an equal protection claim may be all but insurmountable. Putting aside the unquestionably expensive and time-consuming process of assembling statistical evidence, it is debatable whether the requisite data would even be available. Supreme Court precedent also suggests that minority motorists alleging that a pretextual traffic stop constituted a denial of equal protection must show that similarly situated white motorists could have been stopped, but were not.

[The petitioners in *Whren*] urged the adoption of an objective standard by which to judge police exploitation of arbitrary traffic code enforcement to conduct investigative stops: whether a reasonable police officer, under the circumstances, would have made the stop for the reasons given. Despite the objective nature of that test, the Supreme Court's primary reason for rejecting it was that it was "driven by subjective considerations" — that is, the improper motivation of the seizing officer to conduct an otherwise unjustified investigative stop. . . . This criticism, in our view, misses the mark. The petitioners in *Whren* claimed that the officers' seizure was unreasonable because it was arbitrary, not because it was either unjustified or improperly motivated. . . .

The *Whren* Court offered only two other reasons for rejecting the test suggested by the petitioners. The first was that "police enforcement practices, even if they could be practicably assessed by a judge, vary from place to place and from time to time. We cannot accept that the search and seizure protections of the Fourth Amendment are so variable . . . and can be made to turn upon such trivialities." Under well-established Federal and State search and seizure doctrine, however, the . . . the basic determination of reasonable suspicion or even probable cause to support a search or seizure will almost always vary from place to place and time to time, depending on the particular circumstances confronting an officer.

[The opinion in *Whren*] also claimed in substance that accepting petitioners' position would place Judges in the role of deciding what traffic code provisions are to be enforced at all. . . . Adoption of the [reasonable officer standard] would do nothing of the sort. It does nothing more than set an objective standard, the violation of which would deprive law enforcement officers only of the use of evidence of crimes unrelated to the traffic infraction obtained in investigative stops effected through arbitrary enforcement of the traffic laws. As to the infraction itself, . . . prosecution of the underlying traffic infraction is not based upon evidence obtained through exploitation of the initial stop, but upon observations made before the stop. . . .

Next to be addressed on these appeals is the standard we would adopt to determine whether the stops in these cases were pretextual. . . . Defendants urge that we adopt a subjective test, whether the "primary motivation" for the stop was to investigate criminal activity rather than to prosecute the traffic offense ostensibly justifying the seizure. We would reject that test [because] courts and commentators have noted the difficulty, if not futility, of basing the constitutional validity of searches or seizures on judicial determinations of the subjective motivation of police officers. . . . Thus, we prefer an objective [standard:] would a reasonable officer assigned to Vehicle and Traffic Law enforcement in the seizing officer's department have made the stop under the circumstances presented, absent a purpose to investigate serious criminal activity of the vehicle's occupants[?] Whether the stop was carried out in accordance with standard procedures of the officer's department would be a highly relevant inquiry in that regard. . . .

Problem 2-2. Asset Management

Under state and federal asset forfeiture laws, the police can seize any "proceeds" or "instrumentalities" of a crime. After a streamlined process to confirm that the assets are indeed connected to a crime, the assets typically are sold; if the asset is cash, it is converted to government use. Under most of these forfeiture laws, the proceeds from the sale go directly into the coffers of the law enforcement agency that seized the asset, not into general revenue to support all governmental operations. This arrangement allows some law enforcement agencies to purchase equipment and support programs without drawing on tax dollars.

In Barbour County, Alabama, Chief Deputy Eddie Ingram specializes in traffic stops that lead to asset forfeiture. He estimates that he and the officers he supervises have discovered more than $11 million in drug assets over the past 15 years. The sheriff's department has used asset forfeiture money to buy bulletproof vests, gun belts, guns, and 9 out of the 14 cars in the department's fleet.

When Ingram is deciding which cars to stop on the U.S. highway that serves as the main north-south thoroughfare through the county, he looks for "things that just are different, and there's no one way to explain it, there's no one indicator. I just look for people that try to fit in that make themselves stand out." For instance, he says, if the speed limit is 65 mph, most people will drive 75 mph. But someone who is committing a crime will travel at 65 mph or less, and avoid eye contact with a deputy who pulls up alongside. Ingram calls these "stress-induced indicators."

Other departments in the region noticed the high levels of asset forfeiture in Barbour County and became interested in Ingram's techniques. He formed his own training academy, which has allowed him to train thousands of officers, some of whom now run their own seminars. After the classroom portion of the training, the students in Ingram's academy go out on the highway to practice the techniques. If they make a stop and find hidden currency, the Barbour County Sheriff's Office keeps 40 percent of the cash.

Several years ago, when Ingram worked on the highway interdiction team at the Villa Rica Police Department in Georgia, the police received complaints of racial profiling. The U.S. Department of Justice investigated and found problems.

Suppose you are a trial judge in Barbour County and you periodically hear claims from defendants about the alleged lack of reasonable suspicion to support a traffic stop that produced evidence of a drug crime. Would the larger pattern of reliance on asset forfeiture by the sheriff's department have any effect on your evaluation of reasonable suspicion in the case at hand? What other forum might be available for motorists to challenge the adequacy of reasonable suspicion to support a stop?

Notes

1. *Pretextual stops: majority position.* Under the federal constitution, courts refuse to question the legitimacy of allegedly pretextual stops, so long as the officer "could have" properly stopped the vehicle based on evidence of a traffic offense. According to the Supreme Court in Whren v. United States, 517 U.S. 806 (1996), any effort to determine whether a reasonable officer "would have" stopped a vehicle for traffic violations alone would be too uncertain: "While police manuals and standard procedures may sometimes provide objective assistance, ordinarily one would be reduced to speculating about the hypothetical reaction of a hypothetical constable — an exercise that might be called virtual subjectivity." The *Whren* decision convinced most states that at one time employed the "would have" doctrine to change approaches for purposes of the state constitution. At this point, over 40 states follow the *Whren* decision. See Mitchell v. State, 745 N.E.2d 775 (Ind. 2001); State v. Pagotto, 762 A.2d 97 (Md. 2000).

One of the few remaining exceptions is the state of Washington. In State v. Ladson, 979 P.2d 833 (Wash. 1999), officers on proactive gang patrol noticed a driver who was rumored to be involved in gang and drug activity. They followed the car and stopped the driver after noticing that the license plate tabs had expired. Their primary reason for the stop was to investigate drug activity, and they found drugs in the passenger's possession. The Washington Supreme Court called pretextual stops "a triumph of form over substance" and worried that approving such searches would mean that "nearly every citizen would be subject to a *Terry* stop simply because he or she is in his or her car." As for how to determine whether a given stop is pretextual, the court adopted a "totality of the circumstances" approach. Trial courts may inquire both about the subjective intent of the officer as well as the objective reasonableness of the officer's behavior to determine whether a stop was pretextual or not. If you wanted to learn whether judicial controls of pretextual stops are workable in practice, what aspect of the Washington system would you study most closely?

2. *State constitutions and the federal constitution.* In *Robinson,* the New York court pointed out that both the state and federal constitutions contain provisions to limit police searches and seizures and to protect privacy. State courts must interpret both constitutional provisions when a litigant presents the issue. The state courts must adhere to the decisions of the U.S. Supreme Court as to the meaning of the federal constitution. State law enforcement officers must comply with certain provisions of the federal constitution — those applicable to the states because the due process clause of the Fourteenth Amendment "incorporates" them. Today, most of the specific Bill of Rights protections for criminal defendants and for citizens generally have been "incorporated" to apply against the states and their agents. See Akhil Reed Amar, The Bill of Rights: Creation and Reconstruction (1998) and Michael Kent Curtis, No State Shall Abridge: The Fourteenth Amendment and the Bill of Rights (1986).

However, a state's supreme court has the ultimate judicial authority over the meaning of its own state constitution. It might interpret the state constitution (or some other provision of state law, such as a statute) to place restrictions on law enforcement officers different from what the federal constitution might require. The federal courts, including the U.S. Supreme Court, must allow a state supreme court's decision in a criminal case to stand so long as the decision does not flatly conflict with binding federal law and rests on "independent and adequate" state law grounds. Periodically, we will consider cases about procedural issues in which state law gives different answers from federal law or asks different procedural questions altogether. This variety in criminal procedure in different jurisdictions makes it possible for lawyers to argue for procedural innovations that might not be apparent from studying federal law alone.

3. *Reading minds.* Do judicial controls on pretextual stops require the judge to read the officer's mind? Is it truly possible to declare that a stop was pretextual based on "objective" evidence (such as the prevalence of traffic stops in that situation, or the officer's compliance with a police department's internal rules about traffic stops)? Or is some finding about subjective intent implicit in any pretext case? Perhaps a court's position on the pretext doctrine reflects an underlying assumption about the trustworthiness of police officers. If a court is unwilling to attempt to control pretextual stops, is it implicitly deciding that the police ordinarily make good faith decisions that ought to be encouraged? Is it making any implicit claims about the truthfulness of police testimony in the ordinary case? See Angela Davis, Race, Cops, and Traffic Stops, 51 U. Miami L. Rev. 425 (1997). Consider how defense attorneys and prosecutors might explain the relevance of a particular officer's habits in making traffic stops. See "State Highway Patrol Trooper Barry Washington Is on the Prowl for Drugs," San Antonio Express-News, July 25, 1996 (trooper seizes more than 1,000 pounds of marijuana and 20,000 grams of cocaine each year; stops up to 40 drivers daily, spending about four minutes with each; sends average of two drug suspects per week into court system).

4. *Highways as a special arena.* The pretext issue takes on special urgency on the highways. Over half of all contacts between adults and police officers take place during traffic stops. In a given year, the police stop about 9 percent of all drivers. See Bureau of Justice Statistics, Characteristics of Drivers Stopped by Police, 2002 (June 2006, NCJ 211471). The vehicle's equipment and the driver's conduct are also regulated in minute detail, allowing a wide variety of stops. The potential grounds for stops cover everything from bumper height, to tire tread, to a burned-out license tag light, or the ever-popular "changing lanes without signaling." In 2005, speeding was the stated reason given to 53 percent of the stopped drivers; 10 percent were stopped for a burned-out light or other vehicle defect; 6 percent were stopped for an improper turn or lane change. Bureau of Justice Statistics, Contacts Between Police and the Public, 2005 (April 2007, NCJ 215243).

Does a healthy legal system depend on lax enforcement of certain laws? In this imperfect world, how many cars and drivers can go for long without some minor violation, such as tag lights or lane violations? If police officers can develop reasonable suspicion against any driver if they persist in the effort, does the *Whren* decision effectively repeal the reasonable suspicion limit for police power on the highways? How does the majority opinion in the New York case answer this question?

5. *Arbitrary enforcement.* Is the pretext doctrine necessary to prevent arbitrary enforcement decisions by the police (including possible harassment of racial minorities), or are other legal doctrines available to prevent arbitrary policing? See Jones v. Sterling, 110 P.3d 1271 (Ariz. 2005) (criminal defendants can assert racial profiling as defense to charges and not rely solely on civil rights claims); David Harris, "Driving While Black" and All Other Traffic Offenses: The Supreme Court and Pretextual Traffic Stops, 87 J. Crim. L. & Criminology 544 (1997) (describing

disproportionate stops of African Americans and Hispanics in Colorado, Florida, Illinois, and Maryland; large-scale study in Florida showed almost 70 percent of drivers stopped were African American or Hispanic, although they constitute about 5 percent of drivers on that highway). Would a challenge based on the equal protection clause of the Constitution be available (or sufficient) to respond to any police use of race as a basis for selecting drivers to stop? See Tracy Maclin, Race and the Fourth Amendment, 51 Vand. L. Rev. 333 (1998).

Would the pretext doctrine give a court a basis to respond to a claim that police officers stop cars on an equal basis, but then treat drivers differently during the stop on the basis of race? See Jeffrey Fagan and Amanda Geller, Profiling and Consent: Stops, Searches and Seizures after *Soto*, available at *http://www.ssrn.com/abstract=1641326* (based on New Jersey data, black and Hispanic drivers when stopped are more than twice as likely as white drivers to be searched).

6. *Police responses to pretext claims.* If you were legal counsel to a police department in a jurisdiction adopting the reasonable officer "would" test for pretext (such as Washington state), what advice would you give the department? For instance, what charges should the arresting officer file — the original offense justifying the stop or the more serious offense or both? What sorts of reasons should an officer give to justify an initial stop? Will the officer fare better if he identifies some grounds for stopping a car other than a traffic violation? See Scott v. State, 877 P.2d 503 (Nev. 1994) (officer stopped car because vehicle might have been stolen). Can the officer overcome the claim of pretext by arguing that he routinely stops several vehicles per month based on similar traffic violations? State v. Wilson, 867 P.2d 1175 (N.M. 1994) (officer testifies that he stops six to eight cars every month for failure to use seat belts; stop upheld).

7. *Department-level pretexts.* Some individual police officers use traffic stops as a means to enforce drug laws. Are pretext claims by defendants stronger or weaker when the use of pretext (such as traffic stops to look for drugs) is a department policy instead of just an individual officer's decision? Other departments (for example, the Kansas City Police Department) use reasonable suspicion stops of cars and persons as a general policy with the goal of finding weapons and enforcing firearms laws. A study of the Kansas City program, which began in 1991, concluded that gun seizures in the 80-by-10-block target area increased by 65 percent, while seizures in a comparable beat went down slightly. Gun crimes in the target beat decreased by 49 percent and increased slightly in the comparison beat. See Lawrence Sherman, James Shaw & Dennis Rogan, The Kansas City Gun Experiment, National Institute of Justice, Research in Brief (Jan. 1995 NCJ 150855). Would a challenge to this Kansas City practice be more difficult than the challenges to the various individual stops in *Robinson*?

4. *Criminal Profiles and Race*

The police officer in the field is not left entirely to her own devices when deciding whether apparently innocent facts are actually indicators of criminal activity. Both police departments and legislative bodies offer guidance on the types of conduct that might create grounds for a stop. Police departments periodically create "criminal profiles," which are lists of personal characteristics and behaviors said to be associated with particular types of crime (most commonly drug trafficking).

Sometimes these profiles are quite specific, while at other times they are relatively short and general. An officer hoping to explain after the fact why she stopped a person might describe the features of the profile that the suspect matched.

The criminal profiles developed in police departments often remain informal and unwritten. Do these "profiles" — collective judgments about suspicious activity — add any weight to the individual police officer's expert judgment in the field as the officer tries to establish reasonable suspicion? Does your response to a criminal profile change if it places some weight on the racial or ethnic identification of the suspect?

■ SAMIR QUARLES v. STATE

696 A.2d 1334 (Del. 1997)

WALSH, J.

In this appeal from the Superior Court, the appellant, Samir Quarles, seeks a reversal of a ruling that denied his motion to suppress evidence of illegal drugs seized from his person during a street encounter with police. . . . We conclude that under a totality of circumstances test the conduct of the appellant, measured from the perspective of experienced police officers, provided a specific and articulable basis for a limited investigative stop. . . .

At approximately 10:00 P.M. on the date in question, Officers Looney and Solge went to the terminal to meet a bus arriving from New York City. Based on their past experience, the officers were aware that the bus in question was often used by persons acting as drug couriers. It was their intention to conduct surveillance of persons departing the bus with the hope of intercepting the flow of drugs into the city. As they watched, fifteen to twenty passengers disembarked from the bus with two individuals, later identified as Quarles and Thomas, exiting last.

Although Quarles and Thomas were conversing as they left the bus, their conversation "came to an abrupt halt" as soon as they observed two uniformed officers standing nearby. The conversation was not reinitiated once the pair passed the officers. The pair then stood motionless on the sidewalk for a few moments before turning to walk north toward Second Street in the opposite direction of the police. The police observed as Quarles began walking at a faster pace ahead of Thomas, who eventually caught up with Quarles after some distance. As Quarles and Thomas proceeded quickly toward Second Street, Quarles looked back on three different occasions to determine the location of the police officers. When Quarles and Thomas reached the intersection of Second and French Streets they turned west on Second Street. After they turned the corner, Quarles observed a third officer, Officer Cunningham, sitting in his patrol car in a parking lot a short distance ahead on Second Street. Upon observing Cunningham's vehicle, Quarles backtracked to the corner and looked around to determine where the two officers on foot were located. According to the officers, Quarles and Thomas seemed "kind of surprised" and in a quandary as to what direction to proceed. At that point Officers Looney and Solge approached the pair and Officer Solge asked if he could speak to them. Quarles and Thomas agreed to speak with the officers.

In the meantime, Officer Cunningham, who had been in radio contact with the other two officers, proceeded the wrong way on Second Street, against traffic, and parked his vehicle partially on the sidewalk prior to joining the group gathered at the corner. The defendants gave inconsistent statements as to their destination and appeared nervous in answering questions about their origin and destination. They were advised that the police were checking for drugs and/or weapons couriers and were asked if they had any drugs or contraband on their persons. The police requested permission to conduct a search of their persons as well as of a bag carried by Quarles. . . . The police proceeded to search both Quarles' bag and his person, uncovering a large quantity of cocaine in Quarles' boot. . . .

Under the Fourth Amendment, a police seizure can be justified only when, based upon specific and articulable facts which, taken together with rational inferences from those facts, reasonably warrant the belief that a crime is being or has been committed. Under this standard, the courts must look for a minimal level of objective "justification" for making the stop. United States v. Sokolow, 490 U.S. 1 (1989). This burden of proof is "considerably less" than proof by a preponderance of the evidence and less demanding than probable cause. When conducting its analysis, the court must consider the totality of the circumstances, the "whole picture," as viewed through the eyes of a police officer who is experienced in discerning the ostensibly innocuous behavior that is indicative of narcotics trafficking.

The United States Supreme Court has stated that the circumstances must be evaluated under an objective/subjective standard as opposed to a purely objective standard. This reflects the reality that:

> [much] of the drug traffic is highly organized and conducted by sophisticated criminal syndicates. The profits are enormous. And many drugs . . . may be easily concealed. As a result, the obstacles to detection of illegal conduct may be unmatched in any other area of law enforcement.

It logically follows that a pattern of behavior interpreted by an untrained observer as innocent could justify an investigatory stop when viewed by experienced law enforcement agents who are cognizant of current drug trafficking operations. United States v. Cortez, 449 U.S. 411 (1981). In *Cortez*, the United States Supreme Court cautioned that terms like "articulable reasons" and "founded suspicion" are not self-defining. But the Court noted that any assessment of police conduct must be two-pronged, based upon: (1) "all the circumstances," including objective observations and "consideration of the modes or patterns of operation of certain kinds of lawbreakers"; and (2) the inferences and deductions that a trained officer could make which "might well elude an untrained person." We believe that standard is an appropriate one for use by courts reviewing the conduct of detaining officers, and we adopt it here.

In our case, the officers relied upon specific factors together with a "drug courier profile" to justify their articulable suspicion. Although the use of "profiling" is vigorously debated in academic circles, it has been accepted by the United States Supreme Court. The Court has stated that a "profile," alone, will not justify a seizure, but when considered in conjunction with police observations, a seizure could be warranted even though the "non-profile" observations by themselves would not justify an investigatory stop. Moreover, the fact that the articulated factors "may be set forth in a 'profile' does not somehow detract from their evidentiary significance as seen by a trained agent." *Sokolow,* 490 U.S. at 9-10.

Here the "profile" characteristics were: (1) the defendants came into Wilmington via bus from New York (a known drug source city); (2) they carried no luggage;

(3) they came in at night, typically when law enforcement activity is at a minimum; and (4) they traveled as a pair. This profile was compiled relying upon police experience, based on past arrests of individuals bringing drugs into the City of Wilmington. The "non-profile" factors relied upon by police were: (1) the defendants' startled reaction to uniformed police officers upon exiting the bus (ceasing their conversation); (2) quickly leaving the bus terminal in a direction away from the officers; (3) . . . repeated glances over their shoulders to see if the officers were following them both before and after turning the corner; (4) rapid stride; and (5) abrupt about face upon seeing a marked police car.

When assessing the relevance of these factors the focus is not on whether the particular conduct is "innocent" or "guilty" but the degree of suspicion that attaches to particular types of conduct. Courts have recognized that wholly lawful and innocent conduct descriptive of a large segment of the population can justify the suspicion that criminal activity is afoot.

When Quarles exited the New York bus in Wilmington, he and his companion satisfied a number of well-known "drug courier profile" characteristics. While this fact alone would not justify a seizure, when combined with the other specific instances of suspicious and odd behavior, police were justified in effectuating a seizure. This Court notes that the conclusions reached by the officers as to Quarles' behavior were based in large part upon their personal experiences in conducting drug courier surveillance at the bus station. Combined, the officers conducted surveillance at the bus station over 90 times, approximately two to three times a month, with, over the past year, Officer Looney personally arresting 12 people for carrying drugs through the station.

The two arresting officers, drawing on their experience of observing hundreds of people move through the bus station, were able to conclude that Quarles' behavior was abnormal and suspicious when compared to other passengers.[5] Quarles' suspicious behavior and the "drug profile," when taken as a whole from the perspective of one who is trained in narcotics detection, produces a reasonable articulable suspicion that a crime was afoot. We therefore conclude that the police officers had a sufficient basis upon which to support an initial stop to question Quarles.

The safeguarding of a citizen's rights against unreasonable stops and seizures by police officers is a cherished protection under the Fourth Amendment and this Court's obligation to advance those rights is clear. But this Court should not turn a blind eye to the realities of society's war against drugs and the experience of the police in combating that problem. We are entitled to test the actions of the police by the exacting standards of the Fourth Amendment jurisprudence, but we should be reluctant to substitute an academic analysis for the on the spot judgment of trained law enforcement officers. . . .

VEASEY, C.J., dissenting.

. . . I submit, respectfully, that the majority opinion rests on a novel rationale — unprecedented deference to subjective police observations based solely

5. With over 90 surveillance operations at the bus station, if each night only one bus carrying twenty passengers came into the station, the two arresting officers would have witnessed the behavior of over 1800 passengers. This vast experience gave the officers an adequate frame of reference for detecting abnormal or suspicious behavior.

upon law enforcement experience. The majority correctly states that . . . "any curtailment of a person's liberty by the police must be supported at least by a reasonable and articulable suspicion that the person seized is engaged in criminal activity." The key words here are "reasonable" and "articulable." These are objective tests. . . . Hunches and subjective impressions of experienced police officers will not suffice. . . .

In this case police did not rely on intelligence reports that drugs were being carried on the bus or that defendant, or anyone fitting his description, was transporting drugs to Wilmington. . . . There were no suspicious hand signals or papers passed secretly. [The] data available to Officers Cunningham, Looney, and Solge at the time they seized Quarles completely lacked specificity and could not have raised a justifiable suspicion that Quarles was engaged in wrongdoing. . . .

Moreover, I question whether the four benign facts cited by the majority establish a profile. . . . These four facts taken as a whole might well describe a number of innocent people. New York City is only 120 miles from Wilmington. Nighttime travel with a companion and without luggage is hardly remarkable. As for New York City being a "known drug source city," what city is not infested with drugs and drug suppliers? Even the trial judge here concluded, "The mere fact that they exited a bus coming from New York City would not give rise to a reasonable suspicion." . . .

At bottom, the majority opinion attaches a novel, and outcome-determinative, deference to experienced police eyes without any expert or empirical evidence. . . . If the precedent embodied in the majority opinion is taken to its logical extreme, police experience alone, and without articulable expert analysis or meticulous police work . . . , will almost always support the seizure. . . .

This case is about constitutional protections that the judicial branch of government is obliged to enforce for the protection of innocent citizens, as well as reprehensible drug traffickers who poison our citizens. With the utmost deference, I must state my concern that the rationale and the unprecedented reach of the majority opinion is dangerous and could lead to a pernicious erosion of our liberty.

Notes

1. *Criminal profiles in the courts: majority position.* The strong majority of courts presented with stops based on facts listed in a criminal profile will not allow the match with the profile, standing alone, to constitute reasonable suspicion. However, courts also often say that the appearance of an observed fact in a profile gives that fact added weight in the reasonable suspicion calculus. See State v. Staten, 469 N.W.2d 112 (Neb. 1991) (airline passengers fitting drug courier profile may be detained up to one hour). A significant minority of states have rejected or criticized any reliance on the use of profiles to add any weight to facts observed in the field. Commonwealth v. Lewis, 636 A.2d 619 (Pa. 1994). The federal law on profiles seems agnostic, placing no independent weight — positive or negative — on the existence of a profile. See United States v. Sokolow, 490 U.S. 1 (1989); Florida v. Royer, 460 U.S. 491 (1983) (reasonable suspicion established). Some state courts reject particular components of a profile without rejecting the reliance on profiles generally. See State v. Gonzalez-Gutierrez, 927 P.2d 776 (Ariz. 1996) (characteristic of being Mexican did not add weight to reasonable suspicion analysis); Derricott v. State, 611 A.2d 592 (Md. 1992) (criticizing profile that apparently included race of suspect);

Crockett v. State, 803 S.W.2d 308 (Tex. Crim. App. 1991) (no evidence that drug dealers purchase train tickets with cash more frequently than other people).

2. *Dueling profiles and discretion.* Courts seem especially skeptical about profiles phrased broadly enough to "describe a very large category of presumably innocent travelers, who would be subject to virtually random seizures" if a mere match to such a profile were enough to justify a search or seizure. Reid v. Georgia, 448 U.S. 438 (1980). Drug courier profiles sometimes are written broadly enough to attach suspicion both to a particular characteristic (such as exiting a plane first or making eye contact with another passenger) and to its opposite (exiting a plane last or avoiding eye contact with another passenger). What exactly is the problem with a declaration that a particular behavior and its opposite are both suspicious? Judicial opinions dealing with challenges to the use of a criminal profile almost never list the complete provisions of the profile. What does this mean to the attorney hoping to challenge the reliability of the profile as a method of establishing reasonable suspicion?

3. *Officer expertise and subjective standards.* Should the particular expertise of the investigating officer have any bearing on a finding of reasonable suspicion? Or should the court accept only those inferences that any "reasonable person" (that is, a citizen) would draw from the observed facts? If you are willing to account for the special experience of a particular police officer in establishing reasonable suspicion, is this consistent with your views on the "reasonable person" standard we encountered earlier, dealing with the definition of a "stop"? See United States v. Cortez, 449 U.S. 411 (1981) ("when used by trained law enforcement officers, objective facts, meaningless to the untrained, can be combined with permissible deductions from such facts to form a legitimate basis for suspicion of a particular person"); Harris v. State, 806 A.2d 119 (Del. 2002) (to establish reasonable suspicion for stop on basis of drug courier profile, state and federal constitutions require officer to explain how training makes apparently innocent conduct suspicious).

4. *Collective judgments and expertise.* Stops based on criminal profiles differ from other reasonable suspicion stops because they attempt to give the officer on the street the benefit of the collective experience of other officers or the collective judgments of political authorities. The officer makes the stop not only based on his own expertise in law enforcement but also because the "profile" places significance on certain facts. Which is a stronger basis for believing that certain apparently innocent facts are actually indications of criminal activity: the individual training and experience of the officer making the stop, or the statistical and collective experience of police in the department? As the attorney for a person stopped, which of the two bases would you prefer to test on cross-examination? See Wayne LaFave, Controlling Discretion by Administrative Regulations: The Use, Misuse, and Nonuse of Police Rules and Policies in Fourth Amendment Adjudication, 89 Mich. L. Rev. 442 (1990).

5. *Package profiles.* Recall that courts distinguish between "consensual" encounters that do not involve a seizure at all (and therefore require no justification) and stops that do require reasonable suspicion. If the seizure amounts to a full arrest, the government must show probable cause. The same framework applies to property. When the government takes possession (temporary or permanent) of property and the owner later challenges that control as an unconstitutional seizure, courts ask whether the governmental control amounted to a "stop" of the property that required reasonable suspicion.

The U.S. Supreme Court has held that postal authorities must have reasonable suspicion to detain a mail package for a short time and probable cause to seize it outright. United States v. Van Leeuwen, 397 U.S. 249 (1970). The postal service has developed profiles for identifying packages carrying illegal narcotics: packages meeting the profile are delayed for further inspection (often by drug-sniffing dogs) and for controlled delivery to the addressee. One such profile lists the following characteristics: (1) size and shape of the package; (2) package taped to close or seal all openings; (3) handwritten or printed labels; (4) unusual return name and address; (5) unusual odors coming from the package; (6) fictitious return address; and (7) destination of the package. See State v. Cooper, 652 A.2d 995 (Vt. 1994).

Often the challenges to detentions of property involve delays in delivering luggage to airline passengers waiting in baggage claims areas. A brief detention of the luggage also effectively detains the person. Should this make a difference in a court's evaluation of the government's handling of the property?

6. *Efficiency in proof?* Is the problem with criminal profiles that the government has not written specific profiles and has not shown rigorously how the profile features are common to a great number of criminal defendants? Consider a profile constructed as follows. A group of more than 40 representatives from law enforcement agencies in the Phoenix area developed a profile for stopping suspected automobile thieves transporting stolen vehicles to Mexico. The profile was based on an analysis of 10,000 auto thefts in the area over a 17-month period. The profile indicated which vehicles were targeted most often by the thieves: sedans and pickup trucks manufactured by Ford and Chevrolet within the last three years. In addition, the records indicated that the driver of a stolen car would probably be a male between 17 and 27 years of age; he would usually be alone; he would have no apparent luggage; if there was a passenger, there would be no children; and the car's license plate would show a registration to either Pima or Maricopa County. This profile fit only a small percentage of those people driving between Tucson and Nogales. See State v. Ochoa, 544 P.2d 1097 (Ariz. 1976). Could profiles, when carefully constructed and meticulously proven in early cases, prevent duplicative presentation of evidence in later cases?

Problem 2-3. Race and Witness Descriptions

On February 21, at approximately 4:15 A.M., Nancy Henderson approached an automatic teller machine on Main Street. While she was operating the teller machine, but before completing her transaction, someone grabbed her from behind and said, "this is a stick-up" and "I want your money." During a brief struggle, the man pressed a hard, blunt object into her back. He forced Henderson from the front of the bank to a parking lot in back of the building. She gave her money to the man. The man then declared that he planned to rape Henderson. He forced her to walk to the front of the bank and ordered her to get into the driver's seat of her car, threatening to "blow her brains out" if she did not comply. The man positioned himself next to Henderson in the front passenger seat, and directed her where to drive the car.

As Henderson drove, she noticed a pizza shop that appeared to be open. She accelerated the car in that direction and jumped the curb. Then she got out of the car and ran screaming for help. Several people emerged from the shop. During the confusion, the assailant walked away. The police were called, and arrived at the pizza shop within minutes. Henderson described her assailant as "a black male, 5'11" to 6'2", wearing a ski cap, had a mustache, was wearing a light-colored coat, dark pants, white tennis shoes and had medium to dark skin." The police dispatcher sent this description to all officers on patrol.

At 5:25 A.M., another officer on patrol stopped Daniel Coleman in the parking lot of a restaurant located approximately one-half of a mile from the pizza shop. Coleman fit the general description of the assailant, except that he had a goatee as well as a mustache and was not wearing a coat or a cap. The officer questioned Coleman briefly about his identity and destination. Coleman stated that he was coming from his girlfriend's home and that he was on his way to work. During this discussion, another officer drove by with Henderson in the car. She was unable to identify Coleman as her assailant. The officer detained Coleman for a total of about 10 minutes, then released him.

Later that morning, the police viewed a videotape taken by a camera installed near the automatic teller machine. Both of the police officers who had seen Coleman earlier that morning during his brief detention viewed the videotape and identified the assailant on the videotape as Coleman. Coleman was arrested at his place of employment and charged with robbery and attempted rape. When the officers first stopped Coleman, did they have reasonable suspicion? If they ignored information about the race of the suspect, would they have reasonable suspicion? See Coleman v. State, 562 A.2d 1171 (Del. 1989).

Notes

1. *Race and witness descriptions: majority position.* Most courts allow the police to rely on race as one among many components of reasonable suspicion, particularly if the police use the racial element of a description received from a victim or witness of the crime. Note, Developments in the Law — Race and the Criminal Process, 101 Harv. L. Rev. 1473 (1988). Can you imagine a jurisdiction that would bar any use of race in establishing reasonable suspicion, thus requiring the police to point to other factors? For witness identifications, could the police rely on descriptions of clothing or facial hair, while being barred from using information about skin color?

On the other hand, police officers will at times rely on a suspect's race in cases where no witness has described the perpetrator, or even where there is no report of a crime at all. This most often occurs when a person appears to be "out of place": for instance, a black person in a predominantly white neighborhood. Courts have divided on whether such a fact can be the primary component of reasonable suspicion. See, e.g., State v. Dean, 543 P.2d 425 (Ariz. 1975) (Mexican male in dented car in predominantly white neighborhood, reasonable suspicion); State v. Mallory, 337 N.W.2d 391 (Minn. 1983) (black male stopped in white neighborhood where burglary by a black male had occurred recently, reasonable suspicion); State v. Barber, 823 P.2d 1068 (Wash. 1992) (presence of black person in white neighborhood can never amount to reasonable suspicion standing alone).

Officers also sometimes rely on the race of the suspect when it is difficult to articulate other specific grounds for suspicion; courts now tend to invalidate stops in such cases. See United States v. Bellamy, 619 A.2d 515 (D.C. 1993) (no reasonable suspicion where officer stops four black youths in car who teased him about violence against police); Commonwealth v. Phillips, 595 N.E.2d 310 (Mass. 1992) (no reasonable suspicion where Boston police implement policy to "search on sight" young black males suspected of membership in gangs). If most American jurisdictions allow race as one "factor" that contributes to a finding of reasonable suspicion, won't there necessarily be cases where race provides the extra marginal evidence to obtain reasonable suspicion? Would this be objectionable discrimination, or a plausible reaction to probabilities familiar to the police? See Sheri Lynn Johnson, Race and the Decision to Detain a Suspect, 93 Yale L.J. 214 (1983).

2. *Patterns of discrimination in stops.* When the Supreme Court first considered the validity of stops based on reasonable suspicion, in Terry v. Ohio, 392 U.S. 1 (1968), advocates and commentators objected to the police practice, pointing to evidence that police used stops in a discriminatory manner to harass African Americans. More recent observers of police practices argue that officers still choose to stop a disproportionate number of black males. Michael Brown, Working the Street: Police Discretion and the Dilemmas of Reform 166 (1981) ("Race, the field observations [of police] reveal, is one of the most salient criteria to patrolmen in deciding whether or not to stop someone"). An analysis of data concerning traffic stops between 1995 and 2000 concluded that the Maryland State Police "stopped and searched cars with black and Hispanic drivers much more often than cars with white drivers; it is hard to see how they could have produced these results without taking race into account in deciding who to stop and who to search." Although this practice "seems to increase the probability of finding large hauls of drugs," the large hauls are rare, and about "two-thirds of all drivers searched were not carrying any illegal drugs." Most of the drivers who had any drugs in the car were found with trace amounts; among black and Hispanic drivers, "a larger minority of the searches uncovered substantial quantities of illegal drugs." See Samuel R. Gross & Katherine Y. Barnes, Road Work: Racial Profiling and Drug Interdiction on the Highway, 101 Mich. L. Rev. 651 (2002). How might the attorney for an individual who is stopped go about establishing this sort of claim?

Defendants have only rarely convinced courts to outlaw the use of pretextual stops or criminal profiles, but a related claim has achieved more success outside the courts. The related claim is that police stop motorists based at least partly on their race. Such claims are often described in public debates as the creation of a crime called "driving while black" or "DWB."

Claims of DWB are difficult for a criminal defendant to litigate, but state and federal governments now regularly investigate patterns of traffic and drug stops on highways. The New Jersey Attorney General conducted one such investigation. Law enforcement officials prepared the report excerpted below in the aftermath of a tragic shooting incident in 1998 on the New Jersey Turnpike. Troopers were accused of firing 11 shots into a van containing four young men on their way to a basketball tryout. The shots wounded two black men and a Hispanic man. The officers said that they initially stopped the van because it was speeding, and opened fire when the van backed up to hit them. The shooting triggered protests and an internal investigation of claims that officers used racial profiling during stops and investigations on the highway.

■ PETER VERNIERO, ATTORNEY GENERAL INTERIM REPORT OF THE STATE POLICE REVIEW TEAM REGARDING ALLEGATIONS OF RACIAL PROFILING

(April 20, 1999)

. . . This Interim Report specifically focuses on the activities of state troopers assigned to patrol the New Jersey Turnpike. [The] Turnpike is widely believed to be a major drug corridor, thereby providing the State Police with both the impetus and the opportunity to engage in drug interdiction tactics that appear to be inextricably linked to the "racial profiling" controversy. [Based] upon the information that we reviewed, minority motorists have been treated differently than nonminority motorists during the course of traffic stops on the New Jersey Turnpike. For the reasons set out fully in this Report, we conclude that the problem of disparate treatment is real — not imagined. This problem . . . is more complex and subtle than has generally been reported.

[We] define "racial profiling" broadly to encompass any action taken by a state trooper during a traffic stop that is based upon racial or ethnic stereotypes and that has the effect of treating minority motorists differently than nonminority motorists. . . .

Our review has revealed two interrelated problems that may be influenced by the goal of interdicting illicit drugs: (1) willful misconduct by a small number of State Police members, and (2) more common instances of possible de facto discrimination by officers who may be influenced by stereotypes and may thus tend to treat minority motorists differently during the course of routine traffic stops. . . .

Our review has shown that over the years, conflicting messages have been sent regarding the official policy to prohibit any form of race-based profiling. This situation should be rectified by developing a clear and consistent message. We propose that as a matter of policy for the New Jersey State Police, race, ethnicity, and national origin should not be used at all by troopers in selecting vehicles to be stopped or in exercising discretion during the course of a stop (other than in determining whether a person matches the general description of one or more known suspects). In making this recommendation, we propose going beyond the minimum requirements of federal precedent because, simply, it is the right thing to do and because the Executive Branch, no less than its judicial counterpart, has an independent duty to ensure that our laws are enforced in a constitutional, efficient, and even-handed fashion. . . .

Stops. We have received and compiled information regarding stops by troopers assigned to the Moorestown and Cranbury stations from the monthly stop data. . . . Four of every ten stops (40.6 percent) made during the period for which data are available involved black, Hispanic, Asian or other nonwhite people. . . .

Searches. It is obvious from the data provided that very few stops result in the search of a motor vehicle. For example, in those instances for which we have data permitting comparisons between stops and searches, only 627 (0.7 percent) of 87,489 stops involved a search. [The] available data indicate that the overwhelming majority of searches (77.2 percent) involved black or Hispanic persons. Specifically, of the 1,193 searches for which data are available, 21.4 percent involved a white person, more than half (53.1 percent) involved a black person, and almost one of every four (24.1 percent) involved a Hispanic person.

. . . Not surprisingly, most consent searches do not result in a "positive" finding. . . . Specifically, 19.2 percent of the searches we considered resulted in an arrest or seizure of contraband. Accounting for race and ethnicity, 10.5 percent of the searches that involved white motorists resulted in an arrest or seizure of contraband, 13.5 percent of the searches that involved black motorists resulted in an arrest or seizure, and 38.1 percent of the searches of Hispanic motorists resulted in an arrest or seizure.

Arrests. [During the years 1996 through 1998], there were a total of 2,871 arrests [for crimes other than drunk driving]. Of these, 932 (32.5 percent) involved white persons, 1,772 (61.7 percent) involved black persons, and 167 (5.8 percent) involved persons of other races.

Interpretations of the Data and Areas of Special Concern

. . . Information and analysis compiled by the Public Defender's Office . . . suggests that troopers who enjoyed a wider ambit of discretion, by virtue of the nature of their duty assignment, stopped and ticketed minority motorists more often. Specifically, the Public Defender's statistical expert compared the tickets issued on 35 randomly selected days by three different State Police units: (1) the Radar Unit, which uses radar-equipped vans and chase cars and exercises comparatively little discretion; (2) the Tactical Patrol Unit, which focuses on motor vehicle enforcement in particular areas and exercises somewhat greater discretion; and (3) the Patrol Unit, which is responsible for general law enforcement and exercises the most discretion. [The] Radar Unit was found to have issued 18% of its tickets to African-Americans, the Tactical Patrol Unit issued 23.8% of its tickets to African-Americans, and the Patrol Unit issued 34.2% of its tickets to African-Americans. . . . We are concerned by what may be a pattern that when state troopers are permitted more discretion by virtue of their duty assignment, they tended during the time periods examined to ticket African-Americans more often. . . .

The potential for the disparate treatment of minorities during routine traffic stops may be the product of an accumulation of circumstances that can contribute to the use of race- or ethnicity-based criteria by creating the unintended message that the best way to catch drug traffickers is to focus on minorities. To some extent, the State Police as an organization may have been caught up in the martial rhetoric of the "war on drugs," responding to the call to arms urged by the public, the Legislature, and the Attorney General's Statewide Narcotics Action Plans of 1987 and 1993.

[The] officially stated policy has always been to condemn reliance upon constitutionally impermissible factors. . . . The State Police official policy prohibiting racial profiling was announced in a 1990 Standard Operating Procedure. Ironically, the problem of the reliance upon stereotypes may have unwittingly been exacerbated by the issuance of this [1990 Procedure. It] included a discussion of the "sufficiency of objective facts to establish reasonable suspicion or probable cause," explaining that . . . personal characteristics such as race, age, sex, length of hair, style of dress, type of vehicle, and number of occupants of a vehicle "may not be utilized as facts relevant to establish reasonable suspicion or probable cause *unless the [State Police] member can identify and describe the manner in which a characteristic is directly and specifically related to particular criminal activity*." (Emphasis added.) [This] portion of the Standard Operating Procedure, read literally, suggests that a person's race *may* be relied upon by a State Police member if he or she is able to identify and describe the manner in which race is directly and specifically related to a particular criminal activity. This exception has the very real capacity to swallow the rule, and opens the door (or at least fails to shut the door) to the use of stereotypes, especially those that have been "validated" by tautological and self-serving intelligence reports and profiles. . . .

With respect to training programs, . . . inadequate attention may have been paid to the possibility that subtle messages in these lectures and videos would reinforce preexisting stereotypes by, for example, focusing mostly on criminal groups that happen to be comprised of minority citizens or foreign nationals. These kinds of messages may have been further reinforced by statistics compiled by State Police and disseminated to troopers in seminars and bulletins. The very fact that information concerning the racial characteristics of drug traffickers was provided to troopers assigned to patrol duties could have suggested that such characteristics are a legitimate, relevant factor to be taken into account or "kept in mind" in exercising police discretion during a traffic stop.

The State Police reward system, meanwhile, gave practical impetus to the use of these inappropriate stereotypes about drug dealers. [Evidence] has surfaced that minority troopers may also have been caught up in a system that rewards officers based on the quantity of drugs that they have discovered during routine traffic stops. (An internal audit of State Police motor vehicle stops recorded on the Moorestown Station radio logs between May 1, 1996 and July 31, 1996 shows that 34.3% of the 3,524 stops that were conducted by nonminority troopers involved minority motorists. An essentially identical proportion (33.3%) of the 1,751 total stops that were conducted by minority troopers involved minority motorists.) . . . The typical trooper is an intelligent, rational, ambitious, and career-oriented professional who responds to the prospect of rewards and promotions as much as to the threat of discipline and punishment. The system of organizational rewards, by definition and design, exerts a powerful influence on officer performance and enforcement priorities. . . .

The Critical Distinction Between Legitimate Crime Trend Analysis and Impermissible Racial Profiling

[We] start with a discussion of the legitimate use of law enforcement's "collective knowledge and experience." Sophisticated crime analysis is sorely needed if police agencies are to remain responsive to emerging new threats and enforcement opportunities. The law is thus well-settled that in appropriate factual circumstances, police may piece together a series of acts, which by themselves seem innocent, but to a trained officer would reasonably indicate that criminal activity is afoot. State v. Patterson, 270 N.J. Super. 550, 557 (Law Div. 1993). As the court in *Patterson* correctly noted, "it is appropriate and legitimate police work to develop a so-called 'profile' based upon observations made in investigating the distribution or transportation of illicit drugs." Using these and other means, the police can develop a pattern of criminal wrongdoing that justifies their suspicions when they observe features that are in accord with the principal aspects of that pattern. . . . This regularized police experience reflects the collection of historical and intelligence information, careful crime trend analysis, and an examination of the methods of operations, the so-called "modus operandi," of drug traffickers and others engaged in various types of criminal activity. . . .

While police agencies are permitted, indeed are expected, to conduct crime trend analysis and to train officers as to those facts and circumstances that, while innocent on their face, provide a reasonable basis for suspecting criminal activity, the law also provides that certain factors may not be considered by law enforcement. In State v. Kuhn, 213 N.J. Super. 275 (App. Div. 1986), the court held that police are not permitted to draw any inferences of criminal activity from a suspect's race. The court in State v. Patterson expounded on this point, noting that "[certainly] the police cannot conclude that all young, male African-Americans are suspected of involvement in the illicit drug trade." . . .

One need not be a constitutional scholar to understand that race, ethnicity, or national origin cannot be the sole basis for initiating a motor vehicle stop. On this point, everyone seems to agree. The law is far less clear, and opinions within and outside the criminal justice system become far more diverse, with respect to the question whether there are any circumstances when police may legitimately consider these kinds of personal traits and characteristics in drawing rational inferences about criminal activity. No one disputes, of course, that police can take a person's race into account in deciding whether the person is the individual who is described in a "wanted" bulletin; in this instance, race or ethnicity is used only as an "identifier." The issue, rather, and one that has not yet been definitely or at least uniformly resolved by the courts, is whether race, ethnicity, or national origin may be considered as one among an array of factors to infer that a particular individual is more likely than others to be engaged in criminal activity.

We believe that when finally confronted with this issue, the New Jersey Supreme Court would likely . . . hold, based upon independent state constitutional grounds if necessary, that race may play no part in an officer's determination of whether a particular person is reasonably likely to be engaged in criminal activity. In any event, . . . we need not wait for the courts to reach this conclusion before we propose a clear rule to be followed by state troopers assigned to patrol duties. . . .

The Importance of Perceptions

[Law] enforcement policy cannot be divorced from public opinion and public perceptions. The New Jersey State Police, no less than any other law enforcement agency, [must] remain responsive to public needs and expectations if it is to achieve its ultimate mission to protect and to serve.

[A] *Star Ledger/Eagleton* poll that was conducted in early May 1998 . . . showed that while the overall job performance rating of the State Police is quite positive in New Jersey, there is a major racial divide among Garden State residents. Black and white New Jerseyans have markedly different views of troopers' fairness in the enforcement of the laws, even-handed treatment of all drivers, judgment in deciding whom to pull over, and courteousness in dealing with stopped motorists. The poll revealed that the vast majority of African-Americans in New Jersey feel that State Police members treat minorities worse than others, and that troopers target cars to pull over based on the race and age of the people in the cars. In stark contrast, the majority of white New Jerseyans feel that troopers treat all motorists the same and seem highly satisfied with all aspects of their job performance. . . .

The Circular Illogic of Race-Based Profiles

. . . We turn now to the specific assumption that is at the heart of the racial profiling controversy: the notion that a disproportionate percentage of drug traffickers and couriers are black or Hispanic, so that race, ethnicity, or national origin can serve as a reliable, accurate predictor of criminal activity. The proponents of this view point to empirical evidence, usually in the form of arrest and conviction statistics, that would appear at first blush to demonstrate quite conclusively that minorities are disproportionately represented among the universe of drug dealers.

The evidence for this conclusion is, in reality, tautological and reflects as much as anything the initial stereotypes of those who rely upon these statistics. . . .

Arrest statistics, by definition, do not show the number of persons who were detained or investigated who, as it turned out, were not found to be trafficking drugs or carrying weapons. Consistent with our human nature, we in law enforcement proudly display seized drug shipments or "hits" as a kind of trophy, but pay scant attention to our far more frequent "misses," that is, those instances where stops and searches failed to discover contraband. . . .

Remedial Steps

[The] State Police has already undertaken a series of initiatives to address these issues, beginning in 1990 with a comprehensive Standard Operating Procedure governing the conduct of motor vehicle stops. That SOP included a number of important and innovative safeguards, including a requirement that state troopers have a reasonable, articulable suspicion to believe that evidence of a crime would be found before asking for permission to conduct a consent search, and a requirement that all consents to search be reduced to writing.

The State Police have also issued policies and procedures that require troopers to advise the dispatcher as to the racial characteristics of motorists who are stopped, that require troopers to record this information on patrol logs, and that prohibit the practice of "spotlighting" vehicles to ascertain the racial characteristics of the occupants of vehicles that have not yet been ordered to pull over. . . . Most recently, pursuant to the Governor's and Attorney General's initiative, State Police vehicles were equipped with video cameras that can be used to provide conclusive evidence of the conduct of motor vehicle stops. . . .

[A] trooper who is bent on finding drugs will . . . engage in comparatively protracted patrol stops, since his or her objective would not be simply to issue a summons or warning, but rather to undertake a full-blown criminal investigation. For this reason, we propose the establishment of a system that would allow supervisors and the State Police hierarchy to monitor the duration of road stops. If, for example, the median length of patrol stops by a given officer is shown to be correlated to the race, ethnicity, or national origin of motorists, that circumstance would trigger the "early warning system" and require appropriate follow-up investigation and explanation. . . .

The Department of Law and Public Safety should prepare and make public on a quarterly basis aggregate statistics compiled pursuant to the databases created in accordance with the recommendations of this Interim Report, detailing by State Police station the proportion of minority and nonminority citizens who were subject to various actions taken by State Police members during the course of traffic stops.

The Superintendent should [establish] a protocol for the use of an "early warning system" to detect and deter the disparate treatment of minority citizens by State Police members assigned to patrol duties. . . . The protocol for use of the "early warning system" should provide for the routine supervisory review of videotapes, patrol officer logs, Traffic Stop Report forms, Search Incident forms, and any other patrol work product. The protocol should also provide for regularly conducted audits of enforcement patterns including traffic stops, the issuance of motor vehicle summons, and search and arrest activity. . . .

The Superintendent should within 90 days of this Report issue a single, comprehensive Standard Operating Procedure [regarding traffic stops]. In preparing the Standard Operating Procedure, the following should be considered:

1. Before exiting his or her police vehicle, a State Police member will inform the dispatcher of the exact reason for the stop (e.g., speeding, 70 mph), a description of the vehicle and, when possible, a description of its occupants (i.e., the number of occupants and the apparent race and gender).
2. A system should be established to monitor the exact duration of all stops.
3. When the patrol vehicle is equipped with a video camera, the State Police person will ensure that the camera is activated before exiting the patrol vehicle and will not turn the camera off until the detained vehicle has been released and departs the scene.
4. In the case of routine stops, the State Police member will at the outset of the stop, introduce him or herself by name, and inform the driver as to the reason for the stop. . . .
5. At the conclusion of the vehicle stop, the State Police person will inform the dispatcher as to the stop outcome (e.g., warning, summons, etc.). . . .
6. All State Police members conducting a motor vehicle traffic stop must utilize a Traffic Stop Report form, which shall record all officer action information necessary for immediate supervisory review or to supplement information recorded by the Computer Aided Dispatch System. . . .
7. All Traffic Stop Report forms are to be reviewed by supervisory personnel at the conclusion of all duty shifts. The information contained in the reports should be entered into the "early warning system" database. . . .

Although the racial profiling issue has gained state and national attention recently, the underlying conditions that foster disparate treatment of minorities have existed for decades in New Jersey and throughout the nation, and will not be changed overnight. Even so, we firmly believe that this Interim Report represents a major step, indeed a watershed event, signaling significant change. We thus hope that this Report, once fully implemented through the issuance of new and comprehensive Standard Operating Procedures, a monitoring system, training, and other reforms, will ensure that New Jersey is a national leader in addressing the issue of racial profiling.

U.S. DEPARTMENT OF JUSTICE, RACIAL PROFILING FACT SHEET

(June 17, 2003)

. . . Racial profiling sends the dehumanizing message to our citizens that they are judged by the color of their skin and harms the criminal justice system by eviscerating the trust that is necessary if law enforcement is to effectively protect our communities.

America has a moral obligation to prohibit racial profiling. Race-based assumptions in law enforcement perpetuate negative racial stereotypes that are harmful to our diverse democracy, and materially impair our efforts to maintain a fair and just society. As Attorney General John Ashcroft said, racial profiling creates a "lose-lose" situation because it destroys the potential for underlying trust that "should support the administration of justice as a societal objective." . . .

The guidance in many cases imposes *more* restrictions on the use of race and ethnicity in federal law enforcement than the Constitution requires. This guidance prohibits racial profiling in federal law enforcement practices without hindering the important work of our nation's public safety officials, particularly the intensified anti-terrorism efforts precipitated by the attacks of September 11, 2001.

Prohibiting Racial Profiling in Routine or Spontaneous Activities in Domestic Law Enforcement: In making routine or spontaneous law enforcement decisions, such as ordinary traffic stops, federal law enforcement officers may *not* use race or ethnicity to any degree, except that officers may rely on race and ethnicity if a specific suspect description exists. This prohibition applies even where the use of race or ethnicity might otherwise be lawful.

Routine Patrol Duties Must Be Carried Out Without Consideration of Race. Federal law enforcement agencies and officers sometimes engage in law enforcement activities, such as traffic and foot patrols, that generally do not involve either the ongoing investigation of specific criminal activities or the prevention of catastrophic events or harm to the national security. Rather, their activities are typified by spontaneous action in response to the activities of individuals whom they happen to encounter in the course of their patrols and about whom they have no information other than their observations. These general enforcement responsibilities should be carried out without *any* consideration of race or ethnicity.

Example: While parked by the side of the highway, a federal officer notices that nearly all vehicles on the road are exceeding the posted speed limit. Although each such vehicle is committing an infraction that would legally justify a stop, the officer may not use race or ethnicity as a factor in deciding which motorists to pull over. Likewise, the officer may not use race or ethnicity in deciding which detained motorists to ask to consent to a search of their vehicles.

Stereotyping Certain Races as Having a Greater Propensity to Commit Crimes Is Absolutely Prohibited. Some have argued that overall discrepancies in crime rates among racial groups could justify using race as a factor in general traffic enforcement activities and would produce a greater number of arrests for non-traffic offenses (*e.g.*, narcotics trafficking). We emphatically reject this view. It is patently unacceptable and thus prohibited under this guidance for federal law enforcement officers to engage in racial profiling.

Acting on Specific Suspect Identification Does Not Constitute Impermissible Stereotyping. The situation is different when a federal officer acts on the personal identifying characteristics of potential suspects, including age, sex, ethnicity or race. Common sense dictates that when a victim or witness describes the assailant as being of a particular race, authorities may properly limit their search for suspects to persons of that race. In such circumstances, the federal officer is not acting based on a generalized assumption about persons of different races; rather, the officer is helping locate a specific individual previously identified as involved in crime.

Example: While parked by the side of the highway, a federal officer receives an "All Points Bulletin" to be on the look-out for a fleeing bank robbery suspect, a man of a particular race and particular hair color in his 30s driving a blue automobile. The officer may use this description, including the race of the particular suspect, in deciding which speeding motorists to pull over.

Prohibiting Racial Profiling in Federal Law Enforcement Activities Related to Specific Investigations: In conducting activities in connection with a specific investigation, federal law enforcement officers may consider race and ethnicity only to the extent that there is trustworthy information, relevant to the locality or time frame, that links persons of a particular race or ethnicity to an identified criminal incident, scheme, or organization. This standard applies even where the use of race or ethnicity might otherwise be lawful. . . .

Example: In connection with a new initiative to increase drug arrests, federal authorities begin aggressively enforcing speeding, traffic, and other public area laws in a neighborhood predominantly occupied by people of a single race. The choice of neighborhood was not based on the number of 911 calls, number of arrests, or other pertinent reporting data specific to that area, but only on the general assumption that more drug-related crime occurs in that neighborhood because of its racial composition. This effort would be *improper* because it is based on generalized stereotypes. . . .

Reliance Upon Generalized Stereotypes Continues to Be Absolutely Forbidden. Use of race or ethnicity is permitted only when the federal officer is pursuing a specific lead concerning the identifying characteristics of persons involved in an *identified* criminal activity. The rationale underlying this concept carefully limits its reach. In order to qualify as a legitimate investigative lead, the following must be true:

- The information must be relevant to the locality or time frame of the criminal activity;
- The information must be trustworthy; and,
- The information concerning identifying characteristics must be tied to a particular criminal incident, a particular criminal scheme, or a particular criminal organization.

Example: The FBI is investigating the murder of a known gang member and has information that the shooter is a member of a rival gang. The FBI knows that the members of the rival gang are exclusively members of a certain ethnicity. This information, however, is not suspect-specific because there is no description of the particular assailant. But because authorities have reliable, locally relevant information linking a rival group with a distinctive ethnic character to the murder, federal law enforcement officers could properly consider ethnicity in conjunction with other appropriate factors in the course of conducting their investigation. Agents could properly decide to focus on persons dressed in a manner consistent with gang activity, but ignore persons dressed in that manner who do not appear to be members of that particular ethnicity.

Example: While investigating a car theft ring that dismantles cars and ships the parts for sale in other states, the FBI is informed by local authorities that it is common knowledge locally that most car thefts in that area are committed by individuals of a particular race. In this example, although the source (local police) is trustworthy, and the information potentially verifiable with reference to arrest statistics, there is no particular incident- or scheme-specific information linking individuals of that race to the particular interstate ring the FBI is investigating. Thus, agents could not use ethnicity as a factor in making law enforcement decisions in this investigation. . . .

Federal Law Enforcement Will Continue Terrorist Identification. Since the terrorist attacks on September 11, 2001, the President has emphasized that federal law enforcement personnel must use every legitimate tool to prevent future attacks, protect our nation's borders, and deter those who would cause devastating harm to our country and its people through the use of biological or chemical weapons, other weapons of mass destruction, suicide hijackings, or any other means.

Therefore, the racial profiling guidance recognizes that race and ethnicity may be used in terrorist identification, but only to the extent permitted by the nation's laws and the Constitution. The policy guidance emphasizes that, even in the national security context, the constitutional restriction on use of generalized stereotypes remains. . . .

Given the incalculably high stakes involved in such investigations, federal law enforcement officers who are protecting national security or preventing catastrophic events (as well as airport security screeners) may consider race, ethnicity, alienage, and other relevant factors. Constitutional provisions limiting government action on the basis of race are wide-ranging and provide substantial protections at every step of the investigative and judicial process. Accordingly, this policy will honor the rule of law and promote vigorous protection of our national security. . . .

Example: U.S. intelligence sources report that Middle Eastern terrorists are planning to use commercial jetliners as weapons by hijacking them at an airport in California during the next week. Before allowing men appearing to be of Middle Eastern origin to board commercial airplanes in California airports during the next week, Transportation Security Administration personnel, and other federal and state authorities, may subject them to heightened scrutiny. . . .

Problem 2-4. Borderline State

In 2010 the Arizona legislature enacted the highly controversial state immigration law known as SB 1070. One aspect of the law that attracts the most public commentary is whether it allows, mandates, invites, or forbids the use of race in police decisions whether to stop a suspect, or whether to investigate their immigration status. The leadership of the Tucson Police Department has hired you to advise them on the relationship between SB 1070 and racial profiling.

Your client asks you to address separately two distinct conceptions of racial profiling: (1) when police officers use race as one element in a decision whether to stop or search, and (2) when race is an unconstitutional or otherwise illegal element in a decision whether to stop or search. With these two definitions in mind, consider the text of A.R.S. §11-1051(B):

> For any lawful stop, detention or arrest made by a law enforcement official or a law enforcement agency of this state or a law enforcement official or a law enforcement agency of a county, city, town or other political subdivision of this state in the enforcement of any other law or ordinance of country, city or town or this state where reasonable suspicion exists that the person is an alien and is unlawfully present in the United States, a reasonable attempt shall be made, when practicable, to determine the immigration status of the person, except if the determination may hinder or obstruct an investigation. Any person who is arrested shall have the person's immigration status determined before the person is released. The person's immigration status shall be verified with the federal government. . . . A law enforcement official or agency of this state or a county, city, town or other political subdivision of this state may not consider race, color or national origin in implementing the requirements of this subsection except to the extent permitted by the United States or Arizona Constitution.

SB 1070 also prohibits government agencies from restricting enforcement of immigration law "to less than the full extent permitted by federal law." A.R.S. §1151(A). The statute creates a citizen suit provision, allowing a judicial challenge of any policy that interferes with the full enforcement of federal law. A.R.S. §11-1051(H).

Arizona Governor Jan Brewer stated that it is "crystal clear and undeniable that racial profiling is illegal, and will not be tolerated in Arizona." The primary author of SB 1070, Arizona State Senator Russell Pearce, wrote that SB 1070 "explicitly prohibits racial profiling." The Arizona Police Office Standards and Training Board, AZPOST, which issues training materials but has no enforcement power, issued training materials and videos stating that race and ethnicity cannot be used in police decisions about whether to investigate immigration status. See *http://www.azpost.state.az.us/SB1070infocenter.htm*.

In United States v. Brignoni-Ponce, 422 U.S. 873, 886-887 (1975), the Supreme Court of the United States held that the U.S. Constitution allows race to be considered in immigration enforcement: "The likelihood that any given person of Mexican ancestry is an alien is high enough to make Mexican appearance a relevant factor." The Arizona Supreme Court has agreed that "enforcement of immigration laws often involves a relevant consideration of ethnic factors." State v. Graciano, 653 P.2d 683, 687 n.7 (Ariz. 1982). In 1996, the Arizona Supreme Court reaffirmed the relevance of race in determinations of reasonable suspicion:

> Mexican ancestry alone, that is, Hispanic appearance, is not enough to establish reasonable cause, but if the occupants' dress or hair style are associated with people currently living in Mexico, such characteristics may be sufficient. The driver's behavior may be considered if the driving is erratic or the driver exhibits an "obvious attempt to evade officers." The type or load of the vehicle may also create a reasonable suspicion.

State v. Gonzalez-Gutierrez, 927 P.2d 776 (Ariz. 1996). See also United States v. Soto-Cervantes, 138 F.3d 1319, 1325 (10th Cir. 1998) (affirming trial court finding of reasonable suspicion of immigration violations based on factors including "the defendant's presence in an area known to be frequented by illegal aliens from

Mexico"); but cf. United States v. Montero-Camargo, 208 F.3d 1122, 1131 (9th Cir. 2000) (en banc) (in a case arising in El Centro, 50 miles north of the Mexican border, "The likelihood that in an area in which the majority — or even a substantial part — of the population is Hispanic, any given person of Hispanic ancestry is in fact an alien, let alone an illegal alien, is not high enough to make Hispanic appearance a relevant factor in the reasonable suspicion calculus"). Notably, modern cases on the question of the explicit relevance of race to stops or searches arise in immigration cases and overwhelmingly involve persons of apparent Hispanic or Mexican origin.

Your counsel to the Tucson Police Department will likely expose the city to lawsuits, regardless of what you say. The Police Department plans to share your advice with other police departments and sheriff's offices throughout Arizona. What is your advice?

Notes

1. *DWB claims.* Claims that police officers stop drivers because of their race and not their behavior are not new, but have become much more prominent over the past several years after a series of prominent law review articles, and some litigation in New Jersey and Maryland. These civil lawsuits, along with defenses raised in criminal proceedings, have produced only modest success. Based on cases such as Whren v. United States, 517 U.S. 806 (1996), described above, most courts have found no constitutional violation. See Tracey Maclin, The Fourth Amendment on the Freeway, 3 Rutgers Race & L. Rev. 117, 117-28 (2001).

2. *DWB legislation.* With DWB making little or no headway as a constitutional claim, state legislatures have taken the lead in efforts to monitor, limit, and sanction racially biased traffic stops. See David A. Harris, Addressing Racial Profiling in the States: A Case Study of the "New Federalism" in Constitutional Criminal Procedure, 3 Pa. J. Const. L. 367 (2001). The statutes pursue different strategies. An Oklahoma statute, 22 Okla. Stat. §34.3, directly forbids the use of race as the "sole" basis for stopping or detaining a person, and makes racial profiling a misdemeanor. The statute also calls for law enforcement agencies to adopt and publicize "a detailed written policy that clearly defines the elements constituting racial profiling." A California statute, Penal Code §13519.4, requires training of officers in topics related to cultural diversity. A Missouri statute, Mo. Stat. §590.650, provides for mandatory collection of data about the race of motorists whom the police stop and search. Which of these strategies is most likely to reduce the amount of racial profiling?

Apart from legislation on the subject, many police departments have now adopted internal guidelines calling on officers to record the age, gender, and race or ethnicity of every person they stop in traffic. See Bureau of Justice Statistics, Traffic Stop Data Collection Policies for State Police, 2004 (2005, NCJ 209156) (22 of 49 state police agencies require officers to record race or ethnicity of motorist in all traffic stops). What (or who) might convince a police department to adopt such a policy?

3. *Race and prevention of terrorism.* Note that the Department of Justice policy on racial profiling creates a special set of rules for terrorism investigations. What justification does the statement offer for creating an exception in this area? Does the legitimacy of such a policy depend on the actual number of terrorist acts committed by Muslim noncitizens, as compared to the number of terrorist acts committed by

Christian citizens (such as the Oklahoma City bombing of 1995)? For a sample of the debates in this fast-changing area, see the web extension for this chapter at *http://www.crimpro.com/extension/ch02*.

4. *Race in immigration enforcement*. For enforcement of general criminal laws, such as drug crimes, race plays a shadowy, often implicit role as a factor in reasonable suspicion or probable cause determinations. For immigration enforcement, both federal law (as in *Brignoni-Ponce*) and state law (as illustrated by the Arizona cases cited in Problem 2-4) allow *explicit* reliance on race or ethnicity. But only one race (or ethnicity) has been at issue in these cases — being Hispanic. Explicit reliance on race for immigration enforcement has become more awkward, as suggested by the battles over the text and effect of Arizona Senate Bill 1070. Professor Gabriel (Jack) Chin and Dean Kevin Johnson, in a July 13, 2010, *Washington Post* op-ed, suggested that

> [we] suspect that *Brignoni-Ponce* and its incorporation into S.B. 1070 have escaped the notice of many Americans because of the ways in which racial sensibilities have evolved since the 1954 ruling in *Brown v. Board of Education*. Modern American values and most of modern constitutional law are simply inconsistent with the equation of race and suspicion authorized and encouraged by *Brignoni-Ponce*. Today, being subject to questioning by law enforcement for no other reason than that others of your race, religion or national origin are supposed to commit more of a particular type of crime is nothing short of un-American.

Has *Brignoni-Ponce* been overruled by social norms? Has the United States Supreme Court simply not taken an opportunity to bring doctrine into a more modern line?

5. *Executive branch policies on race*. Arizona Senate Bill 1070 provoked a national controversy, copycat statutes, and federal litigation. On July 28, 2010, a day before the law was to take effect, a federal judge in Phoenix enjoined the most controversial provisions of the law, including §11-1051(B). If race or ethnicity — appearing to be Hispanic or Mexican — are no longer legitimate factors in immigration enforcement, then federal and state executive branch agencies (including police and prosecutors) could choose not to rely on race without waiting for a court order on the issue. Federal authorities and authorities in other states could forbid reliance on race in criminal or immigration enforcement, even without new constitutional rulings. This option might not be available in Arizona under SB 1070, which included provisions requiring state agents to "fully enforce federal law" and made state agencies subject to lawsuits by citizens who could challenge any state or local policy that failed to do so. The federal government, however, has not forbidden reliance on race or ethnicity. To the contrary, the Obama Administration Department of Justice regularly relies on apparent race and ethnicity in federal immigration enforcement. See United States v. Bautista-Silva, 567 F.3d 1266, 1270 (11th Cir. 2009) (reasonable suspicion existed based on seven factors, including that "the driver and all five passengers were Hispanic adult males"), and federal courts regularly accept them. See United States' Response in Opposition to Defendant's Motion to Suppress and Memorandum of Law, in United States v. Gustavo Telles-Montenegro, 2009 WL 6478237, 7 (M.D. Fl. Dec. 21 2009) (reasonable suspicion supported by "the apparent Mexican ancestry of the occupants of the vehicle"), defendant's motion denied, United States v. Telles-Montenegro, 2010 WL 737640, *7 (M.D. Fl. Feb. 4, 2010) ("Agent Fiorita testified that, in his experience, Hispanic

males are typically the drivers of alien smuggling vehicles. Therefore, this is also a relevant consideration.").

B. BRIEF ADMINISTRATIVE STOPS

Among the brief stops and searches that government agents carry out, some are subject to less restrictive rules because of their routine administrative nature. These brief stops are carried out on large numbers of people and further government interests apart from criminal law enforcement. The U.S. Supreme Court determined, in Camara v. Municipal Court, 387 U.S. 523 (1967), that the Fourth Amendment could place limits on government activities even when they are not directed at enforcement of the criminal laws. These "administrative" stops and searches sometimes take place even when the government agents have no reasonable suspicion to believe that a law has been violated. We begin with non-individualized stops of drivers.

■ CITY OF INDIANAPOLIS v. JAMES EDMOND

531 U.S. 32 (2000)

O'CONNOR, J.*

. . . I.

. . . In August 1998, the city of Indianapolis began to operate vehicle checkpoints on Indianapolis roads in an effort to interdict unlawful drugs. The city conducted six such roadblocks between August and November that year, stopping 1,161 vehicles and arresting 104 motorists. Fifty-five arrests were for drug-related crimes, while 49 were for offenses unrelated to drugs. The overall "hit rate" of the program was thus approximately nine percent.

The parties stipulated to the facts concerning the operation of the checkpoints by the Indianapolis Police Department (IPD) for purposes of the preliminary injunction proceedings instituted below. At each checkpoint location, the police stop a predetermined number of vehicles. Approximately 30 officers are stationed at the checkpoint. Pursuant to written directives issued by the chief of police, at least one officer approaches the vehicle, advises the driver that he or she is being stopped briefly at a drug checkpoint, and asks the driver to produce a license and registration. The officer also looks for signs of impairment and conducts an open-view examination of the vehicle from the outside. A narcotics-detection dog walks around the outside of each stopped vehicle.

The directives instruct the officers that they may conduct a search only by consent or based on the appropriate quantum of particularized suspicion. The officers must conduct each stop in the same manner until particularized suspicion develops,

* [Justices Stevens, Kennedy, Souter, Ginsburg, and Breyer joined in this opinion. — EDS.]

and the officers have no discretion to stop any vehicle out of sequence. . . . According to Sergeant [Marshall] DePew, checkpoint locations are selected weeks in advance based on such considerations as area crime statistics and traffic flow. The checkpoints are generally operated during daylight hours and are identified with lighted signs reading, "NARCOTICS CHECKPOINT _______ MILE AHEAD, NARCOTICS K-9 IN USE, BE PREPARED TO STOP." Once a group of cars has been stopped, other traffic proceeds without interruption until all the stopped cars have been processed or diverted for further processing. Sergeant DePew also stated that the average stop for a vehicle not subject to further processing lasts two to three minutes or less.

Respondents James Edmond and Joell Palmer were each stopped at a narcotics checkpoint in late September 1998. Respondents then filed a lawsuit on behalf of themselves and the class of all motorists who had been stopped or were subject to being stopped in the future at the Indianapolis drug checkpoints. Respondents claimed that the roadblocks violated the Fourth Amendment of the United States Constitution and the search and seizure provision of the Indiana Constitution. Respondents requested declaratory and injunctive relief for the class, as well as damages and attorney's fees for themselves. . . .

II.

The Fourth Amendment requires that searches and seizures be reasonable. A search or seizure is ordinarily unreasonable in the absence of individualized suspicion of wrongdoing. While such suspicion is not an irreducible component of reasonableness, we have recognized only limited circumstances in which the usual rule does not apply. For example, we have upheld certain regimes of suspicionless searches where the program was designed to serve "special needs, beyond the normal need for law enforcement." See, e.g., Vernonia School Dist. 47J v. Acton, 515 U.S. 646 (1995) (random drug testing of student-athletes); Treasury Employees v. Von Raab, 489 U.S. 656 (1989) (drug tests for United States Customs Service employees seeking transfer or promotion to certain positions). We have also allowed searches for certain administrative purposes without particularized suspicion of misconduct, provided that those searches are appropriately limited. See, e.g., New York v. Burger, 482 U.S. 691 (1987) (warrantless administrative inspection of premises of "closely regulated" business).

We have also upheld brief, suspicionless seizures of motorists at a fixed Border Patrol checkpoint designed to intercept illegal aliens, United States v. Martinez-Fuerte, 428 U.S. 543 (1976), and at a sobriety checkpoint aimed at removing drunk drivers from the road, Michigan Dept. of State Police v. Sitz, 496 U.S. 444 (1990). In addition, in Delaware v. Prouse, 440 U.S. 648 (1979), we suggested that a similar type of roadblock with the purpose of verifying drivers' licenses and vehicle registrations would be permissible. In none of these cases, however, did we indicate approval of a checkpoint program whose primary purpose was to detect evidence of ordinary criminal wrongdoing. . . .

In *Sitz*, we evaluated the constitutionality of a Michigan highway sobriety checkpoint program. The *Sitz* checkpoint involved brief suspicionless stops of motorists so that police officers could detect signs of intoxication and remove impaired drivers from the road. Motorists who exhibited signs of intoxication were diverted for a license and registration check and, if warranted, further sobriety tests. This checkpoint program was clearly aimed at reducing the immediate hazard posed by the presence of drunk drivers on the highways, and there was an obvious connection between the imperative of highway safety and the law enforcement practice at issue. The gravity of the drunk driving problem and the magnitude of the State's interest in getting drunk drivers off the road weighed heavily in our determination that the program was constitutional.

In *Prouse,* we invalidated a discretionary, suspicionless stop for a spot check of a motorist's driver's license and vehicle registration. The officer's conduct in that case was unconstitutional primarily on account of his exercise of "standardless and unconstrained discretion." We nonetheless acknowledged the States' "vital interest in ensuring that only those qualified to do so are permitted to operate motor vehicles, that these vehicles are fit for safe operation, and hence that licensing, registration, and vehicle inspection requirements are being observed." Accordingly, we suggested that "questioning of all oncoming traffic at roadblock-type stops" would be a lawful means of serving this interest in highway safety.

We further indicated in *Prouse* that we considered the purposes of such a hypothetical roadblock to be distinct from a general purpose of investigating crime. [We considered the State's primary interest in this setting to be roadway safety.] Not only does the common thread of highway safety thus run through *Sitz* and *Prouse,* but *Prouse* itself reveals a difference in the Fourth Amendment significance of highway safety interests and the general interest in crime control.

III.

It is well established that a vehicle stop at a highway checkpoint effectuates a seizure within the meaning of the Fourth Amendment. The fact that officers walk a narcotics-detection dog around the exterior of each car at the Indianapolis checkpoints does not transform the seizure into a search. See United States v. Place, 462 U.S. 696 (1983). Just as in *Place,* an exterior sniff of an automobile does not require entry into the car and is not designed to disclose any information other than the presence or absence of narcotics. . . . Rather, what principally distinguishes these checkpoints from those we have previously approved is their primary purpose.

As petitioners concede, the Indianapolis checkpoint program unquestionably has the primary purpose of interdicting illegal narcotics. In their stipulation of facts, the parties repeatedly refer to the checkpoints as "drug checkpoints" and describe them as "being operated by the City of Indianapolis in an effort to interdict unlawful drugs in Indianapolis." In addition, the [operating] directives instruct officers to "advise the citizen that they are being stopped briefly at a drug checkpoint." . . . Because the primary purpose of the Indianapolis narcotics checkpoint program is to uncover evidence of ordinary criminal wrongdoing, the program contravenes the Fourth Amendment.

Petitioners propose several ways in which the narcotics-detection purpose of the instant checkpoint program may instead resemble the primary purposes of the checkpoints in *Sitz* and *Martinez-Fuerte.* Petitioners state that the checkpoints in those cases had the same ultimate purpose of arresting those suspected of committing crimes. Securing the border and apprehending drunk drivers are, of course, law enforcement activities, and law enforcement officers employ arrests and criminal prosecutions in pursuit of these goals. If we were to rest the case at this high level of generality, there would be little check on the ability of the authorities to construct roadblocks for almost any conceivable law enforcement purpose. Without drawing the line at roadblocks designed primarily to serve the general interest in crime control, the Fourth Amendment would do little to prevent such intrusions from becoming a routine part of American life. . . .

Nor can the narcotics-interdiction purpose of the checkpoints be rationalized in terms of a highway safety concern similar to that present in *Sitz.* The detection and punishment of almost any criminal offense serves broadly the safety of the community, and our streets would no doubt be safer but for the scourge of illegal drugs. Only with respect to a smaller class of offenses, however, is society confronted with the type of immediate, vehicle-bound threat to life and limb that the sobriety checkpoint in *Sitz* was designed to eliminate. . . .

Of course, there are circumstances that may justify a law enforcement checkpoint where the primary purpose would otherwise, but for some emergency, relate to ordinary crime control. For example, . . . the Fourth Amendment would almost certainly permit an appropriately tailored roadblock set up to thwart an imminent terrorist attack or to catch a dangerous criminal who is likely to flee by way of a particular route. The exigencies created by these scenarios are far removed from the circumstances under which authorities might simply stop cars as a matter of course to see if there just happens to be a felon leaving the jurisdiction. . . .

Petitioners argue that our prior cases preclude an inquiry into the purposes of the checkpoint program. For example, they cite Whren v. United States, 517 U.S. 806 (1996) . . . to support the proposition that "where the government articulates and pursues a legitimate interest for a suspicionless stop, courts should not look behind that interest to determine whether the government's 'primary purpose' is valid." These cases, however, do not control the instant situation.

In *Whren,* we held that an individual officer's subjective intentions are irrelevant to the Fourth Amendment validity of a traffic stop that is justified objectively by probable cause to believe that a traffic violation has occurred. . . . In so holding, we expressly distinguished cases where we had addressed the validity of searches conducted in the absence of probable cause. [While] subjective intentions play no role in ordinary, probable-cause Fourth Amendment analysis, programmatic purposes may be relevant to the validity of Fourth Amendment intrusions undertaken pursuant to a general scheme without individualized suspicion. . . .

Petitioners argue that the Indianapolis checkpoint program is justified by its lawful secondary purposes of keeping impaired motorists off the road and verifying licenses and registrations. If this were the case, however, law enforcement authorities would be able to establish checkpoints for virtually any purpose so long as they also included a license or sobriety check. For this reason, we examine the available evidence to determine the primary purpose of the checkpoint program. While we recognize the challenges inherent in a purpose inquiry, courts routinely engage in this enterprise in many areas of constitutional jurisprudence as a means of sifting abusive governmental conduct from that which is lawful. . . .

Because the primary purpose of the Indianapolis checkpoint program is ultimately indistinguishable from the general interest in crime control, the checkpoints violate the Fourth Amendment. . . .

REHNQUIST, C.J., dissenting.*

The State's use of a drug-sniffing dog, according to the Court's holding, annuls what is otherwise plainly constitutional under our Fourth Amendment jurisprudence: brief, standardized, discretionless, roadblock seizures of automobiles, seizures which effectively serve a weighty state interest with only minimal intrusion on the privacy of their occupants. Because these seizures serve the State's accepted and significant interests of preventing drunken driving and checking for driver's licenses and vehicle registrations, and because there is nothing in the record to indicate that the addition of the dog sniff lengthens these otherwise legitimate seizures, I dissent.

I.

... Petitioners acknowledge that the "primary purpose" of these roadblocks is to interdict illegal drugs, but this fact should not be controlling. [The] question whether a law enforcement purpose could support a roadblock seizure is not presented in this case. The District Court found that another "purpose of the checkpoints is to check driver's licenses and vehicle registrations," and the written directives state that the police officers are to "look for signs of impairment." ... That the roadblocks serve these legitimate state interests cannot be seriously disputed, as the 49 people arrested for offenses unrelated to drugs can attest. ...

Because of the valid reasons for conducting these roadblock seizures, it is constitutionally irrelevant that petitioners also hoped to interdict drugs. In Whren v. United States, we held that an officer's subjective intent would not invalidate an otherwise objectively justifiable stop of an automobile. The reasonableness of an officer's discretionary decision to stop an automobile, at issue in *Whren*, turns on whether there is probable cause to believe that a traffic violation has occurred. The reasonableness of highway checkpoints, at issue here, turns on whether they effectively serve a significant state interest with minimal intrusion on motorists. ... Once the constitutional requirements for a particular seizure are satisfied, the subjective expectations of those responsible for it, be it police officers or members of a city council, are irrelevant. It is the objective effect of the State's actions on the privacy of the individual that animates the Fourth Amendment. Because the objective intrusion of a valid seizure does not turn upon anyone's subjective thoughts, neither should our constitutional analysis. ...

[The] checkpoints' success rate — 49 arrests for offenses unrelated to drugs [or 4.2 percent of the motorists stopped] — only confirms the State's legitimate interests in preventing drunken driving and ensuring the proper licensing of drivers and registration of their vehicles. These stops effectively serve the State's legitimate interests; they are executed in a regularized and neutral manner; and they only minimally intrude upon the privacy of the motorists. They should therefore be constitutional.

* [Justice Thomas joined this opinion; Justice Scalia joined in Part I. — EDS.]

II.

[Expectations] of privacy in an automobile and of freedom in its operation are significantly different from the traditional expectation of privacy and freedom in one's residence. This is because automobiles, unlike homes, are subjected to pervasive and continuing governmental regulation and controls. The lowered expectation of privacy in one's automobile is coupled with the limited nature of the intrusion: a brief, standardized, nonintrusive seizure. . . .

Because of these extrinsic limitations upon roadblock seizures, the Court's newfound non-law-enforcement primary purpose test is both unnecessary to secure Fourth Amendment rights and bound to produce wide-ranging litigation over the "purpose" of any given seizure. Police designing highway roadblocks can never be sure of their validity, since a jury might later determine that a forbidden purpose exists. . . .

IOWA CODE §321K.1

1. The law enforcement agencies of this state may conduct emergency vehicle roadblocks in response to immediate threats to the health, safety, and welfare of the public; and otherwise may conduct routine vehicle roadblocks only as provided in this section. Routine vehicle roadblocks may be conducted to enforce compliance with the law regarding any of the following:

a. The licensing of operators of motor vehicles.

b. The registration of motor vehicles.

c. The safety equipment required on motor vehicles.

d. The provisions of chapters 481A and 483A [dealing with fish and game conservation].

2. Any routine vehicle roadblock conducted under this section shall meet the following requirements:

a. The location of the roadblock, the time during which the roadblock will be conducted, and the procedure to be used while conducting the roadblock, shall be determined by policymaking administrative officers of the law enforcement agency.

b. The roadblock location shall be selected for its safety and visibility to oncoming motorists, and adequate advance warning signs, illuminated at night or under conditions of poor visibility, shall be erected to provide timely information to approaching motorists of the roadblock and its nature.

c. There shall be uniformed officers and marked official vehicles of the law enforcement agency or agencies involved, in sufficient quantity and visibility to demonstrate the official nature of the roadblock.

d. The selection of motor vehicles to be stopped shall not be arbitrary.

e. The roadblock shall be conducted to assure the safety of and to minimize the inconvenience of the motorists involved.

Notes

1. *Automobile checkpoints: majority position.* As the opinion in *Edmond* makes clear, the federal constitution imposes different requirements on sobriety checkpoints and drug enforcement checkpoints. In Michigan Department of Police v. Sitz, 496 U.S. 444 (1990), the Court upheld a sobriety checkpoint where officers stopped vehicles without reasonable suspicion. The opinion emphasized the importance of neutral guidelines for carrying out the roadblock, formulated by supervisors or others besides the officers in the field. Those guidelines reduced both the "objective" intrusion (the duration of the stop and the intensity of the questioning) and the "subjective" intrusion of the stop (the anxiety of law-abiding drivers who are unaware of the purpose of the stop). On the other hand, after the ruling in *Edmond,* governments may not conduct suspicionless stops at drug enforcement checkpoints.

State courts are split on whether suspicionless sobriety checkpoints violate their state constitutions, with a strong majority (nearly 40 states) mirroring the federal position. See State v. Mikolinski, 775 A.2d 274 (Conn. 2001). A minority (about 10) require individualized suspicion before a vehicle stop may occur at a sobriety checkpoint. This group includes Michigan, the state whose appeals court decision was reversed in *Sitz,* which in turn rejected the U.S. Supreme Court's *Sitz* opinion on state constitutional grounds. Sitz v. Department of Police, 506 N.W.2d 209 (Mich. 1993).

2. *Driver's license and other safety reasons for checkpoints.* Police in many jurisdictions stop vehicles without individualized suspicion at a checkpoint to verify the validity of the operators' licenses, following much the same procedures for license checkpoints as they do for sobriety checkpoints. The Iowa statute above approves of roadblocks for purposes of enforcing safety equipment laws but not for purposes of enforcing drunk driving laws. Does this distinction make sense?

The U.S. Supreme Court has approved of license checkpoints so long as they are carried out in a way that does not leave officers in the field with discretion to select the vehicles to stop. Delaware v. Prouse, 440 U.S. 648 (1979). Some states have rejected license checkpoints under their state constitutions. State v. Sanchez, 856 S.W.2d 166 (Tex. Crim. App. 1993) (license and insurance checkpoint set up by four officers); State v. Hicks, 55 S.W.3d 515 (Tenn. 2001) (license checkpoint).

Government agents enforcing health and safety laws other than traffic laws also find it useful to stop and question motorists and persons outside their cars. See People v. McHugh, 630 So. 2d 1259 (La. 1994) (upholding statute authorizing suspicionless stops of hunters who are leaving state wilderness area to inspect hunting license and to request permission to inspect game); but see State v. Medley, 898 P.2d 1093 (Idaho 1995) (disallowing, in an opinion by Justice Trout, a game management checkpoint because of officer discretion in stopping vehicles and presence of criminal law enforcement officials). What set of safety and health concerns convinced the Iowa legislature to pass Section 321K.1?

3. *Which programmatic purpose?* Justice O'Connor, in her majority opinion in *Edmond,* says that "programmatic purposes may be relevant" even though an officer's subjective intentions normally do not matter in evaluating the reasonableness of a seizure. We encountered this issue earlier, in discussing "pretextual" stops. Is it any easier for courts to determine the purpose of a program than to determine the

intentions of a particular officer? What sources of evidence are available to the court making this factual finding? See Crowell v. State, 994 P.2d 788 (Okla. Crim. App. 2000) (use of narcotics detection dog to sniff cars not enough to show that safety roadblock was a pretext for drug enforcement); State v. Sigler, 687 S.E.2d 391 (W. Va. 2009) (police conducting equipment safety checks must follow the same guidelines as they do for sobriety checkpoints; different rules for checkpoints carrying different labels would invite "pretextual" checkpoints).

4. *Warrant clause and reasonableness clause.* A court ruling on the constitutionality of a suspicionless checkpoint stop confronts a question of legal text that we will encounter time and again in search and seizure issues. Recall that the text of the Fourth Amendment provides as follows: "The right of the people to be secure . . . against unreasonable searches and seizures, shall not be violated, and no Warrants shall issue, but upon probable cause. . . . " The first phrase (up to the word "violated") is known as the "reasonableness clause"; the second, the "warrant clause." What is the proper relationship between these clauses? Is the warrant clause a modifier to the reasonableness clause, defining the quintessential "reasonable" search and seizure, or do the clauses have independent meaning? If we are free to define reasonableness apart from the presence of a warrant and probable cause, then courts will need to determine in many different settings the proper measure of reasonableness. But if reasonableness is defined only in light of the warrant and probable cause requirements, then reasonableness in most settings becomes only a matter of determining how feasible it is to require police to show probable cause and obtain warrants.

Sobriety checkpoints take place in the absence of any probable cause or reasonable suspicion to believe that a driver being stopped is violating the law. The Supreme Court in *Sitz* and the other courts that have upheld sobriety checkpoints have used a "balancing" methodology to determine that individualized suspicion is not necessary. These courts balance the needs of law enforcement against the intrusiveness of the search and the individual's interest in privacy. Did the majority opinion in *Edmond* also balance interests? Should courts engage in balancing at all when it comes to constitutionally protected privacy interests? Or should they conclude that the Fourth Amendment and its equivalents have already struck a balance for all cases, requiring individualized suspicion for any "seizure" or "search"?

5. *Effectiveness of checkpoints.* Is it relevant in weighing the government's interest to determine the effectiveness of a particular set of roadblock guidelines in catching drunk drivers or meeting the other objectives of the checkpoint? Would a roadblock that produces one arrest for every 100 cars stopped be more constitutionally suspect than a roadblock that produces one arrest for every 20 cars stopped? How might police supervisors change guidelines to increase the number of arrests? Perhaps courts, police, and legislatures could consider some measure of effectiveness besides the number of arrests. Would courts be more likely to validate sobriety checkpoints if the government shows decreases in alcohol-related fatal crashes?

Consider the type of evidence that supports a decision to establish a random checkpoint and the evidence that supports "individualized" suspicion. Don't both sorts of judgments depend on assessments of similar groups or situations from the past to predict a "hit rate" for future stops? See Christopher Slobogin, Government Dragnets, 73 Law and Contemporary Problems 107 (2010); Bernard E. Harcourt and Tracey L. Meares, Randomization and the Fourth Amendment, 78 Univ. Chi. L. Rev. (forthcoming 2011), available at *http://www.ssrn.com/abstract =1665562.*

6. *Advance notice and neutral plans.* The guidelines for conducting roadblocks often provide for two types of notice. First, there are markers at the scene of the roadblock, announcing to oncoming drivers the purpose of the stop. Second, some guidelines require advance notice in the local media that roadblocks will be taking place in the area on particular days, without announcing the exact locations of the roadblocks. This advance notice is designed to increase the deterrent effect of the roadblocks by influencing the choices of all potential drivers who hear about the stops and to decrease the anxiety of drivers who encounter a roadblock. Such notice was part of the Michigan guidelines considered by the Supreme Court in *Sitz.*

If you were writing roadblock guidelines for a police department, would you include provisions for advance notice? Some courts have concluded that advance notice is not constitutionally required. See People v. Banks, 863 P.2d 769 (Cal. 1993). A few states modify the typical procedures by allowing random stops and giving officers more discretion. See State v. Mitchell, 592 S.E.2d 543 (N.C. 2004) (approves checkpoints based on standing permission from supervisor to operate under unwritten guidelines). Who is in a position to know if the police adequately follow the plan for stopping and questioning drivers? Should the plan be written? If the state's legislature has passed a statute similar to the Iowa statute above, is any further written plan necessary?

The necessary conditions for valid automobile checkpoints have attracted the attention of many state and federal courts. For a sample of these debates, see the web extension for this chapter at *http://www.crimpro.com/extension/ch02*.

7. *Roadblocks to find particular criminal suspects.* Police will occasionally receive information about the location of a suspect for a serious crime and will search all vehicles leaving the area. At least 10 states give police explicit statutory authority to set up roadblocks to find criminal suspects. See Idaho Code §19-621. Courts evaluating these roadblocks tend to approve them more readily if the crime is serious and the officers administer the roadblock in an evenhanded way that minimizes the delay and other intrusions.

What if a car approaching a roadblock makes a U-turn or exits the highway in an apparent attempt to avoid the roadblock? Does that give the police reasonable suspicion to pursue and stop the vehicle? See Commonwealth v. Scavello, 734 A.2d 386 (Pa. 1999) (properly executed turn to avoid passing through roadblock not a basis for stop).

The Supreme Court created a specialized version of the checkpoint rules to apply when the roadblock is designed to obtain information about people other than the motorist stopped. In Illinois v. Lidster, 540 U.S. 419 (2004), a police department seeking information about a fatal hit-and-run accident stopped motorists passing by the scene of the accident several days later. Although one of the stopped motorists was discovered to be driving while intoxicated, the Court ruled that the suspicionless stop was reasonable because the checkpoint sought information rather than arrests of intoxicated drivers.

After this decision, is it still fair to characterize suspicionless searches as "exceptional" techniques that will be approved only under "special" circumstances? Or has the law now evolved (or devolved) to the point that suspicionless searches are regulated and approved on the same basis as more traditional searches?

8. *Fixed and roving stops for immigration enforcement.* Customs and immigration officials routinely stop vehicles crossing the border into the country, and vehicles passing fixed checkpoints near the border. There are criminal sanctions for certain

violations of the immigration laws; indeed, immigration crimes have become some of the most common charges encountered in the federal courts (along with drug and fraud cases).

While the Supreme Court has disapproved of "roving" suspicionless stops of vehicles, it has upheld suspicionless stops of cars for brief questioning at fixed checkpoints at or near the border. See United States v. Martinez-Fuerte, 428 U.S. 543 (1976) (approves fixed checkpoint stops for brief questioning); United States v. Brignoni-Ponce, 422 U.S. 873 (1975) (disapproves roving stops in interior for questioning about immigration status); United States v. Ortiz, 422 U.S. 891 (1975) (disapproves roving immigration stops away from border to search interior of car); cf. United States v. Villamonte-Marquez, 462 U.S. 579 (1983) (approves suspicionless boarding of vessels at sea to inspect documentation). The Court has required reasonable suspicion for unusually long detentions of persons at the border. See United States v. Montoya de Hernandez, 473 U.S. 531 (1985); but cf. United States v. Flores-Montano, 541 U.S. 149 (2004) (Customs officials do not need individualized suspicion before removing, dismantling, and searching fuel tank of vehicle crossing the border, despite the fact that such searches were not routine).

9. *Legislative intent in statutory construction.* Does the Iowa statute reprinted above require each of the listed conditions for a roadblock to be valid? Courts faced with questions about the meaning of a statute will often look beyond the actual language of the statute and will read the language in light of the "legislative intent." Sometimes this legislative intent will be expressed in the "legislative history," a set of documents such as committee reports that discuss the statute before its passage or statements of legislators during floor debates on the bill. Such materials occupy a prominent place in federal statutory construction, although Justice Scalia and several other federal judges have argued for less reliance on legislative history. See INS v. Cardoza-Fonseca, 480 U.S. 421, 452 (1987) (Scalia, J., concurring).

Legislative history is generally less influential in most states. Many state courts do not consider legislative history at all because the state does not even maintain or publish such materials. Other state courts have legislative history available but discount it because it is difficult to know when statements of a single committee or a single legislator reflect the collective views of all those voting for a bill. Nevertheless, even those state courts that ignore or discount legislative history will inquire into the "purpose" of the statute. They might surmise this purpose from the language and structure of the statute (perhaps contained in the title of the statute or in a preamble explicitly stating the statute's purpose) or from a familiarity with the general history of the perceived problem and the statutory solution.

This effort to identify a statutory "purpose" gives courts the opportunity to read different statutes, perhaps passed and amended at different times, as a coherent and rational whole, furthering social purposes of the current day. In an influential text from 1958, Henry Hart and Albert Sacks expressed the interpreting judge's obligation this way: A judge interpreting a statute with ambiguous language "must resolve the uncertainty . . . in a way which is consistent with other established applications of [the statute.] And he must do so in the way which best serves the principles and policies it expresses. If the policy of the [statute] is open to doubt, the official should interpret it in the way which best harmonizes with more basic principles and policies of law." The Legal Process: Basic Problems in the Making and Application of Law 147 (William Eskridge and Phillip Frickey eds., 1994) (1958).

What was the intent of the Iowa legislature in passing its roadblock statute? What would a court need to know to answer this question? If a court determines the general "purpose" of the statute and applies the statute in a way that furthers that purpose, whose "intent" is it furthering?

Problem 2-5. Airport Checkpoints After September 11

You are an associate in a firm representing Los Angeles International Airport (LAX). Airport authorities have decided to install the Secure 2000 scanner. The Secure 2000 is a back-scatter X-ray system for detecting weapons and contraband hidden under a person's clothing. The Secure 2000 covertly scans persons for hidden weapons and explosives as they walk down a hallway. Almost immediately, an image of the person and any concealed objects appears on the monitor. Metal guns and knifes can be detected, as well as nonmetallic objects such as drugs and explosives. The image allows a view under clothes and, indeed, under the skin's surface.

Airport officials ask whether they can implement the Secure 2000 in all of the hallways leading to the terminals. If so, do they need to post a notice, and what does any notice need to say? They ask what authorities should do if the scanner reveals drugs, but not weapons.

Notes

1. *Airport and mass transit security checks.* Passengers who fly on commercial airlines must submit to unusually thorough inspections of their persons and belongings before they may approach the gate for boarding the airplane. What theory best explains this commonly accepted practice? Is it that the inspections do not amount to a "search" for Fourth Amendment purposes? That all passengers "consent" to the search when they purchase their tickets (including all the fine print buried on the back of the ticket or in the recesses of the airline websites)? See United States v. Hartwell, 296 F. Supp. 2d. 596, 602 (E.D. Pa. 2003) ("no consensus has been reached as to the grounds justifying" an airport search). As we saw earlier, drivers do not consent to random searches for any and all of their travels on the road; some special justification is required for searches of cars that are not based on individualized suspicion. Would the rationale for airport searches apply equally well to searches of subway trains and other forms of mass transit? Does the choice of method of travel reflect different levels of privacy expectations?

2. *Changing airport security, changing reasonableness.* The security practices at airports change constantly, in response to the latest efforts by terrorists and criminals to bring weapons and explosives on board flights. If the consent of the people, at least in some broad sense, is necessary to make a search "reasonable," how might the government get feedback from the public about the reasonableness of its ever-changing intrusions into traveler privacy in airports? See Andrew E. Taslitz, Fortune-Telling and the Fourth Amendment: Of Terrorism, Slippery Slopes, and Predicting the Future, 58 Rutgers L. Rev. 195 (2005).

C. GATHERING INFORMATION WITHOUT SEARCHING

Thus far, we have focused on various stops (that is, brief seizures) of persons and their property. We now turn to brief searches, the least intrusive efforts by government agents to collect private information from individuals.

Just as there are some encounters with police that do not count as a "seizure," there are some government efforts to gather information from individuals that do not amount to a "search" at all. Where there is no search, there is no constitutional requirement for the government to justify its efforts to gather information. Under the Fourth Amendment and most of its state equivalents, there is no search within the meaning of the Constitution when the government intrudes into some place or interest where the person has no "reasonable expectation of privacy." The definition contains both a subjective and an objective component. The target of the search must actually expect privacy, and that expectation must be one that society is prepared to recognize as reasonable.

This definition of a "search," now prominent in the case law of every state, derives from Katz v. United States, 389 U.S. 347 (1967). Before *Katz*, searches were defined in terms of property rights. A government agent performed a "search" within the meaning of the constitution when he or she "trespassed" on a protected area. Now under the *Katz* "reasonable expectation of privacy" test, a search might occur even if there is no trespass into a protected place. In the materials that follow, ask yourself what factors might make an expectation of privacy "reasonable."

One of the least intrusive forms of information-gathering occurs when the police simply notice what is in open view of others. Under the Fourth Amendment and its equivalents, there is no reasonable expectation of privacy in matters left within open view. Hence, no "search" has occurred to be evaluated under federal or state law. But when is an item in "open" or "plain" view?

■ STATE v. MIHAI BOBIC

996 P.2d 610 (Wash. 2000)

TALMADGE, J.

We are asked in this case to determine whether an officer's warrantless search of a commercial storage unit was constitutional when the search was made through a small, preexisting hole in an adjoining storage unit. . . . Under the circumstances of this case, we agree the evidence the officers obtained from the storage unit was in open view. . . .

Mihai Bobic and Igor Stepchuk were charged with numerous crimes arising from a sophisticated auto theft conspiracy. Bobic, Stepchuk, or their confederates stole vehicles and stripped them of their contents and key parts. They stored the stolen car parts and other stolen goods in various commercial storage facilities. Insurance carriers subsequently sold the hulks of the cars left by the thieves at auto auctions. Bobic, Stepchuk, or their confederates then purchased the hulks at those auto auctions, giving them clear tide to the vehicles. They then reassembled the vehicles with the stolen car parts and sold them.

Detective Kelly Quirin became suspicious about certain auto thefts and his investigation uncovered a possible connection between auto thefts and storage facilities. On March 1, 1994, Quirin obtained and executed a search warrant to examine certain units at a Shurgard Storage facility. After searching the units in accordance with the warrant, the facility's manager told Quirin that one of the units at his facility, unit E-71, might be connected with stolen vehicles. . . . On March 8, Quirin went to the storage facility with another officer and asked to look at unit E-71, which was locked. The manager let the officers into an unrented, unlocked storage unit next door to unit E-71. Upon entering the unit, the officers saw a preexisting hole, "maybe big enough to stick your pinky finger in or a little bigger," about four feet off the ground. (The walls of the units go up to the ceiling.) Quirin looked through the hole, and without aid of a flashlight was able to see items in unit E-71. Based on this information, Quirin obtained a search warrant for unit E-71 and recovered stolen goods.

[Stepchuk and Bobic were charged with theft, trafficking in stolen property, and conspiracy.] Prior to trial, Bobic moved to suppress the evidence recovered during the search of unit E-71. During his pretrial suppression hearing, Bobic testified [that a friend rented unit E-71, but he and the friend shared the unit. Bobic placed a lock on the door of the unit. The rental agreement] permitted the manager to open a unit at any time to uncover illegal activities.[1] . . . After a lengthy trial in King County Superior Court, Bobic and Stepchuk were convicted [and Bobic] appealed the lower court's denial of both his motion to suppress evidence seized from unit E-71. . . .

Washington's constitution provides that "[no] person shall be disturbed in his private affairs, . . . without authority of law." Const. Art I, §7. A violation of this right turns on whether the State has unreasonably intruded into a person's private affairs. In contrast, a search occurs under the Fourth Amendment if the government intrudes upon a reasonable expectation of privacy. Thus, Washington's "private affairs inquiry" is broader than the Fourth Amendment's "reasonable expectation of privacy inquiry."

Detective Quirin's observations do not constitute a search because the objects under observation were in "open view." Under the open view doctrine, when a law enforcement officer is able to detect something by utilization of one or more of his senses while lawfully present at the vantage point where those senses are used, that detection does not constitute a search. Here, the detective was lawfully inside the adjoining unit because the manager had given him permission to enter. Furthermore, it appears from the record that the detective's observations were made without extraordinary or invasive means and could be seen by anyone renting the unit. [Detective Quirin was able to "look into the hole with one eye"; not utilizing a flashlight because the hole "wasn't big enough to be able to look at to have the flashlight and your eye next to it to see in."]

Bobic contends the search here must nonetheless fail because it invaded a protected privacy interest and was more intrusive than the search in *State v. Rose,* 909 P.2d 280 (1996). In *Rose,* the officer's search was likely *more* intrusive because he

1. The rental agreement states, in pertinent part: ". . . The Storage Unit may not be used for any unlawful purpose . . . nor will Tenant keep in the Storage Unit any . . . substances whose storage or use is regulated or prohibited by local, state or federal law or regulation. . . . Tenant shall give the Landlord permission to enter the Storage Unit at any time for the purpose of removing and disposing of any property in the Storage Unit in violation of this provision. . . . Tenant represents to Landlord that all personal property to be stored by Tenant in the Storage Unit will belong to Tenant only, and not to any third parties. . . ."

looked with the aid of a flashlight through a window into the defendant's residence during the evening. Here, the detective did not peer through a curtained window; he did not wait until something incriminating came into sight or hearing; and he did not attempt to create a better vantage point.

Moreover, a commercial storage unit is not the kind of location entitled to special privacy protection. For example, a person's home is entitled to heightened constitutional protection relative to other locations. We decline to determine that a commercial storage unit has any special protected status. . . .

In this case, notwithstanding the troubling image of a police officer peering through a peephole in a storage unit, the trial court did not err in denying Bobic's motion to suppress because there was no "search"; the contents of the unit were in open view as that doctrine is understood in our law where the officer was legally at the vantage point, the vantage point was not artificially improved, and the officer perceived what he did with his unaided vision. . . .

STEVEN DEWAYNE BOND v. UNITED STATES

529 U.S. 334 (2000)

REHNQUIST, C.J.*

This case presents the question whether a law enforcement officer's physical manipulation of a bus passenger's carry-on luggage violated the Fourth Amendment's proscription against unreasonable searches. We hold that it did.

Petitioner Steven Dewayne Bond was a passenger on a Greyhound bus that left California bound for Little Rock, Arkansas. The bus stopped, as it was required to do, at the permanent Border Patrol checkpoint in Sierra Blanca, Texas. Border Patrol Agent Cesar Cantu boarded the bus to check the immigration status of its passengers. After reaching the back of the bus, having satisfied himself that the passengers were lawfully in the United States, Agent Cantu began walking toward the front. Along the way, he squeezed the soft luggage which passengers had placed in the overhead storage space above the seats.

Petitioner was seated four or five rows from the back of the bus. As Agent Cantu inspected the luggage in the compartment above petitioner's seat, he squeezed a green canvas bag and noticed that it contained a "brick-like" object. Petitioner admitted that the bag was his and agreed to allow Agent Cantu to open it. Upon opening the bag, Agent Cantu discovered a "brick" of methamphetamine. The brick had been wrapped in duct tape until it was oval-shaped and then rolled in a pair of pants.

Petitioner was indicted for conspiracy to possess, and possession with intent to distribute, methamphetamine. . . . He moved to suppress the drugs, arguing that Agent Cantu conducted an illegal search of his bag. Petitioner's motion was denied, and the District Court found him guilty on both counts and sentenced him to 57 months in prison.

* [Justices Stevens, O'Connor, Kennedy, Souter, Thomas, and Ginsburg joined in this opinion. — EDS.]

[It] is undisputed here that petitioner possessed a privacy interest in his bag. But the Government asserts that by exposing his bag to the public, petitioner lost a reasonable expectation that his bag would not be physically manipulated. The Government relies on our decisions in California v. Ciraolo, 476 U.S. 207 (1986), and Florida v. Riley, 488 U.S. 445 (1989), for the proposition that matters open to public observation are not protected by the Fourth Amendment. In *Ciraolo,* we held that police observation of a backyard from a plane flying at an altitude of 1,000 feet did not violate a reasonable expectation of privacy. Similarly, in *Riley,* we relied on *Ciraolo* to hold that police observation of a greenhouse in a home's curtilage from a helicopter passing at an altitude of 400 feet did not violate the Fourth Amendment. We reasoned that the property was "not necessarily protected from inspection that involves no physical invasion," and determined that because any member of the public could have lawfully observed the defendants' property by flying overhead, the defendants' expectation of privacy was "not reasonable and not one that society is prepared to honor."

But *Ciraolo* and *Riley* are different from this case because they involved only visual, as opposed to tactile, observation. Physically invasive inspection is simply more intrusive than purely visual inspection. For example, in Terry v. Ohio, 392 U.S. 1 (1968), we stated that a "careful [tactile] exploration of the outer surfaces of a person's clothing all over his or her body" is a "serious intrusion upon the sanctity of the person, which may inflict great indignity and arouse strong resentment, and is not to be undertaken lightly." Although Agent Cantu did not "frisk" petitioner's person, he did conduct a probing tactile examination of petitioner's carry-on luggage. Obviously, petitioner's bag was not part of his person. But travelers are particularly concerned about their carry-on luggage; they generally use it to transport personal items that, for whatever reason, they prefer to keep close at hand.

Here, petitioner concedes that, by placing his bag in the overhead compartment, he could expect that it would be exposed to certain kinds of touching and handling. But petitioner argues that Agent Cantu's physical manipulation of his luggage "far exceeded the casual contact [petitioner] could have expected from other passengers." The Government counters that it did not.

Our Fourth Amendment analysis embraces two questions. First, we ask whether the individual, by his conduct, has exhibited an actual expectation of privacy; that is, whether he has shown that he sought to preserve something as private. Here, petitioner sought to preserve privacy by using an opaque bag and placing that bag directly above his seat. Second, we inquire whether the individual's expectation of privacy is "one that society is prepared to recognize as reasonable."[2] When a bus passenger places a bag in an overhead bin, he expects that other passengers or bus employees may move it for one reason or another. Thus, a bus passenger clearly expects that his bag may be handled. He does not expect that other passengers or bus employees will, as a matter of course, feel the bag in an exploratory manner. But this is exactly what the agent did here. We therefore hold that the agent's physical manipulation of petitioner's bag violated the Fourth Amendment.

2. The parties properly agree that the subjective intent of the law enforcement officer is irrelevant in determining whether that officer's actions violate the Fourth Amendment. See Whren v. United States, 517 U.S. 806 (1996) (stating that "we have been unwilling to entertain Fourth Amendment challenges based on the actual motivations of individual officers"). This principle applies to the agent's acts in this case as well; the issue is not his state of mind, but the objective effect of his actions.

BREYER, J., dissenting.*

Does a traveler who places a soft-sided bag in the shared overhead storage compartment of a bus have a "reasonable expectation" that strangers will not push, pull, prod, squeeze, or otherwise manipulate his luggage? Unlike the majority, I believe that he does not.

Petitioner argues . . . that even if bags in overhead bins are subject to general "touching" and "handling," this case is special because Agent Cantu's physical manipulation of petitioner's luggage far exceeded the casual contact he could have expected from other passengers. But the record shows the contrary. . . . On the occasion at issue here, Agent Cantu "felt a green bag" which had "a brick-like object in it." He explained that he felt "the edges of the brick in the bag," and that . . . "when squeezed, you could feel an outline of something of a different mass inside of it." Although the agent acknowledged that his practice was to "squeeze [bags] very hard," he testified that his touch ordinarily was not "[hard] enough to break something inside that might be fragile." Petitioner also testified that Agent Cantu "reached for my bag, and he shook it a little, and squeezed it."

How does the "squeezing" just described differ from the treatment that overhead luggage is likely to receive from strangers in a world of travel that is somewhat less gentle than it used to be? I think not at all. Eagan, Familiar Anger Takes Flight with Airline Tussles, Boston Herald, Aug. 15, 1999, p.8 ("It's dog-eat-dog trying to cram half your home into overhead compartments"). The trial court . . . viewed the agent's activity as "minimally intrusive touching." . . .

Privacy itself implies the exclusion of uninvited strangers, not just strangers who work for the Government. Hence, an individual cannot reasonably expect privacy in respect to objects or activities that he knowingly exposes to the public. . . . Of course, the agent's purpose here — searching for drugs — differs dramatically from the intention of a driver or fellow passenger who squeezes a bag in the process of making more room for another parcel. But in determining whether an expectation of privacy is reasonable, it is the effect, not the purpose, that matters. Few individuals with something to hide wish to expose that something to the police, however careless or indifferent they may be in respect to discovery by other members of the public. Hence, a Fourth Amendment rule that turns on purpose could prevent police alone from intruding where other strangers freely tread. . . .

Nor can I accept the majority's effort to distinguish "tactile" from "visual" interventions, even assuming that distinction matters here. Whether tactile manipulation (say, of the exterior of luggage) is more intrusive or less intrusive than visual observation (say, through a lighted window) necessarily depends on the particular circumstances.

If we are to depart from established legal principles, we should not begin here. At best, this decision will lead to a constitutional jurisprudence of "squeezes," thereby complicating further already complex Fourth Amendment law, increasing the difficulty of deciding ordinary criminal matters, and hindering the administrative guidance (with its potential for control of unreasonable police practices) that a less complicated jurisprudence might provide. At worst, this case will deter law enforcement officers searching for drugs near borders from using even the most non-intrusive touch to help investigate publicly exposed bags. At the same time, the

* [Justice Scalia joined in this opinion. — EDS.]

ubiquity of nongovernmental pushes, prods, and squeezes (delivered by driver, attendant, passenger, or some other stranger) means that this decision cannot do much to protect true privacy. Rather, the traveler who wants to place a bag in a shared overhead bin and yet safeguard its contents from public touch should plan to pack those contents in a suitcase with hard sides, irrespective of the Court's decision today. For these reasons, I dissent.

Notes

1. *Items in plain view: majority position.* If an officer sees an item in plain view, no search has occurred under state or federal law. To qualify for plain view treatment, the police officer must view the item from a place where she has a right to be. The officer might have legal access to the place because it is open to the general public — some state courts, such as those in Florida and Hawaii, call this situation "open view" rather than "plain view." An officer might also have reason to view some item from a vantage point not open to the general public. For instance, the officer might be executing an arrest warrant or might be present in a "community caretaker" capacity. If the officer has a proper reason to be in that non-public location, the discovery of new information from that vantage point is not considered a search. In either setting, plain view or open view, the courts conclude that the target of the investigation has no reasonable expectation of privacy in the item within view of the officer.

What matters other than the location of the officer making the observation? As the Washington court indicates in *Bobic,* the amount of police effort involved in reaching the location might matter. The use of technological enhancements such as flashlights might matter. The nature of the location (a home versus a commercial storage facility) could matter. The U.S. Supreme Court has indicated in several cases that any physical movement of an item makes it much more difficult to claim that the item observed was in plain view. See Arizona v. Hicks, 480 U.S. 321 (1987) (stereo receiver moved inches to observe serial number was not in plain view). Does the opinion in Bond v. United States offer any guidance on the relevance of the *purpose* of the person observing or touching an item? Do you think that Bobic or Bond makes the stronger case that the government conducted a search?

2. *Location of the item; seizing versus viewing.* After an officer has seen some contraband or evidence of a crime in plain view, he may want to seize the item. Even when there has been no "search" of an item in plain view, there are some additional requirements the officer must meet before seizing the item. His ability to complete the seizure will depend primarily on where the item is located. If it is located in an unprotected area (such as the open bed of a pickup truck or an apartment where the officer already has obtained legal access) the officer may seize the item so long as there is probable cause to believe that it is contraband or evidence of a crime or otherwise subject to seizure. If the item is located in a protected area (such as the interior of a building that the officer observes from a point outside), most courts require the officer to obtain a search warrant or to explain why an exception to the warrant requirement is necessary. See Coolidge v. New Hampshire, 403 U.S. 443 (1971) (warrantless seizure of item in plain view is acceptable if officer observes item from lawful location, the discovery is inadvertent, its incriminating nature is immediately apparent, and officer has lawful right of access to the object).

3. *Incriminating nature of the item in plain view.* State and federal courts also require that the incriminating nature of the item in plain view be "immediately apparent" before the officer can seize an item in plain view. When the item in plain view is an illicit drug or other contraband, the incriminating nature of the item is easy to see. In other cases, the incriminating nature of the item might not be apparent to the average observer, but the police officer conducting the search will often know enough about the ongoing investigation to link the items she sees to the crime she is investigating. See State v. Chrisman, 514 N.W.2d 57 (Iowa 1994) (tennis shoes incriminating in light of footprints at crime scene). The incriminating nature of the item is "immediately apparent" if there is probable cause to believe that it is evidence of a crime.

4. *Police "inadvertence" in obtaining the plain view.* Under federal law and the law of most states, the police may observe and seize an item in plain view, even if the officer intended to find it. See Horton v. California, 496 U.S. 128 (1990):

> Evenhanded law enforcement is best achieved by the application of objective standards of conduct, rather than standards that depend upon the subjective state of mind of the officer. The fact that an officer is interested in an item of evidence and fully expects to find it in the course of a search should not invalidate its seizure if the search is confined in area and duration by the terms of a warrant or a valid exception to the warrant requirement.

Roughly 20 states take up a suggestion in older U.S. Supreme Court cases and insist that the police officer "inadvertently" discover the item in plain view before the officer can seize it. If the officer had reason to expect the discovery, he cannot seize the item. See Commonwealth v. Balicki, 762 N.E.2d 290 (Mass. 2002). Why don't most courts care about the motives of the police officer in obtaining the plain view? See State v. Nieves, 999 A.2d 389 (N.H. 2010). What police purpose might be objectionable? Is this debate over "inadvertence" the same as the disagreement reviewed above over "pretextual" stops, or are different interests at stake here?

5. *Plain smell and plain hearing.* If it is possible for an officer to notice an object in "plain view" without conducting a search, is it possible for the officer to notice a "plain smell" without conducting a search? There are cases in which the officer, standing in a proper location, smells something that creates some suspicion or evidence of a crime. State v. Rodriguez, 945 A.2d 676 (N.H. 2008) (officers who smell burning marijuana from exterior of residence need no warrant before entering; reviews divided case law on issue). The same can be said of an investigation based on something an officer hears when standing in a legally sanctioned location (plain hearing): There is no "search" here in the constitutional sense. We will consider the "plain feel" doctrine in section D of this chapter.

Problem 2-6. Plain View from a Ladder

Special Agent Forsythe became aware that football gambling forms were circulating in the town of Farrell. After receiving a tip about the source of the gambling forms, Forsythe began to keep watch at a local print shop. During one October evening, Forsythe noticed that the presses inside the shop were operating, but due to the location and size of the windows, he was unable to observe what was being printed from his position off the premises. The sills of the windows were 7 feet off the ground, so they prevented any view into the shop by someone standing on the ground outside the building. To remedy this problem, Forsythe mounted a 4-foot ladder that he placed on the railroad tracks abutting the print shop property. From a distance of 15 to 20 feet, he observed through a side window some "Las Vegas" football parlay sheets being run off the press. Did Agent Forsythe conduct a "search" within the meaning of state or federal constitutions? Compare Commonwealth v. Hernley, 263 A.2d 904 (Pa. Super. Ct. 1970).

Problem 2-7. The Friendly Skies

Officer Greg Bohlen, an undercover narcotics investigator, received an anonymous telephone call informing him that Bernard Henderson was cultivating and selling marijuana from his home. Bohlen watched the residence carefully for several days but did not observe any illegal activity. Several months later, another officer received a second anonymous call implicating Henderson in marijuana trafficking. Bohlen was unable to obtain a law enforcement helicopter to fly over the property, so he arranged for the use of a helicopter operated by a television station, KUSA. KUSA agreed to provide a helicopter to Officer Bohlen in exchange for the right to report on the drug investigation. On the morning of the scheduled flyover, Bohlen received another anonymous telephone call about Henderson, indicating that Henderson was growing five-foot-tall marijuana plants in a shed behind his house. Officer Bohlen, the helicopter pilot, and a photographer for KUSA made four or five passes over Henderson's residence during a period of approximately five minutes. Officer Bohlen observed a shed, located about 100 yards away from the house. The shed had a plastic roof with "green plant material" (as Bohlen later described it in a warrant application) growing underneath the plastic. Bohlen stated that the helicopter stayed between 500 and 700 feet in altitude. He based his altitude estimate on his experience flying in helicopters. Although he could not describe the plants in detail, based on his special education in drug identification and on his law enforcement experience, Officer Bohlen concluded that the plants were marijuana. A later warranted search of the property and the house produced marijuana plants, along with guns, scales, and other drug paraphernalia. The defendant has filed a motion to suppress the evidence. Will the judge grant it? Compare Henderson v. People, 879 P.2d 383 (Colo. 1994).

Notes

1. *Flyovers and reasonable expectations of privacy: majority position.* Recall that under the Fourth Amendment and its state equivalents, the government has not engaged in a search if it has invaded no "reasonable expectation of privacy." One difficult question about the definition of a search arises when government agents place themselves in unusual — but not necessarily illegal — positions for observing wrongdoing. A situation of this sort that appears frequently in appellate cases is the "flyover" of property by police officers searching for evidence of a crime.

In Florida v. Riley, 488 U.S. 445 (1988), the Supreme Court determined that police observing the defendant's backyard from a helicopter flying in legal airspace did not conduct a search for Fourth Amendment purposes. The defendant lived in a mobile home located on five acres of property. A greenhouse near the residence was obscured from view by a fence, trees, and shrubs. As the result of an anonymous tip, a police helicopter made two passes over the property at an altitude of 400 feet. The observing officer viewed what he thought was marijuana growing in the greenhouse, because two roof panels were missing. One of the primary factors in determining whether the defendant's expectation of privacy was unreasonable was that the helicopter was flying in navigable airspace within the Federal Aviation Administration guidelines. Thus, the Court relied on the fact that the observation itself was legal. The Court also considered the minimal intrusiveness of the observations: the helicopter never "interfered with respondent's normal use of the greenhouse or other parts of the curtilage." Furthermore, "no intimate details connected with the use of the home or curtilage were observed, and there was no undue noise, and no wind, dust, or threat of injury." See also California v. Ciraolo, 476 U.S. 207 (1986) (no search when police officer observes property from fixed-wing aircraft 1,000 feet above property in legal airspace). Do you believe the Supreme Court should have ruled in *Ciraolo* and *Riley* that the government conducted a search? Should the answer depend on whether the police have routine access to helicopters and planes?

Virtually all state courts have agreed with the U.S. Supreme Court's view that a flyover is not a "search" so long as the police aircraft stays within airspace where private aircraft could travel and does not create too much noise, dust, or threat of injury. But see State v. Bryant, 2008 VT 39 (Vt. 2008) (police needed to obtain warrant before helicopter flyover of residential property in search of marijuana, based on reading of state constitution). How might a defendant dispute the government's factual claim about the flight pattern of the aircraft?

2. *Subjective expectations of privacy.* Many courts asking whether government agents have engaged in a search employ a two-part analysis taken from the concurring opinion of Justice Harlan in Katz v. United States, 389 U.S. 347 (1967). A litigant hoping to establish a "search" under the Fourth Amendment must meet "a twofold requirement, first that a person [has] exhibited an actual (subjective) expectation of privacy and, second, that the expectation be one that society is prepared to recognize as 'reasonable.'" Later opinions of the U.S. Supreme Court and of state courts repeat this formulation, but they also suggest that the objective component alone might be enough: a subjective expectation of privacy will not always be a precondition to a conclusion that a search has occurred. See United States v. White, 401 U.S. 745 (1971). Could you imagine courts holding otherwise, that is, insisting on a subjective expectation of privacy before finding that a search took place?

3. *Legal entitlement versus likelihood of observation.* Suppose a litigant could show that flyovers at 500 feet above the property in question are very rare. In what way would this be relevant to the definition of a search? Would such a defendant need to argue that there is a legitimate expectation of lax enforcement of the narcotics laws? Could there be some moral (but extralegal) objection to the police conduct that makes more reasonable an expectation of avoiding such scrutiny?

4. *Police observation versus public observation.* Let us assume that reasonable and law-abiding people leave some things visible to a few members of the public that they would rather not expose to the sustained scrutiny of the police. Can police officers make observations from any place open to the public, or should they be expected to remain outside some areas open to some members of the public? Does the defendant's argument on the "search" issue get stronger when police officers

flying over a property must apply their expertise to interpret what they see below (such as an assertion that a building is "typical" of those used to grow marijuana)?

5. *Other sense enhancements.* So long as the government agent remains in a position properly available to her, many state courts allow the agent to use various devices to get a clearer or closer look at the items in plain view. The clearest cases involve commonly used devices such as flashlights. See State v. Brooks, 446 S.E.2d 579 (N.C. 1994) (officer walking up to car and shining light inside is not a search). A few state and federal courts have been willing to go farther, allowing government agents to use vision-enhancing devices not readily available to most viewers. See Dow Chemical Co. v. United States, 476 U.S. 227 (1986) (no search when agents in airplane over chemical plant use precision aerial-mapping camera). See Chapter 7.

6. *Garbage and abandoned property.* Reasonable expectations of privacy do not attach to property or activities in "plain view" or "open view." Thus, efforts to see such property are not searches in the constitutional sense. The same can be said for property that a person has abandoned, even though it does not lie within plain view of the public or government agents.

The U.S. Supreme Court in California v. Greenwood, 486 U.S. 35 (1988), held that there is no reasonable expectation of privacy in trash put out for collection; thus, there is no constitutionally relevant search if government agents inspect the trash. Over half the states have adopted this same view. See State v. Sampson, 765 A.2d 629 (Md. 2001) (officer collected trash left at curb by suspected drug dealer for six days; not a search). A smaller group (fewer than a dozen) have held in various contexts that there is a reasonable expectation of privacy in garbage, while a good number of high state courts still have not confronted the issue. See Beltz v. State, 221 P.3d 328 (Alaska 2009) (expectation of privacy in garbage placed by curb is reasonable under state constitution).

Privacy interests in a home or building also extend to the area under the eaves and immediately surrounding the building, an area known as the "curtilage." Thus, it could matter where the trash is placed. If the police inspect garbage kept in containers beside a home prior to the day appointed for collection, have they conducted a "search"? For a survey of various state court holdings regarding garbage searches, see the web extension for this chapter at *http://www.crimpro.com/extension/ch02*.

Some have pointed out that the government, under the reasoning of *Greenwood*, can defeat a widely shared expectation of privacy simply by announcing that it plans to conduct a particular form of investigation, thus defeating any expectation of privacy. See Anthony G. Amsterdam, Perspectives on the Fourth Amendment, 58 Minn. L. Rev. 349, 384 (1974). If most Americans today still have an expectation of privacy in their curbside garbage bags, isn't there a reasonable expectation of privacy regardless of what the Supreme Court held in *Greenwood*? See Christopher Slobogin & Joseph Schumacher, Reasonable Expectations of Privacy and Autonomy in Fourth Amendment Cases: An Empirical Look at "Understandings Recognized and Permitted by Society," 42 Duke L.J. 727 (1993) (public survey measuring perceived intrusiveness of various investigative techniques). Should the courts announce decisions about reasonable expectations of privacy on a tentative basis, and overrule themselves if most people don't take the decision to heart?

7. *Computer "trash" cans.* Most electronic message systems allow the computer user to delete messages, but the deleted messages are recoverable until further events take place (e.g., the user turns off the system, or some manager of the

computer system empties the electronic "trash can"). Similarly, it is possible under some circumstances to recover copies of electronic documents or files that a user has attempted to delete. If the government discovers evidence of a crime in these deleted but recoverable messages or files, was there a search at all? If there was a search, was it justified by implied consent?

D. BRIEF SEARCHES OF INDIVIDUALS

The police conduct a great variety of searches, ranging from brief and less intrusive searches of persons or property, up to extensive and very invasive searches. The number of legal standards — constitutional and otherwise — available to limit these searches is not nearly so large. As you read in this section about brief searches of individuals, consider whether the fit between police practices and available legal standards is sufficiently tight and whether different legal standards are likely to change actual behavior.

1. *Frisks for Weapons*

Police encounter people every day who carry hidden handguns. One time-honored police response to this threat is the "frisk," a brief search of a suspect's body. The frisk was a reality long before American courts resolved the question of whether or how the law would regulate the practice. The following case lays out the constitutional controls over frisks, controls at work in every U.S. jurisdiction.

■ JOHN TERRY v. OHIO

392 U.S. 1 (1968)

WARREN, C.J.*

This case presents serious questions concerning the role of the Fourth Amendment in the confrontation on the street between the citizen and the policeman investigating suspicious circumstances.

Petitioner Terry was convicted of carrying a concealed weapon. [The] prosecution introduced in evidence two revolvers and a number of bullets seized from Terry and a codefendant, Richard Chilton, by Cleveland Police Detective Martin McFadden. At the hearing on the motion to suppress this evidence, Officer McFadden testified that while he was patrolling in plain clothes in downtown Cleveland at approximately 2:30 in the afternoon, [he noticed two men, Chilton and Terry, who "didn't look right."] His interest aroused, Officer McFadden took up a post of observation in the entrance to a store 300 to 400 feet away from the two men. "I get more purpose to watch them when I seen their movements," he testified. [One of the men walked away from the corner and past some stores, paused for a moment

* [Justices Black, Brennan, Stewart, Fortas, and Marshall joined in this opinion. Justices Harlan and White concurred in the result. — EDS.]

and looked in a store window, then walked on a short distance, turned around and walked back toward the corner, pausing once again to look in the same store window. Then the second man went through the same series of motions. Each of the two men repeated this ritual five or six times. A third man, Katz, approached them and engaged them briefly in conversation, then walked away. Chilton and Terry resumed their earlier routine. After this had gone on for 10 to 12 minutes, the two men walked off together, following the route taken earlier by Katz.]

By this time Officer McFadden had become thoroughly suspicious. He testified that . . . he suspected the two men of "casing a job, a stick-up," and that he considered it his duty as a police officer to investigate further. He added that he feared "they may have a gun." Thus, Officer McFadden followed Chilton and Terry and saw them stop in front of Zucker's store to talk to [Katz]. Deciding that the situation was ripe for direct action, Officer McFadden approached the three men, identified himself as a police officer and asked for their names. . . . When the men "mumbled something" in response to his inquiries, Officer McFadden grabbed petitioner Terry, spun him around so that they were facing the other two, with Terry between McFadden and the others, and patted down the outside of his clothing. In the left breast pocket of Terry's overcoat Officer McFadden felt a pistol. He reached inside the overcoat pocket, but was unable to remove the gun. At this point, keeping Terry between himself and the others, the officer ordered all three men to enter Zucker's store. As they went in, he removed Terry's overcoat completely, removed a .38-caliber revolver from the pocket and ordered all three men to face the wall with their hands raised. Officer McFadden proceeded to pat down the outer clothing of Chilton and [Katz]. He discovered another revolver in the outer pocket of Chilton's overcoat, but no weapons were found on Katz. The officer testified that he only patted the men down to see whether they had weapons, and that he did not put his hands beneath the outer garments of either Terry or Chilton until he felt their guns. . . . Chilton and Terry were formally charged with carrying concealed weapons.

[The trial court concluded that McFadden did not have probable cause to search or arrest the men, but nonetheless upheld the validity of the search.] The court distinguished between an investigatory "stop" and an arrest, and between a "frisk" of the outer clothing for weapons and a full-blown search for evidence of crime. The frisk, it held, was essential to the proper performance of the officer's investigatory duties, for without it "the answer to the police officer may be a bullet, and a loaded pistol discovered during the frisk is admissible." [The court found Terry and Chilton guilty in a bench trial.]

I.

The Fourth Amendment provides that "the right of the people to be secure in their persons, houses, papers, and effects, against unreasonable searches and seizures, shall not be violated. . . ." This inestimable right of personal security belongs as much to the citizen on the streets of our cities as to the homeowner closeted in his study to dispose of his secret affairs. [However,] what the Constitution forbids is not all searches and seizures, but unreasonable searches and seizures. Unquestionably petitioner was entitled to the protection of the Fourth Amendment as he walked down the street in Cleveland. The question is whether in all the circumstances of this on-the-street encounter, his right to personal security was violated by an unreasonable search and seizure.

[It] is frequently argued that in dealing with the rapidly unfolding and often dangerous situations on city streets the police are in need of an escalating set of flexible responses, graduated in relation to the amount of information they possess. For this purpose it is urged that distinctions should be made between a "stop" and an "arrest" (or a "seizure" of a person), and between a "frisk" and a "search." Thus, it is argued, the police should be allowed to "stop" a person and detain him briefly for questioning upon suspicion that he may be connected with criminal activity. Upon suspicion that the person may be armed, the police should have the power to "frisk" him for weapons. If the "stop" and the "frisk" give rise to probable cause to believe that the suspect has committed a crime, then the police should be empowered to make a formal "arrest," and a full incident "search" of the person. This scheme is justified in part upon the notion that a "stop" and a "frisk" amount to a mere minor inconvenience and petty indignity, which can properly be imposed upon the citizen in the interest of effective law enforcement on the basis of a police officer's suspicion.

On the other side the argument is made that the authority of the police must be strictly circumscribed by the law of arrest and search as it has developed to date in the traditional jurisprudence of the Fourth Amendment. It is contended with some force that there is not — and cannot be — a variety of police activity which does not depend solely upon the voluntary cooperation of the citizen and yet which stops short of an arrest based upon probable cause to make such an arrest. The heart of the Fourth Amendment, the argument runs, is a severe requirement of specific justification for any intrusion upon protected personal security, coupled with a highly developed system of judicial controls to enforce upon the agents of the State the commands of the Constitution. Acquiescence by the courts in the compulsion inherent in the field interrogation practices at issue here, it is urged, would constitute an abdication of judicial control over, and indeed an encouragement of, substantial interference with liberty and personal security by police officers whose judgment is necessarily colored by their primary involvement in the often competitive enterprise of ferreting out crime. This, it is argued, can only serve to exacerbate police-community tensions in the crowded centers of our Nation's cities.

In this context we approach the issues in this case mindful of the limitations of the judicial function in controlling the myriad daily situations in which policemen and citizens confront each other on the street. . . . Street encounters between citizens and police officers are incredibly rich in diversity. They range from wholly friendly exchanges of pleasantries or mutually useful information to hostile confrontations of armed men involving arrests, or injuries, or loss of life. Moreover, hostile confrontations are not all of a piece. Some of them begin in a friendly enough manner, only to take a different turn upon the injection of some unexpected element into the conversation. Encounters are initiated by the police for a wide variety of purposes, some of which are wholly unrelated to a desire to prosecute for crime. . . .

II.

Our first task is to establish at what point in this encounter the Fourth Amendment becomes relevant. That is, we must decide whether and when Officer McFadden "seized" Terry and whether and when he conducted a "search." There is some suggestion in the use of such terms as "stop" and "frisk" that such police conduct is outside the purview of the Fourth Amendment because neither action rises to the level of a "search" or "seizure" within the meaning of the Constitution. We emphatically reject this notion. It is . . . nothing less than sheer torture of the English language to suggest that a careful exploration of the outer surfaces of a person's clothing all over his or her body in an attempt to find weapons is not a "search." . . . It is a serious intrusion upon the sanctity of the person, which may inflict great indignity and arouse strong resentment, and it is not to be undertaken lightly.

The danger in the logic which proceeds upon distinctions between a . . . "frisk" and a "search" is twofold. It seeks to isolate from constitutional scrutiny the initial stages of the contact between the policeman and the citizen. And by suggesting a rigid all-or-nothing model of justification and regulation under the Amendment, it obscures the utility of limitations upon the scope, as well as the initiation, of police action as a means of constitutional regulation. [A] search which is reasonable at its inception may violate the Fourth Amendment by virtue of its intolerable intensity and scope. The scope of the search must be strictly tied to and justified by the circumstances which rendered its initiation permissible. . . .

In this case there can be no question, then, that Officer McFadden "seized" petitioner and subjected him to a "search" when he took hold of him and patted down the outer surfaces of his clothing. We must decide whether at that point it was reasonable for Officer McFadden to have interfered with petitioner's personal security as he did. And in determining whether the seizure and search were "unreasonable" our inquiry is a dual one — whether the officer's action was justified at its inception, and whether it was reasonably related in scope to the circumstances which justified the interference in the first place.

III.

If this case involved police conduct subject to the Warrant Clause of the Fourth Amendment, we would have to ascertain whether "probable cause" existed to justify the search and seizure which took place. However, that is not the case. We do not retreat from our holdings that the police must, whenever practicable, obtain advance judicial approval of searches and seizures through the warrant procedure, or that in most instances failure to comply with the warrant requirement can only be excused by exigent circumstances. But we deal here with an entire rubric of police conduct — necessarily swift action predicated upon the on-the-spot observations of the officer on the beat — which historically has not been, and as a practical matter could not be, subjected to the warrant procedure. Instead, the conduct involved in this case must be tested by the Fourth Amendment's general proscription against unreasonable searches and seizures.

Nonetheless, the notions which underlie both the warrant procedure and the requirement of probable cause remain fully relevant in this context. In order to assess the reasonableness of Officer McFadden's conduct as a general proposition, it is necessary first to focus upon the governmental interest which allegedly justifies official intrusion upon the constitutionally protected interests of the private citizen, for there is no ready test for determining reasonableness other than by balancing the need to search [or seize] against the invasion which the search or seizure entails. And in justifying the particular intrusion the police officer must be able to point to specific and articulable facts which, taken together with rational inferences from those facts, reasonably warrant that intrusion. [When a judge assesses the reasonableness of a search or seizure,] it is imperative that the facts be judged against an objective standard: would the facts available to the officer at the moment of the seizure or the search warrant a man of reasonable caution in the belief that the action taken was appropriate? Anything less would invite intrusions upon constitutionally guaranteed rights based on nothing more substantial than inarticulate hunches, a result this Court has consistently refused to sanction. And simple good faith on the part of the arresting officer is not enough. If subjective good faith alone were the test, the protections of the Fourth Amendment would evaporate, and the people would be secure in their persons, houses, papers, and effects, only in the discretion of the police.

Applying these principles to this case, we consider first the nature and extent of the governmental interests involved. One general interest is of course that of effective crime prevention and detection; it is this interest which underlies the recognition that a police officer may in appropriate circumstances and in an appropriate manner approach a person for purposes of investigating possibly criminal behavior even though there is no probable cause to make an arrest. [In this case, it] would have been poor police work indeed for an officer of 30 years' experience in the detection of thievery from stores in this same neighborhood to have failed to investigate this behavior further.

The crux of this case, however, is not the propriety of Officer McFadden's taking steps to investigate petitioner's suspicious behavior, but rather, whether there was justification for McFadden's invasion of Terry's personal security by searching him for weapons in the course of that investigation. We are now concerned with more than the governmental interest in investigating crime; in addition, there is the more immediate interest of the police officer in taking steps to assure himself that the person with whom he is dealing is not armed with a weapon that could unexpectedly and fatally be used against him. Certainly it would be unreasonable to require that police officers take unnecessary risks in the performance of their duties. American criminals have a long tradition of armed violence, and every year in this country many law enforcement officers are killed in the line of duty, and thousands more are wounded. Virtually all of these deaths and a substantial portion of the injuries are inflicted with guns and knives.

In view of these facts, we cannot blind ourselves to the need for law enforcement officers to protect themselves and other prospective victims of violence in situations where they may lack probable cause for an arrest. When an officer is justified in believing that the individual whose suspicious behavior he is investigating at close range is armed and presently dangerous to the officer or to others, it would appear to be clearly unreasonable to deny the officer the power to take necessary measures to determine whether the person is in fact carrying a weapon and to neutralize the threat of physical harm.

We must still consider, however, the nature and quality of the intrusion on individual rights which must be accepted if police officers are to be conceded the right to search for weapons in situations where probable cause to arrest for crime is lacking. Even a limited search of the outer clothing for weapons constitutes a severe, though brief, intrusion upon cherished personal security, and it must surely be an annoying, frightening, and perhaps humiliating experience. . . .

Petitioner does not argue that a police officer should refrain from making any investigation of suspicious circumstances until such time as he has probable cause to make an arrest; nor does he deny that police officers in properly discharging their investigative function may find themselves confronting persons who might well be armed and dangerous. Moreover, he does not say that an officer is always unjustified in searching a suspect to discover weapons. Rather, he says it is unreasonable for the policeman to take that step until such time as the situation evolves to a point where there is probable cause to make an arrest. When that point has been reached, petitioner would concede the officer's right to conduct a search of the suspect for weapons, fruits or instrumentalities of the crime, or "mere" evidence, incident to the arrest.

[The problem with this line of reasoning, however, is that] it fails to take account of traditional limitations upon the scope of searches, and thus recognizes no distinction in purpose, character, and extent between a search incident to an arrest and a limited search for weapons. The former, although justified in part by the acknowledged necessity to protect the arresting officer from assault with a concealed weapon, is also justified on other grounds, and can therefore involve a relatively extensive exploration of the person. A search for weapons in the absence of probable cause to arrest, however, must, like any other search, be strictly circumscribed by the exigencies which justify its initiation. Thus it must be limited to that which is necessary for the discovery of weapons which might be used to harm the officer or others nearby, and may realistically be characterized as something less than a "full" search, even though it remains a serious intrusion. . . .

Our evaluation of the proper balance that has to be struck in this type of case leads us to conclude that there must be a narrowly drawn authority to permit a reasonable search for weapons for the protection of the police officer, where he has reason to believe that he is dealing with an armed and dangerous individual, regardless of whether he has probable cause to arrest the individual for a crime. The officer need not be absolutely certain that the individual is armed; the issue is whether a reasonably prudent man in the circumstances would be warranted in the belief that his safety or that of others was in danger. And in determining whether the officer acted reasonably in such circumstances, due weight must be given, not to his inchoate and unparticularized suspicion or "hunch," but to the specific reasonable inferences which he is entitled to draw from the facts in light of his experience.

IV.

We must now examine the conduct of Officer McFadden in this case to determine whether his search and seizure of petitioner were reasonable, both at their inception and as conducted. He had observed Terry, together with Chilton and another man, acting in a manner he took to be preface to a "stick-up." We think on the facts and circumstances Officer McFadden detailed before the trial judge a reasonably prudent man would have been warranted in believing petitioner was armed and thus presented a threat to the officer's safety while he was investigating his suspicious behavior. The actions of Terry and Chilton were consistent with McFadden's hypothesis that these men were contemplating a daylight robbery — which, it is reasonable to assume, would be likely to involve the use of weapons. . . . We cannot say his decision at that point to seize Terry and pat his clothing for weapons was the product of a volatile or inventive imagination, or was undertaken simply as an act of harassment; the record evidences the tempered act of a policeman who in the course of an investigation had to make a quick decision as to how to protect himself and others from possible danger, and took limited steps to do so.

The manner in which the seizure and search were conducted is, of course, as vital a part of the inquiry as whether they were warranted at all. The Fourth Amendment proceeds as much by limitations upon the scope of governmental action as by imposing preconditions upon its initiation. . . . We need not develop at length in this case, however, the limitations which the Fourth Amendment places upon a protective seizure and search for weapons. These limitations will have to be developed in the concrete factual circumstances of individual cases. Suffice it to note that such a search, unlike a search without a warrant incident to a lawful arrest, is not justified by any need to prevent the disappearance or destruction of evidence of crime. The sole justification of the search in the present situation is the protection of the police officer and others nearby, and it must therefore be confined in scope to an intrusion reasonably designed to discover guns, knives, clubs, or other hidden instruments for the assault of the police officer.

The scope of the search in this case presents no serious problem in light of these standards. Officer McFadden patted down the outer clothing of petitioner and his two companions. He did not place his hands in their pockets or under the outer surface of their garments until he had felt weapons, and then he merely reached for and removed the guns. He never did invade Katz' person beyond the outer surfaces of his clothes, since he discovered nothing in his pat-down which might have been a weapon. Officer McFadden confined his search strictly to what was minimally necessary to learn whether the men were armed and to disarm them once he discovered the weapons. He did not conduct a general exploratory search for whatever evidence of criminal activity he might find.

V.

We conclude that the revolver seized from Terry was properly admitted in evidence against him. . . . Each case of this sort will, of course, have to be decided on its own facts. We merely hold today that where a police officer observes unusual conduct which leads him reasonably to conclude in light of his experience that criminal activity may be afoot and that the persons with whom he is dealing may be armed and presently dangerous, where in the course of investigating this behavior he identifies himself as a policeman and makes reasonable inquiries, and where nothing in the initial stages of the encounter serves to dispel his reasonable fear for his own or others' safety, he is entitled for the protection of himself and others in the area to conduct a carefully limited search of the outer clothing of such persons in an attempt to discover weapons which might be used to assault him. Such a search is a reasonable search under the Fourth Amendment, and any weapons seized may properly be introduced in evidence against the person from whom they were taken. Affirmed.

HARLAN, J., concurring.

[If] the frisk is justified in order to protect the officer during an encounter with a citizen, the officer must first have constitutional grounds to insist on an encounter, to make a forcible stop. . . . Where such a stop is reasonable, however, the right to frisk must be immediate and automatic if the reason for the stop is, as here, an articulable suspicion of a crime of violence. Just as a full search incident to a lawful arrest requires no additional justification, a limited frisk incident to a lawful stop must often be rapid and routine. There is no reason why an officer, rightfully but forcibly confronting a person suspected of a serious crime, should have to ask one question and take the risk that the answer might be a bullet. . . . Upon the foregoing premises, I join the opinion of the Court.

DOUGLAS, J., dissenting.

[Frisking] petitioner and his companions for guns was a "search." But it is a mystery how that "search" . . . can be constitutional by Fourth Amendment standards, unless there was "probable cause" to believe that (1) a crime had been committed or (2) a crime was in the process of being committed or (3) a crime was about to be committed.

The opinion of the Court disclaims the existence of "probable cause." If loitering were in issue and that was the offense charged, there would be "probable cause" shown. But the crime here is carrying concealed weapons; and there is no basis for concluding that the officer had "probable cause" for believing that that crime was being committed. Had a warrant been sought, a magistrate would, therefore, have been unauthorized to issue one, for he can act only if there is a showing of "probable cause." We hold today that the police have greater authority to make a "seizure" and conduct a "search" than a judge has to authorize such action. We have said precisely the opposite over and over again.

In other words, police officers up to today have been permitted to effect arrests or searches without warrants only when the facts within their personal knowledge would satisfy the constitutional standard of probable cause. At the time of their "seizure" without a warrant they must possess facts concerning the person arrested that would have satisfied a magistrate that "probable cause" was indeed present. The term "probable cause" rings a bell of certainty that is not sounded by phrases such as "reasonable suspicion." Moreover, the meaning of "probable cause" is deeply imbedded in our constitutional history. . . .

The infringement on personal liberty of any "seizure" of a person can only be "reasonable" under the Fourth Amendment if we require the police to possess "probable cause" before they seize him. Only that line draws a meaningful distinction between an officer's mere inkling and the presence of facts within the officer's personal knowledge which would convince a reasonable man that the person seized has committed, is committing, or is about to commit a particular crime. . . .

To give the police greater power than a magistrate is to take a long step down the totalitarian path. Perhaps such a step is desirable to cope with modern forms of lawlessness. But if it is taken, it should be the deliberate choice of the people through a constitutional amendment. Until the Fourth Amendment . . . is rewritten, the person and the effects of the individual are beyond the reach of all government agencies until there are reasonable grounds to believe (probable cause) that a criminal venture has been launched or is about to be launched.

There have been powerful hydraulic pressures throughout our history that bear heavily on the Court to water down constitutional guarantees and give the police the upper hand. That hydraulic pressure has probably never been greater than it is today. Yet if the individual is no longer to be sovereign, if the police can pick him up whenever they do not like the cut of his jib, if they can "seize" and "search" him in their discretion, we enter a new regime. The decision to enter it should be made only after a full debate by the people of this country.

Notes

1. *Frisks for weapons: majority position.* The *Terry* opinion addressed both stops and frisks, and approved a framework already in place in some states at that point. It allowed the police to seize a person for a short time based on reasonable suspicion. We explored this question in section A of this chapter. But the Court considered the brief search — the frisk — to be the "crux" of this case. On the question of frisks, *Terry* has been very influential in the state systems; all the states now approve of frisks for weapons based on some justification less than probable cause. The majority take this position by statute, while others authorize such frisks through judicial rulings. An elaborate body of law in the state courts defines the boundaries of where an officer may search during a frisk, and what techniques he or she may use to identify what they feel inside the clothing. An exploration of these topics appears on the web extension for this chapter at *http://www.crimpro.com/extension/ch02*.

2. *Grounds for a* Terry *search.* Exactly what justification must an officer have before she performs a pat-down search? Why do both Chief Justice Warren and Justice Harlan distinguish between the justification needed for the initial stop and the justification needed for the brief search? Was Justice Douglas right to be concerned that government agents could manipulate too easily any standard less than probable cause?

Some state courts have declared that the police automatically have reasonable suspicion to frisk a person suspected of involvement in drug crimes and burglary. See State v. Evans, 618 N.E.2d 162, 169 (Ohio 1993); State v. Scott, 405 N.W.2d 829, 832 (Iowa 1987). Does the *Terry* opinion leave room for courts to make categorical judgments about reasonable suspicion to frisk, or does it require individualized findings in each case?

3. *Prevalence of frisks.* How often do frisks happen? According to a nationwide survey in 2005, police officers searched 4.8 percent of the drivers they stopped. Bureau of Justice Statistics, Contacts Between Police and the Public, 2005 (April 2007). Police officers in the New York City Police Department conducted 575,304 stops during 2009. The number was up from 97,296 in 2002, more than a fivefold increase in stops during a period when crime rates remained flat. Almost 490,000 of the people stopped were black or Latino, numbers disproportionate to the racial composition of the city population. See *http://www.nyc.gov/html/nypd/html/analysis_and_planning/stop_question_and_frisk_report.shtml.* A spokesperson for the NYPD explained that the stops increased because of a deliberate increased emphasis on enforcement of weapons laws. See Al Baker, Minorities Frisked More But Arrested at Same Rate, N.Y. Times, May 10, 2010. How would you go about determining how often your local police department conducts frisks?

4. Terry *searches before* Terry. Do you believe that police officers frisked suspects based on something less than probable cause before Detective McFadden decided to do so in Cleveland in 1963? Police officers in some states had statutes or department rules explicitly authorizing them to search for weapons without probable cause to arrest. The Uniform Arrest Act of 1942 provided that a "peace officer may search for a dangerous weapon any person whom he has stopped or detained to question . . . whenever he has reasonable ground to believe that he is in danger if the person possesses a dangerous weapon." Rule 470 of the Chicago Police Department

in 1933 also recognized a brief search for weapons without having probable cause: "[When] stopping and questioning a suspicious character [the police officer] shall be on guard against the use of any concealed or deadly weapon by such person. He shall be justified at such times in passing his hands over the clothing for the purpose of finding any deadly weapons." Many other police departments allowed frisks based on grounds less than probable cause but never openly acknowledged the practice.

Only a handful of state courts before 1968 ever explicitly addressed whether police could perform these brief searches without probable cause, with a slight majority of courts approving of the practice. Why did the issue not arise in the Supreme Court until 1968? See Wayne LaFave, "Street Encounters" and the Constitution: *Terry, Sibron, Peters,* and Beyond, 67 Mich. L. Rev. 40 (1968).

5. *The law and self-preservation.* Did the Supreme Court have any choice other than to approve of brief searches for weapons? If police officers felt that their lives were in jeopardy, would they not carry out the search regardless of the legal consequences? If Justice Douglas had written the opinion for the Court, what would have been the impact of the decision on police behavior and on the law of criminal procedure?

6. *Frisks in foreign systems.* In Great Britain, the Police and Criminal Evidence Act of 1984 provides that a constable can stop and search a person in a "public place" based on "reasonable grounds for suspecting" a search will reveal stolen or contraband articles. This level of justification is the same for a full-blown arrest, but it seems to correspond more closely to the American "reasonable suspicion" standard than to the "probable cause" standard. According to the government-issued Code of Practice for the Exercise by Police Officers of the Statutory Powers of Stop and Search, §3.5, a "search" occurring in a "public place" must be limited to a search of the outer garments, while a more thorough search can occur at the police station. In what ways do these legal provisions differ from the law of frisks in the United States? Do you believe that police practices in Great Britain reflect these differences in law? The law in France authorizes the police to conduct an identity check procedure that resembles the American stop and frisk, but the French procedure does not require individualized suspicion and may last up to four hours. See Richard S. Frase, Comparative Criminal Justice as a Guide to American Law Reform: How Do the French Do It, How Can We Find Out, and Why Should We Care? 78 Cal. L. Rev. 542, 576 (1990).

2. *The Scope of a Terry Search*

The frisk for weapons in *Terry* proceeds on a reduced level of justification (reasonable suspicion) because of the especially urgent nature of the government's objective in that setting (the safety of the officer and others in the area) and the limited nature of the search. Could a search based on reasonable suspicion also serve other, non-safety purposes, such as collecting evidence of a crime? What if the search is a bit more intrusive than a weapons frisk? In short, how far do *Terry* searches extend?

COMMONWEALTH v. ROOSEVELT WILSON

805 N.E.2d 968 (Mass. 2004)

COWIN, J.

. . . On the night of October 24, 2000, the Brockton police received a telephone call from a person who stated, "This is Stella's Pizza." The caller reported that a person was being beaten with a hammer or being stabbed in a group of ten people huddled across the street from the small commercial area where the pizza parlor was located. A police radio dispatch was broadcast containing this information, and State Trooper Francis Walls, alone in his unmarked vehicle and dressed in plain clothes, was the first officer to arrive at the scene. Walls stopped a short distance from the commercial area, saw a group of nine or ten men standing in a circle, but detected no suspicious activity. He was familiar with the area as one where he had made numerous arrests for drug and weapon violations and fights.

When he saw a backup vehicle close by, Walls pulled up to the group of men. As he got out of his vehicle, Walls made eye contact with the defendant. On making eye contact, the defendant turned, started walking away from Walls, and put his hand "to his waist area." The defendant's back was toward Walls, who, at this point, was concerned that the defendant possessed a gun. Walls grabbed the defendant by the back of his shirt and simultaneously placed his hand on "the area of the defendant's waist" where the defendant's hand had been. As soon as Walls put his hand on the defendant's waist, he felt a bundle of smaller packages, which he recognized by feel as "dime" bags of marijuana. Walls immediately asked the defendant, "You did that for weed? I thought you were putting a gun in your pants." The defendant responded that he did not "mess with guns." Walls retrieved the bag from the defendant's waist and handcuffed him.

Two backup officers, also in an unmarked vehicle and in plain clothes, were getting out of their vehicle as Walls stopped and frisked the defendant. No evidence was found of the assault or beating that had been the subject of the radio dispatch. The defendant was arrested, and an inventory search revealed that in addition to the seized "dime" bags of marijuana, a pager, a cellular telephone, and $476 in cash were in his possession. . . .

The defendant claims that the police lacked the requisite reasonable suspicion to stop him and to initiate a patfrisk. In "stop and frisk" cases our inquiry is two-fold: first, whether the initiation of the investigation by the police was permissible in the circumstances, and, second, whether the scope of the search was justified by the circumstances. In both aspects, the inquiry is whether the police conduct was reasonable under the Fourth Amendment.

In regard to the stop, a police officer may make an investigatory stop where suspicious conduct gives the officer reasonable ground to suspect that a person is committing, has committed, or is about to commit a crime. Concerning the second part of the analysis, a *Terry*-type patfrisk incident to the investigatory stop is permissible where the police officer reasonably believes that the individual is armed and dangerous. Terry v. Ohio, 392 U.S. 1 (1968). The officer's action in both the stop and the frisk must be based on specific and articulable facts and reasonable inferences therefrom, in light of the officer's experience.

Applying these principles to the facts in this case, we first consider the stop. The defendant was seized (or stopped) when Walls grabbed the back of his shirt. At that time, specific and articulable facts supported Walls's belief that the defendant had committed a crime. Walls was responding to a radio dispatch that described ten people involved in a stabbing or beating with a weapon outside Stella's Pizza. On arriving at the location, an area of Brockton where Walls had made numerous arrests for fights and weapon violations, Walls's observations confirmed a group of men huddled on the sidewalk, just as the caller had described. As he left his vehicle, Walls made eye contact with the defendant, who immediately turned away from him, walked away from the group, and simultaneously moved his hand into his "waist area." [Walls testified at the motion hearing that "As soon as he looked at me, he turned around and took his right hand and placed it into his pant line . . . ."] The totality of these facts supports a reasonable belief that the defendant had been involved in a fight with a weapon, and therefore, the stop was proper. The same facts justify the patfrisk, as they establish a reasonable belief that the defendant was armed and dangerous and presented a threat to the officer or others. . . .

The defendant next argues that Walls exceeded the scope of the patfrisk by "exploring" and seizing the package of marijuana he discovered in the defendant's waistband after he had determined it contained no weapon. The scope of a *Terry* search cannot be general; rather it is strictly tied to the circumstances that render its initiation permissible. The Fourth Amendment permits a police officer to conduct a patfrisk for concealed weapons, provided that such a search is confined to what is minimally necessary to learn whether the suspect is armed and to disarm him should weapons be discovered. Terry v. Ohio, 392 U.S. 1, 29-30 (1968).

In Minnesota v. Dickerson, 508 U.S. 366 (1993), the Supreme Court concluded that a police officer may also seize nonthreatening contraband discovered during a *Terry*-type frisk if the "police officer lawfully pats down a suspect's outer clothing and feels an object whose contour or mass makes its identity [as contraband] immediately apparent." If the officer must manipulate or otherwise further physically explore the concealed object in order to discern its identity, then an unconstitutional search has occurred.

The scope of a *Terry* search is not exceeded if, during a lawful patfrisk, it is immediately apparent to the police officer, in light of the officer's training and experience, that a concealed item is contraband. The "plain feel" doctrine is grounded on the same premise that authorizes an officer to frisk the suspect for concealed weapons, i.e., that the weapon will be immediately detected through touch during the patfrisk. As long as the object's contraband identity is immediately apparent to the officer, there is no further "invasion of the suspect's privacy beyond that already authorized by the officer's search for weapons." The "plain feel" doctrine is limited; it does not permit an officer to conduct a general exploratory search for whatever evidence of criminal activity he might find. The contraband nature of the item must be immediately apparent on touch. For these reasons, we conclude that the "plain feel" doctrine is consistent with art. 14, as well as with the Fourth Amendment.

[Several States have adopted the "plain feel" doctrine. See, e.g., People v. Mitchell, 650 N.E.2d 1014 (Ill. 1995); People v. Champion, 549 N.W.2d 849 (Mich. 1996); Commonwealth v. Zhahir, 751 A.2d 1153 (Pa. 2000). Although the Court of Appeals of New York rejected the doctrine, that court did so prior to the Supreme Court's decision in Minnesota v. Dickerson. See People v. Diaz, 612 N.E.2d 298 (N.Y. 1993).]

We consider "plain feel" as analogous to "plain view." As long as the initial search is lawful, the seizure of an item whose identity is already known occasions no further invasion of privacy. The only difference between the two doctrines is the sensory perception used to identify the contraband nature of the object. The "plain feel" doctrine merely recognizes that if contraband is immediately apparent by sense of touch, rather than sight, the police are authorized to seize it.

The "plain feel" doctrine is no more susceptible to fabrication than the "plain view" doctrine. The initial requirement, that the officer be conducting a valid pat-frisk of the suspect, ensures that the officer is lawfully in the position immediately to identify the contraband. Once an otherwise lawful search is in progress, the police may inadvertently discover contraband. Requiring an officer who recognizes contraband by "plain feel" to ignore this fact and walk away from the suspect without seizing the object flies in the face of logic. . . .

When we apply these principles to the facts here, Walls did not exceed the scope of the search because the judge found that it was immediately apparent to Walls when he touched the defendant's waist area that the object in the defendant's waistband was bundles of marijuana, and no manipulation was necessary to determine that fact. Contrast Minnesota v. Dickerson, 508 U.S. at 378-379 (scope of search unconstitutional where officer manipulated contents of defendant's pocket before discerning lump was contraband).

The defendant also contests the judge's finding that Walls knew the item in the defendant's waistband was drugs as soon as he touched it and did not manipulate it. The judge's finding is supported by record evidence. Walls repeatedly stated, despite thorough examination by the defense attorney, that he knew the identity of the object as soon as he touched it, without any manipulation ("The second I hit it, that's what I felt" . . .). Other testimony by Walls supports this finding: his seven years of experience as a State trooper, and his inquiry to the defendant made immediately on touching the object, "You did that for weed?"

Contrary to the defendant's argument that there was no evidence concerning Walls's training and experience in tactile detection of marijuana or its packaging, Walls stated that he has made numerous arrests for drug violations, has seized drugs, and was serving in the "gang unit." From all of this evidence, the judge could reasonably infer that Walls had sufficient personal experience in narcotics packaging and detection to identify immediately the object in the defendant's waistband. . . .

Holding

ARKANSAS RULE OF CRIMINAL PROCEDURE 3.4

If a law enforcement officer who has detained a person under Rule 3.1 reasonably suspects that the person is armed and presently dangerous to the officer or others, the officer or someone designated by him may search the outer clothing of such person and the immediate surroundings for, and seize, any weapon or other dangerous thing which may be used against the officer or others. In no event shall this search be more extensive than is reasonably necessary to ensure the safety of the officer or others.

■ MONTANA CODE §46-5-401(2)

A peace officer who has lawfully stopped a person [may] frisk the person and take other reasonably necessary steps for protection if the officer has reasonable cause to suspect that the person is armed and presently dangerous to the officer or another person present. The officer may take possession of any object that is discovered during the course of the frisk if the officer has probable cause to believe that the object is a deadly weapon until the completion of the stop, at which time the officer shall either immediately return the object, if legally possessed, or arrest the person.

Notes

1. *"Plain feel": majority position.* Under the "plain feel" or "plain touch" doctrine, if an officer conducts a properly circumscribed *Terry* search for weapons and feels an object that is not a weapon, the officer can seize the item if it is "immediately apparent" that the item is contraband or evidence of a crime. Minnesota v. Dickerson, 508 U.S. 366 (1993). Most state courts to consider the question also have adopted a "plain feel" doctrine under their state constitutions. See People v. Champion, 549 N.W.2d 849 (Mich. 1996). While accepting the basic contours of the doctrine, courts in about half the states apply it strictly. Courts have declared that commonplace items touched during a frisk cannot be seized, because it cannot be "immediately apparent" that the item is contraband or evidence. Murphy v. Commonwealth, 570 S.E.2d 836 (Va. 2002) ("plain feel" doctrine does not permit seizure of baggie containing marijuana felt during pat of outside surface of pants pocket); but cf. State v. Rushing, 935 S.W.2d 30 (Mo. 1996) (applying doctrine more leniently; confiscation of roll of breath mints felt during pat-down was justified because officer's training and experience revealed that breath mint rolls were common cocaine containers).

The high court in New York rejected the "plain touch" doctrine entirely under its state constitution. The court in People v. Diaz, 612 N.E.2d 298 (N.Y. 1993) explained its position as follows:

> The identity and criminal nature of a concealed object are not likely to be discernible upon a mere touch or pat within the scope of the intrusion authorized by *Terry.* While in most instances seeing an object will instantly reveal its identity and nature, touching is inherently less reliable and cannot conclusively establish an object's identity or criminal nature. Moreover, knowledge concerning an object merely from feeling it through an exterior covering is necessarily based on the police officer's expert opinion. . . .
>
> Finally, an opinion of a police officer that the object touched is evidence of criminality will predictably, at least in some circumstances, require a degree of pinching, squeezing or probing beyond the limited intrusion allowed under *Terry.* The proposed "plain touch" exception could thus invite a blurring of the limits to *Terry* searches and the sanctioning of warrantless searches on information obtained from an initial intrusion which, itself, amounts to an unauthorized warrantless search.

What kind of training — formal and informal — would you expect to occur within police departments in jurisdictions that adopt a "plain feel" rule? Should courts evaluate plain feel cases based on what a reasonable officer would know or on what the officer in question knew?

2. *Reasonable suspicion for non-weapons frisks?* The Supreme Court has insisted that a frisk of a person designed to obtain evidence of a crime cannot be based on reasonable suspicion; the officer must have probable cause that the evidence will be on the person, even if the brief search is no more intrusive than a weapons frisk. See Ybarra v. Illinois, 444 U.S. 85 (1979) (frisk of customer in bar where search warrant was being executed). How exactly will the courts make the distinction between permissible weapons frisks and impermissible evidence frisks?

3. *Frisk statutes.* Would the court in *Wilson* have decided the case any differently if a statute identical to the Arkansas statute had been in effect in Massachusetts? What outcome under the Montana statute? Are the police in a better position, generally speaking, in states with a frisk statute or in those where the authority to frisk is based entirely on judicial opinions?

4. *Are courts the agents of legislators or independent interpreters?* Suppose a court is convinced that a state statute regarding the scope of frisks is badly flawed because it does not authorize a frisk beyond the "outer clothing." Should the court feel free to "fix" the problem created by the legislature? Are there canons of construction that would allow a court to read this statute to allow more intrusive (and effective) frisks?

As we have seen earlier, courts look to several different sources of guidance in interpreting the meaning of ambiguous statutory language. They sometimes resort to canons of construction to determine the "plain meaning" of the statutory text. They also often consult the legislative history to determine the legislature's intent in passing the statute. Alternatively, they may refer to the statute's title or language to ascertain the legislative purpose. These different sources may point in different directions in a particular case. What weight will a court give to the various sources of guidance?

The answer to such a question depends on the court's objective: Does the court view itself as an agent of the legislature, or is the court to exercise its own best judgment about how to give meaning to the language? Courts have not agreed on this question. On the one hand, most probably adhere to the view that they interpret statutes as agents of the legislature, to put into effect what the legislators intended in a specific setting (or what they *would have* intended for the setting if they had thought of it). As Justice Oliver Wendell Holmes once stated, "If my fellow citizens want to go to Hell I will help them. It's my job." 1 Holmes-Laski Letters 249 (Mark DeWolfe Howe ed., 1953).

On the other hand, many courts *act* as if they have an independent responsibility to make sense of statutory language. Professor Ernst Freund captured this independent view of courts as interpreters of statutes with the following advice in 1917: "In cases of genuine ambiguity courts should use the power of interpretation consciously and deliberately to promote sound law and sound principles of legislation." Ernst Freund, Interpretation of Statutes, 65 U. Pa. L. Rev. 207 (1917). What objective of statutory interpretation would a court be endorsing if it were to interpret the Arkansas frisk statute to allow frisks of the person beyond the outer clothing?

5. *Purses, briefcases, and bags.* Police also commonly extend protective *Terry* searches to purses, briefcases, and other items a suspect might be holding at the time of a stop. Although the officer might reduce the danger of any weapons in a purse or bag by placing it well out of reach of the suspect, courts and police department rules have not uniformly required the police to do so. Cf. State v. Peterson, 110

P.3d 699 (Utah 2005) (officers could not pat down a jacket before giving it to detained person, who did not request jacket before going outdoors). The search must start with a "frisk" of the exterior of a cloth bag, and the officer may not open the bag to search its contents if the initial frisk confirms that there is no weapon inside.

Problem 2-8. Frisking Car and Driver

Around 12:30 A.M., police officers Josephine Copland and Jess Segundo were patrolling West Oliwood, investigating narcotics sales in that area. As they waited at an intersection for a traffic signal to change, they saw a red Lexus drive through the intersection with a taillight burned out. Officers Copland and Segundo immediately stopped the Lexus, although they typically would not stop a car based only on a problem with the taillight.

When the driver, Steven Worth, pulled over and stopped, he started to move about the inside the vehicle, back and forth in the front seat, and ducked down below the seat. When Officers Copland and Segundo exited their cruiser and approached on foot, they ordered Worth to step out of his vehicle.

Officer Copland ordered Worth to move away from his vehicle, and began examining the interior of the Lexus. She looked around and under the seats and found nothing suspicious. Officer Copland then opened the glove compartment and found what looked to her like a hand-rolled cigarette. Upon picking up and examining the cigarette, she discovered it was filled with tobacco. Officer Copland reached over and lifted the lever next to the driver's seat to disengage the trunk latch. Moving outside to the back of the car, she looked inside the trunk and found an expensive-looking set of golf clubs inside a golf bag. Officer Copland noticed a number of bulges within the golf bag, and she began to unzip the bag's various pockets. In the largest pocket, which ran the length of the bag, Copland discovered a sawed-off shotgun.

Meanwhile, Officer Segundo was examining Worth. She performed a pat-down search of Worth's outer clothing. As part of this frisk, Officer Segundo patted down the knit stocking cap Worth wore, which was rolled over on the edges. Officer Segundo felt a hard object on the right side of Worth's hat. Officer Segundo was not sure what this hard object was, and she reached inside the hat. Grabbing the hard object with her fingers, she felt what she believed (based upon her previous experience) to be crack cocaine. Officer Segundo then removed two pieces of suspected crack cocaine from the hat and arrested Worth for possession of that illegal substance.

Steven Worth was charged with possession of crack cocaine and with possession of an illegal firearm. He filed a motion prior to trial asking the court to suppress the gun recovered from the golf bag and the drugs recovered from his stocking cap. How would you argue in support of the motion?

Problem 2-9. Duty to Cooperate?

The sheriff's department in Humboldt County, Nevada, received an afternoon telephone call reporting an assault. The caller reported seeing a man assault a woman in a red and silver GMC truck on Grass Valley Road. Deputy Sheriff Lee

Dove was dispatched to investigate. When Dove arrived at the scene, he found the truck parked on the side of the road. A man was standing by the truck, and a young woman was sitting inside it. Dove observed skid marks in the gravel behind the vehicle, leading him to believe it had come to a sudden stop.

The officer approached the man, Larry Dudley Hiibel, and explained that he was investigating a report of a fight. Hiibel appeared to be intoxicated. The officer asked him if he had "any identification." Hiibel refused to provide any identification and asked why the officer wanted to see it. Dove responded that he was conducting an investigation (but did not specify the alleged crime he was investigating) and needed to see some identification. Hiibel became agitated and insisted he had done nothing wrong. The officer insisted that he needed to find out who Hiibel was and what he was doing there. After repeated refusals to give the officer any identification, Hiibel became more belligerent, placing his hands behind his back and telling the officer to arrest him and take him to jail, because he would not provide any identification. This routine kept up for several minutes: the officer asked for identification 11 times and was refused each time. During this time, two other officers arrived on the scene. After warning Hiibel that he would be arrested if he continued to refuse to comply, Dove placed Hiibel under arrest.

When Hiibel's daughter shouted her protests over the arrest of her father, three officers removed her from the pickup, pushed her to the ground, handcuffed her, and placed her under arrest as well.

The state charged Hiibel with "willfully resisting, delaying, or obstructing a public officer in discharging or attempting to discharge any legal duty of his office" in violation of Nev. Rev. Stat. (NRS) §199.280. In the trial court, Deputy Dove explained his thinking this way:

> During my conversation with Mr. Hiibel, there was a point where he became somewhat aggressive. I felt based on me not being able to find out who he was, to identify him, I didn't know if he was wanted or what his situation was, I wasn't able to determine what was going on crimewise in the vehicle, based on that I felt he was intoxicated, and how he was becoming aggressive and moody, I went ahead and put him in handcuffs so I could secure him for my safety, and put him in my patrol vehicle.

The government reasoned that Hiibel had obstructed Deputy Dove in carrying out his duties under §171.123:

> 1. Any peace officer may detain any person whom the officer encounters under circumstances which reasonably indicate that the person has committed, is committing or is about to commit a crime. . . .
>
> 3. The officer may detain the person pursuant to this section only to ascertain his identity and the suspicious circumstances surrounding his presence abroad. Any person so detained shall identify himself, but may not be compelled to answer any other inquiry of any peace officer.

Roughly 20 states have enacted similar "stop and identify" statutes. They permit an officer to ask or require a suspect to disclose his identity. A few states model their statutes on the Uniform Arrest Act, a model code that permits an officer to stop a person reasonably suspected of committing a crime and "demand of him his name, address, business abroad and whither he is going."

Hiibel was convicted and fined $250. Does the constitutional bar on "unreasonable searches and seizures" prevent this prosecution of Hiibel? Cf. Hiibel v. Sixth Judicial District Court, 542 U.S. 177 (2004).

Notes

1. Terry *searches of stopped cars.* Although a pat-down search of a person should expose any guns or other large weapons hidden in the clothing, a person stopped while riding in a car might hide a weapon somewhere in the vehicle. How can an officer protect herself from a suspect who keeps a weapon somewhere nearby, but not on his person? The U.S. Supreme Court, in Michigan v. Long, 463 U.S. 1032 (1983), stated that police officers who stop a vehicle and frisk the driver standing outside the car may conduct a further "protective" search of the passenger compartment and any containers inside it that might contain a large weapon such as a gun. Under the federal constitution, the police must have a reasonable suspicion that there may be weapons in the vehicle before the protective search takes place. Most state courts (all but about a half dozen) allow police to conduct protective searches of stopped cars, on terms identical to federal law. They allow the officers to conduct a protective search of the interior and any containers inside (but only those large enough to contain a weapon) if the officers reasonably suspect that there are dangerous weapons in the vehicle. These courts reason that the search of a vehicle is just as important to the officer's safety as a frisk of the person under *Terry.* See State v. Wilkins, 692 A.2d 1233 (Conn. 1997). However, the high court in New York decided in People v. Torres, 543 N.E.2d 61 (N.Y 1989), that police officers could not search the interior of a stopped vehicle for weapons based only on reasonable suspicion. The *Torres* court suggested that the officer stopping the vehicle can reduce any risk by separating the suspect from the vehicle. How might the majority of courts respond to this argument? Would you draw a distinction between a pat-down search of the driver and placing the driver into the patrol car during the stop? See Wilson v. State, 745 N.E.2d 789 (Ind. 2001) (pat-down search of motorist prior to placing him in police car during routine traffic stop violated Fourth Amendment; pat-down search was not supported by particularized reasonable suspicion that motorist was armed).

2. *Orders to exit a vehicle.* When an officer stops a vehicle, he will sometimes but not always ask the driver to get out of the vehicle, out of concern for his own safety. The U.S. Supreme Court has concluded that this intrusion on the driver is minimal and that the officer needs no justification (other than the reasonable suspicion necessary to stop the car) for ordering the driver to get out of the car. Pennsylvania v. Mimms, 434 U.S. 106 (1977); but see State v. Sprague, 824 A.2d 539 (Vt. 2003) (under state constitution, officer conducting routine traffic stop may not automatically order driver to exit vehicle). In Maryland v. Wilson, 519 U.S. 408 (1997), the court extended *Mimms* to hold that officers may order a *passenger* in the car to get out, without any grounds to believe that the passenger is dangerous. Some states previously had rejected that position. See State v. Smith, 637 A.2d 158 (N.J. 1994) (order to passenger to get out of car stopped for minor traffic infraction must be based on articulable suspicion that passenger poses danger). The great majority of

state courts follow both *Mimms* and *Wilson*. Cf. People v. Jackson, 45 P.3d 1237 (Colo. 2002) (police may request identification of passenger in stopped vehicle without individualized suspicion); but see State v. Mendez, 970 P.2d 722 (Wash. 1999). Should the police treat the driver and the passenger differently? Is one any more or less dangerous than the other? Is the intrusion on drivers and passengers the same?

Arizona v. Johnson, 129 S. Ct. 781 (2009), confirms that passengers in a stopped vehicle are also subject to frisk if officer has reasonable suspicion to believe a passenger is armed and dangerous, even if there is no reasonable suspicion that a passenger is involved in crime. In that case, an officer frisked a passenger suspected of membership in a gang whose members frequently carried weapons.

3. Terry *stops and requests for identification.* The Supreme Court in Hiibel v. Sixth Judicial District Court, 542 U.S. 177 (2004), upheld a suspect's conviction for failure to provide his name to an officer during an otherwise valid investigative stop:

> The request for identity has an immediate relation to the purpose, rationale, and practical demands of a *Terry* stop. The threat of criminal sanction helps ensure that the request for identity does not become a legal nullity. On the other hand, the Nevada statute does not alter the nature of the stop itself: it does not change its duration or its location. A state law requiring a suspect to disclose his name in the course of a valid *Terry* stop is consistent with Fourth Amendment prohibitions against unreasonable searches and seizures.

Before *Hiibel*, there was surprisingly little precedent (in either state or federal courts) on the question of whether the state could punish a citizen's refusal to answer an officer's questions during an investigatory stop. Does an effort to investigate and prevent acts of terrorism — an objective of criminal law enforcement that gained new urgency after September 11, 2001 — make this sort of questioning more common and more valuable?

Many states have enacted statutes that compel some level of cooperation with police officers during crime investigations. For a detailed discussion of these statutes, see Margaret Raymond, The Right to Refuse and the Obligation to Comply: Challenging the Gamesmanship Model of Criminal Procedure, 54 Buffalo L. R. 1483 (2007). Related questions involve the subjects a police officer may discuss with occupants of a vehicle after making a stop. An exploration of these topics appears on the web extension for this chapter at *http://www.crimpro.com/extension/ch02*.

The controversial Arizona immigration law enacted in 2010, SB 1070 (codified at A.R.S. §11-1051), creates a presumption of legal residency for people who carry specific identification. The text describes the presumption in these terms:

> A person is presumed to not be an alien who is unlawfully present in the United States if the person provides to the law enforcement officer or agency any of the following:
>
> 1. A valid Arizona driver license.
> 2. A valid Arizona non-operating identification license.
> 3. A valid tribal enrollment card or other form of tribal identification.
> 4. If the entity requires proof of legal presence in the United States before issuance, any valid United States federal, state or local government issued identification.

Arizona legislators declared that they did not intend for SB 1070 to enact a state version of the "Real ID" law, a 2005 federal law that set forth requirements for state driver's licenses and identification cards to be accepted by the federal government for "official purposes," as defined by the Secretary of Homeland Security. Is the new Arizona law in effect a statute requiring people to carry identification? Would it be a good idea for the law to require this of all people?

III

Full Searches of People and Places: Basic Concepts

We now move from brief searches and stops to more extended and complete searches. This chapter describes the origins of the Fourth Amendment and the language of analogous provisions in state constitutions. Then it introduces the three concepts that dominate the case law governing full searches: probable cause, warrants, and consent. Probable cause is the usual justification required to validate a full search. The judicial warrant is the procedure meant to ensure careful and early assessment of probable cause. To obtain a warrant, a government agent must demonstrate to a judge or magistrate, before the search happens, that the plan is justified. The last of the basic concepts, consent, may be the most important of all because police obtain consent from private parties for a large proportion of the searches they conduct. Following this chapter's survey of the most important tools for analyzing full searches, Chapter 4 applies these concepts in several contexts that recur time and again in judicial decisions and in the field.

A. ORIGINS OF THE FOURTH AMENDMENT AND ITS ANALOGS

The police force is a nineteenth-century invention; the repressive government officers that most infuriated the colonists were tax and customs inspectors. These officials often carried out their work by using general warrants, which were broad grants of authority from the king of England or his representatives to search homes and businesses. One goal of this section is to identify the characteristics of government searches that constitutional drafters found most objectionable. Many historians and judges say that Americans were especially concerned with "general warrants." Why were general warrants troubling to colonial lawyers? Did any other characteristics of government searches, apart from their reliance on general warrants, also draw colonial criticism?

1. General Search Warrants

In the 1760s, a series of English cases addressed the validity of general search warrants. The cases were civil tort actions against the individuals who issued and executed the warrants. The plaintiff in the following case, John Entick, published a series of pamphlets critical of the government. A minister of the government, Lord Halifax, considered the pamphlets libelous. He issued to his subordinates a "warrant" authorizing them to search for Entick (without specifying a place where they could look) and to seize him and his papers (without specifying which ones). Halifax's subordinates (or "messengers") executed the warrant and seized a great many of Entick's papers. Entick later brought a tort suit against Carrington, one of the messengers who had executed the warrant. The issue on appeal was whether the warrant was authorized by law (giving the searcher a legal defense) or was beyond the scope of the law, perhaps exposing those who created and executed the warrant to liability for the improper search.

■ JOHN ENTICK v. NATHAN CARRINGTON

95 Eng. Rep. 807 (K.B. 1765)

In trespass; the plaintiff declares that the defendants . . . broke and entered the dwelling-house of the plaintiff . . . and continued there four hours without his consent and against his will, and all that time disturbed him in the peaceable possession thereof, and . . . searched and examined all the rooms, &c. in his dwelling-house, and all the boxes &c. so broke open, and read over, pryed into, and examined all the private papers, books, &c. of the plaintiff there found, whereby the secret affairs, &c. of the plaintiff became wrongfully discovered and made public; and took and carried away . . . printed pamphlets, &c. &c. of the plaintiff there found. [The defendants say] the plaintiff ought not to have his action against them, because they say, that before the supposed trespass . . . the Earl of Halifax was, and yet is, one of the Lords of the King's Privy Council, and one of his principal Secretaries of State, and that the earl . . . made his warrant under his hand and seal directed to the defendants, by which the earl did in the King's name authorize and require the defendants, taking a constable to their assistance, to make strict and diligent search for the plaintiff, mentioned in the said warrant to be the author . . . of several weekly very seditious papers . . . containing gross and scandalous reflections and invectives upon His Majesty's Government, and upon both Houses of Parliament, and him the plaintiff having found, to seize and apprehend and bring together with his books and papers in safe custody, before the Earl of Halifax to be examined. [The defendants argued that such warrants have frequently been granted by Secretaries of State since the Glorious Revolution of 1688 and have never been controverted. The jury found that the agents of Lord Halifax had committed the acts described by the plaintiff and was willing to award damages of 3,000 pounds if the court concluded that these facts constituted a trespass.]

[We] shall now consider the special justification, whether [the defense to a tort claim for trespass] can be supported in law, and this depends upon the jurisdiction of the Secretary of State; for if he has no jurisdiction to grant a warrant to break open doors, locks, boxes, and to seize a man and all his books, &c. in the first instance upon an information of his being guilty of publishing a libel, the warrant will not justify the defendants: it was resolved . . . in the case of Shergold v. Holloway, that a justice's warrant expressly to arrest the party will not justify the officer, there being no jurisdiction. The warrant in our case was an execution in the first instance, without any previous summons, examination, hearing the plaintiff, or proof that he was the author of the supposed libels; a power claimed by no other magistrate whatever . . . ; it was left to the discretion of these defendants to execute the warrant in the absence or presence of the plaintiff, when he might have no witness present to see what they did; for they were to seize all papers, bank bills, or any other valuable papers they might take away if they were so disposed; there might be nobody to detect them.

[In the case of Wilkes v. Wood (1763), involving a member of the House of Commons who had published an attack on the King and his ministers], all his books and papers were seized and taken away; we were told by one of these messengers that he was obliged by his oath to sweep away all papers whatsoever; if this is law it would be found in our books, but no such law ever existed in this country; our law holds the property of every man so sacred, that no man can set his foot upon his neighbour's close without his leave; if he does he is a trespasser, though he does no damage at all; if he will tread upon his neighbour's ground, he must justify it by law. [We] can safely say there is no law in this country to justify the defendants in what they have done; if there was, it would destroy all the comforts of society; for papers are often the dearest property a man can have. This case was compared to that of stolen goods; . . . but in that case the justice and the informer must proceed with great caution; there must be an oath that the party has had his goods stolen, and his strong reason to believe they are concealed in such a place; but if the goods are not found there, he is a trespasser; the officer in that case is a witness; there are none in this case, no inventory taken; if it had been legal many guards of property would have attended it. We shall now consider the usage of these warrants since the [Glorious] Revolution [of 1688]; if it began then, it is too modern to be law; the common law did not begin with the Revolution; the ancient constitution which had been almost overthrown and destroyed, was then repaired and revived; the Revolution added a new buttress to the ancient venerable edifice. [This] is the first instance of an attempt to prove a modern practice of a private office to make and execute warrants to enter a man's house, search for and take away all his books and papers in the first instance, to be law, which is not to be found in our books. It must have been the guilt or poverty of those upon whom such warrants have been executed, that deterred or hindered them from contending against the power of a Secretary of State and the Solicitor of the Treasury, or such warrants could never have passed for lawful till this time. We are . . . all of opinion that it cannot be justified by law. [If] a man is punishable for having a libel in his private custody, as many cases say he is, half the kingdom would be guilty in the case of a favourable libel, if libels may be searched for and seized by whomsoever and wheresoever the Secretary of State thinks fit. . . . Our law is wise and merciful, and supposes every man accused to be innocent before he is tried by his peers: upon the whole, we are all of opinion that this warrant is wholly illegal and void. One word more for ourselves; we are no advocates for libels, all

Governments must set their faces against them, and whenever they come before us and a jury we shall set our faces against them; and if juries do not prevent them they may prove fatal to liberty, destroy Government and introduce anarchy; but tyranny is better than anarchy, and the worst Government better than none at all. Judgment for the plaintiff.

The English controversy in the 1760s over general warrants was familiar to American colonists. A similar practice was creating a popular uproar in the colonies at about this time. Customs agents of the English government, who enforced the highly unpopular and widely flouted tax laws for imports and exports, had all the powers of their English counterparts as they searched for taxable goods. Their power to search for goods sometimes took the form of "writs of assistance." Like a general warrant, the writ of assistance authorized the agent to search private premises, without specifying the place to search or the things to seize. These writs contained no real time limitation, for they expired only upon the death of the king. The writs also obligated all government officials and all subjects of the Crown to assist the customs agent in the search. A reporter of proceedings in the court in the Massachusetts Bay colony offers the following example of a 1755 application for a writ of assistance.

■ THE WRITS OF ASSISTANCE

Quincy's Rep. (Mass.) App., 1:402-04, 453

To the Honourable his Majestys Justices of his Superiour Court for said Province to be held at York in and for the County of York on the third Tuesday of June 1755.

HUMBLY SHEWS Charles Paxton Esqr: That he is lawfully authorized to Execute the Office of Surveyor of all Rates Duties and Impositions arising and growing due to his Majesty at Boston in this Province & cannot fully Exercise said Office in such Manner as his Majestys Service and the Laws in such Cases Require Unless Your Honours who are vested with the Power of a Court of Exchequer for this Province will please to Grant him a Writ of Assistants, he therefore prays he & his Deputys may be Aided in the Execution of said office within his District by a Writ of Assistants under the Seal of this Superiour Court in Legal form & according to Usage in his Majestys Court of Exchequer & in Great Britain, & your Petitioner &Ca:

CHAS PAXTON

[The court issued the writ in the following form:]

GEORGE the Second by the Grace of God of Great Britain, France and Ireland King, Defender of the Faith &c — To all and singular Justices of the Peace, Sheriffs and Constables, and to all other our officers and Subjects within said Prov. & to each of you Greeting —

WHEREAS the Commissioners of our Customs have by their Deputation dated the 8th day of Jany 1752, assignd Charles Paxton Esqr Surveyor of all Rates, Duties, and Impositions arising and growing due within the Port of Boston in said Province as by said Deputation at large appears, WE THEREFORE command you and each of you that you permit ye said C.P. and his Deputies and Servants from Time to time at his or their Will as well in the day as in the Night to enter and go on board any Ship, Boat or other Vessell riding lying or being within or coming to the said Port or any Places or Creeks appertaining to said Port, such Ship, Boat or Vessell then & there found to View & Search & strictly to examine in the same, touching the Customs and Subsidies to us due, And also in the day Time together with a Constable or other public officer inhabiting near unto the Place to enter and go into any Vaults, Cellars, Warehouses, Shops or other Places to search and see whether any Goods, Wares or Merchandises, in ye same Ships, Boats or Vessells, Vaults, Cellars, Warehouses, Shops or other Places are or shall be there hid or concealed, having been imported, ship't or laden in order to be exported from or out of the said Port or any Creeks or Places appertain'g to the same Port; and to open any Trunks, Chests, Boxes, fardells [packages] or Packs made up or in Bulk, whatever in which any Goods, Wares, or Merchandises are suspected to be packed or concealed and further to do all Things which of Rt and according to Law and the Statutes in such Cases provided, is in this Part to be done: And We strictly command you and every of you that you, from Time to Time be aiding and assisting to the said C.P. his Deputies and Servants and every of them in the Execution of the Premises in all Things as becometh: Fail not at your Peril.

Notes

1. *The battle over general warrants and writs of assistance.* The English legal system was rejecting general warrants at the same time colonial officials in America were relying on such warrants more heavily. Lord Camden's decision in Entick v. Carrington is one of several decisions to declare that there was no statutory or other legal authority for general warrants in England. An equally famous decision, Wilkes v. Wood, 19 Howell's State Trials 1153 (C.P. 1763), involved a member of Parliament (John Wilkes) who wrote a series of pamphlets critical of the government and, like John Entick, became the target of government agents executing a general warrant. Did the *Entick* court simply want to encourage Parliament to enact clearer legislation authorizing such warrants? Does the opinion reveal any deeper concerns about their use?

Writs of assistance issued in the American colonies in the 1760s provoked arguments and protests similar to those found in the *Entick* decision. In a now famous (but at the time losing) argument against the validity of writs of assistance, James Otis criticized the writs in these terms:

> Now one of the most essential branches of English liberty, is the freedom of one's house. A man's house is his castle; and while he is quiet, he is as well guarded as a prince in his castle. This writ, if it should be declared legal, would totally annihilate this privilege. Custom house officers may enter our houses when they please — we are commanded to permit their entry — their menial servants may enter — may break locks, bars and every thing in their way — and whether they break through malice or revenge, no man, no court can inquire — bare suspicion without oath is sufficient.

2 Legal Papers of John Adams 113, 142 (L. Wroth and H. Zobel eds., 1965); see generally M. H. Smith, The Writs of Assistance Case (1978).

2. *Fourth Amendment history in the Supreme Court.* The concerns of the Constitution's framers figure into current interpretations of the Fourth Amendment. While the role of history rises and falls in different eras of the Supreme Court's search and seizure jurisprudence, history appears to be on the upswing lately. Consider this assertion by Justice Scalia in Wyoming v. Houghton, 526 U.S. 295, 299-300 (1999): "In determining whether a particular governmental action violates [the Fourth Amendment] provision, we inquire first whether the action was regarded as an unlawful search or seizure under the common law when the Amendment was framed. Where that inquiry yields no answer, we must evaluate the search or seizure under traditional standards of reasonableness. . . ." See David A. Sklansky, The Fourth Amendment and Common Law, 100 Colum. L. Rev. 1739, 1745-70 (2000) (Justices in earlier periods focused on general warrants and writs of assistance and generalized from those controversies to the underlying evils; current justices read the Constitution in light of eighteenth-century common law practices).

3. *What were the offensive characteristics of searches?* In its condemnation of general warrants, did the *Entick* court express concern about the lack of an explanation for a proposed search before it began? Was it concerned with the fact that a government official issued the warrant to his own subordinates? Why does it matter that the general warrants and writs of assistance name no particular target or place for a search? Notice also that the *Entick* court seemed troubled by the fact that the searches under these warrants took place with no witnesses present. What evils would witnesses help prevent? How did the *Entick* court describe a search for "stolen goods"? Was that sort of search more palatable than a search under a general warrant? Try to identify, from these materials, a definition of general warrants that will enable you to spot their possible reemergence in modern doctrine and practice.

4. *Warranted searches and reasonable searches.* The incidents discussed most during constitutional debates involved *warranted* searches rather than warrantless searches. See Thomas Y. Davies, Recovering the Original Fourth Amendment, 98 Mich. L. Rev. 547, 551 (1999) ("the Framers understood 'unreasonable searches and seizures' simply as a pejorative label for the inherent illegality of any searches or seizures that might be made under general warrants"). Warrants issued from an authority with proper jurisdiction became a legal defense for the government officer in any tort suit against him for trespass during the search or seizure. As William Blackstone put it in his influential treatise on the common law of the period, "a lawful warrant will at all events indemnify the officer, who executes the same ministerially." 4 William Blackstone, Commentaries on the Laws of England *286. A messenger executing a warrant could defend against a tort suit by proving that the search was successful. Thus, warrants diminished the power of the jury in a tort suit to control government officers. See Akhil Amar, Fourth Amendment First Principles, 107 Harv. L. Rev. 757 (1994); compare Ronald J. Alien & Ross M. Rosenberg, The Fourth Amendment and the Limits of Theory: Local Versus General Theoretical Knowledge, 72 St. John's L. Rev. 1149, 1169 (1998) (arguing that juries were not granted general power to determine reasonableness of searches).

The various uses of history in the interpretation of the Fourth Amendment will be a recurring theme over the next few chapters of this book. For additional resources in answering these questions, see the web extension for this chapter at *http://www.crimpro.com/extension/ch03*.

5. *Recent appearance of police departments.* The creators of the Fourth Amendment and the earliest analogs in state constitutions did not anticipate possible abuses by

professional police officers, because police departments did not exist at the time. Most law enforcement was carried out by amateurs: citizens who volunteered (or who grudgingly took their turn) as constable or night watchman. There were local sheriffs, but they had no professional staff. Police departments as we think of them did not appear, even in the largest American cities, until late in the nineteenth century. See Lawrence M. Friedman, Crime and Punishment in American History 27-30 (1993); Carol Steiker, Second Thoughts About First Principles, 107 Harv. L. Rev. 820, 830-38 (1994). Does this major change in circumstance make history less relevant for interpreting the Fourth Amendment than it is for other constitutional language? See Anthony Amsterdam, Perspectives on the Fourth Amendment, 58 Minn. L. Rev. 349 (1974) (treating history as unhelpful).

2. *American Limits on General Warrants and Other Searches*

In June 1776, just before the American colonies declared their independence, Virginia adopted a Declaration of Rights that included this provision:

> That general warrants, whereby any officer or messenger may be commanded to search suspected places without evidence of a fact committed, or to seize any person or persons not named, or whose offense is not particularly described and supported by evidence, are grievous and oppressive, and ought not to be granted.

The Maryland constitution expanded the concern from general warrants to "all warrants." The Pennsylvania Declaration of Rights in the Constitution of 1776 explained the connection between the limits on searches and warrants, and the basic rights of the people:

> That the people have a right to hold themselves, their houses, papers, and possessions free from search and seizure, and therefore warrants without oaths or affirmations first made, affording a sufficient foundation for them, and whereby "any officer or messenger may be commanded or required to search suspected places, or to seize any person [or his] property, not particularly described, are contrary to that right, and ought not to be granted.

When the debate shifted from state constitutions to the new proposed federal constitution, many of the ratifying conventions in the states stipulated that they were approving the proposed federal constitution under the assumption that individual rights were implicit within the document and that an express Bill of Rights would soon be added. The First Congress elected under the new constitution immediately took up the task of drafting constitutional amendments dealing with basic liberties. James Madison presented to the House of Representatives a package of amendments, including one that addressed the problem of improper warrants:

> The rights of the people to be secured in their persons, their houses, their papers, and their other property, from all unreasonable searches and seizures, shall not be violated by warrants issued without probable cause, supported by oath or affirmation, or not particularly describing the places to be searched, or the persons or things to be seized.

After a House committee made some slight changes in language, the amendment came to the full House for a vote. At this point, some remarkable things happened. Rep. Egbert Benson of New York suggested that the provision was "good as far as it went" but was not sufficient. He proposed inserting the phrase "and no warrant shall issue" after the word "violated," so as to create two clauses, one addressing unreasonable searches and seizures generally and the other focused on warrants. Voting records of the convention showed that the House voted down Benson's proposed change "by a considerable majority." After the vote, the House appointed a committee to collect and summarize the various amendments it had approved over several days of debate. This so-called Committee of Three (which included Benson) placed on its list the search and seizure provision — as Benson had proposed amending it! The Senate and House both approved the language in this form, and the state conventions also ratified the text as follows:

> The right of the people to be secure in their persons, houses, papers, and effects, against unreasonable searches and seizures, shall not be violated, and no Warrants shall issue, but upon probable cause, supported by oath or affirmation, and particularly describing the place to be searched, and the persons or things to be seized.

See Nelson Lasson, The History and Development of the Fourth Amendment to the United States Constitution 100-03 (1937); Edward Dumbauld, The Bill of Rights and What It Means Today 35-42 (1957).

3. The Language of the Fourth Amendment and Its Analogs

Courts did not treat the Fourth Amendment as a limit on the power of *state* governments (where most crimes are prosecuted) until Wolf v. Colorado, 338 U.S. 25 (1949). Although the federal Bill of Rights originally applied only to the federal government, the Fourteenth Amendment (passed after the Civil War) declared that "no state shall deprive any person of . . . liberty without due process of law." During the 1940s and 1950s, the Supreme Court decided a series of cases, declaring that many of the rights guaranteed in the federal Bill of Rights were such a fundamental part of "due process" that they should apply to the states. The due process clause selectively "incorporated" these rights against state governments. See George C. Thomas, III, When Constitutional Worlds Collide: Resurrecting the Framers' Bill of Rights and Criminal Procedure, 100 Mich. L. Rev. 145 (2001). Before and after *Wolf,* however, states had their own constitutional limitations on state government action, parallel to the Fourth Amendment.

Today all states have a constitutional provision limiting the power of the government to conduct searches and seizures. About half of the states have a provision that tracks the language of the Fourth Amendment, some with only minor modifications. Other states have variations on the Fourth Amendment language that include additional procedural requirements. A typical requirement appears in article II, section 7 of the Colorado constitution, which says that affidavits must be in writing and that the person or thing to be seized must be described "as near as may be." A few states take aim at the specific problem of general warrants. For example, article I, section 7 of the Tennessee constitution states that "general warrants, whereby an officer may be commanded to search suspected places, without evidence of the fact committed, or to seize any person or persons not named, whose offenses are not particularly described and supported by evidence, are dangerous to liberty and ought not to be granted."

Other states emphasize the range of protected privacy rights of individuals. Article I, section 5 of the Louisiana constitution guarantees that the "person, property, communications, houses, papers, and effects" of every person shall be secure against "invasions of privacy." Arizona and Washington State frame the protection even more generally: "No person shall be disturbed in his private affairs, or his home invaded, without authority of law." The constitutions of about ten states contain express protections for individual "privacy" rights. A number of these state constitutional provisions grew out of recent constitutional conventions, some as recent as the 1990s. See Robert Williams, Are State Constitutional Conventions a Thing of the Past? The Increasing Role of the Constitutional Commission in State Constitutional Change, 1 Hofstra L. & Pol'y Symp. 1 (1996).

The varying language of these Fourth Amendment analogs creates room for differing interpretations of the scope of the rights they protect. But variation in language is not determinative: Some states with provisions identical to the Fourth Amendment have interpreted their language differently from one another and differently from federal law; other states with substantially different language in their constitutions have interpreted it in the same way that the U.S. Supreme Court interprets the Fourth Amendment.

In light of the Fourth Amendment and these state provisions, consider three basic issues that underlie many difficult questions regarding the law of search and seizure:

- *The interaction between probable cause and reasonableness.* Do the Fourth Amendment and its state constitutional analogs provide one standard to determine the validity of government searches and seizures? Is that standard probable cause or reasonableness? Are searches without probable cause presumptively (or conclusively) unreasonable? If reasonableness is not defined by reference to probable cause, how should it be defined?
- *The preference for warrants.* Do you think the Fourth Amendment or its state analogs were meant to require that all (or most) searches and seizures take place only after the issuance of a warrant? Or are warrants merely a mechanism for obtaining prior review of the "reasonableness" of searches and seizures, but otherwise not preferred? In other words, how strong is the presumption for warrants?
- *The nature of warrants.* For searches based on warrants, what limits should be placed on the issuance, content, or effect of warrants? Can warrants be issued for more than one person or place? Do warrants need to specify the crime suspected or the nature of the evidence to be sought? Should time limits be placed on the execution of warrants?

What information, principles, or logic should interpreters use to answer these questions? Should the intent of the framers of each provision matter? Can definitions change over time or in different contexts? The remainder of this chapter explores these questions.

B. PROBABLE CAUSE

The two most important standards in modern criminal procedure for justifying stops, searches, and seizures are reasonable suspicion (examined in Chapter 2) and probable cause. Probable cause is the central standard of traditional search and seizure law, and it continues to govern a large portion of full-fledged searches and seizures, including those based on warrants.

1. *Defining Probable Cause*

Probable cause is constantly applied but only rarely defined. Perhaps this is because the assessment of probable cause is an inherently fact-laden, case-specific sort of judgment. While some situations arise frequently enough for standards to develop (for example, how information from an unnamed informant should be assessed to determine probable cause), general principles are difficult to deduce.

A close analysis of case law and a handful of statutes suggest that general definitions of probable cause do exist and that there is some interesting variation among those definitions. The most common definition emerges from language used by the Supreme Court in Brinegar v. United States, 338 U.S. 160, 175-76 (1949), reprinted below. Four elements, not all of which are present in every definition, tend to capture the variation in definitions of probable cause.

Reasonable to whom. Most jurisdictions focus on the assessment that a "reasonably prudent" or "cautious" person would make in deciding whether probable cause exists. Some jurisdictions, however, focus on the information that a *police officer* knows. Would officers make the same connections and assessment as a citizen without law enforcement experience or training? Kentucky requires the assessment of probable cause to be reasonable to the magistrate. Would experienced magistrates make the same assessments as police?

Strength of inference. Several formulations define the required strength of the link between the facts offered and the conclusion that criminal activity has occurred. One common formulation says the magistrate must determine whether the facts suggest a "probability of criminal activity." Another says the magistrate must determine whether the facts are sufficient "to believe an offense has been committed." Yet another standard requires that the investigator "believe or consciously entertain a strong suspicion that the person is guilty." A few jurisdictions require merely that there be a "substantial basis for concluding that the articles mentioned are probably present" at the place to be searched.

Can these formulations be translated into probabilities of criminal activity? For example, do some of them mean less than 50 percent, while others mean a 50-50 chance, and still others mean more likely than not? Alone among the states, Oregon answers this question by statute. Oregon Rev. Stat. §131.005(11) states that probable cause "means that there is a substantial objective basis for believing that more likely than not an offense has been committed and a person to be arrested has committed it."

Comparison to other standards. Some jurisdictions not only define the probable cause standard but also suggest its limits through comparison with other procedural standards. For example, several states say that probable cause is "more than mere suspicion or possibility but less than certainty." Some states note that the determination of probable cause requires less confidence that a crime has occurred than is required for guilt (that is, proof beyond a reasonable doubt). As we saw in Chapter 2, the "reasonable suspicion" demands less of a showing by police than probable cause.

Quality of information. Some jurisdictions enhance their general definition of probable cause by requiring that the assessment be based on evidence that is reliable, trustworthy, or credible. The following chart excerpts typical language from the case law, constitutional provisions, and statutes in selected states.

State	*Information to Be Considered*	*Quality of Information*	*Perspective*	*Nature of Belief*	*Degree of Certainty*
Arizona	Facts and circumstances,	based on trustworthy information [such that a]	person of reasonable caution [would believe that]	items are related to criminal activity and likely to be found at the place described.	The showing is one of criminal activity, not the rigorous standard required for admissibility of evidence at trial.
California	A particularized suspicion or facts [sufficient]	to entertain a strong suspicion [such that a]	person of ordinary caution [would find that the]	object of the search is in the particular place to be searched.	The government need not demonstrate certainty.
Colorado	Sufficient facts [that a]		person of reasonable caution [would conclude that]	contraband or evidence of criminal activity is located at the place to be searched.	This judgment is one of reasonableness, not pure mathematical probability.
Connecticut	All information set forth in affidavit [such that the]	totality of the circumstances [could lead a]	magistrate [to conclude that]	contraband or evidence will be found in a particular place [with a]	fair probability.
South Dakota	The existence of facts and circumstances within the knowledge of the magistrate [such that a]		reasonable prudent man [would conclude that]	an offense has been or is being committed and the property exists at the place designated [to a]	probability.

Problem 3-1. Applying Different Probable Cause Standards

Consider the following two searches in light of the California and Connecticut standards.

Case 1: One afternoon, Captain Lee and Sergeant Hurter were on patrol in what they described as a "high crime area." Lee, Hurter, and four other officers in two other patrol cars stopped at 1225 6th Alley East, where five or six persons were gathered in front of a shot house (a private residence where illegal whiskey is sold by the shot). Officers had executed a search warrant at this residence two to three weeks earlier. As a result of that search, the owner of the residence had been arrested and charged with the illegal sale of alcohol. Officers during that earlier search found a small quantity of illegal drugs on the front porch, presumably left by people sitting there who dispersed when the police arrived at the house.

The house was located in a mostly African American neighborhood, and the people gathered in front of the house were African American men. Between the porch of the house and the roadway there was a small yard, and there was no sidewalk. Some of the men, including Eddie Tucker, were standing in the yard abutting the roadway, and some were in the roadway leaning on a parked car. There had been no calls or complaints to the police that day concerning any illegal activity at the house or pertaining to any of the people gathered in front of the house. Neither Lee nor Hurter knew Tucker at that point.

The officers testified that they were not aware of anything illegal occurring among the men, but as Lee exited the car, he noticed that Tucker (who was about three feet away from him) had a large bulge in one of his front pants pockets. For safety reasons, Lee asked Tucker what was in his pocket and told him to take whatever it was out so that it could be seen. Tucker took from his pocket a black 35mm film canister with its lid closed. Both officers knew at this point that the object was a film canister and was not a weapon.

Lee then directed his attention to another of the persons present, and Hurter asked Tucker what was in the canister. In response, Tucker put the canister behind his back. Sergeant Hurter then asked to see the canister. Tucker handed the canister to Hurter, who opened it and found five $10 bags of marijuana packaged in cellophane. Did Officer Hurter have probable cause to search the canister? Compare Ex parte Tucker, 667 So. 2d 1339 (Ala. 1995).

Case 2: At 3:20 A.M. on June 10, the Dothan Police Department received a call saying that shots had been fired at the Johnson Homes apartment complex. Officer Jerry Watkins responded to the call. As Watkins arrived, he saw four people standing outside behind the apartments, arguing. The people yelled for Officer Watkins to stop, but when he did, one of the people standing in the group started running. A second man in the group told Watkins that the person who ran away was Kenneth Moffitt, and that Moffitt "had a gun." Watkins followed Moffitt because he believed that he "would probably be pretty dangerous if he was out there shooting." Moffitt ran into the back door of an apartment, and Watkins followed a few seconds later. Watkins searched the kitchen and the living room, and noticed some cocaine on a television, but Moffitt was not in either of those rooms. Officer Watkins then went into the bedroom across the hall, where a small child was sitting on a bed pointing under the bed. Watkins found Moffitt on the floor under the bed. Did Officer

Watkins have probable cause to enter the apartment? Compare Ex parte Moffitt, 844 So. 2d 531 (Ala. 2002).

VIRGIL BRINEGAR v. UNITED STATES

338 U.S. 160 (1949)

RUTLEDGE, J.*

. . . At about six o'clock on the evening of March 3, 1947, Malsed, an investigator of the Alcohol Tax Unit, and Creehan, a special investigator, were parked in a car beside a highway near the Quapaw Bridge in northeastern Oklahoma. The point was about five miles west of the Missouri-Oklahoma line. Brinegar drove past headed west in his Ford coupe. Malsed had arrested him about five months earlier for illegally transporting liquor; had seen him loading liquor into a car or truck in Joplin, Missouri, on at least two occasions during the preceding six months; and knew him to have a reputation for hauling liquor. As Brinegar passed, Malsed recognized both him and the Ford. He told Creehan, who was driving the officers' car, that Brinegar was the driver of the passing car. Both agents later testified that the car, but not especially its rear end, appeared to be "heavily loaded" and "weighted down with something." Brinegar increased his speed as he passed the officers. They gave chase. After pursuing him for about a mile at top speed, they gained on him as his car skidded on a curve, sounded their siren, overtook him, and crowded his car to the side of the road by pulling across in front of it. The highway was one leading from Joplin, Missouri, toward Vinita, Oklahoma, Brinegar's home. [The officers searched the car and found 13 cases of liquor. Brinegar was charged with importing intoxicating liquor into Oklahoma from Missouri in violation of the federal statute that forbids such importation contrary to the laws of any state. The trial judge denied the motion to suppress. Even though the facts described above did not constitute probable cause, the judge believed that certain statements Brinegar made after he was stopped gave the officers probable cause to search].

The crucial question is whether there was probable cause for Brinegar's arrest, in the light of prior adjudications on this problem, more particularly Carroll v. United States, 267 U.S. 132 (1925), which on its face most closely approximates the situation presented here. The *Carroll* [court ruled] that the facts presented amounted to probable cause for the search of the automobile there involved.

In the *Carroll* case three federal prohibition agents and a state officer stopped and searched the defendants' car on a highway leading from Detroit to Grand Rapids, Michigan, and seized a quantity of liquor discovered in the search. About three months before the search, the two defendants and another man called on two of the agents at an apartment in Grand Rapids and, unaware that they were dealing with federal agents, agreed to sell one of the agents three cases of liquor. Both agents noticed the Oldsmobile roadster in which the three men came to the apartment and its license number. Presumably because the official capacity of the proposed purchaser was suspected by the defendants, the liquor was never delivered.

* [Chief Justice Vinson and Justices Black, Reed, Douglas, Burton, and Minton joined in this opinion. Justices Jackson, Frankfurter, and Murphy dissented. — EDS.]

About a week later the same two agents, while patrolling the road between Grand Rapids and Detroit on the lookout for violations of the National Prohibition Act, were passed by the defendants, who were proceeding in a direction from Grand Rapids toward Detroit in the same Oldsmobile roadster. The agents followed the defendants for some distance but lost track of them. Still later, on the occasion of the search, while the officers were patrolling the same highway, they met and passed the defendants, who were in the same roadster, going in a direction from Detroit toward Grand Rapids. Recognizing the defendants, the agents turned around, pursued them, stopped them about sixteen miles outside Grand Rapids, searched their car and seized the liquor it carried.

This Court ruled that the information held by the agents, together with the judicially noticed fact that Detroit was "one of the most active centers for introducing illegally into this country spirituous liquors for distribution into the interior," constituted probable cause for the search.

Carroll holding

Variations between the cases

fact

legal

I.

Obviously the basic facts held to constitute probable cause in the *Carroll* case were very similar to the basic facts here. . . . In each instance the officers were patrolling the highway in the discharge of their duty. And in each before stopping the car or starting to pursue it they recognized both the driver and the car, from recent personal contact and observation, as having been lately engaged in illicit liquor dealings. Finally, each driver was proceeding in his identified car in a direction from a known source of liquor supply toward a probable illegal market, under circumstances indicating no other probable purpose than to carry on his illegal adventure.

[There were also variations in details of the proof in the two cases.] In *Carroll* the agent's knowledge of the primary and ultimate fact that the accused were engaged in liquor running was derived from the defendants' offer to sell liquor to the agents some three months prior to the search, while here that knowledge was derived largely from Malsed's personal observation, reinforced by hearsay; . . . and in *Carroll* the Court took judicial notice that Detroit was on the international boundary and an active center for illegal importation of spirituous liquors for distribution into the interior, while in this case the facts that Joplin, Missouri, was a ready source of supply for liquor and Oklahoma a place of likely illegal market were known to the agent Malsed from his personal observation and experience as well as from facts of common knowledge. . . .

There were of course some legal as well as some factual differences in the two situations. Under the statute in review in *Carroll* the whole nation was legally dry. Not only the manufacture, but the importation, transportation and sale of intoxicating liquors were prohibited throughout the country. Under the statute now in question only the importation of such liquors contrary to the law of the state into which they are brought and in which they were seized is forbidden. . . .

[The probable place of market for Brinegar may have been] the State of Oklahoma as a whole or its populous northeastern region. From the facts of record we know, as the agents knew, that Oklahoma was a "dry" state. At the time of the search, its law forbade the importation of intoxicating liquors from other states. . . . This fact, taken in connection with the known "wet" status of Missouri and the location of Joplin close to the Oklahoma line, affords a very natural situation for persons inclined to violate the Oklahoma and federal statutes to ply their trade. The proof therefore concerning the source of supply, the place of probable destination and illegal market, and hence the probability that Brinegar was using the highway for the forbidden transportation, was certainly no less strong than the showing in these respects in the *Carroll* case.

Finally, as for the most important potential distinction, namely, that concerning the primary and ultimate fact that the petitioner was engaging in liquor running, Malsed's personal observation of Brinegar's recent activities established that he was so engaged quite as effectively as did the agent's prior bargaining with the defendants in the *Carroll* case. He saw Brinegar loading liquor, in larger quantities than would be normal for personal consumption, into a car or a truck in Joplin on other occasions during the six months prior to the search. He saw the car Brinegar was using in this case in use by him at least once in Joplin within that period and followed it. And several months prior to the search he had arrested Brinegar for unlawful transportation of liquor and this arrest had resulted in an indictment which was pending at the time of this trial. . . .

II.

Guilt in a criminal case must be proved beyond a reasonable doubt and by evidence confined to that which long experience in the common-law tradition, to some extent embodied in the Constitution, has crystallized into rules of evidence consistent with that standard. These rules are historically grounded rights of our system, developed to safeguard men from dubious and unjust convictions, with resulting forfeitures of life, liberty and property. . . .

In dealing with probable cause, however, as the very name implies, we deal with probabilities. These are not technical; they are the factual and practical considerations of everyday life on which reasonable and prudent men, not legal technicians, act. The standard of proof is accordingly correlative to what must be proved.

The substance of all the definitions of probable cause is a reasonable ground for belief of guilt. And this means less than evidence which would justify condemnation or conviction. [It] has come to mean more than bare suspicion: Probable cause exists where the facts and circumstances within [the officers'] knowledge and of which they had reasonably trustworthy information [are] sufficient in themselves to warrant a man of reasonable caution in the belief that an offense has been or is being committed.

These long-prevailing standards seek to safeguard citizens from rash and unreasonable interferences with privacy and from unfounded charges of crime. They also seek to give fair leeway for enforcing the law in the community's protection. Because many situations which confront officers in the course of executing their duties are more or less ambiguous, room must be allowed for some mistakes on their part. But the mistakes must be those of reasonable men, acting on facts leading sensibly to their conclusions of probability. The rule of probable cause is a practical, nontechnical conception affording the best compromise that has been found for accommodating these often opposing interests. Requiring more would unduly hamper law enforcement. To allow less would be to leave law-abiding citizens at the mercy of the officers' whim or caprice.

The troublesome line posed by the facts in the *Carroll* case and this case is one between mere suspicion and probable cause. That line necessarily must be drawn by an act of judgment formed in the light of the particular situation and with account taken of all the circumstances. No problem of searching the home or any other place of privacy was presented either in *Carroll* or here. Both cases involve freedom to use public highways in swiftly moving vehicles for dealing in contraband, and to be unmolested by investigation and search in those movements. In such a case the citizen who has given no good cause for believing he is engaged in that sort of activity is entitled to proceed on his way without interference. But one who recently and repeatedly has given substantial ground for believing that he is engaging in the forbidden transportation in the area of his usual operations has no such immunity, if the officer who intercepts him in that region knows that fact at the time he makes the interception and the circumstances under which it is made are not such as to indicate the suspect going about legitimate affairs.

This does not mean, as seems to be assumed, that every traveler along the public highways may be stopped and searched at the officers' whim, caprice or mere suspicion. The question presented in the *Carroll* case lay on the border between suspicion and probable cause. But the Court carefully considered that problem and resolved it by concluding that the facts within the officers' knowledge when they intercepted the *Carroll* defendants amounted to more than mere suspicion and constituted probable cause for their action. We cannot say this conclusion was wrong, or was so lacking in reason and consistency with the Fourth Amendment's purposes that it should now be overridden. Nor, as we have said, can we find in the present facts any substantial basis for distinguishing this case from the *Carroll* case. Accordingly the judgment is affirmed.

Notes

1. *Applying different standards?* Which of the cases described in Problem 3-1 offers a stronger basis — in other words, a stronger argument for probable cause — for a search? Does the relative strength of the cases depend on the standard applied to them, or are all the standards stronger for one of the cases? Consider the Connecticut standard. Can you add (or subtract) a fact that would make a weaker case for probable cause? Would you change different facts to make the case for finding probable cause stronger or weaker under the California standard?

2. *Probable cause and probabilities.* Does probable cause translate into a level of certainty the same as the preponderance of the evidence standard at trial? Courts in all jurisdictions have long insisted that probable cause is something less than "beyond a reasonable doubt" and something more than "mere suspicion," but they have shied away from equating it with the preponderance standard. See Illinois v. Gates, 462 U.S. 213 (1983) (probable cause requires "only the probability, and not a prima facie showing of criminal activity"). In a survey of more than 150 federal judges, about one-third believed that "probable cause" required 50 percent certainty, with the next largest groups of judges calling for 40 percent and 30 percent certainty. See C. M. A. McCauliff, Burdens of Proof: Degrees of Belief, Quanta of Evidence, or Constitutional Guarantees? 35 Vand. L. Rev. 1293 (1982). Does this mean that the judges would not sustain the validity of a search of a house when the police know that one of three possible locations contains evidence of a serious crime? Cf. Maryland v. Pringle, 540 U.S. 366 (2003) (officer who found $763 in glove compartment and cocaine behind armrest in back seat had probable cause to

arrest driver, front seat passenger, and rear passengers when all occupants of car denied knowledge of drugs).

3. *Police expertise in assessing probable cause.* Courts often recognize that officers rely on their training and experience in assessing probable cause. See Ornelas v. United States, 517 U.S. 690 (1996) (reviewing court should give due weight to inferences drawn from historical facts by resident judges and local law enforcement officers; officer may draw inferences "based on his own experience"; the loose panel below the backseat armrest in the automobile in this case may suggest to a layman "only wear and tear, but to Officer Luedke, who had searched roughly 2,000 cars for narcotics, it suggested that drugs may be secreted inside the panel"). As a trial judge in a suppression hearing, would you attribute the same level of expertise to all officers or to those within a particular unit of the police department (such as the narcotics squad)? Or would you insist on some particularized showing of experience from each police officer trying to establish probable cause? See Max Minzer, Putting Probability Back into Probable Cause, 87 Tex. L. Rev. 913 (2009) (proposal for the use of empirical evidence of the success of a given investigating officer or investigative technique in assessing the existence of probable cause to search or seize); Commonwealth v. Thompson, 985 A.2d 928 (Pa. 2009) (officer observed defendant standing on street while exchanging small object for cash from driver; in such a setting, characterization of neighborhood as "high crime" and abstract assertion of police expertise would not suffice for probable cause, but officer here made the requisite connection between his experience and facts in case through testimony that he had observed hundreds of similar transactions that turned out to involve illegal narcotics).

4. *Actual knowledge of officer.* Does one assess probable cause based on what the officer(s) on the scene actually relied on to justify the search or on facts that were available to the officer, whether or not she relied on them? Courts have not entirely agreed on this question, but the existence of probable cause usually depends on the facts available to the officer in the field, not just on facts the officer actually relied on to justify a search or seizure.

Most jurisdictions test probable cause based on the collective information the police have, even if the arresting or searching officer does not hold all of that information. See Prince v. United States, 825 A.2d 928 (D.C. 2003). Does this "collective knowledge" doctrine draw the wrong lessons from the institutional reality of police work? Should search and seizure doctrine generally try to account for the way that organizations (police departments) typically shape the actions of individuals (police officers)? For a comparison of the "collective knowledge" rule and the related "fellow officer" doctrine, see the web extension for this chapter at *http://www.crimpro.com/extension/ch03*.

Recall the discussion in Chapter 2 of "pretextual" stops, and the choice discussed there between objective and subjective standards in criminal procedure. It is possible that the collective knowledge doctrine gives the police too much opportunity for *post hoc* rationalization of the individual officer's decision to conduct a search. What, if anything, is wrong with justifying a search after the fact, based on events that truly did occur?

2. *Sources of Information to Support Probable Cause*

The information needed to show probable cause comes from sources as varied as victims, other witnesses, anonymous sources, confidential informants, and police officers themselves. In the abstract, which of these sources would you expect to be most reliable? Can we judge reliability in the abstract? Jurisdictions have reached different conclusions, and have used different standards, in answering these questions. This section considers how courts assess information from different sources, with particular attention to confidential informants and anonymous sources.

a. Confidential Informants

Much as the law of evidence shows a mistrust of hearsay, so the law of probable cause shows a mistrust of informants, who provide information to the police but are often not available to be questioned further when the time comes to assess probable cause. The U.S. Supreme Court has developed a specialized set of rules for judging the reliability of information from informants. The following two cases trace the impact of a major change in the Supreme Court's approach to such questions.

■ STATE v. TIMOTHY BARTON

594 A.2d 917 (Conn. 1991)

PETERS, J.

The sole issue in this appeal is whether . . . article first, §7, of the Connecticut constitution permits a court to determine the existence of probable cause on the basis of the "totality of the circumstances" when it reviews a search warrant application based on information provided to the police by a confidential informant. The state charged the defendant, Timothy Barton, with possession of over a kilogram of marihuana with intent to sell and with possession of marihuana . . . after police, acting under the authority of a warrant, had searched his home and had seized more than fifty pounds of marihuana there. The defendant moved to suppress the seized evidence, and the trial court granted the defendant's motion on the ground that the affidavit accompanying the search warrant application failed to state the informant's "basis of knowledge." The charges were subsequently dismissed with prejudice. [We] reverse.

[Officers] of the Winsted police department, acting on the authority of a search and seizure warrant obtained that day on the basis of information provided by a confidential informant, searched the defendant's apartment. . . . In the course of their search, the police found some fifty-two pounds of marihuana wrapped in clear plastic bags and kept in larger garbage bags in a bedroom. When the defendant returned home after midnight, the police arrested him.

[At the hearing on the defendant's motion to suppress this evidence, the trial court] applied the two-pronged analysis mandated by this court's decision in State v. Kimbro, 496 A.2d 498 (Conn. 1985), which requires a magistrate, in determining whether probable cause exists for a search or seizure, to evaluate both the "basis of knowledge" and the "veracity" or "reliability" of an informant upon whose information the police have relied. Spinelli v. United States, 393 U.S. 410 (1969); Aguilar v. Texas, 378 U.S. 108 (1964). In the circumstances of this case, [the trial court] concluded that the affidavit in support of the search warrant did not adequately set forth the unnamed informant's basis of knowledge and therefore failed to establish probable cause. . . .

In the present appeal, the state urges us to overrule our holding in *Kimbro*, and to adopt the "totality of the circumstances" standard for determining probable cause used in the federal courts pursuant to the decision of the United States Supreme Court in Illinois v. Gates, 462 U.S. 213 (1983). . . . We agree with the state that application of the standards mandated by *Kimbro* has resulted at times in unduly technical readings of warrant affidavits, and we reject such an inappropriate methodology. . . .

In Illinois v. Gates, the United States Supreme Court rejected the "complex superstructure of evidentiary and analytical rules" that had evolved from its earlier decisions in Aguilar v. Texas and Spinelli v. United States. [The] "two-pronged" *Aguilar-Spinelli* test provides a method for evaluating the existence of probable cause consistent with the requirements of the fourth amendment when a search warrant affidavit is based upon information supplied to the police by a confidential informant. The issuing judge must be informed of (1) some of the underlying circumstances relied on by the informant in concluding that the facts are as he claims they are, and (2) some of the underlying circumstances from which the officer seeking the warrant concluded (a) that the informant, whose identity need not be disclosed, was credible, or (b) that the information was reliable. When the information supplied by the informant fails to satisfy the *Aguilar-Spinelli* test, probable cause may still be found if the warrant application affidavit sets forth other circumstances — typically independent police corroboration of certain details provided by the informant — that bolster the deficiencies.

The *Gates* court identified two principal flaws in the *Aguilar-Spinelli* test. First, because courts and commentators had generally regarded the two prongs of the test to be entirely independent of each other, courts had struggled to formulate rules regarding what types of information and what types of corroboration might satisfy each of the prongs. Specifically, some courts had concluded that independent police investigation might corroborate the "reliability" of the information, but could never satisfy the "basis of knowledge" prong of the test, while ample "self-verifying details" might establish that the informant had personal knowledge of the alleged activity and thus could satisfy the "basis of knowledge" prong, but could never compensate for a deficiency in the "veracity" or "reliability" prong. The "elaborate set of legal rules" that had resulted from this emphasis on the independent character of the two prongs had led courts, in many cases, to dissect warrant applications in an excessively technical manner, "with undue attention being focused on isolated issues that [could not] sensibly be divorced from the other facts presented to the magistrate." Such a result was inconsistent with the nature of a probable cause determination, which, as the *Gates* court noted, involves a "practical, nontechnical conception."

The second principal flaw in the application of the *Aguilar-Spinelli* test, according to the *Gates* court, was that the test had caused reviewing courts, both at suppression hearings and at appellate levels, to test the sufficiency of warrant affidavits by de novo review. Such de novo review, in the view of the *Gates* majority, was inconsistent with the constitution's "strong preference for searches conducted pursuant to a warrant." A reviewing court should rather determine whether the magistrate issuing the warrant had a "substantial basis" for concluding that a search would uncover evidence of criminal activity.

In rejecting the complex structure of rules that had evolved from *Aguilar* and *Spinelli,* however, the *Gates* court did not reject out of hand the underlying concerns that had originally been expressed in *Aguilar.* In that case, the United States Supreme Court invalidated a search warrant supported by an affidavit that stated only that the affiants "have received reliable information from a credible person," without stating any of the underlying circumstances that would support a finding of probable cause. The *Aguilar* court ruled that such a conclusory affidavit failed to state a factual basis on which a neutral and detached magistrate could determine the existence of probable cause. In *Gates,* the court reaffirmed that the "veracity" or "reliability" and the "basis of knowledge" inquiries formulated in *Aguilar* remain "highly relevant" in the determination of probable cause and should be regarded as "closely intertwined issues that may usefully illuminate the commonsense, practical question" of the existence of probable cause to believe that contraband or evidence is located in a particular place. The *Gates* court abandoned only a "rigid compartmentalization" of the inquiries and denied that the court had ever intended them to be understood as "entirely separate and independent requirements to be rigidly exacted in every case."

In the place of the "compartmentalized" *Aguilar-Spinelli* test, the *Gates* court directed lower courts to apply a "totality of the circumstances" analysis more consistent with traditional assessments of probable cause. While still employing the analytical frame of reference established in *Aguilar,* a "totality of the circumstances" analysis permits a judge issuing a warrant greater freedom to assess "the relative weights of all the various indicia of reliability (and unreliability) attending an informant's tip." . . . The task of a subsequent court reviewing the magistrate's decision to issue a warrant is to determine whether the magistrate had a "substantial basis" for concluding that probable cause existed. The court's decision in *Gates* emphasized the necessity of a case-by-case analysis of probable cause based on all of the facts presented to the judge issuing the warrant, not merely on those capable of categorization as indicating the "veracity" or "basis of knowledge" of a particular informant.

[We turn now to a reconsideration of our 1985 decision in State v. Kimbro.] *Kimbro* did not rely upon historical analysis to determine the standard by which probable cause should be measured. We relied, rather, upon our determination that the *Aguilar-Spinelli* test, "with its two prongs of 'veracity' or 'reliability' and 'basis of knowledge,' offers a practical and independent test under our constitution that predictably guides the conduct of all concerned, including magistrates and law enforcement officials, in the determination of probable cause." We regarded the *Gates* "totality of the circumstances" analysis as an "amorphous standard" that inadequately safeguarded the rights of individuals to be free from unjustified intrusions. Upon careful review of that determination, we agree with the conclusion of the United States Supreme Court in *Gates* that the two prongs of the *Aguilar-Spinelli* test are highly relevant evidentiary questions that a magistrate issuing the warrant must consider in deciding whether probable cause for a search or seizure exists, but that they are not wholly independent and dispositive constitutional tests for which de novo review exists at a suppression hearing.

In reaching our present conclusion we return to first principles. Article first, §7, of our constitution . . . safeguards the privacy, the personal security, and the property of the individual against unjustified intrusions by agents of the government. One of the principal means by which the warrant requirement protects the privacy and property of the individual is by the interposition of a neutral and detached magistrate who must judge independently the sufficiency of an affidavit supporting an application for a search warrant. Whether applying the fourth amendment or article first, §7, of our own constitution, we have frequently recognized that a magistrate issuing a warrant cannot form an independent opinion as to the existence of probable cause unless the affidavit supporting the warrant application sets forth some of the facts upon which the police have relied in concluding that a search is justified. . . .

When a police officer seeking a search warrant relies on hearsay information supplied by confidential informants rather than on personal knowledge and observations, certain additional facts are necessary to ensure that the magistrate's decision to issue the warrant is informed and independent. [The *Aguilar* decision began with the commonsensical premise] that confidential informants are themselves often "criminals, drug addicts, or even pathological liars" whose motives for providing information to the police may range from offers of immunity or sentence reduction, promises of money payments, or "such perverse motives as revenge or the hope of eliminating criminal competition." Because such an informant's reliance on rumors circulating on the street is not unlikely and the veracity of such an informant is questionable, a magistrate reviewing a search warrant application based on such an informant's word can best assess the probable reliability of the information if she or he is informed of some of the predicate facts that indicate how the informant gained his information and why the police officer believes that the information is reliable in order to decide, independently, whether the police officer's inferences from the informant's statements are reasonable.

In *Kimbro,* we expressed concern that the "fluid" totality of the circumstances analysis approved in the fourth amendment context of Illinois v. Gates would inadequately inform magistrates and law enforcement officials of their obligation to scrutinize the information gathered from confidential police informants with appropriate caution. In construing article first, §7, of our constitution to require continued application of the *Aguilar-Spinelli* test, we sought to make clear certain benchmarks to guide the discretion of our judges in reviewing ex parte applications for search and seizure warrants based on confidential informants' tips.

Nonetheless, over time, the case law applying the *Aguilar-Spinelli* test has come to be encrusted with an overlay of analytical rigidity that is inconsistent with the underlying proposition that it is the constitutional function of the magistrate issuing the warrant to exercise discretion in the determination of probable cause. That discretion must be controlled by constitutional principles and guided by the evidentiary standards developed in our prior cases, but it should not be so shackled by rigid analytical standards that it deprives the magistrate of the ability to draw reasonable inferences from the facts presented. To the extent that *Kimbro* stands for the proposition that the exercise of discretion by a magistrate is reviewable only according to fixed analytical standards, it is overruled.

Our adoption of a "totality of the circumstances" analysis does not mean, however, that a magistrate considering a search warrant application should automatically defer to the conclusion of the police that probable cause exists. Such deference would be an abdication of the magistrate's constitutional responsibility to exercise an independent and detached judgment to protect the rights of privacy and personal security of the people of Connecticut.

In essence, our adoption of a "totality of the circumstances" analysis of the probable cause requirement of article first, §7, of our constitution means simply this: When a search warrant affidavit is based on information provided to the police by confidential informants, the magistrate should examine the affidavit to determine whether it adequately describes both the factual basis of the informant's knowledge and the basis on which the police have determined that the information is reliable. If the warrant affidavit fails to state in specific terms how the informant gained his knowledge or why the police believe the information to be trustworthy, however, the magistrate can also consider all the circumstances set forth in the affidavit to determine whether, despite these deficiencies, other objective indicia of reliability reasonably establish that probable cause to search exists. In making this determination, the magistrate is entitled to draw reasonable inferences from the facts presented. When a magistrate has determined that the warrant affidavit presents sufficient objective indicia of reliability to justify a search and has issued a warrant, a court reviewing that warrant at a subsequent suppression hearing should defer to the reasonable inferences drawn by the magistrate. . . .

In adopting the *Gates* "totality of the circumstances" analysis, as we have here construed it, as the standard of analysis applicable to article first, §7, of our constitution, we do not intend to dilute the constitutional safeguards of the warrant requirement. This court has both the constitutional duty to construe article first, §7, in a way that adequately protects the rights of individuals in Connecticut and also the supervisory responsibility, as the overseer of the judiciary in Connecticut, to ensure that the standards adopted here require law enforcement officers to provide magistrates with adequate information on which to base their decisions in an ex parte context. . . .

We now consider the affidavit presented in this case in light of the proper constitutional standards. [The critical paragraph of the affidavit] provides: "That the affiants state on Sunday, August 7, 1988 Sgt. Gerald O. Peters received information from a confidential informant at police headquarters pertaining to Tim Barton who resides at 232 Perch Rock Trail, Winsted, Connecticut, first floor that Barton has in his apartment a large quantity of marijuana in plastic garbage bags, which are kept in a closet. That the informant also provided Sergeant Peters of [*sic*] a sample of the marijuana that is in the bags. A field test of the marijuana substance that was provided to Sgt. Peters was field tested and the test results was [*sic*] positive for cannibas [*sic*] substance. The informant further stated that Tim Barton operates a Texas registered vehicle and after being away for approximately one week Barton returned home on Saturday, August 6, 1988 and unloaded several large plastic bags in the evening hours. The informant further stated that shortly after that four to five people arrived at the Barton apartment and stayed a short while and then left with plastic garbage bags." . . .

Reviewing the allegations set forth in the third paragraph of the affidavit in this case, the Appellate Court concluded that the affidavit failed to establish probable cause because it was defective under the "basis of knowledge" prong of the *Aguilar-Spinelli* test mandated by *Kimbro*. The Appellate Court cited the following deficiencies: (1) the affidavit did not expressly indicate that the informant had ever been inside the defendant's apartment; (2) the details regarding the truck and the carrying in and out of garbage bags were "innocuous"; (3) the affidavit did not indicate that the informant had said that he had purchased the marihuana from the defendant, or that he had observed the defendant "constantly in possession" of marihuana in the apartment; and (4) the informant did not give a detailed description of the apartment but merely alleged that the garbage bags were in a closet. We agree that the affidavit does not expressly state that the informant had personal knowledge of the facts described. Legitimate law enforcement efforts, however, should not be unduly frustrated because a police officer, in the haste of a criminal investigation, fails to recite his information in particular formulaic phrases. Probable cause does not depend upon the incantation of certain magic words. Having reviewed the circumstances described by the informant, we conclude that the affidavit provided a substantial basis for the magistrate's inference that the informant was reporting events that he had personally observed.

[Details from the affidavit] support an inference that the informant was sufficiently acquainted with the defendant to have known of a week-long absence and to have been present to observe the defendant's activities upon his return. When considered together with the detail that the garbage bags were kept in a closet and with the fact that the informant provided the police with a marihuana sample purportedly from the same bags, these details support a reasonable, commonsense inference that the informant had personally observed the events he reported and had secured the marihuana sample directly from the defendant at his apartment. . . . Although the magistrate could have properly exercised his discretion to reject the warrant application or to require the affiants to supplement it or corroborate some of its details we conclude that the inference drawn by the magistrate that the informant had firsthand knowledge of the defendant's activities was not unreasonable.

[We also conclude] that the affidavit provided a substantial basis for the magistrate's inference that the informant's information was reliable. The first circumstance supporting an inference of "veracity" or "reliability" is the fact that the informant was not anonymous. . . . Because his identity was known to the police, the informant could expect adverse consequences if the information that he provided was erroneous. Those consequences might range from a loss of confidence or indulgence by the police to prosecution for the class A misdemeanor of falsely reporting an incident . . . had the information supplied proved to be a fabrication.

More significantly, however, the informant supplied the police with a sample of a substance that the police tested and confirmed to be marihuana. By entering the police station with the marihuana in his possession and by exhibiting the marihuana to the police, the informant rendered himself liable to arrest, conviction, and imprisonment. . . . Although the warrant application would have unquestionably been stronger if the affiants had bolstered the reliability of the informant by independently corroborating some of the details he reported we conclude that the affidavit sufficiently set forth some of the underlying circumstances from which the police could have concluded that the informant was credible or that his information was reliable.

As our discussion of this affidavit demonstrates, the determination of an informant's "veracity" or "reliability" and "basis of knowledge" remains highly relevant under the constitutional standard announced in this decision. . . . This is a marginal case; the magistrate could reasonably have demanded more information. We will not invalidate a warrant, however, merely because we might, in the first instance, have reasonably declined to draw the inferences that were necessary here. Having reviewed all the circumstances presented to the magistrate in this affidavit, we conclude that the affidavit provided a substantial basis for concluding that probable cause existed. We accordingly reverse the judgment of the Appellate Court [and] remand the case to the trial court for further proceedings.

GLASS, J., concurring in part, dissenting in part.

I concur in the result reached by the majority in this case because, unlike the majority, I conclude that the disputed warrant meets the established requirements of the time honored *Aguilar-Spinelli* test. Because I disagree with the majority's decision to scrap the *Aguilar-Spinelli* test by overruling State v. Kimbro . . . I write separately in dissent. . . .

Dressed today in Connecticut constitutional finery, the *Gates* approach relegates the principles pertinent to the "veracity" and "basis of knowledge" prongs of the *Aguilar-Spinelli* test to the status of "relevant considerations" among the amorphous "totality of the circumstances." The purported relevance of these "considerations," however, is belied by the majority's suggestion that despite "deficiencies" under both prongs of the *Aguilar-Spinelli* test, a warrant may yet derive sufficient sustenance from the "totality of the circumstances" to satisfy the mandates of our constitution. The majority thus appears to have strayed even further beyond the strictures of *Aguilar-Spinelli* than the *Gates* majority, which proposed that "a deficiency in one [of the prongs of the *Aguilar-Spinelli* test] may be compensated for . . . by a strong showing as to the other, or by some other indicia of reliability." Under the majority's evident reading of *Gates,* a warrant deficient under both prongs of the *Aguilar-Spinelli* test, nevertheless, complies with Connecticut constitutional requirements where the "totality of the circumstances" permit. [Magistrates and police officers,] unfettered by meaningful standards by which to discharge their respective functions in the warrant process, are now granted the unbridled play to accord weight to their subjective preferences in determining the "circumstances" whose "totality" permissibly adds up to probable cause. . . .

The *Aguilar-Spinelli* test, in my opinion, allows ample room for the application of common sense and the evaluation of the unique facts presented by particular cases. I do not, therefore, share the majority's desire to strip probable cause determinations of the "fixed, analytical standards" of *Aguilar-Spinelli* that have served to protect the free men and women of Connecticut from unreasonable government intrusion in a way that the standardless *Gates* approach, I submit, will never do. . . . In my view, the Connecticut constitution is not a document so fragile that a swift stroke of the federal pen suffices, as is allowed today, to erode the substantive protections found not six years ago to be afforded thereunder to the citizens of this state.

■ STATE v. RANDALL UTTERBACK

485 N.W.2d 760 (Neb. 1992)

PER CURIAM

[A] search warrant, to be valid, must be supported by an affidavit establishing probable cause [founded on articulable facts.] When a search warrant is obtained on the strength of an informant's information, the affidavit in support of the issuance of the search warrant must (1) set forth facts demonstrating the basis of the informant's knowledge of criminal activity and (2) establish the informant's credibility, or the informant's credibility must be established in the affidavit through a police officer's independent investigation. The affidavit must affirmatively set forth the circumstances from which the status of the informant can reasonably be inferred.

To determine the sufficiency of an affidavit used to obtain a search warrant, this jurisdiction has adopted the "totality of the circumstances" test set forth by the U.S. Supreme Court in Illinois v. Gates, 462 U.S. 213 (1983). The issuing magistrate must make a practical, commonsense decision whether, given the totality of the circumstances set forth in the affidavit before him, including the veracity and basis of knowledge of the persons supplying hearsay information, there is a fair probability that contraband or evidence of a crime will be found in a particular place. . . .

At approximately 7 A.M. on March 1, 1990, a Fremont police detective and six or seven fellow law enforcement officers executed a no-knock search warrant at Utterback's home. Utterback shared his home with his wife and infant child. In various containers discovered at various locales in the Utterback house, police found 25 separate plastic bags which contained a total of 570 grams of marijuana. . . .

The warrant which the officers executed authorized a search for automatic weapons, drug paraphernalia, and various controlled substances. The police detective obtained the warrant on the previous day from a Dodge County judge. The sworn affidavit executed by the police detective to obtain the search warrant states in pertinent part:

> On February 28, 1990, your affiant was advised by an *individual who is neither a paid nor habitual informant* that a second individual named "Randy" was engaged in the distribution and sale of controlled substances at the residence [at 321 North K Street]. The informant advised that "Randy" lived at the above described residence with his wife. The informant gave a physical description of "Randy" which matches the physical description of Randy Utterback contained in Fremont Police Dept. files. *The informant advised your affiant that in the past six months (the informant) had purchased marijuana from "Randy" at the residence described above,* and had observed other sales of illegal drugs at said residence. The informant further advised your affiant that (the informant) had been inside said residence within the last five days, and had seen a large quantity of marijuana, and lesser quantities of hashish, cocaine, LSD, and PCP. The informant indicated to your affiant that (the informant) was very familiar with illegal drugs, and the information furnished to your affiant indicated such knowledge.
>
> The informant further indicated to your affiant that (the informant) had observed what (the informant) believed to be an AK 47 assault rifle and an Uzi submachine gun in said residence, together with other weapons. The informant advised your affiant that (the informant) had personally inspected these weapons, and that they were loaded with ammunition. The informant gave a description of these weapons to your affiant, and that description is consistent with an AK 47 assault rifle and an Uzi submachine gun.
>
> Your affiant personally drove by the above described residence and observed an older model blue station wagon parked in the driveway of said residence bearing Nebraska license plate No. 5-B8618. According to records of the Dodge County Treasurer said vehicle is registered to Randy and/or Maria Utterback. Your affiant personally checked the records of the Fremont Department of Utilities and determined that the utilities were registered to Maria Utterback. . . .

Utterback argues that the search warrant was invalid in that the affidavit failed to establish the veracity of the confidential informant. To credit a confidential source's information in making a probable cause determination, the affidavit should support an inference that the source was trustworthy and that the source's accusation of criminal activity was made on the basis of information obtained in a reliable way.

Among the ways in which the reliability of an informant may be established are by showing in the affidavit to obtain a search warrant that (1) the informant has given reliable information to police officers in the past, see State v. Hoxworth, 358 N.W.2d 208 (Neb. 1984); (2) the informant is a citizen informant, see State v. Duff, 412 N.W.2d 843 (Neb. 1987); (3) the informant has made a statement that is against his or her penal interest, see State v. Sneed, 436 N.W.2d 211 (Neb. 1989); and (4) a police officer's independent investigation establishes the informant's reliability or the reliability of the information the informant has given, see United States v. Stanert, 762 F.2d 775 (9th Cir. 1985).

Nowhere in the detective's affidavit to obtain the search warrant in this case is there an averment that the detective's informant had given reliable information in the past, nor is there an averment that the informant was a "citizen informant."[Our prior cases have defined a citizen informant as]

> a citizen who purports to be the victim of or to have been the witness of a crime who is motivated by good citizenship and acts openly in aid of law enforcement. [E]xperienced stool pigeons or persons criminally involved or disposed are not regarded as "citizen-informants" because they are generally motivated by something other than good citizenship. . . .

The status of a citizen informant cannot attach unless the affidavit used to obtain a search warrant affirmatively sets forth the circumstances from which the existence of the status can reasonably be inferred. Here, there is nothing in the detective's affidavit used to obtain a search warrant even hinting that the informant was "motivated by good citizenship."

The State argues that the assertion in the detective's affidavit that "[t]he informant advised your affiant that in the past six months (the informant) had purchased marijuana from 'Randy' at the residence described above" was a statement against the penal interest of the informant. An admission by an informant that he or she participated in the crime about which the informant is informing carries its own indicia of reliability, since people do not lightly admit a crime and place critical evidence of that crime in the hands of police.

The act of purchasing marijuana is not a statutorily proscribed act in Nebraska. [Statutes] prohibit the possession of marijuana and . . . being under its influence, but nowhere in the statutes of the State of Nebraska is the purchase of marijuana expressly prohibited. There is nothing in the affidavit used to obtain the search warrant in this case that would establish, unequivocally, that the informant could be prosecuted for the crimes of possession or being under the influence of marijuana. [When] the informant in this case admitted to purchasing marijuana he did not make a statement against his penal interest.

The fourth method of determining the veracity of a confidential informant is through corroboration. Here, the affidavit reveals only that the police corroborated that Utterback lived at the described address, that the car in the driveway was registered to him, that the utilities at the house were registered to Utterback's wife, and that Utterback's physical description matched that given by the informant. If the police had chosen to corroborate the information regarding any criminal activities of Utterback's rather than merely corroborating these innocent details of his life, or had the affidavit contained other corroborative sources of information about the same alleged criminal activity of Utterback's, the veracity of the informant might have been established in the affidavit. However, no such corroboration is reflected in the detective's affidavit used to obtain the search warrant in this case.

We conclude that the affidavit in support of obtaining the search warrant herein fails to establish the veracity and reliability of the confidential informant and that the county judge was clearly wrong in determining that it supported a finding of probable cause to issue a search warrant. . . .

Notes

1. Gates *versus* Aguilar-Spinelli: *majority position.* In Illinois v. Gates, 462 U.S. 213 (1983), the Supreme Court upheld a trial court's finding of probable cause on the following facts. The police received an anonymous letter on May 3 alleging that a husband and wife were engaged in selling drugs; that the wife would drive their car to Florida on May 3 to be loaded with drugs, and the husband would fly down in a few days to drive the car back; that the car's trunk would be loaded with drugs; and that the suspects were storing over $100,000 worth of drugs in their basement. A police officer determined the address of the couple and learned that the husband made a reservation on a May 5 flight to Florida. A federal drug enforcement agent confirmed that the husband took the flight, stayed overnight in a motel room registered in the wife's name, and left the following morning with a woman in a car bearing an Illinois license plate issued to the husband, heading north on an interstate highway. These facts were sufficient under the "totality of the circumstances" test. Could they also support probable cause under the *Aguilar-Spinelli* test?

More than 40 states have adopted the *Gates* "totality of the circumstances" standard, though a handful of states such as Massachusetts, New York, and Tennessee (fewer than 10) have retained the *Aguilar-Spinelli* analysis, relying on state constitutions or statutes. See, e.g., People v. Serrano, 710 N.E.2d 655 (N.Y. 1999). Why have these states rejected the *Gates* standard? A few jurisdictions have adopted a "totality of the circumstances" test but have emphasized the continuing relevance of the *Aguilar-Spinelli* analysis. Is this a preferable compromise position?

The *Barton* court in Connecticut switched from its earlier choice of *Aguilar-Spinelli* to the *Gates* standard, saying the *Aguilar-Spinelli* analysis had become "encrusted with an overlay of analytical rigidity." What evidence did the court offer to support this conclusion? If the claim about "encrustation" is hyperbole, what other reasons might have moved the court to the *Gates* standard?

2. *Fact-based probable cause analysis.* Both *Barton* and *Utterback* adopt the "totality of the circumstances" standard of *Gates.* Which set of facts provided stronger support for a finding of probable cause? Which confidential informant provided

greater detail? Which description could a police officer verify more easily? Do you agree with the court in *Utterback* that an admitted purchase of marijuana is not an admission against penal interest because purchasing is not a crime? The web extension for this chapter, at *http://www.crimpro.com/extension/ch03*, offers photographs of Utterback's home.

The "totality" standard, as the court said in *Barton,* is designed to place more responsibility for the probable cause finding in the hands of the factfinder on the scene: the magistrate reviewing the application for a warrant. Should other institutions allow magistrates to make probable cause determinations by their own lights or should they attempt to standardize the probable cause determination? Do you imagine that magistrates see similar fact patterns repeatedly, ones amenable to legal rules? Or do the warrant applications present such different fact patterns that they cannot usefully be compared?

3. *Legal standards and legal cultures.* How different are the alternative legal standards at issue in these cases? If you were concerned about limiting police powers at a time of rising fear about crime, would you rather be in a state with the *Aguilar-Spinelli* standard or in a state with a legal culture suspicious of government abuses where the courts use the *Gates* standard? Attorneys and others who train police officers very often emphasize the facts central to the *Aguilar-Spinelli* standard, even in jurisdictions that have adopted the *Gates* standard under the state constitution. See Corey Fleming Hirokawa, Making the "Law of the Land" the Law on the Street: How Police Academies Teach Evolving Fourth Amendment Law, 49 Emory L. J. 295 (2000). Why do they make such a choice?

4. *Prevalence of confidential informants.* While officers rely heavily on their own observations in unwarranted searches, cases involving search warrants more often turn on evidence obtained from confidential informants. A survey of warrants issued in drug cases in San Diego in 1998 found that 64 percent of the warrant applications included information from confidential informants, and a quarter of the applications offered information from anonymous tips. Most of the applications gave little information about the informant's reliability or track record; the information offered appeared in standard boilerplate language. However, in almost all cases depending on information from confidential informants (95 percent of them), the police corroborated the tip by conducting a "controlled buy" of narcotics. See Laurence A. Benner and Charles T. Samarkos, Searching for Narcotics in San Diego: Preliminary Findings from the San Diego Search Warrant Project, 36 Cal. W. L. Rev. 221, 238-43 (2000).

5. *The presumption in favor of "citizen informants."* As suggested in dicta in *Utterback*, most courts presume information provided by victims and witnesses to be sufficiently reliable to serve as a basis for finding probable cause without additional proof that the source is credible or the information reliable. See Bryant v. State, 901 So. 2d 810 (Fla. 2005). Why? Does a person lose the status of "citizen informant" if she receives a reward for the information? What if the police pay the citizen small amounts of cash for meals or transportation? See People v. Cantre, 95 A.D.2d 522 (N.Y App. Div. 1983). Can victims or witnesses be liable to suspects for the torts of malicious prosecution or false arrest if they file a complaint with an intent other than the investigation or prosecution of the suspect?

6. *Informer's privilege.* Should suspects be able to challenge information provided by a confidential informant, even at the stage of establishing probable cause? Courts and legislatures have long recognized an "informer's privilege" that allows the government to withhold the name of a confidential informant. Drawing on well-established common law roots in the law of evidence, the Supreme Court in McCray v. Illinois, 386 U.S. 300 (1967), explained the privilege in these terms: "Whether an informer is motivated by good citizenship, promise of leniency or prospect of pecuniary award, he will usually condition his cooperation on an assurance of anonymity — to protect himself and his family from harm, to preclude adverse social reactions." . . .

Typically, the law allows a magistrate or judge (but not the suspect) to learn the informer's identity and to examine the informer in camera if there is some reason to disbelieve the informer's statements. Should the informer's privilege apply when *all* the information supporting a search warrant is withheld from the defendant as confidential? Justice Mosk of the California Supreme Court, in a dissenting opinion in People v. Hobbs, 873 P.2d 1246 (Cal. 1994) characterized this problem as follows:

> A search warrant containing no information other than the address of a home to be searched. Not a word as to what the government seeks to discover and seize. A government informer, his — or, indeed, her — identity kept secret from the suspect, the suspect's counsel, and the public. Both the suspect and counsel barred from a closed proceeding before a magistrate. No record of the proceeding given to the suspect or counsel. Based entirely on the foregoing, a court order approving an unrestricted search of the suspect's home. Did this scenario occur in a communist dictatorship? Under a military junta? Or perhaps in a Kafka novel? No, this is grim reality in California in the final decade of the 20th century.

What if another court — say, the Idaho Supreme Court — reads Justice Mosk's observation, then re-reads Kafka and decides to eliminate the informer's privilege? Could a legal system function if it took the position that no deprivation of liberty, including a search or seizure, could take place without full disclosure to the suspect after the search or arrest?

b. Anonymous Sources

Should courts treat anonymous sources like citizen informants, with presumptions of reliability, or like confidential informants, with a requirement that police show the informant is trustworthy or the information is accurate? Consider the following "wanted" poster, soliciting anonymous and confidential informants, along with the case on the next page.

WANTED: Information

Do you want to help keep Anaconda-Deer Lodge County
DRUG FREE . . . ?
HERE'S YOUR CHANCE!
If you know or suspect that someone is dealing in drugs . . .
TURN THEM IN
Fill out the information below, clip it out, and mail to:

Jim Connors, Police Chief
Anaconda, MT

or phone 555-5242
All information will be kept strictly confidential

. . . .

Who? (name) ______________________________ Age __________
Where? (address) ______________________________
City, State ______________________________
What? Coke ______________ Crank ______________ Grass ______________
Any other info ______________________________

■ STATE v. KELLI JOY RAVEYDTS

691 N.W.2d 290 (S.D. 2004)

KONENKAMP, J.

In this appeal, we confront the question of what amount of independent police corroboration is sufficient, when combined with information received from anonymous informants, to establish probable cause for the issuance of a search warrant. . . .

On the morning of July 6, 2003, Deputy Sheriff James Biesheuvel of the Custer County Sheriff's Department received two anonymous telephone calls. The first caller reported that he believed illegal drug activity was taking place in an apartment located in the upstairs portion of his apartment building. Throughout the first caller's explanation of what he thought was suspicious, he stated that he believed the occupant's name was "Kelli," that the address to the apartment building was 886 Montgomery Street, that Kelli had a lot of traffic coming in and out of the building at all hours of the day and night, and that visitors to the apartment complex would only stay for a short period of time. The first caller also indicated that Kelli would whistle to foot and vehicle traffic from her window to signal the visitors. On one occasion, the caller observed a blonde female visit Kelli's apartment at 3 o'clock in the morning. The caller later watched the female leave Kelli's apartment with something in her hand that was small and plastic. Lastly, the first caller provided the officer with a list of vehicle license plate numbers of persons who had visited Kelli's apartment complex within the last few days. The caller did not give his name to the deputy.

The second caller telephoned the sheriff's deputy two hours after the first caller. Like the first caller, this person never gave a name or other identifying information. The second caller, too, claimed to have observed a lot of foot and vehicle traffic coming to and from "Kelli Joy Raveydts's" apartment throughout the middle part of the week. The caller recognized one of Raveydts's visitors as a former, and possibly current, drug dealer. Additionally, a similar list of license plate numbers was provided to the deputy. Finally, because of the caller's claimed experience with illicit drugs, the second caller told the deputy that a particular smell coming from Raveydts's apartment had the odor of marijuana.

Using public records, Deputy Biesheuvel was able to identify the owners of the license plate numbers supplied by the callers. Three of the identified car owners had a questionable, if not criminal, history. Two of the vehicle owners were involved in prior drug violations. Specifically, the deputy indicated in his affidavit that one of the three known vehicle owners and prior arrestees had been recently identified through drug debriefs and interviews as being involved in large marijuana sales throughout the Custer area.

Based on this information provided in the affidavit, a circuit judge issued a search warrant. The warrant authorized law enforcement officers to search Raveydts's apartment, anyone located in the apartment, the urine of anyone located in the apartment, and any vehicle located at the apartment building during the search belonging to Raveydts or any visitor. The search was conducted at approximately 6:40 P.M. the same day that Deputy Biesheuvel received the anonymous telephone calls. Upon entering the apartment, officers apprehended Defendant Robert James Nicholson and seized a hypodermic syringe from his pocket. When Defendants Raveydts and Santana Jean Hansen arrived at the apartment in the course of the search, they were also arrested. Numerous items relating to illegal drugs were found and seized in the apartment, including baggies with residue, documents, prescription tablets, a marijuana pipe, snort tubes, a bindle of opium, plastic bongs, and a small tool with residue. Defendants were all charged with drug-related offenses based on the result of the search and interviews conducted after their arrests. Defendants moved to suppress the evidence obtained, alleging that the warrant and supporting affidavit were deficient for lack of probable cause. The circuit court granted defendants' motion to suppress. . . .

We review the sufficiency of a search warrant by looking at the totality of the circumstances to decide if there was at least a "substantial basis" for the issuing judge's finding of probable cause. State v. Jackson, 616 N.W.2d 412 (S.D. 2000). In Illinois v. Gates, 462 U.S. 213 (1983), a pivotal decision in search and seizure law, the United States Supreme Court abandoned formal application of the two-pronged test enunciated in Aguilar v. Texas, 378 U.S. 108 (1964), and Spinelli v. United States, 393 U.S. 410 (1969). Now the inquiry is whether the information provided to the judge was sufficient for a "common sense" decision that there was a "fair probability" the evidence would be found on the person or at the place to be searched. . . .

Reviewing courts are not empowered to conduct an after-the-fact de novo probable cause determination; on the contrary, the issuing judge's legal basis for granting the warrant is examined with great deference. A deferential standard of review is appropriate to further the Fourth Amendment's strong preference for searches conducted pursuant to a warrant. Under this Court's implementation of the *Gates* standard, we view an anonymous caller's reliability, veracity, and basis of knowledge as relevant considerations in finding probable cause; these considerations, however, are not independent, essential elements. . . .

Two elements are often crucial in deciding whether an anonymous informant's tip provides a "substantial basis" for the issuing court's finding of probable cause. First, an explicit and detailed description of alleged wrongdoing, along with a statement that the event was observed firsthand, entitles the informant's tip to greater weight than might otherwise be the case. Here, the informants provided considerable detail about the activities they personally observed at Raveydts's apartment.

Second, the extent to which the tip is corroborated by the officer's own investigation is important. . . . Deputy Biesheuvel checked the motor vehicle licensing records to identify the individuals who allegedly visited Raveydts's apartment. But he performed no personal surveillance or observation of unusual civilian or vehicular traffic at the address to substantiate either caller's account of presumed illegal conduct. An anonymous tip is insufficient in itself to support a finding of probable cause. See Florida v. J.L., 529 U.S. 266 (2000). The question is whether the checking of the license plate numbers was sufficient independent corroboration.

The case of People v. Titus, 880 P.2d 148, 151-52 (Colo. 1994), provides a helpful counterpoint to our case. Similarly, the issue in *Titus* was law enforcement corroboration of an anonymous informant's list of motor vehicle license plates of alleged drug buyers who frequented a suspect's home. There, the police corroborated that the license plate numbers of the vehicles on the list provided by the anonymous informant matched the description of the vehicles that the informant gave. But this list was innocuous: "There was nothing in the affidavit to suggest . . . that any of these vehicles belonged to known drug offenders. . . ." Thus, the court explained: "The matching of vehicle license plate numbers with vehicle descriptions was not the kind of police corroboration that would serve to establish probable cause in this case. Absent any additional corroboration — for example, that the owners of the vehicles were involved in illegal activity — it was insufficient to support a finding of probable cause."

Here, on the other hand, Deputy Biesheuvel verified that some of the license plate numbers belonged to persons known to have been involved in illegal drug activity. This tended to corroborate the information the two anonymous informants had given. . . . And the two separate anonymous tipsters also tended to corroborate each other. Under the facts of this case, allowing deference to the issuing judge's probable cause determination, we think the corroboration here was sufficient. . . .

MEIERHENRY, J., dissenting.

I respectfully dissent. The majority cites extensively to *Gates*. While *Gates* did abandon the formal application of the two-prong test for anonymous tips in favor of a totality of the circumstances analysis, it still requires "a conscientious assessment of the basis for crediting [anonymous] tips." The Court in *Gates* goes on to state, "Our decisions applying the totality of circumstances analysis outlined above have consistently recognized the value of corroboration of details of an informant's tip by independent police work." . . .

The American Heritage Dictionary defines "corroborate" as follows: "To support or confirm by new evidence; attest the truth or accuracy of." In this case, the officer did nothing to verify that the anonymous caller's information was truthful or accurate. He did not even go to the scene of the alleged criminal activity. It is true that there were two anonymous calls made in this case, but the State acknowledges the calls may have been made by the same person, since they were, after all, anonymous. And while the officer did check the license plate numbers given to him, he never verified that the vehicles had actually been at the apartment. If the "corroboration" that occurred in this case is all we require, an unaccountable, anonymous caller can cause a completely innocent person's home to be raided by simply making up a provocative and entirely untruthful story.

The majority cites to *Titus*. In *Titus* the Colorado Supreme Court found that no probable cause existed where the license plate numbers given by an anonymous tipster were innocuous, and the majority distinguishes it on this basis. However, the majority fails to mention that in *Titus*, the police also sent a police informant to the suspect's home to attempt to purchase drugs, at which time the suspect made a number of suspicious statements, the police performed surveillance of the home, and the officer determined the employment status of the suspect (self-employed). All of this was included in the officer's affidavit. Despite all of this comparatively substantial corroborating evidence, the Colorado court did not believe that probable cause was established. . . .

[In this case, there was no] firsthand observation of the wrongdoing by the tipster or anyone else. Here, the tipster(s) did not claim to have witnessed drug possession, consumption, sales, or purchases. By adopting the majority opinion, we have nearly absolved an officer of the duty to investigate crimes personally, and now allow an officer to rely almost exclusively on unknown, unnamed, and unaccountable tipsters. . . . Simply put, this decision stretches the limits and reduces the requirements for probable cause to a point that puts even the most innocent and law-abiding citizens at risk of a humiliating and demeaning intrusion of their homes.

Problem 3-2. Holding Something Back

During his investigation of a robbery, Detective Sergeant Steven Gibbs received an anonymous phone call telling him that Danny Bradley had committed the crime. He investigated further, then obtained a search warrant based on the following affidavit:

> Det/Sgt Steven T Gibbs of the Marion CSD swears or affirms that he believes and has good cause to believe . . . that certain property hereinafter described is concealed in the following described residence, to wit: a two story yellow frame house with white trim and an enclosed brick porch with the numbers 2021 in the window and located at 2021 N Bellefontaine, Indpls, Marion County, Indiana.
>
> The property is described as follows: A light colored small automatic pistol; a grey sweatshirt with wide red stripes down the sleeves; two diamond rings, a diamond cross necklace, two maroon suitcases, a ladies Gucci watch, a black ladies purse; a maroon John Romaine purse and credit cards and identification in the names of Mary Lou Leonard and Janet M McLaughlin; which constitutes unlawfully obtained property and evidence of an offense.

In support of your affiant's assertion of probable cause, your affiant would show the court that he has received the following facts from a reliable informant which facts the informant stated to be within the informant's personal knowledge, to wit: On 11-6-89 the informant made a phone call to Det/Sgt Steve Gibbs. The informant stated that he knew an armed robbery had occurred at a motel room near Shadeland Ave the previous Friday or Saturday. The informant said that two older white women had a black male force his way into their motel room and display a weapon. The informant stated that luggage, jewelry, cash and credit cards were taken and that one lady had been injured. The informant stated that this robbery had been done by a Denny Bradley who resides at 2021 Bellefontaine, and that Bradley has a prior history of robbery arrests.

Your affiant believes and has probable cause to believe that the informant's information is reliable, based upon the following facts within your affiant's personal knowledge, to wit: On 11-4-89 (the previous Saturday) at about 2:41 A.M. Det/Sgt Gibbs was sent to 7101 E 21st St, the Knights Inn Motel, room 309 (a block east of Shadeland) to investigate an armed robbery. There I found Mary Lou Leonard wf55 and Janet McLaughlin wf56. They stated that a black male forced his way into their motel room and robbed them at gunpoint. They described all the property mentioned above by the informant as being taken with the exception of the credit cards. Mrs. Leonard had her left finger broken by the robber as he took her wedding band. On 11-6-89 Det/Sgt Gibbs phoned both Leonard and McLaughlin and they stated that their credit cards had also been taken. To your affiant's knowledge, there has been no publicity of this incident prior to receiving the informant's phone call. Checking criminal histories Det/Sgt Gibbs found a Danny Bradley living at 2021 N Bellefontaine with prior robbery arrests. Therefore, your affiant respectfully requests the court to issue a search warrant directing the search for and seizure of the above-described property.

The trial court denied the motion to suppress, but the appellate court reversed, because the affidavit did not establish the credibility of the source and the factual basis for the information. Further, in the court's view, the affidavit did not contain information to show that the totality of the circumstances corroborated the hearsay.

Assuming that this case was decided in a *Gates* jurisdiction, can this outcome be reconciled with the court's holding and reasoning in *Raveydts*? Cf. Bradley v. State, 609 N.E.2d 420 (Ind. 1993).

Notes

1. *Anonymous tips and probable cause: majority position.* Courts do not adopt a special framework for assessing probable cause based on information from an anonymous tip. They usually apply the same basic framework — whether it be *Gates* or *Aguilar-Spinelli* — used to assess the reliability of named and confidential informants. A number of the classic cases on the sources of probable cause, including Illinois v. Gates, 462 U.S. 213 (1983), involved tips from anonymous sources. Of course, the police in such cases face the major difficulty of establishing the reliability of the source without knowing the identity of the source. While a track record for the source might not be available, and an "admission against penal interest" cannot bolster the credibility of an anonymous source, it is still possible that the police will be able to corroborate some details of the tip. See State v. Griggs, 34 P.3d 101 (Mont.

2001) (corroborated facts in anonymous tip must be suspicious and associated with criminal activity to establish probable cause).

In a jurisdiction following the *Aguilar-Spinelli* approach to probable cause, how often will information from an anonymous informant satisfy both prongs? In a *Gates* jurisdiction, would you expect the showing for "basis of knowledge" to be much higher than usual in an anonymous informant case? In assessing the reliability of an anonymous source, does it matter to you whether the anonymous tipster uses a telephone call (as in *Bradley*) or submits a written tip (as requested in the "wanted" poster)? Governments, corporations, and "watchdog" organizations often maintain "whistle blower" sites on the internet, to encourage employees and others who know about wrongdoing to share the information. Should those sites allow for anonymous submissions?

2. *Anonymous tips and reasonable suspicion to stop vehicles.* In Chapter 2, we considered the "reasonable suspicion" necessary to justify a police stop of a person or vehicle. Sometimes anonymous tips give the police a reason to stop a person. Typically, courts require the officer to confirm some of the details that the anonymous tipster related before reasonable suspicion is present. In one common fact pattern, an anonymous tip identifies a driver who might be driving while intoxicated. If the officer stops the vehicle on the basis of the anonymous tip without first developing some independent basis for reasonable suspicion, courts will frequently overturn the stop.

The U.S. Supreme Court has addressed the use of anonymous tips to establish reasonable suspicion to stop a driver suspected of drug activity. In Alabama v. White, 496 U.S. 325, 332 (1990), an anonymous caller gave police specific information about the future travel plans of an alleged drug dealer. The Court agreed that the tip, together with police efforts to corroborate the tip by following the vehicle for a time, amounted to reasonable suspicion, despite the anonymity of the source: "[If] a tip has a relatively low degree of reliability, more information will be required to establish the requisite quantum of suspicion than would be required if the tip were more reliable." The fact that the tip predicted future behavior, which the police were able to verify, gave it extra weight. For a glimpse of the rich case law in the state courts on this question, see the web extension for this chapter at *http://www.crimpro.com/extension/ch03*.

3. *Can a Statute or Rule Clarify the Assessment of Probable Cause?*

If a jurisdiction were committed to consistent determinations of probable cause, would it help if a statute or criminal procedure rule specified the factors for assessing probable cause? Do the following statutes adopt the *Aguilar-Spinelli* or the *Gates* standard? Apply the following statutes to the facts in *Barton* and *Utterback.* Would you reach a different outcome in either of those cases?

■ ARKANSAS RULE OF CRIMINAL PROCEDURE 13.1

(b) [If] an affidavit or testimony is based in whole or in part on hearsay, the affiant or witness shall set forth particular facts bearing on the informant's reliability and shall disclose, as far as practicable, the means by which the information was obtained. An affidavit or testimony is sufficient if it describes circumstances establishing reasonable cause to believe that things subject to seizure will be found in a particular place. Failure of the affidavit or testimony to establish the veracity and bases of knowledge of persons providing information to the affiant shall not require that the application be denied, if the affidavit or testimony viewed as a whole, provides a substantial basis for a finding of reasonable cause to believe that things subject to seizure will be found in a particular place.

■ IOWA CODE §808.3

[The] magistrate shall endorse on the application the name and address of all persons upon whose sworn testimony the magistrate relied to issue the warrant together with the abstract of each witness' testimony, or the witness' affidavit. However, if the grounds for issuance are supplied by an informant, the magistrate shall identify only the peace officer to whom the information was given. The application or sworn testimony supplied in support of the application must establish the credibility of the informant or the credibility of the information given by the informant. The magistrate may in the magistrate's discretion require that a witness upon whom the applicant relies for information appear personally and be examined concerning the information.

■ IOWA RULE OF CRIMINAL PROCEDURE 2.36, FORM 2

An application for a search warrant shall be in substantially the following form: . . . Being duly sworn, I, the undersigned, say that at the place (and on the person (s) and in the vehicle (s)) described as follows:

in ______ County, there is now certain property, namely:
which is:
______ Property that has been obtained in violation of law.
______ Property, the possession of which is illegal.
______ Property used or possessed with the intent to be used as the means of committing a public offense or concealed to prevent an offense from being discovered.
______ Property relevant and material as evidence in a criminal prosecution.

The facts establishing the foregoing ground(s) for issuance of a search warrant are as set forth in the attachment(s) made part of this application.

ATTACHMENT
Applicant's name: ______________________________
Occupation: ____________________ No. of years: ____________________
Assignment: ____________________ No. of years: ____________________
Your applicant conducted an investigation and received information from other officers and other sources as follows:
(______ See attached investigative and police reports.) . . .

INFORMANT'S ATTACHMENT (Note: Prepare separate attachment for each informant.)
Peace officer _______________ received information from an informant whose name is: ____________
______ Confidential because disclosure of informant's identity would:
______ Endanger informant's safety;
______ Impair informant's future usefulness to law enforcement.

The informant is reliable for the following reason(s):

______ The informant is a concerned citizen who has been known by the above peace officer for years and who:

______ Is a mature individual.

______ Is regularly employed.

______ Is a student in good standing.

______ Is a well-respected family or business person.

______ Is a person of truthful reputation.

______ Has no motivation to falsify the information.

______ Has no known association with known criminals.

______ Has no known criminal record.

______ Has otherwise demonstrated truthfulness. (State in the narrative the facts that led to this conclusion.)

______ Other:
______ The informant has supplied information in the past ______ times.
______ The informant's past information has helped supply the basis for ______ search warrants.
______ The informant's past information has led to the making of ______ arrests.
______ Past information from the informant has led to the filing of the following charges: ____
______ Past information from the informant has led to the discovery and seizure of stolen property, drugs, or other contraband.
______ The informant has not given false information in the past.
______ The information supplied by the informant in this investigation has been corroborated by law enforcement personnel. (Indicate in the narrative the corroborated information and how it was corroborated.)
______ Other: ____
The informant has provided the following information: ______________________

IOWA RULE OF CRIMINAL PROCEDURE 2.36, FORM 3

An endorsement on a search warrant shall be in substantially the following form: . . .

1. In issuing the search warrant, the undersigned relied upon the sworn testimony of the following person(s) together with the statements and information

contained in the application and any attachments thereto. The court relied upon the following witnesses:

Name	Address
______________________	______________________
______________________	______________________
______________________	______________________

2. Abstract of Testimony. (As set forth in the application and the attachments thereto, plus the following information.)

3. The undersigned has relied, at least in part, on information supplied by a confidential informant (who need not be named) to the peace officer(s) shown on Attachment(s) ______.

4. The information appears credible because (select):

______ A. Sworn testimony indicates this informant has given reliable information on previous occasions; or,

______ B. Sworn testimony indicates that either the informant appears credible or the information appears credible for the following reasons (if credibility is based on this ground, the magistrate MUST set out reasons here):

____

5. The information (is/is not) found to justify probable cause.

6. I therefore (do/do not) issue the warrant.

Notes

1. *Statutes and probable cause determinations: majority position.* Only one state (Oregon) offers a general statutory definition of probable cause. However, most states do have statutes or rules of procedure instructing magistrates how to determine whether probable cause exists before issuing a warrant. The statutes often specify the types of sources a magistrate may consider and the inquiries a magistrate must make when assessing "hearsay" information or other questionable sources.

Iowa courts have concluded that the state legislature, in passing section 808.3, was repudiating the decision of the Supreme Court in Illinois v. Gates, 462 U.S. 213 (1983). See State v. Swaim, 412 N.W.2d 568 (Iowa 1987) (interpreting language in statute, "shall include a determination that the information appears credible," as a rejection of *Gates*). What purposes might the other two provisions reprinted above serve?

2. *Rules as requirements and rules as nonbinding guidance.* What should be the effect of a failure to check any boxes on the Iowa form to show why an informant was reliable, in a case where a reviewing court believes that the information provided to the magistrate was enough for probable cause? See State v. District Court of Black Hawk County, 472 N.W.2d 621 (Iowa 1991) (invalidating search warrant based on form application with no checks indicating informant's basis of knowledge). Such checklists are also developed as part of police and prosecutorial manuals. The lists often take the form of computer software, used to prompt an officer to answer specific questions while constructing an application for a search warrant. Should failure to

follow a written executive branch guideline have the same effect on review of probable cause as failure to follow an identical rule of criminal procedure? Should the question simply be whether probable cause exists, with the forms or checklists, whatever their origins, merely serving as evidence for the court assessing or reviewing the probable cause determination?

C. WARRANTS

The U.S. Supreme Court and state supreme courts say it often: Searches and seizures ordinarily must be carried out under warrants obtained from neutral magistrates. See, e.g., Trupiano v. United States, 334 U.S. 699, 705 (1948) ("It is a cardinal rule that, in seizing goods and articles, law enforcement agents must secure and use search warrants wherever reasonably practicable"). Look back at the language of the Fourth Amendment and its equivalents. How would you respond to an argument that searches can be conducted only pursuant to warrants?

Even if an absolute warrant requirement is not plausible, the constitutional language and the oft-stated judicial "preference" for warrants might lead to the expectation that *most* searches are conducted pursuant to a warrant, with exceptions to the warrant requirement being just that — exceptions, and therefore uncommon. Does a judicial preference for warrants mean that warrants are common in practice? It is difficult to determine what proportion of searches are carried out based on warrants, but the current appellate case law suggests a great majority of searches in most contexts are conducted without first obtaining a warrant.

What advantage might warranted searches offer over searches supported by probable cause but no warrant? The special contributions of the warrant involve the timing of the decision and the identity of the decision maker. For warranted searches, the determination of probable cause must occur before the search begins. By settling the issue early, a warrant prevents the use of hindsight. If the probable cause issue waits until after the search produces evidence, judges may feel pressure to accept a search that was based on nothing more than a lucky guess. Some police officers might also feel tempted to lie about the original basis for their search. And for warranted searches, a judicial officer decides whether probable cause is present, rather than the law enforcement officers who are in the thick of the chase. See William Stuntz, Warrants and Fourth Amendment Remedies, 77 Va. L. Rev. 881 (1991).

1. The Warrant Requirement and Exigent Circumstances

Perhaps the largest "exception" to the preference for warrants is the presence of exigent circumstances. When exigent circumstances appear, there is no need for police to obtain a warrant before conducting a search. Exigent circumstances include situations in which an immediate search or seizure is needed to protect the safety of an officer or the public, or when the suspect might escape or destroy evidence. In what proportion of all searches and seizures would you imagine that there is some risk that one of these events might occur? How much risk must the government accept before the circumstances become "exigent"? Can the government take any actions to decrease (or increase) these risks?

■ JOHNNY MANN v. STATE

161 S.W.3d 826 (Ark. 2004)

CORBIN, J.

The record reflects that on or about May 20, 2001, Mitchell Webb, a United States postal inspector in Little Rock, received information from a postal inspector in California of a suspicious package addressed to Clark Nuss, 424 Ashley 81 West, Hamburg, Arkansas. The package had a return address of Crescent City, California. Webb instructed the California office to forward the package to him, via sealed mail. Once Webb received the package, he ran a drug-detection canine by the package, and the dog alerted on it. Another postal inspector then obtained a federal search warrant for the package, which was then opened and discovered to contain approximately eighteen grams of methamphetamine. Webb contacted officers of the Arkansas State Police to see if they were interested in investigating the matter. They indicated that they were, so Webb re-wrapped the package and transported it to Hamburg the following day.

Officers from the state police discovered that Appellant lived at 424 Ashley 81 West in Hamburg. They also ran criminal histories on Appellant and Clark Nuss and discovered that both men had previously lived in Crescent City, California. Officers then decided to make a controlled delivery of the package, with Inspector Webb posing as a rural route carrier in Hamburg. Prior to the actual delivery, Appellant approached his regular mail carrier and asked if there were any packages for him. The mail carrier told Appellant that the mail route for that day was being split up and that another carrier may possibly have his mail.

At the time of the controlled delivery, officers conducted surveillance of the residence at 424 Ashley 81 West, Hamburg. They watched it from the ground, as well as from the air in a state police helicopter. The residence was a mobile home with a screened-in porch area on the front. There was some construction going on at the front of the residence, in an apparent attempt to convert the mobile home into a permanent structure. There was a screen door on the porch and a metal door on the trailer itself.

On the date of the controlled delivery, May 21, 2001, Inspector Webb drove his postal vehicle into Appellant's driveway and honked his horn. Appellant came out and approached Webb. Webb told him that he had two packages that were too big to fit into the mailbox. Webb then asked Appellant if the packages belonged there, and Appellant said that they did. The police officers remained in their surveillance positions for five to six minutes, to give Appellant time to open up the packages. They then approached the residence, entered the screened-in porch, and announced their presence. The metal door to the trailer was open. At some point, either while they were inside the porch area or in the doorway of the trailer, one of the officers heard someone running down the hallway, and he alerted the others. At least two of the officers pursued the runner toward the bathroom, where they discovered Appellant, who was fully clothed, sitting on the commode, which had just been flushed. Appellant was then taken into custody, and officers subsequently obtained his consent to search the residence. The officers then recovered the methamphetamine from the drain of the commode. . . .

Appellant filed a motion to suppress the evidence found during the search of his residence, on the ground that the warrantless entry violated his Fourth Amendment rights. Following a hearing, the trial court denied the motion to suppress, finding that there were exigent circumstances to justify the warrantless entry. Particularly, the trial court found that when the police entered the screened-in porch and announced that they were police, they heard someone running in the residence. According to the trial court: "That led to the reasonable conclusion that Mr. Mann, who they knew was in possession of these drugs at this time, was trying to do something to dispossess himself of them or destroy them." . . .

We begin our analysis by acknowledging the boilerplate principle that a warrantless entry into a private residence is presumptively unreasonable under the Fourth Amendment. See Welsh v. Wisconsin, 466 U.S. 740 (1984). An exception to the warrant requirement is where, at the time of entry, there exists probable cause and exigent circumstances. Exigent circumstances are those requiring immediate aid or action, and, while there is no definite list of what constitutes exigent circumstances, several established examples include the risk of removal or destruction of evidence, danger to the lives of police officers or others, and the hot pursuit of a suspect. The burden is on the State to prove that the warrantless activity was reasonable. . . .

The testimony of the officers during the suppression hearing was inconclusive as to when the exigent circumstances arose. The record reflects that six officers testified at the suppression hearing; however, only two officers, Dennis Roberts, of the Arkansas State Police, and Deputy Jim Culp, of the Ashley County Sheriff's Department, testified that they entered Appellant's residence before he was taken into custody. Roberts initially testified that he was inside the residence when he heard someone running down the hallway. He explained: "We went into the house, and I was one of the first into the house. I heard running down the wooden floor. I announced, 'State Police.' Continued to hear the running. We pursued the running down the hallway and found Mr. Mann inside of the bathroom." Roberts also stated: "Upon entry of the house, just as I was standing, or just as I was hearing the running down the hallway, I saw our package that had been torn open sitting on a kitchen bar right as you walked into the doorway." On cross-examination, Roberts candidly admitted that he could not be certain where he was when he heard someone running down the hallway. He explained: "Immediately, immediately after I heard the running, and I can't tell you where I was, whether I was in the screened-in area or the doorway where I could see the package, I, when I heard the running, I stated, 'state police.' " . . .

During the suppression hearing, the State maintained that the officers' warrantless entry into Appellant's home was based on the exigent circumstance that they feared that evidence was about to be destroyed. This fear was based on the sound of someone running down the hallway. The record reveals that Roberts was apparently the only officer to actually have heard this noise. His testimony, however, is admittedly uncertain as to when he heard the running, i.e., before or after he had entered the home. Our case law requires us to examine only those exigent circumstances that existed at the time of the entry. Obviously, a warrantless entry that occurs before the exigent circumstance exists violates the Fourth Amendment. It was the State's burden to present evidence proving that the warrantless entry was reasonable under the Fourth Amendment. Based on the record before us, we conclude that the State failed to meet its burden and that the trial court erred in concluding that the warrantless entry was reasonable.

Furthermore, regardless of when the exigent circumstance arose, . . . this particular exigent circumstance was effectively created by the police's chosen strategy in this case. At a minimum, the officers reasonably could have foreseen that their decision to approach Appellant's residence without a warrant immediately after completing a controlled delivery of methamphetamine would likely result in an attempt to destroy the evidence. . . .

Here, there is no doubt that the officers had the opportunity to seek and secure a warrant to search Appellant's residence. The officers had probable cause to believe that Appellant was committing the crime of possession of a controlled substance. They had already determined that the package contained a controlled substance, namely methamphetamine, and they had witnessed Appellant accept the package after telling Postal Inspector Webb that the package belonged at his residence. Moreover, they knew that Appellant and the addressee, Clark Nuss, were previously residents of Crescent City, California, where the package originated. The police had two viable options in this case. First, they could have continued their surveillance of Appellant's residence while one or more of them attempted to secure a search warrant. If Appellant would have left the residence with the package during the time that the police were attempting to secure the warrant, they would have had probable cause to stop Appellant and arrest him at that time.

The second option available to police was to obtain an anticipatory search warrant prior to the time that the controlled delivery was executed. An anticipatory warrant is one that is issued before the item to be seized has arrived at the place to be searched. . . . In the present case, the police could have obtained an anticipatory search warrant conditioned upon the delivery of the controlled substance to Appellant's residence. They knew that the package contained a controlled substance and that the package identified a real person at an accurate address.

[The] situations of urgency protected by this exception cannot be created by police officers. This general holding will not dispose of this case or, in fact, of many cases. For in some sense the police always create the exigent circumstances that justify warrantless entries and arrests. Their discovery of the criminal causes him to flee; their discovery of the contraband causes the criminal's attempt to destroy or divert the evidence. For the claim of exigent circumstances to be adequately evaluated, the better question to ask is: how did those urgent circumstances come about? This antecedent inquiry — into the reasonableness and propriety of the investigative tactics that generated the exigency — seems to be what courts have in fact been doing in these kinds of cases. . . . There is no question that the deliberate creation of urgent circumstances is unacceptable. But bad faith is not required to run afoul of the standard. . . .

[The] test for determining whether the exigent circumstances are of the police's own creation [is whether], regardless of good faith, it was reasonably foreseeable that the investigative tactics employed by the police would create the exigent circumstances relied upon to justify a warrantless entry. Applying that test to the facts of this case, we conclude that it was reasonably foreseeable that the police's chosen strategy of approaching Appellant's residence and announcing their presence, only minutes after a controlled delivery had occurred, would create a situation in which Appellant would attempt to destroy the evidence.

[If we] were to uphold the police's actions even though the exigent circumstances were foreseeable, this type of situation may reoccur repeatedly and might lend itself to too easy a by-pass of the constitutional requirement that probable cause should generally be assessed by a neutral and detached magistrate before the citizen's privacy is invaded. [We] conclude that the trial court erred in denying Appellant's motion to suppress. . . . Accordingly, the warrantless entry was unreasonable under the Fourth Amendment, and all evidence gained as a result of the intrusion must be suppressed. . . .

GLAZE, J., dissenting.

[Based on the testimony] before the trial judge at the suppression hearing, the judge quite properly made the following findings and ruling:

> THE COURT: . . . They entered a porch, which was opened, the door was open and the porch as well and the contents of that front porch were visible to anyone on the outside. And at the time they were on this porch, they announced that they were police. They then heard someone running in the trailer. That led to the reasonable conclusion that Mr. Mann, who they knew was in possession of these drugs at this time, was trying to do something to dispossess himself of them or destroy them. [Thus,] there were exigent circumstances concerning their entry that a warrant was not required. . . .

[In] reviewing a ruling denying a defendant's motion to suppress, this court makes an independent determination based on the totality of the circumstances and views the evidence in the light most favorable to the State; we reverse only if the trial court's ruling is clearly against the preponderance of the evidence. Here, the trial court found that, as the officers approached the open door of the porch, Officer Culp heard footsteps inside the trailer home, announced "there's someone running," and then the officers entered the open door of the trailer. When the officers heard someone running in the trailer, they reasonably concluded Mann was trying to destroy the evidence. The majority court simply ignores the trial judge's reasonable analysis of the evidence that supports his ruling to deny Mann's motion to suppress. . . .

[The majority] contends that the officers had the opportunity to secure a warrant to search Mann's trailer; it opines that the officers had probable cause to believe Mann was committing the crime of possession of a controlled substance, since the package he was handed was accepted by him. . . . [Only when the Arkansas officers made a controlled delivery of the package could they] be certain they had probable cause. The majority court here attempts to challenge the officers' failing to obtain a warrant immediately after Mann approached his regular mail carrier and asked if there were any packages for Mann, and his carrier said another carrier may possibly have his mail. Of course, even if the officers suspected at this point that Mann was referring to the Nuss package, they could not be sure until he accepted the package. . . .

In conclusion, it is my strongly held view (and that of the trial judge, I might add) that the officers had not created the exigency in this case. Instead, Mann himself caused the officers to enter the trailer when he started running and the toilet was flushed after the officers identified themselves as they approached the porch leading to the open door of the trailer. . . . The trial judge was correct in denying Mann's motion to suppress, and I would affirm the judge.

Notes

1. *Exigent circumstances: majority position.* Two of the most common grounds for arguing that the police need not obtain a judicial warrant are the potential destruction of evidence and the potential escape of suspects. Williams v. State, 813 A.2d 231 (Md. 2002). Are there exigent circumstances in all cases dealing with evidence (such as narcotics) that is easy to destroy or remove? In all cases where private parties will have access to the area while the police seek a warrant?

Exigent circumstances might also be based on possible danger to the investigating officers or to citizens in the area where the search is to take place. The danger might involve the use of a weapon on the premises, an item creating a risk of fire or explosion, or the possible presence of persons needing medical care, among other things. See People v. Higbee, 802 P.2d 1085 (Colo. 1990) (search for bomb); Holder v. State, 847 N.E.2d 930 (Ind. 2006) (presence of child and adults in home used as methamphetamine lab, combined with health risk to neighbors when smell of ether was present throughout area). See also Michigan v. Fisher, 130 S. Ct. 546 (2009) (exigent circumstances allowed warrantless entry into home when occupant appeared to be injured and was screaming and throwing objects). For a sample of the rich detail of the cases on this question, see the web extension for this chapter at *http://www.crimpro.com/extension/ch03*.

Exigent circumstances can vary with the seriousness of the crime; the showing becomes more difficult as the crime under investigation becomes less serious. See Welsh v. Wisconsin, 466 U.S. 740 (1984) ("application of the exigent-circumstances exception in the context of a home entry should rarely be sanctioned when there is probable cause to believe that only a minor offense [such as driving while intoxicated] has been committed").

When do inconvenient circumstances become "exigent"? That is, how much extra risk must the police accept before they may conclude that obtaining a warrant would be too difficult? Was it feasible in *Mann* for the police to wait to enter the house only after obtaining a warrant? Could they detain any person leaving the premises until officers returned with a warrant?

Exigent circumstances are not the only cases in which courts will allow a warrantless search. As we saw in Chapter 2, many less intrusive searches may be conducted without a warrant. It is useful to make a list of the variety of justifications for warrantless searches.

2. *Maintaining the status quo while seeking a warrant.* May the police enter or remain on the premises long enough to prevent the destruction of evidence or other harms that could occur while they seek a warrant? See Illinois v. McArthur, 531 U.S. 326 (2001) (police obtain probable cause of presence of illegal narcotics in home; occupant required to remain outside home two hours with police officer present while other officers seek search warrant); Segura v. United States, 468 U.S. 796 (1984) (search valid where police officers remained in apartment 19 hours until warrant was obtained); Posey v. Commonwealth, 185 S.W.3d 170 (Ky. 2006) (officers speaking to occupant of home outside front door noticed through open door some marijuana inside the home, and stepped inside to secure evidence until warrant

could be obtained for more thorough search). If it requires too many police officers too long to maintain the status quo, do the police then have exigent circumstances?

3. *The special status of homes.* Courts strike down warrantless searches most often in the context of searches of homes. Many of the exceptions to the warrant requirement applicable outside the home do not apply in the same way within a home, and courts tend to demand greater justifications for warrantless searches of a house. Some courts extend the special protection provided homes to other areas. Indiana, for example, has found a similar preference for warrants when the police search parked and impounded cars. Brown v. State, 653 N.E.2d 77 (Ind. 1995):

> With respect to automobiles generally, it may safely be said that Hoosiers regard their automobiles as private and cannot easily abide their uninvited intrusion. . . . Americans in general love their cars. It is, however, particularly important, in the state which hosts the Indy 500 automobile race, to recognize that cars are sources of pride, status, and identity that transcend their objective attributes. We are extremely hesitant to countenance their casual violation, even by law enforcement officers who are attempting to solve serious crimes.

2. *Requirements for Obtaining Warrants*

Procedures for obtaining warrants typically appear in state statutes, local code provisions, and local rules of court. These rules specify such things as who can issue warrants, the form and content of warrant applications, and the allowable scope of warrants. Several procedural requirements appear on the face of the Fourth Amendment and its analogs. Most constitutions require the applicant to specify the targeted place and the items or person sought. Some also require that the warrant application be in writing or under oath.

a. Neutral and Detached Magistrate

While there are occasional cases litigating the constitutional requirement of a "neutral and detached magistrate," issues of judicial neutrality are more often litigated under judicial ethics rules. Indeed, ethics rules have become a standard avenue for the regulation of lawyers and judges throughout the criminal process, as influential today in practical terms as constitutional provisions.

■ STATE EX REL. EUSTACE BROWN v. JERRY DIETRICK

444 S.E.2d 47 (W. Va. 1994)

MILLER, J.

[We] consider whether the Circuit Court of Jefferson County was correct in holding that a search warrant issued by a magistrate was void because the magistrate was married to the chief of police and one of his officers had procured the warrant. The lower court determined that because the magistrate was married to the chief of police there was a violation of Canon 3C(1) and 3C(1)(d) of the Judicial Code of Ethics. The former provision requires the recusal of a judge if his impartiality might reasonably be questioned; the latter requires disqualification where the judge's spouse has an interest in the proceeding.[3] We have not had occasion to consider this particular question.

Initially, we note that independent of the Judicial Code of Ethics, the United States Supreme Court has interpreted the Fourth Amendment to the United States Constitution to require that a search warrant be issued by a "neutral and detached magistrate." In Shadwick v. City of Tampa, 407 U.S. 345 (1972), the Supreme Court held that the office of magistrate, in order to satisfy the neutral and detached standard "requires severance and disengagement from activities of law enforcement." By way of illustration, the Supreme Court in *Shadwick* pointed to its earlier case of Coolidge v. New Hampshire, 403 U.S. 443 (1971), where it voided a search warrant issued by the state's attorney general because he "was actively in charge of the investigation and later was to be chief prosecutor at trial." Similarly, in Lo-Ji Sales, Inc. v. New York, 442 U.S. 319 (1979), the magistrate was found not to be neutral and detached when he "allowed himself to become a member, if not the leader, of the search party which was essentially a police operation." In Connally v. Georgia, 429 U.S. 245 (1977), the Supreme Court determined that a magistrate who was compensated based on a fee for the warrants issued could not be considered neutral and detached. It relied on its earlier case of Tumey v. Ohio, 273 U.S. 510 (1927), which invalidated on due process principles the payment of the village mayor, when he acted as a judge, from costs collected in criminal cases brought before him in which there was a conviction.

We afforded the same protection for a neutral and detached magistrate under our search and seizure constitutional provision in . . . State v. Dudick, 213 S.E.2d 458 (W.Va. 1975):

> The constitutional guarantee under W. Va. Const., Article III, §6 that no search warrant will issue except on probable cause goes to substance and not to form; therefore, where it is conclusively proved that a magistrate acted as a mere agent of the prosecutorial process and failed to make an independent evaluation of the circumstances surrounding a request for a warrant, the warrant will be held invalid and the search will be held illegal.

As the foregoing law indicates, where there is a lack of neutrality and detachment in the issuance of the search warrant, it is void. Aside from the constitutional requirements for a neutral and detached magistrate as to warrants, similar standards are imposed by Canon 3C of the Judicial Code of Ethics relating to the disqualification of a judge. The Code defines those situations when a judge may be precluded from presiding over a case. The underlying rationale for requiring disqualification is based on principles of due process. . . .

3. The applicable provisions in 1992 of the Judicial Code of Ethics . . . were in Canon 3C(1) and 3C(1)(d):

A judge should disqualify himself in a proceeding in which his impartiality might reasonably be questioned, including but not limited to instances where: . . .

(d) he or his spouse, or a person within the third degree of relationship to either of them, or the spouse of such a person:

(i) is a party to the proceeding, or an officer, director, or trustee of a party; . . .

(iii) is known by the judge to have an interest that could be substantially affected by the outcome of the proceeding;

(iv) is to the judge's knowledge likely to be a material witness in the proceeding. . . .

Canon 3C(1) contains an initial general admonition that a "judge should disqualify himself in a proceeding in which his impartiality might reasonably be questioned." This admonition is followed by a number of specific instances when disqualification is required. . . . In this case, in addition to the general disqualification standard, it is claimed that the more specific disqualification test contained in Canon 3C(1)(d)(iii) applies. This provision requires disqualification if the judge's spouse has "an interest that could be substantially affected by the outcome of the proceeding." This disqualification is claimed to apply if Chief Boober appeared before his wife to seek a warrant. . . . We have no case law on this point, but we agree with cases from other jurisdictions that support the disqualification.

For example, the Louisiana court in State v. LaCour, 493 So. 2d 756 (La. Ct. App. 1986), set aside a criminal conviction because it found that the judge should have disqualified himself because his son was prosecuting the defendant on another criminal charge in a different county. . . . In Smith v. Beckman, 683 P.2d 1214 (Colo. Ct. App. 1984), the judge's wife was an assistant prosecutor. The record showed that the prosecutor's office had screened her from cases that were before her husband. The court concluded that his disqualification in all criminal cases was warranted because of the appearance of impropriety. . . . The critical point in the court's view was the perception of the closeness created by the marital relationship:

> A husband and wife generally conduct their personal and financial affairs as a partnership. In addition to living together, a husband and wife are also perceived to share confidences regarding their personal lives and employment situations. Generally, the public views married people as "a couple," as "a partnership," and as participants in a relationship more intimate than any other kind of relationship between individuals. In our view the existence of a marriage relationship between a judge and a deputy district attorney in the same county is sufficient to establish grounds for disqualification, even though no other facts call into question the judge's impartiality. . . .

We believe that the foregoing cases and the language in Canon 3C(1) and 3C(1)(d)(i) of the Judicial Code of Ethics relating to the disqualification of a judicial official when his or her impartiality might reasonably be questioned if the official's spouse is a party to the proceeding would foreclose a magistrate from issuing a warrant sought by his or her spouse who is a police officer. However, this situation did not occur here.

The search warrant was issued at the request of Sergeant R. R. Roberts of the Ranson police force. At the hearing below, Magistrate Boober testified that she was the on-call magistrate for emergency matters that might occur after 4:00 P.M. and before 8:00 A.M. the next morning when the magistrate office would be open for normal business.

Magistrate Boober also stated that she was not related to Sergeant Roberts and had no contact with him except through the magistrate system. She also stated that she made an independent review of the affidavit for the search warrant. Her husband's name did not appear on the affidavit nor was there any discussion about her husband with Sergeant Roberts.

There was no evidence to show any actual bias or partiality on the part of Magistrate Boober. The entire argument centered on an implied partiality because of the magistrate's relationship to Chief Boober. We indicated earlier that any criminal matters which the magistrate's husband is involved with cannot be brought before her because of their spousal relationship. We decline to extend such a per se rule with regard to the other members of the Ranson police force. The fact that a magistrate's spouse is the chief of police of a small police force does not automatically disqualify the magistrate, who is otherwise neutral and detached, from issuing a warrant sought by another member of such police force. However, a small police force[14] coupled with the chief's active role in a given case may create an appearance of impropriety that would warrant a right to challenge the validity of a search warrant. Certainly, prudence dictates that Magistrate Boober's involvement with warrants from the Ranson police force should be severely curtailed. . . .

Finally, we are asked to extend the rule of necessity to allow Magistrate Boober to handle warrants when she is the on-call magistrate. The rule of necessity is an exception to the disqualification of a judge. It allows a judge who is otherwise disqualified to handle the case to preside if there is no provision that allows another judge to hear the matter. . . .

The rule of necessity is an exception to the general rule precluding a disqualified judge from hearing a matter. Therefore, it is strictly construed and applied only when there is no other person having jurisdiction to handle the matter that can be brought in to hear it. . . . We would not sanction the use of the rule were it to be offered if Chief Boober appeared seeking the search warrant. In the case of the other police officers from Ranson, we decline to utilize the rule simply because we do not find that Magistrate Boober is automatically barred from issuing warrants at their request. There may be circumstances that can be shown that would cast a shadow over the magistrate's impartiality. In that event, a motion to suppress the evidence obtained under the warrant may be made, and the issue will be resolved at a hearing. . . . The matter is remanded for a further hearing with regard to the warrant if the relators below desire to challenge it on the basis that there are additional facts, other than her marriage to Chief Boober, that demonstrate Magistrate Boober was not neutral and detached. . . .

Notes

1. *Who issues warrants? Majority view.* Most states (more than 30) allow only judges and magistrates to issue warrants. Some state statutes require that magistrates be lawyers, while others list no special statutory qualifications. Judges generally appoint magistrates. They are thus subject to removal by judges or city officials and lack some of the usual privileges accorded to judicial officers. A smaller group of states allow functionaries — who go by titles such as "clerk magistrates," "ministerial recorders," clerks of court, or court commissioners — to issue search warrants. In West Virginia, mayors have the power to issue search warrants pursuant to violations of city ordinances. W. Va. Code §8-10-1.

As noted in *Dietrick,* the Supreme Court, in Connally v. Georgia, 429 U.S. 245 (1977), found unconstitutional a system that compensated magistrates for each warrant they issued. What if, to encourage protection of individual rights, magistrates were paid for warrants they refused to issue?

14. The 1993 West Virginia Blue Book gives the population of the City of Ranson at 2,890. According to the [briefs], there are six other police officers in addition to the Chief of Police.

2. *Neutrality in outcomes.* What if a defendant can show that a particular magistrate has never refused a warrant or approves warrants 98 percent of the time? A major empirical study of the search warrant process in seven jurisdictions made the following observations about the number of warrant applications denied by magistrates:

> It is unfortunate, though not surprising, that documents are not routinely collected that reveal the number of applications that are denied by magistrates. Normally a rejected application is destroyed or revised by the applicant. According to our observations and interviews, the rate of outright rejection is extremely low. Most of the police officers interviewed could not remember having a search warrant application turned down. The estimates by the judges interviewed varied on the number of rejections from almost never to about half. Of the 84 warrant proceedings observed, 7 resulted in denial of the application (8 percent).

Richard van Duizend, Paul Sutton & Charlotte Carter, The Search Warrant Process: Preconceptions, Perceptions, Practices 26-27 (1985). A more recent study of warrant practices in one jurisdiction noted that some judges handled far more than their share of warrant applications. Of the 24 judges available for duty, six judges issued almost three-fourths of the search warrants. Laurence A. Benner and Charles T. Samarkos, Searching for Narcotics in San Diego: Preliminary Findings from the San Diego Search Warrant Project, 36 Cal. W. L. Rev. 221, 226 (2000). Could a defendant strengthen her challenge to the neutrality of a magistrate by demonstrating that the police apply to the particular magistrate in question for search warrants far more often than to other available magistrates?

b. Particularity in Warrants

Remember that the Fourth Amendment, in language echoed in many state provisions, says that "no Warrants shall issue, but upon probable cause, supported by Oath or affirmation, and particularly describing the place to be searched, and the persons or things to be seized." The following classic state cases explore the requirement that warrants be supported by "Oath or affirmation" and that they "particularly" describe the place to be searched and the persons or things to be seized. This "particularity" requirement captures an essential part of the distinction between valid warrants and invalid general warrants.

BELL v. CLAPP

10 Johns. 263 (N.Y. 1813)

PER CURIAM

The matter set forth in the plea is a justification of the trespass. The search warrant was founded on oath, and the information stated that one hundred barrels of flour had been stolen from the wharf, in the first ward, by Richard and Isaac Jaques, and that the same, or a part thereof, was concealed in a cellar of Gideon Jaques. The plea then states that the warrant, being under the hand and seal of the magistrate . . . , and being directed to the constables and marshals, authorized and required them to enter the said cellar, in the day-time, and search for the flour, and to bring it, together with the said Gideon, or the person in whose custody it might be found, before the justice; that in pursuance of the warrant, the defendants, the one being a constable and the other a marshal, did go to the cellar, which was part and parcel of the dwelling-house of the plaintiff, and, after being refused entrance, did open the door by force, and seize the flour in as peaceable a manner as possible. This, then, was a valid warrant duly executed by these officers. The warrant had all the essential qualities of a legal warrant. It was founded on oath, and was specific as to place and object, and the stolen goods were taken, and taken in as peaceable a manner as the nature of the case admitted.

In Entick v. Carrington . . . Lord Camden admitted a search warrant, so well guarded, to be a lawful authority. The warrant did not state in whom the property of the flour resided, nor was this essential to its validity: a person may even be indicted and convicted of stealing the goods of a person unknown. Nor did it affect the legality of the warrant that it directed the officer to bring Jaques, to whom the cellar belonged, or the person in whose custody the flour might be found. It was impossible for any warrant to be more explicit and particular; and it would, probably, have been the duty of the officer to have arrested any person in possession of the stolen goods at the place designated, without any directions in the warrant, and to have carried him before the justice for examination.

Sir Mathew Hale, in one part of his treatise, denies to the officer the right of breaking open the door, on a warrant to search for stolen goods. But he, afterwards, admits this power in the officer, if the door be shut, and if upon demand it is refused to be opened. This past opinion is founded on the better reason, for search warrants are often indispensable to the detection of crimes; and they would be of little or no efficacy without this power attached to them. All the checks which the English law, and which even the constitution of the United States, have imposed upon the operation of these search warrants, and with the manifestation of a strong jealousy of the abuses incident to them, would scarcely have been thought of, or have been deemed necessary, if the warrant did not communicate the power of opening the outer door of a house. . . .

The defendants are, accordingly, entitled to judgment upon the demurrers. Judgment for the defendants.

Notes

1. *Particular description of place to be searched: majority position.* The nineteenth-century opinion in *Bell* reflects some very modern concerns. Both state and federal constitutions require that the warrant name with "particularity" the place to be searched and the things to be seized. When a warrant lists property in an urban setting, the street address (including the apartment number, where relevant) is usually particular enough to allow the searching officer "with reasonable effort [to] ascertain and identify the place intended." Steele v. United States, 267 U.S. 498 (1925). Property in a rural setting might be described without an address.

Another famous case from the early nineteenth century offers a useful comparison to *Bell*. In Grummon v. Raymond, 1 Conn. 40 (1814), the court disapproved of a search warrant authorizing government agents to search for stolen goods; the warrant directed the officials to search for the stolen bags "at Aaron Hyatt's, or some other place" among the houses, stores, shops, and barns of the town of Wilton. The officer also was directed to search suspected persons, and arrest them. The court described the proper contents of a warrant as follows: "There must be an oath by the applicant that he has had his goods stolen, and strongly suspects that they are concealed in such a place; and the warrant cannot give a direction to search any other place than the particular place pointed out." What was the difference between the alternative phrasing in the warrants in *Bell* and *Grummon*? Would a warrant listing more than one place to search ever be valid? Does it matter if different people own or occupy the properties? Compare State v. Mehner, 480 N.W.2d 872 (Iowa 1992) (validating warrant listing two house trailers with different occupants) with State v. Marshall, 974 A.2d 1038 (N.J. 2009) (warrant that listed address of house containing duplex units, leaving officers uncertain which unit to search, violated particularity requirement).

Warrants tend to be more specific about the place to be searched than about any persons to be searched. Why is that? If you were a magistrate, what sort of evidence would convince you to issue a warrant authorizing the search of a specific bar and "all persons" found on those premises? See State v. Thomas, 540 N.W.2d 658 (Iowa 1995) (invalidating warrant; application noted numerous prior arrests and controlled purchases of crack cocaine, and observations by undercover officers that most persons present in bar possessed narcotics or weapons).

2. *Particular description of things to be seized: majority position.* Warrants authorize searches for particular objects. The types of objects that may be seized vary somewhat from state to state, although the general categories are fruits, instrumentalities, and evidence of crime. See Ill. Stat. ch. 725, §5/108-3(a) ("any judge may issue a search warrant for the seizure of [any] instruments, articles or things designed or intended for use or which are or have been used in the commission of, or which may constitute evidence of, the offense in connection with which the warrant is issued; or contraband, the fruits of crime, or things otherwise criminally possessed"). The Fourth Amendment requirement of particularity "makes general searches . . . impossible and prevents the seizure of one thing under a warrant describing another. As to what is taken, nothing is left to the discretion of the officer executing the warrant." Marron v. United States, 275 U.S. 192 (1927). What sort of description in the warrant would leave "nothing" to the discretion of the officer? See People v. Brown, 749 N.E.2d 170 (N.Y. 2001) (warrant naming four particular items plus authorizing search for "any other property the possession of which would be considered contraband" was overbroad); State v. Browne, 970 A.2d 81 (Conn. 2009) (supporting affidavit incorporated by reference in search warrant can cure lack of sufficient particularity in description of items to be seized, even if affidavit does not accompany warrant at scene of search; most important protections of warrant occur before search, not at scene of search).

The consequences are severe when the warrant fails to describe particularly the items to be seized. In Groh v. Ramirez, 540 U.S. 551 (2004), the Supreme Court held that a search warrant failing to describe the items to be seized from a home could not be cured by the agent's inclusion of a list of the items in an unincorporated warrant application, or by his oral description to the homeowners of the items to be seized.

Like the federal constitution, most state constitutions and statutes also require a description of the items (or persons) being sought and an explanation for why the applicant believes that the items (or persons) are at the location sought. See Ohio

Rev. Code §2933.24(A) (search warrant shall "particularly name or describe the property to be searched for and seized, the place to be searched, and the person to be searched").

3. *Warrants "in writing" and telephonic warrants.* A majority of states have statutes requiring that warrants be in writing. A number of state constitutions also expressly provide for written warrants. See Neb. Rev. Stat. §29-830; R.I. Const. Art. 1, §6. Requiring warrants to be in writing does not preclude their electronic transmission. See Mich. Comp. Laws §780.651.

Despite the prevalence of constitutional provisions and statutes calling for warrants obtained by testimony made under oath and "in writing," a growing number of states have statutes authorizing the police to obtain warrants over the telephone. Consider, for example, Kan. Stat. Ann. §22-2502(a):

> A search warrant shall be issued only upon the oral or written statement, including those conveyed or received by telefacsimile communication, of any person under oath or affirmation which states facts sufficient to show probable cause that a crime has been or is being committed and which particularly describes a person, place or means of conveyance to be searched and things to be seized. Any statement which is made orally shall be either taken down by a certified shorthand reporter, sworn to under oath and made part of the application for a search warrant, or recorded before the magistrate from whom the search warrant is requested and sworn to under oath. Any statement orally made shall be reduced to writing as soon thereafter as possible. If the magistrate is satisfied that grounds for the application exist or that there is probable cause to believe that they exist, the magistrate may issue a search warrant.

Why does Kansas insist that the person seeking the warrant swear to the statement under oath? Why does the state go to the trouble and expense of reducing the statements to writing? Does the availability of telephonic warrants mean that police can claim exigent circumstances in far fewer cases? One survey of warrant practices discovered that officers rarely used the available procedures for telephonic and electronic search warrants. Laurence A. Benner & Charles T. Samarkos, Searching for Narcotics in San Diego: Preliminary Findings from the San Diego Search Warrant Project, 36 Cal. W. L. Rev. 221, 223 (2000). Why might police officers decline to use such procedures when they are available?

4. *Plain view seizures.* You may recall, from Chapter 2, the "plain view" doctrine, which declares that the police may seize evidence, contraband, or the fruits or instrumentalities of crime that come within the "plain view" of police officers during proper execution of a valid warrant. See Horton v. California, 496 U.S. 128 (1990) (item in plain view is seizable if its incriminating character is immediately apparent to police). Does this authorization to seize items not named in the warrant effectively eliminate any requirement that the warrant "particularly name" the property to be seized?

5. *The advantage for police of warrants listing small items.* The nature of the items sought will determine the permissible scope of the search. If police are looking for an elephant, the search will be limited to places an elephant might hide. If police are looking for a field mouse, the scope of the search would be much broader. See, e.g., State v. Apelt, 861 P.2d 634 (Ariz. 1993) (because warrant included receipts, police could conduct a very detailed search and had a higher possibility of additional "plain view" discovery of evidence than in a more narrowly circumscribed

search). Would it be ethical to advise police to include small items such as receipts in all warrant applications?

6. *The "four corners" rule.* If a defendant challenges the sufficiency of a warrant during a suppression hearing, statutes and court rules in most jurisdictions (and constitutional rulings in a few others) prevent the government from supplementing the warrant application itself with information that the officers knew at the time but failed to present to the magistrate. Some also prevent the government from relying on any information supplementing the application, even if it was actually presented to the magistrate. Greenstreet v. State, 898 A.2d 961 (Md. 2006). The government's defense of the warrant, in other words, must come from within the "four corners" of the application. Some states allow courts to supplement the "four corners" of the affidavit with information that could be "reasonably inferred" from the document, while others (about 10 states) go further and say that the court is free to use outside information at its discretion. See Moore v. Commonwealth, 159 S.W.3d 325, 328 (Ky. 2005). Various applications of the four corners rule can be found on the web extension for this chapter at *http://www.crimpro.com/extension/ch03*.

7. *Challenges to facially sufficient warrants.* Defendants sometimes will concede that the facts set forth in the affidavit amount to probable cause but contend that the factual basis for the warrant is untrue. The Supreme Court has held (and state courts have largely agreed) that if a defendant makes a preliminary showing of false statements in the warrant application, the trial court must grant a hearing on the question. Under Franks v. Delaware, 438 U.S. 154 (1978), the defendant's preliminary showing must demonstrate that the government "knowingly and intentionally, or with reckless disregard for the truth," included a false statement in the warrant affidavit. The attack must be "more than conclusory," and must point out "specifically with supporting reasons" the portion of the warrant affidavit that is claimed to be false. It also must be accompanied by affidavits or reliable statements of witnesses, or a satisfactory explanation of their absence. If the unreliable evidence was necessary to the government's showing of probable cause, the defendant gets a hearing and must establish his or her claims by a preponderance of the evidence before the fruits of the search or seizure are excluded from evidence. See State v. Chenoweth, 158 P.3d 595 (Wash. 2007) (state constitution, like federal law, requires suppression of evidence only if officer seeking a search warrant makes an omission or misrepresentation through reckless or intentional disregard for the truth; negligence by affiant does not require suppression).

Problem 3-3. Errors in a Facially Valid Warrant

Officer Holden observed a confidential informant make two illegal purchases of weapons at 916 Varney Street. Both times, the informant entered the building, returned with the weapons, and told Holden that he made the purchases in the "last apartment, of two, on the left" in a hallway down a flight of stairs. With this information, Holden applied for and obtained a warrant to search the apartment. The affidavit accompanying the application described the premises as follows:

> First-floor corner apartment, 916 Varney Street, described as a four-story red-brick structure with a green-colored solid door, with the number 916 affixed to the outside of the main entryway. The corner apartment is described as down one flight of stairs

where three apartment doors are situated with two on the left side and one on the right side, the door is tan in color and is the second door on the left side in the main hallway at the end of the hall.

Prior to executing the warrant, Holden sent the informant into the building for a third time. After returning outside, he told Holden that the apartment subject to the warrant had a rug in front of the door. When Holden entered the hallway of the building, he realized that the informant was mistaken: There were two doors on the right side of the hallway and only one on the left. Holden decided to search the sole apartment on the left because there was a rug outside the door. He discovered evidence of weapons violations.

In a suppression hearing, will the court treat the evidence as the product of a valid warranted search? Compare Buckner v. United States, 615 A.2d 1154 (D.C. 1992).

Notes

1. *Awareness of the error.* In this problem, the officer was aware of the inaccuracy in the warrant before executing it. Does it make a difference if the officer remains unaware of the inaccuracy until she has begun the search? See Maryland v. Garrison, 480 U.S. 79 (1987) (warrant listing third floor as single apartment, when it was actually divided into separate apartments, could be executed because officers were reasonable in not discovering the inadvertent error in the warrant). What should police officers do when they obtain new information about the person or place named in the warrant before they execute the warrant? Return to the magistrate for an updated finding of probable cause? See State v. Maddox, 98 P.3d 1199 (Wash. 2004) (officers must return to magistrate for updated ruling only if new facts negate probable cause).

2. *The wrong jurisdiction.* Is an otherwise valid warrant still valid if it is executed by police accidentally acting outside of their jurisdiction? See People v. Martinez, 898 P.2d 28 (Colo. 1995) (error in jurisdiction, despite violating statute, not fatal).

3. *Execution of Warrants*

Once the police have obtained a valid warrant, they must "execute" it. That is, the police carry out a search within the limits described in the warrant, and "return" it to the magistrate who issued the warrant. The return serves as a report about the search. Recall that the court in Entick v. Carrington expressed some concern about the lack of any return for a general warrant, and thus the enforcement officer who conducted the search would not be accountable for completing the job properly. Does a return actually prevent abuses by searchers?

Specific procedure rules and statutes address the details of executing warrants. For instance, rules determine the total time that can elapse between issuance and execution of a search warrant. All but three states prescribe a deadline for serving a warrant, at which time the warrant expires. This period ranges from two days (North Carolina and Pennsylvania) to 60 days (Arkansas). The typical time span is 10 days (the period employed in more than 30 states plus the federal system). As one might expect, searches are far more likely to produce the expected evidence if they are executed promptly. See Laurence A. Benner & Charles T. Samarkos, Searching for Narcotics in San Diego: Preliminary Findings from the San Diego Search Warrant Project, 36 Cal. W. L. Rev. 221, 223 (2000).

STATE v. TANYA MARIE ANYAN

104 P.3d 511 (Mont. 2004)

NELSON, J.

. . . ¶3 In late May 2000, Officer Christopher Nichols of the Thompson Falls Police Department was assigned to investigate suspected illegal drug activity occurring at a rented house in Thompson Falls. During the course of the investigation, Officer Nichols determined that the occupants of the house were involved in operating a clandestine methamphetamine lab. Hence, on July 11, 2000, Officer Nichols requested the assistance of Sergeant Allen Bardwell, an officer with the Kalispell Police Department and team leader of the Kalispell SWAT team, in serving a search warrant. After meeting with Officer Nichols and learning that the house to be searched was a large structure consisting of three levels with numerous rooms and that it might be occupied by as many as fifteen individuals, Sergeant Bardwell contacted the Flathead County Sheriff Department's SWAT team for assistance. The commander of the Flathead County SWAT team, Undersheriff Chuck Curry, agreed to assist in the service of the warrant.

¶4 On July 24, 2000, Officer Nichols obtained a warrant to search the residence. In his application for the search warrant, Officer Nichols related that "out of the ordinary traffic" was seen coming [to] and going from the residence and that a great number of the vehicles were from Washington state. Officer Nichols also stated that he checked the license plates on three of the vehicles that he had seen at the residence. One of them was registered to [Troy Klein]. Officer Nichols then checked with Spokane County and discovered that Klein had been charged in the past with committing drug offenses. According to Officer Nichols, Klein also had three active felony warrants.

¶5 Officer Nichols also related in his search warrant application that several other individuals that had been seen near the residence had been charged with drug offenses. In addition, one of the vehicles seen at the residence was registered to an individual who had felony convictions for burglary and child rape. Officer Nichols also related that during his investigation, he discovered that there was a surveillance camera located in the second story east window of the residence and that it appeared to be pointed at the driveway.

¶6 Officer Nichols had discovered during the course of his investigation that an individual matching Klein's description had purchased ammunition from a local hardware store. While he did not include this information in the application for the search warrant, Officer Nichols did share this information with Sergeant Bardwell and Undersheriff Curry. However, the two-and-a-half month investigation, which included surveillance of the home, had yielded no observation or reports of weapons sighted in the home or in the possession of any of the individuals in the home. Officer Nichols also discovered that Klein had a warrant for his arrest in connection with a nonviolent felony parole violation.

¶7 On the night of July 25, 2000, the two SWAT teams, totaling fifteen men, and officers from several other law enforcement agencies converged on Thompson Falls at approximately 1:45 A.M. . . . Officer Nichols ordered two officers to conduct surveillance on the residence from an upstairs bedroom of the house across the street. Officer Shawna Reinschmidt was watching the activities in the front of the house at 2:20 A.M. when a car, which had left the house about five minutes earlier, returned, and the male driver got out of the car and yelled at everyone to get inside and turn off the lights. Officer Reinschmidt reported her observations to the SWAT team assembled at the police department. . . . Officer Reinschmidt continued to observe the house and although she saw some movement in the kitchen, she later testified that her observations were entirely consistent with the occupants preparing to retire for the night.

¶9 Law enforcement officers executed their no-knock raid at 3:00 A.M. As the officers approached the house they observed that it was quiet and most of the lights were off. None of the officers detected any activity or heard anything consistent with attempts to escape or resist arrest. . . .

¶10 The officers approached the home from the west and the north, outside of the range of the surveillance camera located on the east side of the house. The Kalispell SWAT team was assigned to enter the house at the upper level from an outside stairway and the Flathead County SWAT team was assigned to enter the house from the ground floor. At least six officers from the Kalispell SWAT team entered the top floor by using a steel ram to break the doorjamb. They confronted four of the occupants of the house who were in various stages of sleep and preparation for sleep. Another seven or eight officers from the Flathead County SWAT team entered the house through the downstairs kitchen door confronting the two occupants residing in that portion of the house. Another five to ten officers surrounded the house. The officers did not knock and announce their presence prior to entering the house. . . .

¶12 [Several occupants of the house were charged] with conspiracy to manufacture dangerous drugs; criminal production or manufacture of dangerous drugs; criminal possession of dangerous drugs; and possession of dangerous drugs with intent to sell. [They] each filed motions to suppress the evidence seized during the search of the residence, based in part on the officers' failure to knock and announce their presence prior to entering the house to execute the search warrant. The District Court denied the motions. . . .

¶20 This is an issue of first impression in Montana. Montana has no statutory provisions or case law addressing the knock-and-announce rule. Consequently, we look to the relevant federal law and the laws of our sister states to decide this issue. We also look to the greater protections afforded to Montanans in search and seizure matters under Article II, Sections 10 and 11 of the Montana Constitution. . . .

¶22 Underlying the knock-and-announce rule are concerns for the protection of privacy, reduction in the potential for violence, and the prevention of the destruction of property of private citizens. There is nothing more terrifying to the occupants than to be suddenly confronted in the privacy of their home by a police officer decorated with guns and the insignia of his office. This is why the law protects its entrance so rigidly.

> The fear of a smashing in of doors by government agents is based upon much more than a concern that our privacy will be disturbed. It is based upon concern for our safety

and the safety of our families. Indeed, the minions of dictators do not kick in doors for the mere purpose of satisfying some voyeuristic desire to peer around and then go about their business. Something much more malevolent and dangerous is afoot when they take those actions. . . .

United States v. Lockett, 919 F.2d 585, 592 (9th Cir. 1990). [As] a matter of policy, no-knock warrants are disfavored because of their staggering potential for violence to both the occupants of the residence and the police. "Unannounced breaking and entering into a home could quite easily lead an individual to believe that his safety was in peril and cause him to take defensive measures which he otherwise would not have taken had he known that a warrant had been issued to search his home." State v. Bamber, 630 So. 2d 1048, 1052 (Fla. 1994). . . .

¶25 Because the Fourth Amendment protects property as well as privacy, another purpose of the knock-and-announce rule is to prevent the needless destruction of property. . . .

¶27 [The United States Supreme Court addressed the knock-and-announce principle in Wilson v. Arkansas, 514 U.S. 927 (1995).] After Sharlene Wilson made several narcotics sales to an informant, law enforcement officers with the Arkansas State Police obtained warrants to arrest her and search her home. The affidavit in support of the warrants stated that Wilson's housemate, Bryson Jacobs, had previously been convicted of arson and firebombing. On the afternoon of the search, the officers found the main door to Wilson's home open. As the officers opened an unlocked screen door and entered the residence, they identified themselves as police officers and stated that they had a warrant. They found Wilson in the bathroom flushing marijuana down the toilet. [The Supreme Court held that] the common-law knock-and-announce principle forms a part of the Fourth Amendment reasonableness inquiry. . . .

¶29 In making this determination, the Supreme Court examined in *Wilson* the history of the common-law knock-and-announce rule, noting that although common law generally protected a man's house as "his castle of defense and asylum," common-law courts long held that the sheriff, acting on behalf of the King, could enter a man's house to arrest him "or to do other execution of the King's process," but only after signifying the cause of his coming and requesting that the doors be opened. See 3 W. Blackstone, Commentaries; Semayne's Case, 77 Eng. Rep. 194 (K.B. 1603). . . . In addition, most of the states that ratified the Fourth Amendment enacted constitutional provisions or statutes generally incorporating English common law and a few states enacted statutes specifically embracing the common-law view that the breaking of the door of a dwelling was permitted once admittance was refused. . . . Hence, the Court held that the common-law knock-and-announce principle does form a part of the Fourth Amendment reasonableness inquiry.

¶32 The Court further held, however, that not every entry must be preceded by an announcement. [The] presumption in favor of announcement necessarily would give way to countervailing law enforcement interests. Those interests included circumstances presenting a threat of physical harm to officers, the fact that an officer is pursuing a recently escaped arrestee, and where officers have reason to believe that evidence would likely be destroyed if advance notice were given. . . .

Exigent Circumstances

¶34 Exigent circumstances [are] those circumstances that would cause a reasonable person to believe that entry (or other relevant prompt action) was necessary to prevent physical harm to the officers or other persons, the destruction of relevant evidence, the escape of a suspect, or some other consequence improperly frustrating legitimate law enforcement efforts. . . .

¶35 There are two types of exigencies, those that are foreknown and those unexpected that arise on the scene. . . . In the case before us on appeal, all of the factors that officers actually deemed exigent were actually known well in advance of applying for the search warrant. The SWAT teams became involved in this investigation almost two weeks prior to applying for a search warrant. It was at that point that the decision was made that there would be a no-knock forcible entry into the house. The court issuing the search warrant was never apprised of that decision, nor were any exigent circumstances laid out to the court when the search warrant was applied for.

¶36 Moreover, while peril to officers or the possibility of destruction of evidence or escape may well demonstrate an exigency, mere unspecific fears about those possibilities will not. Were they enough, the knock-and-announce [principle would be inapplicable to virtually all narcotics-based cases. The Supreme Court, however, has] held that the Fourth Amendment does not permit a blanket exception to the knock-and-announce requirement in felony drug investigations. Richards v. Wisconsin, 520 U.S. 385 (1997).

¶37 In *Richards*, law enforcement officers obtained a warrant to search Richards' motel room for drugs and related paraphernalia. One officer, dressed as a maintenance man, knocked on the door and stated that he was with maintenance. With the chain still on the door, Richards cracked it open, but slammed it closed again when he saw a uniformed officer standing behind the "maintenance man." After waiting two or three seconds, the officers kicked in the door. They claimed at trial that they identified themselves as police as they were kicking in the door. The officers caught Richards trying to escape through a window. They found cash and cocaine hidden in plastic bags in the bathroom ceiling.

¶38 Richards sought to have the evidence from his motel room suppressed on the ground that the officers failed to knock and announce their presence prior to forcing entry into the room. The trial court denied the motion. . . . The Wisconsin Supreme Court affirmed, concluding that it was reasonable to assume that all felony drug crimes would involve "an extremely high risk of serious if not deadly injury to the police as well as the potential for the disposal of drugs by the occupants prior to entry by the police." Thus, the Wisconsin Supreme Court concluded that exigent circumstances justifying a no-knock entry are always present in felony drug cases; hence, police officers are never required to knock and announce their presence when executing a search warrant in a felony drug investigation.

¶39 The United States Supreme Court disagreed and determined that the Fourth Amendment does not permit a blanket exception to the knock-and-announce requirement for felony drug investigations. Rather, the Supreme Court held that to justify a no-knock entry, police must have a reasonable suspicion that knocking and announcing their presence, under the particular circumstances, would be dangerous or futile, or that it would inhibit effective investigation of the crime by, for example, allowing the destruction of evidence.

¶40 [The use of blanket exceptions] presented two serious concerns: (1) the exception contains considerable overgeneralization as not every drug investigation poses substantial risks to the officers' safety and the preservation of evidence; and (2) the reasons for creating an exception in one category can, relatively easily, be applied to others and thereby render meaningless the knock-and-announce element of the Fourth Amendment's reasonableness requirement.

¶41 Although the Supreme Court rejected the Wisconsin court's blanket exception to the knock-and-announce requirement in *Richards,* the Supreme Court agreed with the trial court that on the facts of that case, it was reasonable for the officers to believe that Richards knew, after he opened the door, that the men seeking entry to his room were the police and that once the officers reasonably believed that Richards knew who they were, it was reasonable for them to force entry immediately given the disposable nature of the drugs. . . .

Safety Concerns

¶43 Exigent circumstances cannot be predicated upon general fears of the officers executing a search warrant in a narcotics investigation. While peril to officers may well demonstrate an exigency, mere unspecific fears about that possibility will not. [Officers] are concerned about an armed response when they execute any narcotics search warrant. Clearly, though, to expand the exigent circumstances exception to that extent would completely swallow the rule.

¶44 Hence, [evidence] that firearms are within the residence or that a particular defendant is armed is not by itself sufficient to create an exigency. There must be specific information to lead the officers to a reasonable conclusion that the presence of firearms raises concerns for the officers' safety. [Threats] to an officer's safety, a criminal record reflecting violent tendencies, or a verified reputation of a suspect's violent nature can be enough to provide law enforcement officers with justification to forgo the necessity of knocking and announcing their presence.

¶45 In the case sub judice, the officers had no information that any of the occupants of the house possessed weapons. Officer Nichols had information that a person matching Klein's description had purchased ammunition. However, even after months of surveillance, Officer Nichols had no information of weapons being in the residence and no report of anyone seeing any of the occupants of the house, including Klein, with weapons. There was no testimony indicating that any of the occupants of the house were prone to violence or the use of weapons or had ever made threats against law enforcement officers.

¶46 Prior to initiating the raid, Sergeant Bardwell completed a risk analysis report intended to assess the risk associated with specific individuals who the officers anticipate might be present during a raid. Sergeant Bardwell testified that Klein was the only person considered in conjunction with the risk analysis assessment and the only person about whom Sergeant Bardwell had any information prior to the raid. Sergeant Bardwell agreed that the only criterion that applied to Klein from the risk analysis checklist was that he was on probation or parole for a nonviolent offense. . . .

¶48 The State claims that another factor in determining exigency under the safety exception is the inherent danger in methamphetamine labs. In this case, although Officer Nichols expressed concerns regarding the safety of neighborhood residents, he made no attempt to evacuate any residences. . . .

Futility

¶51 The futility exception to the knock-and-announce rule excuses the knock-and-announce requirement where police officers have a reasonable suspicion that the occupants know of the presence and purpose of the police prior to their entry into the residence. . . .

¶55 In the present case, the State conceded in oral argument that the futility exception was not applicable in this case. [The] SWAT teams approached the house from the north and west, thereby effectively remaining outside of the range of the surveillance camera. Additionally, the raid was conducted at night and the officers had no information that the camera was operational, especially in the dark. . . .

Destruction of Evidence

¶58 We also conclude that in this case the possibility of destruction of evidence did not create an exigent circumstance justifying the no-knock entry into Appellants' house. [The] government must prove they had a reasonable belief that the loss or destruction of evidence was imminent. The mere possibility or suspicion that a party is likely to dispose of evidence when faced with the execution of a search warrant is not sufficient to create an exigency. . . . The larger the amount of drugs and the more complex the operation, the less likelihood there is that evidence will be destroyed during the period between the knock and announce and the subsequent entry.

¶60 In this case, both Sergeant Bardwell and Undersheriff Curry testified that the mere fact that the residence contained a meth lab would not justify a no-knock entry. Moreover, Sergeant Bardwell testified that the potential for the destruction of the meth lab was not a concern in deciding to take on the assignment. Both Sergeant Bardwell and Undersheriff Curry agreed that a meth lab cannot be destroyed in a matter of five to ten seconds.

Conclusion

. . . ¶63 [The] decision to make a no-knock entry should ordinarily be made by a neutral and detached magistrate as part of the application for search warrant. An investigating officer may, however, make this decision based on unexpected exigent circumstances that arise on the scene. When law enforcement officers contemplate a no-knock entry in executing a search warrant, that intention must be included in the application for the search warrant along with any foreknown exigent circumstances justifying the no-knock entry. . . .

¶65 In conclusion, we hold that the law enforcement officers' no-knock entry into Appellants' house to execute the search warrant violated Appellants' federal and state constitutional rights to be free from unreasonable searches and seizures. Consequently, the trial court erred in failing to suppress the evidence resulting from that search. . . .

¶72 [The dissent] objects to our analysis, complaining that we have taken the "totality" out of "totality of the circumstances." Contrary to the dissent's contention, in order to examine the "totality" of the circumstances, each circumstance must first be considered on its own strength. [We] cannot agree that just because there are a number of circumstances, not one of which standing alone would create an exigency, the sheer volume of circumstances without something more is sufficient to create exigent circumstances. [Simply] put, zero plus zero can never equal one. . . .

RICE, J., dissenting.

. . . ¶78 [The Supreme Court in] *Richards* held that, although police should be required to make the necessary showing whenever the reasonableness of a no-knock entry is challenged, the showing itself is "not high." Further, it is not necessary to establish a level of proof satisfying the probable cause standard.

¶79 Indeed, the *Richards* "reasonable suspicion" standard is the same standard applied for the reasonableness of an investigative stop. . . .

¶80 Whether particularized suspicion supports an investigative stop is a question of fact that is analyzed in the context of the totality of the circumstances. In order for the State to prove the existence of particularized suspicion, the State must show: (1) objective data from which an experienced officer can make certain inferences; and (2) a resulting suspicion that the occupant of a certain vehicle is or has been engaged in wrongdoing or was a witness to criminal activity. . . .

¶81 . . . Citing to *Richards*' holding that there can be no "blanket exceptions" to the knock-and-announce rule for felony drug investigations, the Court simply dismisses the nature of the crime here as irrelevant to the inquiry. This is an incorrect application of *Richards*, which also concluded that it is "indisputable that felony drug investigations may frequently involve both" the threat of physical violence and the likelihood of destruction of evidence. [Contrary] to this Court's analysis, the nature of the crime being investigated is nonetheless a key factor which must be considered by police. The law has uniformly recognized that substantial dealers in narcotics possess firearms and that entrance into a situs of drug trafficking activity carries all too real dangers to law enforcement officers. . . .

¶82 [The Court also] dismisses the significance of the kind of drugs involved here — a methamphetamine laboratory. The Court should well know by now that "meth labs" are inherently unstable and dangerous, presenting this additional danger to officers. Nonetheless, the Court concludes this factor is not relevant to the inquiry because police made no attempt to evacuate any residences. Unfortunately, the dismissal of this concern by the Court does not accurately reflect the evidence in the record. To the contrary, Officer Bardwell testified that the situation here — "a meth lab with multiple suspects and they had warrants" — weighed significantly in his mind. . . .

¶83 . . . Klein's ammunition purchase may by itself have been insufficient to establish an exigency, but that did not render this evidence irrelevant to the inquiry. The Court reasons as if the evidence did not exist or was completely inconsequential. To the contrary, Officer Bardwell testified that evidence of the ammunition purchase by Klein, a fugitive felon, was significant to his analysis, and the District Court found this fact to be significant.

¶84 The Court . . . repeatedly focuses on the evidence which the police did not have. . . . Here, because the police had "no information" about whether the occupants were armed and "no information" about weapons being in the house, the Court concludes that the ammunition purchase by Klein is simply immaterial. This is a faulty inquiry. The proper focus in determining reasonable suspicion is what police did observe, and whether an experienced police officer can make certain inferences therefrom. Thus, I disagree with the Court's conclusion about this evidence. Purchase of ammunition by a fugitive felon who is associating with a group operating a meth lab is not a "mere unspecific fear." . . .

¶85 [The] Court illogically reasons that because the surveillance camera would be rendered ineffective by the speed of the no-knock entry, the camera was therefore not a factor to be considered in justifying the no-knock entry. Obviously, the camera would not have been rendered ineffective but for the no-knock entry. In addition to this error in logic, the Court again critically misapprehends Officer Bardwell's testimony. Officer Bardwell offered testimony to the precisely opposite conclusion about the significance of the surveillance camera: . . .

> *Defense:* How did [the presence of a surveillance camera] matter in terms of planning your raid?
>
> *Bardwell:* That if they have an operation that they deem the expense and trouble to put up counter-surveillance, it's probably a pretty substantial operation that they have. . . .

¶88 Additional factors could be analyzed, but this is enough. Clearly, there were specifically identifiable, objective factors which indicated to police that the situation required a no-knock entry. However, the Court, engaging in a "divide and conquer" analysis, systematically eliminates the effect of each factor. [The Court's analysis] separates and pigeonholes the factors which the police here considered, thereby eliminating all of them. In effect, it has taken the "totality" out of "totality of the circumstances."

¶90 Police here were faced with executing a felony drug warrant in a large structure in which numerous suspects with violent criminal backgrounds were staying. One suspect was known to have purchased ammunition. The suspects had mounted a surveillance camera. A meth lab was housed in the structure, and the size of the structure would inhibit the ability of police to locate and secure the lab. The numbers of suspects known to be inside could present safety and escape concerns. Shortly before the raid, one suspect yelled suspiciously. From a consideration of the totality of these circumstances, I would conclude that police had objective data from which they could reasonably infer, and from which a reasonable suspicion would arise, that a no-knock entry was necessary.

Notes

1. *Use of force in executing warrants and "knock and announce."* Most states have statutes requiring a police officer executing a search warrant to "knock and announce"—that is, to knock on the door before entering, to identify himself as a police officer, and to explain the purpose for seeking entry. See 18 U.S.C. §3109. Those with no statute on point have recognized the doctrine through judicial opinions. Only after entrance has been refused may the officer use force to enter. The knock-and-announce requirement derives from the common law. See Semayne's Case, 77 Eng. Rep. 194 (K.B. 1603). It also has constitutional dimensions: A failure to knock and announce can have some bearing on the constitutional "reasonableness" of a search or seizure. See Wilson v. Arkansas, 514 U.S. 927 (1995).

Once the officers have knocked on the door and announced their identity and purpose for wanting to enter, they may then enter by force after waiting a reasonable time for the occupants to respond to their knock. The amount of delay required in a given case depends on the nature of the evidence involved, the size of the dwelling, the time of day, and many other factors. In United States v. Banks, 540 U.S. 31 (2003), the Court approved of forceful entry by officers after they knocked, announced, and waited for 15 to 20 seconds. The evidence involved (cocaine) was easily disposable, and the apartment was small.

2. *No-knock entry.* There are important exceptions to the knock-and-announce requirement. Typically, the police may enter without notice if they have enough reason to believe that notice would endanger themselves or some other party, or would allow for the destruction of evidence or the escape of a suspect. What common household sounds might justify a forcible no-knock entry to execute a search? See also United States v. Ramirez, 523 U.S. 65 (1998) ("no knock" searches that cause property damage subject to same reasonableness standard as those causing no damage). A number of courts allow police officers to enter without announcing their true intentions if they can gain entry through a ruse such as pretending to be the "pizza man." Adcock v. Commonwealth, 967 S.W.2d 6 (Ky. 1998); State v. Elerieki, 993 P.2d 1191 (Haw. 2000). Is entry through a ruse consistent with the rationale of the knock-and-announce principle?

According to the opinion in Richards v. Wisconsin, 520 U.S. 385 (1997), the exceptions to the knock-and-announce requirement cannot be phrased too broadly. A blanket exception for "drug cases" will not stand; the police must show case-specific facts to demonstrate the need for a no-knock warrant. However, on the specific facts of that case, the officers' decision to enter the location unannounced might be constitutionally reasonable. An exploration of the cases that evaluate no-knock entry by the police appears on the web extension for this chapter at *http://www.crimpro.com/extension/ch03*.

3. *Limits on nighttime searches.* Another common subject for statutes and codes of criminal procedure is the time of day or night an officer may execute a search warrant. More than a dozen states have rules or statutes explicitly authorizing the execution of a search warrant at night, without any special showing or procedures. See Ind. Code §35-33-5-7(c); Va. Code Ann. §19.2-56. However, more than 30 states have statutes or procedural rules imposing some legal limit on the execution of search warrants at night beyond the usual requirements for daytime warrants. These states often require the government agents to make some special showing to the magistrate before conducting a search at night. See Minn. Stat. §626.14 (search warrant may be served only between 7 A.M. and 8 P.M. unless court "determines on the basis of facts stated in the affidavits that a nighttime search outside those hours is necessary to prevent the loss, destruction, or removal of the objects of the search or to protect the searchers or the public"); State v. Jackson, 742 N.W.2d 163 (Minn. 2007) (Fourth Amendment incorporates common law requirement that law enforcement officers have some justification for executing a search warrant at night). Where detailed statutes or procedure rules loom larger than any constitutional requirements, does that tend to make procedure clearer?

4. *Witnesses and returns.* The law in Germany and France requires searches of a home to be witnessed by a resident or someone else not working for the police. See Richard S. Frase & Thomas Weigend, German Criminal Justice as a Guide to American Law Reform: Similar Problems, Better Solutions?, 18 B.C. Int'l & Comp. L. Rev. 317 (1995). In the United States, officers executing a search warrant must fill out the "return," describing to the issuing judge the results of the search. Do these two requirements provide comparable protections to the owner of property that is searched?

5. *Burden of proof.* Most jurisdictions encourage greater police use of search warrants by shifting the burden of proof at a suppression hearing. While the government bears the burden of proof for warrantless searches that are challenged at a suppression hearing, the defendant must carry the burden of proof for warranted searches. Ford v. State, 158 S.W.3d 488 (Tex. Crim. App. 2005) (defendant bears burden of production in motions to suppress, but burden of proof shifts to state if defendant shows that search was warrantless); People v. Syrie, 101 P.3d 219 (Colo. 2004). There is, however, a sizable group of states placing the burden of coming forward and the burden of persuasion on the prosecution for all motions to suppress. See Kan. Stat. Ann. §22-3216 ("the burden of proving that the search and seizure were lawful shall be on the prosecution").

6. *Physical detentions during execution of warrant.* Can the police insist that those present at the location of a warranted search remain there while the search goes forward? Can they use force to prevent those present from moving about? See Muehler v. Mena, 544 U.S. 93 (2005) (execution of search warrant was not unreasonable where officers entered home at 7 A.M., detained occupants of home in handcuffs during hours-long search of home for weapons and gang member, and questioned occupants about their immigration status); Michigan v. Summers, 452 U.S. 692 (1981); Cotton v. State, 872 A.2d 87 (Md. 2005) (officers executing search warrant at residence used to sell drugs may detain person found standing outside the home).

7. *Warrants for computer searches.* Some magistrates place specialized conditions on how computer warrants are executed. The conditions address the on-site seizure of computers, the timing of a later off-site search, the method of the off-site search, and the return of the seized computers after searches are complete. Does the nature of the storage medium for information justify a specialized set of practices for executing a warrant? See Orin S. Kerr, Ex Ante Regulation of Computer Search and Seizure, 96 Va. L. Rev. 1241 (2010).

4. *So You Like Warrants?*

There is surprisingly little empirical literature on how often warrants are actually used across different jurisdictions and for different kinds of searches (for example, for different suspected crimes). The general perception, supported by the limited evidence now available, is that the police conduct most searches, across most crime categories, in most jurisdictions, without obtaining warrants. Consider the following introduction from the van Duizend et al. study of the warrant process:

> [Warrants] do not serve as a primary safeguard of privacy because they are sought in relatively few cases. . . . The most detailed study of warrants prior to this one — the American Bar Foundation's survey of the Administration of Criminal Justice conducted in the late 1950s — found 29 search warrants issued in Detroit, 30 in Milwaukee, and 17 in Wichita during 1956. Following the application of the "exclusionary rule" to state court decisions, there was a substantial increase in the use of search warrants, although the number remains a small proportion of all criminal cases. In Boston, for example, the number of search warrants issued annually averaged 693 between 1961 and 1976. Moreover, the types of cases in which warrants were used appear to be quite limited, according to the literature. . . . Krantz, Gilman, Benda and

> Hallstrom (1979), in their study of Boston police practices, found that 83 percent of the warrants issued during 1976 in the city's three busiest district courts "were to investigate suspected violations of the narcotic drug laws or vice laws." Such offenses accounted for less than 12 percent of all arrests nationally for that year.

What could courts or legislatures or police departments do to encourage police officers to use warrants more often and to make warrants a more significant form of protection against improper searches and seizures? One possibility is to make the warrant requirement a true requirement, subject only to an exception for necessity. In other words, if a warrant can be obtained, it must be obtained or the search will be held invalid. Another approach would be to judge warrantless searches under a different, tougher standard than searches conducted pursuant to a warrant. A third possibility would be to encourage the use of telephonic or electronic warrants. For example, a jurisdiction might allow oral statements to support warrant requests, put cellular phones in police cars, and arrange to have a magistrate available "on call." Consider as well the two approaches we explore in this section, both of which might encourage the use of search warrants.

a. Anticipatory Warrants

The prototypical application for a search warrant describes events that have already occurred and infers from those facts the probable cause to believe that a crime has been committed and that the items sought will be found at the named location. But this creates a timing problem. The officer completes the application after gathering the relevant facts establishing probable cause and before the search takes place. The minutes or hours necessary to obtain a warrant may not be available after the confirmation of probable cause but before the search must happen. To relieve this problem, can the application anticipate future events?

■ MICHAEL DODSON v. STATE

150 P.3d 1054 (Okla. Crim. App. 2006)

C. JOHNSON, J.

. . . ¶3 On September 29, 2003, a Tulsa police drug interdiction officer noticed a suspicious package at the Federal Express facility in Tulsa, Oklahoma. After the officer's drug dog "hit" on the package, the officer obtained a search warrant to open the package. Upon opening the package, the officer found the package contained a manila envelop with Mike Dodson's name on it. Inside the manila envelope was some rolled up tissue paper. Inside the rolled up tissue paper was a baggie. Inside the baggie was approximately one ounce of white crystal substance which field-tested positive for methamphetamine.

¶4 The officer prepared an affidavit for an anticipatory search warrant requesting to search Mike Dodson's residence upon delivery of the package and presented it to a Tulsa County magistrate. After the officer obtained a search warrant, he dressed as a Federal Express driver and delivered the package to Michael Dodson's address. Dodson answered the door, signed for the package and took it inside his residence.

¶5 Tulsa police officers served the search warrant about fifteen minutes later. During the search, they located the baggie containing the white crystal substance and a small quantity of marijuana in the house. No tax stamps were found on either the marijuana or the methamphetamine. . . .

¶6 . . . Mr. Dodson contends the Oklahoma Constitution prohibits the issuance of a warrant based upon future contingent events, making the "house warrant" illegal, and the fruits of its execution inadmissible at trial. This Court has not previously addressed the constitutionality of anticipatory search warrants under our state constitution, but recently the United States Supreme Court, in United States v. Grubbs, 547 U.S. 90 (2006) upheld the constitutionality of anticipatory search warrants under the Fourth Amendment to the United States Constitution.

¶7 Art.2, §30 of the Oklahoma Constitution provides:

> The right of the people to be secure in their persons, houses, papers, and effects against unreasonable searches or seizures shall not be violated; and no warrant shall issue but upon probable cause supported by oath or affirmation, describing as particularly as may be the place to be searched and the person or thing to be seized.

The language of Article II, Section 30 is almost an exact copy of the fourth amendment of the Constitution of the United States and while the language is not in all respects the same in the two provisions, the substance is identical.

¶8 Nothing in the text of Article II, Section 30 requires a showing that the evidence must be in the place to be searched at the time the warrant issues. On the contrary, the provision does not say anything about whether a finding of probable cause can or cannot be based upon the anticipation of some future event. Nothing in the plain language of Article II, Section 30 prohibits the issuance of an anticipatory search warrant and they do not run afoul of plain language of Oklahoma's constitution.

¶9 While anticipatory search warrants may not run afoul of the United States Constitution or the Oklahoma Constitution, we find merit to Mr. Dodson's second proposition that Oklahoma statutes prohibit the issuance of a warrant based upon future contingent events. Sections 1221-1238 of Title 22 outline the requisites for the issuance of a search warrant. Absent specific statutory authority for a separate procedure prior to the filing of a complaint in a criminal case, the State's ability to search for and seize evidence of a crime is limited to the procedure set forth in [the statutes listing] the requisites of a search warrant.

¶10 . . . The plain language of Title 22, Section 1222 requires that the object of the search be currently in the possession of the person or at the location to be searched. It provides that a search warrant may be issued and property seized upon any of the following grounds:

> First: When the property was stolen or embezzled, in which case it may be taken on the warrant, from any house or other place in which it is concealed, or from the possession of the person by whom it was stolen or embezzled, or of any other person in whose possession it may be.
>
> Second: When it was used as the means of committing a felony, in which case it may be taken on the warrant from any house or other place in which it is concealed, or from the possession of the person by whom it was used in the commission of the offense, or of any other person in whose possession it may be.

> Third: When it **is in the possession of any person,** with the intent to use it as the means of committing a public offense, or in the possession of another to whom he may have delivered it for the purpose of concealing it or preventing its being discovered, in which case it may be taken on the warrant from such person, or from a house or other place occupied by him, or under his control, or from the possession of the person to whom he may have so delivered it.
>
> Fourth: When the property constitutes evidence that an offense was committed or that a particular person participated in the commission of an offense.

¶11 The language used in "First," "Second," and "Fourth" subsections clearly presuppose a crime has already been committed which is shown by the use of the past tense in those subsections — *i.e.* "when the property *was stolen or embezzled.*" . . . The language in the "Third" subsection is plain and clear, and is in the present tense — a warrant may be issued when the property "is in the possession of" — which specifically requires the property to currently be in the possession of the person.

¶12 The wording of the "Third" subsection of Section 1222 is applicable to this case. The anticipatory search warrant was issued based upon an affidavit which claimed the defendant "has placed the following described property for concealment, *does now* unlawfully, illegally, knowingly and willfully *keep,* and *does* unlawfully *have in his possession* and under his control certain dangerous substances." Although the affiant expected that certain events (Dodson's possession of illegal substances) would occur *after* the issuance of the warrant, it is that future event which created all of the probable cause for the issuance of the warrant. . . .

¶14 While we recognize that a majority of states have found anticipatory search warrants to be constitutional, several have held they are invalid upon statutory grounds. [The court cited cases from Maryland, Colorado, and Iowa.] Other states which have found the anticipatory search warrants were constitutional but were not permitted by statute subsequently amended their statutes to specifically provide for such warrants. [The court cited cases from Illinois, Alabama, and Hawaii.]

¶15 . . . The utility of anticipatory search warrants in drug investigations, especially when dealing with the activities of persons who traffic in narcotics cannot be ignored. However, it is incumbent upon our legislature to amend §1222 of Title 22 to provide a legal statutory basis for such anticipatory warrants to be issued. . . .

¶21 [Because] the evidence of drug trafficking, possession of marijuana, and failure to affix tax stamp was obtained pursuant to a statutorily invalid warrant, the trial court should have granted the Motion to Suppress. There being no evidence remaining upon which to sustain Mr. Dodson's convictions, his convictions must be reversed and remanded with instructions to dismiss. . . .

LUMPKIN, V.P.J., dissenting.

¶1 I see absolutely no reason — legal, moral, practical, or otherwise — to apply the exclusionary rule's harsh sanction to the facts of this case, for there is no overreaching police conduct to deter. Therefore, I dissent to the Court's opinion and its narrow reading of 22 O.S.2001, §1222.

¶2 Time after time, this Court has instructed police officers who are actively investigating crimes and seeking to conduct a search in that regard to first "obtain your warrants." The policy reason, of course, is that warrantless searches are to be the exception not the rule. Our statutes strongly encourage the participation of a neutral magistrate, detached from the underlying investigation and applying an objective eye to the facts and law involved. This protects all parties involved.

¶3 On this occasion, however, the authorities followed our advice and obtained not one warrant, but two. Through the use of good police work, drugs that were in the process of being illegally distributed from one person to another through a private mail delivery service were intercepted while in transit. After a drug dog hit on a suspicious package, authorities obtained a warrant to open the package. And there they found exactly what they had suspected: methamphetamine, located inside an envelope with Appellant's name written on it.

¶4 At this point, officers had probable cause to search the place where these illegal drugs were scheduled to be delivered, i.e., Appellant's residence. Exercising extreme caution, they obtained another warrant and prepared to serve the warrant at a time when they knew beyond a shadow of a doubt that drugs would be located on the premises. This was extraordinary.

¶5 So now we will punish those same officers for their good work by dismissing the case and allowing another drug trafficker back on the street. And we do this by taking an unconvincing position on the law, a position that is both ill-advised and not required under the statutory language. In other words, the Court is, for some inexplicable reason, straining a gnat's hair to reverse this case.

¶6 Under paragraph two of section 1222, a search warrant may issue and property seized when that property "was used as the means of committing a felony, in which case it may be taken on the warrant from any house or other place in which it is concealed, or from the possession of the person by whom it was used in the commission of the offense, or of any other person in whose possession it may be." It takes no legal gymnastics to find this section may be used to support the warrants issued here. Likewise, the fourth paragraph may be used as the "property" here, the mailed package of drugs, "constitutes evidence that an offense was committed or that a particular person participated in the commission of an offense."

¶7 . . . Officers could have had the magistrate ready to issue the warrant once the drugs were on the property and then executed it minutes later. However, the problem with that scenario is that drugs are too often easily destroyed, i.e. flushing down the toilet, and time, as well as stealth, is of the essence. That is why this case is evidence of nothing more than good, professional police work and that type of professionalism should be commended, not condemned. . . .

time & stealth of the essence

Problem 3-4. A New Look

On July 1, an anonymous informant telephoned Detective Wygnanski of the Washoe County Consolidated Narcotics Unit. The informant told Wygnanski that Craig Parent would arrive at the Reno Airport on a Continental Airlines flight from New Orleans on July 3. The informant stated that Parent would be with two women named "Jody" and "Stephanie" and he would have cocaine concealed inside a baby powder bottle in his baggage. The informant also provided Wygnanski with a physical description of Parent, saying that he was 6'1" tall, with brown "wavy" hair, green eyes, and a moustache. The caller knew Parent's social security number, his FBI number, and his date of birth, and said that he had an extensive criminal record. Wygnanski confirmed the fact that Parent was scheduled to fly on Continental Airlines to Reno on July 3 and determined that he had several criminal convictions on his record. On July 2, Wygnanski obtained a search warrant. Execution of the warrant was conditioned upon the arrival of Continental Airlines flight number 781 from New Orleans on July 3.

On July 3, Parent and two women arrived at the Reno Airport. Police officers observed the threesome as they exited the airplane, and heard Parent call one of the two women "Karen." They noted that his hair was shortly trimmed rather than wavy, and he had no moustache, but Parent otherwise met the description that the informant had provided. The police officers arrested Parent shortly after he retrieved his luggage. A police officer found 3.7 grams of cocaine in a baby powder bottle located inside one of Parent's bags.

The state charged Parent with narcotics crimes, and Parent moved to suppress the evidence. He argues that the justice of the peace improperly issued the search warrant because the Nevada constitution prohibits anticipatory warrants under the circumstances presented in this case. As defense counsel, how would you distinguish the facts in this case from the controlled delivery situation in the *Dodson* case from Oklahoma? Cf. State v. Parent, 867 P.2d 1143 (Nev. 1994).

Notes

1. *Anticipatory warrants: majority position.* The courts in over half of the states upheld the use of anticipatory search warrants, even before the Supreme Court addressed the question in United States v. Grubbs, 547 U.S. 90 (2006). The majority opinion in *Grubbs* drew the following comparison between anticipatory warrants and traditional search warrants:

> An anticipatory warrant is a warrant based upon an affidavit showing probable cause that at some future time (but not presently) certain evidence of crime will be located at a specified place. Most anticipatory warrants subject their execution to some condition precedent other than the mere passage of time — a so-called "triggering condition." . . .
>
> In the typical case where the police seek permission to search a house for an item they believe is already located there, the magistrate's determination that there is probable cause for the search amounts to a prediction that the item will still be there when the warrant is executed. . . . Anticipatory warrants are, therefore, no different in principle from ordinary warrants. They require the magistrate to determine (1) that it is now probable that (2) contraband, evidence of a crime, or a fugitive will be on the described premises (3) when the warrant is executed. It should be noted, however, that where the anticipatory warrant places a condition (other than the mere passage of time) upon its execution, the first of these determinations goes not merely to what will probably be found if the condition is met. . . . Rather, the probability determination for a conditioned anticipatory warrant looks also to the likelihood that the condition will occur, and thus that a proper object of seizure will be on the described premises. In other words, for a conditioned anticipatory warrant to comply with the Fourth Amendment's requirement of probable cause, two prerequisites of probability must be satisfied. It must be true not only that if the triggering condition occurs there is a fair probability that contraband or evidence of a crime will be found in a particular place, but also that there is probable cause to believe the triggering condition will occur. The supporting affidavit must provide the magistrate with sufficient information to evaluate both aspects of the probable-cause determination.

As the *Dodson* court mentioned, a number of state courts (about a half dozen) decided over the years that anticipatory warrants violated state *statutes* defining the use of search warrants. In some jurisdictions, the legislature responded right away with new statutory language authorizing the use of anticipatory warrants. See Ex parte Turner, 792 So. 2d 1141, 1151 (Ala. 2000). Would you expect the federal constitutional ruling in *Grubbs* to influence the way that state courts interpret these state statutes?

2. *Predicting the future.* Are anticipatory warrants likely to involve magistrates in reviewing a larger number of searches? Do they remove the magistrate from effective review, or do they involve the magistrate even more closely than usual in examining warrant applications? Suppose that investigators plan to send a paid informant into two specific locations to purchase illegal drugs. They are confident that the informant will be able to purchase the drugs at one of the two locations, but they are uncertain which location is correct. Could they obtain an anticipatory search warrant for the two locations, conditioned on a positive field test showing that the substance purchased was indeed cocaine? See State v. Gillespie, 530 N.W.2d 446 (Iowa 1995). Would the names of the targets contribute to the showing of probable cause? The dates or the addresses? Does this application amount to a request for the magistrate to pre-approve a standard police operating procedure?

Suppose you serve as counsel to the judicial conference of a state. What guidelines might you set for magistrates to avoid abuse of anticipatory warrants? Would you insist that the magistrate include as a condition in the warrant every detail that the police relate in the application? Over what time span might an anticipatory warrant be valid?

3. *Anticipatory warrants and exigent circumstances.* If anticipatory warrants are both allowed and encouraged in a particular state, what might that do to the state's doctrines regarding exigent circumstances? Should courts require police to obtain anticipatory search warrants and anticipate exigent circumstances that might arise? See Commonwealth v. Killackey, 572 N.E.2d 560 (Mass. 1991) (rejecting requirement that police obtain anticipatory warrant if they can). Will anticipatory warrants reinvigorate the warrant requirement?

b. Administrative Warrants

Anticipatory warrants, considered in the preceding section, encourage the *use* of warrants. Another way to encourage the use of warrants is to allow a standard lower than probable cause (or a different kind of probable cause) for searches when the investigators obtain prior review and approval by magistrates, leaving the ordinary probable cause standard for warrantless searches.

The following case is pivotal in Fourth Amendment jurisprudence. Not only did it open up the possibility of a reduced standard of probable cause in certain settings, but it also established the importance of "balancing" the competing interests in different categories of Fourth Amendment cases. The balancing methodology enables a court to decide what level of justification the government must present to support a valid search in different contexts.

ROLAND CAMARA v. MUNICIPAL COURT OF SAN FRANCISCO

387 U.S. 523 (1967)

WHITE, J.*

... On November 6, 1963, an inspector of the Division of Housing Inspection of the San Francisco Department of Public Health entered an apartment building to make a routine annual inspection for possible violations of the city's Housing Code. The building's manager informed the inspector that appellant, lessee of the ground floor, was using the rear of his leasehold as a personal residence. Claiming that the building's occupancy permit did not allow residential use of the ground floor, the inspector confronted appellant and demanded that he permit an inspection of the premises. Appellant refused to allow the inspection because the inspector lacked a search warrant.

[The inspector returned on several later occasions without a search warrant. When Camara refused to allow him to enter, he was charged with refusing to permit a lawful inspection, a misdemeanor. Camara argued that the charges against him were unconstitutional, because they derived from illegitimate power of government agents to search without probable cause or a warrant.]

[In this Court's cases interpreting the Fourth Amendment,] one governing principle, justified by history and by current experience, has consistently been followed: except in certain carefully denned classes of cases, a search of private property without proper consent is "unreasonable" unless it has been authorized by a valid search warrant....

In Frank v. Maryland, 359 U.S. 360 (1959), this Court upheld the conviction of one who refused to permit a warrantless inspection of private premises for the purposes of locating and abating a suspected public nuisance.... We proceed to a re-examination of the factors which persuaded the *Frank* majority to adopt this construction of the Fourth Amendment's prohibition against unreasonable searches.

To the *Frank* majority, municipal fire, health, and housing inspection programs "touch at most upon the periphery of the important interests safeguarded by the Fourteenth Amendment's protection against official intrusion," because the inspections are merely to determine whether physical conditions exist which do not comply with minimum [regulatory standards]. We may agree that a routine inspection of the physical condition of private property is a less hostile intrusion than the typical policeman's search for the fruits and instrumentalities of crime.... But we cannot agree that the Fourth Amendment interests at stake in these inspection cases are merely "peripheral." It is surely anomalous to say that the individual and his private property are fully protected by the Fourth Amendment only when the individual is suspected of criminal behavior. For instance, even the most law-abiding citizen has a very tangible interest in limiting the circumstances under which the sanctity of his home may be broken by official authority, for the possibility of criminal entry under the guise of official sanction is a serious threat to personal and family security. ... Like most regulatory laws, fire, health, and housing codes are enforced by criminal processes....

* [Chief Justice Warren and Justices Black, Douglas, Brennan, and Fortas joined this opinion. — EDS.]

The *Frank* majority suggested, and appellee reasserts, two other justifications for permitting administrative health and safely inspections without a warrant. First, it is argued that these inspections are "designed to make the least possible demand on the individual occupant." The ordinances authorizing inspections are hedged with safeguards, and at any rate the inspector's particular decision to enter must comply with the constitutional standard of reasonableness even if he may enter without a warrant. [For instance, the San Francisco Code requires that the inspector display proper credentials, that he inspect "at reasonable times," and that he not obtain entry by force except in emergencies.] In addition, the argument proceeds, the warrant process could not function effectively in this field. The decision to inspect an entire municipal area is based upon legislative or administrative assessment of broad factors such as the area's age and condition. Unless the magistrate is to review such policy matters, he must issue a "rubber stamp" warrant which provides no protection at all to the property owner.

In our opinion, these arguments unduly discount the purposes behind the warrant machinery contemplated by the Fourth Amendment. Under the present system, when the inspector demands entry, the occupant has no way of knowing whether enforcement of the municipal code involved requires inspection of his premises, no way of knowing the lawful limits of the inspector's power to search, and no way of knowing whether the inspector himself is acting under proper authorization. These are questions which may be reviewed by a neutral magistrate without any reassessment of the basic agency decision to canvass an area.... The practical effect of [the current] system is to leave the occupant subject to the discretion of the official in the field. This is precisely the discretion to invade private property which we have consistently circumscribed by a requirement that a disinterested party warrant the need to search. We simply cannot say that the protections provided by the warrant procedure are not needed in this context; broad statutory safeguards are no substitute for individualized review, particularly when those safeguards may only be invoked at the risk of a criminal penalty....

In summary, we hold that administrative searches of the kind at issue here are significant intrusions upon the interests protected by the Fourth Amendment, [and] that such searches when authorized and conducted without a warrant procedure lack the traditional safeguards which the Fourth Amendment guarantees to the individual.... Because of the nature of the municipal programs under consideration, however, these conclusions must be the beginning, not the end, of our inquiry....

The Fourth Amendment provides that, "no Warrants shall issue, but upon probable cause." Borrowing from more typical Fourth Amendment cases, appellant argues not only that code enforcement inspection programs must be circumscribed by a warrant procedure, but also that warrants should issue only when the inspector possesses probable cause to believe that a particular dwelling contains violations of the minimum standards prescribed by the code being enforced. We disagree.

In cases in which the Fourth Amendment requires that a warrant to search be obtained, "probable cause" is the standard by which a particular decision to search is tested against the constitutional mandate of reasonableness. To apply this standard, it is obviously necessary first to focus upon the governmental interest which allegedly justifies official intrusion upon the constitutionally protected interests of the private citizen....

Unlike the search pursuant to a criminal investigation, the inspection programs at issue here are aimed at securing city-wide compliance with minimum physical standards for private property. The primary governmental interest at stake is to prevent even the unintentional development of conditions which are hazardous to public health and safety. Because fires and epidemics may ravage large urban areas, because unsightly conditions adversely affect the economic values of neighboring structures, numerous courts have upheld the police power of municipalities to impose and enforce such minimum standards even upon existing structures. . . . There is unanimous agreement among those most familiar with this field that the only effective way to seek universal compliance with the minimum standards required by municipal codes is through routine periodic inspections of all structures.

[Camara contends, first], that his probable cause standard would not jeopardize area inspection programs because only a minute portion of the population will refuse to consent to such inspections, and second, that individual privacy in any event should be given preference to the public interest in conducting such inspections. The first argument, even if true, is irrelevant to the question whether the area inspection is reasonable within the meaning of the Fourth Amendment. The second argument is in effect an assertion that the area inspection is an unreasonable search. Unfortunately, there can be no ready test for determining reasonableness other than by balancing the need to search against the invasion which the search entails. But we think that a number of persuasive factors combine to support the reasonableness of area code-enforcement inspections. First, such programs have a long history of judicial and public acceptance. Second, the public interest demands that all dangerous conditions be prevented or abated, yet it is doubtful that any other canvassing technique would achieve acceptable results. Many such conditions — faulty wiring is an obvious example — are not observable from outside the building and indeed may not be apparent to the inexpert occupant himself. Finally, because the inspections are neither personal in nature nor aimed at the discovery of evidence of crime, they involve a relatively limited invasion of the urban citizen's privacy. . . .

Having concluded that the area inspection is a "reasonable" search of private property within the meaning of the Fourth Amendment, it is obvious that "probable cause" to issue a warrant to inspect must exist if reasonable legislative or administrative standards for conducting an area inspection are satisfied with respect to a particular dwelling. Such standards, which will vary with the municipal program being enforced, may be based upon the passage of time, the nature of the building (e.g., a multi-family apartment house), or the condition of the entire area, but they will not necessarily depend upon specific knowledge of the condition of the particular dwelling. It has been suggested that so to vary the probable cause test from the standard applied in criminal cases would be to authorize a "synthetic search warrant" and thereby to lessen the overall protections of the Fourth Amendment. But we do not agree. The warrant procedure is designed to guarantee that a decision to search private property is justified by a reasonable governmental interest. But reasonableness is still the ultimate standard. If a valid public interest justifies the intrusion contemplated, then there is probable cause to issue a suitably restricted search warrant. Such an approach [recognizes] the competing public and private interests here at stake and, in so doing, best fulfills the historic purpose behind the constitutional right to be free from unreasonable government invasions of privacy.

[Most] citizens allow inspections of their property without a warrant. Thus, as a practical matter and in light of the Fourth Amendment's requirement that a warrant specify the property to be searched, it seems likely that warrants should normally be sought only after entry is refused unless there has been a citizen complaint or there is other satisfactory reason for securing immediate entry. . . .

In this case, [there was no emergency demanding immediate access, yet] no warrant was obtained and thus appellant was unable to verify either the need for or the appropriate limits of the inspection. [We] conclude that appellant had a constitutional right to insist that the inspectors obtain a warrant to search and that appellant may not constitutionally be convicted for refusing to consent to the inspection. . . .

CLARK, J., dissenting.*

Today the Court renders . . . municipal experience, which dates back to Colonial days, for naught by . . . striking down hundreds of city ordinances throughout the country and jeopardizing thereby the health, welfare, and safety of literally millions of people. But this is not all. It prostitutes the command of the Fourth Amendment that "no Warrants shall issue, but upon probable cause" and sets up in the health and safety codes area inspection a newfangled "warrant" system that is entirely foreign to Fourth Amendment standards. . . .

There is nothing here that suggests that the inspection was unauthorized, unreasonable, for any improper purpose, or designed as a basis for a criminal prosecution; nor is there any indication of any discriminatory, arbitrary, or capricious action affecting the appellant. . . . The majority say, however, that under the present system the occupant has no way of knowing the necessity for the inspection, the limits of the inspector's power, or whether the inspector is himself authorized to perform the search. [All] of these doubts raised by the Court could be resolved very quickly. Indeed, the inspectors all have identification cards which they show the occupant and the latter could easily resolve the remaining questions by a call to the inspector's superior or, upon demand, receive a written answer thereto. . . .

The Court then addresses itself to the propriety of warrantless area inspections. [These] boxcar warrants will be identical as to every dwelling in the area, save the street number itself. I daresay they will be printed up in pads of a thousand or more — with space for the street number to be inserted — and issued by magistrates in broadcast fashion as a matter of course. I ask: Why go through such an exercise, such a pretense? As the same essentials are being followed under the present procedures, I ask: Why the ceremony, the delay, the expense, the abuse of the search warrant? In my view this will not only destroy its integrity but will degrade the magistrate issuing them and soon bring disrepute not only upon the practice but upon the judicial process. It will be very costly to the city in paperwork incident to the issuance of the paper warrants, in loss of time of inspectors and waste of the time of magistrates and will result in more annoyance to the public. . . .

* [Justices Harlan and Stewart joined this opinion. — EDS.]

Notes

1. *Do administrative warrants honor the Fourth Amendment or undermine it?* Does the majority or dissent in *Camara* do greater honor to the Fourth Amendment? Would the Court have been truer to the Fourth Amendment if it had allowed unwarranted administrative searches on the basis of their reasonableness, modest intrusion, and general applicability, subject to careful guidelines, rather than craft a new kind of warrant? Would the Court have been truer still to the Fourth Amendment if it had barred administrative searches absent consent or individualized suspicion of a civil or criminal violation?

Have you seen administrative warrants before, in another context? Review now the eighteenth-century writ of assistance reprinted in section A of this chapter. Are there significant differences between that writ and the administrative warrants described in the *Camara* decision?

2. *Statutory guidance.* The authority for such warrants is often in statutes. Does a legislative imprimatur help to validate the idea of administrative warrants? Does the legislative approval of the practice answer concerns about the discretion or priorities of police supervisors or field officers? Consider the following language from Mich. Stat. §333.7504(2):

> A magistrate . . . upon proper oath or affirmation showing probable cause, may issue a warrant for the purpose of conducting an administrative inspection authorized by this article or the rules promulgated under this article and seizures of property appropriate to the inspection. Probable cause exists upon showing a valid public interest in the effective enforcement of this article or the rules promulgated under this article sufficient to justify administrative inspection of the area, premises, building, or conveyance in the circumstances specified in the application for the warrant. . . .

3. *Sliding scales.* One of the justifications for allowing administrative search warrants appears to be the modestly invasive nature of the searches they justify. The Supreme Court has declared that the balancing method of determining the reasonableness of a search is available whenever there is a "special need" beyond the normal need for law enforcement. New York v. Burger, 482 U.S. 691 (1987).

Should this "lesser invasion/lesser justification" idea be limited to the context of administrative searches, or should the principle be taken more broadly to require a rough correlation between the intrusiveness of any search (warranted or warrantless) and the justification the government must offer? Is a sliding scale of searches a workable concept? Can it be reconciled with the traditional limits of a warrant requirement and probable cause?

4. *Administrative warrants in highly regulated industries.* There is an important exception to the requirement that the government obtain an administrative warrant. If the target of the search is engaged in a "highly regulated industry," the Supreme Court and an overwhelming number of state courts have concluded that an administrative warrant is not necessary. Instead, the government must show that the warrantless search is necessary, that there is an adequate substitute for the warrant to limit the discretion of the field agent, and that the inspection is limited in time, place, and scope. Donovan v. Dewey, 452 U.S. 594 (1981) (statute authorizing warrantless safety inspections of coal mines). The regulation in question must apply to a focused group of people or enterprises; regulations covering all or most employers, however

intrusive, do not eliminate the need for an administrative warrant. Marshall v. Barlow's, Inc., 436 U.S. 307 (1978) (inspection to enforce OSHA workplace safety rules invalid). Is this exception available because of the consent of the targets? That is, does a liquor or firearms retailer understand when going into the business that warrantless searches will occur? See State v. Larsen, 650 N.W.2d 144 (Minn. 2002) (conservation officer needed warrants to search recreational "ice fishing houses" on frozen lakes; court rejected analogy to closely regulated industries); Scott E. Sundby, Protecting the Citizen "Whilst He Is Quiet": Suspicionless Searches, "Special Needs" and General Warrants, 74 Miss. L. J. 501-52 (2004).

D. CONSENSUAL SEARCHES

The police can conduct a full search *without a warrant and without probable cause* if the target of the search consents. In most jurisdictions, the police conduct far more consensual searches than those justified by probable cause or a search warrant. Indeed, one might ask whether a consensual search is a "search" (within the meaning of the constitution) at all. As you read these materials, compare consensual searches with intrusions, covered in Chapter 2, that are not considered "searches" at all.

1. Components of a Voluntary Choice

Any valid consent to search must be "voluntary," yet this choice rarely takes place in a setting ideally suited to rational deliberation of all available options. What are the minimum elements of voluntariness necessary to make a consensual search legally acceptable?

■ MERLE SCHNECKLOTH v. ROBERT BUSTAMONTE

412 U.S. 218 (1973)

STEWART, J.*

. . . I.

[While on routine patrol in Sunnyvale, California, at approximately 2:40 A.M., Police Officer James Rand stopped an automobile when he observed that one headlight and its license plate light were burned out. Six men were in the vehicle. When the driver, Joe Gonzalez, could not produce a driver's license, Rand asked the others for identification. Only Joe Alcala produced a license,] and he explained that the car was his brother's. After the six occupants had stepped out of the car at the officer's request and after two additional policemen had arrived, Officer Rand asked Alcala if he could search the car. Alcala replied, "Sure, go ahead." Prior to the search

* [Chief Justice Burger and Justices White, Blackmun, Powell, and Rehnquist joined in this opinion. — EDS.]

no one was threatened with arrest and, according to Officer Rand's uncontradicted testimony, it "was all very congenial at this time." [The police officer asked Alcala, "Does the trunk open?" Alcala said, "Yes," and opened up the trunk.] Wadded up under the left rear seat, the police officers found three checks that had previously been stolen from a car wash.

[Bustamonte was brought to trial in a California court on a charge of possessing a check with intent to defraud. The trial judge denied the motion to suppress the checks, and on the basis of the checks and other evidence he was convicted. After his failure to obtain relief on appellate review in state court, Bustamonte challenged his conviction in federal habeas corpus proceedings.]

II.

[The] State concedes that when a prosecutor seeks to rely upon consent to justify the lawfulness of a search, he has the burden of proving that the consent was, in fact, freely and voluntarily given. The precise question in this case, then, is what must the prosecution prove to demonstrate that a consent was "voluntarily" given. . . .

B.

[The] question whether a consent to a search was in fact "voluntary" or was the product of duress or coercion, express or implied, is a question of fact to be determined from the totality of all the circumstances. While knowledge of the right to refuse consent is one factor to be taken into account, the government need not establish such knowledge as the sine qua non of an effective consent. As with police questioning, two competing concerns must be accommodated in determining the meaning of a "voluntary" consent — the legitimate need for such searches and the equally important requirement of assuring the absence of coercion.

In situations where the police have some evidence of illicit activity, but lack probable cause to arrest or search, a search authorized by a valid consent may be the only means of obtaining important and reliable evidence. . . . And in those cases where there is probable cause to arrest or search, but where the police lack a warrant, a consent search may still be valuable. If the search is conducted and proves fruitless, that in itself may convince the police that an arrest with its possible stigma and embarrassment is unnecessary, or that a far more extensive search pursuant to a warrant is not justified. In short, a search pursuant to consent may result in considerably less inconvenience for the subject of the search, and, properly conducted, is a constitutionally permissible and wholly legitimate aspect of effective police activity.

But the Fourth and Fourteenth Amendments require that a consent not be coerced, by explicit or implicit means, by implied threat or covert force. For, no matter how subtly the coercion was applied, the resulting "consent" would be no more than a pretext for the unjustified police intrusion against which the Fourth Amendment is directed. . . .

The problem of reconciling the recognized legitimacy of consent searches with the requirement that they be free from any aspect of official coercion cannot be resolved by any infallible touchstone. To approve such searches without the most careful scrutiny would sanction the possibility of official coercion; to place artificial restrictions upon such searches would jeopardize their basic validity. . . . In examining all the surrounding circumstances to determine if in fact the consent to search was coerced, account must be taken of subtly coercive police questions, as well as the possibly vulnerable subjective state of the person who consents. Those searches that are the product of police coercion can thus be filtered out without undermining the continuing validity of consent searches. In sum, there is no reason for us to depart in the area of consent searches, from the traditional definition of "voluntariness."

The approach of [those courts ruling] that the State must affirmatively prove that the subject of the search knew that he had a right to refuse consent, would, in practice, create serious doubt whether consent searches could continue to be conducted. There might be rare cases where it could be proved from the record that a person in fact affirmatively knew of his right to refuse — such as a case where he announced to the police that if he didn't sign the consent form, "[you] are going to get a search warrant;" or a case where by prior experience and training a person had clearly and convincingly demonstrated such knowledge. But more commonly where there was no evidence of any coercion, explicit or implicit, the prosecution would nevertheless be unable to demonstrate that the subject of the search in fact had known of his right to refuse consent. . . .

One alternative that would go far toward proving that the subject of a search did know he had a right to refuse consent would be to advise him of that right before eliciting his consent. That, however, is a suggestion that has been almost universally repudiated by both federal and state courts, and, we think, rightly so. For it would be thoroughly impractical to impose on the normal consent search the detailed requirements of an effective warning. Consent searches are part of the standard investigatory techniques of law enforcement agencies. They normally occur on the highway, or in a person's home or office, and under informal and unstructured conditions. The circumstances that prompt the initial request to search may develop quickly or be a logical extension of investigative police questioning. . . . These situations are a far cry from the structured atmosphere of a trial where, assisted by counsel if he chooses, a defendant is informed of his trial rights. And, while surely a closer question, these situations are still immeasurably far removed from "custodial interrogation" where, in Miranda v. Arizona, 384 U.S. 436 (1966), we found that the Constitution required certain now familiar warnings as a prerequisite to police interrogation. . . .

C.

It is said, however, that a "consent" is a "waiver" of a person's rights under the Fourth and Fourteenth Amendments. The argument is that by allowing the police to conduct a search, a person "waives" whatever right he had to prevent the police from searching. It is argued that under the doctrine of Johnson v. Zerbst, 304 U.S. 458 (1938) to establish such a "waiver" the State must demonstrate "an intentional relinquishment or abandonment of a known right or privilege." But these standards were enunciated in *Johnson* in the context of the safeguards of a fair criminal trial [such as waiver of counsel at trial or] the right to confrontation, to a jury trial, and to a speedy trial, and the right to be free from twice being placed in jeopardy. . . .

The protections of the Fourth Amendment are of a wholly different order, and have nothing whatever to do with promoting the fair ascertainment of truth at a criminal trial. [The] Fourth Amendment protects the security of one's privacy against arbitrary intrusion by the police. . . . It is no part of the policy underlying the Fourth and Fourteenth Amendments to discourage citizens from aiding to the utmost of their ability in the apprehension of criminals. Rather, the community has a real interest in encouraging consent, for the resulting search may yield necessary evidence for the solution and prosecution of crime, evidence that may insure that a wholly innocent person is not wrongly charged with a criminal offense. [It] would be unrealistic to expect that in the informal, unstructured context of a consent search, a policeman, upon pain of tainting the evidence obtained, could make the detailed type of examination demanded by *Johnson*. . . .

D.

It is . . . argued that the failure to require the Government to establish knowledge as a prerequisite to a valid consent, will relegate the Fourth Amendment to the special province of "the sophisticated, the knowledgeable and the privileged." We cannot agree. The traditional definition of voluntariness we accept today has always taken into account evidence of minimal schooling, low intelligence, and the lack of any effective warnings to a person of his rights; and the voluntariness of any statement taken under those conditions has been carefully scrutinized to determine whether it was in fact voluntarily given.

E.

Our decision today is a narrow one. We hold only that when the subject of a search is not in custody and the State attempts to justify a search on the basis of his consent, the Fourth and Fourteenth Amendments require that it demonstrate that the consent was in fact voluntarily given, and not the result of duress or coercion, express or implied. Voluntariness is a question of fact to be determined from all the circumstances, and while the subject's knowledge of a right to refuse is a factor to be taken into account, the prosecution is not required to demonstrate such knowledge as a prerequisite to establishing a voluntary consent. . . .

MARSHALL, J., dissenting.

[I would] have thought that the capacity to choose necessarily depends upon knowledge that there is a choice to be made. But today the Court reaches the curious result that one can choose to relinquish a constitutional right — the right to be free of unreasonable searches — without knowing that he has the alternative of refusing to accede to a police request to search. I cannot agree, and therefore dissent.

I.

[The Court] imports into the law of search and seizure standards developed to decide entirely different questions about coerced confessions. . . . The inquiry in a case where a confession is challenged as having been elicited in an unconstitutional manner is . . . whether the behavior of the police amounted to compulsion of the defendant. [No] sane person would knowingly relinquish a right to be free of compulsion. Thus, the questions of compulsion and of violation of the right itself are inextricably intertwined. The cases involving coerced confessions, therefore, pass over the question of knowledge of that right as irrelevant, and turn directly to the question of compulsion.

[When] a search is justified solely by consent . . . , the needs of law enforcement are significantly more attenuated, for probable cause to search may be lacking but a search permitted if the subject's consent has been obtained. Thus, consent searches are permitted, not because such an exception to the requirements of probable cause and warrant is essential to proper law enforcement, but because we permit our citizens to choose whether or not they wish to exercise their constitutional rights. . . .

↳ Consent searches are OK b/c citizens choose if they want to exercise their © Rights

II.

If consent to search means that a person has chosen to forgo his right to exclude the police from the place they seek to search, it follows that his consent cannot be considered a meaningful choice unless he knew that he could in fact exclude the police. . . . I can think of no other situation in which we would say that a person agreed to some course of action if he convinced us that he did not know that there was some other course he might have pursued. . . .

If one accepts this view, the question then is a simple one: must the Government show that the subject knew of his rights, or must the subject show that he lacked such knowledge? I think that any fair allocation of the burden would require that it be placed on the prosecution. . . . If the burden is placed on the defendant, all the subject can do is to testify that he did not know of his rights. And I doubt that many trial judges will find for the defendant simply on the basis of that testimony. [The government, however, might demonstrate the subject's knowledge of his rights by showing his responses at the time of the search.] Denials of knowledge may be disproved by establishing that the subject had, in the recent past, demonstrated his knowledge of his rights, for example, by refusing entry when it was requested by the police. The prior experience or training of the subject might in some cases support an inference that he knew of his right to exclude the police.

The burden on the prosecutor would disappear, of course, if the police, at the time they requested consent to search, also told the subject that he had a right to refuse consent and that his decision to refuse would be respected. . . . The Court contends that if an officer paused to inform the subject of his rights, the informality of the exchange would be destroyed. I doubt that a simple statement by an officer of an individual's right to refuse consent would do much to alter the informality of the exchange, except to alert the subject to a fact that he surely is entitled to know. It is not without significance that for many years the agents of the Federal Bureau of Investigation have routinely informed subjects of their right to refuse consent, when they request consent to search. . . .

I must conclude, with some reluctance, that when the Court speaks of practicality, what it really is talking of is the continued ability of the police to capitalize on the ignorance of citizens so as to accomplish by subterfuge what they could not achieve by relying only on the knowing relinquishment of constitutional rights. Of course it would be "practical" for the police to ignore the commands of the Fourth Amendment, if by practicality we mean that more criminals will be apprehended, even though the constitutional rights of innocent people also go by the board. But such a practical advantage is achieved only at the cost of permitting the police to disregard the limitations that the Constitution places on their behavior, a cost that a constitutional democracy cannot long absorb. . . .

■ PITTSFIELD, MAINE, POLICE DEPARTMENT CONSENT-TO-SEARCH FORM

I, ______, have been informed by ______ and ______ who made proper identification as (an) authorized law enforcement officers of the Pittsfield PD . . . of my CONSTITUTIONAL RIGHT not to have a search made of the premises and property owned by me and/or under my care, custody and control, without a search warrant. Knowing of my lawful right to refuse to consent to such a search, I willingly give my permission to the above named officers to conduct a complete search of the premises and property, including all buildings and vehicles, both inside and outside of the property located at ______.

The above said officers further have my permission to take from my premises and property, any letters, papers, materials or any other property or things which they desire as evidence for criminal prosecution in the case or cases under investigation. This written permission to search without a search warrant is given by me to the above officers voluntarily and without any threats or promises of any kind, at ______ A.M./P.M. on this ______ day of ______, at ______ (place).

PHILADELPHIA POLICE DEPARTMENT DIRECTIVE 7, APPENDIX A

[Officers] will ensure they provide the consenting party with the following warnings:

1. that the consenting party has the right to require the police to obtain a search warrant, and
2. that he/she has the right to refuse to consent to a search. . . .

If the person is in police custody, three additional warnings must be provided:

1. that any items found can and will be confiscated and may be used against them in court;
2. they have the right to consult with an attorney before making a decision to consent; and
3. that they have the right to withdraw their consent at any time.

Problem 3-5. Consent After a Traffic Stop

Robert Robinette was driving his car at 69 miles per hour in a 45-mile-per-hour construction zone on the Interstate. Deputy Roger Newsome, who was on drug interdiction patrol at the time, stopped Robinette for a speeding violation. Before Newsome approached Robinette's vehicle, he decided to issue Robinette only a verbal warning, which was his routine practice regarding speeders in that construction zone. Newsome approached Robinette's vehicle and requested his driver's license. Robinette handed over his license, and Newsome returned to his vehicle to check it. Finding no violations, Newsome returned to Robinette's vehicle. Newsome then asked Robinette to get out of his car and step to the rear of the vehicle. Robinette complied with Newsome's request and stood between his car and the deputy's cruiser. Newsome returned to his vehicle to activate the cruiser's video camera so that he could videotape his interaction with Robinette. Newsome then issued a verbal warning regarding Robinette's speed and returned Robinette's driver's license.

After returning the license, Newsome said to Robinette, "One question before you go: Are you carrying any illegal contraband in your car? Any weapons of any kind, drugs, anything like that?" When Robinette said that he did not have any contraband in the car, Newsome asked if he could search the vehicle. Robinette hesitated briefly, then answered "yes." Upon his search of Robinette's vehicle, Newsome found a small amount of marijuana. Newsome then put Robinette and his passenger in the back seat of the cruiser and continued the search. As a result of this extended search, Newsome found a pill inside a film container; the pill was later determined to be an illegal narcotic. Newsome always asked permission to search the cars he stopped for speeding violations. He had followed this procedure more than 800 times during the previous 12 months. Was Robinette's consent valid? Compare State v. Robinette, 653 N.E.2d 695 (Ohio 1995); Ohio v. Robinette, 519 U.S. 33 (1996).

Notes

1. *Voluntariness of consent: majority position.* Almost all state courts agree with *Bustamonte* that a "totality of the circumstances" determines whether a person consented to a search, and that it is not necessary to inform the person of the right to refuse consent. See Commonwealth v. Cleckley, 738 A.2d 427 (Pa. 1999); but see State v. Johnson, 346 A.2d 66 (N.J. 1975) (party consenting to search must understand right to refuse consent). Whose perceptions of the totality of the circumstances will determine whether the choice was voluntary? Should a court adopt the viewpoint of the person being searched, the officer, or an objective "reasonable person"? Both subjective and objective perspectives operate here. Courts ask about the subjective features of the target of the search, focusing specifically on the consenting person's age, education, and intelligence. Then they consider any objective evidence of coercion, deception, threats, or other undue influence by the police. In light of the police conduct and the defendant's particular subjective circumstances, the court ultimately decides whether the police conduct could have appeared to be coercive to a reasonable person in the defendant's circumstances. See Krause v. Commonwealth, 206 S.W.3d 922 (Ky. 2006) (consent to search was coerced when officer knocked at 4:00 A.M. and requested permission to enter apartment as part of an investigation of a roommate not present at the time, accused of rape of young girl; no sexual assault had occurred, officer's intent was to look for drugs in plain view, but knew that college-educated suspects would refuse consent to search for drugs). Should a person with more education and worldliness have more difficulty arguing that her consent to a search was involuntary? Indeed, after taking this course, would you be able to claim your consent to a search was involuntary on any grounds short of torture?

2. *Why consent?* Why would a "reasonable" person who knows that evidence of a crime is present on the premises ever consent to a search? There is considerable evidence in psychological studies that people unreflectively defer to the wishes of authority figures, including police officers. Is this a sufficient explanation? For a review of the empirical basis for consent doctrine, see Steven L. Chanenson, Get the Facts, Jack! Empirical Research and the Changing Constitutional Landscape of Consent Searches, 71 Tenn. L. Rev. 399 (2004).

3. *Proof of knowledge.* As a prosecutor, how would you try to prove that a person who consented to a search knew that she had the power to refuse? As police counsel, would you recommend that your officers use a consent form in all cases when they

wish to search on the basis of consent? Would it increase the chance that the courts would validate consent searches? Would this practice result in a loss of too many searches? Should the form contain explicit notice that the person can refuse to consent? Note that Directive 7 from the Philadelphia Police Manual provides for some warnings not required as a matter of federal constitutional law. The manual also calls for consent searches only when there is no probable cause and no chance to get a warrant. Why would a police manual contain such provisions?

4. *Consent based on inevitability of a search.* Is consent voluntary when the police claim to have the authority to search immediately, or as soon as they obtain a warrant? In Bumper v. North Carolina, 391 U.S. 543 (1968), the police officer said to a homeowner, "I have a warrant," but the prosecution later justified the search as a consensual search rather than relying on a warrant. The court held that the homeowner's consent to the search was not voluntary because it was induced by a "show of authority" by the police. Was the consent involuntary because of some knowledge the homeowner did not have, such as the invalidity of the warrant? Or was it because the police affirmatively misrepresented the range of options open to her?

Suppose the officer had said, "I can get a warrant if you don't consent." Would your answer change if she had said, "I will seek a warrant"? See State v. Brown, 783 P.2d 1278 (Kan. 1989). Would consent be voluntary if the police ask to search a home while saying that if the owner insists that they obtain a warrant, they plan to return with their "blue lights and sirens blazing" for the benefit of the neighbors?

5. *"Knock and talk" practices.* Police departments encourage their officers to obtain consent to search in many settings. The practice provokes some serious challenges in the setting of searches in a home. When police officers approach a home with no probable cause to search, and plan to request consent to search, this "knock and talk" practice raises difficult factual issues about whether the resident's consent is truly voluntary. Given the special sensitivity of searches in a home, a few jurisdictions declare that officers who approach a home for the sole purpose of obtaining consent to search the home must inform the resident that he or she does not have to consent. State v. Brown, 156 S.W.3d 722 (Ark. 2004) (state constitution requires police officers conducting "knock and talk" to inform home dweller that consent may be refused). Most jurisdictions, however, leave the voluntariness of such consensual searches to the factfinding of the trial judge in the individual case. State v. Smith, 488 S.E.2d 210 (N.C. 1997) ("knock and talk" policy of police department does not violate constitution per se).

6. *Consent while in custody.* Does the driver of a vehicle stopped for a traffic violation voluntarily consent to a search of the car if told that the alternative is to be arrested and taken to jail (and the officer has lawful authority to do just that for traffic violators)? Can a suspect already in custody consent to a search? In United States v. Watson, 423 U.S. 411 (1976), the court approved of a consensual search of a car owned by a person who had been taken into custody in a restaurant and was being held on a public street. As in *Bustamonte,* the Court held that the lack of notice about the right to refuse consent did not make the choice involuntary in this setting. See United States v. Drayton, 536 U.S. 194 (2002) (when armed and uniformed officers of drug interdiction team boarded bus and worked down the aisle questioning passengers, suspect agreed to allow pat-down search of his baggage and person; consent was valid); People v. Anthony, 761 N.E.2d 1188 (Ill. 2001) (suspect wordlessly assuming frisk position after officer's request to search his person is too ambiguous to establish consent; actions might indicate acquiescence to authority).

7. *Consent after a traffic stop.* The Supreme Court held, in Ohio v. Robinette, 519 U.S. 33 (1996), that a police officer asking for consent to search the car at the conclusion of a valid traffic stop need not inform the motorist that he is free to leave and may refuse to consent to the search. However, the Ohio Supreme Court on remand held that the officer's failure to inform the motorist that the stop was over still amounted to one important factor showing lack of consent in the case. State v. Robinette, 685 N.E.2d 762 (Ohio 1997). Roughly 15 states follow Ohio's lead and list a lack of warning as one important component of the voluntariness issue. See Harris v. Commonwealth, 581 S.E.2d 286 (Va. 2003). Courts in other jurisdictions state that consent obtained at the end of any traffic stop deserves heightened review to ensure the voluntariness of the consent. Ferris v. State, 735 A.2d 491 (Md. 1999). In fact, a small group of states (fewer than a half dozen) insist that police may not request consent to search a car stopped for traffic violations unless they have reasonable suspicion of some criminal activity other than the traffic matter. See State v. Smith, 184 P.3d 890 (Kan. 2008). Are these decisions consistent with Schneckloth v. Bustamonte? Is knowledge about the power to refuse consent more important for stopped automobile drivers than for others who are asked to consent to a search? A sampling of consent-to-search cases in the automobile context appears on the web extension of this chapter at *http://www.crimpro.com/extension/ch03*.

Problem 3-6. Scope of Consent

Just past midnight, Sergeant William Planeta and his partner, Officer Joseph Agresta, spotted a 10-year-old black Honda with tinted windows. A computer check on the car failed to turn up any negative information. After following the car for about 20 blocks, the officers pulled it over for excessively tinted windows — a violation of the state motor vehicle code. While his partner spoke with the driver (Gomez), Planeta approached the vehicle, looked through the passenger window, and then inspected the undercarriage of the car for evidence of a hidden compartment. In Planeta's experience, the undercarriage of a vehicle can offer telltale signs of secret compartments used in narcotics trafficking.

Planeta noticed fresh undercoating around the gas tank. Meanwhile, the driver handed Agresta a registration card for the vehicle that showed signs of tampering. The word "Company" had been removed from the name on the card so that it read "Anna Teodora Fermin" rather than "Anna Teodora Fermin Company." The darkly tinted windows, fresh undercoating near the gas tank, and altered registration led Planeta to suspect that the vehicle was being used to transport drugs. Planeta then asked the driver whether he had any guns, knives, cocaine, heroin, or marijuana, and the driver responded, "No." Planeta then asked, "May I search your car, sir?" and the driver said, "Yeah."

Planeta instructed Gomez to stand at the rear of the car, where Officer Agresta patted him down; he then told him to sit on the rear bumper and wait. Planeta unlocked the rear seat and pulled it back. He observed gray "non-factory" carpet in the location above the area where he had spotted the fresh undercoating. He then pulled up the glued carpeting and discovered a cut in the floorboard. Planeta used his pocket knife to pry up the sheet metal. After struggling to reach what he thought was a plastic bag, Planeta returned to his cruiser and retrieved a crowbar, which he brought back to the Honda. Gomez remained silent as Sergeant Planeta began his search again. The crowbar finally enabled him to open part of the gas tank, where he discovered seven bags of cocaine weighing over 1.5 pounds in a hidden compartment.

Gomez has moved to suppress the drugs. He does not contest the voluntariness of his consent to search the vehicle but claims that Planeta's search went beyond the scope of his consent. Will the trial judge grant to motion? Cf. People v. Gomez, 838 N.E.2d 1271 (N.Y. 2005).

Notes

1. *Scope of consent: majority position.* A consent search is valid only if the government agent conducting the search remains within the bounds of the consent granted. The Supreme Court has held that "[t]he standard for measuring the scope of a suspect's consent under the Fourth Amendment is that of 'objective' reasonableness — what would the typical reasonable person have understood by the exchange between the officer and the suspect?" Florida v. Jimeno, 500 U.S. 248 (1991). Virtually all state courts deciding this question have reached the same conclusion.

Scope of Consent

A court will determine the exact coverage of the agreement by reviewing the language that the officer and the target of the search used, much as a court would examine the language used by contractual parties to determine the meaning of their agreement. Would the use of written consent forms tend to help or hurt police departments in this inquiry? If a person consents generally to a search of his "person" or his "vehicle," does that general statement include consent to search all areas within those bounds? A court will typically find it significant if the government agent tells the search target what he is looking for. If the officer is seeking illegal narcotics, the search might be more thorough and intrusive while still remaining within the bounds of the consent. But a number of courts have insisted that an officer obtain specific consent before searching the crotch area. See Davis v. State, 594 So. 2d 264 (Fla. 1992).

2. *Withdrawal of consent.* A person who has consented to a search can withdraw that consent (or restrict its scope) at any time before the completion of the search. However, the person must make an unequivocal withdrawal, through words or actions or both. An action withdrawing consent must be clearly inconsistent with the prior consent, such as a refusal to open a door or a container. See State v. Smith, 782 N.W.2d 913 (Neb. 2010) (person entering a nightclub requiring all patrons to submit to frisk withdrew that consent when officer tried to reach into his pocket and he grabbed officer's wrist and knocked his hand away).

3. *Duration of consent.* While it is clear that a person must withdraw consent through clear language or action, does that mean that a consent to search remains effective indefinitely, allowing a search several days after the grant of consent? Most courts conclude that an open-ended consent to search contains an implied time limitation: The search must be conducted as soon as it is reasonably possible to do so. But do some circumstances suggest a consent with longer duration? In Caldwell v. State, 393 S.E.2d 436 (Ga. 1990), the defendant called the police at 3:00 P.M. to report the stabbing of her children, invited the police into her apartment, and asked them to search for evidence that would lead to the arrest of the murderer. She then left the premises to spend the night with relatives. The search

continued until 10:00 P.M. the day of the murder, and for several hours the next day. The court concluded that the consent remained valid for the entire period of the search.

2. *Third-Party Consent*

The police can obtain the consent to search property either from the target of the search herself or from some third party. Of course, the third party's consent must be voluntary, just as with the target of the search. In addition, the third party must have the authority (or at least the apparent authority) to consent to the search. The third party's authority to consent to a search of property "does not rest upon the law of property, with its attendant historical and legal refinements, but rests rather on mutual use of the property by persons generally having joint access or control for most purposes." In such a setting, the target of the search has "assumed the risk" that another person with access to the property will consent to a search. United States v. Matlock, 415 U.S. 164 (1974). How might this standard apply in the following problems? Would any recurring fact make a difference to a reviewing court?

Problem 3-7. Co-tenant Consenting for Co-tenant

Gina owned a house, which she rented to her son Dale and another man, Thomas. At about 2:00 A.M. on August 30, several acquaintances of Dale and Thomas were at the house. Two of the guests left for about 30 minutes and returned with more than a half pound of marijuana. Thomas was upset that there was marijuana in the house and complained to Dale, but Dale seemed unconcerned.

Thomas went to the police, where he signed a consent to search the house for the marijuana. Several officers went to the house, drew their weapons, and entered the house without knocking or announcing their purpose or authority. They found marijuana in baggies in a black leather jacket in the kitchen and arrested the guest who owned the jacket. In plain view in the living room was a "sawed off" or "short barreled" shotgun belonging to Dale. Was this a valid consensual search? Compare In re Welfare of D.A.G., 474 N.W.2d 419 (Minn. 1991).

Problem 3-8. Parent Consenting for Child

During a murder investigation, police officers went to a suspect's house and asked his mother for consent to search his room. The suspect, who was 23 years old, slept and stored his clothes and other property in a bedroom upstairs in the house and sporadically paid his mother rent for the room. His mother had regular access to the room for purposes of collecting his laundry. She also stored her sewing machine in the room. Although the room was usually unlocked, on this day it was locked. The suspect's mother opened the door with a key and allowed the police to search his room. They found in the closet a jacket with blood stains matching the blood of the murder victim. Was this a valid consensual search?

Problem 3-9. Child Consenting for Parent

Deputy Sheriff Joe Brown and Officer Chris Nichols planned to arrest Jonathan Lowe. Nichols learned that Lowe was staying at the home of Karen Schwarz, so the two officers drove to Schwarz's home on a Friday night to carry out the arrest. Brittany Glazier, Schwarz's 13-year-old daughter, who had just arrived home from the movies with two girlfriends, answered the door. The three friends had been watching a video while waiting for one girl's ride home; the other friend had permission to spend the night at Brittany's house. Brittany had met Officer Brown at a Girl Scout event. Officer Brown explained to Brittany, who he believed to be either 13 or 14 years old, that he was looking for Lowe. The officers asked for permission to come into the home and "look around" while they waited for Lowe. Brittany agreed.

During the search, Officer Nichols discovered a marijuana pipe and a small plastic container containing a white substance, later determined to be methamphetamine. At some point, Schwarz, who was out bowling, called home and learned of the officers' presence. She immediately drove home. When Schwarz arrived, Officer Nichols told her that he had discovered drugs. Schwarz admitted to owning the pipe and methamphetamine and provided written consent to another search of the entire house. Was this a valid consensual search? Cf. State v. Schwarz, 136 P.3d 989 (Mont. 2006).

ARKANSAS RULE OF CRIMINAL PROCEDURE 11.2

The consent justifying a search and seizure can only be given, in the case of: (a) search of an individual's person, by the individual in question or, if the person is under 14 years of age, by both the individual and his parent, guardian, or a person in loco parentis; (b) search of a vehicle, by the person registered as its owner or in apparent control of its operation or contents at the time consent is given; and (c) search of premises, by a person who, by ownership or otherwise, is apparently entitled to give or withhold consent.

Notes

1. *Presence or absence of target and consenting party.* In Problem 3-7, the target of the search was present during the search and did not consent. This situation arises frequently during investigations of alleged domestic abuse. In Georgia v. Randolph, 547 U.S. 103 (2006), Janet Randolph complained to the police that her husband, Scott, had taken their son away after a domestic dispute. She went with an officer to the home she shared with Scott to reclaim the child. When they arrived, Scott said that he had removed the child to a neighbor's house out of concern that Janet might take the boy out of the country. Janet mentioned that her husband used cocaine and left evidence of his use in the bedroom. She gave her consent for the police to search the home, but when an officer asked Scott for permission to search the house, he

unequivocally refused. The Supreme Court held that "a physically present co-occupant's stated refusal to permit entry prevails" over the consent of the other occupant.

Would the analysis change if the target of a search leaves explicit instructions to others with joint control over the property that she does not wish for them to authorize any searches? Or if the consenting party is not at the scene of the search? The court in United States v. Matlock, 415 U.S. 164 (1974), addressed these questions obliquely when it spoke of valid third-party consent against an "absent, nonconsenting" person with an interest in the property. State and federal courts have almost always upheld third-party consents when they contradicted the explicit instructions of the absent search target.

2. *Unequal interests in property.* Parties with different legal interests in a location, such as landlords and tenants, will typically have powers to consent to a search only when contractual terms and other reasonable expectations allow such consent. See State v. Licari, 659 N.W.2d 243 (Minn. 2003) (landlord's contractual right to inspect rented storage unit did not provide actual or apparent authority to consent to police search); Stoner v. California, 376 U.S. 483 (1964) (unwarranted search of hotel room without consent of defendant was unlawful even though police obtained consent of hotel clerk). What happens if the consenting party has a clearly lesser interest in the property than the target of the search? Suppose the target of the search pays rent on an apartment, while the consenting third party is a frequent long-term guest. Should the third party in that setting be able to override the objections of the party with the stronger claim on the property? A few courts require a third party to have at least an equal interest with other owners before allowing that person to consent to a search of the property, at least when the superior interest holder is present and objecting to the search. See Silva v. State, 344 So. 2d 559 (Fla. 1977). Is the principle here that the third party's interests derive from the first party's and therefore cannot override the first party's privacy?

3. *Family member consent.* Family members frequently consent to a search of the shared family home during an investigation of some other occupant of the home, particularly when they are victims of the alleged crime. State v. Ellis, 210 P.3d 144 (Mont. 2009) (police obtained consent from 13-year-old to search her bedroom for evidence of sexual assault by father; state constitutional rule limiting third-party consent for search to those 16 and older provides for no exception for child's own bedroom).

Many third-party consent cases involve spouses or others in a similar relationship. Sometimes one spouse will consent to a search in an effort to injure a partner during a time of conflict. Is it reasonable for the police to rely on consent if it is clear that one party intends only to harm the target of the search? For a perusal of third-party consent cases from the family context, consult the web extension of this chapter at *http://www.crimpro.com/extension/ch03*.

4. *Consent forms and policies.* Would you advise a police department to adopt a special version of its consent-to-search forms for third-party consent searches? Would you advise the police to adopt any rules regarding the proper procedure for obtaining third-party consent?

COMMONWEALTH v. PORTER P.

923 N.E.2d 36 (Mass. 2010)

GANTS, J.

The Commonwealth was granted leave to appeal from an order entered in the Juvenile Court suppressing a gun seized by the police during a search of a room in a transitional family shelter occupied by the juvenile and a statement that he made after his arrest. Having been notified by the shelter's director that the juvenile allegedly possessed a gun, the police officers determined that the director had the authority to consent to their entry and conducted a warrantless search of the juvenile's room with her consent. After the police found the gun, the . . . juvenile was charged with delinquency by reason of the unlawful possession of a firearm and ammunition. [The trial] judge ordered suppression of the gun and the statement to the police. . . . We affirm the allowance of the motion to suppress.

Background. . . . The juvenile and his mother moved into a room at the Roxbury Multi-Service Center, Inc., Family House Shelter in March, 2006. The shelter [contracts with the Commonwealth to provide] temporary housing for otherwise homeless families. . . . Families may remain at the shelter until they find a permanent living situation, unless they commit a violation of the shelter's rules and regulations. The typical stay is between four and eight months. Apart from a key deposit fee of thirty dollars, the families do not pay to live at the shelter.

Each new resident of the shelter, including the juvenile and his mother, as part of the intake procedure, is given a manual setting forth the shelter's rules and regulations. According to the manual, residents . . . are not permitted to enter another resident's room at any time for any purpose. Because residents must commit to being actively engaged at least twenty hours per week in employment, education, or job training, or looking for employment or housing, the residents are required to be out of the shelter from 9 A.M. to 3 P.M. every weekday. . . . Each resident and his or her family is provided a furnished room and given a key to his or her room. The director, however, has a master key that opens every door in the shelter, and the staff members have a master key that opens every resident's room. Members of the shelter's staff have the right to enter any room "for professional business purposes (maintenance, room inspections, etc.)," but only with the knowledge of the director. If a "business professional," such as a repair person or exterminator, requires entry to a resident's room, he or she must be escorted by a staff member, with the director's approval. The shelter staff may conduct "room checks" at any time without warning to monitor compliance with the shelter's "Good Housekeeping Standard" and other rules and regulations, including those affecting health and safety. The manual has a "zero tolerance policy in regards to violent acts committed by residents" and the possession of any weapon; "any resident in possession of a weapon will be terminated immediately." The shelter "reserves the right to contact the Police should the situation warrant," but the manual does not state that the shelter director or a staff member may consent to a police search of a resident's room.

On October 25, 2006, the shelter's director, Cynthia M. Brown, after having heard rumors that the juvenile had a gun, . . . contacted the Boston police department and arranged a meeting for the following morning "to figure out how to proceed." On October 26, 2006, at approximately 10:30 A.M., Detective Frank McLaughlin and four other police officers met with Brown at the shelter. . . . Brown told the officers that the resident's manual authorized her to enter residents' rooms to conduct room checks and that she had inspected residents' rooms several days earlier after reports of suspected drug use. The officers reviewed the portions of the manual authorizing staff to make controlled room entries. Detective McLaughlin confirmed with Brown that her authority to search residents' rooms included the ability to search closets, drawers, bureaus, and other places not in plain view. The detective testified at the evidentiary hearing that he "absolutely" believed that Brown had the authority to consent to a police search of the juvenile's room. He based this belief on the shelter's rules and regulations in the resident's manual, as well as Brown's possession of a master key to the residents' rooms.

Brown and the officers . . . proceeded upstairs to the room, where Brown knocked on the door and announced that she was conducting a room check. When no one answered, she used her master key to open the door. The juvenile was in the room, and it appeared that he had been lying in bed moments before. Brown explained that she was there to conduct a room check and had the police with her because of allegations that the juvenile had a gun in his possession. Detective McLaughlin asked the juvenile to step out of the room into the hallway, and the juvenile complied. Two or three officers began to search the room while the detective and Brown attempted to speak with the juvenile, who denied having a gun. When Brown asked why he was not in school, he stated that he was home sick that day. During their search of the room, the officers found a Glock .40 caliber firearm containing hollow point bullets in the clip underneath a duffel bag in the closet. The juvenile was then handcuffed and placed under arrest. . . .

Discussion. The juvenile argues that the warrantless search of his room at the shelter and the seizure of his firearm violated the Fourth Amendment to the United States Constitution; art. 14 of the Massachusetts Declaration of Rights; and G.L. c. 276, §1. . . .

2. . . . A third party has actual authority to consent to a warrantless search of a home by the police when the third party shares common authority over the home. See Georgia v. Randolph, 547 U.S. 103, 106 (2006); United States v. Matlock, 415 U.S. 164, 171 (1974). The authority which justifies the third-party consent does not rest upon the law of property but rests rather on "mutual use of the property by persons generally having joint access or control for most purposes," so that it is reasonable to recognize that any of the co-inhabitants has the right to permit the inspection in his own right and that the others have assumed the risk that one of their number might permit the common area to be searched.

The reasonableness of a consent search is in significant part a function of commonly held understanding about the authority that co-inhabitants may exercise in ways that affect each other's interests. [Common] authority does not mean simply the right to enter the premises that the police wish to search. Landlords often contractually retain that right, and hotels routinely do, but that does not allow the landlord or hotel manager to consent to a police search of a defendant's apartment or hotel room. United States v. Jeffers, 342 U.S. 48 (1951) (hotel patron gives "implied or express permission [to enter] to such persons as maids, janitors or repairmen in the performance of their duties" but not to police). We have held that, when a college student executes a residence hall contract that permits college officials to enter the student's dormitory room "to inspect for hazards to health or personal safety," the college officials' authority to enter the room to conduct a health and safety inspection does not entitle those officials to consent to a police search for evidence of a crime. Commonwealth v. Neilson, 666 N.E.2d 984 (1996). Here, the shelter's manual allowed shelter staff to enter the room for "professional business purposes," such as to make repairs, exterminate insects and rodents, and monitor compliance with the shelter's "Good Housekeeping Standard," and to escort "business professionals" into the room to accomplish these purposes, but it did not permit shelter staff to allow the police to enter to search for and seize contraband or evidence. . . .

We understand that the police need clear guidance as to who has common authority over a residence and therefore who is entitled to give actual consent, because, as here, they rely on such consent in deciding to conduct a warrantless search, as opposed to securing the residence and applying for a search warrant. Therefore, we declare under art. 14 that a person may have actual authority to consent to a warrantless search of a home by the police only if (1) the person is a co-inhabitant with a shared right of access to the home, that is, the person lives in the home, either as a member of the family, a roommate, or a houseguest whose stay is of substantial duration and who is given full access to the home; or (2) the person, generally a landlord, shows the police a written contract entitling that person to allow the police to enter the home to search for and seize contraband or evidence. No such entitlement may reasonably be presumed by custom or oral agreement.

Co-inhabitancy need not be defined by any legal relationship, such as that of spouses or cotenants on a lease. Rather, it should be defined by the person's demonstrated intent to make a residence his or her home for some substantial period of time. Therefore, an overnight houseguest would lack the authority to consent, unless his or her stay is substantial in its duration, and he or she is given "the run of the house."

Under this standard, Brown did not have actual authority to consent to the police entry into the room to search for a firearm. She was not a co-inhabitant of the room, and the shelter manual did not permit her to allow the police to enter the room to search for contraband or evidence. . . .

3. Having concluded that Brown did not have actual authority to consent to the search of the room by the police, we turn to whether she had the apparent authority to consent.

In Illinois v. Rodriguez, 497 U.S. 177, 179 (1990), the United States Supreme Court held that the Fourth Amendment's proscription of "unreasonable searches and seizures" is not violated when a warrantless entry of a home is based on the consent of a third party who the police, at the time of entry, reasonably, but mistakenly, believed had common authority over the premises. The Court reasoned, "to satisfy the reasonableness requirement of the Fourth Amendment, what is generally demanded of the many factual determinations that must regularly be made by agents of the government — whether the magistrate issuing a warrant, the police officer executing a warrant, or the police officer conducting a search or seizure under one of the exceptions to the warrant requirement — is not that they always be correct, but that they always be reasonable." The Court concluded that "the Constitution is no more violated when officers enter without a warrant because they reasonably (though erroneously) believe that the person who has consented to their entry is a resident of the premises, than it is violated when they enter without a warrant because they reasonably (though erroneously) believe they are in pursuit of a violent felon who is about to escape." Apparent authority is judged against an objective standard: "would the facts available to the officer at the moment . . . warrant a man of reasonable caution in the belief that the consenting party had authority over the premises?"

Federal courts have universally limited apparent authority to reasonable mistakes of fact, not mistakes of law. The *Rodriguez* decision thus applies to situations in which an officer would have had valid consent to search if the facts were as he reasonably believed them to be. An officer's mistaken belief as to the law, even if reasonable, cannot establish apparent authority.

The police officers' mistake in this case was one of law, not of fact. Detective McLaughlin and the other officers took considerable care to ascertain whether Brown had the authority to consent to a search of the room. Prior to entering the room, Detective McLaughlin conferred with Brown and reviewed the portions of the manual pertaining to staff searches of the rooms. They accurately understood the relevant facts regarding Brown's authority to consent to the search. They erred not in their understanding of the facts or in the diligence of their inquiry into Brown's authority to consent to the search, but in their understanding of the law; they believed that these facts gave them valid consent to search the room when, as a matter of law, they did not. Because Brown did not have actual or apparent authority to consent to the search, the warrantless search of the room was not reasonable under the Fourth Amendment or art. 14.

4. [Although the Court concluded that the officers' search of the room was unconstitutional, the Justices went on to decide under art. 14 whether a warrantless search of a home may ever be justified by apparent authority.]

We evaluate the reasonableness of a police officer's conduct based on the information available to him at the time, not on what we later learn to be true. If probable cause in a search warrant affidavit is based on information from a reliable source with personal knowledge, we do not conclude that there has been a violation of art. 14 if the information turns out to be inaccurate, provided the affiant did not know the information to be false or show reckless disregard for its truthfulness. . . . By this same reasoning, we do not believe that art. 14 is violated if a warrantless search of a home occurs after a police officer obtains the voluntary consent of a person he reasonably believes, after diligent inquiry, has common authority over the home, but it turns out that the person lacked common authority. See Illinois v. Rodriguez, 497 U.S. 177, 186 (1990). Apparent authority in the context of consent to search is a police officer's finding of actual authority based on a reasonable mistake of fact.

While we conclude that a search of a home does not violate art. 14 if the police officer has the voluntary consent of an individual with the apparent authority to give such consent, we do so only if the reasonable mistake of fact occurs despite diligent inquiry by the police as to the consenting individual's common authority over the home. To conduct a diligent inquiry, a police officer must take two basic steps. First, the police officer must base his conclusion of actual authority on facts, not assumptions or impressions. He must continue his inquiry until he has reliable information on which to base a finding of actual authority to consent. . . .

Second, even when the consenting individual explicitly asserts that he lives there, if the surrounding circumstances could conceivably be such that a reasonable person would doubt its truth, the police officer must make further inquiry to resolve the ambiguity. The police officer owes a duty to explore, rather than ignore, contrary facts tending to suggest that the person consenting to the search lacks actual authority. Police must not only thoroughly question the individual consenting to the search with respect to his or her actual authority, but also pay close attention to whether the surrounding circumstances indicate that the consenting individual is truthful and accurate in asserting common authority over the premises. . . .

5. Having concluded that the warrantless search was justified by neither Brown's actual authority to consent to the search nor her apparent authority to do so, the firearm seized by the police during the search must be suppressed as fruit of the poisonous tree. . . .

COWIN, J., dissenting.

[Shelter rules regulate the] residents' use of their rooms. Residents "are not allowed access or permitted to enter another resident's room at any time," and they may meet with outside visitors only during stated times at designated locations in the building. The shelter's rules even forbid residents from rearranging the furniture in their rooms, limit the number of suitcases present in the room to "two . . . per family member," and prohibit residents from placing items "on the windowsills." Alcohol and firearms are strictly forbidden in the facility, as are sexual activities (except between residents "coupled" together). [The] shelter requires residents to perform weekly chores and clean their rooms according to enumerated housekeeping standards.

The manual reveals a special concern for eliminating the presence of weapons in the shelter. The shelter forbids possession of "weapons of any kind." The manual defines a weapon as "any item that can be used to threaten or cause physical damage or harm." . . .

[The] shelter director possessed sufficient common authority over the premises to consent to a police search. The staff's plenary authority in the circumstances, including the right to conduct unannounced inspections, meaningfully differentiates the shelter from hotels, apartments, and university dormitories.

The court does not dispute that the conditions of the manual grant shelter staff the authority to enter residents' rooms to search for contraband, but it holds that this power does not extend to granting consent to the police to do the same. This is an entirely unwarranted and impractical distinction, requiring that the shelter staff resort to self-help in order to obtain prompt enforcement of the prohibition on firearms. Shelter staff are not trained in dealing with guns or people armed with guns, and they cannot arrest those in possession of weapons. A commonsense reading of the provisions of the manual regarding weapons plainly communicates that shelter staff, at its choosing, may seek police assistance in undertaking their reserved right to control the premises. In sum, there was no objective basis in these circumstances for any expectation that the juvenile may have had that his room would be immune from the kind of entry that occurred.

Problem 3-10. Divide and Conquer

New Jersey State Troopers Frank Trifari and Thomas Colella were patrolling the southbound lane of Interstate 95 when they observed a 1988 Oldsmobile with out-of-state license plates driving in the left-hand lane for approximately one-half mile. The troopers stopped the car for failing to keep right. . . . The troopers approached the car and asked the driver, Gerald Green, for his license and registration. Both Green and the passenger, Reinaldo Maristany, appeared nervous as they searched for the papers. When Green failed to produce credentials, Trifari asked him to step out of the car and walk to the rear of the vehicle. The officers ordered Maristany to get out of the passenger seat and to sit on the front hood, facing forward.

Trifari and Colella questioned Green and Maristany separately. Green explained that he was returning from a visit with his sick aunt in New York. While Colella remained with Green at the rear of the car, Trifari walked to the front of the car to question Maristany, who claimed that he and Green had been visiting Maristany's children in New York. Because of the inconsistent responses and apparent nervousness, Trifari exchanged places with Colella and requested Green's consent to search the car and trunk. When asked if the trunk contained any luggage, Green indicated that a blue canvas bag and brown suitcase were inside. . . .

After Trifari advised Green of his right to refuse consent, Green agreed to the search and signed a consent-to-search form that authorized Trifari to "conduct a complete search of trunk portion of vehicle including blue canvas bag, brown suitcase, also includes interior portion of vehicle." Maristany, still at the front of the car, did not hear Green consent to a search.

Trifari found no contraband in the car's interior. Green removed the keys from the ignition and opened the trunk for the trooper's inspection. In the blue canvas gym bag, Trifari found three kilograms of cocaine. The bag did not have any identification tags and was empty except for the cocaine. A search of the brown suitcase, likewise showing no identification tag, revealed no contraband. . . . A further search of the car uncovered a rental agreement, indicating that the car had been rented to a Bernadette Harvey. After his arrest, Green claimed that the blue bag belonged to Maristany and that he had no knowledge of its contents.

At the suppression hearing, relying on Green's statement at headquarters, defense counsel argued that Green did not own the blue gym bag, and therefore his consent to search was invalid. According to the State, nothing had indicated that Maristany owned the gym bag, and the trooper saw only a driver who showed apparent ownership and control of the car and who consented to its search. How would you rule on the motion to suppress? Cf. State v. Maristany, 627 A.2d 1066 (N.J. 1993).

Notes

1. *Apparent authority: majority position.* In a number of third-party consent cases, the third party does not actually have authority to consent to the search. Several state courts over the years concluded that these searches were still constitutional so long as the officer had a reasonable belief that the third party had authority to consent. The Supreme Court endorsed this "apparent authority" rule in Illinois v. Rodriguez, 497 U.S. 177 (1990). In that case, the police searched an apartment based on the consent of a former lover of the tenant, who did not have actual authority to consent to a search of the apartment; the Court held that the police were reasonable to search based on her apparent authority. The majority of states addressing this question both before and after *Rodriguez* have reached the same conclusion, approving of searches based on apparent rather than actual authority to consent. See State v. McCaughey, 904 P.2d 939 (Idaho 1995). A few states, however, have disagreed. See State v. McLees, 994 P.2d 683 (Mont. 2000).

The Massachusetts court in *Porter P.* was more explicit than most courts in specifying what the police must do when encountering a claim of authority to consent by a third party; most other courts simply say that the policy must act reasonably under the totality of the circumstances. Can you formulate an alternative description of the police officer's duty to investigate?

2. *Are consent searches reasonable?* One might view consent as a method of making any search a reasonable one. Alternatively, one might say that consent makes reasonableness irrelevant because the party consenting to the search decides not to insist on the probable cause or valid warrant or other circumstances that would make a search reasonable. The latter view might lead a court to reject the apparent authority doctrine: If the search is unreasonable, then actual consent is necessary to salvage it. If, on the other hand, police act reasonably when they conduct a consensual search, then consent that is invalid for reasons not apparent to the police does not make their actions any less reasonable. Is there a principled basis for deciding between these two views?

3. *Voluntariness revisited.* While following *Bustamonte,* courts have stated that consent must still be voluntary, even if the consenting party lacks full knowledge of the nature of his rights. By allowing police to proceed on the apparent authority rather than the actual authority of third parties, have the majority of courts effectively eliminated the voluntariness requirement for a sizable group of cases? Are police training policies and practices likely to increase the number of consent searches based on the apparent authority of third parties?

Problem 3-11. Consent Through Lease Provisions

In response to long-standing problems with drug trafficking and handgun violence in public housing developments in the city, organized groups of tenants urge the housing authority to require all public housing residents to sign leases consenting to police searches of their apartments for drugs or weapons at any time during the lease period. The housing authority tentatively agrees to the plan. In any public housing development where a majority of tenants vote to adopt the plan, the housing authority will include in every lease a provision consenting to searches of the apartment during the lease period.

As legal counsel for the housing authority, what advice would you offer about this plan? Would you amend it?

Notes

1. *Prospective consent and conditioning of government benefits.* Courts limit the extent to which a landlord may waive a tenant's privacy rights and consent to police searches. They enforce lease terms allowing the landlord access only for inspections or emergencies. But suppose the lease includes an explicit clause giving prospective consent for weapons or drug searches. Would you allow tenants prospectively to give consent to searches? If so, should the consent be limited to searches of an individual's home or might it extend to searches of the person?

In Wyman v. James, 400 U.S. 309 (1971), the Supreme Court held that governments could condition the provision of social services (in this instance, Aid to Families with Dependent Children) on agreements to allow home access by aid workers on the grounds that home visits were not searches. To the extent the visits had the appearance of searches, they were reasonable. Finally, relying on *Camara,* the Court noted that the penalty for refusing caseworkers access was termination of benefits, not criminal sanctions.

What arguments would you make for and against applying Wyman v. James to a public housing lease condition allowing prospective searches? The general issue raised here — known as the doctrine of "unconstitutional conditions" — is whether the conditions that the government places on receipt of government support are unconstitutional. The question arises in a variety of contexts, including, for example, the ability of a state university to condition participation on an athletic team on a student's willingness to agree to random or periodic drug tests. See Lynn Baker, The Prices of Rights: Toward a Positive Theory of Unconstitutional Conditions, 75 Cornell L. Rev. 1185 (1990).

2. *Group consent.* Can a majority of a defined group consent for all members of the group? In the public housing situation, if a majority of residents sign leases allowing random searches, do the police have to check a list of who has agreed to the searches or can they treat the situation as one of "group consent"? Could a majority of residents agree to install a metal detector at the entrance to the complex? What percentage of residents would be needed to consent to searches in the common areas of the building?

If collective consent is not allowed as a basis to waive the rights of an entire group, could collective behavior, such as a series of gunshots in a project or a group fight, serve as an exigency that justifies multiple apartment searches? See Pratt v. Chicago Housing Authority, 848 F. Supp. 792 (N.D. Ill. 1994) (rejecting broad-scale searches and sweeps of multiple apartment units, including searches of "closets, drawers, refrigerators, cabinets and personal effects," days after multiple, random gunfire was heard throughout a complex, and despite consent from many tenants).

IV

Searches in Recurring Contexts

Chapters 2 and 3 introduced the basic elements of search and seizure analysis. This chapter explores the recurring situations in which courts, legislatures, and executive branch agencies have applied those elements. Most of these situations actually happen quite often; others appear often in court opinions and statutes but happen less frequently in actual practice.

Review of these commonly encountered problems will offer some worthwhile practice in using concepts introduced in the previous two chapters. Will the government practice be considered a "search" within the meaning of the federal or state constitution? What showing does the government need to make to justify the search: reasonable suspicion, probable cause, or something else? Is a warrant necessary? Is the search acceptable because the target (or someone else with authority) consented to the search, either explicitly or implicitly?

This chapter is divided into categories identified in the text of the Fourth Amendment and many of its analogs. Remember that the Fourth Amendment secures the right of the people to be secure "in their persons, houses, papers, and effects, against unreasonable searches and seizures." Section A considers searches of "persons," along with searches of places or objects based on their proximity to persons. Section B considers issues raised during searches of "houses" and then expands the inquiry to cover other searches where the location of the search matters in creating the relevant legal rules. Section C considers a historic debate (with modern statutory echoes) about the proper treatment of private "papers," a debate that goes to the heart of the types of limits our legal system now places (and refuses to place) on government searches. Section D considers searches of personal property (or "effects"), including searches of cars and containers, which are among the most common recurring situations in law enforcement.

A. "PERSONS"

Searches of the human body intrude into privacy more clearly than most other searches. Do the legal rules about searches of the person reflect the special intrusiveness of these searches? Consider what distinctions in principle or policy explain the various search rules adopted.

1. *Searches Incident to Arrest*

When government agents arrest a person, it has long been clear that they may search the person "incident" to the arrest, without any probable cause or reasonable suspicion to believe that the search will produce any weapon or anything else connected to the crime. This automatic "search incident to arrest" was established in English common law and became part of the law of the American colonies from the very earliest times.

The "search incident to arrest" also extends beyond the body of the arrestee to include areas nearby. But just how near? As a matter of both common law and constitutional law, the answer to this question has fluctuated over time. As Judge Learned Hand once wrote, with typical understatement, "When a man is arrested, the extent to which the premises under his direct control may be searched has proved a troublesome question." United States v. Poller, 43 F.2d 911 (2d Cir. 1930).

■ ARKANSAS RULE OF CRIMINAL PROCEDURE 12.2

An officer making an arrest and the authorized officials at the police station or other place of detention to which the accused is brought may conduct a search of the accused's garments and personal effects ready to hand, the surface of his body, and the area within his immediate control.

■ ANNOTATED LAWS OF MASSACHUSETTS CH. 276, §1

A search conducted incident to an arrest may be made only for the purposes of seizing fruits, instrumentalities, contraband and other evidence of the crime for which the arrest has been made, in order to prevent its destruction or concealment; and removing any weapons that the arrestee might use to resist arrest or effect his escape. Property seized as a result of a search in violation of the provisions of this paragraph shall not be admissible in evidence in criminal proceedings.

■ STATE v. MARC HUFNAGEL

745 P.2d 242 (Colo. 1987)

MULLARKEY, J.

. . . On October 21, 1986, Hufnagel was indicted by the grand jury on charges of selling cocaine and a warrant for his arrest was issued. In the afternoon of the same day, Sheriff Masters, Undersheriff Walters, and Sergeant Berg went to Hufnagel's condominium for the purpose of executing the arrest warrant. The officers did not have a search warrant. When the officers arrived at the defendant's condominium, the door to his unit was open and Undersheriff Walters called out the defendant's name. The defendant, who had been asleep on a sofa in the living area downstairs, responded by calling out "Hello" or "Yo." The officers entered the unit at the top of the stairs leading down to the living area. They saw an eighteen-inch billy club in the entry way and a hatchet downstairs near a fireplace. The officers went downstairs, asked Hufnagel to stand up, and told him that he was under arrest for selling cocaine. He did not overtly resist the arrest, but he was slow to follow their instructions. The officers were in plain clothes and, although armed, did not display their weapons.

Within approximately five minutes after the officers first made verbal contact with the defendant, he was arrested, handcuffed, and led out of the condominium unit. The exact sequence of events within the five minutes is not entirely clear from the record or from the trial court's findings. It is apparent that Hufnagel was patted down for weapons shortly after he stood up and, at that time, he was standing near the sofa and an adjacent, octagonal end table about eighteen inches high. One or two of the officers turned Hufnagel around and handcuffed him with his hands behind his back while Sheriff Masters felt around the edge of the sofa for weapons. As the defendant was being handcuffed, Sheriff Masters saw him look at the end table. Concerned by the defendant's glance, the sheriff flipped open a door in the end table and, inside, he saw a white box. Since the box had no lid, he saw that it contained several baggies, each of which held a white substance which he believed was cocaine. He picked up the box and examined its contents without removing them. He then put the box back into the end table and closed the door.

At approximately the same time that Sheriff Masters searched the sofa and end table, Sergeant Berg made a cursory search of the rest of the condominium to make sure no one else was present. Two of the officers then took the defendant to the sheriff's office; the third remained behind to guard the premises. Later on the same day, Sheriff Masters executed an affidavit for a search warrant, based in part on his observation of the cocaine in the defendant's end table. The warrant was executed, and additional evidence was found and seized.

The defendant moved to suppress the evidence found during the warrantless search incident to his arrest. He conceded that the arrest had been valid, but argued that because he could not have reached into the end table, the search had not been limited to the area within his immediate control. After a hearing, the trial court found as matters of fact that the defendant had been handcuffed before Sheriff Masters searched the sofa and end table and that the door to the end table had been completely closed prior to the search. Based on his finding that the defendant was handcuffed with his hands behind his back, the judge reasoned that the defendant would not have been able to reach into the end table to remove a weapon or to destroy evidence. Therefore, he concluded that the search violated the fourth amendment's prohibition on unreasonable searches and granted the defendant's first motion to suppress. [Because the search warrant was issued on the basis of information obtained in the search incident to the arrest, the trial court concluded that all evidence obtained in the warranted search should also be suppressed.]

As the defendant notes, a warrantless search is generally presumed to be unreasonable and in violation of the fourth amendment. The prosecution has the burden of showing that such a search falls within an exception to the warrant requirement.

In this case, the People rely on the well-settled rule that, when making a lawful arrest, law enforcement officers may search the arrestee's person and the area within the arrestee's immediate control. See Chimel v. California, 395 U.S. 752 (1969). In *Chimel,* the Supreme Court explained that:

> It is entirely reasonable for the arresting officer to search for and seize any evidence on the arrestee's person in order to prevent its concealment or destruction. And the area into which an arrestee might reach in order to grab a weapon or evidentiary items must, of course, be governed by a like rule. A gun on a table or in a drawer in front of one who is arrested can be as dangerous to the arresting officer as one concealed in the clothing of the person arrested. There is ample justification, therefore, for a search of the arrestee's person and the area "within his immediate control" — construing that phrase to mean the area from within which he might gain possession of a weapon or destructible evidence.

The trial court found that the end table door was within "lunging" distance of the defendant and its finding is supported by the record. The end table was directly adjacent to the sofa on which the defendant had been sleeping. When he sat up, he was approximately one to two feet from the end table. He stood up when the officers came downstairs, but did not leave "a very narrow confinement of [the] vicinity" of the end table, according to Sheriff Masters' testimony, and moved only "a few feet," according to his own testimony. This evidence indicates that, prior to being handcuffed, the defendant could have reached the end table and grabbed a weapon or destructible evidence from inside it.

In spite of this, the trial court found that the search was unreasonable because the defendant was handcuffed. We disagree. The search was reasonable in scope and time and was confined to items within the defendant's immediate control. First, it is clear that the police did not engage in a general search of the defendant's home. The search was limited to two items, the sofa and the adjacent end table, which were brought to the officers' attention by the defendant's conduct. As discussed above, Hufnagel had been sleeping on the sofa when the police arrived and he stared at the end table while he was being arrested. Second, the events occurred within a very short time span; the officers spent a total of only about five minutes in the condominium unit. The defendant was not secured when he looked at the end table but he was secured by the time Sheriff Masters flipped open the door. As these findings demonstrate, whether the handcuffs clicked shut before or after the end table search is a matter of split-second timing. We think it would be unwise and highly artificial to make the validity of a search incident to an arrest turn on such a fine point of timing.[2]

Third, the sofa and end table were within the defendant's immediate control. It is well established that, when a search of the arrestee and the area immediately around him or her is incident to a valid, custodial arrest, no additional justification is required for the search. The United States Supreme Court has stated that "the

2. This position has been persuasively explained by Professor LaFave: . . . "A highly sophisticated set of rules, qualified by all sorts of ifs, ands, and buts and requiring the drawing of subtle nuances and hairline distinctions, may be the sort of heady stuff upon which the facile minds of lawyers and judges eagerly feed, but [such rules] may be 'literally impossible of application by the officer in the field.'" LaFave, "Case-by-Case Adjudication" Versus "Standardized Procedures": The *Robinson* Dilemma, 1974 Sup. Ct. Rev. 127.

potential dangers lurking in all custodial arrests make warrantless searches of items within the 'immediate control' area reasonable without requiring the arresting officer to calculate the probability that weapons or destructible evidence may be involved." United States v. Chadwick, 433 U.S. 1 (1977); see also United States v. Robinson, 414 U.S. 218 (1973). This court also has stated that such a search requires no independent justification. Therefore, we have declined to make a separate determination in each case as to whether the arresting officers had reason to believe that the arrestee would grab a weapon or evidence from the surrounding area. As explained below, the danger inherent in any custodial arrest also leads us to hold that a search incident to arrest is constitutional even if the arrestee is handcuffed prior to the search.

Chimel did not decide the exact boundaries of the search incident to arrest exception to the warrant requirement. Therefore, courts have interpreted the exception in a variety of ways. Many courts have considered the fact that the arrestee was handcuffed as one factor in determining the reasonableness of the search. To determine the legal effect of handcuffing an arrestee, courts using this approach have considered the practical effects handcuffs have on the arrestee's "lunging" distance. For example, handcuffs do not completely eliminate an arrestee's ability to reach and grab items. Further, since handcuffs can fail, it is reasonable for the arresting officer to search the area the arrestee could reach after breaking free from them.

Other courts have adopted a rule that a search of the area immediately around the arrestee, made contemporaneously with or immediately following the arrest, is constitutional even if the arrestee is physically unable to reach the area searched at the time of the search.

We believe the second approach, permitting officers to make a reasonable search incident to arrest regardless of whether the arrestee is handcuffed, is the most realistic approach and serves the purposes behind *Chimel.* Arrests are necessarily tense, risky events when many things are happening at once. The difficulty of imposing an orderly chronology after the fact is apparent in this case. Police officers, who must act quickly, cannot reasonably be expected to pay attention to the exact time at which the arrestee is handcuffed and then to make an accurate guess as to how much a reviewing court will think the handcuffs restrict that particular arrestee's "lunging" distance under all the circumstances. . . .

A case-by-case analysis considering all the circumstances of such a search would be impracticable. Further, a case-by-case analysis is not required by *Chimel.* In *Chimel,* the United States Supreme Court rejected the prosecution's argument that an unlimited, warrantless search of an arrestee's house was justified whenever an individual was arrested at home, explaining that "under such an unconfined analysis, Fourth Amendment protection in this area would approach the evaporation point." Instead, the Court concluded that, while legitimate needs of arresting officers to protect themselves and to preserve evidence made warrantless searches "of the person arrested and the area within his reach" reasonable, those needs did not justify "more extensive searches." The Court's goal was to develop a rule that would allow police officers to protect themselves and to preserve evidence without eviscerating arrestees' fourth amendment rights. This goal can be met by limiting searches incident to arrests to the area immediately around the arrestee and the time contemporaneous with or immediately following the arrest.

Rule

Therefore, we hold that the People need not show that the arrestee was physically able to reach the exact place searched at the exact second it was searched in order to justify a search incident to arrest. Instead, the prosecution can meet its burden of showing that a warrantless search was reasonable by showing, as it did here, that it was contemporaneous with or immediately following the defendant's arrest and was limited to the area immediately around him. Because we conclude that Sheriff Masters' observation of the contents of the end table was made during a valid search incident to a lawful arrest, we reverse the trial court's order suppressing the evidence found in both searches. . . .

Problem 4-1. Sweeping the Upstairs

The sheriff's office of Shelby County, Tennessee, notified the Stamford Police Department that it had intercepted a Federal Express parcel containing 27 pounds of marijuana, and that the parcel was addressed to a "Sylvia Sloan" at 16 Lipton Place in Stamford. On the basis of this information, the Stamford police went to the address, which appeared to be a multifamily house. Further investigation showed that the house contained three apartments and was owned by an elderly woman who occupied the first-floor apartment. There were also apartments on the second and third floors. Department records revealed that two months earlier officers had responded to a call at that address concerning a domestic disturbance involving Michael Spencer and his wife.

The following morning, the police took possession of the parcel from the Stamford Federal Express office, and a field test revealed that its contents were, in fact, marijuana. They then replaced approximately 5 pounds of the marijuana in the box and resealed it for delivery. Later that morning, working with the statewide narcotics task force, the police conducted a "controlled delivery" of the parcel to 16 Lipton Place. Police officers watched the residence from vantage points 50 to 60 feet away while a task force member, Detective Frederick Caruso, delivered the parcel. Caruso, dressed in a Federal Express coat and carrying the parcel and a pad of delivery invoices, rang the doorbell for the first-floor apartment and knocked on the front door. A man opened the door; in response to Caruso's questions, he verified the address and he told Caruso that his name was Michael Spencer and that he lived on the second floor. When Caruso told him that the delivery was for "Sylvia Sloan," the defendant repeated the name to himself and then told Caruso that he would accept the package. Spencer signed the delivery invoice, took the parcel under his arm and went inside, closing the front door behind him. As Caruso walked away, Spencer came back outside, without the parcel, and looked up and down the street.

At this point, Police Sergeant Eugene Dohmann and three other officers approached the residence and encountered Spencer in the front doorway. They identified themselves as police officers and brought Spencer into the first-floor common hallway, where they saw the Federal Express parcel on a shelf. The officers then read the defendant his *Miranda* rights and placed him under arrest. Spencer denied knowledge of the contents of the parcel or of anybody named Sylvia Sloan, and he claimed that he had accepted the package innocently.

From the bottom of a flight of approximately 12 to 14 steps leading up to the second floor, the officers could see that the door to the defendant's apartment was ajar. Dohmann asked Spencer if anybody else was inside the apartment, but received no response. Two officers then climbed the stairs and entered the second-floor apartment. In Spencer's bedroom in the rear of the apartment, they saw on the bed a homemade "crack" pipe and a dinner plate containing crack cocaine residue, as well as a rolled-up $1 bill containing crack cocaine.

The government charged Spencer with possession of one kilogram or more of a cannabis-type substance with intent to sell and possession of crack cocaine. At trial, the defendant filed a motion to suppress the evidence of crack cocaine seized from his apartment on the ground that the evidence had been obtained illegally as the result of an unconstitutional warrantless search.

The trial court conducted a full evidentiary hearing on the motion to suppress. Sergeant Dohmann testified that the defendant was "kind of reluctant" to tell the officers whether anybody else was in his apartment. According to Dohmann, the defendant "was a bit nervous," and the officers feared that he may have been "hiding something" from them. Therefore, the officers decided to enter the apartment "to make sure no further evidence was being destroyed or possibly other people involved that may be escaping." Dohmann also testified that the officers were concerned for their safety, because weapons often are involved in the narcotics trade:

> It's not unusual for narcotics and weapons to be found in the same building and we wanted to make sure there were no weapons and more importantly nobody up there to use those weapons. I didn't think it was just a coincidence that this package was being delivered there. So, it was our belief that there was somebody in that apartment and we didn't really expect the package to come back to the name on the package because it's not typically done that way for obvious reasons. So, we expected somebody was in that apartment that was expecting a large amount of marijuana and with that we're feeling there's a drug dealer in that apartment. And, if there's a drug dealer in that apartment, we don't know who he is and he could very well be armed.

The sergeant testified that during the search of the apartment the officers did not look in any drawers, and their search was limited to places "where you might find people, human beings."

On cross-examination, Dohmann acknowledged that the investigation prior to the controlled delivery had not revealed that anybody named Sloan was living at 16 Lipton Place. He also acknowledged that his investigation had not indicated that any individual living at that address might be armed or involved in the drug trade. He admitted that there was no other noise in the house: "Nobody came out of their doors to see what was going on or anything else." Finally, defense counsel questioned Dohmann concerning the officers' decision to enter the defendant's apartment:

> *Q.* There came a time when you went up the stairs to go into [the defendant's] home —
> *A.* Uh-huh.
> *Q.* You had a suspicion that there could be somebody armed upstairs?
> *A.* A suspicion? I wouldn't say a suspicion but we had to know.
> *Q.* A hunch?
> *A.* Not a hunch. You don't even think about it. You just have to eliminate — we have to eliminate the possibility so we went up there with the possibility of that being there and we didn't want to be surprised.

As a trial judge, precisely what factual findings would you need to make to support a valid ruling that the search of the apartment was reasonable? Does it matter that the initial arrest happened outside the house? Compare State v. Spencer, 848 A.2d 1183 (Conn. 2004).

Notes

1. *Search incident to arrest: majority position.* Under the long-standing doctrine of "search incident to arrest," the police may search the person of an arrestee, along with some area near the arrestee, without any independent probable cause or warrant to support the search. As for the amount of area the police may search "incident" to the arrest, the federal standard appears in Chimel v. California, 395 U.S. 752 (1969). The search may extend to the area within the "immediate control" of the arrestee, that is, the area in which the arrestee could reach a weapon or destroy evidence. State courts have by and large adopted this same standard under their state constitutions and statutes. See State v. Lamay, 103 P.3d 448 (Idaho 2004) (backpack that was 10 inches from defendant's hand at start of detention was not within area of immediate control of arrestee). However, as the *Hufnagel* case from Colorado makes clear, there are real disagreements over how to apply this standard. *Hufnagel* represents a strong minority position on the question of handcuffs: A larger group of state courts will consider the fact that an arrestee was handcuffed at the time of a search when determining the area within the "immediate control" of an arrestee. For further exploration of the variety of state court applications of this standard, see the web extension for this chapter at *http://www.crimpro.com/extension/ch04*.

Whether a suspect is handcuffed at the time of a search incident to arrest is only one of a host of facts that courts have used to assess the validity of searches in particular cases. Other factors include: (a) whether there are multiple defendants; (b) whether there are confederates of the suspect nearby who might destroy evidence; (c) whether the officers are between the suspect and the area or object to be searched; (d) whether the officers have control over the area or object to be searched; and (e) any postarrest movement by the arrestee (for example, to get dressed). Which of these factors is subject to the control of the officer? Doesn't assessment of these factors depend on the justification underlying searches incident to arrest?

In the *Hufnagel* case from Colorado, what were the critical factors justifying the search of the end table as a search incident to arrest? How far away from Hufnagel was the end table when the officers entered the apartment? When Hufnagel gave the fatal glance?

2. Chimel *and its predecessors.* The law defining the permissible scope of searches incident to arrest has gone through many changes over the past 70 years. Flexible as *Chimel* may seem, it narrowed the prior rule of Harris v. United States, 331 U.S. 145 (1947), and United States v. Rabinowitz, 339 U.S. 56 (1950), which allowed searches of multiple-room dwellings as searches incident to arrest. An earlier strand of Supreme Court cases — notably Go-Bart Importing Co. v. United States, 282 U.S. 344 (1931), and Trupiano v. United States, 334 U.S. 699 (1948) (rejected by *Rabinowitz)* — suggested that where a search warrant could be obtained before the arrest, it should be.

The court in *Hufnagel*, echoing the U.S. Supreme Court in *Chimel*, justified searches incident to arrest based on the need to find relevant evidence before it is destroyed and the need to protect officers from harm by discovering possible weapons. Which of the two basic justifications supports a more expansive view of searches incident to arrest? What additional theories might justify expansion or contraction of searches incident to arrest? Do the justifications for searches incident to arrest apply most strongly before, during, or after arrest?

3. *Automatic authorization to search.* The distinctive feature of the search incident to arrest is its automatic quality: The police need no justification for the search beyond the justification for the arrest. See United States v. Robinson, 414 U.S. 218 (1973). There is no need to suspect that the person himself is holding a weapon or evidence of a crime; there is no need to suspect that the area within the arrestee's immediate control holds weapons, contraband, or evidence. Is this another example of the courts adopting a "bright line" rule to make the police officer's job more manageable? See Ronald Dworkin, Fact Style Adjudication and the Fourth Amendment, 48 Ind. L.J. 329 (1973).

Statutes in England allow different searches incident to arrest than does American law. Under section 18 of the Police and Criminal Evidence Act of 1984, the constable may search the *premises* of any arrested person (regardless of where the arrest takes place) if there are "reasonable grounds" to believe that the premises contain evidence of the offense that is the basis of the arrest or some similar offense. Section 32 of the Act allows the constable to search a *person,* if the person to be searched has been arrested at a place other than a police station, and if "the constable has reasonable grounds for believing that the arrested person may present a danger to himself or others." The constable may also search the arrested person for evidence of a crime, or for anything he or she might use to escape custody, but only if the constable has "reasonable grounds for believing" that such items will be found in the search. Finally, section 32 also allows the constable "to enter and search any premises in which [the arrested person] was when arrested . . . for evidence relating to the offence for which he has been arrested," but once again, only if the constable has "reasonable grounds for believing that there is evidence . . . on the premises." If an American jurisdiction were to adopt this statute, would it change the practices of the police during arrests in a significant way? Would the police be in greater danger?

4. *Comparison to* Terry *searches.* Courts allow searches of the person incident to arrest to be more intensive than *Terry* searches. See United States v. Robinson, 414 U.S. at 224-229. Why? How long can a search incident to arrest take? Is there any kind of search, either of the person or of a place, that would not be allowed within the justification of a search incident to arrest?

5. *A "life cycle" for procedure issues?* For some time after *Chimel,* state supreme courts actively explored the scope of the area of "immediate control" of the arrestee, considering issues such as the impact of handcuffing the suspect. In recent years the number of cases involving searches incident to arrest in the U.S. and state supreme courts has decreased, and the validity of such searches has been left to trial courts to decide on the facts of each case, with only occasional appeals to lower appellate courts. What characteristics of a criminal procedure issue will make it appear on the docket of a state supreme court? Is there a "life cycle" for criminal procedure issues, in which they become prominent in different institutions in predictable patterns?

6. *Protective sweeps.* Although *Chimel* rejected searches of entire rooms or multiple rooms as part of a search incident to arrest, such searches may still be allowed at the time of arrest on other grounds. One justification for a full-house search is to discover persons who may pose a threat to officers conducting the arrest. In

Maryland v. Buie, 494 U.S. 325 (1990), the Supreme Court upheld two sorts of "protective sweeps" outside the area within the "immediate control" of the arrestee. First, the arresting officers may look in closets and other places immediately adjoining the place of the arrest from which another person might launch an attack on the officers. This search needs no justification beyond the simple fact of the arrest. Second, the officers may search other areas in the house for any persons who might pose a danger to them, but only if they have a reasonable suspicion that the "sweep" will reveal the presence of such a person. In either case, the search is limited to places where a person may be found.

Almost all state courts addressing this subject also allow police to make "protective sweeps" of the premises where an arrest takes place, under the same two-tier analysis that the *Buie* court used. See Commonwealth v. Robertson, 659 S.E.2d 321 (Va. 2008); cf. State v. Davila, 999 A.2d 1116 (N.J. 2010) (protective sweep also available in nonarrest situation if officers are lawfully on premises). Should multiple-room searches for potential accomplices be allowed even when there are no reasonable grounds to believe such accomplices pose a danger to officers but when there is a reasonable suspicion that parties to a multiparty offense are likely to be present or that persons in the house may destroy evidence?

Problem 4-2. Search Incident to (but After) Arrest

An officer looking through binoculars saw a man with a plaid shirt and a blue backpack leaving a field of marijuana plants in a remote, unpopulated canyon. The officer and his partner followed the man in the plaid shirt, whose name turned out to be Howard Boff, and arrested him on a deserted dirt road after he sat down and placed the backpack on the ground about five feet from his body.

The officers drove Boff and his backpack to the sheriff's office, about 45 minutes away in Dove Creek. Three hours after placing Boff in custody, the police officers opened the backpack without a search warrant and found marijuana. Was the search valid as a search incident to arrest? Compare People v. Boff, 766 P.2d 646 (Colo. 1988).

Notes

1. *Subsequent searches: how much time?* Until 1974 the Supreme Court required that searches incident to arrest be "substantially contemporaneous with the arrest." See, e.g., Vale v. Louisiana, 399 U.S. 30 (1970). In 1974 the Court decided United States v. Edwards, 415 U.S. 800, in which it upheld a search of defendant's clothing for paint chips 10 hours after he was arrested. State courts have generally allowed searches at the police station, well after the time of arrest, of objects "immediately associated with the person" that could have been searched at the time of arrest, including clothing, wallets, and purses. See Commonwealth v. Stallworth, 781 A.2d 110 (Pa. 2001); but see State v. Lamay, 103 P.3d 448 (Idaho 2004) (suspect first encountered in hotel room lying on bed next to backpack on floor, then ordered to step into hallway outside hotel room, where he was arrested; later search of backpack not justified as incident to arrest). Professor Myron Moskovitz, based on telephone interviews with police officers and written training materials from various

police departments, concluded that police officers typically handcuff a suspect before searching the vicinity, but they usually obtain a warrant to search an area if they have already removed the arrestee from the scene. Moskovitz, A Rule in Search of a Reason: An Empirical Re-examination of *Chimel* and *Belton,* 2002 Wis. L. Rev. 657, 666-67. This practice, he concludes, is based on police views about the reasonableness of searches rather than their reading of what the courts might allow.

2. *Searches prior to arrest.* The rationale for a search incident to arrest may be strongest immediately prior to arrest, when officers are searching for the person to be arrested or have reasonable grounds to believe that weapons may be present or that evidence might be destroyed. Courts typically allow pre-arrest searches, on the basis of "exigent circumstances," to find a suspect when police are otherwise lawfully within the premises. Courts may also allow pre-arrest searches of areas too small to conceal the offender but large enough to conceal weapons, at least during a "hot pursuit" of the defendant. See Warden v. Hayden, 387 U.S. 294 (1967) (during search for suspect, officer looks in washing machine and discovers evidence). Should such searches generally be allowed as part of arrests within homes? Should officers be able to conduct a "search incident to arrest" beyond the scope of a *Terry* search if they find a person they believe to be the suspect but are not certain?

2. *Intrusive Body Searches*

Strip searches and body cavity examinations are among the most intrusive searches that government agents perform. The police sometimes conduct these searches in the field, either before an arrest or incident to arrest. Sometimes they conduct these searches with the suspect's consent. At other times, officers carry out strip searches at the police station or in a jail or other detention facility, either as part of standard booking procedures or in response to police concerns about an individual.

In recent years, legislatures rather than courts have created the legal limits for these searches. Most states now have statutes placing some limits on the use of strip searches and body cavity searches, and courts have in turn largely ceased their efforts to regulate such searches. Reprinted below are a few examples of these statutes. They highlight how legislatures develop legal rules different from those that courts develop.

Consider the differences between the legislative and judicial rules governing pre-arrest and postarrest searches. Should the extremely intrusive nature of the search technique require some showing beyond probable cause and a judicial warrant in any setting? Or should the regulation of strip searches be more substantial in the field (because of possible abuse), or in the station house (because of the more controlled setting)? Strip search statutes generally require that any allowable strip or body cavity search take place in clean, private surroundings and that the police officers conducting the search must be of the same sex as the person being examined.

As you examine the following three statutes, consider (1) the different levels of justification required for such searches, (2) any special procedures or additional actors who must approve the search, and (3) the use of alternatives to body cavity and strip searches. Then, based on these elements, rank the following statutes in terms of their potential to minimize the number of strip and body cavity searches. What information would you collect to test your assumptions about the impact of different procedures in actual practice?

■ ARKANSAS RULE OF CRIMINAL PROCEDURE 12.3

(a) Search of an accused's blood stream, body cavities, and subcutaneous tissues conducted incidental to an arrest may be made only:

(i) if there is a strong probability that it will disclose things subject to seizure and related to the offense for which the individual was arrested; and

(ii) if it reasonably appears that the delay consequent upon procurement of a search warrant would probably result in the disappearance or destruction of the objects of the search; and

(iii) if it reasonably appears that the search is otherwise reasonable under the circumstances of the case, including the seriousness of the offense and the nature of the invasion of the individual's person.

■ TENNESSEE CODE §40-7-121

(b) No person shall be subjected to a body cavity search by a law enforcement officer or by another person acting under the direction, supervision or authority of a law enforcement officer unless such search is conducted pursuant to a search warrant. . . .

(c) The issue of whether a person subjected to a body cavity search consented to such search is irrelevant and shall not be considered in determining whether the search was a valid one under the provisions of this section, unless the consent is in writing on a preprinted form and contains the following language:

Waiver of Warrant Requirement and Consent to Search Body Cavities

I knowingly and voluntarily consent to have my body cavities searched immediately by law enforcement personnel in the manner provided by the laws of Tennessee. By signing this consent form, I knowingly and voluntarily waive my right to require that a warrant be obtained from an appropriate judge or magistrate before my body cavities are searched. I understand that a body cavity search may involve both visual and physical probing into my genitals and anus. I understand that I would not be prejudiced or penalized by declining to give my consent to be searched in this manner.

■ REVISED CODE OF WASHINGTON §§10.79.080, 10.79.130, 10.79.140

§10.79.080

(1) No person may be subjected to a body cavity search by or at the direction of a law enforcement agency unless a search warrant is issued. . . .

(2) No law enforcement officer may seek a warrant for a body cavity search without first obtaining specific authorization for the body cavity search from the ranking shift supervisor of the law enforcement authority. Authorization for the body cavity search may be obtained electronically: PROVIDED, That such electronic authorization shall be reduced to writing by the law enforcement officer seeking the authorization and signed by the ranking supervisor as soon as possible thereafter.

(3) Before any body cavity search is authorized or conducted, a thorough pat-down search, a thorough electronic metal-detector search, and a thorough clothing search, where appropriate, must be used to search for and seize any evidence of a crime, contraband, fruits of crime, things otherwise criminally possessed, weapons, or other things by means of which a crime has been committed or reasonably appears about to be committed. No body cavity search shall be authorized or conducted unless these other methods do not satisfy the safety, security, or evidentiary concerns of the law enforcement agency.

(4) A law enforcement officer requesting a body cavity search shall prepare and sign a report regarding the body cavity search. . . .

§10.79.130

(1) No person [in custody at a holding, detention, or local correctional facility, regardless of whether an arrest warrant or other court order was issued before the person was arrested, may] be strip searched without a warrant unless:

(a) There is a reasonable suspicion to believe that a strip search is necessary to discover weapons, criminal evidence, contraband, or other thing concealed on the body of the person to be searched, that constitutes a threat to the security of a holding, detention, or local correctional facility;

(b) There is probable cause to believe that a strip search is necessary to discover other criminal evidence concealed on the body of the person to be searched, but not constituting a threat to facility security; or

(c) There is a reasonable suspicion to believe that a strip search is necessary to discover a health condition requiring immediate medical attention.

(2) For the purposes of subsection (1) of this section, a reasonable suspicion is deemed to be present when the person to be searched has been arrested for:

(a) A violent offense . . . ;

(b) An offense involving escape, burglary, or the use of a deadly weapon; or

(c) An offense involving possession of a drug or controlled substance . . .

§10.79.140

(1) A person [in custody at a holding, detention, or local correctional facility, regardless of whether an arrest warrant or other court order was issued before the person was arrested or otherwise taken into custody] who has not been arrested for an offense within one of the categories specified in RCW 10.79.130(2) may nevertheless be strip searched, but only upon an individualized determination of reasonable suspicion or probable cause as provided in this section.

(2) With the exception of those situations in which reasonable suspicion is deemed to be present under RCW 10.79.130(2), no strip search may be conducted

without the specific prior written approval of the jail unit supervisor on duty. Before any strip search is conducted, reasonable efforts must be made to use other less-intrusive means, such as pat-down, electronic metal detector, or clothing searches, to determine whether a weapon, criminal evidence, contraband, or other thing is concealed on the body, or whether a health condition requiring immediate medical attention is present. The determination of whether reasonable suspicion or probable cause exists to conduct a strip search shall be made only after such less-intrusive means have been used and shall be based on a consideration of all information and circumstances known to the officer authorizing the strip search, including but not limited to the following factors:

(a) The nature of the offense for which the person to be searched was arrested;

(b) The prior criminal record of the person to be searched; and

(c) Physically violent behavior of the person to be searched, during or after the arrest.

Notes

1. *Strip search statutes: majority position.* In most places, state statutes and police department policies place special limits on strip searches and body cavity searches. More states have statutes or rules addressing this sort of search than virtually any other specific search technique (with the exception of electronic eavesdropping, which we consider in Chapter 7). Is it possible to bar all strip searches? Why does the Washington legislature provide so much more guidance for searches conducted once a person is in custody? Apart from responding to abuses in specific cases, what else might explain the willingness of so many legislatures to address this topic? If legislatures were to leave this question to courts, what standards would courts apply?

2. *Strip searches for misdemeanors and infractions.* Public attention is often drawn to strip searches conducted on people suspected only of minor offenses. See Edwards v. State, 759 N.E.2d 626 (Ind. 2001) (warrantless and suspicionless strip search of misdemeanor arrestees violates federal and state constitutions). Legislatures often claim to sharply limit strip searches for minor offenses. Consider the following illustration from California Penal Code §4030 (f):

> No person arrested and held in custody on a misdemeanor or infraction offense, except those involving weapons, controlled substances or violence . . . shall be subjected to a strip search or visual body cavity search prior to placement in the general jail population, unless a peace officer has determined there is reasonable suspicion based on specific and articulable facts to believe such person is concealing a weapon or contraband, and a strip search will result in the discovery of the weapon or contraband. No strip search or visual body cavity search or both may be conducted without the prior written authorization of the supervising officer on duty. The authorization shall include the specific and articulable facts and circumstances upon which the reasonable suspicion determination was made by the supervisor. . . .

How much protection for citizens suspected of minor offenses does this statute provide? Why do some legislatures create different presumptions for drug and violent offenders? In these states, how important for the ultimate impact of these rules is the definition of a drug or violent offender?

Other state legislatures have passed such statutes in response to notorious and newsworthy cases involving strip searches. See Mary Beth G. v. City of Chicago, 723 F.2d 1263 (7th Cir. 1983) (civil suit brought by women arrested for outstanding parking tickets, challenging city policy requiring a strip search and body cavity search of all women arrested and detained in city lockups, regardless of charges; Illinois legislature amended arrest statute to prohibit strip searches of persons arrested for traffic, regulatory, or misdemeanor offenses absent a reasonable belief that the arrestee is concealing weapons or controlled substances on her person). Often the motivation for these statutes is not the facts of a particular case but the judgment in a lawsuit. Hundreds of lawsuits based on strip suits have been filed over the years.

3. *The relative virtues of process and substantive standards.* Among the statutes addressing strip searches and body cavity searches, there are two distinct limiting techniques at work. Some of the statutory provisions contain substantive "standards," describing a subclass of cases not eligible for this type of search (such as those accused of particular offenses or cases where the police do not have adequate reason to believe that the search will succeed). Others focus on the process of authorizing such a search (by requiring a judicial warrant or supervisor approval or a written record of any decision to conduct such a search). Which regulatory technique offers greater protection to citizens: more intricate process requirements or higher substantive standards?

4. *The mouth exception.* Most of the body cavity statutes do not cover searches of the mouth. Would you expect statutes to have separate mouth search statutes? Why or why not? See State v. Peterson, 515 N.W.2d 23 (Iowa 1994) (upholding forced search of mouth as search incident to arrest).

5. *Consent to strip searches.* Some statutes bar consent to strip searches, others allow consent, still others require special procedures for obtaining consent, and several say nothing about consent. In a jurisdiction whose statute says nothing about consent, what arguments would you make to a court that it should enforce special consent rules for strip and body cavity searches?

Probable cause, a term captured in the text of the Fourth Amendment and many of its analogs, is the core standard for determining when the government may search a place or person. But it is not the only standard. The investigatory searches and stops described in Chapter 2 are governed by the "reasonable suspicion" standard, considered to be less demanding than probable cause. A few other searches — often bodily searches of a highly intrusive nature — are allowed only when the government makes a showing that is even more demanding than probable cause.

The strip search statutes suggest that legislatures will sometimes step in to define sharper limits or higher standards for intrusive body searches. Consider, for example, how the Arkansas, Tennessee, and Washington strip search statutes would apply to the following case. Where legislatures have not acted to limit highly intrusive searches, courts have stepped in to fill that gap.

■ PEOPLE v. ERIC MORE

764 N.E.2d 967 (N.Y. 2002)

LEVINE, J.

Defendant was convicted of criminal possession of a controlled substance in the third degree, criminal possession of a controlled substance in the fifth degree, resisting arrest and false personation. The drug possession counts related to 2.37 grams of crack cocaine which the police extracted from defendant's rectum during a strip search incident to his arrest. . . .

Prior to trial, defendant moved to suppress the drugs seized from his person. At the suppression hearing, a detective in the Troy Police Department Special Operations Unit testified that he and several other officers entered an apartment after obtaining the tenant's permission to do so. The tenant told the police that individuals in the apartment were "cutting up cocaine" for sale and that one of the subjects was wanted on an arrest warrant for assaulting a police officer. Upon entering the apartment, the detective saw defendant sitting on a couch with a woman on his lap. He also saw a "crack pipe and small piece of white rocklike substance" on a nearby table. Based upon his training and experience, the detective believed the substance was crack cocaine. The police arrested defendant and the woman, ordered them onto the floor, handcuffed them and conducted a "quick pat-down" search for weapons. No weapons were found.

The police then separated defendant and the female in order to strip search them. Defendant initially cooperated by taking off most of his clothes, but at some point he protested and scuffled with the officers. During the search, which took place in a bedroom, the police removed a plastic bag, an outer portion of which they saw protruding from defendant's rectum. The bag contained several individually wrapped pieces of a white rock-like substance, which later tested positive for cocaine. Drugs were also recovered from defendant's female companion.

In his motion to suppress the drugs seized from his person, defendant focused his challenge on the legality of his arrest and the strip search incident thereto. He claimed that the arrest was effected without probable cause, presumably as a pretext to justify the search of his person. In addition, he specifically averred that the body cavity search was "illegal and effected in the absence of probable cause, in the absence of a warrant and in the absence of any exigency." County Court denied the motion to suppress in all respects. . . .

The Supreme Court of the United States addressed the constitutionality of a seizure involving an intrusion into the human body in Schmerber v. California, 384 U.S. 757 (1966). Recognizing that it was "writing on a clean slate," the Court held that the police were justified in requiring a person arrested for driving while under the influence of alcohol to submit to a blood test to determine blood alcohol level. The Court framed the relevant issues as "whether the police were justified in requiring petitioner to submit to the blood test, and whether the means and procedures employed in taking his blood respected relevant Fourth Amendment standards of reasonableness."

After concluding that the police had probable cause to arrest the petitioner for driving while under the influence of alcohol, the Supreme Court determined that seizures involving intrusions beyond the body's surface cannot be justified simply because they are made incident to a lawful arrest. The Court reasoned that although a "full search" of a person is allowed incident to a lawful arrest in order to disarm the suspect or preserve evidence, the considerations permitting such a search "have little applicability with respect to searches involving intrusions beyond the body's surface." The Fourth Amendment "forbids any such intrusions on the mere chance that desired evidence might be obtained." Rather, there must exist a "clear indication" that desired evidence will be found. In the absence of such an indication, the Fourth Amendment mandates that the police "suffer the risk that such evidence may disappear unless there is an immediate search."

Moreover, even where there is a "clear indication" that incriminating evidence will be retrieved if the bodily intrusion is permitted, search warrants are "ordinarily required for searches of dwellings, and *absent an emergency*, no less could be required where intrusions into the human body are concerned." Indeed, as the Court stressed, the "importance of informed, detached and deliberate determinations of the issue whether or not to invade another's body in search of evidence of guilt is indisputable and great." The police were not required to obtain a search warrant in *Schmerber* only because of the existence of exigent circumstances — the officer there "might reasonably have believed that he was confronted with an emergency, in which the delay necessary to obtain a warrant, under the circumstances, threatened 'the destruction of evidence.'"

Finally, the *Schmerber* Court concluded that the procedure used to extract the blood from the petitioner was itself reasonable and conducted in a reasonable manner. In upholding the seizure, the Court noted that its decision to allow the intrusion into the petitioner's body "under stringently limited conditions" did not indicate that the Fourth Amendment "permits more substantial intrusions, or intrusions under other conditions."

Undoubtedly, body cavity searches incident to an arrest are at least as intrusive as blood test procedures. This Court has referred to them as "invasive" and "degrading," People v. Luna, 535 N.E.2d 1305 (N.Y. 1989), and other courts have similarly described them. [The court cited federal cases from the First and Seventh Circuits.]

On the suppression record before us, we conclude that the body cavity search of defendant incident to his arrest was unreasonable and invalid. Even assuming that the extraction of the drugs satisfied all of *Schmerber*'s other requirements, the People failed to offer any evidence of exigent circumstances to justify dispensing with the warrant requirement — that a neutral, detached magistrate determine that the search is justified and will be conducted in a reasonable manner. This record is devoid of any evidence from which an officer "might reasonably have believed that he was confronted with an emergency, in which the delay necessary to obtain a warrant" posed a threat to the officer's personal safety or of the destruction of the evidence. Notably, no police officer testified that, despite the available means of incapacitating defendant and keeping him under full surveillance, an immediate body cavity search was necessary to prevent his access to a weapon or prevent his disposing of the drugs. Nor was there any evidence the police were concerned that the drugs — which were wrapped in plastic — could have been absorbed into defendant's body. The absence of exigent circumstances dictates the conclusion that the body cavity search here was unreasonable. . . .

Problem 4-3. Blood Test Consent

Melissa Helton drove her two children, along with her friend, Lori Lathrop, and Lathrop's two children, to a local creek to swim. Helton and Lathrop drank alcohol while the children swam and played. That evening, they all got into the van to drive home. Helton drove the van off the road and struck some trees and shrubs. Lathrop and three of the children were killed in the accident.

Helton was admitted to the university hospital. Two deputy sheriffs asked the medical staff to draw a blood sample from Helton for their investigation, in addition to the blood tests the medical staff was performing to prepare Helton for surgery. Helton was unconscious during the visit of the deputies and the drawing of her blood. The deputies did not have a warrant to support their request for a blood test. The sample showed that Helton had a blood alcohol content of 0.16 percent.

Helton was indicted for four counts of wanton murder and one count of first-offense driving under the influence. She moved to suppress the evidence of her blood alcohol level, arguing that the sample was taken in violation of state statutes and the state and federal constitutions. Section 189A.103 of the state code provides as follows:

> The following provisions shall apply to any person who operates a motor vehicle in this State:
>
> (1) He or she has given his or her consent to one or more tests of his or her blood, breath, and urine, for the purpose of determining alcohol concentration or presence of a substance which may impair one's driving ability, if an officer has reasonable grounds to believe that a violation of the impaired driving laws has occurred;
>
> (2) Any person who is dead, unconscious, or otherwise in a condition rendering him or her incapable of refusal is deemed not to have withdrawn the consent provided in subsection (1) of this section, and the test may be given.

Another statute in the same chapter of the code, Section 189A.105, provides as follows:

> (1) A person's refusal to submit to tests under Section 189A.103 shall result in revocation of his driving privilege as provided in this chapter.
>
> (2) (a) At the time a breath, blood, or urine test is requested, the person shall be informed:
>
> first, that if the person refuses to submit to such tests, the fact of this refusal may be used against him in court as evidence and will result in revocation of his driver's license; and second, that if a test is taken, the results of the test may be used against him in court as evidence of violating the impaired driving laws.
>
> (b) Nothing in this subsection shall be construed to prohibit a judge of a court of competent jurisdiction from issuing a search warrant or other court order requiring a blood or urine test of a defendant charged with a violation of the impaired driving laws when a person is killed or suffers physical injury as a result of the incident in which the defendant has been charged. However, if the incident involves a motor vehicle accident

in which there was a fatality, the investigating peace officer shall seek such a search warrant for blood, breath, or urine testing unless the testing has already been done by consent.

What will the prosecution have to prove to demonstrate compliance with all the relevant statutes and constitutional requirements? Will the judge suppress the evidence? Cf. Helton v. Commonwealth, 299 S.W.3d 555 (Ky. 2009).

Notes

1. *Probable cause "plus": majority position.* Some courts require the government to justify the use of an especially intrusive bodily search with something more than probable cause. Does the New York court in *More* require some "plus," in addition to probable cause? When the government uses invasive medical techniques to carry out a bodily search, the relevant standard under the federal constitution appears in Schmerber v. California, 384 U.S. 757 (1966). There the Court approved the use of evidence derived from a blood sample that a physician had taken from a suspect. The Court found the search reasonable because (1) there was a "clear indication" that the blood sample would produce evidence of a crime; (2) the test was "commonplace" and involved almost no risk or trauma; and (3) the test was conducted in a "reasonable manner," carried out by a physician in a hospital environment. See also Rochin v. California, 342 U.S. 165 (1952) (forced administration of emetic solution to induce vomiting in suspect who had swallowed capsules; barred by due process). Some state courts interpret *Schmerber* to require only probable cause, but most take this language to mean that the government must show exigent circumstances or evidence stronger than probable cause to justify the taking of blood. For further exploration of the variety of state court applications of this standard, see the web extension for this chapter at *http://www.crimpro.com/extension/ch04*.

What role will police expertise play in jurisdictions where officers are left with some discretion to conduct highly intrusive searches in the field? For example, in *More,* how could the police determine before the search whether or not any secreted drugs were in a form that might be destroyed or disappear with further delay? Would the plastic bag and its contents "inevitably" be discovered when a strip search was conducted at the station as part of standard processing before placing the suspect in a jail cell?

2. *Orders for nonintrusive identification evidence.* Should nonintrusive nontestimonial requests — for example, for handwriting, voice, saliva, and hair samples — and other evidence involving the physical state of the suspect be governed by a reasonable suspicion standard, since such information does not require intrusive body searches? See Iowa Code §§810.1-.6 (governing collection of nontestimonial identification evidence including "fingerprints, palm prints, footprints, measurements, hair strands, handwriting samples, voice samples, photographs, blood and saliva samples, ultraviolet or black-light examinations, paraffin tests, and lineups"). Under Iowa Code §810.6, nontestimonial identification orders require the government to establish each of the following:

1. That there is probable cause to believe that a felony described in the application has been committed.

2. That there are reasonable grounds to suspect that the person named or described in the application committed the felony and it is reasonable in view of the seriousness of the offense to subject that person to the requested nontestimonial identification procedures.
3. That the results of the requested nontestimonial identification procedures will be of material aid in determining whether the person named or described in the application committed the felony.
4. That such evidence cannot practicably be obtained from other sources.

In Bousman v. District Court, 630 N.W.2d 789 (Iowa 2001), the Iowa Supreme Court held that this statute and the federal and Iowa constitutions required only reasonable suspicion in support of an order to obtain saliva for a DNA test. The court also held that reasonable suspicion was all that is required to support a brief investigatory detention to gather this information. Is the compelled presence of a suspect at the police station for a physical sample an arrest? If so, why don't the federal and state constitutions require probable cause for the suspect's detention or forced presence, even if they do not require probable cause to compel the nontestimonial evidence?

3. *Noninvasive medical search techniques.* The pumping of a stomach is one medical technique that typically requires the probable cause "plus" showing. Would you require the probable cause "plus" only for physically invasive techniques? How about the use of an X-ray, followed by administration of a laxative? See People v. Thompson, 820 P.2d 1160 (Colo. Ct. App. 1991) (higher justification required for laxative but not for X-ray). Would most people rather be subject to an unwanted X-ray or an unwanted laxative? Which of these procedures can go forward without the assistance of a doctor? A number of cases have approved the taking of a blood sample based only on a showing of probable cause. Would a justification higher than probable cause be necessary if the police officer uses a "stun gun" (a weapon that produces 0.00006 of an amp of electricity to cause muscle contractions and a resulting loss of balance) to disable a resisting suspect long enough to draw the blood sample? See McCann v. State, 588 A.2d 1100 (Del. 1991).

B. "HOUSES" AND OTHER PLACES

We move now to searches of "houses" and other common searches in which the location of the search plays a major part in the legal analysis. Recall from Chapter 2 that the Fourth Amendment and most analogous state provisions protect only a "reasonable expectation of privacy." In Katz v. United States, 389 U.S. 347 (1967), the Supreme Court declared that the Fourth Amendment "protects people, not places." Nevertheless, the location of a search still matters a great deal. We consider in this section searches and seizures that take place in several important recurring locations: in or near homes, workplaces, and institutions such as schools and prisons.

1. *The Outer Boundaries of Houses*

Searches of homes have always presented some of the easiest cases for limiting the power of the government to search. Recall that the most infamous searches of the late eighteenth century — which most influenced the framers of the Fourth Amendment — were searches of homes. But it is not always so easy to tell where a home leaves off and where the rest of the world begins. The area immediately surrounding the home, known as the "curtilage," receives the same protection as the home itself. Areas beyond the curtilage, known as "open fields," traditionally received no Fourth Amendment protection at all. The two cases reprinted in this section explore these two concepts.

■ CONSTITUTION OF MICHIGAN ART. I, §11

The person, houses, papers and possessions of every person shall be secure from unreasonable searches and seizures. No warrant to search any place or to seize any person or things shall issue without describing them, nor without probable cause, supported by oath or affirmation. The provisions of this section shall not be construed to bar from evidence in any criminal proceeding any narcotic drug, firearm, bomb, explosive or any other dangerous weapon, seized by a peace officer outside the curtilage of any dwelling house in this state.

■ STATE v. GREGORY FISHER

154 P.3d 455 (Kan. 2007)

NUSS, J.

Gregory C. Fisher was convicted of unlawful manufacture of methamphetamine, possession of ephedrine with the intent to manufacture methamphetamine, possession of anhydrous ammonia in an unapproved container for the production of methamphetamine, possession of methamphetamine, and possession of paraphernalia for use in the manufacture of methamphetamine. [The issue on appeal is as] follows: Did the district court err in failing to suppress evidence obtained pursuant to a search warrant partially based upon the contents of a trash bag seized from Fisher's property? . . .

Issue

FACTS

On August 20, 2001, Detective Shane Jager of the Pottawatomie County Sheriff's Department received information from fellow deputy Paul Hoyt concerning suspicious activity at 12420 Highway 63, Emmett, in Pottawatomie County. The property is located in a rural area approximately 4 miles north of the town of Emmett, on the west side of Highway 63. There are no other houses in the general vicinity on the west side of the highway. On the east side of the highway, the closest neighbor's house is approximately a quarter of a mile away.

The property is bounded on the east by Highway 63 and by barbed wire fencing on the north, south, and west which separates the property from surrounding pasture. Photographs reveal the house is approximately 25 yards west of the highway and sits on the northeast part of the property. Its front porch and door face south. A large shed (barn) is located 50 to 60 yards straight west of the house's western exterior near the barbed wire fence. A second, smaller shed sits equidistant between the house and the barn, but somewhat north, actually forming part of the north fence.

From Highway 63, a driveway runs from east to west on the south of the house, curving to the north and ending in a turn-around near the center of the area bounded by the three buildings. The only apparent walkway or sidewalk leads directly south from the house's front door to the driveway. According to photographs in the record, several large trees surround the house inside of the driveway.

According to Jager's suppression hearing testimony, Deputy Hoyt told him that a concerned citizen noticed a strong or peculiar odor emanating from trash being burned on the property and also observed numerous cars stopping there for short intervals of time. Hoyt further relayed to Jager that on August 28, 2001, he received information from another concerned citizen that a white female driving a van — that had been seen coming and going from the residence — drove to a shed located on the property, emptied boxes, placed more boxes in the van, and then left.

At approximately 1 A.M. on the day after Hoyt relayed the information about the delivery of boxes, Jager, Sergeant Chris Schmidt, and Deputy Shane Van Meter went to the area to determine if they could observe anything. While standing in a grass field to the west of the property, and approximately 30 yards west of the barn, Jager noticed a strong odor of ether. Based on his special training, coupled with the prior information of cars stopping at the residence, Jager suspected that methamphetamine was being manufactured and sold there.

Later that morning, Jager returned to the area twice more, once with the county attorney. From his parked position near Highway 63 about 50 yards south of Fisher's driveway, and once again off of Fisher's property, Detective Jager saw a burn barrel and a white translucent plastic trash bag near the barn. He then used binoculars to observe that the bag contained yellow containers. Based upon his training and experience, he associated the yellow bottles with the manufacture of methamphetamine, i.e., Heet bottles. Jager then walked to the field north of the property, where he again smelled ether. Jager testified that at that point he asked the county attorney how he felt about the trash bag. "He said . . . it was not on curtilage, that I could obtain the trash bag, and I advised him that I would like to try . . . to talk to the residents, see what we could obtain from them, and that's when I went to the door of the residence."

Jager testified that after this discussion with the county attorney he got back in his vehicle and

> I pulled my patrol vehicle in the driveway, went to the front door, knocked on the door several times. [After no answer,] I got back in my vehicle and there's a circle driveway that goes around the back side of the residence there, got in, drove by. When I was driving by the white trash bag I noticed Actifed blister packs, several Heet bottles, [and pseudoephedrine and] that's when I collected that white trash bag. . . .

Jager brought the bag to the sheriff's department for examination. In addition to the Heet bottles and 8 to 10 packs of ephedrine, the bag contained plastic gloves, coffee filters with a pinkish powder residue, and miscellaneous trash, including documents identifying Greg Fisher and Betty Harper.

Based upon the tips and Jager's information observed and obtained at the scene, including the contents of the bag, he [obtained and executed a search warrant for the house, outbuildings, and vehicles. The search produced evidence of the manufacture of methamphetamine].

ANALYSIS

. . . Fisher has consistently maintained that the State unlawfully seized the white trash bag from his property because it was within his curtilage. Because the warrant was issued based in part upon facts gleaned from this alleged unconstitutional seizure, he claims the evidence seized pursuant to the improper warrant was fruit of the poisonous tree and should have been suppressed. At oral arguments, the State responded that the bag was outside the curtilage and, if not, it was seized while in Jager's plain view.

When reviewing a motion to suppress evidence, this court reviews the factual underpinnings of a district court's decision by a substantial competent evidence standard and the ultimate legal conclusion drawn from those facts by a de novo standard. This court will not reweigh the evidence. The ultimate determination of the suppression of evidence is a legal question requiring independent review.

In rejecting Fisher's challenge, the district court examined the totality of the circumstances to justify the issuance of the magistrate's search warrant. During this examination, the court found that the bag was seized from outside the curtilage. . . . The district court stated:

> [The] officers went to the house to inquire. They had a right to be there. They have a right to go to the house and knock and talk to the occupants when they have that kind of information. They weren't trespassing. [This] wasn't curtilage as I see it and under these facts. The Heet bottle that [then] became readily apparent, as did [blister packs of pseudoephedrine, after the attempted knock and talk] which are a known precursor for the manufacturing of methamphetamine. They had a right to take the trash . . . .

While Fisher objects to the seizure of the bag, he does not dispute the propriety of the methods or locations, on and off the premises, used for obtaining information, i.e., ether odor and apparent yellow containers in the bag, up to and including Jager's knock and talk. He essentially argues that lawfully made observations do not equate to the right to seize. While the characterization of an observation as a nonsearch plain view situation settles the lawfulness of the observation itself, it does not determine whether a *seizure* of the observed object would likewise be lawful.

At the scene, however, and now on appeal, the county attorney concluded the bag lawfully observed by Jager could be seized from Fisher's property because (1) it was trash and (2) it was outside the curtilage. Curtilage is the area surrounding the residence, to which historically the Fourth Amendment protection against unreasonable searches and seizures has been extended.

California v. Greenwood, 486 U.S. 35 (1988), is of guidance on the seizure issue. There, the Supreme Court addressed a situation where (1) the trash bag (2) was admittedly outside the curtilage; it determined seizure was proper. Despite the seizure of the bag from outside the curtilage, the Court nevertheless engaged in a reasonable expectation of privacy analysis. Since *Greenwood,* lower courts have struggled with exactly how the concept of curtilage fits into the analysis of trash seizures. In trash cases, this court has not only analyzed whether curtilage exists but also whether the owner has a reasonable expectation of privacy in the trash. . . . To analyze the parties' positions in the instant case, we will therefore examine both curtilage and reasonable expectation of privacy in trash.

CURTILAGE

[The] question of curtilage is a mixed question of fact and law. Accordingly, we review the district court's factual findings for substantial competent evidence and review de novo the district court's legal conclusion whether a particular seizure occurred within the curtilage.

Without elaboration, the district court in the instant case simply concluded that the trash bag was not within the cartilage. [United States v. Dunn, 480 U.S. 294 (1987) holds a central place in the curtilage analysis. The] extent of the curtilage is determined by factors that bear upon whether an individual reasonably may expect that the area in question should be treated as the home itself. [The] central component of this inquiry [is] whether the area harbors the "intimate activity associated with the sanctity of a man's home and the privacies of life." The *Dunn* Court held that curtilage questions should be resolved with particular reference to four factors:

> [1] The proximity of the area claimed to be curtilage to the home, [2] whether the area is included within an enclosure surrounding the home, [3] the nature of the uses to which the area is put, and [4] the steps taken by the resident to protect the area from observation by people passing by.

The *Dunn* Court was also quick to point out, however:

> We do not suggest that combining these factors produces a finely tuned formula that, when mechanically applied, yields a "correct" answer to all extent-of-curtilage questions. Rather, these factors are useful analytical tools only to the degree that, in any given case, they bear upon the centrally relevant consideration — whether the area in question is so intimately tied to the home itself that is should be placed under the home's "umbrella" of Fourth Amendment protection. . . .

The Fisher property is bounded on the east by the highway and on the west, north and south by a barbed wire fence. Outside the fence is farm ground in three directions. According to the photographs, inside the fence is short grass which appears to be mowed and maintained throughout. [Several] large trees surround the house inside of the driveway. Photographs show that vehicles are parked in the area formed by the three buildings. A garden apparently is between the barn and shed in the northwest corner of the property. A power pole with a readable electricity meter is near the curve (from west to north) in the driveway. A "Notice, No Trespassing" sign is on another pole near the entrance to the driveway from the highway. The bag was found between the house and the barn, i.e., within the area bounded by the three buildings.

We begin our determination by observing this is rural property, four miles from the nearest town. There are no other houses in the general vicinity of the house on the west side of the highway. On the east side of the highway, a neighbor's house sits approximately a quarter of a mile away. We next apply the *Dunn* factors.

(1) Proximity of the area claimed to be curtilage to the home: [There] is not any fixed distance at which curtilage ends. Here, although the barn is 50-60 yards west of the house's western edge, the exact distance of the trash bag from any feature is unknown, but it was found between the barn and house, albeit nearer the barn. Several courts have noted that in the context of a rural setting, the area extending to outbuildings may be in the curtilage.

(2) Whether the area is included within an enclosure surrounding the home: There is barbed wire fencing on three sides and highway on another. Moreover, the area within the barbed wire fence appears to be mowed and maintained.

(3) The nature of the uses to which the area is put: the bag was found between the barn and the driveway which splits the area between the house and the barn. Photographs show vehicles are parked on the driveway, between the driveway and the house, and between the driveway and the small shed. Additionally, the barbed wire fence-enclosed area also apparently includes a garden between the barn and shed.

(4) The steps taken by the resident to protect the area from observation by people passing by: The bag was found nearly 100 hundred yards from the highway, *i.e.*, behind the large two-story house whose eastern edge is 25 yards west of the highway and near the barn which, because of the size of the house, is more than 50-60 yards further west of the highway. According to the photographs, from the highway the house would have blocked a direct view of the bag, and the bag would have been observable only from obliques to the house, concomitantly from further distances. Outside of that distance, the house's placement, the remoteness of the house from other rural homes in the area, and a "No Trespassing" sign, however, there is nothing to suggest the residents took any particular precautions to prevent observation. [The] barbed wire fences do not prevent observation. Ether was smelled from outside the property. Yellow containers in the translucent bag were discovered through a detective's use of binoculars while parked near the highway and oblique to the house.

Based upon these facts, particularly this rural environment, we independently conclude the trash bag was found within the curtilage. We hold that in rural Kansas, Fisher's area harbors the "intimate activity associated with the sanctity of a person's home and the privacies of life."

the bag was in the curtilage

REASONABLE EXPECTATION OF PRIVACY

Even though we have concluded that the trash bag was seized from within the curtilage, we still need to examine whether Fisher maintained a reasonable expectation of privacy in the bag. . . .

An important inquiry in applying the *Greenwood* analysis to garbage within the curtilage is whether the garbage was so readily accessible to the public that its contents were exposed to the public for Fourth Amendment purposes. [In this case, the] trash bag was placed almost 100 yards from the public highway, blocked from the direct east view from the highway by the house, obscured from the direct north view by the small shed, and blocked from the direct west view by the barn; . . . the bag's yellow containers were visible only with use of binoculars. The bag was not exposed for the public to see; indeed, it was not left out for commercial trash collection. Rather, it was placed on the ground near a barrel for eventual disposition by Fisher. . . .

it's not out for the garbage man

Under these circumstances, we conclude rural residents in Kansas would be quite surprised to learn that highway travelers, children, scavengers, snoops and other members of the public would be fully justified in pawing through the contents of a resident's trash bag placed approximately 100 yards from the highway and behind a rural home. In short, we conclude that Fisher maintained a reasonable expectation of privacy in his trash bag at its specific location — a subjective expectation that was objectively reasonable. Accordingly, the bag's warrantless seizure was per se unreasonable unless permissible under some recognized exception to the warrant requirement.

PLAIN VIEW

The State [argues that] even if the seizure occurred within the curtilage, as we have determined, that the plain view doctrine still justified the seizure. Under the facts of this case, we disagree for several reasons. . . .

It is first important to keep clear the distinctions between the different types of "plain view." As the Supreme Court has stated: "It is important to distinguish 'plain view' as used in Coolidge v. New Hampshire, 403 U.S. 443 (1971) to justify *seizure* of an object, from an officer's mere observation of an item left in plain view. Whereas the latter generally involves no Fourth Amendment search, . . . the former generally does implicate the Amendment's limitations upon seizures of personal property." Horton v. California, 496 U.S. 128, 133 n.5 (1990).

A number of courts have therefore used the term "open view doctrine" to refer to the rule that no Fourth Amendment search occurs where a law enforcement officer observes incriminating evidence or unlawful activity from a nonintrusive vantage point. Thus, the "open view" terminology distinguishes the analysis applicable to warrantless observations from the legally distinct "plain view" doctrine applicable to seizures. It is unclear, however, which of the doctrines the State applies to which events on the day of the seizure.

As for any State contention that the open view of the bag from the highway justified the seizure, we repeat that lawful observation does not equate to lawful seizure. [Absent] a justifiable intrusion onto Fisher's curtilage, the mere observation of the bag from the highway does not itself allow the bag's seizure.

As for any State contention that its justified intrusion was Jager's knock and talk and that the "plain view" of the bag obtained directly thereafter justified the seizure, we hold that the open observation of the bag from the highway — which led to the knock and talk — cannot also serve as a "plain view" of the bag from within the curtilage authorizing the seizure. . . . We specifically disapprove of any State attempt to "piggyback," i.e., to observe an object in open view from off the premises, to use knock and — in these cases, unsuccessful — talk for justified entry onto the premises, and then assert plain view while on the premises as a legal basis to seize the identical object that had been observed earlier. Such piggybacking under these facts would smear the careful distinctions drawn by the *Horton* Court between the right to merely observe an object (here, from off the premises) and the right to seize that object (on the premises). From a practical standpoint, this piggyback practice would grant law enforcement the right to seize virtually any object initially observed from a distance and subsequently located within plain view of a residential doorway by an officer purposely looking for that identical object.

An additional reason for us to reject the State's request to apply the plain view doctrine for justification of the seizure is that Jager's premises search and seizure of the bag exceeded the scope of his justified intrusion. . . . We acknowledge that the knock and talk allows officers to come within the curtilage to ask questions. We also acknowledge that if no one answers the knock, as here, the officers can be justified in knocking on more doors. We also acknowledge that, as here, while driving to and from the parking spot on the driveway, while walking to and from the front door, and while at the front door, the officer may make lawful observations. However, Jager did not have the run of the entire Fisher property. . . . An officer is permitted the same license to intrude as a reasonably respectful citizen. However, a substantial and unreasonable departure from such an area, or a particularly intrusive method of viewing, will exceed the scope of the implied invitation and intrude upon a constitutionally protected expectation of privacy. Accordingly, any observations Jager made while exceeding the scope of his lawful intrusion into the curtilage are unlawful. As a result, any seizure made while Jager was exceeding the scope of his lawful intrusion into the curtilage was also unlawful.

There is little evidence in the record indicating that at the time Jager observed the bag while on the premises he was performing any legitimate functions, i.e., observing while moving around the house exterior to look for another door or observing while on his way back to his vehicle after no one answered the knock. Admittedly, he testified at one point that he was "circling around to leave the property" when he observed the bag's contents. On this record, however, we find the evidence insufficient for the State to meet its burden that Jager did not exceed his lawful intrusion, i.e., the knock and talk.

[Once] Jager's knock and talk was complete, instead of driving away from the house to the highway, he simply drove deeper into the property on the driveway — according to the photographs, perhaps as much as 50 yards — directly to the previously observed bag. Once there, from his vehicle he noticed that it contained Actifed blister packs and, in confirmation of his earlier opinion, Heet bottles. He got out of the vehicle and seized the bag. . . .

REVIEW OF THE EXCISED AFFIDAVIT

Our analysis of the suppression issue does not end here, however. We now examine the validity of the search warrant's issuance based upon the remaining — and lawfully obtained — evidence. [After reviewing the totality of these circumstances presented to the magistrate, the court held] that he had a substantial basis for concluding that a crime had been or was being committed, and there was a fair probability that contraband or evidence of a crime would be found in the places to be searched. Therefore, even absent evidence of the contents of the trash bag, the search warrant was valid. The district court was correct in denying the motion to suppress, albeit for a somewhat different reason.

DAVIS, J., concurring.

I concur in the result of the majority decision affirming the validity of the search warrant. [But] I respectfully disagree with the conclusion that seizure of the trash bag violated the defendant's rights under the Fourth Amendment and would conclude that Officer Jager, in what amounted to an excellent investigation of a clandestine methamphetamine lab, had the right under the "plain view doctrine" to seize the trash bag in question, thereby providing probable cause for a search and seizure of evidence on the defendant's premises. . . .

Officer Jager was lawfully on the defendant's property for a knock and talk. As he was leaving the property by the way offered by the resident, the circle drive, he observed in plain view the contents of the trash bag, which were immediately known by the officer to contain evidence of a crime. This observation provided probable cause to seize the bag.

Notwithstanding the advice of the county attorney, Officer Jager did not seize the bag immediately and did not engage in an exploratory search of the premises (such as the shed from where the ether smell emanated) but observed from his patrol vehicle incriminating evidence in the translucent bag as he was leaving the premises. I would therefore [hold] that the officer's seizure of the bag from defendant's premises was justified by the plain view doctrine, thereby validating the search warrant based upon the contents of the trash bag lawfully seized and other evidence contained in the affidavit. . . .

■ STATE v. THERESA DIXSON

766 P.2d 1015 (Or. 1988)

GILLETTE, J.

The issue in these criminal cases, combined for purposes of appeal, is whether the search and seizure provision in the Oregon Constitution protects land outside the "curtilage" of a residence. . . .

Sheriff's deputies received an informant's tip that marijuana was growing on heavily forested land owned by the Rogge Lumber Company. . . . The officers requested and received the company's permission to search the property for marijuana. [They] drove onto the property by way of a public road until they reached a dirt logging road the informant had described as leading to the marijuana. Unknown to the officers, this road extended onto property [where Lorin and Theresa Dixson lived]. The dirt road had fallen into disuse and no longer was passable by car. The trunk of a large tree lay across the road and, a little further on, a wire cable with a "No Hunting" sign on it stretched across the road. The officers left their car and walked past the fallen tree and wire cable. Just past the cable was another dirt road running along a fence line. This road also had a wire cable and "No Hunting" sign stretched across it. The officers continued walking down this second road. At a bend in the road, they encountered another "No Hunting" sign. The area was rural and covered with thick brush. The officers were able to see marijuana plants only after pushing aside the brush. The plants, which were on the Dixsons' property, were not visible at ground level except from that property. [The officers returned the next day and arrested the defendants near the plants. After charges were filed, the defendants filed a motion to suppress the evidence, based on both the state and federal constitutions.]

The state argues that this court should adopt an "open fields" exception to Article I, section 9, for the reasons expressed in the majority opinion in Oliver v. United States, 466 U.S. 170 (1984). In *Oliver,* the police, without first obtaining a warrant, went to Oliver's farm to investigate reports that he was raising marijuana there. They drove past Oliver's house to a locked gate with a "No Trespassing" sign on it. On foot, they followed a path around the gate and along the road for several hundred yards. As they passed a barn and a parked camper, they heard someone standing by the camper shout, "No hunting is allowed, come back up here." The officers identified themselves and approached the camper, but found no one. They continued walking until they found a field of marijuana over a mile from Oliver's house. . . .

The *Oliver* majority relied on the following rationale for holding that the Fourth Amendment does not protect land outside the curtilage of a dwelling: First, the language of the amendment expressly protects from unreasonable search and seizure only "persons, houses, papers, and effects." The majority concluded that the framers of the Fourth Amendment "would have understood the term 'effects' to be limited to personal, rather than real, property." Second, at common law, a distinction was drawn between the curtilage of a home and other land surrounding the home. In the majority's view, this distinction bolstered its conclusion that the framers of the Fourth Amendment did not intend to extend its protection to land outside the curtilage; it also demonstrated that society historically has had a reduced expectation of privacy in such land.

Third, land outside the curtilage of a dwelling "do[es] not provide the setting for those intimate activities that the Amendment is intended to shelter from government interference or surveillance"; thus, those who perform the activities typically conducted in such areas do not require or expect a great deal of privacy. Finally, the desirability of a uniform rule and the problems inherent in fashioning and enforcing a case-by-case approach outweigh any privacy interests that may exist in land outside the curtilage of a dwelling.

The state [argues] that the above reasons wholly justify an interpretation of Article I, section 9, that parallels the federal rule. Although in interpreting Article I, section 9, we are not bound either by the Supreme Court's holding in *Oliver* or by its method of tackling the problem, we will examine its underlying rationale, to the extent that they are pertinent to an Article I, section 9, inquiry.

At the outset, [a caveat is] in order. [The term "open fields"] encompasses lands that are neither fields nor, in any fair sense of the word, open; the open fields doctrine denies Fourth Amendment protection to all undeveloped and unoccupied land outside the curtilage of a residence. We therefore frame the question presented by this case in what we believe to be more realistic terms — not whether the requirements of Article I, section 9, are subject to an exception for "open fields," but whether that provision prohibits unreasonable searches and seizures conducted on land that falls outside the curtilage of a dwelling.

THE TEXTUAL ARGUMENT

The state argues that, because Article I, section 9, like the Fourth Amendment, expressly protects "persons, houses, papers, and effects," the state provision should be interpreted the same way that the United States Supreme Court has interpreted the Fourth Amendment. That argument has some obvious validity, because the language of a constitutional provision must have some meaning if it is to be interpreted in any principled manner. On the other hand, Article I, section 9, has acquired a meaning over the years that is hard to reconcile with the literal interpretation advocated by the state.

Our prior decisions establish that Article I, section 9, does not protect property alone; in a broader sense, it also protects an individual's "privacy interest," which we have defined as an interest in freedom from certain forms of governmental scrutiny. [A] literal interpretation of Article I, section 9, would afford no protection from such things as the police interception of a private telephone conversation from a public telephone booth. . . .

There is a second problem with the literal interpretation proposed by the state. If we were to rely on the language of Article I, section 9, to limit its protection to "persons, papers, houses, and effects [i.e., personal property]," that interpretation necessarily would exclude all kinds of real property except houses. There would be no principled way to distinguish, based on the language itself, office buildings, churches, schools, commercial establishments, and the like, from other kinds of real property. The drafters of Article I, section 9, are unlikely to have intended to exclude from its protections all real property except houses, i.e., structures where people customarily reside. The scope of the section is broader than a literal reading of its terms.

We conclude that we cannot rely on a literal reading of Article I, section 9. To hold that the provision applies only to those items specifically enumerated therein would undermine the rationale that we have identified as the touchstone of Article I, section 9 — the right to be free from intrusive forms of government scrutiny — and would open up prior decisions of this court . . . to serious question. We decline to take that step. Article I, section 9, protects the privacy of the individual from certain kinds of governmental scrutiny. If the individual has a privacy interest in land outside the curtilage of his dwelling, that privacy interest will not go unprotected simply because of its location. . . .

The Argument Based on the Uses to Which Land Outside the Curtilage of a Dwelling Is Put

[Under Article I, section 9,] the question is whether governmental intrusions into privately owned land would significantly impair an individual's interest in freedom from scrutiny, i.e., his privacy. The answer is: That depends.

Areas such as "the vast expanse of some western ranches or . . . the undeveloped woods of the Northwest" described by the *Oliver* majority may involve little or no privacy interest. Some areas of this state contain large unmarked tracts of land in which it is difficult to tell where one piece of property ends and another begins. The public may be in the habit of using these areas to hike, fish, hunt or camp. However lonely a person usually may be in such places, he or she has no true privacy in them.

On the other hand, owners of even large tracts may, at some expense, take steps to keep out intruders. In this society, signs, such as "No Trespassing" signs, the erection of high, sturdy fences and other, similar measures are all indications that the possessor wishes to have his privacy respected. Allowing the police to intrude into private land, regardless of the steps taken by its occupant to keep it private, would be a significant limitation on the occupant's freedom from governmental scrutiny. Article I, section 9, does not permit such freewheeling official conduct. The remaining question is whether it is possible to fashion a workable test to enable the police to determine whether a particular intrusion constitutes a search under the state constitution. It is.

Case-by-Case Analysis

The rule we announce today is simple and objective. An individual's privacy interest in land he or she has left unimproved and unbounded is not sufficient to trigger the protections of Article I, section 9. Thus, it is not sufficient that the property in question is privately owned, or that it is shielded from view by vegetation or topographical barriers, because those features do not necessarily indicate the owner's intention that the property be kept private. A person who wishes to preserve a constitutionally protected privacy interest in land outside the curtilage must manifest an intention to exclude the public by erecting barriers to entry, such as fences, or by posting signs. This rule will not unduly hamper law enforcement officers in their attempts to curtail the manufacture of and trafficking in illegal drugs, because it does not require investigating officers to draw any deduction other than that required of the general public: if land is fenced, posted or otherwise closed off, one does not enter it without permission or, in the officers' situation, permission or a warrant.

In the present case, the defendants (or someone) had blocked access to their property with cables and posted "No Hunting" signs. However, on this record there was no objective reason for the officers to believe that, in addition to the restriction on hunting, other uses such as hiking were forbidden. In this state, with its expanses of rough and open country, hiking, camping and the like commonly occur on land that is owned by large companies and individuals. See generally, ORS §105.655-.680, dealing with public recreational use of private lands. Unless they intended to hunt, neither the officers nor anyone else would have understood the posted signs to be intended to exclude them from the property entirely. The state carried its burden of showing that there was no violation of the Oregon Constitution in the officer's actions. . . .

Notes

1. *Open fields: majority position.* Under the federal constitution, there is no "search" when officers discover something in "open fields," land beyond the boundaries of a home and its curtilage. The decision in Oliver v. United States, 466 U.S. 170 (1984), affirming the traditional "open fields" doctrine, came as a surprise. After the Supreme Court declared in Katz v. United States, 389 U.S. 347 (1967), that the Fourth Amendment protected expectations of privacy rather than property interests, most lower courts assumed that the old per se rule allowing warrantless and suspicionless searches of open fields was no longer tenable. The *Oliver* decision, however, reaffirmed the traditional "open fields" doctrine (based on Hester v. United States, 265 U.S. 57 (1924)). See Stephen Saltzburg, Another Victim of Illegal Narcotics: The Fourth Amendment (as Illustrated by the Open Fields Doctrine), 48 U. Pitt. L. Rev. 1 (1986).

State courts considering the "open fields" question since 1984 are divided. A majority of state courts have followed the Supreme Court in *Oliver:* For items discovered on property outside the curtilage, no search takes place and no case-by-case consideration of "expectations of privacy" is necessary. See Commonwealth v. Russo, 934 A.2d 1199 (Pa. 2007) (seizure of bear stomach from ground 150 yards from cabin to obtain proof that hunting camp was baited). Roughly 10 states, including New York, Oregon, Vermont, and Washington, have parted company with the federal rule. These courts have ruled that, under state statutes or constitutions, police must have a warrant to enter private property if the owner has taken enough measures to prevent entry onto the land by the public. The adequacy of the property owner's efforts to maintain privacy on the land might be measured case by case or with a relatively clear rule.

2. *Curtilage.* Many cases, both state and federal, have declared that the constitutional protection of privacy is at its highest in the home and the area immediately surrounding it, known as the "curtilage." Does the Michigan constitution make this distinction between the home and all other places explicit?

As the *Fisher* court indicated, United States v. Dunn, 480 U.S. 294 (1987), announced several factors that are now widely used to determine whether property is curtilage. In that case, federal agents suspected that the defendant was operating a drug laboratory in a barn on a ranch. The barn sat 60 yards from a house; a waist-high wooden fence with locked gates enclosed the front of the barn. A fence surrounded the perimeter of the property, and several barbed-wire fences crossed the interior of the property (including a fence surrounding the ranch house and running between the barn and the house). The agents crossed the perimeter fence, several of the barbed-wire fences, and the wooden fence in front of the barn. The court held that the barn was not within the curtilage of the ranch house. The web extension for this chapter, at *http://www.crimpro.com/extension/ch04*, offers diagrams of the properties in *Oliver*, *Fisher*, and *Dunn*.

The *Dunn* case and many others deal with searches of alleged "curtilage" areas in a rural or wooded setting. Are these definitions based on assumptions about land use and habits that do not apply in urban and suburban areas? For instance, would you conclude that a "search" of an item in the curtilage had occurred if police officers walked onto the front porch of a home, rang the doorbell, and then picked up a pair of boots, covered with plaster dust, sitting on a box on the porch (attempting to match the tread of the boots to white footprints found on the carpet at a burglary scene)? See State v. Portrey, 896 P.2d 7 (Or. Ct. App. 1995). Is a home best characterized as a place of activity and industry?

3. *Impermanent homes.* How long must a person occupy a temporary shelter before it can receive all the protections afforded to "houses" under the constitution? See State v. Pruss, 181 P.3d 1231 (Idaho 2008) (privacy expectation in "hooch," wooden frame enclosing a tent, on public land); State v. Mooney, 588 A.2d 145 (Conn. 1991) (privacy expectation in cardboard box hidden under bridge abutment containing effects of homeless man). Does it matter whether the occupant of the temporary shelter is otherwise homeless? For an argument that protections for traditional housing structures reach farther than necessary to protect genuine privacy interests, see Stephanie Stern, The Inviolate Home: Housing Exceptionalism in the Fourth Amendment, 95 Cornell L. Rev. 905 (2010).

4. *Categories covered by constitutional texts.* The Oregon court in *Dixson* was willing to conclude that real property was included within the "persons, houses, papers, and effects" that are protected from unreasonable searches and seizures. Does it matter what the constitutional framers considered to be the meaning of "effects" or "houses"? Where would a lawyer discover the framers' views on this question? Would it matter if the final category were called "possessions" instead of "effects"? See Falkner v. State, 98 So. 691 (Miss. 1924) (term "possessions" embraces "all of the property of the citizen"); State v. Finder, 514 A.2d 1241 (N.H. 1986) (term "possessions" does not include real property beyond curtilage).

5. *Crime scene searches.* Police often search crime scenes. Do they need to obtain warrants at any point? Officers can secure a crime scene without a warrant. Officers can also conduct an initial search in response to emergency situations such as

assisting a victim, searching for other victims, or searching for an offender. Police may also seize evidence in plain view during their emergency search and while securing the crime scene. However, in Mincey v. Arizona, 437 U.S. 385 (1978), the U.S. Supreme Court rejected a "crime scene exception" to the Fourth Amendment, and said that police should have obtained a warrant before they conducted a detailed four-day search of an apartment following the murder of an undercover officer. In Flippo v. West Virginia, 528 U.S. 11 (1999), the U.S. Supreme Court reaffirmed *Mincey* and rejected the warrantless search of a briefcase found (closed) during a murder scene investigation of a vacation cabin in a state park. The briefcase belonged to the husband of the victim, who had called the police to investigate; it contained pictures that established his motive for the murder. How do defendants and their lawyers know what police do at crime scenes, and when they do it?

6. *The "new judicial federalism."* On many constitutional questions arising in the criminal process, the Oregon Supreme Court and others have taken positions different from the federal view under their own state constitutions. One of the recurring questions — on which state courts have reached a wide range of positions — is how much deference state courts should give to U.S. Supreme Court decisions when the state courts are interpreting state law that is analogous to federal provisions. The degree of deference has shifted in response to highly publicized calls, led by Supreme Court Justice William Brennan, for independent state constitutional decision-making. See William Brennan, Jr., State Constitutions and the Protection of Individual Rights, 90 Harv. L. Rev. 489 (1977); James Gardner, The Failed Discourse of State Constitutionalism, 90 Mich. L. Rev. 761 (1992); Barry Latzer, The New Judicial Federalism and Criminal Justice: Two Problems and a Response, 22 Rutgers L. J. 863 (1991).

7. *Independent and adequate state grounds.* The U.S. Supreme Court reviews questions of federal law but cannot question a state court's interpretation of state law. When a state court discusses both state and federal law in its decision (and you have now seen how commonly that occurs), how does the U.S. Supreme Court decide whether it can review the decision? Under Michigan v. Long, 463 U.S. 1032 (1983), the Court requires a "plain statement" sufficient to show that "the federal cases are being used only for the purpose of guidance, and do not themselves compel the result that the court has reached." An assertion by the state court that it has relied independently on state law will not suffice. If the discussion of state law is "interwoven with the federal law, and . . . the adequacy and independence of any possible state law ground is not clear from the face of the opinion," the Supreme Court will treat the decision as one resting on federal law. Is this an appropriate test for judging the intentions of a state court? Does a state court risk reversal if it cites any U.S. Supreme Court cases at all? See Pennsylvania v. Labron, 518 U.S. 938 (1996) (taking jurisdiction and reversing in case where state court cited two federal decisions along with multiple state decisions); Commonwealth v. Labron, 690 A.2d 228 (Pa. 1997) (on remand, reinstating earlier decision and "explicitly noting that it was, in fact, decided upon independent state grounds").

2. *Workplaces*

Although the Fourth Amendment and its state analogs extend to "homes," all courts have extended the protection against unreasonable searches and seizures to other locations. The nature of the place can profoundly influence the reasonableness of the search. Given the amount of time many people spend in the workplace, it should come as no surprise that police searches of the workplace generate plenty of disputes. In addition to the location of the search, these cases also sometimes raise questions about the relationship between the government and a private employer who participates to some degree in a search.

■ PEOPLE v. CARLOS CHRISTOPHER GALVADON

103 P.3d 923 (Colo. 2005)

MARTINEZ, J.

. . . Galvadon worked as the night manager of a liquor store owned by his mother-in-law. Galvadon and his mother-in-law were the only employees of the store.

The store is located in a strip shopping center and occupies a narrow rectangular retail space. The front two-thirds of the retail space make up the publicly accessible portion of the store. The back of the store, however, is separated from the front of the store by a large refrigerator to create a separate room . . . used for inventory storage, an office and a bathroom. The only access to the back room from the front of the store is through a narrow corridor between the wall of the store and the refrigerator.

The front of the store consists of large glass windows and a glass-paned door with a checkout counter in front. The store has four surveillance video cameras. One is located in the back room and three others are located throughout the front of the store. The video recorder and monitor are also located in the back room.

As night manager, Galvadon was left by himself to take care of the store. His responsibilities included ordering liquor, making bank deposits, writing checks for the store, and restocking shelves. Galvadon used the back room to conduct all of these activities. According to Galvadon, the only people who had unrestricted access to the back room were himself and the owner. Delivery persons were regularly permitted in the back room, but only if supervised or otherwise granted access.

On November 20, 2003, Galvadon was working at the liquor store as night manager. Two other people, Jeffery Hogan and David Flores, were at the store with him for about an hour. Although the record is not clear as to what exactly transpired, the parties recite the same sequence of events: Shortly before midnight, Flores and Hogan were outside of the store standing in the parking lot. Galvadon stood in the open doorway at the front of the store. Flores was sprayed in the face with pepper spray.

At the same time, or immediately thereafter, Sergeant Juhl of the Colorado Springs Police Department drove by the store. Sergeant Juhl became suspicious when he saw Flores drop to the ground. He called for backup officers, turned around and pulled into the parking lot.

When Sergeant Juhl arrived, Galvadon was inside the store, but Hogan and Flores were still in the parking lot. Hogan explained that he and Flores had been "assaulted" by someone around the corner and that Flores was sprayed with pepper spray. Hogan explained that he wanted to take Flores to get his face washed off and then began to escort Flores into the store. Sergeant Juhl followed them.

Once in the store, Hogan asked if he and Flores could use the bathroom. Galvadon stated that no one was allowed in the back. Hogan urged Galvadon that Flores was in pain and needed to use the bathroom to wash off his face. Galvadon again insisted, several times, that no one was allowed in the back room. Hogan, however, ignored Galvadon and escorted Flores to the back room. Sergeant Juhl followed them. Galvadon followed all three of them into the back room.

While Flores was washing his face, backup officers arrived and went to the back room. Galvadon again told everyone in the back room that no one was allowed in back. Galvadon then returned to the front of the store. The officers stayed in the back room with Flores and Hogan while Sergeant Juhl went to the front of the store to speak with Galvadon. While in the back room, one of the officers discovered a "brick" of marihuana sitting in the bottom of an open cardboard box. Shortly thereafter, another brick was discovered sitting in a bag on the floor of the bathroom. Later, the owner of the store arrived and consented to a search of the store. During the search a third brick of marihuana was discovered in the back room.

After Flores, Hogan and the officers cleared out of the back room, Galvadon went into the back room by himself. Sergeant Juhl followed him. When Sergeant Juhl reached Galvadon, he discovered him attempting to hide a surveillance video tape in his pants. Galvadon explained that he had been drinking in the store earlier that night and was hiding the tape because he did not want the owner to find out. The video was later viewed by the investigating officers and showed Galvadon placing what the officers believed to be the bricks of marihuana in the back room.

Galvadon was subsequently charged with possession of marihuana, possession with intent to distribute marihuana and assault in the third degree. Prior to trial, Galvadon sought to suppress the evidence seized from the liquor store as the fruit of an illegal search. In response, the prosecution . . . claimed that because Galvadon was only an employee he could have no reasonable expectation of privacy. In addition, the prosecution asserted that because others had access to the back room and Galvadon was aware he was being videotaped by the in-store surveillance system while in the back room, . . . Galvadon could not have a reasonable expectation of privacy. The trial court disagreed and found that Galvadon had [a] reasonable expectation of privacy in the back room [and that] the warrantless intrusion into the back room could not be justified by any of the exceptions at law argued by the prosecution. Specifically, the court found there were no exigent circumstances, the intrusion was not based on emergency aid and Galvadon did not give consent. . . .

Analysis

. . . Prior to Katz v. United States, 389 U.S. 347 (1967), the Court struggled with a method of determining when a person is afforded Fourth Amendment protection. Protection at the time was generally based on traditional notions of property law, where one must have a property interest in the place or thing searched. Such an inquiry focused on the place or thing searched, rather than the person asserting protection. The Court in *Katz* rejected this idea because it lost sight of what the Fourth Amendment actually protected. The Court held that the Fourth Amendment protects people and their privacy from government intrusion, not simply places based upon a person's property interests or their right to be in that place. . . .

Based upon privacy expectations set forth in *Katz*, the U.S. Supreme Court found that protection afforded by the Fourth Amendment is not limited to a literal reading of "houses," but instead extends beyond the home and may be asserted in the workplace. . . . In Mancusi v. DeForte, 392 U.S. 364 (1968), the defendant was a union official charged with misusing his office for coercion, extortion and conspiracy. The defendant shared an office with several other union officials. When the defendant refused to comply with a subpoena to produce union records, the state officials that served the subpoena searched the office and seized various records without a warrant. The defendant was present for the search and objected to it. The papers seized did not belong to the defendant. The Court applied the expectation of privacy analysis established in *Katz* to hold in *Mancusi* that the defendant could object to the search on Fourth Amendment grounds. . . . The Court found that despite sharing the office with several others, the defendant maintained a reasonable expectation of privacy from government intrusion in the office. . . .

Where the government search at issue takes place in a highly regulated industry such as the liquor business, under certain circumstances proprietors of such businesses might have a diminished expectation of privacy because of long-standing government oversight and consequently have less Fourth Amendment protection. The expectation of privacy in the liquor industry, however, is only diminished to the extent that searches are specifically authorized pursuant to constitutional administrative inspection regulations and conducted pursuant to the purpose of the regulatory scheme. Where, as here, the search of the liquor store was investigatory in nature and not an administrative search conducted pursuant to any regulation or statute, the defendant maintains his otherwise reasonable expectation of privacy. . . .

In examining the circumstances of a particular case [to determine if the defendant maintained a reasonable expectation of privacy in the place searched], courts have chosen to focus on different factors. Some courts look to the "nexus" between the area searched and the work space of the defendant. Other courts have looked to a defendant's right to exclude others from accessing the area for which the defendant asserts privacy. Regardless of the factors considered, an employee's expectation of privacy must be assessed in the context of the employment relation. O'Connor v. Ortega, 480 U.S. 709 (1987).

We look to several factors to determine whether Galvadon's expectation of privacy against government intrusion would exist absent the in-store surveillance system. . . . First, the back room of the liquor store is an exclusive area reserved for use by the owner and Galvadon. Its physical separation from the rest of the store indicates that public access is restricted in this area. The testimony of Sergeant Juhl indicates that even he assumed upon his first entry to the store that the public was not allowed in the back room. The room was specifically set apart as a private place for the owner and Galvadon to conduct the business affairs for the store shielded from the view and access of the public.

Second, Galvadon had the power to exclude access to the back room. As the night manager, and at the time of the police intrusion in this case, Galvadon was in charge and the only person in the store that controlled access to the back room. Because this incident occurred near midnight and Galvadon was left alone by the owner to manage the store, Galvadon could reasonably expect that only persons to whom he granted permission would be given access to the back room. Furthermore, Galvadon attempted several times to keep out Sergeant Juhl, Flores and Hogan, as well as the emergency medical technicians and other officers that arrived at the liquor store. This is a clear manifestation of Galvadon's belief that he could control access to the back room and maintain an expectation of privacy from intrusion of others into that area.

Despite the prosecution's argument to the contrary, the fact that the back room was accessible by a limited number of people does not eliminate Galvadon's expectation of privacy. Galvadon testified that there was a store policy that no one other than himself and the owner were permitted in the back room. Exceptions were made for delivery persons; however, Galvadon's expectation of privacy was not diminished simply because the space was occasionally accessed by someone else.... Access could only be granted at the instance of Galvadon or the owner, whoever was present. With respect to delivery persons, such access was only granted for the limited purpose of delivering beer and liquor, a circumstance necessary for the continued operation of the liquor store. Because Galvadon, as night manager and sole person operating the store, could control the access of delivery persons, such access has no effect on Galvadon's reasonable expectation of privacy from government intrusion....

Having found that Galvadon could maintain an expectation of privacy in absence of the in-store surveillance system, we now turn to the question of whether his expectation of privacy from government intrusion was diminished by the presence of the surveillance system. The surveillance system consists of four video cameras; one was located in the back room. The video monitor and tape machine were also located in the back room. The prosecution generally asserts that because Galvadon was aware that the back room was under in-store surveillance, any activities that occurred in the back room were "knowingly exposed" to the store owner and the public.... This general assertion, however, ignores the fundamental inquiry supporting Fourth Amendment standing — whether the defendant has a reasonable expectation of privacy from government intrusion....

Galvadon's activities were not exposed to the public through the surveillance system. [There] is no indication that any monitors were viewable from the publicly accessible portions of the store or that the public had access to the video recordings under the normal operation of the store. The owner and Galvadon were the only store employees, the only persons with access to the back room, and thus the only persons with access to the video recording and video monitor located there. The public, under these circumstances, did not have access to view the surveillance monitor or the video recording. As such, we find no support for the proposition that the in-store surveillance system "exposed" Galvadon to the public....

The parties do not dispute that the surveillance system exposed Galvadon's activities in the back room to the owner of the store. As such, we proceed with the analysis to determine if such exposure to the store owner eliminated Galvadon's reasonable expectation of privacy from government intrusion. The U.S. Supreme Court has found that defendant-employees may have little or no expectation of privacy from their employer, but may still maintain a reasonable expectation of privacy from government intrusion. In *Mancusi*, the defendant shared his office with several others. The Court found that this factor alone was insufficient to extinguish the defendant's expectation of privacy from government intrusion.... Similarly, we can assume here that because of the surveillance system, Galvadon had a diminished expectation of privacy from the owner of the store. Although the record is void of any reference to how often, if at all, the owner reviewed the surveillance tapes, such evidence would only demonstrate Galvadon's diminished expectation of privacy from the store owner. This, however, does not indicate that he had no reasonable expectation of privacy from government intrusion....

We conclude under the totality of circumstances that the sole person in control of the store, the night manager, maintained a reasonable expectation of privacy from government intrusion in the back room of the store, an area without public access, such that he may assert protection of the Fourth Amendment. The use of a surveillance system reviewable only by the night manager and the owner of the store did not diminish his reasonable expectation of privacy from government intrusion. . . .

MULLARKEY, C.J., dissenting.

The majority concludes that the defendant, Carlos Galvadon, had a reasonable expectation of privacy in the back room of a retail liquor store based on his exclusive control over the back room of the store. I respectfully dissent. I would find that Galvadon, as an employee of a retail liquor store, had no reasonable expectation in the store's back room because it was a liquor storage place subject to inspection at any time when the liquor store did business. . . .

Determination of this question requires examining the law regulating searches of business premises in highly regulated industries and the law defining an employee's reasonable expectation of privacy in his workplace. With respect to highly regulated industries, the Supreme Court has recognized that searches may be conducted without warrants. The liquor business is perhaps the prime example of a highly regulated industry. In Colorado, a retail liquor store may operate only if it complies with the Liquor Code and its implementing regulations. The relevant regulations require a licensed retail liquor store to be open to warrantless inspection by administrative authorities and by peace officers during normal business hours and at all times when activity is occurring on the premises. 1 C.C.R. 203-2, §47-700 (2001). . . .

The Supreme Court has recognized that not all workplaces have identical levels of Fourth Amendment protection. Indeed, the Colorado regulation is consistent with Supreme Court case law that recognizes an explicit exception to the warrant requirement for inspections of business premises within highly regulated industries in Colonnade Catering Corp. v. United States, 397 U.S. 72 (1970) (warrant exception for inspections of the liquor industry); United States v. Biswell, 406 U.S. 311 (1972) (warrant exception applies to firearms industry); and Donovan v. Dewey, 452 U.S. 594 (1981) (extending exception to inspections conducted pursuant to the Federal Mine Safety and Health Act of 1977). Of course, the constitutional rights at issue in these cases protect persons, not places, and the warrant exception at issue applies to the owners or proprietors of businesses within highly regulated industries. In summarizing the effect of these cases, the Supreme Court flatly stated that owners of businesses in highly regulated industries have no reasonable expectation of privacy in the premises. Marshall v. Barlow's Inc., 436 U.S. 307 (1978) (The liquor industry has "such a history of government oversight that no reasonable expectation of privacy . . . could exist for a proprietor over the stock of such an enterprise."). . . .

An employee of a licensed liquor establishment like Galvadon has even more limited rights. In general, an employee's expectation of privacy in the workplace is subordinate to the employer's interests. See O'Connor v. Ortega, 480 U.S. 709, 717 (1987) ("The operational realities of the workplace, however, may make some employees' expectations of privacy unreasonable when an intrusion is by a supervisor rather than a law enforcement official."). Furthermore, when an employee knows, as Galvadon did, that he or she is being watched by an employer, the affected workers are on clear notice from the outset that any movements they might make and any objects they might display within the work area would be exposed to the employer's sight. In light of employees' reduced expectation of privacy vis-à-vis employers, an employee can never be said to have a greater expectation of privacy than an employer. This lower expectation of privacy vis-à-vis the employer is particularly acute where, as here, the employee takes the risk that the employer will find evidence of wrongdoing by means of the video surveillance system in place and turn over such evidence to law enforcement. . . .

The fact that the police officers in this case were not in the back room of the store to conduct an inspection pursuant to the liquor code may be important in cases where there is evidence of bad faith by the police officers. However, there is no allegation of bad faith in this case, and the Supreme Court has made it clear that such bad faith does not affect the analysis of whether the individuals involved had any reasonable expectation of privacy. . . .

Notes

1. *Privacy interests in the workplace: majority position.* American courts have overwhelmingly decided that workers can hold some reasonable expectation of privacy in items kept at their workplace and in their activities at the workplace. The crucial question, as identified in the *Galvadon* opinion from Colorado, is whether the workers have some control over access to the area. Yet the Fourth Amendment and its state analogs speak only about government searches of "persons, houses, papers, and effects." Is a workplace a "house"? What is the justification for treating the workplace as a protected area? What would a society be like that did not limit searches in workplaces?

The government has plenty of reasons to collect information in the workplace. What begins as routine regulatory enforcement might end in a criminal prosecution. For instance, immigration agents may question employees in their workplace about their immigration status. Because of the limited intrusion involved, the questioning does not amount to a "seizure," even if workplace rules require the employees to remain on the site when the government agents arrive. INS v. Delgado, 466 U.S. 210 (1984). Does the access of regulators to the workplace strengthen or weaken the privacy interest of workers in their place of employment?

2. *Private searches.* The federal and state constitutions reach only searches conducted by government agents. A private employer can conduct any sort of search she chooses without engaging in an "unreasonable" search or seizure within the meaning of the federal constitution. See Burdeau v. McDowell, 256 U.S. 465 (1921); but cf. Texas Code Crim. Proc. Article 38.23 ("No evidence obtained by an officer *or other person* in violation of any provisions of the Constitution or laws of the State of Texas, or of the Constitution or laws of the United States of America, shall be admitted in evidence against the accused on the trial of any criminal case."). Statutes and common law rules (or contracts) may limit the private employer's searching power. However, if a private employer acts at the government's behest, a search can become "state action."

Does the power of private employers to gather information about their employees affect the reasonable expectations of privacy that an employee might have in the workplace? Employers may monitor telephone conversations or read computer files at the workplace. Private parties routinely collect and use information about their customers. Credit card companies can track where and what a consumer buys and can sell that information to merchants. As the editors of The Economist magazine put it, as we lose control over our privacy, the "chief culprit is not so much Big Brother as lots of little brothers, all gossiping with each other over computer networks." The Economist, February 10, 1996, at 27. Are statutory protections for privacy in the workplace likely to be enacted? Would they be effective?

The private security industry employs more personnel than federal, state, and local governments combined. As Professor David Sklansky points out, the growing number of private security forces might entail a shift in some of the most basic tenets of criminal procedure. He suggests that this trend will create a body of criminal procedure law that is deconstitutionalized, defederalized, tort-based, and heavily reliant both on legislatures and on juries. See Sklansky, The Private Police, 46 UCLA L. Rev. 1165 (1999); Elizabeth Joh, Conceptualizing the Private Police, 2005 Utah L. Rev. 573.

3. *Government as employer.* If a government agent wishes to search a workplace in the private sector, she usually needs probable cause and a warrant, or consent. But if the government agent represents a government employer conducting a search of a *government* workplace, different constitutional rules apply. Neither a warrant nor probable cause is necessary when the government employer is conducting (1) a non-investigatory work-related search (such as retrieving a file) or (2) an investigation of work-related misconduct. The Supreme Court in O'Connor v. Ortega, 480 U.S. 709 (1987), concluded that the reasonable suspicion standard was the best method of accommodating the employee's privacy interests with the public employer's interests apart from law enforcement. See also City of Ontario, Cal. v. Quon, 130 S. Ct. 2619 (2010) (police chief ordered review of text messages sent by officers on alphanumeric pagers the department recently purchased to determine source of billing overruns, which revealed that officer used pager during work hours for personal messages; review was reasonable because it was motivated by legitimate work-related purpose, and not excessive in scope). Workplace searches that are based on some neutral criteria, but not on individualized suspicion, may also be acceptable. See State v. Ziegler, 637 So. 2d 109 (La. 1994).

3. Schools and Prisons

When searches take place in institutions such as schools and prisons, courts tend to evaluate them much more generously than searches of homes or workplaces. These searches fall into a category sometimes known as "administrative" searches, where the government has purposes for its search other than enforcement of the criminal law. In such settings, warrants are often unnecessary, and the level of justification required does not rise to the level of probable cause. As you read the following materials, try to identify the elements of these searches that lead courts to place fewer controls on them than they do for searches in other settings. Could the arguments used to explain the looser supervision of searches in these contexts apply more broadly to others?

IN THE MATTER OF GREGORY M.

627 N.E.2d 500 (N.Y. 1993)

LEVINE, J.

... On November 29, 1990 appellant, then 15 years old, arrived at the high school he attended in The Bronx without a proper student identification card. He was directed by a school security officer to report to the office of the Dean to obtain a new card. In accordance with school policy, he was required to leave his cloth book bag with the security officer until he had obtained the proper identification. When appellant tossed the book bag on a metal shelf before proceeding beyond the school lobby to the Dean's office, the security officer heard a metallic "thud" which he characterized as "unusual." He ran his fingers over the outer surface of the bottom of the bag and felt the outline of a gun. The security officer then summoned the Dean who also discerned the shape of a gun upon feeling the outside of appellant's book bag. The bag was brought to the Dean's office and opened by the head of school security, revealing a small hand gun later identified as a .38 Titan Tiger Special. A juvenile delinquency petition was filed in Family Court accusing appellant of [weapons violations]. Family Court denied appellant's motion to suppress the gun....

We affirm [the denial of the appellant's motion to suppress]. Although minimally intrusive, the purposeful investigative touching of the outside of appellant's book bag by the school security officer (i.e., to acquire knowledge about the bag's contents) falls marginally within a search for constitutional purposes. Also, appellant is quite correct in contending that the metallic thud heard by the security officer when appellant put the book bag down was by itself insufficient to furnish a reasonable suspicion that the bag contained a weapon. We conclude, however, that a less rigorous premonition concerning the contents of the bag was sufficient to justify the investigative touching of the outside of the bag. When that touching disclosed the presence of a gun-like object in the bag, there was reasonable suspicion to justify the search of the inside of the bag.

In People v. Scott D., 315 N.E.2d 466 (1974), this Court held that students attending public schools are protected by the constitutional ban against unreasonable searches and seizures. *Scott D.* involved a school search of a student for illegal drugs. We further held in *Scott D.* that inherent in determining whether a school search was reasonable is a "balancing of basic personal rights against urgent social necessities" and that, given the "special responsibility of school teachers in the control of the school precincts and the grave threat, even lethal threat, of drug abuse among school children, the basis for finding sufficient cause for a school search will be less than that required outside the school precincts."

Employing an analysis similar to that of People v. Scott D., the United States Supreme Court in New Jersey v. T.L.O., 469 U.S. 325 (1985), also concluded that the Fourth Amendment of the United States Constitution applies to searches of students by school authorities, but held that less cause is required to justify such a search than is required of law enforcement authorities searching persons or their effects outside school premises. Thus, the Supreme Court held that a determination of the appropriate standard of reasonableness to govern a certain class of searches requires a balancing: "On one side of the balance are arrayed the individual's legitimate expectations of privacy and personal security; on the other, the government's need for effective methods to deal with breaches of public order." The Court in New Jersey v. T.L.O. held that, ordinarily, searches by school authorities of the persons or belongings of students may be made upon "reasonable grounds for suspecting that the search will turn up evidence that the student has violated or is violating either the law or the rules of the school." The Court applied the reasonable suspicion standard in validating a teacher's full search of the inside of a student's purse for cigarettes, during which evidence of her involvement in drug dealing was revealed.

We agree that for searches by school authorities of the persons and belongings of students, such as that conducted in New Jersey v. T.L.O., the reasonable suspicion standard adopted in that case for Fourth Amendment purposes is also appropriate under our State Constitution (N.Y. Const., art. I, §12). In the instant case, however, the investigative touching of the outer surface of appellant's book bag falls within a class of searches far less intrusive than those which, under New Jersey v. T.L.O., require application of the reasonable suspicion standard. Applying the balancing process required under People v. Scott D. and New Jersey v. T. L. O., it is undeniable that appellant had only a minimal expectation of privacy regarding the outer touching of his school bag by school security personnel, even for purposes of learning something regarding its contents, when he left the bag with the security officer pursuant to the school policy requiring this until he obtained a valid identification card. On the other hand, it seems equally undeniable that, in the balancing process, prevention of the introduction of hand guns and other lethal weapons into New York City schools such as this high school is a governmental interest of the highest urgency. The extreme exigency of barring the introduction of weapons into the schools by students is no longer a matter of debate.

Thus, the balancing process ordained by People v. Scott D. and New Jersey v. T.L.O. leads to the conclusion that a less strict justification applies to the limited search here than the reasonable suspicion standard applicable for more intrusive school searches. In this regard, we find it noteworthy that the Supreme Court in New Jersey v. T.L.O. specifically disclaimed that its decision made some quantum of individualized suspicion an essential element of every school search.* The Supreme Court has elsewhere made it clear that, at least outside the context of criminal investigations by law enforcement officers, individualized suspicion is not a constitutional floor below which any search must be deemed unreasonable. There may be circumstances in which, because the privacy interests involved in the case are minimal and are overborne by the governmental interests in jeopardy if a higher standard were enforced, a search may be reasonable despite the absence of such suspicion. See Skinner v. Railway Labor Executives' Assn., 489 U.S. 602 (1989) [approving of drug testing of railway employees involved in train accidents or safety incidents]; United States v. Martinez-Fuerte, 428 U.S. 543 (1976) [brief suspicionless stops of vehicles for questioning at immigration checkpoint at fixed location]. We need not apply these precedents, however, to sustain the actions of the school authorities in the instant case.

* [Footnote 8 of the *T.L.O.* opinion reads as follows: "We do not decide whether individualized suspicion is an essential element of the reasonableness standard we adopt for searches by school authorities. In other contexts, however, we have held that although some quantum of individualized suspicion is usually a prerequisite to a constitutional search or seizure, . . . the Fourth Amendment imposes no irreducible requirement of such suspicion." — EDS.]

Because appellant's diminished expectation of privacy was so clearly outweighed by the governmental interest in interdicting the infusion of weapons in the schools, we think the "unusual" metallic thud heard when the book bag was flung down — quite evidently suggesting to the school security officer the possibility that it might contain a weapon — was sufficient justification for the investigative touching of the outside of the bag, thus rendering that limited intrusion reasonable (and not based on mere whim or caprice) for constitutional purposes. Our application in the instant case of a graduated standard of reasonableness is, of course, sanctioned by and premised on the minimal nature of the search, and that it was conducted by school officials for the special needs of school security and not for a criminal investigative purpose. Once the touching of the outer surface of the bag revealed the presence of a gun-like object inside, school authorities had a reasonable suspicion of a violation of law justifying the search of the contents of the bag.

[Despite] vague professions to the contrary, the dissent is contending that reasonable suspicion is a constitutional floor for purposes of all types of searches, however limited, in a school setting or elsewhere, and irrespective of who conducts the search. [The dissent] supports this position by reliance on Terry v. Ohio, 392 U.S. 1 (1968), and [related New York cases]. The Supreme Court in *Terry* described the intrusion in that case as "a careful exploration of the outer surfaces of a person's clothing all over his or her body in an attempt to find weapons" and characterized it as "a serious intrusion upon the sanctity of the person, which may inflict great indignity."[The Court called the frisk a "limited search" only because] it must be limited to that which is necessary for the discovery of weapons which might be used to harm the officer or others nearby.

People v. Diaz, 612 N.E.2d 298 (N.Y. 1993), declined to extend the *Terry* warrantless search exception to a frisk disclosing other forms of contraband. "Once an officer has concluded that no weapon is present, the search is over and there is no authority for further intrusion." *Diaz* and *Terry* simply do not apply to a less intrusive touching of the outside of a book bag by school personnel, after possession of the bag had been lawfully relinquished. . . . Thus, Family Court's denial of appellant's motion to suppress should be upheld. . . .

TITONE, J., dissenting.

Acknowledging that there was not even a "reasonable suspicion" of criminality, the Court nevertheless holds that the school security guard was entitled to conduct a search of appellant's book bag. In so ruling, the Court has reduced the privacy protections of the Fourth Amendment and of article I, §12 of the State Constitution below all previously recognized minimum thresholds. While I too am horrified by the recent escalation of deadly weapons in the public schools, I cannot agree that the problem should be remedied by a contraction of even the minimal privacy rights that the Supreme Court has accorded to school children, particularly when there exist other, less intrusive remedies. . . .

The teaching of New Jersey v. T.L.O., on which the majority places heavy reliance, is that search warrants are not constitutionally required for school searches and that such searches may be justified by a lesser showing of reasonable suspicion. Nothing in *T.L.O.*, however, suggests that the serious intrusion of a search may be upheld on even less than reasonable suspicion, much less on the gossamer thread of what the Court has labeled an "unusual" metallic thud. . . .

The majority begins its analysis with the premise that the "investigative touching" of the outside of appellant's book bag was somehow "far less intrusive" than other types of searches. [But] an investigative touching of a closed container requires a degree of pinching, squeezing or probing beyond the limited intrusion allowed under Terry v. Ohio. . . .

The majority also attempts to justify its decision on the theory that appellant had only a "minimal" expectation of privacy "regarding the outer touching of his school bag" when he left it with a security officer pursuant to a school policy. This sweeping conclusion, however, remains unexplained. Significantly, the Supreme Court [in *T.L.O.*] has specifically rejected the contention that a child has a drastically diminished expectation of privacy in articles of personal property that are carried into school. . . .

A further reason offered by the majority for reducing the quantum of information necessary to conduct a school search such as this one is the unquestionably compelling need to prevent the introduction of hand guns and other lethal weapons into the schools. I find this aspect of the majority's rationale unconvincing for several reasons. First, the reduction of students' privacy rights that the majority sanctions is not narrowly tailored to address weapon-related criminal activities. While the search in this case happened to disclose a weapon, the sequence of events that led to that disclosure here could just as easily lead in another case to the discovery of some other illegality or rule infraction such as the possession of drugs or cigarettes. Second, there exist other, more effective means of interdicting weapons in public schools, namely, the installation of metal detectors at the front door. . . .

Third, and most importantly, the constitutional privacy guarantees in our Federal and State Constitutions exist precisely to protect citizens from governmental overreaching in the name of the exigencies of law enforcement. [The majority's rationale is] dangerous, since the same rationale may be trotted out to justify virtually any governmental excess that is aimed at a currently troublesome or rampant form of crime. [T]he need for judicial intervention to bolster the privacy protections would concomitantly increase, rather than diminish, with an increase in the public pressure on law enforcement authorities to take all necessary steps to obliterate a new crime threat. . . .

Finally, even if it is assumed that some lesser showing than the reasonable suspicion approved by the Supreme Court is permissible in these circumstances, the majority has not given any indication of the nature of that showing or of what the lower limits of that showing might be. . . . If, as the majority admits, the "thud" was not sufficient to furnish reasonable suspicion that the bag contained a gun, it is difficult to see how that "thud" could have "evidently suggest[ed] to the school security officer the possibility that [the bag] might contain a weapon." The distinction between a "reasonable suspicion" and an "evident suggestion" is not at all clear to me and will probably be even less meaningful to the school authorities who have to implement this new standard. The significance of the majority's reference to a "premonition" that is "less rigorous" than reasonable suspicion is even more opaque.

The closest the majority has come to actually objectifying the standard it has used is its characterization of the "thud" the guard heard as "unusual." However, what made this sound so "unusual" is far from clear. Students' book bags routinely contain such unexceptional items as make-up cases, portable cassette players and other consumer electronic devices, all of which would likely produce a metallic "thud" when dropped on a hard surface such as a counter. Even more importantly, the "unusual" nature of an event or circumstance does not provide a sound basis for a search of an individual's personal effects. Without more, such an amorphous touchstone would permit intrusions on the most arbitrary of predicates, including a student's "unusual" manner of dress, gait or speech.

. . . While we all have a vital interest in preventing weapons from entering our public school classrooms, that interest could have been served in this case without seriously undermining the student's constitutional rights by either asking the student about the contents of his bag upon his return or by insisting that he empty it or leave it with the guard before re-entering the building. In any event, while I do not advocate anything as sweeping as an over-all constitutional floor of "reasonable suspicion" that would be applicable in all situations, I cannot concur in the majority's decision to sustain this search on a showing that falls well below the minimum requirements approved by the Supreme Court for searches conducted on school premises. Accordingly, I dissent. . . .

OKLAHOMA STATUTES TIT. 70, §24-102

The superintendent, principal, teacher, or security personnel of any public school in the State of Oklahoma, upon reasonable suspicion, shall have the authority to detain and search or authorize the search, of any pupil or property in the possession of the pupil when said pupil is on any school premises, or while in transit under the authority of the school, or while attending any function sponsored or authorized by the school, for dangerous weapons, controlled dangerous substances, . . . intoxicating beverages, . . . or for missing or stolen property if said property be reasonably suspected to have been taken from a pupil, a school employee or the school during school activities. The search shall be conducted by a person of the same sex as the person being searched and shall be witnessed by at least one other authorized person, said person to be of the same sex if practicable.

The extent of any search conducted pursuant to this section shall be reasonably related to the objective of the search and not excessively intrusive in light of the age and sex of the student and the nature of the infraction. In no event shall a strip search of a student be allowed. No student's clothing, except cold weather outerwear, shall be removed prior to or during the conduct of any warrantless search. . . .

Pupils shall not have any reasonable expectation of privacy towards school administrators or teachers in the contents of a school locker, desk, or other school property. School personnel shall have access to school lockers, desks, and other school property in order to properly supervise the welfare of pupils. School lockers, desks, and other areas of school facilities may be opened and examined by school officials at any time and no reason shall be necessary for such search. Schools shall inform pupils in the student discipline code that they have no reasonable expectation of privacy rights towards school officials in school lockers, desks, or other school property.

Notes

1. *Lesser protections in school: majority position.* The decision of the U.S. Supreme Court in New Jersey v. T.L.O., 469 U.S. 325 (1985), reached the same conclusion as

had many of the state courts considering earlier challenges to searches by school officials. Because of the special environment of the school, these courts concluded that neither a warrant nor probable cause was necessary to justify a search by school officials, even if the evidence found during the search ultimately led to a criminal or juvenile conviction. Instead, reasonable suspicion was all that was typically necessary to support a valid search. See also Safford Unified School District #1 v. Redding, 129 S. Ct. 2633 (2009) (search of 13-year-old student's underwear for prescription pain killer without probable cause was unreasonable).

State courts and legislatures visiting this question have continued to take the position that warrants and probable cause are unnecessary in this environment; the statutes printed above are typical in this respect. See State v. Best, 987 A.2d 605 (N.J. 2010) (reasonable suspicion can support search of automobile in school lot for drugs); cf. In re Randy G., 28 P.3d 239 (Cal. 2001) (reasonable suspicion not required to justify school security officer's temporary detention of student).

2. *Individualized suspicion, less than reasonable.* The New York court in *Gregory M.* allowed a search to go forward on the basis of information about an individual student (a backpack making a "thud") that did not amount to reasonable suspicion. Do you agree with the court that the "thud" was not enough for reasonable suspicion? Instead of expanding its own definition of reasonable suspicion, the court decided to recognize a lower level of suspicion in the school context, "evident suggestion." What does the court accomplish (if anything) by creating a new category rather than expanding an old one? Should the new standard apply to exterior touching of purses and backpacks outside the school setting?

3. *Searches of school-owned areas.* School authorities grant students access to lockers and other areas for storage of personal property; sometimes school administrators inform students (either by posting signs or by providing individual notice) that they might search the lockers from time to time. See New Jersey v. T.L.O., 469 U.S. at 338 n.5 (reserving question of proper standard for searches of lockers and desks); Md. Educ. Code §7-308 (authorizes searches of school-owned areas); S.C. Stat. §59-63-1120 (search of school property or student's personal belongings). Under such circumstances, is it reasonable for a student to expect any privacy at all in the locker area? What if the school assumes but does not announce its power to search lockers and exercises that power periodically? Would the same analysis apply to searches of dormitory rooms by school officials in state-supported universities?

4. *School officials as criminal law enforcers.* Part of the justification that courts often give for the relaxed requirements for valid searches in schools is the noncriminal purpose of the searches. School administrators can conduct searches based on reasonable suspicion of a violation of "either the law or the rules of the school." *T.L.O.*, 469 U.S. at 341. But what happens if law enforcement officials approach school officials and ask them to conduct the search? What if the law enforcement agent who initiates the search is stationed full time at the school? Most courts have used the probable cause standard for searches carried out by school officials at the request of the police. Courts use the reasonable suspicion standard for searches initiated by a police officer assigned full time or part time as a liaison to the school. See People v. Dilworth, 661 N.E.2d 310 (Ill. 1996). Should it matter whether the searching police officer has a regular relationship with the school? For further exploration of the variety of state court applications of this standard, including the permissible scope of searches in the school context, see the web extension for this chapter at *http://www.crimpro.com/extension/ch04.*

Would your analysis change if school officials have a general duty to cooperate with criminal law enforcement rather than an intent to do so in a particular case? For instance, Tenn. Code Ann. §49-6-4209 imposes on school officials the legal duty to help enforce the criminal law: "It is the duty of a school principal who has reasonable suspicion to believe, either as a result of a search or otherwise, that any student is committing or has committed any violation of [criminal laws against possession of weapons or drugs], upon the school ground . . . to report [the] suspicion to the appropriate law enforcement officer." Searches in the school context have attracted the attention of about 20 state legislatures. A few statutes place limits on who can conduct searches, or the crimes to be investigated. Others require schools to notify parents about any searches, or to develop a standard search "plan."

Problem 4-4. Gun Lockers

One Friday night in November, students at Madison High School reported hearing gunshots as they left the school following a basketball game. School security guards found spent casings on school grounds the next day. By the following Monday morning, the school staff and security personnel were receiving more reports of guns present in the school building and on school buses, and rumors that a shootout would occur at the school that day. Some staff members and students asked to leave the school out of fear for their safety.

The school principal, Jude, ordered school security personnel to begin a random search of student lockers as a preventive measure while he interviewed selected students. The public school handbook indicates that "lockers are the property of the school system and subject to inspection as determined necessary or appropriate." Students are prohibited from putting private locks on their lockers.

Siena, a Madison High School security aide, searched the school lockers. Using a pass key, he opened the lockers and visually inspected the lockers' contents, moving some articles to see more clearly, and patted down coats in the lockers. Siena did not search every student locker. He chose lockers initially on the lower level of the building, where the largest crowds gathered. He also took care to search the lockers of any known "problem" students and any locker where he saw groups of students congregating.

Altogether, Siena conducted between 75 and 100 locker searches before he opened Baker's locker. At the time, Siena did not know who was assigned to the locker. Baker did not have a history of prior weapon violations, nor did the school officials suspect his involvement in the recent gun incidents. Siena removed a coat from the locker and immediately believed it to be unusually heavy. He found a gun in the coat.

Was the search legal? How would you resolve the case under the constitutional standards described in the *Gregory M.* case? Under the Oklahoma statute reprinted above? Would your analysis change if you knew that the FBI estimates that nearly 100,000 students carry guns to school every day? See Isiah B. v. State, 500 N.W.2d 637 (Wis. 1993).

■ BOARD OF EDUCATION OF INDEPENDENT SCHOOL DISTRICT NO. 92 OF POTTAWATOMIE COUNTY v. LINDSAY EARLS

536 U.S. 822 (2002)

THOMAS, J.*

The Student Activities Drug Testing Policy implemented by the Board of Education of Independent School District No. 92 of Pottawatomie County requires all students who participate in competitive extracurricular activities to submit to drug testing. Because this Policy reasonably serves the School District's important interest in detecting and preventing drug use among its students, we hold that it is constitutional.

I.

The city of Tecumseh, Oklahoma, is a rural community located approximately 40 miles southeast of Oklahoma City. . . . In the fall of 1998, the School District adopted the Student Activities Drug Testing Policy (Policy), which requires all middle and high school students to consent to drug testing in order to participate in any extracurricular activity. In practice, the Policy has been applied only to competitive extracurricular activities sanctioned by the Oklahoma Secondary Schools Activities Association, such as the Academic Team, Future Farmers of America, Future Homemakers of America, band, choir, pom pom, cheerleading, and athletics. Under the Policy, students are required to take a drug test before participating in an extracurricular activity, must submit to random drug testing while participating in that activity, and must agree to be tested at any time upon reasonable suspicion. The urinalysis tests are designed to detect only the use of illegal drugs, including amphetamines, marijuana, cocaine, opiates, and barbituates, not medical conditions or the presence of authorized prescription medications. . . .

Respondent Lindsay Earls was a member of the show choir, the marching band, the Academic Team, and the National Honor Society. Respondent Daniel James sought to participate in the Academic Team. Together with their parents, Earls and James brought a 42 U.S.C. §1983 action against the School District, challenging the Policy both on its face and as applied to their participation in extracurricular activities. They alleged that the Policy violates the Fourth Amendment as incorporated by the Fourteenth Amendment and requested injunctive and declarative relief. [The District Court granted summary judgment to the School District, but the Tenth Circuit reversed.]

II. . . .

Searches by public school officials, such as the collection of urine samples, implicate Fourth Amendment interests. We must therefore review the School District's Policy for "reasonableness," which is the touchstone of the constitutionality of a governmental search. In the criminal context, reasonableness usually requires a showing of probable cause. The probable-cause standard, however, is peculiarly

* [Chief Justice Rehnquist and Justices Scalia, Kennedy, and Breyer joined in this opinion. — EDS.]

related to criminal investigations and may be unsuited to determining the reasonableness of administrative searches where the Government seeks to *prevent* the development of hazardous conditions. The Court has also held that a warrant and finding of probable cause are unnecessary in the public school context because such requirements "would unduly interfere with the maintenance of the swift and informal disciplinary procedures [that are] needed." New Jersey v. T.L.O., 469 U.S. 325, 340-41 (1985).

Given that the School District's Policy is not in any way related to the conduct of criminal investigations, respondents do not contend that the School District requires probable cause before testing students for drug use. Respondents instead argue that drug testing must be based at least on some level of individualized suspicion. It is true that we generally determine the reasonableness of a search by balancing the nature of the intrusion on the individual's privacy against the promotion of legitimate governmental interests. But we have long held that the Fourth Amendment imposes no irreducible requirement of individualized suspicion. In certain limited circumstances, the Government's need to discover such latent or hidden conditions, or to prevent their development, is sufficiently compelling to justify the intrusion on privacy entailed by conducting such searches without any measure of individualized suspicion. Treasury Employees v. Von Raab, 489 U.S. 656 (1989) [allowing drug testing of customs employees in drug enforcement positions]; Skinner v. Railway Labor Executives' Assn., 489 U.S. 602 (1989) [allowing drug testing of railway employees after train accidents]. Therefore, in the context of safety and administrative regulations, a search unsupported by probable cause may be reasonable when "special needs, beyond the normal need for law enforcement, make the warrant and probable-cause requirement impracticable." *T.L.O.* at 351.

Significantly, this Court has previously held that "special needs" inhere in the public school context. While schoolchildren do not shed their constitutional rights when they enter the schoolhouse, "Fourth Amendment rights . . . are different in public schools than elsewhere; the 'reasonableness' inquiry cannot disregard the schools' custodial and tutelary responsibility for children." Vernonia School Dist. 47J v. Acton, 515 U.S. 646, 656 (1995). In particular, a finding of individualized suspicion may not be necessary when a school conducts drug testing.

In *Vernonia,* this Court held that the suspicionless drug testing of athletes was constitutional. The Court, however, did not simply authorize all school drug testing, but rather conducted a fact-specific balancing of the intrusion on the children's Fourth Amendment rights against the promotion of legitimate governmental interests. Applying the principles of *Vernonia* to the somewhat different facts of this case, we conclude that Tecumseh's Policy is also constitutional.

A.

We first consider the nature of the privacy interest allegedly compromised by the drug testing. As in *Vernonia,* the context of the public school environment serves as the backdrop for the analysis of the privacy interest at stake and the reasonableness of the drug testing policy in general. A student's privacy interest is limited in a public school environment where the State is responsible for maintaining discipline, health, and safety. Schoolchildren are routinely required to submit to physical examinations and vaccinations against disease. Securing order in the school environment sometimes requires that students be subjected to greater controls than those appropriate for adults.

Respondents argue that because children participating in nonathletic extracurricular activities are not subject to regular physicals and communal undress, they have a stronger expectation of privacy than the athletes tested in *Vernonia.* [However], students who participate in competitive extracurricular activities voluntarily subject themselves to many of the same intrusions on their privacy as do athletes. Some of these clubs and activities require occasional off-campus travel and communal undress. All of them have their own rules and requirements for participating students that do not apply to the student body as a whole. For example, each of the competitive extracurricular activities governed by the Policy must abide by the rules of the Oklahoma Secondary Schools Activities Association, and a faculty sponsor monitors the students for compliance with the various rules dictated by the clubs and activities. . . . We therefore conclude that the students affected by this Policy have a limited expectation of privacy.

B.

Next, we consider the character of the intrusion imposed by the Policy. Urination is an excretory function traditionally shielded by great privacy. But the degree of intrusion on one's privacy caused by collecting a urine sample depends upon the manner in which production of the urine sample is monitored. Under the Policy, a faculty monitor waits outside the closed restroom stall for the student to produce a sample and must "listen for the normal sounds of urination in order to guard against tampered specimens and to insure an accurate chain of custody." . . . This procedure is virtually identical to that reviewed in *Vernonia*. . . .

In addition, the Policy clearly requires that the test results be kept in confidential files separate from a student's other educational records and released to school personnel only on a "need to know" basis. Respondents nonetheless contend that the intrusion on students' privacy is significant because the Policy fails to protect effectively against the disclosure of confidential information and, specifically, that the school "has been careless in protecting that information: for example, the Choir teacher looked at students' prescription drug lists and left them where other students could see them." But the choir teacher is someone with a "need to know," because during off-campus trips she needs to know what medications are taken by her students. . . . This one example of alleged carelessness hardly increases the character of the intrusion.

Moreover, the test results are not turned over to any law enforcement authority. Nor do the test results here lead to the imposition of discipline or have any academic consequences. Rather, the only consequence of a failed drug test is to limit the student's privilege of participating in extracurricular activities. Indeed, a student may test positive for drugs twice and still be allowed to participate in extracurricular activities. . . . Given the minimally intrusive nature of the sample collection and the limited uses to which the test results are put, we conclude that the invasion of students' privacy is not significant.

C.

Finally, this Court must consider the nature and immediacy of the government's concerns and the efficacy of the Policy in meeting them. This Court has already articulated in detail the importance of the governmental concern in preventing drug use by schoolchildren. The drug abuse problem among our Nation's youth has hardly abated since *Vernonia* was decided in 1995. In fact, evidence suggests that it has only grown worse. As in *Vernonia,* "the necessity for the State to act is magnified by the fact that this evil is being visited not just upon individuals at large, but upon children for whom it has undertaken a special responsibility of care and direction." The health and safety risks identified in *Vernonia* apply with equal force to Tecumseh's children. Indeed, the nationwide drug epidemic makes the war against drugs a pressing concern in every school.

Additionally, the School District in this case has presented specific evidence of drug use at Tecumseh schools. Teachers testified that they had seen students who appeared to be under the influence of drugs and that they had heard students speaking openly about using drugs. A drug dog found marijuana cigarettes near the school parking lot. Police officers once found drugs or drug paraphernalia in a car driven by a Future Farmers of America member. And the school board president reported that people in the community were calling the board to discuss the "drug situation." We decline to second-guess the finding of the District Court that "viewing the evidence as a whole, it cannot be reasonably disputed that the School District was faced with a 'drug problem' when it adopted the Policy." . . .

We also reject respondents' argument that drug testing must presumptively be based upon an individualized reasonable suspicion of wrongdoing because such a testing regime would be less intrusive. [We] question whether testing based on individualized suspicion in fact would be less intrusive. Such a regime would place an additional burden on public school teachers who are already tasked with the difficult job of maintaining order and discipline. A program of individualized suspicion might unfairly target members of unpopular groups. The fear of lawsuits resulting from such targeted searches may chill enforcement of the program, rendering it ineffective in combating drug use. In any case, this Court has repeatedly stated that reasonableness under the Fourth Amendment does not require employing the least intrusive means, because the logic of such elaborate less-restrictive-alternative arguments could raise insuperable barriers to the exercise of virtually all search-and-seizure powers. . . .

III.

Within the limits of the Fourth Amendment, local school boards must assess the desirability of drug testing schoolchildren. In upholding the constitutionality of the Policy, we express no opinion as to its wisdom. Rather, we hold only that Tecumseh's Policy is a reasonable means of furthering the School District's important interest in preventing and deterring drug use among its schoolchildren. . . .

BREYER, J., concurring.

. . . When trying to resolve this kind of close question involving the interpretation of constitutional values, I believe it important that the school board provided an opportunity for the airing of these differences at public meetings designed to give the entire community the opportunity to be able to participate in developing the drug policy. The board used this democratic, participatory process to uncover and to resolve differences, giving weight to the fact that the process, in this instance, revealed little, if any, objection to the proposed testing program.

[A] contrary reading of the Constitution, as requiring "individualized suspicion" in this public school context, could well lead schools to push the boundaries of "individualized suspicion" to its outer limits, using subjective criteria that may "unfairly target members of unpopular groups," or leave those whose behavior is slightly abnormal stigmatized in the minds of others. . . .

GINSBURG, J., dissenting.*

Seven years ago, in Vernonia School Dist. 47J v. Acton, 515 U.S. 646 (1995), this Court determined that a school district's policy of randomly testing the urine of its student athletes for illicit drugs did not violate the Fourth Amendment. In so ruling, the Court emphasized that drug use "increased the risk of sports-related injury" and that Vernonia's athletes were the "leaders" of an aggressive local "drug culture" that had reached "epidemic proportions." Today, the Court relies upon *Vernonia* to permit a school district with a drug problem its superintendent repeatedly described as "not major" to test the urine of an academic team member solely by reason of her participation in a nonathletic, competitive extracurricular activity — participation associated with neither special dangers from, nor particular predilections for, drug use. . . . The particular testing program upheld today is not reasonable, it is capricious, even perverse: Petitioners' policy targets for testing a student population least likely to be at risk from illicit drugs and their damaging effects. I therefore dissent.

I.

[The Court points to] the voluntary character of both interscholastic athletics and other competitive extracurricular activities. . . . The comparison is enlightening. While extracurricular activities are "voluntary" in the sense that they are not required for graduation, they are part of the school's educational program; for that reason, the petitioner . . . is justified in expending public resources to make them available. Participation in such activities is a key component of school life, essential in reality for students applying to college, and, for all participants, a significant contributor to the breadth and quality of the educational experience. Students "volunteer" for extracurricular pursuits in the same way they might volunteer for honors classes: They subject themselves to additional requirements, but they do so in order to take full advantage of the education offered them.

Voluntary participation in athletics has a distinctly different dimension: Schools regulate student athletes discretely because competitive school sports by their nature require communal undress and, more important, expose students to physical risks that schools have a duty to mitigate. . . . Competitive extracurricular activities other than athletics, however, serve students of all manner: the modest and shy along with the bold and uninhibited. Activities of the kind plaintiff-respondent Lindsay Earls pursued — choir, show choir, marching band, and academic team — afford opportunities to gain self-assurance. . . .

Finally, the nature and immediacy of the governmental concern faced by the Vernonia School District dwarfed that confronting Tecumseh administrators. Vernonia initiated its drug testing policy in response to an alarming situation: "[A] large segment of the student body, particularly those involved in interscholastic athletics, was in a state of rebellion . . . fueled by alcohol and drug abuse as well as the students' misperceptions about the drug culture." Tecumseh, by contrast, repeatedly

* [Justices Stevens, O'Connor, and Souter joined in this opinion. — EDS.]

reported to the Federal Government during the period leading up to the adoption of the policy that "types of drugs [other than alcohol and tobacco] including controlled dangerous substances, are present [in the schools] but have not identified themselves as major problems at this time." 1998-1999 Tecumseh School's Application for Funds under the Safe and Drug-Free Schools and Communities Program. . . .

Nationwide, students who participate in extracurricular activities are significantly less likely to develop substance abuse problems than are their less-involved peers. See, *e.g.*, N. Zill, C. Nord, & L. Loomis, Adolescent Time Use, Risky Behavior, and Outcomes 52 (1995) (tenth graders "who reported spending no time in school-sponsored activities were . . . 49 percent more likely to have used drugs" than those who spent 1-4 hours per week in such activities). Even if students might be deterred from drug use in order to preserve their extracurricular eligibility, it is at least as likely that other students might forgo their extracurricular involvement in order to avoid detection of their drug use. Tecumseh's policy thus falls short doubly if deterrence is its aim: It invades the privacy of students who need deterrence least, and risks steering students at greatest risk for substance abuse away from extracurricular involvement that potentially may palliate drug problems.

II.

[Schools'] tutelary obligations to their students require them to "teach by example" by avoiding symbolic measures that diminish constitutional protections. "That [schools] are educating the young for citizenship is reason for scrupulous protection of Constitutional freedoms of the individual, if we are not to strangle the free mind at its source and teach youth to discount important principles of our government as mere platitudes." West Virginia Bd. of Ed. v. Barnette, 319 U.S. 624, 637 (1943). . . .

Notes

1. *Drug testing in schools: majority position.* When the Supreme Court first addressed drug testing in schools in Vernonia School District 47J v. Acton, 515 U.S. 646 (1995), the issue had received little attention in courts or legislatures. The existing statutes and cases validated drug testing of students based on reasonable suspicion of illegal drug use without addressing mandatory random testing. See Tenn. Code Ann. §49-6-4213 (reasonable suspicion testing). In the years between *Vernonia* and *Earls,* very few school districts adopted a policy of random drug testing. See Ronald F. Wright, The Abruptness of *Acton,* 36 Crim. L. Bull. 401 (2000). Do you expect the number of districts adopting this policy to increase more quickly after the *Earls* decision?

A study of 76,000 high school students published in 2003 found that drug testing in schools does not deter drug use among students. Thirty-seven percent of twelfth-graders in schools that tested for drugs said they had smoked marijuana in the last year, compared with 36 percent in schools that did not. The study indicated that about 18 percent of the nation's high schools employed some type of drug testing. See Greg Winter, "Study Finds No Sign That Testing Deters Students' Drug Use," N.Y. Times, May 17, 2003. Does this study suggest to you that schools should spend their limited funds on other forms of drug prevention, or that they should invest more and conduct more reliable and credible urinalysis tests?

If you were sitting on a state supreme court addressing a challenge to a random testing program, would your ruling turn on the types of students subject to the program (for example, all athletes, or all students at particular grade levels)? Would it depend on the uses the school makes of the test results (such as counseling, school sanctions, or criminal prosecution)? See York v. Wahkiakum School District No. 200, 178 P.3d 995 (Wash. 2008) (suspicionless drug testing of student athletes violates state constitution).

2. *Drug testing in other contexts: majority position.* Drug testing occurs more frequently in workplaces than in schools. Some employers require a drug test of all job applicants and probationary employees; among current employees, reasonable suspicion testing is more common. If the employer is a private party, the Fourth Amendment and its state analogs do not apply. Only statutes and common law theories are available to limit the employer's choices, and those statutes tend to regulate but not bar use of random drug testing. See Ariz. Rev. Stat. §23-493.04 (allowing testing "for any job-related purposes"); Minn. Stat. §181.951 (allowing reasonable suspicion testing for all employees and random testing for "safety sensitive" employees). For further exploration of the variety of state court applications of this standard, see the web extension for this chapter at *http://www.crimpro.com/extension/ch04*.

As for public employers, courts have upheld testing programs against most challenges. It is clear that when a public employer has reasonable suspicion of drug use by an employee, drug testing is acceptable. Specific incidents (such as an accident involving a train) might give the employer reasonable suspicion, or at least some individualized suspicion, to test for drug use among the employees involved in the incident. See Skinner v. Railway Labor Executives' Assn., 489 U.S. 602 (1989). Courts have even approved random or routine drug testing, at least for job categories in which drug use presents a special concern for the employer. In National Treasury Employees Union v. Von Raab, 489 U.S. 656 (1989), the Court upheld a program requiring a urinalysis from any Customs Service employee seeking a transfer to a position involving drug interdiction or the carrying of a firearm. Does this opinion suggest that a police department could insist on random drug testing for all of its officers? See McCloskey v. Honolulu Police Department, 799 P.2d 953 (Haw. 1990) (upholding such a program); Guiney v. Police Commissioner of Boston, 582 N.E.2d 523 (Mass. 1991) (striking down such a program). For all members of the Narcotics Bureau within the department? See Delaraba v. Police Dept, 632 N.E. 2d 1251 (N.Y. 1994) (upholding such a program). Collective labor agreements will sometimes limit the power of an employer to implement drug testing. See Fraternal Order of Police, Miami Lodge 20 v. City of Miami, 609 So. 2d 31 (Fla. 1992).

Would you argue that some public employees (within the police department or otherwise) should be subject to drug testing only after officials obtain a warrant based on probable cause? See Chandler v. Miller, 520 U.S. 305 (1997) (Georgia's requirement that candidates for state office pass drug test did not fit within "closely guarded category" of constitutionally permissible suspicionless searches, and was not sufficiently related to requirements of public office).

Problem 4-5. Jail Cell Search

McCoy's first two trials on charges of armed robbery and attempted murder of a police officer ended in mistrials. After his third trial, the jury convicted McCoy, but an appellate court reversed the conviction. On the eve of the scheduled date for the fourth trial, the assistant state attorney assigned to the case, Ketchum, and a police officer, Hagerman, went to McCoy's cell at the local pretrial detention facility.

Hagerman, following instructions from Ketchum, first removed McCoy and his cellmate and then searched the cell for anything McCoy may have written that might contain incriminating statements. As Hagerman searched, Ketchum stood in the doorway of the cell. Hagerman found on a table in the cell a number of depositions, transcripts, offense reports, and personal notes. He seized McCoy's copies of depositions of four state witnesses, which consisted of some 70 pages and included McCoy's copious handwritten notes in the margins. Several of the handwritten notes were incriminating.

McCoy presented no particular security problems at the detention facility, and there was no concrete information suggesting that the papers in his cell would contain incriminating information. How will the trial court rule on his motion to suppress the handwritten notes found on the depositions? Compare McCoy v. State, 639 So. 2d 163 (Fla. Dist. Ct. App. 1994).

Notes

1. *Searches of prison cells: majority position.* State and federal appellate courts have traditionally given a lot of latitude to the decisions of the administrators of prisons, jails, and other detention facilities. They point out the exceptional need for order in such a setting. The Supreme Court in Hudson v. Palmer, 468 U.S. 517 (1984), made a particularly strong statement of this view when it held that the Fourth Amendment does not place any limits on a prison guard's search of the prison cell of a convicted offender. The prisoner in that case claimed that a prison guard had searched his cell and destroyed his property solely to harass the prisoner. The Court replied:

> A right of privacy in traditional Fourth Amendment terms is fundamentally incompatible with the close and continual surveillance of inmates and their cells required to ensure institutional security and internal order. We are satisfied that society would insist that the prisoner's expectation of privacy always yield to what must be considered the paramount interest in institutional security.

468 U.S. at 527-528. A concern for the security and order of prisons led the Court to hold that "the Fourth Amendment has no applicability to a prison cell." Virtually all state courts to consider this question have followed the *Hudson* case and concluded that their analogous state constitutional provisions also have no application to searches of prison cells. Should the exemption from the Fourth Amendment apply only when searches are motivated by the need for order and security in the jail or prison? If so, how should a court determine what motivated the search?

2. *Pretrial detainees versus convicted offenders.* Some persons confined in a cell have been convicted of a crime, while others have only been accused of a crime. Should a

pretrial detainee have a "reasonable expectation of privacy" in a cell when a convicted offender would not? The Supreme Court spoke indirectly to this issue in Bell v. Wolfish, 441 U.S. 520 (1979), when it held that the Fourth Amendment protects neither sentenced nor pretrial detainees from a prison policy requiring inmates to undergo strip and body cavity searches after all contact visits with non-inmates. The Court stated that the security concerns at issue for convicted offenders also exist for pretrial detainees. State courts have split on the question whether constitutional privacy protections apply differently to pretrial detainees and convicted offenders. See DeLancie v. Superior Court, 647 P.2d 142 (Cal. 1982) (invalidating sheriff's routine practice of monitoring conversations between pretrial detainees and visitors); State v. Martin, 367 S.E.2d 618 (N.C. 1988) (search of pretrial detainee's cell by jailer not subject to Fourth Amendment reasonableness test).

In Samson v. California, 547 U.S. 843 (2006), the court heard a challenge to a state law that required parolees to submit to warrantless, suspicionless searches at any time. The Court held that the law did not violate the Fourth Amendment, drawing a parallel between parolees and prisoners, and saying that the public's strong interest in supervising parolees outweighs the parolees' diminished expectation of privacy. Does the lack of a reasonable expectation of privacy, as announced in Hudson v. Palmer, derive from the nature of the person's status (convicted of a crime) or from the nature of the place (a prison)?

3. *Places categorically out of reach of the constitution?* Do *Hudson* and the cases following its lead establish "Fourth-Amendment-free zones"? If prison officials are free to act without legal limits, how will this affect the present or future conduct of the prisoners being punished for violating the criminal law? Are there any alternatives? Consider State v. Berard, 576 A.2d 118 (Vt. 1990) (search and seizure provision in state constitution applies to prison searches, but "special needs" of prison environment allow warrantless random searches of cells). Is *Berard* an improvement over *Hudson* from a prisoner's point of view? From society's point of view? Cf. United States v. Knights, 534 U.S. 112 (2001) (constitution allows police with reasonable suspicion of criminal behavior to conduct a warrantless search of home of a probationer who is subject to a probation condition authorizing warrantless searches).

In Ferguson v. City of Charleston, 532 U.S. 67 (2001), the Supreme Court returned to the question of drug testing in special institutional settings. A state hospital instructed its staff to identify pregnant patients at risk for drug abuse, to test those patients for drug abuse, and to report positive tests to the police. Patients who tested positive for cocaine use were arrested and prosecuted for child abuse. The Court held that this testing was an unreasonable search. Given the amount of cooperation between the hospital and criminal prosecutors in this program, the tests served no "special needs" apart from the State's "general law enforcement interest." The central purpose of the program was the use of criminal law enforcement to coerce patients into substance abuse treatment. Drug testing in these circumstances was a search that was not accomplished through consent and not supported by probable cause.

C. "PAPERS"

There are several methods available to the government to inspect "papers" during criminal law enforcement. One method, which we will explore in Chapter 10, is to issue a subpoena from a grand jury or an administrative agency. The government might also rely on statutory requirements for certain types of businesses to maintain records and to allow the government access to those records. On the other hand, if the government attempts to search and seize papers without using a subpoena or a record-keeping requirement, it must comply with traditional Fourth Amendment requirements: showing probable cause to believe that the papers will provide evidence of a crime, and perhaps obtaining a warrant.

Are there some papers, however, that are so intimately personal that the government cannot obtain them, even if it demonstrates probable cause and obtains a warrant? We start with one of the most important early Supreme Court cases on the Fourth Amendment. The answer that the Court gave in 1886 to the question of "private papers" searches is not the same answer that legal institutions, by and large, give today. This classic opinion, however, does offer us a chance to consider an alternative form of privacy protection, in which rules would absolutely bar the government from searching some areas, regardless of the justifications it might have to conduct the search.

■ EDWARD BOYD v. UNITED STATES

116 U.S. 616 (1886)

BRADLEY, J.*

[The government brought this forfeiture action to obtain 35 cases of glass that Boyd and others allegedly imported from England without paying the proper customs duties. At trial, it became important to show the quantity and value of the glass contained in 29 cases previously imported. The trial court ordered Boyd to produce the invoices for the cases. He did so, but objected to the constitutionality of the 1874 statute giving the judge the power to make such an order. Other provisions of the same statute, which were passed in 1863 and 1867, empowered the judge to issue a warrant to a marshal or customs collector to enter private premises and obtain any papers, books, or invoices that might tend to prove the government's allegations in a civil forfeiture suit under the customs laws. The jury in this case heard the evidence relating to the invoices and rendered a verdict for the United States.]

The clauses of the Constitution, to which it is contended that these laws are repugnant, are the fourth and fifth amendments. . . . The fifth article, amongst other things, declares that no person "shall be compelled in any criminal case to be a witness against himself." . . .

Is a search and seizure, or, what is equivalent thereto, a compulsory production of a man's private papers, to be used in evidence against him in a proceeding to forfeit his property for alleged fraud against the revenue laws — is such a proceeding for such a purpose an "unreasonable search and seizure" within the meaning of the

* [Justices Field, Harlan, Woods, Matthews, Gray, and Blatchford joined in this opinion. — EDS.]

fourth amendment of the Constitution? Or, is it a legitimate proceeding? It is contended by the counsel for the government, that it is a legitimate proceeding, sanctioned by long usage, and the authority of judicial decision. No doubt long usage, acquiesced in by the courts, goes a long way to prove that there is some plausible ground or reason for it in the law. . . .

But we do not find any long usage, or any contemporary construction of the Constitution, which would justify any of the acts of Congress now under consideration. [The] act of 1863 was the first act in this country, and, we might say, either in this country or in England, so far as we have been able to ascertain, which authorized the search and seizure of a man's private papers, or the compulsory production of them, for the purpose of using them in evidence against him in a criminal case, or in a proceeding to enforce the forfeiture of his property. Even the act under which the obnoxious writs of assistance were issued did not go as far as this, but only authorized the examination of ships and vessels, and persons found therein, for the purpose of finding goods prohibited to be imported or exported, or on which the duties were not paid, and to enter into and search any suspected vaults, cellars, or warehouses for such goods.

The search for and seizure of stolen or forfeited goods, or goods liable to duties and concealed to avoid the payment thereof, are totally different things from a search for and seizure of a man's private books and papers for the purpose of obtaining information therein contained, or of using them as evidence against him. . . . In the one case, the government is entitled to the possession of the property; in the other it is not. The seizure of stolen goods is authorized by the common law; and the seizure of goods forfeited for a breach of the revenue laws, or concealed to avoid the duties payable on them, has been authorized by English statutes for at least two centuries past; and the like seizures have been authorized by our own revenue acts from the commencement of the government. . . .

But, when examined with care, it is manifest that there is a total unlikeness of these official acts and proceedings to that which is now under consideration. In the case of stolen goods, the owner from whom they were stolen is entitled to their possession; and in the case of excisable or dutiable articles, the government has an interest in them for the payment of the duties thereon, and until such duties are paid has a right to keep them under observation, or to pursue and drag them from concealment; and in the case of goods seized on attachment or execution, the creditor is entitled to their seizure in satisfaction of his debt. . . . Whereas, by the proceeding now under consideration, the court attempts to extort from the party his private books and papers to make him liable for a penalty or to forfeit his property.

In order to ascertain the nature of the proceedings intended by the fourth amendment to the Constitution under the terms "unreasonable searches and seizures," it is only necessary to recall the contemporary or then recent history of the controversies on the subject, both in this country and in England. The practice had obtained in the colonies of issuing writs of assistance to the revenue officers, empowering them, in their discretion, to search suspected places for smuggled goods, which James Otis [in 1761] pronounced "the worst instrument of arbitrary power, the most destructive of English liberty, and the fundamental principles of law, that ever was found in an English law book;" since they placed "the liberty of every man in the hands of every petty officer." . . .

These things, and the events which took place in England immediately following the argument about writs of assistance in Boston, were fresh in the memories of those who achieved our independence and established our form of government. [The opinion of Lord Camden in the 1765 case of Entick v. Carrington] is regarded as one of the permanent monuments of the British Constitution, and is quoted as such by the English authorities on that subject down to the present time. As every American statesmen, during our revolutionary and formative period as a nation, was undoubtedly familiar with this monument of English freedom, and considered it as the true and ultimate expression of constitutional law, it may be confidently asserted that its propositions were in the minds of those who framed the fourth amendment to the Constitution, and were considered as sufficiently explanatory of what was meant by unreasonable searches and seizures. . . .

The principles laid down in [Entick v. Carrington] affect the very essence of constitutional liberty and security. They reach farther than the concrete form of the case then before the court, with its adventitious circumstances; they apply to all invasions on the part of the government and its employees of the sanctity of a man's home and the privacies of life. It is not the breaking of his doors, and the rummaging of his drawers, that constitutes the essence of the offence; but it is the invasion of his indefeasible right of personal security, personal liberty and private property [that violates the constitutional principle]. Breaking into a house and opening boxes and drawers are circumstances of aggravation; but any forcible and compulsory extortion of a man's own testimony or of his private papers to be used as evidence to convict him of crime or to forfeit his goods, is within the condemnation of that judgment. In this regard the fourth and fifth amendments run almost into each other.

Can we doubt that when the fourth and fifth amendments to the Constitution of the United States were penned and adopted, the language of Lord Camden was relied on as expressing the true doctrine on the subject of searches and seizures, and as furnishing the true criteria of the reasonable and "unreasonable" character of such seizures? [Could the men who proposed those amendments have approved of statutes such as those at issue here?] It seems to us that the question cannot admit of a doubt. They never would have approved of them. The struggles against arbitrary power in which they had been engaged for more than 20 years, would have been too deeply engraved in their memories to have allowed them to approve of such insidious disguises of the old grievance which they had so deeply abhorred. . . .

We have already noticed the intimate relation between the two amendments. They throw great light on each other. For the "unreasonable searches and seizures" condemned in the fourth amendment are almost always made for the purpose of compelling a man to give evidence against himself, which in criminal cases is condemned in the fifth amendment; and compelling a man "in a criminal case to be a witness against himself," which is condemned in the fifth amendment, throws light on the question as to what is an "unreasonable search and seizure" within the meaning of the fourth amendment. And we have been unable to perceive that the seizure of a man's private books and papers to be used in evidence against him is substantially different from compelling him to be a witness against himself. We think it is within the clear intent and meaning of those terms. . . .

Though the proceeding in question is divested of many of the aggravating incidents of actual search and seizure, yet, as before said, it contains their substance and essence, and effects their substantial purpose. . . . We think that the notice to produce the invoice in this case, the order by virtue of which it was issued, and the law which authorized the order, were unconstitutional and void, and that the inspection by the district attorney of said invoice, when produced in obedience to said notice, and its admission in evidence by the court, were erroneous and unconstitutional proceedings. . . .

MILLER, J., concurring.*

. . . While the framers of the Constitution had their attention drawn, no doubt, to the abuses of this power of searching private houses and seizing private papers, as practiced in England, it is obvious that they only intended to restrain the abuse, while they did not abolish the power. Hence it is only unreasonable searches and seizures that are forbidden, and the means of securing this protection was by abolishing searches under warrants, which were called general warrants, because they authorized searches in any place, for the thing. This was forbidden, while searches founded on affidavits, and made under warrants which described the thing to be searched for, the person and place to be searched, are still permitted. . . .

Notes

1. *The erosion of* Boyd: *property and privacy.* The *Boyd* court notes that the government could seize contraband or proceeds of a crime but not papers containing evidence of a crime, because only in the former cases does the government have a proprietary interest in the item stronger than that of the private party. The constitution, under this reading, reinforces the protections of property law.

The linkage between property law and unreasonable searches has changed. For one thing, as we have seen, the definition of a "search" now depends on the "reasonable expectations of privacy" of the target of the search, and not on whether the government has trespassed on any property interest of the target. Katz v. United States, 389 U.S. 347 (1967). For another thing, most courts have now abandoned a traditional limitation on the search power known as the "mere evidence" rule. Under that rule, the government could search for and seize contraband, instrumentalities, or fruits of crime but not mere evidence of crime. Again, the reasoning was grounded in property law: The government had a superior claim to contraband and the like (which the private party had no right to own), but the private party had a superior claim to innocent property that provided evidence of a crime. The U.S. Supreme Court abandoned the mere evidence rule in Warden v. Hayden, 387 U.S. 294 (1967). Every state now interprets its own constitution to allow such searches.

Why might searches of papers become more common after the rejection of the mere evidence rule? Does the mere evidence rule offer more protection to some classes of search targets than to others? See Eric Schnapper, Unreasonable Searches and Seizures of Papers, 71 Va. L. Rev. 869 (1985).

2. *The erosion of* Boyd: *self-incrimination and unreasonable searches.* The *Boyd* court also suggested that the Fourth and Fifth Amendments throw light on each other, or provide mutually reinforcing protections. A search of a person's papers is equivalent to a demand that the person make incriminating testimony. This aspect of the *Boyd* case has also fallen by the wayside. In several cases, such as Andresen v. Maryland, 427 U.S. 463 (1976), the Supreme Court has declared that a search of a person's

* [Chief Justice Waite joined in this opinion. — EDS.]

documents does not amount to compelled "testimony" because the person created the documents voluntarily and does not have to participate in the government's later search or seizure of the documents. Again, state courts have followed suit.

3. *The erosion of* Boyd: *private papers.* Federal and state courts have left more room to wonder if there is still an absolute bar to the search or seizure of private papers such as diaries. The Supreme Court has allowed searches and seizures of business records, see Andresen v. Maryland, but has not squarely addressed private papers. See Daniel Solove, The First Amendment as Criminal Procedure, 82 N.Y.U.L. Rev.112 (2007).

By and large, state courts have taken the next step to conclude that there is no absolute bar to the search of private papers. See State v. Andrei, 574 A.2d 295 (Me. 1990). Every so often, a court says or intimates that some private papers (so long as the papers themselves were not used to commit a crime) might be beyond the reach of a government search, even if supported by probable cause and a warrant. See State v. Bisaccia, 213 A.2d 185 (N.J. 1965). Georgia has passed an unusual statute protecting "private papers" from searches:

> [A judicial officer] may issue a search warrant for the seizure of the following: (1) Any instruments, articles, or things, including the private papers of any person, which are designed, intended for use, or which have been used in the commission of the offense in connection with which the warrant is issued; . . . or (5) Any item, substance, object, thing, or matter, other than the private papers of any person, which is tangible evidence of the commission of the crime for which probable cause is shown.

Ga. Code Ann. §17-5-21(a). Cf. King v. State, 577 S.E.2d 764 (Ga. 2003) (declines to extend to search warrants an earlier holding that use of subpoena to obtain medical records offends Georgia constitution's privacy protection). Does this statutory protection from searches re-create the now-abandoned requirements of *Boyd*? Would it prevent a search for an illegal lottery ticket? For a list of telephone numbers of purchasers of illegal narcotics? If you were restricting the scope of this statute, how might you define "private" papers? See Sears v. State, 426 S.E.2d 553 (Ga. 1993) (interpreting section to bar search for documents only when covered by privilege, such as attorney-client or doctor-patient).

4. *Extra particularity in search warrants for private papers.* While it is not often that a legal system will absolutely bar all searches for private papers, it is more common to see judges insist on extra particularity in a warrant authorizing a search for books or papers. See Lo-Ji Sales, Inc. v. New York, 442 U.S. 319 (1979); Tattered Cover, Inc. v. City of Thornton, 44 P.3d 1044 (Colo. 2002); compare In re C.T., 999 A.2d 210 (N.H. 2010) (when law enforcement seeks privileged medical records, providers must comply with search warrant by producing records for in camera review, allowing patient and provider opportunity to object; state must demonstrate "essential need" for record). Will a more specific warrant address the special intrusiveness of a search for papers? Consider this argument by Telford Taylor, from his renowned essay on the Fourth Amendment:

> [Where] personal papers are concerned, specificity of category is no real safeguard against the most grievous intrusions on privacy, as was pointed out over two hundred years ago during the House of Commons debates on general warrants: "Even a particular warrant to seize seditious papers alone, without mentioning the titles of them, may

> prove highly detrimental, since in that case, all a man's papers must be indiscriminately examined. . . ." Of course, a search for a tiny object, such as a stolen or smuggled diamond, which can be concealed among papers or in some other small recess, may involve much the same kind of ransacking search. But at least in such a case it is unnecessary to read papers. [Two Studies in Constitutional Interpretation 67-68 (1969).]

5. *Private records held by third parties: banking records.* Many types of sensitive personal documents, such as banking records or medical records, are held by institutions on behalf of their customers. When government agents investigating a crime try to obtain these records, does the legal system allow the institution to deny the request? Under the Fourth Amendment, the Supreme Court in United States v. Miller, 425 U.S. 435 (1976), decided that a bank's customer has no reasonable expectation of privacy in records relating to the customer's account:

> All of the documents obtained, including financial statements and deposit slips, contain only information voluntarily conveyed to the banks and exposed to their employees in the ordinary course of business. . . . The depositor takes the risk, in revealing his affairs to another, that the information will be conveyed by that person to the Government.

Two years earlier, the California Supreme Court in Burrows v. Superior Court, 529 P.2d 590 (Cal. 1974), set out an argument in favor of giving bank customers standing to challenge unreasonable searches of bank records relating to their accounts:

> A bank customer's reasonable expectation is that, absent compulsion by legal process, the matters he reveals to the bank will be utilized by the bank only for internal banking purposes. . . . For all practical purposes, the disclosure by individuals or business firms of their financial affairs to a bank is not entirely volitional, since it is impossible to participate in the economic life of contemporary society without maintaining a bank account. In the course of such dealings, a depositor reveals many aspects of his personal affairs, opinions, habits and associations. . . .

State courts have divided on the constitutional question, with a strong minority following *Burrows.* See State v. Thompson, 810 P.2d 415 (Utah 1991) (following *Burrows*); State v. Schultz, 850 P.2d 818 (Kansas 1993) (following *Miller*). See Stephen E. Henderson, Learning from All Fifty States: How to Apply the Fourth Amendment and Its State Analogs to Protect Third Party Information from Unreasonable Search, 55 Cath. U. L. Rev. 373 (2006).

Several legislatures have also declared that banking customers may challenge the reasonableness of government efforts to search their banking records. Congress adopted the Right to Financial Privacy Act, 12 U.S.C. §§3401 et seq., as a repudiation of the *Miller* decision: "The Court did not acknowledge the sensitive nature of these records." 1978 U.S.C.C.A.N. 9305. The act requires that the bank customer have notice and an opportunity to object before the financial institution complies with a subpoena seeking the records. About one-third of the states have enacted an equivalent of the Right to Financial Privacy Act. See, e.g., Mo. Rev. Stat. §§408.683 et seq. We will explore the subpoena power and the gathering of documents in complex investigations in Chapter 10.

Do these statutes and cases provide enough protection by allowing the customer to insist that any search of records be reasonable? Should they provide instead for a much higher level of justification by the government to support a search of banking records (similar to bank secrecy provisions in some other nations)? Would a reinvigorated *Boyd* present an absolute bar to a search of banking records? Would you take the same position on a proposed statute protecting the records relating to movie rentals?

D. "EFFECTS"

We now turn to the final interest mentioned in the text of the Fourth Amendment, "effects." Given the variety of property that falls within the meaning of this phrase, and the variety of places where a search of effects could take place, it is difficult to find a unifying theme for all these searches. There are a few settings, however, in which courts and others have created special search rules about personal property. We begin with the "inventory" practices of police departments, the routine methods they use to process the property of those who are taken into custody. We then survey the complex rules surrounding that most American form of personal property, the automobile.

1. Inventory Searches

When police officers take a person into custody, some of his personal property comes with him. When the government holds a person's property, it must use ordinary care to maintain the property; the department therefore may need to keep records of the property. This process of examining and storing personal property can often produce evidence of a crime.

PEOPLE v. CURTIS GIPSON

786 N.E.2d 540 (Ill. 2003)

THOMAS, J.

At issue are two questions concerning inventory searches: (1) whether a police officer's unrebutted testimony about police policy on inventory searches can be sufficient evidence of such a policy if the State does not introduce a written policy into evidence; and (2) whether a policy requiring the police to inventory items of value is sufficient to allow the opening of closed containers if the policy does not specifically mention closed containers.

BACKGROUND

. . . Defendant moved to quash his arrest and to suppress the evidence that was found during a search of his car. At the hearing on the motion to suppress, defendant testified as follows. At 12:25 A.M. on January 8, 1998, defendant was driving home from work. When defendant reached the intersection of Jackson and Homan in Chicago, a police car began to follow him. The police car followed him for several minutes. The police car's lights went on when defendant crossed Kedzie, and defendant pulled over. The police officer approached defendant's car and told defendant that he was driving on a revoked license. Defendant gave the officer his identification and proof of insurance, following which the officer put defendant into the backseat of his squad car and locked it. The officer put some information into his computer and told defendant that if he did not have any outstanding warrants, he was free to go.

According to defendant, the officer never told him that he was under arrest. The officer then got out of the squad car and looked under the hood of defendant's car. He searched the passenger compartment of the car and then came back to the squad car. The officer started typing on his computer again and then went back to defendant's car, took the keys out of the ignition, and opened the trunk. Defendant testified that he had a yellow plastic Ameritech bag tied closed in the trunk. Inside of the Ameritech bag was a black plastic bag, containing rocks of cocaine, that was also tied closed. According to defendant, he never gave the officer permission to search his car, and the officer never told him that the car would be towed or that the officer was conducting an inventory search. The officer never told defendant he was under arrest before he searched the car.

The State presented the testimony of Sergeant David Byrd of the Illinois State Police. Byrd testified that he initially began following defendant's car because it had a cracked windshield. A "registration response" on defendant's license plate revealed that the owner's name was Curtis Gipson and that Gipson's driver's license had been revoked. Byrd pulled over defendant and informed him that the reason for the stop was that the car had a defective windshield and that the car's owner had a revoked license. When defendant confirmed that he was Curtis Gipson, Byrd placed defendant in the back of his squad car.

Once defendant was in the car, Byrd called a tow truck and conducted an inventory search of defendant's vehicle. Byrd explained that the State Police policy is to tow the vehicle when someone is arrested for driving on a revoked license. When a vehicle is towed following an arrest, the police policy is that a tow inventory search should be conducted. When asked to explain the police policy on tow inventory searches, Byrd responded: "We are required to check the passenger compartment and trunk area for any valuables, or just for our own — we don't want anything to leave us that might be of value without checking it first and putting it down on the tow sheet."

When Byrd opened the trunk, he found a yellow Ameritech bag. He opened the bag and noticed two smaller bags inside. He opened these and observed what appeared to be crack cocaine. Byrd testified that he never told defendant that he would be free to go at some point. Rather, defendant was arrested and taken into custody. Byrd gave defendant a ticket for having a cracked windshield and driving on a revoked license.

Following arguments by the attorneys, the trial judge recalled Sergeant Byrd to the stand. The following colloquy ensued:

The Court: You are still under oath, sergeant. Is there a printed procedure regarding towing by the Illinois State police?
The Witness: Yes, there is, your Honor. It's in our policy manual.
The Court: It's in the policy manual?
The Witness: Right, and we teach it to all our cadets when they come out on the road.
The Court: Is it a manual that you might have handy?
The Witness: No, it's a —
The Court: Big?
The Witness: Six hundred pages.
The Court: But it is printed in the police procedure?
The Witness: It is printed, tow searches and vehicles being towed and if I may, the reason we do that is because even if somebody is revoked and if they just said, okay, okay, you are going to write the ticket —
Mr. Draper [defendant's attorney]: Objection, judge.
The Court: Okay, all right.

Following further arguments from counsel, the trial court decided to reserve ruling on the motion until the parties submitted further case law. Two months later, the court granted defendant's motion to suppress. The trial judge stated that the police had no right to tow the car and that State Police policy could not supersede the law. The State filed a motion to reconsider, [arguing] that a lawful inventory search pursuant to State Police policy had occurred. The trial judge responded that he was not sure what the State Police policy was because he had never seen it and the officer might have just given his own interpretation. The trial judge then stated that the police could not use a minor traffic ticket to create a basis for a search and that defendant had only been stopped for "a little, minor thing like a cracked windshield." . . . The court denied the motion to reconsider. . . .

ANALYSIS

On review of a trial court's ruling on a motion to suppress, we accord great deference to the trial court's factual findings, and we will reverse those findings only if they are against the manifest weight of the evidence. However, we review de novo the ultimate legal question of whether suppression is warranted.

The State first argues . . . that there is no constitutional requirement that the State produce the actual written policy. We agree with the State.

An inventory search of a lawfully impounded vehicle is a judicially created exception to the warrant requirement of the fourth amendment. In South Dakota v. Opperman, 428 U.S. 364 (1976), the Supreme Court identified three objectives that are served by allowing inventory searches: (1) protection of the owner's property; (2) protection of the police against claims of lost or stolen property; and (3) protection of the police from potential danger.

In conducting such a search, the police must be acting pursuant to standard police procedures. Colorado v. Bertine, 479 U.S. 367 (1987). A single familiar standard is essential to guide police officers, who have only limited time and expertise to reflect on and balance the social and individual interests involved in the specific circumstances they confront. However, as Professor LaFave has noted, the courts have generally not read *Bertine* as requiring that these procedures be in writing. 3 W. LaFave, Search & Seizure §7.4(a), at 550 (3d ed. 1996). Rather, a police officer's testimony that he was following standard procedure is generally deemed to be sufficient. See, e.g., United States v. Lage, 183 F.3d 374, 380 (5th Cir. 1999) (officer's unrebutted testimony that he acted in accordance with standard inventory procedures is sufficient); United States v. Lozano, 171 F.3d 1129, 1132 (7th Cir. 1999) (lack of written policy not dispositive; evidence of "well-honed" police department routine may be sufficient). . . .

We agree . . . that there is no requirement that the procedures be in writing. The Supreme Court requires only that, in conducting inventory searches, the police act in accordance with standardized department procedures. Although it may be easier for the State to show that it was acting in accordance with standard procedures if it can produce a written policy, the Supreme Court has not required, as a matter of constitutional law, that such policies be reduced to writing.

The precise issue we face here is somewhat different. Here, the issue is whether, if the police do have a written policy on inventory searches, the policy itself has to be admitted into evidence, or if an officer's testimony describing the standard procedure can be sufficient. The State contends that the appellate court's decision in this case effectively creates a rule that the State must always produce a written policy on inventory searches if one exists. Defendant contends that we do not need to decide the issue as a matter of law. Rather, the question in any case is simply whether the State introduced sufficient evidence of standardized procedures. Defendant argues that Officer Byrd's testimony was insufficient.

[We] disagree with defendant's assertion that the State did not meet its burden in this case. The defendant bears the burden of proof at a hearing on a motion to suppress. A defendant must make a prima facie case that the evidence was obtained by an illegal search or seizure. If a defendant makes a prima facie case, the State has the burden of going forward with evidence to counter the defendant's prima facie case. However, the ultimate burden of proof remains with the defendant.

Here, defendant made his prima facie case by showing that Sergeant Byrd searched the trunk of defendant's car without a warrant. The State, however, met its burden of going forward with the evidence by establishing that Sergeant Byrd searched defendant's trunk as part of a routine tow inventory search. Sergeant Byrd gave clear, unrebutted testimony of the standard procedures for inventory searches that he was following. Sergeant Byrd testified that it was department policy to tow the vehicle whenever a person is arrested for driving on a revoked license. Before the vehicle is towed, the arresting officer is supposed to do an inventory search of the vehicle and to record anything of value on the tow inventory sheet. The officer is supposed to check the passenger compartment and trunk area for valuables.

Defendant never attempted to challenge this testimony. His attorney did not ask a single question of Sergeant Byrd about the policy and presented no rebuttal testimony on the issue. The attorney did absolutely nothing to cast doubt on Sergeant Byrd's testimony. In his arguments to the trial court, the defense attorney's principal contention was that the police had no right to tow the car. The trial court, not the defense attorney, asked further questions about the policy. But the trial court seemed satisfied with Sergeant Byrd's answer. The trial court asked Sergeant Byrd if the procedure was written down, and Byrd responded that it was in the policy manual that was taught to all cadets. When the trial court asked Byrd if he had the manual handy, Byrd began to answer the question by saying, "No, it's a —," following which the trial court finished Byrd's sentence for him by saying, "Big?" When Byrd tried to give more information about the policy, the court cut him off.

The court later ruled that it did not know what the police policy was because it had not seen the policy. This was error. Sergeant Byrd explained the police policy and defendant did not cross-examine him on the issue or offer any rebuttal to the testimony. The State met its burden of going forward with evidence to rebut the defendant's prima facie case. Sergeant Byrd's testimony established that defendant's trunk was searched as part of a routine tow inventory search. The ultimate burden of proof remained with defendant, and defendant offered nothing to show that the inventory search was improper. . . .

Of course, it would be the better practice for the State to produce the written policy. If it does not, the State leaves itself open to the possibility that the defense will be able to cast doubt on the officer's testimony either through cross-examination or rebuttal testimony. Here, defense counsel did not attempt to do so. Defendant had the burden of proof, and he failed to show that he was subjected to an illegal search.

The [defendant also contends] that Sergeant Byrd was not entitled to open the plastic bags because the State failed to produce any evidence that the inventory search policy allowed the opening of closed containers. In Florida v. Wells, 495 U.S. 1 (1990), the United States Supreme Court upheld the suppression of marijuana found in the trunk of a car during an inventory search. The marijuana was in a locked suitcase in the trunk, and the police forced open the suitcase as part of the inventory search. The record contained no evidence of a police policy on the opening of closed containers during inventory searches. The Supreme Court held that it would be permissible for the police policy to mandate the opening of all containers or no containers, or to allow the police the discretion to decide which containers should be opened, based on the nature of the search and the characteristics of the container. However, because there was no evidence of any policy with respect to closed containers in that case, the Supreme Court held that the search was not sufficiently regulated to satisfy the fourth amendment.

In People v. Hundley, 619 N.E.2d 744 (Ill. 1993), this court held that the general order of the State Police was sufficient to allow the opening of closed containers during an inventory search. The policy introduced into evidence in *Hundley* . . . did not use the words "closed containers." Rather, it required the police to inventory the contents of towed vehicles and to look wherever the owner or operator would ordinarily place or stow property. The officer testified in *Hundley* that he opened a cigarette case because, in his experience, women often put their drivers' licenses and money in such cases. This court held that the general order of the State Police was "adequate to the situation."

Hundley is controlling on this issue. Although defendant is correct that Sergeant Byrd did not specifically mention a closed container policy, he did testify that the policy required the police to check the passenger compartment and the trunk for valuables and to list any valuables on the tow inventory sheet. Obviously, such a policy requires the police to open any containers that might contain valuables. The policy that Sergeant Byrd testified to was more specific than the one at issue in *Hundley*. The *Hundley* policy merely referred to an inventory of the contents of the vehicle. Here, Sergeant Byrd specifically testified that he was supposed to search the trunk and passenger area for "valuables" and to inventory anything of value on the tow sheet. We believe this policy was sufficient to allow Sergeant Byrd to open the plastic bags in the trunk of defendant's car. . . .

Notes

1. *Inventory searches: majority position.* Inventory searches serve "administrative caretaking functions" of protecting against property damage claims and protecting police from dangerous items rather than enforcing criminal law. As a result, the Supreme Court has held that the federal constitution allows a routine (and warrantless) inventory search of impounded automobiles or other personal property without probable cause or individualized suspicion. South Dakota v. Opperman, 428 U.S. 364 (1976). The government must satisfy three requirements for a valid warrantless inventory search of a vehicle: (1) the original impoundment of the vehicle must be lawful; (2) the purpose of the inventory search must be to protect the owner's property or to protect the police from claims of lost, stolen, or vandalized property and to guard the police from danger; and (3) the inventory search must be conducted in good faith pursuant to reasonable standardized police procedures and not as a pretext for an investigatory search. The Supreme Court, in cases such as Colorado v. Bertine, 479 U.S. 367 (1987), has insisted that the inventory search occur under the guidance of "standardized" regulations. According to Florida v. Wells, 495 U.S. 1 (1990), the rules must address the proper treatment of containers found in a car, although those rules may leave some discretion to the officer conducting the inventory to open some containers and to leave others unopened. Most state courts also allow the police to conduct inventory searches without any special justification, so long as the inventory proceeds according to standard rules. The recurring issues in litigation deal with the specificity of the inventory rules and the amount of discretion those rules leave to the police officer in deciding whether to impound a vehicle and whether to open containers.

The issue is not as straightforward as it sounds. Consider this policy of the Illinois State Police, mentioned in the *Gipson* case:

> An examination and inventory of the contents of all vehicles/boats towed or held by authority of Division personnel shall be made by the officer who completes the Tow-In Recovery Report. This examination and inventory shall be restricted to those areas where an owner or operator would ordinarily place or store property or equipment in the vehicle/boat; and would normally include front and rear seat areas, glove compartment, map case, sun visors, and trunk and engine compartments.

Different officers, with different levels of experience, might have very different ideas about where owners "ordinarily" place property. What property do owners normally store in the engine compartment? Do police departments need inventory rules at all? Would consensual inventory searches (and routine requests for that consent) address the problems of safeguarding property in vehicles?

2. *The impoundment decision.* Some jurisdictions address the inventory process at the first possible point and impose various limits on the initial decision whether to impound a vehicle or to leave it at the scene. See Fair v. State, 627 N.E.2d 427 (Ind. 1993) (prosecution must demonstrate (1) that the belief that the vehicle posed some threat or harm to the community or was itself imperiled was consistent with objective standards of sound policing, and (2) that the decision to combat that threat by impoundment was in keeping with established departmental routine or regulation); State v. Huisman, 544 N.W.2d 433 (Iowa 1996) (impoundment decision must be made "according to standardized criteria," and "an administrative or care-taking

reason to impound" must exist). Others, such as the Colorado rules reviewed in *Bertine,* leave some discretion to the individual officer to act within guidelines in deciding whether to impound a car in the first place.

3. *Least intrusive means and investigatory intent.* Defendants often argue that their vehicle was impounded, or the contents inventoried, despite less intrusive means to achieve the stated goals of inventory searches, such as leaving the car where it sits, leaving it with another person, or getting the defendant to sign liability waivers (thus removing the interest in protecting officers against a lawsuit for harm to the personal property). Only a handful of jurisdictions (fewer than a half dozen) recognize such claims when it comes to closed containers; however, a larger group (about 15) require police to give an arrestee a reasonable chance to provide for alternative custody of a vehicle before it is impounded. See, e.g., State v. Perham, 814 P.2d 914 (Haw. 1991) (closed containers). Most courts focus only on whether the administrative rules were followed and whether those rules provide adequate guidance. Isn't a "least intrusive means" test one way to guarantee that officers do not use inventory searches to investigate crimes? Are less intrusive methods easier to see in hindsight than at the moment of decision? The Supreme Court has rejected the argument that the "least intrusive means" is a requirement of the federal constitution. Illinois v. Lafayette, 462 U.S. 640 (1983).

In Colorado v. Bertine, the Supreme Court said that inventory searches could be challenged if they were conducted "in bad faith or for the sole purpose of investigation." Is examination of "bad faith" consistent with the general rejection of "pretext" claims? See Chapter 2. Most state courts discussing inventory searches require that the officer conducting the inventory show "good faith" and prohibit use of the inventory as a "pretext" for a search for incriminating evidence. See State v. West, 862 P.2d 192 (Ariz. 1993). How will this "bad faith" come to light? What if an officer admits to "dual" purposes for an inventory search? See State v. Hauseman, 900 P.2d 74 (Colo. 1995).

4. *Inventory searches of personal belongings at the station.* Inventory searches apply to personal items carried by a person who is arrested and placed in detention. What arguments can you make that the justification for inventory searches is stronger for inventory of personal belongings than for cars? What arguments can you make that the privacy interest of the individual is stronger for personal belongings, especially those held in pockets, outside of public view (such as the content of wallets or purses)? Most states impose fewer restrictions on inventory searches of personal belongings than on inventory searches of cars. See Oles v. State 993 S.W.2d 103 (Tex. Crim. App. 1999) (police did not need probable cause or warrant to take a second look at clothing that had been seized from a defendant a week earlier as part of inventory of his belongings after his arrest). Should similar rules apply to the personal property of civil detainees, such as those who are extremely intoxicated or who suffer from mental illness? See State v. Carper, 876 P.2d 582 (Colo. 1994).

5. *Procedures whose validity turns on the adequacy of executive rules.* There are several types of searches, like inventory searches, in which courts have approved of procedures only when there is a regularized process for police to follow. Consider, for example, the legitimacy of sobriety checkpoints, where the U.S. Supreme Court and state courts have approved only of checkpoints governed by detailed rules. See Chapter 2; Wayne LaFave, Controlling Discretion by Administrative Regulations: The Use, Misuse, and Nonuse of Police Rules and Policies in Fourth Amendment Adjudication, 89 Mich. L. Rev. 442 (1990). Who should issue inventory rules?

Should they be determined by statute? If you were the general counsel to a police department, would you have a responsibility to maximize police power to conduct inventory searches? If police officers are concerned about the length and complexity of the inventory forms and process, how might you address that concern?

Problem 4-6. Personal Inventories

Pursuant to a search warrant, officers entered a house where they found four individuals, including Nancy Filkin, who did not reside there. Filkin and the other three individuals were arrested and removed from the premises. The officer who placed her under arrest did not notice whether Filkin was carrying a purse. However, Deputy Richard McKinny, who transported Filkin to the county jail, testified that she had it with her when he transported her to the jail.

Upon arrival at the county jail, McKinny took Filkin to the female booking area, removed her handcuffs, and remained present during the booking process. The standard operating procedure during the booking process at the county jail was to inventory personal items, to assure that the detainee carries no contraband objects into the jail, and to produce an accurate record so that the prisoner gets everything back when she is released. The search is also designed to protect the safety of the officers. The standard operating procedure for a purse is to remove all items to ensure that it contains no money or valuables.

A female corrections officer inventoried Filkin's closed purse under the watchful eye of McKinny. In the process, the officers discovered and opened a black film canister. The canister contained, among other things, a small self-seal bag holding .05 grams of methamphetamine.

Filkin has filed a motion to suppress the drugs found in the black film canister. How would you rule? Compare State v. Filkin, 494 N.W.2d 544 (Neb. 1993).

STOP

2. *Cars and Containers*

Of all the forms of personal property protected from unreasonable searches and seizures, cars and the containers inside them have generated the most litigation. There are distinctive constitutional and statutory rules involving car searches. When reading the following cases, be sure to distinguish the various rationales available to the police to search a car and its contents, and note the ways that the analysis changes because the search involves a car.

304, 342

■ ARIZONA v. RODNEY GANT

129 S. Ct. 1710 (2009)

STEVENS, J.*

After Rodney Gant was arrested for driving with a suspended license, handcuffed, and locked in the back of a patrol car, police officers searched his car and

* [Justices Scalia, Souter, Thomas, and Ginsburg joined in this opinion. — EDS.]

discovered cocaine in the pocket of a jacket on the backseat. Because Gant could not have accessed his car to retrieve weapons or evidence at the time of the search, the Arizona Supreme Court held that the search-incident-to-arrest exception to the Fourth Amendment's warrant requirement, as defined in Chimel v. California, 395 U.S. 752 (1969), and applied to vehicle searches in New York v. Belton, 453 U.S. 454 (1981), did not justify the search in this case. We agree with that conclusion.

Under *Chimel*, police may search incident to arrest only the space within an arrestee's "immediate control," meaning "the area from within which he might gain possession of a weapon or destructible evidence." The safety and evidentiary justifications underlying *Chimel*'s reaching-distance rule determine *Belton*'s scope. Accordingly, we hold that *Belton* does not authorize a vehicle search incident to a recent occupant's arrest after the arrestee has been secured and cannot access the interior of the vehicle. Consistent with the holding in Thornton v. United States, 541 U.S. 615 (2004), . . . we also conclude that circumstances unique to the automobile context justify a search incident to arrest when it is reasonable to believe that evidence of the offense of arrest might be found in the vehicle.

I.

On August 25, 1999, acting on an anonymous tip that the residence at 2524 North Walnut Avenue was being used to sell drugs, Tucson police officers Griffith and Reed knocked on the front door and asked to speak to the owner. Gant answered the door and, after identifying himself, stated that he expected the owner to return later. The officers left the residence and conducted a records check, which revealed that Gant's driver's license had been suspended and there was an outstanding warrant for his arrest for driving with a suspended license.

When the officers returned to the house that evening, they found a man near the back of the house and a woman in a car parked in front of it. After a third officer arrived, they arrested the man for providing a false name and the woman for possessing drug paraphernalia. Both arrestees were handcuffed and secured in separate patrol cars when Gant arrived. The officers recognized his car as it entered the driveway, and Officer Griffith confirmed that Gant was the driver by shining a flashlight into the car as it drove by him. Gant parked at the end of the driveway, got out of his car, and shut the door. Griffith, who was about 30 feet away, called to Gant, and they approached each other, meeting 10-to-12 feet from Gant's car. Griffith immediately arrested Gant and handcuffed him.

Because the other arrestees were secured in the only patrol cars at the scene, Griffith called for backup. When two more officers arrived, they locked Gant in the backseat of their vehicle. After Gant had been handcuffed and placed in the back of a patrol car, two officers searched his car: One of them found a gun, and the other discovered a bag of cocaine in the pocket of a jacket on the backseat.

Gant was charged with two offenses — possession of a narcotic drug for sale and possession of drug paraphernalia (i.e., the plastic bag in which the cocaine was found). He moved to suppress the evidence seized from his car on the ground that the warrantless search violated the Fourth Amendment. Among other things, Gant argued that *Belton* did not authorize the search of his vehicle because he posed no threat to the officers after he was handcuffed in the patrol car and because he was arrested for a traffic offense for which no evidence could be found in his vehicle. When asked at the suppression hearing why the search was conducted, Officer Griffith responded: "Because the law says we can do it."

The trial court rejected the State's contention that the officers had probable cause to search Gant's car for contraband when the search began, but it denied the motion to suppress. Relying on the fact that the police saw Gant commit the crime of driving without a license and apprehended him only shortly after he exited his car, the court held that the search was permissible as a search incident to arrest. A jury found Gant guilty on both drug counts, and he was sentenced to a 3-year term of imprisonment. . . .

II.

. . . Among the exceptions to the warrant requirement is a search incident to a lawful arrest. The exception derives from interests in officer safety and evidence preservation that are typically implicated in arrest situations. In *Chimel*, we held that a search incident to arrest may only include "the arrestee's person and the area within his immediate control — construing that phrase to mean the area from within which he might gain possession of a weapon or destructible evidence." That limitation, which continues to define the boundaries of the exception, ensures that the scope of a search incident to arrest is commensurate with its purposes of protecting arresting officers and safeguarding any evidence of the offense of arrest that an arrestee might conceal or destroy. If there is no possibility that an arrestee could reach into the area that law enforcement officers seek to search, both justifications for the search-incident-to-arrest exception are absent and the rule does not apply.

In *Belton*, we considered *Chimel*'s application to the automobile context. A lone police officer in that case stopped a speeding car in which Belton was one of four occupants. While asking for the driver's license and registration, the officer smelled burnt marijuana and observed an envelope on the car floor marked "Supergold" — a name he associated with marijuana. Thus having probable cause to believe the occupants had committed a drug offense, the officer ordered them out of the vehicle, placed them under arrest, and patted them down. Without handcuffing the arrestees, the officer "split them up into four separate areas of the Thruway . . . so they would not be in physical touching area of each other" and searched the vehicle, including the pocket of a jacket on the backseat, in which he found cocaine.

The New York Court of Appeals found the search unconstitutional, concluding that after the occupants were arrested the vehicle and its contents were "safely within the exclusive custody and control of the police." The State asked this Court to consider whether the exception recognized in *Chimel* permits an officer to search "a jacket found inside an automobile while the automobile's four occupants, all under arrest, are standing unsecured around the vehicle." We granted certiorari because courts had found no workable definition of "the area within the immediate control of the arrestee" when that area arguably includes the interior of an automobile.

[We] held that when an officer lawfully arrests "the occupant of an automobile, he may, as a contemporaneous incident of that arrest, search the passenger compartment of the automobile" and any containers therein. That holding was based in large part on our assumption that articles inside the relatively narrow compass of the passenger compartment of an automobile are in fact generally, even if not inevitably, within "the area into which an arrestee might reach." . . .

III.

[Our opinion in *Belton*] has been widely understood to allow a vehicle search incident to the arrest of a recent occupant even if there is no possibility the arrestee could gain access to the vehicle at the time of the search. [Although] it is improbable that an arrestee could gain access to weapons stored in his vehicle after he has been handcuffed and secured in the backseat of a patrol car, cases allowing a search in this precise factual scenario are legion. Indeed, some courts have upheld searches under *Belton* even when the handcuffed arrestee has already left the scene.

Under this broad reading of *Belton*, a vehicle search would be authorized incident to every arrest of a recent occupant notwithstanding that in most cases the vehicle's passenger compartment will not be within the arrestee's reach at the time of the search. To read *Belton* as authorizing a vehicle search incident to every recent occupant's arrest would thus untether the rule from the justifications underlying the *Chimel* exception — a result clearly incompatible with our statement in *Belton* that it "in no way alters the fundamental principles established in the *Chimel* case regarding the basic scope of searches incident to lawful custodial arrests." Accordingly, we reject this reading of *Belton* and hold that the *Chimel* rationale authorizes police to search a vehicle incident to a recent occupant's arrest only when the arrestee is unsecured and within reaching distance of the passenger compartment at the time of the search.[4]

Although it does not follow from *Chimel*, we also conclude that circumstances unique to the vehicle context justify a search incident to a lawful arrest when it is "reasonable to believe evidence relevant to the crime of arrest might be found in the vehicle." *Thornton*, 541 U.S., at 632 (Scalia, J., concurring). In many cases, as when a recent occupant is arrested for a traffic violation, there will be no reasonable basis to believe the vehicle contains relevant evidence. But in others, including *Belton* and *Thornton*, the offense of arrest will supply a basis for searching the passenger compartment of an arrestee's vehicle and any containers therein.

Neither the possibility of access nor the likelihood of discovering offense-related evidence authorized the search in this case. Unlike in *Belton*, which involved a single officer confronted with four unsecured arrestees, the five officers in this case outnumbered the three arrestees, all of whom had been handcuffed and secured in separate patrol cars before the officers searched Gant's car. Under those circumstances, Gant clearly was not within reaching distance of his car at the time of the search. An evidentiary basis for the search was also lacking in this case. Whereas Belton and Thornton were arrested for drug offenses, Gant was arrested for driving with a suspended license-an offense for which police could not expect to find evidence in the passenger compartment of Gant's car. Because police could not reasonably have believed either that Gant could have accessed his car at the time of the

4. Because officers have many means of ensuring the safe arrest of vehicle occupants, it will be the rare case in which an officer is unable to fully effectuate an arrest so that a real possibility of access to the arrestee's vehicle remains. But in such a case a search incident to arrest is reasonable under the Fourth Amendment.

search or that evidence of the offense for which he was arrested might have been found therein, the search in this case was unreasonable.

IV. . . .

The State argues that *Belton* searches are reasonable regardless of the possibility of access in a given case because that expansive rule correctly balances law enforcement interests, including the interest in a bright-line rule, with an arrestee's limited privacy interest in his vehicle. For several reasons, we reject the State's argument. First, the State seriously undervalues the privacy interests at stake. Although we have recognized that a motorist's privacy interest in his vehicle is less substantial than in his home, the former interest is nevertheless important and deserving of constitutional protection. It is particularly significant that *Belton* searches authorize police officers to search not just the passenger compartment but every purse, briefcase, or other container within that space. A rule that gives police the power to conduct such a search whenever an individual is caught committing a traffic offense, when there is no basis for believing evidence of the offense might be found in the vehicle, creates a serious and recurring threat to the privacy of countless individuals. Indeed, the character of that threat implicates the central concern underlying the Fourth Amendment — the concern about giving police officers unbridled discretion to rummage at will among a person's private effects.

At the same time as it undervalues these privacy concerns, the State exaggerates the clarity that its reading of *Belton* provides. Courts that have read *Belton* expansively are at odds regarding how close in time to the arrest and how proximate to the arrestee's vehicle an officer's first contact with the arrestee must be to bring the encounter within *Belton*'s purview and whether a search is reasonable when it commences or continues after the arrestee has been removed from the scene. The rule has thus generated a great deal of uncertainty, particularly for a rule touted as providing a "bright line."

Contrary to the State's suggestion, a broad reading of *Belton* is also unnecessary to protect law enforcement safety and evidentiary interests. Under our view, *Belton* and *Thornton* permit an officer to conduct a vehicle search when an arrestee is within reaching distance of the vehicle or it is reasonable to believe the vehicle contains evidence of the offense of arrest. Other established exceptions to the warrant requirement authorize a vehicle search under additional circumstances when safety or evidentiary concerns demand. For instance, Michigan v. Long, 463 U.S. 1032 (1983), permits an officer to search a vehicle's passenger compartment when he has reasonable suspicion that an individual, whether or not the arrestee, is "dangerous" and might access the vehicle to "gain immediate control of weapons." If there is probable cause to believe a vehicle contains evidence of criminal activity, United States v. Ross, 456 U.S. 798 (1982), authorizes a search of any area of the vehicle in which the evidence might be found. . . . *Ross* allows searches for evidence relevant to offenses other than the offense of arrest, and the scope of the search authorized is broader. Finally, there may be still other circumstances in which safety or evidentiary interests would justify a search. Cf. Maryland v. Buie, 494 U.S. 325 (1990) (holding that, incident to arrest, an officer may conduct a limited protective sweep of those areas of a house in which he reasonably suspects a dangerous person may be hiding).

These exceptions together ensure that officers may search a vehicle when genuine safety or evidentiary concerns encountered during the arrest of a vehicle's recent occupant justify a search. Construing *Belton* broadly to allow vehicle searches incident to any arrest would serve no purpose except to provide a police entitlement, and it is anathema to the Fourth Amendment to permit a warrantless search on that basis. For these reasons, we are unpersuaded by the State's arguments that a broad reading of *Belton* would meaningfully further law enforcement interests and justify a substantial intrusion on individuals' privacy. [The court noted that at least eight states — Vermont, New Jersey, New Mexico, Nevada, Pennsylvania, New York, Oregon, and Wyoming have declined to follow a broad reading of *Belton* under their state constitutions, and that a Massachusetts statute provides that a search incident to arrest may be made only for the purposes of seizing weapons or evidence of the offense of arrest. See Commonwealth v. Toole, 448 N.E.2d 1264, 1266-1267 (Mass. 1983) (citing Mass. Gen. Laws, ch. 276, §1).]

V.

Our dissenting colleagues argue that the doctrine of stare decisis requires adherence to a broad reading of Belton even though the justifications for searching a vehicle incident to arrest are in most cases absent. The doctrine of stare decisis is of course essential to the respect accorded to the judgments of the Court and to the stability of the law, but it does not compel us to follow a past decision when its rationale no longer withstands careful analysis.

We have never relied on stare decisis to justify the continuance of an unconstitutional police practice. And we would be particularly loath to uphold an unconstitutional result in a case that is so easily distinguished from the decisions that arguably compel it. The safety and evidentiary interests that supported the search in *Belton* simply are not present in this case. Indeed, it is hard to imagine two cases that are factually more distinct, as *Belton* involved one officer confronted by four unsecured arrestees suspected of committing a drug offense and this case involves several officers confronted with a securely detained arrestee apprehended for driving with a suspended license. This case is also distinguishable from *Thornton*, in which the petitioner was arrested for a drug offense. . . .

We do not agree with the contention in Justice Alito's dissent that consideration of police reliance interests requires a different result. Although it appears that the State's reading of *Belton* has been widely taught in police academies and that law enforcement officers have relied on the rule in conducting vehicle searches during the past 28 years,[11] many of these searches were not justified by the reasons underlying the *Chimel* exception. Countless individuals guilty of nothing more serious than a traffic violation have had their constitutional right to the security of their private effects violated as a result. The fact that the law enforcement community may view the State's version of the *Belton* rule as an entitlement does not establish the sort of reliance interest that could outweigh the countervailing interest that all individuals share in having their constitutional rights fully protected. If it is clear that a practice is unlawful, individuals' interest in its discontinuance clearly outweighs any law enforcement "entitlement" to its persistence. . . .

11. Because a broad reading of *Belton* has been widely accepted, the doctrine of qualified immunity will shield officers from liability for searches conducted in reasonable reliance on that understanding.

The dissent also ignores the checkered history of the search-incident-to-arrest exception. Police authority to search the place in which a lawful arrest is made was broadly asserted in Marron v. United States, 275 U.S. 192 (1927), and limited a few years later in Go-Bart Importing Co. v. United States, 282 U.S. 344 (1931), and United States v. Lefkowitz, 285 U.S. 452 (1932). The limiting views expressed in *Go-Bart* and *Lefkowitz* were in turn abandoned in Harris v. United States, 331 U.S. 145 (1947), which upheld a search of a four-room apartment incident to the occupant's arrest. Only a year later the Court in Trupiano v. United States, 334 U.S. 699 (1948), retreated from that holding, noting that the search-incident-to-arrest exception is "a strictly limited" one that must be justified by "something more in the way of necessity than merely a lawful arrest." And just two years after that, in United States v. Rabinowitz, 339 U.S. 56 (1950), the Court again reversed course and upheld the search of an entire apartment. Finally, our opinion in *Chimel* overruled *Rabinowitz* and what remained of *Harris* and established the present boundaries of the search-incident-to-arrest exception. Notably, none of the dissenters in *Chimel* or the cases that preceded it argued that law enforcement reliance interests outweighed the interest in protecting individual constitutional rights so as to warrant fidelity to an unjustifiable rule.

The experience of the 28 years since we decided *Belton* has shown that the generalization underpinning the broad reading of that decision is unfounded. We now know that articles inside the passenger compartment are rarely "within the area into which an arrestee might reach," and blind adherence to *Belton*'s faulty assumption would authorize myriad unconstitutional searches. The doctrine of stare decisis does not require us to approve routine constitutional violations.

VI.

Police may search a vehicle incident to a recent occupant's arrest only if the arrestee is within reaching distance of the passenger compartment at the time of the search or it is reasonable to believe the vehicle contains evidence of the offense of arrest. When these justifications are absent, a search of an arrestee's vehicle will be unreasonable unless police obtain a warrant or show that another exception to the warrant requirement applies. . . .

SCALIA, J., concurring.

To determine what is an "unreasonable" search within the meaning of the Fourth Amendment, we look first to the historical practices the Framers sought to preserve; if those provide inadequate guidance, we apply traditional standards of reasonableness. Since the historical scope of officers' authority to search vehicles incident to arrest is uncertain, traditional standards of reasonableness govern. It is abundantly clear that those standards do not justify what I take to be the rule set forth in *Belton* and *Thornton*: that arresting officers may always search an arrestee's vehicle in order to protect themselves from hidden weapons. When an arrest is made in connection with a roadside stop, police virtually always have a less intrusive and more effective means of ensuring their safety — and a means that is virtually always employed: ordering the arrestee away from the vehicle, patting him down in the open, handcuffing him, and placing him in the squad car.

Law enforcement officers face a risk of being shot whenever they pull a car over. But that risk is at its height at the time of the initial confrontation; and it is not at all reduced by allowing a search of the stopped vehicle after the driver has been arrested and placed in the squad car. I observed in *Thornton* that the government had failed to provide a single instance in which a formerly restrained arrestee escaped to retrieve a weapon from his own vehicle; Arizona and its *amici* have not remedied that significant deficiency in the present case.

It must be borne in mind that we are speaking here only of a rule automatically permitting a search when the driver or an occupant is arrested. Where no arrest is made, we have held that officers may search the car if they reasonably believe "the suspect is dangerous and . . . may gain immediate control of weapons." Michigan v. Long. In the no-arrest case, the possibility of access to weapons in the vehicle always exists, since the driver or passenger will be allowed to return to the vehicle when the interrogation is completed. The rule of Michigan v. Long is not at issue here. . . .

No other Justice . . . shares my view that application of *Chimel* in this context should be entirely abandoned. It seems to me unacceptable for the Court to come forth with a 4-to-1-to-4 opinion that leaves the governing rule uncertain. I am therefore confronted with the choice of either leaving the current understanding of *Belton* and *Thornton* in effect, or acceding to what seems to me the artificial narrowing of those cases adopted by Justice Stevens. The latter, as I have said, does not provide the degree of certainty I think desirable in this field; but the former opens the field to what I think are plainly unconstitutional searches-which is the greater evil. I therefore join the opinion of the Court.

ALITO, J., dissenting.*

Twenty-eight years ago, in New York v. Belton, this Court held that "when a policeman has made a lawful custodial arrest of the occupant of an automobile, he may, as a contemporaneous incident of that arrest, search the passenger compartment of that automobile." Five years ago, in Thornton v. United States — a case involving a situation not materially distinguishable from the situation here — the Court not only reaffirmed but extended the holding of Belton, making it applicable to recent occupants. Today's decision effectively overrules those important decisions. . . .

To take the place of the overruled precedents, the Court adopts a new two-part rule under which a police officer who arrests a vehicle occupant or recent occupant may search the passenger compartment if (1) the arrestee is within reaching distance of the vehicle at the time of the search or (2) the officer has reason to believe that the vehicle contains evidence of the offense of arrest. The first part of this new rule may endanger arresting officers and is truly endorsed by only four Justices; Justice Scalia joins solely for the purpose of avoiding a "4-to-1-to-4 opinion." The second part of the new rule is taken from Justice Scalia's separate opinion in Thornton without any independent explanation of its origin or justification and is virtually certain to confuse law enforcement officers and judges for some time to come. The Court's decision will cause the suppression of evidence gathered in many searches carried out in good-faith reliance on well-settled case law, and although the Court purports to base its analysis on the landmark decision in Chimel, the Court's

* [Chief Justice Roberts and Justice Kennedy joined in this opinion; Justice Breyer joined in the opinion except for Part II E. — EDS.]

reasoning undermines Chimel. I would follow Belton, and I therefore respectfully dissent.

I.

Although the Court refuses to acknowledge that it is overruling *Belton* and *Thornton*, there can be no doubt that it does so. In *Belton*, an officer on the New York Thruway removed the occupants from a car and placed them under arrest but did not handcuff them. The officer then searched a jacket on the car's back seat and found drugs. . . .

Viewing . . . disagreement about the application of the *Chimel* rule as illustrative of a persistent and important problem, the *Belton* Court concluded that a single familiar standard was essential to guide police officers who make roadside arrests. The Court acknowledged that articles in the passenger compartment of a car are not always within an arrestee's reach, but in order to establish the workable rule this category of cases requires, the Court adopted a rule that categorically permits the search of a car's passenger compartment incident to the lawful arrest of an occupant. . . . The Court stated unequivocally: "[W]e hold that when a policeman has made a lawful custodial arrest of the occupant of an automobile, he may, as a contemporaneous incident of that arrest, search the passenger compartment of that automobile."

Despite this explicit statement, the opinion of the Court in the present case curiously suggests that *Belton* may reasonably be read as adopting a holding that . . . an officer arresting a vehicle occupant may search the passenger compartment "when the passenger compartment is within an arrestee's reaching distance." . . .

II.

Because the Court has substantially overruled *Belton* and *Thornton*, the Court must explain why its departure from the usual rule of stare decisis is justified. I recognize that stare decisis is not an inexorable command, and applies less rigidly in constitutional cases. But the Court has said that a constitutional precedent should be followed unless there is a "special justification" for its abandonment. Relevant factors identified in prior cases include whether the precedent has engendered reliance, whether there has been an important change in circumstances in the outside world, whether the precedent has proved to be unworkable, whether the precedent has been undermined by later decisions, and whether the decision was badly reasoned. These factors weigh in favor of retaining the rule established in *Belton*.

A.

Reliance. While reliance is most important in "cases involving property and contract rights," the Court has recognized that reliance by law enforcement officers is also entitled to weight. . . .

B.

Changed circumstances. Abandonment of the *Belton* rule cannot be justified on the ground that the dangers surrounding the arrest of a vehicle occupant are different today than they were 28 years ago. The Court claims that we now know that articles inside the passenger compartment are rarely within "the area into which an arrestee might reach," but surely it was well known in 1981 that a person who is taken from a vehicle, handcuffed, and placed in the back of a patrol car is unlikely to make it back into his own car to retrieve a weapon or destroy evidence.

C.

Workability. The *Belton* rule has not proved to be unworkable. On the contrary, the rule was adopted for the express purpose of providing a test that would be relatively easy for police officers and judges to apply. The Court correctly notes that even the *Belton* rule is not perfectly clear in all situations. Specifically, it is sometimes debatable whether a search is or is not contemporaneous with an arrest, but that problem is small in comparison with the problems that the Court's new two-part rule will produce.

The first part of the Court's new rule — which permits the search of a vehicle's passenger compartment if it is within an arrestee's reach at the time of the search — reintroduces the same sort of case-by-case, fact-specific decisionmaking that the *Belton* rule was adopted to avoid. As the situation in *Belton* illustrated, there are cases in which it is unclear whether an arrestee could retrieve a weapon or evidence in the passenger compartment of a car.

Even more serious problems will also result from the second part of the Court's new rule, which requires officers making roadside arrests to determine whether there is reason to believe that the vehicle contains evidence of the crime of arrest. What this rule permits in a variety of situations is entirely unclear.

D.

Consistency with later cases. The *Belton* bright-line rule has not been undermined by subsequent cases. On the contrary, that rule was reaffirmed and extended just five years ago in *Thornton*.

E.

Bad reasoning. The Court is harshly critical of *Belton*'s reasoning, but the problem that the Court perceives cannot be remedied simply by overruling *Belton*. *Belton* represented only a modest — and quite defensible — extension of *Chimel*, as I understand that decision.

Prior to *Chimel*, the Court's precedents permitted an arresting officer to search the area within an arrestee's "possession" and "control" for the purpose of gathering evidence. Based on this "abstract doctrine," the Court had sustained searches that extended far beyond an arrestee's grabbing area.

The *Chimel* Court, in an opinion written by Justice Stewart, overruled these cases. Concluding that there are only two justifications for a warrantless search incident to arrest — officer safety and the preservation of evidence — the Court stated that such a search must be confined to "the arrestee's person" and "the area from within which he might gain possession of a weapon or destructible evidence."

Unfortunately, *Chimel* did not say whether "the area from within which [an arrestee] might gain possession of a weapon or destructible evidence" is to be measured at the time of the arrest or at the time of the search, but unless the *Chimel* rule was meant to be a specialty rule, applicable to only a few unusual cases, the Court must have intended for this area to be measured at the time of arrest.

This is so because the Court can hardly have failed to appreciate the following two facts. First, in the great majority of cases, an officer making an arrest is able to handcuff the arrestee and remove him to a secure place before conducting a search incident to the arrest. Second, because it is safer for an arresting officer to secure an arrestee before searching, it is likely that this is what arresting officers do in the great majority of cases. (And it appears, not surprisingly, that this is in fact the prevailing practice.) Thus, if the area within an arrestee's reach were assessed, not at the time of arrest, but at the time of the search, the *Chimel* rule would rarely come into play.

Moreover, if the applicability of the *Chimel* rule turned on whether an arresting officer chooses to secure an arrestee prior to conducting a search, rather than searching first and securing the arrestee later, the rule would create a perverse incentive for an arresting officer to prolong the period during which the arrestee is kept in an area where he could pose a danger to the officer. If this is the law . . . the law would truly be, as Mr. Bumble said, "a ass."

I do not think that this is what the *Chimel* Court intended. Handcuffs were in use in 1969. The ability of arresting officers to secure arrestees before conducting a search — and their incentive to do so — are facts that can hardly have escaped the Court's attention. I therefore believe that the *Chimel* Court intended that its new rule apply in cases in which the arrestee is handcuffed before the search is conducted.

The *Belton* Court, in my view, proceeded on the basis of this interpretation of *Chimel*. [If] we are going to reexamine *Belton*, we should also reexamine the reasoning in *Chimel* on which *Belton* rests. . . .

F.

The second part of the Court's new rule . . . raises doctrinal and practical problems that the Court makes no effort to address. Why, for example, is the standard for this type of evidence-gathering search "reason to believe" rather than probable cause? And why is this type of search restricted to evidence of the offense of arrest? It is true that an arrestee's vehicle is probably more likely to contain evidence of the crime of arrest than of some other crime, but if reason-to-believe is the governing standard for an evidence-gathering search incident to arrest, it is not easy to see why an officer should not be able to search when the officer has reason to believe that the vehicle in question possesses evidence of a crime other than the crime of arrest.

Nor is it easy to see why an evidence-gathering search incident to arrest should be restricted to the passenger compartment. The *Belton* rule was limited in this way because the passenger compartment was considered to be the area that vehicle occupants can generally reach, but since the second part of the new rule is not based on officer safety or the preservation of evidence, the ground for this limitation is obscure. . . .

Notes

1. *Search of automobile incident to arrest: majority position*. Before *Gant*, states were divided on whether to apply an expansive view of the search-incident-to-arrest to cars. About 30 states explicitly adopted New York v. Belton, 453 U.S. 454 (1981), and in doing so they overwhelmingly adopted a broad reading of its rule. About half as many states rejected *Belton* and applied a case-by-case analysis of the scope of searches of cars incident to arrest. To a lesser extent, states and federal courts wrestled with the outer boundaries of the *Belton* line, looking at time, distance, and

other factors to determine when a search was no longer "incident" to arrest. See Crawford v. State, 138 P.3d 254 (Alaska 2006) (center console is "immediately associated with the person" and therefore appropriate for search incident to arrest made after defendant was removed from the car and placed in police cruiser in handcuffs). In *Gant* the Supreme Court rejected the majority reading on *Belton* and adopted a test in line with narrower state constitutional provisions.

How much of a practical barrier will this ruling be to law enforcement? What exactly does the government have to show under the "reasonable to believe" standard? Does this amount to probable cause, reasonable suspicion, or something else?

2. *Passengers and searches of cars incident to arrest.* There was some doubt over the years whether a search of a car incident to the arrest of the driver could also reach property that clearly belonged to a passenger who is not arrested. The Supreme Court resolved this question in Wyoming v. Houghton, 526 U.S. 295 (1999). In that case, an officer stopped a vehicle for speeding and noticed a hypodermic syringe in the driver's shirt pocket. When the driver admitted that he used the syringe to take drugs, the officer arrested him and ordered two female passengers out of the car. He searched the passenger compartment of the car for contraband and discovered drugs in a purse on the back seat belonging to one of the passengers. The Court upheld the search, emphasizing once again the need for bright-line rules that are easy for officers to apply in the field. Do you predict that state courts will follow *Houghton* as they interpret their own constitutions? See State v. Ray, 620 N.W.2d 83 (Neb. 2000) (officer may inspect passenger's knapsack found in passenger compartment, although passenger not arrested at the time). Will this pre-*Gant* decision stand?

3. *Let's be honest: deference to precedent.* Is it better for the Court to admit a change of direction, or to claim a strong foundation in precedent when the prior doctrine was at best questionable in support of the current ruling? Which approach gives greater credibility to the idea of the rule of law? Were *Belton* and *Thornton* as much of a "bright line" as Justice Alito suggests in dissent?

4. *Changing search-incident landscape.* The many variations on car searches will doubtlessly lead to a new wave of litigation on these questions in state and federal courts. For instance, will the second prong of the rule apply to searches of hatchback and trunk areas? You can track developments in this fast-changing area of the law by consulting the web extension of this chapter at *http://www.crimpro.com/extension/ch04*.

Justice Alito highlights the situation of an officer who arrests some but not all of the occupants of a vehicle. He also points out that persons who were not passengers in the car might attempt to retrieve a weapon or evidence from the car while the officer is still on the scene. How would you counsel a police department to respond to these situations? What are the prospects that *Gant* will influence the search-incident-to-arrest doctrine beyond the vehicle context? See State v. Henning, 209 P.3d 711 (Kan. 2009) (suppressing evidence obtained from search of automobile console after arrest of passenger on outstanding arrest warrant; court overturned statute allowing search incident to arrest for evidence of any crime).

■ CALIFORNIA v. CHARLES ACEVEDO

500 U.S. 565 (1991)

BLACKMUN, J.*

This case requires us once again to consider the so-called "automobile exception" to the warrant requirement of the Fourth Amendment and its application to the search of a closed container in the trunk of a car.

I.

On October 28, 1987, Officer Coleman of the Santa Ana Police Department received a telephone call from a federal drug enforcement agent in Hawaii. The agent informed Coleman that he had seized a package containing marijuana which was to have been delivered to the Federal Express Office in Santa Ana and which was addressed to J. R. Daza at 805 West Stevens Avenue in that city. The agent arranged to send the package to Coleman instead. Coleman then was to take the package to the Federal Express office and arrest the person who arrived to claim it.

Coleman received the package on October 29, verified its contents, and took it to the Senior Operations Manager at the Federal Express office. At about 10:30 A.M. on October 30, a man, who identified himself as Jamie Daza, arrived to claim the package. He accepted it and drove to his apartment on West Stevens. He carried the package into the apartment.

At 11:45 A.M., officers observed Daza leave the apartment and drop the box and paper that had contained the marijuana into a trash bin. Coleman at that point left the scene to get a search warrant. About 12:05 P.M., the officers saw Richard St. George leave the apartment carrying a blue knapsack which appeared to be half full. The officers stopped him as he was driving off, searched the knapsack, and found 11/2 pounds of marijuana.

At 12:30 P.M., respondent Charles Steven Acevedo arrived. He entered Daza's apartment, stayed for about 10 minutes, and reappeared carrying a brown paper bag that looked full. The officers noticed that the bag was the size of one of the wrapped marijuana packages sent from Hawaii. Acevedo walked to a silver Honda in the parking lot. He placed the bag in the trunk of the car and started to drive away. Fearing the loss of evidence, officers in a marked police car stopped him. They opened the trunk and the bag, and found marijuana.

Respondent was charged in state court with possession of marijuana for sale. . . . He moved to suppress the marijuana found in the car. The motion was denied. He then pleaded guilty but appealed the denial of the suppression motion. We granted certiorari to reexamine the law applicable to a closed container in an automobile, a subject that has troubled courts and law enforcement officers since it was first considered in United States v. Chadwick, 433 U.S. 1 (1977). . . .

* [Chief Justice Rehnquist and Justices O'Connor, Kennedy, and Souter joined in this opinion. — EDS.]

II.

. . . In Carroll v. United States, 267 U.S. 132 (1925), this Court established an exception to the warrant requirement for moving vehicles, for it recognized "a necessary difference between a search of a store, dwelling house or other structure in respect of which a proper official warrant readily may be obtained, and a search of a ship, motor boat, wagon or automobile, for contraband goods, where it is not practicable to secure a warrant because the vehicle can be quickly moved out of the locality or jurisdiction in which the warrant must be sought." It therefore held that a warrantless search of an automobile, based upon probable cause to believe that the vehicle contained evidence of crime in the light of an exigency arising out of the likely disappearance of the vehicle, did not contravene the Warrant Clause of the Fourth Amendment. . . .

In United States v. Ross, 456 U.S. 798 (1982), we held that a warrantless search of an automobile under the *Carroll* doctrine could include a search of a container or package found inside the car when such a search was supported by probable cause. The warrantless search of Ross' car occurred after an informant told the police that he had seen Ross complete a drug transaction using drugs stored in the trunk of his car. The police stopped the car, searched it, and discovered in the trunk a brown paper bag containing drugs. We decided that the search of Ross' car was not unreasonable under the Fourth Amendment. [If] probable cause justifies the search of a lawfully stopped vehicle, it justifies the search of every part of the vehicle and its contents that may conceal the object of the search. . . .

Ross distinguished the *Carroll* doctrine from the separate rule that governed the search of closed containers. The Court had announced tins separate rule, unique to luggage and other closed packages, bags, and containers, in United States v. Chadwick, 433 U.S. 1 (1977). In *Chadwick,* federal narcotics agents had probable cause to believe that a 200-pound double-locked footlocker contained marijuana. The agents tracked the locker as the defendants removed it from a train and carried it through the station to a waiting car. As soon as the defendants lifted the locker into the trunk of the car, the agents arrested them, seized the locker, and searched it. In this Court, the United States did not contend that the locker's brief contact with the automobile's trunk sufficed to make the *Carroll* doctrine applicable. Rather, the United States urged that the search of movable luggage could be considered analogous to the search of an automobile. The Court rejected this argument because, it reasoned, a person expects more privacy in his luggage and personal effects than he does in his automobile. Moreover, it concluded that as "may often not be the case when automobiles are seized," secure storage facilities are usually available when the police seize luggage.

In Arkansas v. Sanders, 442 U.S. 753 (1979), the Court extended *Chadwick*'s rule to apply to a suitcase actually being transported in the trunk of a car. In *Sanders,* the police had probable cause to believe a suitcase contained marijuana. They watched as the defendant placed the suitcase in the trunk of a taxi and was driven away. The police pursued the taxi for several blocks, stopped it, found the suitcase in the trunk, and searched it. Although the Court had applied the *Carroll* doctrine to searches of integral parts of the automobile itself (indeed, in *Carroll,* contraband whiskey was in the upholstery of the seats), it did not extend the doctrine to the warrantless search of personal luggage "merely because it was located in an automobile lawfully stopped by the police." Again, the *Sanders* majority stressed the heightened privacy expectation in personal luggage and concluded that the presence of luggage in an automobile did not diminish the owner's expectation of privacy in his personal items.

In *Ross*, the Court endeavored to distinguish between *Carroll*, which governed the *Ross* automobile search, and *Chadwick*, which governed the *Sanders* automobile search. It held that the *Carroll* doctrine covered searches of automobiles when the police had probable cause to search an entire vehicle, but that the *Chadwick* doctrine governed searches of luggage when the officers had probable cause to search only a container within the vehicle. Thus, in a *Ross* situation, the police could conduct a reasonable search under the Fourth Amendment without obtaining a warrant, whereas in a *Sanders* situation, the police had to obtain a warrant before they searched. . . .

III.

The facts in this case closely resemble the facts in *Ross*. In *Ross*, the police had probable cause to believe that drugs were stored in the trunk of a particular car. Here, the [California courts] concluded that the police had probable cause to believe that respondent was carrying marijuana in a bag in his car's trunk. Furthermore, for what it is worth, in *Ross*, as here, the drugs in the trunk were contained in a brown paper bag.

This Court in *Ross* rejected *Chadwick*'s distinction between containers and cars. It concluded that the expectation of privacy in one's vehicle is equal to one's expectation of privacy in the container, and noted that "the privacy interests in a car's trunk or glove compartment may be no less than those in a movable container." [T]he time and expense of the warrant process would be misdirected if the police could search every cubic inch of an automobile until they discovered a paper sack, at which point the Fourth Amendment required them to take the sack to a magistrate for permission to look inside. We now must decide the question deferred in *Ross:* whether the Fourth Amendment requires the police to obtain a warrant to open the sack in a movable vehicle simply because they lack probable cause to search the entire car. We conclude that it does not.

IV.

[A] container found after a general search of the automobile and a container found in a car after a limited search for the container are equally easy for the police to store and for the suspect to hide or destroy. In fact, we see no principled distinction in terms of either the privacy expectation or the exigent circumstances between the paper bag found by the police in *Ross* and the paper bag found by the police here. Furthermore, by attempting to distinguish between a container for which the police are specifically searching and a container which they come across in a car, we have provided only minimal protection for privacy and have impeded effective law enforcement.

The line between probable cause to search a vehicle and probable cause to search a package in that vehicle is not always clear, and separate rules that govern the two objects to be searched may enable the police to broaden their power to make warrantless searches and disserve privacy interests. . . . At the moment when officers stop an automobile, it may be less than clear whether they suspect with a high degree of certainty that the vehicle contains drugs in a bag or simply contains drugs. If the police know that they may open a bag only if they are actually searching the entire car, they may search more extensively than they otherwise would in order to establish the general probable cause required by *Ross*. . . . We cannot see the benefit of a rule that requires law enforcement officers to conduct a more intrusive search in order to justify a less intrusive one.

To the extent that the *Chadwick-Sanders* rule protects privacy, its protection is minimal. Law enforcement officers may seize a container and hold it until they obtain a search warrant. . . . And the police often will be able to search containers without a warrant, despite the *Chadwick-Sanders* rule, as a search incident to a lawful arrest. . . .

Finally, the search of a paper bag intrudes far less on individual privacy than does the incursion sanctioned long ago in *Carroll*. In that case, prohibition agents slashed the upholstery of the automobile. This Court nonetheless found their search to be reasonable under the Fourth Amendment. If destroying the interior of an automobile is not unreasonable, we cannot conclude that looking inside a closed container is. In light of the minimal protection to privacy afforded by the *Chadwick-Sanders* rule, and our serious doubt whether that rule substantially serves privacy interests, we now hold that the Fourth Amendment does not compel separate treatment for an automobile search that extends only to a container within the vehicle.

V.

The *Chadwick-Sanders* rule not only has failed to protect privacy but also has confused courts and police officers and impeded effective law enforcement. The conflict between the *Carroll* doctrine cases and the *Chadwick-Sanders* line has been criticized in academic commentary. One leading authority on the Fourth Amendment, after comparing *Chadwick* and *Sanders* with *Carroll* and its progeny, observed: "These two lines of authority cannot be completely reconciled, and thus how one comes out in the container-in-the-car situation depends upon which line of authority is used as a point of departure." 3 W. LaFave, Search and Seizure 53 (2d ed. 1987).

The discrepancy between the two rules has led to confusion for law enforcement officers. For example, when an officer, who has developed probable cause to believe that a vehicle contains drugs, begins to search the vehicle and immediately discovers a closed container, which rule applies? The defendant will argue that the fact that the officer first chose to search the container indicates that his probable cause extended only to the container and that *Chadwick* and *Sanders* therefore require a warrant. On the other hand, the fact that the officer first chose to search in the most obvious location should not restrict the propriety of the search. The *Chadwick* rule, as applied in *Sanders*, has devolved into an anomaly such that the more likely the police are to discover drugs in a container, the less authority they have to search it. We have noted the virtue of providing clear and unequivocal guidelines to the law enforcement profession. The *Chadwick-Sanders* rule is the antithesis of a "clear and unequivocal" guideline.

[Justice Stevens argues in dissent] that law enforcement has not been impeded because the Court has decided 29 Fourth Amendment cases since *Ross* in favor of the government. . . . In each of these cases, the government appeared as the petitioner. The dissent fails to explain how the loss of 29 cases below, not to mention the many others which this Court did not hear, did not interfere with law enforcement. The fact that the state courts and the Federal Courts of Appeals have been reversed in their Fourth Amendment holdings 29 times since 1982 further demonstrates the extent to which our Fourth Amendment jurisprudence has confused the courts. . . .

VI.

The interpretation of the *Carroll* doctrine set forth in *Ross* now applies to all searches of containers found in an automobile. In other words, the police may search without a warrant if their search is supported by probable cause. [However, probable] cause to believe that a container placed in the trunk of a [vehicle] contains contraband or evidence does not justify a search of the entire [vehicle]. In the case before us, the police had probable cause to believe that the paper bag in the automobile's trunk contained marijuana. That probable cause now allows a warrantless search of the paper bag. The facts in the record reveal that the police did not have probable cause to believe that contraband was hidden in any other part of the automobile and a search of the entire vehicle would have been without probable cause and unreasonable under the Fourth Amendment. . . .

Until today, this Court has drawn a curious line between the search of an automobile that coincidentally turns up a container and the search of a container that coincidentally turns up in an automobile. The protections of the Fourth Amendment must not turn on such coincidences. We therefore interpret *Carroll* as providing one rule to govern all automobile searches. . . .

SCALIA, J., concurring in the judgment.

I agree with the dissent that it is anomalous for a briefcase to be protected by the "general requirement" of a prior warrant when it is being carried along the street, but for that same briefcase to become unprotected as soon as it is carried into an automobile. On the other hand, I agree with the Court that it would be anomalous for a locked compartment in an automobile to be unprotected by the "general requirement" of a prior warrant, but for an unlocked briefcase within the automobile to be protected. I join in the judgment of the Court because I think its holding is more faithful to the text and tradition of the Fourth Amendment, and if these anomalies in our jurisprudence are ever to be eliminated that is the direction in which we should travel.

The Fourth Amendment does not by its terms require a prior warrant for searches and seizures; it merely prohibits searches and seizures that are "unreasonable." What it explicitly states regarding warrants is by way of limitation upon their issuance rather than requirement of their use. For the warrant was a means of insulating officials from personal liability assessed by colonial juries. An officer who searched or seized without a warrant did so at his own risk; he would be liable for trespass, including exemplary damages, unless the jury found that his action was "reasonable." If, however, the officer acted pursuant to a proper warrant, he would be absolutely immune. See Bell v. Clapp, 10 Johns. 263 (N.Y. 1813). By restricting the issuance of warrants, the Framers endeavored to preserve the jury's role in regulating searches and seizures. . . .

Even before today's decision, the "warrant requirement" had become so riddled with exceptions that it was basically unrecognizable. . . . Our intricate body of law regarding "reasonable expectation of privacy" has been developed largely as a means of creating these exceptions, enabling a search to be denominated not a Fourth Amendment "search" and therefore not subject to the general warrant requirement.

Unlike the dissent, therefore, I do not regard today's holding as some momentous departure, but rather as merely the continuation of an inconsistent jurisprudence that has been with us for years. . . . In my view, the path out of this confusion should be sought by returning to the first principle that the "reasonableness" requirement of the Fourth Amendment affords the protection that the common law afforded. I have no difficulty with the proposition that that includes the requirement of a warrant, where the common law required a warrant; and it may even be that changes in the surrounding legal rules (for example, elimination of the common-law rule that reasonable, good-faith belief was no defense to absolute liability for trespass) may make a warrant indispensable to reasonableness where it once was not. But the supposed "general rule" that a warrant is always required does not appear to have any basis in the common law, and confuses rather than facilitates any attempt to develop rules of reasonableness in light of changed legal circumstances. . . .

STEVENS, J., dissenting.*

. . . I.

The Fourth Amendment is a restraint on Executive power. The Amendment constitutes the Framers' direct constitutional response to the unreasonable law enforcement practices employed by agents of the British Crown. Over the years — particularly in the period immediately after World War II and particularly in opinions authored by Justice Jackson after his service as a special prosecutor at the Nuremburg trials — the Court has recognized the importance of this restraint as a bulwark against police practices that prevail in totalitarian regimes. This history is, however, only part of the explanation for the warrant requirement. The requirement also reflects the sound policy judgment that, absent exceptional circumstances, the decision to invade the privacy of an individual's personal effects should be made by a neutral magistrate rather than an agent of the Executive.

[In United States v. Chadwick, we] concluded that neither of the justifications for the automobile exception could support a similar exception for luggage. We first held that the privacy interest in luggage is substantially greater than in an automobile. Unlike automobiles and their contents, we reasoned, luggage contents are not open to public view, except as a condition to a border entry or common carrier travel; nor is luggage subject to regular inspections and official scrutiny on a continuing basis. Indeed, luggage is specifically intended to safeguard the privacy of personal effects, unlike an automobile, whose primary function is transportation. We then held that the mobility of luggage did not justify creating an additional exception to the Warrant Clause. Unlike an automobile, luggage can easily be seized and detained pending judicial approval of a search. . . .

* [Justice Marshall joined this opinion. — EDS.]

II.

In its opinion today, the Court recognizes that the police did not have probable cause to search respondent's vehicle and that a search of anything but the paper bag that respondent had carried from Daza's apartment and placed in the trunk of his car would have been unconstitutional. Moreover, as I read the opinion, the Court assumes that the police could not have made a warrantless inspection of the bag before it was placed in the car. Finally, the Court also does not question the fact that, under our prior cases, it would have been lawful for the police to seize the container and detain it (and respondent) until they obtained a search warrant. Thus, all of the relevant facts that governed our decisions in *Chadwick* and *Sanders* are present here whereas the relevant fact that justified the vehicle search in *Ross* is not present.

The Court does not attempt to identify any exigent circumstances that would justify its refusal to apply the general rule against warrantless searches. Instead, it advances these three arguments: First, the rules identified in the foregoing cases are confusing and anomalous. Second, the rules do not protect any significant interest in privacy. And, third, the rules impede effective law enforcement. None of these arguments withstands scrutiny.

The "Confusion"

... In the case the Court decides today, the California Court of Appeal ... had no difficulty applying the critical distinction. Relying on *Chadwick,* it explained that "the officers had probable cause to believe marijuana would be found only in a brown lunch bag and nowhere else in the car. We are compelled to hold they should have obtained a search warrant before opening it." The decided cases ... provide no support for the Court's concern about "confusion." The Court instead relies primarily on predictions that were made by Justice Blackmun in his dissenting opinions in *Chadwick* and *Sanders.* The Court, however, cites no evidence that these predictions have in fact materialized....

To the extent there was any "anomaly" in our prior jurisprudence, the Court has "cured" it at the expense of creating a more serious paradox. For surely it is anomalous to prohibit a search of a briefcase while the owner is carrying it exposed on a public street yet to permit a search once the owner has placed the briefcase in the locked trunk of his car. One's privacy interest in one's luggage can certainly not be diminished by one's removing it from a public thoroughfare and placing it — out of sight — in a privately owned vehicle. Nor is the danger that evidence will escape increased if the luggage is in a car rather than on the street. In either location, if the police have probable cause, they are authorized to seize the luggage and to detain it until they obtain judicial approval for a search. Any line demarking an exception to the warrant requirement will appear blurred at the edges, but the Court has certainly erred if it believes that, by erasing one line and drawing another, it has drawn a clearer boundary.

The Privacy Argument

... To support its argument that today's holding works only a minimal intrusion on privacy, the Court suggests that "[i]f the police know that they may open a bag only if they are actually searching the entire car, they may search more extensively than they otherwise would in order to establish the general probable cause required by *Ross*." [T]his fear is unexplained and inexplicable. Neither evidence uncovered in the course of a search nor the scope of the search conducted can be used to provide post hoc justification for a search unsupported by probable cause at its inception.

The Court also justifies its claim that its holding inflicts only minor damage by suggesting that, under New York v. Belton, 453 U.S. 454 (1981), the police could have arrested respondent and searched his bag if respondent had placed the bag in the passenger compartment of the automobile instead of in the trunk. In *Belton,* however, the justification for stopping the car and arresting the driver had nothing to do with the subsequent search, which was based on the potential danger to the arresting officer. The holding in *Belton* was supportable under a straightforward application of the automobile exception. I would not extend *Belton's* holding to this case, in which the container — which was protected from a warrantless search before it was placed in the car — provided the only justification for the arrest. Even accepting *Belton's* application to a case like this one, however, the Court's logic extends its holding to a container placed in the trunk of a vehicle, rather than in the passenger compartment. And the Court makes this extension without any justification whatsoever other than convenience to law enforcement.

THE BURDEN ON LAW ENFORCEMENT

The Court's suggestion that *Chadwick* and *Sanders* have created a significant burden on effective law enforcement is unsupported, inaccurate, and, in any event, an insufficient reason for creating a new exception to the warrant requirement. Despite repeated claims that *Chadwick* and *Sanders* have "impeded effective law enforcement," the Court cites no authority for its contentions. Moreover, all evidence that does exist points to the contrary conclusion. In the years since *Ross* was decided, the Court has heard argument in 30 Fourth Amendment cases involving narcotics. In all but one, the government was the petitioner. All save two involved a search or seizure without a warrant or with a defective warrant. And, in all except three, the Court upheld the constitutionality of the search or seizure.

In the meantime, the flow of narcotics cases through the courts has steadily and dramatically increased. No impartial observer could criticize this Court for hindering the progress of the war on drugs. On the contrary, decisions like the one the Court makes today will support the conclusion that this Court has become a loyal foot soldier in the Executive's fight against crime.

Even if the warrant requirement does inconvenience the police to some extent, that fact does not distinguish this constitutional requirement from any other procedural protection secured by the Bill of Rights. It is merely a part of the price that our society must pay in order to preserve its freedom. . . . I respectfully dissent.

Notes

1. *Searches of containers in cars: majority position.* In California v. Acevedo, the Court resolved the tension between two lines of its earlier cases. It allowed warrantless searches of containers within automobiles so long as the police have probable cause to believe that either the car as a whole or the container itself holds contraband or evidence. Very few state courts have rejected the Court's holding in *Acevedo* as they have interpreted their state constitutions. But see State v. Sawa, 616 A.2d 774 (Vt. 1991). Even in the handful of courts that do require exigent circumstances for

containers in cars, the rule applies only to containers in the trunk or other areas not covered by a search incident to arrest.

The Court made it clear in Wyoming v. Houghton, 526 U.S. 295 (1999), that the *Acevedo* rule also applied to any containers owned by passengers rather than the driver. Police officers with probable cause to search a car may inspect a passengers' belongings inside the car if they are capable of concealing the object of the search. Passengers, just like drivers, possess a reduced expectation of privacy when it comes to property inside cars. Would requiring a warrant in this setting encourage drivers to hide contraband in containers belonging to passengers?

2. *Containers (effects) not in cars.* The decision in the federal courts to apply the automobile exception to containers in cars creates an inconsistency between the status of the containers inside and outside a car. For containers outside of cars, police apparently must find one of the many familiar exigencies to justify a warrantless examination of its contents. In jurisdictions that follow the federal rule, a container becomes subject to warrantless search, so long as the officer has probable cause, as soon as it is placed in a car. Will this wrinkle in the law change a police officer's strategy for the timing of an arrest of a suspect holding a container?

3. *Grounds for searching cars: inventory searches.* As in many areas of search and seizure law, the government may use a number of justifications for a search of an automobile and its contents. A lawyer must assess all the possible theories.

As we saw earlier in this chapter, the justifications for a vehicle search include the need for an inventory of the contents of a vehicle when the vehicle is impounded, or a search of the vehicle when an officer is arresting one of its occupants. See State v. Hundley, 619 N.E.2d 744 (Ill. 1993).

4. *Grounds for searching cars: automobile exception to the warrant requirement.* In Carroll v. United States, 267 U.S. 132 (1925), the Supreme Court upheld a warrantless search by two federal prohibition agents looking for liquor hidden in the upholstery of an automobile. The Court allowed warrantless searches, based on probable cause, of automobiles and other vehicles because "the vehicle can be quickly moved out of the locality or jurisdiction." A second theory justifying reduced Fourth Amendment protection for cars, developed in a series of later cases, is that cars are subject to public view and to pervasive state regulation. Car owners have lower reasonable expectations of privacy than, for example, homeowners.

The power of the police to search cars and other conveyances without a warrant has become known as the "automobile exception." This is an exception to the warrant requirement but not to the probable cause requirement: To exercise this power, police must have probable cause to believe that the car contains evidence or contraband. If police have probable cause, under the automobile exception they may stop the car and conduct a search. A search may be rejected if it exceeds the scope justified by objects which police, based on their finding of probable cause, expect to discover.

The largest group of state courts (about half) have fully embraced the federal view and require no warrant for any search of an automobile. In effect, these courts conclusively presume that exigent circumstances are present for any search of a car, even if the particular car in question was unlikely to move while the officers sought a warrant. A minority of state courts (roughly 15) still explicitly or implicitly require the government to show exigent circumstances to support a warrantless search of a car. The mobility of a car makes this showing quite easy in the ordinary case, but defendants can rebut a presumption of exigency by showing that the car

was parked and locked or was otherwise not mobile. See State v. Tibbles, 236 P.3d 885 (Wash. 2010). For a glimpse of the rich case law in the state courts on the automobile exception to the warrant requirement, see the web extension for this chapter at *http://www.crimpro.com/extension/ch04*.

5. *Grounds for searching cars: the application of* Terry. A separate justification for car searches stems from the application of *Terry* searches to cars. As we saw in Chapter 2, the Supreme Court approved such searches in Michigan v. Long. Such searches must satisfy the requirements of *Terry*. In other words, the officer must have a proper basis for stopping the car. Then the officer may automatically order the driver and any passengers out of the car. At that point, if the officer has reasonable suspicion to believe there are weapons in the car, she can search in the passenger compartment, in any areas that could contain an accessible weapon, such as under the seats and inside containers large enough for a weapon. How would this doctrine apply in a case where the driver of a vehicle informs a police officer during a vehicle stop that he is carrying a concealed weapon under the terms of a license allowing him to do so?

6. *Viewing the exterior of cars.* The rules for searching the interior of cars do not apply to examination of the exterior of cars. Following the familiar expectation of privacy analysis of *Katz,* courts have held that no Fourth Amendment issue is raised when police examine the outside of a car or take a picture of it. Courts have also typically refused to apply the Fourth Amendment to examinations of the tread, tire wear, and even the removal of dirt or small samples of paint. See, e.g., Cardwell v. Lewis, 417 U.S. 583 (1974); State v. Skeleton, 795 P.2d 349 (Kan. 1990). Examination of the contents of a car from the outside, including the use of sight, smell, or even a flashlight to enhance the view, usually falls outside the limits of the Fourth Amendment so long as the car is parked in a place that is otherwise accessible to the police.

What about the viewing of the VIN (vehicle identification number)? In cases involving police efforts to obtain the VIN, courts agree that if the VIN is visible through the front windshield (as it is on all modern cars), and the officer simply reads it, there is no search. If the officer must reach into the car, open the door, lift the hood, or look under the vehicle to read the VIN or inspect some other feature of the car, some courts (a minority) still hold that no search has occurred. See, e.g., New York v. Class, 475 U.S. 106 (1986); Wood v. State, 632 S.W.2d 734 (Tex. Crim. App. 1982). About twice as many states, however, conclude that probable cause is required to move items inside a car, open a door, or lift a hood before viewing a VIN. State v. Larocco, 794 P.2d 460 (Utah 1990).

7. *Warrants reconsidered: what is the exception and what is the rule?* After studying the automobile exception, searches of cars incident to arrest, and inventory searches, look again at the following oft-repeated statement, quoted here from United States v. Ross, 456 U.S. 798 (1982), in a manner that emphasizes the statement's pedigree:

> We reaffirm the basic rule of Fourth Amendment jurisprudence stated by Justice Stewart for a unanimous Court in Mincey v. Arizona, 437 U.S. 385, 390: "The Fourth Amendment proscribes all unreasonable searches and seizures, and it is a cardinal principle that 'searches conducted outside the judicial process, without prior approval by judge or magistrate, are per se unreasonable under the Fourth Amendment — subject only to a few specifically established and well-delineated exceptions.' Katz v. United States, 389 U.S. 347, 357."

Consider Justice Scalia's observation in California v. Acevedo, that the warrant requirement has become "so riddled with exceptions" that it is "basically unrecognizable." Is this a problem courts and legislatures should care about, or have they developed an acceptable replacement for a strong warrant requirement? See Joseph Grano, Rethinking the Fourth Amendment Warrant Requirement, 19 Am. Crim. L. Rev. 603 (1982); Tracey Maclin, The Central Meaning of the Fourth Amendment, 35 Wm. & Mary L. Rev. 197 (1993).

Problem 4-7. Mobile . . . Homes

Robert Williams, an agent of the Drug Enforcement Administration, watched Charles Carney approach a youth in downtown San Diego. The youth accompanied Carney to a Dodge Mini Motor Home parked in a nearby lot, a few blocks from the courthouse. Carney and the youth closed the window shades in the motor home. Williams had previously received uncorroborated information that another person who used the same motor home was exchanging marijuana for sex. Williams, with assistance from other agents, watched the motor home for the entire one and one-quarter hours that Carney and the youth remained inside. When the youth left the motor home, the agents followed and stopped him. The youth told the agents that he had received marijuana in return for allowing Carney sexual contacts.

At the agents' request, the youth returned to the motor home and knocked on its door; Carney stepped out. The agents identified themselves as law enforcement officers. Without a warrant or consent, one agent entered the motor home and observed marijuana, plastic bags, and a scale of the kind used in weighing drugs on a table.

Assess the validity of the warrantless search. Compare California v. Carney, 471 U.S. 386 (1985).

V

Arrests

Every year, police in the United States make about 15 million arrests. Arrests are a serious intrusion on liberty, and our legal systems place several types of controls on them. The constraints come from constitutions, statutes, police department rules, the common law of torts, and elsewhere. Despite these multiple limits, police officers in the field still make the most important decisions about arrests.

This chapter surveys the legal rules and institutions that limit the arrest power and studies the operation of that power within (and sometimes outside) those legal boundaries. Section A considers the distinction between arrests and the lesser restraints on liberty known as "stops." Section B identifies the limited situations in which a warrant is necessary to complete a valid arrest. Section C focuses on legal rules dealing with the police officer's decision *not* to make an arrest in certain settings. Section D continues with the theme of police discretion in the arrest decision, looking to the use of the citation power as an alternative to arrests. And finally, Section E introduces the limits on the officer's use of force in carrying out an arrest.

A. STOP OR ARREST?

Police often find it necessary to restrain an individual from moving away from a particular place. They might do so to protect themselves or others from harm. They might do so to investigate a completed crime or to prevent an ongoing or future one. As we saw in Chapter 2, not all of these restraints are equally intrusive, and the different levels of restraint are subject to different legal controls. Some are consensual encounters, some are stops, and some are arrests. How do legal systems distinguish the different types of police efforts to control the movement of citizens?

Answers to this question appear in statutes, in cases, and in the interaction between the two.

NEVADA REVISED STATUTES §171.123

1. Any peace officer may detain any person whom the officer encounters under circumstances which reasonably indicate that the person has committed, is committing or is about to commit a crime. . . .

4. A person must not be detained longer than is reasonably necessary to effect the purposes of this section, and in no event longer than 60 minutes. The detention must not extend beyond the place or the immediate vicinity of the place where the detention was first effected, unless the person is arrested.

ARKANSAS RULE OF CRIMINAL PROCEDURE 3.1

A law enforcement officer lawfully present in any place may, in the performance of his duties, stop and detain any person who he reasonably suspects is committing, has committed, or is about to commit (1) a felony, or (2) a misdemeanor involving danger of forcible injury to persons or of appropriation of or damage to property, if such action is reasonably necessary either to obtain or verify the identification of the person or to determine the lawfulness of his conduct. An officer acting under this rule may require the person to remain in or near such place in the officer's presence for a period of not more than 15 minutes or for such time as is reasonable under the circumstances. At the end of such period the person detained shall be released without further restraint, or arrested and charged with an offense.

ROBERT BAILEY v. STATE

987 A.2d 72 (Md. 2010)

GREENE, J.

Issue

In this case, we are asked to determine whether the search and seizure of the petitioner, Robert Bailey, violated the Fourth Amendment to the United States Constitution and the Maryland Declaration of Rights. . . .

I.

On the night of August 16, 2006, Officer Rodney Lewis of the Prince George's County Police Department was patrolling the 6800 block of Hawthorne Street in Landover, Maryland. The area was known for drug activity, though there were no specific complaints on the night in question. At approximately 11:35 P.M., while patrolling on foot, Officer Lewis spotted the petitioner, Robert Bailey, standing alone on the side of 6890 Hawthorne Street. Officer Lewis testified about the encounter at the suppression hearing:

> I observed the defendant standing on the side of a home, . . . just standing in the shadows, at which time I yelled out to him, "Excuse me, sir, do you live there?" I didn't get

> any acknowledgment from the individual, at which time I assumed that he probably didn't hear me. I repeated the same thing, "Excuse me, sir, do you live there," which again I received no acknowledgment from the suspect, at which time myself, along with another officer, walked over to the individual. At that time, I just happened to step out of the shallow [sic] area on the sidewalk where I could visibly see his hands. And from the area at which he was standing at the time, I could smell a strong odor of ether.

When Officer Lewis smelled the odor of ether, he was within a few feet of the petitioner, close enough to "reach out and touch him." The odor was emanating from the petitioner's "body odor." The odor of ether, according to Officer Lewis's testimony, is associated with phencyclidine, more commonly known as PCP. Officer Lewis acknowledged on cross-examination that it is not illegal to possess ether and that ether is a solvent that is used in several household products. Upon smelling the odor of ether, Officer Lewis "reached over and grabbed both of [the petitioner's] hands and . . . had him place them over top of his head." Officer Lewis then conducted a search of the petitioner, which uncovered a glass vial, approximately three to four inches in length and one inch in diameter, half-full of liquid, in the petitioner's right front pants pocket. Field tests confirmed that the liquid contained PCP, and the petitioner was subsequently taken into custody and charged with possession of a controlled dangerous substance. . . .

In addition to observing the odor of ether, Officer Lewis noted that the petitioner had "glossy eyes" and that the petitioner failed to respond to the inquiries about whether he lived in the house. Officer Lewis did not, however, indicate whether he observed the petitioner's glossy eyes before or after he initially seized the petitioner.

The petitioner moved to suppress the physical evidence recovered from the search, asserting that the glass vial was the fruit of an illegal search and seizure under the Fourth Amendment, as well as the Maryland Declaration of Rights. Following a suppression hearing at which Officer Lewis was the sole witness, the trial court found that Officer Lewis had reasonable articulable suspicion to stop and question the petitioner based on the smell of ether, the petitioner's failure to respond to Officer Lewis's questions, and the petitioner's presence in a "high crime drug area with a number of complaints from citizens." The suppression court also determined that Officer Lewis conducted a valid pat-down of the petitioner for "officer safety" and that, based on the totality of the circumstances, the search and seizure were valid.

The petitioner proceeded to trial on an Agreed Statement of Facts. [The] Circuit Court for Prince George's County entered verdicts of guilty to . . . possession of a controlled dangerous substance, and sentenced the petitioner to four years in prison, all but two years suspended, with three years of supervised probation upon release. . . .

III.

. . . This Court analyzed the applicability of the Fourth Amendment to varying levels of police interaction in Swift v. State, 899 A.2d 867 (Md. 2006):

> Many courts have analyzed the applicability of the Fourth Amendment in terms of three tiers of interaction between a citizen and the police. The most intrusive encounter, an arrest, requires probable cause to believe that a person has committed or is committing a crime. The second category, the investigatory stop or detention, known commonly as a *Terry* stop, is less intrusive than a formal custodial arrest and must be supported by reasonable suspicion that a person has committed or is about to commit a crime and permits an officer to stop and briefly detain an individual. . . . The least intrusive police-citizen contact, a consensual encounter, . . . involves no restraint of liberty and elicits an individual's voluntary cooperation with non-coercive police contact. A consensual encounter need not be supported by any suspicion and because an individual is free to leave at any time during such an encounter, the Fourth Amendment is not implicated; thus, an individual is not considered to have been "seized" within the meaning of the Fourth Amendment.

We will consider how the petitioner's encounter with Officer Lewis proceeded from consensual encounter to custodial arrest, in light of settled Fourth Amendment precedent.

IV. Consensual Encounter or Investigatory Stop

. . . Officer Lewis's initial questioning of the petitioner was not an investigative stop, but rather a "consensual encounter" or accosting. [A] consensual encounter does not implicate the Fourth Amendment because the individual with whom the police are interacting is free to leave at any time. . . .

When the police officers asked the petitioner if he lived at the house in whose shadows he was standing, the petitioner could not have reasonably believed that the police were doing anything more than making a routine inquiry. The officers' inquiry was a request for basic information, not an order. Officer Lewis "yelled" the question because of the distance between the officers and the petitioner, and the officers began to walk toward the petitioner only after he did not respond to their questions, presumably to find out why he had not. In sum, the petitioner was not seized by the officers but merely was accosted at the point at which the officers began to approach him. . . .

V. Seizure and Search

An encounter has been described as a fluid situation, and one which begins as a consensual encounter may lose its consensual nature and become an investigatory detention or arrest once a person's liberty has been restrained and the person would not be free to leave. Officer Lewis's testimony indicates that his encounter with the petitioner proceeded quickly from an accosting, in which he shouted questions to the petitioner from the street, to a physical detention, when he grabbed the petitioner's hands.

As the Supreme Court observed in *Terry*, 392 U.S. at 19 n. 16, when the officer, "by means of physical force or a show of authority, has in some way restrained the liberty of a citizen [we may] conclude that a 'seizure' has occurred." In determining whether a person has been seized, the crucial test is whether, taking into account all of the circumstances surrounding the encounter, the police conduct would have communicated to a reasonable person that he was not at liberty to ignore the police presence and go about his business. . . .

In the present case, it is clear that, once Officer Lewis grabbed the petitioner's hands and placed them over his head, a reasonable person in the petitioner's position would have understood that he was physically detained and thus not free to leave or go about his business. Thus, when Officer Lewis grabbed the petitioner's hands, he seized the petitioner for purposes of the Fourth Amendment.

Because the officer seized and searched the petitioner without a warrant, the seizure was presumptively invalid unless it was supported by a reasonable, articulable suspicion of a threat to officer safety or by an exception to the warrant requirement. We must consider whether this seizure of the petitioner was a temporary detention and protective frisk pursuant to *Terry* . . . or a lawful arrest of the petitioner. . . .

VI. *TERRY* FRISK

We disagree with the Circuit Court's conclusion that the search and seizure of the petitioner was an investigatory stop and protective frisk pursuant to *Terry*.[5] The purpose of a protective *Terry* frisk is not to discover evidence, but rather to protect the police officer and bystanders from harm. Pat-down frisks are proper when the officer has reason to believe that he is dealing with an armed and dangerous individual, regardless of whether he has probable cause to arrest the individual for a crime. The officer has reason to believe that an individual is armed and dangerous if a reasonably prudent person, under the circumstances, would have felt that he was in danger, based on reasonable inferences from particularized facts in light of the officer's experience.

Even if we were to assume that the encounter with the Officer Lewis was a *Terry* stop, the reasonableness of a *Terry* stop is determined by considering whether the officer's action was justified at its inception, and whether it was reasonably related in scope to the circumstances which justified the interference in the first place. Further, assuming *arguendo* that Officer Lewis had reasonable, articulable suspicion to believe that criminal activity was afoot and, accordingly, detain the petitioner, he still lacked the basis for a protective *Terry* frisk. At the suppression hearing, Officer Lewis indicated that he searched the petitioner to "check for weapons," but did not provide any basis for his suspicion that the petitioner was armed and dangerous. Officer Lewis did not testify as to any factors that would lead to a suspicion that the petitioner was carrying a weapon. Further, there are no objective factors in the record that indicate that the petitioner was armed and dangerous. Although the encounter took place at nighttime, the petitioner was alone and the officer "could visibly see his hands," which, presumably because the officer did not indicate otherwise, were empty. There is no indication in the record that the petitioner made

5. This Court need not consider whether Officer Lewis had reasonable articulable suspicion for a *Terry* stop because no investigatory stop took place. Pursuant to Terry v. Ohio, 392 U.S. 1 (1968), and its progeny, a police officer who has reasonable suspicion that a particular person has committed, is committing, or is about to commit a crime may detain that person briefly in order to investigate the circumstances that provoked suspicion. Police conduct a *Terry* investigation by asking the detainee a moderate number of questions to determine his identity and to try to obtain information confirming or dispelling the officer's suspicions. The detainee is not obligated to respond, however, and, unless the detainee's answers provide the officer with probable cause to arrest him, he must be released. In this case, no such questioning took place. Officer Lewis proceeded from an accosting, in which he called out to the petitioner from the street, to a physical detention of the petitioner, when he grabbed the petitioner's hands, without asking any additional questions.

any threatening movements, or any movements at all, nor is there any indication that Officer Lewis suspected that the petitioner was dealing drugs. Thus, we . . . hold that Officer Lewis had no basis to conduct a protective frisk.

Even if Officer Lewis had reasonably believed that the petitioner was armed and dangerous, therefore providing the basis for a proper *Terry* frisk, the search in the present case exceeded the scope of a proper protective frisk. A proper *Terry* frisk is limited to a pat-down of the outer clothing not to discover evidence of a crime, but rather to protect the police officer and bystanders from harm by checking for weapons. . . .

In the present case, Officer Lewis testified that he patted down the petitioner's right front pocket and that he did not manipulate the object contained therein. Officer Lewis testified that he "felt and recognized a glass vial" in the petitioner's pocket. He further testified that generally, in his experience, PCP is "contained in a glass vial." Based on Officer Lewis's testimony, however, the incriminating nature of the object in the defendant's pocket was not immediately apparent upon his initial touch of the object in the pat-down. Rather, Officer Lewis testified that he field-tested the liquid contained in the vial after removing it from the petitioner's pocket, thereby determining that the liquid contained PCP. The removal of the vial from the petitioner's pocket and field test of the liquid contained in the vial constituted a general exploratory search exceeding the permissible scope of a protective *Terry* frisk. Accordingly, we hold that Officer Lewis lacked the proper basis for a *Terry* frisk at the inception of the search, and that the search was a general exploratory search that exceeded the permissible scope of a *Terry* frisk, which serves as a basis to exclude the evidence seized from the petitioner's pocket.

VII. Arrest

We must consider, alternatively, whether Officer Lewis's seizure of the petitioner in the present case constituted a de facto arrest. . . . This Court analyzed what constitutes an arrest in Bouldin v. State, 350 A.2d 130, 133 (Md. 1976).

> It is generally recognized that an arrest is the taking, seizing, or detaining of the person of another . . . by touching or putting hands on him. . . . It is said that four elements must ordinarily coalesce to constitute a legal arrest: (1) an intent to arrest; (2) under a real or pretended authority; (3) accompanied by a seizure or detention of the person; and (4) which is understood by the person arrested.

In Belote v. State, 981 A.2d 1247, 1254 (Md. 2009), this Court further analyzed the factors set forth in *Bouldin:*

> Where a police officer's objective conduct unambiguously reflects an intent to make a custodial arrest, the subjective intent inquiry . . . takes on less significance. In other words, when an arresting officer's objective conduct, which provides significant insight into the officer's subjective intent, is unambiguous, courts need not allocate significant weight to an officer's subjective intent that is revealed partially in the form of his testimony at the suppression hearing; the officer's objective conduct, in effect, will have made his subjective intent clear.

A show of force is objective conduct demonstrating the officer's intent to make an arrest. Generally, a display of force by a police officer, such as putting a person in handcuffs, is considered an arrest. . . . Although the display of force often involves placing the individual who is seized in handcuffs, application of handcuffs is not a necessary element of an arrest. See Grier v. State, 718 A.2d 211, 217 (Md. 1998) ("Once Petitioner was on the ground and in custody and control of the officers, he was certainly under arrest . . . ."); Morton v. State, 397 A.2d 1385, 1388 (Md. 1979) ([arrest occurred] where an officer removed the individual from a recreation center and placed him under guard in a patrol car . . .); Dixon v. State, 758 A.2d 1063, 1073 (Md. App. 2000) (officers exceeded the permissible scope of an investigative *Terry* stop and "arrested appellant at the time they blocked his car, removed him from his vehicle, and handcuffed him").[8]

[Before] the Supreme Court's landmark decision in *Terry*, the Fourth Amendment's guarantee against unreasonable seizures of persons was analyzed in terms of arrest, and probable cause for arrest. *Terry* constituted a limited departure from the requirement of probable cause to support a seizure.[9] If a seizure [amounts to an arrest, it] must be supported by probable cause in order to be lawful.

In this case, Officer Lewis's conduct constituted an unambiguous show of force. He approached the petitioner while in uniform, physically restrained the petitioner, conducted a search of the petitioner's person, and ultimately took the petitioner into physical police custody. [Although] Officer Lewis testified at the suppression hearing that he was checking the petitioner for weapons, this statement is given less weight than his objective conduct on the night in question. . . .

Officer Lewis's conduct on the night in question exceeded the permissible boundaries of an investigative *Terry* stop, both in scope and in duration. A *Terry* stop must be justified both at its inception and be limited in scope, for the specific purpose of searching for weapons to protect the officer's safety, or the safety of bystanders. In the present case, the officer took complete control of the situation in

8. Conversely, even if the officers' physical actions are equivalent to an arrest, the show of force is not considered to be an arrest if the actions were justified by officer safety or permissible to prevent the flight of a suspect. In re David S., 789 A.2d 607, 616 (Md. 2002) (holding that a "hard take down" in which officers forced the individual to the ground and handcuffed him was a limited *Terry* stop, not an arrest, when the "conduct was not unreasonable because the officers reasonably could have suspected that the respondent posed a threat to their safety"). The use of handcuffs in a seizure is not a dispositive factor in determining whether the seizure was a *Terry* stop or an arrest.

9. The Supreme Court of the United States discussed the distinction between an arrest and a *Terry* stop in United States v. Robinson, 414 U.S. 218, 228 (1973):

> An arrest is a wholly different kind of intrusion upon individual freedom from a limited search for weapons, and the interests each is designed to serve are likewise quite different. An arrest is the initial stage of a criminal prosecution. It is intended to vindicate society's interest in having its laws obeyed, and it is inevitably accompanied by future interference with the individual's freedom of movement, whether or not trial or conviction ultimately follows. The protective search for weapons, on the other hand, constitutes a brief, though far from inconsiderable, intrusion upon the sanctity of the person.

The distinction between a *Terry* stop and an arrest is not defined simply by the length of the detention, the investigative activities during the detention, and whether the suspect was removed to a detention or interrogation area. [An] arrest is distinguishable from a *Terry* detention because the *Terry* stop is not only limited in duration, but also has a limited permissible scope. The scope of a *Terry* stop is limited to brief investigatory stops or detentions conducted in furtherance of the goal of protecting the safety of the officer, or the safety of bystanders.

conducting a general exploratory search of the petitioner, removing the vial from his pocket and taking him into custody. . . .

Grabbing the petitioner's wrists when he was not suspected of being armed and dangerous, then conducting a search and removing the vial from his pocket, and, finally, taking him into custody as the initial action leading up to a criminal prosecution, constituted a de facto arrest. Thus, we hold that Officer Lewis's seizure, in which he physically restrained the petitioner and ultimately took him into custody, constituted an arrest.

[The Court went on to conclude that the circumstances present in this case did not create probable cause to support an arrest. Because] Officer Lewis did not make a lawful arrest when he seized the petitioner, the subsequent warrantless search of the petitioner was not within an exception to the warrant requirement and therefore violated the Fourth Amendment. . . .

Notes

1. *Arrest versus stop: majority position.* The difference between an arrest (requiring probable cause) and an investigative detention (requiring reasonable suspicion) turns on several different factors. Courts look to the amount of time the detention lasts, the techniques (such as handcuffs) used to restrain the suspect, the location of the suspect (including the distance covered during any transportation of the suspect), and what the police officers say to the suspect about the purposes of the detention. The judicial opinions often say, using a circular definition, that an arrest takes place when a reasonable person would believe that he or she is under arrest. Medford v. State, 13 S.W.2d 769 (Tex. 2000) (arrest is complete "when a person's liberty of movement is successfully restricted or restrained, whether this is achieved by an officer's physical force or the suspect's submission to the officer's authority [and] only if a reasonable person in the suspect's position would have understood the situation to constitute a restraint on freedom of movement of the degree which the law associates with formal arrest.").

The interaction among all these relevant facts is typically important. In Kaupp v. Texas, 538 U.S. 626 (2003), police officers awakened a 17-year-old boy in his bedroom at 3:00 in the morning, saying, "We need to go and talk." He was taken out in handcuffs, without shoes, dressed only in his underwear in January, driven in a patrol car to the scene of a crime and then to the sheriff's offices, and then taken into an interrogation room and questioned for 10-15 minutes before admitting to participation in a murder. The Court concluded that such police actions were "sufficiently like arrest to invoke the traditional rule that arrests may constitutionally be made only on probable cause."

2. *Time of detention.* The amount of time that the police detain a person is among the most important facts in determining whether a seizure amounted to an arrest or merely a stop. In Florida v. Royer, 460 U.S. 491 (1983), the Supreme Court stated that an investigative detention "must be temporary and last no longer than is necessary to effectuate the purpose of the stop." Most states allow for a flexible determination of the time necessary to convert a stop into an arrest. Why do the Nevada statute and the Arkansas rule choose such different time limits (15 minutes and 60 minutes)? Did the legislators in the two states have different concerns in mind? Courts deciding cases in the absence of a statute also pay close attention to the

amount of time elapsed. While the absolute number of minutes in a detention is important, courts also judge the length of the detention in light of the purposes of the stop and the time reasonably needed to effectuate those purposes, including the diligence of officers in pursuing the investigation. See United States v. Sharpe, 470 U.S. 675 (1985) (approves of 20-minute automobile stop for purpose of investigating potential narcotics violations); People v. Garcia, 11 P.3d 449 (Colo. 2000) (length of valid investigatory stop measured as time required for officers to diligently complete investigation given complexity of situation and protection of personal safety).

Is the amount of time allowed for an investigative stop the kind of factor amenable to bright-line rules? Is it the kind of factor that can be undermined by the use of general standards such as "reasonableness"? If you were to draft a bright-line rule, would you include an "escape" valve for exceptional situations? If you prefer a rule in this situation, would you want that rule to be determined by the legislature or the courts? Do rules as a class tend to favor prosecution or defense?

3. *Conditions of detention.* What can be more typical of arrest than being handcuffed and placed in the back of a police cruiser? If this is true, how can the majority of state courts find that being handcuffed and placed in the back of a cruiser does not, alone, convert an investigative stop into an arrest? See State v. Blackmore, 925 P.2d 1347 (Ariz. 1996) (burglary suspect stopped at gunpoint, handcuffed, placed in back seat of police cruiser; no arrest). Which is more indicative of arrest, the handcuffs or the seat in the police car? Would you support a bright-line rule stating that handcuffs = arrest? For a sampling of the rich case law on this question, consult the web extension for this chapter at *http://www.crimpro.com/extension/ch05*.

4. *Location of detention.* Why do both the Arkansas rule and the Nevada statute require that the detained person remain in the vicinity of the initial stop? Most of the cases on this question allow officers to transport a suspect to some other location nearby to complete an investigation, but longer trips can convert the stop into an arrest. Taking a suspect to the police station is also a key factor in the cases. Can a person be taken to the police station and still not be under arrest? See Dunaway v. New York, 442 U.S. 200 (1979) (recognizing possibility of nonarrest detention based on reasonable suspicion for questioning at police station; however, arrest without probable cause occurred here where defendant was taken to police station for questioning without being told he was under arrest); Collins-Draine v. Knief, 617 N.E.2d 679 (Ill. 2000) (bounds of stop exceeded if officer unnecessarily holds suspect or transports suspect to police station; holding at jail for five hours).

5. *Probable cause to believe what?* Officers need probable cause to justify an arrest. However, an officer might suspect that a person committed one crime although probable cause exists at that time to arrest the person for some other crime. Does it matter which crime the officer has in mind when making the arrest? In Devenpeck v. Alford, 543 U.S. 146 (2004), officers stopped a driver and ultimately arrested him for unlawful audio-taping of a police conversation during the stop, which was later determined not to be a crime. However, the officers on the scene had probable cause to arrest the suspect for impersonating an officer, a sufficient basis to support arrest even though it was not the crime the officers relied upon. Are the arguments in this setting precisely the same as the arguments we encountered in the discussion of "pretextual" stops?

B. ARREST WARRANTS

In Chapter 3, we explored the various ways that the law supposedly encourages the use of a judicial warrant to authorize an officer to conduct a full search. Yet, despite the often-stated "preference" for warrants, most searches take place without a warrant. The same is true for arrests. There are legal rules encouraging or requiring warrants before a police officer can arrest a person in some settings (in particular, arrests made in a home). But in reality, most arrests take place without a warrant. As you read the following materials on the coverage of the warrant requirement for arrests, keep in mind the types of arrests that these rules do not cover.

■ WILLIAM BLACKSTONE, COMMENTARIES ON THE LAWS OF ENGLAND

Vol. 3, p. 288 (1768)

An arrest must be by corporal seising or touching the defendant's body; after which the bailiff may justify breaking open the house in which he is, to take him: otherwise he has no such power; but must watch his opportunity to arrest him. For every man's house is looked upon by the law to be his castle of defence and asylum, wherein he should suffer no violence. Which principle is carried so far in the civil law, that for the most part not so much as a common citation or summons, much less an arrest, can be executed upon a man within his own walls.

■ STATE v. STEVEN THOMAS

124 P.3d 48 (Kan. 2005)

LUCKERT, J.

. . . Just before midnight on March 26, 2002, the Sedgwick County Sheriff's Department received information from a confidential informant that Brandon Prouse was trying to sell the informant 5 or 6 quarts of anhydrous ammonia. Deputies ran a background check on Prouse and discovered that he was wanted on a felony arrest warrant for a probation violation in an aggravated battery case. At around 1:30 A.M. on March 27, 2002, the sheriff's office began surveillance on the house where the informant indicated Prouse might be found. At the time of the surveillance, however, the deputies neither had a search warrant for the house, nor did they know who owned the residence.

At about 2 A.M., Prouse stepped out of the house and walked into the front yard. The uniformed deputies ordered him to stop, but Prouse ran back into the residence through the front door. Four deputies followed Prouse inside. They pursued Prouse through different rooms and then arrested him.

Inside the house, the deputies smelled a strong odor of anhydrous ammonia. As they moved through the residence, the deputies saw in plain view various items that they believed were consistent with a methamphetamine lab. Besides Prouse, the deputies discovered six other individuals inside the house, including Thomas, who owned the residence. A deputy started to open an interior door into the garage to check for more people, but the smell of anhydrous ammonia from the garage was so overwhelming that he immediately shut the door. Because of the strong chemical smell and for safety reasons, the deputies ordered all occupants to go outside onto the front lawn area.

Once the occupants of the house were outside, one of the deputies told his fellow deputies that he would perform a pat-down search of the seven occupants. When the deputy asked Thomas who owned the house, Thomas admitted ownership. During the pat-down search, Thomas said, "You might as well get [my] dope," and indicated that he had methamphetamine in his left front pants pocket. The deputy reached into Thomas' pocket and pulled out a bag containing smaller baggies filled with white rocks. Thomas was then placed under arrest.

At the sheriff's office, [Thomas] admitted ownership of the methamphetamine lab in his house and the drugs found on his person. Thomas told the officers that he learned how to make methamphetamine in prison. He indicated that this was his first attempt at manufacturing methamphetamine and that, sometime before the deputies' arrival at his house, the lab had blown up. . . .

The district court implicitly denied Thomas' motions to suppress, finding Thomas guilty of unlawfully manufacturing a controlled substance, illegal possession of pseudoephedrine, and possession of methamphetamine with intent to sell. . . . The district court found, inter alia, that the deputies intended to wait until Prouse came out of the residence to arrest him. The court also found that the deputies had probable cause to believe that Prouse was the person who came out of the house during the surveillance, that the deputies were in "hot pursuit" of Prouse, and that "exigent circumstances allowed them to enter the house without a warrant." The district court concluded that Thomas' constitutional rights were not violated when the deputies chased Prouse into Thomas' home. . . .

Thomas argues that the arrest warrant upon which the deputies based their chase of Prouse did not authorize their entry without a search warrant into the home of a third party. Further, Thomas contends there were no exigent circumstances to support the entry. . . .

The Fourth Amendment prohibits law enforcement officers from making a warrantless and nonconsensual entry into a home in order to make a routine felony arrest absent exigent circumstances. Payton v. New York, 445 U.S. 573 (1980). The majority in *Payton* noted it was a basic principle of Fourth Amendment law that searches and seizures inside a home without a warrant are "presumptively unreasonable," while "objects . . . found in a public place may be seized by the police without a warrant." The Court concluded that "this distinction has equal force when the seizure of a person is involved" because "an entry to arrest and an entry to search for and to seize property implicate the same interest in preserving the privacy and the sanctity of the home, and justify the same level of constitutional protection." Thus, the Court concluded: "In terms that apply equally to seizures of property and to seizures of persons, the Fourth Amendment has drawn a firm line at the entrance to the house. Absent exigent circumstances, that threshold may not reasonably be crossed without a warrant." . . .

ARREST WARRANT AUTHORIZES ENTRY INTO SUSPECT'S HOME

However, in *Payton* the United States Supreme Court recognized that a search warrant was not constitutionally required if the entry was made into a home where one who was the subject of a felony arrest warrant resided if there was probable cause to believe the subject was present in the home. The Court stated:

> It is true that an arrest warrant requirement may afford less protection than a search warrant requirement, but it will suffice to interpose the magistrate's determination of probable cause between the zealous officer and the citizen. If there is sufficient evidence of a citizen's participation in a felony to persuade a judicial officer that his arrest is justified, it is constitutionally reasonable to require him to open his doors to the officers of the law. Thus, for Fourth Amendment purposes, an arrest warrant founded on probable cause implicitly carries with it the limited authority to enter a dwelling in which the suspect lives when there is reason to believe the suspect is within.

Thus, had the officers followed Prouse into a house in which he resided in order to serve the warrant, the entry would have been constitutional. . . . In the present case, however, there is nothing in the record to indicate that the officers believed Prouse owned or resided at the house.

THIRD PARTY'S HOUSE

An arrest warrant, standing alone, is not a sufficient basis to enter the home of a third party. The United States Supreme Court reached this holding in Steagald v. United States, 451 U.S. 204 (1981). In *Steagald*, a confidential informant contacted an agent of the Drug Enforcement Administration, suggesting he might be able to locate Ricky Lyons, a federal fugitive wanted on drug charges. Agents found the address where they thought Lyons was located and, 2 days later, drove to the residence. Gary Steagald and Hoyt Gaultney stood outside of the house. After the agents frisked the two men and discovered that neither man was Lyons, they went to the front door. Gaultney's wife answered the door and told the agents she was alone. The agents proceeded, without consent, into the house and searched for Lyons. Although they did not find Lyons, the agents found cocaine. They subsequently obtained a search warrant, and ultimately found 43 pounds of cocaine. Steagald was arrested on federal drug charges.

The Supreme Court stated that the agents had neither consent nor exigent circumstances when they made their initial, warrantless search. The Court phrased its narrow issue for consideration as "whether an arrest warrant — as opposed to a search warrant — is adequate to protect the Fourth Amendment interests of persons not named in the warrant, when their homes are searched without their consent and in the absence of exigent circumstances." The *Steagald* Court recognized that different interests are protected by arrest warrants and search warrants. Arrest warrants protect individuals from unreasonable seizures; search warrants protect against the unjustified intrusion of police into one's home. The Court found that the agents wrongly relied on Lyon's arrest warrant to give them the legal authority to enter into a third person's home. Thus, the third person's privacy interests were left unprotected.

The *Steagald* Court feared that allowing officers, without consent or exigent circumstances, to enter into a third party's residence to search for the subject of an arrest warrant would create a significant potential for abuse and pointed out that officers would then be able to use arrest warrants as a pretext for entering the residences of a suspect's friends and acquaintances or as a pretext for entering residences in which police have mere suspicion, not probable cause, that illegal activity is being committed. The Court held that, under the facts of the case, the warrantless search was unconstitutional.

However, the United States Supreme Court was careful to exempt two circumstances from its holding: consent and exigent circumstances. In this case, the State does not allege there was consent. Rather, the State relies upon exigent circumstances. . . .

EXIGENT CIRCUMSTANCES

The Court of Appeals, in holding that the deputies' conduct was justified by exigent circumstances, found that the present case is similar to United States v. Santana, 427 U.S. 38 (1976). Dominga Santana stood in the doorway of her own house when officers arrived to arrest her. When she saw the police, the defendant went inside the vestibule of the house. The officers followed the defendant inside and arrested her.

Santana filed a motion to suppress the incriminating evidence found during and after her arrest. The federal district court granted Santana's motion, [but the Supreme Court] disagreed with the lower court and determined that Santana's pursuit originated in a public place. Further, "the fact that the pursuit here ended almost as soon as it began did not render it any the less a [hot pursuit] sufficient to justify the warrantless entry into Santana's house." As for the police officers' entry into the defendant's house, the Court concluded: "A suspect may not defeat an arrest which has been set in motion in a public place . . . by the expedient of escaping into a private place."

Santana addressed a situation involving police entry into the suspect's house. The current set of facts involves the warrantless entry of police into a third party's house while trying to apprehend a suspect on an arrest warrant. [The *Steagald* Court discussed] the historical basis for the "hot pursuit doctrine," [and] concluded that English common-law "suggests that forcible entry into a third party's house was permissible only when the person to be arrested was pursued to the house." Later in the decision, the Court dismissed the government's argument that practical problems would arise if law enforcement were required to obtain a search warrant before entering the home of a third party. The Court noted these practical problems were largely ameliorated because "the situations in which a search warrant will be necessary are few." As examples, the Court noted that (1) "an arrest warrant alone will suffice to enter a suspect's own residence"; (2) "if probable cause exists, no warrant is required to apprehend a suspected felon in a public place"; (3) "the subject of an arrest warrant can be readily seized before entering or after leaving the home of a third party"; and (4) under the exigent circumstances doctrine, "a warrantless entry of a home would be justified if the police were in [hot pursuit] of a fugitive." . . .

APPLICATION OF HOT PURSUIT DOCTRINE

Without specific discussion of the hot pursuit exception, Thomas contends there were no exigent circumstances and cites to the list of factors this court has recognized which may be considered in determining if exigent circumstances existed, including: (1) the gravity or violent nature of the offense with which the suspect is to be charged; (2) whether the suspect is reasonably believed to be armed; (3) a clear showing of probable cause; (4) strong reasons to believe that the suspect is in the premises; (5) a likelihood that the suspect will escape if not swiftly apprehended; and (6) the peaceful circumstances of entry. The possible destruction of evidence is also a factor which may be considered. Thomas, as the homeowner, contends that these six or seven factors were not met; therefore, the officers violated his constitutional rights.

Although his argument is unclear, it appears that Thomas seeks a factor-by-factor analysis. Prior cases have not required such a review. [In] Warden v. Hayden, 387 U.S. 294, 299 (1967), the Supreme Court noted the search was "necessary to prevent the dangers that the suspect at large in the house may resist or escape." The United States Supreme Court has recognized that hot pursuit alone justifies a warrantless intrusion into a home. This court has also recognized that hot pursuit is one example of an exigent circumstance. . . .

Here, the deputies had an arrest warrant for Prouse, began surveillance of the house where they reasonably believed he could be found, and then spotted Prouse as he first exited and then reentered the house. The district court found that the deputies initially intended to wait for Prouse and to arrest him outside. There is no evidence, or assertion by Thomas, that the deputies used the arrest warrant as a pretext for entering Thomas' house or for searching it for incriminating evidence.

The district court found the doctrine of hot pursuit applied and also found it was impractical to expect the officers to obtain a warrant once Prouse took refuge in Thomas' house. The district court expressed doubt that a search warrant could have been obtained quickly at 2 o'clock in the morning. Unquestionably, if the officers had sought a search warrant, there was a high possibility that the fugitive named in the arrest warrant would escape apprehension. Indeed, requiring such police conduct would negate the essence of the hot pursuit doctrine. . . .

Furthermore, certain facts in this particular case are important to a conclusion that the officers were justified in making a warrantless entry into a third-party residence. The initial entry and search was limited to the apprehension of Prouse, the suspect named in the arrest warrant. Thomas does not contest the officers' quick protective sweep of the home once they discovered that Prouse was not alone. There is no indication that the deputies dug into drawers or looked into places where the suspect obviously could not hide.

In addition, the evidence pertaining to the methamphetamine lab was in plain view as the deputies pursued Prouse and made a protective sweep of the residence. It is clear that any evidence seized in plain view must be located in places lawfully accessible to officers. The strong smell of anhydrous ammonia was prevalent throughout the house, and various items consistent with the manufacture of methamphetamine sat in plain view in the kitchen area. . . . The Court of Appeals' decision affirming the district court's denial of Thomas' motion to suppress evidence based upon the alleged unauthorized entry into a third-party residence is affirmed.

Problem 5-1. Indoor-Outdoor Arrest

Officer Roy Gows of the Boston Police Department responded to the hospital emergency room to investigate the report of a rape. The victim of the alleged rape told Gows that she had been living in an apartment with Antonio Molina for six weeks. She said that Molina had raped her at knifepoint the previous night in the apartment, using a very large knife drawn from a brown sheath. The witness then gave Officer Gows the address of the apartment. Gows returned to the police station to consult with other officers about the case. Then, along with Detective Martin Nee, Gows proceeded to Molina's apartment to make an arrest.

When they arrived at the apartment, Officer Gows knocked on the front door. People had begun to gather outside the house when Molina opened the door. He fit the physical description provided by the victim and, when asked, identified himself as Molina. Detective Nee and Officer Gows stepped into the living room, which is accessible directly from the front door, and Detective Nee handcuffed Molina while saying that he was under arrest. At that point, a young woman who was also standing in the living room became very angry and began screaming at the officers. Concerned that she might have access to Molina's handgun that was sitting on a table in the living room, Detective Nee moved Molina 10 feet through an adjacent doorway into the kitchen while instructing Officer Gows to deal with the young woman.

Detective Nee informed Molina that the complainant had accused him of rape. While in the kitchen, Nee noticed a two-foot-long knife on the counter. The officers then told Molina that he would be spending the night at the station, and asked if he wanted to retrieve a sweater to wear over his muscle shirt. He agreed, and led the officers to his third-floor bedroom. While in the bedroom, the officers saw a brown knife sheath.

Before his trial for rape, Molina filed a motion to suppress the knife and the sheath as evidence. Will the trial court grant the motion? Cf. Commonwealth v. Molina, 786 N.E.2d 1191 (Mass. 2003).

Notes

1. *Warrants for arrests in a home: majority position.* The federal constitution allows a police officer to make an arrest in a public place without a warrant. When the arrest takes place in a home, however, warrants become more important. As the *Thomas* decision from Kansas explained, the federal constitution requires only an arrest warrant to justify entry into a suspect's home to carry out the arrest, along with some "reason to believe" the suspect is within. Payton v. New York, 445 U.S. 573 (1980); Kirk v. Louisiana, 536 U.S. 635 (2002) (reaffirms *Payton*). This is often the first place a police officer will look when trying to execute an arrest warrant. When an officer enters a third party's home to arrest a suspect, he must have a search warrant, based on probable cause to believe that the suspect (the object of the search) is present in that location. Virtually all state courts have used this same framework under their state constitutions. See State v. Chippero, 987 A.2d 555 (N.J. 2009).

In what ways are arrest warrants different from search warrants? Do separate requirements for search warrants and arrest warrants accomplish anything meaningful for suspects? For nonsuspects?

2. *Warrantless arrests in public places.* The U.S. Constitution does not require warrants for arrests made in a public place, even if the arresting officer could easily have obtained a warrant. In United States v. Watson, 423 U.S. 411 (1976), the Court upheld statutes and regulations granting Postal Service officers the power to make warrantless arrests for felonies. The Court deferred to Congress's judgment about

the meaning of the Fourth Amendment and also relied on "the ancient common-law rule that a peace officer was permitted to arrest without a warrant for a misdemeanor or felony committed in his presence as well as for a felony not committed in his presence if there was reasonable ground for making the arrest," noting that the common law rule had prevailed under state and federal law. See N.D. Cent. Code §29-06-15 (allowing warrantless arrests for misdemeanors only when they are committed in the presence of the arresting officer; exceptions for traffic offenses and domestic violence assaults).

3. *Is crime seriousness a basis for exigency?* In Welsh v. Wisconsin, 466 U.S. 740 (1984), the Supreme Court considered the validity of a night entry of a person's home to arrest him for a nonjailable traffic offense. The Court held that no exigent circumstances could support the arrest in Welsh's home, particularly "when the underlying offense for which there is probable cause to arrest is relatively minor." See also State v. Kiper, 532 N.W.2d 698 (Wis. 1995) (executing arrest warrant for failure to pay fine for allowing minor to drive; no exigent circumstances). Why should exigent circumstances for entering homes vary based on the seriousness of the alleged crime committed? For a sense of the interaction among arrest warrants, search warrants, and the exigent circumstances doctrine, consult the web extension for this chapter at *http://www.crimpro.com/extension/ch05*.

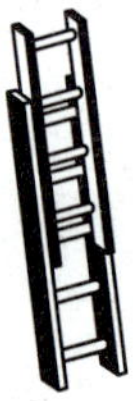

C. POLICE DISCRETION IN THE ARREST DECISION

Police officers remain the critical decisionmakers for arrests. This section considers recent legal reforms that could have contradictory effects on police discretion in arrests. First, statutes have expanded the power of the police to arrest a person without adhering to traditional common law and statutory requirements that the police obtain an arrest warrant in some contexts. In most states, these reforms have eliminated the need for an arrest warrant in most settings. Second, while police officers generally have discretion to decide whether to arrest, statutes and police department rules in special areas now guide the officers in their arrest decisions once there is probable cause to believe that the person has committed a crime. Prominent examples of both of these trends — one expanding the officer's discretion to arrest and the other restricting it — appear in cases involving domestic violence. We begin with the traditional common law rule, which requires a warrant to arrest a person for lesser crimes committed outside the officer's presence.

■ WILLIAM BLACKSTONE, COMMENTARIES ON THE LAWS OF ENGLAND

Vol. 4, p. 287 (1769)

A warrant may be granted . . . ordinarily by justices of the peace. This they may do in any cases where they have a jurisdiction over the offence [and] this extends undoubtedly to all treasons, felonies, and breaches of the peace; and also to all such offences as they have power to punish by statute. [The constable] may, without warrant, arrest any one for a breach of the peace, committed in his view, and carry him before a justice of the peace. And, in case of felony actually committed, or a dangerous wounding whereby felony is likely to ensue, he may upon probable suspicion arrest the felon.

OKLAHOMA STATUTES TIT. 22, §40.3

A. A peace officer shall not discourage a victim of rape, forcible sodomy or domestic abuse from pressing charges against the assailant of the victim.

B. A peace officer may arrest without a warrant a person anywhere, including his place of residence, if the peace officer has probable cause to believe the person within the preceding seventy-two hours has committed an act of domestic abuse . . . although the assault did not take place in the presence of the peace officer. A peace officer may not arrest a person pursuant to this section without first observing a recent physical injury to, or an impairment of the physical condition of, the alleged victim. . . .

CONNECTICUT GENERAL STATUTES §46b-38b

(a) Whenever a peace officer determines upon speedy information that a family violence crime . . . has been committed within his jurisdiction, he shall arrest the person or persons suspected of its commission and charge such person or persons with the appropriate crime. The decision to arrest and charge shall not (1) be dependent on the specific consent of the victim, (2) consider the relationship of the parties or (3) be based solely on a request by the victim.

(b) No peace officer investigating an incident of family violence shall threaten, suggest or otherwise indicate the arrest of all parties for the purpose of discouraging requests for law enforcement intervention by any party. Where complaints are received from two or more opposing parties, the officer shall evaluate each complaint separately to determine whether he should seek a warrant for an arrest.

IOWA CODE §236.12

1. If a peace officer has reason to believe that domestic abuse has occurred, the officer shall use all reasonable means to prevent further abuse including but not limited to the following:

a. If requested, remaining on the scene as long as there is a danger to an abused person's physical safety without the presence of a peace officer, [or] assisting the person in leaving the residence.

b. Assisting an abused person in obtaining medical treatment necessitated by an assault. . . .

c. Providing an abused person with immediate and adequate notice of the person's rights. The notice shall consist of handing the person a copy of the following statement written in English and Spanish, asking the person to read the card and whether the person understands the rights:

> You have the right to ask the court for the following help on a temporary basis:
>
> (1) Keeping your attacker away from you, your home and your place of work.
>
> (2) The right to stay at your home without interference from your attacker.
>
> (3) Getting custody of children and obtaining support for yourself and your minor children if your attacker is legally required to provide such support.
>
> (4) Professional counseling for you, the children who are members of the household, and the defendant.
>
> You have the right to seek help from the court to seek a protective order with or without the assistance of legal representation. . . .
>
> You have the right to file criminal charges for threats, assaults, or other related crimes. You have the right to seek restitution against your attacker for harm to yourself or your property.
>
> If you are in need of medical treatment, you have the right to request that the officer present assist you in obtaining transportation to the nearest hospital or otherwise assist you.
>
> If you believe that police protection is needed for your physical safety, you have the right to request that the officer present remain at the scene until you and other affected parties can leave or until safety is otherwise ensured.

The notice shall also contain the telephone numbers of safe shelters, support groups, or crisis lines operating in the area.

2. a. A peace officer may, with or without a warrant, arrest a person . . . if, upon investigation, . . . the officer has probable cause to believe that a domestic abuse assault has been committed which did not result in any injury to the alleged victim.

b. Except as otherwise provided in subsection 3, a peace officer shall, with or without a warrant, arrest a person [if] the officer has probable cause to believe that a domestic abuse assault has been committed which resulted in the alleged victim's suffering a bodily injury.

c. Except as otherwise provided in subsection 3, a peace officer shall, with or without a warrant, arrest a person [if] the officer has probable cause to believe that a domestic abuse assault has been committed with the intent to inflict a serious injury.

d. Except as otherwise provided in subsection 3, a peace officer shall, with or without a warrant, arrest a person [if] the officer has probable cause to believe that a domestic abuse assault has been committed and that the alleged abuser used or displayed a dangerous weapon in connection with the assault.

3. As described in subsection 2, paragraph "b," "c," or "d," the peace officer shall arrest the person whom the peace officer believes to be the primary physical aggressor. . . . Persons acting with justification . . . are not subject to mandatory arrest. In identifying the primary physical aggressor, a peace officer shall consider the need to protect victims of domestic abuse, the relative degree of injury or fear inflicted on the persons involved, and any history of domestic abuse between the persons involved. A peace officer's identification of the primary physical aggressor shall not be based on the consent of the victim to any subsequent prosecution or on the relationship of the persons involved in the incident, and shall not be based solely upon the absence of visible indications of injury or impairment.

LAWRENCE SHERMAN AND RICHARD BERK, THE MINNEAPOLIS DOMESTIC VIOLENCE EXPERIMENT
(1984)

[The] Minneapolis domestic violence experiment was the first scientifically controlled test of the effects of arrest for any crime. It found that arrest was the most effective of three standard methods police use to reduce domestic violence. The other police methods — attempting to counsel both parties or sending assailants away from home for several hours — were found to be considerably less effective in deterring future violence in the cases examined. [The] preponderance of evidence in the Minneapolis study strongly suggests that the police should use arrest in most domestic violence cases. . . .

Policing Domestic Assaults

Police have typically been reluctant to make arrests for domestic violence, as well as for a wide range of other kinds of offenses, unless a victim demands an arrest, a suspect insults an officer, or other factors are present. [Two surveys] of battered women who tried to have their domestic assailants arrested report that arrest occurred in only ten percent [and] three percent of the cases. Surveys of police agencies in Illinois and New York found explicit policies against arrest in the majority of the agencies surveyed. Despite the fact that violence is reported to be present in one-third to two-thirds of all domestic disturbances police respond to, police department data show arrests in only five percent of those disturbances in Oakland, . . . and six percent in Los Angeles County. . . .

The apparent preference of many police for separating the parties rather than arresting the offender has been attacked from two directions over the past 15 years. The original critique came from clinical psychologists who agreed that police should rarely make arrests in domestic assault cases and argued that police should mediate the disputes responsible for the violence. A highly publicized demonstration project teaching police special counseling skills for family crisis intervention failed to show a reduction in violence, but was interpreted as a success nonetheless. By 1977, a national survey of police agencies with 100 or more officers found that over 70 percent reported a family crisis intervention training program in operation. Although it is not clear whether these programs reduced separation and increased mediation, a decline in arrests was noted for some. Indeed, many sought explicitly to *reduce* the number of arrests.

By the mid 1970's, police practices were criticized from the opposite direction by feminist groups. Just as psychologists succeeded in having many police agencies respond to domestic violence as "half social work and half police work," feminists began to argue that police put "too much emphasis on the social work aspect and not enough on the criminal." Widely publicized lawsuits in New York and Oakland sought to compel police to make arrests in every case of domestic assault, and state legislatures were lobbied successfully to reduce the evidentiary requirements needed for police to make arrests for misdemeanor domestic assaults. Some legislatures are now considering statutes requiring police to make arrests in these cases.

The feminist critique was bolstered by a study showing that for 85 percent of a sample of spouse killings, police had intervened at least once in the preceding two years. For 54 percent of those homicides, police had intervened five or more times. But it was impossible to determine from the data whether making more or fewer arrests would have reduced the homicide rate.

How the Experiment Was Designed

[To] find which police approach was most effective in deterring future domestic violence, . . . the Minneapolis Police Department agreed to conduct a classic experiment. A classic experiment is a research design that allows scientists to discover the effects of one thing on another by holding constant all other possible causes of those effects. The design of the experiment called for a lottery selection, which ensured that there would be no difference among the three groups of suspects receiving the different police responses. The lottery determined which of the three responses police officers would use on each suspect in a domestic assault case. According to the lottery, a suspect would be arrested, or sent from the scene of the assault for eight hours, or given some form of advice, which could include mediation at an offender's discretion. In the language of the experiment, these responses were called the arrest, send, and advice treatments. The design called for a six-month follow-up period to measure the frequency and seriousness of any future domestic violence in all cases in which the police intervened.

The design applied only to simple (misdemeanor) domestic assaults, where both the suspect and the victim were present when the police arrived. Thus, the experiment included only those cases in which police were empowered, but not required, to make arrests under a recently liberalized Minnesota state law. The police officer must have probable cause to believe that a cohabitant or spouse had assaulted the victim within the past four hours. Police need not have witnessed the assault. Cases of life-threatening or severe injury, usually labeled as a felony (aggravated assault), were excluded from the design.

The design called for each officer to carry a pad of report forms, color coded for the three different police responses. Each time the officers encountered a situation that fit the experiment's criteria, they were to take whatever action was indicated by the report form on the top of the pad. The forms were numbered and arranged for each officer in an order determined by the lottery. . . .

Anticipating something of the background of the victims in the experiment, a predominantly minority, female research staff was employed to contact the victims for a detailed, face-to-face interview, to be followed by telephone follow-up interviews every two weeks for 24 weeks. The interviews were designed primarily to measure the frequency and seriousness of victimizations caused by a suspect after police interventions. The research staff also collected criminal justice reports that mentioned suspects' names during the six-month follow-up period.

Conduct of the Experiment

As is common in field experiments, the actual process in Minneapolis suffered some slippage from the original plan. [The experiment ran from March 17, 1981] until August 1, 1982, and produced 314 case reports. . . . Ninety-nine percent of the suspects targeted for arrest actually were arrested; 78 percent of those scheduled to receive advice did; and 73 percent of those to be sent out of the residence for eight hours actually were sent. One explanation for this pattern . . . is that mediating and sending were more difficult ways for police to control a situation. There was a greater likelihood that an officer might have to resort to arrest as a fallback position. . . .

RESULTS

[Two] measures of repeat violence were used in the experiment. One was a police record of an offender repeating domestic violence during the six-month follow-up period. . . . A second kind of measure came from the interviews in which victims were asked if there had been a repeat incident with the same suspect, broadly defined to include an assault, threatened assault, or property damage. . . .

Figure 1 shows the results taken from the police records on subsequent violence. The arrest treatment is clearly an improvement over sending the suspect away, which produced two and a half times as many repeat incidents as arrest. The advice treatment was statistically not distinguishable from the other two police actions.

Figure 2 shows a somewhat different picture. According to the victims' reports of repeat violence, arrest is still the most effective police action. But the advise category, not sending the suspect away, produced the worst results, with almost twice as much violence as arrest. Sending the suspect away produced results that were not statistically distinguishable from the results of the other two actions. It is not clear why the order of the three levels of repeat violence is different for these two ways of measuring the violence. But it is clear that arrest works best by either measure.

Additional statistical analysis showed that these findings were basically the same for all categories of suspects. Regardless of the race, employment status, educational level, criminal history of the suspect, or how long the suspect was in jail when arrested, arrest still had the strongest violence reduction effect. There was one factor, however, that seemed to govern the effectiveness of arrest: whether the police showed interest in the victim's side of the story.

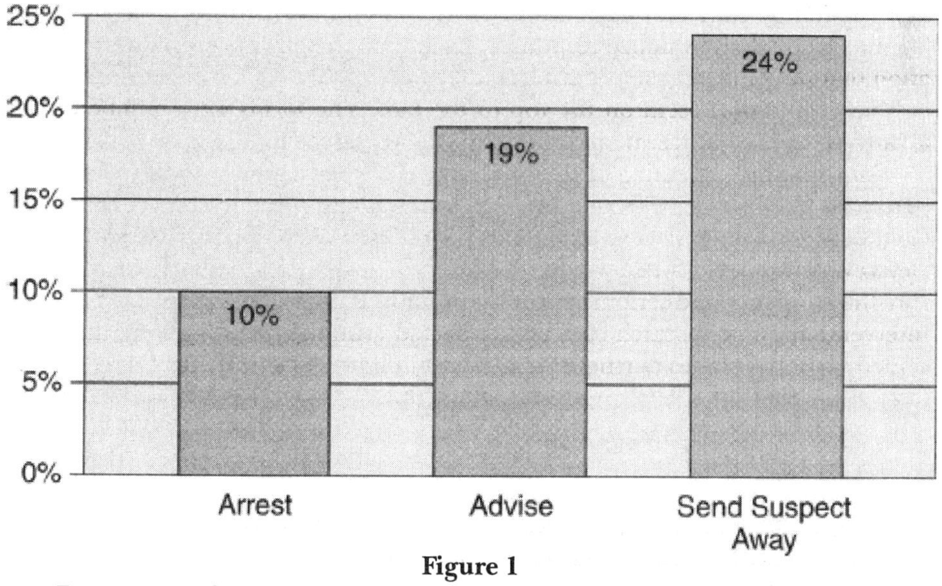

Figure 1
Percentage of Repeat Violence over Six Months for Each Police Action (Office Records N = 314)

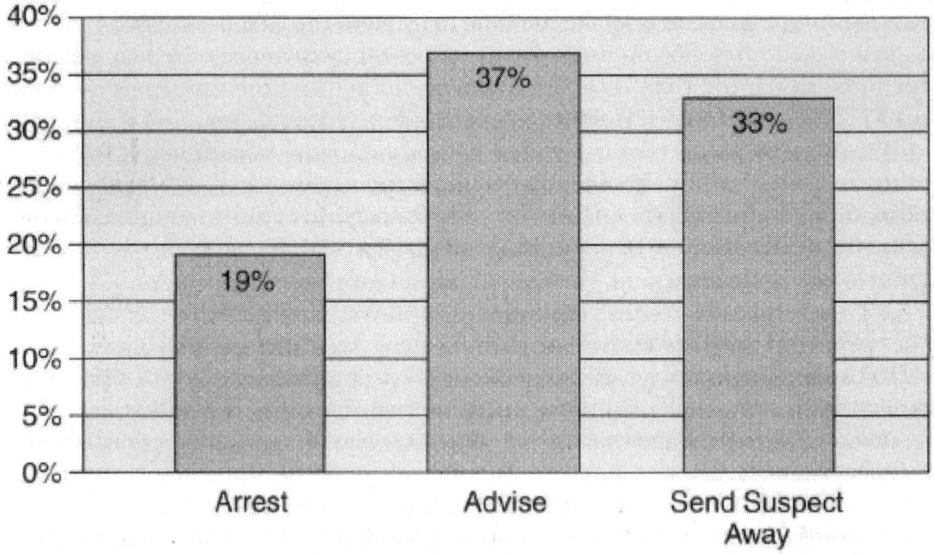

Figure 2
Percentage of Repeat Violence over Six Months for Each Police Action (Victim Interviews N = 161)

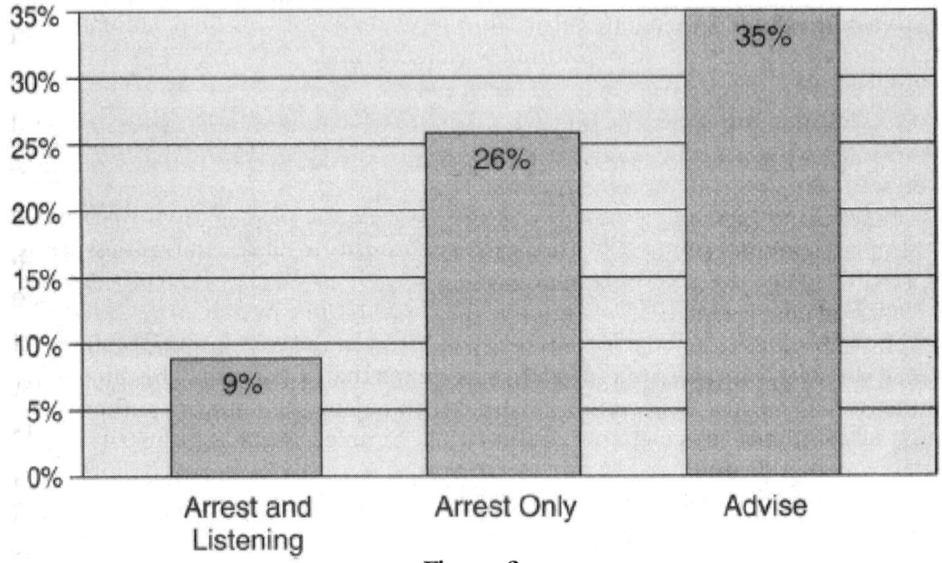

Figure 3
Percentage of Repeat Violence over Six Months for Each Police Action and Listening to Victim (Victim Interviews N = 194)

Figure 3 shows what happens to the effect of arrest on repeat violence incidents when the police do or do not take the time to listen to the victim, at least as the victim perceives it. If police do listen, that reduces the occurrence of repeat violence even more. But if the victims think the police did not take the time to listen, then the level of victim-reported violence is much higher. One interpretation of this finding is that by listening to the victim, the police "empower" her with their strength, letting the suspect know that she can influence their behavior. If police ignore the victim, the suspect may think he was arrested for arbitrary reasons unrelated to the victim and be less deterred from future violence.

Conclusions and Policy Implications

It may be premature to conclude that arrest is always the best way for police to handle domestic violence, or that all suspects in such situations should be arrested. A number of factors suggest a cautious interpretation of the findings, [such as the small sample size, the fact that most arrested suspects in Minneapolis spent the night in jail, and biases in the interview and follow-up process].

But police officers cannot wait for further research to decide how to handle the domestic violence they face each day. They must use the best information available. This experiment provides the only scientifically controlled comparison of different methods of reducing repeat violence. And on the basis of this study alone, police should probably employ arrest in most cases of minor domestic violence. . . .

As a result of the experiment's findings, the Minneapolis Police Department changed its policy on domestic assault in early March of 1984. The policy did not make arrest 100 percent mandatory. But it did require officers to file a written report explaining why they failed to make an arrest when it was legally possible to do so. . . . If the findings are truly generalizeable, the experiment will help ultimately to reduce one of the most common forms of violent crime.

Notes

1. *Common law arrest powers and domestic abuse.* As the passage from Blackstone indicates, officers at common law did not have authority to make a warrantless arrest of a person who committed a misdemeanor out of the presence of the officer, even if the officer had probable cause to believe that the person had committed the crime. This common law limitation often survived in the case law and statutes of states and is still the law in a few locations (fewer than 10 states). This limitation makes it difficult for police officers, without some special statutory authority, to make arrests in the typical domestic abuse call. "Simple assault" is ordinarily classified as a misdemeanor.

2. *The variety of legislative solutions.* Many statutes, like those reprinted above, expand the authority of the officer to arrest an assailant in a domestic abuse setting. Note the different limits that states (for instance, Oklahoma and Connecticut) place on this expanded arrest power. Why do the statutes address the time elapsed between the injury and the arrival of the police? See N.H. Stat. §594:10 (authority to arrest without warrant for misdemeanor domestic abuse occurring within six hours of arrest). Why do some require evidence of a physical injury? See 18 Pa. Cons. Stat. §2711; W. Va. Code §48-27-1002 (listing examples of "credible corroborative

evidence," such as contusions, missing hair, torn clothing, damaged furnishings on premises).

In addition to expanding police authority to arrest in the domestic abuse setting, some of the statutes encourage or require officers to respond in ways other than arresting the assailant. For instance, about a dozen states require the officer on the scene to provide the victim with information about health care and legal protection from further abuse. Why do some statutes call for an automatic warning, such as the one set forth in the Iowa statute? It is also common for statutes to require the officer responding to the call to report the incident to the prosecutor's office, regardless of the arrest decision.

Finally, more than a dozen states have passed statutes encouraging or mandating arrest as the proper police response to evidence of domestic violence. Is the Iowa statute an example of a mandatory statute? While a few statutes only require probable cause that a domestic violence offense has occurred, other statutes impose a number of different preconditions on the mandatory arrest duty of the police. See Utah Code Ann. §77-36-2.2 ("shall arrest" if there is evidence of recent serious injury, or use of dangerous weapon, or probable cause to believe there is potential of continued violence toward victim); Mo. Rev. Stat. §455.085 ("shall" arrest for second incident within 12 hours). Why does Iowa direct a police officer to arrest the person the officer believes to be the "primary physical aggressor," and how does the statute define that term?

The statutes reprinted here do not exhaust the legislative responses to this problem. Other relevant approaches include a Florida statute directing state agencies to collect detailed annual statistics about the enforcement of that state's domestic violence arrest policy and subsequent incidents of violence. See Fla. Stat. §943.1702. Some statutes emphasize training of officers that stresses the criminal nature of domestic abuse rather than the "social work" approach to the problem. Idaho Code §6316.

As the Sherman and Berk study demonstrates, local ordinances or police department policies might adopt a mandatory arrest policy, or a strong preference for arrests, even when state statutes do not. Indeed, almost 90 percent of all police departments have policies dealing with domestic violence. See Bureau of Justice Statistics, Local Police Departments 2003 (June 2006, NCJ 210118).

3. *Arrest statutes for other crimes.* For some other controversial offenses, statutes in many states provide for arrest powers that are broader than common law arrest doctrine would support. One common example is a statute that approves warrantless arrests whenever a driver violates the traffic code or commits related offenses such as driving under the influence. See N.D. Cent. Code §29-06-15(1)(f). These driving violation arrest statutes find additional authority in the quasi-contractual nature of the agreement between the citizen and the state represented by the driver's license: The citizen, it is argued, grants the state additional arrest powers if she exercises the option to drive.

4. *Arrest quotas.* Police department policies *other* than those calling for automatic or presumed arrests in some situations can have a powerful effect on individual officers' arrest decisions. How will officers respond to a departmental policy that evaluates and rewards officers based on the number of arrests they make? See Howie Carr, "Arresting Memo Puts State Cops in a Pinch," Boston Herald, Oct. 21, 1998, at 1 (quoting internal memorandum of Massachusetts State Police, reviewing arrest journal and calling for "corrective action" to "increase the level of activity" because

arrests are a "valid indicator" but not the only indicator of good performance). Is there a plausible legal basis for challenging a system of "arrest quotas" in court? Disputes over these policies more often arise during labor negotiations between police officer unions and department administrators.

5. *History and changes in legal rules.* Lawyers typically face questions about the application or validity of a *current* rule. Because they are not trained as historians and have limited time and resources, it can be difficult for lawyers to trace the evolution of policies and rules. One of the notable aspects of the Sherman and Berk policy paper is its effective use of recent history (the past 20 years) to build an argument for a particular policy position.

The story told by Sherman and Berk offers a telling reminder: Prior policies were passionately supported by smart and principled people, and those policies, too, were bolstered by varying amounts of research. This realization should serve as a warning against assuming that current policies are necessarily an improvement over earlier ones and that the current policy is the best possible policy — the end of the line. About the only thing that can be said with confidence about any policy in effect 10 to 20 years from now is that its proponents will view current policy — the current generation's views — as misguided and ineffective.

6. *The virtues of social science methods.* How persuasive is the bottom line in the analysis of the Minneapolis experiment? If you were the police chief in another city or a legislator in another state, would you change policy on the basis of this publication?

This policy brief, and the movement it captured, is a notable example of the possible influence of social science on criminal procedure. Many states and police departments adopted some version of an "automatic" arrest policy (although most are not truly mandatory arrest policies but strongly encourage such arrests). Despite the warnings about the need for further research, the Minneapolis study was central in promoting these policy changes.

7. *"More research is needed": an important caveat.* A series of replication experiments in six cities only partially confirmed the dramatic findings in Minneapolis. In three cities, the use of arrest actually *increased* later domestic violence. The use of arrest had more of a deterrent effect on suspects who were employed than on those who were unemployed. Arrest also had a positive effect in *neighborhoods* with high rates of employment, and negative effects in neighborhoods with low employment rates. See, e.g., Lawrence W. Sherman, The Police, in James Q. Wilson & Joan Petersilia, Eds., Crime 327, 336-38 (1995) (describing replication studies in Omaha, Charlotte, Milwaukee, Colorado Springs, Bade County). Criminologists remain interested in this topic and continue to generate new data and updated analyses. For references to this sociological literature and a discussion of its ongoing significance, go to the web extension for this chapter at *http://www.crimpro.com/extension/ch05*.

Despite the mixed outcomes of replication studies, policies favoring arrest in domestic assault situations generally have remained in force, and new policies encouraging arrest are still being adopted. Why hasn't the more recent research on domestic assaults and arrest policies produced more targeted policies (for instance, a policy calling for arrest only if the suspect is employed)? Is it easier for police chiefs, mayors, and legislators to apply the gas than the brakes?

Problem 5-2. Arrests and Curfews

The local police department is considering a rule that would require officers to take into custody every juvenile found outdoors after an established curfew hour. The department hopes the new rule will reduce the crime rate by and against juveniles. A recent study found that 40 percent of crimes after curfew are committed against juveniles and that an unknown but significant percentage of all crimes — especially property crimes — are also committed by juveniles.

How would you design a study to test whether the proposed arrest policy would reduce either crimes generally or the percentage of crimes against juveniles? How would you convince the local police department to participate in the study? Would you tell the media about the study?

Problem 5-3. Racial Patterns in Arrests

In the early 1980s, police officers in Georgia arrested more white suspects than black suspects for drug offenses. In a typical year, officers arrested about 10,000 white suspects and 5,000 to 7,000 black suspects. Beginning in the mid-1980s, law enforcement officials decided to increase their emphasis on enforcement of the narcotics laws. As a result, the number of white suspects arrested each year on drug charges increased slightly, while a much steeper increase occurred in arrests of black suspects. Between 1990 and 1995, black suspects accounted for about 119,000 drug arrests; white suspects accounted for about 58,000 arrests, less than a third of the total. The disparity was stronger for cocaine cases than for marijuana cases. About 85 percent of all cocaine arrestees were black, while just over 40 percent of the marijuana arrestees were black.

When these figures are adjusted for the number of blacks and whites in the general population of the state, the arrest rate for African Americans was more than 10,200 arrests (over the five-year period) for every 100,000 black residents of the state. The comparable rate for whites was about 1,600 arrests for every 100,000 white residents. Even for marijuana arrests, where the racial disparities were least pronounced, the adjusted rate of arrest for blacks was about 2,600 per 100,000, while the rate for whites was around 1,200 per 100,000. National surveys at the time suggested that a slightly larger proportion of blacks than whites used illicit drugs. These surveys showed that blacks used drugs at a rate about 20 percent higher than whites.

As a concerned high-ranking police official, how might you react to these developments? Officers in the department tell you that more blacks are arrested for drug trafficking because they tend to make more sales on street corners and other places visible to the public, while white users and sellers tend more often to conduct their operations indoors. Would it address the disparity problem to issue a departmental policy making arrest mandatory whenever a police officer develops probable cause that a narcotics offense has taken place, no matter how small?

Notes

1. *The competing (or complementary) explanations.* For most crimes that generate large numbers of arrests in this country, African Americans are arrested in numbers disproportionate to their percentage of the general population. The disproportion is usually much less dramatic than the numbers described above for drug arrests in Georgia. But the differences are present, nonetheless, for many crimes in many different places (but not for all crimes or places). How might one explain this persistent and discomfiting fact?

Some have postulated racial bias, whether conscious or unconscious, on the part of arresting police officers. See Coramae Richey Mann, Unequal Justice (1993). Consistent with this view, one study of the processing of arrests by prosecutors suggested that blacks were arrested on less stringent legal criteria than whites. John Hepburn, Race and the Decision to Arrest: An Analysis of Warrants Issued, 15 J. Res. Crime & Delinq. 54 (1978). Others conclude that blacks are arrested more often because they more often violate the criminal law. Alfred Blumstein, On the Racial Disproportionality of the United States' Prison Populations, 73 J. Crim. L. & Criminology 1259 (1982). Those who rely on this explanation point to surveys of victims regarding the race of the offenders in their cases (regardless of whether the police were ever involved or whether an arrest was ever made): The information from victims about the race of criminal perpetrators roughly corresponds to the racial makeup of arrestees.

Another line of explanation suggests, based on observations from field studies, that police officers are more likely to arrest suspects who are antagonistic toward them and that black suspects are more likely to meet this description. See Donald Black, The Social Organization of Arrest, 23 Stan. L. Rev. 1087 (1971). Still another group of researchers has argued that police arrest black suspects more frequently because black complainants (who are most often the victims of crimes by black perpetrators) request arrest more often than white complainants. See Richard Lundman, Richard Sykes & John Clark, Police Control of Juveniles: A Replication, 15 J. Res. Crime & Delinq. 74 (1978). Others suggest that blacks are more likely to encounter police officers in poorer neighborhoods and that police officers are more likely to use their discretion to arrest in such neighborhoods. Douglas Smith, Christy Visher & Laura Davidson, Equity and Discretionary Justice: The Influence of Race on Police Arrest Decisions, 75 J. Crim. L. & Criminology 234 (1984). Do these various explanations for racial disparity in arrest rates conflict with one another or are they reconcilable? Further studies of the interaction of race and arrest practices receive attention on the web extension for this chapter at *http://www.crimpro.com/extension/ch05*.

2. *The ethics of police experiments.* Does it trouble you that the Minneapolis police treated similar domestic assault cases differently in the same time period? Do the police have an obligation to apply one, consistent policy at any one time? The recommendation that police officers pursue an arrest policy, in Minneapolis and elsewhere, was not based on a prediction that more arrests would lead to more domestic assault prosecutions. Is there an ethical issue with police using arrest when they know there will not be a prosecution? Does arrest become a form of punishment without trial?

3. *Expungement of arrest records.* Arrests have consequences beyond the initial detention. An arrest record might influence police decisions months or years later about who to investigate, or prosecutorial decisions about whether to charge a person with a new crime. But what if the original arrest was unfounded? Many states provide for "expungement" of arrest records if they do not result in conviction. The state laws vary greatly as to the crimes where they apply (for instance, some make arrests for sex crimes ineligible for expungement). They use different events to judge which arrests were unsubstantiated and therefore subject to expungement: Some use acquittal only, while others include any dismissal without adjudication. Some of them are self-executing, while others depend on a formal request from the arrestee. Should expungement be available automatically (and immediately) whenever a case is dismissed without a prosecution? See Mich. Comp. Laws 28.243 (5); 20 ILCS 2630/5.

D. PAPER ARRESTS: CITATIONS

An arrest is not the only method available to initiate a criminal prosecution or to secure a defendant's presence at judicial proceedings. There are some circumstances when a police officer will issue a "citation" or "appearance ticket" to a person, requiring the person to appear in court regarding a crime the officer believes the person has committed. As in other areas of police officer discretion not to arrest, legal reforms in this field are moving in different directions. On the one hand, the range of offenses where the officer can use citation rather than arrest is expanding. On the other hand, in some limited circumstances the law restricts the officer to using a citation instead of an arrest.

■ NEW YORK CRIMINAL PROCEDURE LAW §§150.10, 150.20, 150.60

§150.10

An appearance ticket is a written notice issued and subscribed by a police officer or other public servant . . . , directing a designated person to appear in a designated local criminal court at a designated future time in connection with his alleged commission of a designated offense. . . .

§150.20

1. Whenever a police officer is authorized . . . to arrest a person without a warrant for an offense other than a class A, B, C or D felony, [the officer may] instead issue to and serve upon such person an appearance ticket.
2. (a) Whenever a police officer has arrested a person without a warrant for an offense other than a class A, B, C or D felony . . . such police officer may, instead of bringing such person before a local criminal court and promptly filing or causing the arresting peace officer or arresting person to file a local

criminal court accusatory instrument therewith, issue to and serve upon such person an appearance ticket. The issuance and service of an appearance ticket under such circumstances may be conditioned upon a deposit of pre-arraignment bail. . . .

§150.60

If after the service of an appearance ticket and the filing of a local criminal court accusatory instrument charging the offense designated therein, the defendant does not appear in the designated local criminal court at the time such appearance ticket is returnable, the court may issue a summons or a warrant of arrest based upon the local criminal court accusatory instrument filed.

Commission Staff Notes on Desk Appearance Ticket Provisions (1970 Comment)*

[An appearance ticket] is issued and served by a police officer or other public servant who has observed the commission of a minor offense, and it requires the offender to appear in a designated court upon a designated return date to answer a charge which the issuer of the ticket will formally file in the court some time after the issuance. In terms of basic function, an appearance ticket is used in some minor cases as a compassionate substitute for an arrest without a warrant, which is also employed to require or compel the court appearance of an offender against whom no formal charges have as yet been lodged.

On a state-wide basis, the use of appearance tickets is at present largely confined to traffic infraction cases. In New York City, however, numerous non-police public officials and employees, such as those of the Sanitation, Fire, Building and Markets Departments, are authorized to issue and serve such tickets in cases involving offenses peculiarly within their ambits. . . .

The theory of the proposed section is that under present law the virtues and advantages of the appearance ticket have not been sufficiently exploited. . . . The results to be expected from the new appearance ticket scheme are (1) an immense saving of police time, (2) elimination of much expense and embarrassment to defendants charged with minor offenses who are excellent risks to appear in court when required, and (3) above all, a significant reduction of that portion of our jail population consisting of unconvicted defendants awaiting trial or other disposition of their cases.

The advantages to the police may be partly appreciated by picturing the predicament of a police officer who observes the commission of a misdemeanor or petty offense by a person whom he either knows to be a resident of the community or whom he finds to have solid roots therein. Absent the appearance ticket device, two very awkward and unsatisfactory courses of action are available to the officer. Normal procedure requires him to arrest the defendant and, dropping his regular duties, take him to the station house to book him, and then to take him to a local criminal court where a formal information must be filed, the defendant arraigned, bail set, and so on. The even less appealing and equally time consuming alternative

* [This is considered the legislative history for these provisions. The following excerpts mix paragraphs from the report for different statutory sections. — Eds.]

entails the officer first going to the court himself, filing an information against the defendant, obtaining a summons or a warrant of arrest and then returning to find the defendant and serve or execute such process; and all this in a case in which the simple issuance of an appearance ticket would almost certainly accomplish the same end result.

■ REVISED STATUTES OF NEBRASKA §§29-435, 29-427

§29-435

Except as provided in section 29-427, for any offense classified as an infraction, a citation shall be issued in lieu of arrest or continued custody. . . .

§29-427

Any peace officer having grounds for making an arrest may take the accused into custody or, already having done so, detain him further when the accused fails to identify himself satisfactorily, or refuses to sign the citation, or when the officer has reasonable grounds to believe that (1) the accused will refuse to respond to the citation, (2) such custody is necessary to protect the accused or others when his continued liberty would constitute a risk of immediate harm, (3) such action is necessary in order to carry out legitimate investigative functions, (4) the accused has no ties to the jurisdiction reasonably sufficient to assure his appearance, or (5) the accused has previously failed to appear in response to a citation.

■ PATRICK KNOWLES v. IOWA

525 U.S. 113 (1998)

REHNQUIST, C.J.*

An Iowa police officer stopped petitioner Knowles for speeding, but issued him a citation rather than arresting him. The question presented is whether such a procedure authorizes the officer, consistently with the Fourth Amendment, to conduct a full search of the car. We answer this question "no."

Issue

Knowles was stopped in Newton, Iowa, after having been clocked driving 43 miles per hour on a road where the speed limit was 25 miles per hour. The police officer issued a citation to Knowles, although under Iowa law he might have arrested him. The officer then conducted a full search of the car, and under the driver's seat he found a bag of marijuana and a "pot pipe." Knowles was then arrested and charged with violation of state laws dealing with controlled substances.

Before trial, Knowles moved to suppress the evidence so obtained. He argued that the search could not be sustained under the "search incident to arrest" exception recognized in United States v. Robinson, 414 U.S. 218 (1973), because he had not been placed under arrest. At the hearing on the motion to suppress, the police officer conceded that he had neither Knowles' consent nor probable cause to conduct the search. He relied on Iowa law dealing with such searches.

* [All the Justices joined in this opinion. — EDS.]

Iowa Code Ann. §321.485(1) (a) provides that Iowa peace officers having cause to believe that a person has violated any traffic or motor vehicle equipment law may arrest the person and immediately take the person before a magistrate. Iowa law also authorizes the far more usual practice of issuing a citation in lieu of arrest or in lieu of continued custody after an initial arrest.[1] Section 805.1(4) provides that the issuance of a citation in lieu of an arrest "does not affect the officer's authority to conduct an otherwise lawful search." The Iowa Supreme Court has interpreted this provision as providing authority to officers to conduct a full-blown search of an automobile and driver in those cases where police elect not to make a custodial arrest and instead issue a citation — that is, a search incident to citation. See State v. Meyer, 543 N.W.2d 876, 879 (Iowa 1996). Based on this authority, the trial court denied the motion to suppress and found Knowles guilty. . . .

In *Robinson,* we noted the two historical rationales for the "search incident to arrest" exception: (1) the need to disarm the suspect in order to take him into custody, and (2) the need to preserve evidence for later use at trial. But neither of these underlying rationales for the search incident to arrest exception is sufficient to justify the search in the present case.

We have recognized that the first rationale — officer safety — is both legitimate and weighty. The threat to officer safety from issuing a traffic citation, however, is a good deal less than in the case of a custodial arrest. In *Robinson,* we stated that a custodial arrest involves "danger to an officer" because of "the extended exposure which follows the taking of a suspect into custody and transporting him to the police station." . . . A routine traffic stop, on the other hand, is a relatively brief encounter and is more analogous to a so-called *Terry* stop than to a formal arrest.

This is not to say that the concern for officer safety is absent in the case of a routine traffic stop. It plainly is not. But while the concern for officer safety in this context may justify the "minimal" additional intrusion of ordering a driver and passengers out of the car, it does not by itself justify the often considerably greater intrusion attending a full field-type search. Even without the search authority Iowa urges, officers have other, independent bases to search for weapons and protect themselves from danger. For example, they may order out of a vehicle both the driver, Pennsylvania v. Minims, 434 U.S. 106, 111 (1977) (per curiam), and any passengers, Maryland v. Wilson, 519 U.S. 408, 414 (1997); perform a "patdown" of a driver and any passengers upon reasonable suspicion that they may be armed and dangerous, Terry v. Ohio, 392 U.S. 1 (1968); conduct a "*Terry* patdown" of the passenger compartment of a vehicle upon reasonable suspicion that an occupant is dangerous and may gain immediate control of a weapon, Michigan v. Long, 463 U.S. 1032 (1983); and even conduct a full search of the passenger compartment, including any containers therein, pursuant to a custodial arrest, New York v. Belton, 453 U.S. 454, 460 (1981).

Nor has Iowa shown the second justification for the authority to search incident to arrest — the need to discover and preserve evidence. Once Knowles was stopped

1. Iowa law permits the issuance of a citation in lieu of arrest for most offenses for which an accused person would be "eligible for bail." See Iowa Code Ann. §805.1(1). In addition to traffic and motor vehicle equipment violations, this would permit the issuance of a citation in lieu of arrest for such serious felonies as second-degree burglary and first-degree theft, both bailable offenses under Iowa law. The practice in Iowa of permitting citation in lieu of arrest is consistent with law reform efforts. See 3 W LaFave, Search and Seizure §5.2(h), p. 99, and n.151 (3d ed. 1996).

for speeding and issued a citation, all the evidence necessary to prosecute that offense had been obtained. No further evidence of excessive speed was going to be found either on the person of the offender or in the passenger compartment of the car.

Iowa nevertheless argues that a "search incident to citation" is justified because a suspect who is subject to a routine traffic stop may attempt to hide or destroy evidence related to his identity (e.g., a driver's license or vehicle registration), or destroy evidence of another, as yet undetected crime. As for the destruction of evidence relating to identity, if a police officer is not satisfied with the identification furnished by the driver, this may be a basis for arresting him rather than merely issuing a citation. As for destroying evidence of other crimes, the possibility that an officer would stumble onto evidence wholly unrelated to the speeding offense seems remote.

In *Robinson,* we held that the authority to conduct a full field search as incident to an arrest was a "bright-line rule," which was based on the concern for officer safety and destruction or loss of evidence, but which did not depend in every case upon the existence of either concern. Here we are asked to extend that "bright-line rule" to a situation where the concern for officer safety is not present to the same extent and the concern for destruction or loss of evidence is not present at all. We decline to do so. . . .

■ GAIL ATWATER v. CITY OF LAGO VISTA

532 U.S. 318 (2001)

SOUTER, J.*

The question is whether the Fourth Amendment forbids a warrantless arrest for a minor criminal offense, such as a misdemeanor seatbelt violation punishable only by a fine. We hold that it does not.

I. . . .

In Texas, if a car is equipped with safety belts, a front-seat passenger must wear one, and the driver must secure any small child riding in front. Violation of either provision is a misdemeanor punishable by a fine not less than $25 or more than $50. Texas law expressly authorizes "any peace officer [to] arrest without warrant a person found committing a violation" of these seatbelt laws, Transp. Code §543.001, although it permits police to issue citations in lieu of arrest.

In March 1997, Petitioner Gail Atwater was driving her pickup truck in Lago Vista, Texas, with her 3-year-old son and 5-year-old daughter in the front seat. None of them was wearing a seatbelt. Respondent Bart Turek, a Lago Vista police officer at the time, observed the seatbelt violations and pulled Atwater over. According to Atwater's complaint (the allegations of which we assume to be true for present purposes), Turek approached the truck and "yelled" something to the effect of "we've

* [Chief Justice Rehnquist and Justices Scalia, Kennedy, and Thomas joined in this opinion. — EDS.]

met before" and "you're going to jail."[1] He then called for backup and asked to see Atwater's driver's license and insurance documentation, which state law required her to carry. When Atwater told Turek that she did not have the papers because her purse had been stolen the day before, Turek said that he had "heard that story two hundred times."

Atwater asked to take her frightened, upset, and crying children to a friend's house nearby, but Turek told her, "you're not going anywhere." As it turned out, Atwater's friend learned what was going on and soon arrived to take charge of the children. Turek then handcuffed Atwater, placed her in his squad car, and drove her to the local police station, where booking officers had her remove her shoes, jewelry, and eyeglasses, and empty her pockets. Officers took Atwater's "mug shot" and placed her, alone, in a jail cell for about one hour, after which she was taken before a magistrate and released on $310 bond.

Atwater was charged with driving without her seatbelt fastened, failing to secure her children in seatbelts, driving without a license, and failing to provide proof of insurance. She ultimately pleaded no contest to the misdemeanor seatbelt offenses and paid a $50 fine; the other charges were dismissed. Atwater and her husband, petitioner Michael Haas, filed suit in a Texas state court under 42 U.S.C. §1983, [alleging that the City] had violated Atwater's Fourth Amendment "right to be free from unreasonable seizure," and sought compensatory and punitive damages.

II.

[An] examination of the common-law understanding of an officer's authority to arrest sheds light on the obviously relevant, if not entirely dispositive, consideration of what the Framers of the Amendment might have thought to be reasonable. . . . Atwater's specific contention is that "founding-era common-law rules" forbade peace officers to make warrantless misdemeanor arrests except in cases of "breach of the peace," a category she claims was then understood narrowly as covering only those nonfelony offenses "involving or tending toward violence." Although her historical argument is by no means insubstantial, it ultimately fails.

A.

We [find that] the common-law commentators (as well as the sparsely reported cases) reached divergent conclusions with respect to officers' warrantless misdemeanor arrest power. . . .

On one side of the divide there are certainly eminent authorities supporting Atwater's position. . . . James Fitzjames Stephen and Glanville Williams both seemed to indicate that the common law confined warrantless misdemeanor arrests to actual breaches of the peace. See 1 J. Stephen, A History of the Criminal Law of England 193 (1883) ("The common law did not authorise the arrest of persons guilty or suspected of misdemeanours, except in cases of an actual breach of the peace either by an affray or by violence to an individual"); G. Williams, Arrest for Breach of the Peace, 1954 Crim. L. Rev. 578, 578 ("Apart from arrest for felony . . . , the only power of arrest at common law is in respect of breach of the peace"). . . .

1. Turek had previously stopped Atwater for what he had thought was a seatbelt violation, but had realized that Atwater's son, although seated on the vehicle's armrest, was in fact belted in. Atwater acknowledged that her son's seating position was unsafe, and Turek issued a verbal warning.

The great commentators were not unanimous, however, and there is also considerable evidence of a broader conception of common-law misdemeanor arrest authority unlimited by any breach-of-the-peace condition. Sir Matthew Hale, Chief Justice of King's Bench from 1671 to 1676, wrote in his History of the Pleas of the Crown that, by his "original and inherent power," a constable could arrest without a warrant "for breach of the peace and some misdemeanors, less than felony." 2 M. Hale, The History of the Pleas of the Crown 88 (1736). . . .

A second, and equally serious, problem for Atwater's historical argument is posed by the "divers Statutes," M. Dalton, Country Justice ch. 170, §4, p. 582 (1727), enacted by Parliament well before this Republic's founding that authorized warrantless misdemeanor arrests without reference to violence or turmoil. [T]he legal background of any conception of reasonableness the Fourth Amendment's Framers might have entertained would have included English statutes, some centuries old, authorizing peace officers (and even private persons) to make warrantless arrests for all sorts of relatively minor offenses unaccompanied by violence. The so-called "nightwalker" statutes are perhaps the most notable examples. From the enactment of the Statute of Winchester in 1285, through its various readoptions and until its repeal in 1827, night watchmen were authorized and charged "as . . . in Times past" to "watch the Town continually all Night, from the Sun-setting unto the Sun-rising" and were directed that "if any Stranger do pass by them, he shall be arrested until Morning. . . ."

B.

An examination of specifically American evidence is to the same effect. Neither the history of the framing era nor subsequent legal development indicates that the Fourth Amendment was originally understood, or has traditionally been read, to embrace Atwater's position. . . . During the period leading up to and surrounding the framing of the Bill of Rights, colonial and state legislatures, like Parliament before them, regularly authorized local peace officers to make warrantless misdemeanor arrests without conditioning statutory authority on breach of the peace. See, e.g., First Laws of the State of Connecticut 214-215 (authorizing warrantless arrests of "all Persons unnecessarily travelling on the Sabbath or Lord's Day"). . . .

Nor does Atwater's argument from tradition pick up any steam from the historical record as it has unfolded since the framing, there being no indication that her claimed rule has ever become woven into the fabric of American law. The story, on the contrary, is of two centuries of uninterrupted (and largely unchallenged) state and federal practice permitting warrantless arrests for misdemeanors not amounting to or involving breach of the peace.

[There are] numerous early- and mid-19th-century decisions expressly sustaining (often against constitutional challenge) state and local laws authorizing peace officers to make warrantless arrests for misdemeanors not involving any breach of the peace. See, e.g., Mayo v. Wilson, 1 N.H. 53 (1817) (upholding statute authorizing warrantless arrests of those unnecessarily traveling on Sunday against challenge based on state due process and search-and-seizure provisions). . . . Small wonder, then, that today statutes in all 50 States and the District of Columbia permit warrantless misdemeanor arrests by at least some (if not all) peace officers without requiring any breach of the peace, as do a host of congressional enactments. . . .

III.

[But] Atwater does not wager all on history. Instead, she asks us to mint a new rule of constitutional law on the understanding that when historical practice fails to speak conclusively to a claim grounded on the Fourth Amendment, courts are left to strike a current balance between individual and societal interests by subjecting particular contemporary circumstances to traditional standards of reasonableness. . . .

If we were to derive a rule exclusively to address the uncontested facts of this case, Atwater might well prevail. She was a known and established resident of Lago Vista with no place to hide and no incentive to flee, and common sense says she would almost certainly have buckled up as a condition of driving off with a citation. In her case, the physical incidents of arrest were merely gratuitous humiliations imposed by a police officer who was (at best) exercising extremely poor judgment. Atwater's claim to live free of pointless indignity and confinement clearly outweighs anything the City can raise against it specific to her case.

But we have traditionally recognized that a responsible Fourth Amendment balance is not well served by standards requiring sensitive, case-by-case determinations of government need, lest every discretionary judgment in the field be converted into an occasion for constitutional review. Often enough, the Fourth Amendment has to be applied on the spur (and in the heat) of the moment, and the object in implementing its command of reasonableness is to draw standards sufficiently clear and simple to be applied with a fair prospect of surviving judicial second-guessing months and years after an arrest or search is made. . . .

At first glance, Atwater's argument may seem to respect the values of clarity and simplicity, so far as she claims that the Fourth Amendment generally forbids warrantless arrests for minor crimes not accompanied by violence or some demonstrable threat of it (whether "minor crime" be defined as a fine-only traffic offense, a fine-only offense more generally, or a misdemeanor). But the claim is not ultimately so simple, nor could it be, for complications arise the moment we begin to think about the possible applications of the several criteria Atwater proposes for drawing a line between minor crimes with limited arrest authority and others not so restricted.

One line, she suggests, might be between "jailable" and "fine-only" offenses, between those for which conviction could result in commitment and those for which it could not. The trouble with this distinction, of course, is that an officer on the street might not be able to tell. It is not merely that we cannot expect every police officer to know the details of frequently complex penalty schemes, but that penalties for ostensibly identical conduct can vary on account of facts difficult (if not impossible) to know at the scene of an arrest. Is this the first offense or is the suspect a repeat offender? Is the weight of the marijuana a gram above or a gram below the fine-only line? Where conduct could implicate more than one criminal prohibition, which one will the district attorney ultimately decide to charge? And so on.

But Atwater's refinements would not end there. She represents that if the line were drawn at nonjailable traffic offenses, her proposed limitation should be qualified by a proviso authorizing warrantless arrests where "necessary for enforcement of the traffic laws or when [an] offense would otherwise continue and pose a danger to others on the road." . . . The proviso only compounds the difficulties.

Would, for instance, either exception apply to speeding? [Is] it not fair to expect that the chronic speeder will speed again despite a citation in his pocket, and should that not qualify as showing that the "offense would . . . continue" under Atwater's rule? . . . Atwater's rule therefore would not only place police in an almost impossible spot but would guarantee increased litigation over many of the arrests that would occur. . . .

An officer not quite sure that the drugs weighed enough to warrant jail time or not quite certain about a suspect's risk of flight would not arrest, even though it could perfectly well turn out that, in fact, the offense called for incarceration and the defendant was long gone on the day of trial. Multiplied many times over, the costs to society of such underenforcement could easily outweigh the costs to defendants of being needlessly arrested and booked. . . .

Just how easily the costs could outweigh the benefits may be shown by asking, as one Member of this Court did at oral argument, "how bad the problem is out there." The very fact that the law has never jelled the way Atwater would have it leads one to wonder whether warrantless misdemeanor arrests need constitutional attention, and there is cause to think the answer is no. [Anyone] arrested for a crime without formal process, whether for felony or misdemeanor, is entitled to a magistrate's review of probable cause within 48 hours. . . . Many jurisdictions, moreover, have chosen to impose more restrictive safeguards through statutes limiting warrantless arrests for minor offenses. [The Court cited statutes from eight states.] It is of course easier to devise a minor-offense limitation by statute than to derive one through the Constitution, simply because the statute can let the arrest power turn on any sort of practical consideration without having to subsume it under a broader principle. It is, in fact, only natural that States should resort to this sort of legislative regulation, for, as Atwater's own *amici* emphasize, it is in the interest of the police to limit petty-offense arrests, which carry costs that are simply too great to incur without good reason.

. . . The upshot of all these influences, combined with the good sense (and, failing that, the political accountability) of most local lawmakers and law-enforcement officials, is a dearth of horribles demanding redress. [The] country is not confronting anything like an epidemic of unnecessary minor-offense arrests. . . . Accordingly, we confirm today [that if] an officer has probable cause to believe that an individual has committed even a very minor criminal offense in his presence, he may, without violating the Fourth Amendment, arrest the offender.

Rule

O'CONNOR, J., dissenting.*

. . . I.

[History] is just one of the tools we use in conducting the reasonableness inquiry. And when history is inconclusive, as the majority amply demonstrates it is in this case, we will evaluate the search or seizure under traditional standards of reasonableness by assessing, on the one hand, the degree to which it intrudes upon an individual's privacy and, on the other, the degree to which it is needed for the promotion of legitimate governmental interests. In other words, in determining reasonableness, each case is to be decided on its own facts and circumstances. . . .

* [Justices Stevens, Ginsburg, and Breyer joined in this opinion. — EDS.]

A custodial arrest exacts an obvious toll on an individual's liberty and privacy, even when the period of custody is relatively brief. The arrestee is subject to a full search of her person and confiscation of her possessions. If the arrestee is the occupant of a car, the entire passenger compartment of the car, including packages therein, is subject to search as well. The arrestee may be detained for up to 48 hours without having a magistrate determine whether there in fact was probable cause for the arrest. Because people arrested for all types of violent and nonviolent offenses may be housed together awaiting such review, this detention period is potentially dangerous. And once the period of custody is over, the fact of the arrest is a permanent part of the public record. . . .

Because a full custodial arrest is such a severe intrusion on an individual's liberty, its reasonableness hinges on the degree to which it is needed for the promotion of legitimate governmental interests. In light of the availability of citations to promote a State's interests when a fine-only offense has been committed, I cannot concur in a rule which deems a full custodial arrest to be reasonable in every circumstance. . . . Instead, I would require that when there is probable cause to believe that a fine-only offense has been committed, the police officer should issue a citation unless the officer is able to point to specific and articulable facts which, taken together with rational inferences from those facts, reasonably warrant the additional intrusion of a full custodial arrest. . . .

At bottom, the majority offers two related reasons why a bright-line rule is necessary: the fear that officers who arrest for fine-only offenses will be subject to personal 42 U.S.C. §1983 liability for the misapplication of a constitutional standard, and the resulting systematic disincentive to arrest where arresting would serve an important societal interest. These concerns are certainly valid, but they are more than adequately resolved by the doctrine of qualified immunity.

If, for example, an officer reasonably thinks that a suspect poses a flight risk or might be a danger to the community if released, he may arrest without fear of the legal consequences. Similarly, if an officer reasonably concludes that a suspect may possess more than four ounces of marijuana and thus might be guilty of a felony, the officer will be insulated from liability for arresting the suspect even if the initial assessment turns out to be factually incorrect. . . .

II.

The record in this case makes it abundantly clear that Ms. Atwater's arrest was constitutionally unreasonable. . . . The Court's error, however, does not merely affect the disposition of this case. The per se rule that the Court creates has potentially serious consequences for the everyday lives of Americans. A broad range of conduct falls into the category of fine-only misdemeanors. In Texas alone, for example, disobeying any sort of traffic warning sign is a misdemeanor punishable only by fine, as is failing to pay a highway toll, and driving with expired license plates. Nor are fine-only crimes limited to the traffic context. In several States, for example, littering is a criminal offense punishable only by fine.

[Unbounded] discretion carries with it grave potential for abuse. The majority takes comfort in the lack of evidence of "an epidemic of unnecessary minor-offense arrests." But the relatively small number of published cases dealing with such arrests proves little and should provide little solace. Indeed, as the recent debate over racial profiling demonstrates all too clearly, a relatively minor traffic infraction may often serve as an excuse for stopping and harassing an individual. After today, the arsenal available to any officer extends to a full arrest and the searches permissible concomitant to that arrest. An officer's subjective motivations for making a traffic stop are not relevant considerations in determining the reasonableness of the stop. But it is precisely because these motivations are beyond our purview that we must vigilantly ensure that officers' poststop actions — which are properly within our reach — comport with the Fourth Amendment's guarantee of reasonableness. . . .

Notes

1. *Citations as supplement to arrest: majority position.* Every state gives its law enforcement officers the authority to issue citations (or "appearance tickets") for the violation of some criminal laws. Citations are ordinarily available to address traffic violations, but they are increasingly available for minor nontraffic violations of the criminal law — sometimes all "infractions" or specified misdemeanors. See Cincinnati Police Department Procedure Manual §12.555 (adults charged with misdemeanor offenses are eligible for Notice to Appear, except for specified misdemeanors such as weapons offense, second DUI offense, and three pending summons). The limited evidence on the use of the citation power suggests that officers do not commonly replace arrests with citations outside the traffic enforcement area.

Some foreign jurisdictions make extensive use of devices such as citations to give police officers an alternative to custodial arrest. For instance, in Queensland, Australia, police can issue a "notice to appear" (NTA) for any criminal offense. The NTA can be issued in the field or after taking the person into custody. It is used most frequently for traffic violations, prostitution, drugs, and weapons charges. If police officers in the United States had similarly broad powers to use citations, do you believe they would use it in similar categories of cases? Would citation in the field or at the station prove more popular?

2. *Citations as replacement for arrest.* Almost half of the states now have statutes that attempt to control the choice between citations and arrests for certain traffic offenses. Some simply state that the officer "shall" use the citation, while others (such as the Nebraska statute reprinted above) require the citation unless the officer can demonstrate one of the designated exceptions. Will a law such as the Nebraska statute effectively limit the use of arrest? On the constitutional level, the *Atwater* decision held that the federal constitution does not limit a police officer's power to arrest for a minor crime. Before *Atwater,* state courts were reluctant to declare that state constitutions required use of a citation rather than an arrest. Relatively few state courts have addressed this question under state law, but about half the courts that took up the question after *Atwater* parted ways with the Supreme Court. See State v. Askerooth, 681 N.W.2d 353 (Minn. 2004); State v. Brown, 792 N.E.2d 175 (Ohio 2003). For a sampling of the rich case law on this question, consult the web extension for this chapter at *http://www.crimpro.com/extension/ch05*.

What concerns, if any, might there be with the extensive use of citations? It might help in answering this question to consider it from a number of different perspectives — police, courts, civil rights groups, minority groups, and various kinds of possible defendants. Another way to think about the policy and justice implications of such a reform is to summarize its effect this way: Citations make arrests easier for the police.

3. *Search incident to citation: majority position.* Prior to the Supreme Court's 1998 ruling in *Knowles*, very few courts addressed the question of whether police could conduct a search incident to citation. Why did state courts develop so little case law on this subject? Was the practice of "search incident to citation" simply too rare to generate much litigation? Or was the practice common but unchallenged because prosecutors used other techniques to avoid appellate rulings on the subject? Here, as with many issues surrounding arrest and detention, police department policies often supplement statutes and judicial doctrine. See Phoenix Police Manual Order No. B-5(5)(D) (prohibiting search incident to issuance of a citation). Does *Knowles* apply outside the traffic stop context? See Lovelace v. Commonwealth, 522 S.E.2d 856 (Va. 1999) (applies to brief detention of pedestrian to issue summons).

4. *Pretextual arrests and limiting factors.* Recall the discussion from Chapter 2 about pretextual stops. Are the arguments any stronger or weaker to place controls on pretextual arrests — arrests motivated by some factor other than a desire to enforce some law that the officer has probable cause to believe the suspect has violated? Courts have given comparable treatment to claims about pretextual stops and arrests. See Arkansas v. Sullivan, 532 U.S. 769 (2001) (arrest based on probable cause does not violate Fourth Amendment even if arrest was motivated by desire to conduct search incident to arrest); State v. Hofmann, 537 N.W.2d 767 (Iowa 1995); but see State v. Sullivan, 74 S.W.2d 215 (Ark. 2002) (state constitution bars pretextual arrests for misdemeanor punishable by 90 days in jail).

The court in *Atwater* mentioned several practical limits on the willingness of police officers to arrest for minor crimes, including the amount of time and effort it takes to process an arrest. Does the arrest actually have to happen before the search incident? Could the officer announce an arrest, conduct the search, and then convert the arrest to a citation? See Wayne A. Logan, An Exception Swallows a Rule: Police Authority to Search Incident to Arrest, 19 Yale L. & Pol'y Rev. 381, 406-14 (2001) (distinguishes custodial and noncustodial arrests; argues that search incident should only happen if the officer actually does carry out a custodial arrest).

The *Atwater* court also mentioned the prospect that legislatures would pass statutes to limit any abuses of the arrest power. Under what political circumstances would a state legislature take action to limit the arrest authority of the police? See People v. McKay, 41 P.3d 59 (Cal. 2002) (state statute allows arrest for improper bicycle riding; even if it did not, arrest in violation of statute would not amount to Fourth Amendment violation).

5. *Arrests for minor crimes and race.* Does the officer's discretion to choose between arrest and citation for minor crimes create more risk of racial discrimination in enforcement? If you were advising a police department about a proposed campaign to stop and ticket more drivers who fail to use seat belts, and you knew that Latino and African American drivers use seat belts less frequently than other drivers, what advice would you give about carrying out this program? In the context of drug crimes, could you exercise arrest discretion in a way that equalizes the impact of enforcement on suburban and urban neighborhoods?

E. USE OF FORCE IN MAKING ARRESTS

The prior sections of this chapter have focused on *whether* an officer should make an arrest. In addition, the legal system pays attention to *how* a police officer makes an arrest. Legal controls are most vigorous when a suspect resists the officer's effort to make the arrest and the officer must use force — either deadly or nondeadly — to complete the arrest.

■ WILLIAM BLACKSTONE, COMMENTARIES ON THE LAWS OF ENGLAND

Vol. 4, p. 289 (1769)

[In] case of felony actually committed, or a dangerous wounding whereby felony is likely to ensue, [the constable] may upon probable suspicion arrest the felon; and for that purpose is authorized (as upon a justice's warrant) to break open doors, and even to kill the felon if he cannot otherwise be taken.

■ TENNESSEE v. EDWARD GARNER

471 U.S. 1 (1985)

WHITE, J.*

This case requires us to determine the constitutionality of the use of deadly force to prevent the escape of an apparently unarmed suspected felon. We conclude that such force may not be used unless it is necessary to prevent the escape and the officer has probable cause to believe that the suspect poses a significant threat of death or serious physical injury to the officer or others.

I.

At about 10:45 P.M. on October 3, 1974, Memphis Police Officers Elton Hymon and Leslie Wright were dispatched to answer a "prowler inside call." Upon arriving at the scene they saw a woman standing on her porch and gesturing toward the adjacent house. She told them she had heard glass breaking and that "they" or "someone" was breaking in next door. While Wright radioed the dispatcher to say that they were on the scene, Hymon went behind the house. He heard a door slam and saw someone run across the backyard. The fleeing suspect, who was [Edward Garner], stopped at a 6-feet-high chain link fence at the edge of the yard. With the aid of a flashlight, Hymon was able to see Garner's face and hands. He saw no sign of a weapon, and, though not certain, was "reasonably sure" and "figured" that Garner was unarmed. He thought Garner was 17 or 18 years old and about 5'5" or 5'7" tall.[2] While Garner was crouched at the base of the fence, Hymon called out "police, halt"

* [Justices Brennan, Marshall, Blackmun, Powell, and Stevens joined in this opinion. — EDS.]

2. In fact, Garner, an eighth-grader, was 15. He was 5'4" tall and weighed somewhere around 100 or 110 pounds.

and took a few steps toward him. Garner then began to climb over the fence. Convinced that if Garner made it over the fence he would elude capture,[3] Hymon shot him. The bullet hit Garner in the back of the head. Garner was taken by ambulance to a hospital, where he died on the operating table. Ten dollars and a purse taken from the house were found on his body.

In using deadly force to prevent the escape, Hymon was acting under the authority of a Tennessee statute and pursuant to Police Department policy. The statute provides that "[if], after notice of the intention to arrest the defendant, he either flee or forcibly resist, the officer may use all the necessary means to effect the arrest." Tenn. Code §40-7-108. The Department policy was slightly more restrictive than the statute, but still allowed the use of deadly force in cases of burglary. The incident was reviewed by the Memphis Police Firearm's Review Board and presented to a grand jury. Neither took any action.

Garner's father then brought this action, [seeking damages for asserted violations of Garner's constitutional rights.] After a 3-day bench trial, the District Court entered judgment for all defendants. [The trial court concluded that] Hymon had employed the only reasonable and practicable means of preventing Garner's escape. Garner had "recklessly and heedlessly attempted to vault over the fence to escape, thereby assuming the risk of being fired upon." . . .

II.

Whenever an officer restrains the freedom of a person to walk away, he has seized that person. While it is not always clear just when minimal police interference becomes a seizure there can be no question that apprehension by the use of deadly force is a seizure subject to the reasonableness requirement of the Fourth Amendment.

A police officer may arrest a person if he has probable cause to believe that person committed a crime. [The state argues] that if this requirement is satisfied the Fourth Amendment has nothing to say about how that seizure is made. This submission ignores the many cases in which this Court, by balancing the extent of the intrusion against the need for it, has examined the reasonableness of the manner in which a search or seizure is conducted. To determine the constitutionality of a seizure "[we] must balance the nature and quality of the intrusion on the individual's Fourth Amendment interests against the importance of the governmental interests alleged to justify the intrusion." We have described "the balancing of competing interests" as "the key principle of the Fourth Amendment." Because one of the factors is the extent of the intrusion, it is plain that reasonableness depends on not only when a seizure is made, but also how it is carried out.

[The balancing process] demonstrates that, notwithstanding probable cause to seize a suspect, an officer may not always do so by killing him. The intrusiveness of a seizure by means of deadly force is unmatched. The suspect's fundamental interest in his own life need not be elaborated upon. The use of deadly force also frustrates the interest of the individual, and of society, in judicial determination of guilt

3. When asked at trial why he fired, Hymon stated . . . that the area beyond the fence was dark, that he could not have gotten over the fence easily because he was carrying a lot of equipment and wearing heavy boots, and that Garner, being younger and more energetic, could have outrun him.

and punishment. Against these interests are ranged governmental interests in effective law enforcement. It is argued that overall violence will be reduced by encouraging the peaceful submission of suspects who know that they may be shot if they flee. Effectiveness in making arrests requires the resort to deadly force, or at least the meaningful threat thereof. "Being able to arrest such individuals is a condition precedent to the state's entire system of law enforcement."

Without in any way disparaging the importance of these goals, we are not convinced that the use of deadly force is a sufficiently productive means of accomplishing them to justify the killing of nonviolent suspects. The use of deadly force is a self-defeating way of apprehending a suspect and so setting the criminal justice mechanism in motion. If successful, it guarantees that that mechanism will not be set in motion. And while the meaningful threat of deadly force might be thought to lead to the arrest of more live suspects by discouraging escape attempts, the presently available evidence does not support this thesis. The fact is that a majority of police departments in this country have forbidden the use of deadly force against nonviolent suspects. If those charged with the enforcement of the criminal law have abjured the use of deadly force in arresting nondangerous felons, there is a substantial basis for doubting that the use of such force is an essential attribute of the arrest power in all felony cases. Petitioners and appellant have not persuaded us that shooting nondangerous fleeing suspects is so vital as to outweigh the suspect's interest in his own life.

The use of deadly force to prevent the escape of all felony suspects, whatever the circumstances, is constitutionally unreasonable. It is not better that all felony suspects die than that they escape. Where the suspect poses no immediate threat to the officer and no threat to others, the harm resulting from failing to apprehend him does not justify the use of deadly force to do so. It is no doubt unfortunate when a suspect who is in sight escapes, but the fact that the police arrive a little late or are a little slower afoot does not always justify killing the suspect. A police officer may not seize an unarmed, nondangerous suspect by shooting him dead. The Tennessee statute is unconstitutional insofar as it authorizes the use of deadly force against such fleeing suspects.

It is not, however, unconstitutional on its face. Where the officer has probable cause to believe that the suspect poses a threat of serious physical harm, either to the officer or to others, it is not constitutionally unreasonable to prevent escape by using deadly force. Thus, if the suspect threatens the officer with a weapon or there is probable cause to believe that he has committed a crime involving the infliction or threatened infliction of serious physical harm, deadly force may be used if necessary to prevent escape, and if, where feasible, some warning has been given. As applied in such circumstances, the Tennessee statute would pass constitutional muster.

III.

It is insisted that the Fourth Amendment must be construed in light of the common-law rule, which allowed the use of whatever force was necessary to effect the arrest of a fleeing felon, though not a misdemeanant. As stated in Hale's posthumously published Pleas of the Crown:

> [If] persons that are pursued by these officers for felony or the just suspicion thereof . . . shall not yield themselves to these officers, but shall either resist or fly before they are apprehended or being apprehended shall rescue themselves and resist or fly, so that they cannot be otherwise apprehended, and are upon necessity slain therein, because they cannot be otherwise taken, it is no felony.

2 M. Hale, Historia Placitoram Coronae 85 (1736). See also 4 W. Blackstone, Commentaries *289. Most American jurisdictions also imposed a flat prohibition against the use of deadly force to stop a fleeing misdemeanant, coupled with a general privilege to use such force to stop a fleeing felon.

The State and city argue that because this was the prevailing rule at the time of the adoption of the Fourth Amendment and for some time thereafter, and is still in force in some States, use of deadly force against a fleeing felon must be "reasonable." It is true that this Court has often looked to the common law in evaluating the reasonableness, for Fourth Amendment purposes, of police activity. On the other hand, it "has not simply frozen into constitutional law those law enforcement practices that existed at the time of the Fourth Amendment's passage." Because of sweeping change in the legal and technological context, reliance on the common-law rule in this case would be a mistaken literalism that ignores the purposes of a historical inquiry.

It has been pointed out many times that the common-law rule is best understood in light of the fact that it arose at a time when virtually all felonies were punishable by death. Though effected without the protections and formalities of an orderly trial and conviction, the killing of a resisting or fleeing felon resulted in no greater consequences than those authorized for punishment of the felony of which the individual was charged or suspected. Courts have also justified the common-law rule by emphasizing the relative dangerousness of felons.

Neither of these justifications makes sense today. Almost all crimes formerly punishable by death no longer are or can be. And while in earlier times the gulf between the felonies and the minor offences was broad and deep, today the distinction is minor and often arbitrary. Many crimes classified as misdemeanors, or nonexistent, at common law are now felonies. These changes have undermined the concept, which was questionable to begin with, that use of deadly force against a fleeing felon is merely a speedier execution of someone who has already forfeited his life. They have also made the assumption that a "felon" is more dangerous than a misdemeanant untenable. Indeed, numerous misdemeanors involve conduct more dangerous than many felonies.

There is an additional reason why the common-law rule cannot be directly translated to the present day. The common-law rule developed at a time when weapons were rudimentary. Deadly force could be inflicted almost solely in a hand-to-hand struggle during which, necessarily, the safety of the arresting officer was at risk. Handguns were not carried by police officers until the latter half of the last century. Only then did it become possible to use deadly force from a distance as a means of apprehension. As a practical matter, the use of deadly force under the standard articulation of the common-law rule has an altogether different meaning — and harsher consequences — now than in past centuries. . . .

In evaluating the reasonableness of police procedures under the Fourth Amendment, we have also looked to prevailing rules in individual jurisdictions. The rules in the States are varied. Some 19 States have codified the common-law rule, though in two of these the courts have significantly limited the statute. Four States, though without a relevant statute, apparently retain the common-law rule. Two States have adopted the Model Penal Code's provision verbatim.* Eighteen others allow, in slightly varying language, the use of deadly force only if the suspect has committed a felony involving the use or threat of physical or deadly force, or is escaping with a deadly weapon, or is likely to endanger life or inflict serious physical injury if not arrested. . . .

It cannot be said that there is a constant or overwhelming trend away from the common-law rule. In recent years, some States have reviewed their laws and expressly rejected abandonment of the common-law rule. Nonetheless, the long-term movement has been away from the rule that deadly force may be used against any fleeing felon, and that remains the rule in less than half the States.

This trend is more evident and impressive when viewed in light of the policies adopted by the police departments themselves. Overwhelmingly, these are more restrictive than the common-law rule. The Federal Bureau of Investigation and the New York City Police Department, for example, both forbid the use of firearms except when necessary to prevent death or grievous bodily harm. For accreditation by the Commission on Accreditation for Law Enforcement Agencies, a department must restrict the use of deadly force to situations where "the officer reasonably believes that the action is in defense of human life . . . or in defense of any person in immediate danger of serious physical injury." A 1974 study reported that the police department regulations in a majority of the large cities of the United States allowed the firing of a weapon only when a felon presented a threat of death or serious bodily harm. Overall, only 7.5 percent of departmental and municipal policies explicitly permit the use of deadly force against any felon; 86.8 percent explicitly do not. In light of the rules adopted by those who must actually administer them, the older and fading common-law view is a dubious indicium of the constitutionality of the Tennessee statute now before us.

Actual departmental policies are important for an additional reason. We would hesitate to declare a police practice of long standing "unreasonable" if doing so would severely hamper effective law enforcement. But the indications are to the contrary. There has been no suggestion that crime has worsened in any way in jurisdictions that have adopted, by legislation or departmental policy, rules similar to that announced today. . . .

Nor do we agree with [the state] that the rule we have adopted requires the police to make impossible, split-second evaluations of unknowable facts. We do not deny the practical difficulties of attempting to assess the suspect's dangerousness.

* [Section 3.07(2) (b) of the Model Penal Code provides:

> The use of deadly force is not justifiable . . . unless (i) the arrest is for a felony; and (ii) the person effecting the arrest is authorized to act as a peace officer or is assisting a person whom he believes to be authorized to act as a peace officer; and (iii) the actor believes that the force employed creates no substantial risk of injury to innocent persons; and (iv) the actor believes that (1) the crime for which the arrest is made involved conduct including the use or threatened use of deadly force; or (2) there is a substantial risk that the person to be arrested will cause death or serious bodily harm if his apprehension is delayed.

— Eds.]

However, similarly difficult judgments must be made by the police in equally uncertain circumstances. See, e.g., Terry v. Ohio, 392 U.S. 1 (1968). Nor is there any indication that in States that allow the use of deadly force only against dangerous suspects, the standard has been difficult to apply or has led to a rash of litigation involving inappropriate second-guessing of police officers' split-second decisions. Moreover, the highly technical felony/misdemeanor distinction is equally, if not more, difficult to apply in the field. An officer is in no position to know, for example, the precise value of property stolen, or whether the crime was a first or second offense. . . .

IV.

The [district court did not determine whether Garner presented a danger of physical harm to Officer Hymon or others.] The court did find, however, that Garner appeared to be unarmed, though Hymon could not be certain that was the case. Restated in Fourth Amendment terms, this means Hymon had no articulable basis to think Garner was armed.

[These facts do not justify the use of deadly force.] Officer Hymon could not reasonably have believed that Garner — young, slight, and unarmed — posed any threat. Indeed, Hymon never attempted to justify his actions on any basis other than the need to prevent an escape. [T]he fact that Garner was a suspected burglar could not, without regard to the other circumstances, automatically justify the use of deadly force. Hymon did not have probable cause to believe that Garner, whom he correctly believed to be unarmed, posed any physical danger to himself or others.

The dissent argues that the shooting was justified by the fact that Officer Hymon had probable cause to believe that Garner had committed a nighttime burglary. While we agree that burglary is a serious crime, we cannot agree that it is so dangerous as automatically to justify the use of deadly force. The FBI classifies burglary as a "property" rather than a "violent" crime. Although the armed burglar would present a different situation, the fact that an unarmed suspect has broken into a dwelling at night does not automatically mean he is physically dangerous. This case demonstrates as much. In fact, the available statistics demonstrate that burglaries only rarely involve physical violence. During the 10-year period from 1973-1982, only 3.8 percent of all burglaries involved violent crime.[23] . . .

V.

[We] hold that the statute is invalid insofar as it purported to give Hymon the authority to act as he did. [The] case is remanded for further proceedings consistent with this opinion. So ordered.

23. The dissent points out that three-fifths of all rapes in the home, three-fifths of all home robberies, and about a third of home assaults are committed by burglars. These figures mean only that if one knows that a suspect committed a rape in the home, there is a good chance that the suspect is also a burglar. That has nothing to do with the question here, which is whether the fact that someone has committed a burglary indicates that he has committed, or might commit, a violent crime. The dissent also points out that this 3.8% adds up to 2.8 million violent crimes over a 10-year period, as if to imply that today's holding will let loose 2.8 million violent burglars. The relevant universe is, of course, far smaller. At issue is only that tiny fraction of cases where violence has taken place and an officer who has no other means of apprehending the suspect is unaware of its occurrence.

O'CONNOR, J., dissenting.*

[Although] the circumstances of this case are unquestionably tragic and unfortunate, our constitutional holdings must be sensitive both to the history of the Fourth Amendment and to the general implications of the Court's reasoning. By disregarding the serious and dangerous nature of residential burglaries and the longstanding practice of many States, the Court effectively creates a Fourth Amendment right allowing a burglary suspect to flee unimpeded from a police officer who has probable cause to arrest, who has ordered the suspect to halt, and who has no means short of firing his weapon to prevent escape. I do not believe that the Fourth Amendment supports such a right, and I accordingly dissent.

I.

The facts below warrant brief review because they highlight the difficult, split-second decisions police officers must make in these circumstances. . . . As Officer Hymon walked behind the house, he heard a door slam. He saw Edward Eugene Garner run away from the house through the dark and cluttered backyard. Garner crouched next to a 6-foot-high fence. Officer Hymon thought Garner was an adult and was unsure whether Garner was armed because Hymon "had no idea what was in the hand [that he could not see] or what he might have had on his person." In fact, Garner was 15 years old and unarmed. Hymon also did not know whether accomplices remained inside the house. . . .

The precise issue before the Court deserves emphasis. . . . The issue is not the constitutional validity of the Tennessee statute on its face or as applied to some hypothetical set of facts. Instead, the issue is whether the use of deadly force by Officer Hymon under the circumstances of this case violated Garner's constitutional rights. Thus, the majority's assertion that a police officer who has probable cause to seize a suspect "may not always do so by killing him," is unexceptionable but also of little relevance to the question presented here. . . . The question we must address is whether the Constitution allows the use of such force to apprehend a suspect who resists arrest by attempting to flee the scene of a nighttime burglary of a residence.

II.

[We must balance] the important public interest in crime prevention and detection and the nature and quality of the intrusion upon legitimate interests of the individual. In striking this balance here, it is crucial to acknowledge that police use of deadly force to apprehend a fleeing criminal suspect falls within the "rubric of police conduct . . . necessarily [involving] swift action predicated upon the on-the-spot observations of the officer on the beat." Terry v. Ohio, 392 U.S. 1 (1968). The clarity of hindsight cannot provide the standard for judging the reasonableness of police decisions made in uncertain and often dangerous circumstances. . . .

The public interest involved in the use of deadly force as a last resort to apprehend a fleeing burglary suspect relates primarily to the serious nature of the crime. Household burglaries not only represent the illegal entry into a person's home, but

* [Chief Justice Burger and Justice Rehnquist joined in this opinion. — EDS.]

also "[pose] real risk of serious harm to others." According to recent Department of Justice statistics, "[three-fifths] of all rapes in the home, three-fifths of all home robberies, and about a third of home aggravated and simple assaults are committed by burglars." During the period 1973-1982, 2.8 million such violent crimes were committed in the course of burglaries. Victims of a forcible intrusion into their home by a nighttime prowler will find little consolation in the majority's confident assertion that "burglaries only rarely involve physical violence." Moreover, even if a particular burglary, when viewed in retrospect, does not involve physical harm to others, the "harsh potentialities for violence" inherent in the forced entry into a home preclude characterization of the crime as [innocuous or nonviolent.]

Because burglary is a serious and dangerous felony, the public interest in the prevention and detection of the crime is of compelling importance. Where a police officer has probable cause to arrest a suspected burglar, the use of deadly force as a last resort might well be the only means of apprehending the suspect. With respect to a particular burglary, subsequent investigation simply cannot represent a substitute for immediate apprehension of the criminal suspect at the scene. Indeed, the Captain of the Memphis Police Department testified that in his city, if apprehension is not immediate, it is likely that the suspect will not be caught. Although some law enforcement agencies may choose to assume the risk that a criminal will remain at large, the Tennessee statute reflects a legislative determination that the [provision will] assist the police in apprehending suspected perpetrators of serious crimes and provide notice that a lawful police order to stop and submit to arrest may not be ignored with impunity. . . .

Against the strong public interests justifying the conduct at issue here must be weighed the individual interests implicated in the use of deadly force by police officers. The majority declares that "[the] suspect's fundamental interest in his own life need not be elaborated upon." This blithe assertion hardly provides an adequate substitute for the majority's failure to acknowledge the distinctive manner in which the suspect's interest in his life is even exposed to risk. [The] officer's use of force resulted because the suspected burglar refused to heed [his command to halt] and the officer reasonably believed that there was no means short of firing his weapon to apprehend the suspect. Without questioning the importance of a person's interest in his life, I do not think this interest encompasses a right to flee unimpeded from the scene of a burglary. The legitimate interests of the suspect in these circumstances are adequately accommodated by the Tennessee statute: to avoid the use of deadly force and the consequent risk to his life, the suspect need merely obey the valid order to halt.

A proper balancing of the interests involved suggests that use of deadly force as a last resort to apprehend a criminal suspect fleeing from the scene of a nighttime burglary is not unreasonable within the meaning of the Fourth Amendment. Admittedly, the events giving rise to this case are in retrospect deeply regrettable. No one can view the death of an unarmed and apparently nonviolent 15-year-old without sorrow, much less disapproval. Nonetheless, the reasonableness of Officer Hymon's conduct for purposes of the Fourth Amendment cannot be evaluated by what later appears to have been a preferable course of police action. [Instead], the question is whether it is constitutionally impermissible for police officers, as a last resort, to shoot a burglary suspect fleeing the scene of the crime. . . .

IV.

I cannot accept the majority's creation of a constitutional right to flight for burglary suspects seeking to avoid capture at the scene of the crime. Whatever the constitutional limits on police use of deadly force in order to apprehend a fleeing felon, I do not believe they are exceeded in a case in which a police officer has probable cause to arrest a suspect at the scene of a residential burglary, orders the suspect to halt, and then fires his weapon as a last resort to prevent the suspect's escape into the night. I respectfully dissent.

Problem 5-4. Ruby Ridge

When Randy Weaver failed to appear in court on federal weapons charges, federal marshals decided to arrest him at his home in Ruby Ridge, Idaho. While several agents were walking around the property before approaching the house, a gun battle erupted between the marshals and Weaver's 14-year-old son, who was out walking and carrying a rifle when he encountered the agents. Weaver's son and one of the marshals died in the firefight.

The federal government was aware that other adults and children were on the Weaver property and that Weaver and his family owned and used a large number of firearms. As a result, the FBI sent several SWAT teams and a hostage rescue team to support the marshals in their effort to apprehend Weaver.

The FBI has general policies regarding the use of deadly force by its agents. The standard FBI rules at that time stated that an agent could use deadly force if the agent or some third party is threatened with "grievous" bodily injury. However, when FBI tactical teams are deployed, specialized "rules of engagement" can supplement the general policy. Rules of engagement are instructions that clearly indicate what action agents should take when confronted, threatened, or fired upon by someone. The on-scene commander formulates the rules of engagement. The special rules of engagement in effect at Ruby Ridge stated:

> If any adult in the compound is observed with a weapon after the surrender announcement is made, deadly force can and should be employed to neutralize this individual. If any adult male is observed with a weapon prior to the announcement, deadly force can and should be employed, if the shot can be taken without endangering any children.

The on-scene commander discussed these rules of engagement with supervisors within the FBI but not with legal counsel for the agency.

There were many interpretations of the rules of engagement among the FBI SWAT teams deployed to the Ruby Ridge site. One SWAT team leader recalled the rules as "if you see Weaver or Harris outside with a weapon, you've got the green light." Another member of a SWAT team remembered the rules as, "if you see 'em, shoot 'em."

During the ensuing siege, a member of the FBI's hostage rescue team shot and killed Weaver's wife while she was standing behind a door, holding her 10-month-old baby. Kevin Harris, a member of the Weaver household, was also shot. After the siege ended, Weaver was acquitted of criminal charges. He brought a civil suit against the government and settled the case for $3.1 million. Kevin Harris also filed a civil action against the government and its agents. See Harris v. Roderick, 126 F.3d 1189 (9th Cir. 1997). During Senate hearings on the matter, the FBI announced a new policy on deadly force. The new policy read as follows:

> *Use of Deadly Force Policy*
>
> a. Deadly Force. Officers may use deadly force only when necessary, that is, when the officer has a reasonable belief that the subject of such force poses an imminent danger of death or serious physical injury to the officer or to another person.
>
> b. Fleeing Felons. Deadly force may be used to prevent the escape of a fleeing subject if there is probable cause to believe:
>
> (1) the subject has committed a felony involving the infliction or threatened infliction of serious physical injury or death; and
>
> (2) the escape of the subject would pose an imminent danger of death or serious physical injury to the officer or to another person.
>
> *Use of Nondeadly Force*
>
> If force other than deadly force reasonably appears to be sufficient to accomplish an arrest or otherwise accomplish the law enforcement purpose, deadly force is not necessary.
>
> *Verbal Warnings*
>
> If feasible and if to do so would not increase the danger to the officer or others, a verbal warning to submit to the authority of the officer shall be given prior to the use of deadly force.

See 60 Fed. Reg. 54,569 (October 24, 1995). The policy applies to all federal law enforcement agents. Is each component of the new federal deadly force policy required by Garner? Were the Ruby Ridge rules of engagement consistent with *Garner*? Would you recommend the same deadly force policy for the police officers in Memphis responding to calls about crimes in progress?

Notes

1. *Deadly force: majority position.* In the wake of *Garner,* most states now have statutes either meeting or surpassing the constitutional minimum described in that decision. More than 30 states follow the Model Penal Code provisions on the use of force; more than a dozen of these states adopted (or reaffirmed) this position after the decision in *Garner.* Other states enforce the constitutional requirements through judicial decisions. Police departments now routinely adopt written policies regarding the use of deadly force, even departments that ordinarily do not maintain written operational guidelines. In fact, 100 percent of the police departments serving jurisdictions with populations greater than 10,000 have adopted written deadly force policies. About 90 percent of all police departments have written policies on nondeadly force. Bureau of Justice Statistics, Local Police Departments 2003 (June 2006, NCJ 210118).

Are the situations in which police can use deadly force after *Garner* sufficiently clear to allow police to anticipate and train for those situations? Does *Garner* create an incentive for perjury by officers being sued for their use of force?

2. *Excessive nondeadly force.* The police need not use deadly force to provoke a claim that they used force improperly to carry out an arrest. Many civil damage claims are founded on incidents involving nondeadly force used during arrests. See, e.g., Samaniego v. City of Kodiak, 2 P.3d 78 (Alaska 2000). The use of nondeadly force raises potential claims under the Fourth Amendment that an unreasonable seizure occurred. But in much of the litigation over nondeadly force, traditional doctrines of tort law govern. Claims are made under state tort law, federal civil rights laws, or both. The question in such cases is often whether the officer reasonably believed such force to be necessary to accomplish a legitimate police purpose. Are civil juries less capable of evaluating claims of negligence or gross negligence by the police than they are in other types of tort cases?

3. *Changing times.* What societal changes since 1985 might be the basis for arguing that the Supreme Court should reverse *Garner*? What about the emergence of methamphetamine or the presence of Uzis and Mac 10s? The increase in the number of homicides among youth? What if researchers found an increase in the number of killings committed by burglars?

Since the early 1970s, in a trend that *Garner* has reinforced, killings of citizens by police have decreased substantially, as have killings of police by citizens. Documentation of this trend is available on the web extension for this chapter at *http://www.crimpro.com/extension/ch05*. These changes occurred despite a largely stable, high homicide rate nationwide and dramatically increasing levels of homicide among youth in urban centers. To the extent the reduction in police killings (and killings of police) can be attributed to *Garner*, does this positive social change justify the original decision? Should courts intentionally conduct experiments, or is experimentation the sole province of legislatures, executive branch agencies, nonprofit foundations, and academics?

4. *Racial patterns in the use of excessive force.* Criminologists have extensively studied police use of deadly force; one researcher summarized the thrust of the studies as follows: "The literature on police use of deadly force has produced two major findings. First, researchers report extreme variation in rates of police shooting among American jurisdictions. Second, regardless of its geographic scope, the research invariably reports that the percentage of police shootings involving black victims far exceeds the percentage of blacks in the population." James Fyfe, Blind Justice: Police Shootings in Memphis, 73 J. Crim. L. & Criminology 707 (1982); see also Jerome Skolnick & James Fyfe, Above the Law: Police and the Excessive Use of Force (1993). In some places, this pattern might be explained by the disproportionate number of black suspects involved in the most serious violent crimes. In other places, such as Memphis (the location of the shooting in *Garner*) between 1969 and 1976, African Americans were more likely to be injured or killed, even after controlling for seriousness of the suspected crime. Should the *Garner* court have mentioned this sort of evidence as support for its decision?

Police departments have devoted much attention to their policies for the use of force, both deadly and nondeadly. Their efforts go far beyond the constitutional requirements set out in *Garner* or in state constitutional decisions. The following materials suggest, both directly and more obliquely, the forces that compel police departments to develop these rules.

DAVID FRISBY, FLORIDA'S POLICE CONTINUUM OF FORCE

12 Trial Advoc. Q. 37 (1993)

[The] Florida Department of Law Enforcement Bureau of Criminal Justice Standards and Training (FDLE/CJST) in the early 1980's recognized a civil vulnerability of Florida police agencies. [FDLE/CJST created the Use of Force Subcommittee to develop state standards and curricula on use of force]. This committee met formally for the first time in 1986. It completed its initial charge in 1990.

Its product consisted of a use of force matrix and a list of approved police arrest techniques. The arrest techniques had been medically reviewed by a committee of medical doctors and legally reviewed by a committee of attorneys. Both pronounced the techniques appropriate in the context of the use of force matrix. . . . The standard of care established by the police use of force matrix became Florida's official standard of care. . . .

CONTINUUM OF FORCE/LEVELS OF RESISTANCE MATRIX

The matrix defines the relationship between the proper use of force by a police officer and the resistance offered by the offender. The levels of resistance to lawful police authority are broken down into six categories.

RESISTANCE LEVELS

Presence is the first level of resistance. This level of resistance occurs when a person breaks the law by the nature of his very presence in a place, as in a trespass.

The second level of resistance is verbal resistance. A person can violate the law and subject himself to arrest by his speech. Disorderly conduct and variations of "Fire" shouted in a movie theater are typical examples. Verbal resistance, however, is usually a response to a police officer's direction or command.

The third level of resistance is passive physical resistance. Passive physical resistance involves more than mere presence or speech. It occurs when a law breaker, by action or inaction, physically resists the action or direction of a lawful authority. A shoplifter who sits and must be carried away from the store is exhibiting passive resistance.

The fourth level of resistance is active physical resistance. This level includes such behavior as pulling away or fleeing arrest.

The fifth level is aggressive physical resistance. When a person turns his active resistance against the police officer or against another person he achieves this level. Aggressive physical resistance need not necessarily be effective, just threatening.

Florida Use of Force / Levels of Resistance Matrix

Resistance Levels	Arrival	Interview Stance	Touch (consoling)	Verbal Direction	Dialogue	Restraint Devices	Transporters	Take Downs	Pain Compliance	Counter Moves	Intermediate Weapons	Incapacitation	Deadly Force
6 Aggravated Physical	†	†	†	†	†	†	†	†	†	†	†	†	†
5 Aggressive Physical	†	†	†	†	†	†	†	†	†	†	†	†	
4 Active Physical	†	†	†	†	†	†	†	†	†	†	†		
3 Passive Physical	†	†	†	†	†	†	†	†	†				
2 Verbal	†	†	†	†	†	†							
1 Presence	†	†	†	†									
Response Levels	Official Presence 1		Verbal Control 2			Physical Control 3					Inter-mediate Weapons 4	Incapac-itating Conduct 5	Deadly Force 6

Areas with crosses represent suggested, acceptable, beginning response levels. Any response in an area without a cross requires explanation.

The sixth level is aggravated physical resistance. An officer is faced with aggravated physical resistance when a resistor makes overt, hostile, attacking movements, with or without a weapon, with the apparent intent and ability to cause death or great bodily harm.

RESPONSE LEVELS

As the name suggests, the police continuum of force theory defines a spectrum of police response starting at a low level of police response and moving to a high level. It gives rules for escalating and de-escalating the use of force. The police continuum of force sets a standard and makes it clear when a particular example of force is within guidelines or outside acceptable practice. As with the law-breaker's resistance, the police continuum of force defines six levels of police response or police force.

The first and lowest level of police force is presence. Before an officer can even give a lawful command he must establish presence by establishing his identity and authority. He can do this by presenting himself in uniform or by presenting a badge, credentials, and announcing his authority. Presence is often enough force to convince a lawbreaker to stop his unlawful activity.

The second level of force is verbal direction. A police officer uses this force when he requests or commands, verbally or with body language. The third level of force is physical control. Physical control is the most complex level and will be discussed in greater detail later. The fourth level is alternate weapons. This level of force includes the use of police batons, chemical irritants, and stun guns. It is the level automatically in effect whenever the various police specialty weapons are used to obtain compliance. The fifth level of force is incapacitating force. As the name suggests, this level of force is intended to incapacitate a lawbreaker temporarily. Incapacitation techniques include some strikes and blows.

Level six is deadly force. This level of force is reached whenever firearms are used. It is force which is likely to cause serious bodily harm or even death. The deadly force category also includes baton strikes to the head, the use of police vehicles against other occupied vehicles and any other techniques defined as deadly by the local police administration.

The police continuum of force matrix relates these levels of police response to the levels of resistance. It gives a police officer guidance about where to enter the continuum matrix based on the particular bad behavior from the lawbreaker. . . .

Police response in level three is divided into subcategories. Transporters are techniques which are designed to move an arrested person from one place to another. Pain compliance techniques are designed to cause pain but not injury. Such a technique might be appropriate to separate a determined trespasser from a fence when he insists on holding tight. The techniques called takedowns, designed to place an arrestee on the ground for handcuffing, compose another subcategory. The very use of handcuffs, leg irons and other restraint devices is also a level three subcategory. Finally blocks, strikes and reactive techniques designed to control but not incapacitate are classified as level three countermoves. Striking a lawbreaker's hand which is bringing up a weapon is an example of a countermove.

General Rules

There are some general rules for the use of the continuum of force. Usually an officer will escalate up the continuum step by step until the law enforcement goal is achieved. He must then de-escalate as much as possible, consistent with maintaining control. An officer may by-pass steps in the continuum if he can explain why the lesser force would not be effective. An officer who exceeds the recommended level of force must document acceptable justification. For example, an officer might easily justify bypassing intermediate steps and initiating a level four or five response to recapture a desperate escaped murderer. . . .

Local police administrators routinely exercise their legitimate power to set force guidelines different from those of the state. Some department administrators move particular techniques to different places in the continuum because of sensitivity to community feelings. Sometimes they forbid certain types of force. For example, a few police departments in Florida have banned the use of the police baton. This type of practice might lead to increased civil liability if an officer found it necessary to use greater police force because his baton (a level four tool) was not available. Sensitive administrators weigh the benefits of varying from state standards carefully. . . .

Problem 5-5. Bicycle Kicks

Shonna Hobson was the mother of a five-year-old boy, James. Officer Nathan Shoate went to a home in Hobson's neighborhood to interview a child suspected in a bike theft. A child in the neighborhood, Matt, reported to Officer Shoate that he had seen James Hobson riding a bicycle stolen from Matt's sister. When Officer Shoate reached the Hobson home, he saw James near a bicycle. When Shoate got out of his car, James ran into the house.

Officer Shoate met Ms. Hobson at the front door of her home. He told her that her son was seen on a stolen bike and that he would need to talk to James about where he got the bike. Hobson told her son, who was now standing at the front door, to go back into the house. She then told Officer Shoate that James was not on a stolen bicycle, and that he had his own bike. Hobson became a bit irritated and refused to allow Officer Shoate to speak with James. The officer then told Hobson that he would have to take her son to the police station to interview him about the stolen bicycle, and gave her the opportunity to go along to the station. She replied that the officer was not taking her son anywhere.

At that point in the conversation, Officer Shoate called for backup police officers to assist him. When three other officers arrived a few minutes later, Hobson was standing with her son on the front steps of her residence yelling and saying "bullshit" in a loud voice. Officer Shoate then repeated to Hobson that they had to take her son to the police station, to which she again replied, "You aren't taking my son anywhere." Officer Shoate then advised Hobson that she was under arrest for obstructing an officer.

Two officers attempted to handcuff Hobson. When Officer Shoate tried to take hold of Hobson's arm, she pushed him away, saying, "Let me go!" Hobson punched another officer in the face, then was taken to the ground by the three other officers. Once she was on the ground, Hobson continued to flail her arms and legs in an attempt to get away. The officers took her to the police station.

Later investigation determined that the bicycle seen outside the Hobson home did in fact belong to James. Hobson was charged with obstructing an officer, disorderly conduct, and resisting an officer. In an amended complaint filed a few weeks later, the prosecutor added a fourth count: the felony of causing intentional bodily harm (battery) to a peace officer.

Hobson filed a motion to dismiss all the charges because there was no probable cause to support the obstruction or disorderly conduct counts, and her forceful efforts to resist the arrest were legitimate because the arrest was baseless and unlawful. How would you rule? Cf. State v. Hobson, 577 N.W.2d 825 (Wis. 1998).

Notes

1. *Detailed guidance.* Almost all major metropolitan police departments have adopted policies dealing with the use of force, and most of them describe a "continuum" of force similar to the one used in Florida. They vary, however, in the amount of detail they offer to guide police officers in the field. For a point of comparison with the Florida grid reprinted above, you should consult the "Discipline Matrix" of the Tucson Police Department, available on the web extension for this chapter at *http://www.crimpro.com/extension/ch05*.

How do you suppose the law enforcement community received the Florida guidelines on the use of force? If you were one of the attorneys asked to review the guidelines during the drafting process, would you have suggested more or fewer categories? Would you change any of the boxes to add or eliminate a particular response level to a particular resistance level? If you were chief of police in Jacksonville, would you issue cards with this chart for every member of the force? Would you publish this chart in the local newspaper?

2. *Extent of the use of force.* The prescribed responses in the lower and middle range of the grid prove just as important as the higher levels of force and resistance because police officers use the lower levels of force much more frequently. The Department of Justice collects statistics regarding use of "excessive force by law enforcement officers," as required by §210402 of the Violent Crime Control and Law Enforcement Act of 1994. In 2005, an estimated 43.5 million persons had a face-to-face contact with a police officer. The police used or threatened to use force against an estimated 700,000 persons, or about 1.6 percent of the total contacts. In 43 percent of those instances, the police pushed or grabbed the suspect; in 9 percent, the officer hit the suspect; and in 15 percent, the officer pointed a gun. The police sprayed chemical or pepper spray in 3 percent of the cases. See Bureau of Justice Statistics, Contacts between Police and the Public, 2005 at Table 12 (April 2007, NCJ 215243).

3. *High-speed chases.* Sometimes police officers must pursue suspects in automobiles, and those pursuits at high speed sometimes result in injuries to the police officers, the suspect, and third parties. Public scrutiny of police departments often centers on the use of force, particularly the damage that officers cause to third parties during high-speed chases. Newspapers routinely publish articles about high-visibility cases, especially those resulting in the payment of tort damages by the city.

More than 90 percent of law enforcement agencies have policies restricting the use of high-speed chases. Most of those policies appeared in the 1970s; about half of the policies have been updated since then to place tighter controls on the occasions for engaging in a high-speed chase. These policies allow high-speed chases more readily to chase suspects involved in more dangerous crimes. Geoffrey Alpert, Police Pursuit: Policies and Training (1997, NCJ 164831); Cal. Pen. Code §13519.8 (mandating creation of department policies). States must waive their sovereign immunity before they can be held liable in tort for injuries resulting from high-speed chases. In what types of cases would you imagine that states have waived their immunity?

Federal law is not hospitable to constitutional tort claims based on high-speed chases. In Sacramento County, California v. Lewis, 523 U.S. 833 (1998), the court affirmed the lower court's dismissal of a suit brought by the estate of a passenger on a motorcycle who was killed after the police and the driver of the motorcycle engaged in a high-speed chase. The court held that the high-speed police chase there did not amount to a Fourth Amendment "seizure" because the chase did not terminate the passenger's "freedom of movement through means intentionally applied." A plaintiff must show that the officers have an "intent to harm suspects physically."

4. *Resisting unlawful arrest.* Although the common law recognized a privilege for citizens to use reasonable force to resist an unlawful arrest, most states now require citizens to submit to unlawful arrests by police officers — about a dozen through judicial opinions and roughly another 20 states through statutes. See State v. Crawley, 901 A.2d 924 (N.J. 2006) (resisting an unlawful arrest or an unsupported stop by a known officer is a violation of state law); Haw. Rev. Stat. §703-304(4)(a) (use of force not justifiable to "resist an arrest which the actor knows is being made by a law enforcement officer, although the arrest is unlawful"). Courts typically address this criminal procedure topic when interpreting the outer boundaries of the substantive criminal law, such as a statute or ordinance making it a crime to "obstruct a police officer lawfully performing an official function by means of flight." What is the case for allowing citizens to use reasonable efforts to resist an unlawful arrest by a police officer?

VI

Remedies for Unreasonable Searches and Seizures

We have seen how the Fourth Amendment and its analogs, along with many statutes, rules, and internal police policies, condemn certain searches and seizures as unreasonable. We now consider the various methods available to remedy the government's violations of law.

A. ORIGINS OF THE EXCLUSIONARY RULE

The texts of the Fourth Amendment and its state constitutional analogs do not usually specify the remedy for the victim of an illegal search or seizure. Up until the twentieth century, courts remedied these violations of the law by allowing the victims to sue the offending government agents in tort (typically for trespass). But when criminal defendants also asked the courts during criminal proceedings to exclude the wrongfully obtained evidence, state and federal courts rejected the suggestion unanimously. As Justice Joseph Story once put it:

> If it is competent or pertinent evidence, and not in its own nature objectionable, as having been created by constraint, or oppression, such as confessions extorted by threats or fraud, the evidence is admissible on charges for the highest crimes, even though it may have been obtained by a trespass upon the person, or by any other forcible and illegal means. The law deliberates not on the mode, by which it has come to the possession of the party, but on its value in establishing itself as satisfactory proof.

United States v. La Jeune, 26 F. Cas. 832 (C.C.D. Mass. 1822). The Supreme Court suggested for the first time in Boyd v. United States, 116 U.S. 616 (1886), that exclusion of evidence might be the proper remedy for evidence obtained through a violation of both the Fourth and Fifth Amendments. A later case, Adams v. New York, 192 U.S. 585 (1904), curtly dismissed the exclusion remedy for a Fourth Amendment violation alone. The following case was the Court's next word on the subject of remedies for illegal searches and seizures.

■ FREMONT WEEKS v. UNITED STATES

232 U.S. 383 (1914)

DAY, J.*

[The defendant was convicted of using the mails for the purpose of transporting lottery tickets, in violation of §213 of the Criminal Code. At the time of his arrest at the Union Station in Kansas City, Missouri, police officers went to the defendant's house to search it. A neighbor told them where to find the key, and they entered the house and took various papers from his room. Later in the same day police officers returned with the United States Marshal, who thought he might find additional evidence,] and, being admitted by someone in the house, probably a boarder, in response to a rap, the Marshal searched the defendant's room and carried away certain letters and envelopes found in the drawer of a chiffonier. Neither the marshal nor the police officers had a search warrant.

The defendant filed in the cause before the time for trial a "Petition to Return Private Papers, Books and Other Property" [claiming that officers of the government had seized his books and papers] "in violation of Sections 11 and 23 of the Constitution of Missouri and of the 4th and 5th Amendments to the Constitution of the United States." [He further argued that the District Attorney's plans to use the papers and property as evidence in the case against him would violate his constitutional rights. The trial court denied the petition.] Among the papers retained and put in evidence were a number of lottery tickets and statements with reference to the lottery, taken at the first visit of the police to the defendant's room, and a number of letters written to the defendant in respect to the lottery, taken by the Marshal upon his search of defendant's room. . . .

The effect of the Fourth Amendment is to put the courts of the United States and Federal officials, in the exercise of their power and authority, under limitations and restraints as to the exercise of such power and authority, and to forever secure the people, their persons, houses, papers and effects against all unreasonable searches and seizures under the guise of law. This protection reaches all alike, whether accused of crime or not, and the duty of giving to it force and effect is obligatory upon all entrusted under our Federal system with the enforcement of the laws. The tendency of those who execute the criminal laws of the country to obtain conviction by means of unlawful seizures and enforced confessions, the latter often obtained after subjecting accused persons to unwarranted practices destructive of rights secured by the Federal Constitution, should find no sanction in the judgments of the courts which are charged at all times with the support of the Constitution and to which people of all conditions have a right to appeal for the maintenance of such fundamental rights.

* [All the Justices joined in this opinion. — EDS.]

[This case] involves the right of the court in a criminal prosecution to retain for the purposes of evidence the letters and correspondence of the accused, seized in his house in his absence and without his authority, by a United States Marshal holding no warrant for his arrest and none for the search of his premises. . . . If letters and private documents can thus be seized and held and used in evidence against a citizen accused of an offense, the protection of the Fourth Amendment declaring his right to be secure against such searches and seizures is of no value, and, so far as those thus placed are concerned, might as well be stricken from the Constitution. The efforts of the courts and their officials to bring the guilty to punishment, praiseworthy as they are, are not to be aided by the sacrifice of those great principles established by years of endeavor and suffering which have resulted in their embodiment in the fundamental law of the land. The United States Marshal . . . acted without sanction of law, doubtless prompted by the desire to bring further proof to the aid of the Government, and under color of his office undertook to make a seizure of private papers in direct violation of the constitutional prohibition against such action. . . . To sanction such proceedings would be to affirm by judicial decision a manifest neglect if not an open defiance of the prohibitions of the Constitution, intended for the protection of the people against such unauthorized action.

The [Government contends that the correct rule of law is] that the letters having come into the control of the court, it would not inquire into the manner in which they were obtained, but if competent would keep them and permit their use in evidence. Such proposition, the Government asserts, is conclusively established by certain decisions of this court. [This doctrine,] that a court will not in trying a criminal cause permit a collateral issue to be raised as to the source of competent testimony, has the sanction of so many state cases that it would be impracticable to cite or refer to them in detail. [The editor of one legal publication has explained the rule as follows:] "Such an investigation is not involved necessarily in the litigation in chief, and to pursue it would be to halt in the orderly progress of a cause, and consider incidentally a question which has happened to cross the path of such litigation, and which is wholly independent thereof."

It is therefore evident that [our prior cases] afford no authority for the action of the court in this case, when applied to in due season for the return of papers seized in violation of the Constitutional Amendment. [Prior cases were distinguishable, however, because they involved] application of the doctrine that a collateral issue will not be raised to ascertain the source from which testimony, competent in a criminal case, comes. . . . The right of the court to deal with papers and documents in the possession of the District Attorney and other officers of the court and subject to its authority [is clearly established.] That papers wrongfully seized should be turned over to the accused has been frequently recognized in the early as well as later decisions of the courts.

We therefore reach the conclusion that the letters in question were taken from the house of the accused by an official of the United States acting under color of his office in direct violation of the constitutional rights of the defendant; that having made a seasonable application for their return, which was heard and passed upon by the court, there was involved in the order refusing the application a denial of the constitutional rights of the accused, and that the court should have restored these letters to the accused. In holding them and permitting their use upon the trial, we think prejudicial error was committed. . . .

Notes

1. *Evidentiary fruits of illegal searches.* Would the exclusionary rule described in the *Weeks* case prevent the government from introducing evidence *derived* from illegally obtained papers rather than the papers themselves? In Silverthorne Lumber Co. v. United States, 251 U.S. 385 (1920), the government had illegally seized corporate papers, returned them before trial, and then issued a subpoena duces tecum to obtain the documents through proper means. The Court declared that the exclusionary rule prevented such a method of curing the effects of an illegal seizure: Exclusion means "that not merely evidence [illegally] acquired shall not be used before the Court but that it shall not be used at all."

2. *The states and the exclusionary rule after 1949.* Because the *Weeks* opinion was based on the federal Bill of Rights, which did not at that time apply to the states, state courts and legislatures were free to adopt or reject the exclusionary remedy. Only a handful of states adopted an exclusionary rule prior to the *Weeks* opinion. See State v. Sheridan, 96 N.W. 730 (Iowa 1903). The *Weeks* opinion did not change this trend in the state courts. Most took the view of Judge Benjamin Cardozo in People v. Defore, 150 N.E. 585 (N.Y. 1926), in which he tartly summarized the exclusionary rule as follows: "There is no blinking the consequences. The criminal is to go free because the constable has blundered. . . . The pettiest peace officer would have it in his power through overzeal or indiscretion to confer immunity upon an offender for crimes the most flagitious."

Thus, for the first half of this century the exclusionary remedy applied only in the federal system and a handful of states. As of 1926, fewer than 15 states had adopted the exclusionary rule and more than 30 had rejected it. Even after the Supreme Court decided to apply the Fourth Amendment to state law enforcement officers in Wolf v. Colorado, 338 U.S. 25 (1949), it did not insist that state courts exclude improperly seized evidence. They were still free to adopt remedies other than the exclusionary rule. About half of the states continued to rely on civil remedies for victims of illegal searches and on criminal charges against police officers who violated the law. But by the 1950s, judges and commentators started having doubts about the success of alternatives to the exclusionary rule — at that time, not just alternatives but the only remedies available in many states.

■ PEOPLE v. CHARLES CAHAN

282 P.2d 905 (Cal. 1955)

TRAYNOR, J.

Defendant and 15 other persons were charged with conspiring to engage in horse-race bookmaking and related offenses. [After a trial without a jury, the court found one defendant not guilty, and all the other defendants, including Cahan, guilty.]

Most of the incriminatory evidence introduced at the trial was obtained by officers of the Los Angeles Police Department in flagrant violation of the United States Constitution (4th and 14th Amendments), the California Constitution (art. I, §19), and state and federal statutes. Gerald Wooters, an officer attached to the intelligence unit of that department testified that after securing the permission of the chief of police to make microphone installations* at two places occupied by defendants, he, Sergeant Keeler, and Officer Phillips one night at about 8:45 entered one "house through the side window of the first floor," and that he "directed the officers to place a listening device under a chest of drawers." Another officer made recordings and transcriptions of the conversations that came over wires from the listening device to receiving equipment installed in a nearby garage. . . . Section 653h of the Penal Code does not and could not authorize violations of the Constitution. . . .

The evidence obtained from the microphones was not the only unconstitutionally obtained evidence introduced at the trial over defendants' objection. In addition there was a mass of evidence obtained by numerous forcible entries and seizures without search warrants. [The officers testified that they obtained evidence by kicking open a door in one location, and by breaking a window at another.]

Thus, without fear of criminal punishment or other discipline, law enforcement officers, sworn to support the Constitution of the United States and the Constitution of California, frankly admit their deliberate, flagrant acts in violation of both Constitutions and the laws enacted thereunder. It is clearly apparent from their testimony that they casually regard such acts as nothing more than the performance of their ordinary duties for which the city employs and pays them.

[Both] the United States Constitution and the California Constitution make it emphatically clear that important as efficient law enforcement may be, it is more important that the right of privacy guaranteed by these constitutional provisions be respected. [The] contention that unreasonable searches and seizures are justified by the necessity of bringing criminals to justice cannot be accepted. It was rejected when the constitutional provisions were adopted and the choice was made that all the people, guilty and innocent alike, should be secure from unreasonable police intrusions, even though some criminals should escape. Moreover, the constitutional provisions make no distinction between the guilty and the innocent, and it would be manifestly impossible to protect the rights of the innocent if the police were permitted to justify unreasonable searches and seizures on the ground that they assumed their victims were criminals. Thus, when consideration is directed to the question of the admissibility of evidence obtained in violation of the constitutional provisions, it bears emphasis that the court is not concerned solely with the rights of the defendant before it, however guilty he may appear, but with the constitutional right of all of the people to be secure in their homes, persons, and effects.

The constitutional provisions themselves do not expressly answer the question whether evidence obtained in violation thereof is admissible in criminal actions. Neither Congress nor the Legislature has given an answer, and the courts of the country are divided on the question. The federal courts and those of some of the states exclude such evidence. In accord with the traditional common-law rule, the courts of a majority of the states admit it, and heretofore the courts of this state have admitted it.

* [Section 653h of the Penal Code provided: "Any person who, without consent of the owner, lessee, or occupant, installs or attempts to install or use a dictograph in any house . . . is guilty of a misdemeanor; provided, that nothing herein shall prevent the use and installation of dictographs by a regular salaried police officer expressly authorized thereto by the head of his office . . . when such use and installation are necessary in the performance of their duties in detecting crime and in the apprehension of criminals." — EDS.]

The decision of the United States Supreme Court in Wolf v. Colorado, 338 U.S. 25 (1949), that the guarantee of the Fourth Amendment applies to the states through the Fourteenth [Amendment,] does not require states like California that have heretofore admitted illegally seized evidence to exclude it now. The exclusionary rule is not "an essential ingredient" of the right of privacy guaranteed by the Fourth Amendment, but simply a means of enforcing that right, which the states can accept or reject. . . .

The rule admitting the evidence has been strongly supported by both scholars and judges. Their arguments may be briefly summarized as follows:

The rules of evidence are designed to enable courts to reach the truth and, in criminal cases, to secure a fair trial to those accused of crime. Evidence obtained by an illegal search and seizure is ordinarily just as true and reliable as evidence lawfully obtained. The court needs all reliable evidence material to the issue before it, the guilt or innocence of the accused, and how such evidence is obtained is immaterial to that issue. It should not be excluded unless strong considerations of public policy demand it. . . .

Exclusion of the evidence cannot be justified as affording protection or recompense to the defendant or punishment to the officers for the illegal search and seizure. It does not protect the defendant from the search and seizure, since that illegal act has already occurred. If he is innocent or if there is ample evidence to convict him without the illegally obtained evidence, exclusion of the evidence gives him no remedy at all. Thus the only defendants who benefit by the exclusionary rule are those criminals who could not be convicted without the illegally obtained evidence. Allowing such criminals to escape punishment is not appropriate recompense for the invasion of their constitutional rights; it does not punish the officers who violated the constitutional provisions; and it fails to protect society from known criminals who should not be left at large. For his crime the defendant should be punished. For his violation of the constitutional provisions the offending officer should be punished. As the exclusionary rule operates, however, the defendant's crime and the officer's flouting of constitutional guarantees both go unpunished. . . .

Opponents of the exclusionary rule also point out that it is inconsistent with the rule allowing private litigants to use illegally obtained evidence, and that as applied in the federal courts, it is capricious in its operation, either going too far or not far enough. So many exceptions to the exclusionary rule have been granted the judicial blessing as largely to destroy any value it might otherwise have had. . . .

Finally it has been pointed out that there is no convincing evidence that the exclusionary rule actually tends to prevent unreasonable searches and seizures and that the disciplinary or educational effect of the court's releasing the defendant for police misbehavior is so indirect as to be no more than a mild deterrent at best.

Despite the persuasive force of the foregoing arguments, we have concluded that evidence obtained in violation of the constitutional guarantees is inadmissible. We have been compelled to reach that conclusion because other remedies have completely failed to secure compliance with the constitutional provisions on the part of police officers with the attendant result that the courts under the old rule have been constantly required to participate in, and in effect condone, the lawless activities of law enforcement officers.

When, as in the present case, the very purpose of an illegal search and seizure is to get evidence to introduce at a trial, the success of the lawless venture depends entirely on the court's lending its aid by allowing the evidence to be introduced. . . .

Court shouldn't have a hand in the dirty business

Out of regard for its own dignity as an agency of justice and custodian of liberty the court should not have a hand in such dirty business.

Courts refuse their aid in civil cases to prevent the consummation of illegal schemes of private litigants; a fortiori, they should not extend that aid and thereby permit the consummation of illegal schemes of the state itself. It is morally incongruous for the state to flout constitutional rights and at the same time demand that its citizens observe the law. The end that the state seeks may be a laudable one, but it no more justifies unlawful acts than a laudable end justifies unlawful action by any member of the public. Moreover, any process of law that sanctions the imposition of penalties upon an individual through the use of the fruits of official lawlessness tends to the destruction of the whole system of restraints on the exercise of the public force that are inherent in the concept of ordered liberty. . . . "Our Government is the potent, the omnipresent teacher. For good or for ill, it teaches the whole people by its example. Crime is contagious. If the Government becomes a lawbreaker, it breeds contempt for law, it invites everyman to become a law unto himself; it invites anarchy." Olmstead v. United States, 277 U.S. 438 (1928) (Brandeis, J., dissenting).

[If the constitutional guarantees against unreasonable searches and seizures] were being effectively enforced by other means than excluding evidence obtained by their violation, a different problem would be presented. If such were the case there would be more force to the argument that a particular criminal should not be redressed for a past violation of his rights by excluding the evidence against him. Experience has demonstrated, however, that neither administrative, criminal nor civil remedies are effective in suppressing lawless searches and seizures. The innocent suffer with the guilty, and we cannot close our eyes to the effect the rule we adopt will have on the rights of those not before the court. "The difficulty with [other remedies] is in part due to the failure of interested parties to inform of the offense. No matter what an illegal raid turns up, police are unlikely to inform on themselves or each other. If it turns up nothing incriminating, the innocent victim usually does not care to take steps which will air the fact that he has been under suspicion." Irvine v. California, 347 U.S. 128 (1954). Moreover, even when it becomes generally known that the police conduct illegal searches and seizures, public opinion is not aroused as it is in the case of other violations of constitutional rights. Illegal searches and seizures lack the obvious brutality of coerced confessions and the third degree and do not so clearly strike at the very basis of our civil liberties as do unfair trials or the lynching of even an admitted murderer. . . . There is thus all the more necessity for courts to be vigilant in protecting these constitutional rights if they are to be protected at all. People v. Mayen, 205 P. 435 (Cal. 1922) [rejecting the exclusionary rule in California] was decided over 30 years ago. Since then case after case has appeared in our appellate reports describing unlawful searches and seizures against the defendant on trial, and those cases undoubtedly reflect only a small fraction of the violations of the constitutional provisions that have actually occurred. On the other hand, reported cases involving civil actions against police officers are rare, and those involving successful criminal prosecutions against officers are nonexistent. In short, the constitutional provisions are not being enforced.

Granted that the adoption of the exclusionary rule will not prevent all illegal searches and seizures, it will discourage them. Police officers and prosecuting officials are primarily interested in convicting criminals. Given the exclusionary rule and a choice between securing evidence by legal rather than illegal means, officers will be impelled to obey the law themselves since not to do so will jeopardize their objectives. [If] courts respect the constitutional provisions by refusing to sanction their violation, they will not only command the respect of law-abiding citizens for themselves adhering to the law, they will also arouse public opinion as a deterrent to lawless enforcement of the law by bringing just criticism to bear on law enforcement officers who allow criminals to escape by pursuing them in lawless ways.

It is contended, however, that the police do not always have a choice of securing evidence by legal means and that in many cases the criminal will escape if illegally obtained evidence cannot be used against him. This contention is not properly directed at the exclusionary rule, but at the constitutional provisions themselves. It was rejected when those provisions were adopted. In such cases had the Constitution been obeyed, the criminal could in no event be convicted. He does not go free because the constable blundered, but because the Constitutions prohibit securing the evidence against him. . . .

In developing a rule of evidence applicable in the state courts, this court is not bound by the decisions that have applied the federal rule, and if it appears that those decisions have developed needless refinements and distinctions, this court need not follow them. . . . Under these circumstances the adoption of the exclusionary rule need not introduce confusion into the law of criminal procedure. Instead it opens the door to the development of workable rules governing searches and seizures and the issuance of warrants that will protect both the rights guaranteed by the constitutional provisions and the interest of society in the suppression of crime. . . .

SPENCE, J., dissenting.

I dissent. The guilt of the appellant is clearly demonstrated by the record before us. . . . In adopting and adhering to the nonexclusionary rule, the law of the State of California has thereby been kept in harmony with the law of the great majority of the other states and of all the British commonwealths; as well as in line with the considered views of the majority of the most eminent legal scholars. Only the federal courts and the courts of a relatively few states have adopted the judicially created exclusionary rule. . . .

The experience of the federal courts in attempting to apply the exclusionary rule does not appear to commend its adoption elsewhere. The spectacle of an obviously guilty defendant obtaining a favorable ruling by a court upon a motion to suppress evidence or upon an objection to evidence, and thereby, in effect, obtaining immunity from any successful prosecution of the charge against him, is a picture which has been too often seen in the federal practice. . . . Furthermore, under the present federal practice, the trial of the accused is interrupted to try the question of whether the evidence was in fact illegally obtained. This question is often a delicate one, and the main trial is at least delayed while the question of whether some other person has committed a wrong in obtaining the evidence has been judicially determined. . . .

[I cannot] ascertain from the majority opinion in the present case the nature of the rule which is being adopted to supplant the well established nonexclusionary rule in California. Is it the exclusionary rule as interpreted in the federal courts with all its technical distinctions, exceptions, and qualifications . . . ? [Neither] the federal courts nor the courts of any of the few states which adopted the exclusionary rule have apparently found a satisfactory solution to [the] problem of developing "workable rules," and it seems impossible to contemplate the possibility that this court can develop a satisfactory solution. At best, this court would have to work out such rules in piecemeal fashion as each case might come before it. In the meantime, what rules are to guide our trial courts in the handling of their problems? If the nonexclusionary rule can be said to have one unquestioned advantage, it is the advantage of certainty. . . .

If, however, reasons may be said to exist for a change in the established policy of this state, I believe that the Legislature, rather than the courts, should make such change. This is particularly true in a situation such as the present one, when the change of policy should be accompanied by "workable rules" to implement such change. . . . In this connection, it is worthy of note that bills have frequently been introduced in the Legislature to accomplish precisely that which is accomplished by the majority opinion, to wit: the supplanting of the nonexclusionary rule by the so-called exclusionary rule, without prescribing any "workable rules" for the latter's application. In the recent legislative sessions of 1951 and of 1953, such bills have been introduced but none has ever been brought to a vote in either house. Under the circumstances, it would be far better for this court to allow the Legislature to deal with this question of policy. . . .

Returning to the precise situation presented by the record before us, it may be conceded that the illegality in obtaining the evidence was both clear and flagrant. It may be further conceded that the crimes which defendants conspired to commit were not in the class of the more serious public offenses. The fact remains, however, that the exclusionary rule, as adopted by the majority, is a rule for all cases and that it deprives society of its remedy against the most desperate gangster charged with the most heinous crime merely because of some degree of illegality in obtaining the evidence against him. . . .

In my opinion, the cost of the adoption of the exclusionary rule is manifestly too great. It would be far better for this state to adhere to the nonexclusionary rule, and to reexamine its laws concerning the sanctions to be placed upon illegal searches and seizures. If the present laws are deemed inadequate to discourage illegal practices by enforcement officers, the Legislature might well consider the imposition of civil liability for such conduct upon the governmental unit employing the offending officer, in addition to the liability now imposed upon the officer himself. It might also consider fixing a minimum amount to be recovered as damages in the same manner that a minimum has been fixed for the invasion of other civil rights. These methods would be far more effective in discouraging illegal activities on the part of enforcement officers and such methods would not be subject to the objection, inherent in the adoption of the exclusionary rule, that "It deprives society of its remedy against one lawbreaker because he has been pursued by another." Irvine v. California, 347 U.S. 128 (1954). . . .

DOLLREE MAPP v. OHIO

367 U.S. 643 (1961)

CLARK, J.*

On May 23, 1957, three Cleveland police officers arrived at appellant's residence in that city pursuant to information that "a person [was] hiding out in the

* [Chief Justice Warren and Justices Black, Douglas, and Brennan joined in this opinion. — EDS.]

home, who was wanted for questioning in connection with a recent bombing, and that there was a large amount of policy paraphernalia being hidden in the home." Miss Mapp and her daughter by a former marriage lived on the top floor of the two-family dwelling. Upon their arrival at that house, the officers knocked on the door and demanded entrance but appellant, after telephoning her attorney, refused to admit them without a search warrant. They advised their headquarters of the situation and undertook a surveillance of the house.

The officers again sought entrance some three hours later when four or more additional officers arrived on the scene. When Miss Mapp did not come to the door immediately, at least one of the several doors to the house was forcibly opened[2] and the policemen gained admittance. Meanwhile Miss Mapp's attorney arrived, but the officers, having secured their own entry, and continuing in their defiance of the law, would permit him neither to see Miss Mapp nor to enter the house. It appears that Miss Mapp was halfway down the stairs from the upper floor to the front door when the officers, in this highhanded manner, broke into the hall. She demanded to see the search warrant. A paper, claimed to be a warrant, was held up by one of the officers. She grabbed the "warrant" and placed it in her bosom. A struggle ensued in which the officers recovered the piece of paper and as a result of which they handcuffed appellant because she had been "belligerent" in resisting their official rescue of the "warrant" from her person. Running roughshod over appellant, a policeman "grabbed" her, "twisted [her] hand," and she "yelled [and] pleaded with him" because "it was hurting." Appellant, in handcuffs, was then forcibly taken upstairs to her bedroom where the officers searched a dresser, a chest of drawers, a closet and some suitcases. They also looked into a photo album and through personal papers belonging to the appellant. The search spread to the rest of the second floor including the child's bedroom, the living room, the kitchen and a dinette. The basement of the building and a trunk found therein were also searched. The obscene [books and pictures] for possession of which she was ultimately convicted were discovered in the course of that widespread search.

At the trial no search warrant was produced by the prosecution, nor was the failure to produce one explained or accounted for. [The Ohio Supreme Court affirmed the conviction because] the evidence had not been taken "from defendant's person by the use of brutal or offensive physical force against defendant." The State says that even if the search were made without authority, or otherwise unreasonably, it is not prevented from using the unconstitutionally seized evidence at trial. . . .

I.

[In] the year 1914, in the *Weeks* case, this Court for the first time held that in a federal prosecution the Fourth Amendment barred the use of evidence secured through an illegal search and seizure. This Court has ever since required of federal law officers a strict adherence to that command which this Court has held to be a clear, specific, and constitutionally required — even if judicially implied — deterrent safeguard without insistence upon which the Fourth Amendment would have been reduced to a form of words. . . .

2. A police officer testified that "we did pry the screen door to gain entrance"; the attorney on the scene testified that a policeman "tried . . . to kick in the door" and then "broke the glass in the door and somebody reached in and opened the door and let them in. . . ."

II.

[Thirty-five years later, in Wolf v. Colorado, 338 U.S. 25 (1949)], the Court decided that the *Weeks* exclusionary rule would not then be imposed upon the States as "an essential ingredient of the right." The Court's reasons for not considering essential to the right to privacy, as a curb imposed upon the States by the Due Process Clause, that which decades before had been posited as part and parcel of the Fourth Amendment's limitation upon federal encroachment of individual privacy, were bottomed on factual considerations.

While they are not basically relevant to a decision that the exclusionary rule is an essential ingredient of the Fourth Amendment as the right it embodies is vouchsafed against the States by the Due Process Clause, we will consider the current validity of the factual grounds upon which *Wolf* was based.

The Court in *Wolf* first stated that "the contrariety of views of the States" on the adoption of the exclusionary rule of *Weeks* was "particularly impressive"; and, in this connection, that it could not "brush aside the experience of States which deem the incidence of such conduct by the police too slight to call for a deterrent remedy by overriding the States' relevant rules of evidence." While in 1949, prior to the *Wolf* case, almost two-thirds of the States were opposed to the use of the exclusionary rule, now, despite the *Wolf* case, more than half of those since passing upon it, [including California], by their own legislative or judicial decision, have wholly or partly adopted or adhered to the *Weeks* rule.

[The] second basis elaborated in *Wolf* in support of its failure to enforce the exclusionary doctrine against the States was that "other means of protection" have been afforded the right to privacy.[7] The experience of California [described in People v. Cahan] that such other remedies have been worthless and futile is buttressed by the experience of other States. . . . It, therefore, plainly appears that the factual considerations supporting the failure of the *Wolf* Court to include the *Weeks* exclusionary rule when it recognized the enforceability of the right to privacy against the States in 1949, while not basically relevant to the constitutional consideration, could not, in any analysis, now be deemed controlling. . . .

III.

. . . Today we once again examine *Wolf*'s constitutional documentation of the right to privacy free from unreasonable state intrusion, and, after its dozen years on our books, are led by it to close the only courtroom door remaining open to evidence secured by official lawlessness in flagrant abuse of that basic right, reserved to all persons as a specific guarantee against that very same unlawful conduct. We hold that all evidence obtained by searches and seizures in violation of the Constitution is, by that same authority, inadmissible in a state court.

7. Less than half [23] of the States have any criminal provisions relating directly to unreasonable searches and seizures. . . .

IV.

Since the Fourth Amendment's right of privacy has been declared enforceable against the States through the Due Process Clause of the Fourteenth, it is enforceable against them by the same sanction of exclusion as is used against the Federal Government. Were it otherwise, then just as without the *Weeks* rule the assurance against unreasonable federal searches and seizures would be "a form of words," valueless and undeserving of mention in a perpetual charter of inestimable human liberties, so too, without that rule the freedom from state invasions of privacy would be so ephemeral and so neatly severed from its conceptual nexus with the freedom from all brutish means of coercing evidence as not to merit this Court's high regard as a freedom "implicit in the concept of ordered liberty." . . . Therefore, in extending the substantive protections of due process to all constitutionally unreasonable searches — state or federal — it was logically and constitutionally necessary that the exclusion doctrine — an essential part of the right to privacy — be also insisted upon as an essential ingredient of the right newly recognized by the *Wolf* case. . . . To hold otherwise is to grant the right but in reality to withhold its privilege and enjoyment. . . .

This Court has not hesitated to enforce as strictly against the States as it does against the Federal Government the rights of free speech and of a free press, the rights to notice and to a fair, public trial, including, as it does, the right not to be convicted by use of a coerced confession, however logically relevant it be, and without regard to its reliability. And nothing could be more certain than that when a coerced confession is involved, "the relevant rules of evidence" are overridden. . . . Why should not the same rule apply to what is tantamount to coerced testimony by way of unconstitutional seizure of goods, papers, effects, documents, etc.? . . .

V.

Moreover, our holding that the exclusionary rule is an essential part of both the Fourth and Fourteenth Amendments is not only the logical dictate of prior cases, but it also makes very good sense. There is no war between the Constitution and common sense. Presently, a federal prosecutor may make no use of evidence illegally seized, but a State's attorney across the street may, although he supposedly is operating under the enforceable prohibitions of the same Amendment. Thus the State, by admitting evidence unlawfully seized, serves to encourage disobedience to the Federal Constitution which it is bound to uphold. Moreover, . . . the very essence of a healthy federalism depends upon the avoidance of needless conflict between state and federal courts. . . . Federal-state cooperation in the solution of crime under constitutional standards will be promoted, if only by recognition of their now mutual obligation to respect the same fundamental criteria in their approaches. . . .

There are those who say, as did Justice (then Judge) Cardozo, that under our constitutional exclusionary doctrine "the criminal is to go free because the constable has blundered." In some cases this will undoubtedly be the result. But . . . there is another consideration — the imperative of judicial integrity. The criminal goes free, if he must, but it is the law that sets him free. Nothing can destroy a government more quickly than its failure to observe its own laws, or worse, its disregard of the charter of its own existence. . . .

The ignoble shortcut to conviction left open to the State tends to destroy the entire system of constitutional restraints on which the liberties of the people rest. Having once recognized that the right to privacy embodied in the Fourth Amendment is enforceable against the States, and that the right to be secure against rude invasions of privacy by state officers is, therefore, constitutional in origin, we can no longer permit that right to remain an empty promise. Because it is enforceable in the same manner and to like effect as other basic rights secured by the Due Process Clause, we can no longer permit it to be revocable at the whim of any police officer who, in the name of law enforcement itself, chooses to suspend its enjoyment. Our decision, founded on reason and truth, gives to the individual no more than that which the Constitution guarantees him, to the police officer no less than that to which honest law enforcement is entitled, and, to the courts, that judicial integrity so necessary in the true administration of justice. . . .

HARLAN, J., dissenting.*

. . . II.

[It] cannot be too much emphasized that what was recognized in *Wolf* was not that the Fourth Amendment as such is enforceable against the States as a facet of due process, . . . but the principle of privacy "which is at the core of the Fourth Amendment." It would not be proper to expect or impose any precise equivalence, either as regards the scope of the right or the means of its implementation, between the requirements of the Fourth and Fourteenth Amendments. [Unlike the Fourteenth, which states a general principle only, the Fourth] is a particular command, having its setting in a pre-existing legal context on which both interpreting decisions and enabling statutes must at least build. . . .

I would not impose upon the States this federal exclusionary remedy. . . . Our concern here, as it was in *Wolf,* is not with the desirability of that rule but only with the question whether the States are Constitutionally free to follow it or not as they may themselves determine, and the relevance of the disparity of views among the States on this point lies simply in the fact that the judgment involved is a debatable one. . . .

The preservation of a proper balance between state and federal responsibility in the administration of criminal justice demands patience on the part of those who might like to see things move faster among the States in this respect. Problems of criminal law enforcement vary widely from State to State. One State, in considering the totality of its legal picture, may conclude that the need for embracing the *Weeks* rule is pressing because other remedies are unavailable or inadequate to secure compliance with the substantive Constitutional principle involved. Another, though equally solicitous of Constitutional rights, may choose to pursue one purpose at a time, allowing all evidence relevant to guilt to be brought into a criminal trial, and dealing with Constitutional infractions by other means. Still another may consider the exclusionary rule too rough-and-ready a remedy, in that it reaches only unconstitutional intrusions which eventuate in criminal prosecution of the victims. Further, a State after experimenting with the *Weeks* rule for a time may, because of

* [Justices Frankfurter and Whittaker joined in this opinion. — EDS.]

unsatisfactory experience with it, decide to revert to a non-exclusionary rule. And so on. . . . For us the question remains, as it has always been, one of state power, not one of passing judgment on the wisdom of one state course or another. . . .

I regret that I find so unwise in principle and so inexpedient in policy a decision motivated by the high purpose of increasing respect for Constitutional rights. But in the last analysis I think this Court can increase respect for the Constitution only if it rigidly respects the limitations which the Constitution places upon it, and respects as well the principles inherent in its own processes. In the present case I think we exceed both, and that our voice becomes only a voice of power, not of reason.

Notes

1. *Power and reason.* Was *Mapp* an appropriate interpretation of the due process clause? Do you believe that conditions had changed significantly between 1949 (the date of the *Wolf* decision) and 1961 (the date of *Mapp*)? Mapp's attorney did not ask the court to overturn the *Wolf* decision, but the American Civil Liberties Union, appearing as *amicus curiae,* raised the issue.

2. *Empirical evidence on the benefits of the exclusionary rule.* The *Cahan* court stated that "there is no convincing evidence that the exclusionary rule actually tends to prevent unreasonable searches and seizures" and that it was "a mild deterrent at best." It is quite difficult to estimate the real impact of the exclusionary rule on police and magistrate practices because the effect of the rule (if any) would be to produce a nonevent. That is, the exclusionary rule would, in theory, prevent improper searches and seizures from occurring. Some have attempted to measure the effects of the exclusionary rule by tracking either the number of search and arrest warrants sought or the number of arrests completed in the same location before and after the exclusionary rule took effect. In some locations, the number of warrants sought went up and the number of arrests went down after *Mapp,* but in other locations there was little or no change.

Others have estimated the deterrent effect of the exclusionary rule by asking police officers themselves how the prospect of losing evidence in a case would affect their decisions in the field. A 1997 survey of law enforcement officers in Ventura County, California, offered equivocal evidence about the deterrent effects of the exclusionary rule. About 20 percent of the officers responding to the survey said that the risk of exclusion of evidence was their primary concern in deciding whether to conduct a search or seizure, while nearly 60 percent considered suppression to be an "important" concern. Officers who had "lost" evidence because of improper searches or seizures in past cases were no more likely than other officers to give correct answers to hypothetical search and seizure questions. See Timothy Perrin, et al., If It's Broken, Fix It: Moving Beyond the Exclusionary Rule — A New and Extensive Empirical Study of the Exclusionary Rule and a Call for a Civil Administrative Remedy to Partially Replace the Rule, 83 Iowa L. Rev. 669 (1998).

3. *Empirical evidence on the costs of the exclusionary rule.* More effort has gone into measuring the "costs" of the exclusionary rule. A number of studies have estimated the number of convictions that the government loses because of concerns about exclusion of evidence obtained from an improper search or seizure. The estimates of arrests lost range from 0.6 percent to 2.35 percent of all felony arrests, with a

higher proportion (in the range of 3 to 5 percent) of arrests on drug and weapons charges. Thomas Davies, A Hard Look at What We Know (and Still Need to Learn) about the "Costs" of the Exclusionary Rule: The NIJ Study and Other Studies of "Lost" Arrests, 1983 Am. B. Found. Res. J. 611. For an attempt to measure the effects of the exclusionary rule on crime rates (as opposed to conviction rates), see Raymond A. Atkins & Paul H. Rubin, Effects of Criminal Procedure on Crime Rates: Mapping Out the Consequences of the Exclusionary Rule, 46 J. L. & Econ. 157 (2003).

Assuming we knew with some confidence how many cases are lost because of improper searches or seizures, how many would be too many? Perhaps the answer depends on whether the exclusionary rule should function as a "sanction" to signal that conduct is wrong and completely intolerable, or as a "price" that tolerates some of the behavior so long as it produces more good than harm overall. See Sharon Davies, The Penalty of Exclusion — A Price or Sanction? 73 S. Cal. L. Rev. 1275 (2000).

4. *The imperative of judicial integrity.* The courts in *Mapp* and *Cahan* each mentioned that the exclusionary rule would serve multiple purposes. In addition to deterring violations of the Constitution, it would also protect judicial integrity. Today, however, the Supreme Court describes the purpose of the exclusionary rule solely in terms of deterrence. See United States v. Janis, 428 U.S. 433, 458 (1976) ("considerations of judicial integrity do not require exclusion of the evidence"). Is the exclusionary rule necessary to protect the integrity of courts? Do courts undermine their integrity when they accept evidence in *civil* cases that was obtained contrary to law? Is the "truth seeking" function of the criminal process the best guarantee of judicial integrity, and does the exclusionary rule harm the truth-seeking function?

5. *Exclusion for violation of state constitutions, statutes, and procedure rules.* When a state court concludes that a search or seizure violated the state constitution rather than the federal constitution, exclusion is almost always the remedy the court adopts. Although exclusion is not required by federal law in such a case, state courts will typically choose exclusion as the proper remedy under state law.

When a search or seizure violates the provisions of a statute (state or federal) rather than a constitution, courts try to determine which remedy the legislature intended. Sometimes an explicit provision in a statute makes this relatively easy. See Ill. Stat. Ann. ch. 720, §5/14-5 (exclusion of any evidence obtained in violation of eavesdropping statute). . . . In other cases, the statutory language does not address remedies, and the legislative history is unhelpful. In such cases, courts tend to use the exclusion remedy for statutory violations when the search or seizure infringed in a "significant" way on "substantial" rights of the defendant. Compare People v. McKinstry, 843 P.2d 18 (Colo. 1993) (no exclusion for failure to include affiant's name in warrant application, as required by statute) with People v. Taylor, 541 N.E.2d 386 (N.Y. 1989) (exclusion required for violation of statutory requirement of contemporaneous recording of evidence supporting warrant application). What remedy would you expect state courts to select when police officers violate departmental policies as they gather evidence?

6. *Silver platters.* It is clear that a federal court cannot receive evidence that state officers obtain in violation of federal law. That is, the state officers may not present the evidence to their federal counterparts on a "silver platter." See Elkins v. United States, 364 U.S. 206 (1960). The same rule prevents federal officers from presenting

evidence to a state court if they obtained it in violation of the federal constitution. But the "silver platter doctrine" does not operate in all possible combinations. Officers from some other jurisdiction (federal or state) may obtain evidence in violation of state law (constitutional or statutory) and present that evidence in the federal courts or in the courts of another state. Local rules about search and seizure do not export to the courts of other jurisdictions. As the reach of federal criminal law grows and the overlap between state and federal criminal justice increases, does the argument get stronger for applying local search and seizure rules in the courts of other jurisdictions? How would traditional conflicts of laws doctrine resolve this issue?

7. *International adoption of exclusionary rule.* Although judges in the United States sometimes claim that no other country in the world uses an exclusionary rule, the claim is not true. For instance, in Germany, judges must consider whether admission of evidence obtained illegally would violate the constitutionally protected privacy interests of the defendant. German judges balance in each case the defendant's interests in privacy against the importance of the evidence and the seriousness of the offense charged. In practice, however, German judges rarely exclude evidence obtained through improper searches.

In Canada, exclusion happens more frequently. The constitutionally based Charter of Rights and Freedoms gives the accused a basis for excluding evidence that was obtained improperly. Evidence is excluded only if a breach of a Charter right or freedom is demonstrated and if the admission of the evidence in the trial would tend to bring the administration of justice "into disrepute." More serious violations are more likely to result in exclusion. Craig Bradley, *Mapp* Goes Abroad, 52 Case Western Res. L. Rev. 375 (2001). In general, judges in other countries distinguish between "real" evidence and interrogation evidence, and are more likely to exclude interrogation evidence. Why would courts make this distinction? The web extension for this chapter, at *http://www.crimpro.com/extension/ch06*, offers further examples of the use of the exclusionary remedy in other countries.

The basis for the exclusionary rule in these and other countries focuses more on judicial integrity than deterrence of police misconduct. If courts in the United States were to emphasize once again the "imperative of judicial integrity," would that open the way to an exclusionary rule that is applied less consistently than it is today?

B. LIMITATIONS ON THE EXCLUSIONARY RULE

We have traced the history of the adoption of the exclusionary rule as a remedy for illegal searches and seizures. The exclusionary rule was a highly controversial choice of remedies at the time of *Weeks*, *Cahan*, and *Mapp*, and it remains so today. Reservations about the exclusionary rule have not yet led any U.S. legal system to abandon the remedy, but they have led to some serious limitations on its applicability and effects.

1. *Evidence Obtained in "Good Faith"*

COMMONWEALTH v. LOUIS EDMUNDS

586 A.2d 887 (Penn. 1991)

CAPPY, J.

The issue presented to this court is whether Pennsylvania should adopt the "good faith" exception to the exclusionary rule as articulated by the United States Supreme Court in the case of United States v. Leon, 468 U.S. 897 (1984). We conclude that a "good faith" exception to the exclusionary rule would frustrate the guarantees embodied in Article I, Section 8, of the Pennsylvania Constitution. Accordingly, the decision of the Superior Court is reversed. . . .

The pertinent facts can be briefly summarized as follows. On August 5, 1985 State Police Trooper Michael Deise obtained a warrant from a district magistrate to search a white corrugated building and curtilage on the property of the defendant. [The information in the warrant affidavit came from confidential informants and from a later helicopter flyover of the property. When Trooper Deise and three other troopers went to Edmunds's property to execute the warrant, they discovered 17 growing marijuana plants inside the building, rather than outside the building as the informants had alleged. Prior to trial on drug charges, Edmunds moved to suppress the marijuana seized from the building] on the ground that the warrant was constitutionally defective, and probable cause was lacking, because the warrant failed to set forth a time frame in which the informants had observed the marijuana.

Recognizing that the affidavit of probable cause was deficient on its face, the trial court granted the request of the district attorney to convene a supplemental suppression hearing. . . . The express purpose of this hearing was to allow the district attorney to provide oral supplementation of the facts set forth in the written affidavit and warrant, in order to establish a "good faith" exception to the exclusionary rule under the auspices of *Leon.* [District Justice Tlumac] testified that Trooper Deise appeared in her office . . . and related his conversation with the two anonymous informants. She stated that Trooper Deise thereafter dictated the affidavit, which she typed verbatim. She then prepared and issued the search warrant. [She was under the impression that the informants had seen the marijuana the day before Trooper Deise had sought the warrant.]

Upon the close of the supplemental suppression hearing, the trial court found that . . . this warrant would be incapable of establishing probable cause to justify the search of defendant's property. The warrant failed to set forth a time frame from which a neutral and detached magistrate could reasonably infer that the criminal conduct observed was recent and would most likely still be in progress at the time the warrant was requested. [The trial court nevertheless admitted the evidence, because the trooper acted in "good faith" in executing the defective warrant.]

Our starting point must be the decision of the United States Supreme Court in *Leon.* In *Leon,* the Supreme Court in 1984 departed from a long history of exclusionary rule jurisprudence dating back to Weeks v. United States (1914) and Mapp v. Ohio (1961). The Court in *Leon* concluded that the Fourth Amendment does not mandate suppression of illegally seized evidence obtained pursuant to a constitutionally defective warrant, so long as the police officer acted in good faith reliance upon the warrant issued by a neutral and detached magistrate.

In *Leon,* police officers in Burbank, California, had initiated a drug investigation after receiving a tip from a confidential informant that large quantities of cocaine and methaqualone were being sold from a residence. The informant had indicated that he witnessed a sale of methaqualone approximately five months earlier. The Burbank police set up a surveillance of three residences, [and used their observations there to seek a search warrant. A magistrate mistakenly issued the warrant even though the officers had not established probable cause. The search uncovered large quantities of cocaine and methaqualone.]

Justice White, writing for the majority in *Leon,* first indicated that the exclusionary rule was not a "necessary corollary of the Fourth Amendment." Although . . . Mapp v. Ohio had suggested that the exclusion of illegally seized evidence was part-and-parcel of the Fourth Amendment's guaranty, the *Leon* Court took the position that the exclusionary rule operates as "a judicially created remedy designed to safeguard Fourth Amendment rights generally through its deterrent effect, rather than a personal constitutional right of the party aggrieved."

Justice White went on to conclude that the issue of whether the exclusionary rule should be imposed in a particular case "must be resolved by weighing the costs and benefits" of precluding such evidence from the prosecution's case. On the costs side of the analysis, Justice White declared that the exclusionary rule incurs "substantial social costs" in terms of "impeding unacceptably the truthfinding functions of judge and jury." As a result, Justice White noted that "some guilty defendants may go free or receive reduced sentences as a result of favorable plea bargains."

On the benefits side of the analysis, Justice White indicated that the sole purpose of the exclusionary rule under the Fourth Amendment was to "deter police misconduct rather than to punish the errors of judges and magistrates." Given this goal, Justice White concluded that there was no reason to presume that judges or magistrates would be more inclined to "ignore or subvert" the Fourth Amendment if evidence seized pursuant to a defective warrant were admissible. The majority wrote: "Although there are assertions that some magistrates become rubber stamps for the police and others may be unable effectively to screen police conduct . . . we are not convinced that this is a problem of major proportions."

The Court in *Leon* found that the argument that the exclusionary rule "deters future inadequate presentations" by police officers or prevents "magistrate shopping" was "speculative." . . . The *Leon* majority therefore concluded that, where a police officer is acting in objective good faith, based upon a search warrant duly issued by a neutral magistrate or judge, the Fourth Amendment does not require exclusion of such evidence, even where it is later determined that probable cause was lacking for the warrant. Unless the police officer acted "knowingly" or "recklessly" in providing false information to the magistrate, or the affidavit of probable cause is "so lacking in indicia of probable cause as to render official belief in its existence unreasonable," the evidence is admissible. . . .

This Court has long emphasized that, in interpreting a provision of the Pennsylvania Constitution, we are not bound by the decisions of the United States Supreme Court which interpret similar (yet distinct) federal constitutional provisions. [Independent analysis of state constitutions] is a positive expression of the jurisprudence which has existed in the United States since the founding of the nation.

[In Pennsylvania, a court considering differences between state and federal constitutional provisions will analyze] at least the following four factors: 1) text of the

Pennsylvania constitutional provision; (2) history of the provision, including Pennsylvania case-law; (3) related case-law from other states; (4) policy considerations, including unique issues of state and local concern, and applicability within modern Pennsylvania jurisprudence. . . . Depending upon the particular issue presented, an examination of related federal precedent may be useful as part of the state constitutional analysis, not as binding authority, but as one form of guidance. . . .

The text of Article I, Section 8 of the Pennsylvania Constitution [provides:] "The people shall be secure in their persons, houses, papers and possessions from unreasonable searches and seizures, and no warrant to search any place or to seize any person or things shall issue without describing them as nearly as may be, nor without probable cause, supported by oath or affirmation subscribed to by the affiant." Although the wording of the Pennsylvania Constitution is similar in language to the Fourth Amendment of the United States Constitution, we are not bound to interpret the two provisions as if they were mirror images, even where the text is similar or identical.

[Pennsylvania's] Constitution was adopted on September 28, 1776, a full ten years prior to the ratification of the U.S. Constitution. [It] was drafted in the midst of the American Revolution, as the first overt expression of independence from the British Crown. The Pennsylvania Constitution was therefore meant to reduce to writing a deep history of unwritten legal and moral codes which had guided the colonists from the beginning of William Penn's charter in 1681. . . . Thus, contrary to the popular misconception that state constitutions are somehow patterned after the United States Constitution, the reverse is true. The federal Bill of Rights borrowed heavily from the Declarations of Rights contained in the constitutions of Pennsylvania and other colonies. . . .

With respect to Article I, Section 8 of the present Pennsylvania Constitution, which relates to freedom from unreasonable searches and seizures, that provision had its origin prior to the Fourth Amendment, in [the original Commonwealth] Constitution of 1776, drafted by the first convention of delegates chaired by Benjamin Franklin. The primary purpose of the warrant requirement was to abolish "general warrants," which had been used by the British to conduct sweeping searches of residences and businesses, based upon generalized suspicions. Therefore, . . . the issue of searches and seizures unsupported by probable cause was of utmost concern to the constitutional draftsmen. Moreover, as this Court has stated repeatedly in interpreting Article I, Section 8, that provision is meant to embody a strong notion of privacy, carefully safeguarded in this Commonwealth for the past two centuries.

The history of Article I, Section 8, thus indicates that the purpose underlying the exclusionary rule in this Commonwealth is quite distinct from the purpose underlying the exclusionary rule under the Fourth Amendment, as articulated by the majority in *Leon.* The United States Supreme Court in *Leon* made clear that, in its view, the sole purpose for the exclusionary rule under the Fourth Amendment was to deter police misconduct. . . . This reinterpretation differs from the way the exclusionary rule has evolved in Pennsylvania. . . .

Like many of its sister states, Pennsylvania did not adopt an exclusionary rule until the United States Supreme Court's decision in *Mapp* required it to do so. However, at the time the exclusionary rule was embraced in Pennsylvania, we clearly viewed it as a constitutional mandate. . . . During the first decade after *Mapp,* our decisions in Pennsylvania tended to parallel the cases interpreting the Fourth

Amendment. However, beginning in 1973, our case-law began to reflect a clear divergence from federal precedent. The United States Supreme Court at this time began moving towards a metamorphosed view, suggesting that the purpose of the exclusionary rule is not to redress the injury to the privacy of the search victim but, rather, to deter future unlawful police conduct. At the same time this Court began to forge its own path under Article I, Section 8 of the Pennsylvania Constitution, declaring with increasing frequency that Article I, Section 8 of the Pennsylvania Constitution embodied a strong notion of privacy, notwithstanding federal cases to the contrary. . . . Thus, the exclusionary rule in Pennsylvania has consistently served to bolster the twin aims of Article I, Section 8; to-wit, the safeguarding of privacy and the fundamental requirement that warrants shall only be issued upon probable cause. . . .

More protection

Citizens in this Commonwealth possess such rights, even where a police officer in "good faith" carrying out his or her duties inadvertently invades the privacy or circumvents the strictures of probable cause. To adopt a "good faith" exception to the exclusionary rule, we believe, would virtually emasculate those clear safeguards which have been carefully developed under the Pennsylvania Constitution over the past 200 years.

A number of states other than Pennsylvania have confronted the issue of whether to apply a "good faith" exception to the exclusionary rule, under their own constitutions, in the wake of *Leon.* [The court reviewed the decisions of eight states approving of *Leon* and 11 rejecting *Leon* on constitutional or statutory grounds.]

Judicial integrity

We similarly conclude that [allowing] the judicial branch to participate, directly or indirectly, in the use of the fruits of illegal searches would only serve to undermine the integrity of the judiciary in this Commonwealth. From the perspective of the citizen whose rights are at stake, an invasion of privacy, in good faith or bad, is equally as intrusive. This is true whether it occurs through the actions of the legislative, executive or the judicial branch of government.

We recognize that, in analyzing any state constitutional provision, it is necessary to go beyond the bare text and history of that provision as it was drafted 200 years ago, and consider its application within the modern scheme of Pennsylvania jurisprudence. An assessment of various policy considerations, however, only supports our conclusion that the good faith exception to the exclusionary rule would be inconsistent with the jurisprudence surrounding Article I, Section 8.

First, such a rule would effectively negate the judicially created mandate reflected in the Pennsylvania Rules of Criminal Procedure, in [Rule 2003, which] relates to the requirements for the issuance of a warrant, and provides in relevant part:

> (a) No search warrant shall issue but upon probable cause supported by one or more affidavits sworn to before the issuing authority. The issuing authority, in determining whether probable cause has been established, may not consider any evidence outside the affidavits.
>
> (b) At any hearing on a motion for the return or suppression of evidence, or for suppression of the fruits of evidence, obtained pursuant to a search warrant, no evidence shall be admissible to establish probable cause other than the affidavits provided for in paragraph (a).

Rule 2003 thus adopts a "four corners" requirement, and provides that only evidence contained within the four corners of the affidavit may be considered to establish probable cause. . . . Although Rule 2003 is not constitutionally mandated by Article I, Section 8, . . . it reflects yet another expression of this Court's unwavering insistence that probable cause exist before a warrant is issued, and only those facts memorialized in the written affidavit may be considered in establishing probable cause, in order to eliminate any chance of incomplete or reconstructed hindsight. [We] have chosen to adopt that Rule as an administrative matter, and that Rule has now stood in Pennsylvania for 17 years.

In the instant case, probable cause — as defined under Pennsylvania law — is lacking. Two lower courts have so held; we concur. Applying the federal *Leon* test would not only frustrate the procedural safeguards embodied in Rule 2003, but would permit the admission of illegally seized evidence in a variety of contexts where probable cause is lacking, so long as the police officer acted in "good faith." In *Leon* itself probable cause was absent entirely, yet illegally seized evidence was admitted into evidence. We cannot countenance such a wide departure from the text and history of Article I, Section 8, nor can we permit the use of a "good faith" exception to effectively nullify Pa. R. Crim. P. 2003. . . .

A second policy consideration which bolsters our conclusion is that the underlying premise of *Leon* is still open to serious debate. Although it is clear that the exclusionary rule presents some cost to society, in allowing some guilty defendants to go free, the extent of the costs are far from clear. A number of recent studies have indicated that the exclusion of illegally seized evidence has had a marginal effect in allowing guilty criminals to avoid successful prosecution. Nardulli, The Societal Costs of the Exclusionary Rule: An Empirical Assessment, 1983 A. B. Found. Research J. 585. . . . Equally as important, the alternative to the exclusionary rule most commonly advanced — i.e., allowing victims of improper searches to sue police officers directly — has raised serious concern among police officers. Note, The Exclusionary Rule and Deterrence: An Empirical Study of Chicago Narcotics Officers, 54 U. Chi. L. Rev. 1016, 1053 (1987).

A third policy consideration which compels our decisions is that, given the recent decision of the United States Supreme Court in Illinois v. Gates, 462 U.S. 213 (1983), adopting a "totality of the circumstances test" in assessing probable cause, there is far less reason to adopt a "good faith" exception to the exclusionary rule. We have adopted *Gates* as a matter of Pennsylvania law. . . . As a number of jurists have pointed out, the flexible *Gates* standard now eliminates much of the prior concern which existed with respect to an overly rigid application of the exclusionary rule.

Finally, the dangers of allowing magistrates to serve as "rubber stamps" and of fostering "magistrate-shopping," are evident under *Leon.* As the instant case illustrates, police officers and magistrates have historically worked closely together in this Commonwealth. Trooper Deise and District Justice Tlumac prepared the warrant and affidavit with Trooper Deise dictating the affidavit while the magistrate typed it verbatim.

There is no suggestion here that Trooper Deise and District Justice Tlumac acted other than in utmost "good faith" when preparing the warrant. Nevertheless, we are mindful of the fact that both state and federal interpretations of the Fourth Amendment require a warrant to be issued by a "neutral and detached magistrate."

because . . . there is a requirement of an independent determination of probable cause. . . .

It must be remembered that a District Justice is not a member of the executive branch — the police — but a member of the judiciary. By falling within the judicial branch of government, the District Justice is thus charged with the responsibility of being the disinterested arbiter of disputes and is charged further with acting as the bulwark between the police and the rights of citizens. Unless and until a magistrate independently determines there is probable cause, no warrant shall issue.

This is not to say that we distrust our police or district justices; far from it. We, in fact, have no doubt that police officers and district justices in Pennsylvania are intelligent, committed and independent enough to carry out their duties under the scheme which has evolved over the past 30 years, in order to safeguard the rights of our citizens. However, requiring "neutral and detached magistrates" furthers the twin aims of safeguarding privacy and assuring that no warrant shall issue but upon probable cause. As such, we see no reason to eliminate this requirement, for if we did, we would eviscerate the purpose of requiring warrants prior to searches. "If it ain't broke, don't fix it."

Thirty years ago, when the exclusionary rule was first introduced, police officers were perhaps plagued with ill-defined, unarticulated rules governing their conduct. However, the past 30 years have seen a gradual sharpening of the process, with police officers adapting well to the exclusionary rule. . . . Although the exclusionary rule may place a duty of thoroughness and care upon police officers and district justices in this Commonwealth, in order to safeguard the rights of citizens under Article I, Section 8, that is a small price to pay, we believe, for a democracy.

PAPADAKOS, J., concurring.

I am compelled to concur in the result because Rule 2003(a) of the Pennsylvania Rules of Criminal Procedure is absolute in requiring that the affidavit of probable cause supporting the issuance of a search warrant must be complete on its face in every essential detail, and that no testimony is permitted after its execution to fill in the blanks. . . .

In view of the clear, unequivocal command of Rule 2003(a), I see no reason for the majority to reinvent the wheel and re-express the rationale underpinning the judicially created rule of procedure. It's all been said before. . . . Were the rule not so absolute on its face, I would gladly join [Justice McDermott] in dissent, for my sympathies and reason lie in his expression of outrage in the result of cases such as this.

MCDERMOTT, J., dissenting.

Today we have abandoned the 27 year history of this Court's restrictive use of the exclusionary rule to only those instances where its application would deter misconduct by law enforcement authorities. Now that we have ignored that history and have decided to employ it even in cases where police officers have fulfilled their every obligation to protect the individual constitutional rights of citizens, I dissent.

Until this day we have dutifully followed the canons of the Fourth Amendment prescribed by the Supreme Court of the United States through hundreds of cases. We . . . were obliged to ignore a mountain of illegal contraband that otherwise was palpable indicia of guilt. There is no doubt that the social cost has been more than criminals freed to try again. It has generated a disbelief and a growing disrespect in the efficacy of law that stands mute in the presence of incontrovertible evidence of fire and lets the house burn down because the fireman arrived before he was properly called.[2] United States v. Leon, 468 U.S. 897 (1984), does not open the gates to unauthorized search, it does not dissolve the need for probable cause. It simply and properly shifts the responsibility for determining probable cause to a neutral magistrate and frees the police of his or her mistakes. . . .

The instant case is a classic illustration. The defect in the affidavit of probable cause was that the time of the offense was not specified. What was told the magistrate was that the contraband was "growing," a clear indication of present tense. The informants told the police that they saw it growing and the magistrate was told that it was growing and she issued a search warrant on that premise. When the police arrived it was still growing. All concerned acted in good faith. To suppress the evidence because a date was not specified with exactitude under those circumstances dwindles into practiced absurdity.

The United States Supreme Court has made it abundantly clear that suppression of evidence seized without probable cause is not a constitutional right. This Court has made that clear as well. See Commonwealth v. Miller, 518 A.2d 1187 (Pa. 1986). The United States Supreme Court has made it equally clear that suppression of evidence seized without probable cause is mandated to contain police action. Likewise, we have approved the suppression of evidence only where it will have the benefit of deterring similar police misconduct in the future.

In interpreting our Constitution we are, as are our sister states, always free to give more than that allowed under Federal Constitutional interpretation. I would choose to accept the rationale of the Supreme Court and recognize the "good faith exception" of *Leon* to the exclusionary rule as have 18 of our sister states. . . . Like the United States Supreme Court, I find no evidence that the judiciary has run beyond its responsibilities, or that if they do we cannot correct them. The Supreme Court of the United States is a world landmark for the protection of constitutional rights. What they require we enforce; what they allow we ought not deter except upon clear evidence of positive need. The United States Supreme Court has recognized a positive need to allow, under the canons of *Leon,* a good faith exception. To do otherwise is to provide a sanctuary for the lawless elements seeking profit, particularly in the growing human misery of addiction. . . .

Notes

1. *Good faith exception: majority position.* About 15 states have decided, like Pennsylvania, not to adopt a good faith exception to exclusionary rules under their state constitutions. A majority of states have explicitly adopted *Leon* under state constitutions. See State v. Eason, 629 N.W.2d 625 (Wis. 2001). For a richer account of the courts that accept or reject *Leon*, consult the web extension for this chapter at *http://www.crimpro.com/extension/ch06*. Do you agree with the Pennsylvania court that a state rejecting the good faith exception will maintain stronger privacy protections

2. One rationale, other than deterrence, that has been offered for the use of the exclusionary rule is "the imperative of judicial integrity." However, this rationale has been criticized because [the] layman finds the judicial integrity rationale difficult to grasp, [and] many lawyers think the highest integrity of the adjudicative aspect of the criminal process lies in the separation of the guilty from the innocent on the basis of all the relevant evidence available.

and stronger control over the quality of warranted searches? If you were directing a police training program in a state that had adopted *Leon,* would that decision affect your training priorities or your recommendations to police officers?

2. *Objective good faith and perjury.* As the *Edmunds* court mentions, the officer's good faith reliance on the warrant under *Leon* must be "objectively reasonable." There is no objective good faith when (1) the officer gives to the magistrate information that the officer knew or should have known was false; (2) the magistrate "wholly abandon[s]" the judicial role; (3) the affidavit is "so lacking in indicia of probable cause" that it would be "entirely unreasonable" for a well-trained officer to believe probable cause existed; or (4) the warrant is so facially deficient that the officer could not reasonably believe it is valid. *Leon,* 468 U.S. at 923. See People v. Miller, 75 P.3d 1108 (Colo. 2003) (well-trained officer could not rely on month-old tip with no mention of ongoing activity as basis for probable cause in warrant; no good faith exception). How would a criminal defendant prove that an officer gave false information to the magistrate?

The "four corners" rule, mentioned in the *Edmunds* case from Pennsylvania, is one traditional technique to prevent perjury or other inaccurate police testimony. Is it possible to adopt the good faith exception while continuing to insist that any facts related to the reasonableness of the search appear within the warrant application and supporting affidavits? See State v. Davidson, 618 N.W.2d 418 (Neb. 2000) (inquiry into officers' good faith is not limited to four corners of warrant affidavit).

3. *What counts as a cost?* Are criminal convictions lost because the exclusionary rule is the chosen remedy or are the lost convictions simply the cost of having the Fourth Amendment and its analogs? Since the exclusionary rule arguably returns the parties to their relative positions before the constitutional violation took place, one might consider it a backward-looking "tort" remedy. On the other hand, if one is convinced that the value of the remedy to the defendant (avoiding a criminal conviction) far exceeds the value of any lost privacy, then the difference in value between the loss to the defendant and the loss to the government might be considered a "cost" of the exclusionary rule rather than a cost of the constitutional provision. One might prefer a remedy that more closely matches the defendant's actual loss. Which is the most appropriate measure?

4. *Good faith reliance on legislatures and appellate courts.* Rules or statutes can also work in favor of a good faith exception. In Illinois v. Krull, 480 U.S. 340 (1987), the court extended the good faith exception of *Leon* to include searches by officers who relied in good faith during a search or seizure on a statute later declared to be unconstitutional. See State v. De La Cruz, 969 A.2d 413 (N.H. 2009) (adopting *Krull* while rejecting *Leon*). Does the exclusionary rule help to "deter" the legislature from passing unconstitutional legislation regarding searches and seizures? Do the arguments for the good faith exception change when the police rely on established interpretations of the Fourth Amendment by appellate courts that are later overturned? State v. Dearborn, 786 N.W.2d 97 (Wis. 2010) (applying good faith exception to police action in reliance on established but mistaken appellate interpretations of search incident to arrest law).

5. *Good faith reliance on negligent police action.* The *Leon* decision allows police officers to rely on determinations by a magistrate. In Arizona v. Evans, 514 U.S. 1 (1995), the Court allowed a good faith exception to the exclusionary rule when an officer relied on an inaccurate record showing an outstanding arrest warrant for a person he had stopped. The record was inaccurate because an employee of the clerk

of the court had failed to update a computer database. In Herring v. United States, 129 S. Ct. 695 (2009), in a 5-4 decision authored by Chief Justice Roberts, the Court extended this decision and held that the exclusionary rule does not apply when an illegal search is based on "isolated [police] negligence attenuated from the search." In *Herring*, police relied on a faulty police report of an outstanding arrest warrant for failure to appear on a felony change. This false report led to an arrest, a search incident to arrest, and the discovery of methamphetamine in Herring's pocket and an illegal pistol in his car. The Court held:

> To trigger the exclusionary rule, police conduct must be sufficiently deliberate that exclusion can meaningfully deter it, and sufficiently culpable that such deterrence is worth the price paid by the justice system. As laid out in our cases, the exclusionary rule serves to deter deliberate, reckless, or grossly negligent conduct, or in some circumstances recurring or systemic negligence. The error in this case does not rise to that level.

Is *Herring* a logical extension of *Leon* and *Evans*? Or is it another example of death (to exclusion) by a thousand small (doctrinal) cuts? Thomas K. Clancy, The Irrelevancy of the Fourth Amendment in the Roberts Court, 85 Chicago-Kent L.J. 191 (2010) (attributing decline in the number of cases addressing Fourth Amendment questions in part to *Herring*).

Problem 6-1. Objective Good Faith

The Drug Squad of the Boulder Police Department received an anonymous letter, postmarked from Kansas City, which read as follows:

> This letter is to inform you that the person described below is an active drug dealer and warrants investigation. This is based on firsthand knowledge and eyewitness accounts by me and others. Below are some facts that may help you.
>
> Name: Jeff; Age: 35-40; Height: 5'9"; Weight: 170 lbs.; Race: white; Features: Bald on the top of his head. Crooked front teeth. Address: Lives in Boulder, Colorado, and is a student at the university.
>
> Vehicle: Two-door van with a large window on the driver's side. The passenger side has a sliding door. Color is steel blue. License plate number is MXS 518 or MSX 518, Colorado.
>
> Drugs are collected at a music store located in Kansas City just north of the intersection of 39th and Main on the east side of the street. The collection times may coincide with the vacation times of the university in Colorado. The drugs are then taken to Boulder for resale.
>
> We hope that this information will help you and are sorry that we must remain anonymous as other innocent people may get involved.
>
> Your friends in Kansas City.

Detective Kurt Weiler began an investigation, and confirmed that the vehicle described was registered to Jeffrey Leftwich, that Leftwich was 37 years old, and that his appearance matched the description in the letter. A call to the Kansas City Police Department confirmed that the music store described in the letter was in a "high drug" area.

During spring break at the university, officers noted that no vehicles were parked outside Leftwich's trailer residence. The day after spring break ended, an officer observed a car parked in the driveway of the residence. The parked car belonged to a person who had been convicted two years earlier of possessing cocaine. The next day, officers noted that Leftwich's Ford van was parked in the driveway. Further inquiries confirmed that Leftwich had traveled to Kansas City during spring break.

Detective Weiler then prepared an affidavit for a search warrant for Leftwich's home. The chief deputy district attorney reviewed the affidavit and advised Detective Weiler that the affidavit presented a close case and that a judge might not sign it. Weiler nonetheless filed the application and a district court judge issued a warrant. During the search of Leftwich's home, Weiler found a triple-beam balance and some marijuana.

Assuming that a reviewing court would conclude that the warrant was not supported by probable cause, would the good faith exception apply? Recall that the officer's good faith must be "objectively" reasonable. If this officer did not qualify for the good faith exception, how often will the exception apply in those states adopting it? Compare People v. Leftwich, 869 P.2d 1260 (Colo. 1994).

■ TEXAS CODE OF CRIMINAL PROCEDURE ART. 38.23

(a) No evidence obtained by an officer or other person in violation of any provisions of the Constitution or laws of the State of Texas, or of the Constitution or laws of the United States of America, shall be admitted in evidence against the accused on the trial of any criminal case. . . .

(b) It is an exception to the provisions of subsection (a) of this Article that the evidence was obtained by a law enforcement officer acting in objective good faith reliance upon a warrant issued by a neutral magistrate based on probable cause.

■ COLORADO REVISED STATUTES §16-3-308

(1) Evidence which is otherwise admissible in a criminal proceeding shall not be suppressed by the trial court if the court determines that the evidence was seized by a peace officer . . . as a result of a good faith mistake or of a technical violation.

(2) As used in subsection (1) of this section:

(a) "Good faith mistake" means a reasonable judgmental error concerning the existence of facts or law which if true would be sufficient to constitute probable cause.

(b) "Technical violation" means a reasonable good faith reliance upon a statute which is later ruled unconstitutional, a warrant which is later invalidated due to a good faith mistake, or a court precedent which is later overruled. . . .

(4) (a) It is hereby declared to be the public policy of the state of Colorado that, when evidence is sought to be excluded from the trier of fact in a criminal proceeding because of the conduct of a peace officer leading to its discovery, it will be open to the proponent of the evidence to urge that the conduct in question was taken in

a reasonable, good faith belief that it was proper, and in such instances the evidence so discovered should not be kept from the trier of fact if otherwise admissible. . . .

(b) It shall be prima facie evidence that the conduct of the peace officer was performed in the reasonable good faith belief that it was proper if there is a showing that the evidence was obtained pursuant to and within the scope of a warrant, unless the warrant was obtained through intentional and material misrepresentation.

Problem 6-2. Unwarranted Good Faith

Three undercover police officers went to the Brook Hollow Inn to set up a surveillance of possible illegal activities in one of the rooms. The manager checked the officers into a room that she believed to be vacant. However, when the officers entered the room they noticed that clothing and luggage had been left in the room. One officer called the registration desk to confirm that they were in the right room. Another officer opened the doors of the television cabinet and found cocaine there. After the officers had left the room, Charles Farmer arrived at the room and let himself in with his key. He called the manager from the phone in the room and told her that he had paid for another day and still occupied the room. The manager told Farmer that a terrible mistake had been made.

Would a court in Colorado exclude from evidence the cocaine found in the room? What about a court in Texas? Would this evidence be admissible under *Leon?* Compare Fanner v. State, 759 P.2d 1031 (Okla. Crim. App. 1988).

Notes

1. *Statutory exclusion.* A number of states have passed statutes calling in general terms for the exclusion of evidence obtained through illegal searches or seizures. Would this sort of statute make it more difficult for a court to justify the creation of good faith exceptions or other limitations on the state's exclusionary rule? On the other hand, several jurisdictions have passed statutes allowing admission of evidence obtained illegally, so long as the officer acted in good faith. See Zarychta v. State, 44 S.W.3d 155 (Tex. App. 2001) (narrow interpretation of coverage for Texas good faith statute). Would the passage of such a statute affect your analysis in Problem 6-2? Further examples of statutory exclusionary rules and statutory limits to the remedy appear on the web extension for this chapter at *http://www.crimpro.com/extension/ch06.*

2. *Evidence excluded in which proceedings?* The statutes printed above all address admission of evidence in criminal proceedings. Federal and state constitutions require the exclusion of evidence from the government's case-in-chief at a criminal trial. However, the exclusionary rule usually does not operate in other proceedings. For instance, the government can use such evidence in grand jury proceedings and in most administrative proceedings. See INS v. Lopez-Mendoza, 468 U.S. 1032 (1984) (exclusion does not apply in civil deportation proceedings).

Courts deciding whether to follow the exclusionary rule in various types of proceedings have often relied on the reasoning of the Supreme Court in United States v. Calandra, 414 U.S. 338 (1974). The Court there decided that the exclusionary rule would not apply to grand jury proceedings because the rule would have little additional deterrent value on police, given that the evidence was already excludable from any criminal trial. Would this reasoning apply to investigators for the Immigration and Naturalization Service, or others like them, whose principal task is to enforce civil laws? The exclusionary rule is generally applied to "quasi-criminal" proceedings before judges or administrative agencies such as proceedings to forfeit property (because of its connection with criminal activity). See, e.g., Commonwealth v. One 1985 Ford Thunderbird Automobile, 624 N.E.2d 547 (Mass. 1993). But see Pennsylvania Board of Probation and Parole v. Scott, 524 U.S. 357 (1998) (parole boards are not required by federal law to exclude evidence obtained in violation of Fourth Amendment). Is the deterrent value of the exclusionary rule in quasi-criminal proceedings any greater than in other civil proceedings? A number of state statutes and court rules clarify whether illegally obtained evidence may be admitted in various types of proceedings. See, e.g., La. Code Evid. art. 1101.

3. *Impeachment.* The government can also use improperly obtained evidence as the basis for impeaching a defendant if she testifies at a criminal trial. The Court in United States v. Havens, 446 U.S. 620 (1980), reasoned that exclusion in such cases would not deter police because the usefulness of evidence for impeachment purposes is so difficult to predict. At the same time, allowing the evidence to form the basis of impeachment questions would discourage defendants from committing perjury. See also James v. Illinois, 493 U.S. 307 (1990) (illegally obtained evidence may *not* be used to impeach defense witnesses other than defendant; such impeachment not necessary to discourage perjury of witnesses other than defendant).

2. *Causation Limits: Inevitable Discovery and Independent Source*

Long before *Wolf* and *Mapp*, it was clear that the exclusionary rule applied not only to evidence obtained during an improper search or seizure but also to any "fruits," that is, evidence the government later developed on the basis of leads obtained during an improper search or seizure. A common phrase presents a powerful image: The exclusionary rule, it is said, applies to the "fruit of the poisonous tree." But there must be some end to the consequences of error; a government error early in an investigation cannot bar all subsequent investigation. Courts have wrestled over how far to extend the impact of government errors — what harms can be said to be "caused" by, or fairly attributed to, the initial violation?

Federal and state courts have placed several causal limitations on the fruit-of-the-poisonous-tree doctrine. Two widely acknowledged limitations are known as the "independent source" and "inevitable discovery" rules. Though these are often described as "exceptions" to the exclusionary rule, each amounts to a conclusion that the government would have obtained the evidence in question even without the illegal enforcement activity; thus, the violation did not "cause" the government to hold the evidence. Application of the "inevitable discovery" and "independent source" rules raise a host of questions, many spurred by the fundamental problem of asking judges to decide what could or would have happened in a case, rather than what did in fact happen.

STATE v. CHARLES RABON

930 A.2d 268 (Me. 2007)

LEVY, J.

. . . During the summer of 2004, the Rumford Police Department received information indicating that the Rabons were involved in transporting cocaine from Florida for sale in Maine. . . . The information concerning the Rabons' activities came from a confidential informant who was the subject of a pending criminal charge or charges. . . . The confidential informant claimed that Charles Rabon drives to Florida several times during the year to pick up large amounts of cocaine, brings the cocaine back to the apartment that he shares with his wife Sharon in Rumford, and then distributes most of his cocaine to local dealers for sale at local bars where Charles operates a karaoke business.

[On] August 13, five police officers were sent to the Rabons' apartment to secure the scene in anticipation of the issuance of a search warrant that was to be sought by other officers. The officers arrived at the Rabons' apartment at 11:58 A.M. An officer in plain clothes, but wearing a vest that clearly identified him as a police officer, knocked on the closed front door of the apartment. One of the other officers observed a woman peek through the blinds of a window near the door. One of the officers heard the woman say "Oh shit," and observed her run toward the back of the apartment. The officers immediately opened the door and entered the apartment without consent and located both Rabons. Charles was found sitting at a desk on which there was a container of white powder and a digital scale. The officers handcuffed the Rabons, conducted a brief safety search of the house for firearms or other inhabitants, took photographs of the inside of the apartment, and made a list of the telephone numbers listed in the Rabons' telephone's caller ID. The officers then sat with the Rabons to await the issuance of a search warrant.

The Maine Drug Enforcement Agency (MDEA) agent who participated in the preparation of the warrant request included in paragraphs ten and eleven of his affidavit information concerning the other officers' warrantless entry into the Rabons' apartment. The District Court issued a search warrant at 4:31 P.M. The resulting search of the apartment led to the seizure of cocaine and money.

search after warrant

[The warrant affidavit detailed] the initial information provided by the informant in June of 2004, and on August 11 and 13, 2004, and . . . the extent to which the police were able to corroborate the same. The affidavit reports that the police corroborated that the Rabons' blue van was not at their apartment on August 11 and 12, and that it returned on August 13, a period corresponding to the informant's claim that the Rabons were returning from a drug run to Florida. In addition, the affidavit reports police corroboration of the Rabons' names, telephone number, address, car, color of their apartment building, the fact that Charles Rabon had received a summons for excessive noise and had not been subject to a search, and that two bars in the Rumford and Mexico area, named by the informant as locations where Charles Rabon trafficked in drugs, were known to the police as places where drugs are trafficked. . . .

Following their arrest, the Rabons were each charged with aggravated trafficking of scheduled drugs and a count seeking criminal forfeiture. The Rabons filed a joint motion to suppress all of the evidence obtained from their apartment. . . . The

Superior Court denied the motion to suppress [and] approved the Rabons' conditional guilty pleas. . . . The Rabons' central contention is that because the officers lacked probable cause to search the apartment prior to the warrantless entry, no evidence gathered from the initial warrantless entry into the apartment or from the subsequent search of the apartment pursuant to the warrant can be admitted against them. The State contends that the contested evidence was lawfully seized because the officers' initial warrantless entry into the apartment was justified by the exigent circumstances exception to the warrant requirement; was nonetheless justified as a reasonable, temporary seizure in order to secure the premises and preserve any evidence within it pending the issuance of a search warrant; or because . . . the inevitable discovery exception permits the admission of the evidence seized from the Rabons. . . .

Exigent Circumstances. The exigent circumstances justification for warrantless searches applies when there is a compelling need to conduct a search and insufficient time in which to secure a warrant. However, probable cause is a prerequisite for the exigent circumstances justification to apply. Accordingly, the exigent circumstances exception to the warrant requirement authorizes the warrantless entry in this case only if the officers had probable cause to search the Rabons' apartment at the time they made the decision to enter the Rabons' apartment.

Temporary Seizure of the Premises to Secure the Scene. The temporary seizure of a residence for the purpose of preserving evidence pending the issuance of a warrant is another recognized exception to the warrant requirement. Such a seizure is constitutionally sound under certain circumstances, but only if the officers have probable cause to search at the time they entered the residence. As applied here, if the officers did not have probable cause to search the premises at the time they entered the residence, then this exception is inapplicable and cannot support the denial of the motion to suppress.

The Independent Source Exception. The independent source exception to the exclusionary rule permits the use of evidence that has been obtained in violation of the Fourth Amendment to the United States Constitution and article I, section 5 of the Maine Constitution when that evidence "was gained through an independent source as well as the tainted source." State v. Storer, 583 A.2d 1016 (Me. 1990). An independent source exception analysis is appropriate in circumstances where a search warrant was issued, but some of the information used to establish probable cause is determined to have been illegally obtained. If the magistrate would still have had probable cause to issue the warrant without the allegedly unlawfully obtained information, the independent source exception allows the admission of the evidence, and suppression is not justified.

In the present case, most of the evidence sought to be suppressed was discovered during the search of the Rabons' apartment following the issuance of a search warrant. . . . To determine whether the independent source exception will permit admission of the evidence obtained pursuant to the warrant in this case, we: (1) excise from the affidavit used to obtain the warrant all the information believed to have been illegally obtained, and then (2) determine whether the judge or magistrate would have had probable cause to issue the warrant relying solely on the remaining information. . . .

The Inevitable Discovery Exception. The inevitable discovery exception is an additional analytical framework for considering the suppression of the evidence if we conclude that the initial warrantless entry into the Rabons' apartment prior to the issuance of the search warrant was unlawful because there was no probable cause. The inevitable discovery exception to the exclusionary rule permits the use of evidence that has been obtained in violation of the Fourth Amendment to the United States Constitution and article I, section 5 of the Maine Constitution when that evidence "inevitably would have been discovered by lawful means." *Storer*, 583 A.2d at 1020 (quoting Nix v. Williams, 467 U.S. 431 (1984)). The specific question presented here is whether the evidence discovered by the police when they initially entered the Rabons' apartment with the intent of securing it would have been inevitably discovered through lawful means.

If a warrant would not have issued without the information resulting from the initial warrantless entry reported in paragraphs ten and eleven of the affidavit, there would not be a lawful means to enter the apartment, and it would not be inevitable that the police would have lawfully discovered the evidence they discovered during their initial warrantless entry. Accordingly, for the inevitable discovery exception to apply in this case, it requires that the police had probable cause at the time they entered the Rabons' apartment.

All of the above exceptions to the warrant requirement and the exclusionary rule require the existence of probable cause at the time of the initial warrantless entry into the Rabons' apartment. . . . To determine probable cause, a magistrate must apply the "totality-of-the-circumstances approach" articulated in Illinois v. Gates, 462 U.S. 213 (1983). . . .

The warrant affidavit signed by the MDEA agent is based largely on information provided to him by the confidential informant. In viewing the affidavit, as redacted, in its most positive light, we assess the information in the affidavit regarding the informant's: (a) reliability and basis of knowledge; (b) claims regarding the Rabons' criminal activities; and (c) reports of other information concerning the Rabons. We conclude the analysis by applying the totality of the circumstances test.

Informant's Reliability and Basis of Knowledge. The warrant affidavit reveals very little about the informant's background. It reports that the confidential informant contacted the police wishing to share information about drug trafficking occurring in Rumford in order to receive "prosecutorial consideration if any information provided is helpful in a drug trafficking case." The informant is described as not being on probation, but as being on bail for non-drug related offenses; as not receiving any remuneration in exchange for information; and as having provided additional information on other drug trafficking in the area. The affidavit does not provide any details regarding this additional information, or whether it had been found to be accurate.

The affidavit fails to explain the basis for the informant's knowledge that the Rabons were engaged in drug trafficking. The affidavit does not assert that the informant had actually seen firsthand any contraband or criminal activity. The affidavit also does not contain any statement to the effect that the informant has been found or is otherwise believed by the MDEA agent or other law enforcement officials to be a reliable reporter of information. . . .

An affidavit that supplies no information about an informant's reliability or basis of knowledge fails to provide information that is highly relevant to the probable cause determination. The absence of such information does not preclude a finding of probable cause, but . . . absent that information, "something more" is required.

Corroboration of Informant's Claims of Suspicious or Criminal Activity. Our decisions establish that "something more" is frequently supplied by police corroboration of the informant's reports regarding suspicious or criminal activities by the person suspected of wrongdoing. . . . The affidavit in this case reveals that the police corroborated, to a limited degree, the informant's report that Charles and Sharon Rabon had recently left Florida and were en route back to Rumford in their van in possession of cocaine. . . . The absence of the Rabons' van on August 11 and 12, and its return on August 13 was not, however, contextually suspicious.

Corroboration of Other Information Concerning the Rabons. The MDEA agent's affidavit also corroborates other information provided by the informant, such as the Rabons' names, telephone number, address, car, the color of their apartment building, and the fact that Charles Rabon had received a summons for excessive noise and had not been subject to a search. The corroboration of this readily available information reveals that the informant, or the persons providing information to the informant, were familiar with the Rabons. The informant's identification of two bars in the area known to the police as sites where drugs are trafficked establishes that either the informant, or the persons providing information to the informant, were generally familiar with drug activity in the area. The affidavit contains no corroboration of the informant's claim that Charles Rabon has a karaoke business, nor does it contain information that corroborates whether Charles Rabon was ever present at the two bars where the informant alleges the drugs were sold.

None of the preceding information qualifies as "inside information" that would be uniquely available to an informant with direct knowledge of otherwise uncorroborated criminal activity. An informant's accurate description of readily available information establishes reliability in the limited sense that it will help the police correctly identify the person whom the tipster means to accuse, but it does not show that the tipster has knowledge of concealed criminal activity. . . .

Totality of the Circumstances Analysis. When the police saw the Rabons' van return on August 13, they were in the middle of a promising investigation. Considered in its totality, however, the warrant affidavit, as redacted, does not contain information that establishes the informant's reliability or basis of knowledge, or corroborate in any significant way the informant's claim that the Rabons purchased cocaine in Florida for resale in Maine. . . .

Because probable cause did not exist to search the apartment without the information gained from the warrantless entry into the apartment, none of the above discussed exceptions to the warrant requirement or the exclusionary rule apply, and the evidence seized from the Rabons' apartment during the initial warrantless entry and the subsequent search pursuant to the warrant should have been ordered suppressed.

ALEXANDER, J., concurring.

. . . I write separately because I do not concur in the Court's opinion that probable cause to search was not sufficiently established because the information obtained through the confidential informant was not sufficiently corroborated. . . . Although probable cause to search was sufficiently established without reliance on evidence obtained in the illegal entry, I would vacate because the State failed to meet its burden to establish that discovery of the illegally seized evidence was inevitable. See Nix v. Williams, 467 U.S. 431 (1984) (noting that the prosecution has the burden to prove inevitable discovery by a preponderance of the evidence). . . .

The protections of article I, section 5, and the concurrent protections of the Fourth Amendment of the United States Constitution, cannot be easily circumvented by illegally seizing evidence then asserting that its discovery, by legal means, was "inevitable." Our constitutional protections for person and home can be avoided only for special, narrowly construed purposes, and then, only when justified by a high quality of evidence. [The] inevitable discovery doctrine is available only where there is a high level of confidence that each of the contingencies required for the discovery of the disputed evidence would in fact have occurred. . . .

The First Circuit, in a case originating in Lewiston, outlined a three-step analytical framework for examination of inevitable discovery claims, with the prosecution bearing the burden of proof on each point:

> In evaluating inevitable discovery claims, we ask three questions: first, whether the legal means by which the evidence would have been discovered was truly independent; second, whether the use of the legal means would have inevitably led to the discovery of the evidence; and third, whether applying the inevitable discovery rule would either provide an incentive for police misconduct or significantly weaken constitutional protections.

United States v. Almeida, 434 F.3d 25, 28 (1st Cir. 2006).

We have indicated that evidence may be admitted pursuant to the inevitable discovery doctrine if the prosecution proves two criteria: first, the information in the application for the search warrant that is independent of illegally obtained information must be sufficient to provide probable cause to support the issuance of the warrant, and, second, the independent information would have inevitably led to discovery of the evidence through lawful means.

Whether we apply the First Circuit's three-step analysis or our two-step analysis, the first two steps of either analysis are similar and hold the keys to this case. The third step of the First Circuit's analysis is an important reminder of the significance of the constitutional protections at issue and the caution with which the inevitable discovery doctrine must be applied.

I concur with the Chief Justice that . . . independent of the information derived from the warrantless entry, [the record] demonstrates sufficient probable cause to justify issuing a warrant. . . . There is insufficient evidence, however, to support the second element that use of the legal means would have inevitably led to the discovery of the evidence. Pursuant to *Nix*, the prosecution must prove the elements of the inevitable discovery doctrine by a preponderance of the evidence. Applying the preponderance of the evidence standard to inevitable discovery cases, however, requires a higher standard of quality of evidence. This derives from the conceptual difficulty of proving inevitability to a probability. Thus, . . . the government cannot prevail under the inevitable discovery doctrine merely by establishing that it is more probable than not that the disputed evidence would have been obtained without the constitutional violation. [The] First Circuit requires that inevitability must be demonstrated "to a high degree of probability." . . .

The quality of evidence supporting inevitability of legal discovery of the evidence at the Rabons' home [does not satisfy] the First Circuit's "high degree of probability" test. Instead, the State's evidence presents a logical inconsistency. If it was essential to send five officers to prevent disappearance of the Rabons or the contraband before a warrant could be obtained, then it cannot be inevitable that the

Rabons and the contraband would have been at the apartment five hours later when the warrant was obtained. . . .

The trial court found that, shortly before noon, five Rumford officers, some in uniform and at least one wearing a protective vest, appeared "at the [Rabons'] residence" in order to "secure the premises pending the issuance of a warrant." It is quite a stretch to speculate that this heavy police presence would not have been observed at some time over the next five hours, and that the Rabons, observing the police presence, might not have taken some steps to separate themselves from the contraband or from the premises. Even without the observed police presence, it is also a stretch, inconsistent with the "high degree of probability" standard of evidence, to speculate that the Rabons and the contraband, having arrived at the apartment sometime after 7:30 A.M., would "inevitably" have remained there until sometime after 5:00 P.M. . . .

The court's conclusion of inevitability of the legal discovery of this evidence is speculation, unsupported by any evidence in the record. Basically, the court is bootstrapping the fact that the contraband was discovered upon the illegal entry at noon to infer that, but for the illegal entry, the contraband would have remained in the apartment, inevitably, after 5:00 P.M. The strictures imposed by our Constitution to protect persons and their homes from illegal searches cannot be so easily avoided. The contraband in this case was obtained in a search based on a created exigency that the trial court found was an illegal search. The State failed to meet its burden to prove inevitability of discovery by legal means.

SAUFLEY, C.J., dissenting.

. . . A magistrate reviewing the affidavit would have information demonstrating that the authorities were able to independently confirm much of what was given to them by the confidential informant. This information regarded the Rabons' identities and activities, including their real names, their residence, their vehicle, their travels, and when they were and were not present. The information also related to places where cocaine trafficking was known to be occurring on a regular basis. This information was sufficient to establish the confidential informant's bona fides. The extent, detail, and corroborated nature of the information provided by [the confidential informant] would lead a reasonable person to conclude that there was a "fair probability" that cocaine would be found in the Rabons' home on the date of the search. . . .

The inevitable discovery exception has developed as a logical counterpart to the "fruit of the poisonous tree" doctrine, which reaches out to suppress any evidence obtained as a result of earlier illegal action on the part of law enforcement. Because one of the primary purposes of the judicially-created exclusionary rule, and its extension through the suppression of evidence gained as the "fruit" of other illegally obtained evidence, has been to deter police misconduct, exceptions to the application of the exclusionary rule have been recognized in instances where separate, legitimate investigatory tools would inevitably have turned up the evidence at issue. . . .

We recently applied the inevitable discovery doctrine in a situation where a victim's body was recovered as a result of a custodial interrogation that we presumed to be illegal for purposes of the inevitable discovery analysis. See State v. St. Yves, 751 A.2d 1018 (Me. 2000). There, the police had lawfully and independently gathered the following information prior to any alleged misconduct: (1) the defendant's wife had recently given birth to an infant; (2) the defendant had attempted to obtain food stamps for himself, the infant, and his other daughter, but the infant was nowhere to be seen, and the defendant appeared confused and unkempt; (3) the elder daughter appeared uncared for when the police lawfully entered the defendant's trailer to arrest the defendant's wife; (4) a caseworker had attempted to contact the parents on a number of occasions at their trailer and had heard a child inside, though no adult answered the door; (5) when the police arrived to arrest the defendant's wife, the trailer was cold and filled with refuse, dog feces, and urine; and (6) the defendant and his wife provided conflicting explanations to the police as to the whereabouts of the infant and refused to tell them where the infant could be located.

Taking this information into account, we held that the victim's body would inevitably have been discovered because, if the police had not discovered the victim's body as a result of the interrogation, they would have checked the defendant's wife's story and found that the victim was not with her grandparents. We therefore concluded that, even without the information obtained by interrogating the defendant, the police would have been able to establish probable cause for a warrant to search the defendant's trailer and, after seeking and obtaining a warrant, inevitably would have discovered the victim's body. We concluded, "fairness can be assured by placing the State and the accused in the same positions they would have been in had the impermissible conduct not taken place, and, therefore, the court did not err in determining that the inevitable discovery doctrine saved the evidence from suppression."

In contrast to the search conducted in *St. Yves*, here the challenged evidence was not obtained through an illegal interrogation, and the State did obtain a warrant to search the premises. The warrant, however, was tainted by the inclusion of evidence gained through the initial presumed-illegal entry into the Rabons' residence. Thus, the analysis is similar to that used in *St. Yves*, but turns on whether the warrant would have issued without the offending paragraphs. . . .

I would conclude that the warrant would properly have issued even if the officers had not gone first to the Rabons' home, and even if the paragraphs in the affidavit cataloguing the evidence found in that initial entry had not been added to the affidavit. Thus, the remaining question presented is whether the evidence would inevitably have been discovered when the warrant was issued, several hours after the Rabons' home was secured. [The] warrant was issued and executed approximately four-and-one-half hours after the officers' initial entry. Had the police not secured the Rabons' home prior to seeking the warrant, it is very likely that, based on the urgency of the situation, both the police and the court would have acted upon the warrant request much more quickly. . . .

Problem 6-3. The Search Party

Pamela Powers, a 10-year-old child, disappeared from a YMCA building in Des Moines, Iowa, where she had accompanied her parents to watch an athletic contest. Shortly after she disappeared, Robert Williams was seen leaving the YMCA carrying a large bundle wrapped in a blanket; a 14-year-old boy who had helped Williams open his car door reported that he had seen "two legs in it and they were skinny and white."

Williams' car was found the next day 160 miles east of Des Moines in Davenport, Iowa. Later several items of clothing belonging to the child, some of Williams' clothing, and an army blanket like the one used to wrap the bundle that Williams carried out of the YMCA were found at a rest stop on Interstate 80 near Grinnell, between Des Moines and Davenport. A warrant was issued for Williams' arrest.

Police surmised that Williams had left Pamela Powers or her body somewhere between Des Moines and the Grinnell rest stop, where some of the girl's clothing had been found. On December 26, the Iowa Bureau of Criminal Investigation initiated a large-scale search. Two hundred volunteers divided into teams began the search 21 miles east of Grinnell, covering an area several miles to the north and south of Interstate 80. A snowstorm threatened as the volunteers moved westward from Poweshiek County, in which Grinnell was located, into Jasper County. Searchers were instructed to check all roads, abandoned farm buildings, ditches, culverts, and any other place in which the body of a small child could be hidden.

Suppose that police officers learned the location of the body through an illegal search of Williams' home. The officers found the child's body next to a culvert in a ditch beside a gravel road in Polk County, about two miles south of Interstate 80. At that time, one search team near the Jasper-Polk county line was only two and one-half miles from the location of the body. Will the trial court exclude from trial the evidence obtained from the body? Cf. Nix v. Williams, 467 U.S. 431 (1984).

Problem 6-4. Illegal Stop vs. Outstanding Warrant

A Florida officer observed a person make a left turn without signaling, and then saw a white light emanating from a crack in the plastic lens covering the tail light of the left rear of the defendant's vehicle. On these two grounds, the officer stopped the vehicle, checked the driver's identification, and learned that there was an outstanding warrant for his arrest for failure to appear in another proceeding. As a result of the outstanding warrant, the officer arrested the driver. A search incident to the arrest revealed a firearm, which formed the basis for criminal charges against the driver.

The initial traffic stop was unlawful under Florida law. State v. Riley, 638 So.2d 507 (Fla.1994) (failure to use turn signal without driver's conduct creating reasonable safety concern does not constitute violation of statute), and Doctor v. State, 596 So.2d 442 (Fla.1992) (cracked taillight was not violation of law). The arrest warrant also turned out to be erroneous: A later investigation determined that the arrest warrant was issued due to another person's failure to appear.

Imagine that the defendant moves to suppress the seizure of the firearm, contending (1) that the traffic stop preceding the arrest was unlawful and (2) that the warrant that provided the basis for his arrest was wrongfully issued, and therefore that the government should not be allowed to use the fruits of the search incident to arrest. You are the trial judge. How would you rule? See State v. Frierson, 926 S.2d 1139 (Fla. 2006).

Notes

1. *Inevitable discovery: majority position.* Along with the federal system, Nix v. Williams, 467 U.S. 431 (1984), every state except Texas and Washington recognizes an "inevitable discovery" exception to exclusion. See State v. Winterstein, 220 P.3d 1226 (Wash. 2009). Under this doctrine, a court may use evidence obtained as the fruit of an illegal search or seizure if the government would have learned about the evidence through proper techniques or channels without the illegal search or seizure ever taking place. The inevitable discovery exception is a potentially huge limit on exclusion, particularly if one is willing to presume that the police (or interested citizens) are often capable of solving important crimes. The government must argue more than "if we hadn't done it wrong, we would have done it right." State v. Topanotes, 76 P.3d 1159 (Utah 2003). The level of certainty required in predicting the "inevitability" of the discovery is a key issue.

Under federal law, the government must prove by a preponderance of the evidence the underlying facts necessary to conclude that the discovery was inevitable, and most states have embraced the federal position and use a preponderance standard. A few states require the government to show that discovery was inevitable by "clear and convincing" evidence. See Smith v. State, 948 P.2d 473 (Alaska 1997). But as highlighted in the *Rabon* case, especially by the concurring opinion, many states distinguish between the standard of proof necessary to establish the underlying facts and the level of certainty necessary to reach the conclusion that discovery was "inevitable." See Compare State v. Sugar, 527 A.2d 1377 (N.J. 1987) (body buried in shallow ground would have inevitably been discovered because defendant was attempting to sell the property and prospective buyers would have smelled decomposing body; meets clear and convincing evidence requirement of state law) with Commonwealth v. O'Connor, 546 N.E.2d 336, 340 (Mass. 1989) (question is whether specific facts demonstrate that discovery by lawful means was "certain as a practical matter").

In the typical pretrial motion to suppress (for claims other than inevitable discovery), the standard of proof is a preponderance of the evidence. The defendant carries the burden of proof for warranted searches; the government carries the burden for warrantless searches. Do the factual and legal questions surrounding inevitable discovery justify changes in the ordinary rules about standard of proof and burden of proof?

2. *Potential limits on inevitable discovery doctrine.* A number of state courts endorsing the inevitable discovery exception to the exclusionary rule take great pains to say that they do not consider it a "blanket" exception and that it might be used in some circumstances but not in others. See, e.g., State v. Ault, 724 P.2d 545 (Ariz. 1986) (inevitable discovery doctrine does not apply to illegal search or seizure of items in a home); People v. Stith, 506 N.E.2d 911 (N.Y. 1987) (inevitable discovery exception does not apply to "primary evidence" obtained at time of illegal search; applies only to indirect fruits of illegal search). The web extension for this chapter, at *http://www.crimpro.com/extension/ch06*, offers a richer view of the state cases marking limits on the use of inevitable discovery.

3. *Can inevitable discovery cure intentional illegal searches?* What if the police deliberately conduct an illegal search, knowing that discovery of any evidence is inevitable (say, during a later inventory search)? Should courts apply the inevitable

discovery exception only when the police act in "good faith"? How regularized must the investigative process be to count as "inevitable"? Consider State v. Notti, 71 P.3d 1233 (Mont. 2003) (inevitable discovery of identification of suspect who was in state DNA database and who left DNA on cigarette at murder scene, either through a DNA database computer check or when a Crime Lab employee compared profiles in the "forensic unknown" database with the State's DNA Identification Index).

4. *Inevitable discovery and statutory remedies*. Despite the importance of the issue, and the variety of positions a state might take on this exception to the exclusionary rule, very few states have a statute addressing "inevitable discovery." Why have the legislatures remained silent? If the legislature has adopted a statutory form of the exclusionary rule without providing for an inevitable discovery exception, should a court nevertheless be willing to create the exception?

5. *Independent source: majority position*. All but a few states have declared that the exclusionary rule does not apply to evidence obtained after an improper search or seizure if the government also learned of the evidence through an "independent source." The independent source claim is closely related to inevitable discovery, but it is sometimes distinguishable because it is based on an untainted source that actually did lead the police to the evidence in question, rather than a source or process that hypothetically might have done so. A case like *Rabon* sits on the line, but it would be construed as independent source if officers had later in fact obtained a warrant based on information in their possession before they entered the building. The basis for the proper warranted search was "independent" of anything the police learned during the improper search. See Murray v. United States, 487 U.S. 533 (1988); Segura v. United States, 468 U.S. 796 (1984); compare People v. Weiss, 978 P.2d 1257 (Cal. 1999) (prosecution does not have to show that particular magistrate would have issued warrant if affidavit had not contained illegally obtained information; independent source applies if police would have sought warrant even without tainted information, and redacted affidavit was sufficient for probable cause). In light of the independent source doctrine, do police have anything to lose by routinely conducting a "preliminary" search before seeking a search warrant? See William Stuntz, Warrants and Fourth Amendment Remedies, 77 Va. L. Rev. 881 (1991); State v. Krukowski, 100 P.3d 1222 (Utah 2004) (officer's failure to disclose in search warrant application that he had already conducted an illegal entry of premises cannot be basis for refusing to apply independent source doctrine).

6. *Attenuation*. Even when there is a causal linkage between an improper search or seizure and some evidence obtained later, the evidence can still be admitted if the link is sufficiently "attenuated." An analogy from the law of torts might be the concept of "proximate cause." For instance, in United States v. Ceccolini, 435 U.S. 268 (1978), a police officer during a conversation with a friend at her workplace wrongfully peered into an envelope in the room and discovered gambling paraphernalia, which belonged to the friend's boss. The friend agreed months later to testify against her boss in criminal proceedings. Even though the improper search of the package was a "but for" cause of the government's access to this testimony, it was not excluded because the witness's willingness to testify was more important than the improper search. In this type of case, courts will not exclude the evidence because, they say, police are unlikely to anticipate the chain of events linking their illegal search to some later source of evidence and therefore will not be deterred by the threat of exclusion. Could the officer in *Ceccolini* have anticipated that an unlawful search of the envelope might create an opportunity for his friend to provide

evidence in a criminal trial? See also State v. Guillen, 223 P.3d 658 (Ariz. 2010) (possibly improper dog sniff of garage cured by later consent of homeowner unaware of dog sniff; consent was sufficiently attenuated from tainted conduct).

In Hudson v. Michigan, 547 U.S. 586 (2006), the Supreme Court held that violation of the "knock-and-announce" rule does not require suppression. Justice Scalia, writing for the majority, found the connection between the constitutional violation (knocking, but not waiting long enough before entering) and the harm too attenuated to suppress the evidence.

> [Exclusion] may not be premised on the mere fact that a constitutional violation was a "but-for" cause of obtaining evidence. Our cases show that but-for causality is only a necessary, not a sufficient, condition for suppression. In this case, of course, the constitutional violation of an illegal manner of entry was not a but-for cause of obtaining the evidence. Whether that preliminary misstep had occurred or not, the police would have executed the warrant they had obtained, and would have discovered the gun and drugs inside the house. But even if the illegal entry here could be characterized as a but-for cause of discovering what was inside, we have never held that evidence is "fruit of the poisonous tree" simply because it would not have come to light but for the illegal actions of the police. Rather, but-for cause, or causation in the logical sense alone, can be too attenuated to justify exclusion. . . .
>
> Attenuation can occur, of course, when the causal connection is remote. Attenuation also occurs when, even given a direct causal connection, the interest protected by the constitutional guarantee that has been violated would not be served by suppression of the evidence obtained. . . .

7. *Improper stops and arrests that produce additional information.* If an arrest is improper, the defendant might argue that his very presence in the courtroom is the result of illegal government action, and a conviction would be barred. Both state and federal courts have uniformly rejected this argument because the use of properly obtained evidence to obtain a conviction in criminal proceedings cures any error in the arrest. United States v. Crews, 445 U.S. 463 (1980) (illegal arrest does not taint otherwise valid eyewitness identification of arrestee); Frisbie v. Collins, 342 U.S. 519 (1952) (illegal arrest is no bar to prosecution); People v. Jones, 810 N.E.2d 415 (N.Y. 2004) (police improperly arrested defendant in his home without arrest warrant; identification during lineup conducted while in custody was admissible).

Like the inevitable discovery and independent source rules, the *Frisbie* rule is based on the idea that the illegal government action was not a legally sufficient "cause" of any harm to the defendant. States are divided on whether an outstanding arrest warrant can cure an illegal stop. Consistent with the *Frisbie* doctrine, the majority of states hold that discovery of an outstanding warrant and subsequent arrest and search are attenuated from the initial illegal stop that led to the identification and warrant check, and that this holds true even though the warrant check or search would not have occurred but for that stop. See e.g., Myers v. State, 909 A.2d 1049 (Md. 2006); compare State v. Maland, 103 P.3d 430 (Idaho 2004).

3. *Standing to Challenge Illegal Searches and Seizures*

One other major limitation on the exclusionary rule restricts the number of people who can challenge an allegedly illegal search or seizure. In some jurisdictions, this is known as the "standing" doctrine. This limitation applies when the government improperly intrudes on a reasonable privacy expectation of one person and finds evidence implicating a second person in a crime. Can the second person challenge the unreasonable intrusion?

■ LOUISIANA CONSTITUTION ART. I, §5

Any person adversely affected by a search or seizure conducted in violation of this Section shall have standing to raise its illegality in the appropriate court.

■ STATE v. JOHN BRUNS

796 A.2d 226 (N.J. 2002)

STEIN, J.

. . . In the early morning hours of July 27, 1997, Officer John Seidler stopped a vehicle for speeding in Lakewood Township. After effectuating the stop, Seidler [determined that the driver, Barbara Edwards, was operating the car with a suspended license. He also discovered two outstanding arrest warrants for Edwards.] Based on the outstanding warrants, Seidler placed Edwards under arrest, handcuffed her, searched her, and seated her in his patrol car.

Seidler next asked the sole passenger in the vehicle, Walter Evans, to step out of the car. Officer Regan, who had been called to the scene as backup, placed Evans in his patrol car. Seidler conducted a search of the passenger compartment after Evans exited the vehicle. He found a handgun and a large knife under the front passenger seat. The object that appeared to be a handgun was later determined to be a toy handgun. [Those two items later became relevant evidence in the investigation of an armed robbery that Evans and John Bruns allegedly committed seven days before the search of Edwards' car.]

In his subsequent trial for armed robbery defendant made a motion to suppress the evidence seized during the search of Edwards' car, alleging that Seidler's search of the vehicle and seizure of the toy handgun and knife were unlawful. The motion judge concluded that the search was incident to Edwards' lawful arrest and that "the steps that the officers took were necessary given the particular circumstances." . . .

The State argues that defendant did not have a proprietary, possessory, or participatory interest in the vehicle searched or the evidence retrieved from it. Therefore, it asserts that defendant did not have standing to move to suppress the evidence. . . .

II.

In order to contest at trial the admission of evidence obtained by a search or seizure, a defendant must first demonstrate that he has standing. Generally speaking, that requires a court to inquire whether defendant has interests that are substantial enough to qualify him as a person aggrieved by the allegedly unlawful search and seizure.

In Rakas v. Illinois, 439 U.S. 128 (1978), the United States Supreme Court held that a defendant must have a legitimate expectation of privacy in the place searched or items seized to establish Fourth Amendment standing. In State v. Alston, 440 A.2d 1311 (N.J. 1981), this Court established a broader standard to determine when a defendant has the right to challenge an illegal search or seizure, rejecting the line of United States Supreme Court cases culminating with Rakas v. Illinois that effectively resolved standing issues only on the basis of a defendant's expectations of privacy. Instead, before reaching the substantive question whether a defendant has a reasonable expectation of privacy, our courts first determine whether that defendant has a proprietary, possessory or participatory interest in the place searched or items seized.

For the twenty years preceding the United States Supreme Court's adoption of the "legitimate expectation of privacy" standard the leading Fourth Amendment standing case was Jones v. United States, 362 U.S. 257 (1960). In *Jones*, the defendant was arrested for the possession and sale of narcotics after federal officers executed a search warrant for narcotics in an apartment in which the defendant was present. The Court rejected the Government's contention that the defendant lacked standing because he did not claim either ownership of the seized narcotics or a property interest in the apartment, but rather was simply a guest in the apartment. Recognizing the predicament a defendant faces when attempting to establish Fourth Amendment standing by demonstrating that he owned or possessed the seized property while at the same time defending against a charge in which an essential element is possession, the Court adopted the so-called "automatic standing rule." The Court . . . concluded that the allegations of possession that led eventually to defendant's conviction afforded him sufficient standing to challenge the search. In addition, acknowledging that the interests of law enforcement would not "be hampered by recognizing that anyone legitimately on premises where a search occurs may challenge its legality by way of a motion to suppress, when its fruits are proposed to be used against him," the Court concluded that his friend's consent to his presence also gave defendant sufficient standing to challenge the search under the Fourth Amendment. That portion of the *Jones* holding became known as the "legitimately on the premises test."

In Rakas v. Illinois, . . . the defendants argued that any person who was a "target" of a search should have standing to object to the search. Reaffirming the principle that Fourth Amendment rights cannot be vicariously asserted, the Court rejected the defendants' argument and [endorsed the "better analysis" that] forthrightly focuses on the extent of a particular defendant's rights under the Fourth Amendment, rather than any theoretically separate, but invariably intertwined concept of standing. The Court in *Rakas* also considered the appropriate scope of the interest protected by the Fourth Amendment. It determined that the "legitimately on the premises" standard applied in *Jones* was too broad, and instead adopted the standard established in Katz v. United States, 389 U.S. 347 (1967), stating that a defendant must have a "legitimate expectation of privacy in the invaded place." Based on that standard the Court held that the defendants had failed to demonstrate that they had a legitimate expectation of privacy in the glove compartment or the area under the front seat of the car in which they were passengers.

In United States v. Salvucci, 448 U.S. 83 (1980), shortly after its decision in *Rakas*, the Court also abolished the "automatic standing" rule of *Jones* and held that defendants who are charged with crimes that have an element of possession can invoke the exclusionary rule only if their own Fourth Amendment rights have in fact been violated. The defendants in *Salvucci* were charged with unlawful possession of stolen mail, and relied solely on the *Jones* automatic standing rule without asserting that they had a legitimate expectation of privacy in the place where the stolen mail was seized. In assessing the trial court's decision to suppress the evidence the Court concluded: "We are convinced that the automatic standing rule of *Jones* has outlived its usefulness in the Court's Fourth Amendment jurisprudence. The doctrine now serves only to afford a windfall to defendants whose Fourth Amendment rights have not been violated. . . ."

In Rawlings v. Kentucky, 448 U.S. 98 (1980), the companion case to *Salvucci*, the Court addressed an argument by the defendant that his ownership of drugs seized by the police entitled him to invoke his Fourth Amendment rights although he claimed no expectation of privacy in the area from which the drugs were seized. The Court rejected defendant's argument, relying on the Court's observation in *Rakas* that "arcane" concepts of property law should not control the analysis of Fourth Amendment standing. [The Court] explained that prior to *Rakas* the defendant "might have been given 'standing' in such a case to challenge a 'search' that netted those drugs but probably would have lost his claim on the merits. After *Rakas*, the two inquiries merge into one: whether governmental officials violated any legitimate expectation of privacy."

Concluding that the United States Supreme Court's decisions such as *Rakas*, *Salvucci*, and *Rawlings* insufficiently guarded against unreasonable searches and seizures, this Court's decision in State v. Alston, 440 A.2d 1311 (N.J. 1981), applied Article I, paragraph 7 of the New Jersey State Constitution to the standing issue in order to afford our citizens greater protection. . . . The more protective approach adopted by this Court was based on the belief that "adherence to the vague 'legitimate expectation of privacy' standard, subject as it is to the potential for inconsistent and capricious application, will in many instances produce results contrary to commonly held and accepted expectations of privacy. . . ."

In *Alston* four defendants charged with the unlawful carrying and possession of weapons moved to suppress the weapons seized as the result of the warrantless search of the vehicle in which they were the driver and passengers. The State argued that the passengers had no standing to challenge the search because they had no ownership interest in the vehicle, and that the driver legitimately possessed the car but lacked a reasonable expectation of privacy in the areas of the vehicle that were searched. The Court rejected the State's arguments, finding that the privacy interests protected by the federal constitution and our State Constitution "flow from some connection with or relation to the place or property searched" and that "it serves the purposes of clarity to emphasize an accused's relationship to property rather than to attempt a definition of expectations in terms of the person." Accordingly, we reiterated our traditional standing rule that requires a defendant to show that "he has a proprietary, possessory, or participatory interest in either the place searched or the property seized," and found that the automatic standing rule conferred standing on all four defendants.

In State v. Mollica, 554 A.2d 1315 (N.J. 1989), we elaborated on the participatory interest portion of our standing rule. Defendants Mollica and Ferrone were charged with various gambling offenses after the state police discovered bookmaking paraphernalia in their hotel rooms. The warrants to search the rooms were based in part on the telephone records for Ferrone's hotel room that the Federal Bureau of Investigation had previously obtained without a warrant as part of its own bookmaking investigation. The State argued that Mollica had no standing to object to the seizure of Ferrone's telephone records even though those records provided the basis for a search warrant that included his hotel room. The Court acknowledged that our standing rule does not automatically provide a defendant charged with a possessory crime "standing to object to prior or antecedent state action that was directed against another person," and observed that Mollica's standing to object to the search and seizure of evidence found in his hotel room did not necessarily give him standing to object to the seizure of Ferrone's telephone records. Nonetheless, the Court considered whether Mollica had a participatory interest in the seized telephone records, noting that a participatory interest "stresses the relationship of the evidence to the underlying criminal activity and defendant's own criminal role in the generation and use of such evidence," and confers standing on a person who "had some culpable role, whether as a principal, conspirator, or accomplice, in a criminal activity that itself generated the evidence." Based on the State's allegation that Mollica participated in illegal bookmaking that included the use of Ferrone's hotel room telephone and resulted in the generation of the telephone records in question, the Court concluded that [there was a] "sufficient connection between the telephone toll records and the underlying criminal gambling for which this defendant is charged, and a sufficient relationship between the defendant and the gambling enterprise, to establish a participatory interest on the part of defendant in this evidence. . . ."

III.

We see no reason to depart from the broad standing rule that entitles a criminal defendant to challenge an unreasonable search and seizure under Article I, paragraph 7 of the New Jersey Constitution if he or she can demonstrate a proprietary, possessory, or participatory interest in the place searched or items seized. Nonetheless, applying that standard to the facts of this case we find that defendant has failed to demonstrate an interest sufficient to give him standing. In reaching that conclusion, we need not specifically delineate the contours of the interest in evidence seized that will justify standing. Defendant's alleged connection to the place searched and items seized simply is far too attenuated to support a constitutional right to object to the search and seizure.

To begin with, based on the record before us defendant cannot claim a proprietary or possessory interest in the vehicle that was searched. During the suppression hearing defense counsel made a vague claim that Edwards had at one point indicated that the vehicle belonged to Bruns. However, the claim was never substantiated and the record confirms that the vehicle was registered in Edwards' name at the time of the search.

Moreover, defendant has failed to demonstrate either an ownership or possessory interest in the weapons seized. We note defense counsel's assertion that there is no reason to believe defendant divested himself of any possessory interest in the weapons, and his hypothetical statement that "for all we know, Mr. Bruns placed the toy gun under the seat ten minutes before the car was stopped and asked those in the car to keep a close watch on it." However, the record contains no evidence whatsoever to support the contention that defendant retained any interest in the weapons at the time of the search.

With no proprietary or possessory interest established, defendant nevertheless asserts that he had a participatory interest in the weapons seized because they were used to commit the robbery for which he was charged. We note first that the toy handgun and knife seized from Edwards' vehicle implicated defendant and Evans in a robbery that took place seven days before the contested search. The evidence was seized as a result of the search incident to Edwards' arrest that occurred after she was pulled over for speeding and a police officer discovered that there were two outstanding warrants for her arrest. Moreover, defendant was not a passenger in the vehicle and he was not in the vicinity of the vehicle at the time it was searched. In *Mollica,* the only case in which we have had occasion to consider whether a defendant's participatory interest was sufficient to confer standing, the Court emphasized the relationship between the evidence seized and the underlying criminal activity with which the defendant was charged, as well as the extent to which a co-defendant played a role in generating and using that evidence.

Defendant points to the relationship between the weapons seized from Edwards' car and the crime with which he was charged. Accepting that generalized connection, however, we are unpersuaded that that connection is adequate to confer standing based on a participatory interest. That evidence implicates a defendant in a crime is not, in and of itself, sufficient to confer standing. There also must be at a minimum some contemporary connection between the defendant and the place searched or the items seized. [Suppression] of the product of a Fourth Amendment violation can be successfully urged only by those whose rights were violated by the search itself, not by those who are aggrieved solely by the introduction of damaging evidence. . . .

Likewise, the weapons seized in this matter did not relate to any ongoing criminal activity between Edwards and defendant, or between Evans and defendant, at the time the allegedly illegal search occurred. The robbery for which defendant was charged occurred seven days before the items were found in Edwards' vehicle. . . .

Although we recognize that in most cases in which the police seize evidence implicating a defendant in a crime that defendant will be able to establish an interest in the property seized or place searched, our broad standing rule necessarily has limits. If substantial time passes between the crime and the seizure of the evidence, and a proprietary connection between defendant and the evidence no longer exists, the defendant's basis for being aggrieved by the search will have diminished. In addition to the temporal aspects of a specific search or seizure, a showing that the search was not directed at the defendant or at someone who is connected to the crime for which he has been charged also will diminish a defendant's interest in the property searched or seized. . . .

Problem 6-5. Place of Business

A citizen in Eagen, Minnesota, was walking by a ground-floor apartment and saw through the window several people putting white powder into bags. He called the police, and Officer James Thielen went to Apartment 103 to investigate. Thielen looked in the same window through a gap in the closed blinds and observed

Wayne Carter, Melvin Johns, and Kimberly Thompson putting the powder into bags for several minutes. While other officers began to prepare affidavits for a search warrant, Thielen remained at the apartment building to keep watch. He then saw Carter and Johns leave the building and drive away. Police stopped the car, and noticed in the passenger compartment some drug paraphernalia and a handgun. They arrested Carter and Johns, and an inventory search of the vehicle uncovered 47 grams of cocaine in plastic sandwich bags.

After seizing the car, the police returned to Apartment 103 and arrested Thompson. A warranted search of the apartment revealed cocaine residue on the kitchen table and plastic bags similar to those found in the car. Thompson was the lessee of the apartment. Carter and Johns lived in Chicago and had come to the apartment for the sole purpose of packaging the cocaine. They had never been to the apartment before and were in the apartment for less than three hours. In return for the use of the apartment, Carter and Johns had given Thompson one-eighth of an ounce of the cocaine.

Carter and Johns were charged with narcotics crimes, and they moved to suppress all evidence obtained from the apartment and the car. Do they have a sufficient privacy interest in the apartment to challenge any illegal search that may have happened there? Compare Minnesota v. Carter, 525 U.S. 83 (1998).

Notes

1. *Standing: majority position.* A majority of states follow the federal "legitimate expectation of privacy" approach when they determine who may invoke the exclusionary rule to remedy an illegal search or seizure. Others, like the New Jersey court in *Bruns*, use some form of the older "legitimately on the premises" test for standing. Often, these courts say that a defendant challenging an illegal search or seizure must demonstrate a "proprietary, possessory, or participatory interest" in the premises searched or the property seized. Try to imagine situations in which the federal test and the "legitimately on the premises" test produce different results.

The Supreme Court attempted, in Rakas v. Illinois, 439 U.S. 128 (1978), to eliminate any distinction between a person's "standing" to challenge an illegal search and the "extent of a particular defendant's rights" under the Fourth Amendment. Rights against unreasonable searches and seizures, said the Court, are personal rights and third parties may not assert them. See Brendlin v. California, 551 U.S. 249 (2007) (when police officer makes traffic stop, passenger in car is seized and may challenge constitutionality of stop). What would be the consequences of allowing a criminal defendant to challenge an allegedly improper search of a third party's property? Consider the Louisiana constitutional provision reprinted above. Why require standing *at all* for a litigant who hopes to challenge governmental misconduct, particularly if deterrence of government wrongdoing is the central purpose of the exclusionary rule?

2. *Standing for searches of residences and business premises.* Even though a defendant, under the federal (and majority) rule, must show a "legitimate" expectation of privacy in the premises searched or the property seized, this does not preclude challenges by those who do not own or lease property. The easier cases to decide involve the search of a residence, where the defendant lives full time even though another person owns or leases the residence. Courts in that setting have no trouble in

concluding that the person living in the house may challenge a search of any common area in the house or any area within the special control of the defendant. How might these residential cases apply to business premises?

More difficult cases involve guests and others who are present in a residence for shorter periods. In Minnesota v. Olson, 495 U.S. 91 (1990), the Court recognized standing for an overnight guest at an apartment: staying overnight in another's home "is a longstanding social custom that serves functions recognized as valuable by society." On the other hand, the Court in Minnesota v. Carter, 525 U.S. 83 (1998), concluded that defendants present in an apartment only for a few hours did not have a "legitimate expectation of privacy" in the premises. What could be said in favor of allowing dinner guests to challenge the admission of evidence obtained when the police make a warrantless entry of a home to arrest the guest or search her possessions? What if the police illegally search the purse of one person and find inside some contraband belonging to another person? See Rawlings v. Kentucky, 448 U.S. 98 (1980) (denying standing in such a setting). What if the nature of the social arrangement between the resident and a guest is unclear at the time of the search? See State v. Hess, 680 N.W.2d 314 (S.D. 2004) (tenant of apartment testified that she had an intimate relationship with owner of drugs found during search, and he had spent the night at her apartment on previous nights, but on this night her plans were unclear and it was "possible" he would spend night); State v. Filion, 966 A.2d 405 (Me. 2009) (long-time friend of lessee of apartment who was frequent social visitor does not have reasonable privacy expectation; key inquiry is defendant's relationship to property, not to the tenant; defendant had never spent the night at apartment, held no key to dwelling, and never visited apartment when friend was absent).

3. *"Automatic" standing for possessory crimes.* Special rules sometimes apply to defendants charged with possessory offenses, such as possession of stolen property or narcotics. The defendant in such a case faces a dilemma. For purposes of standing, she often must establish some ownership interest in the premises that were illegally searched, but for purposes of defending against the charges, she would prefer to deny any connection with the contraband or the premises searched. At one time, most American courts responded to this difficulty by granting "automatic" standing to any defendant who chose to challenge a search or seizure in a possessory crime case. See Jones v. United States, 362 U.S. 257 (1960). Later, the Supreme Court took a different approach to the problem. It held, in Simmons v. United States, 390 U.S. 377 (1968), that the government could not use at trial the defendant's testimony at a suppression hearing, if it was given for the purpose of establishing standing. Because of this "immunity" for the defendant's testimony, the Court decided that "automatic" standing was no longer necessary to protect a defendant. In addition, a defendant might establish a "legitimate" expectation of privacy in some premises searched without necessarily admitting ownership of contraband. See United States v. Salvucci, 448 U.S. 83 (1980). A sizable minority of states have retained the "automatic" standing rule for possessory offenses. See State v. Carvajal, 996 A.2d 1029 (N.J. 2010) (bus passenger who denied ownership of checked luggage abandoned that property and could not later invoke state's automatic standing rule). Some have explained that the "immunity" for the defendant's testimony at a suppression hearing is not adequate because the testimony still might be used to impeach the defendant's trial testimony. Can you think of any other reasons to retain the "automatic" standing rule?

4. *"Target" standing.* Should a court give any special treatment to a claim that the police *intentionally* conducted an illegal search against one party for the purpose of obtaining evidence against another party? In United States v. Payner, 447 U.S. 727 (1980), the Supreme Court applied its usual rules of standing in such a case. A few other courts, however, have responded to purposefully illegal searches of this sort by granting standing to the "target" of the search, even if the target had no legitimate expectation of privacy (or any other interest) in the premises that were searched. See Waring v. State, 670 P.2d 357 (Alaska 1983). What difficulties might a court encounter in applying the "target" standing rule? How often will the doctrine be relevant?

C. ADDITIONS AND ALTERNATIVES TO THE EXCLUSIONARY RULE

As we have seen, the exclusionary rule is not available in many cases to enforce rights against unreasonable searches and seizures. Are there any credible alternatives to the exclusionary rule? Would you embrace any (or all) of these remedies as replacements to the exclusionary rule, or would you adopt them as *additional* remedies and wait for proof of their viability?

1. Administrative Remedies

Police officers are sworn to uphold the law, and supervisors within a police department must ensure that the rank-and-file officers obey the law during criminal investigations. Many police departments hire legal counsel to train and advise investigating officers. What other steps might a police department or a local government adopt to discourage illegal searches and seizures?

Events in Los Angeles in the late 1990s offer a fascinating window into a police department's efforts to punish and prevent misbehavior by individual officers. In 1998, eight pounds of cocaine was found missing from a police evidence locker in the Los Angeles Police Department's Rampart division. Investigations led to officer Raphael Perez, a member of Rampart's elite anti-gang unit known as CRASH, for Community Resources Against Street Hoodlums. Like criminals everywhere, Officer Perez told prosecutors that he had information about other officers that he would trade for a reduced sentence of five years. The information from Officer Perez (much of it later confirmed from independent sources) revealed one of the largest patterns of police misconduct in U.S. history.

Perez told investigators a wild tale of police conspiring to frame innocent suspects, beating suspects, and covering up unjustified shootings. Hundreds of felony cases were tainted by alleged police misconduct. Dozens of officers were fired, relieved of duty, suspended, or quit. The city faced possible civil damages of hundreds of millions of dollars.

Almost every governmental institution that might respond to police abuse did so, including the police department, the Los Angeles District Attorney, the mayor, the city council, and federal civil rights enforcers. The Los Angeles Police assembled a Board of Inquiry to study the corruption scandal. A 362-page Board of Inquiry report blamed the calamity on poor hiring, the isolation of the special CRASH unit, and "rogue cops." L.A. Police Chief Bernard C. Parks explained:

> [The] Board of Inquiry report . . . points out in graphic detail [that] people with troubling backgrounds have been hired as police officers. We need to tighten up that hiring process. Individuals with criminal records or with histories of violent behavior or narcotics involvement have no place in this department. We need to make sure that field officers are supervised closely and that supervisors have the courage to take corrective action when necessary. I recognize there is a fine line between smothering officers under a stifling bureaucratic blanket and beefing up supervision. The Board of Inquiry report tells us how to walk that fine line and how to do it effectively. . . .
>
> [We] do not need to reinvent the wheel. . . . What we do need to do is emphasize a scrupulous adherence to existing policies and standards. We must enhance our ability to detect any individual or collective pattern of performance that falters. We must have the courage to deal with those who are responsible for failures. If we do not do all those things, another Rampart will surely occur.

Chief Parks issued an 18-page order detailing his response to the Rampart scandal, including abolition of the CRASH name in favor of generic "gang details," a limited three-year tour of duty with the new special anti-gang units, and new requirements for members and supervisors of the units.

Chief Parks fired Brian Hewitt (one of the officers that Perez had specifically accused) for the alleged beating of Ismael Jimenez, a gang member. In doing so, Parks followed the recommendation of the Board of Rights, a panel of officers who hear disciplinary cases. Evidence compiled by LAPD detectives against Hewitt included samples of blood splattered on the walls of the Rampart Station, which were matched to the victim's DNA; testimony from an emergency room doctor detailing the victim's injuries; testimony from several citizens and law enforcement personnel; and a piece of carpet from the Rampart Station that was soaked with the victim's bloody vomit.

But county prosecutors, citing a lack of evidence, twice declined to file charges against Hewitt. The prosecutors concluded that there was insufficient evidence to prove in court that Hewitt assaulted Jimenez. The office argued there were no witnesses, except possibly another gang member, and no photographs of his injuries.

Eventually, the federal government entered the scene with an extensive civil rights investigation of the LAPD. Federal officials wanted to know whether Los Angeles ever implemented the recommendations of the 1991 Christopher Commission report, issued following the Rodney King beating and the trials of the officers who beat him. Los Angeles received federal funds to implement those prior recommendations.

ERWIN CHEMERINSKY, WITH PAUL HOFFMAN, LAURIE LEVENSON, R. SAMUEL PAZ, CONNIE RICE, AND CAROL SOBEL, AN INDEPENDENT ANALYSIS OF THE LOS ANGELES POLICE DEPARTMENT'S BOARD OF INQUIRY REPORT ON THE RAMPART SCANDAL

(September 11, 2000)

On March 1, 2000, The Police Department's Board of Inquiry released its report on the "Rampart Area Corruption Incident." This report, [prepared at the request of the Police Protective League], analyzes the Board of Inquiry report and its recommendations. My overall conclusion is that the Board of Inquiry report unjustifiably minimized the magnitude of the scandal and failed to recommend the major changes necessary to reform the Los Angeles Police Department. The Board of Inquiry report is the management account of the Rampart scandal. . . .

1. The Board of Inquiry Report Fails to Identify the Extent of the Problem and, Indeed, Minimizes Its Scope and Nature

[The] Board of Inquiry minimizes the problem, calling it the "Rampart Incident," saying that the problem was a result of a "few" officers, and declaring that corruption is not a problem throughout the Department. These conclusions are at odds with everything that we learned in preparing this report and with the Justice Department's investigation which concluded that abuses occur "on a regular basis."

To ensure that there is a complete and adequate investigation to determine the full extent of the problem, I recommend [that the City of Los Angeles create an independent commission] with the mandate of thoroughly investigating the Los Angeles Police Department, including assessing the extent and nature of police corruption and lawlessness. . . . The Commission should be external to the Police Department and report to the Mayor, the City Council, the City Attorney, the Police Commission, and the people of Los Angeles. Officers with knowledge of wrongdoing in connection with the Rampart scandal should be encouraged to reveal what they know by granting them immunity from discipline for their failure to reveal wrong-doing previously. . . .

2. The Board of Inquiry Report Fails to Recognize That the Central Problem Is the Culture of the Los Angeles Police Department, Which Gave Rise to and Tolerated What Occurred in the Rampart Division and Elsewhere

The culture within the Los Angeles Police Department gave rise to the Rampart scandal and allowed it to remain undetected for so long. Every police department has a culture — the unwritten rules, mores, customs, codes, values, and outlooks — that creates the policing environment and style. . . . The culture of the Los Angeles Police Department emphasizes control and the exclusion of scrutiny by outsiders, including the Police Commission and its Inspector General, as well as courts and prosecutors. The culture of the Los Angeles Police Department exercises control over the rank and file officers through a highly stratified, elaborate discipline system that enforces voluminous rules and regulations, some of them very petty. The result is a startling degree of alienation and hostility to the management of the Department. The culture of the Los Angeles Police Department, as documented by the Christopher Commission, emphasizes overly aggressive policing, resulting in the use of excessive force.

Code of Silence

Most importantly, a code of silence is deeply embedded in the Los Angeles Police Department. . . . The code of silence is reinforced in many ways, as the Department punishes whistleblowers and those who expose the wrongdoing of others. Changing the culture of the Police Department and reforming its practices will require many dramatic changes, including a shift from overly aggressive police tactics and a mentality that excludes outside oversight, to one that emphasizes community policing and seeks to end the code of silence. This change will not happen voluntarily. [There] must be judicial enforcement of reforms, either through a consent decree or a court order as part of a judgment.

3. The Board of Inquiry Report Fails to Consider the Need for Structural Reforms in the Department, Including Reforming the Police Commission, Strengthening the Independence and Powers of the Inspector General, and Creating Permanent Oversight Mechanisms for the Department

The Board of Inquiry report identifies no problems with the structure of the Police Department and apparently does not see this as in any way responsible for the Rampart scandal. . . . One essential change is to create a full-time, paid Police Commission and to change the manner of selecting and removing Commissioners to ensure greater independence. Under the Los Angeles City Charter, the Police Commission is the manager for all aspects of the Department, except for police discipline which is the responsibility of the Chief of Police. The Police Commission does not exist only for oversight or policy-making; it is the Department's manager. This task cannot be effectively done by a part-time, unpaid Commission.

Under the Charter, all Commissioners are appointed by, and are removable by, the Mayor. The problem is that Commissioners then are much more likely to reflect one philosophy and, at times, refrain from expressing a difference of opinion because of the risk of being removed by the Mayor or not reappointed. . . . The appointment authority should be dispersed (such as by having the Mayor appoint two police commissioners and having one each by the President of the City Council, the City Attorney, and the City Controller). Removal of a commissioner should require approval of the City Council. . . .

There must be a substantial strengthening of the independence of the Inspector General. . . . The first Inspector General saw her role and powers gutted as she was instructed that she could not report to the Police Commission and could not have access to case files. . . . The Inspector General needs more protection from removal and clearer authority to investigate any matter, unimpeded by the Police Commission.

Finally, there must be an external oversight mechanism for the worst abuses by LAPD officers. A permanent special prosecutor should be created, ideally in the Attorney General's office, to conduct criminal investigations and prosecutions of illegal activity by officers.

4. The Board of Inquiry Report Unduly Minimizes the Problems in the Police Department's Disciplinary System

. . . The Board of Inquiry recommends strengthening the disciplinary system, especially by increasing the powers of the Internal Affairs division and the authority of the Chief of Police. These recommendations fail to deal with the serious distrust in the system among officers or with any of the underlying problems in the disciplinary system. . . .

Assignments to Internal Affairs are for limited time periods, usually no more than two or three years for most individuals, some for far shorter time periods. This turnover in personnel in Internal Affairs often results in significant turnover in handling a single case. More insidiously, it means that officers from Internal Affairs soon will be returning to work with the same officers that they were disciplining. . . .

The Charter provides that disciplinary charges against police officers are adjudicated by a Board of Rights comprised of two command officers and one civilian. . . . [One possible reform] . . . would be to reconstitute the Board of Rights to include one command officer, one officer of the rank of Sergeant II or higher, and one civilian. Another would be binding arbitration. Another, likely the most promising, would be a citizen review board. . . .

Conclusion

. . . Reform is not an event, but a process that will take many years to complete. The hope is that this crisis provides a unique opportunity for reform. This opportunity must not be squandered. . . .

ST. PAUL, MINNESOTA, ORDINANCES §§102.01-102.03

Section 102.01

. . . (b) The [police-civilian internal affairs review commission] shall review all complaint investigations concerning members of the police department . . . completed by the internal affairs unit of the police department and subsequent investigations thereof related to alleged acts of excessive force, inappropriate use of firearms, discrimination, . . . poor public relations and such other complaints as may be referred to it by the mayor and/or the chief of police. The commission shall also collect and review summary data on complaints received and report to the mayor and council any patterns which may merit further examination.

Section 102.02

(a) There is hereby created a police-civilian internal affairs review commission consisting of seven voting members to be appointed by the mayor and approved by the council. . . . Five members shall be citizen members and two shall be members of the Saint Paul Police Federation as shall be recommended by the police chief to the mayor for appointment. Members shall, to the extent possible, be representative of the city's diversity of neighborhoods, races and cultures, abilities, incomes and sexual orientations. . . .

Section 102.03

. . . (b) Each member of the commission shall, prior to assuming official duties, participate in a training program which shall include topics related to police work, investigation, relevant law, cultural diversity, gender, sexual orientation, disability and the emotional impact of abuse. They shall also participate in ride-alongs with an officer on actual patrol duties. . . .

(d) The investigatory materials prepared by the internal affairs unit of the police department or independent investigators under contract to the city are considered data collected in furtherance of an active investigation and will be reviewed by the commission. The meetings of the commission on such matters will be closed . . . excepting to members of the commission and such other participants as approved by the chair of the commission and the police chief and that will facilitate the review process of the commission.

(e) The commission may request [that] individuals appear before it to state facts to supplement files. The commission may also request internal affairs staff to gather such additional information as may be needed for a determination by the commission. The commission may . . . hire a private investigator as approved by the mayor or chief of police. The commission shall have the power to subpoena witnesses to compel their appearance before it. . . .

(g) The commission, after review and deliberation of an investigation, shall, by majority vote, make its recommendation on the case. Such recommendation by the commission shall be upon a finding that the complaint be sustained; or the complaint not be sustained; or that the officer be exonerated; or the complaint is unfounded; or that the matter does not involve guilt or a lack thereof, but rather a failure of a departmental policy to address the situation. The commission shall also, by majority vote, make a recommendation as to any action to be taken concerning an involved officer. . . .

(j) In the event the chief of police disagrees with the action recommended by the commission, the chief shall notify the commission, in writing, of the action he or she intends to impose. The commission chair and chief of police shall have five working days to discuss any concerns they may have before any action is finalized. This provision does not prohibit the chief of police from taking immediate action in any case. . . .

Notes

1. *Police review boards.* Most police departments of any size have a section (often called "Internal Affairs" or "IAD") that reviews police officer conduct. Sometimes cities establish review boards to help internal affairs divisions or to reconsider the IAD findings. Sometimes special boards are set up to investigate particular allegations of police abuse. More controversial and less common are review boards entirely outside the police department. What are the advantages of an official review board? Who should be its members? What powers should the board have? Review boards have now operated in some jurisdictions for decades, and policy experts have evaluated their work across several dimensions. You can find a sample of those evaluations on the web extension for this chapter at *http://www.crimpro.com/extension/ch06*.

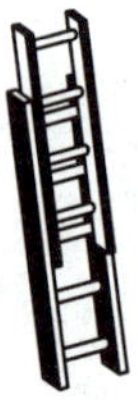

2. *Internal versus external review.* Are internal and external review bodies likely to reach the same results? Two separate reports assessing allegations of "testilying" and other illegal practices by Philadelphia police in the early 1990s reached widely differing conclusions: The internal report identified rogue officers; the external review found fundamental problems with the training and policies of the department. What are the advantages and disadvantages of an "independent" review board? How can internal review efforts be tied to salary raises and promotion decisions?

3. *Review by the media.* Sometimes newspapers or local TV stations will examine allegations of police misconduct. As with unofficial citizen review boards, the formal power of reporters to obtain information is limited, but of course reporters can disclose to the public any refusals to share information. An additional limit on the use of the media to shape officer and department behavior is the risk of libel suits brought by officers against reporters and newspapers. See, e.g., Costello v. Ocean County Observer, 643 A.2d 1012 (N.J. 1994).

4. *Early warning systems.* Police chiefs have a slogan: Ten percent of the officers cause ninety percent of the problems. How can police managers identify the officers who need special training or removal from the field? Some departments (just over a fourth of all departments nationwide) use "early warning" systems (also known as "early intervention" systems) to select officers who might benefit from training or other intervention. See Samuel Walker, Geoffrey P. Alpert & Dennis J. Kenney, Early Warning Systems: Responding to the Problem Police Officer (July 2001, NCJ 188565). Data collection systems flag officers for special attention if they are involved in some requisite number of citizen complaints, firearm discharges, use-of-force reports, civil litigation, high-speed pursuits, or vehicular damage. The supervisor of an officer so identified reviews the incident and counsels the officer; sometimes the department sends the officer to special training classes. Assuming that plaintiffs in civil lawsuits could subpoena this data about individual officers, does it help or hurt the department during the litigation? Do early warning systems encourage inactive policing?

5. *Renegade cops or renegade police culture?* No one defends the brutality of the individual Rampart officers. But is the problem explained by bad cops and weak supervision, or is there a wider problem with the culture of policing? The LAPD has an especially rich history of abuses and breakdowns in supervision, as dramatized in the 1997 movie *L.A. Confidential.* What different responses are called for by the two kinds of problems?

6. *Revocation of officer's license.* State and local police departments hire only individuals who are certified by state licensing authorities to serve as law enforcement officers. Administrative bodies in many states review allegations of police misconduct and sometimes revoke the license of an officer based on that misconduct; the licensing body in Florida is among the most active. The revocation of a license prevents other police forces in the same state from hiring an officer after he or she is fired for misconduct. One database, tracking the work of licensing authorities in 11 states going back to 1973, shows over 5,600 revocations during that time. See Roger L. Goldman, State Revocation of Law Enforcement Officers' Licenses and Federal Criminal Prosecution: An Opportunity for Cooperative Federalism, 22 St. Louis U. Pub. L. Rev. 121 (2003).

2. *Tort Actions and Criminal Prosecutions*

The most common private remedy for illegal searches prior to the use of the exclusionary rule was a tort action against the officer who violated the law during the search. Any victim of a wrongful search (not just those who later face criminal charges) can, in theory, bring a lawsuit against the officer conducting the search, or against the police department or other governmental units, requesting damages or other relief. The search victim might sue in state court based on state common law torts such as false imprisonment or trespass; she might also look to a state statute granting a civil cause of action for wrongful searches or seizures. Some victims also rely on a federal statute, 42 U.S.C. §1983, which creates a cause of action in federal court against any "person" who acts "under color of" state law to deprive another person of federal constitutional or statutory rights.

These lawsuits have not become a common method of dealing with improper searches or seizures. The plaintiffs in such cases face several substantial legal obstacles: The most important are the doctrines of "sovereign immunity" protecting the state or local government from suit, and "qualified immunity," which protects individual police officers who act with "good faith."

The theory behind the tort suit as a remedy for illegal searches and seizures is that civil damages can more precisely measure the violation and the harm. In terms of deterrence, the remedy imposes costs on the officer, the police department, or both; unlike suppression, a tort remedy remains a separate question from whether the suspect committed a criminal offense.

Whether financial costs imposed as result of successful tort claims in fact deter police officers or police departments from unconstitutional actions may turn in part on whether the individual officer (who will often be judgment-proof) or the department (or the county or state government) will pay the damages. One related issue is whether the state is obligated through contract or state law to indemnify the police officer for the costs of defense and any judgment against the officer.

Private enforcement is not the only possibility. In 1994, Congress passed legislation (now codified at 42 U.S.C. §14141) that prohibits state and local governments from engaging in "a pattern or practice of conduct by law enforcement officials" that deprives persons of "rights, privileges, or immunities secured or protected by the Constitution or laws of the United States." The statute authorizes the U.S. Department of Justice to sue in federal court for injunctive and declaratory relief to eliminate the pattern or practice. The Civil Rights Division of the Justice Department filed such a suit against the Los Angeles Police Department in the wake of the Rampart scandal described above; the consent decree resolving that suit is excerpted below. What are the relative merits of public and private civil enforcement?

■ MARK MAIMARON v. COMMONWEALTH

865 N.E.2d 1098 (Mass. 2007)

GREANEY, J.

On November 2, 1998, the plaintiff Mark Maimaron brought an action in the Superior Court under the Massachusetts Tort Claims Act, G.L. c. 258, against State

Trooper David Oxner, several other State troopers, and the Commonwealth, seeking to recover damages for injuries he sustained as the result of an alleged illegal seizure and arrest. The incident involved an altercation in 1995, when Oxner was not on duty. Maimaron asserted that Oxner had violated his civil rights as protected by Federal and State constitutional law and statutes, 42 U.S.C. §1983, and G.L. c. 12, §11I [civil action for violation of constitutional rights], and had committed the intentional torts of assault and battery, malicious prosecution, false arrest, and abuse of process, in making the seizure and arrest. In 2001, the Commonwealth settled Maimaron's claims against it and the State police officers other than Oxner. Thereafter, Maimaron and Oxner agreed to participate in binding arbitration, which resulted in an award and judgment, including attorney's fees, in Maimaron's favor. Unable to satisfy the judgment against him, Oxner entered a settlement agreement and assignment of rights with Maimaron in which Oxner assigned his right to Maimaron to indemnification (of the judgment in the underlying action) by the Commonwealth pursuant to G.L. c. 258, §9A. [The statute] provides, in relevant part:*

> If, in the event a suit is commenced against a member of the state police . . . by reason of a claim for damages resulting from an alleged intentional tort or by reason of an alleged act or failure to act which constitutes a violation of the civil rights of any person under federal or state law, the commonwealth, at the request of the affected police officer, shall provide for the legal representation of said police officer.
>
> The commonwealth shall indemnify members of the state police . . . from all personal financial loss and expenses, including but not limited to legal fees and costs, if any, in an amount not to exceed one million dollars arising out of any claim, action, award, compromise, settlement or judgment resulting from any alleged intentional tort or by reason of an alleged act or failure to act which constitutes a violation of the civil rights of any person under federal or state law; provided, however, that this section shall apply only where such alleged intentional tort or alleged act or failure to act occurred within the scope of the official duties of such police officer.
>
> No member of the state police . . . shall be indemnified for any violation of federal or state law if such member or employee acted in a wilful, wanton, or malicious manner.

Oxner and Maimaron commenced separate actions against the Commonwealth that have been consolidated. In his complaint, Oxner had sought to recover attorney's fees and costs that he incurred defending the underlying action, alleging that the Commonwealth had violated its duty under G.L. c. 258, §9A, in failing to defend him in that action. Maimaron . . . sought to collect the amount of the judgment entered against Oxner in the underlying action, as well as interest, and attorney's fees and costs. . . . A Superior Court judge granted summary judgment in favor of Oxner and Maimaron, and the Commonwealth appealed. . . .

On the evening of November 22, 1995, Oxner and his friend Stephen Roche went to a lounge in Quincy. They were later joined by Oxner's wife and her female friend. Oxner, who was not on duty that evening, had several drinks at the bar.

That same evening, Maimaron, an ironworker, was a patron at the lounge, and had consumed approximately ten beers. Maimaron met Oxner, whom Maimaron believed was actually a coworker from his work site, although Oxner told Maimaron

* [This material was moved from a footnote to text. — Eds.]

that he was a State trooper. Maimaron repeatedly confronted Oxner with this inaccurate belief, despite Oxner's repeated denials.

After midnight, Maimaron and Oxner encountered each other in the parking lot outside the lounge. A heated exchange ensued and Oxner demanded to see Maimaron's identification. Maimaron declined, and was turning to leave, when Oxner hit him on the side of his head and grabbed his shoulder. Fearing for his safety, Maimaron sprayed mace (which he was licensed to carry) into Oxner's face, and then ran down the street.

Oxner pursued Maimaron on foot, holding out his badge, identifying himself as a police officer, whistling, and telling Maimaron to stop because he was under arrest. Roche joined in the pursuit and caught up with Maimaron. Roche struck Maimaron from behind, knocking him to the ground. Maimaron raised his head and tried to get up, at which point Oxner slammed Maimaron down, hitting his face into the pavement.

Oxner and a bystander contacted the Quincy police department. Oxner identified himself as an off-duty officer and requested an ambulance for Maimaron, who was bleeding profusely. Roche disappeared into the crowd of spectators. When Quincy police officers arrived, Oxner told them that he had been assaulted by Maimaron with mace and that an "unknown white male" helped subdue Maimaron by tackling him.

Maimaron suffered extensive injuries, including multiple facial fractures, broken teeth and a detached palate. His jaws were wired shut for six weeks, and he underwent extensive rehabilitation and the implantation of titanium plates in his face. Maimaron sustained long-lasting injuries, including permanent change in his appearance, persistent vertigo and headaches, as well as emotional and psychological distress.

Oxner subsequently filed charges against Maimaron for assault and battery by means of a deadly weapon, as well as for assault and battery on a police officer. The United States Attorney's office conducted an investigation into the altercation. . . . Oxner pleaded guilty to assault and battery of Maimaron and to filing a false written report by a public officer, for which he was sentenced to unsupervised probation for one year.

In January 1997, a trial board of the State police determined that Oxner had violated several State police administrative rules and regulations. The board suspended him without pay for four months, and required that he complete ethics training. On January 3, 1997, the Norfolk County district attorney's office entered a nolle prosequi on the criminal complaint Oxner had filed against Maimaron.

In response to Maimaron's underlying action, Oxner sought defense and indemnification from the Commonwealth during the course of litigation, but the Commonwealth repeatedly declined his requests. After the Commonwealth had settled with Maimaron, Maimaron and Oxner voluntarily entered into binding arbitration. The Commonwealth was notified in writing by Oxner's attorney that the arbitration proceedings were about to begin, and Oxner again demanded that the Commonwealth assume his defense. The Commonwealth responded in writing that it "[declined] to provide . . . indemnification and/or defense of . . . Oxner [and did not] foresee . . . changing its stance on the issue." The Commonwealth did not participate in the arbitration.

In his award, the arbitrator concluded that Oxner had violated Maimaron's civil rights by committing the torts of assault and battery and false arrest. The arbitrator determined that Maimaron was entitled to damages from Oxner in the amount of $363,682. In addition, the arbitrator found the following: at all times during, and after, his confrontation with Maimaron, Oxner was acting within the scope of his employment as a State police officer; Oxner was acting under color of State law throughout the altercation and arrest because, under State police rules and regulations, a State police officer is subject to recall twenty-four hours a day and is instructed to take immediate enforcement action for violations of law observed, and Oxner was following State police regulations in attempting to arrest Maimaron for perceived criminal actions; Oxner violated Maimaron's rights under the Fourth Amendment to the United States Constitution during the assault and battery and subsequent false arrest; Oxner never intended to injure Maimaron during the arrest; and Oxner did not act in a "malicious or wanton" manner. On July 9, 2002, a Superior Court judge entered judgment for Maimaron in the amount of $363,682, and included an award for attorney's fees and costs in the amount of $69,243.52.

In connection with the instant action, the Superior Court judge who ruled on the parties' cross motions for summary judgment . . . concluded that, because the Commonwealth had violated its mandatory duty to defend Oxner against Maimaron's claim in the underlying action, the Commonwealth was bound by the arbitrator's findings and was precluded from arguing that Oxner was not acting within the scope of his official duties or that his conduct was wilful, wanton, or malicious. Judgment entered awarding damages to Maimaron in the amount of $363,682, due to the acts of Oxner; attorney's fees (for litigating the underlying action) to Maimaron in the amount of $69,243.52; attorney's fees (for litigating the instant action) to Maimaron in the amount of $29,951.88; and attorney's fees (for litigating the underlying and instant actions) to Oxner in the amount of $84,879. . . .

1. *Duty to defend.* The judge correctly concluded that the Commonwealth had a mandatory obligation to provide legal representation (the duty to defend) to Oxner under G.L. c. 258, §9A. . . . A review of the plain language of §9A, interpreted in a way to effectuate its purpose, mandates this result.

The first paragraph of G.L. c. 258, §9A, pertains solely to the duty to defend. Its language, "shall provide for the legal representation of said police officer," imposes a mandatory obligation. That obligation arises when (1) a request for legal representation is made by the affected police officer; and (2) a lawsuit is brought against the officer alleging an intentional tort or a violation of civil rights. These requirements were present here.

Relying on language in the second paragraph of G.L. c. 258, §9A, that provides, "this *section* shall apply only where such alleged intentional tort or alleged act or failure to act occurred within the scope of the official duties of such police officer," the Commonwealth maintains that its duty to defend is conditioned on whether the police officer had been acting within the scope of his official duties (emphasis added). We disagree. This language, together with the language also appearing in that paragraph that the indemnification obligation includes "personal financial loss and expenses, including but not limited to legal fees and costs," permits the Commonwealth, if it is *later* determined that the police officer acted outside the scope of his official duties or acted in a wilful, wanton, or malicious manner, to seek reimbursement of legal expenses.[8] To conclude otherwise would undermine the statute's purpose which recognizes that the requirement of mandatory indemnification evidences the Legislature's determination that intentional torts and civil rights violations arise frequently in the scope of police work, and that indemnification of officers against such claims encourages police service. The same applies equally to the duty to defend provision....

2. *Duty to indemnify Maimaron (as assignee).* Under G.L. c. 258, §9A, the Commonwealth is required to indemnify a member of the State police "from all personal financial loss and expenses . . . arising out of any claim, action, award, compromise, settlement or judgment resulting from any alleged intentional tort or by reason of an alleged act or failure to act which constitutes a violation of the civil rights of any person under federal or state law." There are two exclusions: (1) where the alleged act did not occur "within the scope of the official duties of such police officer"; and (2) where the police officer "acted in a wilful, wanton, or malicious manner."

The Commonwealth argues that the judge erred in granting summary judgment on the indemnification issue, maintaining that it should have been permitted to litigate the two exclusions. The judge rejected the Commonwealth's argument on the basis of the rule, applied frequently in insurance cases, that an insurer who has wrongfully refused to defend its insured cannot relitigate coverage issues and, thus, becomes liable to indemnify the damages assessed in the third-party action....

We first address the scope of employment issue as it relates to the color of State law issue that was the concern of the arbitrator in Maimaron's §1983 claim. [The decision in] Pinshaw v. Metropolitan Dist. Comm'n, 524 N.E.2d 1351 (Mass. 1988), established that "the scope of . . . official duties" exclusion in §9A calls for the application of common-law respondeat superior principles. It went on to set forth those principles as follows: . . .

> In determining the scope of employment, the finder of fact must consider whether the conduct complained of is of the kind the employee is hired to perform, whether it occurs within authorized time and space limits, and whether "it is motivated, at least in part, by a purpose to serve the employer." See Restatement (Second) of Agency §228 (1958)....
>
> If an employee acts from purely personal motives . . . in no way connected with the employer's interests, he is considered in the ordinary case to have departed from his employment, and the master is not liable.... If the act complained of was within the scope of the servant's authority, the master will be liable, although it constituted an abuse or excess of the authority conferred. The master . . . is justly held responsible when the servant, through lack of judgment or discretion, or from infirmity of temper, or under the influence of passion aroused by the circumstances and the occasion, goes beyond the strict line of his duty or authority and inflicts an unjustifiable injury on a third person....

8. The Commonwealth's reasons for refusing its duty to defend, such as the fact that Oxner had pleaded guilty to two criminal charges and was found to be in violation of various State police administrative rules and regulations, do not bear on the Commonwealth's duty to provide a defense. Rather, if such reasons later are found to take Oxner's conduct outside the scope of his official duties or to amount to wilful, wanton, or malicious behavior, the Commonwealth would be entitled to seek reimbursement of the legal fees incurred in his defense.

The determination whether a defendant acted under color of State law is one of two essential requirements for an action under 42 U.S.C. §1983. Generally speaking, there are three basic principles that define the scope of "acting under the color of State law" requirement. First, "a public employee acts under color of State law while acting in his official capacity or while exercising his responsibilities pursuant to State law." That is the basic proposition. Second, a public official . . . acts under color of State law if he acts under "pretense" of law, but not when he is acting as a private individual pursuing his own goals.

Third, and of importance to this case, when a public official "misuses" or "abuses" the authority given him by the State (i.e., if he acts outside the scope of his employment) he nevertheless acts under color of State law where he is "clothed with the authority of State law." Monroe v. Pape, 365 U.S. 167, 184 (1961), overruled in part by Monell v. Department of Social Servs. of the City of N.Y., 436 U.S. 658, 663 (1978) (overruling *Monroe* case "insofar as it holds that local governments are wholly immune from suit under §1983"). Under the third principle, a police officer may be acting under color of State law, but *not* acting within the scope of his employment, because he may have "misused" or "abused," in the Supreme Court's language, the authority given to him by the State. [The] two concepts — acting within the scope of employment and acting under color of State law — do not involve precisely parallel considerations (although there may, in a given case, be some overlap). The scope of employment issue bespeaks a narrower inquiry and, in certain cases, would allow a fact finder to conclude that an officer who is acting under color of State law for purposes of §1983 liability is not acting within the scope of his employment for purposes of G.L. c. 258, §9A, indemnification. . . .

In this case, the arbitrator provided no explanation to support his conclusion that Oxner was acting within the scope of employment, and he did not refer to, much less discuss, the standards governing the scope of official duties exception set forth in the *Pinshaw* decision. . . . The facts found by the arbitrator establish that Oxner was subject to recall twenty-four hours a day; that he eventually displayed his police badge to Maimaron thereby officially identifying himself as a police officer; and that he issued an official command to stop, seeking to arrest Maimaron for some undetermined violation of law. These facts do not, however, compel a conclusion that Oxner was acting within the scope of his employment. Rather, because Oxner could be found to have acted unlawfully and with excessive force in subduing Maimaron (after an encounter in the lounge where Maimaron had done nothing unlawful), a fact finder could conclude that Oxner "abused" his authority, namely, that he was acting outside the scope of his employment, even though he was acting under color of State law. . . .

It was also not necessary for the arbitrator to find in connection with the claims before him that Oxner was not acting wilfully, wantonly, or maliciously. There must be a trial on this exclusion as well. The standard for assessing Oxner's conduct under this exclusion was described in *Pinshaw* in these terms:

> For purposes of §9A, in a civil rights context "wilful, wanton, or malicious" conduct means egregious conduct which would warrant imposition of punitive damages in the underlying action. In Federal civil rights actions, which are among the actions for which §9A provides indemnity, the United States Supreme Court has interpreted the terms "malice," "wanton," and "willful" to constitute a standard for punitive damages "when the defendant's conduct is shown to be motivated by evil motive or intent, or when it

> involves reckless or callous indifference to the federally protected rights of others." Linking the exclusion from indemnification to the standard for punitive damages achieves the Legislature's clear intent; it indemnifies officers for intentional torts and civil rights violations occurring within the scope of their official duties, yet excludes indemnification in egregious cases. It also provides a bright line test for precluding indemnification where punitive damages are awarded in the underlying action.

The arbitrator's conclusion that Oxner had not acted wilfully, wantonly, or maliciously does not, on this record, preclude a finding that Oxner took himself outside the coverage of §9A, when he confronted, and viciously attacked, Maimaron outside the lounge. Oxner's conduct could be found by a trier of fact to be "egregious" (and therefore punitive) in the sense described by the *Pinshaw* case.

Finally, we note that *both* exclusions involve the need for a fact finder to ascertain Oxner's state of mind. Summary judgment, when an actor's state of mind is relevant, is strongly disfavored. . . .

This case, particularly with reference to Oxner's defense by the Commonwealth, has not been handled well. The Commonwealth, to satisfy its defense obligations under §9A, should have defended Oxner under a reservation of rights (and litigated the indemnification issue later). . . . The Commonwealth also could have sought a declaratory judgment in advance of the arbitration to determine whether it was obligated under §9A to defend Oxner. This procedure is utilized in insurance cases to determine an insurer's obligation when there is a legitimate question about provision of a defense, and we discern no reason why the procedure would not have utility in this type of case.

The judgment for the plaintiffs is vacated. The case is remanded to the Superior Court for the entry of a new and partial judgment stating that the Commonwealth breached its duty to defend Oxner under G.L. c. 258, §9A . . . . With respect to the Commonwealth's liability for indemnification to Maimaron (as assignee), the case is remanded for further proceedings consistent with this opinion.

■ OFFICE OF THE ATTORNEY GENERAL, STATE OF ARKANSAS, OPINION NO. 2004-188

(September 8, 2004)

The Honorable Larry Jegley
Prosecuting Attorney, Sixth Judicial District
Little Rock, Arkansas

Dear Mr. Jegley:

You have requested my opinion on certain issues related to chemical testing for the purpose of determining alcohol and drug levels in a suspect's body. You indicate that your questions are related to situations in which police officers arrive at the scene of a motor vehicle accident and find a dead or dying victim of a suspected drunk driver. The suspected drunk driver refuses to submit to chemical testing pursuant to A.C.A. §5-65-208. . . .

Your questions are: . . .

(2) [What] action should police take to enforce the provisions of Section 208? (Should they seek a court order or warrant if a driver refuses consent to testing

(although dissipating drugs or alcohol create a time crunch, often late at night)?) May officers use reasonable force, if needed to obtain the sample, either with or without court order or warrant?

(3) If force is permitted either with or without a warrant, are there any civil liability issues for police agencies enforcing the requirements of A.C.A. §5-65-208, assuming it is mandatory? . . .

RESPONSE

[Question 2: What] action should police take to enforce the provisions of Section 208? (Should they seek a court order or warrant if a driver refuses consent to testing (although dissipating drugs or alcohol create a time crunch, often late at night)?) May officers use reasonable force, if needed to obtain the sample, either with or without court order or warrant? . . .

The Arkansas Supreme Court recently stated: "The law is settled that the taking of blood by a law enforcement officer amounts to a Fourth Amendment search and seizure." Haynes v. State, 127 S.W.3d 456, 461 (Ark. 2003), citing Schmerber v. California, 384 U.S. 757 (1966). Accordingly, a warrant is required unless an exception to the warrant requirement can be established. For example, a warrant is not necessary if the suspect gives his consent to the test. Another example of a situation in which a warrant may not be necessary is a situation involving certain exigent circumstances, such as those in which the opportunity to administer the test will exist only for a short time. . . .

Question 3: If force is permitted either with or without a warrant, are there any civil liability issues for police agencies enforcing the requirements of A.C.A. §5-65-208 . . . ?

The answer to this question will depend upon the type of liability to which you are referring. Law enforcement officers, as employees of the state or of political subdivisions of the state, are entitled to certain limited immunity from suit for some types of acts that are performed in the course of their official duties. Law enforcement officers who are employees of the State fall within the provisions of A.C.A. §19-10-305(a), which states: "Officers and employees of the State of Arkansas are immune from liability and from suit, except to the extent that they may be covered by liability insurance, for damages for acts or omissions, other than malicious acts or omissions, occurring within the course and scope of their employment."

It should be noted that the above-quoted grant of immunity applies generally to nonmalicious acts, but that it contains an exception to the extent of liability insurance coverage. Therefore, while law enforcement officers generally cannot be held liable for nonmalicious acts, they can be held liable for such acts to the extent that such acts are covered by liability insurance. They can also, of course, be held liable for malicious acts.

Law enforcement officers who are employees of cities and counties fall within the provisions of A.C.A. §21-9-301, which states:

> It is declared to be the public policy of the State of Arkansas that all counties, municipal corporations, school districts, special improvement districts, and all other political subdivisions of the state shall be immune from liability and from suit for damages, except to the extent that they may be covered by liability insurance. No tort action shall

> lie against any such political subdivision because of the acts of its agents and employees.

Although A.C.A. §21-9-301 speaks only in terms of the immunity of the political subdivision itself, the Arkansas Supreme Court has interpreted the statute as extending immunity to officers and employees of the political subdivisions as well when they negligently commit acts or omissions in their official capacities. Accordingly, a claimant may be able to sue city or county law enforcement officers personally for intentional or malicious acts, or for negligent acts not committed in their official capacities. However, the claimant cannot sue the city or county officer for negligence that was committed in the officer's official capacity (except to the extent that such acts are covered by liability insurance).

In addition to these two types of statutory immunity, law enforcement officers may be entitled to "qualified immunity." Under the doctrine of qualified immunity, an individual is immune from suit if the actions complained of were taken in good faith in the performance of one's duties, and the acts do not violate any clearly established constitutional right. Harlow v. Fitzgerald, 457 U.S. 800 (1982). The test for the applicability of qualified immunity turns upon the "objective legal reasonableness of the action," assessed in light of legal rules that were "clearly established" at the time the action was taken. See Anderson v. Creighton, 483 U.S. 635 (1987). The immunity is "qualified" because it does not obtain where the activity is in violation of clearly established law that a reasonable person would have known.

The question of whether a law enforcement officer is entitled to any type of immunity from a claim arising out of the execution of the testing requirements of A.C.A. §5-65-208 will depend largely upon the facts of each case, including the particular damage claimed, whether that damage resulted from an act committed by the officer in his official capacity, and whether the officer acted negligently or maliciously. . . .

Assistant Attorney General Suzanne Antley prepared the foregoing opinion, which I hereby approve.

Sincerely,
Mike Beebe, Attorney General

■ CONSENT DECREE, UNITED STATES v. CITY OF LOS ANGELES

Civil No. 00-11769 GAF, June 15, 2001

1. The United States and the City of Los Angeles, a chartered municipal corporation in the State of California, share a mutual interest in promoting effective and respectful policing. They join together in entering this settlement in order to promote police integrity and prevent conduct that deprives persons of rights, privileges, or immunities secured or protected by the Constitution or laws of the United States.

2. In its Complaint, plaintiff United States alleges that the City of Los Angeles, the Los Angeles Board of Police Commissioners, and the Los Angeles Police Department (collectively, "the City defendants") are violating 42 U.S.C. §14141 by engaging in a pattern or practice of unconstitutional or otherwise unlawful conduct that

has been made possible by the failure of the City defendants to adopt and implement proper management practices and procedures. In making these allegations, the United States recognizes that the majority of Los Angeles police officers perform their difficult jobs in a lawful manner. . . .

MANAGEMENT AND SUPERVISORY MEASURES TO PROMOTE CIVIL RIGHTS INTEGRITY

39. The City has taken steps to develop, and shall establish a database containing relevant information about its officers, supervisors, and managers to promote professionalism and best policing practices and to identify and modify at-risk behavior (also known as an early warning system). This system shall be a successor to, and not simply a modification of, the existing computerized information processing system known as the Training Evaluation and Management System ("TEAMS"). The new system shall be known as "TEAMS II". . . .

41. TEAMS II shall contain information on the following matters:

a. all non-lethal uses of force that are required to be reported in LAPD "use of force" reports or otherwise are the subject of an administrative investigation by the Department; . . .

c. all officer-involved shootings and firearms discharges, both on-duty and off-duty; . . .

d. all other lethal uses of force;

e. all other injuries and deaths that are reviewed by the LAPD Use of Force Review Board; . . .

f. all vehicle pursuits and traffic collisions; . . .

i. all written compliments received by the LAPD about officer performance;

j. all commendations and awards;

k. all criminal arrests and investigations known to LAPD of, and all charges against, LAPD employees;

l. all civil or administrative claims filed with and all lawsuits served upon the City or its officers . . . resulting from LAPD operations and known by the City, the Department, or the City Attorney's Office; . . .

p. training history and any failure of an officer to meet weapons qualification requirements; and

q. all management and supervisory actions taken pursuant to a review of TEAMS II information, including non-disciplinary actions. . . .

47. The protocol for using TEAMS II shall include the following provisions and elements:

a. The protocol shall require that, on a regular basis, supervisors review and analyze all relevant information in TEAMS II about officers under their supervision to detect any pattern or series of incidents that indicate that an officer, group of officers, or an LAPD unit under his or her supervision may be engaging in at-risk behavior. . . .

c. The protocol shall require that LAPD managers on a regular basis review and analyze relevant information in TEAMS II about subordinate managers and supervisors in their command regarding the subordinate's ability to manage adherence to policy and to address at-risk behavior. . . .

g. The protocol shall require that all relevant and appropriate information in TEAMS II be taken into account when [deciding matters of] pay grade advancement, promotion, assignment as . . . a Field Training Officer, or when preparing annual personnel performance evaluations. . . .

Incidents, Procedures, Documentation, Investigation, and Review

78. The Department shall continue to require officers to report to the LAPD without delay: any conduct by other officers that reasonably appears to constitute (a) an excessive use of force or improper threat of force; (b) a false arrest or filing of false charges; (c) an unlawful search or seizure; (d) invidious discrimination; (e) an intentional failure to complete forms required by LAPD policies and in accordance with procedures; (f) an act of retaliation for complying with any LAPD policy or procedure; or (g) an intentional provision of false information in an administrative investigation or in any official report, log, or electronic transmittal of information. . . . Failure to voluntarily report as described in this paragraph shall be an offense subject to discipline if sustained. . . .

97. [The] City shall develop and initiate a plan for organizing and executing regular, targeted, and random integrity audit checks, or "sting" operations . . . to identify and investigate officers engaging in at-risk behavior, including: unlawful stops, searches, seizures (including false arrests), [or] uses of excessive force. . . . These operations shall also seek to identify officers who discourage the filing of a complaint or fail to report misconduct or complaints. . . . The Department shall use the relevant TEAMS II data, and other relevant information, in selecting targets for these sting audits. . . .

103. LAPD officers may not use race, color, ethnicity, or national origin (to any extent or degree) in conducting stops or detentions, or activities following stops or detentions, except when . . . officers are seeking one or more specific persons who have been identified or described in part by their race, color, ethnicity, or national origin. . . .

104. [The] Department shall require LAPD officers to complete a written or electronic report each time an officer conducts a motor vehicle stop. . . . The report shall include the following: (i) the officer's serial number; (ii) date and approximate time of the stop; (iii) reporting district where the stop occurred; (iv) driver's apparent race, ethnicity, or national origin; (v) driver's gender and apparent age; (vi) reason for the stop . . . ; (vii) whether the driver was required to exit the vehicle; (viii) whether a pat-down/frisk was conducted; (ix) action taken, to include check boxes for warning, citation, arrest, completion of a field interview card, with appropriate identification number for the citation or arrest report; and (x) whether the driver was asked to submit to a consensual search of person, vehicle, or belongings, and whether permission was granted or denied. . . .

105. [The] Department shall require LAPD officers to complete a written or electronic report each time an officer conducts a pedestrian stop. . . .

Community Outreach and Public Information

155. For the term of this Agreement, the Department shall conduct a Community Outreach and Public Information program for each LAPD geographic area. The program shall require . . . at least one open meeting per quarter in each of the 18 geographic Areas for the first year of the Agreement, and one meeting in each

Area annually thereafter, to inform the public about the provisions of this Agreement, and the various methods of filing a complaint against an officer. . . .

156. The LAPD shall prepare and publish on its website semiannual public reports. . . . Such reports shall include aggregate statistics broken down by each LAPD geographic area and for the Operations Headquarters Bureau, and broken down by the race/ethnicity/national origin of the citizens involved, for arrests, information required to be maintained pursuant to paragraphs 104 and 105, and uses of force. Such reports shall include a brief description of [audits completed] and any significant actions taken as a result of such audits or reports, (ii) a summary of all discipline imposed during the period reported by type of misconduct, broken down by type of discipline, bureau and rank, and (iii) any new policies or changes in policies made by the Department to address the requirements of this Agreement. . . .

Notes

1. *The availability of tort remedies for police misconduct.* All states and the federal system offer some kind of tort (or tort-like) remedies for some kinds of police misconduct. In the federal system, private claims can arise under 42 U.S.C. §1983 (civil rights), the Federal Tort Claims Act, or directly under the Constitution in suits known as *Bivens* actions, after Bivens v. Six Unknown Named Agents of Federal Bureau of Narcotics, 403 U.S. 388 (1971). Remedies in federal court may include money damages, injunctive relief, or consent decrees entered between parties in lieu of further litigation. In many states recovery is allowed under statutes providing generally for tort claims against the government and its agents, subject to limitations for sovereign immunity (for governments) and official immunity (for individual officers). Claims may also be made under specialized tort statutes. Surprisingly, very few states have promulgated statutes specifically addressing actions by citizens against the police.

2. *The invisibility of tort claims.* Despite the long history of tort actions to remedy unconstitutional and excessive police action, it is extremely difficult to find any reported cases involving successful claims. Indeed, there are more law review articles discussing tort actions than reported decisions about successful recoveries. See, e.g., John C. Jeffries, Jr., Disaggregating Constitutional Torts, 110 Yale L. J. 259 (2000); Susan Bandes, Patterns of Injustice: Police Brutality in the Courts, 47 Buff. L. Rev. 1275-341 (1999).

The almost complete absence of reported decisions might suggest that tort remedies are entirely illusory, and that the legal barriers to recovery are too high (at least too high to make tort suits a plausible remedy, either for the purposes of the claimant or as a behavior-shaping device). But some plaintiffs who sue the government for improper police conduct do recover damages, despite immunities and other obstacles. Newspapers regularly carry stories of settlements or jury verdicts in civil suits dealing with officer misconduct. The most frequent basis for these claims is excessive use of force.

Cities tend to settle most of these suits for relatively small amounts, with a few high-visibility cases receiving larger settlements or jury verdicts after trial. The unadorned numbers show some large total payments in some cities and much smaller total payments elsewhere. For example, Detroit spent more than 8 percent of its 1993 operating budget, or $27.5 million, on police misconduct damages.

San Francisco paid less than $2 million between 1990 and 1994 to alleged victims of police brutality. Of 31 cases contested in court, city attorneys won all but two, and the city paid $234,600 to the two successful plaintiffs. The city settled 25 cases out of court for $1.54 million, usually in amounts of $10,000 to $20,000. See Dennis Opatrny, Little Danger of Sudden Wealth in Suing the SFPD, City Fights Claims for Misconduct Hard, Rarely Pays Much, San Francisco Examiner, June 11, 1995. Would you devote a major portion of your private practice to representing such clients? What would you need to know before concluding that such a practice would be financially viable?

The news accounts of settlements raise the classic tort question whether civil suits have any impact on police practices. In Pittsburgh, annual civil judgments and settlements exceeding $1 million between 1990 and 1996 convinced the city council to create a citizen police-review board. Many of the settlements, however, include a provision keeping the settlement terms secret. The settlements are often paid from the city's general budget rather than the police department budget, and the officer whose conduct led to the lawsuit is not routinely disciplined as a result of the city's financial loss. Despite these limits, does the amount of money that cities pay to tort plaintiffs each year suggest that civil liability is working reasonably well? Joanna C. Schwartz, Myths and Mechanics of Deterrence: The Role of Lawsuits in Law Enforcement Decisionmaking, 57 UCLA L. Rev. 1023 (2010) (finding that officials rarely have probative information about suits alleging misconduct by their officers). The web extension for this chapter, at *http://www.crimpro.com/extension/ch06*, surveys evidence from a variety of sources about the prevalence and effects of tort suits against police officers.

3. *Qualified good faith immunity for individuals.* The legal barriers to tort claims are very high. State and federal courts have created protections known as a "qualified good faith immunity" or "official immunity" for police officers sued in tort for the illegal acts they commit during the course of their employment. The immunity is "qualified" because an officer loses it when she subjectively knows that she is violating the rights of the victim, or when she objectively should know that she is violating those rights. Does the doctrine of qualified immunity mean that damages will be unavailable in all cases where *Leon* would create a good faith exception to the exclusionary rule? Does it leave plaintiffs without a remedy? See Malley v. Briggs, 475 U.S. 335 (1986) (officer's good faith immunity from tort liability for improper warranted search is same scope as *Leon* good faith exception to exclusionary rule); Hope v. Pelzer, 536 U.S. 730 (2002) (new factual situations calling for new application earlier legal principles could nonetheless violate "clearly established" rights); Pearson v. Callahan, 129 S. Ct. 808 (2009) (judges considering qualified immunity do not face an inflexible requirement to start with question of whether violation occurred, but may begin by asking whether alleged right was clearly established at the time). Practice problems that allow you to apply qualified immunity doctrine in various contexts appear on the web extension of this chapter.

From the standpoint of the plaintiff Maimaron, how sensible are barriers to claims such as qualified immunity? How understandable is the distinction between "acting under color of state law," and acting "outside of" the police officer's authority?

4. *Sovereign immunity and waiver.* Often the victim of an improper search or seizure will prefer to sue the state or local government rather than the judgment-proof individual officer who violated the law. Under traditional common law

principles, such a suit is not possible under state law because of the doctrine of "sovereign immunity," which insulates the government from any monetary claims. Most states have passed statutes that partially waive their sovereign immunity, so they will pay for some wrongdoing committed by state employees (on a respondeat superior basis). Under these tort claims acts, the lawsuit against the state or local government usually becomes the only cause of action for the wrongdoing; the plaintiff can no longer sue the individual employee. However, almost all of these statutes contain exceptions. For instance, most provide that the state or local government will not be liable for "discretionary" actions of officials. Some also exempt any action by officials engaged in the "enforcement" of any law or judicial order. See S.C. Code §15-78-60. Section 1983 does not create respondeat superior liability for state or local government. A plaintiff can sue a local government based on the actions of its police officers only if the officer was acting pursuant to a "policy" or "practice" endorsed by the government.

Beyond the perspective of individual claimants, a more general issue for remedies other than suppression is whether the substantive and procedural barriers to relief make tort claims a plausible and functional alternative. The materials in this chapter only hint at the complexity of Section 1983 and state civil rights and tort claims. That legal complexity is analogous to the complexity involving claims for post-conviction judicial relief, such as claims in habeas corpus. Entire books and law school courses — and entire legal practices — can be built around specialization in these areas. See, e.g., Joseph Cook & John Sobieski, Civil Rights Actions (seven-volume treatise); Sheldon Nahmod, Civil Rights and Civil Liberties Litigation: The Law of Section 1983 (three-volume treatise).

5. *Costs and indemnity for judgments.* Almost all states have statutes that allow the state or local government to pay for the police officer's legal representation so long as the officer was acting within the scope of authority. Many states go further, allowing the state or local government to indemnify the officer for the amount of any judgment paid to the plaintiff. Many states do have statutes authorizing indemnification. See, e.g., Ky. Code §16.185. Do such statutes compromise the power of tort suits to deter officers from making improper searches and seizures? Some states also have statutes authorizing the trial court to order a losing plaintiff to pay the attorney's fees and costs of the defendants if the suit was not substantially justified. See, e.g., Md. State Govt. Code §12-309. In light of the holding of the Massachusetts court in *Maimaron*, would you recommend any amendments to the state laws on indemnity for officers?

6. *Limitations on equitable relief.* Sometimes plaintiffs want injunctive relief rather than, or in addition to, money damages. Although injunctions are now considered a legitimate response to some search and seizure violations, they are still not as widely used as exclusion or damages. When relief is sought in federal court for actions of state actors, federal courts may be reluctant to order or affirm injunctive relief on federalism grounds. Another limitation on the availability of injunctions is the standing doctrine. Who has standing to challenge a police policy or practice? When a plaintiff seeks injunctive relief rather than damages, the Supreme Court has held that the plaintiff must show a likelihood of future harm. In City of Los Angeles v. Lyons, 461 U.S. 95 (1983), a plaintiff who was challenging the use of "chokeholds" by the police department had no standing to obtain injunctive or declaratory relief (as opposed to damages). Although the police had used the chokehold on Adolph Lyons in a situation where the officers faced no threat of injury,

Lyons could not demonstrate a "substantial likelihood" that he personally would be choked again in the future. Is this standing limitation applicable mostly to use of force policies?

State courts may not be constrained by similarly strict standing doctrines, and the federalism concerns will not be present. Is an injunction inherently more intrusive than damage awards or exclusion of evidence in criminal proceedings? Should it be reserved for certain types of violations by law enforcement officials? Keep in mind that an injunction gives a court continuing jurisdiction over the controversy; the court can impose contempt sanctions on any defendant violating the terms of an injunction.

7. *Who benefits from a damages remedy?* Unlike the exclusion remedy, a tort suit can benefit victims of illegal searches and seizures who commit no crime or who are not charged with a crime. This feature of tort suits could make them a better remedy for those injured in the past; does it affect the relative ability of these remedies to prevent future violations? Think about the connection between remedies and rights. If tort suits were the primary method for enforcing the Fourth Amendment, would courts see different types of parties raising these claims? Would the scope of privacy rights change if the remedy were to change?

8. *Federal involvement in police review.* Over the past several years, the U.S. Department of Justice (DOJ) has entered into a series of consent decrees with local and state police departments around the country, focusing on issues such as racial bias in stops, use of deadly force, and mistreatment of citizens. Under 42 U.S.C. §14141, known as the "Police Misconduct Provision," the Department can sue in federal court to prohibit state and local governments from engaging in "a pattern or practice of conduct by law enforcement officials" that deprives persons of "rights, privileges, or immunities secured or protected by the Constitution or laws of the United States." Since 1994, DOJ has investigated dozens of matters under the authority of 14141, and entered several settlements, including the consent decree in Los Angeles. Other consent decrees or "memoranda of understanding" resolved federal lawsuits against Pittsburgh, Cincinnati, the state of New Jersey, Montgomery County (Maryland), and the District of Columbia (see *http://www.usdoj.gov/crt/split/*). Does the Los Angeles consent decree suggest the promise of this new avenue for structural reform? The Los Angeles Consent Decree requires a lot of data, recordkeeping, and monitoring. Can you access this information?

9. *Criminal charges.* It is possible for a prosecutor to file criminal charges against an officer who conducts an illegal search or seizure, either under general criminal statutes (such as false imprisonment or trespass) or under statutes expressly covering police violations of civil rights. See 18 U.S.C. §§241, 242. U.S. Attorneys have to get central DOJ clearance to bring criminal charges against a police officer. Does the potential for criminal charges help prevent illegal searches and seizures? Would these criminal statutes become more effective if they were amended to compel prosecutors to file charges whenever there is probable cause? Local prosecutors are charged with the duty of prosecuting crimes, whether they are committed by citizens or officers. But do prosecutors aggressively prosecute police officers, with whom they work on a daily basis?

Problem 6-6. Legislative Remedies

You work as an adviser to a state senator who wants to limit or abolish the exclusionary rule and to replace it with a genuinely effective, alternative set of tort remedies. Draft a statute creating, to the extent possible, effective remedies for illegal searches and seizures. The remedies can include tort damages, injunctions, and police department training requirements and promotion rules, among other options. The senator has always valued your candid opinion. When you submit this proposal to her, will you recommend that the array of new remedies replace the exclusionary rule?

VII

Technology and Privacy

There was of course no way of knowing whether you were being watched at any given moment. . . . It was even conceivable that they watched everybody all the time. . . . You had to live — did live, from habit that became instinct — in the assumption that every sound you made was overheard, and . . . every moment scrutinized.

George Orwell, *1984*

The cases, statutes, and executive branch policies we have examined thus far have revealed social forces at work, shaping the basic rules constraining searches and seizures. At times and in places where protection of privacy or individual liberty are paramount or where the police are perceived skeptically, the rules of criminal procedure tend to be more restrictive. Where crime control takes the upper hand or where the police are perceived as largely benign, police are given greater power and discretion.

The collective attitudes that influence criminal procedures are constantly shifting. One force that can change attitudes is technology, which alters the ability both to conceal and to detect information. In this chapter, we consider how typical rules governing searches and seizures change when the government uses various technologies to enhance its powers to collect information that no human sense could otherwise detect.

A. ENHANCEMENT OF THE SENSES

New technologies allow searches of vast databases or observation of daily activities such as how people drive and what they say on the phone or online. These technologies raise new questions about the limits on state power and the right to privacy. You should consider not only whether the limits on today's devices (such as wiretaps and infrared) have been resolved wisely but also whether there is a solid foundation of principle and practice that can resolve questions about the flood of new observation and search technologies on the horizon.

Under the widely adopted test in Katz v. United States, 389 U.S. 347 (1967), a "search" subject to constitutional limitations takes place when the government intrudes into a person's "reasonable expectation of privacy." Applying this test, when a government agent sees something in plain view, there is no "search" that is subject to constitutional limits. See Chapter 2, section C. But can the same be said of an item that an officer sees (or smells or hears) with the aid of some device that offers a clearer or closer view or a louder sound or a stronger smell? Since the *Katz* standard first appeared in 1967, federal and state courts have wrestled with a variety of investigative technologies, often on a technology-by-technology basis. Consider whether either of the following two cases provides a useful framework for assessing high technology searches in other contexts.

■ CHARLES KATZ v. UNITED STATES

389 U.S. 347 (1967)

STEWART, J.*

The petitioner was convicted [of] transmitting wagering information by telephone from Los Angeles to Miami and Boston, in violation of a federal statute. At trial the Government was permitted, over the petitioner's objection, to introduce evidence of the petitioner's end of telephone conversations, overheard by FBI agents who had attached an electronic listening and recording device to the outside of the public telephone booth from which he had placed his calls. In affirming his conviction, the Court of Appeals rejected the contention that the recordings had been obtained in violation of the Fourth Amendment, because "there was no physical entrance into the area occupied by [the petitioner]."

[The] parties have attached great significance to the characterization of the telephone booth from which the petitioner placed his calls. The petitioner has strenuously argued that the booth was a "constitutionally protected area." The Government has maintained with equal vigor that it was not. But this effort to decide whether or not a given "area," viewed in the abstract, is "constitutionally protected" deflects attention from the problem presented by this case. For the Fourth Amendment protects people, not places. What a person knowingly exposes to the public, even in his own home or office, is not a subject of Fourth Amendment protection. But what he seeks to preserve as private, even in an area accessible to the public, may be constitutionally protected. . . .

No less than an individual in a business office, in a friend's apartment, or in a taxicab, a person in a telephone booth may rely upon the protection of the Fourth Amendment. One who occupies it, shuts the door behind him, and pays the toll that permits him to place a call is surely entitled to assume that the words he utters into

* [Chief Justice Warren and Justices Brennan, Douglas, Fortas, Harlan, and White joined in this opinion. — EDS.]

the mouthpiece will not be broadcast to the world. To read the Constitution more narrowly is to ignore the vital role that the public telephone has come to play in private communication.

The Government contends, however, that the activities of its agents in this case should not be tested by Fourth Amendment requirements, for the surveillance technique they employed involved no physical penetration of the telephone booth from which the petitioner placed his calls. It is true that the absence of such penetration was at one time thought to foreclose further Fourth Amendment inquiry, Olmstead v. United States, 277 U.S. 438 (1928), for that Amendment was thought to limit only searches and seizures of tangible property. But the premise that property interests control the right of the Government to search and seize has been discredited. Thus, although a closely divided Court supposed in *Olmstead* that surveillance without any trespass and without the seizure of any material object fell outside the ambit of the Constitution, we have since departed from the narrow view on which that decision rested. Indeed, we have expressly held that the Fourth Amendment governs not only the seizure of tangible items, but extends as well to the recording of oral statements, overheard without any technical trespass under local property law. Silverman v. United States, 365 U.S. 505 (1961). Once this much is acknowledged, and once it is recognized that the Fourth Amendment protects people — and not simply "areas" — against unreasonable searches and seizures, it becomes clear that the reach of that Amendment cannot turn upon the presence or absence of a physical intrusion into any given enclosure.

[The] Government's position is that its agents acted in an entirely defensible manner: They did not begin their electronic surveillance until investigation of the petitioner's activities had established a strong probability that he was using the telephone in question to transmit gambling information to persons in other States, in violation of federal law. Moreover, the surveillance was limited, both in scope and in duration, to the specific purpose of establishing the contents of the petitioner's unlawful telephonic communications. The agents confined their surveillance to the brief periods during which he used the telephone booth,[14] and they took great care to overhear only the conversations of the petitioner himself. . . .

The Government urges that, because its agents . . . did no more here than they might properly have done with prior judicial sanction, we should retroactively validate their conduct. That we cannot do. It is apparent that the agents in this case acted with restraint. Yet the inescapable fact is that this restraint was imposed by the agents themselves, not by a judicial officer. . . . Over and again this Court has emphasized that the mandate of the Fourth Amendment requires adherence to judicial processes, and that searches conducted outside the judicial process, without prior approval by judge or magistrate, are per se unreasonable under the Fourth Amendment — subject only to a few specifically established and well-delineated exceptions. . . . These considerations do not vanish when the search in question is

14. Based upon their previous visual observations of the petitioner, the agents correctly predicted that he would use the telephone booth for several minutes at approximately the same time each morning. The petitioner was subjected to electronic surveillance only during this predetermined period. Six recordings, averaging some three minutes each, were obtained and admitted in evidence. They preserved the petitioner's end of conversations concerning the placing of bets and the receipt of wagering information.

transferred from the setting of a home, an office, or a hotel room to that of a telephone booth. Wherever a man may be, he is entitled to know that he will remain free from unreasonable searches and seizures. . . . It is so ordered.

HARLAN, J., concurring.

[As] the Court's opinion states, "the Fourth Amendment protects people, not places." The question, however, is what protection it affords to those people. Generally, as here, the answer to that question requires reference to a "place." My understanding of the rule that has emerged from prior decisions is that there is a twofold requirement, first that a person have exhibited an actual (subjective) expectation of privacy and, second, that the expectation be one that society is prepared to recognize as "reasonable." Thus a man's home is, for most purposes, a place where he expects privacy, but objects, activities, or statements that he exposes to the "plain view" of outsiders are not "protected" because no intention to keep them to himself has been exhibited. On the other hand, conversations in the open would not be protected against being overheard, for the expectation of privacy under the circumstances would be unreasonable. . . .

BLACK, J., dissenting.

[The Fourth Amendment's] first clause protects "persons, houses, papers, and effects, against unreasonable searches and seizures. . . ." These words connote the idea of tangible things with size, form, and weight, things capable of being searched, seized, or both. The second clause of the Amendment still further establishes its Framers' purpose to limit its protection to tangible things by providing that no warrants shall issue but those "particularly describing the place to be searched, and the persons or things to be seized." A conversation overheard by eavesdropping, whether by plain snooping or wiretapping, is not tangible and, under the normally accepted meanings of the words, can neither be searched nor seized. . . . Yet the Court's interpretation would have the Amendment apply to overhearing future conversations which by their very nature are nonexistent until they take place. . . .

Tapping telephone wires, of course, was an unknown possibility at the time the Fourth Amendment was adopted. But eavesdropping (and wiretapping is nothing more than eavesdropping by telephone) was . . . an ancient practice which at common law was condemned as a nuisance. In those days the eavesdropper listened by naked ear under the eaves of houses or their windows, or beyond their walls seeking out private discourse. There can be no doubt that the Framers were aware of this practice, and if they had desired to outlaw or restrict the use of evidence obtained by eavesdropping, I believe that they would have used the appropriate language to do so in the Fourth Amendment. They certainly would not have left such a task to the ingenuity of language-stretching judges. . . .

Since I see no way in which the words of the Fourth Amendment can be construed to apply to eavesdropping, that closes the matter for me. In interpreting the Bill of Rights, I willingly go as far as a liberal construction of the language takes me, but I simply cannot in good conscience give a meaning to words which they have never before been thought to have and which they certainly do not have in common ordinary usage. I will not distort the words of the Amendment in order to "keep the Constitution up to date" or "to bring it into harmony with the times." . . .

With this decision the Court has completed, I hope, its rewriting of the Fourth Amendment, which started only recently when the Court began referring incessantly to the Fourth Amendment not so much as a law against unreasonable searches and seizures as one to protect an individual's privacy. . . . Few things happen to an individual that do not affect his privacy in one way or another. . . .

DANNY LEE KYLLO v. UNITED STATES

533 U.S. 27 (2001)

SCALIA, J.*

This case presents the question whether the use of a thermal-imaging device aimed at a private home from a public street to detect relative amounts of heat within the home constitutes a "search" within the meaning of the Fourth Amendment.

I.

In 1991 Agent William Elliott of the United States Department of the Interior came to suspect that marijuana was being grown in the home belonging to petitioner Danny Kyllo, part of a triplex on Rhododendron Drive in Florence, Oregon. Indoor marijuana growth typically requires high-intensity lamps. In order to determine whether an amount of heat was emanating from petitioner's home consistent with the use of such lamps, at 3:20 A.M. on January 16, 1992, Agent Elliott and Dan Haas used an Agema Thermovision 210 thermal imager to scan the triplex. Thermal imagers detect infrared radiation, which virtually all objects emit but which is not visible to the naked eye. The imager converts radiation into images based on relative warmth — black is cool, white is hot, shades of gray connote relative differences; in that respect, it operates somewhat like a video camera showing heat images. The scan of Kyllo's home took only a few minutes and was performed from the passenger seat of Agent Elliott's vehicle across the street from the front of the house and also from the street in back of the house. The scan showed that the roof over the garage and a side wall of petitioner's home were relatively hot compared to the rest of the home and substantially warmer than neighboring homes in the triplex. Agent Elliott concluded that petitioner was using halide lights to grow marijuana in his house, which indeed he was. Based on tips from informants, utility bills, and the thermal imaging, a Federal Magistrate Judge issued a warrant authorizing a search of petitioner's home, and the agents found an indoor growing operation involving more than 100 plants. Petitioner was indicted on one count of manufacturing marijuana. . . . He unsuccessfully moved to suppress the evidence seized from his home and then entered a conditional guilty plea.

[The] District Court found that the Agema 210 "is a non-intrusive device which emits no rays or beams and shows a crude visual image of the heat being radiated from the outside of the house"; it "did not show any people or activity within the walls of the structure"; "the device used cannot penetrate walls or windows to reveal conversations or human activities"; and "no intimate details of the home were observed." Based on these findings, the District Court upheld the validity of the warrant that relied in part upon the thermal imaging. . . .

* [Justices Souter, Thomas, Ginsburg, and Breyer joined in this opinion. — EDS.]

II.

. . . At the very core of the Fourth Amendment stands the right of a man to retreat into his own home and there be free from unreasonable governmental intrusion. With few exceptions, the question whether a warrantless search of a home is reasonable and hence constitutional must be answered no.

On the other hand, the antecedent question of whether or not a Fourth Amendment "search" has occurred is not so simple under our precedent. The permissibility of ordinary visual surveillance of a home used to be clear because, well into the 20th century, our Fourth Amendment jurisprudence was tied to common-law trespass. See, e.g., Olmstead v. United States, 277 U.S. 438 (1928). Visual surveillance was unquestionably lawful because "the eye cannot by the laws of England be guilty of a trespass." Boyd v. United States, 116 U.S. 616 (1886) (quoting Entick v. Carrington, (K.B. 1765)). We have since decoupled violation of a person's Fourth Amendment rights from trespassory violation of his property, but the lawfulness of warrantless visual surveillance of a home has still been preserved. As we observed in California v. Ciraolo, 476 U.S. 207 (1986), "the Fourth Amendment protection of the home has never been extended to require law enforcement officers to shield their eyes when passing by a home on public thoroughfares."

One might think that the . . . validating rationale would be that examining the portion of a house that is in plain public view, while it is a "search" despite the absence of trespass, is not an "unreasonable" one under the Fourth Amendment. But in fact we have held that visual observation is no "search" at all — perhaps in order to preserve somewhat more intact our doctrine that warrantless searches are presumptively unconstitutional. In assessing when a search is not a search, we have applied somewhat in reverse the principle first enunciated in Katz v. United States, 389 U.S. 347 (1967). [Under *Katz*,] a Fourth Amendment search occurs when the government violates a subjective expectation of privacy that society recognizes as reasonable. We have subsequently applied this principle to hold that a Fourth Amendment search does *not* occur — even when the explicitly protected location of a *house* is concerned — unless the individual manifested a subjective expectation of privacy in the object of the challenged search, and society is willing to recognize that expectation as reasonable. . . .

The present case involves officers on a public street engaged in more than naked-eye surveillance of a home. We have previously reserved judgment as to how much technological enhancement of ordinary perception from such a vantage point, if any, is too much. While we upheld enhanced aerial photography of an industrial complex in Dow Chemical v. United States, 476 U.S. 227 (1986), we noted that we found "it important that this is *not* an area immediately adjacent to a private home, where privacy expectations are most heightened."

III.

It would be foolish to contend that the degree of privacy secured to citizens by the Fourth Amendment has been entirely unaffected by the advance of technology. For example . . . the technology enabling human flight has exposed to public view (and hence, we have said, to official observation) uncovered portions of the house and its curtilage that once were private. The question we confront today is what limits there are upon this power of technology to shrink the realm of guaranteed privacy.

The *Katz* test — whether the individual has an expectation of privacy that society is prepared to recognize as reasonable — has often been criticized as circular, and hence subjective and unpredictable. See Posner, The Uncertain Protection of Privacy by the Supreme Court, 1979 S. Ct. Rev. 173. While it may be difficult to refine *Katz* when the search of areas such as telephone booths, automobiles, or even the curtilage and uncovered portions of residences are at issue, in the case of the search of the interior of homes — the prototypical and hence most commonly litigated area of protected privacy — there is a ready criterion, with roots deep in the common law, of the minimal expectation of privacy that *exists*, and that is acknowledged to be *reasonable*. To withdraw protection of this minimum expectation would be to permit police technology to erode the privacy guaranteed by the Fourth Amendment. We think that obtaining by sense-enhancing technology any information regarding the interior of the home that could not otherwise have been obtained without physical intrusion into a constitutionally protected area, constitutes a search — at least where (as here) the technology in question is not in general public use. This assures preservation of that degree of privacy against government that existed when the Fourth Amendment was adopted. On the basis of this criterion, the information obtained by the thermal imager in this case was the product of a search.

The Government maintains, however, that the thermal imaging must be upheld because it detected "only heat radiating from the external surface of the house." The dissent makes this its leading point, contending that there is a fundamental difference between what it calls "off-the-wall" observations and "through-the-wall surveillance." But just as a thermal imager captures only heat emanating from a house, so also a powerful directional microphone picks up only sound emanating from a house — and a satellite capable of scanning from many miles away would pick up only visible light emanating from a house. We rejected such a mechanical interpretation of the Fourth Amendment in *Katz*, where the eavesdropping device picked up only sound waves that reached the exterior of the phone booth. Reversing that approach would leave the homeowner at the mercy of advancing technology — including imaging technology that could discern all human activity in the home. While the technology used in the present case was relatively crude, the rule we adopt must take account of more sophisticated systems that are already in use or in development.[3] . . .

The Government also contends that the thermal imaging was constitutional because it did not "detect private activities occurring in private areas." . . . In the home, [however], *all* details are intimate details, because the entire area is held safe from prying government eyes. . . . Limiting the prohibition of thermal imaging to "intimate details" would not only be wrong in principle; it would be impractical in

3. The ability to "see" through walls and other opaque barriers is a clear, and scientifically feasible, goal of law enforcement research and development. The National Law Enforcement and Corrections Technology Center, a program within the United States Department of Justice, features on its Internet Website projects that include a "Radar-Based Through-the-Wall Surveillance System," "Handheld Ultrasound Through the Wall Surveillance," and a "Radar Flashlight" that "will enable law officers to detect individuals through interior building walls." Some devices may emit low levels of radiation that travel "through-the-wall," but others, such as more sophisticated thermal imaging devices, are entirely passive, or "off-the-wall" as the dissent puts it.

application, failing to provide a workable accommodation between the needs of law enforcement and the interests protected by the Fourth Amendment. To begin with, there is no necessary connection between the sophistication of the surveillance equipment and the "intimacy" of the details that it observes — which means that one cannot say (and the police cannot be assured) that use of the relatively crude equipment at issue here will always be lawful. The Agema Thermovision 210 might disclose, for example, at what hour each night the lady of the house takes her daily sauna and bath — a detail that many would consider "intimate"; and a much more sophisticated system might detect nothing more intimate than the fact that someone left a closet light on. We . . . would have to develop a jurisprudence specifying which home activities are "intimate" and which are not. And even when (if ever) that jurisprudence were fully developed, no police officer would be able to know *in advance* whether his through-the-wall surveillance picks up "intimate" details — and thus would be unable to know in advance whether it is constitutional. . . .

We have said that the Fourth Amendment draws "a firm line at the entrance to the house." That line, we think, must be not only firm but also bright — which requires clear specification of those methods of surveillance that require a warrant. While it is certainly possible to conclude from the videotape of the thermal imaging that occurred in this case that no "significant" compromise of the homeowner's privacy has occurred, we must take the long view, from the original meaning of the Fourth Amendment forward. . . . Where, as here, the Government uses a device that is not in general public use, to explore details of the home that would previously have been unknowable without physical intrusion, the surveillance is a "search" and is presumptively unreasonable without a warrant. Since we hold the Thermovision imaging to have been an unlawful search, it will remain for the District Court to determine whether, without the evidence it provided, the search warrant issued in this case was supported by probable cause — and if not, whether there is any other basis for supporting admission of the evidence that the search pursuant to the warrant produced. . . .

STEVENS, J., dissenting.*

There is, in my judgment, a distinction of constitutional magnitude between "through-the-wall surveillance" that gives the observer or listener direct access to information in a private area, on the one hand, and the thought processes used to draw inferences from information in the public domain, on the other hand. The Court has crafted a rule that purports to deal with direct observations of the inside of the home, but the case before us merely involves indirect deductions from "off-the-wall" surveillance, that is, observations of the exterior of the home. Those observations were made with a fairly primitive thermal imager that gathered data exposed on the outside of petitioner's home but did not invade any constitutionally protected interest in privacy. . . .

* [Chief Justice Rehnquist and Justices O'Connor and Kennedy joined in this opinion. — EDS.]

I.

. . . What a person knowingly exposes to the public, even in his own home or office, is not a subject of Fourth Amendment protection. That is the principle implicated here.

[The] ordinary use of the senses might enable a neighbor or passerby to notice the heat emanating from a building, particularly if it is vented, as was the case here. Additionally, any member of the public might notice that one part of a house is warmer than another part or a nearby building if, for example, rainwater evaporates or snow melts at different rates across its surfaces. Such use of the senses would not convert into an unreasonable search if, instead, an adjoining neighbor allowed an officer onto her property to verify her perceptions with a sensitive thermometer. Nor, in my view, does such observation become an unreasonable search if made from a distance with the aid of a device that merely discloses that the exterior of one house, or one area of the house, is much warmer than another. Nothing more occurred in this case.

Thus, the notion that heat emissions from the outside of a dwelling is a private matter [covered under] the Fourth Amendment (the text of which guarantees the right of people "to be secure *in* their . . . houses" against unreasonable searches and seizures) is not only unprecedented but also quite difficult to take seriously. Heat waves, like aromas that are generated in a kitchen, or in a laboratory or opium den, enter the public domain if and when they leave a building. A subjective expectation that they would remain private is not only implausible but also surely not one that society is prepared to recognize as reasonable. [Based] on what the thermal imager showed regarding the outside of petitioner's home, the officers concluded that petitioner was engaging in illegal activity inside the home. It would be quite absurd to characterize their thought processes as "searches." . . . For the first time in its history, the Court assumes that an inference can amount to a Fourth Amendment violation.

[Public] officials should not have to avert their senses or their equipment from detecting emissions in the public domain such as excessive heat, traces of smoke, suspicious odors, odorless gases, airborne particulates, or radioactive emissions, any of which could identify hazards to the community. In my judgment, monitoring such emissions with sense-enhancing technology, and drawing useful conclusions from such monitoring, is an entirely reasonable public service. On the other hand, the countervailing privacy interest is at best trivial. [Society will not] suffer from a rule requiring the rare homeowner who both intends to engage in uncommon activities that produce extraordinary amounts of heat, and wishes to conceal that production from outsiders, to make sure that the surrounding area is well insulated.

II.

[The contours of the] new rule are uncertain because its protection apparently dissipates as soon as the relevant technology is "in general public use." Yet how much use is general public use is not even hinted at by the Court's opinion, which makes the somewhat doubtful assumption that the thermal imager used in this case does not satisfy that criterion.[5] In any event, putting aside its lack of clarity, this criterion is somewhat perverse because it seems likely that the threat to privacy will grow, rather than recede, as the use of intrusive equipment becomes more readily available. . . .

Although the Court is properly and commendably concerned about the threats to privacy that may flow from advances in the technology available to the law enforcement profession, it has unfortunately failed to heed the tried and true counsel of judicial restraint. Instead of concentrating on the rather mundane issue that is actually presented by the case before it, the Court has endeavored to craft an all-encompassing rule for the future. It would be far wiser to give legislators an unimpeded opportunity to grapple with these emerging issues rather than to shackle them with prematurely devised constitutional constraints.

Problem 7-1. Beepers

James Karo ordered 50 gallons of ether from a government informant, Carl Muehlenweg of Graphic Photo Design. Muehlenweg told Agent Rottinger of the Drug Enforcement Administration (DEA) that Karo planned to use the ether to extract cocaine from clothing he had imported into the United States. DEA agents obtained a court order authorizing the installation and monitoring of a beeper in one of the cans of ether. With Muehlenweg's consent, agents substituted their own can containing a beeper for one of the cans in the shipment and then painted all 10 cans to give them a uniform appearance.

On September 20, agents saw Karo pick up the ether from Muehlenweg. They followed Karo to his house, using visual and beeper surveillance. At one point later that day, agents determined by using the beeper that the ether was still inside the house, but they later determined that it had been moved undetected to the house of a person named Richard Horton, where they located it by using the beeper. The next day, the beeper was no longer transmitting from Horton's house, and agents traced the beeper to a self-storage facility.

Agents detected the smell of ether coming from locker 15 and learned from the manager that Horton had rented that locker using an alias. The agents obtained consent from the manager of the facility to install a closed-circuit video camera in a locker that had a view of locker 15. On February 6, agents monitoring the video camera saw a man and a woman removing the cans from the locker and loading them onto the rear bed of Horton's pickup truck.

At about 6 P.M. on February 6, the pickup left the driveway and traveled along public highways to Taos. During the trip, the agents kept the pickup under both physical and electronic surveillance. When the truck arrived at a house in Taos rented by Horton, the agents decided not to maintain tight surveillance for fear of detection. When the truck left the Taos residence, agents determined, using the monitor, that the beeper can was still inside the house. Again on February 7, the beeper revealed that the ether can was still on the premises. At one point, agents

5. The record describes a device that numbers close to a thousand manufactured units; that has a predecessor numbering in the neighborhood of 4,000 to 5,000 units; that competes with a similar product numbering from 5,000 to 6,000 units; and that is "readily available to the public" for commercial, personal, or law enforcement purposes. . . .

noticed that the windows of the house were wide open on a cold, windy day, leading them to suspect that the ether was being used. On February 8, the agents obtained a warrant to search the Taos residence based in part on information derived through use of the beeper. DEA agents executed the warrant on February 10, and they seized cocaine and laboratory equipment.

Karo was indicted for conspiracy to possess cocaine with intent to distribute it. The trial court granted Karo's pretrial motion to suppress the evidence seized from the Taos residence on the grounds that the initial warrant to install the beeper in the ether container was invalid as an unauthorized "seizure" and that the continued tracking of the beeper as it moved among and inside various homes and the storage locker constituted an unauthorized "search." How would you rule on appeal?

Problem 7-2. Eye in the Sky

Advances in technology are making it easier for police to use video cameras for surveillance of pedestrian areas and busy street intersections. Earlier technologies used analog videotape and were wired to monitoring locations through fiber-optic cable. New cameras use digital images that can be stored and manipulated more easily. The new cameras can be operated by radio commands and can transmit images wirelessly, saving the cost of installing cable.

Police in many jurisdictions are experimenting with video cameras posted in public places. Over two million cameras have been deployed in Great Britain, at busy intersections and in public gathering areas. Many cities in the United States have installed cameras at intersections to record the license plates of drivers who disobey traffic signals; private firms operate the cameras in exchange for a large portion of the revenues from traffic tickets issued.

In Washington, D.C., the police department now has dozens of cameras mounted in downtown areas, monitoring such sites as the White House, the National Mall, and Union Station, as well as cameras attached to police helicopters. Eventually, the system could include more than 200 cameras in stations of the Washington Metro system, another 200 cameras in public schools, and 100 more to be installed by the city traffic department at busy intersections. The first neighborhood to add camera surveillance will probably be Georgetown, a shopping district popular with tourists and college students.

The signals from the cameras all feed into a control room in police headquarters, called the Joint Operations Command Center. The center has 40 video stations angled around a wall of floor-to-ceiling screens. The cameras are programmed to scan public areas automatically, and officers can assume manual control if they see something they want to examine more closely. Eventually, the system could include "biometric" software that will permit an automated match between a face in the crowd and a computerized photo of a suspect. Compare Jess Bravin, "D.C. Cops Build Surveillance Network; New System Will Link Hundreds of Public Cameras," Wall St. Journal, Feb. 13, 2002.

If you were asked to testify before a state legislature about the legal implications of camera surveillance, what would you say? Does the sheer number of existing cameras make it easier or harder to justify further additions to the surveillance area? Would it change your argument if you could demonstrate to the legislature that cameras at traffic intersections cause as many auto collisions as they prevent, because more drivers stop abruptly when a light turns yellow, resulting in more collisions from behind? It has become clear that traffic cameras generate large revenues, both for the local government installing the cameras and the private contractor operating the cameras. Would a profit motive routinely affect the placement or use of the cameras?

Notes

1. *Thermal imaging: majority position.* State and federal law enforcement authorities started using thermal imaging — also commonly referred to as forward-looking infrared radar or "FLIR" — in the late 1980s. Federal circuit courts mostly upheld the constitutionality of thermal imaging without a warrant, analogizing the examination of the heat emitted from the house to examination of garbage left at the curb, and to the molecules sniffed by a dog during the warrantless external examination of a bag, approved by the Supreme Court in United States v. Place, 462 U.S. 696 (1983). In contrast, three of the four state supreme courts that addressed the constitutionality of thermal imaging deemed it unconstitutional. See Commonwealth v. Gindlesperger, 743 A.2d 898 (Pa. 1999); State v. Young, 867 P.2d 593 (Wash. 1994) (based on state constitution). In *Kyllo*, decided 10 years after the first of the thermal imaging cases appeared in federal courts, the Supreme Court held that thermal imaging of a home is a search under the Fourth Amendment. The decision surprised many observers, who saw many doctrinal avenues in the court's existing doctrine for the court to find that thermal imaging was a not a search at all.

2. *New doctrine for new technology?* Both the majority and dissent in *Kyllo* recognize that the *Katz* test, based on individual and societal expectations of privacy, created an inherent tension with new technologies for observation and investigation. First, as a technology becomes widespread it might become unreasonable for an individual to hold a subjective expectation of privacy. If humans develop Superman's X-ray vision, we will all subjectively need to recognize that our walls (and perhaps our clothes) no longer create a barrier to observation. Second, as technology becomes more widespread, members of society might be less and less willing to recognize individual subjective preferences as reasonable. Is either element of the *Katz* test modified by *Kyllo*, or does the court simply apply *Katz* to find that thermal imaging is a search? Does *Kyllo* provide a doctrinal framework that will help courts, legislatures, and executive agencies to resolve questions about the use of other search technologies in the future?

3. *Technology in general use.* The majority in *Kyllo* limited its holding to devices that are "not in general public use." Will this limitation pose the same kind of continual erosion as the original "expectation" doctrine of *Katz*, since technology often becomes cheaper and more widespread over time? Consider, for example, satellite imaging. Commercial satellite cameras supplement the government's spy satellite cameras, and they monitor domestic as well as foreign sites. Given enough commercial and spy satellites, intelligence and law enforcement agencies could realistically achieve constant surveillance of the entire planet. Combine this network of satellite cameras with the street-level cameras discussed in Problem 7-2, and it becomes possible to record much of daily living — particularly urban living — on

camera. Do you expect the law that governs satellites to change as the presence of the cameras becomes more ubiquitous and access to the images grows? For a flavor of the active news media coverage of surveillance cameras for law enforcement, see the web extension for this chapter at *http://www.crimpro.com/extension/ch07*.

4. *Home sweet home.* The majority in *Kyllo* finds thermal imaging inappropriate for the home, which it calls the "prototypical" area of protected privacy. Does the holding apply only to technological searches of the home? The majority also qualifies its holding by observing that the image here provided information "that would previously have been unknowable without physical intrusion." Will *Kyllo* be limited only to devices that provide information that would have required "physical intrusion"?

5. *Beepers: federal position.* In United States v. Knotts, 460 U.S. 276 (1983), the Court held that no search took place when police attached a beeper to a drum of chloroform (a chemical used for making drugs) and then followed the movements of the car using the beeper when they lost visual contact. The Court held that a person "traveling in an automobile on public thoroughfares has no reasonable expectation of privacy in his movements from one place to another." In United States v. Karo, 468 U.S. 705 (1984), the Court held that no seizure took place when the DEA planted a beeper in a drum of ether (another precursor chemical), finding that there was no "meaningful interference with an individual's possessory interests in that property." The *Karo* Court also held that there was no "search" when the drum was transferred to the defendant. However, the Court found that a search occurred when agents used the beeper to track movements within a house.

> In this case, had a DEA agent thought it useful to enter the Taos residence to verify that the ether was actually in the house and had he done so surreptitiously and without a warrant, there is little doubt that he would have engaged in an unreasonable search within the meaning of the Fourth Amendment. For purposes of the Amendment, the result is the same where, without a warrant, the Government surreptitiously employs an electronic device to obtain information that it could not have obtained by observation from outside the curtilage of the house. . . .

There have been relatively few decisions about beepers by state supreme courts since *Knotts* and *Karo*, suggesting that the use of beepers is limited. Most of the state supreme court decisions have held — contrary to the decisions in *Karo* and *Knotts* — that placing a beeper in a car or commercial object is a search. See People v. Oates, 698 P.2d 811 (Colo. 1985).

In the "beeper" cases, courts often point out that a beeper simply reveals the target's location on public highways, something the police could monitor without the special device (and without violating the Fourth Amendment) if they had enough time and resources to follow in another vehicle. Could the same argument apply to other devices now in use, such as police surveillance cameras mounted at stop signs? Does the analysis change if the observation technologies become pervasive?

A technological variation on beepers is the use of GPS to track vehicle movement and record that movement. Would the precision and detail of GPS information lead to a different analysis than for radio beepers? See State v. Jackson 76 P.3d 217 (Wash. 2003) (requiring warrant under state constitution). The vigorous state court activity on the topic of GPS technology used to track vehicle movement receives further attention on the web extension for this chapter at *http://www.crimpro.com/extension/ch07*.

6. *Beeper statutes.* Mobile tracking devices receive more attention in statutes than in constitutional decisions. The statutes generally treat the use of beepers as a search that must be supported by reasonable suspicion, and some statutes require judicial authorization. For example, a Pennsylvania statute, 18 Pa. Cons. Stat. §5761, authorizes the use of "mobile tracking devices" only after the application for a judicial order and the demonstration of reasonable suspicion. The judicial order authorizes the use of the device only for 90 days. The statute also bars the use of a mobile tracking device to track movement within "an area protected by a reasonable expectation of privacy" unless "exigent circumstances" are present or the government has obtained a judicial order "supported by probable cause."

What explains the prevalence of statutes as opposed to case law on this question? Are statutes of this sort a basis for concluding that legislative procedure tends to create higher barriers than judicial decisions to police action? Has legislation regarding beepers created such onerous conditions that authorities now rarely use the device?

7. *An area ripe for statutory precision?* Do questions about the use of technological enhancement of the senses require answers too precise for judges to give? Can statutes, with their greater possible detail, better limit the misuse of technology? Should police be limited, for example, to use of binoculars of a certain magnification? Statutes have become the most common method of regulating some technological search devices. These include wiretapping and pen registers, which are topics covered later in this chapter.

■ MATTHEW FITZGERALD v. STATE

864 A.2d 1006 (Md. 2004)

RAKER, J.

This case raises the issue of whether a canine sniff of an apartment door is a search under the Fourth Amendment of the United States Constitution. The United States Supreme Court and this Court have held that canine sniffs are non-searches for Fourth Amendment purposes. As the canine sniff doctrine does not depend upon the sniff's location, we shall hold that a sniff of an apartment door from a common area is a permissible non-search under the Fourth Amendment.

I.

In February 2002, an anonymous source informed Detective Leeza Grim of the Howard County Police Department Criminal Investigation Bureau, Vice and Narcotics Division, that Petitioner Fitzgerald and his girlfriend Allison Mancini lived together in an apartment at 3131 Normandy Woods Drive in Ellicott City, Howard County. The source also stated that Fitzgerald and Mancini drove a white pick-up truck and regularly sold a high quality grade marijuana called "Kind Bud." Grim's subsequent investigation confirmed that the couple lived in the building and that the car was registered to Alicia Joy Mancini, apparently Allison Mancini's relative. Grim also learned that Fitzgerald had a juvenile record of separate 1998 arrests for distribution of marijuana near a school and for three first degree burglaries.

Based on these events, Grim met with Officer Larry Brian of the Howard County Police Department's K-9 unit on March 19, 2002. Brian then visited Fitzgerald and Mancini's apartment building accompanied by Alex, Brian's certified drug detecting dog. Alex's olfactory acumen previously had precipitated numerous arrests. Brian and Alex entered the building through unlocked glass doors leading to a vestibule with a stairwell and mailboxes. Brian led Alex to scan apartment doors A, B, C, and D. Alex "alerted" at apartment A, indicating the presence of narcotics. Apartment A was Fitzgerald and Mancini's apartment. Sniffs of the other three apartments did not result in alerts. Alex repeated the sniffs with the identical outcome. Finally, on March 20, the anonymous source contacted Grim again and asserted that Fitzgerald and Mancini continued to sell "Kind Bud" marijuana.

The next day, District Court Judge JoAnn Ellinghaus-Jones issued a search and seizure warrant for Fitzgerald and Mancini's apartment based on Grim's affidavit. The warrant was executed on April 2, 2002. Grim seized substantial amounts of marijuana and other evidence of marijuana use and distribution. Fitzgerald and Mancini were arrested and charged with possession of marijuana with intent to distribute and related offenses. [The trial judge denied Fitzgerald's motion to suppress the evidence, and Fitzgerald was convicted.]

II.

We review first Fitzgerald's contention that a canine sniff of an apartment's exterior is a search under the Fourth Amendment. . . . The United States Supreme Court determined the constitutionality of a warrantless canine sniff in United States v. Place, 462 U.S. 696 (1983). In *Place*, an airline passenger raised the suspicions of law enforcement officers before takeoff. The police officers contacted Drug Enforcement Administration agents in the arrival city. As part of their investigation, the agents had a trained narcotic detection dog sniff the passenger's two pieces of luggage. The Supreme Court held that a canine sniff is not a search under the Fourth Amendment. The Court noted the limited nature of a canine sniff:

> A "canine sniff" by a well-trained narcotics detection dog, however, does not require opening the luggage. It does not expose noncontraband items that otherwise would remain hidden from public view, as does, for example, an officer's rummaging through the contents of the luggage. Thus, the manner in which information is obtained through this investigative technique is much less intrusive than a typical search. Moreover, the sniff discloses only the presence or absence of narcotics, a contraband item. [T]he information obtained is limited [and] ensures that the owner of the property is not subjected to the embarrassment and inconvenience entailed in less discriminate and more intrusive investigative methods. . . . We are aware of no other investigative procedure that is so limited both in the manner in which the information is obtained and in the content of the information revealed by the procedure. . . .

[The Maryland court cited decisions from 28 state courts holding that a canine sniff is not a Fourth Amendment search.]

In United States v. Jacobsen, 466 U.S. 109 (1984), the Supreme Court affirmed the Court's *Place* dog sniff holding. After concluding that federal agents' seizure of a white powdery substance discovered by private freight carrier employees was not unreasonable, the Court held that a chemical test to determine whether the powder was cocaine was not a search. The *Jacobsen* Court . . . based its decision on the test's narrow scope of determining whether or not the powder was cocaine; "It could tell him nothing more, not even whether the substance was sugar or talcum powder." . . .

A review of *Place* and *Jacobsen* indicates that a crucial component of the Supreme Court's holdings is the focus on the scope and nature of the sniff or test, rather than on the object sniffed, in determining whether a legitimate privacy interest exists. . . . The focus . . . is not the object sniffed, the exterior of the luggage in *Place* . . . but rather the narrow yes/no scope of the sniff. The only relevant locational determination is whether the dog was permitted outside the object sniffed.

We applied the binding precedent of *Place* and its progeny in Wilkes v. State, 774 A.2d 420 (Md. 2001). We held, based on *Place* and *Jacobsen*, that a canine scan of a car is not a search under the Fourth Amendment. . . .

Fitzgerald proposes that we differentiate sniffs of the exterior of homes from all other sniffs. . . . To support his argument, he points to United States v. Karo, 468 U.S. 705 (1984) and Kyllo v. United States, 533 U.S. 27 (2001). . . .

In *Karo*, a federal agent learned that Karo and others had ordered 50 gallons of ether from an informant and planned to use the ether to extract cocaine from imported clothing. Pursuant to a court order and the seller's consent, government agents installed a beeper in one can of ether. The agents monitored the beeper through its many travels, including sojourns in private residences. The Court held that monitoring a beeper in a private residence constitutes a Fourth Amendment search.

Fitzgerald is correct that *Karo* emphasized the expectation of privacy in private residences. . . . The Court, though, based its holding on the scope of information a beeper reveals. Comparing the beeper to the obviously impermissible case of an officer entering a private residence to verify the ether's presence, the Court noted:

> For purposes of the [Fourth] Amendment, the result is the same where, without a warrant, the Government surreptitiously employs an electronic device to obtain information that it could not have obtained by observation from outside the curtilage of the house. The beeper tells the agent that a particular article is actually located at a particular time in the private residence and is in the possession of the person or persons whose residence is being watched. . . .

The beeper's broader revelation about the interior of the house is a significant one. In *Karo*, the agents failed to notice that the ether had been moved from one residence to another. Only through using the beeper did they determine that the ether was no longer in the first house and then that the ether was in a second house.

Karo is inapposite to the case sub judice for a number of reasons. First, *Karo*'s rationale does not contradict *Place*'s rationale; the two complement each other. *Place* held that a dog sniff is unique in that it can determine only the presence or absence of contraband, while *Karo* held that a beeper's utility is too broad, because it indicates both the arrival of the ether and its continued presence. Crucial in this respect is *Karo*'s emphasis of the difference between what the government can observe outside the residence and what the beeper tells the government from its presence inside the residence. The dog, Alex in our case, occupied the same position as the government agent; he observed from the public space outside the residence. Were Alex to have entered the residence himself without a warrant, he would have conducted an unconstitutional search.

Second, the object detected in *Karo* was a can of ether. The ether itself was not contraband; it was a potential tool for extracting contraband. In *Place*, the object was contraband itself. A pivotal premise of *Place* was that the sniff "does not expose noncontraband items." . . .

Fitzgerald next cites *Kyllo* for his argument that *Place* and its progeny should not apply to the exterior of residences. In *Kyllo*, the Supreme Court . . . elaborated a "general public use" standard: "We think that obtaining by sense-enhancing technology any information regarding the interior of the home that could not otherwise have been obtained without physical intrusion into a constitutionally protected area constitutes a search — at least where (as here) the technology in question is not in general public use." Fitzgerald argues that this standard includes dog sniffs, which he classifies as "sense-enhancing technology" that is "not in general public use."

Even a perfunctory reading of *Kyllo* reveals that its standard does not apply to dog sniffs. *Kyllo* is an opinion about the need to limit "advancing technology." The *Kyllo* Court sought to draw a line to prevent the police from utilizing continuously advancing technologies to "see" more and more inside the home. . . . The Court viewed the thermal imager as particularly nefarious, even in its crude form, because of its broad potential uses. The imager's utility was not limited to ascertaining whether contraband was present. Instead, the imager could reveal "intimate" details such as "at what hour each night the lady of the house takes her daily sauna and bath."

With this review of *Kyllo*, it is clear that *Kyllo* has no bearing on dog sniffs. First, a dog is not technology — he or she is a dog. A dog is known commonly as "man's best friend." Across America, people consider dogs as members of their family. The same cannot be said of cars, blenders, or thermal imagers. . . .

Second, dogs are not "advancing technology." Even taking into account potential gains from evolution, breeding, and improved nutrition, the limits to dogs' future ability to smell are not far from the current limits. Not so with technology. Technology is constantly advancing; few who have witnessed the computer revolution doubt that technology can advance in the future beyond our wildest dreams today.

Finally, *Kyllo*'s concern with thermal imagers' scope and potential revelation of intimate private details fits neatly with *Place*'s rationale that dog sniffs are unique in their narrow yes/no determination of the presence of narcotic. A person does not have a legitimate expectation of privacy in contraband, but does in bath water. A dog that can determine contraband's existence and nothing else is not a search, even when sniffing the exterior of a home. . . .

In sum, we conclude that binding and persuasive authority compel our holding that a dog sniff of the exterior of a residence is not a search under the Fourth Amendment. To be sure, the dog and police must lawfully be present at the site of the sniff. In the present case, Brian and Alex lawfully were present, as the apartment building's common area and hallways were accessible to the public through an entrance of unlocked glass doors.

Next, we consider Fitzgerald's argument that Alex's sniff was a search because Alex was trained to alert to diazepam tablets, i.e., Valium. . . . Fitzgerald did not raise the diazepam detection issue in either the Circuit Court or the Court of Special Appeals. Consequently, under Maryland Rules of Procedure 8-131(a) and (b), the Court should not review this issue. . . .

III.

Fitzgerald argues that even if Alex's sniff is not a search under the Fourth Amendment, it is a search under Article 26 of the Maryland Declaration of Rights. . . . Fitzgerald argues that his case should be one in which Article 26 holds an action to be a violation (as an illegal search), while the Fourth Amendment permits the action (as a non-search). To support this claim, Fitzgerald argues that Article 26 was designed to protect the sanctity of the home, thus, creating stronger protection than the Fourth Amendment for sniffs outside a residence. . . .

There is no need to determine whether this is a case in which Article 26 mandates our finding an illegal search, . . . because even were we to adopt Fitzgerald's position, we would uphold the sniff's validity. [The] majority of state courts holding a dog sniff to be a search under their constitutions apply a reasonable suspicion standard. There was reasonable suspicion to support a sniff of Fitzgerald's apartment door. . . .

In Terry v. Ohio, 392 U.S. 1 (1968), the Court held that a police officer suspecting criminal activity could conduct a minimally intrusive search for weapons if the officer had a reasonable suspicion that the person was armed and dangerous. In *Place*, Justice Blackmun concurred [and] argued that there were alternative approaches the majority could have taken on dog sniffs. He wrote, . . . "a dog sniff may be a search, but a minimally intrusive one that could be justified in this situation under *Terry* upon mere reasonable suspicion."

Professor LaFave explains the advantage of Justice Blackmun's approach. He notes that narcotics detecting dogs are more likely to alert erroneously when used to sniff "wholesale," such as when a dog sniffs a large group of students in a school. Wayne R. LaFave, Search and Seizure §2.2(f) (3d ed. 1996). Justice Blackmun's reasonable suspicion approach would reduce the likelihood of errors. . . .

Of the states finding a dog sniff to be a search under their state constitutions, almost all have [applied] a reasonable suspicion standard. [The Court cited cases from Alaska, Colorado, Connecticut, Illinois, Minnesota, Montana, New Hampshire, New York, and Pennsylvania.]

The police had reasonable suspicion to conduct a canine sniff of Fitzgerald's door. An anonymous source told Detective Grim Fitzgerald and Mancini's names, their address, and a description of Mancini's truck. The source specified the exact grade of marijuana the source alleged Fitzgerald and Mancini sold on a regular basis. Detective Grim confirmed all the information except the marijuana sales themselves. Further, Detective Grim discovered that Fitzgerald had a juvenile record, including an arrest for distribution of marijuana near a school. These facts confirm that Detective Grim had reasonable suspicion to seek a canine sniff.

Accordingly, we . . . decline to determine whether the Maryland Declaration of Rights deems a dog sniff a search, because even if it did, it would require only reasonable suspicion, which was present in this case.

GREENE, J., dissenting.

. . . One implication of [the Court's] holding is that a canine sniff can never constitute a search provided that the handler and the dog are situated in a place they have a right to be. . . . A far reaching consequence of today's holding is that those who reside in apartment buildings with gated or secured entrances will be afforded greater protections under the law than those who reside in apartment buildings that are left unsecured or open to the public. Moreover, this decision may indeed constitute a logical extension of the rationale of *Place* and *Jacobsen*, resulting, however, in random canine searches in targeted neighborhoods. Because of these and other concerns, I respectfully dissent. . . .

When police intentionally use an investigative technique, in this case a dog, to detect the presence of drugs by directing the dog to a residence or person, that action constitutes a search. I cannot ignore the fact that the police went to that location to detect evidence of criminal activity. . . . For me, the Fourth Amendment draws the line at the entrance to the residence. Absent exigent circumstances, the police may not reasonably cross the threshold without a warrant. The canine sniff at the door of Fitzgerald's apartment was not a detection of something in the hallway, but rather was a detection of something inside Fitzgerald's apartment — a private dwelling.

[The] rationale of *Place* assumes that the dog sniff is accurate and that the privacy interests of those involved will not be compromised. [But mistakes made by the dog and handler sometimes result in a false positive identification of drugs.] One . . . reason dogs may alert falsely is because of the high percentage of cash that contains sufficient quantities of cocaine to trigger a response in a dog. . . . In the present case it was raised on appeal, but not developed at trial, that the dog in this case was trained also to alert on Valium.

[If] the canine sniff is a search, the Fourth Amendment applies requiring a warrant based on probable cause. If is it not a search, the Fourth Amendment is inapplicable. The proper standard, absent exigent circumstances, is a warrant supported by probable cause. . . .

Notes

1. *Are dog sniffs searches? Majority position.* As the court in *Fitzgerald* notes, in United States v. Place, 462 U.S. 696 (1983), the Supreme Court held that dog sniffs are not searches and therefore are not subject to the constraints of the Fourth Amendment. In Illinois v. Caballes, 543 U.S. 405 (2005), the Court confirmed this position, holding that a dog sniff performed on the exterior of a vehicle during a valid traffic stop requires no justification because the dog reveals only the presence or absence of contraband and does not intrude on a reasonable expectation of privacy.

The largest group of state courts read their state constitutions and statutes in a similar fashion to conclude that the use of canines to sniff items in public places does not qualify as a "search." See, e.g., State v. Morrow, 625 P.2d 898 (Ariz. 1981).

A strong minority, however, treat a canine sniff as a "search" under the state constitution. These holdings tend to appear in cases in which the dog is brought into a residence or to the front door of a home. These courts typically require the police to demonstrate reasonable suspicion — not probable cause — to carry out the canine sniff search. See People v. Devone, 931 N.E.2d 70 (N.Y. 2010) (dog sniff of automobile classified as "search" under state constitution, but the government needs only "founded suspicion," less demanding standard than reasonable suspicion, to justify dog sniff). You can sample the state court variety in dealing with canine sniffs on the web extension for this chapter at *http://www.crimpro.com/extension/ch07*.

2. *Plain view and sense enhancements: majority position.* Remember that it is no search for an officer to view objects within "plain" view when the officer is justified in being in a particular place — whether in a home during execution of a warrant or in an area based on consent or some exception to the warrant requirement. See Chapter 2, section C. Most courts draw an analogy between "plain view" and the use of familiar tools that enhance human senses of sight or hearing to provide light, or to change or magnify a view. They often ask whether the officer (or a group of officers) could have made the observation by using normal senses from a permissible location. If the answer to this question is "yes," courts often conclude that the evidence collection is not a search at all; if not, they are more inclined to consider it a search and then evaluate whether the search was reasonable.

More often than not, a court reviewing a police officer's use of sense-enhancing devices will conclude that the officer did not conduct a "search." See Dow Chemical Co. v. United States, 476 U.S. 227 (1986) (no search when government uses $22,000 aerial mapping camera during overflight of industrial plant suspected of environmental crimes). As with other aspects of search and seizure doctrine, the shift in *Katz* from a property-based conception to a privacy-based conception of the Fourth Amendment makes it more difficult for courts to reach categorical conclusions about the use of any particular technological sense-enhancement. The amount of effort a government agent expends in obtaining a "plain" view, the nature of the location observed, the place from which the observation is made, and the public familiarity with a device may all be relevant. For a sample of state court rulings on the use of sense enhancing devices such as high-powered binoculars, flashlights, starscopes, and others, consult the web extension for this chapter at *http://www.crimpro.com/extension/ch07*. Remember that even when use of a sense-enhancing device constitutes a search, a court must address further questions: It must determine what level of justification the government must have to support the search, and then it must evaluate whether the search was reasonable given those particular facts.

3. *Distinguishing beepers from dogs.* Beepers reveal some information that, at least in theory, would be available to an officer observing a suspect from a legal vantage point. In this sense, beepers differ from dog sniffs because the dog accomplishes what even the most diligent or discerning officer could not. But as the Supreme Court recognized in *Karo*, a beeper can also reveal information (such as the presence or movement of objects within a building) that would not be available to an observing officer at the scene. Do you agree that these different sorts of information deserve different protection under the law?

B. WIRETAPPING

Wiretapping is just one of many technologies that provide the capacity to observe or hear more than would be possible with human senses. This section considers the evolution of the procedures governing wiretapping, from judicial doctrine to statute. The first subsection looks at Olmstead v. United States, one of the earliest wiretapping cases. This case, along with Katz v. United States, invited Congress and state legislatures to occupy the wiretapping field, largely unrestricted by precedent and other limits on judicial authority. The remainder of this section highlights the recurring features of these wiretapping statutes, and reviews some difficult choices about how to extend this regulation to some specialized settings.

1. Judicial Limits on Wiretaps

ROY OLMSTEAD v. UNITED STATES
277 U.S. 438 (1928)

TAFT, C.J.*

The petitioners were convicted . . . of a conspiracy to violate the National Prohibition Act by unlawfully possessing, transporting and importing intoxicating liquors and maintaining nuisances, and by selling intoxicating liquors. Seventy-two others in addition to the petitioners were indicted. Some were not apprehended, some were acquitted and others pleaded guilty.

The evidence in the records discloses a conspiracy of amazing magnitude to import, possess and sell liquor unlawfully. . . . Olmstead was the leading conspirator and the general manager of the business. . . . Of the several offices in Seattle the chief one was in a large office building. In this there were three telephones on three different lines. There were telephones in an office of the manager in his own home, at the homes of his associates, and at other places in the city. . . .

The information which led to the discovery of the conspiracy and its nature and extent was largely obtained by intercepting messages on the telephones of the conspirators by four federal prohibition officers. Small wires were inserted along the ordinary telephone wires from the residences of four of the petitioners and those leading from the chief office. The insertions were made without trespass upon any property of the defendants. They were made in the basement of the large office building. The taps from house lines were made in the streets near the houses. The gathering of evidence continued for many months. . . .

The [Fourth] Amendment itself shows that the search is to be of material things — the person, the house, his papers or his effects. The description of the warrant necessary to make the proceeding lawful, is that it must specify the place to be searched and the person or things to be seized. . . . It is plainly within the words of the Amendment to say that the unlawful rifling by a government agent of a sealed letter is a search and seizure of the sender's papers or effects. The letter is a paper, an effect, and in the custody of a Government that forbids carriage except under its

* [Justices McReynolds, Sanford, Sutherland, and Van Devanter joined in this opinion. — EDS.]

protection. The United States takes no such care of telegraph or telephone messages as of mailed sealed letters. The Amendment does not forbid what was done here. There was no searching. There was no seizure. The evidence was secured by the use of the sense of hearing and that only. There was no entry of the houses or offices of the defendants.

By the invention of the telephone, 50 years ago, and its application for the purpose of extending communications, one can talk with another at a far distant place. The language of the Amendment cannot be extended and expanded to include telephone wires reaching to the whole world from the defendant's house or office. The intervening wires are not part of his house or office any more than are the highways along which they are stretched. . . .

Congress may of course protect the secrecy of telephone messages by making them, when intercepted, inadmissible in evidence in federal criminal trials, by direct legislation, and thus depart from the common law of evidence. But the courts may not adopt such a policy by attributing an enlarged and unusual meaning to the Fourth Amendment. . . .

BRANDEIS, J., dissenting.

[At least six] prohibition agents listened over the tapped wires and reported the messages taken. Their operations extended over a period of nearly five months. The typewritten record of the notes of conversations overheard occupies 775 typewritten pages. [The Government concedes] that if wire-tapping can be deemed a search and seizure within the Fourth Amendment, such wire-tapping as was practiced in the case at bar was an unreasonable search and seizure, and that the evidence thus obtained was inadmissible. . . .

When the Fourth and Fifth Amendments were adopted, [force] and violence were then the only means known to man by which a Government could directly effect self-incrimination. It could compel the individual to testify — a compulsion effected, if need be, by torture. It could secure possession of his papers and other articles incident to his private life — a seizure effected, if need be, by breaking and entry. Protection against such invasion of the sanctities of a man's home and the privacies of life was provided in the Fourth and Fifth Amendments by specific language. . . . Subtler and more far-reaching means of invading privacy have become available to the Government. Discovery and invention have made it possible for the Government, by means far more effective than stretching upon the rack, to obtain disclosure in court of what is whispered in the closet.

Moreover, in the application of a constitution, our contemplation cannot be only of what has been but of what may be. The progress of science in furnishing the Government with means of espionage is not likely to stop with wire-tapping. Ways may some day be developed by which the Government, without removing papers from secret drawers, can reproduce them in court, and by which it will be enabled to expose to a jury the most intimate occurrences of the home. Advances in the psychic and related sciences may bring means of exploring unexpressed beliefs, thoughts and emotions. . . . Can it be that the Constitution affords no protection against such invasions of individual security?

[The] tapping of one man's telephone line involves the tapping of the telephone of every other person whom he may call, or who may call him. As a means of espionage, writs of assistance and general warrants are but puny instruments of tyranny and oppression when compared with wire-tapping.

The makers of our Constitution undertook to secure conditions favorable to the pursuit of happiness. They recognized the significance of man's spiritual nature, of his feelings and of his intellect. . . . They conferred, as against the Government, the right to be let alone — the most comprehensive of rights and the right most valued by civilized men. To protect that right, every unjustifiable intrusion by the Government upon the privacy of the individual, whatever the means employed, must be deemed a violation of the Fourth Amendment. . . .

Notes

1. *Constitutional interpretation.* Recall that the Supreme Court overruled *Olmstead* in Katz v. United States, 389 U.S. 347 (1967). Despite their great difference in doctrine and bottom line, *Olmstead* and *Katz* are both splendid examples of constitutional decision making. They each raise some of the foundational issues in any difficult constitutional context: What do the words of the various provisions mean? Should interpretation be limited to the words? If not, what principles limit the power of the court from acting as a superlegislature by interpreting words? On the question of the role a court plays when interpreting the meaning of constitutional terms such as "persons," "houses," or "effects" — much less concepts such as "privacy" and "reasonableness" — consider the following exchange:

> "There's glory for you!"
>
> "I don't know what you mean by 'glory,'" Alice said.
>
> Humpty Dumpty smiled contemptuously. "Of course you don't — till I tell you. I meant there's a nice knock-down argument for you."
>
> "But 'glory' doesn't mean 'a nice knock-down argument,'" Alice objected.
>
> "When I use a word," Humpty Dumpty said in rather a scornful tone, "it means just what I choose it to mean — neither more nor less."
>
> "The question is," said Alice, "whether you can make words mean so many different things."
>
> "The question is," said Humpty Dumpty, "which is to be the master — that's all."

Lewis Carroll, Through the Looking-Glass and What Alice Found There 269 (Martin Gardner ed., 1960).

2. *Wiretap cases between* Olmstead *and* Katz. Even before *Katz*, the Supreme Court had begun to place limits on electronic eavesdropping. In Silverman v. United States, 365 U.S. 505 (1961), the Court found that the government violated the Fourth Amendment when it inserted a "spike mike" into a heating duct. Although the Court concluded that the government had committed a trespass, it emphasized that its decision did "not turn upon the technicality of a trespass upon a party wall as a matter of local law. It is based upon the reality of an actual intrusion into a constitutionally protected area."

3. *Computer searches.* During investigations of certain crimes (think, for instance, of fraud or pornography cases), investigators need to learn about the contents of personal computers. The computer search context calls for some adjustments to traditional search and seizure doctrine. Just as courts in the wiretap context eventually placed less emphasis on whether investigators carried out a physical intrusion

of a protected place, courts that regulate computer searches have placed less weight over time on the physical location where the information is stored.

When the police want access to a personal computer, they typically obtain a warrant. Should the warrant describe the nature of the storage device, or the files or data to be accessed during a later analysis of the storage device? When the government copies data, does that constitute a "search," or does the search occur only when a human being views or analyzes the data? Does the opening or analysis of the data have to occur within a reasonable time from the issuance of the warrant, or is timing relevant only to the physical seizure of the storage device? Thus far, the federal case law is decidedly more developed than the appellate decisions in the state courts. Professor Orin Kerr has explored these topics in a series of law review articles. See Kerr, Searches and Seizures in a Digital World, 119 Harv. L. Rev. 531 (2005). For a glimpse at the evolving answers that courts offer to these questions, see the web extension for this chapter at *http://www.crimpro.com/extension/ch07*.

2. *Statutory Wiretapping Procedures*

Congress took up the Supreme Court's invitation in the *Olmstead* opinion to regulate wiretapping by statute. Indeed, Congress followed the specific recommendation in Chief Justice William Howard Taft's opinion that wiretap evidence be made inadmissible in federal court. Section 605 of the Federal Communications Act of 1934 stated that no person "shall intercept any communication *and* divulge or publish" that communication to any other person, unless the sender authorizes the interception. This ban on divulging wiretap information barred the use in federal court of most intercepted telephone conversations of criminal defendants. Because Congress focused on the admissibility of the evidence and not on its collection, federal agents continued to use wiretaps in investigations. Where the evidence could be used in state prosecutions, federal agents would provide it to the state under what was known as the "silver platter" doctrine (because the federal agents could offer the tainted evidence to the state prosecutors "on a silver platter").

The 1934 statutory limits on federal law enforcement changed when the United States Congress enacted Title III of the Omnibus Crime Control and Safe Streets Act of 1968, which established procedures for authorized wiretapping. The provisions in Title III reflected not only the new constitutional emphasis on privacy in *Katz*, but the specific concerns that led the United States Supreme Court in 1967 — the same year as *Katz* — to reject New York's wiretap statute in Berger v. New York, 388 U.S. 41 (1967). The key provision in the New York statute, authorizing ex parte wiretapping orders, provided as follows:

> An ex parte order for eavesdropping . . . may be issued by any justice of the supreme court or judge of a county court . . . upon oath or affirmation of a district attorney, or of the attorney-general or of an officer above the rank of sergeant of any police department . . . , that there is reasonable ground to believe that evidence of crime may be thus obtained, and particularly describing the person or persons whose communications . . . are to be overheard or recorded and the purpose thereof, and, in the case of a telegraphic or telephonic communication, identifying the particular telephone number or telegraph line involved. . . . Any such order shall be effective for the time specified therein but not for a period of more than two months unless

> extended or renewed by the justice or judge who signed and issued the original order upon satisfying himself that such extension or renewal is in the public interest. . . .

The Court concluded that the statute violated the Fourth Amendment, 388 U.S. at 58-60:

> We believe the statute here is [unconstitutional]. First, . . . eavesdropping is authorized without requiring belief that any particular offense has been or is being committed; nor that the "property" sought, the conversations, be particularly described. The purpose of the probable-cause requirement of the Fourth Amendment . . . is thereby wholly aborted. Likewise the statute's failure to describe with particularity the conversations sought gives the officer a roving commission to "seize" any and all conversations. It is true that the statute requires the naming of "the person or persons whose communications, conversations or discussions are to be overheard or recorded. . . ." But this does no more than identify the person whose constitutionally protected area is to be invaded rather than "particularly describing" the communications, conversations, or discussions to be seized. As with general warrants this leaves too much to the discretion of the officer executing the order.
>
> Secondly, authorization of eavesdropping for a two-month period is the equivalent of a series of intrusions, searches, and seizures pursuant to a single showing of probable cause. Prompt execution is also avoided. During such a long and continuous (24 hours a day) period the conversations of any and all persons coming into the area covered by the device will be seized indiscriminately and without regard to their connection with the crime under investigation. Moreover, the statute permits, and there were authorized here, extensions of the original two-month period — presumably for two months each — on a mere showing that such extension is "in the public interest." . . . This we believe insufficient without a showing of present probable cause for the continuance of the eavesdrop. . . .
>
> Finally, the statute's procedure, necessarily because its success depends on secrecy, has no requirement for notice as do conventional warrants, nor does it overcome this defect by requiring some showing of special facts. On the contrary, it permits unconsented entry without any showing of exigent circumstances. Such a showing of exigency, in order to avoid notice, would appear more important in eavesdropping, with its inherent dangers, than that required when conventional procedures of search and seizure are utilized. Nor does the statute provide for a return on the warrant thereby leaving full discretion in the officer as to the use of seized conversations of innocent as well as guilty parties. In short, the statute's blanket grant of permission to eavesdrop is without adequate judicial supervision or protective procedures.

Before the enactment of Title III in 1968, many states (like the federal government, under the Federal Communications Act of 1934) prohibited wiretapping. After Title III, most states amended their own wiretap laws, authorizing the government to conduct wiretaps under judicial supervision. Wiretapping throughout the United States and in most other countries is now controlled by procedures specified in statutes.

Portions of Title III and selected provisions from several state statutes follow. Title III served as the model for most states. The provisions in state statutes selected for this section highlight only two sets of questions: (1) the basic coverage of the protections for electronic communications and (2) judicial administration of wiretap requests. The statutory schemes governing wiretaps are quite complex and raise many additional issues, a few of which are covered in notes.

Wiretap statutes treat government searches through electronic surveillance differently from other searches. First, the wiretap statutes decide for all cases the question debated as a matter of Fourth Amendment interpretation in *Olmstead* and *Katz:* They declare that wiretaps are searches. Second, Congress and the state legislatures have left little room for the many varieties of exigent circumstances that government agents rely on every day to conduct warrantless searches: If agents want to use wiretaps, they must seek a warrant.

The federal and state statutes do not cover every "intercepted communication." First, most statutes exclude from the wiretap warrant process conversations that are recorded with the consent of one of the parties. Second, the statutes do not apply to all kinds of communications, though the coverage of wiretap statutes has expanded well beyond traditional taps such as those seen in *Olmstead* and *Katz*. The federal wiretap statute originally applied to communications transmitted over a wire, but now it protects wire, oral, and electronic communications, as do most of the state statutes. A wire communication includes any transfer of the human voice by means of a wire, cable, or other connection between the sender and the recipient. See 18 U.S.C. §§2510(4), (18). Electronic communications include those not carried by sound waves, such as electronic mail, video teleconferences, and other data transfers. 18 U.S.C. §2510 (12). Under the federal statute, an "interception" of one of these types of communications occurs when a person uses "any electronic, mechanical, or other device" to make an "aural acquisition" of the "contents" of the communication. How well do these statutory definitions account for future technological changes in communications?

Third, the statutes may not apply to recording of conversations outside the governing jurisdiction or in another country. This question often arises when prosecutors wish to introduce conversations between a party in a different jurisdiction and a second party in the prosecutors' jurisdiction. Should a state statute control law enforcement efforts to intercept calls placed to or from another state? Between two other states? In a federal system, with many different governments intercepting communications (and regulating those interceptions), how will courts resolve conflicts among the different statutory schemes? Will law enforcement agencies convince states to engage in a "race to the bottom" in the regulation of wiretapping? The following two statutes illustrate common features of wiretap statutes.

■ 18 U.S.C. §2511

(1) Except as otherwise specifically provided in this chapter any person who —

(a) intentionally intercepts, endeavors to intercept, or procures any other person to intercept or endeavor to intercept, any wire, oral, or electronic communication; . . .

(c) intentionally discloses, or endeavors to disclose, to any other person the contents of any wire, oral, or electronic communication, knowing or having reason to know that the information was obtained through the interception of a wire, oral, or electronic communication in violation of this subsection;

(d) intentionally uses, or endeavors to use, the contents of any wire, oral, or electronic communication, knowing or having reason to know that the information was obtained through the interception of a wire, oral, or electronic communication in violation of this subsection; . . . shall be punished as provided [elsewhere in this statute] or shall be subject to suit. . . .

(2)(c) It shall not be unlawful under this chapter for a person acting under color of law to intercept a wire, oral, or electronic communication, where such person is a party to the communication or one of the parties to the communication has given prior consent to such interception.

(d) It shall not be unlawful under this chapter for a person not acting under color of law to intercept a wire, oral, or electronic communication where such person is a party to the communication or where one of the parties to the communication has given prior consent to such interception unless such communication is intercepted for the purpose of committing any criminal or tortious act in violation of the Constitution or laws of the United States or of any State.

NEW JERSEY STATUTES §2A:156A-4

It shall not be unlawful under this act for: . . .

b. Any investigative or law enforcement officer to intercept a wire, electronic or oral communication, where such officer is a party to the communication or where another officer who is a party to the communication requests or requires him to make such interception;

c. Any person acting at the direction of an investigative or law enforcement officer to intercept a wire, electronic or oral communication, where such person is a party to the communication or one of the parties to the communication has given prior consent to such interception; provided, however, that no such interception shall be made without the prior approval of the Attorney General or his designee or a county prosecutor or his designee. . . .

STATE v. ALEXANDER FOWLER

139 P.3d 342 (Wash. 2006)

MADSEN, J.

¶1 Petitioner Alexander L. Fowler was convicted by a jury of two counts of incest in the first degree, two counts of incest in the second degree, and one count of rape in the second degree, all stemming from sexual misconduct with his stepdaughter. Fowler asserts that the trial court erred by admitting into evidence recordings of two telephone conversations he had with the victim. The conversations were recorded in Oregon with the consent of and by the victim acting at the request of the Oregon police when they investigated Fowler's possible sexual misconduct. Fowler was in Washington when he spoke on the phone to the victim, and he did not consent to the recordings; the victim was in Oregon at her family home. . . .

Facts

¶3 . . . On September 16, 2002, the alleged victim, M.P., made a telephone call from Oregon to the defendant while the defendant was at a location within Washington State. The alleged victim intentionally and voluntarily recorded the conversation that took place during this phone call without informing the defendant that the recording was being made. On September 26, 2002, the alleged victim made a second call from Oregon to the defendant while the defendant was at a location within Washington State. The alleged victim again intentionally and voluntarily recorded the conversation that occurred during this phone call without informing the defendant that the recording was being made.

¶4 Both telephone calls and the recording of those calls were made by the alleged victim at the request of Detective Mike Wilson of the Oregon State Police for purposes of Detective Wilson's investigation of an alleged sexual offense by the defendant against the victim, which was alleged to have occurred within the state of Oregon. The record does not reflect why Oregon prosecutors did not bring charges against Fowler.

¶5 No Washington State law enforcement officer or other Washington State official requested or in any way encouraged the making of these calls or the recording of these calls. At the time these calls were recorded, there was no investigation ongoing in Washington concerning any alleged offense by the defendant against the alleged victim. In requesting the alleged victim to record these calls, Detective Wilson was following Oregon law, which provided that such a recording is lawful as long as one of the parties gives his or her consent to the recording.

¶6 Based on its findings of fact, the trial court made the following . . . conclusions of law. First, the trial court concluded that RCW 9.73.030 makes it unlawful to record a telephone conversation without the knowledge and consent of both parties to that conversation. Had the alleged victim's recording of her two calls to the defendant been made within the state of Washington, the trial court concluded, such recordings would have been illegal. Second, the trial court held that because the alleged victim consented to the recordings of these two calls and made the recordings while in Oregon, these recordings were lawfully made under Oregon law pursuant to Oregon Revised Statutes §165.540(1)(a). Third, . . . the trial court concluded that because the recordings by the alleged victim were made in Oregon, at the instigation of an Oregon law enforcement officer conducting a criminal investigation within Oregon concerning an offense alleged to have been committed in Oregon, and were made in full conformity with Oregon law, and because there was no request, instigation or involvement by a Washington law enforcement agency or other Washington official with regard to these recordings, the recordings are not rendered inadmissible at the trial of Fowler by the provisions of RCW 9.73.030, and would not be suppressed on that basis.

¶7 At trial, three people testified: M.P., M.P.'s mother, and Detective Wilson of the Oregon police. Fowler did not testify. The State also presented tapes of the two telephone conversations. The jury found Fowler guilty of all charges.

¶8 Fowler appealed, claiming that the trial court erred in denying his motion to suppress the two tape-recorded conversations between him and M.P. . . .

Analysis

¶10 Fowler asserts that taped telephone conversations are unlawful under RCW 9.73.030 and hence inadmissible under RCW 9.73.050. First, Fowler points to RCW 9.73.030(1)(a), which provides that it shall be unlawful for any individual (among others) to intercept or record any "private communication transmitted by telephone, telegraph, radio, or other device between two or more individuals between points within or without the state" by any device designed to record the communication without first obtaining the consent of "all the participants" in the communication. Fowler . . . argues that the fact that the conversations were recorded in Oregon (and were legally recorded in Oregon under Oregon law) is irrelevant because RCW 9.73.030(1)(a) covers telephone calls between two or more persons "within or without the state." Thus, according to Fowler, the recordings are "unlawful" under RCW 9.73.030. . . .

¶12 [The] State argues that Fowler misinterprets the phrase "between points within or without the state" contained in RCW 9.73.030(1)(a). The State claims that that phrase does not refer to the act of intercepting or recording. Rather, the phrase refers to what communications are the concern of RCW 9.73.030. The phrase establishes that "private communications transmitted by telephone, telegraph, radio, or other device" are the concern of RCW 9.73.030 whether those communications are "between points within or without the state." However, according to the State, the phrase "says nothing about what recording location" will bring the recording of communications under the criminal jurisdiction of Washington pursuant to this statute.

¶13 The State points to Kadoranian v. Bellingham Police Department, 829 P.2d 1061 (Wash. 1992), for the proposition that this court has already answered the question as to the relevance of the place of the recordings. In *Kadoranian,* a Canadian citizen sought civil damages in a Washington state court, claiming a violation of RCW 9.73.030. In that case, the Bellingham police recorded the plaintiff's telephone conversation. The call was placed from Washington to Canada, and was tape recorded in Washington with the consent of only one party, the Washington resident. The Canadian citizen first made the argument that the exceptions in the privacy act allowing police to lawfully record conversations with the consent of only one party did not apply to the Bellingham police because the call was received in Canada, not within Washington. This court disagreed, holding that the privacy act does not limit the territory in which telephone calls may be intercepted, as long as the interception occurs in Washington. "Interceptions and recordings occur where made." The court continued and held that "whether the interception of Ms. Kadoranian's conversation was lawful is thus determined according to the laws of the State of Washington, the place where the conversation was intercepted and recorded, not according to the laws of Canada [where the call was received]."

¶14 In reaching this conclusion, the court cited a number of cases which support the view that courts generally determine the validity of a telephone interception by looking to the law of the jurisdiction in which the interception — or the recording — is made. See State v. Fleming, 755 P.2d 725 (Ore. 1988) (Oregon statute requiring 1-party consent controlled the legality of the recording made in Oregon of a call to the defendant in this state from an informant located in Oregon; while the recording was not in accordance with RCW 9.73.030, it was lawful under Oregon law and was thus admissible in Oregon). . . .

¶16 . . . In this case, the two telephone calls were recorded in Oregon with the consent of one of the parties to the call. . . . While Fowler undoubtedly has an expectation of privacy as a Washington resident, he does not have an expectation of privacy related to his behavior in Oregon and the resulting criminal investigation by the Oregon police regarding his sexual misconduct with M.P. while in Oregon.

¶17 Of course, RCW 9.73.030 may be violated by a recording made outside of this state if the recording was made for use of the evidence in Washington by an agent of a Washington official or other person. RCW 9.73.030 makes it clear that it is unlawful for "any individual, partnership, corporation, association, or the state of Washington, its agencies, and political subdivisions" to intercept or record certain recordings. Moreover, RCW 9.73.060 provides that any person "who, directly or by means of a detective agency or any other agent," violates the provisions of this chapter shall be subject to legal action for damages. Thus, when read together, it is clear that these provisions encompass persons acting as "agents" on behalf of someone in Washington.

¶18 In this case, however, the . . . trial court found that no Washington State law enforcement officer or other Washington State official requested or in any way encouraged the making of these calls or the recording of these calls. Thus, because the telephone calls were lawfully recorded in Oregon and were not done at the request of, with the involvement of, or as agents of Washington law enforcement officials otherwise with the intent to use the recordings in Washington, the recordings were not unlawful under RCW 9.73.030 and accordingly are not barred by RCW 9.73.050. See also State v. Brown, 940 P.2d 546 (Wash. 1997) (recording of appellant's statements to California police while appellant was in California did not violate RCW 9.73.030 or .090(1)(b)(i) and were properly admitted in Washington state courts, statements were lawfully recorded under California law, and the California police were not acting as agents of the King County police department). . . .

Notes

1. *Consensual intercepts: majority view.* Most state wiretap statutes follow the federal lead and do not protect interceptions of communications if at least one of the parties to the communication consents to the interception. About a dozen states require the consent of both parties before a conversation maybe recorded (absent judicial authorization). See, e.g., 18 Pa. Cons. Stat. §5704(4) ("It shall not be unlawful under this chapter for [a] person to intercept a wire, electronic or oral communication, where all parties to the communication have given prior consent to such interception"). The New Jersey statute reprinted above takes the unusual position of allowing consensual interceptions only when a government agent provides the consent or directs the interception. Why did the New Jersey legislature require only executive branch review of these interceptions? Will the state attorney general or county prosecutor ever rebuff a police request to seek third-party consent to record a conversation?

2. *Statutes and federalism.* The language of the federal wiretap statute in Title III applies both to federal and state law enforcement officers. The supremacy clause in Article VI of the U.S. Constitution declares that federal legislation is "the supreme Law of the Land." Thus, federal legislation can create binding legal obligations on state law enforcement officials. But is the converse true? Can state statutes (for

instance, those regulating wiretaps more stringently than federal law) create binding obligations on federal law enforcement officers operating within the state? Does it matter whether the evidence that the federal agents collect is presented in a state or federal prosecution? See 18 U.S.C. §2516(2).

3. *Statutes and extraterritorial behavior.* The far-reaching issue in the *Fowler* case was the extraterritorial effect of the state wiretap statute. How important would a state wiretap statute be if it applied only to monitoring of calls between two people located within the state where the crime was committed? Are you satisfied that the Washington court interpreted this statute properly on this issue? Is there any constitutional limitation on the authority of a state legislature to prohibit monitoring activity occurring outside state boundaries? Would you answer questions about extraterritoriality differently if law enforcement agents of another *country* monitored a telephone call between one person in the state and another person in the foreign country and presented the evidence of a criminal violation to state officials? Consider also whether a state court might allow law enforcement agents to follow the law of a foreign jurisdiction, but insist that prosecutors within the state follow domestic law regarding wiretap evidence, such as an obligation to provide defendants with copies of the wiretap warrant. See State v. Capolongo, 647 N.E.2d 1286 (N.Y. 1995). Would the outcome change if both callers were located in the foreign country during the telephone call and discussed a crime that had occurred in the state?

4. *The statutory exclusion remedy.* If a government wiretap violates a constitutional provision, then the constitutional remedy (exclusion of the evidence) will take hold. But what if the government violates statutory limits on wiretapping that are not mandated by the constitution? The state and federal wiretap statutes almost uniformly contain their own exclusionary remedy for at least some statutory violations. See 18 U.S.C. §2515 (designating exclusion as the remedy for unlawful interceptions of wire and oral communications but not electronic communications). In United States v. Giordano, 416 U.S. 505 (1974), the Supreme Court interpreted the federal remedial statute to apply only to violations of provisions that play "a central role in the statutory scheme." How does a court determine which statutory provisions are "central" if the statute itself does not say so? Does it depend on the number of cases in which the government is likely to violate the provision? Is the intent of the investigating officer relevant? Note that the federal statute reprinted above and most state statutes also provide for civil and criminal sanctions against individuals who intentionally violate those statutes.

5. *Statutory procedure.* Congress and state legislatures have taken an active hand in criminal procedure questions. Hardly a legislative session goes by without the passage of some new statute affecting the investigation and prosecution of crime. Wiretap statutes were one of the earliest and most prominent examples of "statutory procedure": an area in which legislatures take the leading role in setting the legal limits on practices in the field.

Legislatures have considerably greater flexibility than courts to fashion procedural rules. Legislatures can, for example, create new institutions or allocate funds to support new procedures. But if legislatures have such flexibility, and are free to adopt or ignore any nonconstitutional precedents on the topic, what principles might legislatures rely on in crafting wise rules?

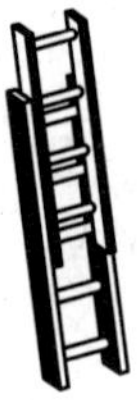

Are there characteristics of new technologies that make them especially strong candidates for legislative procedure? You can follow an active academic debate on this topic on the web extension for this chapter at *http://www.crimpro.com/extension/ch07*. See Orin Kerr, The Fourth Amendment and New Technologies: Constitutional Myths and the Case for Caution, 102 Mich. L. Rev. 801 (2004).

6. *Statutory interpretation in a constitutional area.* Are the principles of statutory interpretation the same for statutes with constitutional dimensions? The statutory text itself is the starting point, of course, and certain interpretive conventions, called "canons of construction," may enable the interpreter to place the language in context or resolve ambiguous language. In American courts, judges also try to apply statutory language in a manner most consistent with the perceived "purpose" of the legislation. In some jurisdictions (especially under federal law), the judge will settle on a statutory purpose by looking to the intent of the legislators who passed the statute, as embodied in specific sources such as committee reports and floor debates. Do any of these interpretive techniques change when a statute deals with a subject that has been the subject of constitutional litigation, such as the law of searches and seizures? Will courts interpreting a wiretap statute tend to be guided more by their own judicial view of prudent legal controls on government investigations, and consider themselves less obliged to carry out the expressed views of legislators who voted for the bill? In other words, does a constitutional aura around a statute increase the judiciary's interpretive powers?

7. *Cell phones and phone-like technologies.* Starting in the 1970s state and federal courts battled over whether wiretap statutes covered conversations made on cordless or cellular phones. The majority of jurisdictions refused to extend the existing statutes governing "wire" communications to wireless exchanges. Federal law now directly addresses these communications. In the Electronic Communications Privacy Act of 1986, 18 U.S.C. §2510(1), Congress protected conversations over cellular phones, and in the Communications Assistance for Law Enforcement Act, 47 U.S.C. §1001, enacted in 1994, Congress extended this protection to conversations on cordless phones. If the problem of unprotected wireless communications first appeared regularly in appellate decisions in the 1970s, and did not lead to specific statutory coverage until 1994, what does this say about the adaptability of the legal system? Do you conclude from this story that statutes are not capable of responding to changing conditions, because they are too rigid and too difficult to amend? Should legislatures address new technologies quickly, or should courts extend laws to cover them unless and until legislatures say otherwise? For example, what privacy should be recognized in voice or data communications conveyed through satellites? Does it matter whether the user knows that the communication bounces off a satellite?

Problem 7-3. Minimization

The Harford County Narcotics Task Force and Baltimore County authorities jointly investigated Carl Briscoe for suspected cocaine distribution. Along the way, the investigators began to suspect that Roland Mazzone, who lived in Baltimore County, was involved in the distribution ring. On June 19, the State's Attorney for Baltimore County filed ex parte applications with the Circuit Court to intercept and record conversations on two telephones (one at Mazzone's home, the other at his business, the Valley View Inn) from June 20 to July 20. A circuit court judge approved the applications and, on June 19, signed orders authorizing the interceptions. The orders authorized the wiretaps, and placed certain conditions on the operation of the wiretap, including a statement in the orders that the interceptions be conducted "in such a way as to minimize the interception of communications not otherwise subject to interception under Title III or the Maryland wiretap provisions."

At the time the orders were signed, the court also approved written "minimization guidelines," formulated by the State's Attorney. The guidelines included a section on privileged communications:

> Under Maryland Law, we will be concerned with privileged communications involving lawyer-client, husband-wife, priest-penitent, accountant-client and psychologist-patient relationship. Contact the above listed Assistant State's Attorneys for Baltimore County for instructions if you anticipate that you are about to monitor such a conversation and cannot affirmatively decide to minimize it completely. If it appears that the communication does discuss the commission of a designated crime itself, the privilege is breached and the whole conversation is to be monitored. If it appears that the communication might discuss the commission of a designated crime then spot monitoring shall be employed. If the communication does not involve the commission of a crime then the privilege applies absolutely and must be completely minimized as soon as the speakers identify themselves. All husband and wife communications are privileged; but discussions which involve the commission of the designated crime may be intercepted. All other communications must be minimized and spot monitoring must be employed carefully.

On July 12, after the State's Attorney filed further ex parte applications, the court issued new orders to continue the interceptions for an additional 30 days. The court approved a new set of written minimization guidelines, prepared by the State's Attorney, which stated that the minimization guidelines approved on June 19 "will also apply to the operational procedures" authorized on July 12, except for the following changes:

> Information garnered from the wiretaps conducted over Roland Mazzone's residence telephone as well as the business telephone of the Valley View Inn has identified Mazzone's wife, Elizabeth Ann, as being involved in this illegal controlled dangerous substance operation. Thus the privilege that is afforded to them under Maryland Law as husband and wife is breached during the interception of conversations that pertain to Mazzone's illegal drug activity.

During the investigation, the investigating officers learned that David Vita was Mazzone's supplier. Specifically, the officers collected evidence that on June 30, Mazzone paid Vita $14,000 and received from Vita a kilo of cocaine. Agents recorded dozens of phone calls between Roland and Elizabeth. Two provided incriminating evidence. In the first conversation, Roland called Elizabeth and she told him that he should not "come home empty-handed," meaning that he should bring some cocaine home with him. In the second conversation, Elizabeth called Roland at his business to inform him that Vita had arrived at their house.

Before trial, Mazzone moved to suppress all communications intercepted pursuant to the wiretap orders. He argued that the wiretap orders were illegal because the minimization guidelines misstated Maryland law on the marital communication privilege and therefore illegally authorized interception of privileged communications. The marital communications privilege is codified at §9-105. It provides that "one spouse is not competent to disclose any confidential communication between the spouses occurring during their marriage." As Mazzone suggests, Maryland courts have indeed interpreted the marital communications privilege to apply even when the communication furthers a crime.

As the trial judge in this case, you must rule on Mazzone's motion to suppress. Section 10-408(i) of the state wiretap law permits suppression of "any intercepted wire, oral, or electronic communication, or evidence derived therefrom" when "the interception was not made in conformity with the order of authorization."

When evaluating the validity of a wiretap order, Maryland courts distinguish between "preconditions" and "post conditions." Preconditions include the actions that investigators must take before a judge may issue an ex parte wiretap order and the inclusion of certain provisions required to be in the wiretap order. One such precondition is the requirement in §10-408(e)(3) that "every order and extension thereof shall contain a provision that the authorization to intercept . . . shall be conducted in such a way as to minimize the interception of communications not otherwise subject to interception under this subtitle." Maryland courts say that failure of a precondition requires suppression of all the evidence obtained under the wiretap.

Post conditions are the actions that must be taken after the judge issues a valid wiretap order, including compliance with the minimization mandate in the order. Imperfect compliance with a post condition does not require suppression of the evidence obtained under the wiretap order, so long as the level of compliance is "reasonable under the circumstances." Maryland case law designates the following ten factors to be considered in determining the reasonableness of minimization:

> (1) the nature and scope of the crime being investigated; (2) the sophistication of those under suspicion and their efforts to avoid surveillance through such devices as coded conversations; (3) the location and the operation of the subject telephone; (4) government expectation of the contents of the call; (5) the extent of judicial supervision; (6) the duration of the wiretap; (7) the purpose of the wiretap; (8) the length of the calls monitored; (9) the existence of a pattern of pertinent calls, which the monitoring agents could discern so as to eliminate the interception of non-pertinent calls; (10) the absence of monitoring of privileged conversations.

As the trial judge, how would you rule? Would you suppress all the wiretap evidence? Only the recorded calls between husband and wife? None of the statements? Compare State v. Mazzone, 648 A.2d 978 (Md. 1994).

Notes

1. *Minimization: majority view.* Wiretap statutes require the government to "minimize" the number of conversations "intercepted." This limitation prevents the government from listening to all conversations at a given telephone. Instead, agents must stop listening to a call if it does not fall within the coverage of the wiretap order. Reviewing courts, however, rarely invalidate a wiretap on the basis of improper minimization. In Scott v. United States, 436 U.S. 128 (1978), the Supreme Court

held that the monitoring and recording of the entirety of virtually all calls received on a tapped phone over a 30-day period was reasonable under the Fourth Amendment and was not a violation of the statute. The Court noted that the extent of the criminal activity under investigation, the extent to which the phone was used for illegal purposes, and the frequent use of ambiguous language in the conversations justified the full monitoring of every call. Admittedly, the officers knew about the "minimization" requirement contained in the statute and in the judge's order and took no steps to reduce the number of conversations they intercepted. Nevertheless, the Supreme Court decided that the relevant question was not the good faith of the officers (or the lack thereof) but the "objective" reasonableness of the scope of the interceptions. If a target suspects the government is listening to her communications, how could she take advantage of a minimization requirement in jurisdictions where it is enforced more strictly?

2. *Special showing of probable cause.* The court issuing a wiretap order under the typical statute must be convinced that probable cause exists as to several facts: (a) an individual has committed, is committing, or is about to commit a crime designated in the statute; (b) communications about that offense will be obtained through an interception; and (c) the particular facility to be monitored will be used in connection with the offense. See 18 U.S.C. §2518(3); Or. Rev. Stat. §133.724(3). How does this compare to the probable cause finding to support an ordinary search warrant?

Wiretap orders are available only to investigate crimes designated in the statute. While the federal statute includes an extensive list of federal and state crimes, some state statutes are far more selective. Most state statutes extend to violent crimes and narcotics offenses. Compare Utah Code §77-23a-8 (extensive list of crimes punishable by more than one year in prison) with Okla. Stat. tit. 13, §176.7 (murder and drug investigations). The applicant has an incentive to list as many crimes as possible to increase the scope of the permissible interceptions that may take place.

3. *Specifying the targeted person and facility.* Wiretap statutes typically require that applications specify the identity of the person whose communications are to be intercepted, "if known." See, e.g., 18 U.S.C. §2518(1)(b)(iv). Do statutory provisions such as these mean that a person specified in the application must take part in every intercepted conversation, or can the government intercept conversations at the specified facility between two people who were not specified in the application? See United States v. Kahn, 415 U.S. 143 (1974) (approving of interception of conversation between two persons not named in application, where application mentioned "others unknown").

Wiretap statutes also require the application to describe the "nature and location" of the facility from which the communication is to be intercepted. In 1986, Congress amended the federal wiretap statute to allow applications for "roving wiretaps" and "roving oral intercepts." See 18 U.S.C. §2518(11). The USA PATRIOT Act, passed soon after the terrorist attacks of September 11, 2001, expanded the authority for roving wiretaps. More than a dozen states followed suit. See, e.g., Fla. Stat. Ann. §§934.09(10), (11). Under these provisions, the government may intercept any communication of a designated individual about a suspected crime, wherever the communication takes place. The application for a roving wiretap must specify, to a greater extent than an ordinary wiretap application, the targeted individuals. It must also set out facts demonstrating that a wiretap at a specific facility would be ineffective because the target has a purpose to thwart interception by changing facilities. Is the "roving wiretap" the equivalent of a search warrant that fails to "particularly describe" the place to be searched? In 2009, no federal wiretaps were designated as roving, while only 16 state wiretaps were authorized as roving. What might explain numbers this low?

4. *Necessity requirement.* Some items included in the wiretap application are analogous to the kinds of information government agents present in typical applications for search warrants. But some of the information required for wiretaps is entirely new. One important example is the requirement in 18 U.S.C. §2518(c) that government agents describe any "other investigative procedures" that have been tried and an explanation of why those procedures failed or why they "reasonably appear" unlikely to succeed or are "likely" to be too dangerous. The provisions are designed to encourage the government to try measures other than wiretapping as the initial steps in an investigation. As the Court stated in United States v. Kahn, 415 U.S. 143 (1974), interceptions should not be permitted if "traditional investigative techniques would suffice to expose the crime." Courts often note that the "other procedures" provisions do not require the government to show that no other means would work, or that all other means have been tried and failed, but only that some reasonable effort has been made. You can find examples of state courts working in the investigative trenches of the wiretapping laws on the web extension for this chapter at *http://www.crimpro.com/extension/ch07*.

5. *Authority to apply for wiretaps.* Although any police officer can typically apply for an ordinary search warrant, a more limited group of law enforcement officials may apply for an interception order. The federal wiretap statute requires a senior Justice Department official or a United States Attorney (or a designee) to approve any application. See 18 U.S.C. §2516. The Oregon statute is typical in requiring the elected district attorney to apply for the interception order. Or. Rev. Stat. §133.724(1). Other statutes allow state-level officials (such as the attorney general) to apply for an order or to comment on the applications of others. Do these provisions successfully promote political accountability for law enforcement decisions? Does a statute create more or less protection for liberty and privacy by centralizing enforcement choices in the hands of politically accountable officials?

6. *Duration of wiretaps.* All wiretap statutes limit the total length of surveillance allowed. For example, 18 U.S.C. §2518(5) provides that wiretap orders should not authorize interceptions "for any period longer than is necessary to achieve the objective of the authorization, nor in any event longer than thirty days." The judge can grant extensions of a wiretap order if the government renews the application, again for no longer than 30 days. Some state statutes authorize shorter periods of time for surveillance. The average duration of a wiretap in 2009 was 42 days.

7. *The dilemma of placing details in the application.* The application will, in most cases, find its way to the target of the wiretap after the interceptions are complete. 18 U.S.C. §2518(8)(d). Thus, details about the investigation and its goals that are included in the application will likely be available to defense counsel at trial. Does this suggest that the applicant should include as few details as possible? On the other hand, wouldn't a wide range of specified individuals, crimes, and conversations lead to a wiretap order with a broader scope?

8. *Wiretap reports.* State and federal wiretap statutes require various types of reports from the prosecutors executing the order. First, they routinely empower the judge issuing the order to require periodic reports from the officers about the progress of the investigation. Some also require the administrative office of the judiciary or the chief prosecutor to assemble periodic statistics on the overall number of

wiretaps and to describe the characteristics of those investigations. The report goes to the legislature. See 18 U.S.C. §2519; Conn. Gen. Stat. §54-41o. If you were a legislator, which features of these investigations would you want to hear about? At the termination of the interception order, the officers must seal the tapes and records and "return" or file them immediately with the court to prevent tampering. Under certain circumstances, particularly if the target of a wiretap later faces criminal charges based on the wiretap evidence, the target must receive notice that the wiretap took place and must be told about its methods and results. If you were a defense attorney, what would you want to know about the wiretap?

9. *The frequency of wiretaps.* The Administrative Office of the U.S. Courts reports the annual number of wiretap orders issued at the request of both federal and state law enforcement officials. A single court order can involve many telephones. The annual number of wiretap orders remained fairly constant during the 1980s, but has increased since the 1990s.

1985: 784	1997: 1,186	2005: 1,773
1989: 763	2001: 1,491	2007: 2,208
1993: 976	2003: 1,442	2009: 2,376

The number of wiretap orders issued each year appears to be remarkably low, at least by comparison to the number of searches (both warranted and warrantless) that take place each year. The federal courts issue the largest number of wiretap orders, followed closely by courts in California, New York, and New Jersey. In 2009, the average cost per wiretap amounted to $52,200. The Administrative Office reported that "no [wiretap] applications were denied" in 2009. Do the multiple statutory requirements for obtaining a court order, one piled on the other, make the overall process so burdensome that government agents rarely find wiretaps worth the effort?

Looking at the number of wiretaps makes wiretapping seem like a fairly modest practical concern. Another perspective, however, is to consider the number of conversations reached by court-ordered wiretaps. According to the Department of Justice, each wiretap request approved in 2005 reached an average of 107 persons and 2,835 conversations. On average, wiretaps produced evidence of a crime in 22 percent of the conversations intercepted. Links to government reports on wiretap practices appear on the web extension for this chapter at *http://www.crimpro.com/extension/ch07*.

Connecticut requires a special showing from any applicant after the courts issue the first 35 interception orders in a given year. The applicant must show the court why any subsequent requests are based on an emergency situation that "may result in imminent peril to the public health, safety and welfare." See Conn. Gen. Stat.§54-41c(12). How do you suppose the legislature settled on the number 35? Would it be possible for judges, in the absence of a statute, to scrutinize government wiretap requests differently if the number of requests gets too large?

3. Bugs on Agents

Katz firmly established that a search occurs when a government agent plants an electronic bug in a flower vase and leaves the vase in a person's home. But what if a government agent attaches the bug to a flower, places the flower in his lapel, and then converses with a suspect? Which should be the determinative fact — that a conversation is taking place between two people (one of whom could be an agent or could choose to recount that conversation to authorities) or that electronic devices are recording the conversation?

■ STATE v. MICHAEL THADDEUS GOETZ

191 P.3d 489 (Mont. 2008)

GRAY, C.J.:

. . . ¶5 On May 19, 2004, Matt Collar, a detective with the Missouri River Drug Task Force, made contact with Suzanne Trusler, who previously had agreed to act as a confidential informant for the Task Force. Trusler informed Collar she had arranged to purchase a gram of methamphetamine from Goetz. Trusler then met with Collar and Detective Travis Swandal and allowed them to outfit her with a body wire receiving device. The detectives did not seek or obtain a search warrant authorizing use of the body wire. Collar gave Trusler $200 with which to purchase the drug. Trusler then went to Goetz's residence and purchased methamphetamine from him. The conversation between Goetz and Trusler during the drug transaction was monitored and recorded by the detectives via Trusler's body wire. Goetz was unaware of, and did not consent to, the electronic monitoring and recording of his conversation with Trusler.

¶6 The State of Montana subsequently charged Goetz by information with the offense of felony criminal distribution of dangerous drugs. . . . Goetz moved the District Court to suppress the evidence derived from the electronic monitoring and recording of the conversation on the basis that it violated his rights to privacy and to be free from unreasonable searches and seizures as guaranteed by Article II, Sections 10 and 11 of the Montana Constitution. The District Court held a hearing and subsequently denied the motion to suppress. . . .

¶7 On August 4, 2004, Collar made contact with Chrystal White, who previously had agreed to act as a confidential informant with the Task Force. White informed Collar that she had arranged to purchase 1/8 ounce of marijuana for $50 from Hamper. White met with Collar and Swandal and allowed the detectives to outfit her with a body wire receiving device. . . . White met Hamper in a parking lot and purchased marijuana from him. The drug transaction took place in White's vehicle and the conversation between White and Hamper was monitored and recorded by the detectives via White's body wire. The following day, White again contacted Collar and informed him she had arranged to purchase another 1/8 ounce of marijuana from Hamper for $50. . . . White then went to Hamper's residence and purchased marijuana from him. Again, the conversation between White and Hamper regarding the drug transaction was electronically monitored and recorded by the detectives via White's body wire. . . .

¶8 The State subsequently charged Hamper by information with two counts of felony criminal distribution of dangerous drugs. [The District Court denied Hamper's motion to suppress.]

¶10 Were the Defendants' rights under Article II, Sections 10 and 11 of the Montana Constitution violated by the warrantless electronic monitoring and recording of their one-on-one conversations with confidential informants, notwithstanding the confidential informants' consent to the monitoring? . . .

¶13 . . . The Defendants do not dispute that, pursuant to United States Supreme Court jurisprudence, warrantless electronic monitoring of face-to-face conversations, with the consent of one party to the conversation, does not constitute a search and, therefore, does not violate the Fourth Amendment. See e.g. United States v. White, 401 U.S. 745 (1971). They assert, however, that Article II, Sections 10 and 11 of the Montana Constitution afford citizens a greater right to privacy which, in turn, provides broader protection than the Fourth Amendment in situations involving searches and seizures occurring in private settings.

¶14 Article II, Section 10 of the Montana Constitution provides that the "right of individual privacy is essential to the well-being of a free society and shall not be infringed without the showing of a compelling state interest." Article II, Section 11 of the Montana Constitution provides that

> [the] people shall be secure in their persons, papers, homes and effects from unreasonable searches and seizures. No warrant to search any place, or seize any person or thing shall issue without describing the place to be searched or the person or thing to be seized, or without probable cause, supported by oath or affirmation reduced to writing.

[In] light of the constitutional right to privacy to which Montanans are entitled, we have held that the range of warrantless searches which may be lawfully conducted under the Montana Constitution is narrower than the corresponding range of searches that may be lawfully conducted pursuant to the federal Fourth Amendment. . . .

II. Analysis Under Current Montana Constitutional Search and Seizure and Right to Privacy Jurisprudence . . .

¶27 We determine whether a state action constitutes an "unreasonable" or "unlawful" search or seizure in violation of the Montana Constitution by analyzing three factors: 1) whether the person challenging the state's action has an actual subjective expectation of privacy; 2) whether society is willing to recognize that subjective expectation as objectively reasonable; and 3) the nature of the state's intrusion. The first two factors are considered in determining whether a search or seizure occurred, thus triggering the protections of Article II, Sections 10 and 11. . . . Under the third factor, we determine whether the state action complained of violated the Article II, Section 10 and 11 protections because it was not justified by a compelling state interest or was undertaken without procedural safeguards such as a properly issued search warrant or other special circumstances. . . .

A. Did the Defendants Have an Actual Subjective Expectation of Privacy? . . .

¶29 . . . What a person knowingly exposes to the public is not protected, but what an individual seeks to preserve as private, even in an area accessible to the public, may be constitutionally protected. Indeed, in Montana, . . .

> when a person takes precautions to place items behind or underneath seats, in trunks or glove boxes, or uses other methods of ensuring that those items may not be accessed

> and viewed without permission, there is no obvious reason to believe that any privacy interest with regard to those items has been surrendered simply because those items happen to be in an automobile.

State v. Elison, 14 P.3d 456 (Mont. 2000). While *Elison* involved physical items stowed within a vehicle, the same rationale applies to a conversation with another person in a vehicle which cannot be overheard by the public outside the vehicle. Thus, where a person has gone to considerable trouble to keep activities and property away from prying eyes, the person evinces a subjective expectation of privacy in those activities and that property. . . .

¶30 Here, the face-to-face conversations between the Defendants and one other individual were within the Defendants' private homes and, in Hamper's case, in the confines of a vehicle. The Defendants did not conduct their conversations where other individuals were present or physically within range to overhear the conversations. . . . We conclude the Defendants exhibited actual subjective expectations of privacy in the face-to-face conversations they held in private settings.

B. IS SOCIETY WILLING TO RECOGNIZE THE DEFENDANTS' EXPECTATIONS OF PRIVACY AS REASONABLE?

¶31 We next address whether society is willing to recognize an individual's subjective expectation that a one-on-one conversation conducted in a private setting is not being surreptitiously electronically monitored and recorded. Stated differently, does society perceive it is reasonable to expect privacy in a personal conversation held in a private setting? . . .

¶33 We have on prior occasions quoted extensively from — and discussed the debates of — the delegates to the constitutional convention with regard to the inclusion of the right to privacy in the 1972 Montana Constitution. Delegate Campbell stated that the Bill of Rights committee "felt very strongly that the people of Montana should be protected as much as possible against eavesdropping, electronic surveillance, and such type of activities. [We] found that the citizens of Montana were very suspicious of such type of activity." Delegate Dahood reported even more strongly: "It is inconceivable to any of us that there would ever exist a situation in the State of Montana where electronic surveillance could be justified. [Within] the area of the State of Montana, we cannot conceive of a situation where we could ever permit electronic surveillance." Thus, the Constitutional Convention delegates were aware of the great value Montana citizens place on the right to privacy and the clear risk to that privacy engendered by the existence and advancement of electronic technology as used by law enforcement. . . .

¶35 The express statements of the delegates to the 1972 Montana Constitutional Convention regarding the government's use of electronic surveillance against Montana's citizens provide direct support for a conclusion that society is willing to recognize as reasonable the expectation that conversations held in a private setting are not surreptitiously being electronically monitored and recorded by government agents. We are convinced that Montanans continue to cherish the privacy guaranteed them by Montana's Constitution. Thus, while we recognize that Montanans are willing to risk that a person with whom they are conversing in their home or other private setting may repeat that conversation to a third person, we are firmly persuaded that they are unwilling to accept as reasonable that the same conversation is being electronically monitored and recorded by government agents without their knowledge.

¶36 Nor should the underlying purpose or content of the conversations at issue reflect upon society's willingness to accept a subjective expectation of privacy in those conversations as reasonable. [All] of us discuss topics and use expressions with one person that we would not undertake with another and that we would never broadcast to a crowd. Few of us would ever speak freely if we knew that all our words were being captured by machines for later release before an unknown and potentially hostile audience. No one talks to a recorder as he talks to a person. . . .
It is, of course, easy to say that one engaged in an illegal activity has no right to complain if his conversations are broadcast or recorded. If, however, law enforcement officials may lawfully cause participants secretly to record and transcribe private conversations, nothing prevents monitoring of those persons not engaged in illegal activity, who have incurred displeasure, have not conformed or have espoused unpopular causes.

¶37 Based on the foregoing, we conclude each Defendant's expectation of privacy in the conversations at issue here is one society is willing to accept as reasonable. . . . Thus, we further conclude that the electronic monitoring and recording of the Defendants' in-person conversations constituted searches within the contemplation of the Article II, Sections 10 and 11 rights to privacy and to be free from unreasonable searches.

C. NATURE OF THE STATE'S INTRUSION . . .

¶39 [The] Article II, Section 10 right to privacy is not absolute, but may be infringed upon a showing of a compelling state interest to do so. Even upon the showing of a compelling state interest, however, state action which infringes upon an individual's privacy right must be closely tailored to effectuate that compelling interest. Thus, the State may not invade an individual's privacy unless the procedural safeguards attached to the right to be free from unreasonable searches and seizures are met.

¶40 . . . Where, as here, a warrantless search has been conducted, the State bears the burden of establishing that an exception to the warrant requirement justifies the search. The State advances alternative arguments in this regard and we address them in turn.

1. Consent

¶41 The State first argues that the warrantless searches at issue here were authorized by the confidential informants' consent to the monitoring and recording of the conversations. . . . The State asserts that, because the confidential informants in these cases arranged with law enforcement to wear the body wires and clearly consented to the electronic monitoring and recording of the conversations, their consents justified the warrantless searches.

¶42 . . . While we interpret Montana's Constitution to provide greater protections for individuals in the context of search and seizure issues than does the Fourth Amendment to the United States Constitution, we use some federal Fourth Amendment analysis in addressing issues under the Montana Constitution. In that regard, we observe that the Supreme Court recently refined the third-party consent exception in Georgia v. Randolph, 547 U.S. 103 (2006).

¶43 In *Randolph,* the defendant's wife contacted law enforcement regarding a domestic dispute she had with Randolph. The wife informed the officers upon their arrival that Randolph was a drug user and items of drug use were located in the house. Randolph, who was present in the house at the time, denied his wife's allegations and unequivocally refused the officers' request for his consent to search the house. The officers then obtained the wife's consent to search. During the search, the officers observed and seized evidence of drug use. Upon being charged with possession of cocaine, Randolph moved to suppress the evidence on the basis that his wife's consent, given over his express refusal to consent, rendered the searches unlawful. . . .

¶44 The United States Supreme Court . . . held that "a warrantless search of a shared dwelling for evidence over the express refusal of consent by a physically present resident cannot be justified as reasonable as to him on the basis of consent given to the police by another resident."

¶45 . . . Here, the search of conversations by means of electronic monitoring and recording, rather than the search of premises, is at issue. Each party to each conversation was physically present at the time of the search and had an interest — that is, an interest in the nature of a co-tenant in physical premises — in the conversation. Under the *Randolph* rationale . . . the confidential informants' consent to the electronic monitoring and recording of the conversations could not override any objection expressed by the Defendants. Furthermore, because both parties to the conversations were present at the time the searches were conducted, both parties must have the opportunity to object to the search. As the Supreme Court observed, law enforcement may not avoid a refusal of consent by removing a potentially objecting individual from the premises prior to requesting consent. . . .

¶46 Similarly, here, the State cannot justify a search under the consent exception as a result of the simple expedient of failing to inform the potential — and physically present — objecting party that the search is being conducted. We conclude that the warrantless searches of the conversations at issue here cannot be justified by the consent exception to the warrant requirement.

2. Particularized Suspicion Standard

¶47 Alternatively, the State contends that, if we conclude the electronic monitoring and recording of a face-to-face conversation constitutes a search, it should be subject to a particularized suspicion standard rather than the Article II, Section 11 probable cause requirement for the issuance of a search warrant. In essence, the argument is that the State's intrusion into the Defendants' privacy expectations by the electronic monitoring and recording of their conversations was minimal and, therefore, did not rise to a level of requiring probable cause.

¶48 [Throughout] this country, but especially in Montana, . . . a person's residence and his homestead are secure from unwarranted government intrusion, be it by physical or technological means. In two of the searches at issue here, the State intruded into the sanctity of the Defendants' homes for the purpose of performing those searches by technological means. We will not countenance such an intrusion under a lesser standard than probable cause.

¶49 We turn, then, to the State's argument that the particularized suspicion standard should apply to the search of the conversation between Hamper and the confidential informant which took place in the confidential informant's vehicle. . . .

¶52 [We have held that] the dog sniff of the exterior of a vehicle constituted a search, but that such a search may be justified by particularized suspicion of wrongdoing, rather than probable cause sufficient for issuance of a search warrant. State v. Tackitt, 67 P.3d 295 (Mont. 2003). Here, the State asserts that, because the electronic monitoring and recording of a conversation is even less intrusive than a dog sniff, particularized suspicion is a sufficient standard here. We disagree.

¶53 In *Tackitt,* law enforcement officers used a drug-detecting canine to sniff the exterior of the defendant's vehicle parked outside his residence and the canine alerted on the trunk of the vehicle, indicating the presence of drugs. [We] determined that, although warrantless searches generally are *per se* unreasonable, the purpose and minimally intrusive nature of such a canine sniff warranted an exception to the warrant requirement, but would "still require particularized suspicion when the area or object subject to the canine sniff is already exposed to the public." Here, however, the private face-to-face conversation in the vehicle was not exposed to the public. Consequently, we decline to adopt a particularized suspicion standard to justify the warrantless electronic monitoring and recording of a one-on-one conversation occurring in a vehicle. . . .

¶54 For the above-stated reasons, we hold that the electronic monitoring and recording of the Defendants' conversations with the confidential informants, notwithstanding the consent of the confidential informants, constituted searches subject to the warrant requirement of Article II, Section 11 of the Montana Constitution. The electronic monitoring and recording of those conversations without a warrant or the existence of an established exception to the warrant requirement violated the Defendants' rights under Article II, Sections 10 and 11. . . .

LEAPHART, J., specially concurring.

¶56 I specially concur in the court's conclusion that evidence obtained through warrantless, consensual participant recording of a conversation in a home or automobile is not admissible in court. Although the court ties its rationale to the private settings (home and automobile) involved in these cases, I would not limit a Montana citizen's reasonable expectation of conversational privacy to "private settings."

¶57 In my view, Montanans do not have to anticipate that a conversation, no matter what the setting, is being secretly recorded by agents of the state acting without benefit of a search warrant. As Justice Harlan noted in his dissent in United States v. White, 401 U.S. 745, 777 (1971), "it is one thing to subject the average citizen to the risk that participants in a conversation with him will subsequently divulge its contents to another, but quite a different matter to foist upon him the risk that unknown third parties may be simultaneously listening in." . . .

¶58 Article II, Section 11, like the Fourth Amendment, protects people not places. . . . Although an individual's expectation of privacy may be more compelling in one setting (e.g., a home) than another, that is not to say that an individual conversing in a more public setting has no expectation of privacy and must reasonably anticipate the risk of warrantless consensual monitoring. As Justice Harlan observed in *White,* warrantless consensual monitoring undermines "that confidence and sense of security in dealing with one another that is characteristic of individual relationships between citizens in a free society." A "free society" is precisely what

Article 10, Section 10, was designed to foster. This constitutional guarantee ensures that our citizens may continue to engage in private discourse, free to speak with the uninhibited spontaneity that is characteristic of our democratic society. . . .

¶61 . . . There is a theme throughout the dissent that someone who chooses to engage in discourse about criminal endeavors, has no expectation of privacy. The examples and rationales cited are all circuitous in that they assume the "risky" or illegal "nature" of the conversation in question. An officer does not know that a call is obscene or that the conversation relates to a drug sale until after the officer listens in or hears the tape of the conversation. If the officer does have prior reason to believe that an individual has already engaged in obscene calling or drug sales, then the officer has probable cause to obtain a warrant. . . .

RICE, J., dissenting. . . .

¶79 . . . The Court's error springs from an incorrect analytical approach to the issue, resulting in an unnecessarily broad and sweeping decision not predicated on the specific facts of this case. . . .

¶88 The facts of this case do not involve the exercise of "complete discretion" by police to wire someone "just to snoop" or to gather information that might be used or not used at all. The facts here do not involve situations where police did not have particularized suspicion and probable cause. Even before wiring the informants, police had probable cause to believe that both defendants had already committed the crime of criminal distribution of dangerous drugs. Authority to wire aside, the police could have *arrested* the defendants because they had already committed a crime. . . .

¶90 [The] Court issues the sweeping proposition that there is an expectation of privacy in "face-to-face conversations" held in "private settings." This conclusion, disconnected from the facts, *will even prohibit a participant in the conversation from testifying* about what the Defendant said or did, unless a warrant is first obtained. . . .

¶91 This was a commercial transaction. In each of the two cases before us, the seller, for the purpose of making a financial profit, offered and then sold a product to a buyer. But for the seller's financial motive, and the buyer's assurance of payment, these parties would not have met at all. . . .

¶92 As in the typical commercial transaction, the sellers here offered their product to members of the public — they intentionally exposed and sold their product to customers who were non-confidants. The length of each transaction is reflective of its impersonal and commercial nature as each lasted only moments — similar to other retail purchases. These meetings were not social occasions between friends or family. The exchange of product and cash was made and the parties immediately went their own way, because the only purpose of their meeting — the sale — was completed. Thus, in these transactions, the defendants first "knowingly exposed" their business by offering to sell and then exposed their product during the actual exchange to someone who was not a confidant to them.

¶93 The place of the transaction is also a relevant fact, though not necessarily determinative. Goetz invited Trusler, described by the District Court as a "mere visitor," into his home on Main Street and there conducted the brief sales transaction. Hamper met Ms. White first in a parking lot on Main Street, where he got into *her* car for the brief conversation and sale. . . .

¶94 [The] Court only considers whether there exists a reasonable expectation of privacy in "a personal conversation held in a private setting." This statement, and others in the opinion, is so broad that it would apply as readily to governmental recording of a conversation among friends or relatives socially gathered around the living room, as to the facts of this case. Indeed, who would disagree that society reasonably expects the government to not record "conversations held in a private setting" such as the confines of one's home during a family Thanksgiving dinner? I certainly would not disagree — but those are not the facts here. The expectation of privacy in a personal family dinner setting is far different than the expectation of privacy in a commercial transaction where a product is sold to a non-confidant in a brief encounter. . . .

¶96 The public and commercial nature of the criminal enterprise at issue here — the sale of illegal drugs to strangers — separates this case from other kinds of crimes, even drug-related, and further illustrates the necessity of a close factual analysis. For instance, a person joining others at a friend's house to smoke pot, though an illegal act, would have a different privacy expectation than a person who undertakes the risk of meeting with a member of the public to consummate a drug transaction. . . .

¶97 Consistent with its approach of over-generalizing, the Court attempts to summarize the statements of the delegates to the 1972 Montana Constitutional Convention in a manner which appears to provide support for its holding. . . . However, the Court considers only some of the delegates' words, and ignores other specifically applicable words altogether, thereby covering up the reality that the delegates' primary concern was over electronic surveillance and eavesdropping undertaken by the government *without the consent of any party*. [The delegates addressed the factual scenario at issue here. As Delegate Campbell put it:]

> I feel that with "oral communications" you are not excluding the legitimate law enforcement people, who, with the consent of one party, the person who is being threatened by phone calls and things like this, to act on behalf of the victim. The privacy of that individual certainly could be waived with his or her consent, and there's certainly no privacy toward the obscene caller. . . .

¶99 [The] Court appears to distinguish between the risk that a conversation will be repeated and the risk that the same conversation will be consensually electronically monitored by government agents. However, if this is the Court's distinction, it is without a constitutional difference because society would not consider a privacy interest in a non-private commercial drug transaction to be reasonable. Indeed, our constitutional convention delegates did not, and neither did some of the greatest legal minds of our time. . . . Accordingly, I would join them and conclude that no "search" took place.

¶100 However, even assuming *arguendo* that a search did occur, the Court's analysis of the "nature of the State's intrusion" again further ignores the facts of the present case and mischaracterizes the role of consent in our search and seizure jurisprudence. . . .

¶101 . . . The *Randolph* situation cannot fairly be likened to the instant case. [A] conversation, unlike a home, is not a shared space. Once the conversation commences, it becomes the individual property of each participant. Neither participant can prevent the other (absent privilege) from sharing or repeating the conversation because each has full control over it. A conversation is not the same as a dwelling space and, accordingly, consent of both conversationalists is not required in order to monitor the conversation. . . .

¶105 [There are other pertinent details about the nature of the state's intrusion here.] First and foremost, the recording did not produce any evidence beyond what the informant herself could have relayed. . . . The facts clearly distinguish the monitoring here from the "sense enhancing" technologies [that] could be used to surreptitiously monitor the heat signatures generated by activities conducted within the confines of Montanans' private homes and enclosed structures for the purpose of drawing inferences about the legality of such activities.

¶106 It could be argued that consensual monitoring enhances the senses of police because officers can hear a conversation which they otherwise could not. However, this distinction is not one of constitutional dimension, because it relates only to the *mode* by which the information is received, not the *content* of that information. Whether the informant testifies, or the officer testifies with the tape, the evidentiary potential is the same. Thus, it is clear that defendants' constitutional privacy claim really boils down to trial strategy: they do not want the daunting task of fighting against the pesky truthfulness of their very own, recorded words. . . .

¶108 [What is the likely impact of this intrusion] on the individual's sense of security? . . . As Goetz stated while selling drugs to Trusler: "[The] real deal is with this sh__, they are all over. The Feds are f___ing everywhere in this town. The DTF, the FBI, there's reason to be superultra-f___ing-freaked!"

¶109 [The] impact of consensual monitoring upon the "sense of security" of people commercially marketing illegal drugs to the public in an environment of active law enforcement is, respectfully, *very* minimal. This activity is a highly risky venture, and, indeed, one engaging in it truly has good reason to be "freaked" because, consistent with Goetz's knowledge of the risk, law enforcement is engaged. . . .

¶111 Truly, it is a different world today, not only in terms of technological advances, but also in the expectation of the use of technology. I would submit . . . that our citizens, especially young people in today's society who have been raised in the age of *Law and Order* and *CSI,* would think it unusual that a drug dealer would have a *reasonable* expectation that his conversations during a drug sale to a non-confidant were not being consensually monitored. . . .

¶112 Moreover, monitoring provides protection for the informant, who risks physical harm to work with police, and provides for accurate recording and preservation of the evidence of the transaction. Thus, . . . the utility of this technology is very high in the furtherance of the state's compelling state interest in enforcing its criminal laws for the benefit and protection of the citizens. . . .

¶114 . . . Our right of privacy has been hijacked by those engaging in activities which the right was clearly not meant to protect, and has thus been devalued — becoming the new refuge of meth dealers selling to the public by means they well knew risked law enforcement involvement. The delegates to the Constitutional Convention did not countenance such a distortion of the right they found "essential to the well-being of a free society."

¶115 And I would not, either. I dissent. . . .

COTTER, J., concurring . . . .

¶125 While the Dissent complains that the Court's decision is unnecessarily broad and sweeping, so too is its own reach. If the Dissent's rationale is intended to apply equally to the criminal and the law-abiding alike — which I submit, it must — then it stands for the proposition that virtually any commercial transaction may be surreptitiously recorded without a warrant and with only one party's consent, with the resulting recording being admissible in evidence against the speaker. It would, in essence, gut any expectation of privacy one might reasonably have in his commercial conversation, regardless of the lawfulness of the transaction. If, on the other hand, the analysis is intended to apply to only those transactions that are criminal in nature . . . then it runs afoul of our duty to treat all persons the same before the law, without distinction for criminal/non-criminal behavior. Respectfully, either result is unacceptable. . . .

Notes

1. *Bugs on government agents: majority position.* A substantial majority of the states take the federal position as stated in United States v. White, 401 U.S. 745 (1971). Under this reasoning, a conversation between a government agent and a suspect does not become a "search," subject to constitutional limitations, when the agent uses a device to transmit or record the conversation. State courts that reject *White* often rely on distinctive language in a state constitution or a distinctive state constitutional history. State v. Geraw, 795 A.2d 1219 (Vt. 2002); State v. Mullens, 650 S.E. 2d 169 (W.Va. 2007).

A number of state courts that originally rejected *White* have reconsidered their decision (sometimes many years later) and have embraced the federal position. See People v. Collins, 475 N.W.2d 684 (Mich. 1991) (overruling 1975 decision that had rejected *White*); Melanie Black Dubis, The Consensual Electronic Surveillance Experiment: State Courts React to *United States v. White*, 47 Vand. L. Rev. 857 (1994). If a state court has rejected the federal view on a constitutional question, does that decision remain a questionable authority for its entire life span? Is there something special about the issue of consensual electronic surveillance that made these courts willing to reconsider their earlier independent stances?

2. *Confusing bugs and people.* Is the tape recording or transmission of a conversation with a government agent a consensual search, or is it no search at all? When a recording device is on an agent, doesn't the microphone simply serve as a more accurate way to capture and re-create statements? Should the rules be different when the technological enhancement changes the listener's capacity for recollection, but not the capacity to hear the evidence in the first place?

4. *Wiretaps to Fight Terrorism and Crime*

Just as wiretaps are useful for criminal investigations, they can also be useful for espionage. During the Cold War, the FBI and the CIA investigated possible agents of foreign governments operating within the United States. Congressional hearings during the 1970s, however, brought to light some abuses of domestic intelligence, including wiretaps and other surveillance of leaders of the civil rights movement and critics of the Vietnam War. In 1978, Congress passed the Foreign Intelligence Surveillance Act (FISA), creating new legal limits on domestic surveillance of suspected foreign agents.

The provisions of FISA require agents of the government to obtain judicial approval for their wiretaps. The order comes from a specialized federal court, known as the FISA court. While FISA does require probable cause to believe that the target is acting as an agent of a foreign power, the application for a surveillance order under FISA does not require the same detailed showing that is necessary for an ordinary criminal wiretap order under Title III. To prevent criminal investigators from using FISA wiretaps to avoid the more burdensome aspects of Title III, federal courts interpreted the statutes to require a clear separation between criminal and foreign intelligence investigations.

After the terrorist attacks of September 11, 2001, Congress passed the USA PATRIOT Act. One set of provisions in the Act made it easier for different groups of investigators to share information obtained from a FISA wiretap order. As you read the following problem, consider whether the new regime for wiretap orders under FISA will become more commonplace in a wide range of criminal investigations.

Problem 7-4. Crack in the Wall?

You are a judge on the Foreign Intelligence Surveillance Court of Review — a special federal appellate court created by Congress in FISA in 1978 to handle appeals from the FISA court. The Foreign Intelligence Surveillance Court of Review did not hear a single case in its first 25 years of statutory existence. After September 11 and the passage of the USA PATRIOT Act, the first appeal arrives, and the government has filed it. The high-stakes questions for the court are these:

1. Is the order of the FISA court setting limits on the government in this case valid?
2. Is the new rule of the FISA court (calling for the government to disclose connections between any FISA application and any ongoing criminal investigations) required by or allowed by the statute?
3. Is the amendment of FISA by the USA PATRIOT Act constitutional?

As part of its investigation into suspected terrorist groups after the September 11 attacks, the government applied to the FISA court for an order authorizing electronic surveillance. The government's application included some detailed information to support its contention that the target, a United States citizen, was conspiring with others in international terrorism. The FISA court granted the order, but it also placed some limits on the government. The order said that

> law enforcement officials shall not make recommendations to intelligence officials concerning the initiation, operation, continuation or expansion of FISA searches or surveillances. Additionally, the FBI and the Criminal Division of the Department of Justice shall ensure that law enforcement officials do not direct or control the use of the FISA procedures to enhance criminal prosecution, and that advice intended to preserve the option of a criminal prosecution does not inadvertently result in the Criminal Division's directing or controlling the investigation using FISA searches and surveillances toward law enforcement objectives.

To ensure the Justice Department followed these strictures, the court also fashioned a "chaperone requirement." A unit of the Justice Department, the Office of Intelligence Policy and Review (OIPR), composed of 31 lawyers and 25 support staff, must be invited to all meetings between the FBI and the Criminal Division to coordinate their efforts "to investigate or protect against foreign attack, international terrorism, or clandestine intelligence activities by foreign powers." If representatives of OIPR are unable to attend such meetings, "OIPR shall be apprized of the substance of the meetings in writing so that the Court may be notified at the earliest opportunity." Finally, the FISA court issued a new procedural rule, Rule 11, stating that "all FISA applications shall include informative descriptions of any ongoing criminal investigations of FISA targets, as well as the substance of any consultations between the FBI and criminal prosecutors at the Department of Justice."

The FISA court's restrictions were designed to build a "wall" between intelligence officials and law enforcement officers in the Executive branch. Drawing on many other judicial interpretations of FISA, the court meant to approve applications only when the "government's objective is not primarily directed toward criminal prosecution of the foreign agents for their foreign intelligence activity."

Under FISA, the court can approve of electronic surveillance to "obtain foreign intelligence information" if the government shows probable cause to believe that the target is "an agent of a foreign power" and that the communication facility to be monitored "is being used, or is about to be used" by the agent. 50 U.S.C. §1805(a)(3). The statute defines "foreign intelligence information" as

> information that relates to, and if concerning a United States person is necessary to, the ability of the United States to protect against — A) actual or potential attack or other grave hostile acts of a foreign power or an agent of a foreign power; B) sabotage or international terrorism by a foreign power or an agent of a foreign power; or C) clandestine intelligence activities by an intelligence service or network of a foreign power or by an agent of a foreign power.

50 U.S.C. §1801(e)(1). It defines an agent of a foreign power to include any person who "knowingly engages in clandestine intelligence gathering activities . . . which activities involve or may involve a violation of the criminal statutes of the United States" or those involving international terrorist acts, defined as "violent acts or acts dangerous to human life that are a violation of the criminal laws of the United States or of any State."

Section 1804 of FISA requires a national security official to certify in the application that "the purpose" of the surveillance is to obtain foreign intelligence information. That same certification must include a statement of "the basis of the certification that (i) the information sought is the type of foreign intelligence information designated." FISA includes "minimization procedures" designed to prevent the acquisition or sharing within the government of material gathered in an electronic surveillance that is unnecessary to the government's need for foreign intelligence information. 50 U.S.C. §1801(h).

Before 2001, the Department of Justice followed some internal procedures that limited contacts between the FBI and the Criminal Division in cases where FISA surveillance or searches were being conducted by the FBI for foreign intelligence purposes. The 1995 version of those internal procedures states that "the FBI and Criminal Division should ensure that advice intended to preserve the option of a criminal prosecution does not inadvertently result in either the fact or the appearance of the Criminal Division's directing or controlling the foreign intelligence investigation toward law enforcement purposes." Under these procedures, OIPR became a "wall" to prevent the FBI intelligence officials from communicating directly with the Criminal Division about their investigations.

The USA PATRIOT Act made some important changes to this statutory structure. It changed the certification requirement of Section 1804 to declare that "a significant purpose" of the surveillance is to obtain foreign intelligence information (as opposed to "the purpose" under FISA). The statute also explicitly authorized federal officers who conduct foreign intelligence surveillance to "consult with Federal law enforcement officers to coordinate efforts to investigate or protect against" attack, sabotage, international terrorism, or clandestine intelligence activities by foreign agents. 50 U.S.C. §1806(k)(1).

In 2002, the Attorney General modified the 1995 internal procedures. The new procedures eliminated the "directing or controlling" language and allowed the exchange of advice among the FBI, OIPR, and the Criminal Division regarding "the initiation, operation, continuation, or expansion of FISA searches or surveillance."

The government has appealed the order of the FISA court in this case, and also challenges the validity of the court's new Rule 11. Is the FISA court's order in this case consistent with the statute, as amended? Is the order compelled by the constitution? Compare In re Sealed Case, 310 F.3d 717 (Foreign Intelligence Surveillance Court of Review 2002).

Notes

1. *Wiretaps outside FISA.* In December 2005, the public learned that in 2001 the president authorized the National Security Agency to intercept and monitor telephone conversations between some callers in the United States and callers outside the country. Although the details of the program were a mystery, it seemed clear that the intercepts happened without any warrant from the FISA court and thus violated the procedures established in that statute. The Bush administration defended the program on two grounds. First, officials argued that the president has "inherent authority" as "commander in chief" of the armed forces under Article II of the Constitution to order wiretaps, outside the statutory framework of FISA, for electronic surveillance related to the prosecution of a war. Second, they argued that Congress had implicitly created an exception to the FISA procedures on September 14, 2001, when it authorized the president to use "all necessary and appropriate military force" against those responsible for the attacks. Without going into details about the program, officials also asserted that the FISA warrant process was impractical because it generated warrants too slowly and prevented the sort of categorical monitoring that the program required. See Eric Lichtau & Adam Liptak, "Bush Aides Press On in Legal Defense for Wiretapping Program," N.Y. Times, Jan. 28, 2006.

During the public debate about this program, several background facts about espionage wiretaps became clear. First, the NSA's scope was quite extensive, reaching the calls of thousands of Americans. Second, the FISA court granted virtually all government requests for espionage wiretaps. Between 1979 and 2003, the government applied for 16,974 surveillance orders from the FISA court, and the court denied the request in only 4 cases.

Does the existence of this NSA surveillance program affect your views about the validity of Rule 11, as described in Problem 7-4?

C. RECORDS IN THE HANDS OF THIRD PARTIES

Just as technology enables government investigators to monitor a suspect's conversations, it can also enable the government to make the most of available information by assembling small bits of scattered information into larger patterns. When electronic documents are in private hands, courts must confront the question whether an individual maintains any expectation of privacy in those documents. Government access to such records may allow collection of a huge range of information because of the sheer quantity of data that business databases contain, together with the ability to computerize a search of that information.

As we have seen, wiretap statutes tightly regulate the government's electronic eavesdropping on telephone conversations, face-to-face conversations, or electronic communications. Wiretaps can occur only after the government invests extraordinary effort in a detailed application to a judge, and the judge approves the application. Both federal and state law place lesser protections on records of communications held in third party storage, including telephone records, e-mail, and voice mail. The statutes in this area, such as 18 U.S.C. §§2701-2709, give law enforcement officers access, ordinarily pursuant to a warrant or court order or under a subpoena in some cases. The warrant or subpoena used in this setting does not include the exceptionally detailed information necessary for a wiretap order.

A less demanding set of restrictions apply to a third form of communications evidence: the government's use of trap and trace devices and "pen registers," which identify the source and destination of calls made to and from a particular telephone. Devices such as pen registers inspired the passage of many statutes that both obligate the telephone company to cooperate in the use of pen registers and limit the cases in which government may seek a pen register.

18 U.S.C. §3121

(a) [N]o person may install or use a pen register or a trap and trace device without first obtaining a court order. . . .

(c) A government agency authorized to install and use a pen register or trap and trace device under this chapter or under State law shall use technology reasonably available to it that restricts the recording or decoding of electronic or other impulses to the dialing, routing, addressing, and signaling information utilized in the processing and transmitting of wire or electronic communications so as not to include the contents of any wire or electronic communications.

18 U.S.C. §3123

(a) . . . Upon an application made under [this statute], the court shall enter an ex parte order authorizing the installation and use of a pen register or trap and trace device . . . if the court finds that the attorney for the Government [or the State law enforcement or investigative officer] has certified to the court that the information likely to be obtained by such installation and use is relevant to an ongoing criminal investigation. [The law enforcement] agency shall ensure that a record will be maintained which will identify —

(i) any officer or officers who installed the device and any officer or officers who accessed the device to obtain information from the network;

(ii) the date and time the device was installed, the date and time the device was uninstalled, and the date, time, and duration of each time the device is accessed to obtain information;

(iii) the configuration of the device at the time of its installation and any subsequent modification thereof; and

(iv) any information which has been collected by the device.

(b) An order issued under this section —

(1) shall specify —

(A) the identity, if known, of the person to whom is leased or in whose name is listed the telephone line to which the pen register or trap and trace device is to be attached;

(B) the identity, if known, of the person who is the subject of the criminal investigation;

(C) the attributes of the communications to which the order applies, including the number or other identifier and, if known, the location of the telephone line or other facility to which the pen register or trap and trace device is to be attached or applied, and, in the case of an order authorizing installation and use of a trap and trace device [requested by state law enforcement officials], the geographic limits of the order; and

(D) a statement of the offense to which the information likely to be obtained by the pen register or trap and trace device relates. . . .

(c) An order issued under this section shall authorize the installation and use of a pen register or a trap and trace device for a period not to exceed sixty days. . . . Extensions of such an order may be granted, but only upon an application for an order under [this statute] and upon the judicial finding required by subsection (a) of this section. The period of extension shall be for a period not to exceed sixty days.

DAMON RICHARDSON v. STATE

865 S.W.2d 944 (Tex. Crim. App. 1993) (en banc)

CLINTON, J.

Appellant was convicted of the offense of engaging in organized criminal activity . . . and the jury assessed punishment at life confinement in the penitentiary and a $10,000 fine. On appeal he contended . . . that the trial court erred in overruling his motion to suppress evidence obtained by use of a pen register because the use of the pen register was a search in contemplation of Article I, §9 of the Texas Constitution; therefore, Article 18.21 [of the Texas Code of Criminal Procedure] is unconstitutional insofar as it authorizes a search without requiring a showing of probable cause.[1] . . .

In March of 1988, officers of the Texas Department of Public Safety were involved in an extensive investigation of a suspected drug ring operating in Lubbock County. The investigation centered around appellant, who was in the Lubbock County Jail awaiting trial for capital murder, and several other individuals residing at the Seven Acres Lodge, a motel in Lubbock. Despite appellant's incarceration, officers believed that he was controlling a cocaine and crack distribution organization using the telephones located in the county jail, by placing calls to a private telephone located at the Seven Acres Lodge. Due to the difficulty in investigating this case through customary investigative techniques, the officers sought court orders authorizing electronic surveillance to assist in their identification of co-conspirators and the modus operandi of the alleged trafficking organization.

On March 30, 1988, in accordance with the provisions of Article 18.21, the officers applied for and received a court order authorizing the installation of a pen register to catalogue the telephone numbers dialed from (806) 555-4729, a telephone at the Seven Acres Lodge. The officers then combined this information with other information outlined in a 56-page affidavit signed by Officer J. A. Randall, and on April 13, 1988, applied for and received a court order authorizing the wiretapping and recording of communications on the same telephone line. The wiretap intercepted numerous incriminating telephone conversations involving appellant and other targeted suspects. [A second pen register was ordered on April 14, and was installed to record numbers dialed from a limited use telephone in the Lubbock County Jail. Prior to trial, Richardson moved to suppress the evidentiary fruit of the pen registers, arguing that the use of a pen register was a search under Article I, §9 of the Texas Constitution.]

Ultimately, in the context of both the Fourth Amendment and Article I, §9, whether the government's installation and use of a pen register constitutes a search necessarily depends upon whether appellant has a "legitimate expectation of privacy" in the numbers he dialed on the telephone. . . . For purposes of the Fourth Amendment, a 5-3 majority of the Supreme Court has held that the installation and use of a pen register is not a search. This is so, the Court observed, because an individual "in all probability" entertains no actual expectation of privacy in the phone numbers he dials, and, even if he did, such an expectation is not "legitimate." Smith v. Maryland, 442 U.S. 735 (1979). The majority reasoned that telephone users "typically know that they must convey numerical information to the phone company; that the phone company has facilities for recording this information; and

1. Article 18.21 authorizes Texas law enforcement's use of pen registers as a means of electronic surveillance. A pen register is a mechanical or electronic device that attaches to a telephone line and is capable of recording outgoing numbers dialed from that line but is not capable of recording the origin of an incoming communication to that line or the content of a communication carried between that line and another line. Although Article 18.21 does establish a number of prerequisites to the issuance of a court order authorizing the use of a pen register, the statute does not require that an applicant show probable cause. The statute merely requires that the application state the installation and utilization of the pen register will be material to the investigation of a criminal offense. . . .

that the phone company does in fact record this information for a variety of legitimate business purposes." Telephone users, therefore, cannot have an actual expectation that the numbers they dial will remain private.

The *Smith* majority further reasoned that even if an individual did have an actual expectation that the numbers he dials would remain secret, such an expectation is not one that society would recognize as reasonable. To the majority, the disclosure of the telephone numbers was similar to other cases in which the Court held that a person has no legitimate expectation of privacy in information he voluntarily turns over to third parties. In particular, the Court noted United States v. Miller, 425 U.S. 435 (1976), which held that the government could access a bank depositor's financial records, including the depositor's monthly statement, checks and deposit slips, without probable cause. The *Miller* Court noted "that the Fourth Amendment does not prohibit the obtaining of information revealed to a third party and conveyed by him to government authorities, even if the information is revealed on the assumption that it will be used only for a limited purpose and the confidence placed in the third party will not be betrayed." Thus, the bank depositor who has voluntarily disclosed certain financial information to the bank and, necessarily, its employees, takes the risk that the information will be conveyed by the bank or its employees to the government. Having assumed this risk, the bank depositor has no legitimate expectation of privacy.

Similarly, the caller who has voluntarily disclosed the telephone number to the telephone company has assumed the risk that the telephone company would reveal these numbers to the police. For this reason the telephone caller has no legitimate expectation of privacy in the telephone numbers dialed. The installation and use of a pen register to record these numbers is therefore not a search under the Fourth Amendment, and no warrant is required.

The Supreme Court's holding in *Smith* has not gone without criticism. Quite the contrary, a number of legal commentators have rejected the Court's holding as making "a mockery of the Fourth Amendment." 1 W. LaFave, Search and Seizure: A Treatise on the Fourth Amendment §2.7(b), at 507 (2d ed. 1987).... LaFave agreed with Justice Marshall's dissent that the mere fact that a telephone user may know the telephone company can monitor his calls for internal reasons does not necessarily mean that he expects "this information to be made available to the public in general or the government in particular." [It] makes no sense to say that the telephone subscriber... is fair game for unrestrained police scrutiny merely because he has surrendered some degree of his privacy for a limited purpose to those with whom he is doing business....

In addition to the commentators, numerous state courts have criticized the Supreme Court's holding in *Smith*. At least seven States have rejected the reasoning of *Smith*, holding that their state constitutions provide an individual with a protected privacy interest in the telephone numbers dialed from a telephone. [The court cited cases from New Jersey, California, Pennsylvania, Colorado, Washington, Idaho, and Hawaii.] All but one of these cases involve construction of a state constitutional provision that is substantially similar to our Article I, §9....

We agree [with these decisions]. The mere fact that a telephone caller has disclosed the number called to the telephone company for the limited purpose of obtaining the services does not invariably lead to the conclusion that the caller has relinquished his expectation of privacy such that the telephone company is free to turn the information over to anyone, especially the police, absent legal process.

Certainly it is true that a general or indiscriminate disclosure of what otherwise may seem private information by its very nature evinces the lack even of a subjective expectation of privacy. Thus, the drug vendor . . . hawking his wares on the street, does not even demonstrate a subjective belief that his activities will remain private. Even if he did, the open nature of the disclosure obviates any possibility that the public would share his belief, and thus he cannot claim an objectively reasonable expectation of privacy. . . .

But whether an individual "assumes the risk" that a more limited disclosure will open the door to public disclosure depends, we think, upon the reasonableness of his subjective belief (if any) that the disclosure will in fact go no further. A selective disclosure may evidence a subjective expectation of privacy; the circumstances in which information is related to a third party may show a unilateral or even a mutual understanding that the information will remain confidential. This is not an understanding that society is invariably willing to recognize as legitimate, however, for society may have no particular stake in the matter. Thus, a subjective expectation of privacy despite a limited disclosure is not always a "reasonable" one.

There are some subjective expectations of privacy, however, that society does sanction as legitimate in spite of limited, confidential disclosure. We would not want to say, for example, that society does not recognize the confidentiality of information imparted to a physician behind the closed doors of an examination room. That certain facts may be revealed in the necessarily candid process of diagnosis and treatment does not mean we no longer have a collective interest in insulating them from public scrutiny. On the contrary, society accepts — indeed, positively insists — that such information, although of necessity partly exposed, should nevertheless retain its essentially private character. In view of this societal imperative, it is hardly fair to reason that the patient "assumed the risk" of public disclosure because of the forthrightness with which he spoke to his doctor.

Although the argument is not quite as compelling, we believe it would be likewise unfair to hold that the customer "assumes the risk" of public disclosure of a number he dials on the telephone. Other than for billing purposes, the telephone company itself has no interest in memorializing that information. Moreover, the telephone company is fiercely protective of what it considers the privacy interest of its customers even in the information it does record in the ordinary course of business — as any private citizen will discover if he attempts to obtain the telephone bill of another customer without that other's express permission.[8] It goes without saying that telecommunications are pervasive in our society. The telephone company's vigilance in protecting from public disclosure the uses to which its customers put their telephones reflects a value that is equally pervasive. As with information imparted to a doctor, we share a common understanding that the numbers we call remain our own affair, and will go no further. Thus, society recognizes as objectively reasonable the expectation of the telephone customer that the numbers he dials as

8. On page 37 of the prefatory pages of the 1992-1993 Greater Austin Telephone Directory printed by Southwestern Bell we find the heading, "Your Rights As a Customer." Under the subheading, "Telecommunications Privacy," we find the following assurance: "We fully safeguard every individual's right to privacy as an essential aspect of our service. We carefully strive to protect communications services from unlawful wiretapping or other illegal interception. Customer service records, credit information and related confidential personal account information are fully protected."

a necessary incident of his use of the telephone will not be published to the rest of the world.

It follows that the use of a pen register may well constitute a "search" under Article I, §9 of the Texas Constitution. The question remaining is whether such a search would be "unreasonable" in the absence of probable cause. If so, then to the extent it authorizes a court ordered pen register without a showing of probable cause, Article 18.21 violates Article I, §9. Because the court of appeals did not decide the question of reasonableness . . . we remand the cause for further disposition.

CAMPBELL, J., dissenting.

The majority perceives the question presented to be the abstract one of whether the State's use of a pen register may constitute a "search" under Article I, §9, of the Texas Constitution. Clearly, however, that is not the question presented. The true question presented is whether appellant has shown that he, as a pretrial detainee in a county jail, had a reasonable expectation of privacy in the telephone numbers he dialed on the jail telephone. [The dissent argued that the appellant had no reasonable expectation of privacy in calls made from jail, and that in any case society would be unwilling to accept such an expectation of privacy.]

Notes

1. *Pen registers as "searches": majority position.* Most state supreme courts ruling on the constitutional question have concluded (unlike the Supreme Court in Smith v. Maryland, 442 U.S. 735 (1979)), that use of a pen register is a "search" within the meaning of the constitution. The cases also conclude that it is a search for the government to compel a telephone company to provide access to *existing* records, as opposed to the creation of new records, which takes place with a pen register. But see Saldana v. State, 846 P.2d 604 (Wyo. 1993) (no violation of state constitution to subpoena toll records for unlisted number).

The federal statute reprinted above has analogs in almost 40 states. The statutes often authorize the use of a pen register after obtaining a court order, based on a showing that the pen register is "likely" to produce information that is "material" or "relevant" to a criminal investigation. See Fla. Stat. §934.33. Are statutes such as these consistent with the conclusion of many state courts that using a pen register is a constitutionally regulated "search"? These statutes also compel the telephone company to cooperate with the government in placing an authorized pen-register device on a telephone. Would telephone companies oppose the passage of a pen-register statute? For discussion of bank secrecy statutes, see Chapter 4, section C.

2. *Electronic Communications Privacy Act.* The Electronic Communications Privacy Act of 1986, 18 U.S.C. §2703, prohibits any "provider of electronic communications" services to the public from disclosing the contents of electronic communications it stores during the transmission process. The statute does not apply to the internal computer networks of computers operated by many employers; it covers instead any provider of electronic communications or computing services to the public, if the transmission occurs on a system that affects interstate or foreign commerce. Despite the statute's general protection from disclosure of electronic message contents, it creates an exception for disclosure to the government. The statute requires the government to obtain a warrant (based on probable cause)

before it can obtain an electronic communication that has been in "electronic storage" for less than 180 days. For communications stored for more than 180 days, the government can obtain them without probable cause if it notifies the owner of the communication and obtains a subpoena or a court order based on "specific and articulable facts showing that there are reasonable grounds to believe that the contents of a wire or electronic communication . . . are relevant and material to an ongoing criminal investigation." Why the different treatment for messages stored longer than 180 days?

Are Internet service providers (ISPs) required to provide the government with records of usage by its users? If the records being requested by the government involve e-mail and communications, they might be covered by the Electronic Communications Privacy Act. But what if the materials sought by the government are not communications, but stored files and documents? Is the delivery of such information by the service provider a matter covered solely by the contractual relationship between the user and the provider?

Problem 7-5. Prescription Privacy

Marcus Brown, a DEA agent, suspected that Nicholas Russo was abusing prescription medicines. Rumor suggested that Santo Buccheri, a Hartford physician, overprescribed pain killers to Russo and failed to maintain proper records. Brown therefore went to pharmacies located near Buccheri's office and Russo's home. Although Brown had no search warrant or probable cause to believe a crime had occurred, he asked each of the pharmacies to provide him with Russo's prescription records. The records contained information about prescriptions that each pharmacy had filled for Russo, including the name of the prescribing physician, the date Russo submitted the prescription to the pharmacy, the type and quantity of drug prescribed, and the price of the drug. The pharmacies complied with Brown's requests. Those records indicated that Russo had obtained a large amount of Tylenol 3, about 8,000 tablets. Brown therefore returned to each pharmacy and requested copies of the actual prescription forms that Russo presented to the pharmacies. Again, the pharmacists cooperated with Brown's request.

The state filed an information charging Russo with 32 counts of obtaining Tylenol with Codeine No. 3 (the active ingredient in Tylenol 3), a controlled substance, by forging a prescription. Russo moved to suppress the records of his prescriptions that the state obtained from the pharmacies without a warrant and without his consent. Russo contended that he had a reasonable expectation of privacy in his prescription records and, therefore, that the state obtained those records in violation of his rights under the federal and state constitutions. A state statute declares that "prescriptions shall be open for inspection only to federal, state, county and municipal officers, whose duty it is to enforce the laws of this state or of the United States relating to controlled substances." How would you rule on the motion to suppress? See State v. Russo, 790 A.2d 1132 (Conn. 2002).

Problem 7-6. Total Information Awareness

After the terrorist attacks on the World Trade Center and the Pentagon in September 2001, the Department of Defense began developing a data system to identify and stop terrorists. The system collected in one database all the publicly available information about an individual's purchases and other electronic transactions. Sophisticated computer programs could then "mine" this data to uncover patterns of behavior by people who make purchases or transactions that raise suspicions of terrorism. For instance, investigators might use the database to identify people who take commercial flying or scuba diving lessons, or people who purchase large amounts of fertilizer.

A government website describes the sorts of "transactional data" for individuals that would be deposited in the Total Information Awareness database: "financial, educational, travel, medical, veterinary, country entry, place/event entry, transportation, housing, critical resources, government, communications." The individual identifiers would be removed from these transactions until the "data mining" process identified persons who called for further investigation.

The columnist William Safire expressed the concerns of civil libertarians and advocates of limited government about this program:

> Every purchase you make with a credit card, every magazine subscription you buy and medical prescription you fill, every Web site you visit and e-mail you send or receive, every academic grade you receive, every bank deposit you make, every trip you book and every event you attend — all these transactions and communications will go into what the Defense Department describes as "a virtual, centralized grand database." To this computerized dossier on your private life from commercial sources, add every piece of information that government has about you — passport application, driver's license and bridge toll records, judicial and divorce records, complaints from nosy neighbors to the F.B.I., your lifetime paper trail plus the latest hidden camera surveillance — and you have the supersnoop's dream: a "Total Information Awareness" about every U.S. citizen.

Safire, "You Are a Suspect," N.Y. Times, Nov. 14, 2002, at 35. He argued that "the government's infinite knowledge about you is its power over you."

Michael Scardaville of the Heritage Foundation, however, supported the program: "Only those already identified as terrorists have anything to fear." He described as follows the safeguards on privacy the system would use:

> Even if they wanted to, TIA employees simply won't have time to monitor who plays football pools, who has asthma, who surfs what websites, or even who deals cocaine or steals cars. They'll begin with intelligence reports about people already suspected of terrorism. . . . Those already identified as terrorists or potential terrorists by the intelligence community then could be monitored through existing public and private databases to build an in-depth portfolio, including contacts and frequent activities. . . . These portfolios should enable authorities to determine whom to watch and where to find them when they suspect a terror strike is imminent.

Scardaville proposed limiting database access to the FBI, the CIA, and the Department of Homeland Security. The TIA program could develop "limited spinoffs" for use by state and local law enforcement and for those working for aviation security or monitoring for epidemics and biological warfare. Scardaville, Targeting Terrorists, National Review, Nov. 25, 2002.

As a member of Congress, would you vote to fund the further development of this program? In 2003 the Department of Defense announced a name change for the program, which was henceforth to be called the "Terrorism Information Awareness" program because the old name "created in some minds the impression that TIA was a system to be used for developing dossiers on U.S. citizens." Despite the change in names, the description of the program remained mostly the same. Congress ultimately cut off most of the funding for the program.

Problem 7-7. Working Texts

Sergeant Jeff Quon works for the Police Department. The Department acquired several alphanumeric pagers capable of sending and receiving text messages. Under the Department's service contract with Arch Wireless, each pager was allotted a limited number of characters sent or received each month. Text messages that exceeded the contract limits would result in additional fees. The Department issued a pager to Quon, which enabled him to communicate more quickly with his fellow employees.

Months before it distributed the new pagers, the Department announced a "Computer Usage, Internet and E-Mail Policy" that applied to all employees. The policy said that the Department "reserves the right to monitor and log all network activity including e-mail and Internet use, with or without notice. Users should have no expectation of privacy or confidentiality when using these resources." Immediately after the release of the Computer Policy, Quon signed a statement acknowledging that he had read and understood the policy.

The Computer Policy did not apply, on its face, to text messaging. Text messages differ from e-mails in an important way. An e-mail sent on a Department computer is transmitted through the Department's own data servers, but a text message sent on one of the Department's pagers is transmitted using wireless radio frequencies from an individual pager to a receiving station owned by Arch Wireless. The text message is routed through Arch Wireless's computer network, where it remains until the recipient's pager or cellular telephone is ready to receive the message, at which point Arch Wireless transmits the message from the station nearest to the recipient. After delivery, Arch Wireless retains a copy on its computer servers. The message does not pass through computers owned by the Department.

Although the Computer Policy did not cover text messages by its explicit terms, the Department made clear to its employees that it would treat text messages the same way as it treated e-mails. At a staff meeting at which Quon was present, Lieutenant Steven Duke, the administrator responsible for the City's contract with Arch Wireless, told officers that messages sent on the pagers "are considered e-mail messages. This means that text messages would be eligible for auditing."

Within the first or second billing cycle after the pagers were distributed, Quon exceeded his monthly text message character allotment. Duke suggested that Quon could reimburse the Department for the overage fee rather than have Duke audit the messages, so Quon wrote a check to the Department for the overage.

Over the next few months, Quon exceeded his character limit three or four times, and reimbursed the Department each time. At this point, Duke declared that he had become "tired of being a bill collector." He decided to determine whether the existing character limit was too low — that is, whether officers such as Quon were having to pay fees for sending work-related messages — or if the overages were for personal messages.

An administrative assistant for the Department requested the transcripts from Arch Wireless for August and September, and the company sent them after verifying that the Department was the subscriber on the accounts. Duke reviewed the transcripts and discovered that many of the messages sent and received on Quon's pager were not work related, and some were sexually explicit. Quon sent or received 456 messages during work hours in the month of August, of which no more than 57 were work related; he sent as many as 80 messages during a single day at work; and on an average workday, Quon sent or received 28 messages, of which only 3 were related to police business. The Department disciplined Quon for misuse of the equipment.

Quon sued the Department, along with several people who had exchanged texts with him, including his ex-wife, a Department employee who was romantically involved with Quon, and a Department employee who worked on a task force with Quon. The plaintiffs raised privacy claims under the Fourth Amendment, 18 U.S.C. §2701 (popularly known as the Stored Communications Act), and state tort laws. The Stored Communications Act amended the federal wiretap laws to prohibit any "person or entity" providing either "an electronic communication service" or a "remote computing service" to the public from "knowingly" divulging to any person or entity "the contents of a communication while in electronic storage by that service," or divulging a "record or other information pertaining to a subscriber or customer of such service." 18 U.S.C. §2702(a).

You are the district court judge. Did Quon have a reasonable expectation of privacy in the content of his text messages? Does the reasonableness of Duke's audit depend on his intent? For instance, would it matter if the purpose of the audit was to determine if Quon was using his pager to play games and waste time, or if the purpose instead was to determine the efficacy of the existing character limits to ensure that officers were not paying hidden work-related costs? Would you ask the parties to explore alternatives to the audit, such as warning Quon at the beginning of the month that his future messages would be audited, or asking Quon himself to redact the transcript of his messages? Finally, consider whether your analysis would change if the Department were a private security firm instead of an entity of municipal government. See City of Ontario, California v. Quon, 130 S. Ct. 2619 (2010).

Notes

1. *Access to transaction records and encryption.* The government can obtain access to transactional information in the hands of third parties (such as retailers) by warrant or subpoena. More frequently, however, the third party consents to provide the information. When it comes to stored communications, however, none of these techniques will give the government access to information that has been "encrypted" to make it unreadable to anyone other than the intended recipient, who holds the encryption "key." From time to time, the federal government asks the creators of encryption software to give the government a "key" to unlock the encryption, a key that the government would be able to use only after demonstrating

probable cause to search. During 1996 congressional hearings on this question, FBI Director Louis Freeh made the case for government access to encrypted messages:

> [Conventional] encryption not only can prevent electronic surveillance efforts, which in terms of numbers are conducted sparingly, but it also can prevent police officers on a daily basis from conducting basic searches and seizures of computers and files. Without an ability to promptly decrypt encrypted criminal or terrorist communications and computer files, we in the law enforcement community will not be able to effectively investigate or prosecute society's most dangerous felons or, importantly, save lives in kidnappings and in numerous other life and death cases. . . .
>
> In a very fundamental way, conventional encryption has the effect of upsetting the delicate legal balance of the Fourth Amendment, since when a judge issues a search warrant it will be of no practical value when this type of encryption is encountered. Constitutionally-effective search and seizure law assumes, and the American public fully expects, that with warrant in hand law enforcement officers will be able to quickly act upon seized materials to solve and prevent crimes, and that prosecutors will be able to put understandable evidence before a jury. Conventional encryption virtually destroys this centuries old legal principle.

What did Director Freeh fear if unbreakable communications were allowed?

2. *Financial, medical, and other personal information held by third parties.* Pharmaceutical records offer just one important instance of a large range of personal information held by third parties. Major categories of information include banking records and other financial records, and health and medical records. The United States Supreme Court has been unwilling to find constitutional privacy limits on government access to such information. See United States v. Miller, 425 U.S. 435 (1976) (no reasonable expectation of privacy in bank records). State courts have divided on the question of constitutional privacy rights in banking records and pharmaceutical records. See State v. Skinner, 10 So.3d 1212 (La. 2009); State v. McAllister, 875 A.2d 866 (N.J. 2005); Stephen E. Henderson, Learning from All Fifty States: How to Apply the Fourth Amendment and Its State Analogs to Protect Third Party Information from Unreasonable Search, 55 Cath. U. L. Rev. 373 (2006).

Both Congress and state legislatures have often stepped in where courts have hesitated to act. To explore some examples, consult the web extension for this chapter at *http://www.crimpro.com/extension/ch07*.

3. *Combinations of government-held information.* Once the government gains access to information, is any search or seizure issue involved in how the government uses the information? The U.S. Department of the Treasury runs an investigative program, known as "FinCEN," designed to make the most of the information scattered in various government files. The records that FinCEN reviews are based on reports that banks and other institutions and individuals must submit to comply with federal statutes and regulations. By using computers to combine and analyze the information held legitimately in various government files, law enforcers can obtain a more complete picture of an individual's activities or can note trends among certain groups of people that could justify closer scrutiny. This particular program focuses on financial crimes, such as tax evasion or money laundering. Does this technique hold promise for other sorts of investigations? How might one construct an argument that the assembling of many existing bits of data about an individual, contained in different records, creates new information that should be deemed a "search" regulated by the constitution?

Most search and seizure law relates to the government's initial access to information. The FinCEN program offers an example of government *use* of information to which it has undeniable access. Is the use of information relevant to the constitutional requirement of "reasonableness"? See Harold Krent, Of Diaries and Data Banks: Use Restrictions Under the Fourth Amendment, 74 Tex. L. Rev. 49 (1995). If a legislature, or some executive policymaker, decided to place some limit on the government's use of legitimately obtained information, what sort of limit would be feasible? Should the statute or policy impose a time limit on the use of the information? Should it force the government to use the information only in the enforcement of specified laws?

4. *DNA databases.* One especially powerful class of information that the government holds is genetic information, revealed through chemical patterns in an individual's DNA. Most states have now firmly established the validity, as an evidentiary matter, of some types of DNA evidence. Beyond the evidentiary and technical aspects of DNA evidence, its use can be quite dramatic. DNA evidence has proven the innocence of some people wrongly convicted.

But individual use of DNA to establish whether a known individual was (or was not) the likely offender is very different from having a broad database that allows the government to match any genetic material to a particular person. A database containing genetic information about many individuals, and perhaps an entire population, might allow investigators who find hairs, blood, semen, or mucus to identify quickly the most likely suspects.

Every state in the country has passed legislation authorizing a DNA database made up of samples from various categories of citizens, most often groups of criminal offenders or suspects. The military obtains genetic information from every member of the armed services. Some states collect identifying information, such as fingerprints, as part of providing basic services, such as a driver's license. It may not be long until the basic elements of citizenship and commerce obligate individuals to provide a sample of their DNA.

The development of genetic databases raises a huge range of issues. Those issues focus on how the information is obtained, how it may be used, and who will have access to it. Take Massachusetts as an example. The statute authorizes collection and analysis of DNA samples from defendants convicted of any of the 33 enumerated felonies, and it applies retroactively to those currently incarcerated, on probation, or on parole as a result of such a conviction. If a conviction is later dismissed, relevant DNA records may be expunged by court order. Law enforcement officers and correction personnel are authorized to use "reasonable force" to collect the DNA samples. Once samples are collected, the state crime laboratory performs "DNA typing tests" to generate numerical identification information. This numerical identifier becomes part of the state DNA database, and is also forwarded to the Federal Bureau of Investigation for storage and maintenance in a national index system.

The crime lab forwards a DNA record to local police departments, to the Department of Correction, to a sheriff's department, to the parole board, or to prosecuting officers on written or electronic request. The crime lab also must disclose DNA records to "local, state and federal criminal justice and law enforcement agencies, including forensic laboratories serving such agencies, for identification purposes in order to further official criminal investigations or prosecutions." Defendants who are charged with crimes as a result of a DNA database search are provided with a copy of their own DNA record. The director of the crime lab also has discretion to release DNA records for identifying victims of mass disasters or for "advancing other humanitarian purposes."

If you, as an attorney in Massachusetts, hoped to challenge the constitutionality of this law, who would be your ideal client? What constitutional texts and doctrines would you invoke? Landry v. Attorney General, 709 N.E.2d 1085 (Mass. 1999). If you were the director of the state crime laboratory, what regulations would you issue to address any potential constitutional or political difficulties? How would you respond to a legislative proposal to expand the DNA database to all arrestees in the state?

5. *Nongovernmental infringement of privacy (or "private privacy").* Criminal procedure and its constitutional superstructure speak to the relationship between citizens' privacy and their government's power to invade that privacy. On the other hand, infringement of privacy rights by nongovernmental actors has historically been left to private law. Tort claims for trespass, conversion, assault, battery, libel, slander, and invasion of privacy allow private parties to recover damages, and a handful of criminal charges reinforce those privacy interests.

There are various private actors who might collect information about criminal suspects, including family members, friends, employers, teachers, or roommates. Private security firms employ a growing number of people to prevent and ferret out crime. Since traditional constitutional limits on searches and seizures do not apply to "private" searches, police and prosecutors might simply encourage private actors to conduct searches and interrogations, and then turn over their evidence to the authorities. However, courts hold private searchers to public standards when the private action is conducted "at the behest of" or "in partnership with" government authorities.

Courts uniformly assess whether there is a sufficiently close link between a private search and government agents in deciding whether evidence found or obtained from a private search should be admitted. Courts look to a variety of factors, including prior agreements between private actors and government agents that a private agent will conduct a search. The application of this loose standard, however, leads to varying outcomes, both across and within jurisdictions. For an exploration of the wide range of issues involving "private privacy," see the web extension for this chapter at *http://www.crimpro.com/extension/ch07*.

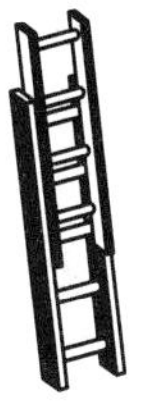

6. *Searches by private security.* Private security agents outnumber sworn law enforcement officers. David Sklansky summarizes the figures as of 1990:

> [There] were 393,000 "proprietary," or in-house, security guards throughout the United States (i.e., guards employed directly by the owner of the property they protect), and 520,000 employees of "contract" guard companies (i.e., companies that hire out guards). [Guards] constitute all but 2-5% of those employed by contract guard companies. The more conservative figure of 5% yields 484,000 contract guards and 877,000 guards overall. There were roughly 600,000 sworn law enforcement officers throughout the country in 1990.

Private Police, 46 UCLA L. Rev. 1165 at n.27 (1999). If the government abolished its police force and a jurisdiction relied entirely on private security, would constitutional limits on search and seizure apply? Should private security agents stay within the same restrictions as other private actors?

7. *Privacy torts in partnership with criminal procedure.* Every state except Rhode Island provides a cause of action for "intentional intrusion upon the solitude or seclusion of another." Some states allow the action as part of common law tort doctrine; in others a cause of action for invasion of privacy appears in state statutes. For instance, Nebraska Statute §20-203 provides that any "person, firm, or corporation that trespasses or intrudes upon any natural person in his or her place of solitude or seclusion, if the intrusion would be highly offensive to a reasonable person, shall be liable for invasion of privacy." Whether based in common law or statutory causes of actions, the law of intentional intrusion on seclusion is relatively unformed. Is this an area of social interaction generally in need of greater legal regulation? If not, are there avenues other than civil tort claims to bolster a sense (and perhaps the reality) of individual privacy, and to limit invasions of privacy by private actors? Are there some actors in particular, such as firms that gather and sell information about individuals, that merit particular regulation?

More familiar than claims for physical invasion of privacy are claims that someone, often a media outlet, has published information that invades the claimant's privacy. It is important to distinguish such claims from claims that another person has reported false information or portrayed the claimant in a false light, which includes causes of action for defamation, libel, and slander.

8. *Web privacy.* Few users of the World Wide Web — a technology whose full name is already an anachronism — know how much information is conveyed when they access a website. Companies and individuals, both legitimate and shady, use the Web to gain information about consumers as a group, and as individuals. The range of issues is substantial. See Daniel J. Solove, Marc Rotenberg & Paul Schwartz, Information Privacy Law (Aspen 2006); The Privacy Law Sourcebook (Marc Rotenberg ed., EPIC 2004). It is helpful to think in terms of the interests and claims that different actors might make in asserting a right to gather information, or the uses of that information, or a right to withhold information. Many websites have privacy policies; when did you last read one?

The technology and its uses shift far more rapidly than existing legal structures. This creates a special challenge for users, lawyers, and courts deciding the limits of existing statutory law and exploring the boundaries of common law claims developed in different times and places. See, e.g., Matthew A. Goldberg, The Googling of Online Privacy: Gmail, Search-Engine Histories and the New Frontier of Protecting Private Information on the Web, 9 Lewis & Clark L. Rev. 249 (2005).

9. *E-mail privacy.* If your employer opens mail that you send from work, the employer may be subject to criminal prosecution under 18 U.S.C. §1702 ("Whoever takes any letter, postal card, or package out of any post office or any authorized depository for mail matter . . . before it has been delivered to the person to whom it was directed, with the design to obstruct the correspondence, or to pry into the business or secrets of another, or opens, secretes, embezzles, or destroys the same, shall be fined under this title or imprisoned not more than five years, or both."). The employer may also be subject to a statutory or common law civil suit for privacy infringement. Add an "e-" to the word "mail," however, and the employer can — and, in the case of many, especially larger employers, probably does — read and review it. See City of Ontario, Cal. v. Quon, 130 S. Ct. 2619 (2010) (review of text messages sent by police officers on departmental pagers to determine source of billing overruns revealed that officer used pager during work hours for personal messages; review was reasonable because it was motivated by legitimate work-related

purpose, and not excessive in scope). The only significant limits on the authority of employers to read employee e-mail come in the contractual relationships between the employee and employer. Of course, employers are not the only potential uninvited readers of a person's e-mail.

The analogy of e-mail to "snail mail" has some vitality with respect to third parties — including the government — seeking to read e-mail without the permission of employers or Internet service providers. However, the analogy has fared poorly with regard to employers or Internet service providers, where the privacy of an individual's communication depends largely on the contract. See Meir S. Hornung, Think Before You Type: A Look at Email Privacy in the Workplace, 11 Fordham J. Corp. & Fin. Law (2005). Should individuals have enforceable privacy interests against nongovernmental parties with respect to e-mail that resides on third-party or corporate computers? Should the answer depend on social norms or laws beyond the scope of any contract between the person and her employer? Limits on employer review of employee e-mail or Web usage may come from quasi-contractual relationships defining professional association, such as the relationship of faculty and students to a university under the principles of academic freedom.

VIII

Interrogations

Some crimes go unsolved unless the perpetrator confesses. Confessions are especially important in some violent crimes, such as murder and robbery; they are less important in possession crimes or transactional crimes (such as drug offenses or fraud), where a greater range of testimonial and physical evidence is often available. Beyond these general observations, however, it is hard to determine the exact number and types of cases in which police interrogation is necessary to solve the crime.

Many police officers are convinced that interrogations and confessions are indispensable in a broad range of cases. Field studies have certainly confirmed that the police interrogate the great majority of all suspects in custody — roughly 80 to 90 percent of them. See Paul Cassell and Bret Hayman, Police Interrogation in the 1990s: An Empirical Study of the Effects of *Miranda,* 43 UCLA L. Rev. 839 (1996); Project, Interrogations in New Haven: The Impact of *Miranda,* 76 Yale L.J. 1519 (1967).

If a suspect does provide the police with incriminating information, this has a considerable effect on the later processing of her case. People who confess to the police are more likely to be charged with a crime, less likely to have the charges against them dismissed, more likely to plead guilty, more likely to be convicted, and more likely to receive a more serious punishment. See Richard Leo, Inside the Interrogation Room, 86 J. Crim. L. & Criminology 266 (1996). Jurors consider evidence of a confession by the defendant to be among the most important types of information that a prosecutor can present. See Saul Kassin & Katherine Neumann, On the Power of Confession Evidence: An Experimental Test of the Fundamental Difference Hypothesis, 21 Law & Hum. Behav. 469 (1997).

In short, the confession of a criminal suspect can be a pivotal moment in the investigation and processing of a criminal case. What are the legal obligations of the police and other government agents who interrogate suspects in the hope of obtaining an outright confession or some admission leading to incriminating evidence?

A. VOLUNTARINESS OF CONFESSIONS

Courts have long declared that an involuntary confession cannot be a valid source of prosecution evidence. However, the precise reasons why involuntary confessions are considered objectionable, and the factors that can demonstrate the involuntariness of the confession, have shifted over the years. The following materials consider the impact of physical abuse, promises, threats, and lies on those courts considering whether a confession is voluntary.

1. Physical Abuse and Deprivations

Not so long ago, police in the United States used physical violence widely when they interrogated suspects. In 1931, the National Commission on Law Observance and Enforcement (known as the Wickersham Commission) collected evidence from current and former police officers and from many observers of police interrogation practices. The Commission concluded as follows:

> The third degree — the inflicting of pain, physical or mental, to extract confessions or statements — is widespread throughout the country. Physical brutality is extensively practiced. The methods are various. They range from beating to harsher forms of torture. The commoner forms are beating with the fists or with some implement, especially the rubber hose, that inflicts pain but is not likely to leave permanent visible scars.
>
> The method most commonly employed is protracted questioning. By this we mean questioning — at times by relays of questioners — so protracted that the prisoner's energies are spent and his powers of resistance overcome. . . . Methods of intimidation adjusted to the age or mentality of the victim are frequently used alone or in combination with other practices. The threats are usually of bodily injury. They have gone to the extreme of procuring a confession at the point of a pistol or through fear of a mob. . . .
>
> In considerably over half of the States, instances of the third degree practice have occurred in the last 10 years. . . . Fifteen representative cities were visited during the last 12 months by our field investigators. In 10 of them there was no doubt as to the existence of third-degree practices at that time.

Some police officers argued that third-degree tactics were justified, for a number of reasons (again, as summarized by the Wickersham Commission):

- [The] third degree is used only against the guilty.
- [Obstacles] in the way of the police make it almost impossible to obtain convictions except by third-degree methods. [Through] intimidation, bribery, and all kinds of political connections criminals are often set free. . . . Consequently they hope to build up such a solid case on the basis of a confession that the prisoner will, in spite of all obstacles, be convicted.
- [Police] brutality is an inevitable and therefore an excusable reaction to the brutality of criminals.
- [Restrictions] on the third degree may impair the morale of the police.

- [The] existence of organized gangs in large cities renders traditional legal limitations outworn.

How might you reply to each of these arguments? Could these same arguments be relevant in discussing other interrogation techniques that do not involve physical violence or intimidation?

Five years after the Wickersham Commission report appeared, the Supreme Court issued a major ruling on the question of coerced confessions. As early as 1897, the Court had considered the validity of confessions obtained by federal law enforcement officers, concluding in Bram v. United States, 168 U.S. 532 (1897), that the Fifth Amendment's self-incrimination clause limited coercive police interrogations. However, the Fifth Amendment did not apply to the states at that point, and it was unclear whether federal law placed any limits on the use of an involuntary confession in state court.

■ ED BROWN v. MISSISSIPPI

297 U.S. 278 (1936)

HUGHES, C.J.*

The question in this case is whether convictions, which rest solely upon confessions shown to have been extorted by officers of the State by brutality and violence, are consistent with the due process of law required by the Fourteenth Amendment of the Constitution of the United States.

[Ed Brown, Henry Shields, and Yank Ellington] were indicted for the murder of one Raymond Stewart, whose death occurred on March 30, 1934. They were indicted on April 4, 1934, and were then arraigned and pleaded not guilty. Counsel were appointed by the court to defend them. Trial was begun the next morning and was concluded on the following day, when they were found guilty and sentenced to death.

Aside from the confessions, there was no evidence sufficient to warrant the submission of the case to the jury. [Defendants testified] that the confessions were false and had been procured by physical torture. The case went to the jury with instructions, upon the request of defendants' counsel, that if the jury had reasonable doubt as to the confessions having resulted from coercion, and that they were not true, they were not to be considered as evidence.

[The state supreme court refused to overturn the convictions on appeal.] The grounds of the decision were (1) that immunity from self-incrimination is not essential to due process of law, and (2) that the failure of the trial court to exclude the confessions after the introduction of evidence showing their incompetency, in the absence of a request for such exclusion, did not deprive the defendants of life or liberty without due process of law. . . .

That the evidence established that [the confessions] were procured by coercion was not questioned. . . . There is no dispute as to the facts upon this point and as they

* [Justices Van Devanter, McReynolds, Brandeis, Sutherland, Butler, Stone, Roberts, and Cardozo joined in this opinion. — EDS.]

are clearly and adequately stated in the dissenting opinion of Judge Griffith . . . — showing both the extreme brutality of the measures to extort the confessions and the participation of the state authorities — we quote this part of his opinion in full, as follows:

> The crime with which these defendants, all ignorant negroes, are charged, was discovered about one o'clock P.M. on Friday, March 30, 1934. On that night one Dial, a deputy sheriff, accompanied by others, came to the home of Ellington, one of the defendants, and requested him to accompany them to the house of the deceased, and there a number of white men were gathered, who began to accuse the defendant of the crime. Upon his denial they seized him, and with the participation of the deputy they hanged him by a rope to the limb of a tree, and having let him down, they hung him again, and when he was let down the second time, and he still protested his innocence, he was tied to a tree and whipped, and still declining to accede to the demands that he confess, he was finally released and he returned with some difficulty to his home, suffering intense pain and agony. The record of the testimony shows that the signs of the rope on his neck were plainly visible during the so-called trial. A day or two thereafter the said deputy, accompanied by another, returned to the home of the said defendant and arrested him, and departed with the prisoner towards the jail in an adjoining county, but went by a route which led into the State of Alabama; and while on the way, in that State, the deputy stopped and again severely whipped the defendant, declaring that he would continue the whipping until he confessed, and the defendant then agreed to confess to such a statement as the deputy would dictate, and he did so, after which he was delivered to jail.
>
> The other two defendants, Ed Brown and Henry Shields, were also arrested and taken to the same jail. On Sunday night, April 1, 1934, the same deputy, accompanied by a number of white men, one of whom was also an officer, and by the jailer, came to the jail, and the two last named defendants were made to strip and they were laid over chairs and their backs were cut to pieces with a leather strap with buckles on it, and they were likewise made by the said deputy definitely to understand that the whipping would be continued unless and until they confessed, and not only confessed, but confessed in every matter of detail as demanded by those present; and in this manner the defendants confessed the crime, and as the whippings progressed and were repeated, they changed or adjusted their confession in all particulars of detail so as to conform to the demands of their torturers. When the confessions had been obtained in the exact form and contents as desired by the mob, they left with the parting admonition and warning that, if the defendants changed their story at any time in any respect from that last stated, the perpetrators of the outrage would administer the same or equally effective treatment. . . .
>
> The evidence upon which the conviction was obtained was the so-called confessions. Without this evidence a peremptory instruction to find for the defendants would have been inescapable. The defendants were put on the stand, and by their testimony the facts and the details thereof as to the manner by which the confessions were extorted from them were fully developed, and it is further disclosed by the record that the same deputy. Dial, under whose guiding hand and active participation the tortures to coerce the confessions were administered, was actively in the performance of the supposed duties of a court deputy in the courthouse and in the presence of *the* prisoners during what is denominated, in complimentary terms, the trial of these defendants. This deputy was put on the stand by the state in rebuttal, and admitted the whippings. It is interesting to note that in his testimony with reference to the whipping of the defendant Ellington, and in response to the inquiry as to how severely he was whipped, the deputy stated, "Not too much for a negro; not as much as I would have done if it were

left to me." Two others who had participated in these whippings were introduced and admitted it — not a single witness was introduced who denied it. . . .

I.

The State stresses the statement in Twining v. New Jersey, 211 U.S. 78 (1908), that "exemption from compulsory self-incrimination in the courts of the States is not secured by any part of the Federal Constitution." . . . But the question of the right of the State to withdraw the privilege against self-incrimination is not here involved. The compulsion to which the quoted statements refer is that of the processes of justice by which the accused may be called as a witness and required to testify. Compulsion by torture to extort a confession is a different matter.

The State is free to regulate the procedure of its courts in accordance with its own conceptions of policy, unless in so doing it "offends some principle of justice so rooted in the traditions and conscience of our people as to be ranked as fundamental." The State may abolish trial by jury. It may dispense with indictment by a grand jury and substitute complaint or information. But the freedom of the State in establishing its policy is the freedom of constitutional government and is limited by the requirement of due process of law. Because a State may dispense with a jury trial, it does not follow that it may substitute trial by ordeal. The rack and torture chamber may not be substituted for the witness stand. The State may not permit an accused to be hurried to conviction under mob domination — where the whole proceeding is but a mask — without supplying corrective process. The State may not deny to the accused the aid of counsel. Nor may a State, through the action of its officers, contrive a conviction through the pretense of a trial which in truth is "but used as a means of depriving a defendant of liberty through a deliberate deception of court and jury by the presentation of testimony known to be perjured." Mooney v. Holohan, 294 U.S. 103 (1935). And the trial equally is a mere pretense where the state authorities have contrived a conviction resting solely upon confessions obtained by violence. . . . It would be difficult to conceive of methods more revolting to the sense of justice than those taken to procure the confessions of these petitioners, and the use of the confessions thus obtained as the basis for conviction and sentence was a clear denial of due process. . . .

II.

. . . In the instant case, the trial court was fully advised by the undisputed evidence of the way in which the confessions had been procured. The trial court knew that there was no other evidence upon which conviction and sentence could be based. Yet it proceeded to permit conviction and to pronounce sentence. The conviction and sentence were void for want of the essential elements of due process. . . .

Notes

1. *Disappearance of the third degree.* Thirty-six years after the appearance of the Wickersham Commission report, another national commission reported the virtual disappearance of physical coercion as an interrogation technique: "today the third

degree is almost non-existent." President's Commission on Criminal Justice and the Administration of Justice, The Challenge of Crime in a Free Society (1967). Physical brutality and intimidation disappeared in part because of political pressure from the public, outraged by the findings of the Wickersham Commission and countless similar news accounts. Would these practices have disappeared, even without the Supreme Court's ruling in *Brown*? During the 30 years following *Brown,* due process claims of involuntary confessions became a staple of the Supreme Court docket. The Court ultimately decided more than 30 such cases. Over time, the nature of the police conduct in question shifted away from physical violence or threats of violence to more subtle physical deprivations and psychological coercion. However, the move away from physical deprivation happened slower in some places than others. In particular, physical abuse of black defendants in Southern states continued through the 1940s. See Michael Klarman, Is the Supreme Court Sometimes Irrelevant? Race and the Southern Criminal Justice System in the World War II Era, 89 J. Am. Hist. 119 (2002). The allegations also still arise in rare cases from the present day. See People v. Richardson, 917 N.E.2d 501 (Ill. 2009) (confession from teenage suspect was voluntary, even though it was obtained a few hours after he was punched by an officer in the jail; interrogating officers worked with separate subdivision of department and in different part of the building from the jail).

2. *Physical deprivations: modern limits.* Although physical abuse such as striking a suspect has largely disappeared from interrogations in this country, one can still find examples of physical deprivations, such as depriving a suspect of food or sleep for some period of time. Courts say that some deprivations are tolerable while others are not. Up to a point, interrogators can limit the sleep or food available to the suspect. See Payne v. Arkansas, 356 U.S. 560 (1958) (confession coerced when defendant given two sandwiches during 40-hour detention and interrogations). What if the interrogator fails to provide the suspect with cigarettes?

After the physical coercion in police interrogations withered away, the legal system still faced questions about psychological manipulation during interrogations. If the *Brown* court prohibited the use of "coerced" or "involuntary" confessions, what types of psychological pressures might qualify under that standard? One recurring source of psychological pressure that has been influential with courts has been the extended isolation of the defendant from family, friends, legal counsel, and other support. See Fikes v. Alabama, 352 U.S. 191 (1957) (isolation for more than a week, confession involuntary).

3. *Length of interrogation.* Interrogators find greater success with suspects after lengthier interrogation sessions. In one survey, 631 police investigators estimated that the mean length of interrogations of suspects is 1.6 hours. See Saul M. Kassin, et al., Police Interviewing and Interrogation: A Self-Report Survey of Police Practices and Beliefs, 31 Law and Human Behavior 381-400 (2007). Criminologist Richard Leo, who observed about 180 police interrogations, conducted a statistical study concluding that the length of an interrogation is one of the strongest determinants of its success. Richard Leo, Inside the Interrogation Room, 86 J. Crim. L. & Criminology 266 (1996). At the same time, lengthy interrogations create a risk that a court will later find any confession to be involuntary. Ashcraft v. Tennessee, 322 U.S. 143 (1944) (continuous 36-hour interrogation, confession involuntary); cf. State v. Harris, 105 P.3d 1258 (Kan. 2005) (detention of a suspect by shackling him to floor of interrogation room for seven hours did not render his subsequent confession involuntary; suspect was questioned for two and a half hours and denied

access to telephone, but allowed to take bathroom breaks). There is no clear time limit that will create an involuntary confession under the "totality of the circumstances," but many interrogators believe that the risk goes up once the session extends past three or four hours.

4. *Delay in presenting a suspect to a judicial officer.* The rules of criminal procedure in most jurisdictions require the police to arrange for the suspect's prompt appearance before a judicial officer. The rules in some states specify a time period. See Ariz. R. Crim. Proc. 4.1 ("A person arrested shall be taken before a magistrate without unnecessary delay. If the person is not brought before a magistrate within 24 hours after arrest, he or she shall immediately be released"); Cal. Penal Code §825 (defendant shall "be taken before the magistrate without unnecessary delay, and, in any event, within 48 hours after his or her arrest, excluding Sundays and holidays").

The Supreme Court has declared that any violation of the time rules contained in the Federal Rules of Criminal Procedure will require suppression of confessions obtained as a result of that delay. This requirement (declared under the Court's so-called supervisory power over federal law enforcement) is known as the *McNabb-Mallory* rule, after McNabb v. United States, 318 U.S. 332 (1943), and Mallory v. United States, 354 U.S. 449 (1957). See also Corley v. United States, 129 S. Ct. 1558 (2009) (federal statute addressing voluntariness of confessions used in federal court did not supplant Federal Rule of Criminal Procedure 5(a), which embodies the "prompt presentment" requirement of *McNabb-Mallory*; statute makes *McNabb-Mallory* inapplicable to voluntary statements obtained within six hours of arrest, but leaves the rule otherwise intact).

Although most states have a time-limit provision in their rules of procedure, most state courts have rejected the *McNabb-Mallory* rule and have declared instead that a violation of the timeliness requirement will not lead to automatic suppression but will be one part of the "totality of the circumstances" that could indicate an involuntary confession. Fewer than 10 states follow the per se federal rule. See Commonwealth v. Perez, 845 A.2d 779 (Pa. 2004) (disavowed state's bright-line rule with a "totality of the circumstances" test for determining the admissibility of statements made during delays in arraignment). Some states have special rules (embodied in statutes, court rules, or constitutional due process rulings) requiring prompt presentation of *juveniles* to a judicial officer. See W. Va. Code, §49-5-8(d); In re Steven William T., 499 S.E.2d 876 (W. Va. 1997).

5. *Vulnerability of suspect.* The Court in *Brown* mentioned the "ignorance" of the suspects. Many other cases assessing the voluntariness of a confession for due process purposes have also considered the vulnerability of the suspect. A suspect who is especially young or who is suffering from illness or injury will be more likely to succeed in claiming that a confession was involuntary. See Beecher v. Alabama, 408 U.S. 234 (1972) (suspect confesses while under influence of morphine and in pain from gunshot wound, confession involuntary); Haley v. Ohio, 332 U.S. 596 (1948) (15-year-old interrogated with no advice from family or friends, confession involuntary). Conversely, a suspect who is mature and well educated will find it more difficult to sustain a claim of involuntariness.

6. *Torture, truth, and need.* Exactly what is objectionable about relying on confessions obtained through torture? If the problem is unreliable information, could that be cured by an evidentiary rule requiring independent corroboration of anything learned through physical abuse of a suspect? If the objection is abuse of police powers, could that risk be addressed through procedures specifying when physical

coercion would be allowed, and the types of physical techniques the police could use? Are there situations in criminal law enforcement that could justify torture? What if the life of a hostage is at stake, or there is a possibility of great loss of life from an act of terror? See John Langbein, Torture and the Law of Proof (1977).

These questions are not merely academic. In the aftermath of the terrorist attacks in New York City and Washington on September 11, 2001, lawyers and government officials started to anticipate settings where torture might be appropriate. During military operations in Afghanistan in 2001 and 2002, U.S. armed forces captured enemy combatants. Agents of the Central Intelligence Agency interrogated the detainees at locations near the fighting, and for months after their capture at the military detention facility at Guantanamo Bay in Cuba. The interrogators used "stress and duress" and "waterboarding" techniques. For instance, detainees who refused to cooperate were kept standing or kneeling for hours while wearing black hoods or spray-painted goggles. Some were allegedly held in awkward and painful positions, or were subjected to 24-hour lighting to disrupt their sleep. In some cases, the United States turned captured combatants over to foreign governments known to use torture during interrogations. News developments related to this topic appear on the web extension for this chapter at *http://www.crimpro.com/extension/ch08*. Do the techniques described above make any confessions of the detainees involuntary? Are such techniques acceptable so long as the government pursues no criminal charges against the detainee? So long as the interrogation takes place outside the territory of the United States?

2. *Promises and Threats*

Only rarely does a suspect volunteer a confession without any effort by the police to convince the suspect that a confession would be worthwhile. When an interrogator tries to convince a suspect of the value of a confession, is it proper to make promises or threats of any type? Are these techniques objectionable for the same reasons that one might object to physical torture during interrogations?

■ STATE v. JAMI DEL SWANIGAN

106 P.3d 39 (Kan. 2005)

NUSS, J.

. . . Shortly before 4 A.M. on October 26, 2000, the Kwik Shop on West Cloud Street in Salina was robbed. According to clerk Krystal Keefer, she saw a black man put his hand up to the glass of the front window and look inside. He then rushed in the front door with a gun. Several times the robber told her to hurry and at one point told her that he would shoot her or kill her if she did not go faster. She opened the cash drawer, grabbed the bills, and handed them to the robber. As she began to grab the change, the robber turned and ran out the front door to the east. The robber stole $100 to $102. . . .

Surveillance cameras at the Kwik Shop captured video images of the robber. The man was wearing a blue bandana over his nose and mouth, blue denim shorts, a long-sleeved black or blue shirt, tennis shoes, and white socks. A photograph of the robber taken from the video was posted at the police station, and Lieutenant Christopher Trocheck believed the person shown to be Jami Swanigan.

Five days after the robbery, Shari Lanham, the lead investigator, [went to Swanigan's home and asked] if he would come to the police department to answer questions about this robbery and other recent convenience store robberies in Salina. He agreed and rode in a patrol car to the station. Upon his arrival, he was placed in a locked waiting room for 30 to 45 minutes before the interrogation began.

The interrogation lasted from 5:03 P.M. until 6:20 P.M., with all but the first few minutes recorded on audiotape. . . . Swanigan first denied knowing anything about the robberies, but eventually said he had heard Marcus Brown was involved. Lanham falsely told Swanigan that his fingerprints had been found at the scene. She also informed him that he had been caught on the surveillance camera. Swanigan had no explanation for either fact, except that he had possibly been at the store before.

After Swanigan took a bathroom break, Lieutenant Mike Sweeney, who was in charge of criminal investigations and who supervised Lanham, joined the interrogation. Swanigan gave Sweeney and Lanham several different stories, but each version contained facts that were contrary to what the officers knew from the eyewitnesses. When confronted with the discrepancies, Swanigan then denied any involvement in the robbery.

Investigator James Feldman then joined the interrogation. Right after Feldman's comments, Swanigan confessed to the robbery. When a discrepancy arose over the clothes the robber had worn, Feldman showed Swanigan a photo from the surveillance video. Swanigan immediately denied the photo was of him and denied that he had any involvement in the robbery. Based primarily upon his interrogation — since latent fingerprints taken from the store, including the front window, were found not to be his — he was arrested and charged with aggravated robbery. . . .

In Swanigan's motion to suppress, he alleged that his statements were not voluntary, knowing, or intelligent under the totality of the circumstances. Specifically, Swanigan alleged that the police used coercive and deceptive tactics, including providing him false information that his fingerprints matched those found at the crime scene and promising that his cooperation in the investigation would help him. [The court denied his motion to suppress the confession.]

In reviewing a district court's decision regarding suppression, this court reviews the factual underpinnings of the decision by a substantial competent evidence standard and the ultimate legal conclusion by a de novo standard with independent judgment. This court does not reweigh evidence, pass on the credibility of witnesses, or resolve conflicts in the evidence. We stated additional considerations specifically concerning confessions in State v. Sanders, 33 P.3d 596 (Kan. 2001):

> In determining whether a confession is voluntary, a court is to look at the totality of the circumstances. The burden of proving that a confession or admission is admissible is on the prosecution, and the required proof is by a preponderance of the evidence. Factors bearing on the voluntariness of a statement by an accused include the duration and manner of the interrogation; the ability of the accused on request to communicate with the outside world; the accused's age, intellect, and background; and the fairness of the officers in conducting the interrogation. The essential inquiry in determining the

voluntariness of a statement is whether the statement was the product of the free and independent will of the accused.

[The court heard] evidence at the suppression hearing concerning the officers' alleged promises, threats, or both. Regarding promises, the trial court found that "Swanigan was told several times that if he cooperated that that would be conveyed to anybody who might pursue the case." The court further found that although "there was . . . an allegation made that you were promised leniency," that "no specific promises of leniency were made," and that several times "Lieutenant Sweeney indicated that there couldn't be any promises made by those in authority." . . .

Regarding threats, the trial court found: "At no time were any threats uttered." We agree no express threats were uttered, but find that evidence of implied threats exists on the audiotape. The implicit threats are occasionally intertwined with the officers' urgings that Swanigan cooperate. Examples from both categories of interrogation techniques are italicized below:

> [Lanham:] So you need to come clean. You know what's gonna happen after I get done talking with you Jami. I've gotta do a report. Right? You know that. That's all we do here is reports. *And I need to go and put in my report that Jami cooperated. I need to be able to tell Parrish that you, that you cooperated with me and that you came clean and that you got it straight. And that you weren't involved in all of them because you know what Jami? I don't think you're involved in all of them. I think you had a small part in one of them, and that's what I want from you. That's what we need to know from you so that you don't go down for all these robberies. We just want to know your involvement in yours. That's all we want to know from you, so that you don't get charged with all of them. . . .*

Later in the interview Lanham said: "I just need you to tell me how you was involved. Jami, you know it's the right thing to do. *It's gonna help you in the long run and you know it. 'Cause I guarantee there's a lot of difference between going to jail for five robberies than there is for one.*"

[When] Investigator Feldman entered the room, he told Swanigan:

> *You're going to jail. It's guaranteed. You are going to jail. You got one of two options. You can sit there and B.S. and act like we're, we're idiots and tell these lame stories and we'll write every word you say down and send it over to the county attorney and you'll have every lawyer reading that going, "Jesus Christ, this is bullshit!" And you know what they're [county attorney] gonna say? Well, when your lawyer comes up and goes, "Hey, can we get a deal?" You know what they're gonna say? "Read the report. He, he played games the whole time. He doesn't deserve a break. He hasn't learned from any of the mistakes he made."* . . .
>
> *You can show that you made a mistake and you want to take responsibility for your actions and you apologize for it. Or you sit there and play stupid. And then you're gonna fry. Because when the county attorney comes to Sweeney or Lanham and goes, "What do you think? Here's the deal [plea bargain] that I'm being offered." You know what we're gonna say if you're playing games? "Screw ya."*

Lanham then told Swanigan, "And if you don't think they [county attorney] ask our opinion you're crazy cause they do."

Immediately after these comments by officers Feldman and Lanham, the following exchange occurred:

> [*Swanigan:*] Everything happened so fast. I was standing up at the window. I looked in, put my hand up on the window and looked in. I walked inside the store with a gun in my hand. And I pointed it at the um, clerk and asked, and tell him give me all your money. . . . "Give me your money or I'll kill you." So he finally gave me the money. . . .
>
> *F:* What were you wearing?
>
> *S:* I was wearing, I was wearing tan pants and, um, tan shirt that's over at Jessica's house. . . .
>
> *L:* So that outfit that you have on, the other one. There's another outfit there just like this one you have on, right? That what you were wearing?
>
> *S:* Yeah. . . .

In an apparent attempt to wrap up Swanigan's confession, Feldman produced a photograph of the robber from the surveillance video and asked, "That you?" Swanigan vehemently denied it: "Hell no! I can tell you that's not me. I can tell you that's not me." Among other things, Swanigan pointed out that the figure in the photograph was not wearing tan pants and a tan shirt, contrary to what he had just confessed.

From that point until the interrogation ended, Swanigan denied that he was involved in the robbery. When Lanham asked Swanigan how he would therefore know exactly how the robbery happened, he replied, "Because you guys done gave me tips behind how it done happened." When Lanham asked why he would make up the story that he committed the robbery when he actually had not, Swanigan responded, "Because you guys are forcing me to do this." When she denied forcing him into saying anything, he said, "When I try to tell you the truth you guys say it's me."

[The court also heard evidence at the suppression hearing concerning Swanigan's intellect and psychological state.] Dr. Schulman's report on Swanigan was reviewed by the trial court, and in a section titled "examination findings" it states:

> *Estimated intellectual functioning is in the borderline range of intellectual abilities with an estimated IQ of 76.* He says that he missed a lot of school, that he was in regular classes and did not enjoy going to high school. The clinical examination is essentially within normal limits. *He shows some mild depression. He also shows difficulty in dealing with anxiety and is susceptible to being overcome by anxiety but in this setting he shows good control.* There are no indications of any underlying associative thought disturbance. . . .

Swanigan argues the police used [unfair tactics] to overbear his will [by] repeatedly telling him that he would be helping or hurting himself by what he told them. According to him, they urged him to confess to the crime so that they could report that he had cooperated. He claims that when he told them he did not commit the crime, they threatened to report that he was not cooperating, occasionally suggesting that he would be charged with more robberies if he did not confess. At the time, Swanigan was on probation.

Investigator Lanham mentioned the other robberies and the need for Swanigan's cooperation, adding she "needed" to put in her report that he cooperated. . . . Sweeney repeated the need for police to show that Swanigan had cooperated and indicated what would happen if Swanigan did not. "We can write the report where it shows that you're willing to get this straightened out" and, if not,

"Jami, we're going to charge you with aggravated robbery. We're gonna show [the county attorney] that you're not cooperating with us." . . .

Like Lanham and Sweeney, Feldman suggested positive consequences for Swanigan admitting his mistake, i.e., confessing to the robbery, but suggested negative consequences if he did not so "cooperate." He specifically mentioned the influence the interrogators have with the county attorney's office, including what they write in their report. . . .

This court has held that, without more, a law enforcement officer's offer to convey a suspect's cooperation to the prosecutor is insufficient to make a confession involuntary. State v. Banks, 927 P.2d 456 (Kan. 1996) ("it will be noted by the authorities that you did cooperate"). Likewise, we have declined to find a confession involuntary when the police encourage the accused to tell the truth. Kansas appellate courts, however, have not addressed the other side of the same coin, law enforcement conveying a suspect's lack of cooperation to the prosecutor. A growing number of courts have disapproved this tactic. Those not finding that it is coercive per se regard it as another circumstance to be considered in determining the voluntariness of the confession.

[We] fail to see how law enforcement can be . . . allowed to warn [Swanigan] of punishment for his "noncooperation" when [the Fifth Amendment gives him a privilege against self-incrimination]. On the other hand, we do not regard this tactic as one which makes the confession involuntary per se, but rather as one factor to be considered in the totality of circumstances.

Turning now to the assertion that detectives told Swanigan he would be charged for five convenience store robberies instead of just one unless he confessed, we first examine general statements of Kansas law. K.S.A. 60-460(f) provides in relevant part:

> Evidence of a statement which is made other than by a witness while testifying at the hearing, offered to prove the truth of the matter stated, is hearsay evidence and inadmissible except: . . .
>
> (f) *Confessions.* In a criminal proceeding as against the accused, a previous statement by the accused relative to the offense charged, but only if the judge finds that the accused . . . (2) was not induced to make the statement . . . (B) *by threats or promises concerning action to be taken by a public official with reference to the crime, likely to cause the accused to make such a statement falsely, and made by a person whom the accused reasonably believed to have the power or authority to execute the same.*

No Kansas cases have addressed this specific issue. However, Aguilar v. State, 751 P.2d 178 (N.M. 1988), is directly on point. Among other things, during Aguilar's interrogation the police chief implied that if Aguilar did not confess to the burglary, he would be charged in connection with unrelated incidents of vandalism in town. Aguilar then confessed. In examining interrogation techniques quite similar to those in the instant case, the New Mexico Supreme Court held:

> Chief Barela's interrogation alternated between threatening the defendant with charges in connection with unrelated incidents of vandalism in Dexter and assuring the defendant that a confession to the burglary would be looked upon favorably by all concerned. In the totality of the circumstances, this interrogation technique is preponderant. In comparison with all evidence to the contrary, these implied threats

and promises, especially when knowingly made to a defendant with diminished mental capacity, rendered the confession involuntary as a matter of law.

[The] trial court did not specifically assess Swanigan's IQ of 76 as a factor in the voluntariness determination. Nor did the court consider his psychological state during the interrogation, finding only that it was insufficient to make the police interrogation improper at all. Our review of the record, including the audiotape of the October 31 interrogation, discloses that Swanigan's relatively low IQ and his susceptibility to being overcome by anxiety played a part in his alternating denials and confessions (which themselves varied considerably). His confession began to unravel for the last time when the robber in the photo was wearing the wrong clothes. . . .

Although any one of these factors which Swanigan asserts — his low intellect and susceptibility to being overcome by anxiety, the officers' repeated use of false information, and their threats and promises — may not be sufficient to show coercion, the combination of all of them in this case leads us to conclude as a matter of law that Swanigan's October 31 statement was not the result of his free will, but was involuntary. . . .

We acknowledge that there must be a link between the coercive conduct of the State and the confession. A thorough review of the record, as partly evidenced by the facts set forth in this opinion, clearly shows that Swanigan's numerous changes in story, whether in denial or in confession, usually occurred shortly after the officers lied to or threatened him. As such, his October 31 statement should have been excluded as evidence at trial. . . .

Notes

1. *Police promises: majority position.* Most jurisdictions have not taken literally the Supreme Court's prohibition on the use of confessions obtained through "any sort of threats or . . . any direct or implied promises, however slight." Bram v. United States, 168 U.S. 532 (1897). Some promises or threats, standing alone, are indeed enough to render a confession "involuntary." These would include promises to reduce (or decline to file) charges, threats to file more serious charges, or promises to seek more or less serious punishment for the crime. See Lynumn v. Illinois, 372 U.S. 528 (1963) (suspect told that cooperation could lead to lesser charges; failure to cooperate would mean loss of custody of children, confession involuntary); State v. Rezk, 840 A.2d 758 (N.H. 2004) (interrogator said that if defendant confessed, the officer "wouldn't charge him with all the felonies"; confession was involuntary because defendant and police engaged in "station house plea-bargaining" without benefit of defense counsel for the suspect). Improper statements could also include threats to refuse to protect the suspect from mob violence or from a dangerous co-conspirator.

Interrogators can, however, make many other promises or threats without invalidating a confession. They can promise to inform the prosecutor about the defendant's cooperation in making a statement, to ask the prosecutor to discuss lesser charges, or to arrange for treatment programs or similar activities. What distinguishes the acceptable from the unacceptable promises? See People v. Holloway,

91 P.3d 164 (Cal. 2004) (detectives' mention of a possible death penalty and suggestions that defendant would benefit from giving a truthful, mitigated version of the crimes was not an improper promise or threat; court compared these facts to improper interrogations where detectives falsely suggested that suspect would be subject to death penalty, or that statements could not be used in court).

When the police make promises or threats to a *juvenile* suspect, the government has a somewhat more difficult burden to meet in showing that the confession was voluntary. See State v. Presha, 748 A.2d 1108 (N.J. 2000) (courts should consider parent's absence during interview as a highly significant factor in judging voluntariness of juvenile's statement); In re G.O., 727 N.E.2d 1003 (Ill. 2000) (juvenile's confession should not be suppressed simply because he was denied the opportunity to confer with a parent during interrogation, but that factor may be relevant in determining voluntariness).

2. *Proving causation.* The government carries the burden of proving that a confession was voluntary, and the standard of proof is preponderance of the evidence. State v. Agnello 593 N.W.2d 427 (Wis. 1999) (voluntariness of confession need be shown only by a preponderance, not beyond reasonable doubt). As the Kansas court in *Swanigan* indicated, even after a defendant demonstrates that the police made an improper promise or threat, his statement still might be admissible if the promise or threat did not "induce" or "cause" the confession. How would a prosecutor typically prove this causal link?

3. *Do innocent people confess?* Do innocent people really confess to crimes they did not commit? A number of psychologists have investigated the circumstances that lead people to make false confessions. A Royal Commission in Great Britain summarized the findings as follows:

> [There] is now a substantial body of research which shows that there are four distinct categories of false confession:
>
> (i) people may make confessions entirely voluntarily as a result of a morbid desire for publicity or notoriety; or to relieve feelings of guilt about a real or imagined previous transgression; or because they cannot distinguish between reality and fantasy;
>
> (ii) a suspect may confess from a desire to protect someone else from interrogation and prosecution;
>
> (iii) people may see a prospect of immediate advantage from confessing (e.g., an end to questioning or release from the police station), even though the long-term consequences are far worse (the resulting confessions are termed "coerced-compliant" confessions); and
>
> (iv) people may be persuaded temporarily by the interrogators that they really have done the act in question (the resulting confessions are termed "coerced-internalized" confessions).

Report of the Royal Commission on Criminal Justice 57 (1993) (Runciman Commission); see also Saul M. Kassin, Inside Interrogation: Why Innocent People Confess, 32 Am. J. Trial Advoc. 525 (2009).

Two developments over the last generation cast a new light on the question of false confessions. First, the availability of video recordings of many interrogations has created a rich field for psychological and sociological research. Richard Ofshe and Richard Leo have used these materials to develop a model of true and false confessions that emphasizes the misuse of standard interrogation techniques as a major cause of false confessions. They pay particular attention to the "post-admission" portion of an interrogation, when a suspect provides the details that can corroborate or repudiate the suspect's admission of guilt. See Ofshe & Leo, The Decision to Confess Falsely: Rational Choice and Irrational Action, 74 Denv. U. L. Rev. 979 (1997).

Second, the use of DNA evidence to identify clear cases of wrongful convictions allows careful assessments of confessions in cases that go wrong. The research of Brandon Garrett indicates that false confessions account for a substantial number of wrongful conviction cases, and those confessions include many convincing details about the crime that were likely suggested to the suspect by the questioners. See Garrett, The Substance of False Confessions, 62 Stan. L. Rev. 1051 (2010). For a review of the sources, effects, and frequency of false confessions, consult the web extension for this chapter at *http://www.crimpro.com/extension/ch08*.

3. Police Lies

Police often know facts that suspects do not know and can use those facts to expose a suspect's false story or to encourage a silent suspect to talk. Sometimes police only pretend to know something: They make assertions that are untrue or unsupported, such as stating that a co-defendant has confessed or that a victim has died. Other times police create props, in the form of physical evidence, to increase the chance of obtaining a confession. Are all police lies in the interrogation room a fair and legal part of the "often competitive enterprise of ferreting out crime"? If not, where should courts or police agencies draw the line?

■ RONALD BRISBON v. UNITED STATES

957 A.2d 931 (D.C. App. 2008)

RUIZ, Associate Judge

Appellants Ronald Brisbon and Michael Wonson appeal their convictions for first-degree murder, assault with intent to kill and related offenses. Brisbon challenges the admission of his videotaped confession claiming it was involuntary. . . . Although we consider that the deceptive tactic used by the officers in interrogating Brisbon make the question of voluntariness a close question, we conclude that admission of his videotaped confession was harmless in light of the government's otherwise overwhelming evidence against him.

[Dana Route was "Ronnie T" Brisbon's ex-girlfriend; they remained friends and worked together in Fort Washington, Maryland. On the evening of May 17, she saw Brisbon cleaning two rifles with WD-40 while his friend "Pretty B" Wonson stood nearby. Brisbon and Wonson left the house with the firearms, then returned in under twenty-five minutes, guns still in hand. After they came into the house, Brisbon said to Wonson, "I can't believe that your gun jammed."]

The following day, Thursday, May 18, 2000, Ms. Route was watching the news on TV while at work when she saw a report "that two people were killed on East Capitol Street." . . . Ms. Route put two and two together and confronted Brisbon, [who] told her that "Pretty B was looking for somebody," and when he and Brisbon spotted the target, "Pretty B had got out of the truck and fired [bullets] into a crowd." . . .

Brisbon was arrested at 11:30 A.M. on May 24 at his place of work (C & T Auto Shop) by the Prince George's County, Maryland police. . . . Once they arrived at the D.C. police station, Detective Irving took Brisbon to an interrogation room and told him that he was under arrest for two murders on May 17, and had been "identified as being a shooter that night." [Detectives Credle and Irving began interrogating him. During] the first fifteen minutes, Brisbon denied everything. Detective Irving told him that they had searched the house where Brisbon lived with his mother and grandmother and "that the police recovered drugs and a shotgun out of his grandmother's house," — which was true — and "that his grandmother had got upset and was rushed to the hospital and that his mother was placed under arrest" — which was false. According to the detectives, Brisbon dropped his head and was quiet for a few seconds, then admitted that he "did it," saying that he did not "want anyone else to get in trouble." Detectives Irving and Credle insisted that Brisbon give them all of the details of the crime, because a blanket confession would not convince them that he had told the truth. The detectives denied promising Brisbon that confessing would aid his mother or grandmother. The interrogation continued for two hours, until, at around 9:30 P.M., Brisbon consented to a videotaped confession. . . .

Brisbon moved to suppress the admission of his confession into evidence, claiming that it was an involuntary statement elicited in violation of the Fifth Amendment. . . . Brisbon then took the stand and testified about how he felt pressured to confess when the police had lied to him about the fate of his mother and grandmother. [The] trial judge stated that "even taking into account Mr. Brisbon's testimony, I would find that [the confessed] statements were wholly voluntary."

Once a motion has been made to suppress a confession as involuntary, the burden is on the government to prove that the statements of the accused were voluntarily given without police coercion. Generally, the factors for consideration in determining voluntariness include (1) the circumstances surrounding the questioning, (2) the accused's age, education, and prior experiences with the law, (3) his physical and mental condition at the time the statement was made, (4) other factors showing coercion or trickery, and (5) the delay between the suspect's arrest and the confession. The government must prove voluntariness by a preponderance of the evidence.

[We are] troubled by the deception used by the police officers and its coercive potential. . . . In early Supreme Court jurisprudence, involuntary confessions were held inadmissible, stressing their inherent untrustworthiness.[13] See Brown v. Mississippi, 297 U.S. 278 (1936). In Rogers v. Richmond, 365 U.S. 534 (1961), the Court explained that the reliability of a confession — although obviously important to the truth-seeking purpose of a criminal trial — is not the touchstone of the inquiry:

13. In this case, the record corroborates that Brisbon's confession was truthful because it both contained details that only a participant would be reasonably expected to know and matched up with the eyewitness evidence presented at trial. At the time Brisbon confessed, for example, the detectives were unaware there had been a second shooter.

> [Convictions] following the admission into evidence of confessions which are involuntary, *i.e.,* the product of coercion, either physical or psychological, cannot stand. This is so not because such confessions are unlikely to be true but because the methods used to extract them offend an underlying principle in the enforcement of our criminal law: that ours is an accusatorial and not an inquisitorial system — a system in which the State must establish guilt by evidence independently and freely secured and may not by coercion prove its charge against an accused out of his own mouth. . . .

The Court . . . has never abandoned this due process jurisprudence and its focus on . . . "whether a defendant's will was overborne" by the circumstances surrounding the giving of a confession. To implement these principles, and recognizing the inherent difficulty in ascertaining whether a suspect has been coerced into confessing, we have said that confessions generally are not vitiated when they are obtained by deception or trickery, as long as the means employed are not *calculated* to produce an untrue statement. This short-form guideline reflects the dual due process concerns that a confession may not be obtained by means that are offensive to due process (inquisitorial methods that overbear the suspect's will) and that such undue coercion is likely to lead to a false confession. Thus, we have affirmed a conviction based on a confession obtained after the police used a technique where the police ran a fake lie-detector test on the defendant. Contee v. United States, 667 A.2d 103 (D.C.1995). As we explained, the suspect in a *Contee*-type situation retains ultimate control over his statements because he privately knows whether they are in fact lies. Similarly, in Davis v. United States, 724 A.2d 1163 (D.C.1998), we concluded that the trickery (falsely telling the suspect that his co-perpetrator had said that Davis was carrying a particular weapon) did not require suppression of a confession in part "because it was inconsistent with Davis's own first-hand knowledge," and, therefore, as the defendant himself testified, he was not fooled.

Here, on the other hand, Brisbon was subjected to a very different kind of psychological pressure, unrelated to the evidence the police purport to have that a suspect is guilty of the charged crime. After being told by the officers that his mother and grandmother had been arrested[15] as a result of the discovery of drugs and a shotgun during a search of their house, Brisbon testified, he felt coerced to tell the police "what they wanted to hear," so that his mother and grandmother would be released. The truth of the premise underlying the officers' deception — the existence of contraband of which Brisbon would have known — gave force to the officers' deception. We have not previously been presented with the question whether the technique used here — which could be taken by a suspect in custody as an implicit threat or a promise involving family members — was calculated to exert so much pressure on a suspect as to lead to a confession, whether true or false. Unlike the suspects in *Contee* and *Davis*, . . . Brisbon was confronted with a lie unrelated to the government's evidence of his guilt that had consequences to others, not solely to his own fate. See Holland v. McGinnis, 963 F.2d 1044, 1052 (7th Cir. 1992) (noting that the police tactic used in Lynumn v. Illinois, 372 U.S. 528 (1963), where the suspect was threatened with loss of her children and federal benefits "also distorted

15. While, according to the police, the detectives told Brisbon that his mother was arrested and his grandmother was taken to the hospital, Brisbon testified that he was told that his grandmother also was arrested and had to be taken to the hospital.

the suspect's rational choice . . . by introducing a completely extrinsic consideration: an empty but plausible threat to take away something to which she and her children would otherwise be entitled"). A defendant who is completely innocent might well confess in the latter circumstances for fear of the extraneous adverse consequences; by contrast, an innocent defendant in the former circumstances would have little incentive to render a false confession. This is at least in part because a suspect who is "in the dark" about what he is told is more susceptible to the coercive pressure of trickery, as he is dependent on what the police tell him, than one who can, as in *Contee* and *Davis,* use his own resources to test what he knows against what the police tell him, which would help him withstand the psychological manipulation. Extrinsic pressure not only impairs free choice, but also casts doubt upon the reliability of the resulting confession.

The detectives in this case candidly testified that they lied to Brisbon in order to get him "to admit his involvement in the case" and to "lure the truth" from him. When the officers who question a suspect by using trickery demonstrate an "undeviating intent . . . to extract a confession . . . the confession obtained must be examined with the most careful scrutiny." Spano v. New York, 360 U.S. 315, 324 (1959). We apply that close scrutiny here.

We begin by cautioning that the kind of deception employed here, involving supposed harm to vulnerable family members, could well cross the line beyond the type of tactics *vel non* that a court will tolerate because they are so offensive to a civilized system of justice that they must be condemned under the Due Process Clause. This is especially true if such tactics are used on a suspect particularly susceptible to police pressure. We have already expressed doubt about the police's use of deceptive tactics to "persuade" a suspect that a confession is in his best interest, in light of the evidence already amassed by the government when, in fact, there is no such evidence. See Beasley v. United States, 512 A.2d 1007, 1016 (D.C. 1986) ("We do not condone certain of the tactics used by the police in this case [promise of leniency and deception concerning strength of the government's evidence], and such tactics have made this a close case"). But the use of deception to exert psychological pressure that exploits vulnerabilities extraneous to the offense charged, such as the threat of adverse consequences to family members if the suspect does not confess or cooperate with the investigation, is in a different category that has been singled out for condemnation. See *Rogers,* 365 U.S. at 549 (expressing view that "issue of voluntariness might fairly have gone either way in the whole of the testimony" where detained suspect who initially denied involvement in shooting confessed after being told that his wife would be brought into custody for questioning); *Spano,* 360 U.S. at 324 (confession involuntary where the police used the suspect's "childhood friend," who falsely stated that the suspect's "telephone call [to him] had gotten him into trouble, that his job was in jeopardy, and that loss of his job would be disastrous to his three children, his wife and his unborn child").[17]

Here, the trial court denied Brisbon's motion to suppress without taking note of the questionable mode of psychological pressure employed in this case, and found that his statements were "wholly voluntary," without detailing the factors that

17. Some courts draw a distinction between deceptive and truthful pressure tactics involving family members. See Armstead v. Mississippi, 978 So.2d 642, 648 (Miss. 2008) (finding that "threats to arrest a defendant's family member(s) do not render a confession involuntary so long as probable cause exists to arrest such persons").

led to that determination. We know from the record that the court had just heard the testimony of the officers, who admitted that they lied to Brisbon about his mother's arrest and grandmother's hospitalization in order to get him to confess, but said that they did not promise Brisbon that his confession would result in the exoneration of his mother or Brisbon's ability to see his grandmother. Brisbon, on the other hand, testified that he felt pressured to confess by the officers' deception which included that even his frail elderly grandmother had not only been hospitalized, but also arrested along with his mother. The effect that the officers' tactics reasonably had on Brisbon is a critical element of the voluntariness inquiry. . . . The trial judge's determination, made after hearing the testimony of Brisbon and the officers and seeing the videotape of the confession, where Brisbon denied any coercion,[19] apparently was that the officers' calculated play on his emotional attachment to his mother and grandmother did not equate to unconstitutional coercion. It is of course possible that the unwelcome "news" about his mother's arrest and grandmother's hospitalization, rather than being something that overcame his will and coerced him to confess, could have instead shocked Brisbon into taking responsibility for his actions. In other words, the *truthful* information Brisbon had received about the seizure of drugs and a shotgun from their house might have induced him to want to spare them the "trouble" of being linked to his criminal activities. Brisbon testified that his mother had been arrested the year before on his account; and his mother confirmed in her testimony that she had been arrested, jailed and released, after which Brisbon became very protective of her and his ill grandmother.[20] This previous experience — and whether the officers who interrogated him were aware of it — would be relevant both to an evaluation of the officers' tactics and Brisbon's foreseeable reaction to the officers' deception involving yet another arrest of his mother for which he was to blame. The issue, however, was not explored on the record. Moreover, the officers' exchange with Brisbon about his mother and grandmother preceded the videotaped confession, so the trial judge was not able to evaluate from the tape itself Brisbon's reaction and his statements to the officers when he first confessed.

From our own review of the record, we note other factors that arguably would weigh in favor of a finding of voluntariness. First, although this was the first time Brisbon had been charged and prosecuted, he had a previous arrest, a fact indicating that he had some familiarity with the criminal justice system. But we do not know anything else about the circumstances of Brisbon's prior arrest, or whether he was subject to interrogation at that time. Second, . . . there is no indication based on the record that due to Brisbon's age (twenty-two), educational background, or physical or mental condition, he was particularly susceptible to psychological pressure, save for the obvious emotional "hot buttons" — his concern for his mother and grandmother — that the police sought to manipulate. . . . Finally, Brisbon confessed not only to the murder and assault of two innocent persons in a hail of bullets

19. According to the transcript of the confession, Brisbon denied being coerced by the police: . . .

[Detective]: Has anyone forced you, coerced you, tricked you or did anything in order for you to give this statement?
[Brisbon]: No, sir. . . .

20. Brisbon testified that he was very close to his mother and felt "disturbed" about her situation and that of his grandmother, who was then eighty-two years old and has Alzheimer's disease. Brisbon testified he would be "willing to sacrifice [his] life" for them.

fired into a group at Eastern High, but also went on to confess to other, unrelated crimes — going well beyond what even he testified the officers told him they "wanted to hear." In light of these indications that Brisbon may well have been able to resist the officers' deceptive pressure tactics, we are inclined to conclude that Brisbon did not in fact succumb to them, and that his videotaped confession was therefore voluntary and admissible.

We recognize that the question of voluntariness in this case is a close one, however, and do not decide it, because we can conclude beyond a reasonable doubt that even if the confession should have been suppressed, its admission was harmless. See Arizona v. Fulminante, 499 U.S. 279 (1991) (admission of involuntary confession is "trial error" subject to harmless error analysis). We recognize that a defendant's confession is uniquely powerful evidence and that its erroneous admission will be deemed harmless only rarely, by an overwhelming government case. For the following reasons, we think that even if we assume that Brisbon's confession was involuntary, and its admission unconstitutional, it was nevertheless harmless beyond a reasonable doubt.

This is a case where the government's evidence was not merely sufficient, or even strong, but presented overwhelming evidence of guilt. Apart from the challenged confession, the evidence arrayed against Brisbon consisted of the testimony of several witnesses and other confessions the admissibility of which is not challenged. An eyewitness to the shooting, Jameice Phillips identified Brisbon, who she knew as "Ronnie T," as the shooter. She testified that she had known him through "friends and family," for five years. . . . Nor was Brisbon's videotaped confession to the officers his only admission of guilt. Dana Route testified that Brisbon had also confessed to her, shortly after the shooting. . . .

Even after Brisbon's videotaped confession to the officers was admitted, the issue of its voluntariness and credibility remained for the jury. The jurors were instructed to weigh the credibility of Brisbon's confession in light of his testimony that it had been coerced. . . . Accordingly, we affirm Brisbon's convictions. . . .

Notes

1. *Police lies: majority position.* Most jurisdictions take the view that some police lies will produce a per se "coerced" confession, while others will ordinarily not be enough standing alone to make the confession inadmissible under the "totality of the circumstances." See Frazier v. Cupp, 394 U.S. 731 (1969) (confession voluntary even though police lied to defendant in telling him that another suspect had already confessed and implicated him). Do you agree with the court in *Brisbon* that police lies are especially likely to produce false confessions if they are "unrelated to the government's evidence of his guilt" and relate instead to "extrinsic" considerations? See State v. Kelekolio, 849 P.2d 58 (Haw. 1993) (treating "extrinsic" lies as per se violations of due process and leaving more latitude for police to tell lies regarding matters "intrinsic" to their investigation). If intrinsic lies are more tolerable, why did the *Brisbon* court express doubt about the validity of police efforts to persuade a suspect to confess "in light of the evidence already amassed by the government when, in fact, there is no such evidence"?

Some courts are especially troubled about police lies that relate to the purpose of the interrogation. See State v. McConkie, 755 A.2d 1075 (Me. 2000) (involuntary statement when officer said during police station interview that suspect's statement would "stay confidential"; officers may not affirmatively mislead suspects about the uses to which their statements may be put). Are police falsehoods of this sort more likely to coerce a confession? More detailed treatment of the categories of deception that produce a skeptical judicial response appears on the web extension for this chapter at *http://www.crimpro.com/extension/ch08*. What would be the impact of a legal rule barring the use of a confession obtained because of police lies of *any* sort? See Deborah Young, Unnecessary Evil: Police Lying in Interrogations, 28 Conn. L. Rev. 425 (1996).

2. *False physical evidence and false friends.* Is there any relevant difference between verbal lies about evidence against a defendant and the creation of false physical evidence against a suspect (for instance, forging a report from the forensics laboratory)? Courts seem especially concerned about the latter form of deception. See Commonwealth v. DiGiambattista, 813 N.E.2d 516 (Mass. 2004) (confession coerced by use of fake videotape and forged documentary evidence); Wilson v. State, 311 S.W.3d 452 (Tex. Crim. App. 2010) (use of fictional fingerprint report requires suppression of confession under statutory bar).

Another type of lie that especially troubles courts is the use of "false friends," when the questioner asks the suspect to confess out of friendship or sympathy. In Spano v. New York, 360 U.S. 315 (1959), the questioner was a friend of the suspect and stated (falsely) that if he did not obtain a statement, he would lose his job and his source of support for his family. The resulting confession was held to be involuntary.

3. *Bad confessions or bad police?* Over time the Supreme Court has shifted its views on the role of blameworthy police conduct in evaluating an "involuntary" confession. In Bram v. United States, 168 U.S. 532 (1897), the Court concluded that a coerced confession was a violation of the Fifth Amendment's self-incrimination clause. Hence, the emphasis was on the state of mind of the suspect — the question was whether the statement was "compelled." By 1936, in Brown v. Mississippi, the Court shifted its emphasis to the due process clause as the relevant limitation on the use of coerced confessions. But the Court still seemed most concerned with interrogation practices, such as physical torture in *Brown*, that made the confession, as a matter of fact, "involuntary" and therefore quite possibly false. Later decisions indicated that the state of mind of the defendant, and the consequent risk of false confessions, was not the only concern of courts evaluating the "voluntariness" of a confession. In cases such as Rogers v. Richmond, 365 U.S. 534 (1961), the Court barred use of confessions that were obtained through trickery (a false order to arrest the suspect's ill wife). Even if police conduct does not create a risk of false confession from the defendant, some morally objectionable interrogation tactics might still lead a court to conclude that the confession was "involuntary" based on the totality of the circumstances. The Supreme Court has suggested that wrongful police coercion is "a necessary predicate to the finding that a confession is not 'voluntary' under federal law. Colorado v. Connelly, 479 U.S. 157 (1986). If the interrogators have not acted wrongfully (for instance, in failing to appreciate a suspect's unusually limited mental capacity), then the fact that the suspect was coerced is not sufficient.

4. *How common is police lying?* One criminologist who observed more than 180 police interrogations noted that police officers lied to the suspect in about 30 percent of all the interrogations he observed. This technique, he concluded, was among

the most effective methods of obtaining a confession or admission but it was less effective than appeals to the suspect's conscience, identifying contradictions in the story the suspect was telling, or offering excuses for the suspect's alleged conduct. Richard Leo, Inside the Interrogation Room, 86 J. Crim. L. & Criminology 266, 278 (1996). What obstacles might prevent one from learning how often police lie during interrogations? See Laurie Magid, Deceptive Police Interrogation Practices: How Far Is Too Far?, 99 Mich. L. Rev. 1168 (2001) (arguing that deception should be permitted unless it creates an unreasonable risk that an innocent person would falsely confess; until statistically sound research on random sample of confession cases demonstrates the size of this problem, no drastic limit on deceptive techniques is justified).

5. *Training police to lie.* A widely used training manual for police interrogators advises readers to accuse the suspect of committing the crime and if necessary to lie about the evidence available to the police or about other matters: Such "trickery and deceit" is necessary to successful interrogations in the majority of cases. Fred Inbau, et al., Criminal Interrogation and Confessions 484 (4th ed. 2004). Is there a difference between this line of argument and the arguments used to justify the "third degree"? What ethical boundaries should limit police lies or unenforceable (but legally valid) promises? Consider the ethics implicit in the observation of Justice Hugo Black dissenting in a case involving the enforcement of treaties with Native Americans: "Great nations, like great men, should keep their word," FPC v. Tuscarora Indian Nation, 362 U.S. 99 (1960) (Black, J., dissenting).

STOP

481 540 - 6PA

B. *MIRANDA* WARNINGS

It can be very difficult for a court to determine after the fact whether a confession was "voluntary." In a series of cases between 1936 and 1964, the Supreme Court attempted to highlight the various facts that might, in the "totality of the circumstances," deprive the suspect of the "power of resistance." Fikes v. Alabama, 352 U.S. 191 (1957). As the cases proliferated, it became clear that a great many facts could be relevant to the question of voluntariness. The Supreme Court, perhaps out of frustration with the repeated and difficult application of the "voluntariness" test it had created under the due process clause, began a search in the late 1950s for a more effective and easily administered method of stopping interrogation abuses.

The Court turned first to the possibility of requiring defense lawyers to be present during at least some interrogations. In a series of opinions, several members of the Court indicated that due process required that any suspect in custody should be able to obtain an attorney from the moment of arrest. See Spano v. New York, 360 U.S. 315 (1959). These tentative suggestions soon led to a holding, under the Sixth Amendment right to counsel (rather than the due process clause), that defendants in at least some interrogations had the right to have an attorney present. In Massiah v. United States, 377 U.S. 201 (1964), the defendant had already been indicted for violating narcotics laws and had retained defense counsel when the government recruited his friend to collect more evidence against him. The government placed a radio transmitter in his friend's car. Then the friend struck up a conversation with Massiah in the car about the crimes.

The Court invalidated the use of the confession that Massiah made in the car. The use of the confession at trial, the Court said, violated Massiah's Sixth Amendment right to counsel in all "criminal proceedings." Although these circumstances did not amount to physical or psychological coercion under the customary due process analysis, the Court said that an effective right to counsel "must apply to indirect and surreptitious interrogations as well as those conducted in the jailhouse." The *Massiah* decision created a method for courts to invalidate confessions on the basis of a clear rule, one that could apply regardless of the conditions during the interrogation. But if the rule were applied only to suspects who have already been indicted or to those who are tricked into a confession outside the police station, its impact would be small.

The right to counsel during custodial interrogations occurring *before* indictment received its clearest declaration in Escobedo v. Illinois, 378 U.S. 478 (1964), decided just weeks after *Massiah*. The investigators in that murder case obtained a confession from Escobedo by preventing him from consulting with his retained attorney (who was present at the police station) during the interrogation. The investigators kept Escobedo handcuffed and standing during the interrogation, and they arranged a confrontation with a second suspect, who accused Escobedo of the killing.

Some of the language in the opinion referred broadly to the importance of the presence of counsel at interrogation, which the Court now called a "critical stage" in the criminal process and which was thus covered by the Sixth Amendment right to counsel during a "prosecution." The opinion suggested that all interrogations of persons in custody would have to take place in the presence of counsel:

> The right to counsel would indeed be hollow if it began at a period when few confessions were obtained. There is necessarily a direct relationship between the importance of a stage to the police in their quest for a confession and the criticalness of that stage to the accused in his need for legal advice. [No] system worth preserving should have to fear that if an accused is permitted to consult with a lawyer, he will become aware of, and exercise, these rights. [378 U.S. at 488.]

However, the opinion also lent itself to a narrower reading by emphasizing some of the distinctive facts of the case in its holding:

> We hold, therefore, that where, as here, the investigation is no longer a general inquiry into an unsolved crime but has begun to focus on a particular suspect, the suspect has been taken into police custody, the police carry out a process of interrogations that lends itself to eliciting incriminating statements, the suspect has requested and been denied an opportunity to consult with his lawyer, and the police have not effectively warned him of his absolute constitutional right to remain silent, the accused has been denied "the Assistance of Counsel" in violation of the Sixth Amendment to the Constitution . . . and that no statement elicited by the police during the interrogation may be used against him at a criminal trial. [378 U.S. at 490-91.]

Escobedo suggested the possibility that the Sixth Amendment might require the government to provide suspects with counsel before any interrogation, and the decision sparked a national debate among state courts. Most states restricted the holding to situations in which a defendant had requested counsel, but some states tried to forecast the direction of the Supreme Court and required the government to provide counsel when an interrogation reached the "accusatory" or "critical" stage. See People v. Dorado, 394 P.2d 952 (Cal. 1964) ("The defendant who does not realize his rights under the law and who therefore does not request counsel is the very defendant who most needs counsel"); Neuenfeldt v. State, 138 N.W.2d 252 (Wis. 1965). A few states went in a different direction, requiring police to advise suspects about their right to assistance of counsel and their right to remain silent. See State v. Mendes, 210 A.2d 50 (R.I. 1965). In 1966, two years after *Escobedo,* the Supreme Court decided Miranda v. Arizona.

1. *The* Miranda *Revolution*

■ ERNESTO MIRANDA v. ARIZONA
384 U.S. 436 (1966)

WARREN, C.J.*

The cases before us raise questions which go to the roots of our concepts of American criminal jurisprudence: the restraints society must observe consistent with the Federal Constitution in prosecuting individuals for crime. More specifically, we deal with the admissibility of statements obtained from an individual who is subjected to custodial police interrogation and the necessity for procedures which assure that the individual is accorded his privilege under the Fifth Amendment to the Constitution not to be compelled to incriminate himself.

We dealt with certain phases of this problem recently in Escobedo v. Illinois, 378 U.S. 478 (1964). We granted certiorari in these cases [to explore some facets of the problems] of applying the privilege against self-incrimination to in-custody interrogation, and to give concrete constitutional guidelines for law enforcement agencies and courts to follow. . . .

We start here, as we did in *Escobedo,* with the premise that our holding is not an innovation in our jurisprudence, but is an application of principles long recognized and applied in other settings. . . . Our holding will be spelled out with some specificity in the pages which follow but briefly stated it is this: the prosecution may not use statements, whether exculpatory or inculpatory, stemming from custodial interrogation of the defendant unless it demonstrates the use of procedural safeguards effective to secure the privilege against self-incrimination. By custodial interrogation, we mean questioning initiated by law enforcement officers after a person has been taken into custody or otherwise deprived of his freedom of action in any significant way. As for the procedural safeguards to be employed, unless other fully effective means are devised to inform accused persons of their right of silence and to assure a continuous opportunity to exercise it, the following measures are required. Prior to any questioning, the person must be warned that he has a right to remain silent, that any statement he does make may be used as evidence against him, and that he has a right to the presence of an attorney, either retained or appointed. The defendant may waive effectuation of these rights, provided the waiver is made voluntarily, knowingly and intelligently. If, however, he indicates in

* [Justices Black, Douglas, Brennan, and Fortas joined in this opinion. — EDS.]

any manner and at any stage of the process that he wishes to consult with an attorney before speaking there can be no questioning. Likewise, if the individual is alone and indicates in any manner that he does not wish to be interrogated, the police may not question him. The mere fact that he may have answered some questions or volunteered some statements on his own does not deprive him of the right to refrain from answering any further inquiries until he has consulted with an attorney and thereafter consents to be questioned.

I.

The constitutional issue we decide in each of these cases is the admissibility of statements obtained from a defendant questioned while in custody or otherwise deprived of his freedom of action in any significant way. In each, the defendant was questioned by police officers, detectives, or a prosecuting attorney in a room in which he was cut off from the outside world. In none of these cases was the defendant given a full and effective warning of his rights at the outset of the interrogation process. In all the cases, the questioning elicited oral admissions, and in three of them, signed statements as well which were admitted at their trials. They all thus share salient features — incommunicado interrogation of individuals in a police-dominated atmosphere, resulting in self-incriminating statements without full warnings of constitutional rights.

An understanding of the nature and setting of this in-custody interrogation is essential to our decisions today. . . . From extensive factual studies undertaken in the early 1930's . . . it is clear that police violence and the "third degree" flourished at that time. [These practices] are undoubtedly the exception now, but they are sufficiently widespread to be the object of concern. Unless a proper limitation upon custodial interrogation is achieved — such as these decisions will advance — there can be no assurance that practices of this nature will be eradicated in the foreseeable future. [Furthermore, this] Court has recognized that coercion can be mental as well as physical, and that the blood of the accused is not the only hallmark of an unconstitutional inquisition.

Interrogation still takes place in privacy. Privacy results in secrecy and this in turn results in a gap in our knowledge as to what in fact goes on in the interrogation rooms. A valuable source of information about present police practices, however, may be found in various police manuals and texts which document procedures employed with success in the past, and which recommend various other effective tactics. These texts are used by law enforcement agencies themselves as guides. . . .

The officers are told by the manuals that the "principal psychological factor contributing to a successful interrogation is privacy — being alone with the person under interrogation." The efficacy of this tactic has been explained as follows:

> [The subject] is more keenly aware of his rights and more reluctant to tell of his indiscretions or criminal behavior within the walls of his home. Moreover his family and other friends are nearby, their presence lending moral support. In his own office, the investigator possesses all the advantages. The atmosphere suggests the invincibility of the forces of the law.

To highlight the isolation and unfamiliar surroundings, the manuals instruct the police to display an air of confidence in the suspect's guilt and from outward appearance to maintain only an interest in confirming certain details. The guilt of the subject is to be posited as a fact. The interrogator should direct his comments toward the reasons why the subject committed the act, rather than court failure by asking the subject whether he did it. Like other men, perhaps the subject has had a bad family life, had an unhappy childhood, had too much to drink, had an unrequited desire for women. The officers are instructed to minimize the moral seriousness of the offense, to cast blame on the victim or on society. These tactics are designed to put the subject in a psychological state where his story is but an elaboration of what the police purport to know already — that he is guilty. Explanations to the contrary are dismissed and discouraged. . . .

Good Cop/ Bad Cop

When the techniques described above prove unavailing, the texts recommend they be alternated with a show of some hostility. One ploy often used has been termed the "friendly-unfriendly" or the "Mutt and Jeff" act:

> In this technique, two agents are employed. Mutt, the relentless investigator, who knows the subject is guilty and is not going to waste any time. . . . Jeff, on the other hand, is obviously a kindhearted man. He has a family himself. He has a brother who was involved in a little scrape like this. He disapproves of Mutt and his tactics and will arrange to get him off the case if the subject will cooperate. He can't hold Mutt off for very long. The subject would be wise to make a quick decision. . . .

The manuals also contain instructions for police on how to handle the individual who refuses to discuss the matter entirely, or who asks for an attorney or relatives. The examiner is to concede him the right to remain silent. "This usually has a very undermining effect. [A] concession of this right to remain silent impresses the subject with the apparent fairness of his interrogator." After this psychological conditioning, however, the officer is told to point out the incriminating significance of the suspect's refusal to talk:

> Joe, you have a right to remain silent. That's your privilege and I'm the last person in the world who'll try to take it away from you. . . . But let me ask you this. Suppose you were in my shoes and I were in yours and you called me in to ask me about this and I told you, "I don't want to answer any of your questions." You'd think I had something to hide, and you'd probably be right in thinking that. That's exactly what I'll have to think about you, and so will everybody else. So let's sit here and talk this whole thing over. . . .

In the event that the subject wishes to speak to a relative or an attorney, the following advice is tendered:

> The interrogator should respond by suggesting that the subject first tell the truth to the interrogator himself rather than get anyone else involved in the matter. If the request is for an attorney, the interrogator may suggest that the subject save himself or his family the expense of any such professional service, particularly if he is innocent of the offense under investigation. The interrogator may also add, "Joe, I'm only looking for the truth, and if you're telling the truth, that's it. You can handle this by yourself."

From these representative samples of interrogation techniques, the setting prescribed by the manuals and observed in practice becomes clear. . . . Even without employing brutality, the "third degree" or the specific stratagems described above, the very fact of custodial interrogation exacts a heavy toll on individual liberty and trades on the weakness of individuals. . . .

In these cases, we might not find the defendants' statements to have been involuntary in traditional terms. Our concern for adequate safeguards to protect precious Fifth Amendment rights is, of course, not lessened in the slightest. In each of the cases, the defendant was thrust into an unfamiliar atmosphere and run through menacing police interrogation procedures. The potentiality for compulsion is forcefully apparent, for example, in State v. Miranda, 401 P.2d 721 (Ariz. 1965), where the indigent Mexican defendant was a seriously disturbed individual with pronounced sexual fantasies, and in People v. Stewart, 400 P.2d 97 (Cal. 1965), in which the defendant was an indigent Los Angeles Negro who had dropped out of school in the sixth grade. [In] none of these cases did the officers undertake to afford appropriate safeguards at the outset of the interrogation to insure that the statements were truly the product of free choice. . . .

The current practice of incommunicado interrogation is at odds with one of our Nation's most cherished principles — that the individual may not be compelled to incriminate himself. Unless adequate protective devices are employed to dispel the compulsion inherent in custodial surroundings, no statement obtained from the defendant can truly be the product of his free choice. From the foregoing, we can readily perceive an intimate connection between the privilege against self-incrimination and police custodial questioning. . . .

II.

[The] constitutional foundation underlying the privilege is the respect a government — state or federal — must accord to the dignity and integrity of its citizens. To maintain a fair state-individual balance, to require the government to shoulder the entire load, to respect the inviolability of the human personality, our accusatory system of criminal justice demands that the government seeking to punish an individual produce the evidence against him by its own independent labors, rather than by the cruel, simple expedient of compelling it from his own mouth. In sum, the privilege is fulfilled only when the person is guaranteed the right to remain silent unless he chooses to speak in the unfettered exercise of his own will.

The question in these cases is whether the privilege is fully applicable during a period of custodial interrogation. . . . An individual swept from familiar surroundings into police custody, surrounded by antagonistic forces, and subjected to the techniques of persuasion described above cannot be otherwise than under compulsion to speak. As a practical matter, the compulsion to speak in the isolated setting of the police station may well be greater than in courts or other official investigations, where there are often impartial observers to guard against intimidation or trickery. . . .

Our holding [in *Escobedo*] stressed the fact that the police had not advised the defendant of his constitutional privilege to remain silent at the outset of the interrogation. . . . A different phase of the *Escobedo* decision was significant in its attention to the absence of counsel during the questioning, [And] *Escobedo* explicated another facet of the pre-trial privilege, noted in many of the Court's prior decisions: the protection of rights at trial. That counsel is present when statements are taken from an individual during interrogation obviously enhances the integrity of the fact-finding processes in court. . . . Without the protections flowing from adequate warnings and the rights of counsel, all the careful safeguards erected around the giving of testimony, whether by an accused or any other witness, would become empty formalities in a procedure where the most compelling possible evidence of guilt, a confession, would have already been obtained at the unsupervised pleasure of the police. . . .

III.

It is impossible for us to foresee the potential alternatives for protecting the privilege which might be devised by Congress or the States in the exercise of their creative rule-making capacities. Therefore we cannot say that the Constitution necessarily requires adherence to any particular solution for the inherent compulsions of the interrogation process as it is presently conducted. Our decision in no way creates a constitutional straitjacket which will handicap sound efforts at reform, nor is it intended to have this effect. . . . However, unless we are shown other procedures which are at least as effective in apprising accused persons of their right of silence and in assuring a continuous opportunity to exercise it, the following safeguards must be observed.

At the outset, if a person in custody is to be subjected to interrogation, he must first be informed in clear and unequivocal terms that he has the right to remain silent. For those unaware of the privilege, the warning is needed simply to make them aware of it — the threshold requirement for an intelligent decision as to its exercise. More important, such a warning is an absolute prerequisite in overcoming the inherent pressures of the interrogation atmosphere. It is not just the subnormal or woefully ignorant who succumb to an interrogator's imprecations, whether implied or expressly stated, that the interrogation will continue until a confession is obtained or that silence in the face of accusation is itself damning and will bode ill when presented to a jury. . . . The Fifth Amendment privilege is so fundamental to our system of constitutional rule and the expedient of giving an adequate warning as to the availability of the privilege so simple, we will not pause to inquire in individual cases whether the defendant was aware of his rights without a warning being given. . . .

The warning of the right to remain silent must be accompanied by the explanation that anything said can and will be used against the individual in court. This warning is needed in order to make him aware not only of the privilege, but also of the consequences of forgoing it. It is only through an awareness of these consequences that there can be any assurance of real understanding and intelligent exercise of the privilege. Moreover, this warning may serve to make the individual more acutely aware that . . . he is not in the presence of persons acting solely in his interest.

The circumstances surrounding in-custody interrogation can operate very quickly to overbear the will of one merely made aware of his privilege by his interrogators. Therefore, the right to have counsel present at the interrogation is indispensable to the protection of the Fifth Amendment privilege under the system we delineate today. Our aim is to assure that the individual's right to choose between silence and speech remains unfettered throughout the interrogation process. A once-stated warning, delivered by those who will conduct the interrogation, cannot itself suffice to that end among those who most require knowledge of their rights. . . . Even preliminary advice given to the accused by his own attorney can be swiftly overcome by the secret interrogation process. Thus, the need for counsel to protect the Fifth Amendment privilege comprehends not merely a right to consult with counsel prior to questioning, but also to have counsel present during any questioning if the defendant so desires.

The presence of counsel at the interrogation may serve several significant subsidiary functions as well. If the accused decides to talk to his interrogators, the assistance of counsel can mitigate the dangers of untrustworthiness. With a lawyer present the likelihood that the police will practice coercion is reduced, and if coercion is nevertheless exercised the lawyer can testify to it in court. The presence of a lawyer can also help to guarantee that the accused gives a fully accurate statement to the police and that the statement is rightly reported by the prosecution at trial.

[An individual's] failure to ask for a lawyer does not constitute a waiver. No effective waiver of the right to counsel during interrogation can be recognized unless specifically made after the warnings we here delineate have been given. The accused who does not know his rights and therefore does not make a request may be the person who most needs counsel. . . .

Accordingly we hold that an individual held for interrogation must be clearly informed that he has the right to consult with a lawyer and to have the lawyer with him during interrogation under the system for protecting the privilege we delineate today. As with the warnings of the right to remain silent and that anything stated can be used in evidence against him, this warning is an absolute prerequisite to interrogation. . . .

If an individual indicates that he wishes the assistance of counsel before any interrogation occurs, the authorities cannot rationally ignore or deny his request on the basis that the individual does not have or cannot afford a retained attorney. The financial ability of the individual has no relationship to the scope of the rights involved here. The privilege against self-incrimination secured by the Constitution applies to all individuals. . . . In fact, were we to limit these constitutional rights to those who can retain an attorney, our decisions today would be of little significance. The cases before us as well as the vast majority of confession cases with which we have dealt in the past involve those unable to retain counsel. . . .

In order fully to apprise a person interrogated of the extent of his rights under this system then, it is necessary to warn him not only that he has the right to consult with an attorney, but also that if he is indigent a lawyer will be appointed to represent him. Without this additional warning, the admonition of the right to consult with counsel would often be understood as meaning only that he can consult with a lawyer if he has one or has the funds to obtain one. . . .

Once warnings have been given, the subsequent procedure is clear. If the individual indicates in any manner, at any time prior to or during questioning, that he wishes to remain silent, the interrogation must cease. At this point he has shown that he intends to exercise his Fifth Amendment privilege; any statement taken after the person invokes his privilege cannot be other than the product of compulsion, subtle or otherwise. Without the right to cut off questioning, the setting of in-custody interrogation operates on the individual to overcome free choice in producing a statement after the privilege has been once invoked. If the individual states that he wants an attorney, the interrogation must cease until an attorney is present. At that time, the individual must have an opportunity to confer with the attorney and to have him present during any subsequent questioning. If the individual cannot obtain an attorney and he indicates that he wants one before speaking to police, they must respect his decision to remain silent.

This does not mean, as some have suggested, that each police station must have a "station house lawyer" present at all times to advise prisoners. It does mean, however, that if police propose to interrogate a person they must make known to him that he is entitled to a lawyer and that if he cannot afford one, a lawyer will be provided for him prior to any interrogation. . . . If the interrogation continues without the presence of an attorney and a statement is taken, a heavy burden rests on the government to demonstrate that the defendant knowingly and intelligently waived his privilege against self-incrimination and his right to retained or appointed counsel. . . .

An express statement that the individual is willing to make a statement and does not want an attorney followed closely by a statement could constitute a waiver. But a valid waiver will not be presumed simply from the silence of the accused after warnings are given or simply from the fact that a confession was in fact eventually obtained. . . . Moreover, where in-custody interrogation is involved, there is no room for the contention that the privilege is waived if the individual answers some questions or gives some information on his own prior to invoking his right to remain silent when interrogated.

Whatever the testimony of the authorities as to waiver of rights by an accused, the fact of lengthy interrogation or incommunicado incarceration before a statement is made is strong evidence that the accused did not validly waive his rights. . . . Moreover, any evidence that the accused was threatened, tricked, or cajoled into a waiver will, of course, show that the defendant did not voluntarily waive his privilege. The requirement of warnings and waiver of rights is a fundamental with respect to the Fifth Amendment privilege and not simply a preliminary ritual to existing methods of interrogation. . . .

The principles announced today deal with the protection which must be given to the privilege against self-incrimination when the individual is first subjected to police interrogation while in custody at the station or otherwise deprived of his freedom of action in any significant way. It is at this point that our adversary system of criminal proceedings commences, distinguishing itself at the outset from the inquisitorial system recognized in some countries. . . .

Our decision is not intended to hamper the traditional function of police officers in investigating crime. When an individual is in custody on probable cause, the police may, of course, seek out evidence in the field to be used at trial against him. Such investigation may include inquiry of persons not under restraint. General on-the-scene questioning as to facts surrounding a crime or other general questioning of citizens in the fact-finding process is not affected by our holding. . . .

In dealing with statements obtained through interrogation, we do not purport to find all confessions inadmissible. Confessions remain a proper element in law enforcement. Any statement given freely and voluntarily without any compelling influences is, of course, admissible in evidence. . . .

IV.

In announcing these principles, we are not unmindful of the burdens which law enforcement officials must bear, often under trying circumstances. [Our] decision does not in any way preclude police from carrying out their traditional investigatory functions. Although confessions may play an important role in some convictions, the cases before us present graphic examples of the overstatement of the "need" for confessions. In each case authorities conducted interrogations ranging up to five days in duration despite the presence, through standard investigating practices, of considerable evidence against each defendant. . . .

Over the years the Federal Bureau of Investigation has compiled an exemplary record of effective law enforcement while advising any suspect or arrested person, at the outset of an interview, that he is not required to make a statement, that any statement may be used against him in court, that the individual may obtain the services of an attorney of his own choice and, more recently, that he has a right to free counsel if he is unable to pay. . . .

The experience in some other countries also suggests that the danger to law enforcement in curbs on interrogation is overplayed. The English procedure since 1912 under the Judges' Rules is significant. As recently strengthened, the Rules require that a cautionary warning be given an accused by a police officer as soon as he has evidence that affords reasonable grounds for suspicion; they also require that any statement made be given by the accused without questioning by police. The right of the individual to consult with an attorney during this period is expressly recognized. . . .

It is also urged upon us that we withhold decision on this issue until state legislative bodies and advisory groups have had an opportunity to deal with these problems by rule making. We have already pointed out that the Constitution does not require any specific code of procedures for protecting the privilege against self-incrimination during custodial interrogation. Congress and the States are free to develop their own safeguards for the privilege, so long as they are fully as effective as those described above in informing accused persons of their right of silence and in affording a continuous opportunity to exercise it. In any event, however, the issues presented are of constitutional dimensions and must be determined by the courts. . . .

V.

Because of the nature of the problem and because of its recurrent significance in numerous cases, we have to this point discussed the relationship of the Fifth Amendment privilege to police interrogation without specific concentration on the facts of the cases before us. We turn now to these facts to consider the application to these cases of the constitutional principles discussed above. . . .

On March 13, 1963, petitioner, Ernesto Miranda, was arrested at his home and taken in custody to a Phoenix police station. He was there identified by the complaining witness. The police then took him to Interrogation Room No. 2 of the detective bureau. There he was questioned by two police officers. The officers admitted at trial that Miranda was not advised that he had a right to have an attorney present. Two hours later, the officers emerged from the interrogation room with a written confession signed by Miranda. At the top of the statement was a typed paragraph stating that the confession was made voluntarily, without threats or promises of immunity and "with full knowledge of my legal rights, understanding any statement I make may be used against me." [One of the officers testified that he read this paragraph to Miranda. Apparently, however, he did not do so until after Miranda had confessed orally.]

At his trial before a jury, the written confession was admitted into evidence over the objection of defense counsel, and the officers testified to the prior oral confession made by Miranda during the interrogation. Miranda was found guilty of kidnapping and rape. He was sentenced to 20 to 30 years' imprisonment on each count, the sentences to run concurrently. On appeal, the Supreme Court of Arizona held that Miranda's constitutional rights were not violated in obtaining the confession and affirmed the conviction. In reaching its decision, the court emphasized heavily the fact that Miranda did not specifically request counsel.

We reverse. From the testimony of the officers and by the admission of respondent, it is clear that Miranda was not in any way apprised of his right to consult with an attorney and to have one present during the interrogation, nor was his right not to be compelled to incriminate himself effectively protected in any other manner. Without these warnings the statements were inadmissible. The mere fact that he signed a statement which contained a typed-in clause stating that he had "full knowledge" of his "legal rights" does not approach the knowing and intelligent waiver required to relinquish constitutional rights. . . .

HARLAN, J., dissenting.*

[The] new rules are not designed to guard against police brutality or other unmistakably banned forms of coercion. Those who use third-degree tactics and deny them in court are equally able and destined to lie as skillfully about warnings and waivers. Rather, the thrust of the new rules is to negate all pressures, to reinforce the nervous or ignorant suspect, and ultimately to discourage any confession at all. The aim in short is toward "voluntariness" in a Utopian sense, or to view it from a different angle, voluntariness with a vengeance. To incorporate this notion into the Constitution requires a strained reading of history and precedent and a disregard of the very pragmatic concerns that alone may on occasion justify such strains. . . .

It is most fitting to begin an inquiry into the constitutional precedents by surveying the limits on confessions the Court has evolved under the Due Process Clause of the Fourteenth Amendment. This is so because these cases show that there exists a workable and effective means of dealing with confessions in a judicial manner. . . .

The earliest confession cases in this Court emerged from federal prosecutions and were settled on a nonconstitutional basis, the Court adopting the common-law rule that the absence of inducements, promises, and threats made a confession voluntary and admissible. [A] new line of decisions, testing admissibility by the Due Process Clause, began in 1936 with Brown v. Mississippi, and must now embrace somewhat more than 30 full opinions of the Court. While the voluntariness rubric was repeated in many instances, the Court never pinned it down to a single meaning but on the contrary infused it with a number of different values. To travel quickly over the main themes, there was an initial emphasis on reliability, supplemented by concern over the legality and fairness of the police practices, in an "accusatorial" system of law enforcement, and eventually by close attention to the individual's state of mind and capacity for effective choice. The outcome was a continuing re-evaluation on the facts of each case of how much pressure on the suspect was permissible.

Among the criteria often taken into account were threats or imminent danger, physical deprivations such as lack of sleep or food, repeated or extended interrogation, limits on access to counsel or friends, length and illegality of detention

* [Justices Stewart and White joined in this opinion. — EDS.]

under state law, and individual weakness or incapacities. Apart from direct physical coercion, however, no single default or fixed combination of defaults guaranteed exclusion, and synopses of the cases would serve little use because the overall gauge has been steadily changing, usually in the direction of restricting admissibility. . . .

There are several relevant lessons to be drawn from this constitutional history. The first is that with over 25 years of precedent the Court has developed an elaborate, sophisticated, and sensitive approach to admissibility of confessions. It is "judicial" in its treatment of one case at a time, flexible in its ability to respond to the endless mutations of fact presented, and ever more familiar to the lower courts . . . . The second point is that in practice and from time to time in principle, the Court has given ample recognition to society's interest in suspect questioning as an instrument of law enforcement . . . .

I turn now to the Court's asserted reliance on the Fifth Amendment, an approach which I frankly regard as a *trompe l'oeil.* The Court's opinion in my view reveals no adequate basis for extending the Fifth Amendment's privilege against self-incrimination to the police station. Far more important, it fails to show that the Court's new rules are well supported, let alone compelled, by Fifth Amendment precedents. . . .

Examined as an expression of public policy, the Court's new regime proves so dubious that there can be no due compensation for its weakness in constitutional law. . . . Without at all subscribing to the generally black picture of police conduct painted by the Court, I think it must be frankly recognized at the outset that police questioning allowable under due process precedents may inherently entail some pressure on the suspect and may seek advantage in his ignorance or weaknesses. . . . The Court's new rules aim to offset these minor pressures and disadvantages intrinsic to any kind of police interrogation. . . .

What the Court largely ignores is that its rules impair, if they will not eventually serve wholly to frustrate, an instrument of law enforcement that has long and quite reasonably been thought worth the price paid for it. There can be little doubt that the Court's new code would markedly decrease the number of confessions. To warn the suspect that he may remain silent and remind him that his confession may be used in court are minor obstructions. To require also an express waiver by the suspect and an end to questioning whenever he demurs must heavily handicap questioning. And to suggest or provide counsel for the suspect simply invites the end of the interrogation. . . .

– this will lower # of confessions

While passing over the costs and risks of its experiment, the Court portrays the evils of normal police questioning in terms which I think are exaggerated. Albeit stringently confined by the due process standards interrogation is no doubt often inconvenient and unpleasant for the suspect. However, it is no less so for a man to be arrested and jailed, to have his house searched, or to stand trial in court, yet all this may properly happen to the most innocent given probable cause, a warrant, or an indictment. Society has always paid a stiff price for law and order, and peaceful interrogation is not one of the dark moments of the law. . . .

It is also instructive to compare the attitude in this case of those responsible for law enforcement with the official views that existed when the Court undertook . . . major revisions of prosecutorial practice prior to this case. . . . In Mapp v. Ohio, 367 U.S. 643 (1961), which imposed the exclusionary rule on the States for Fourth Amendment violations, more than half of the States had themselves already adopted some such rule. In Gideon v. Wainwright, 372 U.S. 335 (1963), . . . an amicus brief was filed by 22 States and Commonwealths urging that [the Court extend the right to counsel to indigents in state court]; only two States besides that of the respondent came forward to protest. By contrast, in this case new restrictions on police questioning have been opposed by the United States and in an amicus brief signed by 27 States and Commonwealths, not including the three other States which are parties. No State in the country has urged this Court to impose the newly announced rules, nor has any State chosen to go nearly so far on its own. [The] FBI falls sensibly short of the Court's formalistic rules. For example, there is no indication that FBI agents must obtain an affirmative "waiver" before they pursue their questioning. . . .

In closing this [discussion] of policy considerations attending the new confession rules, some reference must be made to their ironic untimeliness. There is now in progress in this country a massive re-examination of criminal law enforcement procedures on a scale never before witnessed. [Legislative] reform is rarely speedy or unanimous, though this Court has been more patient in the past. But the legislative reforms when they come would have the vast advantage of empirical data and comprehensive study, they would allow experimentation and use of solutions not open to the courts, and they would restore the initiative in criminal law reform to those forums where it truly belongs. . . .

WHITE, J., dissenting.*

Decisions like these cannot rest alone on syllogism, metaphysics or some ill-defined notions of natural justice, although each will perhaps play its part. . . . First, we may inquire what are the textual and factual bases of this new fundamental rule. [The] Court concedes that it cannot truly know what occurs during custodial questioning, because of the innate secrecy of such proceedings. It extrapolates a picture of what it conceives to be the norm from police investigatorial manuals. . . . Judged by any of the standards for empirical investigation utilized in the social sciences the factual basis for the Court's premise is patently inadequate. . . .

Even if one were to postulate that the Court's concern is not that all confessions induced by police interrogation are coerced but rather that some such confessions are coerced and present judicial procedures are believed to be inadequate to identify the confessions that are coerced and those that are not, it would still not be essential to impose the rule that the Court has now fashioned. Transcripts or observers could be required, specific time limits, tailored to fit the cause, could be imposed, or other devices could be utilized to reduce the chances that otherwise indiscernible coercion will produce an inadmissible confession.

On the other hand, even if one assumed that there was an adequate factual basis for the conclusion that all confessions obtained during in-custody interrogation are the product of compulsion, the rule propounded by the Court would still be irrational, for, apparently, it is only if the accused is also warned of his right to counsel and waives both that right and the right against self-incrimination that the inherent compulsiveness of interrogation disappears. But if the defendant may not answer without a warning a question such as "Where were you last night?" without having his answer be a compelled one, how can the Court ever accept his negative answer

* [Justices Harlan and Stewart joined in this opinion. — EDS.]

to the question of whether he wants to consult his retained counsel or counsel whom the court will appoint? . . .

The obvious underpinning of the Court's decision is a deep-seated distrust of all confessions. As the Court declares that the accused may not be interrogated without counsel present, absent a waiver of the right to counsel, and as the Court all but admonishes the lawyer to advise the accused to remain silent, the result adds up to a judicial judgment that evidence from the accused should not be used against him in any way, whether compelled or not. . . . I see nothing wrong or immoral, and certainly nothing unconstitutional, in the police's asking a suspect whom they have reasonable cause to arrest whether or not he killed his wife or in confronting him with the evidence on which the arrest was based, at least where he has been plainly advised that he may remain completely silent. . . . Particularly when corroborated, as where the police have confirmed the accused's disclosure of the hiding place of implements or fruits of the crime, such confessions have the highest reliability and significantly contribute to the certitude with which we may believe the accused is guilty. . . .

Much of the trouble with the Court's new rule is that it will operate indiscriminately in all criminal cases, regardless of the severity of the crime or the circumstances involved. It applies to every defendant, whether the professional criminal or one committing a crime of momentary passion. [If] further restrictions on police interrogation are desirable at this time, a more flexible approach makes much more sense than the Court's constitutional straitjacket which forecloses more discriminating treatment by legislative or rule-making pronouncements. . . .

LOUISIANA CONSTITUTION ART. 1, §13

When any person has been arrested or detained in connection with the investigation or commission of any offense, he shall be advised fully of the reasons for his arrest or detention, his right to remain silent, his right against self incrimination, his right to the assistance of counsel and, if indigent, his right to court appointed counsel.

MASSACHUSETTS GENERAL LAWS, CH. 276, §33A

The police official in charge of the station or other place of detention having a telephone wherein a person is held in custody, shall permit the use of the telephone, at the expense of the arrested person, for the purpose of allowing the arrested person to communicate with his family or friends, or to arrange for release on bail, or to engage the services of an attorney. Any such person shall be informed forthwith upon his arrival at such station or place of detention, of his right to so use the telephone, and such use shall be permitted within one hour thereafter.

Notes

1. *The constitutional basis for* Miranda. What is the legal basis of the *Miranda* decision? The Court indicated that the warnings and the right to counsel it was

announcing were requirements of the Fifth Amendment's self-incrimination clause. Later, the Court refined this position and stated that the *Miranda* rights were "prophylactic" rules that were not, strictly speaking, required by the Fifth Amendment but were necessary to prevent violations of the self-incrimination privilege. See Michigan v. Tucker, 417 U.S. 433 (1974). Why do you suppose the Court based its ruling on the Fifth Amendment rather than the Sixth Amendment's right to counsel? If the *Miranda* warnings are a prophylactic rule rather than a constitutional requirement, did the Court have the authority to impose this requirement on state as well as federal law enforcement officers?

The opinion in *Miranda* creates a relatively detailed set of obligations. Some states and law enforcement agencies, prior to 1966, used warnings to increase the likelihood that a confession would be found voluntary. Would the Court have been wiser to announce more general principles and hope for legislation or police rules to appear before providing any needed specification? See Mark A. Godsey, Rethinking the Involuntary Confession Rule: Toward a Workable Test for Identifying Compelled Self-Incrimination, 93 Cal. L. Rev. 465 (2005) (argues for replacing voluntariness with self-incrimination as basic criterion for admission of confessions; proposes asking whether confession was obtained by using an objective penalty on the suspect to punish silence or provoke speech).

2. *State adoption and modification of* Miranda. The *Miranda* requirements apply to law enforcement officials in all the states. What would occur if the Supreme Court were to modify the *Miranda* decision? A few states, such as Louisiana and Massachusetts, have independently adopted under their state constitutions or statutes a set of required warnings similar to those in *Miranda.* See Traylor v. State, 596 So. 2d 957 (Fla. 1992). Others declare that *Miranda* has no basis in the state constitution. See State v. Bleyl, 435 A.2d 1349 (Me. 1981). Does the Louisiana provision reprinted above impose any requirements different from what the Court required in *Miranda*?

3. *The coercive environment and the "infinite regress" problem.* The *Miranda* opinion is premised on the view that interrogation of a suspect in a police station is inherently coercive. Do you agree with this premise? If so, what makes the interrogation coercive? Is there any legal or practical consequence if a suspect refuses to speak? Consider again the words of the Fifth Amendment: Are you convinced that interrogation in a police station "compels" a person to be a "witness" against himself? As you answer these questions, keep in mind the physical environment of a typical custodial interrogation. The interrogation rooms are designed to isolate suspects, for instance, by locating the rooms in the rear of the building, often with no windows for viewing persons outside the room. The room will contain only a table and a few chairs. Consider also the subject matter of the conversation, and the assertions a questioner will often make. If interrogation is inherently coercive, isn't the decision to waive the right to counsel also made in the same setting? Could the Court respond to this problem by requiring a more specific warning about waiver? A warning about the warning?

4. *Liberal or conservative?* Was *Miranda* a liberal or conservative ruling? Did it legitimize police interrogation through the use of a routine and inconsequential warning? Did it foreclose more intrusive and less predictable judicial supervision of interrogation techniques? See also Charles D. Weisselberg, Mourning *Miranda*, 96 Calif. L. Rev. 1519 (2008) (safeguards of *Miranda* have become ineffective because police training now instructs officers in how to take advantage of court rulings that have weakened the case; *Miranda*'s hollow ritual often forecloses a searching inquiry

into the voluntariness of a statement). Early opinions among police officers about the wisdom of *Miranda* were mixed. Some officers believed that it was a damaging and unnecessary impediment to effective interrogations; others believed that the required warnings were appropriate and would further the professionalism of police work. See Otis Stephens, Robert Flanders & Lewis Cannon, Law Enforcement and the Supreme Court: Police Perceptions of the *Miranda* Requirements, 39 Tenn. L. Rev. 407 (1972). Over the years, police opinion about the decision has become markedly more positive. Various empirical studies of the reception of *Miranda* among law enforcement officers and other groups are discussed on the web extension for this chapter at *http://www.crimpro.com/extension/ch08*.

5. *Constitutional foundations of* Miranda, *revisited.* Soon after the *Miranda* decision, Congress enacted 18 U.S.C. §3501, stating that the admissibility of statements made by federal defendants while in police custody should turn only on whether or not they were voluntarily made. While the statute instructed the judge to consider any warnings given to the suspect about the right to silence or to consult an attorney, the "presence or absence" of any such warnings "need not be conclusive on the issue of voluntariness of the confession." For many years and through many administrations, federal prosecutors appear to have made only modest use of §3501. See Paul Cassell, The Statute That Time Forgot: 18 U.S.C. §3501 and the Overhauling of *Miranda*, 85 Iowa L. Rev. 175, 197-225 (1999). The most likely explanation is that §3501 was such a stark rejection of the Supreme Court's decision that most federal prosecutors felt they should not, and perhaps could not, rely upon it, since they are sworn to uphold the constitution.

The Supreme Court finally spoke to the issue in Dickerson v. United States, 530 U.S. 428 (2000). The defendant in the case gave incriminating evidence against himself in an interview that proceeded without proper *Miranda* warnings (although the interrogation was not otherwise coercive). The key question was whether *Miranda* announced a constitutional rule or was merely a regulation of evidence used in federal court.

The Court held that *Miranda*, "being a constitutional decision of this Court, may not be in effect overruled by an Act of Congress, and we decline to overrule *Miranda* ourselves." Over the years, the Court made conflicting statements about the constitutional basis for *Miranda*. Many later decisions referred to *Miranda* as a "prophylactic" rule rather than a constitutional requirement in its own right. See New York v. Quarles, 467 U.S. 649 (1984) (warnings not required when questions were necessitated by an immediate threat to public safety). But in the end, the fact that *Miranda* applied to proceedings in state court demonstrated that the rule was constitutionally required.

6. *Real* Miranda *reforms.* Again and again courts and commentators have noted that the *Miranda* court left open "potential alternatives for protecting the privilege which might be devised by Congress or the States," and allowed legislative solutions different from *Miranda* warnings, so long as the alternatives were "at least as effective in apprising accused persons of their right of silence and in assuring a continuous opportunity to exercise it." If *Miranda* warnings are problematic for law enforcement, why hasn't Congress or a state legislature enacted alternatives more substantial than §3501? What form might this legislation take?

2. *"Triggering"* Miranda *Warnings*

Miranda warnings do not need to be given before *every* conversation between police and citizens. There are two conditions that trigger a need for warnings: First, the suspect must be in custody, and second, the officers must be conducting an interrogation. Even though judges, police, and commentators often join the concepts in the phrase "custodial interrogation," it is important to evaluate custody and interrogation separately.

a. "Custody"

The police are required to give *Miranda* warnings only to suspects who are interrogated while in custody. One study of police work in Salt Lake City found that 30 percent of all interviews occurred in noncustodial settings, including examinations at the crime scene, during field investigations, and during arranged interviews. See Paul Cassell & Bret Hayman, Police Interrogation in the 1990s: An Empirical Study of the Effects of *Miranda,* 43 UCLA L. Rev. 839 (1996). The 30 percent figure relates to full-blown interrogations: It substantially understates the total amount of questions, inquiries, comments, and exchanges that police conduct outside of custodial settings.

■ STATE v. KEVIN FRANKLIN ELMARR

181 P.3d 1157 (Colo. 2008)

RICE, J.

In this interlocutory appeal . . . we review an order from the Boulder County District Court suppressing statements the defendant made in response to police interrogation. We find that the trial court properly suppressed the defendant's statements because the defendant was in custody while interrogated, and it is conceded that he did not receive proper *Miranda* warnings before that custodial interrogation. We therefore affirm the trial court's suppression order and remand for further proceedings.

I. Facts and Procedural History

On Sunday, May 24, 1987, Detectives Ferguson and Haugse of the Boulder Sheriff's Department and Officer Stiles of the Longmont Police Department visited Defendant Kevin Franklin Elmarr at his home to inform him that his ex-wife, Carol Murphy, was found dead the day before. According to the testimony before the trial court, the detectives were not in uniform, and their weapons were holstered. Officer Stiles was in uniform, but was present more as a friend of Elmarr's family to aid in the notification of death. Two other police officers — Captain Epp and Lieutenant Hopper — later arrived at Elmarr's home in another unmarked police car and were seen there by Elmarr, but they stayed outside.

Detectives Ferguson and Haugse spoke with Elmarr at his home and Elmarr disclosed that he had visited with his ex-wife the day before she was found dead, and had taken her for a ride on his motorcycle. Shortly after this disclosure, Detective Ferguson said the police had more questions for him, and asked him if he would mind accompanying them to the Sheriff's Department at the Boulder Justice Center for further questioning; Elmarr agreed. The detectives drove Elmarr to the Sheriff's Department in their unmarked police car, with Elmarr in the back seat. The detectives did not provide Elmarr the option of driving himself to the station. Elmarr was not handcuffed.

During the drive to the Sheriff's Department, Elmarr volunteered that he had not been entirely truthful in his earlier conversation with the detectives, and provided further information regarding his meeting with his ex-wife the day before she was found dead. The detectives did not say anything while in the car.

The detectives arrived at the Sheriff's Department through the garage in the basement, which is a secure area not open to the public. They escorted Elmarr into an elevator that led to the Sheriff's Department Detective Bureau, which is also not open to the public. Witnesses were unable to recall whether Elmarr was searched before entering the building, but Captain Epp testified that it was standard procedure for persons to be patted down before being transported. Based on this testimony, the trial court found that Elmarr was subjected to a pat-down search upon arrival at the Sheriff's Department. The trial court also found that Elmarr was then placed in a closed interview room measuring seven by ten feet, and told to stay there until officers returned. Captain Epp and Lieutenant Hopper subsequently interrogated Elmarr in that interview room. During the interrogation, Elmarr was seated against the wall, while Captain Epp and Lieutenant Hopper were seated in front of the door. The officers were dressed casually, but the trial court found that they were carrying their weapons. . . . Though the interview room door had a lock on it, no one could recall if it was locked while Elmarr was in the room.

Witnesses testified that Elmarr was never handcuffed or otherwise directly physically restrained, but no one ever told Elmarr that he was free to leave or that he was not under arrest. The interrogation was audio- and video-taped, and the recording shows that Captain Epp began his interrogation by advising Elmarr that he did not have to talk to the police, that he had a right to remain silent, that anything he said that incriminated him would be taken down, and that he had a right to an attorney. Captain Epp then asked if Elmarr wanted to talk to them then. Elmarr answered "sure," and then began speaking about the last time he saw his ex-wife.

Captain Epp then questioned Elmarr about the details of that last meeting with his ex-wife. Though Captain Epp spoke rather slowly and softly, he soon began expressing his doubts about Elmarr's story. For instance, early in the interview Captain Epp told Elmarr, "I hope you're telling me the truth." Later he inspected what he thought were scratches on Elmarr's arms.

Approximately halfway into the interview, Lieutenant Hopper took over much of the questioning, and his tone was more aggressive. He asked Elmarr if he ever thought of hurting his ex-wife; why witnesses would say they saw his ex-wife on a motorcycle matching Elmarr's near the place where her body was found; and whether his ex-wife was "all right" the last time he saw her. Lieutenant Hopper again asked Elmarr why he initially lied when interviewed at his house. [Elmarr said] that he felt he was being accused of murder, and Lieutenant Hopper answered, "You've lied to us already. . . . Put yourself in our place. What would you, what would you think if you were us?"

The recording also shows that near the end of the interrogation, which lasted almost an hour, Captain Epp resumed his questioning, telling Elmarr, "I just get the feeling that you are holding something back." When Elmarr wondered aloud whether he should get a lawyer[2] and protested that he was telling the truth, Captain Epp responded, "Well, I'm not sure. I've got reason to believe that something, that some points here that you're not." Shortly thereafter Lieutenant Hopper explicitly asked Elmarr whether he killed his ex-wife, and Elmarr denied it. Elmarr then said, "I think I would like to talk to a lawyer." At this point the officers stated the interview was over, opened the door, and left the room. They testified that the entire interrogation lasted approximately fifty minutes.

However, Elmarr remained in the Sheriff's Department. The recording shows that he was kept in the interview room for a period of time, after which one of the officers returned and asked him if he would like to take a polygraph test. Elmarr demurred and again stated he wanted to talk to an attorney. The officer left. After a further wait, yet another officer entered the interview room, stated that he wanted to take some photographs of Elmarr, and asked if Elmarr would mind removing his clothes for those pictures, adding, "You really don't have a choice right now." Elmarr complied, after which he asked, "When do I get to go home?" The officer responded, "Shortly here, I hope." Elmarr then asked to make some calls to his family and the officer left, returning later to escort Elmarr out of the interview room to make his calls. Afterwards, Elmarr was escorted back into the interview room, and in the videotape one can hear the door close again. Elmarr again asked how long he would be there, and was told, "At least until your lawyer calls." After a further wait, Elmarr's attorney entered the interview room and the videotape ended, almost an hour after Captain Epp and Lieutenant Hopper had terminated their formal interrogation. . . .

Elmarr was not charged with a crime until almost twenty years later, when in January 2007 he was arrested and charged with first degree murder for the murder of his ex-wife Carol Murphy. [The trial court] suppressed all of the statements Elmarr made at the Sheriff's Department, finding that they were all the product of custodial interrogation.

Because there was no dispute that Elmarr was interrogated, the trial court focused on whether Elmarr was in custody while at the Sheriff's Department. In concluding that Elmarr was indeed in custody, the trial court made the following findings: (1) Elmarr was subjected to a pat-down search upon arrival at the Sheriff's Department; (2) Elmarr was provided with (albeit deficient) *Miranda*-type warnings typically given when a suspect is in custody; (3) Elmarr was placed in a seven-by-ten-foot interview room and told to stay there until the officers returned; (4) Elmarr was interrogated for at least fifty minutes by officers carrying weapons; (5) Captain Epp likely suspected that Elmarr was involved in Carol Murphy's murder and was attempting to elicit incriminating statements from him; (6) Captain Epp and Lieutenant Hopper used a "good-cop-bad-cop" technique upon Elmarr; (6) Elmarr was never handcuffed or overtly restrained, but was never told he was free to leave. . . .

2. The People conceded that this was a sufficient invocation of the right to counsel, and that interrogation should have ceased at this point.

II. Analysis

In their interlocutory appeal, the People . . . argue that Elmarr was not in custody when he was interrogated at the Sheriff's Department, and that the trial court made erroneous factual findings and considered irrelevant evidence in reaching its conclusion. We find that the trial court erroneously considered the police officers' subjective intent in determining whether Elmarr was in custody, but that the court's other factual findings are supported by the record. We hold that those findings, coupled with the undisputed evidence in the record, establish that Elmarr was in custody when he was interrogated at the Sheriff's Department. . . .

For purposes of determining whether *Miranda* warnings are required, a suspect is in custody when his or her "freedom of action is curtailed to a degree associated with formal arrest." People v. Polander, 41 P.3d 698, 705 (Colo.2001) (quoting Berkemer v. McCarty, 468 U.S. 420, (1984)). In assessing the question of custody, we consider such factors as the time, place, and purpose of the interrogation; the persons present during the interrogation; the words the officers spoke to the suspect; the officers' tone of voice and general demeanor; the length and mood of the interrogation; whether any restraint or limitation was placed on the suspect's movement during interrogation; the officers' response to any of the suspect's questions; whether directions were given to the suspect during interrogation; and the suspect's verbal or nonverbal responses to such directions. None of these factors is determinative, and the question of custody is determined in light of the totality of the circumstances.

However, because the test of custody is an objective one, unarticulated thoughts or views of the officers and suspects are irrelevant. See Stansbury v. California, 511 U.S. 318 (1994) (The "initial determination of custody depends on the objective circumstances of the interrogation, not on the subjective views harbored by either the interrogating officers or the person being questioned."). Thus, the People are correct in their argument that the trial court erred when, in determining whether Elmarr was in custody, it relied (in part) upon the finding that Captain Epp likely suspected that Elmarr was involved in Carol Murphy's murder and attempted to elicit incriminating statements from him. That finding has no relevance to the custody question. We therefore review de novo whether the trial court's other factual findings, and the undisputed evidence in the record, establish that Elmarr was in custody.

Our analysis is guided by precedent considering somewhat analogous facts. For instance, in California v. Beheler, 463 U.S. 1121 (1983), officers asked the suspect to accompany them to the police station, transported him there, informed him he was not under arrest, and questioned him for less than thirty minutes before he voluntarily left the police station. The court found that these facts established that the suspect was not in custody. Similarly, in Oregon v. Mathiason, 429 U.S. 492 (1977), the officers asked the suspect to come to the police station to be interviewed. The suspect drove himself to the station, was immediately told he was not under arrest, was told that he was a suspect in a crime, and interviewed for approximately thirty minutes behind closed doors in an interview room before he left the station voluntarily. Again, the court found the suspect was not in custody. We came to the same conclusion in People v. Matheny, 46 P.3d 453 (Colo. 2002), where the suspect was asked to come to the police station to be interviewed, drove himself and the police officers to the station, was escorted to an interview room, was told he was free to leave and not under arrest, and then was interviewed for approximately an hour and a half.

In People v. Trujillo, 784 P.2d 788 (Colo. 1990), however, we found that a suspect was in custody where he was asked to come to the police station for an interview and drove himself to the station; upon arrival, he was never told he was free to leave or not under arrest, was asked accusatory questions for over an hour and a half, was asked to submit to a mug shot and a polygraph test, and was asked to produce certain evidence to the police. Similarly, in People v. Dracon, 884 P.2d 712 (Colo. 1994), we found the suspect was in custody where she agreed to accompany officers to the police station, riding in the front seat of the police car, and was taken through a non-public area to an office and questioned for almost three hours; she was never told she was free to leave or not under arrest, and was made to wait for another three hours in the police station before being interviewed yet again. Finally, we found that a suspect was in custody in People v. Minjarez, 81 P.3d 348 (Colo. 2003), where police officers came to the hospital where the suspect's child was being treated, asked nurses to bring him to a hospital interview room the officers had procured, directed the suspect to sit in a chair away from the closed door, and told the suspect he was free to go but then subjected him to aggressive interrogation — consisting of leading questions and accusations of guilt — for twenty of the forty-five minutes of the interview.

Precedent doesn't provide a neat formula

Precedent does not provide a neat formula for deciding the case at hand, and indeed there can be no such formula as each case will present novel factual patterns not previously addressed. We have provided some general rules, however. On the one hand, we have heeded the warning that one is not in custody simply because the questioning takes place in the station house. On the other hand, an officer's statement that a suspect is "free to leave" is not sufficient to establish that an interview is non-custodial, when all the external circumstances appear to the contrary.

Though the case at hand presents a close question, we find that Elmarr was in custody while interrogated by officers in the Sheriff's Department in 1987. No one fact leads us to this conclusion, but rather the totality of the circumstances combine to create a custodial atmosphere. Though Elmarr was asked to accompany police officers to the station for questioning, such a question does not necessarily make the event voluntary, as one could interpret the question to be one where "no" is not an available answer — especially in the circumstances present here. It is significant that Elmarr was transported in the back of a police car to the non-public area of the Sheriff's Department, where he was directed to wait and then interrogated in a small, closed-door interview room. Importantly, he was never told he was not under arrest, or that he was free to leave. In fact, the trial court found that Elmarr was instructed to wait for officers in a closed room, and was thereafter interrogated at length in that room.

Furthermore, it is significant that Elmarr was subjected to aggressive interrogation, where the interrogators expressed doubts regarding his truthfulness, discounted his denials, confronted him with potential evidence of his guilt, and accused him of committing murder. Such interrogation by multiple officers in a small room isolated from others helped create a sense of custody. The custodial atmosphere continued after Elmarr requested an attorney — even then, he was kept in the closed-door interview room and was asked about his willingness to submit to a polygraph test, and then was directed to disrobe for photographs, about which he was told, "You really don't have a choice." All of these factors combined to prompt Elmarr to ask the reasonable question, "When do I get to go home?" All of these facts lead to the conclusion that Elmarr's freedom of action was curtailed to a degree associated with formal arrest, and a reasonable person under those circumstances would feel that he was in custody.[5]

We conclude that all of Elmarr's statements to the police at the Boulder Sheriff's Department in 1987 were the product of custodial interrogation. Because it is conceded that Elmarr did not receive a proper *Miranda* warning, all of those statements must be suppressed. Accordingly, we affirm the trial court's suppression order, and remand for further proceedings consistent with this opinion.

COATS, J., dissenting.

Almost a quarter-century ago, the United States Supreme Court made clear that a suspect is not placed in custody for purposes of the *Miranda* requirements merely by being seized and subjected to an investigatory stop. Berkemer v. McCarty, 468 U.S. 420 (1984). Rather, the prophylactic *Miranda* warnings are triggered only when a suspect's liberty has been infringed upon to an extent commensurate with a formal arrest. And interrogation at a police station, as long as it is consensual, does not constitute a seizure of any kind, much less a seizure tantamount to an arrest.

This jurisdiction was late in acknowledging the distinction between a seizure of the defendant's person and custody for purposes of *Miranda,* and when finally forced to acknowledge the Supreme Court's holdings in *Berkemer* . . . and *Beheler,* we dismissed them as merely reflecting a "fact-specific approach" to the question of custody. Despite grudgingly conceding that *Miranda* is triggered only by a show of force traditionally associated with an arrest, characterized by actions like drawing and pointing weapons, handcuffing, and conducting searches that exceed the limits of a weapons pat-down, and eventually even coming to mouth the words of the Supreme Court's standard, we seem never (as evidenced by today's holding) to have fully embraced the concept.

Once again the majority fails to distinguish objective indications that a suspect has effectively been arrested from indications of a potential suspect's interest in avoiding that eventuality. In the former case, any statements made without an effective waiver of *Miranda* warnings are presumptively the product of police coercion. In the latter, whether motivated more by a desire to assist the investigation or to avoid attracting further suspicion, no such presumption arises. Comparing voluntary witness statements and real evidence is not only a legitimate but in fact a highly desirable and effective technique for solving crimes.

In the absence of actual indicia of an arrest, the majority marshals a laundry list of circumstances or factors, indicative of little more than an interview at the police station. The fact that interview rooms are typically neither large nor public, that two officers are present for an interview, or that they close the door for privacy indicate virtually nothing about the voluntariness of an interviewee's presence. As the

5. The People argue that if the interrogation of Elmarr was custodial, it only became so toward the end of the interview, so that only statements after that point could be suppressed. However, there is no discrete point at which one could say that a non-custodial interview suddenly became custodial. It is the totality of the circumstances, from the time Elmarr was put in a police car until the time he was finally released hours later, that makes the encounter custodial.

Supreme Court has expressly noted, the fact that questioners carry holstered side-arms indicates only that they are police officers, which is understood by the interviewee when he consents to a stationhouse interview. And rather than being an indication of arrest, riding in a police car, only after giving consent and without having been patted-down or handcuffed, would suggest to any reasonable person precisely the opposite.

In the absence of an objectively manifested change in circumstances, the fact that a defendant who is present by agreement is not expressly told that he is free to leave has little meaning; and it seems more than a little disingenuous to suggest it as a worthy practice in light of the trial court's adverse reaction to the police reminder that the defendant was free not to speak with them. To the extent that circumstances actually did change at some point as a result of the defendant's responses, he clearly felt free to, and did, terminate the interview, and only his earlier statements are at issue here. In fact, the majority's substantial reliance on events following termination of the interview is a further indication of its failure to grasp, or at least its failure to apply, the objective standard dictated by the Supreme Court. In the absence of any indication that they already intended, and had already communicated their intent, to arrest him, the subsequent actions of the officers could have no bearing whatsoever on the defendant's perception of his status at the time of his statements.

With its mechanical counting of virtually meaningless factors and its comparisons with fact patterns considered by this court long before the Supreme Court's modern custody jurisprudence became clear to us, I can only assume the majority either fails to appreciate the import of that jurisprudence or despite it, continues to harbor reservations about the use of a defendant's own words to establish his guilt. In either case, I believe the majority's holding today conflicts with the Supreme Court's interpretation of the United States Constitution; can serve only to dissuade law enforcement officers from seeking and preserving a record of voluntary witness interviews; and needlessly hinders the search for truth in the criminal process. I therefore respectfully dissent.

EID, J., dissenting.

. . . In my view, the trial court made two significant and fundamental errors in this case. First, the court found that the incomplete *Miranda* warnings given by the officers created custody: "Defendant was advised of *Miranda* at the very beginning of the questioning, which would indicate to someone familiar with the criminal process that he was being deprived of his freedom." In so holding, the court got it exactly backwards. *Miranda* warnings do not create custody. Instead, custody triggers *Miranda*. [It] would be bizarre to penalize police officers for attempting to give *Miranda* warnings in situations that were later determined by a court to be noncustodial.

The second fundamental error committed by the trial court is the fact that it relied on the officers' subjective intentions in its analysis of whether Elmarr was in custody, concluding that "Captain Epp likely suspected that Defendant was involved in the murder and intended to attempt to elicit incriminating statements from Defendant." As the majority recognizes, and Elmarr acknowledges, the subjective intentions of the officers in questioning the defendant have no role in determining whether the defendant was in custody.

These two errors tainted the entirety of the trial court's analysis and render its fact-finding, upon which the majority relies, suspect. In my view, we should correct the trial court's errors and remand the case for further proceedings. For this reason, I respectfully dissent from the majority's opinion.

Problem 8-1. (Non)Custody: Police Assistance

Shortly after midnight, Police Officer Gene Sheldon was dispatched to the residence of Marvin and Linda Dyer on an emergency call. Ms. Dyer was reportedly suffering from a pleurisy attack. Officer Sheldon arrived at the same time as an ambulance. He followed the ambulance crew into the house and found Ms. Dyer seated on the floor of the bathroom. Emergency medical technicians convinced her to leave the house to seek medical attention. After the rescue unit had left to take Ms. Dyer to the clinic, Officer Sheldon asked Mr. Dyer what had happened, and Mr. Dyer admitted that he had hit his wife. While Sheldon spoke with Mr. Dyer in one room, a volunteer firefighter stayed with the six children in the next room. After a few moments of conversation, Mr. Dyer said that he wanted to go to bed and "if anybody comes back to the bedroom, all they are going to hear is a loud bang." Sheldon stopped Mr. Dyer from leaving the room by standing in the hallway. He convinced Mr. Dyer to sit down. About two hours after Officer Sheldon had arrived at the house, Ms. Dyer returned in the ambulance. Mr. Dyer went outside and Officer Sheldon placed him under arrest. Did Mr. Dyer make his statements while in custody? See State v. Dyer, 513 N.W.2d 316 (Neb. 1994).

Problem 8-2. Blunt Questions

Joseph Turmel and one passenger were traveling northbound on Interstate 89 in New Hampshire. At approximately 5:00 P.M., Trooper James Mayers approached Turmel's car in an unmarked State Police pickup truck. Mayers had five years of experience with undercover narcotics investigations. As Mayers passed Turmel's car at about 70 mph, he noticed that Turmel was holding an unusual cigar in an unusual manner. Based on his training as a drug recognition expert, Mayers believed that the cigar was a "blunt," having part of its tobacco replaced by marijuana. Turmel held the cigar between his thumb and index finger, and "cupped" it inside his hand. Mayers then saw Turmel put the cigar to his mouth, inhale, and pass the cigar to his passenger, who also put the cigar to his mouth and inhaled.

Mayers radioed for a marked police cruiser to assist him. He pulled ahead of Turmel's car and monitored it for three miles until Sgt. Scott Sweet caught up to pursue. Sweet then followed Turmel for six miles, at which point two other marked police cruisers joined the pursuit. Neither Mayers nor Sweet saw Turmel drive erratically or violate any traffic laws. The three police cruisers and Mayers' unmarked truck then pulled the car over to investigate.

Sweet approached on the driver's side and asked Turmel to step out of the car. Sweet and Mayers then took him to the back of the car. Two other officers took the passenger to the front of the car. Mayers smelled marijuana coming from the interior of the car. Mayers introduced himself to Turmel as an officer with the Narcotics Investigation Unit of the State Police, and explained that he had watched him smoking marijuana in the car. Mayers told Turmel that he wanted him to cooperate and asked him if he had been smoking marijuana. Turmel replied, "Yes." Mayers told him that he was not under arrest and asked him whether there were any weapons or drugs in the car. Turmel said there were none, and then Mayers asked for consent to search the vehicle, saying that if no weapons or drugs were found in the car, Turmel and his passenger would "probably" be free to leave. Mayers told Turmel that he did not have to consent to the search, but if he did not consent, Mayers would pursue "other avenues" to search the car. Turmel consented to the search.

Mayers' initial search did not produce any contraband. Following the discovery of a large amount of cash in the trunk, however, a trooper with a drug-sniffing dog were summoned and arrived at the scene 10 minutes later, and the butt of a marijuana cigarette was eventually found in the car's ashtray. Neither Sweet nor Mayers read a *Miranda* warning to Turmel before the questioning or before his consent to search the car. Will the trial court grant a motion to suppress the cash and the marijuana cigarette butt? Does the legal analysis here differ at all from the "stop versus arrest" question explored in Chapter 5? Cf. State v. Turmel, 838 A.2d 1279 (N.H. 2003).

Notes

1. *Subjective versus objective test for custody: majority position.* Federal and state courts determine whether a suspect is in "custody" for purposes of *Miranda* by using an objective test: Would a reasonable person in the suspect's position believe that she has been constrained in a manner akin to an arrest? See Berkemer v. McCarty, 468 U.S. 420 (1984). The particular officer's intentions about the suspect's freedom to leave, and the suspect's actual views about whether she was free to leave, are not controlling under this approach. Many circumstances — the location of the interrogation, the suspect's reason for coming there, the number of officers present, the defendant's conduct after the interrogation — can have a bearing on this objective test. An interrogation does not have to occur in a police station to be custodial. See Orozco v. Texas, 394 U.S. 324 (1969) (custodial interrogation when four police officers wake suspect in bedroom at 4 A.M. and question him). By the same token, an interrogation does not become custodial whenever it occurs within a police station. See California v. Beheler, 463 U.S. 1121 (1983) (suspect arrives at station voluntarily, is told he is not under arrest, and leaves after brief interrogation). When a suspect is "asked" to come to the station, is it a voluntary appearance? If a police officer asks a suspect "to have a seat" in the patrol car, is the suspect in custody? See People v. Taylor, 41 P.3d 681 (Colo. 2002) (roadside stop of driver became custodial for *Miranda* purposes after passenger was arrested on outstanding warrant, officers searched car without consent, and one officer kept driver standing in one place outside car). The dizzying level of detail that seems relevant in answering the custody question gets further attention in the web extension for this chapter at *http://www.crimpro.com/extension/ch08*.

The labels "objective" and "subjective" may not be a reliable guide to which facts will figure in the outcome. See Yarborough v. Alvarado, 541 U.S. 652 (2004) (defendant's age or experience with law enforcement do not qualify as "objective circumstances of the interrogation" in determining the question of custody); Rigterink v. State, 2 So.3d 221 (Fla. 2009) (if reasonable person in suspect's position would understand that the police have probable cause to arrest the suspect for a serious crime, that circumstance militates strongly toward the conclusion that the suspect is in custody).

While the Colorado Supreme Court seems to apply a relatively broad definition of "custody," it is equally easy to find high state courts more skeptical of custody determinations. See State v. Smith, 546 N.W. 2d 916) (Iowa 1996) (no custody where four juveniles under probation in Missouri were brought to a juvenile center by their mothers, interviewed by Iowa officers about a murder because while the interviews took place over many hours, the interview center was "family-centered" and "warm" and had a fish tank, food and drinks were provided, and the questioning was "non-coercive"). Indeed, both high state and lower federal courts sometimes work hard to distinguish United States Supreme Court precedent on the question of custody. See, e.g., Herrera v. State, 241 S.W.3d 520 (Tex. Crim. App. 2007) (no custody for purposes of *Miranda* where suspect already in jail on unrelated charges); cf. Mathis v. United States, 391 U.S. 1 (1968) (custody for purposes of *Miranda* when Internal Revenue Service agents questions suspect in prison serving sentencing for another offense).

2. *"Stop" versus "custody."* Recall that, for purposes of the Fourth Amendment, a "stop" occurs when a reasonable person would not "feel free to leave" (see Chapter 2). If an officer questions a person during such an investigative stop, has a custodial interrogation occurred for purposes of *Miranda*? In Berkemer v. McCarty, 468 U.S. 420 (1984), the Supreme Court decided that a traffic stop does not amount to "custody" under *Miranda*. State courts both before and after *Berkemer* reached the same conclusion. How is an investigative stop different from interrogation in the police station? How are they similar?

3. *Compelled appearances in legal proceedings.* Is a person in "custody" when a court orders her to appear in legal proceedings to answer questions? Under the U.S. Constitution, the courts have concluded that compulsory process is not "custody" for purposes of *Miranda*. See United States v. Mandujano, 425 U.S. 564 (1976) (no *Miranda* warnings required for witnesses compelled to appear before grand jury); State v. Monteiro, 632 A.2d 340 (R.I. 1993) (same); Minnesota v. Murphy, 465 U.S. 420 (1984) (no warnings necessary during required interview with probation officer); but see Estelle v. Smith, 451 U.S. 454 (1981) (suspect is in custody when compelled to attend interview with state-paid psychologist who will testify at sentencing). Given that a refusal to comply with an order to appear can lead to a jail term for contempt, how is this situation different from custodial interrogation in a police station?

b. "Interrogation"

A suspect's conversations while in custody might not rise to the level of interrogations and therefore might not require *Miranda* warnings. Of the many conversations taking place between police officers and suspects, which qualify as "interrogations" that trigger *Miranda* warnings in custodial settings? Again, have the courts drawn the line wisely?

RHODE ISLAND v. THOMAS INNIS

446 U.S. 291 (1980)

STEWART, J.[*]

In Miranda v. Arizona, 384 U.S. 436 (1966), the Court held that, once a defendant in custody asks to speak with a lawyer, all interrogation must cease until a lawyer is present. The issue in this case is whether the respondent was "interrogated" in violation of the standards promulgated in the *Miranda* opinion.

I.

[Shortly] after midnight, the Providence police received a telephone call from Gerald Aubin, . . . a taxicab driver, who reported that he had just been robbed by a man wielding a sawed-off shotgun [near Mount Pleasant]. While at the Providence police station waiting to give a statement, Aubin noticed a picture of his assailant on a bulletin board [on a poster relating to the murder of a taxicab driver five days earlier. That picture was of Innis].

At approximately 4:30 A.M. on the same date, Patrolman Lovell, while cruising the streets of Mount Pleasant in a patrol car, spotted [Innis, arrested him, and advised him of his *Miranda* rights. Within minutes, Sergeant Sears and Captain Leyden arrived at the scene, and each of them also gave Innis *Miranda* warnings.] The respondent stated that he understood those rights and wanted to speak with a lawyer. Captain Leyden then directed that the respondent be placed in a "caged wagon," a four-door police car with a wire screen mesh between the front and rear seats, and be driven to the central police station. Three officers, Patrolmen Gleckman, Williams, and McKenna, were assigned to accompany the respondent to the central station. They placed the respondent in the vehicle and shut the doors. Captain Leyden then instructed the officers not to question the respondent or intimidate or coerce him in any way. The three officers then entered the vehicle, and it departed.

While en route to the central station, Patrolman Gleckman initiated a conversation with Patrolman McKenna concerning the missing shotgun. As Patrolman Gleckman later testified:

> At this point, I was talking back and forth with Patrolman McKenna stating that I frequent this area while on patrol and [that because a school for handicapped children is located nearby,] there's a lot of handicapped children running around in this area, and God forbid one of them might find a weapon with shells and they might hurt themselves.

Patrolman McKenna apparently shared his fellow officer's concern: "I more or less concurred with him [Gleckman] that it was a safety factor and that we should, you know, continue to search for the weapon and try to find it." While Patrolman Williams said nothing, he overheard the conversation between the two officers: "He [Gleckman] said it would be too bad if the little — I believe he said a girl — would

* [Justices White, Blackmun, Powell, and Rehnquist joined in this opinion. — EDS.]

pick up the gun, maybe kill herself." The respondent then interrupted the conversation, stating that the officers should turn the car around so he could show them where the gun was located. . . . At the time the respondent indicated that the officers should turn back, they had traveled no more than a mile, a trip encompassing only a few minutes. The police vehicle then returned to the scene of the arrest where a search for the shotgun was in progress. There, Captain Leyden again advised the respondent of his *Miranda* rights. The respondent replied that he understood those rights but that he "wanted to get the gun out of the way because of the kids in the area in the school." The respondent then led the police to a nearby field, where he pointed out the shotgun under some rocks by the side of the road.

[The trial court denied Innis's motion to suppress the evidence regarding the gun, concluding that Innis had waived his *Miranda* rights. The jury returned a verdict of guilty on all counts.] We granted certiorari to address for the first time the meaning of "interrogation" under Miranda v. Arizona. . . .

II.

. . . The starting point for defining "interrogation" in this context is, of course, the Court's *Miranda* opinion. There the Court observed that "[by] custodial interrogation, we mean questioning initiated by law enforcement officers after a person has been taken into custody or otherwise deprived of his freedom of action in any significant way." This passage and other references throughout the opinion to "questioning" might suggest that the *Miranda* rules were to apply only to those police interrogation practices that involve express questioning of a defendant while in custody.

We do not, however, construe the *Miranda* opinion so narrowly. The concern of the Court in *Miranda* was that the "interrogation environment" created by the interplay of interrogation and custody would "subjugate the individual to the will of his examiner" and thereby undermine the privilege against compulsory self-incrimination. The police practices that evoked this concern included several that did not involve express questioning. For example, [the Court mentioned] the use of psychological ploys, such as to posit "the guilt of the subject," to "minimize the moral seriousness of the offense," and "to cast blame on the victim or on society." It is clear that these techniques of persuasion, no less than express questioning, were thought, in a custodial setting, to amount to interrogation.

This is not to say, however, that all statements obtained by the police after a person has been taken into custody are to be considered the product of interrogation. [It is clear] that the special procedural safeguards outlined in *Miranda* are required not where a suspect is simply taken into custody, but rather where a suspect in custody is subjected to interrogation. "Interrogation," as conceptualized in the *Miranda* opinion, must reflect a measure of compulsion above and beyond that inherent in custody itself.

We conclude that the *Miranda* safeguards come into play whenever a person in custody is subjected to either express questioning or its functional equivalent. That is to say, the term "interrogation" under *Miranda* refers not only to express questioning, but also to any words or actions on the part of the police (other than those normally attendant to arrest and custody) that the police should know are reasonably likely to elicit an incriminating response from the suspect. The latter portion of this definition focuses primarily upon the perceptions of the suspect, rather than the intent of the police. This focus reflects the fact that the *Miranda* safeguards were designed to vest a suspect in custody with an added measure of protection against coercive police practices, without regard to objective proof of the underlying intent of the police. A practice that the police should know is reasonably likely to evoke an incriminating response from a suspect thus amounts to interrogation.[7] But, since the police surely cannot be held accountable for the unforeseeable results of their words or actions, the definition of interrogation can extend only to words or actions on the part of police officers that they should have known were reasonably likely to elicit an incriminating response.[8]

Turning to the facts of the present case, we conclude that the respondent was not "interrogated" within the meaning of *Miranda.* It is undisputed that the first prong of the definition of "interrogation" was not satisfied, for the conversation between Patrolmen Gleckman and McKenna included no express questioning of the respondent. Rather, that conversation was, at least in form, nothing more than a dialogue between the two officers to which no response from the respondent was invited.

Moreover, it cannot be fairly concluded that the respondent was subjected to the "functional equivalent" of questioning. It cannot be said, in short, that Patrolmen Gleckman and McKenna should have known that their conversation was reasonably likely to elicit an incriminating response from the respondent. There is nothing in the record to suggest that the officers were aware that the respondent was peculiarly susceptible to an appeal to his conscience concerning the safety of handicapped children. Nor is there anything in the record to suggest that the police knew that the respondent was unusually disoriented or upset at the time of his arrest.

The case thus boils down to whether, in the context of a brief conversation, the officers should have known that the respondent would suddenly be moved to make a self-incriminating response. Given the fact that the entire conversation appears to have consisted of no more than a few offhand remarks, we cannot say that the officers should have known that it was reasonably likely that Innis would so respond. This is not a case where the police carried on a lengthy harangue in the presence of the suspect. Nor does the record support the respondent's contention that, under the circumstances, the officers' comments were particularly "evocative." It is our view, therefore, that the respondent was not subjected by the police to words or actions that the police should have known were reasonably likely to elicit an incriminating response from him. . . .

MARSHALL, J., dissenting.*

I am substantially in agreement with the Court's definition of "interrogation" within the meaning of Miranda v. Arizona, 384 U.S. 436 (1966). In my view, the

7. This is not to say that the intent of the police is irrelevant, for it may well have a bearing on whether the police should have known that their words or actions were reasonably likely to evoke an incriminating response. In particular, where a police practice is designed to elicit an incriminating response from the accused, it is unlikely that the practice will not also be one which the police should have known was reasonably likely to have that effect.

8. Any knowledge the police may have had concerning the unusual susceptibility of a defendant to a particular form of persuasion might be an important factor in determining whether the police should have known that their words or actions were reasonably likely to elicit an incriminating response from the suspect.

* [Justice Brennan joined in this opinion. — EDS.]

Miranda safeguards apply whenever police conduct is intended or likely to produce a response from a suspect in custody. [The] Court requires an objective inquiry into the likely effect of police conduct on a typical individual, taking into account any special susceptibility of the suspect to certain kinds of pressure of which the police know or have reason to know.

I am utterly at a loss, however, to understand how this objective standard as applied to the facts before us can rationally lead to the conclusion that there was no interrogation. . . . Since the car traveled no more than a mile before Innis agreed to point out the location of the murder weapon, Officer Gleckman must have begun almost immediately to talk about the search for the shotgun. . . . One can scarcely imagine a stronger appeal to the conscience of a suspect — any suspect — than the assertion that if the weapon is not found an innocent person will be hurt or killed. And not just any innocent person, but an innocent child — a little girl — a helpless, handicapped little girl on her way to school. The notion that such an appeal could not be expected to have any effect unless the suspect were known to have some special interest in handicapped children verges on the ludicrous. . . . I firmly believe that this case is simply an aberration, and that in future cases the Court will apply the standard adopted today in accordance with its plain meaning.

STEVENS, J., dissenting.

. . . I.

[In] my view any statement that would normally be understood by the average listener as calling for a response is the functional equivalent of a direct question, whether or not it is punctuated by a question mark. The Court, however, takes a much narrower view. It holds that police conduct is not the "functional equivalent" of direct questioning unless the police should have known that what they were saying or doing was likely to elicit an incriminating response from the suspect. This holding represents a plain departure from the principles set forth in *Miranda*.

[Once a suspect cuts off questioning,] the police are prohibited from making deliberate attempts to elicit statements from the suspect. Yet the Court is unwilling to characterize all such attempts as "interrogation," noting only that "where a police practice is designed to elicit an incriminating response from the accused, it is unlikely that the practice will not also be one which the police should have known was reasonably likely to have that effect."[8]

[In] order to give full protection to a suspect's right to be free from any interrogation at all, the definition of "interrogation" must include any police statement or conduct that has the same purpose or effect as a direct question. Statements that appear to call for a response from the suspect, as well as those that are designed to do so, should be considered interrogation. By prohibiting only those relatively few statements or actions that a police officer should know are likely to elicit an incriminating response, the Court today accords a suspect considerably less protection. Indeed, since I suppose most suspects are unlikely to incriminate themselves even when questioned directly, this new definition will almost certainly exclude every

8. This factual assumption is extremely dubious. I would assume that police often interrogate suspects without any reason to believe that their efforts are likely to be successful in the hope that a statement will nevertheless be forthcoming.

statement that is not punctuated with a question mark from the concept of "interrogation."

The difference between the approach required by a faithful adherence to *Miranda* and the stinted test applied by the Court today can be illustrated by comparing three different ways in which Officer Gleckman could have communicated his fears about the possible dangers posed by the shotgun to handicapped children. He could have:

1. directly asked Innis: "Will you please tell me where the shotgun is so we can protect handicapped schoolchildren from danger?"
2. announced to the other officers in the wagon: "If the man sitting in the back seat with me should decide to tell us where the gun is, we can protect handicapped children from danger," or
3. stated to the other officers: "It would be too bad if a little handicapped girl would pick up the gun that this man left in the area and maybe kill herself."

In my opinion, all three of these statements should be considered interrogation because all three appear to be designed to elicit a response from anyone who in fact knew where the gun was located. Under the Court's test, on the other hand, the form of the statements would be critical. The third statement would not be interrogation because in the Court's view there was no reason for Officer Gleckman to believe that Innis was susceptible to this type of an implied appeal; therefore, the statement would not be reasonably likely to elicit an incriminating response. Assuming that this is true, then it seems to me that the first two statements, which would be just as unlikely to elicit such a response, should also not be considered interrogation. But, because the first statement is clearly an express question, it would be considered interrogation under the Court's test. The second statement, although just as clearly a deliberate appeal to Innis to reveal the location of the gun, would presumably not be interrogation because (a) it was not in form a direct question and (b) it does not fit within the "reasonably likely to elicit an incriminating response" category that applies to indirect interrogation.

As this example illustrates, the Court's test creates an incentive for police to ignore a suspect's invocation of his rights in order to make continued attempts to extract information from him. If a suspect does not appear to be susceptible to a particular type of psychological pressure, the police are apparently free to exert that pressure on him despite his request for counsel, so long as they are careful not to punctuate their statements with question marks. And if, contrary to all reasonable expectations, the suspect makes an incriminating statement, that statement can be used against him at trial. The Court thus turns *Miranda*'s unequivocal rule against any interrogation at all into a trap in which unwary suspects may be caught by police deception. . . .

II.

. . . In any event, I think the Court is clearly wrong in holding, as a matter of law, that Officer Gleckman should not have realized that his statement was likely to elicit an incriminating response. The Court implicitly assumes that, at least in the absence of a lengthy harangue, a criminal suspect will not be likely to respond to indirect appeals to his humanitarian impulses. [This assumption] is directly contrary to the teachings of police interrogation manuals, which recommend appealing to a suspect's sense of morality as a standard and often successful interrogation technique. . . .

Moreover, there is evidence in the record to support the view that Officer Gleckman's statement was intended to elicit a response from Innis. Officer Gleckman, who was not regularly assigned to the caged wagon, was directed by a police captain to ride with respondent to the police station. . . . The record does not explain why, notwithstanding the fact that respondent was handcuffed, unarmed, and had offered no resistance when arrested by an officer acting alone, the captain ordered Officer Gleckman to ride with respondent. It is not inconceivable that two professionally trained police officers concluded that a few well-chosen remarks might induce respondent to disclose the whereabouts of the shotgun. This conclusion becomes even more plausible in light of the emotionally charged words chosen by Officer Gleckman. . . .

Problem 8-3. Blurting

A suspect in a shooting was taken into custody. The suspect asked to talk with the detectives investigating the case, but they told him that he could do so only after his fingerprints were taken and after he had executed a written waiver of his *Miranda* rights. While a different detective was taking the prints, the suspect blurted out, "This is really going to fuck me up." The detective immediately asked why, and the suspect said that he had handled the gun in question on the previous day but that it had jammed. The detective stopped the defendant from saying anything further. Later tests of the gun yielded no identifiable fingerprints. Was the suspect "interrogated"? Compare Commonwealth v. Diaz, 661 N.E.2d 1326 (Mass. 1996).

Problem 8-4. Public Safety Motivation

At approximately 12:30 A.M., a young woman approached Police Officers Frank Kraft and Sal Scarring and told them that she had just been raped by a black male, approximately six feet tall, who was wearing a black jacket with the name "Big Ben" printed in yellow letters on the back. She told the officers that the man, who was carrying a gun, had just entered a nearby supermarket.

The officers drove the woman to the supermarket, and Officer Kraft entered the store while Officer Scarring radioed for assistance. Officer Kraft quickly spotted Benjamin Quarles, who matched the description given by the woman, approaching a checkout counter. When Quarles saw Kraft, he turned and ran toward the rear of the store, and Kraft pursued him with a drawn gun. Kraft lost sight of him for several seconds but spotted him again and ordered him to stop and put his hands over his head.

Although more than three other officers had arrived on the scene by that time, Officer Kraft was the first to reach Quarles. He frisked him and discovered an empty shoulder holster. After handcuffing him, Officer Kraft asked him where the gun was. Quarles nodded in the direction of some empty cartons and responded, "The gun is over there." Officer Kraft then retrieved a loaded. 38-caliber revolver from one of the cartons, formally placed Quarles under arrest, and read him his *Miranda* rights from a printed card. Quarles indicated that he would be willing to answer questions without an attorney present. Officer Kraft then asked him if he owned the gun and where he had purchased it. Quarles answered that he did own it and that he had purchased it in Miami.

If you were a judge convinced that all of Quarles's statements should be admitted into evidence, how might you draft an opinion to explain this position? Compare New York v. Quarles, 467 U.S. 649 (1984).

Notes

1. *Interrogation by known government agents: majority position.* Virtually all jurisdictions follow the *Innis* definition of "interrogation": words or actions that the police "should know are reasonably likely to elicit an incriminating response from the suspect." See State v. Grant, 944 A.2d 947 (Conn. 2008) (statement to defendant that defendant's blood had been found at murder scene did not constitute interrogation; conduct here was of the sort "normally attendant to arrest" and "a per se rule that confronting a suspect with incriminating evidence constitutes interrogation is not required under *Innis*"). Did the Court apply this test appropriately on the facts of *Innis*? If not, what definition of "interrogation" could better account for the outcome of the case? This definition applies not only in those cases when the police initiate a conversation; it also reaches some cases in which the suspect asks a question or makes a statement, and the officer responds in a way that leads the suspect to make an incriminating reply.

2. *Booking questions.* The definition of an "interrogation" sometimes becomes an issue when a police officer who processes the routine paperwork and fingerprints as part of the suspect's detention makes some comment that elicits an incriminating response from the suspect. In Pennsylvania v. Muniz, 496 U.S. 582 (1990), the Supreme Court determined that some, but not all, of the questions asked of a defendant during a routine booking on DWI charges were "interrogations" that required *Miranda* warnings. Routine questions asking for the suspect's name, address, height, weight, eye color, date of birth, and current age were not considered interrogations. When, however, the booking officer asked the suspect the date of his sixth birthday and the suspect was unable to calculate it, the officer's question qualified as an interrogation. What is it about most of the booking questions that takes them outside the coverage of *Miranda*? Is it the routine nature of booking questions? Consider again the facts of Problem 8-3. See also State v. Goseland, 887 P.2d 1109 (Kan. 1994) (during booking paperwork, officer remarks to suspect in narcotics case, "You need to find something else to do with your life" and suspect replies "No, I'll not stop selling dope, because then you all would not have anything to do"; no interrogation, because officer always makes this remark to suspects being booked).

3. *Interrogation by unknown government agents: majority position.* In all the interrogations we have considered so far, the suspect was aware that the person asking questions was a police officer. But is there an "interrogation" when a suspect in custody is talking with a person that he does not believe to be an agent of the police? The Supreme Court and state high courts say no. In Illinois v. Perkins, 496 U.S. 292 (1990), the Supreme Court held that no *Miranda* warnings were necessary when police placed an undercover agent in same cellblock with a murder suspect detained on other charges, and during discussion of possible escape, the agent asked if the

suspect had ever "done" anybody. The Court held that conversations between suspects and undercover agents "do not implicate the concerns underlying *Miranda*." But weren't the undercover agent's words "reasonably likely to elicit an incriminating response"? If so, what explains the inapplicability of *Miranda* when undercover agents ask the questions?

4. *"Public safety" exception to* Miranda: *majority position.* In New York v. Quarles, the Court concluded that even though the officer had conducted a custodial interrogation without giving *Miranda* warnings, the suspect's confession was not obtained contrary to the Constitution. The officer's questions about the gun were necessary not only to solve a completed crime but to prevent future crimes or accidents involving the missing gun. The need for "answers to questions in a situation posing a threat to the public safety outweighs the need for the prophylactic rule protecting the Fifth Amendment's privilege against self-incrimination." 467 U.S. at 657. Even if the officer did not ask the questions with the actual purpose of preventing a future mishap with the weapon, a court could later infer a public safety purpose for the questions from the surrounding circumstances. More than half the states allow a "public safety" or related "rescue" exception to *Miranda*. See People v. Davis, 208 P.3d 78 (Cal. 2009) (state's "rescue doctrine" still applies after more than two months elapsed between abduction of young girl and interrogation of suspect, because defendant told others he was "only doing this for the money," raising possibility that victim might still be alive).

Although *Quarles* was partly justified by the idea that warnings about the right to silence are a "prophylactic" rule rather than an actual requirement, the Court has now rejected that reasoning in Dickerson v. United States, 530 U.S. 428 (2000). The uncertain doctrinal footing of Quarles, together with the embrace of the concept in the state courts, deserves further attention. Materials on these questions appear on the web extension for this chapter at *http://www.crimpro.com/extension/ch08*.

3. *Form of Warnings*

The *Miranda* decision designated four topics that warnings would need to cover before a custodial interrogation could take place. However, the Court did not specify the precise language that the police must use to convey these warnings. How much variation in the language of the warnings is tolerable? When is variation necessary?

In California v. Prysock, 453 U.S. 355 (1981), the Supreme Court confirmed that a "verbatim recital" of the words in the *Miranda* opinion is not necessary to give an adequate warning to a suspect before an interrogation. The warning in that case told the suspect of his right to have an attorney present prior to and during questioning, and of his "right to have a lawyer appointed at no cost if he could not afford one." This was sufficient, even though it might have left the suspect with the impression that an appointed lawyer would become available only after questioning. In Duckworth v. Eagan, 492 U.S. 195 (1989), the Supreme Court considered the constitutionality of an Indiana *Miranda* warning that said, among other things, "we have no way of giving you a lawyer, but one will be appointed for you, if you wish, if and when you go to court." The Court held the warning complied with *Miranda*, noting that "*Miranda* does not require that attorneys be producible on call, but only that the suspect be informed, as here, that he has the right to an attorney before and during questioning, and that an attorney would be appointed for him if he could not afford one."

State courts have also determined that their constitutions allow for some variety (and some ambiguity) in the way the warnings are phrased. A few state statutes provide for additional warnings to some suspects (especially juveniles) before interrogation, but state courts have hesitated to conclude that statutes dealing with warnings for suspects require a particular verbal formula. See, e.g., State v. Bittick, 806 S.W.2d 652 (Mo. 1991) (interpreting warnings listed in Mo. Rev. Stat. §600.048.1). Why haven't more state courts insisted on a uniform and unambiguous method of conveying the *Miranda* warnings? Wouldn't an "inflexible" rule be both realistic and easy to administer because police officers could simply read the warnings from a pocket-sized card?

Some situations might call for additional warnings. A suspect may waive the right to counsel because the prospect of waiting in custody may be unappealing, or because no specific attorney has been identified, or because the suspect doubts that the attorney ultimately assigned to the case will be capable. But what if counsel retained for a specific suspect is available at the police station? Do the interrogating officers have to tell the suspect of the presence of a particular attorney when the additional warning could affect the waiver decision?

■ STATE v. JOHN REED

627 A.2d 630 (N.J. 1993)

HANDLER, J.

In this case, the jury convicted defendant, John Reed, of knowing murder and aggravated criminal sexual contact. Defendant had confessed to those crimes and that confession constituted critically important evidence. The admissibility of defendant's confession presents the sole issue on this appeal. The police refused, before and during defendant's interrogation, to inform defendant that an attorney, who had been brought to police headquarters by a friend of defendant, was present and sought to confer with him. The issue is whether that refusal by the police violated defendant's constitutional rights, including the privilege against self-incrimination, and therefore rendered defendant's confession inadmissible.

[Fran Varga called the police Monday at 8:00 A.M. to inform them that her roommate and boyfriend, John Reed, had found the dead body of Susan Green, one of Reed's coworkers. He found Green's body on the floor of her own apartment, with 53 stab wounds. When detectives Shedden and Importico arrived at the scene, they asked Reed some questions, but had difficulty understanding his answers because Reed suffered from a speech impediment and tended to stutter severely when nervous. He told them that the victim had called him the previous Friday night, afraid because a stranger had been trying to enter her apartment. The stranger had disappeared by the time Reed had arrived to help. He found the body, he said, when he stopped by her apartment on his way to work on Monday morning.

The detectives asked Reed to go to the prosecutor's office to give a statement and provide "elimination" fingerprints. Varga drove him to the prosecutor's office, where they arrived just before 11:00 A.M. The detectives isolated Reed in an interrogation room, and asked Varga to remain in the waiting room. Varga called an attorney, and told him that she and Reed were at the prosecutor's office, that the police were about to question Reed, and that she and Reed needed an attorney. The attorney, William Aitken, agreed to come to the station immediately. Varga informed a police officer that Aitken was on the way.

Meanwhile, Chief Richard Thornburg instructed detectives Shedden and Importico to move Reed to the Major Crimes Building, located a few blocks away. Instead of taking Reed past the area where Varga was waiting and down the elevator, the officers led him down four flights of stairs near the interrogation room and out the back door of the building. Reed signed a *Miranda* waiver form, then gave a different account of the events than he had given earlier.

At approximately 11:25 A.M., Aitken arrived at the prosecutor's office and consulted with Varga. He approached the prosecutor who would eventually present the case against Reed and told him that he was there to represent both Varga and Reed. The prosecutor informed Aitken that Reed was a witness and not a suspect, and stated that, in any event, Aitken had "no right to walk into an investigation." Aitken gave the prosecutor a business card, and the prosecutor assured Aitken that the police would call him if and when Reed requested an attorney. No one informed Reed that a lawyer retained by Varga was waiting to see him.

After a second waiver of *Miranda* rights around noon, Reed spoke with another interrogator, Lt. Mazzei, and told a story markedly different from the second account he had provided. In Reed's third version of the story, he had actually witnessed Green being murdered when, looking through Green's front window, he had seen a "black man" repeatedly stabbing her. After detectives confronted him with the inconsistency, and after further questioning, Reed admitted that he had killed Green. After waiving his *Miranda* rights for a third time, Reed confessed on tape. He explained that he had killed Green in self-defense during a heated argument. The confession was taped at 3:52 P.M.]

Prior to trial, defense counsel moved to suppress defendant's confession on the ground that defendant had not knowingly, voluntarily, and intelligently waived his *Miranda* rights. [The trial court denied the motion because] the police had no duty to inform defendant of the attorney's presence.

[In] Moran v. Burbine, 475 U.S. 412 (1986), [the U.S. Supreme Court] held, as a matter of federal constitutional law, that the police had no obligation to advise a defendant that a third party had summoned an attorney to advise him and that, in the absence of a request by the defendant himself, an attorney's presence at the police station does not affect the right of the police to interrogate him.

In *Moran,* the defendant was in police custody for a burglary. While the defendant was in custody, the police received information connecting the defendant with a murder. The police proceeded to interrogate the defendant about the murder, even though they were aware that a public defender, retained by the defendant's sister in connection with the burglary charge, had called to say that she would act as the defendant's attorney if the police placed him in a lineup or interrogated him. Although the police assured the public defender that they had no plans to question the defendant that evening, nevertheless, shortly after the phone call, the police began interrogating the defendant about the murder. Before each interrogation session, the police informed the defendant of his *Miranda* rights and had him sign waiver forms, but they never informed him that his sister had retained a public defender to assist him or that the public defender was trying to reach him.

Writing for the majority, Justice O'Connor held that the actions of the police did not violate the defendant's fifth, sixth, or fourteenth amendment rights. After noting that the voluntariness of the waiver was not at issue, the Court found that there was no question concerning the defendant's understanding of the *Miranda* warnings and of the consequences of waiving them. In the Court's view, the failure of the police to inform the defendant that an attorney was available to assist him was irrelevant to the question whether he had knowingly waived his rights. . . .

The majority decision in *Moran* signaled a marked departure from the fifth amendment jurisprudence that state and federal courts had established prior to *Moran.* At the time *Moran* was decided, many courts had held that when the police fail to inform a suspect that an attorney is actually available and seeking to render assistance, any subsequent waiver of the suspect's *Miranda* rights was invalid. [The court cited cases from Colorado, Delaware, Florida, Illinois, Louisiana, Massachusetts, North Carolina, Ohio, Oklahoma, Oregon, Pennsylvania, and West Virginia. Since 1986], several state courts have had occasion to consider or reconsider the issue presented in *Moran.* Some of those courts . . . have expressly rejected *Moran* on the grounds that its holding offends state-constitutional provisions protecting the privilege against self-incrimination and due process rights. [The court cited cases from California, Connecticut, Delaware, Florida, Oregon, and Texas. The California case was subsequently overruled by a constitutional amendment.]

In New Jersey, the right against self-incrimination is founded on a common-law and statutory — rather than a constitutional — basis. . . . The common-law right against self-incrimination was first codified in New Jersey in 1855. Subsequently, the Legislature incorporated the right against self-incrimination in its enactment of the Rules of Evidence. Thus, although lacking a constitutional provision expressly establishing the right, the privilege against self-incrimination has been an integral thread in the fabric of New Jersey common law. . . .

The right to counsel has been the object of special judicial solicitude [in New Jersey]. The significance of the right to counsel as an adjunct of the privilege against self-incrimination is evidenced by the special requirements that are affixed to that right. It is not sufficient to advise a suspect subjected to custodial interrogation only that he or she has a generalized right to an attorney. It is essential to inform the suspect that, if the suspect cannot afford one, an attorney will be provided at State expense. It is also essential that the suspect be clearly informed that he or she may ask for counsel at any time during custodial interrogation, and, additionally, that interrogation will be stopped any time the defendant desires counsel. Further, a suspect need not be articulate, clear, or explicit in requesting counsel; any indication of a desire for counsel, however ambiguous, will trigger entitlement to counsel. State v. Bey, 548 A.2d 887 (N.J. 1988).

Our decisional law on the state right against self-incrimination is based on the understanding that the privilege is defined by the ancillary rights, like the right to counsel during custodial interrogation. Moreover, the protections afforded by those ancillary rights provide a metric by which to measure the strength of the privilege. The history of our case law reflects a strong commitment to enhance those ancillary rights to forestall the possible use of coerced confessions. . . .

Many state courts, as already noted, have interpreted their respective state constitutions to require that a suspect exposed to custodial interrogation be apprised of the presence of an attorney seeking to render assistance. Courts have offered different rationales for imposing that duty. Some have based the duty on the fundamental constraints that govern the waiver of the right against self-incrimination. Those constraints are invariably expressed in terms of whether the waiver is "knowing, intelligent, and voluntary."[2] . . . Other courts have derived the duty from notions of due process that insist on reasonable police conduct. . . .

However, we need not engage in an extended debate over the different approaches to dealing with the standards governing the validity of a waiver in this context. For while courts may differ on the rationale for imposing the duty to inform a suspect that an attorney is waiting to confer, they agree on one supervening principle: the atmosphere of custodial interrogation is inherently coercive and protecting the right against self-incrimination entails counteracting that coercion. . . .

The lesson to be drawn from this debate is that a waiver of the right against self-incrimination which, by all subjective indicia, appears knowing, intelligent, and voluntary, may still be deemed invalid when elicited in an atmosphere of coercion. That is because the determination of the subjective mental state that leads to a waiver is often so problematic. [A warning is a clear-cut fact.] Accordingly, the most practical means to overcome coercion will be through normative rules that apply reasonable, specific, and objective standards. . . .

[Our] decision today should be governed by a two-fold purpose: to enhance the reliability of confessions by reducing the inherent coercion of custodial interrogation and diminish the likelihood of unreasonable police conduct in those situations where police, knowing that an attorney has been retained for the suspect and is asking for contact with his or her client, are desperate to acquire a confession before the suspect speaks with the attorney.

The State nevertheless contends that the police had no duty to inform defendant about Aitken's presence because Aitken could not be considered defendant's attorney. The State stresses that defendant never requested an attorney and that Aitken had no legal authority to invoke defendant's rights, and could not exercise, for defendant, the right to counsel. The State thus claims that because no attorney-client relationship existed between defendant and Aitken, law-enforcement authorities could not possibly have interfered in that relationship and defendant's right to counsel. . . .

We are satisfied that an attorney-client relationship should be deemed to exist under such circumstances between the suspect and an attorney when the suspect's family or friends have retained the attorney or where the attorney has represented or is representing the suspect on another matter. When, to the knowledge of the police, such an attorney is present or available, and the attorney has communicated a desire to confer with the suspect, the police must make that information known to the suspect before custodial interrogation can proceed or continue. Further, we hold that the failure of the police to give the suspect that information renders the suspect's subsequent waiver of the privilege against self-incrimination invalid per se.

Our holding is essential to give effect to the right to counsel that, in turn, effectuates the privilege against self-incrimination. Moreover, our holding is supported

2. At least one commentator has argued that in order for a suspect's confession to be valid, the suspect should be provided with "as complete an understanding of his tactical position as possible." See George Dix, Mistake, Ignorance, Expectation of Benefit and the Modern Law of Confessions, 1975 Wash. U. L.Q. 275, 330-331. On this view, deprivation of "crucial information" can convert what otherwise would be a noncoercive situation into a coercive situation. . . . The difficulty with this position is that it is unacceptably overinclusive: it would encompass information such as the death of a critical witness, the successful escape of an accomplice, and the destruction of crucial evidence. Certainly, each of these bits of information would play an important part in the suspect's understanding of his or her "tactical position" and, accordingly, in the suspect's decision to confess.

in large measure by the special and essential role lawyers play in realizing the purpose of the right against self-incrimination. . . . Our holding is also consistent with the Rules of Professional Conduct of the American legal profession. The American Bar Association's Standards for Criminal Justice are unequivocally clear about the need for the earliest possible provision of counsel for an accused in custody. Standards 5-5.1; 5-7.1. . . .

Although we have, today, undoubtedly made explicit an additional responsibility of the State in its conduct toward criminal defendants, we do not believe that burden to be a heavy one. The duty to inform, that we place upon the State, is narrow and specific. It arises only where counsel has made known that he or she has been retained to represent the person held in custody, is present or readily available, and makes a request to consult with the suspect in a reasonably diligent, timely and pertinent fashion.

We do not make incumbent upon the attorney the duty to communicate directly with the interrogating officers. That communication will not, most times, be possible. Rather, whenever the attorney has communicated his presence and desire to confer with the suspect to an agent of the State in a position to contact the interrogating officers, we will impute to those officers knowledge of the attorney's presence and desire to confer with the suspect. . . .

We are satisfied that our holding will fully serve considerations of public policy and not undermine the proper and effective administration of criminal justice. . . . Prior to *Moran,* a majority of states followed a rule similar to the one we enunciate today, without any apparent diminishment in the effectiveness of their law-enforcement agencies. In the states, since 1986, that have rejected *Moran,* no evidence exists that the police have been seriously hindered in their efforts to uphold the law.

[We reject] the dissent's contention that the rule we enunciate today is unfairly biased against the "indigent defendant with no previous experience with law enforcement who is arrested while alone." It is probably true that such a person will be less likely to have a lawyer contacted to see him or her. In an ideal world, every defendant would have the family, friends, financial means, time, energy, and personal resources to mount the best defense. But we do not live in an ideal world.

Regrettably, reality compels us to tolerate significant differences in the empirical operation of the constitutional rules we enunciate. Would anyone dispute, after all, that the Sixth Amendment right to counsel is experienced differently by a well educated defendant with access to any trial lawyer in the country and unlimited financial resources to present a defense, than by an illiterate and indigent defendant, without family or friends, who must rely on a highly competent and committed, but overworked, public defender? Yet we have never taken a disparity in the actual ability of differently-situated defendants to make use of a right as an argument against affording that right.

[The] police conduct in this case illustrates the close correlation between police conduct that can increase the inherently coercive atmosphere of custodial interrogation and conduct that is excessive, shocking, and fundamentally unfair and therefore violative of due process. We are presented with a prosecutor misstating to an attorney retained to represent a client that the client was a witness not a suspect, and refusing to allow that attorney access to the client, thus violating the rules of his profession. In turn, the police hurried defendant down a back stairway to prevent defendant from seeing his girlfriend or the attorney retained to represent him.

This, in turn, prompted the police to aver that taking four flights of stairs to exit a building was "more convenient" than using the elevator next to which defendant's girlfriend was coincidentally sitting. We think that in this case the law-enforcement officers were under great pressure to secure a confession. To prevent defendant from speaking with his attorney, the police engaged in conduct that, if not egregious, exemplifies the ways in which the inherently coercive atmosphere of custodial interrogation can be materially increased in the efforts to obtain a confession.

[Police] and prosecutorial behavior, in denying defendant access to counsel, did not well serve the investigative function. Such conduct does not promote public esteem for the law, and it substantially increases the possibility that a suspect's confession will be involuntary. At a minimum, such conduct must not be encouraged by the courts. . . .

CLIFFORD, J., dissenting.

The importance of the right to counsel in protecting suspects against compelled self-incrimination can hardly be overstated. This Court has traditionally been most solicitous of that right. We have determined that any indication of a suspect's desire for counsel — even if not articulate, clear, or explicit — triggers the right. But today the Court extends that treasured right even farther, concluding that the right to counsel can attach even if a suspect expressly and voluntarily waives that right. That goes too far. . . .

Reed, a quality-control inspector whose work required the reading of complex manuals and engineering drawings, understood that he had the right to an attorney. He understood that an attorney would be provided if he could not afford one. He understood that he could ask for counsel at any time during the investigation and that the interrogation would cease at that point. Fully understanding all of the foregoing, defendant waived those rights — three times. Therefore, the failure to inform defendant of attorney Aitken's desire to communicate cannot be viewed as a violation of defendant's *Miranda* rights. And it should not be viewed as contrary to New Jersey's equivalent common-law protections. . . .

Δ understood his rights

Philosophical as well as practical concerns lead me to disagree with my colleagues' conclusion. First, [a] mentally-competent person's constitutional rights may be asserted only by that person. Therefore, I part company with the Court in its conclusion that a third party — in this case, the attorney in waiting — can assert a suspect's right against self-incrimination.

people who are competent may only assert their rights

Moreover, the Court's rule creates an illogical or unfair advantage for some suspects. Those suspects who are taken into custody in the presence of others, or who have previously obtained a private attorney, or who have previously required the services of a public defender — and therefore are more likely to be the beneficiaries of someone's call to an attorney on their behalf — will be found to have been coerced if not alerted should an attorney arrive at the station house. On the other hand, the indigent defendant with no previous experience with law enforcement who is arrested while alone — and hence "out of the loop" as far as legal assistance is concerned — although subjected to identical interrogation techniques will have knowingly and voluntarily waived the right to counsel. The rule therefore results in two classes of suspects and favors those who are more likely to have access to counsel. Such intolerable incongruities result when the emphasis shifts to events entirely unrelated to the suspect's knowledge rather than focusing on the sole person who matters in evaluating the validity of a suspect's waiver — the suspect.

Furthermore, the rule the Court fashions today risks increasing the likelihood of police coercion. Police officers of flexible rectitude who know that the right to question a suspect may terminate once an attorney makes known his or her availability to assist a suspect may be tempted to "turn up the heat" to secure a confession in what the officers may perceive as a limited window of opportunity. . . .

I need hardly add that my resolution of this case in no way constitutes an endorsement of the deplorable bumbling of the law-enforcement personnel who lied to Ms. Varga and Aitken and who scurried through the basement to hide defendant from the attorney who sought to confer with him. I join the majority in its denouncement of such foolishness. However, [the purpose of the majority's decision — to enhance the reliability of confessions by reducing the inherent coercion of custodial interrogation — is] adequately served by careful administering of the *Miranda* warnings, fully complied with in this case, and punctilious observance of the procedures laid out in our case law. . . .

Notes

1. *Informing a suspect about an available retained attorney: majority position.* The Supreme Court decided in Moran v. Burbine, 475 U.S. 412 (1986), that the police had no obligation to tell a suspect about an available attorney if the suspect has already waived the *Miranda* rights. Supreme courts in more than half the states have now faced this issue; a clear majority have disagreed with the Supreme Court and taken the same position as the *Reed* court. Compare Commonwealth v. Mavredakis, 725 N.E.2d 169 (Mass. 2000) (rejecting *Moran*) with Ajabu v. State, 693 N.E.2d 921 (Ind. 1998) (following *Moran* and collecting cases). If an elected prosecutor lived in a jurisdiction following the approach of the Supreme Court in *Moran,* how might she explain this position to a civic organization — say, the Elks Club or the high school's Honor Society? How might an elected prosecutor explain a decision such as the one in *Reed*? Do these questions help to explain why so many states have rejected *Moran*?

2. *Weighting decisions.* If most state courts reject a position taken by the U.S. Supreme Court, what weight should a later state court place on the Supreme Court opinion when interpreting its own state constitution? Should it carry less weight than recent opinions from the highest courts of sister states? Equivalent weight? On what theory of inter-court relations might such a Supreme Court opinion carry greater weight than later decisions from other state courts?

3. *Other variations in the warning.* Some police officers tell suspects that anything they say during an interrogation can be used "for or against" the suspect. Why do you suppose they phrase the warning this way? Is it an acceptable variation on the *Miranda* warnings? See State v. Stanley, 613 A.2d 788 (Conn. 1992) (approving of "for or against" statement on printed waiver form when it is accompanied by other "against" statements); Dunn v. State, 721 S.W.2d 325 (Tex. Crim. App. 1986) (error to give "for or against" warning).

The *Miranda* opinion, after describing the four warnings now known as the *Miranda* warnings, added the following: If the suspect "indicates in any manner that he does not wish to be interrogated, the police may not question him." 384 U.S. at 445. The opinion also refers to "the right to refrain from answering any further inquiries." Should the police be expected to warn suspects about this "fifth right" to cut off questioning? Courts considering this question have almost uniformly said no. See, e.g., State v. Mitchell, 482 N.W.2d 364 (Wis. 1992). If the suspect does indeed have the right to cut off questioning, why should the police be obliged to tell suspects about some of their rights but not this one? Would warnings about this right have any greater effect than the four existing warnings? Cf. United States v. Lombera-Camorlinga, 206 F.3d 882 (9th Cir. 2000) (failure to inform arrested non-citizen of Vienna Convention right to contact consul does not require suppression of statement).

In Florida v. Powell, 130 S. Ct. 1195 (2010), the police informed a suspect before a custodial interrogation that "You have the right to talk to a lawyer before answering any of our questions" and "You have the right to use any of these rights at any time you want during this interview." The suspect waived *Miranda* rights and admitted ownership of a firearm. Although the warning informed a suspect about access to an attorney *before* questioning rather than *during* an interrogation, the Supreme Court held that this combination of warnings satisfied the requirements of *Miranda*. The Court reiterated its view that no particular formulation of words is necessary to convey the essential information about rights of a suspect during custodial interrogation. The two statements that police used in this case, taken together, address the *Miranda* Court's concern that the "circumstances surrounding in-custody interrogation can operate very quickly to overbear the will of one merely made aware of his privilege [to remain silent] by his interrogators."

For an exploration of other variations in the precise wording of the *Miranda* warnings, see the web extension for this chapter at *http://www.crimpro.com/extension/ch08*.

4. *Translation of* Miranda *warnings.* A suspect who has difficulty understanding English must receive the warnings in her own language. For this reason, some police departments maintain a standardized translation of the *Miranda* warnings in languages commonly spoken in the area. See State v. Santiago, 556 N.W.2d 687 (Wis. 1996).

C. INVOCATION AND WAIVER OF *MIRANDA* RIGHTS

After the police give a *Miranda* warning, a suspect may invoke the right to counsel or to silence, or waive these rights and submit to the interrogation. Most suspects waive the right to counsel and the right to silence after receiving *Miranda* warnings. Waiver occurs in at least three-quarters of all custodial interrogations (and probably more). Thus, the legal rules dealing with waiver and invocation of interrogation rights affect more cases than any other aspect of the vast legal doctrine surrounding *Miranda.* In this section, we review how courts determine whether a suspect has invoked or waived *Miranda* rights.

Suspects typically use language that leaves some doubt about their invocation or waiver of the right to counsel or silence. The rules for handling ambiguous words or actions suggesting invocation or waiver can have a huge practical impact: If only crystal clear invocation is valid, there will be more waivers, while if courts insist that government agents treat a range of ambiguous statements or actions as assertions of *Miranda* rights, assertion will be more common. When the suspect makes an ambiguous statement or takes action that might be a waiver of *Miranda* rights, when must the police clarify the waiver before proceeding with the interrogation?

VERMONT STATUTES TIT. 13, §§5234, 5237

§5234

(a) If a person who is being detained by a law enforcement officer . . . is not represented by an attorney under conditions in which a person having his own counsel would be entitled to be so represented, the law enforcement officer, magistrate, or court concerned shall:

(1) Clearly inform him of the right of a person to be represented by an attorney and of a needy person to be represented at public expense; and

(2) If the person detained or charged does not have an attorney and does not knowingly, voluntarily and intelligently waive his right to have an attorney when detained or charged, notify the appropriate public defender that he is not so represented. . . .

(d) Information . . . given to a person by a law enforcement officer under this section gives rise to a rebuttable presumption that the information was effectively communicated if:

(1) It is in writing or otherwise recorded;

(2) The recipient records his acknowledgment of receipt and time of receipt of the information; and

(3) The material so recorded under paragraphs (1) and (2) of this subsection is filed with the court next concerned.

§5237

A person who has been appropriately informed under section 5234 of this title may waive in writing, or by other record, any right provided by this chapter, if the court, at the time of or after waiver, finds of record that he has acted with full awareness of his rights and of the consequences of a waiver and if the waiver is otherwise according to law. The court shall consider such factors as the person's age, education, and familiarity with the English language, and the complexity of the crime involved.

MARY BERGHUIS v. VAN CHESTER THOMPKINS

130 S. Ct. 2250 (2010)

KENNEDY, J.*

. . . I.

On January 10, 2000, a shooting occurred outside a mall in Southfield, Michigan. Among the victims was Samuel Morris, who died from multiple gunshot wounds. . . . Thompkins, who was a suspect, fled. About one year later he was found in Ohio and arrested there.

* [Justices Alito, Scalia, and Thomas and Chief Justice Roberts joined in this opinion. — EDS.]

Two Southfield police officers traveled to Ohio to interrogate Thompkins, then awaiting transfer to Michigan. The interrogation began around 1:30 P.M. and lasted about three hours. The interrogation was conducted in a room that was 8 by 10 feet, and Thompkins sat in a chair that resembled a school desk (it had an arm on it that swings around to provide a surface to write on). At the beginning of the interrogation, one of the officers, Detective Helgert, presented Thompkins with a form derived from the *Miranda* rule. It stated:

> 1. . . . You have the right to remain silent.
> 2. Anything you say can and will be used against you in a court of law.
> 3. You have a right to talk to a lawyer before answering any questions and you have the right to have a lawyer present with you while you are answering any questions.
> 4. If you cannot afford to hire a lawyer, one will be appointed to represent you before any questioning, if you wish one.
> 5. You have the right to decide at any time before or during questioning to use your right to remain silent and your right to talk with a lawyer while you are being questioned.

Helgert asked Thompkins to read the fifth warning out loud. Thompkins complied. Helgert later said this was to ensure that Thompkins could read, and Helgert concluded that Thompkins understood English. Helgert then read the other four *Miranda* warnings out loud and asked Thompkins to sign the form to demonstrate that he understood his rights. Thompkins declined to sign the form. The record contains conflicting evidence about whether Thompkins then verbally confirmed that he understood the rights listed on the form. . . . Compare [Record on Appeal] at 9a (at a suppression hearing, Helgert testified that Thompkins verbally confirmed that he understood his rights), with *id.*, at 148a (at trial, Helgert stated, "I don't know that I orally asked him" whether Thompkins understood his rights).

Officers began an interrogation. At no point during the interrogation did Thompkins say that he wanted to remain silent, that he did not want to talk with the police, or that he wanted an attorney. Thompkins was largely silent during the interrogation, which lasted about three hours. He did give a few limited verbal responses, however, such as "yeah," "no," or "I don't know." And on occasion he communicated by nodding his head. Thompkins also said that he "didn't want a peppermint" that was offered to him by the police and that the chair he was "sitting in was hard."

About 2 hours and 45 minutes into the interrogation, Helgert asked Thompkins, "Do you believe in God?" Thompkins made eye contact with Helgert and said "Yes," as his eyes welled up with tears. Helgert asked, "Do you pray to God?" Thompkins said "Yes." Helgert asked, "Do you pray to God to forgive you for shooting that boy down?" Thompkins answered "Yes" and looked away. Thompkins refused to make a written confession, and the interrogation ended about 15 minutes later.

Thompkins was charged with first-degree murder, assault with intent to commit murder, and certain firearms-related offenses. He moved to suppress the statements made during the interrogation. He argued that he had invoked his Fifth Amendment right to remain silent, requiring police to end the interrogation at once, see

Michigan v. Mosley, 423 U.S. 96, 103 (1975), that he had not waived his right to remain silent, and that his inculpatory statements were involuntary. The trial court denied the motion. . . . The jury found Thompkins guilty on all counts. He was sentenced to life in prison without parole. . . .

III.

A.

Thompkins makes various arguments that his answers to questions from the detectives were inadmissible. He first contends that he invoked his privilege to remain silent by not saying anything for a sufficient period of time, so the interrogation should have ceased before he made his inculpatory statements.

Must be crystal clear in your statement

This argument is unpersuasive. In the context of invoking the *Miranda* right to counsel, the Court in Davis v. United States, 512 U.S. 452, 459 (1994), held that a suspect must do so "unambiguously." If an accused makes a statement concerning the right to counsel "that is ambiguous or equivocal" or makes no statement, the police are not required to end the interrogation or ask questions to clarify whether the accused wants to invoke his or her *Miranda* rights. . . .

The Court has not yet stated whether an invocation of the right to remain silent can be ambiguous or equivocal, but there is no principled reason to adopt different standards for determining when an accused has invoked the *Miranda* right to remain silent and the *Miranda* right to counsel at issue in *Davis*. Both protect the privilege against compulsory self-incrimination by requiring an interrogation to cease when either right is invoked.

There is good reason to require an accused who wants to invoke his or her right to remain silent to do so unambiguously. A requirement of an unambiguous invocation of *Miranda* rights results in an objective inquiry that avoids difficulties of proof and provides guidance to officers on how to proceed in the face of ambiguity. If an ambiguous act, omission, or statement could require police to end the interrogation, police would be required to make difficult decisions about an accused's unclear intent and face the consequence of suppression if they guess wrong. Suppression of a voluntary confession in these circumstances would place a significant burden on society's interest in prosecuting criminal activity. Treating an ambiguous or equivocal act, omission, or statement as an invocation of *Miranda* rights might add marginally to *Miranda*'s goal of dispelling the compulsion inherent in custodial interrogation. But as *Miranda* holds, full comprehension of the rights to remain silent and request an attorney are sufficient to dispel whatever coercion is inherent in the interrogation process.

Thompkins did not say that he wanted to remain silent or that he did not want to talk with the police. Had he made either of these simple, unambiguous statements, he would have invoked his "right to cut off questioning." Here he did neither, so he did not invoke his right to remain silent.

B.

We next consider whether Thompkins waived his right to remain silent. Even absent the accused's invocation of the right to remain silent, the accused's statement during a custodial interrogation is inadmissible at trial unless the prosecution can establish that the accused in fact knowingly and voluntarily waived

Miranda rights when making the statement. The waiver inquiry has two distinct dimensions: waiver must be voluntary in the sense that it was the product of a free and deliberate choice rather than intimidation, coercion, or deception, and made with a full awareness of both the nature of the right being abandoned and the consequences of the decision to abandon it.

Some language in *Miranda* could be read to indicate that waivers are difficult to establish absent an explicit written waiver or a formal, express oral statement. *Miranda* said "a valid waiver will not be presumed simply from the silence of the accused after warnings are given or simply from the fact that a confession was in fact eventually obtained." . . . In addition, the *Miranda* Court stated that "a heavy burden rests on the government to demonstrate that the defendant knowingly and intelligently waived his privilege against self-incrimination and his right to retained or appointed counsel."

The course of decisions since *Miranda,* informed by the application of *Miranda* warnings in the whole course of law enforcement, demonstrates that waivers can be established even absent formal or express statements of waiver that would be expected in, say, a judicial hearing to determine if a guilty plea has been properly entered. . . .

One of the first cases to decide the meaning and import of *Miranda* with respect to the question of waiver was North Carolina v. Butler, 441 U.S. 369 (1979). . . . *Butler* interpreted the *Miranda* language concerning the "heavy burden" to show waiver in accord with usual principles of determining waiver, which can include waiver implied from all the circumstances. . . .

The prosecution therefore does not need to show that a waiver of *Miranda* rights was express. An implicit waiver of the right to remain silent is sufficient to admit a suspect's statement into evidence. *Butler* made clear that a waiver of *Miranda* rights may be implied through the defendant's silence, coupled with an understanding of his rights and a course of conduct indicating waiver. . . .

If the State establishes that a *Miranda* warning was given and the accused made an uncoerced statement, this showing, standing alone, is insufficient to demonstrate "a valid waiver" of *Miranda* rights. The prosecution must make the additional showing that the accused understood these rights. Where the prosecution shows that a *Miranda* warning was given and that it was understood by the accused, an accused's uncoerced statement establishes an implied waiver of the right to remain silent.

Although *Miranda* imposes on the police a rule that is both formalistic and practical when it prevents them from interrogating suspects without first providing them with a *Miranda* warning, it does not impose a formalistic waiver procedure that a suspect must follow to relinquish those rights. As a general proposition, the law can presume that an individual who, with a full understanding of his or her rights, acts in a manner inconsistent with their exercise has made a deliberate choice to relinquish the protection those rights afford. . . . *Miranda* rights can therefore be waived through means less formal than a typical waiver on the record in a courtroom, given the practical constraints and necessities of interrogation and the fact that *Miranda*'s main protection lies in advising defendants of their rights.

The record in this case shows that Thompkins waived his right to remain silent. There is no basis in this case to conclude that he did not understand his rights; and on these facts it follows that he chose not to invoke or rely on those rights when he did speak. [First, there] was more than enough evidence in the record to conclude that Thompkins understood his *Miranda* rights. Thompkins received a written copy of the *Miranda* warnings; Detective Helgert determined that Thompkins could read and understand English; and Thompkins was given time to read the warnings. Thompkins, furthermore, read aloud the fifth warning, which stated that "you have the right to decide at any time before or during questioning to use your right to remain silent and your right to talk with a lawyer while you are being questioned." He was thus aware that his right to remain silent would not dissipate after a certain amount of time and that police would have to honor his right to be silent and his right to counsel during the whole course of interrogation. . . . Helgert, moreover, read the warnings aloud.

Second, Thompkins's answer to Detective Helgert's question about whether Thompkins prayed to God for forgiveness for shooting the victim is a course of conduct indicating waiver of the right to remain silent. If Thompkins wanted to remain silent, he could have said nothing in response to Helgert's questions, or he could have unambiguously invoked his *Miranda* rights and ended the interrogation. [His] course of conduct indicating waiver . . . is confirmed by the fact that before then Thompkins had given sporadic answers to questions throughout the interrogation.

Third, there is no evidence that Thompkins's statement was coerced. Thompkins does not claim that police threatened or injured him during the interrogation or that he was in any way fearful. The interrogation was conducted in a standard-sized room in the middle of the afternoon. It is true that apparently he was in a straight-backed chair for three hours, but there is no authority for the proposition that an interrogation of this length is inherently coercive. Indeed, even where interrogations of greater duration were held to be improper, they were accompanied, as this one was not, by other facts indicating coercion, such as an incapacitated and sedated suspect, sleep and food deprivation, and threats. The fact that Helgert's question referred to Thompkins's religious beliefs also did not render Thompkins's statement involuntary. The Fifth Amendment privilege is not concerned with moral and psychological pressures to confess emanating from sources other than official coercion. In these circumstances, Thompkins knowingly and voluntarily made a statement to police, so he waived his right to remain silent.

C.

Thompkins next argues that, even if his answer to Detective Helgert could constitute a waiver of his right to remain silent, the police were not allowed to question him until they obtained a waiver first. *Butler* forecloses this argument. The *Butler* Court held that courts can infer a waiver of *Miranda* rights "from the actions and words of the person interrogated." This principle would be inconsistent with a rule that requires a waiver at the outset. . . . Any waiver, express or implied, may be contradicted by an invocation at any time. . . .

Interrogation provides the suspect with additional information that can put his or her decision to waive, or not to invoke, into perspective. As questioning commences and then continues, the suspect has the opportunity to consider the choices he or she faces and to make a more informed decision, either to insist on silence or to cooperate. When the suspect knows that *Miranda* rights can be invoked at any time, he or she has the opportunity to reassess his or her immediate and long-term interests. Cooperation with the police may result in more favorable treatment for the suspect; the apprehension of accomplices; the prevention of continuing injury and fear; beginning steps towards relief or solace for the victims; and the beginning of the suspect's own return to the law and the social order it seeks to protect. . . .

SOTOMAYOR, J., dissenting.*

The Court concludes today that a criminal suspect waives his right to remain silent if, after sitting tacit and uncommunicative through nearly three hours of police interrogation, he utters a few one-word responses. The Court also concludes that a suspect who wishes to guard his right to remain silent against such a finding of "waiver" must, counterintuitively, speak — and must do so with sufficient precision to satisfy a clear-statement rule that construes ambiguity in favor of the police. Both propositions mark a substantial retreat from the protection against compelled self-incrimination that Miranda v. Arizona, 384 U.S. 436 (1966), has long provided during custodial interrogation. . . .

I.

. . . The strength of Thompkins' *Miranda* claims depends in large part on the circumstances of the 3-hour interrogation, at the end of which he made inculpatory statements later introduced at trial. The Court's opinion downplays record evidence that Thompkins remained almost completely silent and unresponsive throughout that session. One of the interrogating officers, Detective Helgert, testified that although Thompkins was administered *Miranda* warnings, the last of which he read aloud, Thompkins expressly declined to sign a written acknowledgment that he had been advised of and understood his rights. There is conflicting evidence in the record about whether Thompkins ever verbally confirmed understanding his rights. The record contains no indication that the officers sought or obtained an express waiver.

As to the interrogation itself, Helgert candidly characterized it as "very, very one-sided" and "nearly a monologue." Thompkins was "peculiar," "sullen," and "generally quiet." Helgert and his partner "did most of the talking," as Thompkins was "not verbally communicative" and "largely" remained silent. To the extent Thompkins gave any response, his answers consisted of "a word or two. A 'yeah,' or a 'no,' or 'I don't know.' And sometimes he simply sat down with his head in his hands looking down. Sometimes he would look up and make eye-contact would be the only response." After proceeding in this fashion for approximately 2 hours and 45 minutes, Helgert asked Thompkins three questions relating to his faith in God. The prosecution relied at trial on Thompkins' one-word answers of "yes."

Thompkins' nonresponsiveness is particularly striking in the context of the officers' interview strategy, later explained as conveying to Thompkins that "this was his opportunity to explain his side" of the story because everybody else, including his co-defendants, "had given their version," and asking him "who is going to speak up for you if you don't speak up for yourself?" Yet, Helgert confirmed that the "*only* thing" Thompkins said relative to his involvement in the shooting occurred near the end of the interview — *i.e.,* in response to the questions about God. The only other responses Helgert could remember Thompkins giving were that he "didn't want a peppermint" and "the chair that he was sitting in was hard." Nevertheless, the Michigan court concluded on this record that Thompkins had not invoked his right to remain silent because "he continued to talk with the officer, albeit sporadically," and that he voluntarily waived that right. . . .

* [Justices Breyer, Ginsburg, and Stevens joined this opinion. — EDS.]

Miranda and our subsequent cases . . . require police to respect the accused's decision to exercise the rights outlined in the warnings. If an individual indicates in any manner, at any time prior to or during questioning, that he wishes to remain silent or if he states that he wants an attorney, the interrogation "must cease." . . . A heavy burden rests on the government to demonstrate that the defendant knowingly and intelligently waived his privilege against self-incrimination and his right to retained or appointed counsel. . . .

The question whether a suspect has validly waived his right is entirely distinct as a matter of law from whether he invoked that right. The questions are related, however, in terms of the practical effect on the exercise of a suspect's rights. A suspect may at any time revoke his prior waiver of rights — or, closer to the facts of this case, guard against the possibility of a future finding that he implicitly waived his rights — by invoking the rights and thereby requiring the police to cease questioning.

II.

. . . Even in concluding that *Miranda* does not invariably require an express waiver of the right to silence or the right to counsel, this Court in North Carolina v. Butler, 441 U.S. 369 (1979), made clear that the prosecution bears a substantial burden in establishing an implied waiver. The Federal Bureau of Investigation had obtained statements after advising Butler of his rights and confirming that he understood them. When presented with a written waiver-of-rights form, Butler told the agents, "I will talk to you but I am not signing any form." He then made inculpatory statements, which he later sought to suppress on the ground that he had not expressly waived his right to counsel.

[The] question is whether the defendant in fact knowingly and voluntarily waived the rights delineated in the *Miranda* case. *Miranda,* we observed, "unequivocally said . . . mere silence is not enough." While we stopped short in *Butler* of announcing a *per se* rule that the defendant's silence, coupled with an understanding of his rights and a course of conduct indicating waiver, may never support a conclusion that a defendant has waived his rights, we reiterated that courts must presume that a defendant did not waive his rights; the prosecution's burden is "great." . . .

Together, *Miranda* and *Butler* establish that a court must presume that a defendant did not waive his rights; the prosecution bears a "heavy burden" in attempting to demonstrate waiver; the fact of a "lengthy interrogation" prior to obtaining statements is "strong evidence" against a finding of valid waiver; "mere silence" in response to questioning is not enough; and waiver may not be presumed "simply from the fact that a confession was in fact eventually obtained."

It is undisputed here that Thompkins never expressly waived his right to remain silent. His refusal to sign even an acknowledgment that he understood his *Miranda* rights evinces, if anything, an intent not to waive those rights. That Thompkins did not make the inculpatory statements at issue until after approximately 2 hours and 45 minutes of interrogation serves as strong evidence against waiver. *Miranda* and *Butler* expressly preclude the possibility that the inculpatory statements themselves are sufficient to establish waiver.

In these circumstances, Thompkins' actions and words preceding the inculpatory statements simply do not evidence a "course of conduct indicating waiver" sufficient to carry the prosecution's burden. . . . Unlike in *Butler*, Thompkins made no initial declaration akin to "I will talk to you." . . .

Today's decision thus ignores the important interests *Miranda* safeguards. The underlying constitutional guarantee against self-incrimination reflects many of our fundamental values and most noble aspirations, our society's preference for an accusatorial rather than an inquisitorial system of criminal justice; a fear that self-incriminating statements will be elicited by inhumane treatment and abuses and a resulting distrust of self-deprecatory statements; and a realization that while the privilege is sometimes a shelter to the guilty, it is often a protection to the innocent. For these reasons . . . a criminal law system which comes to depend on the confession will, in the long run, be less reliable and more subject to abuses than a system relying on independent investigation. By bracing against the possibility of unreliable statements in every instance of in-custody interrogation, *Miranda*'s prophylactic rules serve to protect the fairness of the trial itself. Today's decision bodes poorly for the fundamental principles that *Miranda* protects.

III.

Thompkins separately argues that his conduct during the interrogation invoked his right to remain silent, requiring police to terminate questioning. . . . I cannot agree with the Court's much broader ruling that a suspect must clearly invoke his right to silence by speaking. Taken together with the Court's reformulation of the prosecution's burden of proof as to waiver, today's novel clear-statement rule for invocation invites police to question a suspect at length — notwithstanding his persistent refusal to answer questions — in the hope of eventually obtaining a single inculpatory response which will suffice to prove waiver of rights. . . .

In Michigan v. Mosley, 423 U.S. 96 (1975), the Court said that a critical safeguard of the right to remain silent is a suspect's "right to cut off questioning." . . . Thompkins contends that in refusing to respond to questions he effectively invoked his right to remain silent, such that police were required to terminate the interrogation prior to his inculpatory statements. . . .

The Court [extends] *Davis* to hold that police may continue questioning a suspect until he unambiguously invokes his right to remain silent. Because Thompkins neither said "he wanted to remain silent" nor said "he did not want to talk with the police," the Court concludes, he did not clearly invoke his right to silence.

I disagree with this novel application of *Davis*. Neither the rationale nor holding of that case compels today's result. *Davis* involved the right to counsel, not the right to silence. [A request to have counsel present and a request to remain silent each trigger different procedural safeguards. The police may reapproach a suspect who invokes the right to remain silent under certain circumstances; the same does not hold true for a suspect who invokes the right to counsel.] The different effects of invoking the rights are consistent with distinct standards for invocation. . . .

In addition, the suspect's equivocal reference to a lawyer in *Davis* occurred only *after* he had given express oral and written waivers of his rights. . . . The Court ignores this aspect of *Davis,* as well as the decisions of numerous federal and state courts declining to apply a clear-statement rule when a suspect has not previously given an express waiver of rights. . . .

The suspect's right to cut off questioning must be "scrupulously honored." Such a standard is necessarily precautionary and fact specific. The rule would acknowledge that some statements or conduct are so equivocal that police may scrupulously honor a suspect's rights without terminating questioning — for instance, if a suspect's actions are reasonably understood to indicate a willingness to listen before deciding whether to respond. But other statements or actions — in particular, when a suspect sits silent throughout prolonged interrogation, long past the point when he could be deciding whether to respond — cannot reasonably be understood other than as an invocation of the right to remain silent. Under such circumstances, "scrupulous" respect for the suspect's rights will require police to terminate questioning.[8] . . .

Davis' clear-statement rule is also a poor fit for the right to silence. Advising a suspect that he has a "right to remain silent" is unlikely to convey that he must speak (and must do so in some particular fashion) to ensure the right will be protected. By contrast, telling a suspect he has the right to the presence of an attorney, and that if he cannot afford an attorney one will be appointed for him prior to any questioning if he so desires, implies the need for speech to exercise that right. . . .

Conversely, the Court's concern that police will face difficult decisions about an accused's unclear intent and suffer the consequences of "guessing wrong," is misplaced. If a suspect makes an ambiguous statement or engages in conduct that creates uncertainty about his intent to invoke his right, police can simply ask for clarification. It is hardly an unreasonable burden for police to ask a suspect, for instance, "Do you want to talk to us?" . . . Police may well prefer not to seek clarification of an ambiguous statement out of fear that a suspect will invoke his rights. But our system of justice is not founded on a fear that a suspect will exercise his rights. If the exercise of constitutional rights will thwart the effectiveness of a system of law enforcement, then there is something very wrong with that system.

The Court asserts in passing that treating ambiguous statements or acts as an invocation of the right to silence will only "marginally" serve *Miranda*'s goals. Experience suggests the contrary. In the 16 years since *Davis* was decided, ample evidence has accrued that criminal suspects often use equivocal or colloquial language in attempting to invoke their right to silence. A number of lower courts that have (erroneously, in my view) imposed a clear-statement requirement for invocation of the right to silence have rejected as ambiguous an array of statements whose meaning might otherwise be thought plain. At a minimum, these decisions suggest that differentiating "clear" from "ambiguous" statements is often a subjective inquiry. [When] a suspect "understands his (expressed) wishes to have been ignored in contravention of the rights just read to him by his interrogator, he may well see further objection as futile and confession (true or not) as the only way to end his interrogation. . . .

Today's decision turns *Miranda* upside down. Criminal suspects must now unambiguously invoke their right to remain silent — which, counterintuitively, requires them to speak. At the same time, suspects will be legally presumed to have waived their rights even if they have given no clear expression of their intent to do so. Those results, in my view, find no basis in *Miranda* or our subsequent cases and

8. Indeed, this rule appears to reflect widespread contemporary police practice. Thompkins' *amici* collect a range of training materials that instruct police not to engage in prolonged interrogation after a suspect has failed to respond to initial questioning. One widely used police manual, for example, teaches that a suspect who indicates, "even by silence itself," his unwillingness to answer questions "has obviously exercised his constitutional privilege against self-incrimination."

are inconsistent with the fair-trial principles on which those precedents are grounded. . . .

Problem 8-5. Ambiguous Assertion?

The police were investigating the murder of a woman and her two young children. The killer had used a knife and a shotgun, and had stolen several items from the home, including an automobile. The police identified the stolen car on the road at 10:15 P.M., several hours after the murders. They arrested the driver, 16-year-old Jason Williams, and took him to the police station.

At 5:20 A.M., the police took Williams from his detention cell to an interview room located across the hall. Detectives Bozovsky and Christensen were waiting in the interview room when Williams arrived. They introduced themselves and sat at opposite ends of the table, while Williams sat between them with his back to the door. Williams was not wearing handcuffs. After Williams sat down, Detective Bozovsky recited a full *Miranda* warning and asked Williams if he understood the rights. Williams said yes. Bozovsky then asked Williams if he was willing to talk with them, and Williams replied "Yes, I'll talk with you." He signed a waiver of his *Miranda* rights.

Williams had not yet been informed about the homicide investigation. Instead, he was questioned about being in a stolen car. Williams initially maintained that he had stolen the car from a man who had left the keys in its ignition while parked outside of a liquor store. Approximately 45 minutes into the interview, Detective Bozovsky informed Williams that the car had been stolen from the home of people who had been murdered. Bozovsky noticed an injury to Williams' hand, and said that he suspected Williams had injured his hand during the murders. Williams denied any involvement in the homicides. Detective Christensen then explained that the homicide scene would be processed for fingerprints and blood analysis, and hypothesized that if the adult female victim had been sexually assaulted, physical evidence, such as semen, could be traced back to the assailant. Williams emphatically denied his involvement in anything like that, and Christensen accused him of lying. Williams then lost his composure, stood up from his chair, turned toward Christensen and said, "I don't have to take any more of your bullshit." Then Williams walked out of the interrogation room, into the hall, and back to his detention cell, where he was placed by the detention officer. This episode occurred approximately one hour into the interview.

Detectives Christensen and Bozovsky allowed Williams about five minutes to cool down. They would like to continue the interrogation with Williams. You are an attorney working for the police department, and you approach the detectives in the police station at this point. Bozovsky and Chritensen want to know what they should do next. Has Williams now invoked his right to silence? What advice will you give the detectives? Cf. State v. Williams, 535 N.W.2d 277 (Minn. 1995).

Suppose instead that Williams had said, "That's the end of this conversation, I'm done!" as he left the room. Would your advice change? Cf. State v. Schroeder, 777 N.W.2d 793 (Neb. 2010).

Notes

1. *Unambiguous assertion of* Miranda *rights: majority position.* The judicial opinions on assertions of *Miranda* rights divide into three groups. A small group holds that any statements that might be interpreted as an assertion of rights puts an end to the interrogation. A second group says that when a suspect makes an ambiguous statement that could be an assertion of rights, the interrogator must stop the questioning about the crime and obtain a clarification about the meaning of the statement. The largest group, represented by Davis v. United States, 512 U.S. 452 (1994), declares that a suspect must make a clear and unequivocal statement to invoke the *Miranda* right to counsel.

The *Thompkins* case expanded *Davis* to cover both the right to silence and the right to counsel. State courts and lower federal courts are wrestling with the question of which words or actions of a suspect amount to an "unambiguous" invocation of the right to silence. Will the courts encounter greater ambiguity in the invocation of the right to silence than they find in the invocation of the right to counsel? You can track current developments on this question on the web extension for this chapter at *http://www.crimpro.com/extension/ch08*.

2. *Interaction among supreme courts.* In Davis v. United States, 512 U.S. 452 (1994), the Supreme Court addressed an issue that many state courts had already answered, and it adopted a position taken by a minority of state courts until that time. Should the positions of state courts on a question of federal constitutional law have any significance when the U.S. Supreme Court considers the question? If so, is their significance any different from that of lower federal courts? After *Davis,* the state courts moved decisively toward the "unambiguous assertion" position. See State v. Eastlack, 883 P.2d 999 (Ariz. 1994) (follows *Davis,* although officer asked clarifying questions). A few courts, however, reaffirmed their earlier allegiance to some other approach. See State v. Hoey, 881 P.2d 504 (Haw. 1994). How would you explain the apparent, but incomplete, influence of the U.S. Supreme Court on state supreme courts deciding this question, one that arises often in every jurisdiction?

3. *Timing of invocation.* Even if the suspect uses unambiguous words, she must use them at the right time. Courts have not allowed suspects to make "anticipatory assertions" of rights, before interrogation begins. See, e.g., Sapp v. State, 690 So. 2d 581 (Fla. 1997); People v. Villalobos, 737 N.E.2d 639 (Ill. 2000). Although a questioner may continue questioning after an ambiguous statement from a suspect, courts sometimes require them to respond to clear questions from the suspect that do not invoke *Miranda* rights. See Almeida v. State, 737 So. 2d 520 (Fla. 1999) (suspect asks "Well, what good is a lawyer going to do?"; questioner must reply that decision belongs to suspect).

Some courts apply different tests for invocation, depending on whether the invocation happens at the start of the interrogation or in mid-stream, after an initial waiver of *Miranda* rights. See State v. Turner, 305 S.W.3d 508 (Tenn. 2010) (the *Davis* rule requiring unambiguous assertion of right to counsel applies only after a suspect initially waived *Miranda* rights). Does the nature of the interaction between the suspect and questioner change during an interview in ways that justifies a change in the standard for invoking *Miranda* rights?

4. *Ambiguous waiver: majority position.* There are many instances in which a defendant says or does something that might be interpreted to constitute a waiver (rather

than an assertion) of *Miranda* rights. This could be something as simple as refusing to answer any questions about waiver but discussing the crime with the interrogating officer. In North Carolina v. Butler, 441 U.S. 369 (1979), the Court said that "an explicit statement of waiver is not invariably necessary to support a finding that the defendant waived the right to remain silent or the right to counsel guaranteed by the *Miranda* case." Virtually all state courts have agreed that a suspect can implicitly waive *Miranda* rights through conduct or ambiguous statements. Garvey v. State, 873 A.2d 291 (Del. 2005) (suspect who responded to *Miranda* advisory by saying, "Depends on what you ask me," effectively waived interrogation rights, indicating intent to selectively waive rights and an understanding of those rights).

Does the *Thompkins* case mean that any suspect responses to questions during an interrogation will now amount to a waiver of the right to silence? Do you predict any serious changes in interrogation techniques based on this opinion?

Consider how legislation on the topic of waiver might look different from constitutional rulings on the subject. Does the Vermont statute reprinted above prevent the use of a confession obtained after a suspect orally waives his rights but refuses to sign any waiver form? See State v. Caron, 586 A.2d 1127 (Vt. 1990). The Vermont statute is taken in large part from the Model Public Defender Act, adopted in 1970 by the National Conference of Commissioners on Uniform State Laws.

5. *Standard of proof for waiver.* In Lego v. Twomey, 404 U.S. 477 (1972), the Court ruled that the constitution requires the government to show that a confession was voluntary by a preponderance of the evidence. The same standard of proof applies when the government must prove the knowing and intelligent waiver of *Miranda* rights. Colorado v. Connelly, 479 U.S. 157 (1986). In both cases, the Court emphasized the distinction between proving the essential elements of a crime (which bears directly on the reliability of the jury's verdict) and establishing the voluntariness of a confession (which bears on the admissibility of evidence). Most state courts have also adopted the preponderance standard. See, e.g., People v. Clark, 857 P.2d 1099 (Cal. 1993); but see State v. Gerald, 549 A.2d 792 (N.J. 1988) (beyond reasonable doubt). Do doubts about the validity of a waiver of *Miranda* rights translate into doubts about the accuracy of the prosecution's evidence?

6. *Why do suspects waive their rights?* Can a suspect gain anything by talking to the police? Perhaps suspects believe they can convince the officers to look elsewhere for the culprit or to drop the investigation. Observers of interrogations say that it is standard practice for police interrogators at the beginning of an interrogation to encourage the suspect to speak with the officer as a way of telling "his side" of the story and to learn more about the evidence the police have collected. The officer will be careful to engage in small talk, to cover routine booking questions, and to talk about the advantages of waiver before allowing the suspect to answer any questions about *Miranda* rights. At that point, the questioner will often speak of the *Miranda* waiver as a formality that is surely very familiar to the suspect. If the suspect announces a decision about waiver too early, the officer has no opportunity to persuade the suspect to waive, and the relevant legal rules make it difficult to follow up after an invocation of rights. David Simon, Homicide: A Year on the Killing Streets (1991). Suspects with a prior felony record are far less likely than other suspects to waive their *Miranda* rights. The web extension for this chapter, at *http://www.crimpro.com/extension/ch08*, reviews the legal and criminological studies of interrogation practices. In hindsight, if the Warren Court was concerned about the

coercive nature of the interrogation environment in the police station, was it a mistake to allow a suspect to waive the right to silence without an attorney present?

Problem 8-6. Capacity to Waive

Donald Cleary forced his way into a home, struggled with the occupant, held her at gunpoint, and fled. About an hour later, an investigator from the state's attorney's office and a sergeant from the sheriff's department stopped defendant as he was driving his truck because he fit the general description of the assailant. The sergeant read Cleary his *Miranda* rights twice, and Cleary signed a statement purporting to waive those rights. He then confessed, admitting that he had entered the victim's house and accosted her, and that he had intended to rape her.

At the hearing on the defense motion to suppress this statement, Cleary relied on expert testimony from a psychiatrist, Dr. Robert Linder. Linder had evaluated Cleary in connection with several prior criminal charges. He estimated that Cleary had an IQ of 65, which translated into a mental age between ten and twelve, and only a limited ability to read and write. Cleary was 26 years old at the time of the hearing. Dr. Linder testified that Cleary had difficulty thinking abstractly and anticipating future events, which would limit his ability to comprehend the language of the *Miranda* warnings. He conceded, however, that Cleary could understand that he did not have to talk to the police, that he could speak with an attorney if he wished, and that he could stop answering questions whenever he chose. However, he believed that Cleary might have difficulty understanding the future legal impact of waiving his rights. Dr. Linder believed that Cleary would not be able to look beyond his immediate concerns to a future court proceeding in which comments he had made earlier would be used against him. Instead, Cleary would speak to police to take the shortest route to his immediate needs — to please the officers, to make himself feel better, and to go home.

Under cross-examination, Dr. Linder conceded that defendant had undergone a learning process through his prior contacts with the police and court system. Cleary had been questioned in previous arson and sexual assault investigations, and now understood that the prosecutor sought to put him in jail. Those previous charges had all been dismissed. He was declared incompetent to stand trial for one of the charges.

Cleary's former mental health services counselor also testified, and estimated his mental capacity to be that of a seven- or eight-year-old child and his emotional level to be that of a four- or five-year-old child. Cleary himself testified at the hearing that he spoke to the officers because he thought they would help him and because he could not leave until he spoke to them.

According to the U.S. Supreme Court in Fare v. Michael C., 442 U.S. 707, 725 (1979), an analysis of a defendant's capacity to waive *Miranda* rights requires a "totality-of-the-circumstances approach," that mandates an evaluation of the defendant's "age, experience, education, background, and intelligence," and an inquiry into "whether he has the capacity to understand the warnings given him, the nature of his Fifth Amendment rights, and the consequences of waiving those rights." Courts typically say that a suspect's mental impairment is a highly significant circumstance to be considered among all the others in deciding the voluntariness question.

The trial judge found that Cleary had attended special education classes in school through the eleventh grade and had limited ability to read, write, and do mathematics. He read at a second-grade level. He had also participated in programs for mentally retarded adults and continued to work actively with two counselors. She stated that Cleary, "in spite of his intellectual limitations, has the ability to learn and puts his learning to practical use." For example, Cleary operated his own logging business for seven years. He purchased and maintained equipment for the business and negotiated bank loans, timber contracts, and truck transportation for his timber. Cleary had a driver's license, maintained a vehicle, was knowledgeable about how it worked, and purchased parts for it.

Assume that the trial court rules that Cleary voluntarily waived his *Miranda* rights. Recall that the government carries the burden of proof on questions of the voluntariness of a waiver. As an appellate judge, would you conclude that this ruling was an abuse of discretion? Cf. State v. Cleary, 641 A.2d 102 (Vt. 1994).

Notes

1. *Capacity to waive under* Miranda: *majority position.* Analysis of the capacity of suspects to waive their *Miranda* rights is highly case-specific. Courts assess a variety of factors to resolve these frequently litigated claims of incapacity, such as the defendant's prior experience with the criminal justice system, the defendant's intelligence and education, mental illness, vocabulary and literacy, state of intoxication, and emotional state. Courts also look at the conduct of the police in eliciting a confession. For example, the U.S. Supreme Court in Colorado v. Connelly, 479 U.S. 157 (1986), considered a case involving the confession of a suspect who suffered from a psychosis. Because the police could not reasonably have known about the condition and did not engage in any "overreaching" conduct during the interrogation, the Court held that the waiver of *Miranda* rights was knowing and voluntary. See also State v. Chapman, 605 A.2d 1055 (N.H. 1992). How are the police interrogators to determine whether and to what degree a suspect is mentally disabled?

Note that a suspect's capacity to waive *Miranda* rights is distinct from the voluntariness of the confession. The mental illness of a suspect might interfere with that person's ability to understand *Miranda* rights even if the police do nothing blameworthy to affect the voluntariness of the confession. Capacity questions are also connected to the accuracy of confessions. The availability of DNA evidence has uncovered a number of wrongful convictions over the years, some based substantially on false confessions. It is quite common in these false-confession cases to find that the defendant had some form of mental impairment that raised questions about the capacity to waive *Miranda* rights.

Appellate courts defer to trial court judgments of capacity; the appellate case law is full of decisions affirming a trial court's finding of waiver, even on fairly dramatic facts. Is a per se rule or rebuttable presumption of incapacity appropriate for some defendants? See Morgan Cloud, George B. Shepherd, Alison Nodvin Barkoff & Justin V. Shur, Words Without Meaning: The Constitution, Confessions, and Mentally Retarded Suspects, 69 U. Chi. L. Rev. 495 (2002) (authors tested sample of mentally impaired individuals to determine if they could understand *Miranda* warnings; mentally impaired suspects do not understand legal consequences of confessing or meaning of sentences comprising warnings).

2. *Intoxication and capacity to waive.* Suspects under the influence of alcohol or drugs very rarely convince a court that they did not have the capacity to waive their *Miranda* rights. In State v. Keith, 628 A.2d 1247 (Vt. 1993), for example, the court affirmed a finding of valid waiver where defendant had a blood-alcohol level of .203 at the time he was interrogated and gave several inconsistent stories of his whereabouts at the time of a suspicious fire. James Keith had refused to sign the waiver form, saying, "every time I sign something I get in trouble," but he was willing to talk to Sergeant Bombardier of the arson squad, who later expressed his belief that the defendant was just "playing head games." Courts in these cases often point out that the defendant voluntarily got himself into the intoxicated condition. Does the blameworthiness of the defendant have any bearing on her capacity to waive rights? Is a claim that intoxication negates the capacity to waive *Miranda* rights different from the claim that the influence of alcohol or drugs eliminates criminal responsibility for purposes of substantive criminal law?

3. *Juveniles and* Miranda *waivers.* The youth of a suspect in custody can be an important factor for courts determining whether the suspect has the capacity to make a knowing and voluntary waiver. Most states follow the totality-of-the-circumstances rule of Fare v. Michael C., 442 U.S. 707 (1979). See Commonwealth v. Williams, 475 A.2d 1283 (Pa. 1984). A few states, however, require that a juvenile consult with an "interested adult" before she can waive *Miranda* rights. See In re K.W.B., 500 S.W.2d 275 (Mo. 1973); Conn. Gen. Stat. Ann. §46b-137(a). Is a per se consultation rule appropriate for juveniles as a group? Perhaps your answer to this question will depend on how many juveniles you believe will misunderstand the rights explained to them. One empirical study, which sought to determine the capacity of juveniles to comprehend the meaning and significance of their *Miranda* rights, concluded that juveniles younger than 15 years old typically did not adequately comprehend their *Miranda* rights and that one-third to one-half of 15-year-olds showed an inadequate understanding of the *Miranda* warnings. The study further found that 55.3 percent of the children demonstrated an inadequate understanding of at least one of the four warnings, and that 63.3 percent of the juveniles misunderstood at least one of the crucial words used in the standard *Miranda* warnings. Adequate understanding of the warnings was achieved by only 20.9 percent of the juveniles. See Thomas Grisso, Juveniles' Capacities to Waive *Miranda* Rights: An Empirical Analysis, 68 Cal. L. Rev. 1134 (1980).

4. *Language barriers.* Courts have also treated language barriers as one circumstance that might contribute to a finding of incapacity. See People v. Jiminez, 863 P.2d 981 (Colo. 1993) (suspect spoke no English and little Spanish, mostly Kickapoo; no valid waiver when warnings were delivered in Spanish). How might you argue for resolving language-barrier cases with a more clear-cut rule than the approach taken for alcohol, mental disability, or youthfulness claims?

D. EFFECT OF ASSERTING *MIRANDA* RIGHTS

The *Miranda* opinion appeared to bar police efforts to change a suspect's decision after he or she invoked *Miranda* rights during an interrogation: "If the individual indicates in any manner, at any time prior to or during questioning, that he wishes to remain silent, the interrogation must cease. At this point, he has shown that he intends to exercise his Fifth Amendment privilege; any statement taken after the person invokes his privilege cannot be other than the product of compulsion, subtle or otherwise." It later became clear, however, that a suspect could waive *Miranda* rights even after initially invoking them. Indeed, the police in some circumstances can take actions to encourage this later waiver.

The U.S. Supreme Court distinguished between the effects of invoking the *right to silence* and the *right to counsel.* In Michigan v. Mosley, 423 U.S. 96 (1975), the Court upheld the use of a confession despite the fact that the suspect earlier invoked his right to silence. Under the circumstances of that case, the Court concluded that the police "scrupulously honored" Mosley's initial invocation of the privilege, even though they had initiated a later conversation about the criminal investigation that led to his waiver and confession. In Edwards v. Arizona, 451 U.S. 477 (1981), however, the Court insisted on a different rule for those who invoke the right to counsel: Such a person "is not subject to further interrogation, by the authorities until counsel has been made available to him, unless the accused himself initiates further communication, exchanges or conversations with the police." 451 U.S. at 484. Consider the following judicial efforts to apply these rules regarding waiver after an initial invocation.

CHARLES GLOBE v. STATE

877 So.2d 663 (Fla. 2004)

PER CURIAM.

. . . Globe was convicted of the July 3, 2000, first-degree murder of Elton Ard. Ard was a fellow inmate at the Columbia Correctional Institution (CCI). Globe and his codefendant and fellow inmate, Andrew D. Busby, had been planning to murder an inmate or correctional officer for two weeks before Ard's murder. Ard was Busby's cellmate and was one of seven potential victims targeted by Globe and Busby because he was harassing Busby. Globe and Busby talked for days about killing Ard and devised a plan to do so. Using part of a linen sheet and broken ballpoint pens, Globe made two garrotes approximately two weeks prior to the murder. Globe intended to use these garrotes to strangle his victim.

On the morning of July 3, 2000, at approximately 7 A.M., Globe slipped into the prison cell shared by Ard and Busby. After locking the cell door and covering the window, Globe grabbed Ard around the neck and they began to struggle. Globe placed one of the garrotes around Ard's neck, but it broke as he and Busby were strangling Ard. Ard pled for his life, offering to give Globe all of his money, a total of forty-five dollars. Globe told Ard that he didn't want his money "but his fucking life." Globe then struck Ard in the face, causing him to bleed. Globe flushed the broken garrote down the toilet and after discovering that Ard was still alive tied the second garrote around Ard's neck. Globe then lit a cigarette and watched Ard gasp for air six times before he finally died. After Ard died, Globe took the garrote from Ard's neck and tied it around Ard's wrist. He put a cigarette in Ard's mouth and placed a lighter in his hand. . . .

Evidence recovered from the murder scene included photographs of writing on the prison wall, photographs of bloody fingerprints, the cigarette lighter found in Ard's hand, the cigarette from Ard's mouth, the magic marker used to write on the wall, and the wingtip piece from a pair of glasses. The phrases "Call FDLE" and

"Remember Andy and K.D., 7/3/2000," were written in magic marker on the cell door. "Don't forget to look on the door" was written in magic marker on the cell wall. Karen Smith, a crime laboratory analyst and forensic document examiner with FDLE, testified that Globe had written "Call FDLE" and "Remember Andy and K.D., 7/3/2000." . . .

Several hours after the murder, FDLE agent Bill Gootee met with Globe, advised him of his *Miranda* rights, and asked Globe if he wanted to make a statement. Globe replied, "Not at this time," but did not request an attorney. Gootee terminated the interview and passed this information on to FDLE Agent Don Ugliano. Approximately seven hours later, Ugliano was standing in a hallway and heard Globe say something to the effect of "that guy doesn't need to be here." Globe had just finished being photographed and Busby was a short distance away inside the inspector's office talking to his father on the phone. Ugliano asked Globe "why," and Globe said, "The whole place is just screwed up. It is all messed up." Ugliano then asked Globe if he was willing to make a statement. Globe answered that he would, if he could be with Busby. After Globe and Busby were advised of their *Miranda* rights, they gave a tape recorded statement in which they admitted to killing Ard. After the statement was taken, Globe was moved to Florida State Prison and placed under a higher level of security than was available at CCI.

Inspector Jack Schenck, a senior inspector with the Florida Department of Corrections, Office of the Inspector General, interviewed Globe on July 7, 2000, at Florida State Prison. Schenck was present for Globe's July 3, 2000, statement. After being advised of his *Miranda* rights, Globe discussed how he had been planning to murder an inmate and how he had actually murdered Ard. Counsel was appointed for Globe, and he was arraigned on September 7, 2000. While sitting outside the judge's chambers that day, Globe said to Ugliano, "It's stupid to have to go through all this bullshit. I know I am going to get the needle for killing him." Ugliano told Globe that he was not allowed to speak to him anymore because Globe was represented by an attorney. Globe replied, "Shit. We have already confessed to killing the dude. What's it matter?" . . .

The jury convicted Globe of first-degree murder on September 11, 2001, and on September 14, 2001, recommended death by a vote of nine to three. The trial court followed the jury's recommendation and imposed a death sentence, finding and weighing four aggravating factors, no statutory mitigating factors, and eleven nonstatutory mitigating factors. . . .

Globe argues that the trial court erred by denying his motion to suppress the July 3 and July 7 statements. The court denied Globe's motion to suppress his statements "upon a finding that the statements were made freely, voluntarily, and knowingly after full and complete advisal and waiver of *Miranda* rights." . . .

The State must establish, by a preponderance of the evidence, that the waiver of *Miranda* rights is knowing, intelligent, and voluntary. Whether *Miranda* rights were validly waived must be ascertained from two separate inquiries. . . . First, the relinquishment of the right must have been voluntary in the sense that it was the product of free and deliberate choice rather than intimidation, coercion, or deception. Second, the waiver must have been made with a full awareness of both the nature of the right being abandoned and the consequences of the decision to abandon it. Only if the "totality of the circumstances surrounding the interrogation" reveal both an uncoerced choice and the requisite level of comprehension may a court properly conclude that the *Miranda* rights have been waived. . . .

[Police-initiated] questioning of a person in custody is not absolutely foreclosed if he or she invokes the right to remain silent but not the right to counsel. We implicitly recognized the distinction between assertion of the two rights in Traylor v. State, 596 So. 2d 957, 966 (Fla. 1992):

> If the suspect indicates in any manner that he or she does not want to be interrogated, interrogation must not begin or, if it has already begun, must immediately stop. If the suspect indicates in any manner that he or she wants the help of a lawyer, interrogation must not begin until a lawyer has been appointed and is present or, if it has already begun, must immediately stop until a lawyer is present. Once a suspect has requested the help of a lawyer, no state agent can reinitiate interrogation on any offense throughout the period of custody unless the lawyer is present, although the suspect is free to volunteer a statement to police on his or her own initiative at any time on any subject in the absence of counsel.

In Michigan v. Mosley, 423 U.S. 96 (1975), the United States Supreme Court held that resolution of the question of the admissibility of statements obtained after a person in custody has invoked his or her right to remain silent depends upon whether the person's decision to assert his or her "right to cut off questioning" was "scrupulously honored." In holding that no *Miranda* violation occurred in *Mosley*, the Court stated:

> This is not a case, therefore, where the police failed to honor a decision of a person in custody to cut off questioning, either by refusing to discontinue the interrogation upon request or by persisting in repeated efforts to wear down his resistance and make him change his mind. In contrast to such practices, the police here immediately ceased the interrogation, resumed questioning only after the passage of a significant period of time and the provision of a fresh set of warnings, and restricted the second interrogation to a crime that had not been a subject of the earlier interrogation.

We applied *Mosley* in Henry v. State, 574 So. 2d 66, 69 (Fla. 1991), when analyzing the resumption of questioning on the same offense after invocation of the right to silence. We recognized that in *Mosley* the Supreme Court neither set out "precise guidelines" for what constitutes scrupulous adherence to *Miranda* nor stated that "any factor standing by itself would be dispositive of the issue." However, we recognized five factors the Court in *Mosley* found to be relevant:

> First, Mosley was informed of his rights both times before questioning began. Second, the officer immediately ceased questioning when Mosley unequivocally said he did not want to talk about the burglaries. Third, there was a significant lapse of time between the questioning on the burglary and the questioning on the homicide. Fourth, the second episode of questioning took place in a different location. Fifth, the second episode involved a different crime.

In *Henry*, we determined that variance as to one or more of the five factors was not dispositive, and therefore applied a totality of the circumstances approach. We apply the same analysis in this case.

Globe argues that his right to remain silent was not "scrupulously honored" because of Agent Ugliano's request for a statement approximately seven hours after he declined to give a statement to Agent Gootee. The trial court's factual findings are supported by competent, substantial evidence and are entitled to a presumption of correctness. Applying the five factors set out in *Mosley* and *Henry* to the facts in this case, it is evident that four of the five factors are present: (1) *Miranda* warnings were given several times, including right before each request for a statement; (2) interrogations ceased immediately when Globe expressed his desire to remain silent; (3) there was a significant time lapse between the questioning in that the second request for a statement was made seven and a half hours after the first request; and (4) the second questioning took place at a different location. We conclude that it is not dispositive that the second questioning involved the same crime. We consider not only that four of the five factors weigh in favor of admissibility but also that when Globe initially invoked his right to silence he said only that he did not want to make a statement "at this time," leaving open the prospect of future questioning on the crime. We hold that Globe's right to remain silent was scrupulously honored. Accordingly, the trial court did not err when it denied Globe's motion to suppress the July 3, 2000, statement.

The July 7 statement was taken at Florida State Prison, where Globe had been moved for security reasons. Globe alleges that the July 7 statement was the fruit of the illegally obtained July 3 statement; that it was not made voluntarily, intelligently, or knowingly; and that it was taken in violation of Florida Rule of Criminal Procedure 3.130.

Globe's first argument fails because the July 3 statement was not illegally obtained, as discussed above. Globe's second argument also is without merit. Before making his July 7 statement, Globe was advised of his *Miranda* rights by Agent Ugliano. [The] proper inquiry is whether the "totality of the circumstances surrounding the interrogation" reveal both an uncoerced choice and the requisite level of comprehension. In this case, Globe was read his rights. He was asked if he understood his rights and responded, "Sure." He was then asked, "With your rights in mind, would you like to answer questions and make a statement at this time?" Although Globe's response was inaudible on the tape recording, he proceeded to make a statement. All of this occurred after Globe had been read his rights twice before on July 3. The trial court's factual findings are supported by competent, substantial evidence and are entitled to a presumption of correctness. The totality of the circumstances in this case demonstrate that Globe voluntarily waived his rights and was fully aware of the consequences of his decision. Globe's right to remain silent was scrupulously honored.

Globe also argues that the July 7 statement is inadmissible because he was in custody on July 3 and should have been brought before a judge within twenty-four hours pursuant to Florida Rule of Criminal Procedure 3.130. Florida Rule of Criminal Procedure 3.130 states that "every arrested person shall be taken before a judicial officer . . . within 24 hours of arrest." Globe asserts that although he was not formally arrested, he was de facto arrested when he was removed from the open population at Columbia Correctional and was taken to Florida State Prison. The State argues that Globe was in custody pursuant to a lawful conviction unrelated to the murder for which he was under investigation.

[We] noted in Chavez v. State, 832 So. 2d 730 (Fla. 2002), that where a defendant has been sufficiently advised of his rights, a confession that would otherwise be admissible is not subject to suppression merely because the defendant was deprived of a prompt first appearance. "When a defendant has been advised of his rights and makes an otherwise voluntary statement, the delay in following the strictures of

[Rule 3.130] must be shown to have induced the confession." A first appearance "serves as a venue for informing the defendant of certain rights, and provides for a determination of the conditions for the defendant's release."

In this case, Globe was repeatedly advised of his *Miranda* rights, would not have been subject to release because of his prior convictions, and did not invoke his right to counsel. Additionally, Globe made his most incriminating statement, the July 3 statement, less than twenty-four hours after he alleges he was de facto arrested. There is no showing that the delay in following the strictures of rule 3.130 induced the confession. Therefore, under the narrow circumstances in this case, we hold that the trial court did not err in denying the motion to suppress. However, we remind the State of its obligation under rule 3.130 to take every arrested person, including those already in custody on other grounds, before a magistrate within twenty-four hours of arrest. . . .

MARYLAND v. MICHAEL BLAINE SHATZER

130 S. Ct. 1213 (2010)

SCALIA, J.*

We consider whether a break in custody ends the presumption of involuntariness established in Edwards v. Arizona, 451 U.S. 477 (1981).

I.

In August 2003, a social worker assigned to the Child Advocacy Center in the Criminal Investigation Division of the Hagerstown Police Department referred to the department allegations that respondent Michael Shatzer, Sr., had sexually abused his 3-year-old son. At that time, Shatzer was incarcerated at the Maryland Correctional Institution-Hagerstown, serving a sentence for an unrelated child-sexual-abuse offense. Detective Shane Blankenship was assigned to the investigation and interviewed Shatzer at the correctional institution on August 7, 2003. Before asking any questions, Blankenship reviewed Shatzer's *Miranda* rights with him, and obtained a written waiver of those rights. When Blankenship explained that he was there to question Shatzer about sexually abusing his son, Shatzer expressed confusion — he had thought Blankenship was an attorney there to discuss the prior crime for which he was incarcerated. Blankenship clarified the purpose of his visit, and Shatzer declined to speak without an attorney. Accordingly, Blankenship ended the interview, and Shatzer was released back into the general prison population. Shortly thereafter, Blankenship closed the investigation.

Two years and six months later, the same social worker referred more specific allegations to the department about the same incident involving Shatzer. Detective Paul Hoover, from the same division, was assigned to the investigation. He and the social worker interviewed the victim, then eight years old, who described the incident in more detail. With this new information in hand, on March 2, 2006, they went to the Roxbury Correctional Institute, to which Shatzer had since been transferred,

* [Chief Justice Roberts and Justices Kennedy, Ginsburg, Breyer, Alito, and Sotomayor joined in this opinion; Justice Thomas joined in part III. — EDS.]

and interviewed Shatzer in a maintenance room outfitted with a desk and three chairs. Hoover explained that he wanted to ask Shatzer about the alleged incident involving Shatzer's son. Shatzer was surprised because he thought that the investigation had been closed, but Hoover explained they had opened a new file. Hoover then read Shatzer his *Miranda* rights and obtained a written waiver on a standard department form.

Hoover interrogated Shatzer about the incident for approximately 30 minutes. Shatzer denied ordering his son to perform fellatio on him, but admitted to masturbating in front of his son from a distance of less than three feet. Before the interview ended, Shatzer agreed to Hoover's request that he submit to a polygraph examination. At no point during the interrogation did Shatzer request to speak with an attorney or refer to his prior refusal to answer questions without one.

Five days later, on March 7, 2006, Hoover and another detective met with Shatzer at the correctional facility to administer the polygraph examination. After reading Shatzer his *Miranda* rights and obtaining a written waiver, the other detective administered the test and concluded that Shatzer had failed. When the detectives then questioned Shatzer, he became upset, started to cry, and incriminated himself by saying, "I didn't force him. I didn't force him." After making this inculpatory statement, Shatzer requested an attorney, and Hoover promptly ended the interrogation.

The State's Attorney for Washington County charged Shatzer with second-degree sexual offense, sexual child abuse, second-degree assault, and contributing to conditions rendering a child in need of assistance. Shatzer moved to suppress his March 2006 statements pursuant to *Edwards*. The trial court held a suppression hearing and later denied Shatzer's motion. The *Edwards* protections did not apply, it reasoned, because Shatzer had experienced a break in custody for *Miranda* purposes between the 2003 and 2006 interrogations. . . . Based on the proffered testimony of the victim and the "admission of the defendant as to the act of masturbation," the trial court found Shatzer guilty of sexual child abuse of his son. . . .

II.

. . . In Miranda v. Arizona, 384 U.S. 436 (1966), the Court adopted a set of prophylactic measures to protect a suspect's Fifth Amendment right from the "inherently compelling pressures" of custodial interrogation. . . . Critically, however, a suspect can waive [*Miranda*] rights. To establish a valid waiver, the State must show that the waiver was knowing, intelligent, and voluntary under the high standard of proof for the waiver of constitutional rights set forth in Johnson v. Zerbst, 304 U.S. 458 (1938). In *Edwards,* the Court determined that *Zerbst*'s traditional standard for waiver was not sufficient to protect a suspect's right to have counsel present at a subsequent interrogation if he had previously requested counsel; "additional safeguards" were necessary. The Court therefore superimposed a second layer of prophylaxis. *Edwards* held:

> [When] an accused has invoked his right to have counsel present during custodial interrogation, a valid waiver of that right cannot be established by showing only that he responded to further police-initiated custodial interrogation even if he has been advised of his rights. [He] is not subject to further interrogation by the authorities until

> counsel has been made available to him, unless the accused himself initiates further communication, exchanges, or conversations with the police.

The rationale of *Edwards* is that once a suspect indicates that he is not capable of undergoing custodial questioning without advice of counsel, any subsequent waiver that has come at the authorities' behest, and not at the suspect's own instigation, is itself the product of the "inherently compelling pressures" and not the purely voluntary choice of the suspect. Arizona v. Roberson, 486 U.S. 675, 681 (1988). Under this rule, a voluntary *Miranda* waiver is sufficient at the time of an initial attempted interrogation to protect a suspect's right to have counsel present, but it is not sufficient at the time of subsequent attempts if the suspect initially requested the presence of counsel. The implicit assumption, of course, is that the subsequent requests for interrogation pose a significantly greater risk of coercion. That increased risk results not only from the police's persistence in trying to get the suspect to talk, but also from the continued pressure that begins when the individual is taken into custody as a suspect and sought to be interrogated — pressure likely to "increase as custody is prolonged," Minnick v. Mississippi, 498 U.S. 146 (1990). The *Edwards* presumption of involuntariness ensures that police will not take advantage of the mounting coercive pressures of prolonged police custody by repeatedly attempting to question a suspect who previously requested counsel until the suspect is badgered into submission.

We have frequently emphasized that the *Edwards* rule is not a constitutional mandate, but judicially prescribed prophylaxis. Because *Edwards* is our rule, not a constitutional command, it is our obligation to justify its expansion. Lower courts have uniformly held that a break in custody ends the *Edwards* presumption. . . .

A judicially crafted rule is justified only by reference to its prophylactic purpose, and applies only where its benefits outweigh its costs. We begin with the benefits. *Edwards*' presumption of involuntariness has the incidental effect of conserving judicial resources which would otherwise be expended in making difficult determinations of voluntariness. Its fundamental purpose, however, is to preserve the integrity of an accused's choice to communicate with police only through counsel, by preventing police from badgering a defendant into waiving his previously asserted *Miranda* rights. Thus, the benefits of the rule are measured by the number of coerced confessions it suppresses that otherwise would have been admitted.

It is easy to believe that a suspect may be coerced or badgered into abandoning his earlier refusal to be questioned without counsel in the paradigm *Edwards* case. That is a case in which the suspect has been arrested for a particular crime and is held in uninterrupted pretrial custody while that crime is being actively investigated. After the initial interrogation, and up to and including the second one, he remains cut off from his normal life and companions, thrust into and isolated in an unfamiliar, police-dominated atmosphere, where his captors appear to control his fate. That was the situation confronted by the suspects in *Edwards, Roberson,* and *Minnick,* the three cases in which we have held the *Edwards* rule applicable. Edwards was arrested pursuant to a warrant and taken to a police station, where he was interrogated until he requested counsel. The officer ended the interrogation and took him to the county jail, but at 9:15 the next morning, two of the officer's colleagues reinterrogated Edwards at the jail. Roberson was arrested at the scene of a just-completed burglary and interrogated there until he requested a lawyer. A different officer interrogated him three days later while he was still in custody pursuant to the arrest. Minnick was arrested by local police and taken to the San Diego jail, where two FBI agents interrogated him the next morning until he requested counsel. Two days later a Mississippi Deputy Sheriff reinterrogated him at the jail. None of these suspects regained a sense of control or normalcy after they were initially taken into custody for the crime under investigation.

When, unlike what happened in these three cases, a suspect has been released from his pretrial custody and has returned to his normal life for some time before the later attempted interrogation, there is little reason to think that his change of heart regarding interrogation without counsel has been coerced. He has no longer been isolated. He has likely been able to seek advice from an attorney, family members, and friends. And he knows from his earlier experience that he need only demand counsel to bring the interrogation to a halt; and that investigative custody does not last indefinitely. In these circumstances, it is far fetched to think that a police officer's asking the suspect whether he would like to waive his *Miranda* rights will any more wear down the accused than did the first such request at the original attempted interrogation — which is of course not deemed coercive. His change of heart is less likely attributable to "badgering" than it is to the fact that further deliberation in familiar surroundings has caused him to believe (rightly or wrongly) that cooperating with the investigation is in his interest. Uncritical extension of *Edwards* to this situation would not significantly increase the number of genuinely coerced confessions excluded. . . .

At the same time that extending the *Edwards* rule yields diminished benefits, extending the rule also increases its costs: the in-fact voluntary confessions it excludes from trial, and the voluntary confessions it deters law enforcement officers from even trying to obtain. Voluntary confessions are not merely a proper element in law enforcement, they are an unmitigated good, essential to society's compelling interest in finding, convicting, and punishing those who violate the law.

The only logical endpoint of *Edwards'* disability is termination of *Miranda* custody and any of its lingering effects. Without that limitation — and barring some purely arbitrary time-limit — every *Edwards* prohibition of custodial interrogation of a particular suspect would be eternal. The prohibition applies, of course, when the subsequent interrogation pertains to a different crime, *Roberson,* when it is conducted by a different law enforcement authority, *Minnick,* and even when the suspect has met with an attorney after the first interrogation, *ibid.* And it not only prevents questioning *ex ante*; it would render invalid *ex post,* confessions invited and obtained from suspects who (unbeknownst to the interrogators) have acquired *Edwards* immunity previously in connection with any offense in any jurisdiction. In a country that harbors a large number of repeat offenders, this consequence is disastrous.

We conclude that such an extension of *Edwards* is not justified; we have opened its protective umbrella far enough. The protections offered by *Miranda,* which we have deemed sufficient to ensure that the police respect the suspect's desire to have an attorney present the first time police interrogate him, adequately ensure that result when a suspect who initially requested counsel is reinterrogated after a break in custody that is of sufficient duration to dissipate its coercive effects.

If Shatzer's return to the general prison population qualified as a break in custody (a question we address in Part III), there is no doubt that it lasted long enough (2 1/2 years) to meet that durational requirement. But what about a break that has lasted only one year? Or only one week? It is impractical to leave the answer to that question for clarification in future case-by-case adjudication; law enforcement officers need to know, with certainty and beforehand, when renewed interrogation is lawful. . . .

We think it appropriate to specify a period of time to avoid the consequence that continuation of the *Edwards* presumption will not reach the correct result most of the time. It seems to us that period is 14 days. That provides plenty of time for the suspect to get reacclimated to his normal life, to consult with friends and counsel, and to shake off any residual coercive effects of his prior custody.

The 14-day limitation meets Shatzer's concern that a break-in-custody rule lends itself to police abuse. He envisions that once a suspect invokes his *Miranda* right to counsel, the police will release the suspect briefly (to end the *Edwards* presumption) and then promptly bring him back into custody for reinterrogation. But once the suspect has been out of custody long enough (14 days) to eliminate its coercive effect, there will be nothing to gain by such gamesmanship — nothing, that is, except the entirely appropriate gain of being able to interrogate a suspect who has made a valid waiver of his *Miranda* rights.[7] . . .

III.

The facts of this case present an additional issue. . . . After the 2003 interview, Shatzer was released back into the general prison population where he was serving an unrelated sentence. The issue is whether that constitutes a break in *Miranda* custody.

We have never decided whether incarceration constitutes custody for *Miranda* purposes. . . . Whether it does depends upon whether it exerts the coercive pressure that *Miranda* was designed to guard against — the danger of coercion that results from the *interaction* of custody and official interrogation. . . . Without minimizing the harsh realities of incarceration, we think lawful imprisonment imposed upon conviction of a crime does not create the coercive pressures identified in *Miranda*.

Interrogated suspects who have previously been convicted of crime live in prison. When they are released back into the general prison population, they return to their accustomed surroundings and daily routine — they regain the degree of control they had over their lives prior to the interrogation. Sentenced prisoners, in contrast to the *Miranda* paradigm, are not isolated with their accusers. They live among other inmates, guards, and workers, and often can receive visitors and communicate with people on the outside by mail or telephone.

Their detention, moreover, is relatively disconnected from their prior unwillingness to cooperate in an investigation. The former interrogator has no power to increase the duration of incarceration, which was determined at sentencing. And even where the possibility of parole exists, the former interrogator has no apparent power to decrease the time served. . . .

7. A defendant who experiences a 14-day break in custody after invoking the *Miranda* right to counsel is not left without protection. *Edwards* establishes a *presumption* that a suspect's waiver of *Miranda* rights is involuntary. Even without this second layer of prophylaxis, a defendant is still free to claim the prophylactic protection of *Miranda* — arguing that his waiver of *Miranda* rights was in fact involuntary under Johnson v. Zerbst.

Shatzer's experience illustrates the vast differences between *Miranda* custody and incarceration pursuant to conviction. At the time of the 2003 attempted interrogation, Shatzer was already serving a sentence for a prior conviction [in a medium-security correctional facility]. Inmates in these facilities generally can visit the library each week, have regular exercise and recreation periods, can participate in basic adult education and occupational training, are able to send and receive mail, and are allowed to receive visitors twice a week. His continued detention after the 2003 interrogation did not depend on what he said (or did not say) to Detective Blankenship, and he has not alleged that he was placed in a higher level of security or faced any continuing restraints as a result of the 2003 interrogation. The "inherently compelling pressures" of custodial interrogation ended when he returned to his normal life.

IV.

A few words in response to Justice Stevens' concurrence. [We] are not talking about "reinterrogating" the suspect; we are talking about *asking his permission* to be interrogated. An officer has in no sense lied to a suspect when, after advising, as *Miranda* requires, "You have the right to remain silent, and if you choose to speak you have the right to the presence of an attorney," he promptly ends the attempted interrogation because the suspect declines to speak without counsel present, and then, two weeks later, reapproaches the suspect and asks, "Are you now willing to speak without a lawyer present?" . . .

The concurrence also accuses the Court of ignoring that when a suspect asks for counsel, until his request is answered, there are still the same "inherently compelling" pressures of custodial interrogation on which the *Miranda* line of cases is based. We do not ignore these pressures; nor do we suggest that they disappear when custody is recommenced after a break. But if those pressures are merely "the same" as before, then *Miranda* provides sufficient protection — as it did before. The *Edwards* presumption of involuntariness is justified only in circumstances where the coercive pressures have increased so much that suspects' waivers of *Miranda* rights are likely to be involuntary most of the time. . . .

THOMAS, J., concurring in part and concurring in the judgment.

I join Part III of the Court's opinion, which holds that release into the general prison population constitutes a break in custody. I do not join the Court's decision to extend the presumption of involuntariness established in *Edwards* for 14 days after custody ends.

It is not apparent to me that the presumption of involuntariness the Court recognized in *Edwards* is justifiable even in the custodial setting to which *Edwards* applies it. Accordingly, I would not extend the *Edwards* rule beyond the circumstances present in *Edwards* itself. But even if one believes that the Court is obliged to apply *Edwards* to any case involving continuing custody, the Court's opinion today goes well beyond that. It extends the presumption of involuntariness *Edwards* applies in custodial settings to interrogations that occur after custody ends. . . .

Our precedents insist that judicially created prophylactic rules like those in *Edwards* and *Miranda*, maintain the closest possible fit between the rule and the Fifth Amendment interests they seek to protect. The Court's 14-day rule does not satisfy this test. The Court relates its 14-day rule to the Fifth Amendment simply by asserting that 14 days between release and recapture should provide "plenty of time for the suspect . . . to shake off any residual coercive effects of his prior custody."

This *ipse dixit* does not explain why extending the *Edwards* presumption for 14 days following a break in custody — as opposed to 0, 10, or 100 days — provides the closest possible fit with the Self-Incrimination Clause. Nor does it explain how the benefits of a prophylactic 14-day rule (either on its own terms or compared with other possible rules) outweigh its costs (which would include the loss of law enforcement information as well as the exclusion of confessions that are in fact voluntary). . . .

STEVENS, J., concurring in the judgment.

While I agree that the presumption from *Edwards* is not eternal, and does not mandate suppression of Shatzer's statement made after a 2 1/2-year break in custody, I do not agree with the Court's newly announced rule: that *Edwards always* ceases to apply when there is a 14-day break in custody. . . .

I.

The most troubling aspect of the Court's time-based rule is that it disregards the compulsion caused by a second (or third, or fourth) interrogation of an indigent suspect who was told that if he requests a lawyer, one will be provided for him. When police tell an indigent suspect that he has the right to an attorney, that he is not required to speak without an attorney present, and that an attorney will be provided to him at no cost before questioning, the police have made a significant promise. If they cease questioning and then reinterrogate the suspect 14 days later without providing him with a lawyer, the suspect is likely to feel that the police lied to him and that he really does not have any right to a lawyer.[2] [The detainee] may well see further objection as futile and confession (true or not) as the only way to end his interrogation. . . .

II.

The Court never explains why its rule cannot depend on, in addition to a break in custody and passage of time, a concrete event or state of affairs, such as the police having honored their commitment to provide counsel. Instead, the Court simply decides to create a time-based rule, and in so doing, disregards much of the analysis upon which *Edwards* and subsequent decisions were based. . . . The Court, moreover, ignores that when a suspect asks for counsel, until his request is answered, there are still the same "inherently compelling" pressures of custodial interrogation on which the *Miranda* line of cases is based, and that the concern about compulsion is especially serious for a detainee who has requested a lawyer, an act that signals his inability to cope with the pressures of custodial interrogation.

2. The Court states that this argument rests on a fallacy because "we are not talking about 'reinterrogating' the suspect; we are talking about asking his permission to be interrogated." Because, however, a suspect always has the right to remain silent, this is a distinction without a difference: Any time that the police interrogate or reinterrogate, and read a suspect his *Miranda* rights, the suspect may decline to speak. . . .

Instead of deferring to these well-settled understandings of the *Edwards* rule, the Court engages in its own speculation that a 14-day break in custody eliminates the compulsion that animated *Edwards.* But [he has asked for a lawyer, he does not have one, he is in custody, and] police are still questioning him. A 14-day break in custody does not change the fact that custodial interrogation is inherently compelling. It is unlikely to change the fact that a detainee considers himself unable to deal with the pressures of custodial interrogation without legal assistance. . . .

The Court [speculates] that once a suspect has been out of *Miranda* custody for 14 days, "he has likely been able to seek advice from an attorney, family members, and friends." . . . As a factual matter, we do not know whether the defendant has been able to seek advice: First of all, suspects are told that if they cannot afford a lawyer, one will be provided for them. Yet under the majority's rule, an indigent suspect who took the police at their word when he asked for a lawyer will nonetheless be assumed to have been able to seek advice from an attorney. Second, even suspects who are not indigent cannot necessarily access legal advice (or social advice as the Court presumes) within 14 days. Third, suspects may not realize that they *need* to seek advice from an attorney. Unless police warn suspects that the interrogation will resume in 14 days, why contact a lawyer? . . .

The many problems with the Court's new rule are exacerbated in the very situation in this case: a suspect who is in prison. Even if, as the Court assumes, a trip to one's home significantly changes the *Edwards* calculus, a trip to one's prison cell is not the same. A prisoner's freedom is severely limited, and his entire life remains subject to government control. Such an environment is not conducive to "shaking off any residual coercive effects of his prior custody." Nor can a prisoner easily seek advice from an attorney, family members, and friends, especially not within 14 days; prisoners are frequently subject to restrictions on communications. [For] a person whose every move is controlled by the State, it is likely that his sense of dependence on, and trust in, counsel as the guardian of his interests in dealing with government officials intensified. . . .

III.

Because, at the very least, we do not know whether Shatzer could obtain a lawyer, and thus would have felt that police had lied about providing one, I cannot join the Court's opinion. I concur in today's judgment, however, on another ground: Even if Shatzer could not consult a lawyer and the police never provided him one, the 2 1/2-year break in custody is a basis for treating the second interrogation as no more coercive than the first. Neither a break in custody nor the passage of time has an inherent, curative power. But certain things change over time. An indigent suspect who took police at their word that they would provide an attorney probably will feel that he has been denied the counsel he has clearly requested, when police begin to question him, without a lawyer, only 14 days later. But, when a suspect has been left alone for a significant period of time, he is not as likely to draw such conclusions when the police interrogate him again. . . .

Notes

1. *Effect of invoking right to counsel: majority position.* The Supreme Court now applies the two-part test elaborated in Oregon v. Bradshaw, 462 U.S. 1039 (1983), to determine whether a suspect's statement is admissible when made after an earlier invocation of the right to counsel. First, the court asks who "initiated" any post-invocation conversation about the crime. If the police initiate the conversation (by word or deed), then they violate Edwards v. Arizona, 451 U.S. 477 (1981), and the confession must be suppressed. If the suspect initiates "a generalized discussion about the investigation," a court will proceed to the second step and ask whether the defendant waived the right to counsel knowingly and intelligently, despite the earlier invocation of the right. In *Bradshaw,* the defendant "initiated" the conversation by asking, "Well, what is going to happen to me now?" This basic approach has also met with approval in most state courts. See, e.g., Ex parte Williams, 31 So. 3d 670 (Ala. 2010). However, it is not always easy to determine who "initiates" a "generalized" conversation about the investigation. For instance, what should a police officer do if a suspect who has invoked the right to counsel asks, after a lineup procedure, "What happened?"

The Supreme Court has been unwilling to recognize many alternative methods of reopening an interrogation of the suspect who has asked for an attorney. See also Arizona v. Roberson, 486 U.S. 675 (1988) (*Edwards* rule applies even when the second interrogation deals with unrelated crime). Does the *Edwards* rule sufficiently protect the suspect's privilege against self-incrimination? New York provides that a suspect who has invoked the right to counsel should never be allowed to initiate a conversation with the police about the crime unless counsel is present. See People v. Cunningham, 400 N.E.2d 360 (N.Y 1980) (barring any interrogation after invocation of right to counsel unless waiver made with attorney present). This position has attracted virtually no following among the other states. State v. Piorkowski, 700 A.2d 1146 (Conn. 1997) (rejects New York rule on waiver, defendant may make post-arraignment waiver of counsel in counsel's absence). Why do you suppose so many jurisdictions decline to take this approach?

2. *Effect of invoking right to silence: majority position.* As the *Globe* case from Florida indicates, it is easier for the police to initiate a new interrogation after a suspect has invoked the right to silence, as opposed to the right to counsel. Most state courts have read their state constitutions to reach results consistent with the holding in Michigan v. Mosley, 423 U.S. 96 (1975). As the *Globe* case suggests, it is still not entirely clear which of the various facts in *Mosley* were essential to the holding there. See Wilson v. State, 562 S.E.2d 164 (Ga. 2002) (reinterrogation under *Mosley* not available for same crime after 17-hour interval; later interrogation must address different crime). A sampling of the complex state court rulings on this topic appear on the web extension for this chapter at *http://www.crimpro.com/extension/ch08*.

Is it appropriate to place different obligations on the police, depending on which right the defendant invokes? What practical differences are there, if any, between the invocation of the right to counsel and the right to silence? Consider People v. Pettingill, 578 P.2d 108 (Cal. 1978) (rejecting the *Mosley* rule and disallowing any government initiation of interrogation after invocation of right to silence).

3. *Effect of invoking rights: foreign practice.* Under the government-issued Code of Practice in Great Britain, authorities may continue to question a suspect even after

he has asserted a right to silence, so long as the continued questioning is not oppressive. They may question suspects who request a solicitor only under "exigent circumstances" and a few other exceptional cases. Code of Practice for the Detention, Treatment, and Questioning of Persons by the Police, para. 6.6. See also Craig Bradley, The Emerging International Consensus as to Criminal Procedure Rules, 14 Mich. J. Int'l L. 171 (1993).

E. SIXTH AMENDMENT RIGHT TO COUNSEL DURING INVESTIGATIONS

The Fifth Amendment to the U.S. Constitution, as interpreted in *Miranda,* is not the only source of a right to counsel during the investigative stage of the criminal process. Indeed, the Sixth Amendment provides an explicit right to counsel: "In all criminal prosecutions, the accused shall enjoy the right to . . . have the Assistance of Counsel for his defence." Recall that shortly before it decided *Miranda,* the U.S. Supreme Court suggested, in Escobedo v. Illinois, 378 U.S. 478 (1964), that the Sixth Amendment right to counsel might apply before the start of any formal criminal process. But it eventually became clear that the Sixth Amendment right to counsel attaches only after the initiation of formal proceedings, which typically means some form of charging (initial arraignment, indictment or information). State courts have given the same meaning to state constitutions.

The Sixth Amendment thus provides an alternative — and indeed a clear, textually-based alternative — right to counsel after charging. This separate source of a right to counsel for some defendants raises the fundamental question whether the scope and impact of the Fifth and Sixth Amendment rights to counsel are the same. For example, must defendants be informed of the Sixth Amendment right to counsel, or is the notice regarding the Fifth Amendment right to counsel — through *Miranda* — sufficient? Must a defendant assert the Sixth Amendment right, or does it automatically attach after charging? Will the detailed rules that govern notice, assertion and waiver of the right to counsel under *Miranda* also apply after indictment?

Part D examined the effect of assertion of the Fifth Amendment right to counsel under *Miranda.* The following case and problem examine the effect of asserting a Sixth Amendment right to counsel after charges are filed. Notice any differences between the standards applied under the two constitutional clauses. The specific legal question is whether a government agent can ask subsequent questions to the defendant after the Sixth Amendment counsel right attaches.

■ STATE v. BENJAMIN APPLEBY

221 P.3d 525 (Kan. 2009)

Luckert, J.

Benjamin A. Appleby was convicted of the attempted rape and capital murder of A.K., a 19-year-old college student, in Johnson County, Kansas.

Factual and Procedural Background

On June 18, 2002, A.K. was murdered while working alone as an attendant at a swimming pool near her family's home. Her [father] found A.K. in the pool's pump room, lying face down under a pool cover. . . .

Soon after this tragic discovery, police arrived and secured the pool area. In doing so, an officer recorded the name of everyone present at the scene, including a "Teddy Hoover" who was later identified as Appleby. The police also secured evidence, some of which was tested for DNA. This testing revealed DNA that did not match A.K.'s. Few other leads developed from the initial investigation. . . .

Several months after A.K.'s death, Sergeant Scott Hansen of the Leawood Police Department went to Appleby's home in Kansas City, Kansas. At that point in time, the police knew Appleby by his alias of Teddy Hoover. Appleby agreed to speak with Sergeant Hansen and indicated that he was a self-employed pool maintenance contractor. Hansen requested a DNA elimination sample from Appleby, who said he would talk to his attorney about providing a sample. When Hansen tried to follow up later, he discovered that Appleby had left town.

Subsequent leads caused police to seek more information from Appleby, who they still knew as Teddy Hoover. In November 2004, the investigation led Kansas detectives to Connecticut, where Appleby was living. Connecticut State Police discovered an outstanding arrest warrant for Appleby from 1998 and agreed to execute the warrant when Kansas detectives could be present. The purpose of this arrest was to give Kansas detectives an opportunity to question Appleby. . . .

Connecticut police arrested Appleby at his home and executed the residential search warrant. While the search warrant was being executed, Appleby was transported to a nearby Connecticut police station by Connecticut Detective Daniel Jewiss. On the way, Appleby volunteered that after some "trouble" in his past, he had taken on the name of his childhood friend, Teddy Hoover, who had died in an accident.

At the police station, [detectives processed Appleby on the Connecticut arrest warrant and executed a search warrant that allowed swabbing Appleby's inner mouth for purposes of DNA testing. Detective Jewiss then] told Appleby that other detectives wanted to speak to him about "an unrelated matter" and asked if Appleby was willing to talk to them. Appleby agreed and was taken upstairs to an interrogation room where the Kansas detectives waited. The detectives asked Appleby if he would answer some questions about A.K.'s murder. Up to this point, Appleby had not been told that Kansas detectives were involved or that some of the warrants were related to the A.K. murder investigation.

Appleby told the Kansas detectives he wanted to speak with them and straighten out some details from the time Sergeant Hansen interviewed him at his home in Kansas City. [The] detectives repeatedly asked Appleby if he had been at the pool where A.K. died, but Appleby told them he had never been there. After approximately one hour, the detectives moved him to an adjoining interview room. The second room contained items from the police investigation, such as a time line of the investigation, A.K.'s photograph and obituary, an aerial photograph of the pool, a videotape, a notebook labeled with the name Teddy Hoover, and two additional notebooks labeled as crime scene and autopsy photographs. The detectives then confronted Appleby with the fact that an officer at the pool on the day of the murder had logged the presence of a man who gave the name Teddy Hoover and a telephone number. At that point, Appleby acknowledged he had been at the pool that day.

About 15 or 20 minutes later, Appleby admitted he had killed A.K. Appleby told the detectives A.K. was in the pump room when he arrived at the pool. Finding A.K. attractive, Appleby tried to "hit on her," but A.K. rejected his advances and tried to leave the pump room. Appleby stood in her way and tried to grab her breasts and her waist. A.K. pushed Appleby and then punched him. This angered Appleby, who "lost it" and, in his own words, "just beat the shit out of her." [He attempted to have sex with her after she lost consciousness, but could not obtain an erection.]

DNA testing performed by two crime labs matched Appleby's DNA to the DNA found mixed with A.K.'s. . . . The State charged Appleby with capital murder for the death of A.K. . . . and attempted rape. The jury found Appleby guilty of both charges. The trial court imposed a hard 50 life imprisonment sentence for the murder conviction and a consecutive sentence of 228 months' imprisonment for the attempted rape conviction. Appleby now appeals. . . .

SUPPRESSION OF CONFESSION

. . . Appleby contends the trial court erred by admitting into evidence the incriminating statements he made to Kansas detectives. Appleby argues the statements must be suppressed because he asked about an attorney while he was being booked on the Connecticut arrest warrant. . . .

This argument differs from the typical issue arising from the application of Miranda v. Arizona, 384 U.S. 436 (1966), in that Appleby was arrested in another state on unrelated charges, and the arresting officer, Detective Jewiss, had no intention of interrogating Appleby; typically a *Miranda* issue arises when there is custodial interrogation related to the crime on which the arrest was based. Under the circumstances of this case, the State argues Appleby's questions about whether he would be allowed to talk to an attorney were, at most, an invocation of Sixth Amendment rights related to the Connecticut charges. Appleby argues that he was asserting his Fifth Amendment rights and the assertion applied to both cases. To understand these arguments, a more detailed discussion of the interaction is necessary.

When Appleby was arrested in Connecticut, he was arrested on the Connecticut charges only, even though the arrest was timed to occur when Kansas detectives were in Connecticut and the arrest may not have occurred if Kansas law enforcement had not contacted the Connecticut State Police Department to request assistance in investigating Appleby. But this involvement was behind the scene; the Kansas detectives did not directly participate when Detective Jewiss took Appleby into custody at his home, and Appleby was not aware of their presence until after he had asked the Connecticut detectives the four questions about whether he could talk to an attorney. Appleby did ask Detective Jewiss why there were so many officers at his house, and the detective explained a search warrant was being executed and the officers were going to search the home. Appleby questioned what the search was about, and Jewiss replied that he "wasn't going to talk to him any further about the case; that somebody else would talk to him." . . .

When Detective Jewiss and Appleby arrived at the station, Detective Jewiss began the routine book-in process on the Connecticut arrest warrant. At this point, before Appleby had been *Mirandized,* Appleby asked "if he was going to have the opportunity to talk to an attorney." Detective Jewiss replied "absolutely." Detective Jewiss testified he understood this to be a question regarding procedure, not an invocation of the right. While testifying at the suppression hearing, Detective Jewiss was asked if he was questioning Appleby at this point in time. He answered: "Not at all. I even informed him that I wouldn't be questioning him, and that I wouldn't talk to him about either of these cases."

After Appleby asked about an attorney, he was read a notice of rights form that listed the three Connecticut charges — risk of injury to a minor, disorderly conduct, and public indecency. The form also advised of *Miranda* rights and stated in part: "You may consult with an attorney before being questioned; you may have an attorney present during questioning, and you cannot be questioned without your consent." Appleby signed the notice of rights form, which was an acknowledgment, not a waiver of rights.

Soon after that exchange, another Connecticut detective advised Appleby of the search warrant that authorized the officer to swab the inside of Appleby's mouth in order to obtain a DNA sample. Detective Jewiss testified that Appleby asked if he had the right to say "no" and then asked if he could speak to an attorney about his right to refuse the testing. According to Detective Jewiss, the detectives advised Appleby he could not talk to an attorney at that point regarding a search that had been authorized by a judge.

Following the DNA swabbing, Detective Jewiss continued with the book-in process on the Connecticut charges. Appleby was fingerprinted and photographed, the property on his person was inventoried, and a personal information data sheet was completed. During that process, Appleby asked two more times whether he would have an opportunity to talk to an attorney.

At the suppression hearing, Detective Jewiss repeatedly testified that he understood Appleby to be "asking about our procedure as in . . . will he have the opportunity to talk to an attorney." According to Detective Jewiss, the question was never in the context of, "I don't want to talk to you" or "I don't want to talk to anybody without an attorney here."

Detective Jewiss testified that during the book-in process he asked Appleby his name, date and place of birth, residence, and similar book-in questions. The only other question he asked came about 30 minutes after they arrived at the police station when Detective Jewiss asked Appleby if he wanted to talk to some people about an unrelated matter. Appleby said he would. Detective Jewiss was asked if Appleby brought up the word "attorney" at that time, and he replied, "No, he didn't."

Detective Jewiss was also asked why he did not give Appleby the opportunity to speak to an attorney before sending him upstairs to be interrogated by the Kansas detectives. Detective Jewiss, who had repeatedly stated that he had understood Appleby to be asking about procedure and had explained that a defendant would typically be allowed to contact an attorney only after the book-in process was complete, testified that "there was still some processing that I had to continue with."

When Detective Jewiss transferred Appleby to the Kansas detectives, he reported that Appleby had not invoked his right to counsel, "but he has asked something about an attorney when the [DNA] search warrant was being conducted." Detective Jewiss did not tell the Kansas detectives about the other instances when Appleby asked whether he would be able to talk to an attorney.

After Detective Jewiss left, the two Kansas detectives asked Appleby if he wanted to answer some questions about the murder of A.K. He said he wanted to talk to them, and the detectives then told him he would be read his *Miranda* rights again since he was being interviewed "on a different charge from what he was arrested." After being read his rights, Appleby said he understood them and was willing to answer some questions. He was questioned for approximately 2 and 1/2 hours, the final 20 minutes on videotape. At no point during the questioning by the Kansas detectives did Appleby indicate he wished to speak to or have the assistance of an attorney. . . .

Appleby filed three pretrial motions to suppress the statements he made to the Kansas detectives. . . . The trial court recognized there are two questions to ask in the determination of whether a suspect has invoked his or her Fifth Amendment right to counsel: (1) whether the suspect articulated a desire to have an attorney present sufficiently clearly that a reasonable officer in the circumstances would understand the statement to be a request for an attorney and (2) whether an attorney is being requested for purposes of interrogation rather than in regard to later hearings or proceedings. See State v. Walker, 80 P.3d 1132 (Kan. 2003). The trial court concluded Appleby clearly requested an attorney, but he did not make it clear he wanted the attorney to assist with questioning rather than to have assistance with his case. . . .

Appleby argues his requests for an attorney were clear and sufficient to require the Kansas detectives to refrain from questioning him until his requests were honored or until he had initiated contact with them. Appleby . . . argues the trial court's reasoning imposes too exacting a standard, essentially requiring the suspect to use the specific words of "I want an attorney to assist me with your purposed custodial interrogation," and that his statements to Detective Jewiss were sufficiently clear to invoke his Fifth Amendment right to counsel.

In making these arguments, Appleby groups together all of the instances where he referred to an attorney during the book-in process. Nevertheless, as we analyze his arguments, we recognize that one of the instances was of a different character than the others; that was the one made in response to the execution of the search warrant for purposes of obtaining DNA swabs. In that instance, Appleby clearly asked if he could talk to his attorney about whether he could refuse to allow the swabbing. In the three other instances, his questions were more general, as he asked whether he would have the opportunity to talk to an attorney.

[The] State contends that Appleby's requests for an attorney are more akin to a Sixth Amendment invocation of the right to counsel than a Fifth Amendment invocation of the right to counsel. It argues Appleby's requests could not reasonably be construed to be requests for assistance with custodial interrogation because he was not being interrogated at the time he made those requests. In addition, the State asserts that the *Miranda* right to counsel may not be anticipatorily invoked.

The State's arguments bring into issue the interrelationship of Fifth and Sixth Amendment rights, which was discussed by the United States Supreme Court in McNeil v. Wisconsin, 501 U.S. 171 (1991), under circumstances similar to those in this case — *i.e.,* where an arrest is made in one case and an interrogation relates to another. In *McNeil,* the defendant was arrested in Omaha, Nebraska, pursuant to a Wisconsin warrant based on charges of an armed robbery outside Milwaukee. Milwaukee detectives went to Omaha to retrieve McNeil. The detectives advised McNeil of his *Miranda* rights and began to ask questions. McNeil refused to answer any questions, the interview ended, and he was taken to Wisconsin where an attorney was appointed to represent him.

Later that day, McNeil was visited by officers from a different Wisconsin county. The county detectives advised McNeil of his *Miranda* rights, and McNeil signed a form waiving those rights. The county detectives then asked McNeil about charges of murder, attempted murder, and armed robbery. McNeil denied any involvement in the crimes. Two days later the county detectives returned and again advised McNeil of his *Miranda* rights. McNeil again waived his rights and this time confessed.

McNeil sought suppression of his statement to the county detectives asserting a Sixth Amendment right to counsel, but the Supreme Court determined his confession was admissible. The ruling was based on the distinction between McNeil's Fifth and Sixth Amendment rights. The Supreme Court explained that the Sixth Amendment right to counsel had attached in the Milwaukee case [because the] Sixth Amendment right to counsel attaches on filing of formal charges, indictment, [information or] arraignment. . . . But that right, the Court explained, is offense specific and cannot be invoked once for all future prosecutions. As a result, "incriminating statements pertaining to other crimes, as to which the Sixth Amendment right has not yet attached, are, of course, admissible at the trial of those offenses."

A similar dividing line is not drawn, however, when the Fifth Amendment right to counsel — which is protected by Miranda v. Arizona, 384 U.S. 436 (1966) — is invoked (which McNeil did not do in arguing his appeal). In other words, Fifth Amendment rights are not offense specific. Thus, the *McNeil* Court noted that "once a suspect invokes the *Miranda* right to counsel for interrogation regarding one offense, he may not be reapproached regarding *any* offense unless counsel is present." Further, Edwards v. Arizona, 451 U.S. 477 (1981), established a second layer of prophylaxis for the *Miranda* right to counsel: Once a suspect asserts the right, not only must the current interrogation cease, but he may not be approached for further interrogation until counsel has been made available to him — which means . . . that counsel must be present, Minnick v. Mississippi, 498 U.S. 146 (1990). If the police do subsequently initiate an encounter in the absence of counsel (assuming there has been no break in custody), the suspect's statements are presumed involuntary and therefore inadmissible as substantive evidence at trial, even where the suspect executes a waiver and his statements would be considered voluntary under traditional standards. This is designed to prevent police from badgering a defendant into waiving his previously asserted *Miranda* rights.

Recently, in Montejo v. Louisiana, 129 S. Ct. 2079 (2009), the Supreme Court reaffirmed this Fifth Amendment jurisprudence, concluding the three layers of protection — *Miranda, Edwards,* and *Minnick* — are sufficient. However, the *Montejo* Court modified some aspects of its Sixth Amendment jurisprudence. Specifically, it overruled Michigan v. Jackson, 475 U.S. 625 (1986), because of that decision's "wholesale importation of the *Edwards* rule into the Sixth Amendment."

However, . . . the *Montejo* Court did not modify *McNeil's* dividing lines between Fifth and Sixth Amendment analysis. . . . In particular, the *Montejo* Court did not alter the *McNeil* requirement that, even if Sixth Amendment rights have been invoked, a defendant must affirmatively assert Fifth Amendment rights if subjected to a custodial interrogation in another case. As a result, if Appleby asserted Sixth Amendment rights, as the State suggests, the assertion was effective only in the Connecticut case. . . .

Because the accused's purpose in requesting an attorney must be determined in order to sort the interplay of these rights, the *McNeil* Court concluded that an effective invocation of the Fifth Amendment right to counsel applies only when the suspect has expressed his wish for the particular sort of lawyerly assistance that is the subject of *Miranda*. It requires, at a minimum, "some statement that can reasonably be construed to be an expression of a desire for the assistance of an attorney *in dealing with custodial interrogation by the police.*" *McNeil*, 501 U.S. at 178.

[Some] courts have been very restrictive in defining "imminent," allowing no intervening activity between the invocation of the right and the planned initiation of questioning. . . . This restrictive view is supported by the statements in *Montejo* that the Court had "in fact never held that a person can invoke his *Miranda* rights anticipatorily, *in a context other than custodial interrogation.*" . . .

Yet the Court did not clearly explain what was meant by the context of a custodial interrogation or a context other than a custodial interrogation, and the facts of *Montejo* are very different from those in this case and therefore do not help to explain the meaning as it would be applied in this case. As in *McNeil*, the focus in *Montejo* was whether there had been an assertion of Sixth Amendment rights that prevented further interrogation. In fact, upon his arrest, Montejo waived his *Miranda* rights and gave police various versions of events related to the crime. A few days later at a preliminary hearing, known in Louisiana as a "72-hour hearing," counsel was appointed for Montejo even though he had not requested the appointment and had stood mute when asked if he wanted the assistance of an attorney. Later that same day, police approached Montejo, *Mirandized* him again, and asked him to accompany them to locate the murder weapon. During the drive, Montejo wrote an inculpatory letter of apology to the victim's widow. After the drive, Montejo met his attorney for the first time. At trial, he objected to the admission of the letter, basing his objection on *Jackson*. The Supreme Court held that the letter need not be suppressed based on an objection under *Jackson*, which it overruled. The Court concluded Montejo had not asserted his Sixth Amendment right to counsel. Yet, the Court concluded the case should be remanded to allow Montejo to assert an objection under *Edwards*, in other words, a Fifth Amendment objection. . . .

Here, Appleby does not assert that a Sixth Amendment right to counsel requires the suppression of his confession. Nor did the trial court suppress on that basis. The trial court merely pointed to the possibility of a Sixth Amendment assertion in another case — or perhaps even the Kansas case — as a circumstance that caused Appleby's assertion to be ambiguous. He relies on a Fifth Amendment right to counsel and suggests his questions during the book-in process asserted that right. This argument brings us to the State's position that the right was not effectively asserted because Appleby was not in the interrogation room. . . .

This approach is similar to that followed by the trial court in this case and in past decisions of this court where the context of a statement regarding an attorney has been analyzed to view whether an objective law enforcement officer would understand there had been an invocation of Fifth Amendment rights. For example, in State v. Gant, 201 P.3d 673 (Kan. 2009), . . . this court recently held a defendant did not assert his Fifth Amendment rights when he yelled to his companions while being arrested that they should call a lawyer. Although we did not consider the question of whether interrogation must be imminent, we did conclude the factual context revealed the defendant was directing his comments toward his companions, not police, and was not clearly and unambiguously asserting his right to counsel.

Now, we explicitly recognize what was implicit in many of our prior decisions: The timing as well as the content and context of a reference to counsel may help determine whether there has been an unambiguous assertion of the right to have the assistance of an attorney in dealing with a custodial interrogation by law enforcement officers.

This is the approach adopted by the trial court. In reaching the conclusion that the context in this case created ambiguity, the trial court made several findings that are supported by substantial competent evidence. Specifically, the trial court found that Appleby was aware he was being arrested by Connecticut authorities and was being charged for crimes committed in Connecticut. Further, Appleby had not been subjected to interrogation at that point in time about anything, in either the Connecticut or the Kansas case, and no one had indicated to him that his arrest was in any way connected the murder of A.K. Moreover, Detective Jewiss had informed Appleby that he would not be questioning him and that someone else would be talking to him about "the case." At that point in time, Appleby only knew of the Connecticut case. Hence, when Appleby asked whether he would have a chance to talk to an attorney, he knew he was not going to be questioned by Detective Jewiss. At that point in time, interrogation was clearly not imminent or impending.

It was not until minutes before the custodial interrogation with the Kansas detectives that Appleby was asked by Detective Jewiss if he would talk to some people about an unrelated matter. The trial court concluded that at that time: "Appleby undoubtedly believed that matter to be the [A.K.] murder investigation." Yet Appleby agreed without hesitation to speak to the detectives. Then Appleby was given his *Miranda* rights, which he clearly waived. He never asked about an attorney again. Thus, when questioning was imminent — when Appleby was approached for interrogation — he clearly waived his right to counsel.

We agree with the conclusion reached by the trial court that Appleby's references to an attorney during the book-in process on the Connecticut charges did not constitute a clear and unambiguous assertion of his Fifth Amendment right as protected by *Miranda*. The trial court did not err in denying Appleby's motion to suppress his custodial statements made to the Kansas detectives. . . .

JOHNSON, J., concurring in part and dissenting in part:

. . . I would not require a detainee to possess the knowledge of a constitutional scholar well-versed in Fifth and Sixth Amendment jurisprudence. Rather, I would view the circumstances from the perspective of an objectively reasonable layperson interacting with an objectively reasonable law enforcement officer. In that context, even though only the officer knew that the arrest was pretextual, both could not have questioned that Appleby was actually in custody on the 6-year-old Connecticut charges, so as to trigger the protections applicable to custodial interrogations.

In that setting, Appleby asked Detective Jewiss about consulting with an attorney not once, but four times. The trial court found that Appleby had asserted his right to an attorney, albeit perhaps only for Sixth Amendment purposes. The majority questions, but does not decide, whether the wording of Appleby's requests was sufficient to support the trial court's finding. Without belaboring the point, I would simply submit that one might expect a detainee, who has been confronted in his home by a multitude of armed officers, arrested, and taken to jail, to propound a request for an attorney in a most polite and nonconfrontational manner. Moreover, Appleby's persistence in making a number of requests in a short period of time belies any equivocation as to his desire to have an attorney present or as to Detective Jewiss' understanding of that desire.

[A] detainee would need to possess excellent clairvoyance — or astute constitutional acumen — to ascertain that, if there is any way in which the detainee's request for an attorney might be construed as being for Sixth Amendment purposes, then the right would not actually accrue or the request become effective until some undisclosed later time, after the detainee has been subjected to a custodial interrogation. . . .

Problem 8-7. Christian Burial Speech

On the afternoon of December 24, 1968, 10-year-old Pamela Powers went with her family to the YMCA in Des Moines, Iowa, to watch a wrestling tournament in which her brother was participating. When she failed to return from a trip to the washroom, a search for her began; it was unsuccessful.

Robert Williams, who had recently escaped from a mental hospital, was a resident of the YMCA. Soon after the girl's disappearance Williams was seen in the YMCA lobby carrying some clothing and a large bundle wrapped in a blanket. As Williams placed the bundle into his car, a witness noticed a body under the blanket. Williams immediately drove away. His abandoned car was found the following day in Davenport, Iowa, roughly 160 miles east of Des Moines. A warrant was then issued in Des Moines for his arrest on a charge of abduction.

On the morning of December 26, a Des Moines lawyer named Henry McKnight went to the Des Moines police station and informed the officers present that he had just received a long-distance call from Williams and that he had advised Williams to turn himself in to the Davenport police. Williams did surrender that morning to the police in Davenport, and they booked him on the charge specified in the arrest warrant and gave him the warnings required by Miranda v. Arizona. The Davenport police then telephoned their counterparts in Des Moines to inform them that Williams had surrendered. McKnight, the lawyer, was still at the Des Moines police headquarters, and Williams spoke with McKnight on the telephone. McKnight advised Williams that Des Moines police officers would be driving to Davenport to pick him up, that the officers would not interrogate him or mistreat him, and that Williams was not to talk to the officers about Pamela Powers until after consulting with McKnight upon his return to Des Moines. As a result of these conversations, McKnight and the Des Moines police officials agreed that Detective Cleatus Learning and a fellow officer would drive to Davenport to pick up Williams, that they would bring him directly back to Des Moines, and that they would not question him during the trip.

In the meantime Williams was arraigned before a judge in Davenport on the outstanding arrest warrant. The judge advised him of his *Miranda* rights and committed him to jail. Before leaving the courtroom, Williams conferred with a lawyer named Thomas Kelly, who advised him not to make any statements until consulting with McKnight back in Des Moines.

Soon after Detective Learning and his fellow officer arrived in Davenport, they met with Williams and Kelly. Detective Learning repeated the *Miranda* warnings, and told Williams: "We both know that you're being represented here by Mr. Kelly and you're being represented by Mr. McKnight in Des Moines, and I want you to remember this because we'll be visiting between here and Des Moines." Kelly reiterated to Detective Learning that Williams was not to be questioned about the disappearance of Pamela Powers until after he had consulted with McKnight back in Des Moines. When Learning expressed some reservations, Kelly firmly stated that the agreement with McKnight was to be carried out — that there was to be no interrogation of Williams during the journey to Des Moines. Kelly was denied permission to ride in the police car back to Des Moines with Williams and the two officers. The two detectives, with Williams in their charge, then set out on the 160-mile drive. Williams said several times during the trip that "when I get to Des Moines and see Mr. McKnight, I am going to tell you the whole story."

Detective Learning knew that Williams was a former mental patient, and knew also that he was deeply religious. Learning and Williams soon embarked on a conversation covering a variety of topics, including the subject of religion. Learning addressed Williams as "Reverend." He then made this speech:

> I want to give you something to think about while we're traveling down the road. Number one, I want you to observe the weather conditions, it's raining, it's sleeting, it's freezing, driving is very treacherous, visibility is poor, it's going to be dark early this evening. They are predicting several inches of snow for tonight, and I feel that you yourself are the only person that knows where this little girl's body is, that you yourself have only been there once, and if you get a snow on top of it you yourself may be unable to find it. And, since we will be going right past the area on the way into Des Moines, I feel that we could stop and locate the body, that the parents of this little girl should be entitled to a Christian burial for the little girl who was snatched away from them on Christmas Eve and murdered. And I feel we should stop and locate it on the way in rather than waiting until morning and trying to come back out after a snow storm and possibly not being able to find it at all.

Williams asked Detective Learning why he thought their route to Des Moines would be taking them past the girl's body, and Learning responded that he knew the body was in the area of Mitchellville — a town they would be passing on the way to Des Moines. (In fact, Learning did not know where the body was.) Learning then added, "I do not want you to answer me. I don't want to discuss it any further. Just think about it as we're riding down the road."

As the car approached Grinnell, a town approximately 100 miles west of Davenport, Williams asked whether the police had found the victim's shoes. When Detective Learning replied that he was unsure, Williams directed the officers to a service station where he said he had left the shoes; a search for them proved unsuccessful. As they continued toward Des Moines, Williams asked whether the police had found the blanket, and directed the officers to a rest area where he said he had disposed of the blanket. Nothing was found. The car continued toward Des Moines, and as it approached Mitchellville, Williams said that he would show the officers where the body was. He then directed the police to the body of Pamela Powers.

Williams was indicted for first-degree murder. Because a warrant had been issued for Williams' arrest, and because he had been arraigned and confined to jail, Williams' Sixth Amendment right to counsel attached. Before trial, his counsel moved to suppress all evidence resulting from any statements Williams had made during the automobile ride from Davenport to Des Moines. Should the judge grant the motion? Compare Brewer v. Williams, 430 U.S. 387 (1977); Yale Kamisar, Brewer v. Williams — A Hard Look at a Discomfiting Record, 66 Geo. L.J. 209 (1977).

Notes

1. *The Sixth Amendment right to counsel and "deliberately eliciting" a confession.* The Sixth Amendment to the U.S. Constitution provides for a right to counsel "in all criminal prosecutions." The U.S. Supreme Court, along with most states applying analogous state constitutional provisions, has held that Sixth Amendment counsel rights attach after the initiation of formal proceedings, whether by way of indictment, information, or initial arraignment.

In Brewer v. Williams, 430 U.S. 387 (1977), the case on which Problem 8-7 is based, the Court held that Detective Learning violated that right by "deliberately eliciting" information from Williams while his counsel was absent, and that Williams had not waived his right to counsel: "It is true that Williams had been informed of and appeared to understand his right to counsel. But waiver requires not merely comprehension but relinquishment, and Williams's consistent reliance upon the advice of counsel in dealing with the authorities refutes any suggestion that he waived that right." How do the facts compare in the *Innis* case, reprinted in Part B, where the Court held that no interrogation occurred, and in *Williams,* where the Court concluded that the police deliberately elicited information? Are the Fifth and Sixth Amendment definitions of "interrogation" comparable? Compare Fellers v. United States, 540 U.S. 519 (2004) (officer who went to home of indicted defendant to arrest him violated right to counsel by discussing charge in absence of attorney; contact need not amount to an "interrogation" to violate Sixth Amendment).

2. *Waiver and invocation of Sixth Amendment rights.* In Michigan v. Jackson, 475 U.S. 625 (1986), the Court explained that Sixth Amendment rights deserve at least as much protection as Fifth Amendment rights, and applied Edwards v. Arizona, 451 U.S. 477 (1981), to hold that government agents could not initiate a conversation with a defendant after the Sixth Amendment right to counsel had attached. As with *Edwards,* the Court did not preclude a later confession where the defendant initiated a later conversation. In Montejo v. Louisiana, 129 S. Ct. 2079 (2009), however, the Court overruled *Jackson*. After defendant Montejo had been assigned counsel, two police detectives visited him at the prison and asked him to help them locate the murder weapon. During the search for the weapon, Montejo wrote an inculpatory letter of apology to the victim's widow. The Court held that a defendant may waive the Sixth Amendment right to counsel — so long as relinquishment of the right is voluntary, knowing, and intelligent — even if the government initiates the conversation after the assignment of counsel to the defendant. The majority considered the *Edwards* rule to be sufficient to prevent police from badgering a defendant into waiving his previously asserted *Miranda* rights; the Court did not consider it necessary to create any separate protection for Sixth Amendment interests.

3. *Sixth Amendment right to counsel and cellmate confessions.* In Kuhlmann v. Wilson, 477 U.S. 436 (1986), the U.S. Supreme Court deferred to the factual findings of the

trial court that prisoner Benny Lee was not acting as a government interrogator when the government planted Lee in Wilson's cell. *Kuhlmann* addresses the recurring question of whether government agents "deliberately elicit" a confession from a defendant whose Sixth Amendment rights have attached. In this fact-sensitive area, one can find enormous variety in the decisions of state and lower federal courts; a review of some representative holdings appear on the web extension for this chapter at *http://www.crimpro.com/extension/ch08*. Why is there a different standard for assessing when government agents have violated defendants' Fifth Amendment and Sixth Amendment rights to counsel?

4. *Scope of the Sixth Amendment right to counsel for "other" offenses.* Can government agents interrogate a defendant about a crime other than an offense for which the government has initiated formal proceedings? In McNeil v. Wisconsin, 501 U.S. 171 (1991), the Court explained that "The Sixth Amendment right [to counsel] is offense specific. It cannot be invoked once for all future prosecutions, for it does not attach until a prosecution is commenced, that is, at or after the initiation of adversary judicial criminal proceedings — whether by way of formal charge, preliminary hearing, indictment, information, or arraignment." In Texas v. Cobb, 532 U.S. 162 (2001), the Court addressed the issue of what constituted the "same offense." Some state court and lower federal court decisions treated "factually related" crimes as the "same offense." The Supreme Court, however, held that the determination of whether a second offense was the "same offense" under the Sixth Amendment should be determined under the narrow standards applied under federal law to determine whether double jeopardy barred the filing of two separate charges for the "same offence." See Blockburger v. United States, 284 U.S. 299 (1932). Thus, a second offense would not be considered the "same offense" and would allow subsequent interrogation when each of two statutory provisions "requires proof of a fact which the other does not."

F. *MIRANDA* CURES, IMPACTS, AND ALTERNATIVES

The decades-long debate over the wisdom of *Miranda* turns in part on how much of an impact it has on criminal investigations and prosecutions. The first part of this section considers whether a *Miranda* error can be fixed, thus lessening any harm to the prosecution from failure to give proper warnings. The second part considers evidence about the impact of *Miranda* on the criminal justice system. The final part considers whether there are alternatives to giving *Miranda* warnings that would encourage voluntary confessions.

1. *Cures and Remedies for* Miranda *Violations*

In the ordinary case, a *Miranda* violation will mean that the confession obtained as a result of the tainted interrogation will be inadmissible as evidence. But what about physical evidence or testimony of witnesses obtained as a result of the improper interrogation? Will this derivative evidence — the "fruit of the poisonous tree" — be admissible? There are a number of circumstances under which courts will admit evidence obtained after a *Miranda* violation, even if the improper interrogation was the "but for" cause of the police obtaining the evidence. As you read the following materials, try to sort out the various arguments in favor of ignoring the original violation of law.

■ MISSOURI v. PATRICE SEIBERT

542 U.S. 600 (2004)

SOUTER, J.*

This case tests a police protocol for custodial interrogation that calls for giving no warnings of the rights to silence and counsel until interrogation has produced a confession. Although such a statement is generally inadmissible, since taken in violation of Miranda v. Arizona, 384 U.S. 436 (1966), the interrogating officer follows it with *Miranda* warnings and then leads the suspect to cover the same ground a second time. The question here is the admissibility of the repeated statement. Because this midstream recitation of warnings after interrogation and unwarned confession could not effectively comply with *Miranda*'s constitutional requirement, we hold that a statement repeated after a warning in such circumstances is inadmissible.

Respondent Patrice Seibert's 12-year-old son Jonathan had cerebral palsy, and when he died in his sleep she feared charges of neglect because of bedsores on his body. In her presence, two of her teenage sons and two of their friends devised a plan to conceal the facts surrounding Jonathan's death by incinerating his body in the course of burning the family's mobile home, in which they planned to leave Donald Rector, a mentally ill teenager living with the family, to avoid any appearance that Jonathan had been unattended. Seibert's son Darian and a friend set the fire, and Donald died.

Five days later, the police awakened Seibert at 3 A.M. at a hospital where Darian was being treated for burns. In arresting her, Officer Kevin Clinton followed instructions from Rolla, Missouri, officer Richard Hanrahan that he refrain from giving *Miranda* warnings. After Seibert had been taken to the police station and left alone in an interview room for 15 to 20 minutes, Hanrahan questioned her without *Miranda* warnings for 30 to 40 minutes, squeezing her arm and repeating "Donald was also to die in his sleep." After Seibert finally admitted she knew Donald was meant to die in the fire, she was given a 20-minute coffee and cigarette break. Officer Hanrahan then turned on a tape recorder, gave Seibert the *Miranda* warnings, and obtained a signed waiver of rights from her. He resumed the questioning with "Ok, 'trice, we've been talking for a little while about what happened on Wednesday the twelfth, haven't we?," and confronted her with her prewarning statements:

> *Hanrahan:* Now, in discussion you told us, you told us that there was an understanding about Donald.
> *Seibert:* Yes. . . .
> *Hanrahan:* And what was the understanding about Donald?
> *Seibert:* If they could get him out of the trailer, to take him out of the trailer. . . .
> *Hanrahan:* 'Trice, didn't you tell me that he was supposed to die in his sleep?

* [Justices Stevens, Ginsburg, and Breyer joined in this opinion; Justice Kennedy concurred in the judgment. — EDS.]

Seibert: If that would happen, 'cause he was on that new medicine, you know. . . .
Hanrahan: The Prozac? And it makes him sleepy. So he was supposed to die in his sleep?
Seibert: Yes.

After being charged with first-degree murder for her role in Donald's death, Seibert sought to exclude both her prewarning and postwarning statements. At the suppression hearing, Officer Hanrahan testified that he made a "conscious decision" to withhold *Miranda* warnings, thus resorting to an interrogation technique he had been taught: question first, then give the warnings, and then repeat the question "until I get the answer that she's already provided once." He acknowledged that Seibert's ultimate statement was "largely a repeat of information . . . obtained" prior to the warning.

The trial court suppressed the prewarning statement but admitted the responses given after the *Miranda* recitation. A jury convicted Seibert of second-degree murder. . . .

[Giving *Miranda*] warnings and getting a waiver has generally produced a virtual ticket of admissibility; maintaining that a statement is involuntary even though given after warnings and voluntary waiver of rights requires unusual stamina, and litigation over voluntariness tends to end with the finding of a valid waiver. To point out the obvious, this common consequence would not be common at all were it not that *Miranda* warnings are customarily given under circumstances allowing for a real choice between talking and remaining silent.

The technique of interrogating in successive, unwarned and warned phases raises a new challenge to *Miranda.* Although we have no statistics on the frequency of this practice, it is not confined to Rolla, Missouri. [The] Police Law Institute, for example, instructs that "officers may conduct a two-stage interrogation. . . . At any point during the pre-*Miranda* interrogation, usually after arrestees have confessed, officers may then read the *Miranda* warnings and ask for a waiver. If the arrestees waive their *Miranda* rights, officers will be able to repeat any *subsequent* incriminating statements later in court." Police Law Institute, Illinois Police Law Manual 83 (Jan. 2001-Dec. 2003) (hereinafter Police Law Manual). . . .

The inquiry is simply whether the warnings reasonably convey to a suspect his rights as required by *Miranda.* The threshold issue when interrogators question first and warn later is thus whether it would be reasonable to find that in these circumstances the warnings could function "effectively" as *Miranda* requires. Could the warnings effectively advise the suspect that he had a real choice about giving an admissible statement at that juncture? Could they reasonably convey that he could choose to stop talking even if he had talked earlier? For unless the warnings could place a suspect who has just been interrogated in a position to make such an informed choice, there is no practical justification for accepting the formal warnings as compliance with *Miranda,* or for treating the second stage of interrogation as distinct from the first, unwarned and inadmissible segment. . . .

By any objective measure, applied to circumstances exemplified here, it is likely that if the interrogators employ the technique of withholding warnings until after interrogation succeeds in eliciting a confession, the warnings will be ineffective in preparing the suspect for successive interrogation, close in time and similar in content. After all, the reason that question-first is catching on is as obvious as its manifest purpose, which is to get a confession the suspect would not make if he understood his rights at the outset; the sensible underlying assumption is that with one confession in hand before the warnings, the interrogator can count on getting its duplicate, with trifling additional trouble. . . . What is worse, telling a suspect that "anything you say can and will be used against you," without expressly excepting the statement just given, could lead to an entirely reasonable inference that what he has just said will be used, with subsequent silence being of no avail. Thus, when *Miranda* warnings are inserted in the midst of coordinated and continuing interrogation, they are likely to mislead and deprive a defendant of knowledge essential to his ability to understand the nature of his rights and the consequences of abandoning them. . . .

Missouri argues that a confession repeated at the end of an interrogation sequence envisioned in a question-first strategy is admissible on the authority of Oregon v. Elstad, 470 U.S. 298 (1985), but the argument disfigures that case. In *Elstad,* the police went to the young suspect's house to take him into custody on a charge of burglary. Before the arrest, one officer spoke with the suspect's mother, while the other one joined the suspect in a "brief stop in the living room," where the officer said he "felt" the young man was involved in a burglary. The suspect acknowledged he had been at the scene. This Court noted that the pause in the living room "was not to interrogate the suspect but to notify his mother of the reason for his arrest," and described the incident as having "none of the earmarks of coercion." The Court, indeed, took care to mention that the officer's initial failure to warn was an "oversight" that "may have been the result of confusion as to whether the brief exchange qualified as 'custodial interrogation' or . . . may simply have reflected . . . reluctance to initiate an alarming police procedure before [an officer] had spoken with respondent's mother." At the outset of a later and systematic station house interrogation going well beyond the scope of the laconic prior admission, the suspect was given *Miranda* warnings and made a full confession. In holding the second statement admissible and voluntary, *Elstad* rejected the "cat out of the bag" theory that any short, earlier admission, obtained in arguably innocent neglect of *Miranda,* determined the character of the later, warned confession; on the facts of that case, the Court thought any causal connection between the first and second responses to the police was "speculative and attenuated." Although the *Elstad* Court expressed no explicit conclusion about either officer's state of mind, it is fair to read *Elstad* as treating the living room conversation as a good-faith *Miranda* mistake, not only open to correction by careful warnings before systematic questioning in that particular case, but posing no threat to warn-first practice generally.

The contrast between *Elstad* and this case reveals a series of relevant facts that bear on whether *Miranda* warnings delivered midstream could be effective enough to accomplish their object: the completeness and detail of the questions and answers in the first round of interrogation, the overlapping content of the two statements, the timing and setting of the first and the second, the continuity of police personnel, and the degree to which the interrogator's questions treated the second round as continuous with the first. In *Elstad,* it was not unreasonable to see the occasion for questioning at the station house as presenting a markedly different experience from the short conversation at home; since a reasonable person in the suspect's shoes could have seen the station house questioning as a new and distinct experience, the *Miranda* warnings could have made sense as presenting a genuine choice whether to follow up on the earlier admission.

At the opposite extreme are the facts here, which by any objective measure reveal a police strategy adapted to undermine the *Miranda* warnings.[6] The unwarned interrogation was conducted in the station house, and the questioning was systematic, exhaustive, and managed with psychological skill. When the police were finished there was little, if anything, of incriminating potential left unsaid. The warned phase of questioning proceeded after a pause of only 15 to 20 minutes, in the same place as the unwarned segment. [The] police did not advise that her prior statement could not be used. Nothing was said or done to dispel the oddity of warning about legal rights to silence and counsel right after the police had led her through a systematic interrogation. . . . The impression that the further questioning was a mere continuation of the earlier questions and responses was fostered by references back to the confession already given. It would have been reasonable to regard the two sessions as parts of a continuum, in which it would have been unnatural to refuse to repeat at the second stage what had been said before. . . .

Because the question-first tactic effectively threatens to thwart *Miranda*'s purpose of reducing the risk that a coerced confession would be admitted, and because the facts here do not reasonably support a conclusion that the warnings given could have served their purpose, Seibert's postwarning statements are inadmissible. . . .

BREYER, J., concurring.

In my view, the following simple rule should apply to the two-stage interrogation technique: Courts should exclude the "fruits" of the initial unwarned questioning unless the failure to warn was in good faith. I believe this is a sound and workable approach to the problem this case presents. Prosecutors and judges have long understood how to apply the "fruits" approach, which they use in other areas of law. And in the workaday world of criminal law enforcement the administrative simplicity of the familiar has significant advantages over a more complex exclusionary rule.

I believe the plurality's approach in practice will function as a "fruits" test. The truly "effective" *Miranda* warnings on which the plurality insists will occur only when certain circumstances — a lapse in time, a change in location or interrogating officer, or a shift in the focus of the questioning — intervene between the unwarned questioning and any postwarning statement. . . .

KENNEDY, J., concurring in the judgment.

. . . The *Miranda* rule has become an important and accepted element of the criminal justice system. At the same time, not every violation of the rule requires suppression of the evidence obtained. Evidence is admissible when the central concerns of *Miranda* are not likely to be implicated and when other objectives of the criminal justice system are best served by its introduction. . . .

Oregon v. Elstad, 470 U.S. 298 (1985), reflects this approach. . . . In my view, *Elstad* was correct in its reasoning and its result. . . . An officer may not realize that a suspect is in custody and warnings are required. The officer may not plan to question the suspect or may be waiting for a more appropriate time. Skilled investigators often interview suspects multiple times, and good police work may involve referring to prior statements to test their veracity or to refresh recollection. In light

6. Because the intent of the officer will rarely be as candidly admitted as it was here (even as it is likely to determine the conduct of the interrogation), the focus is on facts apart from intent that show the question-first tactic at work.

of these realities it would be extravagant to treat the presence of one statement that cannot be admitted under *Miranda* as sufficient reason to prohibit subsequent statements preceded by a proper warning. That approach would serve "neither the general goal of deterring improper police conduct nor the Fifth Amendment goal of assuring trustworthy evidence." . . .

This case presents different considerations. The police used a two-step questioning technique based on a deliberate violation of *Miranda*. The *Miranda* warning was withheld to obscure both the practical and legal significance of the admonition when finally given. . . . The technique used in this case distorts the meaning of *Miranda* and furthers no legitimate countervailing interest. . . .

The plurality concludes that whenever a two-stage interview occurs, admissibility of the postwarning statement should depend on "whether the *Miranda* warnings delivered midstream could have been effective enough to accomplish their object" given the specific facts of the case. This test envisions an objective inquiry from the perspective of the suspect, and applies in the case of both intentional and unintentional two-stage interrogations. In my view, this test cuts too broadly. *Miranda*'s clarity is one of its strengths, and a multifactor test that applies to every two-stage interrogation may serve to undermine that clarity. I would apply a narrower test applicable only in the infrequent case, such as we have here, in which the two-step interrogation technique was used in a calculated way to undermine the *Miranda* warning. . . .

O'CONNOR, J., dissenting.*

The plurality devours Oregon v. Elstad, 470 U.S. 298 (1985), even as it accuses petitioner's argument of "disfiguring" that decision. I believe that we are bound by *Elstad* to reach a different result, and I would vacate the judgment of the Supreme Court of Missouri. . . . I would analyze the two-step interrogation procedure under the voluntariness standards central to the Fifth Amendment and reiterated in *Elstad*. . . .

Problem 8-8. Hot Load

Officers Mike Hannan and Terry Thomas of the Tennessee Highway Patrol stopped a speeding vehicle driven by Kellie Alisha Jones. When Jones was unable to find the vehicle's registration, Officer Hannan asked her to accompany him to his squad car while he wrote out a traffic citation. While Jones went to the squad car, the passenger, Hosie Smith, looked in the glove compartment for the vehicle's registration. Officer Thomas, who was on the passenger's side of the car, asked Smith questions regarding ownership of the car and the couple's destination. After this brief conversation with Smith, Thomas returned to the squad car and sat in the back seat. While waiting for radio verification of Jones's license and the vehicle's registration, both officers continued to question Jones about the ownership of the car and her destination. When asked who her passenger was, Jones stated that it was her boyfriend, but she could only give the name "Pumpkin" when asked about his name. Because Smith and Jones appeared to be extremely nervous, and had given

* [Chief Justice Rehnquist and Justices Scalia and Thomas joined in this opinion. — EDS.]

inconsistent answers to the questions about their destination and the ownership of the car, the officers became suspicious and asked Jones if she was carrying any illegal items, weapons, or contraband. Jones denied knowledge of such cargo, and consented to a search of the car.

Officer Thomas re-approached the station wagon on the passenger side and asked Smith if there were any illegal items in the car. Smith denied knowledge of any such contraband. Thomas then told Smith that he had permission to look through the vehicle, and asked again about any illegal items in the car. Smith said, "Yes, it was probably a hot load." Thomas then asked, "By a hot load, do you mean cash, marijuana, or cocaine, one of the three?" Smith responded, "Probably." Thomas searched the car and found 22 pounds of pure cocaine in the locked glove compartment. At 6:25 P.M., the officers placed both Smith and Jones under arrest, read them their *Miranda* rights, and transported them to Highway Patrol Headquarters.

At 9:45 P.M., Smith was questioned by Officer Lonnie Hood. Before he was questioned, Smith was read his *Miranda* rights again and signed a written waiver of those rights. During the course of the interrogation, Smith gave Officer Hood an incriminating account of his employment to drive the station wagon with Jones from Oklahoma City, Oklahoma, to Fayetteville, North Carolina. This statement was reduced to writing by Officer Hood and signed by Smith.

Smith filed a motion to suppress the cocaine found in the car, his statements to Thomas beside the road, and those to Hood at Highway Patrol Headquarters.

Instead of following *Elstad* under state law, the court (like about 15 other state courts) embraced the earlier "cat out of the bag" theory of United States v. Bayer, 331 U.S. 532 (1947). In *Bayer,* the Court recognized:

> Of course, after an accused has once let the cat out of the bag by confessing, no matter what the inducement, he is never thereafter free of the psychological and practical disadvantages of having confessed. He can never get the cat back in the bag. The secret is out for good. In such a sense, a later confession always may be looked upon as fruit of the first.

The Tennessee court rejected the idea that all subsequent warnings could cure prior invalid confessions, but it also rejected the idea that all invalid confessions tainted all later confessions. State v. Smith, 834 S.W.2d 915 (Tenn. 1992). The Tennessee court held that unwarned confessions raised a "rebuttable presumption" that a subsequent confession is tainted by the initial illegality." The prosecution can overcome that presumption by establishing that "the taint is so attenuated as to justify admission of the subsequent confession."

Under the state constitution, the "crucial inquiry" for the courts is "whether the events and circumstances surrounding and following the initial, illegal conduct of the law enforcement officers prevented the accused from subsequently (1) making a free and informed choice to waive the State constitutional right not to provide evidence against one's self, and (2) voluntarily confessing his involvement in the crime." In addressing these questions, Tennessee courts examine the following factors:

1. The use of coercive tactics to obtain the initial, illegal confession and the causal connection between the illegal conduct and the challenged, subsequent confession;
2. The temporal proximity of the prior and subsequent confessions;
3. The reading and explanation of *Miranda* rights to the defendant before the subsequent confession;
4. The circumstances occurring after the arrest and continuing up until the making of the subsequent confession including, but not limited to, the length of the detention and the deprivation of food, rest, and bathroom facilities;
5. The coerciveness of the atmosphere in which any questioning took place including, but not limited to, the place where the questioning occurred, the identity of the interrogators, the form of the questions, and the repeated or prolonged nature of the questioning;
6. The presence of intervening factors including, but not limited to, consultations with counsel or family members, or the opportunity to consult with counsel, if desired;
7. The psychological effect of having already confessed, and whether the defendant was advised that the prior confession may not be admissible at trial;
8. Whether the defendant initiated the conversation that led to the subsequent confession; and
9. The defendant's sobriety, education, intelligence level, and experience with the law, as such factors relate to the defendant's ability to understand the administered *Miranda* rights.

If you were arguing this motion for Smith, how would you try to persuade the trial court that the state constitutional standard is more protective of *Miranda* rights than the more recent *Seibert* case? What would be the outcome of the *Smith* facts under *Seibert*? Will states like Tennessee now revert to the new federal position?

Notes

1. *Out-of-court statements obtained after earlier* Miranda *violations: majority position.* Unlike illegal searches and seizures, an unwarned interrogation will not necessarily require a later court to exclude all the evidence derived from the tainted statement. Although any statement made during an unwarned interrogation must not come into evidence, later statements of the suspect might still be admissible — even though the statements appear to be the "fruit of the poisonous tree."

In Oregon v. Elstad, 470 U.S. 298 (1985), the Supreme Court held that the state could use as evidence a subsequent confession. According to the Court, when the initial unwarned statement was given voluntarily,

> a careful and thorough administration of *Miranda* warnings serves to cure the condition that rendered the unwarned statement inadmissible. The warning conveys the relevant information and thereafter the suspect's choice whether to exercise his privilege to remain silent should ordinarily be viewed as an act of free will.

470 U.S. at 310. Before *Seibert* was decided, a significant minority of states (around 15) rejected the *Elstad* decision, placing a burden on the government to overcome a presumption of compulsion for subsequent confessions. See, e.g., Commonwealth v. Smith, 593 N.E.2d 1288 (Mass. 1992). Do you expect those states to revise their state constitutional doctrine in light of *Seibert*? For a glimpse of the vigorous state court rulings on the question of "cures" for improper *Miranda* warnings, see the web extension for this chapter at *http://www.crimpro.com/extension/ch08*.

2. *Use of statements for impeachment at trial.* Although state and federal courts exclude *Miranda*-tainted statements from the prosecution's case in chief, they allow the prosecution to use such statements (and the evidentiary fruit of those statements) to impeach a defendant's testimony at trial. See Oregon v. Hass, 420 U.S. 714 (1975); Harris v. New York, 401 U.S. 222 (1971). Again, not all states agree. See Commonwealth v. Triplett, 462 Pa. 244, 341 A.2d 62 (1975) (under Pennsylvania Constitution, statement obtained in violation of an accused's *Miranda* rights cannot be used to impeach his trial testimony).

The Supreme Court authorized a new use of defendant statements for impeachment purposes in Kansas v. Ventris, 129 S. Ct. 1841 (2009). Prior to the murder trial of Ventris, the government planted an informant in his cell; the informant heard him admit to shooting and robbing the victim. When Ventris testified at trial that his co-defendant committed the crimes, the government asked the informant to testify about his alleged confession. The Supreme Court held that such impeachment use of the statement was constitutionally acceptable, even though the statement was obtained in violation of the defendant's Sixth Amendment rights as interpreted in *Massiah*. Justice Scalia's opinion for the Court distinguished between "core" or "substantive" protections and "prophylactic" protections. For the latter category, impeachment uses of illegally obtained evidence are allowed. He argued that violations of the *pretrial* right to counsel belong to the former category, because the violation occurs when the statement is obtained, not when the government attempts to introduce the evidence at trial.

In light of these rulings, will police officers routinely violate *Miranda* after a suspect invokes the right to silence or to an attorney, simply to provide the prosecutor with potential impeachment evidence? See Richard Leo, The Impact of *Miranda* Revisited, 86 J. Crim. L. & Criminology 621 (1996) (in study of more than 180 interrogations, observing only one instance of interrogator pursuing questions in known violation of *Miranda*); Charles Weisselberg, Saving *Miranda*, 84 Cornell L. Rev. 109 (1998) (collecting evidence of training that encourages interrogations outside *Miranda*).

3. *Harmless error.* There are some constitutional errors in a trial that an appellate court will consider "harmless" because the verdict likely would have remained the same even if the errors had not occurred. There are other errors that courts say can never be harmless. For a number of years after the *Miranda* decision, courts said that the introduction into evidence of a coerced confession qualified as one such error. This type of error was said to involve a right so basic to a fair trial that courts would not bother with a harmless-error inquiry. In Arizona v. Fulminante, 499 U.S. 279 (1991), however, the Supreme Court decided that the introduction of coerced confessions could be treated as a harmless error after all.

4. *Section 1983 and coercive questioning*. The remedy for improper efforts to obtain confessions has been exclusion of the confession. If the confession was

coerced (as opposed to a technical violation of the *Miranda* requirements), any evidentiary fruits of the confession are also inadmissible. Is some alternative remedy possible? Are damage suits, injunctions, or administrative sanctions workable alternatives?

Both federal and state law allow criminal suspects to sue police officers for the use of illegal interrogation techniques. Although there are some important barriers to recovery in both state and federal courts (as we saw in Chapter 6), plaintiffs sometimes can recover damages after they have been subjected to illegal interrogations, including *Miranda* violations and the use of physical deprivations.

Problem 8-9. Inevitable Discovery

Elizabeth Reed, an attendant at a county landfill, died from a shotgun wound fired at close range as she was preparing to leave work. The killer left Reed's body hidden in some brush beside a dirt road, approximately 95 feet from the landfill office. The police soon began to focus their investigation on Kenneth DeShields, who had been seen that day driving Reed's car. They arrested him the morning after the murder.

Before any questioning began, DeShields requested an attorney and said that he did not wish to speak about the incident. However, the investigating officers persisted in their questions, and DeShields ultimately gave a series of statements. Although DeShields initially denied any knowledge of the murder, he eventually told the police that he had been with a man named "Blair" when Blair had killed Reed during an attempt to rob her. DeShields also said that after he and Blair had left the landfill, Blair had thrown a rake into a ditch and driven down a dirt road in the nearby woods to discard several items from the robbery. Detective Hudson then searched the dirt road that DeShields had described. He found an expended shotgun shell casing and the victim's wallet approximately 15 feet east of the dirt road and approximately 1,000 feet from the dump site.

At trial, the state did not introduce any of DeShields's postarrest statements into evidence. However, the shell casing and wallet were admitted into evidence, and an expert testified that the shell casing had been fired from DeShields's shotgun. The shell casing was the only direct evidence linking the killing to his shotgun. Two police officers testified that it was routine police practice to search the general area extensively in a homicide case and that this practice was followed in this case. By the time Hudson found the evidence, the police had already searched the landfill compound and several county roads that crisscrossed the area.

Did the trial court rule correctly in admitting the shell casing and wallet into evidence? Compare DeShields v. State, 534 A.2d 630 (Del. 1987).

Note

1. *Tainted leads to witnesses and physical evidence.* An improper interrogation might give the authorities information that can lead them to other witnesses or to physical evidence. In Michigan v. Tucker, 417 U.S. 433 (1974), the Supreme Court allowed the use of prosecution witnesses whose names had been obtained during an interrogation where proper *Miranda* warnings had not been given. While recognizing

that a truly involuntary confession, obtained in violation of the due process clause, could be remedied only by complete exclusion of all evidentiary "fruits" of the confession, this was not such a case. The failure to give proper *Miranda* warnings was merely a violation of a "prophylactic" rule rather than a constitutional violation as such. For *Miranda* violations that do not create an involuntary (and thus unconstitutional) confession, the Court believed that exclusion of evidence would be too costly. See also United States v. Patane, 542 U.S. 630 (2004) (physical evidence produced through unwarned but voluntary statements was admissible, even though police deliberately violated *Miranda*).

State courts have not often rejected this analysis explicitly, but many seem to assume that any evidentiary "fruit" from a confession obtained in violation of *Miranda* must be excluded unless one of the traditional exceptions to the "fruits" rule is present. A deliberate violation of *Miranda* by interrogators also has led some state courts to limit the use of evidentiary fruit. See Commonwealth v. Martin, 827 N.E.2d 198 (Mass. 2005) (rejects *Patane*; state constitution requires suppression of physical evidence derived from unwarned statements); State v. Peterson, 923 A.2d 585 (Vt. 2007) (state constitution requires suppression of tangible fruits of *Miranda* violation).

2. *Systemwide Impacts*

Miranda has been criticized on both doctrinal and practical grounds. The practical critiques take many forms, but they boil down to the question of how many convictions are "lost" because *Miranda* warnings were given. Before reading the following study, it is worth thinking in the abstract about the challenge of measuring the impact of *Miranda.* The article illustrates recent efforts, 30 years after the decision, to study its continuing impact. Is it possible to reach a conclusion about the impact of *Miranda,* either 30 years ago or today? Can the benefits of *Miranda* be quantified?

PAUL CASSELL AND BRET HAYMAN, POLICE INTERROGATION IN THE 1990S: AN EMPIRICAL STUDY OF THE EFFECTS OF *MIRANDA*

43 UCLA L. Rev. 839 (1996)

[We] undertook an empirical survey of confessions and their importance [in Salt Lake City, Utah]. We collected the basic data for the study by attending "screening" sessions held at the Salt Lake County District Attorney's office during a six-week period in the summer of 1994. Prosecutors in the District Attorney's Office screen all felony cases for prosecutive merit. . . . The screening session is a forty-five-minute interview by the prosecutor of the police officer concerning the evidence supporting the filing of charges. . . . There were 219 suspects in our sample. . . .

A. The Frequency of Questioning, Waivers, and Confessions

One important issue that has not been the subject of much empirical study is the frequency with which suspects are questioned. Not every person who is arrested will be questioned. In our sample, police questioned 79.0% of the suspects. This means that a surprisingly large percentage (21.0%) were not questioned.

[We also] collected information on why police failed to interrogate suspects (as reported by the officer at screening). [In] two cases (4.9% of the nonquestioning cases), the reason for not questioning was a belief that the suspect would invoke *Miranda.* In two other cases (4.9% of the nonquestioning cases), the police cited the fact that a suspect had an attorney as the obstacle to questioning, a reason that has a possible connection with *Miranda.* . . . The most often-given reason for nonquestioning [accounting for 34.1% of the nonquestioning cases] was that a suspect's whereabouts was unknown at the time police screened the case. The second most common reason [26.8%] for failure to question was the officer's belief that the case against the suspect was overwhelming. . . .

One of the most important questions about the *Miranda* regime is how often suspects invoke their *Miranda* rights, preventing any police questioning. A suspect can claim *Miranda* rights in two ways. First, he can refuse at the start of an interview to waive his rights (including the right to remain silent and the right to counsel), thus precluding any interview. Second, even if he initially waives his rights, he can assert them at any point in the interview. If a suspect asserts *Miranda* rights, police questioning must stop. . . . Surprisingly very little information is available on such a fundamental subject. The previously published evidence . . . suggests that about 20% of all suspects invoke their *Miranda* rights.

We gathered data on how often and in what ways suspects asserted their *Miranda* rights. [Of] suspects given their *Miranda* rights, 83.7% waived them. Reflecting the practices of the local law enforcement agencies, virtually all of these waivers were verbal rather than written. At the same time, 16.3% invoked their rights. Of the twenty-one suspects who invoked their rights, nine invoked their right to an attorney (two even before *Miranda* warnings could be read), six invoked their right not to make a statement, and six either refused to execute a waiver or otherwise invoked their rights.

[Five] suspects who initially waived their rights [3.9% of the total] changed their minds later and invoked their rights during the interview. Of these five suspects, three asked for an attorney during the interview (two after giving incriminating statements, one after giving a denial with an explanation), and two asserted their right to remain silent during the interview (one after giving a flat denial, one after giving a denial with an explanation). . . . If these three are added to suspects who invoked their rights initially, then a total of 18.6% of the suspects in our sample who were given *Miranda* rights invoked them before police succeeded in obtaining incriminating information. . . .

Perhaps the critical issue in the debate over *Miranda* is how often today suspects confess or otherwise make incriminating statements. Surprisingly little information is available on this subject, despite frequent definitive pronouncements that many suspects still confess.

[We] divided the outcomes into "successful" and "unsuccessful" categories — looking at the results from law enforcement's point of view. The result of questioning was "successful" when the police: (1) obtained a written confession;

(2) obtained a verbal confession; (3) obtained an incriminating statement; or (4) locked a suspect into a false alibi.

A written or verbal "confession" was "any substantial acknowledgment by the suspect that he or she committed the crime." Simply put, the suspect had to say in essence "I did it." . . . A "confession" could include statements in mitigation. . . .

Our next category was for "incriminating statements." Because this category is somewhat subjective and because its scope makes a critical difference in determining the scope of police success statistics, it is worth explaining in detail. An "incriminating statement" was "any statement that tends to establish guilt of the accused or from which with other facts guilt may be inferred or which tends to disprove some anticipated defense."

We found that such statements generally occurred in one of three situations. First, a suspect might give a statement that linked him to the crime or crime scene without admitting his guilt. For example, in an attempted homicide case the police asked the suspect if a certain car, known to have been involved in the crime, was his. He responded that it was, but denied any involvement in the crime. . . . A second kind of incriminating statement was a partial admission of guilt. For example, in one case involving a burglary, a suspect admitted being in the house unlawfully, but said he was there because of something the victim had done to his girlfriend, not to steal anything. . . .

Table 4 — Results
(N = 219 overall; 173 for those questioned)

	No.	*Questioned Only* %	*Overall* %
Invoked rights	21	12.1	9.5
Successful	73	42.2	33.3 . . .
Unsuccessful	79	45.7	36.1 . . .
Not questioned	46	—	21.0
Total	219	100	100

Third, a suspect might make statements to the police that tended to call into question his truthfulness or make him appear suspicious. For example, in one case an officer suspected a car was stolen and pulled over the suspect. The officer asked the suspect certain questions concerning his license, registration, and his relationship to the car. The suspect was visibly shaken by the questions and gave stammering and sometimes contradictory answers. We classified these statements as "incriminating."

After confessions and incriminating statements, the final category of "successful" outcomes was for a suspect who was "locked into a false alibi." . . .

The number of incriminating statements and denials we found are shown in Table 4. Overall, 9.5% of the suspects invoked their rights, 33.3% were successfully questioned, 36.1% were questioned unsuccessfully, and 21.0% were not questioned. Because some might argue that only suspects who were in fact questioned should be included in determining a confession rate, we also report percentages for only those suspects who were questioned. As can also be seen in Table 4, of all police interviews, 12.1% produced an immediate invocation of *Miranda* rights, 42.2% were successful, and 45.7% were unsuccessful. It should also be noted that, however measured, our "success" rate is artificially inflated because of the point at which our sample was drawn. We sampled cases from screening sessions where police officers believed they had gathered sufficient evidence for prosecution. As a consequence, our sample excludes a significant number of cases that police thought were too weak to warrant prosecution — including cases that were too weak because of an unsuccessful outcome of police questioning. . . .

[We] also examined whether suspects for particular types of crimes were more likely to confess. The limited previous research on this issue, from studies conducted in the 1960s, suggests that suspects are less likely to confess to violent crimes than to property crimes. Our data trend in this direction; . . . police were less successful in interrogating suspects for crimes of violence than for property crimes, although the result is not statistically significant at the conventional . . . confidence level. . . .

Although our success rate is inflated, it is lower than success rates found in this country before *Miranda,* suggesting that *Miranda* has hampered law enforcement efforts to obtain incriminating statements. [The] available pre- and post-*Miranda* information on confession rates in this country . . . suggests that interrogations were successful, very roughly speaking, in about 55% to 60% of interrogations conducted before the *Miranda* decision. For example, the earliest academic study in this country reported confession rates of 88.1% and 58.1% in two cities in California in 1960.[149] Similarly, a 1961 survey in Detroit reported a 60.8% confession rate, which fell slightly to 58.0% in 1965. [These figures] avoid the problem of anticipatory implementation of *Miranda* in various jurisdictions. In particular, confession rates after June 1964 might be dampened by the Supreme Court's *Escobedo* decision, which led some police to adopt *Miranda*-style warnings even before the decision. Our 33.3% overall success rate (and even our 42.2% questioning success rate) is well below the 55%-60% estimated pre-*Miranda* rate and, therefore, is consistent with the hypothesis that *Miranda* has harmed the confession rate.

B. Questioning Inside and Outside the *Miranda* Regime

One question that has not been the subject of any substantial empirical research is the extent to which police questioning falls inside or outside the *Miranda* regime and whether this makes any difference to ultimate outcomes. . . .

The *Miranda* rules cover only "custodial" interrogation. Evidence suggests that police have adjusted to *Miranda* by shifting to noncustodial "interviews" to skirt *Miranda*'s requirements. In talking to police officers, the researchers found some anecdotal evidence supporting this view. In a few screenings, officers (mostly from one large department) referred to giving suspects a *"Beheler"* warning, as in "I gave him *Beheler.*" This is a reference to the Supreme Court's decision in California v. Beheler, 463 U.S. 1121 (1983), which held that a suspect was not in custody when he "voluntarily agreed to accompany police to the station house [and] the police specifically told [him] that he was not under arrest." . . . On the other hand, in a few cases in our sample it appeared that officers Mirandized when not required to do so. . . .

149. Edward Barren, Jr., Police Practices and the Law — from Arrest to Release or Charge, 50 Cal. L. Rev. 11 (1962).

To date, no one has quantified how often police interview in noncustodial settings. In our sample, 69.9% of the interviews were custodial while 30.1% were noncustodial. Of the noncustodial interviews, 40.3% were at the scene, 26.9% were field investigations, and 32.7% were arranged interviews (that is, interviews where police officers had previously contacted the suspects to set up an interview time).

Even if police are able to avoid *Miranda*'s requirements by conducting various noncustodial interviews, the question would remain whether such interviews are less effective in obtaining incriminating information. We found that police were less successful in noncustodial interviews [with a 30% success rate, compared to 56.9% in custodial interrogations].

Notes

1. *Number of attempted interrogations.* Would the *Miranda* decision be likely to affect the number of cases in which the police at least attempt an interrogation? Should a study of the impact of *Miranda* include cases in which the suspect was not available for questioning? The Salt Lake City study did so. One prominent *Miranda*-era study — of the pseudonymous "Seaside City," California — concluded that officers failed to interrogate only 2 percent of the suspects "actually arrested and incarcerated." James Witt, Non-Coercive Interrogation and the Administration of Criminal Justice: The Impact of *Miranda* on Police Effectuality, 64 J. Crim. L. & Criminology 320 (1973).

2. *Number of waivers.* The most current studies have concluded that roughly 80 percent of all suspects waive their *Miranda* rights and make statements without counsel present. Some studies have found waiver rates in excess of 90 percent. See Paul Cassell, *Miranda*'s Social Costs: An Empirical Reassessment, 90 Nw. U. L. Rev. 387 (1996) (collecting studies of waiver rate). A study in Great Britain suggested that about 68 percent of suspects in 1991 requested legal advice, after receiving warnings similar to those in *Miranda.* David Brown, Tom Ellis & Karen Larcombe, Changing the Code: Police Detention Under the Revised PACE Codes of Practice, Home Office Research and Planning Unit, London HMSO (1992). The tendency to waive the right to counsel or the right to silence is especially strong among suspects with no prior criminal convictions. Richard Leo, Inside the Interrogation Room, 86 J. Crim. L. & Criminology 266 (1996). Would the repeat offenders who tend more often to invoke their rights be more or less likely than the average offender to provide an incriminating statement in the absence of a warning? If so many suspects waive their rights, is that an indication of *Miranda*'s failure or success? See George Thomas, Is *Miranda* a Real-World Failure? A Plea for More (and Better) Empirical Evidence, 43 UCLA L. Rev. 821 (1996).

3. *Number of confessions or admissions.* The major concern of *Miranda*'s critics is that the warnings change the dynamic between the questioner and the suspect and reduce the number of successful interrogations, even when the suspect agrees to talk to the police. A number of empirical studies attempt to measure the "success rate" for interrogations immediately before and after the *Miranda* decision. A Pittsburgh study concluded that 48.5 percent of suspects confessed before *Miranda* while 32.3 percent confessed after *Miranda.* Richard Seeburger & Stanton Wettick, *Miranda* in Pittsburgh — A Statistical Analysis, 29 U. Pitt. L. Rev. 1 (1967). The "Seaside City"

(California) study noted above pointed to a pre-*Miranda* confession rate of 68.9 percent and a post-*Miranda* rate of 66.9 percent. This study included only suspects who were arrested and incarcerated; it excluded cases in which suspects were detained for questioning but never incarcerated. The Salt Lake City study, based on cases investigated in 1994, found a success rate of 33.3 percent overall and 42.2 percent of cases where questioning actually occurred. In contrast, a study of interrogations in three California cities in 1992-1993 concluded that 64 percent of all the observed interrogations produced a confession or incriminating admission. Richard Leo, Inside the Interrogation Room, 86 J. Crim. L. & Criminology 266 (1996).

One difficulty in studying this issue is defining what constitutes a "successful" interrogation. The studies all include outright confessions, in which the suspect tells the police that he committed the crime. Many also include some partially successful interrogations leading to "admissions": statements that police and prosecutors can use to prove one or more elements of the crime. Do you agree with the way Cassell and Hayman resolved this issue in the Salt Lake City study? A second difficulty in this debate comes from the (possibly) changing effects of *Miranda* over the 30-plus years since the decision appeared. Is it plausible to think that the confession rate "rebounded" after an initial drop, once police officers adjusted their practices to the new requirements and found the best ways to prevent lost confessions? A reporter who spent one year with homicide detectives in Baltimore (research that later formed the basis for the television series *The Wire*) concluded that the police are able to use the *Miranda* warnings to create an atmosphere of cooperation with at least some suspects. He observed cases in which the suspect's act of acknowledging an understanding of the rights, followed by a waiver of those rights, created some momentum for cooperation during the interrogation. David Simon, Homicide: A Year on the Killing Streets (1991). At the same time, early studies may have *understated* the current effects of *Miranda* because over the years the nature of *Miranda* rights have become more broadly known and understood.

Another difficulty in measuring the effects of *Miranda* on the confession rate is that the warnings and a request for waiving the rights might simultaneously discourage and encourage confessions. Some suspects will refuse to talk once they hear the warnings, while the process of explaining the *Miranda* rights and obtaining a waiver may create a more cooperative atmosphere and lead to more (or more damaging) admissions. George Thomas reviewed the available empirical studies and concluded that they are inconclusive, but still consistent with the view that *Miranda* helps as much as it hurts. Thomas, Plain Talk About the *Miranda* Empirical Debate: A "Steady-State" Theory of Confessions, 43 UCLA L. Rev. 933 (1996).

4. *Number of convictions.* Another measurement of *Miranda*'s effects might come from estimating its impact on the conviction rate. There are two methods of arriving at this number. First, one might compare the percentage of all suspects convicted of crimes in the same location immediately before and after the Court's decision, and presume that some or all of the change in conviction rates was attributable to *Miranda.* Using this method, the Pittsburgh study concluded that the conviction rate was unchanged after the *Miranda* decision. The Seaside City study found a 9 percent decline in the conviction rate (from 92 percent to 83 percent). Is there any problem with this method of estimating the decision's impact on convictions? Second, one might start with an estimate of the number of confessions lost and combine it with some estimate of the proportion of cases in which a confession is essential to obtain a conviction. Multiplying the lost confessions by the number of

cases in which confessions are necessary results in a final estimate. A researcher might estimate the number of cases in which a confession is important by asking for the opinion of prosecutors and others involved in the case. She might also review the case files herself to imagine which cases might have ended differently if a confession were or were not available. Using these methods (or a combination of them), most studies have estimated that confessions are essential in 13 percent to 28 percent of all cases. See Paul Cassell, *Miranda*'s Social Costs, 90 Nw. U. L. Rev. 387 (1996) (summarizing studies and reaching average of 23.8 percent). In choosing which studies of this question are most reliable, what would you want to know?

5. *Number of reversals on appeal.* Yet another measure of *Miranda*'s effects is the number of convictions overturned on appeal because of *Miranda* violations. All the evidence suggests that a trivial number of cases are lost on appeal because of *Miranda.* Peter Nardulli, The Societal Costs of the Exclusionary Rule Revisited, 1987 U. Ill. L. Rev. 223 (confessions suppressed in 0.04 percent of all cases). Why might this be the case when other measures show evidence of a larger *Miranda* impact?

6. *Clearance rates.* An ideal measurement of *Miranda*'s costs over time (such as a reliable account of confession rates before *Miranda* and during the years since) is not available. One indirect measurement of the effects is the "clearance rate," that is, the percentage of reported crimes that the police declare "solved." Those rates, which have been collected and reported since at least 1950, declined just after the *Miranda* decision and have remained at the lower levels since that time. Paul Cassell and Richard Fowles analyzed this data. After attempting to control for other possible explanations for the lower clearance rates, they conclude that "without *Miranda,* the number of crimes cleared would be substantially higher — by as much as 6.6-29.7% for robbery, 6.2-28.9% for burglary, 0.4-11.9% for larceny, and 12.8-45.4% for vehicle theft." Cassell & Fowles, Handcuffing the Cops? A Thirty-Year Perspective on *Miranda*'s Harmful Effects on Law Enforcement, 50 Stan. L. Rev. 1055, 1126 (1998). For what crimes would you expect *Miranda* to have the greatest effect? Would you expect clearance rates to show more or less of an impact than confession rates? See Floyd Feeney, Police Clearances: A Poor Way to Measure the Impact of *Miranda* on the Police, 32 Rutgers L.J. 1 (2000).

7. *Acceptable costs and benefits.* After resolving all the factual disputes about the actual effects of the *Miranda* decision, one is left with a different type of question: How much of the undesirable effect is too much? If the effects of *Miranda* described thus far could be considered the "costs" of the decision, are there any corresponding benefits? What are those benefits and how might one measure them and compare them to the costs?

3. Alternatives to Miranda

Miranda continues to be the subject of criticism, though law enforcement officers in particular have become more supportive of *Miranda* as they have made it part of their routine. Remember that the Court in *Miranda* expressly invited legislatures to find alternative methods for protecting the privilege against self-incrimination.

> It is impossible for us to foresee the potential alternatives for protecting the privilege which might be devised by Congress or the States in the exercise of their creative

rule-making capacities. Therefore we cannot say that the Constitution necessarily requires adherence to any particular solution for the inherent compulsions of the interrogation process as it is presently conducted. Our decision in no way creates a constitutional straitjacket which will handicap sound efforts at reform, nor is it intended to have this effect. . . . Congress and the States are free to develop their own safeguards for the privilege, so long as they are fully as effective as those described above in informing accused persons of their right of silence and in affording a continuous opportunity to exercise it.

What are the alternatives to *Miranda*? The Court in Dickerson v. United States, 530 U.S. 428 (2000), struck down one such effort, a federal statute instructing judges to judge the admissibility of confessions only by the traditional standards of voluntariness. What sort of alternatives might succeed where the 1968 federal statute failed?

Perhaps a legislature could revise the *Miranda* warning to remove aspects most often criticized as obstacles to proper crime-solving techniques. Perhaps interrogations should occur before a judicial officer. Or perhaps a trial jury might later be told of any refusal to make a statement to the magistrate, or the refusal to make a statement to the judicial officer might be punishable as contempt of court. See Akhil Amar & Renee Lettow, Fifth Amendment First Principles: The Self-Incrimination Clause, 93 Mich. L. Rev. 857 (1995); Donald Dripps, Foreword: Against Police Interrogation — And the Privilege Against Self-Incrimination, 78 J. Crim. L. & Criminology 699 (1988). Consider the following approach to interrogations, made possible by technological advances.

■ TEXAS CODE OF CRIMINAL PROCEDURE ART. 38.22

Sec. 2. No written statement made by an accused as a result of custodial interrogation is admissible as evidence against him in any criminal proceeding unless it is shown on the face of the statement that:

(a) the accused, prior to making the statement, . . . received from the person to whom the statement is made a warning that:

(1) he has the right to remain silent and not make any statement at all and that any statement he makes may be used against him at his trial; (2) any statement he makes may be used as evidence against him in court; (3) he has the right to have a lawyer present to advise him prior to and during any questioning; (4) if he is unable to employ a lawyer, he has the right to have a lawyer appointed to advise him prior to and during any questioning; and (5) he has the right to terminate the interview at any time; and

(b) the accused, prior to and during the making of the statement, knowingly, intelligently, and voluntarily waived the rights set out in the warning prescribed by Subsection (a) of this section.

Sec. 3. (a) No oral or sign language statement of an accused made as a result of custodial interrogation shall be admissible against the accused in a criminal proceeding unless:

(1) an electronic recording, which may include motion picture, video tape, or other visual recording, is made of the statement; (2) prior to the statement

but during the recording the accused is given the warning in Subsection (a) of Section 2 above and the accused knowingly, intelligently, and voluntarily waives any rights set out in the warning; (3) the recording device was capable of making an accurate recording, the operator was competent, and the recording is accurate and has not been altered; (4) all voices on the recording are identified; and (5) not later than the 20th day before the date of the proceeding, the attorney representing the defendant is provided with a true, complete, and accurate copy of all recordings of the defendant made under this article. . . .

(c) Subsection (a) of this section shall not apply to any statement which contains assertions of facts or circumstances that are found to be true and which conduce to establish the guilt of the accused, such as the finding of secreted or stolen property or the instrument with which he states the offense was committed. . . . (e) The courts of this state shall strictly construe Subsection (a) of this section and may not interpret Subsection (a) as making admissible a statement unless all requirements of the subsection have been satisfied by the state, except that: (1) only voices that are material are identified; and (2) the accused was given the warning in Subsection (a) of Section 2 above or its fully effective equivalent.

Sec. 4. When any statement, the admissibility of which is covered by this article, is sought to be used in connection with an official proceeding, any person who swears falsely to facts and circumstances which, if true, would render the statement admissible under this article is presumed to have acted with intent to deceive and with knowledge of the statement's meaning for the purpose of prosecution for aggravated perjury. . . . No person prosecuted under this subsection shall be eligible for probation.

Sec. 5. Nothing in this article precludes the admission of a statement made by the accused in open court at his trial, before a grand jury, or at an examining trial . . . , or of a statement that does not stem from custodial interrogation, or of a voluntary statement, whether or not the result of custodial interrogation, that has a bearing upon the credibility of the accused as a witness, or of any other statement that may be admissible under law.

DONALD STEPHAN v. STATE

711 P.2d 1156 (Alaska 1985)

BURKE, J.

More than five years ago, in Mallott v. State, 608 P.2d 737 (Alaska 1980), we informed Alaska law enforcement officials that "it is incumbent upon them to tape record, where feasible, any questioning [of criminal suspects,] and particularly that which occurs in a place of detention." This requirement (hereinafter the *Mallott* rule) was again noted in S.B. v. State, 614 P.2d 786 (Alaska 1980), with the observation that an electronic record of such interviews "will be a great aid" when courts are called upon to determine "the circumstances of a confession or other waiver of [a suspect's] *Miranda* rights." In a third case, McMahan v. State, 617 P.2d 494 (Alaska 1980), the recording requirement was repeated, with the further statement that "if *Miranda* rights are read to the defendant, this too should be recorded." Today, we hold that an unexcused failure to electronically record a custodial interrogation conducted in a place of detention violates a suspect's right to due process, under the Alaska Constitution, and that any statement thus obtained is generally inadmissible.[2]

The relevant facts in the two cases now before us are similar. Malcolm Scott Harris and Donald Stephan, petitioners, were arrested on unrelated criminal charges, taken to police stations and questioned by police officers. Harris was interrogated on two separate occasions; Stephan was interrogated only once. Both men made inculpatory statements. In each instance, a working audio or video recorder was in the room and was used during part, but not all, of the interrogation. The officers, in each case, offered no satisfactory excuse for their clear disregard of the *Mallott* rule.[3]

Prior to their respective trials, Harris and Stephan both moved to suppress confessions made during their interrogations. At the suppression hearings there was conflicting testimony about what occurred during the unrecorded portions of the interviews. Harris claimed that, in his first interrogation, he was not informed of his *Miranda* rights at the beginning of the session, that the questioning continued after he asserted his right to remain silent, and that the officer made threats and promises during the untaped portions. Stephan claimed that his ultimate confession was induced by promises of leniency and was obtained in the absence of an attorney, after he requested one. In both cases, the officers' testimony was to the contrary. Without a full recording to resolve the conflict, the superior court was required to evaluate the credibility of the witnesses and choose which version of the unrecorded events to believe. In each case, the court chose the police officers' recollections and determined that the confession was voluntary and, thus, admissible at trial. Harris and Stephan were ultimately found guilty and filed notices of appeal. . . .

In its decision, the court of appeals acknowledged: "The supreme court has clearly stated in three separate cases that the police are under a duty to record statements which suspects make where recording is feasible. That admonition cannot be ignored." The court, nevertheless, refused to adopt a general exclusionary rule, stating:

> We believe that the issue of what sanction is appropriate is best approached on a case by case basis. . . . Exactly what sanction, if any, to apply for the failure to record a defendant's statement in a given case is a decision which is best left to the sound discretion of the trial court. . . .

The court of appeals' refusal to adopt an exclusionary rule in these circumstances is perhaps due to failure on our part to adequately explain the full significance of our prior decisions. Electronic recording of suspect interrogations was

2. We are not alone in recognizing the importance of recording custodial interrogations. See Hendricks v. Swenson, 456 F.2d 503 (8th Cir. 1972) (suggesting that videotapes of interrogations protect a defendant's rights and are a step forward in the search for truth); Ragan v. State, 642 S.W.2d 489 (Tex. Crim. App. 1982) (Tex. Code Crim. Proc. Ann. art. 38.22, §3, requiring that oral statements of the accused during custodial interrogations must be recorded in order to be admissible); Model Code of Pre-Arraignment Procedure §130.4 (Proposed Official Draft 1975) (requiring sound recordings of custodial interviews). . . .

3. One officer stated that it was "normal practice" to get the suspect's statement "laid out in the desired manner," and only then record the full, formal confession. Another officer explained that a suspect is more at ease and likely to talk without a tape recorder running.

described in those cases, rather ambiguously, as "part of a law enforcement agency's duty to preserve evidence." Today, we resolve that ambiguity. Such recording is a requirement of state due process when the interrogation occurs in a place of detention and recording is feasible. We reach this conclusion because we are convinced that recording, in such circumstances, is now a reasonable and necessary safeguard, essential to the adequate protection of the accused's right to counsel, his right against self incrimination and, ultimately, his right to a fair trial. . . . Thus, as we have done on previous occasions, we construe Alaska's constitutional provision, in this instance, as affording rights beyond those guaranteed by the United States Constitution. . . .

The contents of an interrogation are obviously material in determining the voluntariness of a confession. The state usually attempts to show voluntariness through the interrogating officer's testimony that the defendant's constitutional rights were protected. The defendant, on the other hand, often testifies to the contrary. The result, then, is a swearing match between the law enforcement official and the defendant, which the courts must resolve.

> The difficulty in depicting what transpires at such interrogations stems from the fact that in this country they have largely taken place incommunicado. . . . Interrogation still takes place in privacy. Privacy results in secrecy and this in turn results in a gap in our knowledge as to what in fact goes on in the interrogation rooms. [Miranda v. Arizona, 384 U.S. at 445, 448.]

Thus, we believe a recording requirement is justified, because a tape recording provides an objective means for evaluating what occurred during interrogation. . . .

In the absence of an accurate record, the accused may suffer an infringement upon his right to remain silent and to have counsel present during the interrogation. Also, his right to a fair trial may be violated, if an illegally obtained, and possibly false, confession is subsequently admitted. An electronic recording, thus, protects the defendant's constitutional rights, by providing an objective means for him to corroborate his testimony concerning the circumstances of the confession.

The recording of custodial interrogations is not, however, a measure intended to protect only the accused; a recording also protects the public's interest in honest and effective law enforcement, and the individual interests of those police officers wrongfully accused of improper tactics. A recording, in many cases, will aid law enforcement efforts, by confirming the content and the voluntariness of a confession, when a defendant changes his testimony or claims falsely that his constitutional rights were violated. In any case, a recording will help trial and appellate courts to ascertain the truth.

The concept of due process is not static; among other things, it must change to keep pace with new technological developments. For example, the gathering and preservation of breath samples was previously impractical. Now that this procedure is technologically feasible, many states require it, either as a matter of due process or by resort to reasoning akin to a due process analysis. The use of audio and video tapes is even more commonplace in today's society. The police already make use of recording devices in circumstances when it is to their advantage to do so. Examples would be the routine video recording of suspect behavior in drunk driving cases and, as was done in these cases, the recording of formal confessions. Furthermore, media reports indicate that many Alaska police officers have purchased their own recorders, carry them while on duty and regularly record conversations with suspects or witnesses, in order to protect themselves against false accusations. When a portable recorder has not been available, some officers have even used their patrol car radio to record conversations through the police dispatch center.

In both of the cases before us, the police were engaged in custodial interrogations of suspects in a place of detention. A working recording device was readily available, but was used to record only part of the questioning. Compliance with the recording rule is not unduly burdensome under these circumstances. Turning the recorder on a few minutes earlier entails minimal cost and effort. In return, less time, money and resources would have been consumed in resolving the disputes that arose over the events that occurred during the interrogations.

The only real reason advanced by police for their frequent failure to electronically record an entire interrogation is their claim that recordings tend to have a "chilling effect" on a suspect's willingness to talk. Given the fact that an accused has a constitutional right to remain silent, under both the state and federal constitutions, and that he must be clearly warned of that right prior to any custodial interrogation, this argument is not persuasive.

In summary, the rule that we adopt today requires that custodial interrogations in a place of detention, including the giving of the accused's *Miranda* rights, must be electronically recorded. To satisfy this due process requirement, the recording must clearly indicate that it recounts the entire interview. Thus, explanations should be given at the beginning, the end and before and after any interruptions in the recording, so that courts are not left to speculate about what took place.

Since its announcement, the *Mallott* rule has always included a proviso, "when feasible." The failure to electronically record an entire custodial interrogation will, therefore, be considered a violation of the rule, and subject to exclusion, only if the failure is unexcused. Acceptable excuses might include an unavoidable power or equipment failure, or a situation where the suspect refuses to answer any questions if the conversation is being recorded. We need not anticipate all such possible excuses here, for courts must carefully scrutinize each situation on a case-by-case basis. Any time a full recording is not made, however, the state must persuade the trial court, by a preponderance of the evidence, that recording was not feasible under the circumstances, and in such cases the failure to record should be viewed with distrust.

[We] adopt a general rule of exclusion. While other remedies may each have their merits, we believe an exclusionary rule will best protect the suspects' constitutional rights, provide clear direction to law enforcement agencies and lower courts, and preserve the integrity of our justice system.

[Law] enforcement agencies and lower courts have repeatedly failed to give due regard to the protections the *Mallott* rule is intended to provide, even though the rule was first announced over five years ago. We believe that a strong and certain remedy will have a considerable deterrent effect in future cases. Compliance imposes such minimal costs and burdens on law enforcement agencies that they will have little to gain from noncompliance. . . .

The imposition of sanctions against an individual officer will not necessarily solve what appears to be a systemic problem. Agency policy and operations must change, not simply individual behaviors. Once they are fully aware of the consequences of unexcused violations of the *Mallott* rule, we are confident that law enforcement agencies will establish effective procedures to implement the rule and provide adequate training for their personnel. Suppression of statements taken in violation of the rule will, therefore, deter continued disregard of its requirements by officers, agencies and courts.

Another purpose is also served by the rule that we now adopt. The integrity of our judicial system is subject to question whenever a court rules on the admissibility of a questionable confession, based solely upon the court's acceptance of the testimony of an interested party, whether it be the interrogating officer or the defendant. This is especially true when objective evidence of the circumstances surrounding the confession could have been preserved by the mere flip of a switch. Routine and systematic recording of custodial interrogations will provide such evidence, and avoid any suggestion that the court is biased in favor of either party.

Most importantly, an exclusionary rule furthers the protection of individual constitutional rights. Strong protection is needed to insure that a suspect's right to counsel, his privilege against self incrimination, and due process guarantees are protected. A confession is generally such conclusive evidence of guilt that a rule of exclusion is justified, when the state, without excuse, fails to preserve evidence of the interchange leading up to the formal statement. [E]xclusion of the defendant's statement is the only remedy which will correct the wrong that has been done and place the defendant in the same position he or she would have been in had the evidence been preserved and turned over in time for use at trial. . . .

Thus, we conclude that exclusion is the appropriate remedy for an unexcused failure to electronically record an interrogation, when such recording is feasible. A general exclusionary rule is the only remedy that provides crystal clarity to law enforcement agencies, preserves judicial integrity, and adequately protects a suspect's constitutional rights. The necessity for this strong remedy remains, even when we consider society's interests in crime prevention and the apprehension of criminal offenders. Exclusion of reliable, yet unrecorded, statements will not occur frequently when compliance is widespread.[33]

Despite what we have said thus far, we recognize that nearly every rule must have its exceptions, and that exclusion of a defendant's statements in certain instances would be wholly unreasonable. A violation of the *Mallott* rule does not, therefore, require exclusion of the defendant's statements in all cases. Thus, the holding in this case does not bar the admission of statements obtained before a violation of the recording rule occurs. Where recording ceases for some impermissible reason, properly recorded statements made prior to the time recording stops may be admitted, even when the failure to record the balance of the interrogation is unexcused, since such prior statements could not be tainted by anything that occurred thereafter. Also, failure to record part of an interrogation does not bar the introduction of a defendant's recorded statements, if the unrecorded portion of the interrogation is, by all accounts, innocuous. In such cases, there is no reason to

33. Caveat: We recognize that many custodial interrogations must take place in the field, where recording may not be feasible. Because of this, the rule that we announce today has limited application; it applies only to custodial interrogations conducted in a place of detention, such as a police station or jail, where it is reasonable to assume that recording equipment is available, or can be made available with little effort. In a future case, however, we may be persuaded to extend the application of this rule, particularly if it appears that law enforcement officials are engaging in bad faith efforts to circumvent the recording requirement set forth in this opinion.

exclude the defendant's recorded statements, because no claim of material misconduct will be presented. See Alaska R. Crim. P. 47(a) (errors which do not affect substantial rights shall be disregarded). For the same reason, a defendant's unrecorded statement may be admitted if no testimony is presented that the statement is inaccurate or was obtained improperly, apart from violation of the *Mallott* rule. . . .

Notes

1. *Video recording as a constitutional requirement: majority position.* Only the Alaska Supreme Court has required that interrogations be recorded as a constitutional matter. Compare In re Jerrell C.J., 699 N.W.2d 110 (Wis. 2005) (under judicial supervisory power, court requires all station house custodial interrogations of juveniles to be electronically recorded). While the argument has been made in a number of jurisdictions, courts typically have not received it with any sympathy. See, e.g., Brashars v. Commonwealth, 25 S.W.3d 58 (Ky. 2000); State v. Lockhart, 4 A.3d 1176 (Conn. 2010). After *Stephan* was decided the Minnesota Supreme Court, relying on its supervisory authority, mandated recordings of "custodial interrogations" when they occur "at a place of detention." See State v. Scales, 518 N.W.2d 587, 592 (Minn. 1994). Other courts have indicated that recording will weigh strongly in favor of findings of voluntariness.

Was it appropriate for the Alaska Supreme Court to "warn" police and prosecutors about the possibility of a judicially mandated rule unless a recording rule was adopted voluntarily? Would a long history *of Miranda* and voluntariness violations in a particular state provide a justification for a state court to mandate a recording rule? Can constitutional remedies be supported by the failure of all other remedies to end or diminish serious constitutional violations? See People v. Cahan, reprinted in Chapter 6 (arguing that the exclusionary rule was necessary because no other remedy had worked to control police searches and seizures).

2. *Video recording as a statutory requirement.* Texas is one of only a few states in which the legislature has implemented a statutory video recording requirement. See Brandon Garrett, Judging Innocence, 108 Colum. L. Rev. 55, 123 (2008) (documents spreading use of video recorded interrogations in police departments, and legislation in six jurisdictions — the District of Columbia, Illinois, Maine, New Mexico, Texas, and North Carolina — requiring video recording of interrogations for at least some categories of investigations). It may be easy to understand why other states have not been swayed by the Alaska decision in *Stephan* to mandate recording as a constitutional matter, but why have states been reluctant to mandate recording by statute? Why not video record every interrogation and confession? Do police departments think use of video recording will lead to fewer confessions? Do legislatures think that video recording policies should be left to local police and prosecutors to implement? If you drafted a new law requiring that in general interrogations and confessions be video recorded, what requirements, exceptions, and limitations would you include?

3. *Police discretion to video record interrogations and confessions.* A 1990 survey showed that about one-sixth of the 14,000 police and sheriffs' departments, and one-third of the 710 departments serving populations over 50,000, video recorded some interrogations or confessions. William Geller, Videotaping Interrogations and Confessions: NIJ Research in Brief (NCJ 139962, 1993). Given the prevalence of the

technology and prominent recommendations for its use, video recording of interrogations and confessions may now be even more likely to happen. The use of DNA evidence to establish definitively that false confession led to a surprising number of wrongful convictions has added momentum to the voluntary adoption of video recording by police departments. See Jeremy W. Peters, "Wrongful Conviction Prompts Detroit Police to Videotape Certain Interrogations," N.Y. Times, April 11, 2006 (at least 450 police departments in United States record interrogations, in some cases prompted by concerns about false confessions).

Periodic surveys of law enforcement agencies find that they record interrogations most often in homicide and rape investigations and for other serious crimes. The officers in jurisdictions that use video recording believe that it leads to better preparation by detectives and better monitoring of detectives' work by supervisors. They also believe that it produces stronger evidence of guilt and induces more guilty pleas. Most agencies find suspects less willing to talk when video recording takes place. Not surprisingly, surveys find that video recording leads to fewer claims against police that they had coerced or intimidated a suspect or fabricated a confession. Prosecutors are generally more supportive of video recording interrogations than are defense attorneys, who find video recordings harder to attack than written or audio recorded confessions. Detectives tend at first to disapprove of recording, but most jurisdictions find a strong shift among detectives in favor of recording once they had experience with its use. See Thomas P. Sullivan, et al., The Case for Recording Police Interrogations, Litigation, Volume 34, Number 3 (Spring 2008) (telephone survey of more than 600 departments that record interrogations).

4. *Administrative issues in recording.* Most police departments record interrogations openly or ask the subject about recording. Some police departments, however, use surreptitious recording equipment. Such practices reduce the chance that the use of video recording will discourage suspects from confessing (since they will not know they are being recorded). What reasons might there be not to record surreptitiously? See Matthews v. Commonwealth, 168 S.W.3d 14 (Ky. 2005) (police interrogators may lie to suspect about whether they are recording his statements). Must police record the whole interrogation, or is it necessary to record only the defendant's confession and summary after interrogation? Suppose the interrogation takes seven hours but the summary only 30 minutes. Should the cost of the recording medium factor into the decision whether to record the entire confession? What about the cost of making transcripts? Does the emergence of technology that automatically makes a rough transcription of speech ironically make recording interrogations more functional? See State v. Barnett, 789 A.2d 629 (N.H. 2001) (under supervisory power, court requires any video recording of interrogation admitted into evidence to be complete). In some jurisdictions defense counsel are not given immediate access to recorded interrogations and confessions. Some prosecutors show defense counsel recorded confessions but object to making copies. Other jurisdictions do not give defense counsel access to video recordings until after indictment or for a period of time after the interrogation.

5. *Is video recording an "alternative" to* Miranda? What would be the judicial response to fully video recorded but unwarned confessions in a jurisdiction whose legislature took the U.S. Supreme Court's invitation and passed a mandatory recording statute expressly to take the place of *Miranda* warnings in protecting each suspect's Fifth Amendment rights? Is there any reason not to record interrogations and confessions along with providing *Miranda* warnings? Would you expect foreign

jurisdictions, without the constraints or protections of *Miranda,* to be more or less hesitant to adopt recording procedures? The 1991 Code of Practice for Interrogation in England requires that all interviews be recorded, wherever they occur, unless it is impracticable to do so. See M. McConville & P. Morrell, Recording the Interrogation: Have the Police Got It Taped?, 1983 Crim. L. Rev. 159 (noting an increase after appearance of Code of Practice in spontaneous confessions allegedly spoken before the video was running); Paul Marcus & Vicki Waye, Australia and the United States: Two Common Criminal Justice Systems Uncommonly at Odds, 12 Tulane J. Int'l & Comp. L. 27 (2004).

6. *Confessions, lies, and video recording.* Recording interrogations and confessions seems to solve a number of problems, such as reducing or eliminating the frequent claims by suspects that they were threatened or that they did not in fact confess or say what the police say they did. But does recording make all confessions look voluntary even when they have been compelled by forces not visible (or audible) on the recording? Won't recording create a whole new set of factual issues about whether the recording is complete? Is taping of interrogations and confessions a great reform for a past era?

Perhaps it is not the requirement of warnings but the content of the warnings that needs rethinking. Consider the following reform in Great Britain and its implications for the warnings offered suspects during investigations.

■ UNITED KINGDOM, CRIMINAL JUSTICE AND PUBLIC ORDER ACT OF 1994, §34

(1) Where, in any proceedings against a person for an offence, evidence is given that the accused . . . at any time before he was charged with the offence, on being questioned under caution by a constable trying to discover whether or by whom the offence had been committed, failed to mention any fact relied on in his defence in those proceedings . . . being a fact which in the circumstances existing at the time the accused could reasonably have been expected to mention when so questioned, charged or informed, as the case may be, subsection (2) below applies.

(2) Where this subsection applies . . . the court, in determining whether there is a case to answer; [or] the court or jury, in determining whether the accused is guilty of the offence charged, may draw such inferences from the failure as appear proper.

Notes

1. *Warnings in Great Britain and elsewhere in Europe.* Great Britain changed the law relating to the warnings that suspects must receive before interrogation. Under the old law (which goes back to the nineteenth century and was embodied in the Police and Criminal Evidence Act of 1984), suspects were told, "You do not have to say anything unless you wish to do so, but what you say may be given in evidence." The 1984 act (and the related Code of Practice promulgated by the government a year later) also required that the police inform suspects in custody that they have a right to consult an attorney before any interrogation, that the police make available a

"duty solicitor" for suspects who want advice, and that the warnings be given both orally and in writing. How does the 1994 statute, reprinted above, change these practices?

Some form of warnings about the right to silence and the consequences of speaking (or not speaking) are now standard practice in many European nations. For instance, suspects in France are informed of the right to silence and to consult counsel during detention, but they are not entitled to have counsel present during interrogation. In Germany, police must inform suspects of the right to remain silent when they become the focus of an investigation. The warnings also inform suspects of their right to consult a defense attorney *prior* to interrogation, although there is no right to counsel during interrogation. If the suspect chooses to remain silent, police may continue to question the suspect. German courts prohibit the police from making affirmative misrepresentations during interrogations. See Christopher Slobogin, An Empirically Based Comparison of American and European Regulatory Approaches to Police Investigation, 22 Mich. J. Int'l L. 423, 442-45 (2001); Stephen C. Thaman, *Miranda* in Comparative Law, 45 St. Louis U. L.J. 581 (2001).

2. *Warnings about silence.* Would the 1994 English statute be consistent with the Fifth Amendment to the U.S. Constitution? Would it have any effect on the everyday practices of criminal investigators? Should the Fifth Amendment also require a warning to a suspect that "silence cannot be used against you"?

IX

Identifications

Eyewitnesses to crime can provide some of the most convincing evidence to support a conviction. This is especially true when the physical evidence linking the defendant to the crime is thin, or when the offender is a stranger to others at the scene (as in many robbery cases). All too often, however, this important evidence turns out to be unreliable. How do legal institutions respond to the special value and risks of eyewitness identifications?

This chapter explores this question. Section A reviews some of the psychological literature detailing the risks of eyewitness identifications. Section B surveys the conditions that lead courts to exclude evidence coming from in-person identifications (both in the field and at the police station) and from identifications of photographs. Section C considers the remedies other than exclusion of evidence that are available to a defendant who believes that an identification procedure was unreliable.

A. RISKS OF MISTAKEN IDENTIFICATION

Eyewitnesses are wrong in a disturbing number of cases. One famous example involves the case of Ronald Cotton. One night in 1984, a man broke into the apartment of Jennifer Thompson, who was then a 22-year-old college student in Burlington, North Carolina. The intruder raped Thompson. When police received an anonymous tip in the case, they showed Thompson several photographs of potential suspects, and she picked the photograph of Ronald Cotton. Cotton was a plausible suspect, who had been convicted in 1980 of attempted rape and had recently been released from prison. Although there was no physical evidence linking

Cotton to the crime, the jury convicted based on Thompson's confident identification of Cotton during the trial as the man who had raped her. The judge sentenced him to 50 years in prison. Eleven years later, lawyers for Cotton arranged for DNA tests on some of the physical evidence in the case. The tests conclusively established that Cotton was the wrong man. The evidence pointed instead to Bobby Poole — already convicted and serving a prison term for another sexual assault — and Poole later confessed to the rape of Thompson. Jennifer Thompson-Cannino, Ronald Cotton, & Erin Torneo, Picking Cotton: Our Memoir of Injustice and Redemption (2009).

One famous example, of course, does not tell us how often the problem arises in criminal justice systems that produce millions of criminal convictions each year. How often does a mistaken identification lead to an erroneous conviction? Nobody really knows since we have no convincing way to identify all the wrongful convictions.

It is possible, however, to estimate the importance of mistaken identifications *relative to other causes* of the wrongful convictions we have learned about over the years. Over the last few years, the widespread availability of DNA testing has confirmed many examples of wrongful convictions. Far and away the most common cause of these errors is mistaken identifications by eyewitnesses. See Brandon L. Garrett, Convicting the Innocent: Where Criminal Prosecutions Go Wrong (2011).

Psychologists have studied witness memory in great detail over the years. The following summary of psychological research may suggest some of the reasons why eyewitness identifications sometimes lead to erroneous convictions. Given the commonplace nature of these identification errors, what are the implications for legal systems? What changes in the pertinent rules might address these predictable failures of witnesses?

■ RALPH NORMAN HABER AND LYN HABER, EXPERIENCING, REMEMBERING AND REPORTING EVENTS

6 Psychol. Pub. Pol'y & L. 1057-91 (2000)

[Consider] the following description of a bank robbery, drawn from actual cases. Several men entered a bank, tied up the only guard in the lobby, told the customers to lie down on the floor, and demanded that the tellers hand over all their money. The robbers then left. There were five tellers, two officers, one guard, and five customers in the bank at the time. When the police took their statements over the next hour, there was little consensus among the thirteen witnesses as to the number of robbers, what they looked like, what they did, the presence of weapons, or the duration of the robbery.

Video cameras in the bank recorded the robbery. Comparing these recordings to the descriptions provided by the witnesses, it was found that no single witness gave an accurate report of the sequence of events, nor did any single witness provide a consistently accurate description of any of the robbers. Further, in subsequent photo identification line-ups, half of the witnesses made serious errors: Four of the thirteen witnesses erroneously selected as a perpetrator one of the other people who had been in the bank at the time of the robbery (a teller or a customer), and three of the thirteen erroneously selected a photograph of someone who had not been there at all at the time. All seven of these witnesses asserted that they were sure they had correctly identified one of the robbers and that they were willing to so testify. . . .

The purpose of this article is to summarize the scientific evidence on the accuracy of eyewitness testimony, with specific attention to the factors that enhance or impair the likelihood of accuracy. . . .

OBSERVING AND ENCODING EVENTS INTO MEMORY

In this first section, we consider the factors that might lead witnesses to make and remember differing observations of the same event. . . .

Observational point of view. In the bank robbery described earlier, the customers forced to lie down on the floor had less opportunity to view from the front those robbers who approached the teller booths, whereas some of the tellers had frontal views. Therefore, those tellers should be able to give more detailed descriptions of the appearance of those robbers, and in the absence of other factors, those descriptions are more likely to be accurate. It is critical in evaluating a witness's statements about an event to be sure that the witness had a sufficient opportunity to view the event from a position consistent with the statements being given. . . . In addition to distance, lighting conditions, especially back lighting, reflections, and shadows impact the ability to see fine details. . . .

Allocation of Attention. Attention is memory's gatekeeper. At any moment your five senses are bombarded with vast amounts of external stimulation. [For] encoding to occur, you must attend to [stimulation] during the time it impinges on your senses. [The] deployment of attention has two consequences: it allows you to encode and retain memory of some aspects of what happens to you, and it allows the remainder to slip away and be lost forever.

[You] can switch attention quickly. Any change in stimulation, such as a loud noise, or a movement off to the side, will cause you to orient your attention to it. That re-orientation allows you to encode sudden changes in what is happening, though at the expense of what you had been attending to just previously, which then stops being accessible for encoding into memory. When driving comfortably, it is possible to divide your attention so you can control the car while conversing with a passenger. However, a sudden squeal of brakes refocuses your attention exclusively on the emergency, and you cannot remember what your passenger said during that interval.

This focusing is not simply like moving your eyes. [What] you as an observer will encode about an event depends on where and how your attention is focused, not just where you happen to be looking. Most important, it is possible for events to occur directly in front of you, well within your range of seeing and hearing, and yet make no impact on your memory if you were attending to something else at the time. . . .

Bias in Attentional Focus. [Frequently] some aspect of an event causes an involuntary narrowing of attention to some particular detail, so much so that other parts of the event are not attended to at all, and therefore not encoded into memory. One area of great legal importance concerns the narrowing of attention that occurs for most witnesses when they detect the presence of a weapon. People focus their attention on the weapon so much that almost everything else that's happening goes unnoticed and therefore unremembered. . . . Specifically, scientific research on "weapon focus" has shown that, when a weapon is present, witnesses are far less able to remember distinctive features of the people present, including those of the person holding the weapon. Hence, a witness's chances of making a correct identification of a person are reduced if that person held a weapon.

It is equally likely that a narrowing of attention will occur, with its concomitant loss in encoding, whenever any component of the event is highly dramatic, frightening, violent, or distasteful to the witness. It should always be assumed that violence in any form narrows attention, and that which is outside the resultant narrowed attention is encoded less completely, if at all. . . .

Knowledge, Familiarity, and Expertise with the Content of the Event. In the course of everyday life, you are highly familiar with aspects of your work, both inside your home and at your jobsite. If you work as a supermarket clerk, you are likely to be far more knowledgeable than most people about a wide range of edible products; if you are a car salesman, you know a lot about the makes of cars. Within your own sphere, you are an expert. Bystander-witnesses are often required to testify about details of what they observed, such as the characteristics of a vehicle or a weapon. If the eyewitness has little knowledge of that class of objects, the witness's reports about the object are often incomplete or simply wrong. . . .

Similarly, lack of familiarity has been demonstrated in scientific experiments to lead to inaccurate identification of people. The adage that "all Asians look alike (to non-Asians)" is in fact mostly true. In experiments on cross-racial identification, in which the race of the criminal is different from that of the witness and the witness has few close interactions with people of that race, the witness cannot provide as many identifying features of the criminal he observed, thereby making it less likely that subsequent identifications will be accurate. . . .

Witness Expectations and Interpretation of the Event. Research has shown that the beliefs of the witness produce fundamental changes in the reports of what was observed. For example, one study [from 1947] concerned with racial prejudice asked subjects/witnesses to view a scene depicting two men in which one man held a knife: The witnesses were to describe the scene to other people who had not seen it. The two critical contents of the scene that were varied were whether both men were the same race and which one held the knife. When both men were of the same race, nearly all witnesses correctly described the critical element of who held the knife, as well as most of the details of dress and the position of the two men. However, if one man was Black and one White, most witnesses (Black and White alike) reported that the Black man held the knife even when it was held by the White man. Some witnesses who correctly described who held the knife incorrectly added that the White man was defending himself (there was nothing in either man's posture or position to suggest this conclusion). All of the witnesses stated that they believed that crimes were more likely to be committed by Blacks than by Whites. The results suggest that eyewitnesses sometimes encode and remember the event so as to be consistent with their beliefs rather than the way it actually happened. . . .

REMEMBERING EVENTS

Experts on memory research refer to a witness's first report of an observed event, when it is given after the event, as an independent memory. . . . A witness's independent memory report of an event is normally the most accurate description the witness will ever be able to produce. . . .

In normal life, your own independent memories often undergo influences that, in psychological parlance, "taint" them: You dress your stories up for your listeners who did not observe the events, and you discuss the events with other people who also observed them and you incorporate what they say as part of your memory. A tainted memory is not necessarily a false or inaccurate memory, but it is no longer your own, original, independent encoding of the event. It is a compendium of information and detail, some of which you yourself did not see or remember. In this respect, it is analogous to hearsay. . . .

The Inevitably Wrong Focus of Autobiographical Memory. . . . Typically, as an event unfolds, you as an observer are not thinking about describing the other people and their actions: you see the event in terms of how it affects you. The event has all of the properties of a story, with a beginning, middle, and end, and a sequence of actions with one or more actors. The most important actor — the protagonist in your story — is you. . . . As an example of how an eyewitness describes events from a personal point of view, consider one of the eyewitness accounts from a woman who was in the bank described above:

> I stopped at the bank to cash a check. I was putting the money in my purse when armed men ran into the bank, waved their guns at everyone and ordered me to lie down on the floor. One gigantic man, who looked like a football player, stepped over me and I was afraid he would take all of the money I just got I was so scared he would hurt me. He went to the same teller who had just helped me, threatened her with his pistol, and stuffed what she handed him into his bag. After what seemed like hours of terror, all the robbers ran out. They didn't take my money.

This report has little helpful content for the policeman who wants to identify the robbers. The policeman asked her: How many robbers were there? Which ones had guns? What did each of the robbers look like? What were they wearing? What did each of the other robbers do? Every investigator and every interrogator forces the witness to switch from "What happened to you?" to "What happened in the bank?" Hence, almost immediately, the eyewitness is required to change from an autobiographical and psychological focus to an objective focus. This translation usually produces changes in the report, changes that may introduce inaccuracies about the physical reality. . . . In trying to answer the interrogator's questions, the witness often adds content and details that "must have happened" — details not present in independent memory. . . .

Systematic Changes in the Content of Memory with Each Repetition. Unlike a video recording, which remains the same each time it is played, memory undergoes changes with rehearsal. [Each] further repetition of the report produces predictable changes in the report. These predictable changes are, first, that many of the details drop out of the subsequent reports altogether and are never reported again and, second, that other details are altered or additions are made to fit more consistently with the overall description provided by the observer. . . . Further, not surprisingly, observers also are shown to alter their descriptions depending on the audience to whom they are speaking. . . .

These facts about alterations of memory produced by rehearsal are particularly relevant to testimony made by witnesses in court. By the time the witness reaches the stand and is questioned by counsel, she has told her story dozens of times. Often, the first time the story is told is to other observers or to the first new arrivals at the scene. That description, the closest one available from the independent memory of the observer, is usually unrecorded. The first recorded description, taken down by one of the officers at the scene, may already have undergone many changes after several prior rehearsals, each with its smoothings, rearrangements of facts, and attempts to be congruent with what has been learned from other witnesses. This is only the beginning of the rehearsals required of the witness. More than one policeman will demand a repetition; then come the investigators and the lawyers. . . .

Post-Event Information Can Create New (and Potentially) False Memories. The single most dramatic finding in recent memory research concerns changes in reports made by witnesses when other people give them information. Two insidious facts have emerged: First, witnesses are unaware that they have acquired new information from somebody else — the information is treated as if it were part of what they themselves originally observed; and second, witnesses usually are unaware that they have changed their report based on that new information. . . .

Consider some findings from recent research: (a) Embedding a false presupposition into a question (asking "Did the red car stop or run the light just before the crash?" when the car's color has not been previously specified) will often change the witness's subsequent testimony as to the color of the car; (b) varying the intensity of verbs in a question (asking "Did the car hit . . . , Did the car collide . . . , Did the car smash . . . , Did the car demolish . . . ?") will often change the witness's subsequent testimony about the speed of the car; (c) showing a witness line-up pictures of people not involved in the observed event will often result in the witness subsequently choosing one of those innocent people as the criminal, even when the real criminal is present in the later line-up; (d) allowing the witness to overhear a new or different description about the event or about the persons involved will often lead the witness to include the divergent information in subsequent testimony. . . .

Why is it so easy for post-event information to become incorporated into memory? Research has shown that the main reason is that human beings do not have a particularly good memory for the sources of their knowledge about events. When you acquire information about an event from several sources, regardless of how accurate you are in remembering the information itself, you are less accurate about remembering from which source you acquired it. . . .

Encoding, Remembering, and Identifying Strangers

In the preceding sections, we have discussed memory processes without differentiating between memory of events and memory of people. An eyewitness is frequently required to identify an unfamiliar person who might have perpetrated a crime. Such identifications often comprise the only evidence against the defendant. In this section, we focus specifically on what is known about the accuracy of a witness's identification of unfamiliar people from memory. . . .

In a large number of controlled experiments, witnesses have been asked to observe a realistic enactment of a crime committed by a stranger and then to give descriptions of the criminal. Then, after differing periods of time, these witnesses have been asked to attempt to identify whether the perpetrator they observed is present in a line-up. The observation factors studied have included the type of event being observed, length of time of observation, distance and viewing conditions, amount of activity by the stranger, presence of a weapon, presence of frightening events, number of different strangers, amount of stress felt by the eyewitness, and post-event exposure to other people who had been present at the event or who talk to the eyewitness about the event.

[Consider] identification accuracy for research line-ups that are constructed with the known perpetrator present. The first kind of accuracy of concern is whether the witness can discriminate between the true perpetrator and the remaining foils who are innocent of the crime. Based on a large number of experiments, about 75% of the time the perpetrator is correctly selected (true positive); the remaining 25% of the time the witness identifies someone who either was not present at the crime scene, or was a bystander at the scene, but not the criminal (false positive). If no weapon is present, no violence, no bystanders, no post-event contamination, and little delay, true-positive rates can approach 90% (with false-positive rates dropping to a low of about 10%). Conversely, if a weapon is present, the scene is violent, bystanders are present, post-event information is available, the witness feels great stress, and there is a long time delay between observation and identification, the true-positive rate for correct identification of the perpetrator drops well below 50%, with the false-positive rate exceeding 50%. These percentages just quoted are rough consensual estimates, based on the results of perhaps 100 experiments with line-ups. . . .

The fallibility of the eyewitness becomes even more evident when results of lineup research are considered in which the perpetrator is known not to be in the lineup. Now the correct response for the eyewitness is to say "no," none of the people in the line-up is the perpetrator. The results show that, on average, under normal observation conditions, eyewitnesses still say "yes" (that someone present is the perpetrator) about 60% of the time when the perpetrator is known to be absent! All of these "yes" responses are false positives: The eyewitness has identified an innocent person. Only under the most favorable observation conditions (as described in the previous section) is there some reduction in the false-positive rates (with the perpetrator absent). Even more seriously, "yes" responses are found to increase to a high of 90% (a 90% false-positive rate of identifying an innocent person incorrectly as the perpetrator who committed the crime) when the observation conditions are poor, and the eyewitness is led to believe that the perpetrator is present. . . .

We have presented an array of scientific research evidence showing that, by the time an eyewitness testifies in court, the identification and testimony offered may not accurately reflect either what actually happened, or what was originally observed. . . . The recent examples of DNA evidence being used to reverse convictions that had been originally based on only eyewitness identifications suggest that there are in fact many innocent people who have been wrongly convicted on the basis of erroneous eyewitness testimony. . . .

Notes

1. *Relative importance of different memory problems.* The psychological studies described above identify problems at the encoding, storage, and retrieval phases of memory that might affect the accuracy of an eyewitness identification. Which of the various problems a witness might encounter will have the largest impact on the memory? In one effort to answer this question, researchers performed a statistical analysis (known as a "meta-analysis") on the results of more than 190 studies of eyewitness performance. The analysis measured the relative effects of many different obstacles and aids to accurate memory. The authors concluded that "context

reinstatement" was among the most important contributing factors to an accurate identification: For instance, if the target was placed in the same pose at the initial exposure and at the later time of recognition (or asked to wear a distinctive piece of clothing or speak words that the witness recalled from the original incident), the accuracy of the witness identifications increased. The other factors having the largest effect on witness accuracy include the distinctiveness of the target, exposure time, age of the witness, cross-racial identification, and amount of time elapsed between the original event and the recognition exercise. See Peter Shapiro & Steven Penrod, Meta-Analysis of Facial Identification Studies, 100 Psychol. Bull. 139 (1986). For a sampling of the rich psychological literature on eyewitness observation and memory, consult the web extension for this chapter at *http://www.crimpro.com/extension/ch09*.

The psychological experiments described above test human memory, but they often take place in a setting different from what an actual crime victim might face. What might those differences be? Would they make a crime witness more or less likely than an experimental "subject" to give an accurate identification?

2. *Cross-racial identifications.* Unfortunately, there is some truth to the distasteful phrase, "They [people of another race] all look alike." Research studies for over thirty years have found an empirical basis for saying that people of one race find it more difficult to identify people of another race. A witness's difficulty in making such identifications seems to be tied to unfamiliarity: People who have more regular contact with those of another race have less difficulty making such identifications. The so-called "own-race bias" accounts for about 15 percent of the variation in the ability of witnesses to identify another person. See Christian A. Meissner & John C. Brigham, Eyewitness Identification: Thirty Years of Investigating the Own-Race Bias in Memory for Faces: A Meta-Analytic Review, 7 Psychol. Pub. Pol'y & L. 3 (2001).

3. *Individual recognition skills and witness certainty.* It is important to remember that these difficulties with memory address only trends and averages: Any individual witness might be affected less (or more) by such problems. Unfortunately, it is difficult to determine whether a particular witness is above average or below average in her ability to identify a crime suspect. The age of a witness is one of the few consistently helpful indicators: Children tend to make less accurate identifications, mostly because they are substantially more suggestible than adults. See M. Bruck & S. J. Ceci, The Description of Children's Suggestibility, in Memory for Everyday and Emotional Events (Stein, Ornstein, Tversky & Brainerd eds., 1997). Witnesses over 70 are less accurate when describing events that are especially unfamiliar, or those that unfold quickly with many distractions present. See Daniel Yarmey, The Elderly Witness, in Psychological Issues in Eyewitness Identification (Sporer, Malpass & Koehnken eds., 1996).

One might be tempted to rely on the witness's level of certainty to identify the most "able" witnesses, i.e., the witness who says, "I'm absolutely sure it was him." But witness certainty, it turns out, is not a good measure of accuracy. As one summary of the psychological literature put it, "[The] eyewitness accuracy-confidence relationship is weak under good laboratory conditions and functionally useless in forensically representative settings." Gary Wells & Donna Murray, Eyewitness Confidence, in Eyewitness Testimony: Psychological Perspectives 155 (Gary Wells & Elizabeth Loftus eds., 1984).

4. *Police officers as witnesses.* Sometimes the witness to a crime is a police officer, who may have special training in facial recognition techniques. Does the special training and experience of police officers increase their accuracy as eyewitnesses? The evidence on this question is equivocal. On the one hand, police officers (as well as untrained witnesses) tend to have more complete and accurate memories if they are able to anticipate an event and know that they will later need to recall it accurately. A police officer may be in a good position to anticipate the need for later recall. On the other hand, a number of studies have concluded that police officers and others with special training fare no better than other witnesses under realistic eyewitness conditions.

5. *Early forgetting.* Some of the earliest research in memory showed that more forgetting happens early. We forget very rapidly immediately after an event — usually within a few hours — but forgetting becomes more and more gradual as time passes. See Elizabeth Loftus, Eyewitness Testimony 21-83 (1979). What are the implications of this research for police work?

6. *Words and memory.* Some memory problems arise simply from the fact that investigators ask the witness to express the memory in words. Laboratory studies found that memories for a mock criminal's face were much poorer among eyewitnesses who had described what the perpetrator looked like shortly after seeing him compared with those who had not formulated a description in words. The problem is known as "verbal overshadowing of visual memories." Bruce Bower, Words Get in the Way: Talk Is Cheap, but It Can Tax Your Memory, Science News, April 19, 2003.

B. EXCLUSION OF IDENTIFICATION EVIDENCE

Witnesses identify potential suspects in several settings. The most formal identification procedures — and the easiest to subject to legal controls — occur in the police station. The "lineup" places a small group of persons before the witness; the witness is asked if any person in the lineup is the person who committed the crime. In another identification technique that often takes place in a police station, the witness reviews photographs of different persons to identify a suspect. Finally, there are "confrontations" or "showups," in which the police ask the witness to view the suspect alone. This sort of identification occurs most frequently in the field, near the crime scene, but it can also occur at the station.

Until the mid-1960s, the legal system relied on adversarial testing of evidence to control these identification procedures. If a "showup" produced unreliable evidence, defense counsel was expected to point this out. But in recent decades, federal and state constitutions (and to a lesser extent, statutes and court rules) have required the exclusion of some evidence obtained during identification procedures. The constitutional controls derive from (1) the right to counsel clauses and (2) the due process clauses of the federal and state constitutions. Courts have declared a select group of identification procedures invalid unless they take place with counsel for the defendant present. For a larger group of identification procedures, defendants make claims based on the due process clause, arguing that the identifications were too unreliable to be admitted as evidence. The following materials explore the right-to-counsel and due process limitations in several common settings.

1. Exclusion on Right to Counsel Grounds

The Sixth Amendment to the U.S. Constitution provides that "In all criminal prosecutions, the accused shall . . . have the Assistance of Counsel for his defence." Every state constitution except one (Virginia's) also provides explicitly for legal counsel in criminal cases. A number describe the point at which the right to counsel attaches by using phrases such as "appear" or "defend," as in New York's article I, section 6: "In any trial in any court whatever the party accused shall be allowed to appear and defend in person and with counsel. . . . " Others speak in terms of a right to be "heard" through counsel, as in New Hampshire's article 15: "Every subject shall have a right . . . to be fully heard in his defense, by himself, and counsel." In what way are these constitutional provisions relevant to police efforts to obtain eyewitness identifications of suspects?

■ UNITED STATES v. BILLY JOE WADE

388 U.S. 218 (1967)

BRENNAN, J.*

The question here is whether courtroom identifications of an accused at trial are to be excluded from evidence because the accused was exhibited to the witnesses before trial at a post-indictment lineup conducted for identification purposes without notice to and in the absence of the accused's appointed counsel.

The federally insured bank in Eustace, Texas, was robbed on September 21, 1964. A man with a small strip of tape on each side of his face entered the bank, pointed a pistol at the female cashier and the vice president, the only persons in the bank at the time, and forced them to fill a pillowcase with the bank's money. [Wade was indicted for the robbery on March 23, 1965, and arrested on April 2. Counsel was appointed to represent him on April 26.] Fifteen days later an FBI agent, without notice to Wade's lawyer, arranged to have the two bank employees observe a lineup made up of Wade and five or six other prisoners and conducted in a courtroom of the local county courthouse. Each person in the line wore strips of tape such as allegedly worn by the robber and upon direction each said something like "put the money in the bag," the words allegedly uttered by the robber. Both bank employees identified Wade in the lineup as the bank robber.

At trial, the two employees, when asked on direct examination if the robber was in the courtroom, pointed to Wade. The prior lineup identification was then elicited from both employees on cross-examination. At the close of testimony, Wade's counsel moved for a judgment of acquittal or, alternatively, to strike the bank officials' courtroom identifications on the ground that conduct of the lineup, without notice to and in the absence of his appointed counsel, violated his . . . Sixth Amendment right to the assistance of counsel. The motion was denied, and Wade was convicted. . . .

* [Justice Clark joined in this opinion. Chief Justice Warren and Justices Douglas and Fortas joined in this opinion except for part I, which is not reprinted here. Justice Black joined in parts II through IV of this opinion. Justices White, Harlan, and Stewart joined in parts I and III of this opinion. — EDS.]

II.

. . . The Framers of the Bill of Rights envisaged a broader role for counsel than under the practice then prevailing in England of merely advising his client in "matters of law," and eschewing any responsibility for "matters of fact." The constitutions in at least 11 of the 13 States expressly or impliedly abolished this distinction. . . .

When the Bill of Rights was adopted, there were no organized police forces as we know them today. The accused confronted the prosecutor and the witnesses against him, and the evidence was marshalled, largely at the trial itself. In contrast, today's law enforcement machinery involves critical confrontations of the accused by the prosecution at pretrial proceedings where the results might well settle the accused's fate and reduce the trial itself to a mere formality. In recognition of these realities of modern criminal prosecution, our cases have construed the Sixth Amendment guarantee to apply to "critical" stages of the proceedings. The guarantee reads: "In all criminal prosecutions, the accused shall enjoy the right . . . to have the Assistance of Counsel for his defence." The plain wording of this guarantee thus encompasses counsel's assistance whenever necessary to assure a meaningful "defence." . . . The presence of counsel at such critical confrontations, as at the trial itself, operates to assure that the accused's interests will be protected consistently with our adversary theory of criminal prosecution. . . .

III.

The Government characterizes the lineup as a mere preparatory step in the gathering of the prosecution's evidence, not different — for Sixth Amendment purposes — from various other preparatory steps, such as systematized or scientific analyzing of the accused's fingerprints, blood sample, clothing, hair, and the like. We think there are differences which preclude such stages being characterized as critical stages at which the accused has the right to the presence of his counsel. Knowledge of the techniques of science and technology is sufficiently available, and the variables in techniques few enough, that the accused has the opportunity for a meaningful confrontation of the Government's case at trial through the ordinary processes of cross-examination of the Government's expert witnesses and the presentation of the evidence of his own experts. . . .

IV.

But the confrontation compelled by the State between the accused and the victim or witnesses to a crime to elicit identification evidence is peculiarly riddled with innumerable dangers and variable factors which might seriously, even crucially, derogate from a fair trial. The vagaries of eyewitness identification are well-known; the annals of criminal law are rife with instances of mistaken identification. . . . A major factor contributing to the high incidence of miscarriage of justice from mistaken identification has been the degree of suggestion inherent in the manner in which the prosecution presents the suspect to witnesses for pretrial identification. [It] is a matter of common experience that, once a witness has picked out the accused at the lineup, he is not likely to go back on his word later on, so that in practice the issue of identity may (in the absence of other relevant evidence) for all practical purposes be determined there and then, before the trial.

[As] is the case with secret interrogations, there is serious difficulty in depicting what transpires at lineups and other forms of identification confrontations. [The] defense can seldom reconstruct the manner and mode of lineup identification for judge or jury at trial. Those participating in a lineup with the accused may often be police officers; in any event, the participants' names are rarely recorded or divulged at trial. The impediments to an objective observation are increased when the victim is the witness. Lineups are prevalent in rape and robbery prosecutions and present a particular hazard that a victim's understandable outrage may excite vengeful or spiteful motives. In any event, neither witnesses nor lineup participants are apt to be alert for conditions prejudicial to the suspect. . . . Improper influences may go undetected by a suspect, guilty or not, who experiences the emotional tension which we might expect in one being confronted with potential accusers. Even when he does observe abuse, if he has a criminal record he may be reluctant to take the stand and open up the admission of prior convictions. Moreover, any protestations by the suspect of the fairness of the lineup made at trial are likely to be in vain; the jury's choice is between the accused's unsupported version and that of the police officers present. In short, the accused's inability effectively to reconstruct at trial any unfairness that occurred at the lineup may deprive him of his only opportunity meaningfully to attack the credibility of the witness' courtroom identification. . . .

The potential for improper influence is illustrated by the circumstances, insofar as they appear, surrounding the prior identifications in the three cases we decide today. [The companion cases were Gilbert v. California, 388 U.S. 263 (1967), and Stovall v. Denno, 388 U.S. 293 (1967).] In the present case, the testimony of the identifying witnesses elicited on cross-examination revealed that those witnesses were taken to the courthouse and seated in the courtroom to await assembly of the lineup. The courtroom faced on a hallway observable to the witnesses through an open door. The cashier testified that she saw Wade "standing in the hall" within sight of an FBI agent. . . . The lineup in *Gilbert* was conducted in an auditorium in which some 100 witnesses to several alleged state and federal robberies charged to Gilbert made wholesale identifications of Gilbert as the robber in each other's presence, a procedure said to be fraught with dangers of suggestion. And the vice of suggestion created by the identification in *Stovall,* was the presentation to the witness of the suspect alone handcuffed to police officers. It is hard to imagine a situation more clearly conveying the suggestion to the witness that the one presented is believed guilty by the police. . . .

Insofar as the accused's conviction may rest on a courtroom identification in fact the fruit of a suspect pretrial identification which the accused is helpless to subject to effective scrutiny at trial, the accused is deprived of that right of cross-examination which is an essential safeguard to his right to confront the witnesses against him. . . . The trial which might determine the accused's fate may well not be that in the courtroom but that at the pretrial confrontation, with the State aligned against the accused, the witness the sole jury, and the accused unprotected against the overreaching, intentional or unintentional, and with little or no effective appeal from the judgment there rendered by the witness — "that's the man." . . .

No substantial countervailing policy considerations have been advanced against the requirement of the presence of counsel. Concern is expressed that the requirement will forestall prompt identifications and result in obstruction of the confrontations. As for the first, we note that in the two cases in which the right to counsel is today held to apply, counsel had already been appointed and no argument is made in either case that notice to counsel would have prejudicially delayed the confrontations. [Law] enforcement may be assisted by preventing the infiltration of taint in the prosecution's identification evidence. That result cannot help the guilty avoid conviction but can only help assure that the right man has been brought to justice.[29] Legislative or other regulations, such as those of local police departments, which eliminate the risks of abuse and unintentional suggestion at lineup proceedings and the impediments to meaningful confrontation at trial may also remove the basis for regarding the stage as "critical." But neither Congress nor the federal authorities have seen fit to provide a solution. What we hold today in no way creates a constitutional straitjacket which will handicap sound efforts at reform, nor is it intended to have this effect.

V.

We come now to the question whether the denial of Wade's motion to strike the courtroom identification by the bank witnesses at trial because of the absence of his counsel at the lineup required . . . the grant of a new trial at which such evidence is to be excluded. We do not think this disposition can be justified without first giving the Government the opportunity to establish by clear and convincing evidence that the in-court identifications were based upon observations of the suspect other than the lineup identification. [T]he appropriate procedure to be followed is to vacate the conviction pending a hearing to determine whether the in-court identifications had an independent source, or whether, in any event, the introduction of the evidence was harmless error, and for the District Court to reinstate the conviction or order a new trial, as may be proper. . . .

WHITE, J., dissenting in part and concurring in part.*

The Court has again propounded a broad constitutional rule barring use of a wide spectrum of relevant and probative evidence, solely because a step in its ascertainment or discovery occurs outside the presence of defense counsel. This was the approach of the Court in Miranda v. Arizona, 384 U.S. 436 (1966). I objected then to what I thought was an uncritical and doctrinaire approach without satisfactory factual foundation. I have much the same view of the present ruling and therefore dissent. . . .

The Court's opinion is far-reaching. . . . It matters not how well the witness knows the suspect, whether the witness is the suspect's mother, brother, or long-time associate, and no matter how long or well the witness observed the perpetrator at the scene of the crime. . . .

To find the lineup a "critical" stage of the proceeding and to exclude identifications made in the absence of counsel, the Court must [assume] that there is now no adequate source from which defense counsel can learn about the circumstances

29. Many other nations surround the lineup with safeguards against prejudice to the suspect. In England the suspect must be allowed the presence of his solicitor or a friend; Germany requires the presence of retained counsel; France forbids the confrontation of the suspect in the absence of his counsel; Spain, Mexico, and Italy provide detailed procedures prescribing the conditions under which confrontation must occur under the supervision of a judicial officer who sees to it that the proceedings are officially recorded to assure adequate scrutiny at trial.

* [Justices Harlan and Stewart joined in this opinion. — EDS.]

of the pretrial identification in order to place before the jury all of the considerations which should enter into an appraisal of courtroom identification evidence. But [I am not willing to assume] that the police and the witnesses will forget or prevaricate, that defense counsel will be unable to bring out the truth and that neither jury, judge, nor appellate court is a sufficient safeguard against unacceptable police conduct occurring at a pretrial identification procedure. I am unable to share the Court's view of the willingness of the police and the ordinary citizen-witness to dissemble. . . .

Identifications frequently take place after arrest but before an indictment is returned or an information is filed. The police may have arrested a suspect on probable cause but may still have the wrong man. Both the suspect and the State have every interest in a prompt identification at that stage, the suspect in order to secure his immediate release and the State because prompt and early identification enhances accurate identification and because it must know whether it is on the right investigative track. Unavoidably, however, the absolute rule requiring the presence of counsel will cause significant delay and it may very well result in no pretrial identification at all. . . . Nor do I think the witnesses themselves can be ignored. They will now be required to be present at the convenience of counsel rather than their own. Many may be much less willing to participate if the identification stage is transformed into an adversary proceeding not under the control of a judge. . . .

Finally, I think the Court's new rule is vulnerable in terms of its own unimpeachable purpose of increasing the reliability of identification testimony. Law enforcement officers have the obligation to convict the guilty and to make sure they do not convict the innocent. . . . To this extent, our so-called adversary system is not adversary at all; nor should it be. But defense counsel has no comparable obligation to ascertain or present the truth. Our system assigns him a different mission. [As] part of our modified adversary system and as part of the duty imposed on the most honorable defense counsel, we countenance or require conduct which in many instances has little, if any, relation to the search for truth. [Defense counsel] will not only observe what occurs and develop possibilities for later cross-examination but will hover over witnesses and begin their cross-examination then, menacing truthful factfinding as thoroughly as the Court fears the police now do. . . . In my view, the State is entitled to investigate and develop its case outside the presence of defense counsel. . . .

■ PEOPLE v. JONATHAN HICKMAN

684 N.W.2d 267 (Mich. 2004)

CORRIGAN, C.J.

In this case, we must determine when the right to counsel attaches to corporeal identifications. We adopt the analysis of Moore v. Illinois, 434 U.S. 220 (1977), and hold that the right to counsel attaches only to corporeal identifications conducted at or after the initiation of adversarial judicial criminal proceedings. To the extent that People v. Anderson, 205 N.W.2d 461 (Mich. 1973), goes beyond the constitutional text and extends the right to counsel to a time before the initiation of adversarial criminal proceedings, it is overruled. . . .

FACTUAL HISTORY AND PROCEDURAL POSTURE

Defendant was convicted of possession of a firearm during the commission or attempted commission of a felony, conspiracy, and armed robbery, for robbing the complainant of $26 and two two-way radios. The complainant testified that two men approached him from behind and robbed him. He testified that one of the men, later identified as defendant, pointed a gun at his face while the other person took the radios and money. The complainant then called the police and gave a description of the two men, as well as a description of the gun.

An officer soon saw a man fitting the description of the man with the gun. The man, later identified as defendant, was caught after a foot chase. During the chase, the police saw defendant throw something and they later recovered a chrome handgun that matched the complainant's description of the gun. Defendant was carrying one of the two-way radios.

Approximately ten minutes later, an officer took the complainant to a police car in which defendant was being held. The officer asked the complainant if the person sitting in the police car was involved in the robbery. The complainant immediately responded that defendant was the man who had the gun.

Defendant's motion to suppress an on-the-scene identification by the victim on the ground that defendant was not represented by counsel at the time of the identification was denied, and defendant was convicted. The Court of Appeals affirmed defendant's conviction. The Court held that the prompt on-the-scene identification did not offend the requirements set forth in *Anderson* and rejected defendants due process claim, holding that the identification was not unduly suggestive. Defendant appealed, and this Court granted leave, limited to the issue whether counsel is required before an on-the-scene identification can be admitted at trial. . . .

PEOPLE V. ANDERSON

In *Anderson,* the right to counsel was extended to all pretrial corporeal identifications, including those occurring before the initiation of adversarial proceedings. This extension of United States v. Wade, 388 U.S. 218 (1967), to all pretrial identification procedures was based on "psychological principles," and "social science." Notably absent was any grounding in our federal constitution or state constitution. In People v. Jackson, 217 N.W.2d 22 (Mich. 1974), this Court acknowledged that the *Anderson* rules were not [mandated under the federal constitution]. The *Jackson* Court affirmed the *Anderson* rules, however, as an exercise of the Court's "constitutional power to establish rules of evidence applicable to judicial proceedings in Michigan courts and to preserve best evidence eyewitness testimony from unnecessary alteration by unfair identification procedures." Finally, in People v. Cheatham, 551 N.W.2d 355 (Mich. 1996), this Court noted in obiter dictum that the right to counsel under Const. 1963, art. 1, §20 "attaches only at or after the initiation of adversary judicial proceedings by way of formal charge, preliminary hearing, indictment, information, or arraignment." Thus, the *Anderson* rules lack a foundation in any constitutional provision, whether state or federal. Instead, the rules reflect the policy preferences of the *Anderson* Court. . . .

MOORE V. ILLINOIS

In *Moore,* the United States Supreme Court adopted the plurality opinion in Kirby v. Illinois, 406 U.S. 682 (1972), holding:

> [The] right to counsel announced in *Wade* and Gilbert v. California, 388 U.S. 263 (1967), attaches only to corporeal identifications conducted at or after the initiation of adversary judicial criminal proceedings — whether by way of formal charge, preliminary hearing, indictment, information, or arraignment . . . because the initiation of such proceedings marks the commencement of the criminal prosecutions to which alone the explicit guarantees of the Sixth Amendment are applicable.

The Court further noted that identifications conducted before the initiation of adversarial judicial criminal proceedings could still be challenged: "In such cases, however, *due process* protects the accused against the introduction of evidence of, or tainted by, unreliable pretrial identifications obtained through unnecessarily suggestive procedures." Therefore, it is now beyond question that, for federal Sixth Amendment purposes, the right to counsel attaches only at or after the initiation of adversarial judicial proceedings.

This conclusion is also consistent with our state constitutional provision, Const. 1963, art. 1, §20, which provides: "*In every criminal prosecution,* the accused shall have the right . . . to have the assistance of counsel for his or her defense. . . ." This Court has already noted . . . that a defendant's right to counsel under art. 1, §20 attaches only at or after the initiation of adversarial judicial proceedings. This Court also held in People v. Reichenbach, 587 N.W.2d 1 (Mich. 1998) [that] no peculiar state or local interests exist in Michigan to warrant a different level of protection with regard to the right to counsel in the instant case. Both the federal and the state provisions originated from the same concerns and to protect the same rights.

Because the *Moore* analysis is consistent with both U.S. Const., Am. VI and Const. 1963, art. 1, §20, which expressly apply only to criminal prosecutions, we adopt that analysis and hold that the right to counsel attaches only to corporeal identifications conducted at or after the initiation of adversarial judicial criminal proceedings.

[The] *Anderson* decision generated considerable confusion regarding its proper application. [There is no] simple, practical standard regarding on-the-scene corporeal identifications. In People v. Dixon, 271 N.W.2d 196 (Mich. App. 1978), the Court held that if the police have "more than a mere suspicion" that the suspect is wanted for the crime, there can be no on-the-scene corporeal identification; rather, the suspect must be taken to the police station and participate in a lineup with counsel present. In People v. Turner, 328 N.W.2d 5 (Mich. App. 1982), however, the Court found the *Dixon* rule too difficult and, instead, held that police may conduct on-the-scene identifications without counsel unless the police have "very strong evidence" that the person stopped is the perpetrator. "Very strong evidence" was defined as "where the suspect has himself decreased any exculpatory motive, *i.e.,* where he has confessed or presented the police with either highly distinctive evidence of the crime or a highly distinctive personal appearance."

[The] *Turner* "strong evidence" rule is hardly more workable than *Dixon's* "more than a mere suspicion" rule. Rather than perpetuate the confusion in this area, we take this opportunity to adopt the *Moore* analysis and clarify that the right to counsel attaches only to corporeal identifications conducted at or after the initiation of adversarial judicial criminal proceedings. This eliminates any unwarranted confusion and allows the focus to be on whether the identification procedure used violates due process. . . .

The on-the-scene identification in this case was made before the initiation of any adversarial judicial criminal proceedings; thus, counsel was not required. . . .

The *Anderson* rule, extending the right to counsel to all pretrial identifications, is without constitutional basis. Consistently with both the United States Constitution and the Michigan Constitution, we adopt the straightforward analysis of Moore v. Illinois and hold that the right to counsel attaches only to corporeal identifications conducted at or after the initiation of adversarial judicial criminal proceedings. . . .

KELLY, J., dissenting.

To the casual reader, the rationale for today's majority decision may be elusive. After all, as the majority correctly notes, the case deals with law that has been relatively well-settled for close to thirty years: a potential criminal defendant does not have a Sixth Amendment right to counsel during identifications that occur before the initiation of adversarial judicial proceedings, such as a formal charge or preliminary hearing. Moore v. Illinois, 434 U.S. 220, 226-227 (1977); People v. Jackson, 217 N.W.2d 22 (Mich. 1974).

Nor has this Court held that the protective rules enumerated by People v. Anderson and its progeny apply to on-the-scene identification procedures and require counsel during those procedures. In fact, the opposite is true.

Yet the majority undertakes today ostensibly to resolve these issues. Its purpose is to take away the potential defendant's entitlement to counsel during all preindictment proceedings by overruling *Anderson* and its progeny. Hereafter, a defendant, in custody but not yet indicted, will no longer have the practical ability to challenge photographic or corporeal identification procedures. The police will be able to conduct such procedures without allowing a defendant's attorney to be present. Moreover, even after the initiation of adversarial judicial procedures, a criminal defendant will no longer have the right to counsel during a photographic showup. Because I do not see any good reason to depart from longstanding precedent, I must respectfully dissent.

The majority is not correct in its assertion that, under *Anderson,* "the right to counsel was extended to all pretrial corporeal identifications, including those occurring before the initiation of adversarial proceedings." *Anderson,* which itself dealt with the right to counsel for pretrial custodial photographic showup procedures, set forth "justified" exceptions, albeit arguably in dicta, for the absence of counsel at eyewitness identification procedures. Notably included as exceptions were emergency situations requiring immediate identification and "prompt, on-the-scene corporeal identifications within minutes of the crime. . . ." We have since specifically affirmed the *Anderson* exception for prompt on-the-scene identifications. City of Troy v. Ohlinger, 475 N.W.2d 54 (Mich. 1991).

The majority could reaffirm the *Anderson* exception for prompt on-the-scene identifications, or perhaps enlarge the explanation of the exception to provide a workable framework for the lower courts. Instead, it unnecessarily chooses to remove the *Anderson* protections from all preindictment identification procedures.

It is an ill-conceived decision that ignores principles of stare decisis. It also fails to consider the adverse effect on defendants' rights to be assured that pretrial identifications are not obtained through mistake or unnecessarily suggestive procedures. . . .

Apparently the majority's own "policy preferences" outweigh those of the members of the *Anderson* Court and the *Jackson* Court, as well as other members of this Court. Unlike the majority, I believe *Anderson* was decided with due deference to the practical problems of ensuring accurate identifications. I am concerned that the majority's policy decision gives insufficient thought to the underlying rationale for our long-existing decision to grant counsel to defendants where practicable.

Anderson discussed at length the scope of the problem of misidentifications, particularly in the use of photographic identification procedures. These concerns have certainly not diminished with time. [The] past century has seen the accumulation of literally thousands of studies on the weakness of eyewitness testimony.

[After] DNA identification techniques became more common, the United States Justice Department conducted a study of exonerated defendants and prepared a research report. Connors, *Convicted by juries, exonerated by science: Case studies in the use of DNA evidence to establish innocence after trial* (1996). The study was commissioned by the National Institute of Justice. It reviewed twenty-eight cases where the defendants had been exonerated through the use of DNA identification techniques.

Among the conclusions reached was that, in the majority of cases, "eyewitness testimony was the most compelling evidence. Clearly, however, those eyewitness identifications were wrong." Notably, one of the significant factors of misidentification listed in the Justice Department report involves an issue directly raised in the instant case and the majority's decision to overrule *Anderson:* the potential susceptibility of eyewitnesses to suggestions from the police, whether intentional or unintentional.

One of the major underpinnings of the *Anderson* decision, and the later affirmation in *Jackson,* was the recognition of difficulties with obtaining reliable identification evidence. Courts and scholars have recognized the continued validity of these concerns. Nonetheless, this Court refuses to recognize that *Anderson's* rules were, in fact, grounded on more than a transient notion of what the Sixth Amendment requires.

The majority does so with barely a nod to the principle of stare decisis. . . . Even if this Court has found that an error occurred, before it overrules a decision deliberately made, it should be convinced not merely that the case was wrongly decided, but also that less injury will result from overruling than from following it. . . .

In the instant case, the injury done by unnecessarily overruling *Anderson* is grave. Conversely, the continued use of its precedent would harm no one but those who fail in their duty to ensure that identifications are made under circumstances that render them reliable. The use of counsel during preindictment procedures has become part of the accepted practice in Michigan courts. I see nothing even approaching a special justification to depart from precedent here. . . .

The fact that the majority has seen fit to unnecessarily overturn *Anderson* creates a Catch-22 for defendants during other preindictment identification procedures. Until today, a defendant who was not "formally" charged but in custody was entitled to an attorney during any identification procedure. Now, the only required persons in the room will be the investigating officer and the witness. Where the defendant is presented to a potential witness during an on-the-scene identification, the defendant himself is present to observe the actions and words of the officer. Arguably, a defendant who has been subjected to an unnecessarily suggestive on-the-scene identification procedure has the opportunity to present a coherent rationale for his arguments.

In contrast, a defendant who seeks to challenge a corporeal identification procedure will be effectively unable to do so. He must stand before the one-way glass and trust the competence and conscience of the investigating officer. I doubt that J.R.R. Tolkien's image of Wormtongue whispering quietly into the ear of Theoden, King of Rohan will be one that is frequently repeated in practice. However, even an inadvertent suggestion will be imperceptible to a defendant who remains precluded from witnessing it. The majority is essentially creating a black box into which the defendant will not be allowed to peer. It then requires him to refute the premise that what occurred inside did not violate his right to due process....

I agree wholeheartedly with Justice Brennan's dissenting statement in Kirby v. Illinois, 406 U.S. 682, 699 n.8 (1972):... "the establishment of the date of formal accusation as the time wherein the right to counsel at lineup attaches could only lead to a situation wherein substantially all lineups would be conducted prior to indictment or information." Until today, Michigan has not known this to occur. However, I seriously doubt that it will long be the case after the majority's ruling....

In conclusion,... the decision to overrule *Anderson* is misguided. It has been made without due deference to the principles of stare decisis and without a comprehension of the practical realities of frequent eyewitness misidentifications.

U.S. DEPARTMENT OF JUSTICE, TECHNICAL WORKING GROUP FOR EYEWITNESS EVIDENCE

Eyewitness Evidence: A Guide for Law Enforcement (1999)

Procedures for Eyewitness Identification of Suspects

A. Composing Lineups ...

Procedure [for Live Lineups]:

In composing a live lineup, the investigator should:

1. Include only one suspect in each identification procedure.
2. Select fillers who generally fit the witness' description of the perpetrator. When there is a limited/inadequate description of the perpetrator provided by the witness, or when the description of the perpetrator differs significantly from the appearance of the suspect, fillers should resemble the suspect in significant features.
3. Consider placing suspects in different positions in each lineup, both across cases and with multiple witnesses in the same case. Position the suspect randomly unless, where local practice allows, the suspect or the suspect's attorney requests a particular position.
4. Include a *minimum* of four fillers (nonsuspects) per identification procedure.
5. When showing a new suspect, avoid reusing fillers in lineups shown to the same witness.

6. Consider that complete uniformity of features is not required. Avoid using fillers who so closely resemble the suspect that a person familiar with the suspect might find it difficult to distinguish the suspect from the fillers.
7. Create a consistent appearance between the suspect and fillers with respect to any unique or unusual feature (e.g., scars, tattoos) used to describe the perpetrator by artificially adding or concealing that feature. . . .

B. INSTRUCTING THE WITNESS PRIOR TO VIEWING A LINEUP . . .

Procedure [for Live Lineup]:

Prior to presenting a live lineup, the investigator should:

1. Instruct the witness that he/she will be asked to view a group of individuals.
2. Instruct the witness that it is just as important to clear innocent persons from suspicion as to identify guilty parties.
3. Instruct the witness that individuals present in the lineup may not appear exactly as they did on the date of the incident because features such as head and facial hair are subject to change.
4. Instruct the witness that the person who committed the crime may or may not be present in the group of individuals.
5. Assure the witness that regardless of whether an identification is made, the police will continue to investigate the incident.
6. Instruct the witness that the procedure requires the investigator to ask the witness to state, in his/her own words, how certain he/she is of any identification. . . .

C. CONDUCTING THE IDENTIFICATION PROCEDURE . . .

Procedure: [Simultaneous Live Lineup]

When presenting a simultaneous live lineup, the investigator/lineup administrator should: . . .

2. Instruct all those present at the lineup not to suggest in any way the position or identity of the suspect in the lineup.
3. Ensure that any identification actions (e.g., speaking, moving) are performed by all members of the lineup.
4. Avoid saying anything to the witness that may influence the witness' selection.
5. If an identification is made, avoid reporting to the witness any information regarding the individual he/she has selected prior to obtaining the witness' statement of certainty. . . .
7. Document the lineup in writing, including [identification] information of lineup participants, [names] of all persons present at the lineup, [and date] and time the identification procedure was conducted.
8. Document the lineup by photo or video. This documentation should be of a quality that represents the lineup clearly and fairly.
9. Instruct the witness not to discuss the identification procedure or its results with other witnesses involved in the case and discourage contact with the media.

Sequential Live Lineup:

When presenting a sequential live lineup, the lineup administrator/investigator should: . . .

2. Provide the following additional viewing instructions to the witness:
   a. Individuals will be viewed one at a time.
   b. The individuals will be presented in random order.
   c. Take as much time as needed in making a decision about each individual before moving to the next one.
   d. If the person who committed the crime is present, identify him/her.
   e. All individuals will be presented, even if an identification is made; or the procedure will be stopped at the point of an identification (consistent with jurisdictional/departmental procedures).
3. Begin with all lineup participants out of the view of the witness.
4. Instruct all those present at the lineup not to suggest in any way the position or identity of the suspect in the lineup.
5. Present each individual to the witness separately, in a previously determined order, removing those previously shown.
6. Ensure that any identification actions (e.g., speaking, moving) are performed by all members of the lineup.
7. Avoid saying anything to the witness that may influence the witness' selection.
8. If an identification is made, avoid reporting to the witness any information regarding the individual he/she has selected prior to obtaining the witness' statement of certainty. . . .

D. RECORDING IDENTIFICATION RESULTS . . .

Procedure:

When conducting an identification procedure, the investigator should:

1. Record both identification and nonidentification results in writing, including the witness' own words regarding how sure he/she is.
2. Ensure results are signed and dated by the witness.
3. Ensure that no materials indicating previous identification results are visible to the witness.
4. Ensure that the witness does not write on or mark any materials that will be used in other identification procedures.

Summary:

Preparing a complete and accurate record of the outcome of the identification procedure improves the strength and credibility of the identification or nonidentification results obtained from the witness. This record can be a critical document in the investigation and any subsequent court proceedings.

Notes

1. *Availability of counsel during in-person identifications: majority position.* The decisions in *Wade* and Gilbert v. California, 388 U.S. 263 (1967), gave a dramatic debut to the constitutional right to counsel for identification procedures. The Supreme Court spoke broadly of the unreliability of this type of evidence and of the need for defense counsel to help counter this problem. But five years later, in Kirby v. Illinois, 406 U.S. 682 (1972), the Court sharply limited the type of lineup procedures in which counsel would be required under the Constitution: The *Wade-Gilbert* rule applied only to lineups occurring "at or after the initiation of adversary judicial criminal proceedings." For purposes of the federal constitution, that point arrives as early as the pre-indictment "preliminary hearing" in which a magistrate determines if there is probable cause to bind the defendant over to the grand jury. Moore v. Illinois, 434 U.S. 220 (1977).

Most states have adopted the *Kirby* rule to determine which identification procedures fall within the reach of the constitutional right to counsel. Fewer than a half dozen states extend the right to counsel to lineups occurring earlier in the process. In these states, counsel must be present at any postarrest in-person identification. See State v. Mitchell, 593 S.W.2d 280 (Tenn. 1980) (applies to all warranted arrests).

No state has applied the right to counsel to field confrontations or showups, in which the police bring the crime victim together with a single suspect near the time and place where the crime occurred. To require counsel in such a setting would amount to a constitutional ban on the use of evidence from a field confrontation. How much does the refusal of the legal system to require counsel at field interrogations diminish the counsel requirement of *Wade*?

2. *How much does counsel see?* If you were a lawyer, would you want to know where the witness had been in the station prior to the lineup? Whom she had seen? What route your client took to get to the station? In light of the importance of what the witness has to say immediately after the lineup, can a defense attorney be excluded from the interview? Is this consistent with the reasoning of *Wade*? Cases that address this question generally uphold police efforts to exclude defense counsel from these conversations.

3. *The role of counsel in creating a record.* What should an attorney do at a lineup? Silently observe any suggestive police practices, or object to them? If the attorney takes an observer role, does he have to terminate representation of the defendant later in order to become a witness in the case? If the primary function of the defense counsel is to create a record for possible challenges to the use of the identification evidence at trial, could a state conduct a lineup without counsel present, so long as it is recorded? See Utah Code §77-8-4: "The entire lineup procedure shall be recorded, including all conversations between the witnesses and the conducting peace officers. The suspect shall have access to and may make copies of the record and any photographs taken of him or any other persons in connection with the lineup." In addition, Utah Code §77-8-2 provides suspects with a right to counsel during post-indictment lineups.

4. *Police rules as substitute for counsel? Wade* addressed the possibility of statutes or police regulations as a substitute for a right to counsel: "Legislative or other regulations, such as those of local police departments, which eliminate the risks of abuse

and unintentional suggestion at lineup proceedings and the impediments to meaningful confrontation at trial may also remove the basis for regarding the stage as 'critical.' " Could a police department adopting regulations along the lines of the Department of Justice recommendations reprinted above make an argument that the lineup is no longer a "critical" stage and therefore that the right to counsel does not apply? Are there any reasons to believe that police will not follow the procedures that the department's legal counsel drafts?

5. *Best practices during lineups.* The extensive academic research on the subject of eyewitness testimony produces a long list of possible improvements to current police practices. The U.S. Department of Justice sponsored a Technical Working Group that published the recommended practices reprinted above. Under the guidelines, witnesses should be told that the perpetrator may or may not be present in the lineup. Research indicates that this latter instruction greatly decreases the number of false positives. See Gary L. Wells, Police Lineups: Data, Theory, and Policy, 7 Psychol. Pub. Pol'y & L. 791 (2001).

However, the Department of Justice recommendations stop short of imposing two further requirements that find strong support in the academic research. It is clear that "blind presentations" of the lineup (that is, the officer conducting the lineup procedure does not know which participant is the suspect) improve the accuracy of witness identification. Officers who know the identity of the suspect can signal to the witness, either through words or subtle body language, which is the "correct" choice. A second technique involves "sequential" lineups, where the officer presents to the witness one person at a time, asking each time whether he or she is the perpetrator. Sequential lineups encourage witnesses to compare each person to their memory of the events, rather than asking which lineup participant (relatively speaking) most closely resembles the original description. Dawn McQuiston-Surrett, Roy S. Malpass, & Colin G. Tredoux, Sequential vs. Simultaneous Lineups: A Review of Methods, Data, and Theory, 12 Psychol. Pub. Pol'y & L. 137 (2006).

What might prevent the Department of Justice from recommending these two techniques that so clearly contribute to more accurate identifications? See Kate Zernike, "Study Fuels a Growing Debate Over Police Lineups," N.Y. Times, April 19, 2006 (describing experiment by Chicago Police Department to use sequential lineups and blind presentations for some eyewitness identifications; sequential lineups made witnesses less likely to choose any suspect, and when they did pick, they were more likely to select an innocent person). The debates among local actors about the best identification procedures are lively and have not thus far led to a consensus about best practices. For examples of such debates, see the web extension for this chapter at *http://www.crimpro.com/extension/ch09.*

6. *Right to counsel for photographic identifications: majority position.* Rather than arranging an acceptable in-person encounter, it is often easier for police investigators to show pictures of potential suspects to a witness. Furthermore, pictures can be matched on more features. Are concerns about the reliability of the witness's identification different when investigators use photographs or other recorded images of a suspect? Do different types of legal regulation then become more or less feasible?

In United States v. Ash, 413 U.S. 300 (1973), the Court held that the federal Constitution does not require the presence of counsel at *any* photographic identification, whether it is conducted before or after the start of adversarial criminal proceedings. It reasoned that a photographic display, unlike an in-person lineup, does not involve a "trial-like confrontation" between the defendant and the witness.

Thus, the presence of a lawyer is less important to a defendant whose picture is used in a photo array. Is this distinction convincing?

Most state courts have followed *Ash* and concluded that there is no right to counsel for photographic identifications. See Barone v. State, 866 P.2d 291 (Nev. 1993) (reversing a 1969 decision that had granted right to counsel for photo identification). A handful do require the presence of defense counsel for at least some photo identifications.

7. *The exclusion remedy.* If police fail to allow counsel to be present during identification when such presence is constitutionally required, then the judge must exclude at trial any evidence of the pretrial identification. In addition, any identification of the defendant by the witness *at trial is* excludable unless the prosecution can demonstrate that the witness's ability to recognize the defendant at trial has an "independent basis" apart from the tainted pretrial identification. Justice White's dissent in *Wade* predicted that trial identifications would rarely meet this standard, but one limited survey of case law in the years immediately after *Wade* found that courts still routinely allowed at-trial identifications, Joseph Quinn, In the Wake of *Wade:* The Dimensions of the Eyewitness Identification Cases, 42 U. Colo. L. Rev. 135 (1970) (citing six cases as illustrations of larger trend).

8. *Counsel at identification procedures in foreign practice.* Several legal systems outside the United States rely on counsel at formal identification procedures more heavily than the U.S. system does. For instance, in England and Wales, Code D of the Police and Criminal Evidence Act of 1984 provides for defense counsel at any formal "identification parade." Case law in Israel provides that a suspect must be informed of the right to counsel during a lineup. See Eliahu Harnon and Alex Stein, Israel, in Criminal Procedure: A Worldwide Study (Craig Bradley, 2d ed. 2007). In civil law systems (said to be less "adversarial" than common law systems), would you expect defense counsel to take part in lineups?

2. *Exclusion on Due Process Grounds*

As we saw in the preceding subsection, federal and state constitutions generally require the presence of counsel only for lineups taking place after the initiation of adversary criminal proceedings (typically post-indictment lineups). This accounts for a small number of the identification procedures that take place. Are there any limitations — constitutional or otherwise — on the larger number of lineups and "field confrontations" that occur earlier in the investigative process?

For more than a generation, courts have insisted that due process will prevent the use of the least reliable identification procedures, regardless of the presence or absence of counsel. In Stovall v. Denno, 388 U.S. 293 (1967), decided the same day as United States v. Wade, the Supreme Court refused to exclude evidence of a pretrial identification under the due process clause because the identification was unduly "suggestive." While investigating a stabbing case, the police entered the victim's hospital room with the suspect handcuffed to an officer and asked the victim if the suspect was the person who had committed the crime. Because the police had no viable alternative to the procedure used here, it was not "unnecessarily suggestive."

The Supreme Court appeared to shift its emphasis in two later cases, Neil v. Biggers, 409 U.S. 188 (1972), and Manson v. Brathwaite, 432 U.S. 98 (1977). While the Court had focused in *Stovall* on the suggestiveness of the identification procedures used, that was not enough to show a due process violation in *Biggers* or *Brathwaite*. Even though the police had used suggestive "showups" to identify suspects in those cases, the Court reasoned that a witness with an adequate memory of the original crime could reliably identify the criminal despite the suggestive procedure followed at the time of the identification. The Court went on to describe the factors it would consider, as part of the "totality of the circumstances," that could outweigh a suggestive identification procedure. Thus, the Court rejected a "per se" rule that would exclude all evidence obtained through unduly suggestive identification procedures, in favor of a "reliability test" that would allow some identification evidence to stand because other factors supported its accuracy. The following case describes this "totality" approach to identification evidence obtained at the police station and offers an alternative version of the legal standard.

STATE v. TYRONE DUBOSE

699 N.W.2d 582 (Wis. 2005)

N. PATRICK CROOKS, J.

¶1 Petitioner Tyrone Dubose [argues that] the circuit court erred in denying Dubose's motion to suppress the victim's out-of-court identifications of him. . . .

¶2 We agree with Dubose that the circuit court erred in denying his motion to suppress the out-of-court identification evidence. However, we decline to adopt his proposed per se exclusionary rule regarding such evidence. Instead, we adopt standards for the admissibility of out-of-court identification evidence similar to those set forth in the United States Supreme Court's decision in Stovall v. Denno, 388 U.S. 293 (1967). . . .

I.

¶3 Timothy Hiltsley and Ryan Boyd left the Camelot Bar in Green Bay, Wisconsin, at approximately 1:00 A.M. on January 9, 2002. Hiltsley had been drinking at the bar and admitted to being "buzzed" when he left. In the parking lot, Hiltsley and Boyd encountered a group of men, some of whom Hiltsley recognized as regular customers of a liquor store where he worked. Dubose, an African-American, was one of the men he allegedly recognized. After a brief conversation, Hiltsley invited two of the men, along with Boyd, to his residence to smoke marijuana.

¶4 When they arrived at Hiltsley's apartment, Hiltsley sat down on the couch to pack a bowl of marijuana. At that time, Dubose allegedly held a gun to Hiltsley's right temple and demanded money. After Hiltsley emptied his wallet and gave the men his money, the two men, both African-Americans, left his apartment.

¶5 Within minutes after the incident, at approximately 1:21 A.M., one of Hiltsley's neighbors called the police to report a possible burglary. She described two African-American men fleeing from the area, one of whom was wearing a large hooded flannel shirt. At the same time, Hiltsley and Boyd attempted to chase the men. . . . During his search, Hiltsley flagged down a police officer that was responding to the burglary call. Hiltsley told the officer that he had just been robbed at gunpoint. He described the suspects as African-American, one standing about 5-feet 6-inches, and the other man standing a little taller.

¶6 Another police officer also responded to the burglary call. As he neared the scene, he observed two men walking about one-half block from Hiltsley's apartment. This officer, Jeffrey Engelbrecht, was unable to determine the race of the individuals, but noted that one of the men was wearing a large hooded flannel shirt. When the officer turned his squad car around to face the men, they ran east between two houses. The police quickly set up a one-block perimeter in order to contain the suspects.

¶7 The officer subsequently requested headquarters to dispatch a canine unit to help search for the men. While he waited at the perimeter for the canine unit, police headquarters reported another call in regard to an armed robbery at Hiltsley's apartment. The report indicated that the two suspects were African-American males, that one was possibly armed, and that the two calls were probably related. Upon their arrival, the canine unit officer and his dog began tracking the suspects within the perimeter. The dog began barking near a wooden backyard fence, and the officer demanded that the person behind the fence come out and show his hands. A male voice responded that he was going to surrender and asked why the police were chasing him. The male who came out from behind the fence was Dubose, who was subsequently arrested.

¶8 Dubose, who was not wearing a flannel shirt, told the police that he had been in an argument with his girlfriend and that he had just left her house. He thought she might have called the police on him, which is why he ran when he saw the squad car. After his arrest, he was searched. The search did not uncover any weapons, money, or contraband. Dubose was then placed in the back of a squad car and driven to an area near Hiltsley's residence.

¶9 At this location, the officers conducted a showup procedure, giving Hiltsley the opportunity to identify one of the alleged suspects. The officers placed Hiltsley in the backseat of a second squad car, which was parked so that its rear window was three feet apart from the rear window of the squad car containing Dubose. The dome light was turned on in the car containing Dubose. The officers told Hiltsley that Dubose was possibly one of the men who had robbed him at gunpoint, and asked Hiltsley if he could identify the man in the other squad car. Hiltsley told the police that he was 98 percent certain that Dubose, who sat alone in the back seat of the other squad car, was the man who held him at gunpoint. Hiltsley also told the police that he recognized him due to his small, slender build and hairstyle.

¶10 The squad cars separated and took both Hiltsley and Dubose to the police station. Approximately 10 to 15 minutes after the first showup, the police conducted a second showup. There, Hiltsley identified Dubose, alone in a room, through a two-way mirror. Hiltsley told police that Dubose was the same man he observed at the previous showup, and that he believed Dubose was the man who robbed him. A short time after the second showup, the police showed Hiltsley a mug shot of Dubose, and he identified him for a third time.

¶11 The State of Wisconsin charged Dubose with armed robbery. Dubose filed a motion to suppress all identifications of him in connection with the case. . . . The [trial judge] denied Dubose's motion and scheduled a jury trial. At trial, Hiltsley testified about the events and subsequent showups that occurred on January 9, 2002. He also identified Dubose in the courtroom as the man who held him at gunpoint on the night in question. The jury convicted Dubose of armed robbery on September 5, 2002. . . .

III.

¶17 Our analysis begins with a summary of the law relating to the right to due process in out-of-court identification procedures. In Stovall v. Denno, 388 U.S. 293 (1967), the United States Supreme Court considered for the first time whether, and under what circumstances, out-of-court identification procedures could implicate a defendant's right to due process. The defendant in that case, an African-American male, was arrested for murder. Without time to consult with or retain counsel, the defendant was taken to the hospital room of the only surviving witness to the alleged crime. The witness had been stabbed multiple times and was awaiting surgery. The defendant was handcuffed to one of five police officers who, along with two prosecutors, brought him into the hospital room. He was the only African-American in the room. The witness subsequently identified the defendant from her hospital bed after a police officer asked her if he "was the man," and the defendant uttered a few words for the purpose of voice identification. The witness later recovered, and testified at the defendant's trial as to the events that occurred in her hospital room. At that time, she also made an in-court identification of the defendant.

¶18 The United States Supreme Court considered whether the confrontation in the hospital room was "so unnecessarily suggestive and conducive to irreparable mistaken identification that he was denied due process of law." . . . The Court determined that necessity is a key factor in reviewing whether a showup violates due process. Although the identification was suggestive, the Court determined that it did not violate the defendant's right to due process because the procedure was necessary. It held:

> Here was the only person in the world who could possibly exonerate Stovall. Her words, and only her words, "He is not the man" could have resulted in freedom for Stovall. The hospital was not far distant from the courthouse and jail. No one knew how long Mrs. Behrendt might live. Faced with the responsibility of identifying the attacker, with the need for immediate action and with the knowledge that Mrs. Behrendt could not visit the jail, the police followed the only feasible procedure and took Stovall to the hospital room. Under these circumstances, the usual police station line-up, which Stovall now argues he should have had, was out of the question.

Thus, while the out-of-court identification was not suppressed in that case, *Stovall* established a due process right of criminal suspects to be free from confrontations that, under all circumstances, are unnecessarily suggestive. The right was enforceable by exclusion at trial of evidence of the constitutionally invalid identification. . . .

¶20 [The] United States Supreme Court next considered the identification issue in Simmons v. United States, 390 U.S. 377 (1968). In that case, the defendant was convicted of armed robbery based on in-court identification. However, the in-court identification witnesses had been shown photographs of the defendant prior to trial. The defendant argued that the in-court identifications were tainted, because the out-of-court photo identification was suggestive.

¶21 The Court, attempting to follow the "totality test" developed in *Stovall*, determined that the in-court identification was not tainted. [The Court held] "that convictions based on eyewitness identification at trial following a pretrial identification by photograph will be set aside . . . only if the photographic identification procedure was so impermissibly suggestive as to give rise to a very substantial likelihood of irreparable misidentification." In so holding, however, the Supreme Court [replaced] "conducive to irreparable mistaken identification" with "a very substantial likelihood of irreparable misidentification" [and thus required] a much higher level of proof on the part of the defendant. . . .

¶23 In Neil v. Biggers, 409 U.S. 188 (1972), the United States Supreme Court shifted away from its reliance on the "necessity" of the out-of-court identification as set forth in *Stovall* and, instead, emphasized the standard of reliability established in *Simmons*. In *Biggers*, the police conducted a showup that consisted of two detectives walking the defendant past the victim at the police station. At the victim's request, the police directed the respondent to say "shut up or I'll kill you." The victim identified the defendant after the showup and then later at trial. The defendant objected to the admissibility of the out-of-court identification.

¶24 The Supreme Court determined that . . . evidence from a suggestive identification would be admissible if a court can find it reliable under the totality of the circumstances. In order to determine if an identification is reliable under the totality of the circumstances, the Court developed a five-part test: (1) the opportunity of the witness to view the defendant at the time of the crime; (2) the witness' degree of attention; (3) the accuracy of the witness' prior description of the defendant; (4) the level of certainty demonstrated by the witness at the confrontation; and (5) the length of time between the crime and the confrontation.

¶25 The United States Supreme Court's next significant eyewitness identification case was Manson v. Brathwaite, 432 U.S. 98 (1977). In that case, a police officer made a positive out-of-court photo identification of the defendant two days after he conducted an undercover purchase of drugs from the defendant. Both parties agreed that the identification was improperly suggestive. The Supreme Court held that, under the totality of the circumstances, the identification was reliable even though the confrontation procedure was suggestive. The Court reaffirmed *Biggers* and held that "reliability is the linchpin in determining the admissibility of identification testimony. . . ."

¶26 With guidance from the United States Supreme Court, this court has adopted the test set forth in *Biggers* and *Brathwaite* in an attempt to minimize the misidentification of defendants in Wisconsin. See State v. Wolverton, 533 N.W.2d 167 (Wis. 1995); Fells v. State, 223 N.W.2d 507 (Wis. 1974) (in a case involving lineup and photo identifications, the proper procedure is to first determine if the identification was "unnecessarily suggestive," and, if so, decide whether, under the totality of circumstances, the identification was nevertheless reliable). In *Wolverton*, this court decided a case that presented similar factual circumstances to the case presently before us. There, the police conducted showups in driveways of different witnesses to different incidents. The suspect was positively identified while sitting alone in the back of a squad car. The identifications took place shortly after the alleged incidents, and the witnesses later identified the suspect at trial.

¶27 In relying on *Biggers* and *Brathwaite*, we held that if the criminal defendant demonstrates that the showup was impermissibly suggestive, the burden shifts to the state to demonstrate that under the totality of the circumstances the identification was reliable. Accordingly, we upheld the admissibility of the out-of-court identifications, not under standards involving due process and necessity as set forth in *Stovall*, but because under the totality of the circumstances, such identifications were determined to be reliable.

IV.

¶28 . . . Dubose asks us to abandon [our reliability test] and apply a per se exclusionary rule in cases where out-of-court identifications were impermissibly suggestive.

¶29 We begin our assessment by recognizing that much new information has been assembled since we last reviewed the showup procedure in *Wolverton*. Over the last decade, there have been extensive studies on the issue of identification evidence, research that is now impossible for us to ignore. See Nancy Steblay, et al., Eyewitness Accuracy Rates in Police Showup and Lineup Presentations: A Meta-Analytic Comparison, 27 Law & Hum. Behav. 523 (2003); U.S. Department of Justice, Eyewitness Evidence: A Guide for Law Enforcement (1999), available at *http://www.ncjrs.org/pdffiles1/nij/178240.pdf*.

¶30 These studies confirm that eyewitness testimony is often hopelessly unreliable. The research strongly supports the conclusion that eyewitness misidentification is now the single greatest source of wrongful convictions in the United States, and responsible for more wrongful convictions than all other causes combined. In a study conducted by . . . the Innocence Project at the Benjamin Cardozo School of Law, mistaken identifications played a major part in the wrongful conviction of over two-thirds of the first 138 postconviction DNA exonerations. . . .

¶31 In light of such evidence, we recognize that our current approach to eyewitness identification has significant flaws. [It] is extremely difficult, if not impossible, for courts to distinguish between identifications that were reliable and identifications that were unreliable. . . . Because a witness can be influenced by the suggestive procedure itself, a court cannot know exactly how reliable the identification would have been without the suggestiveness. . . .

¶33 With *Stovall* as our guide, we now adopt a different test in Wisconsin regarding the admissibility of showup identifications. We conclude that evidence obtained from an out-of-court showup is inherently suggestive and will not be admissible unless, based on the totality of the circumstances, the procedure was necessary. A showup will not be necessary, however, unless the police lacked probable cause to make an arrest or, as a result of other exigent circumstances, could not have conducted a lineup or photo array. A lineup or photo array is generally fairer than a showup, because it distributes the probability of identification among the number of persons arrayed, thus reducing the risk of a misidentification. . . .

¶34 We emphasize that our approach . . . is not a per se exclusionary rule like Dubose requests. Showups have been a useful instrument in investigating and prosecuting criminal cases, and there will continue to be circumstances in which such a procedure is necessary and appropriate.

¶35 If and when the police determine that a showup is necessary, special care must be taken to minimize potential suggestiveness. We recommend procedures similar to those proposed by the Wisconsin Innocence Project to help make showup identifications as non-suggestive as possible. For example, it is important that showups are not conducted in locations, or in a manner, that implicitly conveys to the witness that the suspect is guilty. Showups conducted in police stations, squad cars, or with the suspect in handcuffs that are visible to any witness, all carry with them inferences of guilt, and thus should be considered suggestive. Next, officers investigating the matter at issue should proceed with caution in instructing the witness. [An] eyewitness should be told that the real suspect may or may not be present, and that the investigation will continue regardless of the result of the impending identification procedure. Finally, it is important that a suspect be shown to the witness only once. If a suspect is identified, the police have no reason to conduct further identification procedures. Conversely, if the suspect is not identified by the witness, he or she should not be presented to that witness in any subsequent showups. While this list is far from complete, a showup conducted in accord with these standards will do much to alleviate the inherent suggestiveness of the procedure.

¶36 Applying this approach to the facts before us, it is clear that the showups conducted were unnecessarily suggestive, and that the admission of identification evidence denied Dubose a right to due process under Article I, Section 8 of the Wisconsin Constitution. First, there existed sufficient facts at the time of Dubose's arrest to establish probable cause for his arrest. It was not necessary for the police to conduct the showups, since they had sufficient evidence against Dubose to arrest him without such showups. Next, the officers handcuffed Dubose and placed him in the back seat of a squad car. . . . Third, the police officers told the witness, Hiltsley, that they may have caught "one of the guys" who had robbed him. . . .

¶37 Finally, after the first showup was conducted and Dubose was positively identified, the police still conducted two more identification procedures, another showup and a photo of Dubose, at the police station shortly after Dubose's arrival. These subsequent identification procedures were unnecessarily suggestive. . . .

¶38 On remand, we recognize that the exclusion of evidence of the out-of-court identifications does not deprive the prosecutor of reliable evidence of guilt. The witness would still be permitted to identify the defendant in court if that identification is based on an independent source. And properly conducted pretrial viewings can still be proven at trial and would be encouraged by the rule prohibiting use of suggestive ones. . . . The in-court identification is admissible if the State carries the burden of showing by clear and convincing evidence that the in-court identifications were based upon observations of the suspect other than the out-of-court identification. . . .

¶42 We gain support for our reliance on the Wisconsin Constitution by noting that the federal standard in out-of-court eyewitness identifications has also not been accepted, on state constitutional grounds, in two prominent states — New York and Massachusetts. See Commonwealth v. Johnson, 650 N.E.2d 1257 (Mass. 1995); People v. Adams, 423 N.E.2d 379 (N.Y. 1981). Although these states have adopted a per se exclusionary rule under their respective state constitutions, and thus provide a different approach than this court, we recognize nevertheless that Wisconsin does not stand alone on out-of-court identification issues.

¶43 We also recognize that this case is not the first to result in a change in principles based on extensive new studies completed after a court decision that was premised on constitutional interpretation and application. For example, in Brown v. Board of Education, 347 U.S. 483 (1954), the United States Supreme Court relied on comprehensive studies to support its legal conclusion that the doctrine of separate but equal was violative of the United States Constitution and, thus, that Plessy v. Ferguson, 163 U.S. 537 (1896) should be overruled. For support of this much-needed shift in constitutional law, the United States Supreme Court based its decision on several modern studies and on the effects of segregation in public education. . . .

LOUIS B. BUTLER, JR., J., concurring.

. . . ¶47 I agree with Justice Roggensack that with respect to identification testimony in criminal trials, reliability should be the key to admissibility. . . . However, I part ways with the dissent precisely because showup identifications have been shown to be unreliable, thereby undercutting the legal fiction that we have operated under with respect to eyewitness testimony.

¶48 Some of the very research relied upon by the dissent to illustrate the disagreements about the unreliability of showups sets forth an overall accuracy rate of 69 percent for showups, compared to 51 percent for lineups. Nancy Steblay, et al., Eyewitness Accuracy Rates in Police Showup and Lineup Presentations: A Meta-Analytic Comparison, 27 Law and Human Behavior 523, 535 (2003). Although not mentioned by the dissent, that research further indicates that when the target is in the display, a correct identification occurs only 47 percent of the time in showups, compared to 45 percent of the time in lineups. Moreover, when the target is not in the display, a false identification of an innocent suspect . . . occurs 23 percent of the time in showups, as opposed to 17 percent of the time in lineups.

¶49 This is not "disputed social science theory." This is data relied upon by the dissent. What we are dealing with is a serious failure rate with respect to eyewitness identifications. Whether we are looking at the dissent's failure rate for showups of 53 percent, 31 percent, 23 percent, or 16 percent, that rate is simply unacceptable. The dissent cannot seriously argue that any of these statistical misidentification rates lead to the conclusion that eyewitness identifications are inherently reliable. What we have here is a legal fiction that is simply not borne out by the facts. Unless, and until, we improve eyewitness identification procedures so that the likelihood of irreparable misidentification is significantly reduced, we can no longer proceed as though all is good in the Land of Oz. . . .

¶51 The reasons supporting our approach should be readily apparent. If the wrong person is incorrectly identified, an innocent person faces potential prosecution, incarceration, and conviction. More important, however, is the fact that the guilty perpetrator remains at large, able to wreak havoc upon an unsuspecting populace. No one wants that. I therefore join the majority opinion in this matter. . . .

JON P. WILCOX, J., dissenting.

¶61 Today the majority [abandons a] long line of well-established precedent, contending that the Due Process Clause of the Wisconsin Constitution now affords greater protections than its federal counterpart. In doing so, the majority provides no legal justification for its decision other than its raw power to do so. The majority . . . fails to articulate a rationale for how identical language in the two documents can mean the same thing for a number of years and now suddenly mean something different. . . .

¶65 Furthermore, I, too, am troubled by the majority's reliance on recent social science "studies," presented by advocacy groups, to justify its departure from stare decisis. Not only is such data disputed, . . . but, more importantly, it is not a valid basis to determine the meaning of our constitution. The majority fails to adequately explain how the meaning of the text of the constitution can change every time a new series of social science "studies" is presented to the court. If the text is so fluid, then our constitution is no constitution at all, merely a device to be invoked whenever four members of this court wish to change the law.

¶66 It is not the function of this court to create what it considers to be good social policy based on data from social science "studies." That is the province of the legislature. Our task is to render decisions based on legal principles and constitutional authority.

DAVID T. PROSSER, J., dissenting.

¶69 As in any case, the facts are critical. After committing an armed robbery against Timothy Hiltsley, two men fled from Hiltsley's residence in Green Bay. A few minutes later, at about 1:21 A.M., a neighbor called the police to report the two men fleeing the scene. Police officers arrived immediately, and one of the responding officers observed two men walking near the apartment. When the officer turned his vehicle around to investigate, the men fled between two houses, into the middle of a residential block.

¶70 The police immediately set up a perimeter around the block. By all accounts, this took less than 90 seconds. Upon searching the area, the police quickly discovered Dubose. The officers placed Dubose in the back of a squad car and drove him to Hiltsley's location, where they conducted a showup. Hiltsley immediately identified Dubose as the man who robbed him at gunpoint, mentioning that he recognized Dubose due to his build and hairstyle. . . . All of this occurred within minutes after the robbery.

¶72 Shortly thereafter, other officers located a semi-automatic pistol within the perimeter, near the houses where the two unidentified men ran after being pursued by the police. . . .

¶74 The facts in this case are not sufficient to justify the majority's conclusion that this defendant's due process rights were violated. Nothing in these facts is so inherently unfair or suggestive that it justifies this court-ordered sea change in the law. . . .

¶76 By sheer volume of cases, the Supreme Court has developed substantial experience interpreting constitutional provisions. Matters reaching the Supreme Court are of such import that they are also likely to be better briefed and argued than issues in the state court system. When state courts adopt myriad different interpretations of state constitutions, the level of uncertainty rises exponentially. A suspect's constitutional rights may change dramatically depending on which side of a state line he robs an acquaintance. . . .

PATIENCE DRAKE ROGGENSACK, J., dissenting.

¶79 [The] majority requires the suppression of identifications of defendants charged with crimes, no matter how reliable the identification. This holding substitutes a search for the truth, which should form the foundation for every criminal prosecution, with one social science theory that showup identifications are "unnecessarily suggestive." . . . I dissent because reliability, and not a disputed social science theory, must be the key to admissibility of all identification testimony in criminal trials and because I conclude that the totality of circumstances bearing on the identification in this case resulted in a reliable identification of Dubose as the perpetrator of the armed robbery of which he was convicted. . . .

¶80 The term "due process of law" comes from the Magna Charta's promise of a trial directed by the "law of the land" as established by the legislative body of government. One of the four paintings in the Wisconsin Supreme Court hearing room depicts the signing of the Magna Charta. . . . I note this because constitutional principles are not to change depending on what social science theory is in fashion. . . .

¶83 There are many factors that bear on whether an identification is reliable. Showup identifications that are done soon after the commission of the crime, while the appearance of the perpetrator is fresh in a witness's mind, have more reliability than identifications done after the passage of considerable time. Additionally, showup identifications are done in-person, and corporeal identifications are generally held more reliable than photo identifications. *Simmons*, 390 U.S. at 386 n.6 (citing P. Wall, Eye-Witness Identification in Criminal Cases 83 (1965); Williams, Identification Parades, [1955] Crim. L. Rev. 525, 531).

¶87 The rule of law announced today is not based on constitutional principle. This is demonstrated in part by the majority opinion's decision that if officers lack probable cause to arrest, then a showup is permissible. [This places] a defendant in the unusual position of arguing that law enforcement had probable cause to arrest, so the showup identification was unnecessary and accordingly should be suppressed. This is an odd position in which to place a defendant whose defense is, "It wasn't me." . . .

¶90 The research cited by the majority does not represent the only social science theory on the subject of identifications. Hard data that social scientists have analyzed have resulted in disagreements about the unreliability of showups. One social science study reports that "overall, the results present surprising commonality in outcome between [showups and lineups] and . . . an apparent contradiction of the ambient knowledge that showups are more dangerous for innocent suspects than are lineups." Nancy Steblay, et al., Eyewitness Accuracy Rates in Police Showup and Lineup Presentations: A Meta-Analytic Comparison, 27 Law and Human Behavior 523, 535 (2003). Steblay reported that

> when overall identification decisions are tabulated, showups produce an accuracy advantage over lineups (69% vs. 51%). This initial result is qualified by subsequent analyses. As anticipated, a consideration of specific subject choices provides a more complete picture. Correct identification (hit) rate within the context of a target-present condition is nearly identical for the two types of procedures: Approximately 46% of witnesses shown either a lineup or a showup correctly identified the perpetrator when he or she was present. False suspect identification rates in a target-absent display are also approximately equal between showups and lineups, at about 16%. . . .

¶94 No one wants the wrong person identified as the perpetrator of a crime. However, where I part company with the majority opinion and the concurrence is that I am not willing to throw out identifications like the one now before us that are reliable, as the means of addressing those identifications that are not reliable. . . .

¶95 All identification procedures, from showups to lineups to photo arrays, can be improved by crafting better techniques for these methods to reduce suggestiveness and increase reliability. Proposed improvements include videotaping eyewitness identifications and making standard the need for officers to inform eyewitnesses that the suspect in the showup may not be the perpetrator or that the perpetrator may not be included in the lineup or array. See Gary L. Wells & Elizabeth A. Olson, Eyewitness Testimony, 54 Ann. Rev. Psychol. 277, 286 (2003). . . . Other proposed enhancements include allowing expert testimony on the reliability of eyewitness identifications or jury instructions on eyewitness identification. None of these well-respected sources advocate the ban of showup identifications as the majority opinion has done. Instead, they advocate for law enforcement education on how to better conduct eyewitness identifications and for a more complete presentation of the problems with eyewitness identification at trial.

¶96 In sum, because reliability, and not a disputed social science theory, must be the key to admissibility of all identification testimony in criminal trials and because I conclude that the totality of circumstances bearing on the identification in this case resulted in a reliable identification of Dubose as the perpetrator of the armed robbery of which he was convicted, I would affirm the court of appeals. . . .

Problem 9-1. The Pizza Hut Robbery

Shortly before 1:00 A.M., Kathy Davis was preparing to leave the Pizza Hut where she worked as manager. Her husband, John Davis, and her brother, Gerald Wilson, had come to visit her and accompany her home. As they left the building, they were accosted by a man wearing a white scarf across his face and carrying a metal pipe ("the pipe man"). He demanded that they give him the bank bag with the day's receipts. Wilson attempted to grapple with the robber. The robber hit Wilson with the pipe and then told a second robber ("the gunman") that if Wilson moved again, the gunman should kill him.

This was the first indication that a second robber was present. The gunman was crouched near the corner of the building, about 25 feet away from the victims, holding a gun. The man, who wore a hat and covered the lower part of his face with a scarf, held the gun on Wilson while Kathy and John went back into the building. They brought the bank bag out to the robbers, who then fled. The victims reported the robbery to the police, who responded within a few minutes.

Wilson described the gunman as a male Mexican, five feet nine inches to six feet tall, wearing a blue sweater and jeans, with a white scarf around the lower part of his face. He described the pipe man in more detail: male Mexican, 21 to 22 years old, five feet seven inches to five feet eight inches tall, 155 to 160 pounds, shaggy brown hair, brown eyes, wearing a blue sweater and Levi's and a white scarf over the lower part of his face, one front tooth missing, and a bald spot on the side of his head.

A short time after the robbery, police officers apprehended Livio Ramirez, who had been walking with another man, who fled at the sight of a police car. Ramirez was wearing jeans, a blue sweatshirt with paint spattered on the front, and a brown baseball cap. Ramirez also had readily visible tattoos on his arms. They searched Ramirez and handcuffed him to the fence by placing a second set of handcuffs through the fence and attaching them to the handcuffs Ramirez was wearing.

Roughly 45 minutes after the end of the robbery, the police drove Kathy Davis, John Davis, and Gerald Wilson to the location where Ramirez was handcuffed to the fence to determine whether they could identify him as one of the robbers. The police told them they had found someone who matched the description of one of the robbers.

Ramirez, a dark-complexioned Apache Indian with long hair, was the only suspect present and was surrounded by police officers. The police turned the headlights and spotlights from the police cars on Ramirez to provide adequate light. The witnesses viewed Ramirez by looking at him from the back seat of a police car. Of the three witnesses, only Wilson identified Ramirez as the masked man with the gun; the other two witnesses were unable to identify him as one of the robbers. Following the identification, Ramirez was placed under arrest and was charged with the robbery.

Assume that the state Supreme Court has interpreted the state constitution to diverge from the federal test of Neil v. Biggers when it comes to the reliability of suggestive identification procedures. Under the modified state rule, trial courts considering a motion to suppress identification evidence should not consider the level of certainty expressed by the witness, and should consider whether the identification remained consistent over time. Wilson mentioned tattoos and a hat in his description of the gunman for the first time during the suppression hearing. If the trial court admitted this evidence into the trial, could an appellate court fairly apply this modified test to affirm? Compare State v. Ramirez, 817 P.2d 774 (Utah 1991).

Suppose now that Kathy Davis, John Davis, and Gerald Wilson had their first opportunity to identify a suspect during a lineup at the police station two days after the Pizza Hut robbery. Would the due process clause (federal or state) bar the introduction at trial of any evidence of the pretrial identification or an at-trial identification under the following circumstances?

(a) Before the lineup takes place, a police officer mentions to the witnesses that "we have arrested someone for this crime and have included that person in this lineup."
(b) During the lineup, John says (in the presence of Kathy and Gerald), "It's definitely the third guy — I can tell by his eyes." Kathy and Gerald agree that the third lineup participant was the gunman in the robbery.
(c) After the three witnesses have identified a lineup participant as the gunman, a detective says, "You picked out the guy we had arrested for the crime."

NEW YORK CITY POLICE DEPARTMENT, LEGAL BUREAU, EYEWITNESS IDENTIFICATION PROCEDURES: SHOWUPS

A. The one-on-one display of a suspect to a victim is *generally prohibited* as being unnecessarily suggestive, *except:*

1. where it is conducted promptly on-the-scene; or,

2. where there is an emergency hospital situation (witness critically injured and likely to die). . . .

C. Showup Procedures — A police officer should consider the following factors when determining if a prompt on-the-scene showup is permissible:

1. The time elapsed since crime [was] committed. There is no set time limit. However, if more than a few hours have elapsed since the commission of the crime, a showup should *not* be employed. Usually, the apprehension of a suspect and return to the scene for viewing will be within minutes, not hours, of the crime. . . .

4. Showups should not be conducted at a stationhouse.

5. Manner in which suspect is displayed.

a. Never tell the witness that the perpetrator has been "caught," and that the witness must view him for identification purposes.

b. If a witness becomes aware that a "suspect" is in custody, emphasize before the viewing that it is *only a suspect,* and that the witness must not assume it is the perpetrator before even viewing the suspect. . . .

D. Group Identifications

1. Occasions will arise where an officer will ask a witness if he can pick out the suspect from a group of persons not in police custody. [For example, an officer may ask the witness to] observe suspect among a group of individuals (unarranged confrontation). [An officer also might accompany] a witness to an area where suspect is likely to be with other persons, i.e., let witness watch person coming and going from suspect's place of employment, at a park, playground, etc. Procedures:

a. Allow witness to view area, with instructions to look carefully at people on street, in doorways or in stores, etc.

b. If police officer sees a possible suspect, he may draw witness' attention in that direction.

c. Avoid pointing out a single individual, or if necessary, do so in a non-suggestive manner. Don't say, "That looks like him, doesn't it?"

E. There is no right to counsel at any showup procedure.

Notes

1. *Due process limits on suggestive identifications: majority position.* Virtually all jurisdictions have followed the federal position set out in the *Biggers* case and in Manson v. Brathwaite, 432 U.S. 98 (1977). When applying state constitutions to suggestive identifications, courts look to the totality of the circumstances, emphasizing the five factors listed in *Biggers* to determine the "reliability" of an identification despite suggestiveness in the identification procedure. A growing number of state courts, however, now de-emphasize the importance of witness certainty. Courts applying this test refuse to overturn convictions in the overwhelming majority of due process challenges to "suggestive" identifications, although there are exceptions.

Massachusetts employs a per se rule and excludes from evidence *any* identification produced by an unduly suggestive process. See Commonwealth v. Johnson, 650 N.E.2d 1257 (Mass. 1995). The *Johnson* court explained its decision as follows:

> [Mistaken] identification is believed widely to be the primary cause of erroneous convictions. Compounding this problem is the tendency of juries to be unduly receptive to eyewitness evidence. We have stated that "the law has not taken the position that a jury can be relied on to discount the value of an identification by a proper appraisal of the unsatisfactory circumstances in which it may have been made." . . . The "reliability test" is unacceptable because it provides little or no protection from unnecessarily suggestive identification procedures, from mistaken identifications and, ultimately, from wrongful convictions.

Do you agree? Does the per se rule make a defendant better off than she would have been in the absence of any suggestive identification procedure at all?

2. *Unreliable measures of reliability.* Some state courts have criticized the federal "reliability" factors from Neil v. Biggers, 409 U.S. 188 (1972), because they are inconsistent with "empirical" findings of psychologists studying eyewitness memory. One "reliability" factor said to be overrated is the level of certainty a witness displays: Many studies have suggested a very weak correlation, at best, between witness certainty and witness accuracy. A second questionable "reliability" factor is the amount of time a witness originally has to view the suspect. Although the amount of initial exposure is indeed related to the accuracy of memory, most people tend to overestimate the amount of time that elapsed during events that they witness. Did the Wisconsin court in *Dubose* respond adequately to these alleged problems with the federal "reliability" test? Is the court's modified test more empirically grounded? Will it lead to different results?

3. *Showups and lineups.* All other factors being equal, showups are thought to be more suggestive than lineups. Does the due process limitation on the use of identification evidence give police enough reason to avoid showups in favor of lineups whenever possible? Note that the New York City police policy allows showups in the field, but only those occurring within a "reasonable time" (ordinarily within a few hours) of the crime. What proportion of total identification procedures would you imagine occur in this setting? In light of the rapid deterioration of human memory, does the short time lapse between the crime and the identification make the showup, on balance, as reliable as a lineup occurring several hours, days, or weeks later? See Nancy Steblay, Jennifer Dysart, Solomon Fulero & R. C. L. Lindsay, Eyewitness Accuracy Rates in Police Showup and Lineup Presentations: A Meta-Analytic Comparison, 27 Law & Hum. Behav. 523 (2003) (in target-present conditions, showups and lineups yield approximately equal hit rates, whereas in target-absent conditions, showups produce a higher level of correct rejections; false identifications are more numerous for showups when innocent suspect resembles perpetrator).

The recommended procedures for eyewitness evidence issued by the U.S. Department of Justice allow police officers to conduct a showup. Because of the "inherent suggestiveness" of the showup, the witness should be cautioned that the person may not be the perpetrator. According to the guidelines, if one witness identifies a suspect during a showup, the police should use other identification procedures for other witnesses.

4. *Statutory limits on lineups.* For many years, few jurisdictions passed statutes or court rules addressing the use of identification procedures by police. Exonerations based on DNA evidence, however, pointed to identification procedures as a major source of errors in criminal justice and convinced many state legislatures to address

the question. See, e.g., North Carolina General Statutes §15A-284.52 (specifying "warning" statements to be given to witnesses before making identification, and requiring extensive documentation of identification procedures used during investigation). For recent legislative developments in this field, see the web extension for this chapter at *http://www.crimpro.com/extension/ch09*. How do legislatures compare to state appellate courts as the institution to take the lead in changing identification procedures? See Sandra Guerra Thompson, Eyewitness Identifications and State Courts as Guardians Against Wrongful Conviction, 7 Ohio St. J. Criminal Law 603 (2010).

5. *Detention for identification.* Do the police have the power to compel a person who is not currently in custody to participate in a lineup? Many states do address this question by statute and court-issued rules of procedure. See Model Code of Pre-Arraignment Criminal Procedure, art. 170. Nebraska Revised Statutes §29-3303 is typical. It authorizes a judge to order a person to submit to a lineup or some other identification procedure (such as fingerprinting). The order may issue upon a showing that (1) there is probable cause to believe that an offense has been committed; (2) identification procedures may contribute to the identification of the individual who committed the offense; and (3) the identified or described individual has refused, or will refuse, to participate voluntarily.

Such a court order is not necessary if a suspect is already in police custody. A few state rules and statutes allow the detention of persons for the purpose of participating in lineups or other identification procedures, even in the absence of probable cause to believe the detained person committed the crime. See State v. Rodriguez, 921 P.2d 643 (Ariz. 1996). Courts have approved of this practice even in the absence of a statute or rule authorizing it. See State v. Hall, 461 A.2d 1155 (N.J. 1983) (court can compel participation in lineup without probable cause). Are identification procedures sufficiently similar to fingerprinting to allow a judicial order of detention based on less than probable cause? Note that detention for fingerprinting at the station house, based on less than probable cause, would likely be an unconstitutional "seizure" if it took place without a judicial order. See Davis v. Mississippi, 394 U.S. 721 (1969). In a state allowing the police to detain a suspect for identification purposes, should a defendant have a comparable power to obtain a court order forcing *another* suspect to attend a lineup? Should citizens generally have an obligation to take part in a lineup along with a suspect who physically resembles them? Would you willingly take part in a lineup? For modest compensation, say, $100?

■ JOHN J. FARMER, ATTORNEY GENERAL GUIDELINES FOR PREPARING AND CONDUCTING PHOTO AND LIVE LINEUP IDENTIFICATION PROCEDURES

Attorney General of New Jersey, April 18, 2001

I. Composing the Photo or Live Lineup

The following procedures will result in the composition of a photo or live lineup in which a suspect does not unduly stand out. An identification obtained through a lineup composed in this manner should minimize any risk of misidentification and have stronger evidentiary value than one obtained without these procedures.

A. In order to ensure that inadvertent verbal cues or body language do not impact on a witness, whenever practical, considering the time of day, day of the week, and other personnel conditions within the agency or department, the person conducting the photo or live lineup identification procedure should be someone other than the primary investigator assigned to the case. The Attorney General recognizes that in many departments, depending upon the size and other assignments of personnel, this may be impossible in a given case. In those cases where the primary investigating officer conducts the photo or live lineup identification procedure, he or she should be careful to avoid inadvertent signaling to the witness of the "correct" response.

B. The witness should be instructed prior to the photo or live lineup identification procedure that the perpetrator may not be among those in the photo array or live lineup and, therefore, they should not feel compelled to make an identification.

C. When possible, photo or live lineup identification procedures should be conducted sequentially, i.e., showing one photo or person at a time to the witness, rather than simultaneously.

D. In composing a photo or live lineup, the person administering the identification procedure should ensure that the lineup is comprised in such a manner that the suspect does not unduly stand out. However, complete uniformity of features is not required.

E. *Photo Lineup.* In composing a photo lineup, the lineup administrator or investigator should:

1. Include only one suspect in each identification procedure.
2. Select fillers (non-suspects) who generally fit the witness' description of the perpetrator. When there is a limited or inadequate description of the perpetrator provided by the witness, or when the description of the perpetrator differs significantly from the appearance of the suspect, fillers should resemble the suspect in significant features.
3. Select a photo that resembles the suspect's description or appearance at the time of the incident if multiple photos of the suspect are reasonably available to the investigator.
4. Include a minimum of five fillers (nonsuspects) per identification procedure.
5. Consider placing the suspect in different positions in each lineup when conducting more than one lineup for a case due to multiple witnesses.
6. Avoid reusing fillers in lineups shown to the same witness when showing a new suspect. . . .

9. Preserve the presentation order of the photo lineup. In addition, the photos themselves should be preserved in their original condition. . . .

II. Conducting the Identification Procedure . . .

B. *Sequential Photo Lineup.* When presenting a sequential photo lineup, the lineup administrator or investigator should:

1. Provide viewing instructions to the witness as outlined in subsection I B, above.

2. Provide the following additional viewing instructions to the witness:

a. Individual photographs will be viewed one at a time.

b. The photos are in random order.

c. Take as much time as needed in making a decision about each photo before moving to the next one.

d. All photos will be shown, even if an identification is made prior to viewing all photos; or the procedure will be stopped at the point of an identification (consistent with jurisdiction/departmental procedures).

3. Confirm that the witness understands the nature of the sequential procedure.

4. Present each photo to the witness separately, in a previously determined order, removing those previously shown.

5. Avoid saying anything to the witness that may influence the witness' selection.

6. If an identification is made, avoid reporting to the witness any information regarding the individual he or she has selected prior to obtaining the witness' statement of certainty.

7. Record any identification results and witness' statement of certainty. . . .

9. Instruct the witness not to discuss the identification procedure or its results with other witnesses involved in the case and discourage contact with the media.

Problem 9-2. Photo Lineups

On August 8, a man robbed the Fort Gratiot branch of the People's Bank in Port Huron, Michigan, of more than $22,000 (including approximately $600 in Canadian currency). Three bank tellers, the branch manager, and a customer witnessed the robbery and gave descriptions of the robber and his car to investigators. Bank teller Mary Kamendat described the robber as approximately 45 or 46 years old, almost six feet tall, weighing about 210 pounds, with dust or some other substance on his face. She also described him as needing a haircut. Another bank teller, Cindy Dortman, noticed that the robber was wearing a light-colored shirt, a baseball cap, dark sunglasses, and had longer hair than normal for a man of his age. She also described him as wearing flared jeans, with a chain hanging out of his pocket and his shirt pulled over his pants. She said that the robber had a "long, very distinguished" nose.

The bank's surveillance camera took photographs of the robber. After the local newspaper published two of the surveillance photographs a few days after the crime, the St. Glair County Sheriff's Department received several phone calls regarding the robbery. One caller identified Albin Kurylczyk as the man in the photographs. This information prompted a detective and an FBI agent to visit Kurylczyk at his home on August 17. At their request, Kurylczyk permitted the officers to search his house and his car, which was similar to the getaway car the eyewitnesses had described. He also agreed to accompany the investigators to the local police station for further interviews. Once there, he consented to be photographed. At that time, he was not represented by counsel, nor did he request an attorney.

On the same day, other deputies responded to a call from the bank. The bank tellers Dortman and Kamendat believed the robber had returned when a customer dressed like the robber entered the bank and attempted to exchange some

Canadian currency. The tellers detained him by delaying his transaction until the deputies arrived. However, after an investigation, the law enforcement authorities were satisfied that this customer was not the bank robber. He was not included in any of the identification procedures used later in the investigation.

Two days later, on August 19, a detective assembled an array of six photographs, including the photograph he had taken of Kurylczyk and one of another suspect. Kurylczyk was the only man in the photographic array dressed in clothing that matched the description of the eyewitnesses. In particular, his photo showed him wearing a chain attached to his belt and extending to a wallet in the rear pocket of his jeans. None of the others in the photographic lineup wore such a trucker's wallet. This same type of wallet was visible in the bank's surveillance photographs, as published in the local paper. In addition, Kurylczyk's photograph was taken from a closer distance, so that his image appeared larger than the others. Three of the men in the array had mustaches; Kurylczyk did not have a mustache, and none of the witnesses described the robber as having a mustache.

The detective showed the photo array to Kamendat and Dortman, and both identified Kurylczyk as the bank robber. As a result, the government charged him with the crime. Before trial, Kurylczyk moved to exclude the identification testimony of the eyewitnesses. First, he contended that he was entitled to the assistance of counsel during the photographic lineup. Second, he argued that the photographic lineup was impermissibly suggestive in violation of his Fourteenth Amendment right of due process. How should the trial court rule? Compare People v. Kurylczyk, 505 N.W.2d 528 (Mich. 1993).

Problem 9-3. Videorecorded Lineups

At 2:20 A.M., a man entered a gas station and asked Roy Beals, the attendant, for permission to use the telephone. He was followed by a second man, holding what appeared to be a .45-caliber automatic pistol, and by a third man, whom Beals was unable to see. The three men robbed the gas station. Beals told police after the robbery that the gunman was approximately 5"6' or 5"7' tall, and wore a knee-length brown vinyl coat, with a fleecy lining and collar. From the loose fit of the coat, Beals assumed the man was thin. The man wore what appeared to be uniform pants and a security guard's cap, with a badge, and had a second badge pinned on his collar. The fleecy coat collar was turned up around the man's face, and the bill of his cap came down to his eyebrows. Beals was therefore able to observe only a portion of the man's face. From his observation, Beals could tell that the gunman was a black man and that he was not wearing glasses, but could not describe him further. He could not describe the man's hair or estimate his age.

The gunman told Beals to turn around, go into a back room, and lie face down on the floor. Following Beals into the backroom, the gunman then asked where "the money" was. Beals answered that the money was in a locked box on a post outside. The man demanded a key, but Beals did not have one. At one point, the gunman struck him with the weapon he was carrying. The robbers were in the station for about five minutes, and Beals spent most of this time face down on the floor.

Later that same day, the police stopped a car containing four young black men, including Oscar McMillian. The four occupants of the car were taken into custody. At some point, the police staged a lineup, consisting of these four men, in connection with the investigation of an unrelated crime, a purse-snatching. The lineup was recorded on videotape with an audio recording of the men speaking. No attorney was present at this lineup.

Several days later, McMillian was charged with armed robbery. Soon thereafter, the police showed the videotaped lineup to Beals. McMillian was given no notice that Beals was to view the recorded lineup, and defense counsel was not present at the viewing. Based on the defendant's height, build, and voice, Beals identified McMillian as the gunman in the gas station robbery. Was it error to allow Beals to view the videotape without McMillian's attorney being present? Will the trial court allow Beals to identify McMillian at trial? Compare McMillian v. State, 265 N.W.2d 553 (Wis. 1978).

Notes

1. *Due process limits on photo identifications.* As with in-person identifications, the due process clause creates a second constitutional restraint on photographic identifications. If the photo array is unduly suggestive, *and* if the totality of the circumstances suggests that the improper identification procedure created an undue risk of misidentification, the court will exclude at trial any evidence based on that tainted identification. See Commonwealth v. Silva-Santiago, 906 N.E.2d 299 (Mass. 2009) (court described the preferred procedures for presenting photographic arrays to eyewitnesses, and declared that it expected law enforcement agencies to follow these protocols in future; double-blind procedure is best practice but not required in every case; no suppression of identification in this case).

Many of the claims of unduly "suggestive" photo arrays derive from the showing of multiple photo arrays to the witness when the suspect's picture appears in each of the arrays. Courts virtually always reject challenges based on these claims. See, e.g., State v. Rezk, 609 A.2d 391 (N.H. 1992) (approves an identification in second photo lineup when defendant was the only subject pictured also in first photo lineup and was the only person pictured in prison overalls).

2. *Departmental policies and photospreads.* The New Jersey Attorney General policy on photo identifications reprinted above is based in part on recommendations from the U.S. Department of Justice. What would motivate a law enforcement official to recommend procedures that are more specific than what the courts have required in constitutional litigation? The New Jersey policy differs from the DOJ policy in stating a preference for sequential lineups and "blind" presentations. What are the arguments against these two requirements?

3. *Whose pictures?* When the police have no suspect, they will sometimes ask the witness to review a large number of photos in the hope that the perpetrator's picture will appear. Which pictures can the police show to a witness? Can the photos include only those who have been convicted of a crime similar to the one now at issue? Any arrested person? Any person at all? Suppose the police collect pictures of persons from one ethnic group, awaiting those occasions when a crime victim is attempting to identify, say, an Asian perpetrator? See San Jose Recorder, Jan. 31, 1996 (lawsuit settlement by the town of San Jose, California, paying $150,000 in damages to person who spent three months in jail after being identified by witness to armed robbery; witness selected photograph from mug book containing pictures

only of Asians, many of whom — like plaintiff — had never been arrested or convicted). More recently, computer programs have enabled the police to create a digitized image based on the description by a witness, and to match that digitized image to photographs in existing databases such as arrest files or drivers' license pictures. For a survey of the typical features of this software, see the web extension of this chapter at *http://www.crimpro.com/extension/ch09*.

C. OTHER REMEDIES FOR IMPROPER IDENTIFICATION PROCEDURES

As we have seen, one remedy for improper pretrial identification procedures is the exclusion at trial of any evidence of the pretrial identification, along with the possible exclusion of any at-trial identification based on the earlier procedure. But the exclusion remedy is extreme. Recall that identifications tend to be important to the prosecution in cases charging very serious crimes such as rape and robbery. Perhaps for this reason, courts invoke the remedy in only a small number of cases. Whatever problems might be present with the identification procedure, courts have concluded most of the time that the improper identification method was a "harmless error" of sorts — that it did not cause the witness to make an improper identification.

In sum, the exclusion remedy is available to very few defendants who have legitimate complaints about improper identification procedures. Is there some way other than exclusion for these defendants to reduce the chances of an erroneous conviction?

The following case considers the need for a jury instruction that highlights the difficulties of cross-racial identifications. Do you believe that the arguments in favor of such an instruction are basically the same as those supporting instructions about identifications more generally, or is there something distinctively difficult about cross-racial identifications? Will jury instructions of the sort described in this opinion actually change juror conduct?

STATE v. McKINLEY CROMEDY

727 A.2d 457 (N.J. 1999)

COLEMAN, J.

This appeal involves a rape and robbery in which a cross-racial identification was made of defendant as the perpetrator seven months after the offenses occurred. The identification of the perpetrator was the critical issue throughout the trial. The trial court denied defendant's request to have the jury instructed concerning the cross-racial nature of the identification. . . . The novel issue presented is whether a cross-racial identification jury instruction should be required in certain cases before it is established that there is substantial agreement in the scientific community that cross-racial recognition impairment of eyewitnesses is significant enough to warrant a special jury instruction. Our study of the recommendations of a Court-appointed Task Force, judicial literature, and decisional law from other jurisdictions persuades us that there exists a reliable basis for a cross-racial identification charge. We hold that the trial court's failure to submit to the jury an instruction similar to the one requested by defendant requires a reversal of defendant's convictions.

On the night of August 28, 1992, D.S., a white female student then enrolled at Rutgers University in New Brunswick, was watching television in her basement apartment. While she was relaxing on the couch, an African-American male entered the brightly lit apartment and demanded money from D.S., claiming that he was wanted for murder and that he needed funds to get to New York. After D.S. told the intruder that she had no money, he spotted her purse, rifled through it, and removed money and credit cards.

The intruder then [demanded that she remain quiet and led her by the arm into the brightly lit kitchen. He sexually assaulted her.] Throughout the sexual assault, D.S. was facing the kitchen door with her eyes closed and hand over her mouth to avoid crying loudly. Once the assault was over, D.S. faced her attacker who, after threatening her again, turned around and left the apartment. At the time of the second threat, D.S. was standing approximately two feet away from her assailant. The attacker made no attempt to conceal his face at any time. D.S. immediately called the New Brunswick Police Department after the intruder left the apartment. . . .

D.S. described her assailant as an African-American male in his late 20s to early 30s, full-faced, about five feet five inches tall, with a medium build, mustache, and unkempt hair. She stated that the intruder was wearing a dirty gray button-down short-sleeved shirt, blue warm-up pants with white and red stripes, and a Giants logo on the left leg. . . . Three days later, a composite sketch was drawn by an artist with her assistance. The following day at police headquarters, D.S. was shown many slides and photographs, including a photograph of defendant, in an unsuccessful attempt to identify her assailant.

On April 7, 1993, almost eight months after the crimes were committed, D.S. saw an African-American male across the street from her who she thought was her attacker. She spotted the man while she was standing on the corner of a street in New Brunswick waiting for the light to change. As the two passed on the street, D.S. studied the individual's face and gait. Believing that the man was her attacker, D.S. ran home and telephoned the police, giving them a description of the man she had just seen. Defendant was picked up by the New Brunswick police and taken to headquarters almost immediately. Within fifteen minutes after seeing defendant on the street, D.S. viewed defendant in a "show-up" from behind a one-way mirror and immediately identified him as the man she had just seen on the street and as her attacker. Defendant was then arrested and, with his consent, saliva and blood samples were taken for scientific analysis. [The State Police Laboratory was unable to determine whether those samples matched the samples obtained from D.S. at the time of the crime.]

Because of the nature of the crimes, the races of the victim and defendant, and the inability of the victim to identify defendant from his photograph, and because defendant was not positively identified until almost eight months after the date of the offenses, defense counsel sought a cross-racial identification jury charge. The following language was proposed:

> [Y]ou know that the identifying witness is of a different race than the defendant. When a witness who is a member of one race identifies a member who is of another race we say there has been a cross-racial identification. You may consider, if you think it is

> appropriate to do so, whether the cross-racial nature of the identification has affected the accuracy of the witness's original perception and/or accuracy of a subsequent identification.

In support of that request, defendant cited the June 1992 New Jersey Supreme Court Task Force on Minority Concerns Final Report, 131 N.J. L.J. 1145 (1992) (Task Force Report).

The trial court denied the request because this Court had not yet adopted the Task Force Report and because there had been no expert testimony with respect to the issue of cross-racial identification. The trial court instead provided the jury with the Model Jury Charge on Identification. The jury convicted defendant of first-degree aggravated sexual assault. . . .

For more than forty years, empirical studies concerning the psychological factors affecting eyewitness cross-racial or cross-ethnic identifications have appeared with increasing frequency in professional literature of the behavioral and social sciences. People v. McDonald, 690 P.2d 709, 717-18 (Cal. 1984). [Studies] have concluded that eyewitnesses are superior at identifying persons of their own race and have difficulty identifying members of another race. See generally Gary Wells & Elizabeth Loftus, Eyewitness Testimony: Psychological Perspectives 1 (1984); Elizabeth Loftus, Eyewitness Testimony (1979). This phenomenon has been dubbed the "own-race" effect or "own-race" bias. Its corollary is that eyewitnesses experience a "cross-racial impairment" when identifying members of another race. Studies have consistently shown that the "own-race effect" is strongest when white witnesses attempt to recognize black subjects.

Although researchers generally agree that some eyewitnesses exhibit an own-race bias, they disagree about the degree to which own-race bias affects identification. In one study, African-American and white "customers" browsed in a convenience store for a few minutes and then went to the register to pay. Researchers asked the convenience store clerks to identify the "customers" from a photo array. The white clerks were able to identify 53.2% of the white customers but only 40.4% of the African-American subjects. Stephanie Platz & Harmon Hosch, Cross-Racial/Ethnic Eyewitness Identification: A Field Study, 18 J. Applied Soc. Psychol. 972, 977-78 (1988). . . .

Many studies on cross-racial impairment involve subjects observing photographs for a few seconds. Because the subjects remembered the white faces more often than they recalled the African-American faces, researchers concluded that they were biased towards their own race. See Paul Barkowitz & John C. Brigham, Recognition of Faces: Own-Race Bias, Incentive, and Time Delay, 12 J. Applied Soc. Psychol. 255 (1982). Yet, there is disagreement over whether the results of some of the tests can be generalized to real-world situations in which a victim or witness confronts an assailant face-to-face and experiences the full range of emotions that accompany such a traumatic event.

The debate among researchers did not prevent the Supreme Court of the United States, in the famous school desegregation case of Brown v. Board of Education of Topeka, 347 U.S. 483, 494 n.11 (1954), from using behavioral and social sciences to support legal conclusions without requiring that the methodology employed by those scientists have general acceptance in the scientific community. . . . Thus, Brown v. Board of Education is the prototypical example of an appellate court using modern social and behavioral sciences as legislative evidence to support its choice of a rule of law.

In United States v. Telfaire, 469 F.2d 552 (D.C. Cir. 1972), Chief Judge Bazelon urged in his concurring opinion that juries be charged on the pitfalls of cross-racial identification. He believed that the cross-racial nature of an identification could affect accuracy in the same way as proximity to the perpetrator and poor lighting conditions. He felt that a meaningful jury instruction would have to apprise jurors of that fact. . . . Judge Bazelon rejected the notion that instructions on interracial identifications "appeal to racial prejudice." Rather, he believed that an explicit jury instruction would safeguard against improper uses of race by the jury and would delineate the narrow context in which it is appropriate to consider racial differences. . . .

The Supreme Court of the United States has acknowledged that problems exist with eyewitness identifications in general and cross-racial identifications in particular. Manson v. Brathwaite, 432 U.S. 98 (1977). Although there have been no reported decisions in our own State addressing the propriety of requiring a cross-racial identification jury instruction, decisions have been rendered by courts in other jurisdictions. The majority of courts allowing cross-racial identification charges hold that the decision to provide the instruction is a matter within the trial judge's discretion. Omission of such a cautionary instruction has been held to be prejudicial error where identification is the critical or central issue in the case, there is no corroborating evidence, and the circumstances of the case raise doubts concerning the reliability of the identification. See United States v. Thompson, 31 M.J. 125 (C.M.A. 1990) (calling for cross-racial identification instruction when requested by counsel and when cross-racial identification is a "primary issue"); People v. Wright, 755 P.2d 1049 (Cal. 1988). . . .

Courts typically have refused the instruction where the eyewitness or victim had an adequate opportunity to observe the defendant, there was corroborating evidence bolstering the identification, and/or there was no evidence that race affected the identification. See Commonwealth v. Hyatt, 647 N.E.2d 1168 (Mass. 1995) (declining instruction in rape and robbery case where victim was terrorized for fifteen to twenty minutes in broad daylight and could see the attacker's face).

A number of courts have concluded that cross-racial identification simply is not an appropriate topic for jury instruction. See State v. Willis, 731 P.2d 287, 292-93 (Kan. 1987); People v. McDaniel, 630 N.Y.S.2d 112, 113 (N.Y. App. Div. 1995). Those courts have determined that the cross-racial instruction requires expert guidance, and that cross-examination and summation are adequate safeguards to highlight unreliable identifications. Other jurisdictions have denied the instruction, finding that the results of empirical studies on cross-racial identification are questionable. People v. Bias, 475 N.E.2d 253, 257 (Ill. App. Ct. 1985) (rejecting instruction in robbery case where eyewitness failed to describe key distinguishing facial features and gave inconsistent descriptions because empirical studies are not unanimous). One jurisdiction has even rejected cross-racial identification instructions as improper commentary on "the nature and quality" of the evidence. See State v. Hadrick, 523 A.2d 441, 444 (R.I. 1987) (rejecting such instruction in robbery case where victim viewed perpetrator for two to three minutes at close range during robbery and identified him from a line-up). . . .

It is well-established in this State that when identification is a critical issue in the case, the trial court is obligated to give the jury a discrete and specific instruction that provides appropriate guidelines to focus the jury's attention on how to analyze and consider the trustworthiness of eyewitness identification. State v. Green, 430 A.2d 914 (N.J. 1981). *Green* requires that as a part of an identification charge a trial court inform the jury that [it] should consider, among other things, "the capacity or the ability of the witness to make observations or perceptions . . . at the time and under all of the attendant circumstances for seeing that which he says he saw or that which he says he perceived with regard to his identification." What defendant sought through the requested charge in the present case was an instruction that informed the jury that it could consider the fact that the victim made a cross-racial identification as part of the "attendant circumstances" when evaluating the reliability of the eyewitness identification.

The Court-appointed Task Force discussed and debated the issue of the need for a cross-racial and cross-ethnic identification jury instruction for more than five years. That Task Force was comprised of an appellate judge, trial judges, lawyers representing both the prosecution and defense, social scientists, and ordinary citizens. . . . Task Force sessions were conducted in much the same way as legislative committees conduct hearings on proposed legislation. . . . Ultimately, in 1992 the Task Force submitted its final report to the Court in which it recommended, among other things, that the Court develop a special jury charge regarding the unreliability of cross-racial identifications.

The Court referred that recommendation to the Criminal Practice Committee. . . . The Criminal Practice Committee has submitted that proposed charge to the Model Jury Charge Committee for its review. That Committee is withholding further consideration of the proposed charge pending the Court's decision in the present case.

We reject the State's contention that we should not require a cross-racial identification charge before it has been demonstrated that there is substantial agreement in the relevant scientific community that cross-racial recognition impairment is significant enough to support the need for such a charge. This case does not concern the introduction of scientific evidence to attack the reliability of the eyewitness's identification. Defendant's requested jury instruction was not based upon any "scientific, technical, or other specialized knowledge" to assist the jury. N.J.R.E. 702. He relied instead on ordinary human experience and the legislative-type findings of the Task Force because the basis for his request did not involve a matter that was beyond the ken of the average juror.

[I]n a prosecution in which race by definition is a patent factor, race must be taken into account to assure a fair trial. At the same time, we recognize that unrestricted use of cross-racial identification instructions could be counter-productive. Consequently, care must be taken to insulate criminal trials from base appeals to racial prejudice. An appropriate jury instruction should carefully delineate the context in which the jury is permitted to consider racial differences. The simple fact pattern of a white victim of a violent crime at the hands of a black assailant would not automatically give rise to the need for a cross-racial identification charge. More is required.

A cross-racial instruction should be given only when, as in the present case, identification is a critical issue in the case, and an eyewitness's cross-racial identification is not corroborated by other evidence giving it independent reliability. Here, the eyewitness identification was critical; yet it was not corroborated by any forensic evidence or other eyewitness account. The circumstances of the case raise some doubt concerning the reliability of the victim's identification in that no positive identification was made for nearly eight months despite attempts within the first five days following the commission of the offenses. Under those circumstances, turning over to the jury the vital question of the reliability of that identification without acquainting the jury with the potential risks associated with such identifications could have affected the jurors' ability to evaluate the reliability of the identification. We conclude, therefore, that it was reversible error not to have given an instruction that informed the jury about the possible significance of the cross-racial identification factor, a factor the jury can observe in many cases with its own eyes, in determining the critical issue — the accuracy of the identification. . . .

Because of the widely held commonsense view that members of one race have greater difficulty in accurately identifying members of a different race, expert testimony on this issue would not assist a jury, and for that reason would be inadmissible. We request the Criminal Practice Committee and the Model Jury Charge Committee to revise the current charge on identification to include an appropriate statement on cross-racial eyewitness identification that is consistent with this opinion. . . .

Notes

1. *Jury instructions about eyewitness testimony: majority position.* Judicial instructions to the jury can remind jurors about the vagaries of human memory. Such instructions are sometimes called *Telfaire* instructions, after one of the first cases to approve of their use. See United States v. Telfaire, 469 F.2d 552 (D.C. Cir. 1972) (describing a suggested jury instruction). Most states leave it to the trial judge to decide whether to grant a defense request for such an instruction. About 30 states allow (but do not require) the trial judge to grant a request for such jury instructions. Roughly 10 states do require jury instructions, at least when there is some special reason to question the identification. See State v. Ledbetter, 881 A.2d 290 (Conn. 2005) (under supervisory power, court requires jury instructions whenever police fail to tell witness that suspect might not be present in the lineup); Brodes v. State, 614 S.E.2d 766, 769 (Ga. 2005) (jury instructions on factors affecting reliability of eyewitness testimony may not state that witness certainty is an indicator of accuracy).

As the court in *Cromedy* discussed, there may be special reasons to instruct the jury on this issue when the prosecution depends on a cross-racial identification. However, a small but growing number of states prohibit the use of such instructions. See Graham v. Commonwealth, 250 Va. 79 (1995). If jury instructions provide enough specific information about the circumstances that tend to produce less reliable eyewitness testimony, are they an adequate replacement for exclusion? See Edith Greene, Eyewitness Testimony and the Use of Cautionary Instructions, 8 U. Bridgeport L. Rev. 15 (1987) (study of impact of standard jury instructions regarding eyewitness memory, concluding they do not improve juror performance).

2. *Admissibility of expert testimony on eyewitness memory.* Starting in the early 1980s, a few defendants asked courts to allow experts to testify about recurring problems with witness memory. At first, very few courts allowed those experts to testify. Since then, the trend has been toward allowing such testimony. The high state courts addressing this question fall into several different groups. Appellate courts in fewer than 10 states still instruct trial courts that such expert testimony is not admissible

in the ordinary criminal case because it invades the province of the jury. The largest group of appellate courts (over 30 states) now allow the trial court the discretion to admit or exclude the testimony. See Weatherred v. State, 15 S.W.3d 540 (Tex. Crim. App. 2000) (trial court excluded, affirmed on appeal); State v. Clopten, 223 P.3d 1103 (Utah 2009) (expert testimony regarding the reliability of eyewitness identification is admissible under the general standard that governs all expert testimony). There are still very few appellate courts that will overturn a trial court's decision to exclude such testimony as an abuse of discretion. Under what circumstances might a court conclude that such testimony is necessary to a fair trial? See People v. LeGrand, 867 N.E.2d 374 (N.Y. 2007) (it can be an abuse of discretion for the trial court to exclude expert testimony about "weapon focus" if guilt or innocence turns on accuracy of eyewitness identifications and there is little or no corroborating evidence connecting defendant to the crime).

3. *The experts on expert testimony.* Social scientists have concluded that there is a great need for expert testimony about eyewitness identifications. Studies of jurors have indicated (with the usual ambiguity of social science studies) that jurors (1) place great weight on eyewitness testimony as they deliberate and reach their verdicts and (2) often have misconceptions about the reliability of eyewitness testimony and the conditions that pose the greatest risks for misidentification. See Brian Cutler, Steven Penrod, & Hedy Dexter, Juror Sensitivity to Eyewitness Identification Evidence, 14 Law & Hum. Behav. 185 (1990) (study showing jurors remain unaffected by factors that should influence accuracy of witness's memory); but cf. Rogers Elliott, B. Farrington, & H. Manheimer, Eyewitnesses Credible and Discredible, 18 J. Appl. Soc. Psychol. 1411 (1988) (recounts difficulty in replicating early studies showing that jurors rely heavily on eyewitness testimony). Social scientists are split on the question of whether expert testimony can correct juror misconceptions about eyewitness memory without affecting their overall willingness to believe eyewitness testimony. Compare Brian Cutler, Steven Penrod, & Hedy Dexter, The Eyewitness, the Expert Psychologist, and the Jury, 13 Law & Hum. Behav. 311 (1989); with E. B. Ebbesen & V. J. Konecni, Eyewitness Memory Research: Probative v. Prejudicial Value, 5 Expert Evidence 2-28 (1997) (prejudicial outweighs probative value).

4. *Expert testimony as a substitute for exclusion.* In light of the rare use of the exclusion remedy, is expert testimony a more effective method of preventing wrongful convictions? Is due process satisfied whenever the defense can counter any prosecution eyewitness testimony with expert testimony about human memory? Must the government pay for such experts to testify for indigent criminal defendants? See Espinosa v. State, 589 So. 2d 887 (Fla. 1991) (trial court did not abuse discretion in refusing to order state to pay for defense expert on eyewitness memory); State v. Broom, 533 N.E.2d 682 (Ohio 1988) (refusal to appoint eyewitness identification expert to aid in indigent's defense was no due process violation; defendant made no particularized showing of reasonable probability that such an expert would aid in his defense).

5. *Corroboration.* Would it make sense to exclude identification evidence — regardless of any violations of due process or right to counsel — unless there is independent evidence to corroborate the identification evidence? See Regina v. Turnbull, [1977] 1 Q.B. 224 (1976):

> When, in the judgment of the trial judge, the quality of the identifying evidence is poor, as for example when it depends solely on a fleeting glance or on a longer observation

> made in difficult conditions, [the] judge should then withdraw the case from the jury and direct an acquittal unless there is other evidence which goes to support the correctness of the identification. [For] example, X sees the accused snatch a woman's handbag; he gets only a fleeting glance of the thief's face as he runs off but he does see him entering a nearby house. [Although this is poor identification evidence, the judge need not withdraw the case from the jury] if there was evidence that the house into which the accused was alleged by X to have run was his father's.

6. *Prosecutors as the cure.* Is the prosecutor's power to decline to file charges against a defendant the ultimate remedy for weak identification evidence? Do prosecutors have adequate incentives and ability to screen out cases with the most questionable eyewitness-identification evidence? When Samuel Gross studied the records available in a large number of misidentification cases, he reached the following conclusions:

> (1) More often than not, a misidentified defendant was originally suspected because of his appearance. (2) A misidentified defendant is more likely to be cleared before his case comes to trial than after. (3) If he is not exonerated before trial, a misidentified defendant will almost certainly go to trial rather than plead guilty, even in return for an attractive plea bargain. (4) A misidentified defendant who is convicted at trial may still be exonerated, but the chances decrease over time.

Gross, Loss of Innocence: Eyewitness Identification and Proof of Guilt, 16 J. Legal Stud. 395 (1987).

X

Complex Investigations

Most crime investigations last for a short time and involve the efforts of only a few law enforcement officers. Different procedural issues crop up when investigations last longer and involve more people. In this chapter, we consider two central issues that arise in complex investigations. In the first section, we consider whether the legal system places any limits on the government's choice and pursuit of targets. In the second section, we consider the power of the grand jury to investigate crimes and the legal and practical limits on that power.

A. SELECTION AND PURSUIT OF TARGETS

1. Selective Investigations

The typical crime investigation is reactive: It aims to collect evidence of a known and completed crime. What if an investigation focuses instead on a person when there is no evidence of wrongdoing, or on a specific area where crimes might be committed? Does the government ever have to justify its decision to investigate, so long as it does not conduct a "search" or "seizure"? In this section, we consider whether targets of investigations can object to the criteria that the government uses to select places or persons to investigate.

What criteria *should* government agents use — or not use — to focus attention on settings when there is not yet any evidence that a crime has taken place? The Department of Justice memorandum below represents one internal effort by a law enforcement agency to select the highest priority investigative targets. The following two cases identify the possible grounds for constitutional challenges to investigators' choices. Keep selective investigation claims distinct from claims of "selective prosecution": challenges to the decision of a prosecutor (as opposed to an investigator) to file criminal charges in some but not all similar cases when there is sufficient evidence of a crime.

■ MEMORANDUM FOR SELECTED UNITED STATES ATTORNEYS

FROM: David W. Ogden, Deputy Attorney General
SUBJECT: Investigations and Prosecutions in States Authorizing the Medical Use of Marijuana
DATE: October 19, 2009

This memorandum provides clarification and guidance to federal prosecutors in States that have enacted laws authorizing the medical use of marijuana. These laws vary in their substantive provisions and in the extent of state regulatory oversight, both among the enacting States and among local jurisdictions within those States. Rather than developing different guidelines for every possible variant of state and local law, this memorandum provides uniform guidance to focus federal investigations and prosecutions in these States on core federal enforcement priorities.

The Department of Justice is committed to the enforcement of the Controlled Substances Act in all States. Congress has determined that marijuana is a dangerous drug, and the illegal distribution and sale of marijuana is a serious crime and provides a significant source of revenue to large-scale criminal enterprises, gangs, and cartels. One timely example underscores the importance of our efforts to prosecute significant marijuana traffickers: marijuana distribution in the United States remains the single largest source of revenue for the Mexican cartels.

The Department is also committed to making efficient and rational use of its limited investigative and prosecutorial resources. In general, United States Attorneys are vested with "plenary authority with regard to federal criminal matters" within their districts. USAM 9-2.001. In exercising this authority, United States Attorneys are "invested by statute and delegation from the Attorney General with the broadest discretion in the exercise of such authority." This authority should, of course, be exercised consistent with Department priorities and guidance.

The prosecution of significant traffickers of illegal drugs, including marijuana, and the disruption of illegal drug manufacturing and trafficking networks continues to be a core priority in the Department's efforts against narcotics and dangerous drugs, and the Department's investigative and prosecutorial resources should be directed towards these objectives. As a general matter, pursuit of these priorities should not focus federal resources in your States on individuals whose actions are in clear and unambiguous compliance with existing state laws providing for the medical use of marijuana. For example, prosecution of individuals with cancer or other serious illnesses who use marijuana as part of a recommended treatment regimen consistent with applicable state law, or those caregivers in clear and unambiguous compliance with existing state law who provide such individuals with marijuana, is unlikely to be an efficient use of limited federal resources. On the other hand, prosecution of commercial enterprises that unlawfully market and sell marijuana for profit continues to be an enforcement priority of the Department. To be sure, claims of compliance with state or local law may mask operations inconsistent with the terms, conditions, or purposes of those laws, and federal law enforcement should not be deterred by such assertions when otherwise pursuing the Department's core enforcement priorities.

Typically, when any of the following characteristics is present, the conduct will not be in clear and unambiguous compliance with applicable state law and may indicate illegal drug trafficking activity of potential federal interest:

- Unlawful possession or unlawful use of firearms;
- Violence;
- Sales to minors;
- Financial and marketing activities inconsistent with the terms, conditions, or purposes of state law, including evidence of money laundering activity and/or financial gains or excessive amounts of cash inconsistent with purported compliance with state or local law;
- Amounts of marijuana inconsistent with purported compliance with state or local law;
- Illegal possession or sale of other controlled substances; or
- Ties to other criminal enterprises.

Of course, no State can authorize violations of federal law, and the list of factors above is not intended to describe exhaustively when a federal prosecution may be warranted. . . .

This guidance regarding resource allocation does not "legalize" marijuana or provide a legal defense to a violation of federal law, nor is it intended to create any privileges, benefits, or rights, substantive or procedural, enforceable by any individual, party or witness in any administrative, civil, or criminal matter. Nor does clear and unambiguous compliance with state law or the absence of one or all of the above factors create a legal defense to a violation of the Controlled Substances Act. Rather, this memorandum is intended solely as a guide to the exercise of investigative and prosecutorial discretion.

Finally, nothing herein precludes investigation or prosecution where there is a reasonable basis to believe that compliance with state law is being invoked as a pretext for the production or distribution of marijuana for purposes not authorized by state law. Nor does this guidance preclude investigation or prosecution, even when there is clear and unambiguous compliance with existing state law, in particular circumstances where investigation or prosecution otherwise serves important federal interests.

Your offices should continue to review marijuana cases for prosecution on a case-by-case basis, consistent with the guidance on resource allocation and federal priorities set forth herein, the consideration of requests for federal assistance from state and local law enforcement authorities, and the Principles of Federal Prosecution.

■ AH SIN v. GEORGE WITTMAN
198 U.S. 500 (1905)

McKenna, J.*

[Ah Sin filed a petition] alleging that he was a subject of the Emperor of China, and was restrained of his liberty by . . . the chief of police of the city and county of San Francisco, under a judgment of imprisonment rendered in the police court of said city for the violation of one of its ordinances. [Defendant was convicted under a city ordinance making it "unlawful for any person within the limits of the city and county of San Francisco to exhibit or expose to view in . . . any place built or protected in a manner to make it difficult of access or ingress to police officers when three or more persons are present, any cards, dice, dominoes, fan-tan table or layout, or any part of such layout, or any gambling implements whatsoever." The ordinance also made it unlawful to "visit or resort to" such a house or room, and provided for punishment upon conviction by a fine not to exceed five hundred dollars, or by imprisonment in the county jail for not more than six months, or both.]

Plaintiff in error avers "That said ordinance and the provisions thereof are enforced and executed by the said municipality of San Francisco, and said State of California, solely and exclusively against persons of the Chinese race, and not otherwise." The contention is that Chinese persons are thereby denied the equal protection of the law in violation of the Fourteenth Amendment of the Constitution of the United States. Yick Wo v. Hopkins, 118 U.S. 356 (1886), is cited to sustain the contention. . . . That case concerned the use of property for lawful and legitimate purposes. The case at bar is concerned with gambling, to suppress which is recognized as a proper exercise of governmental authority, and one which would have no incentive in race or class prejudice or administration in race or class discrimination. In the *Yick Wo* case there was not a mere allegation that the ordinance attacked was enforced against the Chinese only, but it was shown that not only the petitioner in that case, but two hundred of his countrymen, applied for licenses, and were refused, and that all the petitions of those not Chinese, with one exception, were granted. The averment in the case at bar is that the ordinance is enforced "solely and exclusively against persons of the Chinese race and not otherwise." There is no averment that the conditions and practices to which the ordinance was directed did not exist exclusively among the Chinese, or that there were other offenders against the ordinance than the Chinese as to whom it was not enforced. No latitude of intention should be indulged in a case like this. There should be certainty to every intent.

Plaintiff in error seeks to set aside a criminal law of the State, not on the ground that it is unconstitutional on its face, not that it is discriminatory in tendency and ultimate actual operation as the ordinance was which was passed on in the *Yick Wo* case, but that it was made so by the manner of its administration. This is a matter of proof, and no fact should be omitted to make it out completely, when the power of a Federal court is invoked to interfere with the course of criminal justice of a State. We think, therefore, the judgment of the Superior Court should be and it is hereby affirmed.

* [Chief Justice Fuller and Justices Harlan, Brewer, Brown, White, Holmes, and Day joined in this opinion. — Eds.]

DENNIS BALUYUT v. SUPERIOR COURT

911 P.2d 1 (Cal. 1996)

BAXTER, J.

Petitioners below are defendants charged with violation of Penal Code section 647(a)[1] in the Municipal Court for the Santa Clara County Judicial District. They sought dismissal of the charges on the ground that the Mountain View police who arrested them engaged in a pattern of discriminatory arrest and prosecution of homosexuals under this statute, thereby denying them equal protection of the law. [The trial court denied the motion to dismiss.]

In support of their motion to dismiss, defendants presented ten arrest reports spanning a two-year period. The reports described decoy officers' arrests of men in and outside an adult bookstore in Mountain View for violations of section 647(a). The arrests involved a decoy officer who had engaged a person in small talk. [After] the person eventually made it clear that he was interested in a sexual encounter the officer suggested that the person accompany the officer to the officer's car. Once at the officer's car, the person was arrested for soliciting a lewd act to be performed in a public place. . . . Other evidence was offered that the modus operandi of the decoy officers was typical of a "cruising" pattern of homosexual men and that it invited homosexual men to make contact with the decoy officer.

Mountain View police records for the two years prior to the arrest of defendants were reviewed by the municipal court which also heard testimony about the decoy operation. The court concluded that the operation was focused solely on persons who had a proclivity to engage in homosexual conduct, [and that] it did so without any relationship to the alleged problems at that location for which the citizen complaint had been initially lodged.

Based on these factual conclusions, and applying this court's decision in Murgia v. Municipal Court, 540 P.2d 44 (Cal. 1975), the municipal court ruled that defendants had established there was improper selectivity — discrimination — in prosecution and that the discrimination had an invidious basis. It was unjustifiable, arbitrary, and without a rational relationship to legitimate law enforcement interests. Notwithstanding these conclusions and the court's belief that the complaints should be dismissed, the court felt bound by People v. Smith, 155 Cal. App. 3d 1103 (1984) to deny the motion to dismiss because defendants had not established that the Mountain View police had a specific intent to punish the defendants for their membership in a particular class. . . .

Although referred to for convenience as a "defense," a defendant's claim of discriminatory prosecution goes not to the nature of the charged offense, but to a defect of constitutional dimension in the initiation of the prosecution. The defect lies in the denial of equal protection to persons who are singled out for a prosecution that is "deliberately based upon an unjustifiable standard such as race, religion, or other arbitrary classification." When a defendant establishes the elements of discriminatory prosecution, the action must be dismissed even if a serious crime is charged unless the People establish a compelling reason for the selective enforcement.

1. . . . Section 647: "Every person who commits any of the following acts is guilty of disorderly conduct, a misdemeanor: (a) Who solicits anyone to engage in or who engages in lewd or dissolute conduct in any public place or in any place open to the public or exposed to public view."

Unequal treatment which results simply from laxity of enforcement or which reflects a nonarbitrary basis for selective enforcement of a statute does not deny equal protection and is not constitutionally prohibited discriminatory enforcement. However, the unlawful administration by state officers of a state statute that is fair on its face, which results in unequal application to persons who are entitled to be treated alike, denies equal protection if it is the product of intentional or purposeful discrimination.

In *Murgia* this court explained the showing necessary to establish discriminatory prosecution: "In order to establish a claim of discriminatory enforcement a defendant must demonstrate [1] that he has been deliberately singled out for prosecution on the basis of some invidious criterion, [and (2) that] the prosecution would not have been pursued except for the discriminatory design of the prosecuting authorities." The *Smith* court elaborated on these elements and in so doing appeared to hold that the defendant must show not only that an invidious discriminatory purpose underlies the prosecution, but also that this purpose is to punish the defendant for his membership in a particular class. . . .

Nothing in *Murgia* . . . or the controlling decisions of the United States Supreme Court supports the imposition of this additional burden on a defendant. Showing an intent to punish for membership in a group or class is not necessary to establish a violation of an individual's right to equal protection under the Fourteenth Amendment to the United States Constitution. There must be discrimination and that discrimination must be intentional and unjustified and thus "invidious" because it is unrelated to legitimate law enforcement objectives, but the intent need not be to "punish" the defendant for membership in a protected class or for the defendant's exercise of protected rights. . . .

Murgia arose in the context of a motion for discovery by defendants who claimed that they were being discriminatorily prosecuted under various statutes on the basis of their membership in or support of the United Farm Workers Union (UFW) and sought information relevant to that claim. Discovery had been denied on the ground that the evidence sought was irrelevant as defendants had violated the laws under which they were charged. [We held as follows:] "Neither the federal nor state Constitution countenances the singling out of an invidiously selected class for special prosecutorial treatment, whether that class consists of black or white, Jew or Catholic, Irishman or Japanese, United Farm Worker or Teamster. If an individual can show that he would not have been prosecuted except for such invidious discrimination against him, a basic constitutional principle has been violated, and such prosecution must collapse upon the sands of prejudice."

[*Murgia* recognized that] an equal protection violation does not arise whenever officials prosecute one and not [another] for the same act; instead, the equal protection guarantee simply prohibits prosecuting officials from purposefully and intentionally singling out individuals for disparate treatment on an invidiously discriminatory basis. [But the suggestion] that discriminatory enforcement is not established unless the defendant establishes that the law enforcement officers responsible had a specific intent to punish the defendants for their membership in a particular classification finds no support in [*Murgia*]. Rather, the purpose or intent that must be shown is simply intent to single out the group or a member of the group on the basis of that membership for prosecution that would not otherwise have taken place. When there is no legitimate law enforcement purpose for singling out those persons for prosecution, the prosecution is arbitrary and unjustified and thus results in invidious discrimination. . . .

Subsequent to *Murgia* and the United States Supreme Court decisions on which it relied, the high court again visited the question and reaffirmed the factors which establish a violation of a defendant's right to equal protection, noting that ordinary equal protection principles apply in assessing discriminatory prosecution claims. In Wayte v. United States, 470 U.S. 598 (1985), the court considered a "passive enforcement" policy under which the federal government prosecuted persons who failed to register for the draft. Under that policy the government prosecuted only persons who reported themselves as unwilling to register. Those who reported themselves were known by the government as likely to be persons who for moral or religious reasons were vocal opponents of the registration requirement. At the time the policy existed, the Selective Service system was unable to develop a more active enforcement system.

Wayte . . . was one of the first persons indicted under the passive enforcement policy. He claimed to be a victim of selective or discriminatory enforcement and asserted that the indictment violated his First Amendment rights. The district court dismissed the indictment, ruling that the government had not rebutted Wayte's prima facie case of selective prosecution. [The Supreme Court held, however, that the prosecution could go forward because Wayte had failed to show that the government focused its investigation on him because of his protest activities.]

The court held that even if the government's passive enforcement policy had a discriminatory effect, Wayte had not shown that the government intended that result. Although he had shown that the government was aware that the likely impact of its passive enforcement policy was prosecution of vocal objectors, a showing of "discriminatory purpose" required more. That showing is that the government selected the course of action "at least in part 'because of,' not merely 'in spite of,' its adverse effects upon an identifiable group." . . .

We are not free to adopt a narrower construction of the protection afforded by the equal protection clause of the Fourteenth Amendment than that enunciated by the United States Supreme Court. Requiring a defendant to show that the government had a specific intent to punish a person singled out as a member of a class for criminal prosecution finds no support in the controlling precedent of the United States Supreme Court cases. . . .

Problem 10-1. Selection of Participants

A Brockton police officer arrested Ann O'Connor for two violations of the city ordinance against prostitution. After being charged with these offenses, she filed a motion to dismiss the complaints, arguing that the police had engaged in improper selective enforcement of the prostitution laws. O'Connor claimed that no male was arrested with her on either charge, because it is the police department's policy and practice to arrest only prostitutes and not their clients.

The ordinance in question was amended three years prior to O'Connor's arrest, to apply both to the prostitute and the client:

> Any person who engages, agrees to engage, or offers to engage in sexual conduct with another person in return for a fee, or any person who pays, agrees to pay or offers to

pay another person to engage in sexual conduct, or to agree to engage in sexual conduct with another natural person may be punished by imprisonment in a jail or house of correction for not more than one year, or by a fine of not more than five hundred dollars, or by both such fine and imprisonment.

One Brockton police detective testified at the motion hearing about the department's typical methods of surveillance of female suspects on certain streets in Brockton. The police officer typically would observe (1) females on the street waving at males in cars, (2) a female entering a vehicle and driving off with a male, (3) both returning after an interval, and then (4) a repetition of the process with a different male. The detective testified that, in such circumstances, "ordinarily" the police do not arrest the driver of the vehicle. In cases in which the officer follows the vehicle and discovers two passengers in the vehicle engaged in a sexual act, only the female is arrested.

The detective stated that the basic reason for the policy was that complaints from area citizens related "mainly to the girls," and that the women arrested are known to the police whereas the men are not. The department's arrest records for the previous year show that 36 of the 37 persons arrested for prostitution were female and that 23 of the 25 persons arrested for soliciting prostitution were female.

Will the court grant O'Connor's motion to dismiss? On the basis of a constitutional provision, or on some other basis? Compare Commonwealth v. An Unnamed Defendant, 492 N.E.2d 1184 (Mass. 1986) (constitutional violation for selective enforcement of prostitution laws) with City of Minneapolis v. Buschette, 240 N.W. 2d 500 (Minn. 1976) (no constitutional violation).

Notes

1. *Discriminatory selection of investigative targets: majority position.* Courts in almost all jurisdictions agree about the basic steps to follow in resolving a constitutional challenge to an investigator's selection of a target. Under the equal protection clause of the federal Constitution, "no state shall" make any law denying persons "the equal protection of the laws." When criminal defendants have claimed that the government's "selective enforcement" of a law violates the equal protection clause, courts have asked the defendant to address several issues. First, the defendant must show that others similarly situated were treated differently (that is, the police did not make an arrest or follow up on a viable investigative lead). Second, the defendant must show that differences between the groups receiving different treatment are legally significant (for instance, different treatment of racial or gender groups). Finally (and this is the most difficult showing), a defendant must demonstrate that the government agents intentionally discriminated against the group — that is, they chose the target *because of* the group membership, and not *in spite of* the group membership. See Wayte v. United States, 470 U.S. 598 (1985).

2. *Proving intent.* If the investigator's state of mind is critical to a claim of discriminatory investigation, how would a defendant get evidence of such a state of mind? Courts have created a difficult standard for defendants to satisfy before they can obtain discovery on such questions. See United States v. Armstrong, 517 U.S. 456 (1996) (defendant must show that the government declined to prosecute similarly situated suspects of other races). What showings do the courts in *Ah Sin* and

Baluyut require of a defendant challenging an alleged discriminatory investigation? Note the California court's use of the doctrine of "specific intent," drawn from substantive criminal law. Although the term is slippery, courts speaking of specific intent usually mean (a) an awareness of some specific circumstance surrounding the crime (e.g., knowledge that property is stolen, to be convicted of receiving stolen property), or (b) an intent to do some future act beyond the act that forms the basis for a crime (e.g., a specific intent to deprive the owner of property permanently, as an element of larceny). See Joshua Dressier, Understanding Criminal Law §10.06 (5th ed. 2009). Exactly what state of mind of the investigator does the California court in *Baluyut* require the defendant to prove?

3. *Public selection of enforcement priorities.* Recall from Chapter 1 the discussion of "community policing" and its emphasis on public input into enforcement priorities. Is it adequate for the police to explain their enforcement policy by saying that they enforce certain laws only in situations when a citizen complains about a possible violation? In *Baluyut,* suppose all the complaints about violations of the public lewdness ordinance dealt with homosexual activity. Is there any danger in a police policy that ensures responsiveness to public concerns? Compare State v. Anonymous, 364 A.2d 244 (Conn. C.P. 1976) (invalidating police policy of enforcing Sunday "blue laws" only upon receiving a citizen complaint) with State v. Russell, 343 N.W.2d 36 (Minn. 1984) (denying challenge to police policy of concentrating enforcement efforts in burglary cases in one predominantly black precinct receiving most reports of burglary).

State and local law enforcement agencies often face a choice of whether to treat federal immigration laws as an enforcement priority. Some police departments routinely refer arrestees to federal immigration authorities when they have reason to believe that they are in violation of the immigration laws. In some states, such as Arizona, state legislators instruct law enforcement agencies throughout the state to pursue this strategy. In other jurisdictions, local law enforcement does not routinely cooperate with federal immigration authorities, and instead cultivates cooperation in immigrant communities in the detection and prevention of other crimes. See Jesse McKinley, "San Francisco Alters When Police Must Report Immigrants", N.Y. Times, October 21, 2009.

4. *Resources as a selection criterion.* Police departments and other criminal investigators, just like everyone else, must economize on a limited budget. Is the resource constraint, in the end, the best constraint on investigative decisions? Will budgetary considerations, like Adam Smith's invisible hand, lead investigators to direct their efforts to solve and prevent the greatest number of crimes that are of greatest concern to the community? Could the rules of legal ethics effectively supplement prosecutorial budgets by requiring prosecutors to advise criminal investigators to go forward only when the investigation is "proportional" to the suspected conduct?

For some special investigators, resource questions essentially do not exist. So-called special prosecutors (formerly known in the federal system as the "independent counsel") are typically appointed to investigate politically sensitive cases in which the public might not trust the judgment of the ordinary prosecutors or investigators. Special prosecutors do not have to apportion a limited investigative budget over a large number of potential criminal cases. If there is no effective limit on the amount of time government agents can spend investigating a single person, do the legal and political systems have any workable way to prevent abuses of the investigative power? See Julie O'Sullivan, The Independent Counsel Statute: Bad Law, Bad Policy, 33 Am. Crim. L. Rev. 463 (1996).

5. *Impact of written guidelines.* Written guidelines to govern the selection of investigative targets are the exception rather than the rule. Typically, the criteria for the selection of investigative targets are informal and unwritten, although federal investigators put these policies in writing more often than state investigators, and they tend to appear in white-collar crime settings. For examples of such policies in the investigation of immigration violations, environmental crimes, and corporate crimes, see the web extension for this chapter at *http://www.crimpro.com/extension/ch10*.

Although written policies are exceptional, law enforcement agencies routinely make decisions about how to allocate their resources. Some of these choices involve "proactive" efforts to uncover crimes that have not yet been committed or reported to the police. Is the guidance provided by the Department of Justice memorandum on case selection better than the ad hoc, oral standards recounted in Problem 10-1? If so, what are the differences between them? Or are these policies all equally futile or misleading because a certain amount of arbitrariness in enforcement is inevitable?

2. *Entrapment Defenses*

Some crimes, such as prostitution, drug trafficking, or price fixing, involve voluntary transactions that are difficult for anyone other than the participants to observe. Sometimes government agents investigate such crimes through "undercover" operations, not revealing to their targets the fact that they are law enforcement officers. The undercover agent might pretend to participate in a crime as it takes place rather than inquiring after a crime has happened. The agent might also create the opportunity for some person to commit a crime under "simulated" conditions. How should judges, legislators, and enforcement officials respond to the dangers — and perhaps the necessity — of these enforcement techniques? When will a defendant escape a conviction because the government "entrapped" him? The case and statutes that follow take up the central question surrounding the entrapment doctrine: whether the defendant's state of mind, the activities of the government, or some combination of the two should be the key concept in resolving entrapment claims.

■ PEOPLE v. JESSIE JOHNSON

647 N.W.2d 480 (Mich. 2002)

YOUNG, J.

This case involves the defense of entrapment. The circuit court found that defendant was entrapped by the police and dismissed two charges of possession with intent to deliver more than 225, but less than 650, grams of cocaine. The Court of Appeals affirmed in a split decision. We conclude that the lower courts clearly erred in finding that defendant was entrapped under Michigan's current entrapment test. . . .

FACTS AND PROCEEDINGS

Defendant was a police officer in the city of Pontiac. He also owned a house in the city of Pontiac that he rented out as a residence.

Defendant became the subject of a criminal investigation after one of defendant's former tenants turned informant and reported to the Pontiac police department that defendant was instrumental in operating his rented house as a drug den. The informant indicated that he sold crack cocaine from defendant's house with defendant's full knowledge and consent. Further, according to the informant, defendant arranged, oversaw, and protected the drug-selling operation. In exchange, defendant received a substantial portion of the profits from the drug sales.

The Pontiac police called in the state police for assistance in their investigation of defendant. An undercover officer from the state police department, Lieutenant Sykes, was introduced by the informant to defendant as a major drug dealer in Detroit and Mount Clemens who wished to expand his operations into Pontiac. Defendant agreed to meet with Sykes, but not pursuant to any police investigation he was conducting himself. Defendant was propositioned by Sykes to serve as protection and security from "rip-offs" and police raids for Sykes' drug operations, as well as to identify potential locations for drug dens in Pontiac. Defendant was to be compensated for his services. Defendant agreed to participate only after he determined that Sykes was not an undercover officer known to defendant's fellow Pontiac officers. Defendant made no attempt to arrest Sykes or report his illegal activities for further investigation.

At Sykes' request, defendant agreed to accompany Sykes to a mall on February 7, 1992, to assist him in purchasing drugs from a supplier. The supplier was in reality another undercover state police officer.

Defendant and Sykes arrived at the mall parking lot in different vehicles. After some preliminary discussions, Sykes drove over to the undercover officer to make the staged drug deal, while defendant walked. Armed with a gun in his pocket, defendant stood one and a half car lengths from the passenger side of the second undercover officer's vehicle. After the transaction began, Sykes directed defendant to come to the driver's side of the undercover officer's vehicle. Sykes then handed defendant the package of drugs received from the supplier in the staged drug deal. Defendant took the package and returned to Sykes' vehicle and waited for Sykes. At that time, defendant expressed some confusion regarding the exact procedures he was to follow, stating that he needed to know what to do "from A to Z." Sykes testified, and audiotapes of the February 7, 1992, drug deal confirm, that Sykes wanted defendant to take the drugs back to his car, check them, ensure that the package was correct, and notify Sykes of any problems. Sykes stated that in order for defendant to fulfill his duty to protect against "rip-offs," defendant would be required to hold and examine the drugs purchased. Sykes explained that he could not watch the supplier and the package at the same time. After this conversation, while defendant and Sykes weighed the cocaine, defendant indicated that as a result of their discussion he had a better understanding of what Sykes wanted him to do. Defendant did not express his unwillingness to perform the duties explained by Sykes. Sykes then paid defendant $1,000 for his assistance.

Sometime after this first drug deal, Sykes asked defendant if he wished to participate in future drug deals and told him that it was okay if he no longer wanted to participate. Defendant indicated that he wanted to be included in future transactions. As a result, a second, similarly staged drug deal occurred on March 4, 1992, immediately after which defendant was arrested.

Defendant was charged with two counts of possession with intent to deliver more than 225, but less than 650, grams of cocaine. [Johnson] moved to dismiss the charges on the basis of an entrapment theory. The trial court granted defendant's motion to dismiss, reasoning that Sykes had changed defendant's duty during the first transaction from one of protection to one of actual drug possession, thus entrapping defendant into the drug possessions.

As indicated, the Court of Appeals affirmed in a split decision. The majority wrote that "because many of the factors indicative of entrapment existed in this case, we hold that defendant has met his burden of proving that the police conduct would have induced an otherwise law-abiding person in similar circumstances as defendant to commit the offenses charged." It also concluded that "Sykes' conduct in this case was so reprehensible as to constitute entrapment."...

Analysis

Under the current entrapment test in Michigan, a defendant is considered entrapped if either (1) the police engaged in impermissible conduct that would induce a law-abiding person to commit a crime in similar circumstances or (2) the police engaged in conduct so reprehensible that it cannot be tolerated. People v. Ealy, 564 N.W.2d 168 (Mich. App. 1997). However, where law enforcement officials present nothing more than an opportunity to commit the crime, entrapment does not exist.

Inducing Criminal Conduct

When examining whether governmental activity would impermissibly induce criminal conduct, several factors are considered: (1) whether there existed appeals to the defendant's sympathy as a friend, (2) whether the defendant had been known to commit the crime with which he was charged, (3) whether there were any long time lapses between the investigation and the arrest, (4) whether there existed any inducements that would make the commission of a crime unusually attractive to a hypothetical law-abiding citizen, (5) whether there were offers of excessive consideration or other enticement, (6) whether there was a guarantee that the acts alleged as crimes were not illegal, (7) whether, and to what extent, any government pressure existed, (8) whether there existed sexual favors, (9) whether there were any threats of arrest, (10) whether there existed any government procedures that tended to escalate the criminal culpability of the defendant, (11) whether there was police control over any informant, and (12) whether the investigation was targeted. People v. Juillet, 475 N.W.2d 786 (Mich. 1991).

In holding that defendant was entrapped, the Court of Appeals found that defendant had not previously committed the possession with intent to deliver offenses charged, the procedures employed by the government escalated defendant's conduct to the charged offense, and the offer of consideration was excessive. On the basis of these three factors, it held that "because many of the factors indicative of entrapment existed," the defendant "met his burden of proving that the police conduct would have induced an otherwise law-abiding person in similar circumstances as defendant to commit the offenses charged." We respectfully disagree.

First, while the Court of Appeals noted that defendant had "merely owned" a crack house and that no evidence existed that defendant was a drug dealer or even a drug user, it ignored ample evidence presented that defendant had in fact previously committed the offense of possession with intent to deliver. To be convicted of the charge of possession with intent to deliver, the defendant must have knowingly possessed a controlled substance, intended to deliver that substance to someone else, and the substance possessed must have actually been cocaine and defendant must have known it was cocaine. Actual physical possession is unnecessary for a conviction of possession with intent to deliver; constructive possession will suffice. Constructive possession exists when the totality of the circumstances indicates a sufficient nexus between defendant and the contraband. Possession is attributed not only to those who physically possess the drugs, but also to those who control its disposition. In addition, possession may be either joint or exclusive.

Defendant owned a home that he rented to tenants who operated it as a drug house. Despite being a police officer in the jurisdiction in which the house was located, defendant knew and consented to the house being used for drug sales. Further, defendant provided protection for the operation and received a portion of the profits from the drug sales, specifically $200 for each quarter ounce of drugs sold from the house. . . .

Our conclusion that defendant previously possessed cocaine is one that we make as a matter of law. [We] do not limit our review of whether the lower courts clearly erred to the hearing testimony, but rather review the entire record. While the hearing testimony arguably lends itself to different conclusions, the audio tapes admitted into the record . . . undisputedly establish that defendant played a role in the drug operation:

> *[Informant]:* So I can take the hundred and invest it or what?
> *[Defendant]:* Alright, man, I'm gonna give you one more shot.
> *[Informant]:* Okay, dig, the same arrangement, the two off every quarter?
> *[Defendant]:* Yeah.

As far as corroboration of defendant's past participation in drug activities, this first taped telephone conversation between the informant and defendant is clear evidence that defendant previously received $200 for every quarter ounce of cocaine sold by the informant at the house and that defendant wished and agreed to continue this arrangement.

Under these circumstances, it is clear these alleged previous actions by defendant could serve as the foundation for a conviction for possession with intent to deliver under a constructive possession theory. Defendant had a duty to arrest the informant, yet not only did he permit the informant to sell drugs, he accepted money to provide protection for the operation. Without such protection, drugs would not have been sold from the house. Accordingly, defendant controlled the disposition of drugs at the house he owned and shared in the profits in so doing. For these reasons, we find clear error in the lower court's deduction that there was insufficient evidence to surmise that defendant had not previously committed the offense of possession with intent to deliver cocaine. [The] defendant's prior actions, at the very least, are sufficient to establish the charge of possession with intent to deliver cocaine as an aider and abettor.

Second, contrary to the Court of Appeals majority, we are not convinced that the procedures employed by the police escalated defendant's criminal culpability. The Court of Appeals majority wrote:

> The procedures employed by the police escalated defendant's conduct from merely owning a drug house to possession with intent to deliver cocaine. Sykes initially "hired" defendant to protect against arrest and theft and to inform Sykes of any potential drug raids. At the first staged drug buy, however, Sykes called defendant over and handed defendant the package of cocaine. It was only after the first transaction that defendant was informed that he was expected to handle the drugs, check them, and ensure that the package was "right." This active involvement was not contemplated prior to the buy. Sykes' actions, therefore, served to escalate defendant's passive involvement in the enterprise to active participation beyond the scope of what defendant had agreed to beforehand and pressured defendant into complying with Sykes' requests in order to remain a part of the enterprise. . . .

As discussed above, defendant's previous actions concerning his drug house operation amounted to possession with intent to deliver. Both offenses charged as a result of the undercover operation were possession with intent to deliver. Therefore, no conduct by the state police in the undercover operation could serve to escalate defendant's prior criminal activity. Rather, the government simply provided defendant with an additional opportunity to commit a crime that he had previously committed. . . .

Similarly, defendant's culpability was not escalated at the scene of the first transaction in regard to the role defendant agreed to play in the undercover drug transaction. The touchstone of the Court of Appeals opinion in this regard was that placing the drugs in the hands of defendant at the scene of the first drug deal was a violation of what defendant had agreed to do. However, our review of the record leads us to conclude that touching the drugs should not have come as a surprise to defendant.

Although the taped recording of the first drug transaction suggests that defendant was unsure precisely what he was to do beyond providing "protection," that confusion was not based on defendant's lack of agreement to do more. [Defendant] was hired by Sykes to protect and secure against arrests, police raids, and "rip-offs." While the Court of Appeals construed "rip-off" as narrowly as possible by equating it with "theft," protecting against a "rip-off" would seem to include ensuring that drug packages received at drug deals contain actual drugs in the negotiated quantity and quality, a task that necessarily requires taking possession of the drugs in order to properly inspect them. A recorded audiotape of defendant and Sykes discussing their arrangement before the first staged drug transaction demonstrates that Sykes informed defendant that he would have to handle the drugs on occasion:

> *Sykes:* . . . And probably on occasion, I'm gonna need your expertise to accompany me to pick up a package or two, okay. . . . So if, you know, just run here, run there, pick up some, and we'll be straight, okay. That's, that's basically all that you got to do, I'll run the rest.
>
> *Defendant:* Okay.

In addition, defendant's willingness to participate in the crimes charged is evidenced by his agreement to participate in further transactions after he participated in the first transaction, which included his taking possession of the drugs. We further note that the second drug transaction between defendant and the undercover police officers exposes a consideration that the lower courts appear to have overlooked during their review. Initial entrapment does not immunize a defendant from criminal liability for subsequent transactions that he readily and willingly undertook. . . .

For these reasons, it is apparent that Sykes' handing the drugs to defendant for inspection during the first transaction failed to escalate defendant's criminal culpability. As a result, the Court of Appeals clearly erred in concluding otherwise.

Finally, the Court of Appeals majority clearly erred in holding that the amount of money offered for defendant's services was excessive and unusually attractive. [Given] defendant's understanding that he would receive $1,000 for each transaction, the compensation was neither excessive or unusually attractive. Each transaction involved approximately ten ounces of cocaine, which had an estimated street value of $75,000. A $1,000 fee for a transaction involving almost $75,000, roughly one percent of the street value, is not excessive. This is especially evident given that defendant previously earned a $200 profit, or nearly thirty percent of the street value, for the sale of one quarter ounce of cocaine at his crack house, which the record reflects had a street value of approximately $700. Thus, the Court of Appeals clearly erred in ascertaining that defendant was impermissibly induced because the consideration for his illegal services was excessive or unusually attractive.

In sum, we have concluded that the Court of Appeals clearly erred in regard to each of the three factors that persuaded that Court to conclude that the police engaged in conduct that would induce a law-abiding person to commit a crime in similar circumstances. Therefore, because none of the remaining *Juillet* factors are at issue, we hold that defendant failed to establish by a preponderance of the evidence that the police engaged in conduct that would induce a law-abiding person to commit a crime in similar circumstances.

Reprehensible Conduct

The Court of Appeals alternatively held that the police conduct was so reprehensible that, as a matter of public policy, it could not be tolerated regardless of its relationship to the crime and therefore constituted entrapment. The majority based its reasoning primarily on its escalation analysis. . . .

As we discussed above, defendant was hired to protect against arrests, raids, and "rip-offs." In light of his alleged familiarity with drug operations, defendant should have expected that ensuring against "rip-offs" would include, among other things, examining the drugs for their legitimacy and holding the drugs to prevent a theft at the scene of the drug deal. More importantly, as indicated above, the negotiations between defendant and Sykes before the first transaction support this understanding. [Further, defendant willingly participated in the criminal enterprise and even met with Sykes at the Pontiac police department station before these drug deals in order to determine whether Sykes was an undercover officer who would be recognized by defendant's fellow officers.] Given our conclusion that defendant had previously committed the offense of possession with intent to deliver and that he agreed to provide protection against "rip-offs," which clearly includes handling the drugs in order to inspect them, the police did nothing more than provide defendant with an opportunity to commit a crime. Such conduct was not reprehensible and does not establish entrapment.

For these reasons, we conclude that the Court of Appeals clearly erred in finding that defendant established by a preponderance of the evidence that the police conduct in this case was so reprehensible as to constitute entrapment.

The Entrapment Test in Michigan

We originally granted leave to appeal in this case to consider whether the current entrapment test in Michigan, a modified objective test, is the most appropriate one. Accordingly, we asked the parties to address whether this Court should adopt the federal subjective test for entrapment. Sorrells v. United States, 287 U.S. 435 (1932). However, because defendant's case fails to meet even the current, more lenient modified objective test, we do not need to reach that question.

Nevertheless, after review of our entrapment defense law, we note that Chief Justice Corrigan has raised serious questions regarding the constitutionality of any judicially created entrapment test in Michigan. People v. Maffett, 633 N.W.2d 339 (Mich. 2001) (Corrigan, C. J., dissenting). Accordingly, we urge the Legislature to consider these questions and determine whether a legislative response is warranted. . . .

Cavanagh, J., dissenting.

I concur in the majority's holding that the police conduct did not entrap defendant into the second transaction. However, I would conclude that the police conduct did entrap defendant into the first transaction; therefore, I respectfully dissent.

The majority's conclusion that defendant constructively possessed cocaine and, therefore, was not entrapped into committing the possession crimes is based on repeated references to the informant's claim that defendant "arranged, oversaw, and protected" the drug sales at the home defendant owned. [The informant, however,] did not testify at the entrapment hearing. Rather, the information that the informant allegedly relayed to the police came into evidence through the police officer the informant contacted about defendant. This officer testified as follows:

> *Q.* Now did this [informant] tell you how he [defendant] was involved? . . .
> *A.* He said he was running a dope house. [The defendant] owned the house and [the informant] was selling crack out of the house with [defendant's] full knowledge and consent and more or less participation; not in the actual sale, but in setting it up and providing protection and in running the operation. . . .

The most crucial part of the officer's testimony, which sheds light on the Court of Appeals reasoning, is omitted.

> *Q.* Did you ever run across any . . . evidence other than [the informant's] statements that [defendant] had been involved in the — this purported dope house? . . .
> *A.* Yes.
> *Q.* And what was that?

A. I checked records on the house that was pointed out and [defendant] did in fact own that house; to me that was corroboration. . . .

The police officer initially stated that the informant told him defendant set up, ran, and supervised the drug house. However, when asked what information corroborated what the informant allegedly said, the officer pointed to only the fact that defendant owned the home and accepted money to look the other way. The trial court made its credibility determination on this testimony that defendant had no other involvement beyond owning the drug house and bribery. Contrary to the picture the majority paints of defendant's part in the drug sales occurring in the home he owned, the record supports the Court of Appeals conclusion that defendant did nothing more than own a crack house and accept money to keep silent. Thus, the majority's mischaracterization of defendant's involvement directly conflicts with this Court's duty to give deference to credibility determinations in light of direct testimony supporting them.[1] . . .

I cannot join a decision that not only mischaracterizes the facts in favor of a result, but also strips the deference that is due credibility determinations made by lower courts in such a way as the majority does today. Accordingly, I would reverse in part the decision of the Court of Appeals holding defendant was entrapped into the second possession transaction and affirm in part the decision of the Court of Appeals holding defendant was entrapped into the first.

■ MODEL PENAL CODE §2.13

American Law Institute (1962)

(1) A public law enforcement official or a person acting in cooperation with such an official perpetrates an entrapment if for the purpose of obtaining evidence

1. [The] following is an excerpt from the body recordings of the undercover officer and defendant, which again proves that the majority's heavy reliance upon ambiguous dialog between defendant and the undercover officer before the February 7 audio tape is suspect. Even after the ambiguous discussion, which the majority quoted, defendant clearly stated that he thought his involvement was to protect.

[Undercover Officer]: Ah man, alright, alright look, the reason, the reason I got you there is so that you there not eight places away. If you eight places away, you ain't doing me no good.
[Defendant]: Two cars away.
[Undercover Officer]: That ain't doing me no good. [You] got to be there, that's why I said ride up in the car with me. That way I can, if something happens man, I'm still stuck with the Goddamn package. I want to pitch it. . . . That's, that's what I want.
[Defendant]: Oh, you want me to handle it.
[Undercover Officer]: I don't want, no, no, no, no, I, but if you're in the car, just roll down the window. I can pitch it in there. I ain't got, I ain't holding nothing. That's what I'm talking about, see? But you standing way over there, now I got to hold it and hold it, and hold it, until you get there because I, I, I can't check the package and check him too. Alright. That's my boy, but business is business.
[Defendant]: I thought you wanted protection, that's what I was under the impression that you wanted me for.

This conversation took place after the first transaction, thus revealing that defendant did not know he was to "handle" the drugs, but only thought he was to protect the undercover officer before the first transaction.

of the commission of an offense, he induces or encourages another person to engage in conduct constituting such offense by either:

(a) making knowingly false representations designed to induce the belief that such conduct is not prohibited; or

(b) employing methods of persuasion or inducement that create a substantial risk that such an offense will be committed by persons other than those who are ready to commit it.

(2) Except as provided in Subsection (3) of this Section, a person prosecuted for an offense shall be acquitted if he proves by a preponderance of evidence that his conduct occurred in response to an entrapment. The issue of entrapment shall be tried by the Court in the absence of the jury.

(3) The defense afforded by this Section is unavailable when causing or threatening bodily injury is an element of the offense charged and the prosecution is based on conduct causing or threatening such injury to a person other than the person perpetrating the entrapment.

■ MISSOURI REVISED STATUTES §562.066

1. The commission of acts which would otherwise constitute an offense is not criminal if the actor engaged in the prescribed conduct because he was entrapped by a law enforcement officer or a person acting in cooperation with such an officer.

2. An "entrapment" is perpetuated if a law enforcement officer or a person acting in cooperation with such an officer, for the purpose of obtaining evidence of the commission of an offense, solicits, encourages or otherwise induces another person to engage in conduct when he was not ready and willing to engage in such conduct.

3. The relief afforded by subsection 1 is not available as to any crime which involves causing physical injury to or placing in danger of physical injury a person other than the person perpetrating the entrapment.

4. The defendant shall have the burden of injecting the issue of entrapment.

Notes

1. *Entrapment: majority position.* The Supreme Court first recognized an entrapment defense in Sorrells v. United States, 287 U.S. 435 (1932). In that case, a government agent posed as a tourist and befriended Sorrells. The agent asked Sorrells to get him some illegal liquor. At first, Sorrells declined. Eventually, however, Sorrells obtained a half gallon of whiskey for the agent. The Supreme Court stated that improper entrapment occurs when "the criminal design originates with the officials of the Government, and they implant in the mind of an innocent person the disposition to commit the alleged offense and induce its commission in order that they may prosecute." The concurring opinions focused on the objective conduct of law enforcement personnel rather than on the subjective predisposition of the defendant.

The opinions in *Sorrells* were the origins of the "subjective" and "objective" approaches to entrapment. See also Sherman v. United States, 356 U.S. 369 (1958) (improper entrapment sets a "trap for the unwary innocent [rather than a] trap for the unwary criminal"); United States v. Russell, 411 U.S. 423 (1973) (also recognizing due process defense of "outrageous governmental conduct"). The *Sorrells* and *Sherman* cases were not constitutional rulings. The courts instead based the entrapment defense on the presumed intent of the legislators that had passed the criminal statutes involved. The courts reasoned that Congress did not mean to criminalize acts that were entirely the creations of government action.

More than 30 states follow the "subjective" test developed in the federal courts. Roughly 10 states apply the "objective" approach, exemplified in the Michigan opinion in *Johnson*. See People v. Barraza, 591 P.2d 947 (Cal. 1979). Another group of about a half dozen states use a "hybrid" approach, combining both subjective and objective elements. England v. State, 887 S.W.2d 902 (Tex. Crim. App. 1994); State v. Vallejos, 945 P.2d 957 (N.M. 1997). The subjective component of this mixed test requires evidence that the accused himself was actually induced to commit the charged offense by the persuasiveness of the police conduct. As for the objective component, the issue becomes whether the persuasion was enough to cause an ordinarily law-abiding person nevertheless to commit the offense.

If you were a prosecutor, would you systematically prefer one test over the other or would you guess that each test will be favorable to you in some factual settings and not in others? State courts sometimes adopt the entrapment doctrine (whether subjective or objective) through constitutional rulings or through their supervisory powers, whereas in many states the legislature codifies the defense. Section 2.13 of the Model Penal Code, which opts for the objective approach, has been influential. What might lead a legislature to adopt instead the subjective standard for entrapment? Could it be that those who are entrapped lack the criminal intent that the legislature was targeting when it defined the crime? If one reason to adopt an objective entrapment standard is to protect the integrity of the courts, should the legislatures attempt to address this question or should they leave it to the courts themselves?

2. *The pliability of subjective standards.* Under the "subjective" version of the entrapment defense, a defendant must demonstrate that the government "induced" him to commit the crime and that he was not "predisposed" to commit the crime. In Jacobson v. United States, 503 U.S. 540 (1992), the Supreme Court applied once again its subjective standard of entrapment. The opening words of the opinion tell the reader right away about the Court's view of the case:

> In February 1984, petitioner, a 56-year-old veteran-turned-farmer who supported his elderly father in Nebraska, ordered two magazines and a brochure from a California adult bookstore. The magazines . . . contained photographs of nude preteen and teenage boys. The contents of the magazines startled petitioner, who testified that he had expected to receive photographs of "young men 18 years or older." [Postal] inspectors found petitioner's name on the mailing list of the California bookstore. . . . There followed over the next two and one half years, repeated efforts by two Government agencies, through five fictitious organizations and a bogus pen pal, to explore petitioner's willingness to break the new [child pornography] law by ordering sexually explicit photographs of children through the mail.

The Court explained that the evidence must demonstrate predisposition both prior to and independent of the government's acts. On the evidence presented, the Court found that neither Jacobson's prior behavior nor his response to the agencies' inducements was enough to establish predisposition. Does this mean that the government must have reasonable suspicion of wrongdoing before proceeding with a sting operation against a target? See Foster v. State, 13 P.3d 61 (Nev. 2000) (undercover police need not have grounds for believing that target is predisposed; overrules earlier case requiring reasonable cause).

3. *Physical injury limitation.* Note that the Model Penal Code provision on entrapment makes the defense unavailable when the crime threatens violence to someone other than the government agent making the proposition. Why does the code make this exception? Does the threat of violence have any bearing on the defendant's predisposition? On the acceptability of the government's conduct? This statutory limitation appears in many state codes and is equally common in statutes adopting subjective and objective standards for entrapment. Ky. Rev. Stat. §505.010 (subjective standard); Utah Code Ann. §76-2-303 (objective standard). Would this exception cover drug trafficking cases?

4. *Entrapment and trial strategy.* When a defendant raises the entrapment defense, it has some important consequences at trial. Perhaps most important is the effect on the usual rules of evidence. Once a defendant claims entrapment, the rules barring the introduction of evidence of a defendant's prior criminal conduct are suspended. That evidence becomes relevant to proving predisposition; it also may be relevant to the reasonableness of the government's actions if government agents knew about the conduct. Because of this change in the rules of evidence, many defense lawyers consider entrapment to be a high-risk defense. Raising entrapment also affects the instructions a trial jury could receive about possible defenses, the allocation of authority between judge and jury, and other procedural issues. For an exploration of these trial issues, see the web extension for this chapter at *http://www.crimpro.com/extension/ch10.*

Problem 10-2. Outrageous Government Conduct

During the summer of 1988, defendants Jerome Johnson, a New Jersey state trooper, and Wanda Bonet, Johnson's girlfriend, met a person who became their cocaine supplier. On one occasion, Johnson told his supplier, "I would like to rip off a drug dealer with a lot of cocaine and then I could turn around and sell it and make some money." Some months later, Johnson's supplier was arrested while delivering a large quantity of cocaine to an undercover agent of the Drug Enforcement Administration Task Force. The supplier decided to cooperate with law enforcement authorities by becoming an informant. He told DEA agents that Johnson was willing to "rip off" drugs from a drug dealer and then sell those drugs for money.

The federal agents and the New Jersey State Police jointly developed a plan to give Johnson the opportunity to steal drugs from a drug dealer and to sell those drugs. The plan contemplated that the informant would tell Johnson that he knew of an opportunity for Johnson to steal drugs from a drug courier and make a lot of money; that he, the informant, was acting as a broker for the sale of a kilogram of cocaine; that he had arranged for a "mule," a paid courier, to transport the drugs by car to a meeting place with a prospective buyer; and that the informant and the seller of the cocaine would be in a second car following the mule. According to the plan, Johnson, wearing his state trooper uniform, would pretend to make a traffic stop of the mule's car at a prearranged location and then would seize the cocaine.

The seller of the cocaine, following in the car with the broker-informant, would see the seizure and chalk up the loss of the cocaine as a cost of doing business. Johnson then would meet the broker at Johnson's apartment and sell the cocaine to the mule for $5,000.

When the informant presented and explained the scheme to Johnson, he agreed to participate and added new elements to the plan. He requested $1,000 cash in advance, an unmarked car, and a portable flashing red light to use to make the traffic stop. Johnson also indicated he would change shifts so that he would be off-duty at the time of the stop. On December 22, 1988, the informant and a detective, acting as the mule, met with Johnson and Bonet in their Newark apartment. The parties reviewed and discussed the details of the plan. The next day Johnson stopped the mule as planned and seized one kilogram of cocaine. The informant and a special agent, posing as the seller, drove off. Johnson drove to his apartment, followed by the mule. On his arrival at approximately 12:05 P.M., Johnson was arrested.

Johnson was indicted for drug offenses and for crimes related to the abuse of his office. He moved to dismiss the indictment on two grounds. First, he argued that the sting involved such outrageous government conduct that it violated state due process standards. Second, he claimed that the sting violated the New Jersey statutory entrapment defense, N.J. Stat. Ann. §2C:2-12, which provides as follows:

> A public law enforcement official or a person engaged in cooperation with such an official or one acting as an agent of a public law enforcement official perpetrates an entrapment if for the purpose of obtaining evidence of the commission of an offense, he induces or encourages and, as a direct result, causes another person to engage in conduct constituting such offense by [employing] methods of persuasion or inducement which create a substantial risk that such an offense will be committed by persons other than those who are ready to commit it.

How would you rule? Compare State v. Johnson, 606 A.2d 315 (N.J. 1992).

CINCINNATI POLICE DIVISION, PROCEDURE MANUAL §12.131 CONFIDENTIAL INFORMANT MANAGEMENT AND CONTROL

A. A person must meet three criteria to establish them as a CI: (1) the person is in a unique position to help the Division in a present or future investigation, (2) the person will not compromise Division interests or activities, (3) the person will accept the direction necessary to effectively use their services.

B. Precautions when dealing with CIs:

1. Never provide CIs with knowledge of police facilities, operations, activities, or personnel.
2. Two police officers must be capable of contacting a CI. Two officers will be present at all contact with CIs unless otherwise approved by a supervisor. [When] dealing with CIs of the opposite sex or homosexual CIs, two officers will always be present. [T]wo officers will always be present when paying CIs.

3. Immediately document initial debriefing contacts with CIs on the Confidential Informant Registration and Reliability Report.

4. Document all significant contacts with CIs on the Controlling District/Section/Unit Debriefing Report. Examples of significant contact are: (a) receiving information about criminals or criminal activity including information from phone conversations, (b) any compensation made to CIs, (c) any contact that results in an arrest or the execution of a search warrant. . . .

D. Undesirable CIs are those who (1) commit an act which could endanger the life or safety of a police officer, (2) reveal the identity of a police officer to suspects, or in any other way compromise an official investigation, (3) try to use the Division to further criminal goals, (4) provide false or misleading information to police officers, (5) engage in conduct that brings discredit or embarrassment upon the Division. . . .

L. Controlled Purchases Using Confidential Informants:

(1) Get permission from an immediate supervisor before making controlled purchases.

(2) When possible, use CIs to introduce police officers to make purchases.

(3) Use a concealed body transmitting device and/or recording devices on CIs whenever possible. Never destroy recordings before the conclusion of court proceedings, including appeals.

(4) Search all CIs before and after conducting a controlled purchase of drugs. The Strip Search Law does not apply to the voluntary search of CIs. . . .

(5) Currency used in controlled purchases: (a) photocopy and record serial numbers, (b) two officers will witness buy money given to CIs.

(6) When possible, use two or more officers for surveillance of CIs during controlled purchases.

Notes

1. *Outrageous conduct: majority position.* Most state and federal courts recognize, at least theoretically, a constitutional defense to criminal charges based on the overly aggressive tactics of government investigators. In some jurisdictions, it is called "due process entrapment," while in others (including the federal system) it is known as "outrageous governmental conduct." United States v. Russell, 411 U.S. 423 (1973). However, the defense rarely succeeds. There is no clear consensus among courts on the elements necessary to prove the defense, although many courts consider the four issues raised by the New Jersey Supreme Court in State v. Johnson, 606 A.2d 315 (N.J. 1992), the case on which Problem 10-2 was based.

> Relevant factors are (1) whether the government or the defendant was primarily responsible for creating and planning the crime, (2) whether the government or the defendant primarily controlled and directed the commission of the crime, (3) whether objectively viewed the methods used by the government to involve the defendant in the commission of the crime were unreasonable, and (4) whether the government had a legitimate law enforcement purpose in bringing about the crime. Although courts have used varying formulations of the primary factors governing due process entrapment,

> the factors most invoked center around two major recurrent concerns: the justification for the police in targeting and investigating the defendant as a criminal suspect; and the nature and extent of the government's actual involvement in bringing about the crime.

606 A.2d at 323. The defense commonly appears in drug cases because it would be difficult to prosecute many narcotics violations (which are often consensual transactions leaving behind little evidence and few willing witnesses) without undercover operations.

Most courts and commentators note that there is some overlap between the defenses of subjective entrapment, objective entrapment, and due process "outrageous conduct." See Elizabeth E. Joh, Breaking the Law to Enforce It: Undercover Police Participation in Crime, 62 Stan. L. Rev. 155 (2009). The various tests all allow for some inquiry into both the predisposition of the defendant and the reasonableness of the government's conduct.

Most courts declare that they will assess outrageous misconduct claims by weighing factors on a case-by-case basis. On occasion, a court will declare a particular government tactic, regardless of the other circumstances in the case, to be outrageous conduct per se. One court has declared the use of contingency fees for informants to be outrageous governmental conduct per se. See State v. Glosson, 462 So. 2d 1082 (Fla. 1985); but see State v. Florez, 636 A.2d 1040 (N.J. 1994) (court considers contingency fee for confidential informant a troubling tactic, but not enough standing alone to warrant dismissal of charges). For a sampling of the judicial reaction to government involvement in crimes as part of the investigative enterprise, see the web extension for this chapter at *http://www.crimpro.com/extension/ch10*.

2. *Regulation or ban on undercover operations?* Are undercover operations simply too corrosive to tolerate in an open and democratic society? Consider this description of the use of informants in Communist East Germany: "Of all aspects of the MfS [Ministry for State Security], the generation of an army of individuals, willing to report suspicious information about acquaintances, friends, and family roused the fiercest resentment — and fear. The end result was to turn citizens against one another and to create an atmosphere of debilitating apprehension." Nancy Travis Wolfe, Policing a Socialist Society: The German Democratic Republic 78 (1992).

Police forces in nations other than the United States have been slower to adopt undercover techniques in the enforcement of ordinary criminal laws. For instance, Italian law evaluates the actions of government agents under the ordinary complicity doctrines of criminal law, meaning that an agent must not aid or abet a crime. See Jacqueline E. Ross, Impediments to Transnational Cooperation in Undercover Policing: A Comparative Study of the United States and Italy, 52 Am. J. Comparative Law 569 (2004). What would a society look like if the law prohibited undercover police operations? Conversely, what if the law gave judges no role in regulating undercover operations? See Richard H. McAdams, The Political Economy of Entrapment, 96 J. Crim. L. & Criminology 107 (2005).

3. *Confidential informant guidelines.* The use of a confidential informant raises special difficulty for law enforcement agencies because the government has less control over the actions of its agent. The problem is most pronounced when the informant participates in a crime while being paid by the government, as opposed to simply telling a police officer about past crimes. The Cincinnati police guidelines regarding confidential informants illustrate how executive branch agencies respond

to these special concerns. What dangers were the drafters of the Cincinnati guidelines trying to prevent? See Alexandra Natapoff, Snitching: The Institutional and Communal Consequences, 73 U. Cin. L. Rev. 645 (2004) (use of informants is usually framed as a threat to accuracy, but practice is understood through its connections to plea bargaining, prosecutorial discretion, administrative nature of American criminal justice; all of these realities threaten principles of accountability, consistency, predictability, and other rule of law precepts).

4. *Undercover operations guidelines.* The Federal Bureau of Investigation has guidelines on undercover operations that involve government agents rather than informants. They address the selection of targets for sting operations and the methods used to carry them out. The guidelines require a field agent to obtain prior authorization for certain undercover operations, including those that will last more than six months, target public officials or the news media, or require government agents to engage in a felony. See S. Rep. No. 682, 97th Cong., 2d Sess. 536-52 (1982). A review by the Inspector General for the Department of Justice in 2005 concluded that the FBI complied effectively with the undercover operation guidelines, but deviations from the Department's guidelines on confidential informants were more common. Office of the Inspector General, The Federal Bureau of Investigation's Compliance with the Attorney General's Investigation Guidelines (September 2005). Why might one expect to find more violations of confidential informant guidelines than undercover operation guidelines?

Most large police departments also have policies that address undercover operations, especially for narcotics and vice officers. For instance, the narcotics division of the Dallas Police Department requires written approval for all "long-term undercover operations" (longer than one to two hours). The undercover officer works with a partner whenever possible; when the officer must work undercover alone, a partner is still assigned to maintain daily contact, "cover" the undercover officer during sales, and maintain records and chain of custody for all evidence. The policy also forbids the officer to consume any narcotic unless forced to do so "under threat of immediate bodily injury." If you were drafting police guidelines on the subject of undercover investigations, what criteria would you set out for selecting the targets of undercover investigations? If you were drafting a statute on the subject, as opposed to internal guidelines, would the content of the provisions change?

5. *Supervision by prosecutors.* Prosecutors are often involved in planning and executing undercover operations. Although prosecutors have absolute immunity from any tort suit for their "prosecutorial" decisions, that immunity does not extend to a prosecutor's actions when advising criminal investigators about an undercover operation. See Burns v. Reed, 500 U.S. 478 (1991) (granting qualified "good faith" immunity but not absolute immunity to prosecutors for participation in investigations). What tort claims might arise against a prosecutor who is advising criminal investigators?

Problem 10-3. The Mayor

Federal prosecutors and FBI investigators became convinced in the early 1980s that Mayor Marion Barry of the District of Columbia was involved in various illegal activities. Over an eight-year period, federal law enforcement agencies carried out

10 separate investigations of potential illegal actions by Barry, including bribery, campaign finance fraud, prostitution, and drug use. A grand jury heard accusations from several of Barry's associates (some of them convicted for selling drugs) that the mayor had purchased and used cocaine, but Barry testified before the grand jury that he never used cocaine. None of these investigations resulted in any criminal charges.

In December 1988, district police were notified that Charles Lewis, a friend of Barry, had offered drugs to a maid at a downtown hotel. The detectives were on their way to Lewis's room but left the hotel when they learned that Barry was in the room with Lewis. That incident renewed the government's interest in the mayor's long-rumored drug use.

To create an opportunity for Barry to commit a crime, the government asked for help from a former intimate friend of Barry's, Rasheeda Moore. Moore was willing to cooperate because she was facing criminal charges herself. In January 1990, the government flew Moore to Washington from California and got her a room at the Vista International Hotel. They paid to have her hair styled. On January 18, three days before Barry planned to announce his plans to seek reelection, the agents asked Moore to invite the mayor to her hotel room.

When Barry met Moore in the hotel lobby, he was at first reluctant to go up to her room. She convinced him to accompany her to the room, along with a woman she described as her cousin, Wanda. Wanda was actually an FBI agent. Once in the room, Barry engaged Moore in small talk and drank cognac. Then Barry asked, "Can we make love before you leave, before you leave town?" Moore complained that Barry wasn't sufficiently romantic: "I can't just jump into it." Then she said, "So what are you going to do? Let's do something."

A few minutes later, Barry asked Moore about Wanda, who had left the room a few minutes earlier: "Your friend mess around?" Moore, taking the question as one about drugs, responded, "She has some, yeah, sometimes. . . . She toots [snorts cocaine] more than she'll do anything else." Soon afterward, Barry said, "I don't have anything. What about you?" A short time later, Wanda returned to the room with crack cocaine. Moore presented Barry with a pipe loaded with crack cocaine, and Barry paid for it. Then Barry looked at the pipe and said "How does this work? . . . I never done it before."

Moore replied, "That's what we used to do all the time, what are you talking about?" Barry, however, insisted that he had never "done that before." Moore then said, "Put it in there. . . . Let me give you a lighter." Barry replied "You do it," but Moore said "No, I'm not doing nothing." Each insisted several more times that the other light the pipe. Moore asked, "Are you chicken?"

Eventually Barry lit the crack pipe, put it to his mouth and inhaled twice. Almost immediately, the mayor picked up his jacket and started for the door, as Moore asked if he wanted to smoke more of the crack. "No. You're crazy," Barry responded. Barry then turned for the door, and law enforcement agents burst in from the adjoining room.

A medic told Barry that he had been exposed to a dangerous substance and asked whether the mayor wanted to go to the hospital. Barry said no. "Man, I should have followed my first instincts, I tell you," he said. Then D.C. Police Sergeant James Pawlik said, "I mean, we really didn't want this to happen."

"I didn't want it to happen, either," Barry replied. "I should, if I had followed my instincts tonight, I'd have been all right. I should have stayed downstairs.

Bitch kept insisting coming up here." After complaining about the tightness of the handcuffs, Barry spoke further about Moore: "She was slick, though. I should have known better when she wouldn't do it first. I should have known something was up." He repeatedly muttered, "Damn bitch set me up."

Pawlik asked Barry if he hadn't expected to be caught in a sting sooner or later. "I don't know," Barry said. "I guess you all been checking on me for a long time, huh?" "Obviously," Pawlik responded. "Some day it's got to happen."

"I guess you all figured that I couldn't resist that lady," Barry said. As the agents prepared to lead Barry from the room, Pawlik said, "When it's all over, it'll be better for everybody." Barry responded, "You think so?"

The government brought charges against Barry for perjury (based on his testimony to the grand jury that he had never used cocaine) and for possession of cocaine (a misdemeanor). The FBI's guidelines on undercover operations state that sting operations should be directed toward obtaining evidence of serious crimes by major criminal figures. The same guidelines suggest that officers should ordinarily arrest a suspect immediately after taking possession of cocaine (or making a purchase) and before the suspect smokes or inhales the drug.

Why did the prosecutors decide to give Barry an opportunity to commit only a misdemeanor (possession of a small amount of crack cocaine)? What form of the entrapment defense (if any) would you advise Barry to pursue? What outcome would you predict?

B. THE INVESTIGATIVE GRAND JURY

Efforts by police officers to gather information about criminal suspects have occupied most of our attention thus far. The police are indeed the government agents who gather information in most criminal law enforcement. But in more complex investigations, other institutions such as grand juries and regulatory bodies, often acting under prosecutorial guidance, become important players in the effort to build a file that could lead to criminal charges. These investigations typically pursue suspicions about alleged white-collar crimes such as fraud. Such complex investigations, although making up only a tiny fraction of the criminal cases ultimately filed, require an enormous amount of resources for both the prosecution and defense, and receive much media attention.

The grand jury is the central investigative tool in these complex cases. Unlike police departments, which emerged in this country late in the nineteenth century, the grand jury is an ancient institution. It can trace its heritage at least as far back as twelfth-century England. The grand jury began as a body of citizens that the courts empowered to investigate criminal violations in the vicinity. Initially, the criminal charges that the grand jury issued were based on the personal knowledge of grand jurors. Only later did they acquire the power to call witnesses and to consider evidence that representatives of the Crown placed before them.

The grand jury thrived when first transplanted to England's American colonies. Each state entering the Union prior to the Civil War created grand juries and gave them broad powers to call witnesses and to gather documents. Later in the nineteenth century, voters grew less enthusiastic about the institution (especially in new states, such as Colorado and Nebraska) and passed constitutional provisions allowing the legislature to abolish the grand jury altogether. Although many of the newer states no longer *required* indictments as the method of initiating charges in serious criminal cases, they retained the grand jury as one method of investigating important cases, particularly those involving political corruption, where the independence of the police or prosecutor might be in question. Because of special investigative powers given to grand juries, prosecutors found it convenient to rely on them to gather evidence in cases, such as those involving conspiracies and documentary material, where routine police work could not produce enough evidence.

The grand jury is technically an arm of the court, and a judge supervises some of its activities. For instance, a judge hears any motions to quash a grand jury subpoena and will enforce a subpoena if a witness refuses to comply. The court instructs the grand jurors at the beginning of their term about their general responsibilities. Despite this supervisory power, the judge is generally not present during grand jury proceedings, and state and federal courts have proven reluctant to interfere in the affairs of the grand jury.

In this section, we consider issues relating to the special investigative powers of grand juries and similar governmental bodies to subpoena testimony and evidence. We do not consider here the charging functions of the grand jury.

1. Grand Jury Secrecy

A witness who receives a subpoena to testify before a grand jury enters an unfamiliar room where the prosecuting attorney asks most of the questions, the grand jurors listen, and the stenographer records everything said. The witness usually knows very little about the grand jury's overall investigation or her place in that investigation. In this setting, most of the information flows in one direction. The grand jury can obtain a lot of information without revealing much of its investigative strategy.

Witnesses, however, often have legal counsel who can make the grand jury less intimidating. In an ordinary criminal case, an attorney enters the scene only after the government already has gathered most of its evidence. But lawyers have the opportunity to become involved earlier in more complex investigations because of the long time period involved: A white-collar crime case will often take months, or even years, to investigate. Lawyers also get involved earlier in the more complex cases because larger amounts of money are often at stake, and the targets of the investigation can afford to hire an attorney. As you read the statutes and notes below, consider the intricate game that occurs when counsel and sophisticated grand jury witnesses face off against prosecutors trying to get the most information from witnesses without revealing too much about the grand jury's investigation.

FEDERAL RULE OF CRIMINAL PROCEDURE 6

. . . (d) Who May Be Present.

(1) While the Grand Jury Is in Session. The following persons may be present while the grand jury is in session: attorneys for the government, the witness being

questioned, interpreters when needed, and a court reporter or an operator of a recording device.

(2) During Deliberations and Voting. No person other than the jurors, and any interpreter needed to assist a hearing-impaired or speech-impaired juror, may be present while the grand jury is deliberating or voting.

(e) Recording and Disclosing the Proceedings.

(1) Recording the Proceedings. Except while the grand jury is deliberating or voting, all proceedings must be recorded by a court reporter or by a suitable recording device. But the validity of a prosecution is not affected by the unintentional failure to make a recording. Unless the court orders otherwise, an attorney for the government will retain control of the recording, the reporter's notes, and any transcript prepared from those notes.

(2) Secrecy. . . .

(B) Unless these rules provide otherwise, the following persons must not disclose a matter occurring before the grand jury: (i) a grand juror; (ii) an interpreter; (iii) a court reporter; (iv) an operator of a recording device; (v) a person who transcribes recorded testimony; (vi) an attorney for the government; or (vii) [government personnel who assists the attorney for the government].

■ COLORADO REVISED STATUTES §16-5-204(4)(d)

Any witness subpoenaed to appear and testify before a grand jury or to produce books, papers, documents, or other objects before such grand jury shall be entitled to assistance of counsel during any time that such witness is being questioned in the presence of such grand jury, and counsel may be present in the grand jury room with his client during such questioning. However, counsel for the witness shall be permitted only to counsel with the witness and shall not make objections, arguments, or address the grand jury. Such counsel may be retained by the witness or may, for any person financially unable to obtain adequate assistance, be appointed in the same manner as if that person were eligible for appointed counsel. An attorney present in the grand jury room shall take an oath of secrecy. If the court, at an in camera hearing, determines that counsel was disruptive, then the court may order counsel to remain outside the courtroom when advising his client. No attorney shall be permitted to provide counsel in the grand jury room to more than one witness in the same criminal investigation, except with the permission of the grand jury.

Problem 10-4. Selecting Witnesses

Janet Terreton has contacted the federal government with information about possible corruption in New Jersey's state and local governments. Terreton's former employer, Anderson Hagelman, is the sole proprietor of two companies that do business with various units of local governments in New Jersey. She alleges that Hagelman, along with many others who sell goods and services to state and local governments, have bribed governmental contracting officials to obtain the government contracts. Terreton resigned from her management position in Hagelman's firm two months before she contacted the government, after a dispute over her retirement compensation. Terreton's information ultimately arrives in the office of the U.S. Attorney. As the government attorney assigned to this matter, how would you begin the investigation? Should you, or the agents working with you, attempt to interview any witnesses outside the presence of the grand jury?

Notes

1. *Grand jury secrecy.* The proceedings of grand juries traditionally are secret. The federal rules of criminal procedure, like the rules and statutes of most states, codify the traditional practice: Only the grand jurors, attorneys for the government, the witness, and (sometimes) a court reporter can be present in the room. Each of these parties except for the witness has an obligation not to disclose what happens in the grand jury room. A classic explanation for the secrecy of grand jury proceedings appears in United States v. Amazon Industrial Chemical Corp., 55 F.2d 254, 261 (D. Md. 1931):

> The reasons which lie behind the requirement of secrecy may be summarized as follows: (1) To prevent the escape of those whose indictment may be contemplated; (2) to insure the utmost freedom to the grand jury in its deliberations, and to prevent persons subject to indictment or their friends from importuning the grand jurors; (3) to prevent subornation of perjury or tampering with the witnesses who may testify before the grand jury and later appear at the trial of those indicted by it; (4) to encourage free and untrammeled disclosures by persons who have information with respect to the commission of crimes; (5) to protect the innocent accused who is exonerated from disclosure of the fact that he has been under investigation, and from the expense of standing trial where there was no probability of guilt.

About 20 states have statutes or court rules, like the Colorado statute reprinted above, that allow a grand jury witness to bring an attorney into the grand jury room. See also Fla. Stat. §§905.17(1), (2). Rules of evidence do not apply to grand jury proceedings, and the witness's attorney typically may not object to any questions. What, then, is the attorney's function? Will the presence of an attorney in the grand jury room influence the type of questions asked or the witnesses selected to testify?

2. *Makeup and selection of the grand jury.* At common law, a grand jury had anywhere between 12 and 23 members. Federal grand juries have 16 to 23 members, and most state grand juries stay within the common-law size limits. See Alaska Stat. §12.40.020 (12 to 18 jurors). Some jurisdictions have grand juries that sit routinely, and the court impanels such a grand jury on its own initiative; elsewhere, the prosecutor requests the court to impanel a grand jury for some special purpose. The clerk of the court summons the potential grand jurors, typically (as in the federal system) from the list of registered voters. The judge may excuse some potential jurors if service would be particularly burdensome to them. See Sara Sun Beale, et al., Grand Jury Law and Practice §§3:04, 3:05, 4:8 (2d ed. 1997). What sorts of document requests will an investigative body of this type tend to make? How might the grand jury's requests for testimony and documents change if the court assigned staff members or experts to advise the grand jurors?

3. *Witness debriefing.* Although attorneys for grand jury witnesses are not allowed in the grand jury room in a majority of American jurisdictions, they still obtain

information about the grand jury's questions and the witness's answers by debriefing their clients immediately after the testimony. Many attorneys also encourage their clients to step outside the grand jury room periodically (perhaps after each question) for a consultation. See Sara Sun Beale, et al., Grand Jury Law and Practice §6:28 (2d ed. 1997) (surveying statutory and common law protections for witnesses' ability to consult counsel outside grand jury room). Some attorneys attempt to debrief witnesses who are not their clients. Statutes and rules of criminal procedure typically impose an obligation of secrecy on the grand jurors and the government attorneys but not on grand jury witnesses. See Fed. R. Crim. P. 6(e)(2); Ill. Code Crim. Proc. §112-6. About a dozen states have statutes or rules that prevent a grand jury witness from discussing her testimony with anyone other than her attorney. See N.C. Gen. Stat. §§15A-623(e), (g). What would be the likely attitude of government attorneys about witness debriefing? Is there anything government attorneys can or should do about it? See In re Grand Jury Proceedings, 558 F. Supp. 532 (W.D. Va. 1983) (defense lawyers may debrief all witnesses, but government attorneys may request grand jury witnesses not to discuss their testimony with others).

4. *Warnings to grand jury witnesses: constitutional requirements.* The witness who receives a subpoena to testify before the grand jury can be held in contempt of court for failing to appear, even if the witness plans only to invoke the Fifth Amendment privilege. Despite this element of coercion, the Supreme Court has decided (along with the great majority of state courts) that prosecutors need not give *Miranda* warnings to grand jury witnesses. United States v. Mandujano, 425 U.S. 564 (1976); State v. Driscoll, 360 A.2d 857 (R.I. 1976). Would you require a warning only for those witnesses who become "targets" of a grand jury investigation? Again, most jurisdictions have not required such warnings as a constitutional matter. See United States v. Washington, 431 U.S. 181 (1977) (no warning of "target" status is required by federal Constitution); People v. J.H., 554 N.E.2d 961 (Ill. 1990) (same for Illinois constitution); but see People ex rel. Gallagher v. District Court, 601 P.2d 1380 (Colo. 1979) (Colorado constitution requires warnings).

5. *Nonconstitutional requirements of warnings.* Despite a lack of success on the constitutional front, witnesses still often receive various warnings before appearing in front of the grand jury. In the federal system, the U.S. Attorney's Manual requires prosecutors to inform witnesses of their right to silence, the fact that statements to the grand jury can be used against the witness, and the fact that those who have retained attorneys may consult with their attorneys outside the grand jury room. See §9-11.151. The manual also requires prosecutors to inform grand jury witnesses (and some nonwitnesses) of their status as "targets" of the investigation. See §§9-11.151 to 155. What would be the remedy for a violation of this written prosecutorial policy? In a strong minority of states, statutes require the prosecutor to inform grand jury witnesses of their right to silence, especially when the witness is a target of the investigation. Ill. Rev. Stat. ch. 38, para. 112-4(b); Tex. Code Crim. Proc. art. 20.17. Some state statutes also require the state to notify subpoena recipients if they are targets of the investigation. See Ind. Code Ann. §35-34-2-5. Why would a potential witness want to know if he is a target of the investigation? Some state statutes provide certain advantages (such as the right to consult with counsel in the grand jury room) only to targets and not to other witnesses.

6. *Grand jury witnesses versus police interrogation.* The question of warnings for grand jury witnesses calls for a comparison between interrogation during grand jury proceedings and custodial interrogation in a police station. There are certain

similarities in the two experiences: In both cases, the witness is confined against her will, and the questioning takes place in isolation and in an unfamiliar setting. The two forms of questioning are also different: A person in police custody can end all questioning by invoking the right to silence, while a grand jury witness has no general right to silence and can be imprisoned for contempt of court for refusing to answer questions (unless the answers would be self-incriminating). Can you think of other parallels and differences between the two forms of questioning? Who goes to the grand jury and who goes to the police station?

7. *The legal ethics of contacting represented persons.* There may be times when a prosecutor would prefer to speak to witnesses outside the grand jury room. Such an interview can save the witness the trouble of appearing at a specific time and place to testify, and it allows the prosecutor to screen out all but the most relevant inculpatory evidence from the grand jury. But if the witness is represented by counsel, can the prosecutor accomplish these purposes? Can the prosecutor (or an investigator working with the prosecuting attorney) interview the witness without the witness's attorney present? The Model Rule of Professional Conduct 4.2 has some bearing on this question: "In representing a client, a lawyer shall not communicate about the subject of the representation with a person the lawyer knows to be represented by another lawyer in the matter, unless the lawyer has the consent of the other lawyer or is authorized by law to do so."

In light of this ethical rule, will criminal suspects be able to protect themselves from interrogation by placing a lawyer on retainer and notifying the government of that fact? There is a lively debate about whether state bar authorities can appropriately enforce this rule against federal prosecutors. For a sample of the arguments, see the web extension for this chapter at *http://www.crimpro.com/extension/ch10*.

2. *Immunity for Witnesses*

Although the grand jury can ask for a very broad range of testimony and documents, there is still some evidence beyond its reach. For instance, a grand jury cannot obtain information protected by common law privileges, such as the attorney-client privilege. There is also an important constitutional limit on the statements that a grand jury may obtain from a witness. The Fifth Amendment to the U.S. Constitution, and analogous provisions in almost every state constitution (all but two), create a privilege against self-incrimination:

> No person . . . shall be compelled in any criminal case to be a witness against himself. . . . [U.S. Const., amend. 5]
> No subject shall be . . . compelled to accuse or furnish evidence against himself. [N.H. Const., pt. I, art 15]

A witness who receives a subpoena to appear and testify before a grand jury (or before a magistrate, administrative agency, or congressional committee, as the case may be) can invoke this constitutional privilege and refuse to answer questions when the answers would incriminate the witness. But this does not end the matter. Once the witness has invoked the privilege against self-incrimination, the prosecutor has another option. She can ask a court to order the witness to testify despite the risk of self-incrimination; in exchange, the prosecutor promises that no government agent will use the "compelled" testimony to further a later criminal prosecution against the witness. This promise is known as "immunity."

The question of immunity offers a useful vantage point for studying the privilege against self-incrimination. Just as the nature of a contract can be understood by exploring remedies for breach of contract, so the nature of the privilege against self-incrimination becomes clear when one explores the nature of the immunity necessary to overcome that privilege. The following case explores exactly what sort of promises a prosecutor must make to an immunized witness. Although the case deals with witnesses at trial, the same constitutional reasoning would apply to the immunity offered to grand jury witnesses.

■ COMMONWEALTH v. PATRICIA SWINEHART

664 A.2d 957 (Pa. 1995)

CAPPY, J.

This case presents the question of whether the use and derivative use immunity provided in 42 Pa. C.S. §5947,[1] is consistent with the Pennsylvania constitutional privilege at Article I, Section 9, against compelled self-incrimination. For the reasons that follow we find that use and derivative use immunity is consistent with the protection provided under our state constitution.

[After the murder of David Swinehart, authorities charged his nephew, Thomas DeBlase, with the crime. Preliminary rulings and interlocutory appeals delayed his trial for several years. In the meantime,] Patricia Swinehart, the wife of the decedent, was arrested and charged with the murder of her husband, and with being a co-conspirator of DeBlase. DeBlase was subpoenaed as a witness in the Patricia Swinehart trial and offered a grant of immunity pursuant to 42 Pa. C.S. §5947. DeBlase moved to quash the subpoena and objected to the grant of immunity. . . . The trial court refused to quash the subpoena, approved the grant of immunity to DeBlase, and then when DeBlase still refused to answer, found him to be in both civil and criminal contempt. [Without DeBlase's testimony, the trial of Patricia Swinehart resulted in an acquittal. This is DeBlase's appeal of his contempt conviction.]

DeBlase asserts that the Act, which grants an immunized witness use and derivative use immunity, offers insufficient safeguards in exchange for the considerable protection guaranteed under Article I, Section 9 of the Pennsylvania Constitution which the immunized witness is forced to forsake. DeBlase acknowledges that the United States Supreme Court has upheld use and derivative use immunity as sufficient protection under the Fifth Amendment to the United States Constitution in

1. The pertinent portions of the immunity statute that are at issue provide: . . .

(c) Whenever a witness refuses, on the basis of his privilege against self-incrimination, to testify or provide other information in a [judicial proceeding, and the judge] communicates to the witness an immunity order, that witness may not refuse to testify based on his privilege against self-incrimination.

(d) No testimony or other information compelled under an immunity order, or any information directly or indirectly derived from such testimony or other information, may be used against a witness in any criminal case, except that such information may be used . . . in a prosecution [for perjury or false swearing.]

Kastigar v. United States, 406 U.S. 441 (1972). He argues, however, that the Pennsylvania Constitutional protection is broader and can only be satisfied by a grant of transactional immunity.[5]

[We] will begin our analysis with a review of the text of the constitutional provision at issue, the history of that provision as related through legislative enactments and prior decisions of this Court, related case law from our sister states, and finally, policy considerations which include matters unique to our Commonwealth.

Article I, Section 9 [says that] "In all criminal prosecutions the accused... cannot be compelled to give evidence against himself.... A comparison of the actual language in Article I, Section 9 and the Fifth Amendment does not reveal any major differences in the description of the privilege against self-incrimination within the two Constitutions. As the words themselves are not persuasive of either interpretation on the issue at bar, we turn to the prior decisions of this Court which interpreted the right against self-incrimination as contained within the Pennsylvania Constitution.

[It] was not until after the United States Supreme Court decision in Counselman v. Hitchcock, 142 U.S. 547 (1892), that this Court addressed the question of immunity in relation to the privilege against self-incrimination. In *Counselman,* the United States Supreme Court rejected a federal statute which conferred only use immunity as being an insufficient substitute for the privilege guaranteed under the Fifth Amendment.... The Court then went on to conclude that a statutory grant of immunity, in order to be valid as against the Fifth Amendment, "must afford absolute immunity against future prosecution for the offense to which the question relates." In the wake of *Counselman,* only those legislative grants of immunity which compelled testimony from a witness in exchange for transactional immunity were found to be valid.

Thus, from 1892 until 1978, Pennsylvania recognized only transactional immunity as a sufficient exchange for compelling a witness to forsake the privilege against self-incrimination. The courts in Pennsylvania followed the lead of the United States Supreme Court on this issue.

The Pennsylvania Legislature also adhered to the dictates of the United States Supreme Court when drafting legislation on the issue of immunity grants for witnesses. Prior to the 1978 revisions, which are at issue in this case, the immunity conferred under the Act was transactional immunity. This shift in the type of immunity authorized by the Act can easily be traced to the United States Supreme Court decision in Kastigar v. United States, 406 U.S. 441 (1972).

In *Kastigar,* the United States Supreme Court found use and derivative use immunity to adequately protect the privilege against compulsory self-incrimination contained within the Fifth Amendment. The Court reconsidered its opinion in

5. Generally three types of immunity are recognized, although some scholars treat "use" and "use and derivative use" immunity as one and the same. "Use" immunity provides immunity only for the testimony actually given pursuant to the order compelling said testimony. "Use and derivative use" immunity enlarges the scope of the grant to cover any information or leads that were derived from the actual testimony given under compulsion. Thus, under either "use" or "use and derivative use" immunity a prosecution against the witness is not foreclosed; any prosecution must, however, arise from evidence unrelated to the information which is derived from the witness's own mouth. "Transactional" immunity is the most expansive, as it in essence provides complete amnesty to the witness for any transactions which are revealed in the course of the compelled testimony.

Counselman and determined that although use immunity offers insufficient protection under the Fifth Amendment, transactional immunity offers greater protection than is necessary and thus concluded that use and derivative use immunity would thereafter be sufficient.

> [The] privilege has never been construed to mean that one who invokes it cannot subsequently be prosecuted. Its sole concern is to afford protection against being forced to give testimony leading to the infliction of penalties affixed to criminal acts. Immunity from the use of compelled testimony, as well as evidence derived directly and indirectly therefrom, affords this protection. It prohibits the prosecutorial authorities from using the compelled testimony in any respect, and it therefore insures that the testimony cannot lead to the infliction of criminal penalties on the witness.

This shift by the United States Supreme Court away from transactional immunity in favor of use and derivative use immunity was commented upon by this Court in [1975. Following the *Kastigar* decision and our 1975 decision commenting favorably on *Kastigar,*] the immunity statute was revised to its present form wherein transactional immunity was replaced with use and derivative use immunity. [It] is clear that Pennsylvania, for the most part, followed the lead of the United States Supreme Court....

Turning to our sister states, we find that they are evenly split on the issue of whether their state constitutions afford protection against compulsory self-incrimination greater than the Fifth Amendment in the wake of *Kastigar.* The six states that have rejected *Kastigar* and found their constitutions to require transactional immunity are [Alaska, Hawaii, Massachusetts, Mississippi, Oregon, and South Carolina].[13]

In each of [these six states], the state courts, relying upon their constitutional self-incrimination clauses, rejected legislation that had been developed post-*Kastigar* replacing transactional immunity with use/derivative use immunity. South Carolina and Alaska found the protection of use/derivative use immunity to be too cumbersome to enforce, citing the practical problems in determining whether or not later prosecutions stemmed from the immunized testimony. Mississippi had the same practical reasons for rejecting *Kastigar* as South Carolina and Alaska. Mississippi more bluntly phrased the problem as being one of having to rely upon the good faith of the prosecutor in use/derivative use situations.... Oregon found the rationale of *Kastigar* unpersuasive and chose to remain consistent with their case law which had always followed the reasoning of *Counselman*....

The six states which have found use and derivative use immunity consistent with the self-incrimination clauses in their state constitutions are [Arizona, Indiana, Maryland, New Jersey, New York, and Texas].[14] [These courts] accepted use and derivative use immunity grants as consistent with their state constitutions [because

13. Eleven jurisdictions provide for transactional immunity through legislation. [These include California, Idaho, Illinois, Maine, Michigan, Nevada, New Hampshire, Rhode Island, Utah, Washington, and West Virginia.]

14. Eighteen jurisdictions have provided for use/derivative use immunity through legislation passed after *Kastigar.* [These include Arkansas, Colorado, Connecticut, Delaware, Florida, Georgia, Iowa, Kansas, Louisiana, Minnesota, Montana, Nebraska, New Mexico, North Carolina, North Dakota, South Dakota, Vermont, and Wisconsin.]

they] found the state constitutional privilege at issue to be coextensive with the Fifth Amendment.

In reviewing the relevant opinions and legislation from our sister states we find no clear preference among the jurisdictions. "What appears most striking among the courts which reject use/derivative use immunity is the concern for the practical effect of separating out the information garnered from the compelled testimony when later prosecuting the individual. It is this fear that the individual will be condemned by his/her own words, even inadvertently, which caused South Carolina, Alaska, Mississippi, and to some extent, Oregon, to reject use/derivative use immunity as inconsistent with the protection from self-incrimination found within their state constitutions.... To complete our analysis of this issue we now turn to a consideration of policy concerns which would affect our conclusion.

This case involves the juxtaposition of the privilege against self-incrimination and the need to compel testimony. The inherent conflict between these two important concepts is the heart of this case. Each of these concepts [carries] historical baggage of considerable proportion. Our system of jurisprudence abhors the ancient star chamber inquisitions which forced a witness into "the cruel trilemma of self-accusation, perjury or contempt." On the other hand, of equal importance to our system of justice is the ancient adage that "the public has a right to every man's evidence." The concept of compelling a witness to testify has been recognized in Anglo-American jurisprudence since the Statute of Elizabeth, 5 Eliz. 1, c.9, §12 (1562). Immunizing a witness has always been a feature of Pennsylvania jurisprudence. The dilemma in balancing these competing concerns centers on the type of immunity which can best provide the public with the information to which it is entitled in order to ferret out criminal activity and at the same time protect the rights of the witness being forced to testify under compulsion.

In urging this Court to declare the present immunity statute unconstitutional, DeBlase places great emphasis on the fact that Pennsylvania has historically required transactional immunity as the only adequate safeguard for compelling a witness's testimony in violation of the right against self-incrimination. As with most critics of use/derivative use immunity, DeBlase asserts that only transactional immunity can truly protect a witness from later being condemned by his own words. The strongest argument for rejecting use/derivative use immunity is what has been commonly referred to as the "web effect." ...

In fact in the instant case DeBlase argues that if forced to testify against his co-conspirator he will forever be caught within the web and his ability to receive a fair trial forever tainted. Specifically, the untraceable effects of his immunized testimony will impact upon the selection of his jury, the presentation of a defense, the ability to utilize character witnesses and infringe upon his decision to testify in his own behalf. The practical consequences of rejecting transactional immunity and leaving a witness clothed in only the protection of use/derivative use immunity constitutes the most salient argument against the constitutionality of 42 Pa. C.S. §5947.

On the other hand, there is no dispute that immunization of a witness is a necessary, effective and ancient tool in law enforcement. As the United States Supreme Court stated in *Kastigar,* "many offenses are of such a character that the only persons capable of giving useful testimony are those implicated in the crime." The very nature of criminal conspiracies is what forces the Commonwealth into the Hobson's choice of having to grant one of the parties implicated in the criminal scheme immunity in order to uncover the entire criminal enterprise. Thus, in order to serve justice an accommodation must be made; however, that arrangement should not place the "witness" in a better position as to possible criminal prosecution than he had previously enjoyed. A grant of immunity should protect the witness from prosecution through his own words, yet it should not be so broad that the witness is forever free from suffering the just consequences of his actions, if his actions can be proven by means other than his own words.

Clearly, there are compelling "pros" and "cons" on the question of the right against self-incrimination versus the need to immunize the witness. However, to elevate the right against self-incrimination above the right of the public to every person's evidence would not achieve a proper balance of these competing interests. Transactional immunity offers complete amnesty to the witness, a measure of protection clearly greater than the privilege against self-incrimination. The practical consequences, otherwise known as the "web effect," created by immunizing a witness should not tip the balance so far in favor of the witness that the Commonwealth is only left with the option of granting complete amnesty to a witness in order to fully investigate criminal enterprises and serve the public need for justice. Use/derivative use immunity strikes a better balance between the need for law enforcement to ferret out criminality and the right of the witness to be free of self-incrimination.

In this case we find that Article I, Section 9 is, in fact, more expansive than the Fifth Amendment; it is not, however, so expansive that the privilege against self-incrimination would require greater protection than that provided within the Act. . . . Recognizing the serious practical concerns which almost always accompany a later prosecution of the immunized witness, we hold that in the later prosecution, the evidence offered by the Commonwealth shall be reviewed with the most careful scrutiny. That is, the Commonwealth must prove, of record, by the heightened standard of clear and convincing evidence, that the evidence upon which a subsequent prosecution is brought arose wholly from independent sources. Accordingly, . . . the decision of the Superior Court is affirmed and this matter is remanded to the trial court for further proceedings consistent with this opinion. . . .

Notes

1. *Transactional and use immunity: majority position.* As the *Swinehart* court indicates, "use/derivative use" immunity is sufficient to satisfy the federal constitution, while states are divided over the type of immunity that prosecutors must offer to witnesses before a court will compel the witness to give self-incriminating testimony. Roughly 20 states require use immunity, while a slightly smaller group requires transactional immunity. In other states, the type of immunity needed varies, depending on factors such as the seriousness of the offense being investigated. Note that more states resolve this question by statute than by a constitutional court ruling. Immunity orders do not occur in a large number of cases. For instance, in 2007, prosecutors in the federal system requested immunity for 1,134 witnesses. U.S. Dept. of Justice, Sourcebook of Criminal Justice Statistics, table 5.1.2007, available at *http://www.albany.edu/sourcebook/pdf/t512007.pdf*

2. *Simple use immunity.* The Supreme Court's *Kastigar* decision approved of "use/derivative use" immunity: Later prosecution of an immunized witness is possible, but only if the prosecution's case is not based on the witness's statements or on any

investigative leads obtained from that testimony. But was the Court correct to insist on this form of immunity, instead of "simple" use immunity? Simple use immunity would prevent use of immunized testimony in a later prosecution, but it would leave the prosecution free to use evidence obtained from investigative leads created by the witness's compelled testimony. For instance, the judicially compelled testimony of a murder suspect could not be introduced at the suspect's trial, but the murder weapon found through leads obtained during compelled testimony might come into evidence. Simple use immunity was an acceptable form of overcoming the self-incrimination privilege in most states during the nineteenth century. See State ex rel. Hackley v. Kelly, 24 N.Y. 74 (1861). Courts in England today do not exclude the fruits of testimony compelled under an immunity order. Does this approach, which bars only the use of a witness's actual statements, make the most sense of the Fifth Amendment's language: "No person . . . shall be compelled . . . to be a *witness* against himself"? Would your attitude about simple use immunity be different if you were interpreting a state provision such as the one in Texas, "[The] accused . . . shall not be compelled to give evidence against himself"? Tex. Const, art. I, §10. For a constitutional defense of simple use immunity, see Akhil Amar & Renee Lettow, Fifth Amendment First Principles: The Self-Incrimination Clause, 93 Mich. L. Rev. 857 (1995).

3. *The history of the privilege against self-incrimination.* What exactly does the privilege against self-incrimination — in a federal or state constitution — protect? Because an immunity order must substitute for the privilege against self-incrimination, it creates an occasion for addressing this question. What are the relevant sources for an answer? The precise words of the constitutional provision surely should have some role. What is the relevance of the *history* of the self-incrimination concept? See generally Richard Helmholtz et al., The Privilege Against Self-Incrimination: Its Origins and Development (1997).

The Latin maxim *nemo tenetur seipsum prodere* ("no one is obliged to accuse himself") originated in the medieval law of the Roman Catholic Church: It confirmed that even though a believer had a duty to confess sins to a priest, that obligation did not extend to criminal proceedings. The concept first became prominent in England in the ecclesiastical courts which were investigating and prosecuting those who resisted Anglican religious practice and belief. Puritans and other nonconformists invoked the concept to prevent their investigation and prosecution by ecclesiastical courts. See Michael Macnair, The Early Development of the Privilege Against Self-Incrimination, 10 Oxford J. Legal Stud. 66 (1990). One of the most famous of these crusaders for religious toleration and civil liberties was John Lilburn (a leader in a movement known as the "Levellers"), who invoked the privilege against self-incrimination as a natural right in various pamphlets and at his trial for treason. Lilburn also gave a pragmatic defense of the privilege: The privilege was necessary because "most men once entrusted with authority . . . pervert the same to their own domination and to the prejudice of our Peace and Liberties." Lilburn, An Agreement of the Free People of England (1649).

Despite these early uses in ecclesiastical courts, an evidentiary privilege against the use of self-incriminating statements did not operate in the English common law criminal courts until late in the eighteenth century, when defense counsel first became widely available and it was possible for a defendant to offer a defense without testifying himself. See John Langbein, The Historical Origins of the Privilege Against Self-Incrimination at Common Law, 92 Mich. L. Rev. 1047 (1994).

The American drafters of constitutions in the late eighteenth century all included a privilege against self-incrimination as part of a cluster of rights designed to reinforce the importance of the jury in a criminal trial as the central guarantee against oppressive government. But as Eben Moglen argues, the new constitutional provision was not meant to alter existing practices, and those practices included widespread techniques to encourage an accused to testify. See Eben Moglen, Taking the Fifth: Reconsidering the Origins of the Constitutional Privilege Against Self-Incrimination, 92 Mich. L. Rev. 1086 (1994); cf. Katharine B. Hazlett, The Nineteenth Century Origins of the Fifth Amendment Privilege Against Self-Incrimination, 42 Am. J. Legal Hist. 235 (1998). Defendants in custody had to appear before a magistrate who would routinely question the defendant about his involvement in the alleged crime. If the defendant confessed, the confession could form the basis for a summary conviction before the magistrate (for lesser offenses) or could be introduced at a later trial. If the defendant refused to answer a magistrate's questions, that fact could be revealed at trial. Does this history point in the direction of transactional immunity, use/derivative use immunity, or simple use immunity? Does it point in any direction at all?

4. *The purpose of the privilege.* If the text and history leave some doubt about the proper scope of the privilege, should legislators (who draft immunity statutes) and judges (who apply them) engage in some form of moral or political philosophy to flesh out the meaning of the privilege that is most attractive, or one most in keeping with our governmental structure and traditions? David Dolinko summarized the philosophical support for the privilege as follows:

> The rationales for the privilege fall, very roughly, into two categories. Systemic rationales are policies their proponents believe to be crucial to our particular kind of criminal justice system. Individual rationales are principles claimed to be entailed by a proper understanding of human rights or by a proper respect for human dignity and individuality. Among systemic rationales are the suggestions that the privilege encourages third-party witnesses to appear and testify by removing the fear that they might be compelled to incriminate themselves and removes the temptation to employ short cuts to conviction that demean official integrity. Individual rationales include the arguments that compelled self-incrimination works an unacceptable cruelty or invasion of privacy, as well as the notion of respect for the inviolability of the human personality, and the belief that punishing an individual for silence or perjury when he has been placed in a position in which his natural instincts and personal interests dictate that he should lie is an intolerable invasion of his personal dignity.

Dolinko, Is There a Rationale for the Privilege Against Self-Incrimination? 33 UCLA L. Rev. 1063 (1986). The philosopher Jeremy Bentham criticized some of the leading arguments in favor of the privilege. He listed them as follows:

> 2. The old woman's reason. The essence of this reason is contained in the word *hard:* 'tis hard upon a man to be obliged to criminate himself. Hard it is upon a man, it must be confessed, to be obliged to do any thing that he does not like. That he should not much like to do what is meant by his criminating himself, is natural enough; for what it leads to, is, his being punished. [But] did it ever yet occur to a man to propose a general abolition of all punishment, with this hardship for a reason for it? . . .
>
> You know of such or such a paper; tell us where it may be found. A request thus simple, your tenderness shudders at the thoughts of putting to a man: his

answer might lead to the execution of that justice, which you are looking out for pretences to defeat. This request, you abhor the thought of putting to him: but what you scruple not to do (and why should you scruple to do it?) is, to dispatch your emissaries in the dead of night to his house, to that house which you call his castle, to break it open, and seize the documents by force. . . .

3. The fox-hunter's reason. This consists in introducing upon the carpet of legal procedure the idea of *fairness,* in the sense in which the word is used by sportsmen. The fox is to have a fair chance for his life: he must have . . . leave to run a certain length of way, for the express purpose of giving him a chance for escape. . . . In the sporting code, these laws are rational, being obviously conducive to the professed end. Amusement is that end. [The] use of a fox is to be hunted; the use of a criminal is to be tried. . . .
4. Confounding interrogation with torture: with the application of physical suffering, till some act is done; in the present instance, till testimony is given to a particular effect required. [The] act of putting a question to a person whose station is that of defendant in a cause, is no more an act of torture than the putting the same question to him would be, if, instead of being a defendant, he were an extraneous witness. [If] any thing he says should be mendacious, he is liable to be punished for it. . . .
5. Reference to unpopular institutions. Whatever Titius did was wrong: but this is among the things that Titius did; therefore this is wrong: such is the logic from which this sophism is deduced. In the apartment in which the court called the Court of Star-chamber sat, the roof had stars in it for ornaments. [The] judges of this court conducted themselves very badly: therefore judges should not sit in a room that has had stars in the roof. [Using this reasoning, lawyers claim that the Star Chamber was a bad court because of its] abominable practice of asking questions, by the abominable attempt to penetrate to the bottom of a cause.

5 Bentham, Rationale of Judicial Evidence 230-43 (1827). Which of the possible rationales can best explain limitations on the applicability of the concept (i.e., its use to protect a person from criminal but not civil consequences of wrongdoing, or its application only to "testimony" and not other forms of compelled cooperation with a prosecution, such as participation in a lineup)? Which of the "principled" rationales described above might support transactional immunity? For an assessment of the effect of the self-incrimination privilege in modern practice, where most cases do not go to trial, see Stephanos Bibas, The Right to Remain Silent Helps Only the Guilty, 88 Iowa L. Rev. 421 (2003).

5. *Prosecution based on independent sources.* As the *Swinehart* court indicates, the government might successfully prosecute an immunized witness for the crime that is the subject of the testimony, but only under limited circumstances. The prosecutors must show that the evidence upon which a subsequent prosecution is brought "arose wholly from independent sources" and that they did not use the compelled testimony "in any respect." If you were a prosecutor in such a case, how would you attempt to prove that your evidence was based on "independent" sources? Consider this policy from the U.S. Department of Justice Criminal Resource Manual, §9-706:

> [Prosecutors] should take the following precautions in the case of a witness who may possibly be prosecuted for an offense about which the witness may be questioned

> during his/her compelled testimony: (1) Before the witness testifies, prepare for the file a signed and dated memorandum summarizing the existing evidence against the witness and the date(s) and source(s) of such evidence; (2) ensure that the witness's immunized testimony is recorded verbatim and thereafter maintained in a secure location to which access is documented; and (3) maintain a record of the date(s) and source(s) of any evidence relating to the witness obtained after the witness has testified pursuant to the immunity order.

How often will these procedures be feasible? How often will they suffice when the defendant raises a constitutional challenge to the prosecution?

6. *Effect of immunity in other jurisdictions.* If a state prosecutor immunizes a grand jury witness and compels self-incriminating testimony, what assurance does the witness have that federal prosecutors will not use the testimony as a basis for federal criminal charges? The Supreme Court has declared that the Fifth Amendment requires federal prosecutors to respect the immunity grants of state governments. Murphy v. Waterfront Commission, 378 U.S. 52 (1964). Does this ruling create a potential source of conflict between state and federal authorities? If so, how might the various actors respond to the conflict?

7. *Invoking the privilege based on potential future prosecutions.* Although the Fifth Amendment speaks of a privilege "in any criminal case," a person need not testify in a criminal courtroom to invoke the privilege. In fact, it is extraordinarily easy to invoke Fifth Amendment protections, because they apply to any legally compelled statements that *could* lead to the discovery of incriminating evidence, even though the statements themselves are not incriminating and are not introduced into evidence. Such statements would include grand jury testimony or testimony in a civil trial. For further discussion of the invocation and effects of the privilege in grand jury investigations, see the web extension for this chapter at *http://www.crimpro.com/extension/ch10.*

3. Document Subpoenas

Documents are the stock in trade of an investigative grand jury. The grand jury obtains documents by issuing subpoenas to document holders, compelling them to appear before the grand jury with the documents in hand. In reality, the prosecutor who advises the grand jury draws up the subpoena duces tecum describing the documents the grand jury demands. The terms of the subpoena are often very broad, and courts and legislatures have placed few if any bounds on the document requests. There is no requirement for the grand jury to show probable cause or reasonable suspicion that the documents they request will contain evidence of a crime. Historically, the documents needed only to be relevant to some legitimate grand jury inquiry. In the following case, consider whether the Supreme Court places any limits on the documents a grand jury may request.

UNITED STATES v. R. ENTERPRISES, INC.
498 U.S. 292 (1991)

O'CONNOR, J.*

This case requires the Court to decide what standards apply when a party seeks to avoid compliance with a subpoena duces tecum issued in connection with a grand jury investigation.

I.

Since 1986, a federal grand jury sitting in the Eastern District of Virginia has been investigating allegations of interstate transportation of obscene materials. In early 1988, the grand jury issued a series of subpoenas to three companies — Model Magazine Distributors, Inc. (Model), R. Enterprises, Inc., and MFR Court Street Books, Inc. (MFR). Model is a New York distributor of sexually oriented paperback books, magazines, and videotapes. R. Enterprises, which distributes adult materials, and MFR, which sells books, magazines, and videotapes, are also based in New York. All three companies are wholly owned by Martin Rothstein. The grand jury subpoenas sought a variety of corporate books and records and, in Model's case, copies of 193 videotapes that Model had shipped to retailers in the Eastern District of Virginia. All three companies moved to quash the subpoenas, arguing that the subpoenas called for production of materials irrelevant to the grand jury's investigation and that the enforcement of the subpoenas would likely infringe their First Amendment rights. [The district court denied the motions.]

II.

The grand jury occupies a unique role in our criminal justice system. It is an investigatory body charged with the responsibility of determining whether or not a crime has been committed. Unlike this Court, whose jurisdiction is predicated on a specific case or controversy, the grand jury can investigate merely on suspicion that the law is being violated, or even just because it wants assurance that it is not. The function of the grand jury is to inquire into all information that might possibly bear on its investigation until it has identified an offense or has satisfied itself that none has occurred. As a necessary consequence of its investigatory function, the grand jury paints with a broad brush. A grand jury investigation is not fully carried out until every available clue has been run down and all witnesses examined in every proper way to find if a crime has been committed. [The] Government cannot be required to justify the issuance of a grand jury subpoena by presenting evidence sufficient to establish probable cause because the very purpose of requesting the information is to ascertain whether probable cause exists.

[Any requirement that the government show probable cause or the relevance of a request in a grand jury subpoena] ignores that grand jury proceedings are subject to strict secrecy requirements. See Fed. R. Crim. P. 6(e). Requiring the Government to explain in too much detail the particular reasons underlying a subpoena

* [The Justices were unanimous in joining parts I and II of this opinion. Chief Justice Rehnquist and Justices White, Kennedy, and Souter joined in parts III and IV; Justice Scalia joined in parts IIIA and IV. — EDS.]

threatens to compromise the indispensable secrecy of grand jury proceedings. Broad disclosure also affords the targets of investigation far more information about the grand jury's internal workings than the Federal Rules of Criminal Procedure appear to contemplate.

III.

A.

The investigatory powers of the grand jury are nevertheless not unlimited. Grand juries are not licensed to engage in arbitrary fishing expeditions, nor may they select targets of investigation out of malice or an intent to harass. In this case, the focus of our inquiry is the limit imposed on a grand jury by Federal Rule of Criminal Procedure 17(c), which governs the issuance of subpoenas duces tecum in federal criminal proceedings. The Rule provides that "[the] court on motion made promptly may quash or modify the subpoena if compliance would be unreasonable or oppressive."

This standard is not self-explanatory. [What] is reasonable depends on the context. . . . In the grand jury context, the decision as to what offense will be charged is routinely not made until after the grand jury has concluded its investigation. One simply cannot know in advance whether information sought during the investigation will be relevant and admissible in a prosecution for a particular offense.

To the extent that Rule 17(c) imposes some reasonableness limitation on grand jury subpoenas, however, our task is to define it. In doing so, we recognize that a party to whom a grand jury subpoena is issued faces a difficult situation. As a rule, grand juries do not announce publicly the subjects of their investigations. A party who desires to challenge a grand jury subpoena thus may have no conception of the Government's purpose in seeking production of the requested information. Indeed, the party will often not know whether he or she is a primary target of the investigation or merely a peripheral witness. Absent even minimal information, the subpoena recipient is likely to find it exceedingly difficult to persuade a court that compliance would be unreasonable. . . .

Our task is to fashion an appropriate standard of reasonableness, one that gives due weight to the difficult position of subpoena recipients but does not impair the strong governmental interests in affording grand juries wide latitude, avoiding minitrials on peripheral matters, and preserving a necessary level of secrecy. We begin by reiterating that the law presumes, absent a strong showing to the contrary, that a grand jury acts within the legitimate scope of its authority. Consequently, a grand jury subpoena issued through normal channels is presumed to be reasonable, and the burden of showing unreasonableness must be on the recipient who seeks to avoid compliance. . . . Drawing on the principles articulated above, we conclude that where, as here, a subpoena is challenged on relevancy grounds, the motion to quash must be denied unless the district court determines that there is no reasonable possibility that the category of materials the Government seeks will produce information relevant to the general subject of the grand jury's investigation. . . .

B.

It seems unlikely, of course, that a challenging party who does not know the general subject matter of the grand jury's investigation, no matter how valid that party's claim, will be able to make the necessary showing that compliance would be unreasonable. After all, a subpoena recipient cannot put his whole life before the court in order to show that there is no crime to be investigated. Consequently, a court may be justified in a case where unreasonableness is alleged in requiring the Government to reveal the general subject of the grand jury's investigation before requiring the challenging party to carry its burden of persuasion. We need not resolve this question in the present case, however, as there is no doubt that respondents knew the subject of the grand jury investigation pursuant to which the business records subpoenas were issued. . . .

IV.

Applying these principles in this case demonstrates that the District Court correctly denied respondents' motions to quash. It is undisputed that all three companies — Model, R. Enterprises, and MFR — are owned by the same person, that all do business in the same area, and that one of the three, Model, has shipped sexually explicit materials into the Eastern District of Virginia. The District Court could have concluded from these facts that there was a reasonable possibility that the business records of R. Enterprises and MFR would produce information relevant to the grand jury's investigation into the interstate transportation of obscene materials. Respondents' blanket denial of any connection to Virginia did not suffice to render the District Court's conclusion invalid. A grand jury need not accept on faith the self-serving assertions of those who may have committed criminal acts. Rather, it is entitled to determine for itself whether a crime has been committed. . . .

STEVENS, J., concurring in part and concurring in the judgment.*

Federal Rule of Criminal Procedure 17(c) authorizes a federal district court to quash or modify a grand jury subpoena duces tecum "if compliance would be unreasonable or oppressive." This Rule requires the district court to balance the burden of compliance, on the one hand, against the governmental interest in obtaining the documents on the other. A more burdensome subpoena should be justified by a somewhat higher degree of probable relevance than a subpoena that imposes a minimal or nonexistent burden. Against the procedural history of this case, the Court has attempted to define the term "reasonable" in the abstract, looking only at the relevance side of the balance. Because I believe that this truncated approach to the Rule will neither provide adequate guidance to the district court nor place any meaningful constraint on the overzealous prosecutor, I add these comments.

The burden of establishing that compliance would be unreasonable or oppressive rests, of course, on the subpoenaed witness. . . . This showing might be made in various ways. Depending on the volume and location of the requested materials, the mere cost in terms of time, money, and effort of responding to a dragnet subpoena could satisfy the initial hurdle. Similarly, if a witness showed that compliance with the subpoena would intrude significantly on his privacy interests, or call for the disclosure of trade secrets or other confidential information, further inquiry would

* [Justices Marshall and Blackmun joined in this opinion. — EDS.]

be required. Or, as in this case, the movant might demonstrate that compliance would have First Amendment implications.

The trial court need inquire into the relevance of subpoenaed materials only after the moving party has made this initial showing. And, as is true in the parallel context of pretrial civil discovery, a matter also committed to the sound discretion of the trial judge, the degree of need sufficient to justify denial of the motion to quash will vary to some extent with the burden of producing the requested information. For the reasons stated by the Court, in the grand jury context the law enforcement interest will almost always prevail, and the documents must be produced. I stress, however, that the Court's opinion should not be read to suggest that the deferential relevance standard the Court has formulated will govern decision in every case, no matter how intrusive or burdensome the request.

■ OHIO REVISED CODE §2939.12

When required by the grand jury, prosecuting attorney, or judge of the court of common pleas, the clerk of the court of common pleas shall issue subpoenas and other process to any county to bring witnesses to testify before such jury.

■ ARKANSAS STATUTES §16-43-212

(a) The prosecuting attorneys and their deputies may issue subpoenas in all criminal matters they are investigating and may administer oaths for the purpose of taking the testimony of witnesses subpoenaed before them. Such oath when administered by the prosecuting attorney or his deputy shall have the same effect as if administered by the foreman of the grand jury. . . .

(b) The subpoena provided for in subsection (a) of this section shall be served in the manner as provided by law and shall be returned, and a record made and kept, as provided by law for grand jury subpoenas. . . .

Notes

1. *Breadth of document subpoena.* As *R. Enterprises* states, a recipient of a grand jury subpoena can challenge both the breadth of the subpoena and the burden of compliance. The Supreme Court stated in Oklahoma Press Publishing Co. v. Walling, 327 U.S. 186 (1946), that an unreasonably indefinite or overbroad subpoena might violate the Fourth Amendment or perhaps due process; in many states, such a subpoena would also violate statutes or rules of procedure. Note that in *R. Enterprises,* Federal Rule of Criminal Procedure 17(c) placed the most pertinent limit on the range of documents requested: Compliance must not be "unreasonable or oppressive." What specific facts might convince a court that a particular subpoena is overbroad or too indefinite? Does the subject matter of the grand jury's investigation matter? How about the cost of collecting relevant documents? The proportion of a business's documents falling within the terms of the subpoena (as opposed to the absolute number of documents)?

2. *The justification needed for a subpoena.* The *R. Enterprises* court followed the majority position in concluding that the prosecution does not need to make any preliminary showing of the relevance of testimony or other evidence sought through a grand jury subpoena. The probable cause necessary to support a search warrant is not a prerequisite for a grand jury subpoena. As the Court reasoned in United States v. Dionisio, 410 U.S. 1 (1973), a subpoena is different from an arrest, or even a more limited "stop," because the subpoena is served like any other legal process and involves no stigma and no force. Although the recipient of a subpoena to testify before a grand jury might challenge it on relevance grounds, it is very difficult to succeed on such a claim, in light of the breadth of the grand jury's duties to investigate any violations of the criminal law. Again, the *R. Enterprises* court is typical in its willingness to allow the grand jury to obtain documents and testimony relevant to a broad range of *potentially* criminal conduct. A few jurisdictions have required a modest grand jury showing of relevance. A grand jury subpoena in these courts is enforceable only if the grand jury (or the prosecutor on behalf of the grand jury) affirms that the testimony or documents it seeks will be relevant to a legitimate subject of inquiry. See In re Grand Jury Proceeding, Schofield I, 486 F.2d 85 (3d Cir. 1973); Robert Hawthorne, Inc. v. County Investigating Grand Jury, 412 A.2d 556 (Pa. 1980). Would this preliminary statement from the grand jury make it any easier for the subpoena recipient to show that the subpoena is not relevant to some possible investigation? Should the level of justification to support a grand jury subpoena turn on the type of document involved? See State v. Nelson, 941 P.2d 441 (Mont. 1997) (state constitution requires state to show probable cause to support investigative subpoena for discovery of medical records).

3. *The prosecutor and grand jury subpoenas.* The subpoenas requiring witnesses to appear before a grand jury are, strictly speaking, issued under the authority of the grand jury itself. In practice, however, the prosecutor coordinating the grand jury's investigation has virtually complete control over the subpoenas that issue. Some statutes, such as the Ohio statute above, give independent authority to the prosecutor to issue grand jury subpoenas. State v. Guido, 698 A.2d 729 (R.I. 1997) (prosecutor used subpoena to obtain document for delivery to State Attorney General, grand jury did not see it, information issued on basis of document; no abuse of grand jury power). Others give the prosecutor the power to subpoena a witness only if the grand jury approves of the request, either before or after the subpoena issues.

The Arkansas statute reprinted above is an unusual one, giving the prosecutor the subpoena power completely separate from the grand jury. See also Mich. Comp. Laws 767A.1 et seq. (empowers prosecutors to issue investigatory subpoenas; judge must find probable cause that felony has been committed and that the person subpoenaed "may have knowledge regarding the commission of the felony," before authorizing investigative subpoena); Oman v. State, 737 N.E.2d 1131 (Ind. 2000) (prosecutor acting without grand jury must get court approval to subpoena documents). In the many states where prosecutors have no such subpoena power, do they miss significant investigative opportunities? Must they conduct all their witness interviews in front of the grand jury? How do prosecutors ever speak in private with hostile witnesses during an investigation? Some states (fewer than a dozen) allow a magistrate to issue a subpoena to witnesses during an investigation, requiring the witness to appear before the magistrate rather than a grand jury. This system is sometimes called the "one-man grand jury." See Idaho Code §19-3004. Would you insist on secrecy in such proceedings, as in grand jury proceedings? Would you allow the witness to have counsel present during the testimony?

Problem 10-5. Subpoena Versus Search Warrant

After a violent clash at Stanford University between student antiwar protesters and local police officers, the district attorney's office opened a grand jury investigation to determine the identity of any students who assaulted the officers. Some of the students had assaulted the officers with sticks and clubs, and both students and officers were seriously injured. A few days after the grand jury started to hear testimony, a special edition of the *Stanford Daily,* a student newspaper, carried articles and photographs about the student protest and the violent events of that day. The photographs were the work of a staff photographer for the *Daily.* The police believed that the staff photographer might have taken additional pictures that would help identify the students who had assaulted the officers.

The day after the pictures were published, the district attorney's office secured a warrant to search the *Daily*'s offices for negatives, film, and pictures showing the events and occurrences at the protest. The warrant affidavit contained no allegation that members of the *Daily* staff were in any way involved in unlawful acts during the protest. Four police officers executed the search warrant later the same day. While staff members at the *Daily* looked on, the officers searched photographic laboratories, filing cabinets, desks, and wastepaper baskets. Some of the files they searched contained notes and correspondence. Some of the materials were confidential, although no staff member informed the officers of that fact. The search revealed only the photographs that had already been published in the *Daily,* and the police removed no materials from the *Daily*'s office.

The *Daily* and various members of its staff brought a civil action in federal court against the police officers who conducted the search, the chief of police, the district attorney and one of his deputies, and the judge who had issued the warrant. The complaint alleged that the search of the *Daily's* office was a violation of the First, Fourth, and Fourteenth Amendments of the U.S. Constitution. Assuming there was probable cause to support the search warrant, how would you argue this case on behalf of the *Daily*? Compare Zurcher v. Stanford Daily, 436 U.S. 547 (1978).

Notes

1. *Subpoenas and search warrants.* A prosecutor advising a grand jury during an investigation may have the choice of obtaining documents through a subpoena or a search warrant. What considerations will help the prosecutor make the choice? As we have seen, a subpoena requires the government to show no reasonable suspicion or probable cause to believe that the subpoena will produce evidence of a crime, and it requires virtually no showing of relevance. A search warrant, of course, must be based on probable cause and must particularly describe the place to be searched and the things to be seized. Does a subpoena give the government a way to bypass all the ordinary restraints on searches and seizures? Is the deference to grand jury requests a relic, or are grand jury investigations truly different from investigations that would

require a search warrant? Which method is likely to produce more evidence? Which will be more intrusive and which will cost the recipient more to comply with? State and federal statutes make it a crime for a person to destroy or alter documents that have been subpoenaed by a grand jury. How might these statutes affect a prosecutor's choice about the timing, scope, and recipients of subpoenas?

2. *Searches and freedom of the press.* In Zurcher v. Stanford Daily, 436 U.S. 547 (1978), the Supreme Court considered the validity of a search warrant authorizing the search of a newspaper's offices for photographs of demonstrators who had injured several police officers. The Court concluded that the Constitution imposed no special requirements for "third party" searches: The probable cause necessary to obtain a warrant was sufficient justification for a search, even if the target of the search was a newspaper not itself involved in wrongdoing. Congress responded to this decision by passing the Privacy Protection Act of 1980, 42 U.S.C. §2000aa. The statute, recognizing the special threats to the constitutional freedom of the press that are involved with searches of newspaper offices, creates a presumption in favor of subpoenas rather than search warrants to obtain documents from publishers. It prevents all criminal law enforcement agents (both state and federal) from searching for or seizing any "work-product materials" possessed by a publisher or broadcaster, unless there is probable cause to believe that the publisher has committed a crime relating to the documents or that immediate seizure is necessary to prevent death or serious bodily injury. Is this statute sufficient to protect the special First Amendment concerns involved in the search of newspaper offices? Cf. Branzburg v. Hayes, 408 U.S. 665 (1972) (enforcing grand jury subpoena for testimony of news reporter despite claim of privilege for news sources). Department of Justice regulations establish a similar presumption in favor of subpoenas rather than search warrants for document searches in the offices of attorneys, physicians, and clergy. 28 C.F.R. §59.4(b). Those regulations (unlike the statute) apply only to searches by federal agents. Why treat these categories of document holders any differently from other third parties who hold possible evidence of a crime?

3. *Attorneys as subpoena and search targets.* Internal guidelines at the Department of Justice require special authorization before seeking a subpoena of an attorney to obtain information about that attorney's representation of a client. Before a federal prosecutor may request such a subpoena, the U.S. Attorneys' Manual §9-13.410 requires certification of the following: (1) information is not privileged, (2) information is reasonably necessary to complete investigation, (3) alternative sources of the information are not available, and (4) need for information outweighs "potential adverse effects" on attorney-client relationship. What sorts of harms might flow from issuing a subpoena to an attorney? One of the ABA Model Rules of Professional Conduct, Rule 3.8(f), at one time required a prosecutor to obtain judicial approval after an adversarial hearing before she could issue a grand jury subpoena to a lawyer. The rule has since been revised to remove the requirement of judicial approval, but ethics rules in a handful of states still retain it. Is the requirement consistent with the guidelines in the U.S. Attorneys' Manual?

Section 9-13.420 of the U.S. Attorney's Manual creates special rules for the use of search warrants to search the offices of attorneys who are suspects, subjects, or targets of a criminal investigation. The application may go forward only if there is a "strong need" for material and if alternatives (such as a subpoena) will not work because of a risk of destroyed documents. The rules call for the creation of a "privilege team" consisting of agents and lawyers not involved in the investigation, who must review seized documents to identify those containing possibly privileged information. The privilege team cannot reveal the contents of privileged documents to the investigating agents and attorneys. Why do the rules for search warrants not require a pre-search certification that it will not reach privileged documents?

4. *Negotiations over terms of compliance.* If your client receives a grand jury subpoena for documents, and you conclude that there is no viable constitutional basis for objecting to the subpoena, is there anything left to do except collect the documents and turn them over? Can you negotiate some less onerous form of compliance? What negotiating leverage do you have, if any?

5. *The contents of incriminating documents.* When a grand jury forces a witness to provide documents, including some that the witness created personally, is it forcing him to "witness" against himself? Should the privilege against self-incrimination apply to the contents of all documents a suspect creates? Under federal law, it is now clear that the contents of preexisting documents are not "testimonial" and therefore the privilege against self-incrimination cannot stop the grand jury from obtaining such documents. See Fisher v. United States, 425 U.S. 391 (1976). All the states addressing this question have followed the federal lead. How much documentary evidence would be beyond the reach of a grand jury if the contents of documents were considered privileged when self-incriminating? If the government can force a person to turn over written statements that incriminate, does a privilege against oral testimony mean much at all?

6. *Act of production doctrine.* There is an exception to the *Fisher* rule regarding the contents of incriminating documents. Compliance with a subpoena is an implicit admission that the records requested in the subpoena exist, that they are in the possession or control of the subpoena recipient, and that they are authentic. The U.S. Supreme Court, along with all the state courts to address the issue, recognizes that the *act* of producing documents under a grand jury subpoena can give the government valuable information that might ultimately help convict the document holder of a crime. The contents of the documents, as opposed to the act of producing the documents, remains a valid source of evidence. Is this "act of production" any more "testimonial" than the contents of the documents? See United States v. Doe, 465 U.S. 605 (1984) (act of producing incriminating business records is itself testimonial self-incrimination); Braswell v. United States, 487 U.S. 99 (1988) (individual representative of legal entity must submit subpoenaed documents to grand jury, but prosecution may not use act of production evidence against individual).

This area of law is nuanced, including complex fields such as the "collective entity" doctrine, the self-incrimination privilege for corporate entities, and the "required records" doctrine. For a review of these interconnected doctrines and practices, see the web extension for this chapter at *http://www.crimpro.com/extension/ch10.*

7. *Other acts compelled by the grand jury.* Is a person serving as a "witness" against herself if the grand jury asks for a blood sample for testing? Handwriting exemplars? Are these actions any different from the act of producing documents? In Schmerber v. California, 384 U.S. 757 (1966), the Court held that there is no compelled self-incrimination when a grand jury orders a witness to provide a blood sample. Some states make an exception to the grand jury's broad subpoena power when it comes to the most intrusive grand jury requests for evidence. For instance, grand juries will sometimes subpoena witnesses and ask for fingerprints, hair

samples, or voice exemplars. Compare Woolverton v. Multi-County Grand Jury, 859 P.2d 1112 (Okla. Crim. App. 1993) (requiring showing of probable cause to support request for blood samples, reasonable suspicion for palm prints) with United States v. Dionisio, 410 U.S. 1 (1973) (upholding subpoena for voice exemplar with no special government justification). Is there an argument for treating voice exemplars differently from palm prints? From blood samples?

Table of Cases

Principal Supreme Court cases are in bold. Other principal cases are in italic.

Index